Congressional Elections
1946-1996

Congressional Elections
1946-1996

Congressional Quarterly Inc.
Washington, D.C.

Printed and bound in the United States of America

The paper used in this publication meets the minimum requirements of the American National
Standard for Information Science—Permanence of Paper for Printed Library Materials, ANSI
Z39.48-1984.

Cover illustration credits (clockwise from top right): Scott J. Ferrell; Scott J. Ferrell; courtesy of
League of Women Voters; Scott J. Ferrell; Deborah Kalb

Library of Congress Cataloging-in-Publication Data

Congressional elections, 1946-1996.
     p.   cm.
   Includes bibliographical references and index.
   ISBN 1-56802-248-4 (alk. paper)
   1. United States. Congress—Elections. 2. Elections—United States. 3. United States—Politics
and government—1945-1989. 4. United States—Politics and government—1989- I. Congressional
Quarterly, Inc.

JK1967.C64   1997
324.973'092—dc21   97-35242

Contents

Preface

Swept into power in the 1930s along with Franklin D. Roosevelt and his New Deal, the Democratic Party remained the dominant force in Congress until 1994. During this period the Democrats controlled the House of Representatives every year except during the 80th Congress (1947-1949) and the 83rd Congress (1953-1955), when the Republican Party held the majority. The Republicans fared only slightly better in the Senate—holding the majority there during these same periods and also during a six-year span (1981-1987) when Ronald Reagan was president. When it came to creating and sustaining domestic programs and managing constituent services, the American electorate seemed content to keep the Democrats in charge.

The era of Democratic hegemony in Congress came to a close with the historic 1994 midterm elections that gave the Republican Party control of both houses of Congress for the first time in 40 years. The Republicans had not controlled both the House and Senate since the beginning of President Dwight D. Eisenhower's first term (1953-1955). In 1994 the GOP rode to power on widespread voter discontent over congressional scandals, legislative gridlock and disappointment with the Democratic administration of President Bill Clinton. Although Clinton was reelected to a second term in 1996, the results of the congressional races that year confirmed the ascendancy of the Republican Party in Congress as the GOP maintained its majority in both houses.

Congressional Elections 1946-1996 is a unique collection of vote returns and election data on the U.S. Senate and House of Representatives. General election results are provided for every congressional race (including special elections) during the past fifty years. Election returns prior to 1974 were obtained primarily from the Inter-University Consortium for Political and Social Research (ICPSR) at the University of Michigan. Congressional Quarterly and its *America Votes* series have added to this ICPSR data, supplying the election returns for congressional races from 1974 to 1996.

The introductory section provides a narrative chronology of the political and legislative events that shaped the post-World War II era through 1996. This section, organized by individual Congresses, describes important legislation and interprets the results of each biennial election year. For those congressional elections that occurred during a presidential contest, national issues in the presidential race are also discussed.

The next five sections look at the Senate, the more deliberative chamber of the two legislative houses. The introduction examines the historical changes that have occurred in the choosing U.S. senators. Originally state legislatures decided who became senators; it was not until ratification of the 17th Amendment in 1913 that senators were popularly elected. This section also explains the three classes of U.S. senators and the lengths of congressional sessions. A separate discussion examines the historical significance of Southern primaries. Because of the overwhelming dominance of the Democratic Party in the South during the first half of the 20th century, the party's primaries from the 1940s through the 1960s usually determined the winner of the Senate seat.

Next is a listing of all senators from 1947 to 1997. This list gives the length of the terms and political affiliations of all senators during this period. Notes identify special elections and partial-term appointments. Following this listing is the heart of the Senate data: the general and primary election results. General election returns are provided for all Senate races from 1946 to 1996, including special elections. Results for Senate primaries are given for most states back to 1960; results for Southern primaries are provided back to 1946. All elections results contain the total vote count for each candidate along with political party affiliation and the percentage of the vote received by each candidate.

The people's branch, the U.S. House of Representatives, is the focus of the next three sections. An introduction describes important aspects of election to the House, such as special elections and disputed elections. A separate discussion details the history and current status of reapportionment and redistricting, one of the most important processes in the U.S. political system.

The bulk of the data on House elections is contained in the section listing popular vote returns. All general election results for House races from 1946 to 1996, including special and runoff elections, are provided. Election data include the total vote count for each candidate, political party affiliation and the percentage of the vote received by each candidate. Special elections and circumstances are identified in the notes.

The book concludes with a listing of political party abbreviations, a bibliography, which provides the starting point for further reading about House and Senate elections and four indexes: (1) Senate candidates for general election, (2) Senate candidates for primary election, (3) House candidates for general election, and (4) general subject.

Politics and Issues, 1945-96

Following is a narrative chronology of the political and legislative events of the years after World War II, putting in perspective the national and state elections that took place during that period.

The Postwar Years

By the end of World War II the American people had come to two fundamental decisions that would have a deep influence on the political life of the nation in the postwar years from 1945 through the mid-1960s. In domestic affairs Americans in general had concluded that the social and economic reforms of the New Deal years ought to be preserved and that government had a legitimate role in protecting the individual against economic disaster. On the international front isolationism clearly was rejected in favor of acceptance of a role of active leadership for the United States in world affairs.

These two decisions paved the way for a politics of national consensus in the postwar years. The ideological conflicts of the 1930s were softened, and it was possible for the two major political parties to argue more about means and less about basic national aims.

The main issue usually was which party could best provide for the needs of the people in a steadily expanding economy and at the same time provide firm, reliable leadership for the United States and the free world in a protracted cold war with the Communist bloc. Implicit in both parties' appeals were two basic elements: an acceptance of government's role in the social welfare field and close industry-government ties at home, coupled with a desire to avoid nuclear confrontation with the Soviet Union abroad. When, in 1964, one of the two major national parties sought to deny this postwar consensus in both its domestic and foreign aspects, it encountered the most sweeping electoral repudiation in a quarter-century.

By and large the Democratic Party was more successful than the Republican in presenting itself as the party better able to carry out the national consensus in the postwar years. Three Democrats were elected to the presidency— Harry S. Truman, John F. Kennedy and Lyndon B. Johnson—while only one Republican, Dwight D. Eisenhower, was successful, and then largely because of his status as a hero of World War II. Of the ten Congresses elected in the postwar period, eight had Democratic and only two had Republican majorities. Except for brief periods in 1947-48 and 1951-54

the Democrats held a majority of the state governorships. Democrats maintained regular majorities in most state legislatures. Even the eight-year incumbency of a Republican president failed to strengthen the Republican Party appreciably.

The frequent Democratic victories, however, did not reflect the depth of loyalty to the Democratic Party that had existed in the 1930s, when the fresh recollection of the Great Depression maintained an unwavering Democratic mandate. In fact, the political movements of the postwar period demonstrated a rapidly changing and ambiguous electoral mandate: Republicans scored major victories in 1946 and 1952, but the Democrats achieved significant and far-reaching success in 1948, 1958 and 1964.

Even in the years of party sweeps voters showed an increasing tendency to vote for the candidate rather than the party. The trend toward split tickets was especially evident in 1956, when Eisenhower was reelected by a landslide but the Democrats held Congress, and in 1964, when numerous Republican candidates eked out narrow victories despite the massive national vote for Johnson. Part of the trend toward split tickets could be attributed to an increasingly well educated electorate. But it also seemed to reflect a willingness among the voters to support superior candidates of either party—candidates who represented, in large part, the domestic and foreign policy consensus of the postwar era.

In the early 1960s a new awareness emerged on the issue of civil rights. Civil rights for black citizens had divided Northern and Southern Democrats in Congress for decades and had even caused a rump Southern Dixiecrat Party in the 1948 presidential election. But pressures for equal rights for blacks continued to increase and reached a climax with a series of nationwide demonstrations in 1963. Many white Americans, with church and union groups at the fore, joined the fight for legislative action for equal rights. The result was the comprehensive, bipartisanly sponsored Civil Rights Act of 1964.

Throughout the postwar period Congress was slower to reflect the national consensus on major issues than was the president or the judicial branch of the government. As a rule it was the executive branch that proposed major new programs in fields such as education, welfare and domestic aid—programs that Congress accepted slowly if at all. And it was the Supreme Court that, with its 1954 decision outlawing segregation in the public schools, sparked the movement toward bringing blacks into the mainstream of American life. Other decisions of the Court on constitutional rights, ranging from legislative apportionment to the rights of witnesses and the accused, far outstripped anything Congress was willing to consider.

When Congress did assume a more central role—helping, for instance, to formulate and develop foreign aid programs from the mid-1940s on, pushing aggressively for broader domestic programs while Eisenhower was in the White House, or remolding and expanding the scope of the 1964 Civil Rights Act—its actions stood out as exceptions to the pattern of executive or judicial initiative.

Congress' conservatism and its reticence in initiating programs were based in large part on the committee seniority system and restrictive legislative rules. Committee chairmen often were Southern Democrats or Midwestern Republicans, representing the most rigidly held districts and states. The congressional representatives least able to build up seniority, and thus the least likely to head committees, were those from the politically volatile suburbs and city fringe areas where the major new population movements—and many major problems—of the postwar era occurred.

During this period the House, intended by the Framers of the Constitution to be the chamber closest to the people, actually was the more conservative body, blocking a substantial amount of legislation approved by the Senate. The Senate, especially after the liberal Democratic sweep of 1958, became markedly liberal in its orientation. A principal explanation for the Senate's position was that metropolitan centers, with their pressing demands, had sprung up in virtually every state, prompting senators to be responsive to their needs.

The postwar era might be remembered as one in which both American parties became truly national. Democrats extended their power and influence into Midwestern and northern New England territory that had been unwaveringly Republican in the past. Republicans made significant new breakthroughs in the growing industrial South and in their best years won the votes of millions of Americans who had never voted Republican before.

The 1964 election, at the end of the era, left the Democratic Party in control of most of the power centers, from the presidency to the state legislatures. But many Republicans, noting the somber outcome of an election in which their party had moved far to the right and by implication had repudiated the national stance on most matters, began to work to return the party to a central course. The 1964 election, by underlining the strength of the American consensus on vital issues of domestic economy, civil rights and foreign policy, had demonstrated anew the broad opportunities for a party willing to offer solutions to national needs.

1945-47:
The 79th Congress

The death of a president who had led his country through 12 years of economic and military crisis, the end of the greatest war in history and the inauguration of the atomic age all took place in the two-year interval between Franklin D. Roosevelt's election to a fourth term in 1944 and the 1946 midterm congressional elections.

The president died April 12, 1945, of a cerebral hemorrhage. Two weeks later, on April 25, delegates from Allied powers gathered in San Francisco to write the United Nations charter. (The U.S. Senate ratified the charter July 28, a contrast to the unwillingness of the Senate in 1919 to join the League of Nations.) On April 28 Italian partisans captured and butchered dictator Benito Mussolini. Adolf Hitler was reported to have committed suicide April 29 in his ruined Berlin chancery while Soviet troops poured into the city. Germany surrendered unconditionally on May 7.

In the Pacific, American airplanes administered the coup de grace to the tottering Japanese empire by dropping the first atomic bomb on Hiroshima Aug. 6, 1945; another was used on Nagasaki Aug. 9. World War II ended with the unconditional surrender of Japan on Aug. 14.

In 1944, running on the theme that the nation shouldn't "change horses in the middle of the stream," President Roosevelt had won an unprecedented fourth term with a national vote plurality of 3,594,993 (of 47,976,670 cast) and a total of 432 (of 531) electoral votes. Reversing Democratic losses in the 1942 midterm elections, Congress went heavily Democratic. After the 1944 election 57 Democrats and 38 Republicans were in the Senate, and the House was balanced 243-190 in favor of the Democrats. Less than three months later Roosevelt was dead.

Roosevelt's successor, Harry S. Truman, took office April 12. He faced a perplexing task as he sought to hold together the coalition of big-city machines, organized labor, conservative Southern Democrats, farmers, minority groups, ethnic and religious blocs and intellectual liberals, which FDR had brought together for his successive electoral victories.

Pent-up tensions erupted with the end of World War II. The country was hit by strikes, climaxed in June 1946 by a nationwide rail strike, which President Truman tried to break with a "labor draft," thus incurring deep resentment in the ranks of organized labor. On the right wing Southern Democrats continued to bolt the administration on almost every item of domestic legislation as they had since 1938. Conservative forces in Congress pressed for a relaxation of wartime price controls far more rapidly than Truman thought advisable.

Despite its failure to reach agreement on such basic issues as labor-management relations, a national housing program, federal aid to schools and national health insurance, the 79th Congress produced some notable legislation, including the Atomic Energy Act of 1946, which transferred control over all aspects of atomic energy development from the War Department to a civilian Atomic Energy Commission.

The Employment Act of 1946, considerably weaker than the "Full Employment" bill first proposed—which bordered on a government guarantee of jobs for all—nevertheless broke new ground in fixing responsibility for national economic policies. The Hospital Survey and Construction Act of 1946 authorized a program of matching federal grants to state and local health bodies for hospital construction. The Legislative Reorganization Act of 1946 cut the number of standing committees in the House and the Senate, provided for preparation of an annual legislative budget to complement the president's budget and raised the salaries of senators and representatives from $10,000 to $12,500, plus a $2,500 tax-free expense account. Included in the law, as a separate title, was the Federal Regulation of Lobbying Act, requiring lobbyists to register and report their lobbying expenses.

Congress also authorized a 50-year loan of $3.75 billion to Great Britain, intended to assist the British in removing trade and currency exchange restrictions hampering postwar programs for economic reconstruction and trade liberalization.

1946 Midterm Elections

The 1946 congressional election campaign was marked by two events disadvantageous to the administration. First, President Truman on Sept. 20, 1946, dismissed Secretary of Commerce Henry A. Wallace, former vice president (1941-45) and only original New Dealer still remaining in the cabinet and a spokesperson of labor and progressive groups. The dismissal followed a speech Wallace gave—which Wallace had read to Truman in advance—criticizing the allegedly anti-Soviet tone of the foreign policy of Under Secretary of State James F. Byrnes. The incident encouraged Republicans to pin the "red" label on all candidates for whom Wallace subsequently spoke during the campaign.

A second bad break for the administration came in a seven-week national meat shortage just before the election. Truman was forced to issue an order, Oct. 14, ending all meat price controls. His action drew sharp criticism from organized labor and a charge by the Republican national chairman, Rep. B. Carroll Reece of Tennessee, that he was taking action "after the horse has gone to the butcher shop." The mood of the country was clearly in favor of an early end to all remaining wartime controls. The pent-up frustrations of wartime were directly appealed to in the Republican slogans—"Had enough?" and "It's time for a change." Reece promised that a Republican Congress would restore "orderly, capable and honest government in Washington and replace controls, confusion, corruption and communism."

Symptomatic of the tone of the times—pictured by contemporary observers as a desire to return to "normalcy"—were two election-morning newspaper headlines. One read, "Gay Crowd Hails Return of National Horse Show." A second read, "Crackers, Sugar Back in Stores."

The Democratic congressional campaign was lackadaisical. Democratic national Chairman Robert E. Hannegan did warn the country that a GOP victory would be a "surrender to the will of a few who want only large profits for themselves." But Truman failed to hit the campaign trail and offered scarcely any comment on the important races and issues.

The Democrats appeared to depend in large measure on frequent radio broadcasts of the late president Roosevelt's campaign addresses recorded in earlier years. The most publicized activity for Democratic candidates was carried out by the political action committee of the CIO (Congress of Industrial Organizations), headed by the controversial Sidney Hillman.

Results of the 1946 Elections

The 1946 campaign proved to be the most successful for the Republicans since the 1920s—and the best year they would have for many years to come. Across the nation Republicans swept Senate, House and gubernatorial contests. The Republicans increased their Senate membership from 38 to 51 seats, while the Democrats slipped from 57 to 45 seats.

Among the new Republican senators were John W. Bricker of Ohio, Irving M. Ives of New York, William E. Jenner of Indiana, William F. Knowland of California (who had been appointed to the Senate in 1945), George W. Malone of Nevada, Arthur V. Watkins of Utah and John J. Williams of Delaware. The Progressive candidate, Robert La Follette Jr. of Wisconsin, lost to Republican Joseph R. McCarthy. With the exception of Ives, all represented their party's most conservative wing.

The House Republican delegation rose from 190 seats to 246 seats, while the Democratic delegation dropped from 243 to 188; this was the lowest figure since the 1928 elections. The ratio among the nation's governorships changed from 26-22 in favor of the Democrats to 25-23 in favor of the Republicans.

Important Republican gubernatorial victories included the reelection of Thomas E. Dewey of New York and Earl Warren of California and the elections of Robert F. Bradford of Massachusetts, Alfred E. Driscoll of New Jersey, James H. Duff of Pennsylvania, Thomas J. Herbert of Ohio, Kim Sigler of Michigan and L. W. Youngdahl of Minnesota. The only Democrats to win in generally two-party states were William L. Knous of Colorado, William P. Lane Jr. of Maryland and Lester C. Hunt of Wyoming.

1947-49:
The 80th Congress

In 1947 and 1948 the nation proceeded to shake off most of the remaining wartime economic controls and to enjoy an economic boom marred somewhat by substantial inflation and the beginnings of the first postwar recession in late 1948. Americans began to realize that the postwar period would be one of continuing international tensions rather than a return to "normalcy."

The foreign scene was darkened by increasing Soviet intransigence at the United Nations; by the civil war in Greece and Communist pressures on Turkey, which led to announcement of the Truman Doctrine in 1947; by the ouster of non-Communists from the Hungarian government in May 1947; by the Communist coup d'état in Czechoslovakia in Feb. 1948; and by the beginning of the Soviet blockade of Berlin in April 1948. Faced with the responsibility of formulating new solutions for the new problems of the postwar era, the Republican-controlled 80th Congress wrote some basic laws that governed domestic and foreign policy for many years to come.

On May 15, 1947, Congress approved the Greek-Turkish aid program requested by President Truman (the Truman Doctrine). The concept of massive economic aid to European countries to assist them in their postwar recovery, suggested by Secretary of State George C. Marshall, received final congressional approval in passage of the European Recovery Program (Marshall Plan) April 2, 1948. International tensions paved the way for congressional approval of a peacetime draft law June 19, 1948.

The legislation that placed the most strain on bipartisan foreign policy was extension of the Reciprocal Trade Agreements Act. Congress in 1948 turned down presidential requests for a three-year extension, granting only a single year's extension in a limited form.

During its first session the 80th Congress approved legislation for unifying the armed forces under a single Department of Defense with separate Army, Navy and Air Force departments under the secretary of defense, and for forming the Central Intelligence Agency.

In domestic affairs the Democratic president and Republican Congress generally were at loggerheads. Presidential recommendations to extend New Deal social welfare concepts were largely ignored by Congress. The most significant single piece of domestic legislation approved by the Congress was the Taft-Hartley Labor-Management Relations Act, passed over President Truman's veto June 23, 1947. The bill outlawed the closed shop, jurisdictional strikes and secondary boycotts and was bitterly opposed by organized labor. Its chief provisions were to remain on the statute books throughout the postwar period.

The 80th Congress completed two significant actions concerning the office of president: it passed a bill, approved by Truman on July 18, 1947, making the Speaker and the president pro tempore of the Senate the next two in line of succession to the presidency after the vice president, ahead of the secretary of state and other cabinet members. In a slap at President Roosevelt's four terms, it sent to the states a constitutional amendment limiting the tenure of future presidents to two terms. The 22nd Amendment became law in February 1951. The communist issue monopolized national attention in the summer of 1948, as Elizabeth Bentley and Whittaker Chambers, self-confessed former Communist Party members, spread before the House Un-American Activities Committee charges that numerous high administration officials during the 1930s and war years had been members of communist spy rings. Chambers' Aug. 3 testimony that former State Department aide Alger Hiss had been a communist spy became the most celebrated case of all. It was highly dramatized on nationwide television on Aug. 25, when Hiss and Chambers confronted each other at a hearing of the committee.

The 1948 Campaigns

Truman's underdog victory in the 1948 presidential election set the pattern of rapid and startling reversals in domestic political trends during the postwar years. His victory was accompanied by a Democratic congressional and gubernatorial sweep that reversed, in overwhelming measure, the Republican triumph of 1946.

The year 1947 had appeared to be a favorable one for Truman. The Marshall Plan, his "get-tough-with-Russia" policy, his advocacy of government action to curb rising prices, and his willingness to deal firmly with labor leader John L. Lewis had all increased the president's popularity in sharp contrast to its nadir at the time of the 1946 elections. In November 1947 elections the Democrats were especially successful, electing a governor in Kentucky and winning other important races.

By the late spring of 1948, however, Truman's popularity had plummeted to such depths that leaders of his own party cast about for another nominee to head the Democratic ticket. Several developments contributed to the sharp dip in presidential popularity. Reacting in part to Henry A. Wallace's December 1947 announcement that he was forming a third party, Truman included in his 1948 State of the Union address requests for new social welfare legislation plus a call for a straight $40 tax cut for each individual in the nation. Even some liberal Democrats accused the president of having made a "political harangue" in the most partisan spirit.

In February the president's advocacy of a far-sweeping civil rights program, based on recommendations of his civil rights commission, created a predictably bitter reaction in the Southern wing of his party. The stage was set for the States' Rights ticket, putting four parties in the upcoming presidential campaign. Truman's reelection in the face of open revolts on the left wing (Wallaceites) and the right wing (Dixiecrats) seemed almost impossible.

Fearing defeat for the party in the November elections, an unusual coalition of Democrats began to press in late spring for General Dwight D. Eisenhower's nomination by the Democratic National Convention. The coalition included states' rights southerners, big-city bosses from the North and party liberals. In statements on June 5 and 9,

however, Eisenhower made clear his refusal to consider seeking or accepting the nomination. Neither Eisenhower's political philosophy nor his party were known; it was not until 1952 that he identified himself as a Republican.

A brief effort to draft Supreme Court Justice William O. Douglas also collapsed. No further obstacle remained to Truman's renomination when the Democrats assembled gloomily in Philadelphia July 12 for their 30th national convention.

Truman was nominated on the first ballot on July 15, receiving 947-1/2 votes to 263 for Sen. Richard Russell of Georgia. Senate Democratic leader Alben W. Barkley of Kentucky, who had roused the delegates with a fiery keynote speech July 12, was later nominated for vice president.

Truman's acceptance speech created a sensation. Lashing into the Republicans as "the party of special interests," he called for repeal of the Taft-Hartley Act, criticized Congress for its failure to control prices or pass a housing bill, and said that the tax reduction measure approved was a "Republican rich-man's tax bill." He then announced it was his duty to call Congress back into session on July 26 to act on anti-inflation legislation, housing, aid to education, a national health program, civil rights, an increase in the minimum wage from 40 cents to 75 cents hourly, extension of Social Security, public power and cheaper electricity projects and a new "adequate" displaced-persons bill.

The closing day of the Democratic convention was marked by a walkout of delegations from Mississippi and Alabama, when the convention, at the instigation of Minneapolis mayor Hubert H. Humphrey and other party liberals, adopted a tough substitute civil rights plank. Following an impassioned speech by Humphrey in behalf of the stronger plank, the convention approved it by a 651-1/2 to 582-1/2 vote, substituting it for a noncontroversial plank recommended by the Resolutions (Platform) Committee.

Rebellious southerners from 13 states convened in Birmingham, Alabama, on July 17 as the States' Rights Party and nominated Gov. J. Strom Thurmond, D-S.C., for president and Gov. Fielding L. Wright, D-Miss., for vice president. They urged Southern Democratic parties to substitute Thurmond and Wright for Truman and Barkley as the Democratic candidates on the ballot. The convention adopted a platform terming the national Democratic civil rights plank "this infamous and iniquitous program" that would mean a "police state in a totalitarian, centralized, bureaucratic government." The platform stated, "We stand for the segregation of the races and the integrity of each race."

Another group met in Philadelphia in July. Calling itself the Progressive Party, it nominated Henry A. Wallace for president and Sen. Glen H. Taylor, D-Idaho, for vice president. Party leaders denied that the party was communist-dominated, though most observers considered it heavily influenced by the extreme left. In his acceptance speech Wallace blamed Truman for the Berlin crisis. He said there had been a "great betrayal" following President Roosevelt's death in which the administration inaugurated its "get tough" policy, thus "slamming the door" on peace talks with the Soviet Union. The Progressive platform called for a program of U.S. disarmament, a conciliatory policy toward the Soviet Union, an end to segregation, nationalization of key industries, repeal of Taft-Hartley, high farm price supports and the Townsend plan, giving a $100 monthly pension to everyone at the age of 60.

Scenting victory, Republicans engaged in a lively contest for their party's presidential nomination. The three chief candidates were New York governor Thomas E. Dewey, former Minnesota governor Harold E. Stassen and Sen. Robert A. Taft of Ohio. Taft enjoyed the support of most of the more conservative party regulars.

As the primaries developed during the spring, it first appeared that Stassen might be on his way to the nomination. After losing to Dewey in New Hampshire, he won an overwhelming victory in Wisconsin over Dewey and native son Gen. Douglas MacArthur, who had been considered the strong favorite. Stassen won 19 delegates to eight for MacArthur and none for Dewey. In the Nebraska primary Stassen again won against Dewey, Taft and several other candidates whose names were placed on the ballot.

Observers began to predict Stassen's nomination, but he then made what later appeared to be a serious error. He entered the May 4 Ohio primary, bluntly antagonizing the Taft wing of the party. (He won only nine of the 23 contested delegate spots, the rest going to Taft.) In Oregon, where Stassen had been an early favorite, he lost to Dewey in the May 21 primary (117,554 votes to 107,946), after a radio debate between the two men in which Stassen endorsed and Dewey opposed outlawing the Communist Party. Observers believe the debate and primary returns effectively finished Stassen's chances.

When the 24th Republican National Convention opened in Philadelphia June 21, the Dewey victory already seemed probable. Taft was handicapped because many conservatives considered his stands for federal aid to education and housing too liberal, while many party professionals feared his co-authorship of the Taft-Hartley Act might harm the party among union voters. California governor Earl Warren and Michigan senator Arthur Vandenberg both had hopes that a convention deadlock might turn the delegates toward them, but neither ambition was justified. Dewey began with the solid bloc of New York State and enjoyed substantial support in delegations from every part of the country.

In first ballot voting June 24, with 547 needed to win, Dewey received 434 votes to 224 for Taft and 157 for Stassen. Favorite-son candidates shared the rest. On the second ballot Dewey's total rose to 515 against 274 for Taft and 149 for Stassen. Following this, the other candidates quickly fell behind Dewey. His nomination on the third roll call was merely a formality.

During the following night Dewey conferred with influential party leaders and decided on Governor Warren as his running mate. The party adopted a platform backing a "bipartisan" foreign policy, foreign aid to anti-Communist countries, "full" recognition of Israel, housing, anti-inflation and civil rights legislation, and promised a fight against communists inside and outside government.

The Truman and Dewey campaigns became historic examples. The Truman effort showed how a determined candidate can win by going to the people, even with the odds against him; the Dewey performance was an example of how a supposedly sure candidate can lose by waging a lackluster campaign of overconfidence.

Truman undertook a 31,000-mile "barnstorming" whistle-stop tour by train, appearing before an estimated 6 million persons. At each opportunity the president would appear to give one of his "give-'em-hell" attacks on the Republicans. The "do-nothing Republican 80th Congress" was Mr. Truman's chief target: "When I called them back into session what did they do? Nothing. Nothing. That Congress never did anything the whole time it was in session." If the Republicans win, "they'll tear you apart."

Actions of the ''Do-Nothing'' 80th Congress

The 80th Congress (1947-48), characterized by a hard-campaigning President Truman as the "do-nothing Republican 80th Congress," actually produced a great deal of legislation, some of which Truman wanted, some over his serious objections. A partial list of 80th Congress actions:

- Truman doctrine of aid to Greece and Turkey.
- Marshall Plan for aid to Europe.
- Peace treaties ratified with Italy, Hungary, Bulgaria, and Romania.
- Inter-American Treaty of Mutual Assistance ratified.
- Vandenberg Resolution favoring collective and regional mutual assistance pacts.
- Unification of armed forces under Department of Defense; creation of Central Intelligence Agency.
- $65 million building loan for UN headquarters.
- Peacetime draft law.
- Passage of Taft-Hartley Act, over veto.
- Presidential succession change.
- Constitutional amendment to limit presidential tenure to two terms.
- Hope-Aiken flexible price support bill.
- Newsboys excluded from Social Security system, over veto.
- A tax-reduction bill, over veto.
- Liberalized housing credit terms.
- Extended rent control.

The Republicans are "predatory animals who don't care if you people are thrown into a depression.... They like runaway prices."

Toward the end of the campaign Truman began a special appeal to minority racial and religious groups, calling for strong civil rights legislation and condemning Republican leaders for passing the Displaced Persons Act, which he said discriminated against Catholics and Jews.

Dewey's campaign was characterized by his aloofness and cool manner, his skirting of issues and his diffuse, repetitious calls for "national unity." Dewey called the 80th Congress "one of the best," but he failed to come to the defense of its individual programs even when they were under direct attack from Truman. Assured by the pollsters, campaign strategists, advertising consultants and reporters that he had the election well in hand, Dewey refrained from direct or forceful answers to any of the Truman attacks. Even more than Dewey, vice presidential candidate Warren disdained to enter the partisan fray.

The Dewey program was particularly vague on farm legislation, which was a new field to him as a New York governor. "There are some people who would like to inject politics into the necessities of food raising in our country. I don't believe in that," Dewey said. He expressed a general support for price supports, not indicating whether they should be at parity or close to it or on a flexible or rigid scale. Meanwhile, farm prices were taking a nosedive that was concerning farmers across the Midwest. Also, storage capacity in grain elevators was short, adding to rural dissatisfaction.

Both the Progressive and Dixiecrat movements, meanwhile, were faltering. Wallace became increasingly identified with the communists and few "liberal" leaders joined his cause. His campaign crowds dwindled to a fraction of their size earlier in the year.

The Dixiecrat ticket failed to make substantial headway as most Southern governors and senators—including some who had been most vociferous in denouncing Truman's civil rights proposals—chose the route of party regularity and backed the president. Only four Southern Democratic parties—those in Alabama, Mississippi, South Carolina and Louisiana—followed through on the plea of the Birmingham convention to put Thurmond and Wright on the ballot as the regular Democratic nominees. They went on the ballot as States' Rights Party candidates in ten other states: Arkansas, California, Florida, Georgia, Kentucky, North Carolina, North Dakota, Tennessee, Texas and Virginia.

With the first election eve returns from the Northeastern states, Truman took a lead that he never lost despite the closeness of the election. As the night wore on state after state considered "safe Republican" moved into the Truman column. Dewey carried Pennsylvania, New Jersey, Indiana, Maryland, Michigan and New York (the last three evidently because of usual Democratic voters defecting to Wallace). But the president carried Massachusetts, won the Border states, took all but four Southern states (Alabama, Louisiana, Mississippi and South Carolina) that were in the Dixiecrat column and carried the farm belt. Finally California fell in his column. When Ohio conclusively went for Truman at 11 o'clock Wednesday morning, Nov. 3, Dewey conceded.

The election returns seemed to indicate that the Democratic New Deal philosophy was so generally accepted by the electorate that the president's warnings of a return to "Republican" depression days remained a telling point. On a less philosophical level many observers felt the Truman "Mr. Average" approach, compared to Dewey's "Olympian airs," drew a large sympathy vote from the average people in the street for the conceded "underdog."

Results of the 1948 Elections

With the Truman victory the Democrats took control of Congress with commanding majorities in both the Senate and the House. The Democrats picked up nine Senate seats to make the new balance 54-42 in their favor. Among the new Democratic senators were Lyndon B. Johnson (Texas), Paul H. Douglas (Illinois), Hubert H. Humphrey (Minnesota), Estes Kefauver (Tennessee), Robert S. Kerr (Oklahoma) and Clinton P. Anderson (New Mexico). Republican Margaret Chase Smith was elected senator from Maine. And in House elections Democrats made a net gain of 75 seats; the new total was 263 Democrats and 171 Republicans.

The Democrats also ran strong in gubernatorial contests, winning 20 of the 32 seats up for election and reversing the Republican trend of the immediate past years. The new totals were 30 Democratic and 18 Republican governorships. Among the new Democratic governors were Chester Bowles (Connecticut), Adlai E. Stevenson (Illinois) and G. Mennen Williams (Michigan).

1949-1951:
The 81st Congress

The international situation in the years 1949 and 1950 was marked by stabilization and cooling of tensions in Europe, in sharp contrast to renewed Communist conquest and the threat of nuclear war in Asia. In April 1949 the North Atlantic Treaty was signed by the United States, Canada and 10 European nations, agreeing that "an armed attack against any one or more of them in Europe and North America shall be considered an attack against all." A direct reaction to Communist power moves, which included the 1948 takeover of Czechoslovakia, the NATO treaty laid down a policy of containment of Soviet expansionist ambitions that helped to preserve a territorial status quo on the European continent for years to come. On Sept. 30, 1949, the Soviets lifted a blockade of Berlin, which had been in effect since April 1, 1948.

In Asia, however, the Western position was disintegrating rapidly. On Jan. 22, 1949, the Chinese Communists took Beijing. On April 23 they crossed the Yangtze and captured Nanjing. On Aug. 6 Secretary of State Dean Acheson blamed Generalissimo Chiang Kai-shek's "reactionary" clique for the Communist victory and gave notice that no further aid would be given Chiang's government. On Dec. 7, 1949, the Nationalist Chinese government fled to Formosa.

The takeover of mainland China by a hostile Communist power did not shake the Western world, however, as did the surprise attack of Communist North Korean troops on South Korea June 25, 1950. The UN Security Council immediately ordered a cease-fire. Two days later President Truman ordered U.S. forces under Gen. Douglas MacArthur to repel the North Koreans. This became a UN "peace action" but was largely an American venture. U.S. involvement in Korea led to a near-wartime mobilization of the U.S. economy. It also led to President Truman's dispute with General MacArthur over the proposed bombing of Manchuria, which in turn led to MacArthur's dismissal in April 1951. As the war dragged on for two years with heavy U.S. casualties, it became a source of great frustration for the American people.

In other important developments the Soviet Union in September 1949 exploded its first atomic bomb, ending the U.S. atomic monopoly; India was proclaimed independent in January 1950; Alger Hiss was found guilty of perjury on Jan. 21, 1950; and Truman, in January 1950, authorized the Atomic Energy Commission to produce the hydrogen bomb.

In his inaugural address Jan. 20, 1949, President Truman included a "Point IV" proposal of American foreign policy for "a bold new program for making the benefits of our scientific advances and industrial progress available for the improvement and growth of underdeveloped areas." Over the succeeding years, foreign aid assistance for capital investment to build up the economies of fledgling nations of Africa, Asia and Latin America became a cornerstone of U.S. foreign policy.

When the heavily Democratic 81st Congress assembled in Washington Jan. 3, 1949, liberals had high hopes that it would enact a new body of social welfare legislation such as that proposed by Truman in the 1948 campaign. The first signs for the Truman program seemed bright as the House on Jan. 3 adopted a new rule to break the power of its Rules Committee to bottle up legislation indefinitely. The "21-day rule" provided that if the Rules Committee failed to clear a bill after 21 legislative days the chairman of the legislative committee that originally approved it could ask the House to vote on whether to consider the measure or not, with a majority vote required to bring the bill to the floor. The rule lasted only through the 81st Congress and was rejected by the House when the 82nd Congress organized in 1951.

On Jan. 5 Truman appeared before Congress to urge a sweeping new Fair Deal program of social reform. But Congress in general proved to be a disappointment to the liberal camp on domestic issues. Approval was given to a long-range housing bill providing for expanded federal programs in slum clearance, public housing and farm improvement programs, which Truman signed into law July 15, 1949, "with deep satisfaction." The administration also scored an important victory in passage of the Social Security Expansion Act of 1950 and a limited victory in a 1949 minimum wage increase. But otherwise the Fair Deal program hit formidable obstacles.

Legislation to continue the Marshall Plan, military assistance to friendly foreign nations and a two-year extension of the Trade Agreements Act cleared Congress with some bipartisan support. The Senate on July 21, 1949, ratified the North Atlantic Treaty by a 2-1 margin. In domestic affairs important steps toward streamlining the executive branch of the government were made in the Government Reorganization Act of 1949.

An explosive new issue, meanwhile, had developed on the domestic scene. In a Feb. 11, 1950, speech in Wheeling, W.Va., Sen. Joseph R. McCarthy, R-Wis., charged that there were 57 communists working in the State Department, a charge promptly denied by the department. Until his formal censure by the Senate in 1954, McCarthy and his freewheeling accusations of communist sympathies among high- and low-placed government officials absorbed much of the public attention. The phenomenon of McCarthyism had a major effect on the psychological climate of the early 1950s.

The 1950 Midterm Elections

The liberal Democratic trend apparent in Truman's surprise 1948 victory was sharply reversed in the 1950 elections as Republicans exploited the issues of inflation, Korea, communism and corruption, to make strong comebacks in congressional and gubernatorial elections.

Truman, delivering his only major speech of the campaign Nov. 4, 1950, sought to bolster the Democratic effort with charges similar to those he leveled against the Republicans in 1948: that they were captives of "special interests," that they would undo the country's progress toward peace and prosperity if they gained control of the national government. Truman said the Republicans were "isolationists" and that "any farmer who votes for the Republican Party ought to have his head examined."

The Republican campaign assumed a far more aggressive tone than it had in 1948. Sen. Robert A. Taft, R-Ohio, said the administration was responsible for high prices, high taxes, the loss of China to the Communists and the Korean conflict. (Republicans pointed frequently to a Jan. 12, 1950, speech by Secretary of State Dean Acheson before the National Press Club in which Acheson described the U.S. defensive line in the Far East in such a way as to exclude Korea.)

Typical of other Republican attacks was a Nov. 4 reply to Truman by Harold Stassen, charging that the "blinded, blundering, bewildering" Far East policy of the "spy-riddled" Truman administration was directly to blame for American casualties in Korea.

McCarthy's charges of communism in high places in the government played an important part in the campaign. Whether or not the voters believed all of McCarthy's charges, many seemed to accept the thesis that there was something drastically wrong with U.S. foreign policy and that Acheson was a likely villain.

In Maryland the prominent veteran Democratic senator Millard E. Tydings was defeated by John Marshall Butler, an obscure Republican, after a campaign in which Tydings was accused of having "whitewashed" the State Department as head of a Senate committee investigating McCarthy's charges of communism in the department. Butler was later accused of countenancing distribution of a campaign leaflet with a doctored photograph showing Tydings with U.S. Communist leader Earl Browder.

In California Republican representative Richard M. Nixon ran for the Senate against Rep. Helen Gahagan Douglas, a prominent liberal Democrat. Nixon's charges that Douglas voted frequently with New York representative Vito Marcantonio, a member of the American Labor Party, whose voting record was often depicted as pro-communist, established the image of Nixon as a ruthless campaigner, an image that would harm him in future races.

Another Senate contest with communism as the chief issue took place in North Carolina, where Willis Smith defeated incumbent Frank P. Graham in a June 24 Democratic primary runoff. Smith charged that Graham was badly tainted with socialism because of his alleged "associations with communism."

Among major issues stressed by the Republicans was Truman's program for compulsory health insurance for all, termed "socialized medicine" by doctors who fought it both in the primaries and in the general elections. The issue was thought to have contributed to the defeat of several Democratic senators, including Claude Pepper of Florida and Graham of North Carolina in primaries and Elbert D. Thomas of Utah and Glen H. Taylor of Idaho in the general election. But in each one of these cases and in the California Senate race the "soft-on-communism" issue, at its peak in 1950, played a more important role.

Results of the 1950 Elections

The two most closely watched Senate battles were in Ohio, where Republican senator Robert Taft was the target of an all-out attempt by organized labor to defeat him because of his co-authorship of the Taft-Hartley Act, and in Illinois, where Senate majority leader Scott W. Lucas was challenged by former Republican representative Everett McKinley Dirksen, who campaigned as a conservative near-isolationist. The election returns showed Taft the winner in Ohio by a gigantic 431,184 vote margin (57.5 percent), while Dirksen upset Lucas with 294,354 votes to spare (53.9 percent). Both men later became their party's Senate leader.

Assessment of the election returns showed that, while the Democrats retained nominal control of Congress (the Senate by 2 votes, the House by 35), the Truman-Fair Deal influence on Congress had been virtually nullified. Outside the conservative Southern states, the Democrats elected only 126 House members to 196 for the Republicans.

On the Senate side the Republicans won 18 and the Democrats 9 of the non-Southern contests. Among the new senators were Richard M. Nixon, R-Calif.; George A. Smathers, D-Fla.; Everett McKinley Dirksen, R-Ill.; A. S. Mike Monroney, D-Okla.; and James H. Duff, R-Pa., who was one of the prime movers for the nomination of Eisenhower in 1952.

1951-53: The 82nd Congress

The Korean conflict continued to dominate American life in 1951 and 1952 and led directly to the defeat of the

Democrats in the 1952 elections. On April 11, 1951, President Truman removed General of the Army Douglas MacArthur from his command of UN and U.S. forces in the Far East. MacArthur had wanted to pursue the Chinese Communists across the Yalu River to their sanctuary in Manchuria in order to destroy the air depots and lines of supply being used to sustain their war effort in Korea. On March 25 MacArthur had threatened Communist China with air and naval attack. These steps, running contrary to the Truman administration policy under Secretary of State Dean Acheson, led to MacArthur's removal. Negotiations for a truce along the 38th parallel began July 10, 1951, but the fighting continued for another two years.

In other international developments the Japanese peace treaty was signed in San Francisco on Sept. 8, 1951. War between Germany and the United States was formally ended Oct. 19. On May 26, 1952, a peace contract between Germany and the Western allies was signed. In Nov. 1952 the first hydrogen bomb was exploded by the United States.

A major domestic controversy developed in 1952 when Truman on April 8 ordered seizure of the nation's steel mills to avert a strike by 600,000 CIO steel workers. On June 2, however, the Supreme Court ruled the seizure illegal. The workers struck from June 3 to July 25.

The 82nd Congress accomplished very little outside the realm of foreign and military affairs. None of the Fair Deal proposals expounded by the president and the Democratic leadership in 1948 and 1950—national health insurance, aid to education and increased public health benefits—was enacted into law.

In 1951 the nation's interest was captured by the televised crime hearings of a Senate subcommittee chaired by Sen. Estes Kefauver, D-Tenn. The hearings exposed nationwide criminal organizations that reaped huge illegal profits, influencing local politicians and buying protection.

The 1952 Campaigns

President Truman ended any speculation about his third-term ambitions by announcing March 29 that he would not be a candidate for reelection. The field of possible Democratic nominees included Senator Kefauver; Gov. Adlai E. Stevenson, D-Ill.; W. Averell Harriman of New York; Vice President Alben W. Barkley of Kentucky; Sen. Robert S. Kerr, D-Okla.; and Sen. Richard B. Russell, D-Ga. Stevenson was Truman's personal choice for the nomination and was offered presidential support as early as January. Truman was willing to back Barkley after Stevenson's repeated disavowals of interest in the nomination; however, influential labor leaders vetoed Barkley's nomination, forcing him to withdraw on the eve of the convention.

Stevenson consistently professed his disinterest in the nomination and only submitted to a draft movement in his behalf while the 1952 Democratic convention, which convened in Chicago July 21, was in progress. The support for Stevenson, already strong, began to snowball with the July 24 announcement of Thomas J. Gavin, President Truman's alternate as a delegate from Missouri, that he would vote for Stevenson on Truman's instructions. Stevenson ran second to Kefauver in both the first and second ballots.

Only on the third ballot, not completed until 12:25 a.m. on July 26, did Stevenson move close to nomination as Harriman withdrew in his favor. A unanimous nomination by acclamation was then moved and carried. Following a conference with President Truman, Stevenson chose Sen. John J. Sparkman, D-Ala., a backer of the national Democratic Party on most issues except civil rights, as his running

mate. The convention then confirmed his choice by acclamation.

The contest for the Republican presidential nomination, despite other entries in the field, was fought out between the supporters of two relatively clearly defined groups within the party: Sen. Robert A. Taft of Ohio represented the conservative Midwestern and Southern wing of the party, and Gen. Dwight D. Eisenhower became the candidate of the "internationalist" wing of the party centered on the East and West coasts. Other announcements of candidacy were made by California governor Earl Warren and by Harold E. Stassen.

Eisenhower in early 1952 was on duty in Paris as commanding general of the new North Atlantic Treaty Organization. The major political question as 1952 began was whether he would permit his name to be put forth for the Republican nomination. Previously he had always rejected talk of his running for president, and he had declined to make his political affiliations known. The mystery ended on Jan. 7 when Sen. Henry Cabot Lodge, R-Mass., announced that he was entering Eisenhower's name in the March 11 New Hampshire primary after having received assurances from the general that he was a Republican. In a Jan. 8 statement from Paris, Eisenhower confirmed his Republican loyalties and said he would run for president if he received a "clear-cut call to political duty." Eisenhower said, however, that he would not actively seek the nomination. Despite his refusal to campaign, Eisenhower ran strongly in most of the primaries where his name was entered.

When the 25th Republican National Convention opened in Chicago on July 7, the delegate issue was the hottest—and one of the first—items of business. In a preliminary test the convention voted 658-548 against allowing delegates with disputed seats to vote on other delegate contests until their own credentials were accepted. This resolution, which had been endorsed by 25 of the nation's Republican governors, prevented disputed Taft delegates from the South from voting for each other's seating. The victory of the Eisenhower forces on this issue foreshadowed the general's eventual nomination.

Korea, foreign affairs, corruption in government, internal communism and the domestic economy were the major issues of the 1952 campaign. Of these, only the domestic economy—booming through the stimulation of the Korean War—proved to be in any way a plus for the Democrats. The other issues aided the Republican campaign.

The most dramatic episode of the campaign opened Sept. 18 with an article in the New York Post, charging that GOP vice presidential nominee Nixon had been the beneficiary of an allegedly secret fund financed by California businesses. For a week controversy raged with many demands that Nixon resign from the ticket so that the corruption issue against the Democrats would not be diluted.

Eisenhower declined to take a firm stand on Nixon's continuance on the ticket. Finally, Nixon on Sept. 23 went on nationwide television for a melodramatic defense of the moral rectitude of the fund and to make a complete accounting of his own relatively limited personal assets. In this speech Nixon referred to his wife's "respectable Republican cloth coat" and the gift dog, Checkers—"regardless of what they say about it, we're going to keep it."

Response to Nixon's speech overwhelmingly favored keeping him on the ticket. Eisenhower immediately issued a statement lauding Nixon for his bravery in a "tough situation." At a Sept. 24 meeting between the two men in

Wheeling, W.Va., Eisenhower announced that Nixon had completely "vindicated himself."

Results of the 1952 Elections

In contrast to 1948, when the pollsters and commentators had all foreseen a sweeping Dewey victory, there was a marked reluctance to make a firm prediction on the outcome of the 1952 campaign. But when the returns started to roll in election eve, it was clear that Eisenhower had won by a landslide and that his victory had probably never been in doubt.

Only nine of the 48 states went for Stevenson, and they were in the South or Border areas (West Virginia, Kentucky, Alabama, Arkansas, Georgia, Louisiana, Mississippi, North Carolina and South Carolina). Every state across the East, Midwest and Far West went for Eisenhower. And the tide rolled on into many parts of the South, with the Eisenhower-Nixon ticket carrying Texas, Oklahoma, Florida, Virginia and Tennessee.

The electoral vote count was 442 for Eisenhower, 89 for Stevenson. In popular votes Eisenhower won a 6,621,242-vote plurality. He polled 33,936,234 votes, the highest number of votes ever received by a presidential candidate. But in defeat Stevenson won 27,314,992 votes, the highest number ever received by a losing candidate.

Seeking explanations for the Eisenhower landslide, observers found a multitude of reasons. The doubts, fears and frustrations stemming from the stalemated Korean War, the Hiss case and the communist spy trials, revelations of corruption in the federal government, rising prices and high taxes—all contributed to a strong desire for a change in executive leadership. Stevenson's divorce and wit were thought to be unpopular with many voters. Sparkman's identification with the white supremacy views of the Alabama Democratic Party harmed the ticket among black voters.

The lack of enthusiasm for the Republican congressional leadership, the memory of the depression and fear of reversal of social-economic gains of the Democratic years might have nullified these Republican advantages, however, if the Republicans had not found in Eisenhower an ideal candidate to allay such fears. A national hero, a man whose leadership had already been proven in World War II and in laying the groundwork for the North Atlantic Alliance, Eisenhower also had the invaluable asset of a magic personality that charmed voters and the image of being "above politics." Few could seriously believe that "Ike" would scuttle the New Deal reforms.

The uniquely personal aspect of Eisenhower's victory was underlined by the narrow margins with which Republicans moved into control of Congress, despite the presidential landslide. Republicans made a net gain of 22 House seats to a new total of 221, only three more than the 218 needed to give them control. The Democratic House total slipped from 235 to 213. In Senate elections the Republicans made a net gain of only one seat, just enough to give them a one-seat edge in the new Senate. The new Senate totals were 48 Republicans, 47 Democrats and one Independent (Wayne Morse of Oregon, formerly a Republican).

In what proved to be a significant Senate race 35-year-old Democratic representative John F. Kennedy defeated Republican Henry Cabot Lodge Jr., a top leader in the Eisenhower drive for the GOP presidential nomination, by a 70,737-vote margin in Massachusetts. Other newly elected senators included Barry Goldwater, R-Ariz.; Stuart Symington, D-Mo.; Mike Mansfield, D-Mont.; Henry M. Jackson, D-Wash.; and Albert Gore, D-Tenn.

On the gubernatorial level Republicans solidified the national lead they had achieved in 1950 by winning five new seats. The winners were Christian A. Herter, R-Mass.; William G. Stratton, R-Ill.; J. Caleb Boggs, R-Del.; George N. Craig, R-Ind.; and Hugo Aronson, R-Mont. The new governorship totals were 30 Republicans and 18 Democrats.

1953-55:
The 83rd Congress

Many Americans had hoped that Eisenhower's election to the presidency would usher in an era of domestic tranquillity and international stability. In some respects these wishes were fulfilled. There was a more harmonious relationship between the president and Congress than at any time since World War II. A Korean armistice was finally signed July 27, 1953, with prisoner repatriation following shortly thereafter.

Republicans claimed that President Eisenhower's action in instructing the U.S. Seventh Fleet to stop shielding Communist China from any possible Nationalist Chinese attacks, combined with information relayed to the Chinese that the United States would resort to full-scale war in Korea if the Communists refused to come to peace terms, were decisive factors in persuading the Communists to come to terms. Democrats replied that the terms of the armistice were no better than those the Truman administration had previously rejected.

Even with a return to relative stability in Korea, however, the international situation remained in flux on other fronts. Soviet Premier Joseph Stalin died March 5, setting off a contest for succession in the USSR. On July 7, 1953, an uprising that broke out in Communist-held East Germany was quelled when the Communists called in Soviet troops and tanks, which mowed down civilians revolting in the streets of East Berlin. The United States did not intervene, drawing into question the wisdom of the "liberation" policy spelled out by Republican campaigners in 1952.

On Aug. 20, 1953, the Soviet Union announced the successful testing of its first hydrogen bomb. President Eisenhower went before the United Nations on Dec. 8 to urge the major powers to cooperate in developing the peaceful uses of atomic energy. The United States on Jan. 21, 1954, launched the *Nautilus,* the first atomic-powered submarine.

The curtain began to go down on France's colonial empire as she admitted defeat in the seven-and-a-half-year war against Communist infiltration in Indo-China and submitted to a partition of Vietnam at the spring 1953 Geneva conference on Far Eastern affairs; France subsequently withdrew forces from Vietnam, Cambodia and Laos. Threatened Communist inroads in Central America were reversed, however, by U.S.-supported anti-Communist forces, which invaded Guatemala and overthrew the Communist-oriented government of President Jacobo Arbenz Guzman in June 1954.

The 83rd Congress produced few innovations in domestic or foreign policy, but neither did it reverse New Deal social reforms. During the first session (1953), foreign aid and military appropriations were pared, the controversial Reconstruction Finance Corp. was abolished, legislation was passed giving the states title to the oil-rich coastal lands previously claimed by the federal government, and Congress permitted the president to carry out a governmental reorganization creating a new Department of Health, Education, and Welfare, which it had denied President Truman in 1949 and 1950.

Sen. Joseph R. McCarthy and his unrestrained accusations of communist influence throughout the government remained a domestic issue. Taking over chairmanship of the Senate Government Operations Committee in 1953, McCarthy conducted hearings and investigated the State Department, Voice of America, Department of the Army and other agencies. An opinion-stifling "climate of fear" in many government agencies was said to be one of the results of his probes. The Army-McCarthy hearings, televised in the spring of 1954, were the climax of McCarthy's career and led finally to his censure by the Senate on Dec. 2, 1954. McCarthy's influence waned steadily thereafter. He died May 2, 1957.

The Supreme Court on May 17, 1954, handed down a unanimous decision declaring racial segregation in the public schools to be unconstitutional. The opinion, written by Chief Justice Earl Warren (whom Eisenhower had appointed on the death of Chief Justice Fred M. Vinson in 1953), began a major movement toward racial desegregation across the nation. It inspired bitter hostility in the Southern states.

A potential Democratic comeback with the nation's voters was presaged by special elections held during 1953. The traditional Republican hold on New Jersey was broken by the election of Democrat Robert B. Meyner to the governorship. Special elections in the New Jersey 6th and Wisconsin 9th Districts resulted in the election of two Democrats, Harrison A. Williams Jr. in New Jersey and Lester Johnson in Wisconsin. They were the first members of their party ever to win in either of these districts.

The 1954 Midterm Elections

The Republican success under Eisenhower in winning both houses of Congress in 1952 was not repeated in 1954. Democrats made significant comebacks, recapturing control of both House and Senate and reversing the Republican gubernatorial trend of recent years. But the swing back to the Democrats, while it indicated that the Republican Party was probably much weaker than its popular president, was by no means strong enough to spell a major change in the nation's mood. Although it was in the majority, much of the Democratic Party strength was concentrated in the conservative South.

President Eisenhower appealed to the voters to return a Republican Congress and he campaigned harder and longer than any other president had ever done in a midterm election. He claimed that Congress had enacted 54 of 64 legislative proposals he had submitted and that this "batting average of .830" was "pretty good in any league." (Congressional Quarterly figures showed Congress had approved 150 of 232 specific Eisenhower requests for a batting average of .647.)

In an Oct. 8 televised address he warned that a Democratic congressional victory would start "a cold war of partisan politics between the Congress and the Executive Branch," which would block "the great work" his administration had "begun so well." Congressional Democratic leaders Sam Rayburn and Lyndon B. Johnson, both of Texas, replied in a joint telegram to the president that "there will be no cold war conducted against you by the Democrats" and complained that the president had made an "unjust attack on the many Democrats who have done so much to cooperate with your Administration and to defend your program against attacks by members of your own party."

In a last-minute effort to bolster the Republican vote in critical states, Eisenhower made an unprecedented one-day,

1,521-mile flying trip on Oct. 29, 1954, to address crowds in Cleveland, Detroit, Louisville and Wilmington, Del. In these speeches he implied that Democratic administrations had been able to boast of full employment and prosperity only during war. Following the campaign some observers speculated that Eisenhower may have kept many women's votes by reminding them that the Republicans had put an end to the "futile casualties" in Korea. There was general agreement that his campaign activities averted a still stronger Democratic trend, especially in congressional elections.

Vice President Nixon played a controversial role in the campaign, charging that the Democrats were unfit to govern because of their record on the communist issue.

On the issue of mounting unemployment in several areas of the country, Democrats charged Republicans with a "callous" attitude toward the problem, while Republicans replied that they had provided jobs without war. Public power was also an issue, with Democrats accusing Republicans of "give-aways" to private interests, while Republicans replied that Democratic public power policy had tended toward socialism and government monopoly.

Results of the 1954 Elections

Democrats moved into control of the Senate by a 48-47-1 margin as compared with the 49-46-1 Republican edge before the election. Among the new senators were Richard L. Neuberger, D-Ore., former vice president Alben W. Barkley, D-Ky. and Clifford P. Case, R-N.J.

In the House the new lineup was 232 Democrats and 203 Republicans, a net Democratic gain of 19 seats over the previous Congress, which had had 221 Republicans and 213 Democrats.

The Democratic congressional majorities grew throughout the remainder of the Eisenhower years. Sam Rayburn, D-Texas, again became Speaker of the House, and Lyndon B. Johnson, D-Texas, Senate majority leader—posts they held through the rest of the decade.

Republicans fared even worse in the governorship races. Including the Democratic victory of Edmund S. Muskie in the September 13 Maine election, the Democrats ousted Republicans from eight state governments, and the Republicans failed to take a single Democratic seat. The gubernatorial balance shifted from 29-19 in favor of the Republicans to 27-21 in favor of the Democrats. In the New York governorship election to succeed retiring three-term governor Thomas E. Dewey, a Republican, Democrat Averell Harriman won a narrow 11,125-vote plurality over Republican senator Irving M. Ives. Other Democratic gubernatorial winners included Abraham Ribicoff in Connecticut, Orville Freeman in Minnesota and George M. Leader in Pennsylvania.

1955-57:
The 84th Congress

Cooperation between a middle-of-the-road president and a middle-of-the-road Congress, tension in the Formosa Strait, growing pressures in Africa and Asia for independence from colonial rule, the Geneva "summit" conference, presidential illnesses, "de-Stalinization" in the Soviet empire, revolt in Poland and Hungary, war over the Suez Canal—these events were highlights of the last half of President Eisenhower's first term in office.

Divided responsibility for government brought unexpectedly harmonious sessions of Congress, with nothing resembling the "cold war of partisan politics" predicted in 1954 by Eisenhower if the Democrats were to take control of

Congress. Administration measures fared almost as well as they had during the Republican 83rd Congress, again with substantial aid from Democrats.

Especially in foreign affairs the Democratic leadership cooperated substantially with the president. Early in 1955 Congress approved the resolution Eisenhower had requested to give him authority to employ U.S. armed forces to defend Formosa. Prompted by Communist Chinese bombardment of the off-shore islands of Quemoy and Matsu, the resolution also gave the president authority to defend, in addition to Formosa, "related positions and territories now in friendly hands," an evident reference to Quemoy and Matsu. Senate moves to delete this authority were overwhelmingly rejected.

The Senate ratified, by almost unanimous votes, the Southeast Asia Collective Defense Treaty (which created the Southeast Asia Defense Organization—SEATO), plus protocols ending the occupation of Germany, restoring sovereignty to West Germany and permitting West German rearmament and NATO membership. The peace treaty with Austria, creating an independent, neutral state, was signed in Vienna on May 15 and was ratified by the Senate June 7, 1955. The controversial constitutional amendment offered by Sen. John W. Bricker, R-Ohio, to trim the president's treaty-making powers was reported out of the Senate Foreign Relations Committee in 1956, but it was not brought up for Senate debate because of the president's firm opposition. In 1955 the Reciprocal Trade Agreements Act was extended for three years, the longest single extension since 1945. Foreign aid appropriations came fairly close to matching presidential requests.

Domestic enactments by the politically divided government were less impressive. The two most important measures approved by Congress appeared to be the multibillion dollar federal highway program, providing for a 41,000-mile interstate superhighway program as part of the most extensive public works project in the nation's history, and the Agricultural Act of 1956, which included the soil bank program that supporters hoped would limit farm surpluses and raise farmers' incomes. Congress also voted an increase in the minimum wage to $1 an hour (as opposed to the 90-cent figure recommended by the administration).

On the international scene the first conference of Asian-African countries met April 18-27, 1955, in Bandung, Indonesia. Delegates endorsed an end to colonialism, called for national independence and demanded UN membership for all states qualified in terms of the UN charter (including Communist China). In the following month the Warsaw Treaty, counterpart to NATO for the Communist satellites of Eastern Europe, was ratified.

At the 20th Congress of the Soviet Communist Party in Moscow, Feb. 14-25, 1956, Nikita Khrushchev proclaimed a new party line, which included destruction of Joseph Stalin as a national idol. The rush to "de-Stalinize" however, loosed forces in the Communist world that the Soviet Union was able to control only by bloody repressions of the June 28, 1956, workers revolt in Poznan, Poland, and the revolt of Hungarians in October and November of 1956.

Reacting adversely to Egyptian president Gamal Abdel Nasser's acceptance of Soviet-bloc arms and economic agreements with the Communist world, the United States on July 19, 1956, informed Egypt that it was withdrawing its offer to aid in construction of the Aswan Dam on the Nile River. Britain on July 20 announced it was also withdrawing from the project. On July 26 Egypt seized the British-held Suez Canal and denounced the Western powers. Prolonged negotiations during the summer and fall failed to persuade Egypt to modify its decision on nationalizing the canal, and on Oct. 29 Israel launched an invasion of Egypt. The move was coordinated with the British and French governments, which attacked Egypt on Oct. 31. The Suez Canal was blocked by sunken and scuttled ships. The Soviet Union stepped into the controversy, threatening atomic war if Britain and France refused to retreat. The United Nations, led by the United States, condemned the French, British and Israeli moves. A UN cease-fire ended the fighting Nov. 7, and a UN international peace force moved in to enforce the peace, the terms of which allowed Egypt to regain control of the canal and forced Israeli withdrawal.

The question of President Eisenhower's health hung over the nation for a year before the November 1956 election. On Sept. 24, 1955, the 64-year-old president was stricken by a heart attack, which totally incapacitated him for a period of days and necessitated his hospitalization for almost two months. Republican leaders, who had confidently expected Eisenhower to seek (and easily win) reelection in 1956, suddenly faced the possibility that he might not be available. As the president gradually improved, party leaders, particularly GOP national chairman Leonard W. Hall, repeatedly urged him to run again despite his illness. After thorough physical examinations Eisenhower on Feb. 29, 1956, announced that he was convinced that his health would permit him to carry the "burdens of the Presidency" under a reduced work schedule and that he would seek reelection.

On June 8 the president was again hospitalized, this time with ileitis. He underwent successful surgery on June 9 and was once more hospitalized for several weeks. Again the possibility arose that he might not seek reelection. But on July 10 Eisenhower made it clear he would go ahead with his campaign for reelection.

Without the question of presidential illness, there would probably have been little doubt, at any time, that Ike could achieve reelection. The presidential illness, however, added an element of uncertainty to the entire campaign and made the Democratic nomination appear far more "worth having" than might otherwise have been the case.

The 1956 Campaigns

A familiar cast stepped forward to seek the Democratic presidential nomination: Adlai E. Stevenson, the 1952 nominee; Tennessee senator Estes Kefauver, the popular primary choice of 1952; and New York governor Averell Harriman. Senate majority leader Lyndon B. Johnson of Texas was supported for the nomination by several Southern leaders, but he had little backing outside the South.

Early in the spring it appeared that Kefauver might again sweep the primaries. After winning the New Hampshire Democratic primary without opposition on March 13, he went on to pick up 56 percent of the vote in the March 20 Minnesota primary against Stevenson. The decisive contest came on June 5 in California, where both men had waged vigorous campaigns. The results: Stevenson, 1,139,964; Kefauver, 680,722. The Kefauver campaign limped along for a few more weeks. On July 26 Kefauver announced his withdrawal in favor of Stevenson.

When the Democratic National Convention met in Chicago on Aug. 13, Stevenson and Harriman were the only two serious candidates for the nomination. Harriman's candidacy, discounted by most observers, received a boost when former president Truman on Aug. 11 endorsed him. But in the vital contest for actual delegate votes, Stevenson, with

Kefauver's support, was too far ahead to be stopped. On the first ballot on Aug. 16 Stevenson was nominated with 905-1/2 votes to 210 for Harriman, 80 for Johnson, and the remainder scattered.

Historically, the most significant event at the 1956 convention was the cliff-hanging decision about the Democratic vice-presidential nominee. Following his nomination Stevenson made a brief appearance before the convention to tell the delegates he had decided "to depart from the precedents of the past." He said "the selection of the Vice Presidential nominee should be made through the free processes of this convention."

After a stiff two-ballot contest, Kefauver, on Aug. 17, narrowly won the vice presidential nomination over Massachusetts senator John F. Kennedy. With 686-1/2 votes required for nomination, Kennedy's total moved as high as 648 at one point during the second ballot. But a series of vote switches gave the nomination to Kefauver, who had 755-1/2 votes against 589 for Kennedy and 27-1/2 scattered. Other unsuccessful aspirants for the vice presidential nomination, all of whom received substantial first-ballot votes, were Sen. Hubert H. Humphrey of Minnesota, Sen. Albert Gore of Tennessee and New York mayor Robert F. Wagner.

The vice presidential fight marked Kennedy's entry into presidential politics. The good showing that Kennedy had made, particularly in Southern delegations, convinced his backers that despite his Roman Catholic faith Kennedy could be elected president.

The convention on Aug. 16 adopted a platform including a compromise civil rights plank. It termed Supreme Court rulings "the law of the land" but made no specific pledge to apply the Court's decisions and denounced the use of force to implement them. A move by a Northern liberal group led by Gov. G. Mennen Williams of Michigan, Sen. Paul H. Douglas of Illinois and Sen. Herbert H. Lehman of New York to insert a pledge to "carry out" the Court's decisions, was defeated by voice vote on the convention floor.

On the Republican side from Feb. 29, when Eisenhower announced he would seek a second term, there was no visible opposition to his renomination. Senate minority leader William F. Knowland, R-Calif., had previously announced his "provisional" candidacy, if Eisenhower were not to run, but he quickly withdrew it. The president swept all the primaries where his name was entered.

With the GOP presidential nomination a foregone conclusion, interest centered on the Republican vice presidential nomination. Eisenhower declined to make an early clear-cut endorsement of Richard M. Nixon for renomination as vice president and was reported to have suggested to Nixon that he consider a cabinet assignment or another government post, if Nixon planned to seek the GOP presidential nomination at a later date.

Presidential disarmament adviser Harold E. Stassen on July 25 attempted to spark a "stop Nixon" movement, claiming that Nixon's presence on the ticket might cost Eisenhower as much as 6 percent of the vote in the fall and endanger Republican congressional campaigns. No major Republican leaders came forward to support Stassen and the stop-Nixon move quickly faded. At Eisenhower's request Stassen actually ended by making a seconding speech for Nixon at the convention, which met in San Francisco Aug. 20-23.

The convention adopted without dissent a platform pledging a "continuation of peace, prosperity and progress." Threatened opposition to the civil rights plank evaporated after the Resolutions Committee modified an earlier and "stronger" version and proposed a plank acceptable to both Northern and Southern delegates.

The attack on Egypt and uprisings in Hungary and Poland dominated the news during the last weeks of the 1956 campaign, eclipsing domestic issues and changing the emphasis in international policy debates.

Early in the campaign Eisenhower boasted that his administration had offered, "in all levels of government," an "honest" regime of "good judgment," "tolerance" and "conciliation." The voters were asked to reelect him in order to keep the country "going down the straight road of prosperity and peace." Vice President Nixon, answering Democratic criticisms of Eisenhower administration foreign policy, said the families of "157,000 Americans who were killed, wounded or missing in Korea" could testify "whether we have peace today." Nixon said "the great majority of the American people have enjoyed the best four years of their lives under the Eisenhower Administration."

Stevenson's first approach was to challenge the effectiveness of Eisenhower's executive leadership, putting forth his own gospel of "the New America" under a Democratic Party that "can build as we have to build." He criticized the administration for failing to pass school aid legislation and other vitally needed domestic programs. He said the administration had "pilloried innocent men and women under the pretense of conducting loyalty and security investigations."

The tone of the campaign began to change as debate mounted over Stevenson's proposals to end the draft and stop U.S. testing of hydrogen bombs. The Stevenson proposal to end the draft drew the reply from Eisenhower that he saw "no chance of ending the draft and carrying out the responsibilities for the security of the country."

The debate was disturbed, however, by the beginning of the Hungarian uprising on Oct. 23 and the Israeli attack on Egypt on Oct. 29. Whatever the merits of the Stevenson proposals, they appeared to be badly timed in view of the international situation. Eisenhower again stressed that "we need our military draft for the safety of our nation" and that the country must have the "most advanced military weapons." With war threatening both in the Mideast and in Eastern Europe, the general public reaction seemed to be that it was a bad time to change leaders, especially considering the president's military background.

Results of the 1956 Elections

President Eisenhower was reelected with the largest popular vote in history and a plurality second only to that of Franklin D. Roosevelt in 1936. Eisenhower came out with 35,590,472 votes (457 electoral votes) and Stevenson with 26,022,752 (73 electoral votes). Eisenhower's plurality was 9,567,720 votes.

In the North the president carried or ran unusually well in many urban areas formerly considered safe Democratic areas. More blacks voted Republican than in any election since pre-New Deal days. The only states where Eisenhower pluralities dropped from 1952 were several farm states where Secretary of Agriculture Ezra Taft Benson and administration agricultural policies were highly unpopular.

The presidential election did not have the necessary coattail effect to give Republicans control of Congress. Although the returns indicated Ike's tremendous popularity with voters, the outcome for other offices made it clear that most citizens still identified their interests with those of the Democratic Party. For the first time since 1848 the winning presidential candidate was unable to carry at least one house of Congress for his party.

The Democrats amazingly maintained their 49-47 lead in the Senate, taking Republican seats in Colorado, Idaho, Ohio and Pennsylvania to make up for their losses in New York, West Virginia and Kentucky. Democratic senator Wayne Morse, the man whom the Republicans had wanted most to defeat, won over former secretary of the interior Douglas McKay. Newly elected senators included Thruston B. Morton, R-Ky.; Joseph S. Clark, D-Pa.; Jacob K. Javits, R-N.Y.; Frank Church, D-Idaho; and Frank J. Lausche, D-Ohio.

In the House the Democrats added to the 29-seat margin they had achieved in 1954, bringing their ranks to 234 as against 201 Republicans.

The Democrats made a net gain of one new governorship for a new 28-20 balance in their favor. Important Democratic gubernatorial victories included two in normally Republican farm states: Herschel C. Loveless in Iowa and George Docking in Kansas. Other Democrats winning previously held Republican governorships were Foster Furcolo in Massachusetts and Robert D. Holmes in Oregon. Republicans winning Democratic gubernatorial seats were C. William O'Neill in Ohio, Cecil Underwood in West Virginia and Edwin L. Mechem in New Mexico.

1957-59:
The 85th Congress

The first two years of Eisenhower's second term in office were marked by two major events, one domestic and one foreign, in the fall of 1957.

On Sept. 4 a controversy over admission of black students to the previously all-white Central High School in Little Rock, Arkansas, reached a showdown as the National Guard, ordered out by Gov. Orval Faubus, prevented the black students from entering the school. A federal court on Sept. 21 ordered removal of the National Guard. But when the black students reentered the school two days later, they were ordered to leave by local authorities because of fear of mob violence. Eisenhower then ordered federal troops sent into Little Rock to enforce the court's order, and the school began operation on an integrated basis.

The spectacle of angry, racist crowds in the face of fixed bayonets rioting to prevent black children from entering the school shocked the world. The scene was offset in part by the use of federal troops to enforce the constitutional rights of U.S. citizens. Throughout the South, however, the reaction was one of bitterness toward Eisenhower for using troops to enforce a deeply resented Supreme Court decision.

The second major event in the fall of 1957 was the Soviet Union's successful launching, on Oct. 4, of the first manufactured satellite, Sputnik I, into an orbit around the world. Congress and the nation responded with anger, frustration and alarm, directed chiefly at the Eisenhower administration because it had not pressed the U.S. effort to beat the Soviets into outer space and because it showed, at least initially, little concern about the Soviet achievement. More profound concern developed about the quality of U.S. education, especially in scientific fields. The first successful U.S. satellite, Explorer I, was launched by the Army from Cape Canaveral, Florida, on Jan. 31, 1958.

Other major international events in 1957 and 1958 were the following:

● On March 25, 1957, the Common Market (European Economic Community) and Euratom (European Atomic Energy Community) treaties among six Western European powers were signed in Rome. (The countries were France, Belgium, Netherlands, Luxembourg, Italy and West Germany.) These treaties were significant steps toward the U.S.-supported goal of a united Europe.

● Vice President and Mrs. Nixon narrowly escaped injury from Communist-inspired riots while on a good-will tour in Caracas, Venezuela, on May 13, 1957.

● Great Britain exploded its first hydrogen bomb, May 15, 1957.

● Former premier Georgii M. Malenkov, former foreign minister V. M. Molotov and L. M. Kaganovich were purged by the Soviet Presidium under Nikita Khrushchev's leadership, July 3-4, 1957, for alleged pro-Stalinist activities. On March 27, 1958, Chairman Khrushchev completed solidification of power by succeeding Nikolai A. Bulganin as premier.

● Charles de Gaulle became head of the French government on June 1, 1958, averting threatened civil war.

● At the request of the Lebanese government, U.S. Marines were dispatched to Lebanon on July 15, 1958, to forestall a threatened effort by Egyptian president Gamal Abdel Nasser's United Arab Republic and the Soviet Union to overthrow Lebanon's pro-Western regime. U.S. troops withdrew in August after calm was restored.

● In the fall of 1958 the United States and the Soviet Union began a three-and-one-half-year unpoliced moratorium on nuclear weapons tests.

Major domestic events included the development of the most serious postwar recession, in mid-1957 lasting through 1958; a stroke suffered by President Eisenhower Nov. 25, 1957, from which he was pronounced "completely recovered" on March 1, 1958; and the resignation of Sherman Adams, assistant to the president. Adams' resignation in Sept. 1958 followed revelations before a House subcommittee that he had interceded with various federal agencies in behalf of his friend, Boston industrialist Bernard Goldfine, and that he had received gifts from Goldfine. The Goldfine-Adams episode hurt the Eisenhower administration on the corruption-in-government issue and was one of several elements contributing to the Democratic sweep in the 1958 congressional and gubernatorial elections.

The 85th Congress established a record of moderate productivity, all its chief enactments bearing the "middle-of-the-road" stamp that was the natural result of compromise between a "mildly conservative" president and the "mildly liberal" congressional leadership of House Speaker Sam Rayburn and Senate majority leader Lyndon B. Johnson, both of Texas.

The mounting recession pushed the federal budget increasingly into the red, with a $2.8 billion deficit in fiscal 1958 and a $12.4 billion deficit for the fiscal 1959 budget, approved in mid-1958.

In foreign policy the Senate in 1957 approved the International Atomic Energy treaty (stemming from President Eisenhower's Atoms for Peace program). During its first session Congress approved the Mideast Resolution (Eisenhower Doctrine), in response to the president's request for advance authority to use U.S. troops to protect free Middle East nations from "overt armed aggression" by "power hungry Communists." During the second session Congress acceded readily to the president's request for authority to extend financial aid and technical assistance to the newly formed European Atomic Energy Community.

A military reorganization bill was approved by Congress in 1958. This bill eliminated the "separately administered" provision for Army, Navy and Air Force written into the

1947 National Security Act and made it clear that the three military departments were to operate under the direction and control of the secretary of defense. Legislation passed in July 1958 established a civilian-controlled National Aeronautics and Space Administration. Both houses organized permanent standing committees on space matters.

The major domestic bill passed in 1957 was the Civil Rights Act. The bill created the executive Commission on Civil Rights and empowered the attorney general to seek injunctions when individuals are denied the right to vote. With strengthening amendments in succeeding years, this legislation gave more and more black citizens the power of the ballot, viewed by the bill's advocates as the foundation of most other civil liberties.

The most notable accomplishment of Congress' 1958 session was passage and signature by the president of the Alaska statehood bill, culminating decades of pressure to admit the territory to the Union.

Other important actions of the second session included emergency housing and highway construction legislation to help stem the recession; passage of the National Defense Education Act of 1958, including $295 million for loans to needy college students; the Transportation Act of 1958, designed to revive the failing railroads; and passage of a low-support farm bill with few controls generally in line with administration proposals.

Under the leadership of Democratic national chairman Paul M. Butler, a policy-making Democratic Advisory Committee was organized in November 1956 and became the chief voice for the militantly liberal Democratic point of view. It made sharp partisan attacks on the Eisenhower administration. Democratic congressional leaders Rayburn and Johnson had been asked to join but instead actively opposed it, expressing a preference for policy formulation through regular Democratic congressional leadership channels. Many of the committee's statements reflected severe criticism of the Democratic congressional leadership for alleged lack of sufficiently aggressive opposition to the Eisenhower administration. (The committee was eventually abolished in March 1961 after the Democratic takeover of the executive office. The new Democratic National Chairman, John M. Bailey, said the committee had "served a function" only when the party was out of power.)

The 1958 Midterm Elections

The swing of the political pendulum against the Republicans and in favor of the Democrats was apparent as early as mid-1957. It ended Nov. 25, 1958, with a clean Democratic sweep in Alaska's first election as a state. The over-all national result was the most thorough Democratic victory since the Roosevelt landslide year of 1936.

In August 1957 Democrat William Proxmire easily won the Wisconsin Senate seat of the late Republican senator Joseph R. McCarthy, who had died May 2 of the same year. In the November 1957 off-year elections the Democrats reelected New Jersey Democratic governor Robert B. Meyner by a plurality of nearly 200,000 votes, also scoring important victories in Virginia and New York. In the Sept. 8, 1958, Maine elections the Democrats swept that normally Republican state, electing a Democratic governor, a Democratic senator and two Democratic representatives.

The Republicans began the 1958 campaign with a number of handicaps. The Adams-Goldfine incident had been a source of profound embarrassment for the Eisenhower administration, only partly relieved by Adams' resignation in September. Although recovery from the 1957-58 recession was already under way, the recession had served to weaken seriously voter confidence in the Eisenhower prosperity formula. Another crisis in the Formosa Strait, with renewed Communist shelling of Quemoy and Matsu, reminded voters that the administration had yet to find a solution for the China problem. Sputnik had weakened voter confidence in the Eisenhower administration's defense and space programs.

In many states the Republicans backed ballot initiative proposals for right-to-work laws that were bitterly opposed by organized labor. This inspired labor to work particularly hard to get its members out to vote: against right-to-work and for Democrats. A major portion of the blame for Republican debacles in states such as Ohio and California was attributed to GOP right-to-work stands. Still another incident harming the Republicans was deep Southern resentment against Eisenhower's ordering of paratroops into Little Rock in 1957. This effectively curtailed Republican efforts for new inroads in the South.

In the campaign the Democrats charged that the Republicans had callously allowed the country to slip into a serious recession, showing little regard for the interests of the unemployed. Adlai Stevenson on Oct. 18 said that the crises over Quemoy, desegregation, education and recession "could have been avoided if we had an administration which thought in advance instead of waiting placidly on the fairways until the mortal danger is upon us and then angrily calling out the Marines." "The tragedy of the Eisenhower Administration," Stevenson said, "is that its only weapons seem to be platitudes or paratroops."

Alarmed by the apparent Democratic inroads, the Republicans held an Oct. 6 White House strategy session that produced a manifesto declaring that if a new Democratic Congress were elected, "we are certain to go down the left lane which leads inseparably to socialism." In Baltimore, on Oct. 31, Eisenhower used such terms as "political free spenders," "gloomdoggler," and "extremist" to describe his Democratic opponents.

House Speaker Rayburn on Nov. 1 predicted that a new Democratic-controlled Congress would not fight the president despite "desperation" oratory in which Rayburn said Eisenhower went "pretty far in accusing us of being radicals and left-wingers." Rayburn said that "in the past about 85 percent of the time Eisenhower's programs were just an extension of Democratic principles.... We're not going to hate Eisenhower bad enough for us to change our principles."

Much of the hard campaigning for Republican candidates throughout the country was done by Vice President Nixon. On Oct. 21 Nixon said that the Democratic Party was split between "essentially moderate" Democratic leaders in Congress and the group "which presently controls the Democratic National Committee, which is radical in its approach to economic problems (and) bitterly partisan in its criticism of the Eisenhower foreign policy."

As the campaign progressed, the Republicans came under increasingly heavy Democratic fire for being anti-labor. Eisenhower and Nixon refused to endorse the right-to-work laws, but the president called for legislation to let workers "free themselves of their corrupt labor bosses who have betrayed their trust."

In reply to the potent Democratic "missile gap" issue of allegedly slow U.S. progress in rockets and missiles, Eisenhower repeatedly declared that no more than $1 million had been spent on development of long-range missiles in any year before he became president, but that "the so-called missile gap is being rapidly filled."

Results of the 1958 Elections

As election returns poured in during the evening of Nov. 4, it was clear that the Democratic tide had engulfed Republicans in virtually every area of the nation. Including the Nov. 25 Alaska election, the results showed a new Senate of 64 Democrats and 34 Republicans, a Democratic gain of 15 seats and a Republican loss of 13 from the 49-47 Democratic edge in 1956. Democrats gained seats in California (where Republicans were embroiled in internecine fights and the right-to-work issue), Connecticut, Indiana, Maine, Michigan, Minnesota, Nevada, New Jersey, Ohio, Utah, West Virginia (two seats) and Wyoming and took the two new seats from Alaska.

The new Democratic senators included Eugene J. McCarthy of Minnesota, Thomas J. Dodd of Connecticut, Clair Engle of California and Harrison A. Williams Jr. of New Jersey. New Republicans elected to the Senate were Kenneth B. Keating of New York and Hugh Scott of Pennsylvania.

In the House there were 282 Democrats, 48 more than the previous Congress' total and the highest figure since the 1936 elections. Republicans slipped from 201 to 154 seats. Republican House losses were heaviest in the Midwest, where 23 seats were lost (many in the traditional Republican heartland), and in the East, where 20 were lost. Only two incumbent Democratic House members were defeated: Rep. Coya Knutson of Minnesota, evidently as a result of her marital difficulties, and Rep. Brooks Hays of Arkansas, a moderate on racial issues defeated on a write-in vote by Dale Alford, a Democratic archsegregationist in Arkansas's 5th (Little Rock) District.

In gubernatorial races there was a net switch of five governorships, plus the new Alaska governorship, to the Democrats for a new total of 35 Democratic and 14 Republican governors. Important Democratic gubernatorial victories included Edmund G. Brown in California (over Senate minority leader William F. Knowland); Michael V. DiSalle, Ohio; Ralph G. Brooks, Nebraska; Ralph Herseth, South Dakota; Gaylord A. Nelson, Wisconsin; and J. Millard Tawes, Maryland. Democrats also reelected Gov. Abraham A. Ribicoff in Connecticut by a record majority and re-elected Democratic governor George Docking in traditionally Republican Kansas.

The brightest spot in the entire picture for the Republicans was Nelson A. Rockefeller's New York victory over incumbent governor Averell Harriman by a 573,034-vote margin. Republicans also won the Oregon governorship with Mark Hatfield and the Rhode Island governorship with Christopher Del Sesto.

1959-61:
The 86th Congress

Relations between the United States and the Soviet Union dominated the international news, running the gamut from cordial to extremely bitter during 1959-60.

In November 1958 Soviet premier Nikita S. Khrushchev had demanded an end to the four-power occupation of Berlin and threatened to turn control of Allied supply lines to West Berlin over to East Germany, asking that Berlin be made into a demilitarized "free city." The Soviet Union set May 27, 1959, as the deadline for the end of the occupation of Berlin. An international crisis, threatening atomic war, appeared to develop over the ensuing months. But when the Big Four foreign ministers sat down for consultations in Paris the following May, the Soviet deadline had been lifted and no changes in the Berlin status quo evolved.

Meanwhile, President Eisenhower had lost his key foreign policy adviser when Secretary of State John Foster Dulles was stricken by cancer early in 1959. Dulles resigned by April 15 and died on May 24. Under Secretary Christian A. Herter, former Massachusetts congressman and governor, succeeded Dulles.

A period of moderation in U.S.-Soviet relations followed. Vice President Richard Nixon on July 22 left for a 13-day tour of the Soviet Union. Nixon received a friendly reception by Russian crowds. In September, at Eisenhower's invitation, Khrushchev visited the United States for consultations with the president and a transcontinental tour. But the 1959 "spirit of Camp David" failed to result in a lasting thaw in the cold war.

In May 1960, just before a scheduled Big Four summit conference in Paris, the Soviet Union announced that an American plane had been shot down over its territory. The United States at first said no violation of Soviet air space had been intended. After Khrushchev revealed that the pilot of the U-2 reconnaissance plane had confessed being on an intelligence-gathering flight for the U.S. Central Intelligence Agency, Secretary of State Herter admitted that the United States had engaged in "extensive aerial surveillance of the USSR." President Eisenhower took full responsibility for the flights, terming them a "distasteful but vital necessity."

When the Big Four met May 16, Khrushchev denounced the "spy flight" and demanded a U.S. apology and punishment of responsible officials before the summit conference could continue. He withdrew an already-accepted invitation to Eisenhower to visit the Soviet Union in June 1960. Eisenhower said the flights had been discontinued and would not begin again, but he refused to accept Khrushchev's ultimatum. The conference collapsed, and leaders withdrew to their capitals amid mutual recriminations.

The incident weakened the confidence of many voters in the Republicans' skill in handling foreign affairs. Some observers later speculated that if there had been no U-2 incident, and if the summit conference and the Eisenhower trip to the Soviet Union had proceeded as planned, the country might have been in no mood to replace the Republican hold on the White House in the November elections.

Other important international developments in 1959 and 1960 included the following:

● Fidel Castro assumed power in Cuba after collapse of the Batista dictatorship on Jan. 1, 1959. Communist influence and control over the Castro revolution became increasingly evident in the succeeding years.

● A revolt by the Tibetan people against Chinese Communist rule was crushed in March 1959.

● Eisenhower made good-will visits to Europe, Asia and Africa in December 1959, to Latin America in February-March 1960, and to the Far East in early summer 1960. Leftist riots in Japan protesting the new U.S.-Japanese treaty of mutual security and cooperation forced Eisenhower to cancel plans to include that country in his Far Eastern Tour.

● The French tested their first nuclear device in the Sahara, Feb. 13, 1960.

● The Belgian Congo gained independence, becoming the Republic of the Congo on June 30, 1960; soon thereafter the country was plunged into civil war, resulting in UN intervention in July 1960.

On the domestic front heavy Democratic majorities in the 86th Congress failed to produce the kind of prolabor, liberal legislation for which many observers had seen a mandate in the 1958 election returns. The two major accomplishments of Congress—Hawaiian statehood and a labor reform law—were in fact just as much administration as Democratic bills.

Statehood for Hawaii, signed into law March 18, 1959, after 59 years of territorial status for the one-time island kingdom, added a 50th state to the Union. The new state elected the nation's first two representatives of Chinese and Japanese ancestry: Sen. Hiram L. Fong, a Republican, and Rep. Daniel K. Inouye, a Democrat.

In the waning days of the 1959 session Congress passed a "strong" labor regulation law (the Landrum-Griffin bill), which contained major Taft-Hartley Act amendments favored by business and opposed by organized labor. The continuing exposure of union corruption and labor-management collusion by the Senate Select Committee on Improper Activities in the Labor or Management Field had produced a deluge of letters, telegrams and editorials calling for action.

The relatively mild Kennedy bill for labor regulation was passed by the Senate April 25. The House, on Aug. 13, by a 229-201 roll call, approved a tougher measure, the Landrum-Griffin bill, which incorporated important Taft-Hartley reforms sought by President Eisenhower. The vote was a major victory for Eisenhower and the House Republican leadership under the newly chosen minority leader, Charles A. Halleck, R-Ind. It was a defeat for House Speaker Sam Rayburn, who preferred a milder measure. Most of Landrum-Griffin was incorporated in the conference committee compromise.

Determined to prevent adoption of expensive domestic programs suggested by liberal Democrats, Eisenhower sought to dramatize the issue of "spending" in his press conferences and other public utterances. Grass-roots response was so positive that he was able to galvanize the Republican minority and invigorate the Republican-Southern Democratic coalition, preventing passage of most liberal measures and rallying sufficient strength to sustain his vetoes of all but a handful of those that did pass. Thus Democratic proposals for a wide program of aid for school construction and teachers' salaries, for a massive area redevelopment program, for an increased minimum wage and for medical care for the aged under Social Security all came to naught.

During 1960, however, the liberals found a new issue on which to base their call for increased social welfare legislation: the need for a rapid rate of growth in the national economy. The issue of economic growth developed too late to assist in passage of liberal measures in the 86th Congress, but it provided campaign fodder for Democratic nominee John F. Kennedy in the 1960 presidential campaign.

The failure of many important domestic bills to clear Congress was largely attributed to the continuing party division between the executive and legislative branches and the approaching presidential elections. In 1959, for instance, the Senate took time out for a long and bitter debate that ended in rejection of the president's nomination of Lewis L. Strauss to be secretary of commerce. In 1960 a $750 million pay raise for federal employees was passed over the president's veto. Scenting victory in the upcoming elections, Democrats refused to pass a bill creating 35 badly needed new federal judgeships.

After long debate over the "missile gap" and the general adequacy of the nation's defense effort, Congress passed the president's defense budget with few overall changes in 1959 but in 1960 added $600 million more than Eisenhower had requested. The missile gap became a major issue in the 1960 presidential campaign, only to recede as an apparent mirage early in 1961.

During the postconventions session of Congress that began Aug. 8, 1960, Democratic presidential candidate John F. Kennedy, a Massachusetts senator, and his running mate, Senate majority leader Lyndon B. Johnson, failed in their efforts to complete action on major Democratic legislation planks. The Senate approved the Kennedy minimum wage bill, but the measure died when House conferees refused to budge from their own truncated version. Medical care for the aged under the Social Security system—a second "must" bill—was rejected by the Senate, and a school construction bill expired when the House Rules Committee refused to send it to conference. As Congress adjourned Sept. 1 and the campaign began in earnest, Republicans made the most of their opponents' plight.

The 1960 Campaigns

The 22nd Amendment to the Constitution, placing a two-term limitation on the presidency, meant that Eisenhower was ineligible to seek reelection in 1960. Adlai E. Stevenson's record of two defeats for the presidency appeared to preclude him from choice as the Democrats' candidate, barring a convention deadlock. Thus both parties were faced with the prospect of coming up with new nominees in 1960. For the Republicans the choice appeared relatively easy since Vice President Richard Nixon had been in the public eye for eight full years. Nixon had been an extremely active vice president, he was a tireless campaigner for GOP candidates, and he had strong support in Republican organizations throughout the country. For the Democrats the choice was more difficult because no members of the party had clearly established themselves as leaders of presidential stature.

In a departure from the American tendency to select governors for presidential nominees, all four chief contenders for the Democratic nomination were senators. In order of their announcements they were Hubert H. Humphrey of Minnesota, John F. Kennedy of Massachusetts, Stuart Symington of Missouri and Majority Leader Lyndon B. Johnson of Texas. Of these four only Kennedy and Humphrey chose to campaign in the primaries. In the end the primaries were the decisive factor in Kennedy's victory.

Symington dismissed primary contests as useless and Johnson maintained that he could not carry out his Senate duties properly and simultaneously run in numerous individual primaries. (CQ 1960 Senate Voting Participation scores showed an average of 80 percent for all Democrats. Kennedy scored 35 percent, Humphrey 49 percent; both campaigned extensively during the session. Symington scored 58 percent, and Johnson, 95 percent.)

The issue of Kennedy's religion dominated much of the preconvention and general-election debate and speculation about his chances. Not since 1928, when the Democrats nominated Alfred E. Smith of New York for the presidency, had a Roman Catholic headed a national ticket. Smith had been resoundingly defeated, with many normally Democratic but heavily Protestant states going against him, although other considerations than religion, perhaps equally important, ran against Smith. In the intervening years Roman Catholics had become a far larger segment of the population than before (16 percent in 1928; 22.8 percent by 1960, with especially large concentrations in the urban areas in the biggest states). The consensus was that the nation had become far more tolerant in its religious outlook.

The spring primaries produced a string of unbroken victories for Kennedy. Unopposed, he piled up an impressive 43,372 vote total in the early-bird New Hampshire primary March 8. In May Humphrey withdrew after the West Virginia primary, leaving Symington and Johnson as opponents for Kennedy. Just before the convention it appeared that Stevenson might reenter the race.

At the Democratic National Convention, which opened in Los Angeles on July 11, Kennedy won on the first ballot. After conferring with Democratic leaders, he announced that Lyndon B. Johnson would be his running mate. Most observers were surprised that Johnson, powerful Senate majority leader and almost 10 years Kennedy's senior, would accept the nomination. Most party liberals expressed consternation at Kennedy's selection. Later it became evident that Johnson's presence on the ticket was probably an essential element in holding most of the South behind Kennedy and achieving Democratic victory in one of the closest presidential elections in U.S. history.

Without any significant opposition, Nixon breezed through the primaries and at the Republican National Convention was nominated July 27, receiving 1,321 votes to 10 for Barry Goldwater. He selected UN ambassador and former Massachusetts senator Henry Cabot Lodge as his running mate.

By election day, Nov. 8, Kennedy had covered 75,000 miles and visited 46 states, while Nixon had traveled more than 60,000 miles and appeared in all 50 states. Speaking as often as a dozen times a day, both candidates were seen and heard by millions of voters, in person as well as on radio and television, in what may have been the most talkative as well as the most expensive campaign on record.

The central issue, Kennedy asserted time and again, was the need for strong presidential leadership to reverse the nation's declining prestige abroad and lagging economy at home. Arguing that the position of the United States relative to that of the Soviets had deteriorated under the Eisenhower administration, he called for a stepped-up defense effort and an enlarged federal role in a wide variety of fields at home and abroad "to get America moving again."

In an unprecedented series of face-to-face encounters, candidates Kennedy and Nixon appeared on four nationally televised, hour-long programs during which they were questioned by panels of journalists and permitted to rebut each other's answers. The time was provided free of charge by the networks when Congress suspended the equal time provision of the Communications Act for the duration of the 1960 campaign. The audiences for the four debates were estimated by the Arbitron rating service at 70 to 75 million, 61 million, 65 million and 64 million, respectively.

Republicans generally were dismayed by Nixon's appearance on the first debate, blaming it on poor lighting and their candidate's unaggressive stance, but they found little fault with the remaining three programs. Democrats regarded all the debates as highly successful on grounds that they served to demolish the GOP theme of Kennedy's "immaturity" and to project his personality to millions of undecided voters, many of whom were disturbed by his Catholic faith.

Results of the 1960 Elections

On election day 68,838,219 Americans—the largest number in history—cast ballots for president. Kennedy emerged the victor with a solid majority in the Electoral College. But his popular-vote plurality over Nixon was only 118,574 votes, the smallest vote margin of the 20th century. In 11 states—eight won by Kennedy, three by Nixon—a shift of less than 1 percent of the vote would have switched the state's electoral votes.

The Kennedy-Johnson ticket carried 23 states with 303 electoral votes. They put together a coalition of Eastern states (including New York, Pennsylvania and New Jersey), central industrial states (Illinois, Michigan and Minnesota) and several of the traditionally Democratic Southern states (including Johnson's own Texas) that was sufficient to win, despite loss of almost the entire West and farm belt and several Southern states.

Democrats maintained their heavy majorities in Congress and among the nation's governors in 1960, but Republicans were able to make some important gains, especially in the House of Representatives. Republican gains, taking place in the face of a victory for Democratic candidate Kennedy, appeared due in part to the return of normally Republican seats to the GOP to offset the serious losses suffered by Republicans in the 1958 Democratic sweep.

The continued heavy Democratic congressional majority, especially in the Senate, made it appear unlikely that Republicans would be able to regain control of Congress at any time during President-elect Kennedy's first term in the White House.

The Republicans made a gain of two Senate seats, replacing Democrats in Delaware and Wyoming. Despite advance predictions of possible trouble for Republican Senate incumbents in Massachusetts and New Jersey, both were able to withstand the Kennedy tide in those states. Democrats held their seats in Minnesota, Missouri, Michigan and Montana, where Republican challengers ran energetic campaigns. The new Senate balance was 64 Democrats and 36 Republicans.

The Republican Senate gain was reduced when Senator-elect Keith Thomson, R-Wyo., died on Dec. 9 and was replaced by Democrat J. J. Hickey. But the Senate balance returned to 64-36 in May 1961, when Republican John Tower won the Texas Senate seat vacated by Lyndon B. Johnson, the new vice president.

In House elections Republicans made a net gain of 20 seats. The new House had 263 Democrats and 174 Republicans, as compared to a 283-154 balance in the previous Congress.

In contrast to most presidential elections, the victory of the national Democratic ticket did not appear to play an important part in most congressional contests. If Kennedy coattails existed at all, they were probably evident in New York State, which he carried by a wide margin and where three incumbent GOP congressmen were defeated; in Connecticut, where Democrats held two close seats; and in New Jersey, where one Republican seat went Democratic. All other Democratic House gains appeared to be the result of special local conditions.

The most important Republican congressional gains came in the Midwest, where Nixon ran a strong race. Widespread and deep-seated anti-Catholic sentiment, combined with a marked cooling off of the farm issue, which hurt midwestern Republicans so badly in 1958, appeared to form the basis of much of the increased Republican Midwestern strength in both presidential and local races.

Many Republican gains, through Midwestern farm states but also in Connecticut, Maine, Ohio, Vermont, Oregon and Pennsylvania, seemed to mark the return to the GOP fold of traditionally Republican congressional districts,

Members of Congress Who Became President

From James Madison to George Bush, 24 presidents have served previously in the House of Representatives, or the Senate, or both.

Following is a list of these presidents and the chambers in which they served. Three other presidents — George Washington, John Adams and Thomas Jefferson — had served in the Continental Congress, as had James Madison and James Monroe.

James A. Garfield was elected to the Senate in January 1880 for a term beginning March 4, 1881, but declined to accept in December 1880 because he had been elected president. John Quincy Adams served in the House for 17 years after his term as president, and Andrew Johnson returned to the Senate five months before he died.

House Only

James Madison
James K. Polk
Millard Fillmore
Abraham Lincoln
Rutherford B. Hayes
James A. Garfield
William McKinley
Gerald R. Ford
George Bush

Senate Only

James Monroe
John Quincy Adams
Martin Van Buren
Benjamin Harrison
Warren G. Harding
Harry S. Truman

Both Chambers

Andrew Jackson
William Henry Harrison
John Tyler
Franklin Pierce
James Buchanan

Andrew Johnson
John F. Kennedy
Lyndon B. Johnson
Richard Nixon

Sources: *Biographical Directory of the United States Congress, 1774-1989.* Washington, D.C.: Government Printing Office, 1989; *American Leaders 1789-1994.* Washington, D.C.: Congressional Quarterly Inc., 1994.

which had gone Democratic in 1958 in a temporary protest against Republican policies.

In gubernatorial races the Democrats captured seven seats from the Republicans, and the Republicans captured six from the Democrats. The new lineup was 34 Democrats to 16 Republicans, a net gain of one for the Democrats. Among the governors elected were Democrats Otto Kerner of Illinois, Matthew E. Welsh of Indiana, John B. Swainson of Michigan and Frank B. Morrison of Nebraska. Republican governors elected included John A. Volpe of Massachusetts, Elmer L. Andersen of Minnesota, Norman A. Erbe of Iowa and John Anderson Jr. of Kansas.

1961-63: The 87th Congress

Hopes were high, both in America and abroad, when John F. Kennedy took office as president Jan. 20, 1961. In his inaugural address Kennedy called on Americans and all free people "to bear the burden of a long twilight struggle . . .

against the common enemies of man: tyranny, poverty, disease and war itself." Kennedy urged Americans: "Ask not what your country can do for you—ask what you can do for your country."

Some of this idealism was translated into specific programs and action during the next two years. A Peace Corps was established, sending young Americans to underdeveloped nations, to provide trained personnel for development projects. Fulfilling another campaign promise, Kennedy got congressional approval of a U.S. Arms Control and Disarmament Agency. On March 14, 1961, the president announced an Alliance for Progress with the countries of Latin America, under which the United States would step up aid to the other Americas but expect to see political and social reforms to guarantee true democracy and promote stability and progress in those countries.

In the domestic field several items of "liberal" legislation that had failed passage because of a stalemate between President Eisenhower and a Democratic Congress were enacted into law. Chief among these were a hike in the minimum wage to $1.25, a subsidy program for economically distressed areas in the United States, widening of Social Security benefits, a $4.88 billion omnibus housing bill, stepped-up federal aid to localities to battle water pollution and a vastly increased public works program.

The first two years of Kennedy's term, however, contained disappointments, both foreign and domestic. In January 1961 the administration had high hopes of a period of relaxed tensions with the Soviet world. Congratulating Kennedy on his election, Soviet premier Nikita S. Khrushchev had expressed the "hope that while you are at this post the relations between our countries will again follow the line along which they were developing in Franklin Roosevelt's time." Khrushchev made specific mention of chances for early conclusion of a nuclear test ban treaty and a German peace treaty. During the first week of Kennedy's presidency the Soviet government freed two U.S. Air Force RB-47 pilots who had been held in the USSR since their plane was downed off Soviet shores in July 1960. But the optimism of January 1961 seemed more like overconfidence by late 1961 as the tide of events continued to run almost consistently against the nation's foreign policy objectives.

On April 17, 1961, 1,200 Cuban refugees—recruited, trained and supplied by the U.S. Central Intelligence Agency—landed 90 miles south of Havana; their announced goal was to overthrow the Communist-oriented regime of Fidel Castro. Within three days the invasion had been crushed, inflicting a disastrous blow to American prestige and to that of the new president.

Kennedy met with Khrushchev June 3-4, 1961, in Vienna. At this summit conference Khrushchev made clear his determination to sign a peace treaty with the East German Communist regime, a move long interpreted in the West as part of the effort to force the Western powers out of West Berlin. The Vienna confrontation convinced Kennedy that it was time to muster public support in behalf of a "firm stand" in Berlin. In a July 25 televised report to the nation, he called for an immediate buildup of U.S. and NATO forces along with an extra $3.5 billion in U.S. defense funds. Congress promptly granted his requests.

Khrushchev's reply was to threaten Soviet mobilization and to boast that the Soviets could build a hundred-megaton nuclear warhead. Much more damaging to the West, however, was the Communists' unexpected action on Aug. 13 in sealing off the border between East and West Berlin. The wall virtually stopped the large flow of refugees from East to West that had bled the Communist regime of much of its most valuable personnel during the postwar years.

Adding immeasurably to the tension over Berlin was the Soviet announcement on Aug. 30, 1961, that it would break the three-year voluntary moratorium on testing of nuclear weapons because of the "ever increasing aggressiveness of the policy of the NATO military bloc." The Soviet test series began Sept. 1 and concluded in Nov. 1961. Their tests completed, the Soviets returned to the test ban negotiations in Geneva on Nov. 28. The United States, however, refused to reimpose an uncontrolled moratorium on itself and, between April 25 and Nov. 4, 1962, carried out a series of tests underground and in the atmosphere.

Two Southeast Asian nations, Laos and Vietnam, were thorny problems for the new administration. Fearful that a Communist takeover of Laos would make the Western position in Vietnam untenable, the administration supported establishment of a "neutral" government in Laos, in the hope that the tiny kingdom could serve as a buffer. In Vietnam increased Communist guerrilla activity forced increased commitment of U.S. military "advisers," who soon found themselves in the thick of military engagements.

Cuba, however, remained the chief foreign policy problem of the administration. The Castro regime became increasingly identified as a Soviet satellite and was expelled from the Organization of American States. During the summer of 1962 Soviet arms began to pour into Cuba. On Oct. 22 President Kennedy told the American people in a radio-television address that U.S. aerial surveillance of the Soviet military buildup in Cuba had produced "unmistakable evidence" that "a series of offensive missile sites is now in preparation on that imprisoned island. The purpose of these bases can be none other than to provide a nuclear strike capacity against the Western Hemisphere."

As countermeasures the president announced "a strict quarantine on all offensive military equipment under shipment to Cuba" and said that U.S. ships would begin checking incoming shipments to the island. He called on the Soviet leader to withdraw his offensive weapons from Cuba.

For several days the Soviets continued preparation of their missile sites, and the world wondered whether it might be plunged into war. On Oct. 27 Khrushchev, apparently unwilling to take the ultimate risk, sent a note to Kennedy in which he agreed to remove the offensive weapons systems from Cuba under UN observation and supervision in return for removal of the U.S. quarantine and agreement not to launch an invasion of the islands.

In succeeding weeks the removal of the bases took place at a relatively rapid rate. Castro, however, blocked UN inspection, and the United States never formalized its agreement not to invade Cuba. Thousands of Soviet troops and technical personnel remained on the island, along with a heavy array of "defensive" weapons.

Kennedy's chief domestic problem during his first two years in office was the lagging condition of the U.S. economy. The new administration made clear its commitment to a general monetary and fiscal policy aimed at the inducement of economic growth, even at the price of heavy federal budget deficits. Federal expenditures rose from $81.5 billion in fiscal 1961 to $87.8 billion in fiscal 1962 and $94.3 billion in estimated figures for fiscal 1963. The federal deficit rose from $3.8 billion in 1961 to $6.4 billion in 1962 and dropped slightly to $6.2 billion for fiscal 1963.

Aided in part by the sharply increased federal expenditures under Kennedy, the 1960 recession tapered off by mid-1961. But the basic underlying problems remained.

Although President Kennedy had himself served in the House for six years and in the Senate for eight, relations between his administration and Congress were far from ideal. The change in Democratic leadership in both houses, some congressional apprehension about use of political power by the new administration and a continuing "conservative coalition" between Republicans and Southern Democrats all tended to slow down if not wreck parts of the Kennedy program.

Most apparent and serious was the shift in leadership. The elevation of Lyndon B. Johnson to the vice presidency removed one of the strongest majority leaders in the history of the Senate. He was succeeded by Sen. Mike Mansfield, D-Mont., a mild-mannered man who lacked Johnson's drive.

On Nov. 16, 1961, House Speaker Sam Rayburn, D-Texas, died of cancer. Rayburn had been a member of the House for almost 49 years and had served as Speaker for 17 years (twice interrupted by brief periods of Republican majorities). Any successor would have faced difficulties in filling the shoes of "Mr. Sam," a man who understood the House and, until his later years, could draw together the disparate elements of his party with remarkable success. John W. McCormack of Massachusetts, elevated from the majority leadership to be Speaker, faced the unenviable task of succeeding Rayburn. His first year in office was considered a qualified success.

The 87th Congress ended on an acrimonious note. A year-long feud between the House and Senate on procedural issues regarding appropriation bills was symptomatic of a broader rift between the two chambers that had been growing for several years. The dispute held up several fund bills for months (well beyond July 1, the start of the new fiscal year) and helped prolong the 1962 session to Oct. 13. Not since the Korean War year of 1951 had a session lasted until so late in the autumn.

During the ensuing months increasing discussion was heard of the need to modernize and streamline congressional procedures.

The 1962 Midterm Elections

The Kennedy administration entered the 1962 campaign determined to reinforce the narrow margin by which the president had been elected in 1960 and to prevent serious losses in Democratic congressional strength. The off-year elections of 1961 had produced mixed results. In a May 1961 special election in Texas the Democrats had lost the Senate seat vacated by Vice President Johnson to Republican John Tower. Not since Reconstruction days had Texas sent a Republican to the Senate.

But in the November 1961 elections, Democrat Richard J. Hughes, aided by a personal appearance on his behalf by President Kennedy, won the New Jersey governorship against no less an opponent than Republican James P. Mitchell, secretary of labor in the Eisenhower administration.

Mayor Robert F. Wagner, a political ally of the president, easily won reelection in New York City. The administration felt confident that with sufficient presidential campaigning, the party could fare well in the 1962 elections.

Kennedy set the tone for the 1962 battle in a July 23 press conference. Declaring that the congressional Republicans were almost wholly negative on domestic social legislation, he said that he would go all-out to defeat them in the fall campaign. Kennedy said a Democratic gain of one or two Senate seats and five or ten House seats would make it possible to enact controversial administration bills in such fields as Medicare, public works, mass transit and urban affairs. He said the 1962 elections would give the American people a "clear" choice: to "anchor down" by voting Republican or to "sail" by voting Democratic.

In midsummer the president began to make flying campaign trips to various states every weekend and some weekdays. Until halted by the Cuban crisis Oct. 20, the president's campaigning promised to be the most vigorous of any U.S. president in a midterm election. In every appearance he went down the line for all Democratic candidates. The president was accorded a warm personal reception in most cities, confirming the high degree of personal popularity with the people that had been recorded in Gallup polls. Whether his plea to elect "more Democrats" was making a serious impression remained in doubt, however.

By October public uneasiness over the Communist arms buildup in Cuba was growing. Republicans made a central campaign issue of Cuba, and most observers thought the GOP would make some gains. But the president's Oct. 22 announcement of a naval quarantine of Cuba and his ultimatum to Khrushchev blunted the Republican arguments and rallied the country behind him.

The Republicans began the 1962 campaign in hopes they could win important congressional and gubernatorial gains and thereby increase their effectiveness as an opposition party in Washington and prepare for a possible presidential comeback. They counted on the traditional pattern of midterm gains for the party out of power to help them in the congressional elections.

The party, however, was suffering from image problems. The congressional wing of the GOP, headed by Senate minority leader Everett Dirksen, R-Ill., and House minority leader Charles Halleck, R-Ind., had dominated the news of Republican activity in Washington since Eisenhower's retirement. Deprived of the expertise of the executive branch, Hill Republicans came up with few legislative initiatives and had few counterproposals to the stream of legislative requests that flowed from the White House. The only serious competition to Dirksen and Halleck for the Republican spotlight was Sen. Barry Goldwater of Arizona, whose outspoken conservatism made him the favorite of the right wing throughout the country. Moderate and liberal Republicans received scant attention. Eisenhower had retired; Nixon was embroiled in California politics; New York governor Nelson A. Rockefeller was busy preparing for his own reelection campaign in New York and wrestling with possible adverse effects of his divorce announced late in 1961.

The Republicans waged the 1962 campaign with familiar issues: the need for fiscal responsibility in government, calls for a balanced budget and warnings of the dangers of encroaching federal (especially executive) power. But the GOP lacked any single strong issue, such as the demand for an end to wartime controls in 1946 or alleged Democratic responsibility for the Korean War in 1950, with which to rout the Democrats. For a while they hoped Cuba would be that issue, but the president's firm action in late October effectively deprived them of it. In the end improved Republican organizations, especially in the big cities, helped the party to some victories. But the only region of the country in which they made any significant congressional gains was the South, where they jumped from nine to 14 seats.

Results of the 1962 Elections

The Democratic Party confirmed its heavy majorities in both houses of Congress and among the states' governors. Democrats avoided "normal" midterm losses of the party in power by gaining four Senate seats and suffering only a nominal loss in the House. Not since 1934 had the presidential party fared so well in a midterm election. Democrats said that, in contrast to the familiar patterns of major midterm loses by the presidential party, the 1962 results constituted a real vote of confidence in the administration.

Republicans replied that they saw "no endorsement of the New Frontier and its policies." They pointed out that President Kennedy had not carried Democrats into office with him in 1960, actually losing 20 House seats that year, so that there were fewer vulnerable seats for the GOP to pick off in 1962. The Republicans argued that the national House vote for the GOP had actually risen to 47.7 percent, 4.0 points higher than 1958 and 2.7 points higher than 1960. Privately, however, Republicans expressed deep disappointment that they had not been able to register important gains, especially in the House.

Congressional reapportionment after the 1960 census had caused major shifts in the distribution of seats in the House. The Eastern states lost a net of seven seats; the South, one; and the Midwest, four. The Western states were the beneficiaries, picking up ten new seats; eight of them went to California.

Democrats controlled the California legislature, which redistricted in 1961. As a result they gained eight seats from California in the 1962 elections. A similar Republican gerrymander in New York State misfired, and Republican gains in other areas barely balanced the Democratic bonus from California.

Republicans were especially disappointed by their net loss of four Senate seats. The new Senate was so heavily Democratic that the Republicans had no real hope of regaining control until 1968 or later.

Despite a heavy turnover in the governorship elections (Democrats took seven from the Republicans and lost a like number), the gubernatorial party balance remained 34-16 in favor of the Democrats. The Republicans, however, did seize control of several important state governorships including those of Pennsylvania, Ohio and Michigan.

The most devastating defeat of the year was suffered by former vice president Richard M. Nixon, who was soundly defeated for governor of California only two years after barely missing election to the presidency. Other political veterans retired by the voters included longtime senators Homer E. Capehart, R-Ind. and Alexander Wiley, R-Wis.; Rep. Walter H. Judd, R-Minn.; and Gov. Michael V. DiSalle, D-Ohio.

The potential national leaders elected in 1962 included Republican representative William W. Scranton, elected governor of Pennsylvania by a 486,651-vote majority; former auto maker George W. Romney, a Republican who ended 14 years of Democratic control of the Michigan governorship; youthful Democratic state representative Birch Bayh, who toppled Homer Earl Capehart in the Indiana Senate race; Edward M. "Ted" Kennedy, youngest brother of the president, who was elected U.S. senator from Massachusetts; and Robert Taft Jr., a Republican who was elected congressman at large from Ohio.

Among the new senators elected in 1962 was Democrat Abraham A. Ribicoff, former governor of Connecticut and first secretary of Health, Education, and Welfare in the Kennedy administration. Hawaiian voters sent Rep. Daniel K. Inouye, a Democrat, to the Senate. He was the first U.S. senator of Japanese ancestry. The new governorship roster included James A. Rhodes, R-Ohio; John A. Love, R-Colo.;

Karl Rolvaag, D-Minn.; John B. Connally, D-Texas; and John A. Burns, D-Hawaii.

Among the "miracle men" of 1962 were Philip H. Hoff, who became the first Democratic governor of Vermont in more than a century, and Henry L. Bellmon, who became Oklahoma's first Republican governor since the state joined the Union.

Incumbents who won impressive victories included Sen. Jacob K. Javits, R-N.Y., reelected by a plurality of almost one million; Republican Senate whip Thomas H. Kuchel, R-Calif., reelected by a quarter-million vote margin despite the 296,758-vote triumph of Democratic governor Edmund G. "Pat" Brown over Nixon in the same state's balloting; Sen. Thruston B. Morton, former national chairman of the Republican Party, reelected against powerful Democratic opposition in Kentucky; and New York governor Nelson A. Rockefeller, whose plurality was down slightly from its 1958 level but still big enough to make him appear the top contender for the 1964 Republican presidential nomination.

Across the nation, voters showed a continuing tendency to disregard traditional party lines in choosing people for high office. The success of Democrats in the traditional Republican states of northern New England and break-throughs for the Republicans in the South—including a near miss in the Alabama Senate race—attested to the possible development of significant new voting patterns.

1963-65:
The 88th Congress

The years 1963-64 were good years for most Americans as the nation enjoyed continued economic prosperity and international affairs remained relatively tranquil. These same years, however, witnessed the assassination of a president, the launching of the most profound equal rights drive since the Civil War and seizure of control of one of the major American political parties by a right-wing faction.

John F. Kennedy was shot on Nov. 22, 1963, as his motorcade moved through cheering crowds in downtown Dallas. Approximately one-half hour later the president was pronounced dead. A special presidential commission, headed by Chief Justice Earl Warren, reported Sept. 27, 1964, that Lee Harvey Oswald, "acting alone and without advice or assistance," had shot the president. The report said Jack Ruby was on his own in killing Oswald and that neither was part of "any conspiracy, domestic or foreign," to kill President Kennedy. The report called for an overhauling and modernization of the Secret Service, the group entrusted with physical protection of the president, and of FBI procedures.

At 1:39 p.m., Nov. 22, Vice President Lyndon B. Johnson took the oath of office as the 36th president aboard the presidential jet plane just before its departure from Dallas to Washington. The next few days witnessed President Kennedy's funeral; the confluence in Washington of heads of state, dignitaries and emissaries from governments all over the world to pay their respects to the dead president; and the resolute grasp of the reins of power by Lyndon Johnson.

The new president's political roots reached into the liberalism of the New Deal on the one hand and into the conservatism of political life in his native Texas on the other. His wealth of experience in American political life, especially in Congress, served him well as he moved into the presidency. He quickly embraced the salient features of President Kennedy's program, especially the tax cut bill and

Governors Who Became President

When Bill Clinton was elected president in 1992, he continued the trend in recent years of governors advancing to the White House. Between 1976 and 1992, former governors won four out of five presidential elections. Bill Clinton was the first sitting governor to be elected president since Franklin Roosevelt in 1932. Over the course of U.S. history, 16 presidents have served previously as state governors.

Following is a list of these presidents and the states in which they served as governor. Thomas Jefferson's term of governor of Virginia was during the Revolutionary War. Two other presidents served as governors of territories: Andrew Jackson was the territorial governor of Florida and William Henry Harrison was the territorial governor of Indiana.

President	State
Thomas Jefferson	Virginia
James Monroe	Virginia
Martin Van Buren	New York
John Tyler	Virginia
James K. Polk	Tennessee
Andrew Johnson	Tennessee
Rutherford B. Hayes	Ohio
Grover Cleveland	New York
William McKinley	Ohio
Theodore Roosevelt	New York
Woodrow Wilson	New Jersey
Calvin Coolidge	Massachusetts
Franklin D. Roosevelt	New York
Jimmy Carter	Georgia
Ronald Reagan	California
Bill Clinton	Arkansas

Source: *American Leaders 1789-1994*. Washington, D.C.: Congressional Quarterly Inc., 1994.

civil rights legislation; moved to win the confidence of the liberal community by a well-publicized "war on poverty" in America; and won the confidence of the business community and many conservatives by ordering strict economies in federal spending. Johnson's foes accused him of political sleight-of-hand in being both liberal and conservative at the same time, but opinion polls—and the 1964 elections—indicated the American people approved wholeheartedly.

The issue of civil rights produced a profound domestic crisis for the United States in 1963 and 1964. Discontented with the pace of their advances in all spheres of life, black Americans pressed for full rights in every field from voting to employment, from education to housing.

President Kennedy, in February 1963, had sent his first civil rights legislative program to Congress—one characterized by liberals of both parties as "thin." On April 3 mass demonstrations for equal rights began in Birmingham, Ala. Dramatized by the use of children in the demonstrations and the use of dogs and hoses by the police against the blacks, events in Birmingham sparked a determined nation-wide series of protests. By the end of 1963 demonstrations had taken place in more than 800 cities and towns, climaxed by a gigantic but orderly "March on Washington for Jobs and Freedom" in which more than 200,000 persons participated on Aug. 28.

The demonstrations began primarily with black protesters, but millions of white Americans—most noticeably church groups and college students—took interest in the lot of black Americans. At the same time, however, many Northern whites showed their hostility to the civil rights drive because it appeared to threaten de facto segregation in housing, employment and education. Capitalizing on white Northern fears, Alabama's segregationist governor, George C. Wallace, entered spring 1964 Democratic presidential primaries in Wisconsin, Indiana and Maryland and won 33.8, 29.8 and 42.8 percent of the vote in the respective races. But when the new Republican national leadership sought to cultivate the "white backlash" vote in the 1964 presidential campaign, the effort proved singularly unsuccessful outside a few Deep South states.

In early June 1963 congressional Republicans and liberal Democrats began to press for strong civil rights legislation, and on June 11 President Kennedy told the nation: "We cannot say to 10 percent of the population that . . . the only way they are going to get their rights is to go into the streets and demonstrate." A week later he submitted a new and broadened civil rights program to combat discrimination in public accommodations, schools, jobs and voting, which he urged Congress to enact.

For a while it appeared the bill might go aground, but in November the House Judiciary Committee reported a bipartisan civil rights measure, the fruit of conferences between administration leaders and Republican congressional civil rights advocates. Working under cloture the Senate passed the bill June 19, 1964, by a 73-27 vote. The House passed the amended bill July 2, and President Johnson signed it into law a few hours later. Among other things the bill expanded federal power to protect voting rights; guaranteed access to all public accommodations and public facilities for all races, with federal power to back up the pledge; gave the federal government power to sue for school desegregation; outlawed denial of equal job opportunities in businesses or unions with 25 or more workers; and authorized the federal government to intervene in any court suit alleging denial of equal protection of the laws. It was the most sweeping civil rights measure in American history.

Determined to prevent economic stagnation and give the country's economy a major boost forward, President Kennedy in January 1963 proposed a $10.3 billion personal and corporate income tax cut to take effect July 1, 1963. After protracted hearings in the House and Senate, the final version, reducing taxes $11.5 billion annually, was signed into law by President Johnson Feb. 26, 1964.

In the meantime the economy, which the tax bill had been designed to help, was doing surprisingly well on its own. The 1963 gross national product reached $585 billion, and the Council of Economic Advisers predicted a $623 billion level in 1964. With the exception of unemployment, which remained above 5 percent of the work force, most economic indicators continued a gradual upward rise during 1963 and 1964. In October 1964, 71.2 million Americans were employed. Despite the rise in the economy, only a few economists saw any serious threat of inflation.

In his State of the Union message Jan. 8, 1964, Johnson called for an "unconditional" declaration of "war on poverty in America." The poverty program constituted the chief innovation in the president's legislative proposals. Submitting his specific program to Congress March 16, he called for

a fiscal 1965 outlay of $962.5 million to fight poverty. When Congress finished action on his request in August, it had authorized $947.5 million, only $15 million less than the draft proposal, with approval of almost all the president's requests. As enacted, the bill authorized ten separate programs under the supervision of the Office of Economic Opportunity, created by the bill. Major sections authorized a Job Corps to provide youths with work experience and training in conservation camps and in residential training centers, a work-training program to employ youths locally, a community action program under which the government would assist a variety of local efforts to combat poverty, an adult education program and a "domestic peace corps" program.

The years 1963 and 1964 witnessed a steady relaxation in the tensions of the cold war, perhaps the closest approximation to an East-West detente since 1945. At the beginning of 1963 U.S.-Soviet relations were at a standoff, produced by Russian withdrawal of missiles from Cuba in October 1962. By mid-1963 a Soviet-Chinese rift had deepened, and a lessening of U.S.-Soviet tensions was evident.

In a speech on June 10, 1963, Kennedy announced that the United States, the Soviet Union and Great Britain would begin talks on a partial test ban, apart from the 17-nation Geneva talks that had dragged on intermittently without much hope since 1958. Then, before many realized that progress was at last to be made, a limited treaty was initialed in Moscow July 25. The Senate consented to ratification Sept. 24.

A moderately optimistic tone pervaded U.S.-Soviet relations in 1964. On April 20 both the United States and the Soviet Union announced they were going to cut back their production of nuclear materials for weapons use. The growing tensions between China and the Soviet Union caused the Soviets to turn their attention more and more inward. On Oct. 16 the Western world was shocked to hear that Nikita S. Khrushchev had been ousted from his duties as premier and also as first secretary of the Soviet Communist Party. He was replaced as premier by Aleksei N. Kosygin and as party secretary by Leonid Brezhnev, possibly presaging a prolonged struggle for power within the Soviet hierarchy. The new Soviet leaders quickly made it clear they would follow Khrushchev's policy of "peaceful coexistence" with the West.

The Kennedy-Johnson administration's Alliance for Progress suffered as democratically elected regimes were deposed in Ecuador, Guatemala, Honduras, the Dominican Republic and Bolivia. The Johnson administration faced its first major foreign policy crisis in January 1964 when large-scale violence broke out in Central America as Panamanians protested the 1903 treaty under which the United States administered the Panama Canal and Americans enjoyed special privileges in the Canal Zone. The United States was encouraged, however, when President Joao Goulart of Brazil, accused of conducting a leftist and chaotic administration, was deposed in a bloodless coup on April 1, 1964.

Apparently upset by Vietnam government moves against Buddhists, suicidal burnings by Buddhist monks, corruption within the government and inadequate military success against the Communist Viet Cong, the State Department in 1963 gradually curtailed aid to the Vietnamese regime of Catholic president Ngo Dinh Diem. On Nov. 1 a military coup ended the Diem regime. The State Department denied participation in the coup, but unofficially it admitted that it might have encouraged the "proper climate" for such a revolt. The new ruling junta in Vietnam was itself overturned by a coup in January 1964, starting a series of bewildering governmental shifts that lasted through 1964 as the military situation continued to deteriorate.

The off-year elections of November 1963 provided no definite clue to possible trends for 1964. Democrats maintained control of the Kentucky and Mississippi governorships and the Philadelphia mayoralty in the top three races, but the GOP vote was up sharply in all three areas.

Top Republican takeovers of the year were scored in New Jersey, where the Assembly reverted to GOP hands to give the Republicans majorities in both houses, and in Indiana, where the GOP elected 25 new mayors. The Republicans also scored gains in Virginia and Mississippi legislative elections. Democratic Representative John F. Shelley won election as mayor of San Francisco, ending 55 years of GOP control in technically nonpartisan elections. Suburban New York also showed some Democratic gains.

The 1964 Campaigns

From the beginning of 1964 it was apparent that President Johnson was the strong favorite to win a full four-year White House term in his own right. As the Democrats gathered in Atlantic City for their convention on Aug. 24, Johnson kept silence about his final decision for a running mate. In a move unprecedented in American politics, he appeared before the Democratic National Convention just before his own nomination the same evening to announce to the delegates that Sen. Hubert H. Humphrey of Minnesota was his choice for the vice presidential slot.

The most fascinating story of the 1964 presidential campaign, however, lay in the opposition party. Throughout the postwar years, the Republican Party, despite its conservative inclinations, had generally embraced the wide consensus of U.S. politics: agreement on basic social welfare responsibilities of the government together with a firm but not bellicose policy toward the Communist world. But in 1964 the Republican Party turned abruptly from the moderate course. For president it nominated a militantly conservative two-term Arizona senator, Barry Goldwater, known for his hostile views toward the power of the federal government and his apparent willingness to risk nuclear confrontation with the Soviets to advance the Western cause. The course set by Goldwater brought the Republican Party its most devastating defeat in more than a quarter-century. Republican ranks in Congress and the state legislatures were greatly reduced. Even worse, national confidence in the party was so badly shaken that it might take years to recoup.

Early in 1964, however, only one Republican of national stature was willing to speak out on the possible dangers of Goldwater and his philosophy for the Republican Party. That man was New York governor Nelson A. Rockefeller, who had entered the race for the GOP nomination Nov. 7, 1963. Rockefeller symbolized the Eastern progressive wing of the Republican Party that had dominated Republican National Conventions since 1940. The other leaders of the Republican Party's moderate wing—governors William W. Scranton of Pennsylvania and George W. Romney of Michigan, Ambassador Henry Cabot Lodge and former vice president Richard M. Nixon—all were thought to harbor some presidential ambitions, but none was willing to take the plunge in the presidential primaries or to risk an open challenge to the Goldwater wing of the party.

The "National Draft Goldwater Committee," which organized formally in the spring of 1963, aimed both at nominating Goldwater and at remaking the entire Republican Party into a vehicle for militant conservatism. Their aim appeared to be the reforming of two U.S. political parties along straight liberal versus conservative lines. By the autumn of 1963 the years of Goldwater stewardship within the ranks of the Republican Party had begun to bear fruit. Goldwater supporters held important positions in the Republican Party apparatus. Rep. William E. Miller, R-N.Y., who would later become Goldwater's vice presidential running mate, was the Republican national chairman.

The Republican National Convention, meeting in San Francisco July 13-16, turned sharply to the right, rejecting the party's moderate tone of the postwar years and substituting instead an unabashed conservatism in domestic affairs and all-out nationalism in foreign policy.

Goldwater's controversial stands and his failure to advance meaningful alternative solutions to national problems relieved Johnson of having to spell out in any substantial detail what his plans for the "great society" were. For the most part Johnson confined himself to calls for national unity and remarks aimed at broadening the breach between Goldwater and the bulk of moderate and liberal Republicans. Johnson was so successful in preempting the vital "middle ground" of American politics that a Democratic victory was assured long before election day.

Results of the 1964 Elections

In the Nov. 3 elections President Johnson led the Democratic Party to its greatest national victory since 1936. Not only did Johnson win a four-year White House term in his own right, amassing the largest vote of any presidential candidate in history, but his broad coattails helped the Democrats score major gains in the House of Representatives and increase their already heavy majority in the Senate.

The Johnson-Humphrey ticket ran 15,951,378 votes ahead of the Goldwater-Miller ticket, easily exceeding the record national popular vote plurality of 11,073,102 by which Franklin D. Roosevelt defeated Alfred M. Landon in 1936. The final, official vote for Johnson-Humphrey was 43,129,566; for Goldwater-Miller, 27,178,188.

Johnson won 44 states and the District of Columbia (which voted for the first time for president, under the terms of the 23rd Amendment to the Constitution). His electoral vote total was 486. Goldwater won six states with a total of 52 electoral votes. The Democratic presidential victory began in New England and the East, where Johnson carried every state and chalked up a better than 2-1 majority.

The Democratic sweep continued through the Republican Midwestern heartland, where every state also cast its electoral vote for Johnson. The president was the winner in every mountain and Pacific state except Arizona, Goldwater's home state. California, which had boosted Goldwater to the Republican nomination in the June primary, went for Johnson by over a million votes.

Only an unusual degree of ticket splitting saved the Republican Party from almost total annihilation in races for congressional and state posts. As it was, the Republicans were reduced to their lowest congressional levels since depression days. In elections to the House the Republicans suffered a net loss of 38 seats. The new House balance was 295 Democrats and 140 Republicans, the lowest GOP membership figure since the 1936 elections. Among the more serious Republican House losses were seven seats in New York, five in Iowa and four each in New Jersey, Michigan, Ohio and Washington. Many of the Northern Republican representatives defeated were among their party's most conservative, representing formerly "safe Republican" seats. For example, 54 Republican House members had backed Goldwater's nomination drive in June by signing a statement saying his nomination would "result in substantial increases in Republican membership in both houses of Congress." Of these, 17 were defeated, another three retired but saw their districts go Democratic and all but six saw their winning percentages dwindle. Of the 21 Northern Republicans who had voted with Goldwater against the 1964 Civil Rights Act, 11 were defeated. Republicans who disassociated themselves from Goldwater and his policies were generally more successful. The most spectacular Republican House victory of the year was scored by Rep. John V. Lindsay of New York, who refused to endorse Goldwater but won a 71.5 percent victory in his district, while Johnson was carrying it by more than 2-1.

The only area of significant Republican House gains was the deep South, where Goldwater coattails helped the party elect five new representatives in Alabama and one each in Georgia and Mississippi. They were the first Republican House members from these states since Reconstruction. But at the same time three conservative GOP Southern House members—two in Texas, one in Kentucky—were going down to defeat.

One result of the election was to erode the power base of the "conservative coalition" between Republicans and Southern Democrats. Not only would there be less conservative representation in the House, but the relative strength of Northern liberals in the Democratic House Caucus would be increased substantially.

The Senate elections resulted in a net Democratic gain of two seats, making the new balance 68 Democrats and 32 Republicans. Not since the elections of 1940 had the Democrats held such a heavy majority. But the major story was not the new Democratic Senate gains of 1964 but the fact that the members of the liberal Democratic class of 1958 were all reelected to office. The Democrats' gain of 13 formerly Republican seats in 1958 had effected a basic realignment of power within the Senate, giving it a much more liberal orientation than the House. The Republicans had long looked forward to 1964 as the year when they would win back many of the class of 1958 seats.

The Democrats actually won three GOP Senate seats in 1964: Kenneth Keating's seat in New York, taken by Robert F. Kennedy (thus making Kennedy a potential future contender for the Democratic presidential nomination); J. Glenn Beall's seat in Maryland, won by Democrat Joseph D. Tydings; and the New Mexico seat of interim senator Edwin L. Mechem, won by Rep. Joseph M. Montoya. The sole GOP gain was in California, where George Murphy scored an upset victory over interim senator Pierre Salinger, former presidential press secretary.

A major blow to the GOP was the defeat in Ohio of Robert Taft Jr., who was challenging Democratic senator Stephen M. Young. Before the election Taft had been looked to as a major future leader of his party. But the Goldwater "drag"—Johnson won Ohio by 1,027,466 votes—was too much for Taft to overcome.

In gubernatorial elections the Republicans scored gains in Washington, Wisconsin and Massachusetts and lost seats they had held in Arizona and Utah. The result was a net gain of one for the GOP. But the already heavy Democratic majority was not weakened significantly. The new lineup was 33 Democrats and 17 Republicans.

Without Goldwater at the head of the ticket the Republicans might have scored much better. Their most disap-

pointing defeat came in Illinois, where Charles H. Percy, who had been regarded as a possible future presidential candidate, went down to defeat in the Democratic landslide.

The most spectacular GOP governorship win was scored by Michigan governor George R. Romney, seeking reelection. He withstood a Johnson landslide of more than 2-1 to win reelection. The outcome established Romney, who had refused to endorse Goldwater's candidacy, as a powerful future leader of his party.

Among the new governors elected were Samuel P. Goddard, D-Ariz.; Roger D. Branigin, D-Ind.; Daniel J. Evans, R-Wash.; and Warren P. Knowles, R-Wis.

Democratic governors who won substantial reelection victories despite the Republican complexion of their states included Frank B. Morrison of Nebraska, Harold E. Hughes of Iowa, John W. King of New Hampshire, and Philip H. Hoff of Vermont. But in normally Democratic Rhode Island, Republican governor John H. Chaffee won reelection with 61.3 percent of the vote, while Goldwater received only 19.1 percent of the state's vote.

The Vietnam War Years

The years of the 1960s and 1970s were some of the most turbulent in the nation's history. The seeds of the great upheavals ahead were already sprouting even before President Kennedy's death in November 1963. The country's role in the Vietnam War was inching upward. Black Americans were becoming ever more insistent in demanding an end to all forms of racial discrimination. A huge generation of teenagers, born in the post-World War II baby boom, were reaching college age and were preparing to challenge authority on a scale unprecedented in American history. And there were growing indications of conservative political strength, especially within the Republican Party.

In the late 1960s the nation experienced a series of cataclysmic changes that, while they did not appear to endanger the basic economic health of the nation, did jeopardize the postwar politics of consensus and promise as yet unpredictable changes in the social and political climate of American life. Only when the nation found itself entangled in a seemingly endless and unwinnable war in Vietnam in the mid-1960s did the first major cracks appear in the general national consensus behind U.S. foreign policy. For the first time serious doubts were raised about the role of the nation as a global policeman, and there were indications that a period of limited isolationism might come in the wake of any Vietnam settlement.

Through the 1964 election the United States had enjoyed remarkably stable two-party politics in the postwar years. No major ideological gulfs existed between the parties, and although the Democrats were more frequently victorious at the polls than the Republicans (an apparent legacy of Franklin Roosevelt's New Deal), few Americans were deeply concerned when the party in power changed in Washington or the state capitals. Indeed, two-party politics infused virtually every region of the country for the first time in its history. And as the parties became more competitive, personal allegiances shifted more frequently and ticket splitting became an American electoral pastime.

When Barry Goldwater was repudiated at the polls in 1964, the post-New Deal consensus seemed to have been reaffirmed. Indeed, the year 1965 saw the last major burst of legislative accomplishments and national optimism that the country was to witness for some time. With the large Democratic majorities created by the Johnson landslide,

Congress enacted federal aid to education, a national health insurance program and a voting rights act.

But the Johnson administration's fortunes soon changed. The decision to commit massive American ground forces to Vietnam resulted in increased opposition at home to American participation in the war. The war further stimulated student unrest on the campuses resulting in siege conditions at some universities. Blacks burst forth in anger and destroyed large sections of American cities. And the Rev. Martin Luther King Jr. and Sen. Robert F. Kennedy were assassinated in 1968.

The Democratic Party coalition broke open under these strains in 1968, with the challenge to President Johnson's renomination and the Independent candidacy of Alabama governor George C. Wallace. The result was that Republican Richard Nixon was elected to the presidency.

At the end of the 1960s both parties were clearly in transition. The Democrats, in order to hold their solid base among low-income voters and minorities, would be obliged to remain strong advocates of wide-ranging social reform. But that very course could possibly seal their eventual downfall in the South, even if an increased black vote in that region compensated for some of that loss. And while organized labor had turned out a strong Democratic vote in 1968, its leaders were having increasing difficulty in convincing workers that they should remain unswervingly loyal to the Democratic Party.

The Republicans, even in winning the presidential election of 1968, received only 43 percent of the national vote and had to recognize that in their major base of support—the predominantly white, middle-class rural areas and small cities—they faced a diminishing asset in overall population terms. It was clear that the Republicans' growing strength in the burgeoning white suburban areas of America would hold solidly only as long as the party maintained domestic prosperity and found a way to calm inner-city tensions.

During his first term President Nixon too had to deal with anti-war demonstrations. But his policy of gradual withdrawal of American troops, climaxing with the peace settlement of January 1973, finally removed the war from the top of the American political agenda.

At the same time, with the passage of the baby-boom generation out of college and into the labor market, the nation's campuses became more peaceful. And the movement of many blacks onto the voter rolls, into public office and into more jobs and better housing seemed to relieve some of the racial tension.

But at the very moment when things began looking better, the nation was hit by a fresh series of calamities. Throughout 1973 and 1974 the Watergate scandal implicated several top public officials, including the president himself, in illegal activities. The immediate result was the first presidential resignation in U.S. history, but the deeper ramifications could be found in the weakening of the confidence of the people in their government and leaders.

While the revelations were continuing, the United States was hit with an energy crisis when the Arab states cut off the flow of oil during the October 1973 war in the Middle East. Even when the flow was resumed, the price had been jacked up more than 300 percent, and this increase, combined with other trends in the economy, produced some of the worst inflation in the nation's history. Buffeted by these forces, seemingly beyond their control, many Americans wondered about the future of their country and the stability of their economic and political system.

President Gerald Ford, with his low-key personality and image of personal integrity, helped calm the country after these misfortunes. But he was not seen by many as a strong leader and was almost defeated for the presidential nomination of his own party in the 1976 primaries.

1965-67:
The 89th Congress

Buoyed by the largest party majorities enjoyed by any president in three decades, Lyndon Johnson led the 89th Congress in an amazingly productive 1965 session. The scope of the legislation was even more impressive than the number of major new laws. In the course of the year Congress approved programs that had long been on the agenda of the Democratic Party—in the case of medical care for the aged under Social Security, for as long as 20 years. Other longstanding objectives were met by enactment of aid to primary and secondary schools, college scholarships and immigration reform.

The pace of the 1965 session was so breathless as to cause a major revision of the image, widely prevalent in preceding years, of Congress as structurally incapable of swift decision. The change was because of three primary elements not always present in past years: the decisive Democratic majorities elected in 1965, the personal leadership of President Johnson and the shaping of legislation to obtain maximum political support in Congress.

The expanded Democratic pluralities were most significant in the House, where the Democrats had not only scored a 38-seat net gain over the Republicans in the 1964 elections but had also traded a number of conservative Democratic votes in the South for liberal Democratic votes in the North. The new liberal strength in the House showed itself most dramatically in passage of the aid to education and medical care (Medicare) bills. The Senate had passed similar measures in previous years only to see them blocked by the hitherto powerful coalition of Republicans and conservative Southern Democrats in the House. But the "conservative coalition," where it did appear in House roll call votes, was victorious only 25 percent of the time in 1965, compared with 67 percent in 1962 and 1964 and 74 percent in 1961, the first year of President Kennedy's term.

The president gained maximum political effect from his efforts to build a broad consensus of support. An excise tax cut, designed to keep the economy growing steadily, appealed to business and consumer interests alike. Lack of strong opposition from business circles made it easier for Democrats to mount the Great Society program of greatly increased civil benefits and tended to smother Republican protests that Congress was merely rubber stamping ill-conceived administration proposals.

The Voting Rights Act of 1965, the most comprehensive legislation to ensure the right to vote in 90 years, was prompted by the brutal suppression of demonstrations in Selma, Ala. and other parts of the South. The bill went beyond the milder courtroom remedies of earlier civil rights acts. In the wake of this legislation an additional 500,000 Southern blacks were registered by the time of the 1966 elections.

Other legislation included a housing bill authorizing $7.8 billion to fund new and existing housing programs through 1969 and a bill establishing a cabinet-level Department of Housing and Urban Development.

The year 1965 was punctuated by major crises in Vietnam. Faced with the threat of success by the Viet Cong Communist insurgents in South Vietnam, President Johnson initiated large-scale bombing raids in North Vietnam, which was giving major aid to the Viet Cong. When this tactic failed to turn the unfavorable course of the war, he ordered a vast increase—from about 20,000 to eventually more than 140,000—in American troop strength in the South and an aggressive prosecution of the land war. Both steps required new outlays for personnel and materiel. Despite highly vocal criticism of his Vietnam policy by a small band of senators, Congress overwhelmingly approved Johnson's special request for funds.

The Vietnam budget pressures soon had serious effects on the domestic economy. As 1966 began the U.S. economy was already strained to its noninflationary limit. After 59 months of stable economic growth, it was near full employment. Plant capacity was in full use. Any sizable increase in demand under these conditions would be bound to result in inflation. This is precisely what occurred as the defense budget shot upward, without any significant offsetting measures to cut back on other purchasing power. The cost-of-living index jumped from 111.0 percent in January to 113.8 percent in August. The president early in the year asked and received congressional approval of a $5.9 billion bill to accelerate certain types of tax payments and reimpose 1965 excise tax levies, but the measure was hardly adequate to counter the Vietnam spending boom. Almost every leading economist in the nation called for a general tax increase, but President Johnson refused.

With the public increasingly concerned with inflation and the Vietnam War, congressional Republicans found new Democratic allies in the effort to curb the Great Society—not only its spending programs but almost any measure providing social reform. Despite strong persuasive efforts by the president, the administration was rebuffed on many major bills.

An important reason for the defeat of the administration's new civil rights proposals was a wave of summertime riots in black "ghetto" areas of the large cities. In August 1965 a six-day disturbance had erupted in Los Angeles's 95 percent black Watts area, with about 7,000 youths participating in rioting, looting and arson. The National Guard finally restored order, but only after 34 deaths. In the summer of 1966 other riots followed in the black areas of several other American cities. The 1966 riots were attributed not only to decades of frustration among urban blacks in education, housing and employment fields but to the growth of a new philosophy of "black power," expounded by extremist civil rights groups such as the Congress of Racial Equality (CORE) and the Student Nonviolent Coordinating Committee (SNCC).

In the House, Rep. John William McCormack of Massachusetts continued as Speaker. Sen. Mike Mansfield of Montana remained as Senate majority leader, with Sen. Everett Dirksen of Illinois his Republican counterpart. House minority leader Charles Halleck of Indiana was defeated for reelection to his leadership post by Rep. Gerald R. Ford of Michigan, just before formal opening of the 89th Congress. Ford's election as minority leader was a continuation of the revolt of younger House Republicans that had begun with Ford's election as House GOP Conference chairman two years before. As in 1963 the leadership struggle seemed to be based less on ideological differences than on the question of which representative could give the most forceful leadership to the depleted Republican House ranks.

The 1964 elections had left the Republicans at such a low point that some resurgence seemed inevitable. In 1965 it

began in a spectacular way as Republican-Liberal John V. Lindsay won election as mayor in heavily Democratic New York City. Lindsay's victory, combined with the victories of liberally inclined Republican candidates for district attorney in Philadelphia and mayor in Louisville, Ky., signaled a potential Republican resurgence on the left in the very areas where Goldwater had been weakest—in the major cities and especially among blacks and other minority groups.

In New Jersey, however, the Republican gubernatorial candidate took a conservative tack similar to that of the 1964 Goldwater campaign and found himself defeated by Democratic governor Richard J. Hughes by a record 363,572-vote margin. Democrats also held the Virginia governorship and legislature and easily maintained control of the mayors' offices in major cities such as New Haven, St. Louis, Pittsburgh and Detroit. In Cleveland a black state legislator running as an Independent came within 2,143 votes of upsetting the incumbent Democratic mayor. In the smaller cities some of the most interesting contests took place on June 8 in Hattiesburg and Columbus, Miss., where the first Republicans of the 20th century—all staunch conservatives—were elected mayors.

The 1966 Midterm Elections

From the beginning of the 1966 campaign the Democrats realized that they faced formidable odds if they hoped to maintain their overwhelming margins of control in Congress and in the state governorships and legislatures. Yet at the end of 1965 it looked as if the minority Republicans might be held to minimal gains. The first session of the 89th Congress had passed laws with benefits for almost every segment of the population. President Johnson still enjoyed the wide "consensus" support he had enjoyed in 1964, from every group from organized labor to big business and minorities. And the economy was booming on virtually every front.

By the beginning of the 1966 campaign, however, it was apparent that the odds had shifted significantly to the benefit of the Republicans. Behind the change was the escalation of the Vietnam War, with its heavy toll both in American lives and dollars. The conflict in Vietnam, because of its limited nature, increased frustrations across the country and began to undermine public support of the administration in power.

The war effort generated inflationary pressures that were being felt throughout the country by mid-1966. The Republicans were able to argue with some effectiveness that the Johnson administration should be cutting down, rather than increasing, national expenditures for a wide variety of Great Society programs. Moreover, those very social welfare programs that had looked so politically attractive at the end of 1965 were beginning to encounter serious administrative difficulties, with wide gaps between the administration's promises to improve educational standards, end conditions of poverty and ensure racial peace and its ability to deliver on those promises.

President Johnson's own popularity plummeted during the year; wide splits appeared in the Democratic Party in many important states; and at the same time several attractive Republican candidates appeared to lead the GOP in critical states—in sharp contrast to the unpopularity of Goldwater, the party's 1964 standard bearer.

Early in 1965 the Democrats had launched an ambitious Operation Support from within the Democratic National Committee, designed to reelect a large portion of the 71 freshman Democratic representatives who came into office in the 1964 Democratic sweep—38 of them from formerly Republican districts. But while Operation Support functioned smoothly in 1965, it tended to fall off in 1966 as the national committee obeyed presidential orders to cut back on its activities in order to pay off a heavy debt left from the 1964 campaign.

The Republican congressional effort, on the other hand, was bolstered by a massive fund-raising campaign that made it possible to funnel thousands of dollars into every doubtful congressional district in the country. Reports just before the elections showed national-level gifts of $1.6 million to GOP congressional candidates from their party headquarters, compared with only $250,000 from national-level Democratic committees.

The primary season indicated some significant shifts in the political landscape. In California, long a bastion of liberal Republicanism, actor Ronald Reagan, an outspoken conservative, won a sweeping primary victory over more liberal opposition. In the Virginia primary two aging representatives of traditional conservative Southern Democracy were defeated by younger men of more moderate persuasion. In Florida the mayor of Miami, Robert King High, won the Democratic gubernatorial primary with liberal support over the more conservative incumbent governor. Staunch segregationist candidates, on the other hand, won Democratic gubernatorial primaries in the Deep South: Jim Johnson in Arkansas, Lester Maddox in Georgia and Lurleen Wallace, wife of outgoing governor George C. Wallace (who was ineligible to succeed himself), in Alabama.

As the campaign gathered steam in the fall, the Republicans concentrated their fire increasingly on the issues of inflation, Vietnam, crime and the alleged credibility gap between what President Johnson and his administration said they were doing and their actual performance.

Results of the 1966 Elections

The Republican Party reasserted itself as a major force in American politics by capturing eight new governorships, three new seats in the Senate and 47 additional House seats in the Nov. 8 elections. In a striking comeback from its devastating defeat of 1964, the GOP elected enough new governors to give it control of 25 of the 50 states with a substantial majority of the nation's population. The Senate and House gains left the party still short of a majority but in a position of new power and relevance on the national scene.

A new vigor shown by Republican candidates across the country marked a return to more competitive two-party politics and the possibility that the 1968 presidential election could be closely contested. The vast majority of successful Republican candidates, both for congressional and state offices, appeared to have rejected the ultraconservative ideology espoused by former senator Barry Goldwater. But the winning Republicans did represent a somewhat more conservative philosophy than that of the president and his administration, reflecting a national movement to the right, which many observers felt was reflected in the slowdown on major domestic reforms in the closing session of the 89th Congress. The 1966 elections appeared to lay the groundwork for a strong moderate Republican challenge to Johnson in 1968.

The party control among the state governorships shifted from 33-17 in favor of the Democrats to 25-25, the greatest Republican strength since the early 1950s. The Republicans gained California and held New York, Pennsylvania, Ohio and Michigan to give them control of five of the nation's seven largest states. In addition to California, the

Republicans added Alaska, Arizona, Arkansas, Florida, Maryland, Minnesota, Nebraska, Nevada and New Mexico to the list of governorships under their control. Among the new Republican governors were Winthrop Rockefeller of Arkansas; Claude R. Kirk Jr. (in traditionally Democratic Florida); and Spiro T. Agnew of Maryland, a political moderate who defeated George P. Mahoney, the narrow victor in a three-way Democratic primary who had pitched his campaign to the "white backlash" vote. (In general, "backlash" candidates were unsuccessful in the elections.) Republican gubernatorial candidate Howard Callaway won a plurality of the votes in the one-time impregnable Democratic stronghold of Georgia. But Callaway failed to poll an absolute majority, and under the Georgia constitution, the election was thrown into the state legislature, which chose the Democratic runner-up, Lester Maddox.

The Republicans' most spectacular gain was in the House, where they picked up 52 seats and lost only five to the Democrats. The new party lineup in the House would be 248 Democrats and 187 Republicans. The Republican total in the thirteen Southern states rose to 28 seats, compared with only 14 in 1962. In Senate elections Republicans gained seats in Illinois, Oregon and Tennessee, giving them 36 seats to the Democrats' 64. Democrats failed to take any Senate seats from the Republicans.

In the state legislatures the Republicans scored net gains of 156 senate seats and 401 seats in the lower houses, reflecting not only the strong party trend running in the Republicans' favor but the fact that reapportionment, by adding seats in suburban areas, was helping them as much as it helped the Democrats, if not more.

1967-69:
The 90th Congress

The United States in 1967-68 underwent two of the most trying years in its history as a rising wave of rioting and looting swept over its largely black central cities, the Vietnam War continued to build in human and dollar costs, inflationary pressures mounted and two major national leaders were assassinated. President Johnson, recognizing the inability of his administration to command continued strong popular support, announced in March 1968 that he would not seek reelection to a second full term in the White House.

The Vietnam War became increasingly troublesome. It often overshadowed civil rights and city problems, distorted the U.S. economy and loomed over U.S. foreign policy. Its cost soared to more than $2 billion a month. Reflecting the expense of the war, the federal budget by fiscal 1969 was at a record $186 billion, with $80 billion of that for defense.

Hopes for a political settlement in Vietnam were buoyed on Oct. 31, when President Johnson announced he was ordering a complete halt to all American bombing of the North. Though not officially confirmed, it was believed that the bombing halt was undertaken with tacit agreement that it would last only so long as the North Vietnamese did not use it to their military advantage. A new and complicated round of negotiations then began in Paris on the means and protocol for substantive peace negotiations.

The patterns of violence in American life reasserted themselves when two prominent Americans became victims of assassins' bullets. The first was the Rev. Martin Luther King Jr., who was shot and killed April 4, 1968, in Memphis, Tenn. Following his death, rioting, looting and burning broke out in black districts in more than one hundred cities.

On June 5 another apostle of social progress and reconciliation between the races was struck down. Leaving the Los Angeles hotel ballroom in which he had made his California presidential primary victory statement, Sen. Robert F. Kennedy was shot in the head and died 25 hours later.

The 1968 Campaigns

Few presidential election years in the history of the nation brought as many surprising developments as 1968. Just a year before the election, it appeared likely that the two candidates might be President Johnson for the Democrats and Michigan's governor George W. Romney for the Republicans. But by late winter 1968 both Johnson and Romney were out of the picture, and each of the major parties was plunged into spirited fights for their presidential nominations. During 1968 continued racial tensions in the nation led to fears that Alabama's former governor George C. Wallace, running as the candidate of his own American Independent Party, might win a major share of the national vote or at least cause deadlock in the Electoral College.

For the Democrats the year of surprises began Nov. 30, 1967, when Minnesota's Eugene McCarthy announced that he would enter four 1968 presidential primaries to demonstrate opposition to the Johnson policies. McCarthy's candidacy struck an immediate chord of response, especially among younger Americans who shared his fervent distaste for the war in Vietnam. Most political observers discounted the seriousness of McCarthy's candidacy, but in the March 12 presidential primary in New Hampshire, McCarthy scored an amazing "moral" victory by gathering 42 percent of the vote against the president's 49 percent.

The McCarthy vote in New Hampshire then triggered another major surprise: the entry of Robert Kennedy into the Democratic presidential race, announced March 16. And on March 31 President Johnson stunned the nation by announcing, at the end of a lengthy radio and television address on Vietnam policy, that he would not seek reelection in 1968.

After Johnson withdrew, the race for the Democratic nomination turned into a three-way affair: McCarthy, Kennedy and Vice President Hubert Humphrey, who entered the fray in April. On June 4, in the conclusive California primary, Kennedy emerged the narrow victor over McCarthy, only to be assassinated as he left the hotel ballroom where he had claimed victory.

The death of Kennedy, who had shared McCarthy's Vietnam views while taking a far more aggressive stance on urban and minority problems, was followed by an eerie moratorium in Democratic politics as the shaken party factions sought to decide on their next move. But within weeks Humphrey emerged as the odds-on favorite for the nomination.

While violence flared in the city streets and thousands of police and guards imposed security precautions unprecedented in the annals of American presidential conventions, the 35th Democratic National Convention met Aug. 26-29 in Chicago to nominate Hubert H. Humphrey of Minnesota for the presidency and to endorse the controversial Vietnam policies of the Johnson-Humphrey administration. Humphrey's selection as running mate was Maine's Sen. Edmund S. Muskie. In the campaign that followed Muskie's calm-voiced appeals for understanding between the groups in American society would prove an asset for the Democratic ticket.

In a minority were the anti-war factions that rallied around the candidacies of McCarthy and McGovern. The McCarthy forces mounted a series of challenges to the Humphrey faction, on credentials, rules, the platform and the nomination itself. An unprecedented number of credentials were challenged. McCarthy, McGovern and other liberal factions won their greatest breakthrough on convention rules, obtaining abolition of a mandatory unit rule for the 1968 convention and at every level of party activity leading up to and including the 1972 convention. Many Humphrey-pledged delegates also backed the move. For the first time in recent party history, the functioning of party machinery at every level had been questioned. Humphrey won his party's nomination, but he would lead a bitterly divided party into the autumn campaign.

In the Republican Party George Romney had established himself as the early leader in the race for the nomination, but his liberalism was distasteful to many orthodox Republicans. He was followed into the GOP race by Richard Nixon, who made his long-anticipated candidacy formal on Feb. 1. The two front-runners entered the New Hampshire presidential primary, but it soon became apparent to Romney that he faced a likely loss, and on Feb. 28 he surprised the nation by withdrawing from the contest. Nixon won an overwhelming victory in the March 12 New Hampshire GOP primary. Moderate and liberal Republicans hoped that New York's Gov. Nelson A. Rockefeller would step into the void created by Romney's withdrawal, but Rockefeller declared on March 21 that he would not run because "the majority of (Republican) leaders want the candidacy of Richard Nixon."

Without significant opposition Nixon swept the Wisconsin, Indiana, Nebraska, Oregon and South Dakota primaries, shedding most of the "loser" image he had acquired from his 1960 defeat for president and 1962 defeat for governor of California. Rockefeller reversed his ground once again by entering the race on April 30, but even in the primaries where write-ins were permitted, the vote for him was generally low.

The Republican National Convention, meeting in Miami Beach Aug. 5-8, wrote a moderately progressive party platform and then chose candidates for president and vice president who, at the moment of their selection, seemed to be taking increasingly restrictive attitudes on the sensitive national issues of law, order and civil rights.

Nixon won nomination for the presidency on the first ballot, bearing out the predictions of his campaign organization. For vice president, at Nixon's suggestion, the Republicans selected Spiro T. Agnew, governor of Maryland since his election in 1966. The selection of Agnew, one of the major surprises of the year, was announced by Nixon the morning after his own nomination, and in the wake of almost-solid all-night conferences with Republican leaders, chiefly those of a conservative bent. Liberal Republicans were outraged at Agnew's designation.

Nixon seemed to represent the middle ground of the Republican Party of 1968, substantially to the right of Governor Rockefeller and well to the center of the road compared to the conservative Ronald Reagan. The Republican platform of 1968, adopted by the Convention Aug. 6 without a floor fight or any amendments, was generally moderate in tone and contained a preamble calling for a major national effort to rebuild urban and rural slums and attack the root causes of poverty, including racism.

To conduct his second campaign for the presidency, Nixon assembled a massive—and doubtless the best financed—campaign organization in U.S. history. Nixon was intent on avoiding the mistakes of his 1960 campaign, when a frenetic campaign pace resulted in exhaustion and snap decisions.

A central theme of Nixon's campaign was an appeal to a group he called the "forgotten Americans," whom Nixon defined as "the nonshouters," those who "work in America's factories, run America's business, serve in Government, provide most of the soldiers who died to keep us free." By suggesting that his administration would look chiefly to the interest of this group, Nixon was able to make a strong bid for the support of white suburban and small-town America, the traditional heartland of GOP strength in the nation.

Humphrey's bid for the presidency got off to a depressing start in September 1968 with sparse crowds, disordered schedules and vicious heckling by left-wing, anti-war elements virtually everywhere he sought to speak. Humphrey's first task was to establish some measure of independence from the vastly unpopular Johnson administration. A significant step to win some of the anti-war Democrats to his side came in a Sept. 30 televised address from Salt Lake City, when he said he would stop the bombing of North Vietnam "as an acceptable risk for peace." When President Johnson actually took that step on Oct. 31, Humphrey could hardly restrain his glee. The combination of his own softened stand and the presidential position won him, at least at the last moment, the support of many of the Democrats who had been most disaffected at Chicago.

Humphrey endorsed virtually all the social advances of the Kennedy-Johnson years but called for a substantial broadening of domestic efforts to solve the problems of cities and minorities. He charged that Nixon's economic policies would bring America "back to McKinley," with recessions and unemployment like those the country experienced during the Eisenhower years.

George Wallace had announced on Feb. 8, 1968, that he would run for president as a third party candidate under the banner of the American Independent Party. His campaign had a narrower goal: to win the balance of power in Electoral College voting, thus depriving either major party of the clear electoral majority required for election. Wallace made it clear that he would then expect one of the major party candidates to make concessions in return for sufficient support from the Wallace supporters to win election. Wallace indicated he expected the election to be resolved in the Electoral College and not go to the House of Representatives for resolution. At the end of the campaign, it was revealed that he had obtained affidavits from all his electors in which they promised to vote for Wallace "or whomsoever he may direct" in the Electoral College.

Results of the 1968 Elections

In one of the closest elections of the century Richard Nixon on Nov. 5 was elected president. In percentage terms Nixon had 43.4 percent of the popular vote, the lowest winning percentage for a winning presidential candidate since 1912, when Woodrow Wilson won by 41.9 percent. Humphrey's percentage was 42.7; Wallace's was 13.5.

For the Republican Party Nixon's victory had special significance. He was the first successful GOP presidential contender since the 1920s who was closely identified with the party organization. The victories of Dwight D. Eisenhower in the 1950s, followed by Nixon's defeat in 1960, had raised the possibility that the Republicans might lack the broad appeal ever to win a presidential victory unless their candidate possessed special nonparty appeal.

The Democrats had feared that the election would bring a final dissolution of the grand Democratic coalition that had controlled the federal government in most elections since the 1930s. The election returns did show the South deserting the Democratic Party in presidential voting, the Deep South to Wallace, the border South to Nixon. But the other elements of the Democratic coalition held together remarkably well, helping the party to win the electoral votes of several major states and to return a high proportion of its congressional incumbents.

Preelection surveys of Wallace voters had indicated that if they had been obliged to choose between Nixon and Humphrey, about twice as many would have preferred Nixon as Humphrey. If Wallace had not been on the ballot, Nixon would very possibly have carried some of the five Deep South states that went for Wallace, possibly building up a stronger national vote lead in the process. But it was difficult to tell from the election returns whether Wallace had hurt Nixon or Humphrey the more in the non-Southern states.

Another bright spot for the Republicans was on the governorship level, where the GOP added five seats for a new total of 31. But the Democrats retained control of both houses of the Congress.

In the Senate Republicans gained five new seats, for a total of 42, the largest number they had held since 1956. The gain was a major accomplishment for the GOP. It was the biggest gain since 1950, when the Republicans also won five new seats. The breakdown for the new Senate was 58 Democrats and 42 Republicans. In the 90th Congress, there had been 63 Democrats and 37 Republicans. Republicans actually won seven seats previously held by Democrats, but since Democrats won two seats previously held by Republicans, the net gain for the Republicans was five. No incumbent Republican standing for reelection was defeated, while four incumbent Democrats lost their bids for additional terms.

The makeup of the new Senate was expected to result in a shift, although not a dramatic one, to the right. While liberal strength remained the same as in the 90th Congress, strength among moderate senators dropped and strength among conservative senators rose correspondingly.

The seven Republicans who captured Senate seats previously held by Democrats included Barry Goldwater, former senator from Arizona and unsuccessful Republican presidential candidate in 1964. Goldwater, whose previous service gave him seniority over the other Republican freshmen, replaced retiring Carl Hayden, president pro tempore of the Senate.

Three Republican representatives also won Senate seats previously held by Democrats. They were Edward J. Gurney of Florida, Charles McC. Mathias Jr. of Maryland and Richard S. Schweiker of Pennsylvania. Other Republicans winning seats previously held by Democrats were Henry L. Bellmon of Oklahoma and William B. Saxbe of Ohio. The other two freshman Republicans were Marlow W. Cook of Kentucky and Rep. Robert Dole of Kansas. The two Democrats who won seats previously held by Republicans were Alan Cranston of California and Iowa governor Harold E. Hughes.

In the House the party breakdown when the 91st Congress convened was 243 Democrats and 192 Republicans. In all Republicans took nine seats from the Democrats and lost five of their own for a four-seat net gain. Republicans had scored a net gain of 47 seats in the 1966 elections and had won a special election to fill a Democratic vacancy earlier in 1968. The Republicans had lost 38 seats in the 1964 elections.

Of the 435 representatives elected in November 396 were incumbents (223 Democrats and 173 Republicans), and only 39 (20 Democrats and 19 Republicans) were newcomers. The new winners included two former representatives, one a Democrat and the other a Republican.

The new Congress would have the smallest crop of freshman members in years. Between 1940 and 1948 an average of 96 newcomers were elected to each new House. The average dropped to 68 between 1950 and 1958 but rose to 72 between 1960 and 1966. In 1964 there were 91 newcomers elected and in 1966, 73.

In gubernatorial races the Republican Party, winning 13 of the year's 21 races and capturing seven seats held by Democrats, increased its control of the nation's statehouses from 26 to 31. Even after the selection of a Democrat to succeed Vice President-elect Agnew, the GOP would boast 30 governors, equaling its holdings after the Eisenhower sweep of 1952, when there were two fewer states.

In light of the extremely close presidential race and the continuing, though narrowed, control of Congress by the Democrats, the Republican margin of 10 governorships gave the party its most broad-based mandate for leadership. The GOP scored a net gain of three seats each in the East and the Midwest and lost one in the West. There were no party changes in the South.

Nixon's coattails had a less decisive effect than did Eisenhower's four national elections earlier. Nixon did carry six of the seven states in which Republicans took governorships formerly held by Democrats (including two incumbents). But it was far from clear who helped whom in several of those races. In Montana an easy Nixon win failed to save Gov. Tim M. Babcock, an early Nixon backer. In Rhode Island, the only other race in which a Republican incumbent was beaten, Gov. John H. Chaffee's advocacy of a state income tax appeared to be the major factor in his defeat.

Battling for seats vacated by Democratic incumbents, Republicans won in Indiana, Iowa, West Virginia, New Hampshire and Vermont. State matters, primarily fiscal, were the main issues in all five states. The Democrats suffered particularly through the voluntary retirement of their popular governors in normally Republican Iowa, New Hampshire and Vermont. Except for Montana and Rhode Island the Democrats picked up no seats formerly held by Republicans.

Republicans scored minimal gains in the contests for state legislature seats around the country. As a result of the elections, they would control 20 legislatures, the same number controlled by the Democrats. (The other 10 were split in control or nonpartisan.) The GOP rose in strength from 41.8 to 43.4 percent of the seats in all senate chambers around the country but held static at just over 42 percent of all seats in lower houses.

1969-71:
The 91st Congress

The 91st Congress, which adjourned on Jan. 2, 1971, compiled a substantial record of domestic accomplishments despite drawn-out disputes with President Nixon over foreign policy and spending.

The Senate made the first substantial attempt since World War II to challenge the president's authority on foreign policy and military involvement. Although the House generally agreed to uphold President Nixon's requests to finance new weapons systems and to send money

and troops into Southeast Asia, the Senate engaged in numerous long debates on those issues.

It was in domestic legislation, however, that Congress compiled its most substantial record of accomplishment. This legislation included major air and water pollution control measures, a $25-billion education authorization and a bill extending the 1965 Voting Rights Act and allowing 18-year-olds to vote in national elections. In the final days of the 1970 session Congress completed action on a bill extending the food stamp program that, for the first time, provided free food stamps for the poorest families.

Congress and the administration worked to establish new federal agencies. Foremost among these was the government-owned postal corporation to replace the Post Office Department. Congress also agreed to the president's reorganization plans to set up an independent Environmental Protection Agency and a National Atmospheric and Oceanic Administration in the Commerce Department.

Problems concerning the economy dominated Nixon's first two years in office, and Congress attempted periodically to deal with these problems. In 1969 it enacted a major overhaul of the tax code. It sliced funds from military, foreign aid and space requests and added money to numerous domestic programs, notably education, health, training and pollution control. Congress enacted a federal spending ceiling for fiscal 1971, as it had for fiscal years 1969 and 1970.

Congress engaged in debates over the Vietnam War in attempts to limit deployment of troops and reduce spending. The Senate voted twice to repeal the 1964 Tonkin Gulf resolution, and the House eventually agreed to repeal the resolution.

The 1970 Midterm Elections

Despite the unprecedented off-year campaign efforts of President Nixon and Vice President Agnew, most observers felt the Republicans suffered a net loss in the elections of Nov. 3, 1970. In their drive to improve the Republican position in Congress and in state capitals, the president campaigned for candidates in 23 states during the weeks preceding the election, and the vice president visited 29 states.

Although the effect of a presidential appearance for a candidate was unclear, Nixon and Agnew could point to victories in several states where they campaigned: Senate victories in Maryland, Connecticut, Ohio and Tennessee, for example, and gubernatorial victories in Connecticut, Tennessee, California, Arizona, Iowa, Vermont and Wyoming. Administration efforts failed to pay off in other states on the Republican target list. Democratic candidates were elected to the Senate in Utah, New Mexico, Wyoming, Nevada, North Dakota and Indiana, despite the high-level administration campaigning. And Nixon or Agnew visits failed to persuade voters to elect Republican senators in California, Texas, Illinois, or Florida.

The most spectacular third party victory of the year was that of James L. Buckley of New York, a Conservative who was elected to the Senate with a minority of the votes. Buckley's election was made possible by a division of the votes for the Republican-Liberal incumbent, Charles E. Goodell, and the Democratic candidate, Rep. Richard L. Ottinger.

Another third party success belonged to Sen. Harry F. Byrd Jr of Virginia. In March 1970 the veteran Democrat announced that he would not run as a Democrat because of a party "loyalty oath" that he claimed would force him to commit himself to the Democratic presidential candidate in

1972. Byrd ran as an Independent, easily defeating the Democratic and Republican candidates.

A second incumbent Democratic senator who ran as an Independent was Thomas J. Dodd of Connecticut. Dodd had been censured by the Senate in 1967 for diverting testimonial funds to his personal use. He was regarded as unlikely to win the Senate nomination in a Democratic primary. His Independent candidacy divided the Democratic vote and helped elect a Republican, Rep. Lowell P. Weicker Jr., to his seat.

Results of the 1970 Elections

Republicans registered a net gain of two Senate seats in the Nov. 3 elections, leaving Democrats with a majority of 55 to 45 in the 92nd Congress. Of the 35 Senate seats being contested, 11 were won by Republicans, 22 by Democrats, one by a Conservative Party candidate and one by an Independent. Democrats had held 25 of the seats and Republicans, 10. Republicans who captured Democratic seats were Rep. Weicker, Rep. J. Glenn Beall Jr. of Maryland, Rep. Robert Taft Jr. of Ohio and Rep. W. E. Brock III of Tennessee.

In Minnesota Hubert H. Humphrey won back a seat in the Senate, where he had served from 1949 to 1965, when he became vice president. He defeated Republican representative Clark MacGregor for the seat of retiring Democrat Eugene J. McCarthy. In Texas former Democratic representative Lloyd M. Bentsen Jr. defeated Rep. George Bush for the seat held by Ralph W. Yarborough, a Democrat defeated in the May 2 primary.

The Democratic Party showed renewed strength in the Great Plains and the Far West in the 1970 elections as it gained nine House seats to open up a 255-180 margin for the 92nd Congress. Republicans claimed success in limiting Democratic gains to less than the 38-seat average pickup recorded by the nonpresidential party in off-year elections during this century. Democrats said their gains were significant because President Nixon's 1968 victory carried in few of the marginal candidates, who are normally easy prey to the party out of power in off-year contests.

Registering the most impressive net gain in statehouses by any party since 1938, Democrats in 1970 took 13 governorships from Republican control, while losing only two, in Tennessee and Connecticut. The balance of state power shifted dramatically from 18 Democratic and 32 Republican governors before the election to 29 Democratic and 21 Republican governors.

State-level gains were doubly significant in 1970. Democratic control of a majority of the states furnished vital power bases for the 1972 presidential elections. Democrats won Ohio and Pennsylvania and held Texas, thus controlling three of the most populous states. Democrats also wrested from Republican control Alaska, Florida, Arkansas and Oklahoma and the Western and Midwestern states of Idaho, Minnesota, Nebraska, Nevada, New Mexico, South Dakota and Wisconsin. Republicans continued to hold New York, California, Michigan and Illinois.

Republicans went into the 1970 elections holding 51 of the 99 state legislative bodies (Nebraska has a unicameral legislature). This figure included the two nominally nonpartisan legislatures of Minnesota and Nebraska, which were controlled by conservative, Republican-oriented majorities. Democrats held the other 48 chambers. Following the 1970 elections Democrats gained control of eight new legislative bodies, giving them control of 56.

1971-73:
The 92nd Congress

The years 1971-73 saw some of the boldest and most dramatic presidential initiatives in years. In the summer of 1971 President Nixon imposed wage and price controls on the economy, announced that he would visit Communist China and planned a summit meeting with Soviet leaders. His visits to China and the Soviet Union in 1972 gave Nixon a strong boost in his campaign for reelection.

Dissent over the Vietnam War, which seemed on the rise in the spring of 1971, had waned by midyear following troop withdrawal announcements by Nixon. At year's end 45,000 additional troops were scheduled for withdrawal, practically bringing to an end the offensive combat involvement of U.S. ground forces. By late 1972 it appeared that a settlement of the Vietnam War, or at least a cease-fire and return of U.S. prisoners, was imminent. Presidential aide Henry Kissinger and North Vietnamese officials had hammered out a nine-point agreement, but the Saigon government balked, and the elusive peace had to await a final agreement in January 1973.

In October 1972 Congress gave President Nixon a major legislative victory: passage of a general revenue-sharing measure. The bill was the only one of the president's "six great goals" to pass during the 92nd Congress. In 1972 Congress also approved the Equal Rights Amendment, 49 years after it was introduced. The amendment was sent to the states for ratification March 22 after the Senate passed it 84-8.

On June 17, 1972, five men were arrested in the Democratic national headquarters at the Watergate building in Washington, D.C. This incident was the beginning of a process that was to continue over the next two years and destroy a presidency. The break-in was immediately tagged the "Watergate caper" by the press. But by the time the election arrived it had become the "Watergate affair," and it was being examined seriously. In the months following the celebrated break-in, allegations of a widespread network of political espionage and sabotage engineered by the Republicans were carried in the news media. Charges of involvement were leveled by the Democrats and the press against persons in high positions in the White House and the Committee for the Reelection of the President.

Seven men were indicted on criminal charges, three civil suits were filed and one man was found guilty in a Florida court on a minor charge related to Watergate. Two congressional committees initiated staff investigations of the allegations. And Watergate repeatedly surfaced in the presidential campaign, with Democratic nominee George McGovern and his campaign pursuing the charges and President Nixon and his staff denouncing them. Investigators and reporters began to backtrack: meetings, phone calls, financial transactions and other related events were traced back months before the incident.

The 1972 Campaigns

President Nixon was in a strong position to seek another term as the 1972 presidential election year opened. His wage and price control system had curbed the inflationary spiral, while increased federal spending cut into the unemployment rate. His scheduled trips to Beijing and Moscow promised widespread publicity and a focus on the "peace" half of a peace and prosperity theme. And although he had alienated small groups of Republicans on the left and right wings of his party, Nixon could count on being renominated without much trouble.

The Democrats, meanwhile, headed toward a bruising battle for the nomination that would rip their party apart. Although Maine senator Edmund S. Muskie looked like a strong possibility for the nomination in late 1971, his centrist liberal political stance was not enough to hold the party together. His candidacy soon collapsed in the rush of primary voters toward the left or right wings of the party. Still angry over the Vietnam War, left-wing party activists gathered behind Sen. George McGovern of South Dakota. On the right Alabama governor George C. Wallace gathered voters angry with busing and the rapid pace of social change in general.

Other well-known candidates who entered the fray for the Democratic presidential nomination were Sen. Henry M. Jackson of Washington and Sen. Hubert H. Humphrey of Minnesota. Several other hopefuls failed to gain any significant momentum; among them were former senator Eugene J. McCarthy of Minnesota and Rep. Shirley Chisholm of New York. Chisholm was the first black to run in a series of presidential primaries.

McGovern began his upward climb to the nomination by a stronger than expected showing in the New Hampshire primary. Although Muskie won the popular vote there, he was labeled a loser because he received far fewer votes than expected. From there it was downhill for Muskie, and after he ran fourth in the Pennsylvania primary on April 25, he ceased active campaigning. McGovern, meanwhile, ran first in Wisconsin on April 4, then won Massachusetts, Nebraska, Oregon, and beat Humphrey in a June 6 showdown in California. From there on he was practically assured of the nomination, although there was a last-minute effort at the convention to stop him.

McGovern's highly vocal and longstanding opposition to the Vietnam War caused many political analysts to look on him as a one-issue candidate. But his major problem was one of recognition. Public opinion polls indicated that he had only 2 percent support from the voters in the field of prospective Democratic nominees. By mid-March, after two months of extensive campaigning, McGovern had gained only 3 percentage points in the polls.

Beyond any doubt the reform commission that McGovern had headed after the disastrous Democratic convention of 1968 had changed the face of the Democratic Party. And beyond any doubt the changes favored McGovern's candidacy by expanding the party's base and bringing more women, minorities and youths into the process.

At the convention, McGovern's winning of the nomination was never really in doubt, even before the balloting began, and he moved steadily toward his goal. The Democrats chose Sen. Thomas F. Eagleton of Missouri as their nominee for vice president. But on July 25 Eagleton disclosed that he had voluntarily hospitalized himself three times between 1960 and 1966 for "nervous exhaustion and fatigue." Since 1966, said the candidate, he had "experienced good, solid, sound health." But Eagleton's statement, culminating an investigation by reporters of his past difficulties under stress, started a sequence of developments that included increasing pressure for Eagleton to withdraw from the ticket. After a meeting with McGovern on July 31, Eagleton withdrew from the ticket.

His presidential campaign sidetracked, McGovern announced Aug. 5 that his choice to replace Eagleton was R. Sargent Shriver, former director of the Peace Corps and the Office of Economic Opportunity and U.S. ambassador to France. In a display of unity and anti-Nixon oratory, the newly enlarged Democratic National Committee at an Aug. 8 meeting in Washington nominated Shriver with 2,936 of the 3,013 votes cast.

In the Republican camp the renomination of President Nixon did not go completely unchallenged. He had opposition from both the left and the right. Assailing the president from the left was California representative Paul N. McCloskey Jr., who based his campaign on opposition to administration policies and its deception of the news media. McCloskey withdrew six days after the New Hampshire primary because of insufficient funds, but his name remained on the ballot in 12 other states as a symbolic protest. Nixon's opponent on the right was Ohio representative John M. Ashbrook, who attacked the president for what he called his failure to live up to 1968 promises in fiscal matters, foreign affairs and defense posture. Ashbrook's name was on the ballot in 11 state presidential primaries.

The Republican National Convention was a gigantic television spectacular from start to finish. The main business of the convention, the nomination of President Nixon and Vice President Agnew to a second term, was a preordained ritual.

Nixon did little campaigning for his second term. Because of his strong lead in the polls and lack of speech making, the president also was in the enviable position of making few, if any, concrete campaign pledges to the electorate. He enunciated the major themes of the campaign in his acceptance speech before the Republican convention, emphasizing the divisions in the Democratic Party and urging dissatisfied Democrats to downplay traditional party loyalty.

From almost every standpoint the Democratic campaign contrasted sharply with that of the Republicans. McGovern and his running mate were on the road incessantly from Labor Day until election day. McGovern tried in vain to draw Nixon into debate. His initial tax and welfare reform proposals attracted widespread criticism and helped alienate several traditional sources of Democratic strength, such as ethnic groups and blue-collar workers. When he substituted Shriver for Eagleton, he was attacked for poor judgment and vacillation. His chief issue, administration conduct of the Vietnam War, lost whatever remaining effect it might have had when an administration-negotiated peace appeared to be in sight during the last days of the campaign.

Rather than moving into the offensive against the administration, McGovern was kept on the defensive throughout the campaign, constantly forced to explain earlier positions and rebut Republican charges. The break-in at Democratic headquarters at Watergate in June and ensuing disclosures of the alleged involvement of administration officials in espionage and sabotage directed against the Democrats was potentially damaging, but the charge failed to excite the voters enough to head off the Nixon sweep.

Results of the 1972 Elections

Nixon swept back into the White House on Nov. 7 with a devastating landslide victory over McGovern. He carried a record of 49 states for a total of 520 electoral votes. Only Massachusetts and the District of Columbia, with a meager 17 electoral votes between them, went for McGovern.

The Nixon landslide was the first Republican sweep since Reconstruction of the once solid Democratic South. By runaway margins Nixon took all 11 states of the old Confederacy, plus all the border states.

Americans engaged in massive ticket splitting in the 1972 election. Nixon's landslide victory was not reflected in significant Republican gains in Congress or in governorships. Despite the avalanche of votes for Nixon, the Democrats scored a net gain of two seats in the Senate, thereby increasing their majority to 57-43 in the 93rd Congress. Of the 33 seats contested, the Democrats won 16 and the Republicans won 17. Nineteen of those seats had been controlled by the Republicans in the 92nd Congress, 14 by the Democrats.

The most significant, and surprising, element of the Democratic gain was the upset of four seemingly well entrenched Republican incumbents: Gordon Allott of Colorado, J. Caleb Boggs of Delaware, Jack Miller of Iowa and Margaret Chase Smith of Maine. If it had not been for Republican gains in three Southern states (North Carolina, Oklahoma and Virginia), the Democratic majority in the Senate would have been much larger.

Half of the eight new Democrats were considered significantly more liberal than the incumbent Republicans they upset. In this category were Floyd K. Haskell, who beat Allott in Colorado; Joseph R. Biden Jr., who defeated Boggs in Delaware; Dick Clark, who retired Miller in Iowa; and Rep. William D. Hathaway, who upset Smith in Maine. A fifth Democrat, Rep. James Abourezk, defeated Republican Robert W. Hirsch in South Dakota to take the seat of retiring Republican incumbent Karl E. Mundt. Abourezk was considered far more liberal than the conservative Mundt.

Two more Democrats were conservatives who replaced conservatives. Sam Nunn of Georgia and J. Bennett Johnston Jr. of Louisiana defeated Republican opponents to fill the seats of Democratic incumbents David H. Gambrell of Georgia and the late Allen J. Ellender of Louisiana. The remaining Democrat, Walter "Dee" Huddleston, defied the Southern election trend by winning his race against Republican Louie B. Nunn in Kentucky for the seat of retiring Republican John Sherman Cooper. Both the incumbent and his successor were moderates.

Final returns showed that Republicans gained 13 House seats in the 1972 elections, far short of the number they needed to win control of the House. The 13-seat pickup was slightly more than the four House seats gained when President Nixon first was elected in 1968, but it was far less than the winning party usually has gained in a presidential landslide. A close look at the House figures showed that the president not only lacked coattails, but appeared to have little if any perceptible effect on House races.

The only semblance of coattail effects in the election was in the South, where the Republicans took seven House seats out of Democratic hands. For several states the election of Republican representatives meant drastic breaks with tradition.

The 1972 election was the first to take place after the reapportionment and redistricting that followed the 1970 census. More than a dozen entirely new districts were created, and others had major changes in their boundary lines. Most of these changes tended to favor the Republicans, because many new districts were placed in fast-growing Republican suburbs and because legislatures in several key states drew the lines to partisan Republican advantage.

Redistricting also played a significant part in the defeat of House incumbents. Thirteen incumbents, eight Democrats and five Republicans, were defeated. For nine of these incumbents, seven of them Democrats, redistricting was the dominant factor in their defeat. Three lost because redistricting forced them to run against other incumbents.

The House of Representatives in the 93rd Congress looked quite a bit different from its predecessor, but the reasons were mainly because of redistricting and retirement, not election defeats. The new count was 243 Democrats and 192 Republicans.

Chalking up a net gain of one, the Democrats in 1972 retained the wide margin of statehouse control they won in 1970, holding 31 governorships to the Republicans' 19. (Democrats had gained the Kentucky governorship in the 1971 off-year elections.) Of the 18 seats up for election in 1972, Democrats won 11 and Republicans won seven. Despite upsets in several states, the net result was only a minimal change in party power.

Republicans lost governorships in Delaware, Illinois, and Vermont, while ousting Democrats in Missouri and North Carolina. Close races in New Hampshire, North Carolina, Washington and West Virginia were won by Republicans, who also upset a favored Democratic candidate in Indiana. As expected, Republicans won gubernatorial contests in Iowa and Missouri.

Incumbent or favored Republicans were upset by Democrats in Illinois, North Dakota, Rhode Island and Vermont, while Democratic incumbents were reelected in Arkansas, Kansas, South Dakota and Utah. In Montana and Texas, Democrats were elected to succeed retiring Democratic governors. As expected, the Democratic challenger unseated Delaware's Republican incumbent by capitalizing on the issue of taxes.

In West Virginia's gubernatorial race, which drew national attention, Republican governor Arch A. Moore Jr. put together his general popularity and campaigning ability with Nixon's strong showing in the state—and the obvious incongruity of a millionaire populist candidate running in one of the nation's poorest states—to defeat Democratic challenger John D. "Jay" Rockefeller, the secretary of state.

1973-75:
The 93rd Congress

The legislative activities of the 93rd Congress were overshadowed by one of the nation's greatest political crises: Watergate. Watergate dominated the news from the beginning of the second Nixon administration in January 1973 until the president's resignation on Aug. 9, 1974. The year 1973 opened with the trial of the seven Watergate burglars beginning Jan. 8. Five of the seven defendants pleaded guilty a few days after the trial opened, while the remaining two stood trial and were found guilty by the end of the month. Sentencing was March 23.

From mid-May until early August 1973 American television screens were filled with politicians and former government officials testifying before the Senate Select Committee on Presidential Campaign Activities—the Watergate committee. Most important of all information produced by the hearings was the revelation that tape recordings had been made of many presidential conversations in the White House during the period in which the break-in occurred and the cover-up began. The tapes contained evidence that ultimately led to Nixon's resignation.

Immediately after the existence of the tapes was made public on July 16, a struggle for the recordings began. The legal battle would last a year, from July 23, 1973, to July 24, 1974, when the Supreme Court ruled that Nixon had to turn over the tapes to U.S. District Judge John J. Sirica for use as evidence in the Watergate cover-up trial.

In the midst of the tapes battle, Spiro Agnew, on Oct. 10, 1973, became the second vice president in American history to resign. Under investigation for multiple charges of alleged conspiracy, extortion and bribery, Agnew agreed to resign and avoided imprisonment by pleading nolo contendere to charges of income tax evasion.

Two days after Agnew's resignation President Nixon nominated House Minority Leader Gerald R. Ford of Michigan as his successor. Ford became the 40th vice president of the United States on Dec. 6, 1973.

While Americans were reeling from these events, they were overtaken by an energy crisis, as a result of the Arab oil embargo, and some of the worst inflation to hit the economy in peacetime history.

But even as public attention focused on the presidency and the economic problems of the country, Congress was passing landmark legislation representing an attempt to change the balance of power between the presidency and Congress. Among measures enacted were limits on a president's right to impound money, the establishment of a more thorough method for Congress to consider the federal budget and restrictions on the president's war-making powers.

Investigation of Watergate continued. After two months of closed congressional hearings beginning May 9, 1974, and a series of televised debates beginning July 24, the House Judiciary Committee voted to recommend three articles of impeachment.

On Aug. 5 Nixon released three previously undisclosed transcripts. The conversations showed clearly Nixon's participation in the cover-up. In a written statement the president acknowledged that he had withheld the contents of the tapes despite the fact that they contradicted his previous declarations that he had not known of or participated in the cover-up. These admissions destroyed almost all of Nixon's remaining support in Congress. On Aug. 8 Nixon announced his resignation, to be effective at noon the next day, and Vice President Ford became the nation's 38th president.

A month after assuming office, Ford pardoned Nixon "for all offenses against the United States which he, Richard Nixon, has committed or may have committed" during his years as president.

Ford was succeeded in the vice presidency by Nelson A. Rockefeller, who became vice president Dec. 19, 1974, after the House confirmed his nomination by President Ford, 287-128. The Senate had given its approval Dec. 10, 90-7. Thus the nation for the first time had both a president and a vice president chosen under the 25th Amendment to the Constitution rather than by a national election.

Reacting to presidential campaign abuses, Congress in 1974 enacted a landmark campaign reform bill that radically overhauled the existing system of financing election campaigns. The new measure cleared Congress Oct. 10, 1974, and was signed into law five days later by President Ford. It established the first spending limits ever for candidates in presidential primary and general elections and in primary campaigns for the House and Senate.

Although the Arab nations had lifted their oil embargo, they and other oil producing states refused to lower the posted price for oil. The energy situation became intertwined with the grave economic problems President Ford inherited on taking office. Within months, he and Congress were trying to get together on an economic-energy package that reflected the inseparability of the two crises. The

continuing high oil prices played havoc with the international monetary system and contributed heavily to the deepening worldwide recession.

The 1974 Midterm Elections

Republicans paid the bill in November 1974 for two years of scandal and economic decline, losing heavily in congressional and gubernatorial elections throughout the country and slipping deeper into a minority status. Democrats gained 43 seats in the House, three seats in the Senate and four new governorships.

As soon as the Nov. 5 election returns were in, Republicans began looking for comfort in the fact that parties holding the White House normally lose heavily in midterm elections. But it was a small comfort. Democrats went into the 1974 election with nearly 60 percent of the seats in the Senate and House. For the most part the Democratic gains in the House were not marginal seats won by Republicans in a previous presidential sweep but solid Republican districts.

If there was one region that disappointed Republicans the most, it was the South. Shortly before the election the South was thought to be the one Republican bright spot. Losses were expected to be lightest in that area, and there was a good chance for the party to gain half a dozen House seats. As it turned out Republicans lost 10 House seats in the South and won only 2 Democratic ones.

The Midwest proved even more disastrous for Republicans. Before the election the Midwest had been the only region of the country in which Republicans held a majority of the House seats. But with a net Democratic gain of 14 seats there, that was no longer true.

A look at the demographics of the election yielded another interesting conclusion: Republicans suffered badly in the suburbs, where much of the so-called emerging Republican majority was supposed to lie. The striking fact about these suburban districts was that they were not marginal. In many cases the suburban districts that went Democratic contained thousands of former Democrats who left their party behind as they became prosperous enough to move outside the city limits. The new suburban middle class had been hard hit by recession and inflation, and Republicans may have paid the price.

Perhaps more important, however, was the prevalence in the suburbs of independent and ticket-splitting voters. Surveys had consistently shown a clear majority of independent voters favoring Democratic congressional candidates in 1974, and the switch in the independent vote probably was concentrated in the suburbs.

The heavy turnover decreed by the election—11 new senators, 92 new representatives, 40 incumbent representatives defeated—broke one of the most consistent political patterns of previous years. The tendency since World War II had been for incumbents to seek reelection as long as they were physically able to serve and for nearly all of them to win.

In 1974 that changed. Thanks to the combination of retirement and defeat, there were more first termers elected to the 94th House than to any other since 1949. More than one-third of the new House was elected either in 1972 or 1974.

Results of the 1974 Elections

The Democrats scored a net gain of three Senate seats in the Nov. 5 elections. A fourth gain came later in New Hampshire, where the state ballot law commission had at first declared Republican Louis C. Wyman the winner by two votes. But the Senate refused to seat Wyman, eventually declaring a vacancy which Democrat John Durkin won in a special election in September 1975. In addition, the Democrats had gained a seat in Ohio by appointment early in 1974, which they held in the November balloting.

Two incumbents, both Republicans, were defeated in the election. Marlow W. Cook of Kentucky lost by a substantial margin to Democratic governor Wendell H. Ford. In Colorado, Republican Peter H. Dominick was swamped by Democrat Gary W. Hart.

Democrats also captured two seats from which incumbent Republicans were retiring. In a major upset in Vermont Patrick J. Leahy beat Rep. Richard W. Mallary in a close race and became the first Democratic senator in the state's history. Leahy replaced retiring George D. Aiken, the Senate's senior Republican.

The Republicans' only Senate gain was in Nevada, where former governor Paul Laxalt was the winner by 624 votes.

In other races for vacant seats there were no shifts in party lineup. Democratic representative John C. Culver won the seat of retiring Harold E. Hughes in Iowa. In North Carolina former state attorney general Robert B. Morgan easily held the seat of Sam J. Ervin Jr. Two Democrats who defeated incumbents in primaries, former astronaut John H. Glenn Jr. of Ohio and Gov. Dale Bumpers of Arkansas, won landslide victories over weak Republican opposition.

Republicans, while losing Aiken's seat, held onto the Utah Senate seat of Wallace F. Bennett, who retired. Salt Lake City mayor Jake Garn won easily over Democratic representative Wayne Owens.

The Democratic gain was kept modest because the Republicans managed to hold their vulnerable Utah seat and to reelect three incumbents who had been in serious trouble: Senators Robert Dole of Kansas, Henry L. Bellmon of Oklahoma and Milton R. Young of North Dakota.

Three Democratic incumbents in difficult races won reelection. They were Birch Bayh of Indiana, George McGovern of South Dakota and Mike Gravel of Alaska. Other incumbents in both parties won easily.

In the House Democrats gained 43 seats, pushing their number just above the two-thirds mark. They had already made a net gain of five seats in special elections and a party switch, raising their total in the last days of the 93rd Congress to 248. Thus, after the elections, they had won 291 seats.

The Democratic trend was as broad as it was deep. It took away four Republican seats in New Jersey and four in California. It took five in Indiana, five in New York, three in Illinois, and two in Michigan. In nearly all cases the change to a new member of the House appeared to mean at least a slight shift to the left. There were a few new conservative Democratic representatives in the new House, such as John Birch Society member Lawrence P. McDonald of Georgia, but they were exceptions. For the most part liberal Democrats who retired were replaced by persons of similar persuasion, and conservative Republicans were replaced by Democrats who ran against them from the left.

The Republican group in the House was also expected to shift slightly toward liberalism even as it shrank by 43 members. Nearly every House Republican beaten Nov. 5 was counted among the conservatives; the liberal and moderate Republicans generally had little trouble winning reelection. The only serious casualty among the Republican moderates was John Dellenback of Oregon. Moderates such as John B. Anderson of Illinois and Paul N. McCloskey Jr. of California won without serious contest.

Election night was not pleasant for Republicans who remained loyal to President Nixon in the days just before his resignation. Four Republicans who supported Nixon during the House Judiciary Committee's impeachment inquiry were beaten decisively. They were David W. Dennis of Indiana, Wiley Mayne of Iowa and Joseph J. Maraziti and Charles W. Sandman Jr. of New Jersey. Harold V. Froehlich of Wisconsin, who supported two articles of impeachment against Nixon but opposed the third, also was defeated. All the Republicans on the Judiciary Committee who consistently voted to impeach Nixon were reelected, as were several Nixon defenders.

Democrats increased their firm hold on the nation's governorships from 32 to 36. Of the 35 seats up for election Democrats won 27, Republicans won seven, and an Independent was elected in Maine. The new lineup of governorships was 36 Democrats, 13 Republicans, and one Independent. Not since the 1930s had the Democrats—or any party—held as many as 36 of the nation's governorships.

Republicans lost governorships in three of the nation's ten largest states—New York, California and Massachusetts. They suffered three losses in the mountain states—Wyoming, Colorado and Arizona. Besides these states Republicans also lost control of governorships in Oregon, Connecticut and Tennessee, for a total loss of nine.

The Democrats also suffered some gubernatorial reverses, despite their overall net gain. In Alaska, Ohio, Kansas and South Carolina, Republicans picked up state capitols held by Democrats, leaving the Republicans with a net loss of five. Democrats also lost Maine to an Independent.

Perhaps the two greatest upsets in the gubernatorial races occurred in Maine and Ohio. In Maine voters rejected both major political parties, choosing instead James B. Longley, who ran as an Independent. Longley was the first Independent to be elected governor of any state since 1930. In Ohio, Democratic governor John J. Gilligan lost to former Republican governor James A. Rhodes.

Minority groups fared well in gubernatorial contests. Both Arizona and New Mexico elected Spanish-surnamed governors, Arizona for the first time in history and New Mexico for the first time in 56 years. In Hawaii Democrat George R. Ariyoshi became the first Japanese-American to hold the governorship of any state.

There were 15 other newcomers, for a total of 19 new governors. Among them were Edmund G. Brown Jr., D-Calif.; Ella T. Grasso, D-Conn.; Michael S. Dukakis, D-Mass.; David L. Boren, D-Okla.; James B. Edwards, R-S.C.; and Jay Hammond, R-Alaska.

Years of Uneasy Peace

By the time Jimmy Carter took the oath as president in January 1977, America's confidence had been shaken by almost a decade and a half of violence and scandal. The country had in effect lost its first war; had gone through a series of political assassinations and its first case of presidential resignation; had been besieged by urban, campus and racial violence; and had experienced the strains of an energy crisis and rampant inflation. In large part Carter's victory stemmed from the weariness of the voters with the normal political leadership of the country and their search for a new start. But however great the hopes, President Carter soon became embroiled in national problems and Washington politics. Critics charged him with inflexibility and lack of leadership. His energy bill was stalled and dismantled in Congress. And inflation resumed its seemingly inexorable rise. By mid-1979 few were optimistic that the nation's energy shortages and economic ills would be resolved any time soon. The debate over solutions continued to preoccupy the nation and its leaders.

The Democrats saw a reversal of fortunes in the 1980 election when conservative Ronald Reagan swept Carter from office. Reagan was the first GOP president since Dwight D. Eisenhower to have his party in a majority position in either chamber. The election gave conservatives a chance to control or influence national policy in the executive and legislative branches of government.

In line with his conservative ideology, President Reagan instigated huge tax cuts, which were largely credited with moving the country from recession to prosperity. The president came into office speaking in a traditional Republican manner, calling for a balanced budget. But he presided over the biggest deficits in American history, transforming the United States from the world's biggest creditor nation to the world's biggest debtor nation. During his tenure the national debt increased nearly threefold, from $931 billion to $2.69 trillion.

The Reagan foreign policy took many turns, gradually toning down an early ideological bent and a tendency to exert military muscle—such as in the 1983 invasion of Grenada and the 1986 bombing of Libya. But the focus always was on the Soviet Union. Over the years the United States had grown accustomed to dealing with a Soviet Union that was predictable. Kremlin leaders came and went, but the fundamental Soviet policies remained the same, and Washington did not have to be particularly creative in responding to them. Gorbachev, who came to power in March 1985, during the early stage of Reagan's second term, upset many of the underlying assumptions about Soviet behavior.

At the outset President Reagan vested much of his energy in strengthening the armed forces. He left the presidency as an apostle of superpower disarmament, welcoming U.S.-Soviet summitry that he had once disdained and discarding his earlier belief that the Soviet Union was an "evil empire." Reagan had vowed never to deal with terrorists, but he suffered the humiliation of a White House scandal that involved the secret sale of arms to Iran in an attempt to release American hostages in Lebanon—and the illegal siphoning of the sale proceeds to Central American contra guerrillas.

President Reagan's final year in office was one of warming relations between Washington and Moscow. He took his unique brand of politicking to Moscow May 29-June 2, 1988, for an upbeat summit meeting at which he and Gorbachev exchanged documents ratifying an arms control treaty they had signed the previous December in Washington. It was the first arms treaty ratified by the two countries since 1972 and the first to ban an entire class of nuclear weapons—ground-launched intermediate-range nuclear-force missiles.

Perhaps Reagan's ultimate accolade from the nation's voters was their elevation of his vice president and preferred successor, George Bush, to the Oval Office. In winning the party's nomination and then the presidency in 1988, Bush portrayed himself as the rightful heir to the Reagan legacy.

1975-77:
The 94th Congress

The years 1975-76 gave America a significant respite from the high political temperature of the previous several years. With Richard Nixon gone and the Vietnam War over,

the two great issues that had convulsed the country for so long were gone. But even as the country was cooling off, it found itself stalemated on the prime issues facing it. Congress and the president failed to agree on a workable energy program. A strategic arms limitation treaty with the Soviet Union was put off. And while inflation lessened, unemployment jumped to alarming heights.

As the 94th Congress opened, there were clear differences over what steps to take to cure the continuing economic ills of inflation and recession. The Democrats were calling for a massive tax cut, emergency jobs for the unemployed, housing construction subsidies, an end to certain tax shelters and other proposals aimed at closing tax loopholes.

Ford, who in late 1974 had called for a tax increase to combat inflation, in March 1975 reluctantly agreed to a tax cut package drafted by the Democrats that was retroactive to Jan. 1. He and his advisers insisted that it was just as important to fight inflation as to reduce taxes. For this reason, he vetoed as too inflationary the Democrats' bill to create more than one million jobs; the veto was sustained by Congress even though the national unemployment rate was climbing to its high of 9.2 percent in May. Ford subsequently made an about-face and agreed to a compromise version that had a lower price tag but contained many of the same jobs programs.

No subject consumed more time during the first session of the 94th Congress than energy legislation. But despite the amount of time expended in debate and hearings on energy issues, the legislation enacted fell far short of setting a national energy policy. Congress and the White House were deadlocked on fundamental energy questions, with Ford unable to sell his programs and the Democratic majority unable to draft viable alternatives. After a temporary compromise allowed extension of energy controls until mid-December, a more lasting resolution was attained under which controls would continue until early 1979.

In 1976 Congress generally agreed with the administration's request for increased defense spending. Impressed by evidence of a Soviet military buildup, Congress gave the Defense Department virtually all Ford had requested and accepted the principle that defense spending must continue to grow beyond the amount needed to cover inflation.

The 1976 Campaigns

Both parties witnessed an intense struggle for the presidential nominations in 1976, with President Ford barely surviving an effort by former California governor Ronald Reagan to deny him the Republican nomination and the Democrats selecting an obscure former governor of Georgia, Jimmy Carter.

Because of the scandals of the Nixon regime and the perceived weakness of the Ford administration, Carter was heavily favored to take the presidency at the beginning of the fall campaign. But the race gradually narrowed, until on election day Carter won by only 2.1 percentage points.

Carter's nomination represented a repudiation of the political establishment by Democratic primary voters. Such well-known names as Sen. Henry M. Jackson of Washington, Gov. George C. Wallace of Alabama, 1972 vice presidential nominee Sargent Shriver and Rep. Morris K. Udall of Arizona, all fell before the little-known Georgian who espoused an anti-Washington rhetoric combined with an appeal to the old virtues. Tired of political corruption and what they perceived as too much government interference in their lives, voters responded positively to Carter's appeal, despite his lack of experience in the federal government.

On Dec. 2, 1974, Carter announced his candidacy for the 1976 presidential nomination. His speech before the National Press Club included most of the themes of his campaign: restoration of public trust in government; reforms to make government more open and more efficient; comprehensive energy policy; thorough tax reform; "a simplified, fair, and compassionate welfare program"; and a comprehensive national health program.

Carter won the New Hampshire primary Feb. 24 with 28.4 percent in a field of nine candidates, including write-ins. In Massachusetts on March 2, Carter ran behind Jackson, Udall and Wallace but picked up 16 delegates. The same day he won Vermont's advisory primary with more than 42 percent against three other candidates. His next major test came March 9 in Florida, where he had vowed to defeat Wallace. When all the votes were counted, Carter had beaten Wallace 34.5 to 30.5 percent. Jackson was third with 23.9. Most observers felt that if Jackson had stayed out of the race Carter's victory over Wallace would have been much stronger.

Carter ended the longest primary season ever with 38.8 percent of all votes cast. Of the 27 presidential preference primaries, Carter finished first in 17 and second in eight. On the way to the nomination, he eliminated a dozen candidates who entered the campaign and showed enough strength to block his greatest potential rival, Sen. Hubert H. Humphrey.

Jimmy Carter brought the Democratic Party's diverse elements together in July at its national convention. The four-day convention in New York City was the party's most harmonious in 12 years and a stark contrast to the bitter and divisive conventions of 1968 and 1972.

Balloting for president was merely a formality. Besides Carter, three other names were placed in nomination: Udall, California governor Jerry Brown and anti-abortion crusader Ellen McCormack. The proceedings, however, turned into a love-feast as Udall before the balloting and Brown afterwards appeared at the convention to declare their support for Carter. On the presidential roll call Carter received 2,238½ of the convention's 3,008 votes, topping the needed majority little more than halfway through the balloting with the vote from Ohio. The following morning Carter announced that his choice for vice president was Minnesota senator Walter F. Mondale.

Gerald Ford ran his campaign on his two-year performance record as president. The plan was to cultivate the image of an America healed of its divisive internal wounds, involved in a promising economic recovery, and at peace both at home and abroad. In doing this Ford had many of the incumbent's powers of policy making, media access and patronage. All of these were to be used against Ronald Reagan, who announced his candidacy Nov. 20, 1975.

Ford began early to capitalize on his position, spending considerable time in the fall of 1975 traveling across the country. Knowing that Reagan would have to make bold stands on key issues, Ford hoped to remain presidential in his own low-key manner.

At first the plan seemed to work. Ford won New Hampshire by about 1,500 votes. In Florida, where he was once thought far behind, the president was helped by older voters' fears that Reagan would alter the Social Security system. Ford scored a convincing victory. Following a big win in Illinois March 16, Ford strategists hoped to build a party consensus that would force Reagan to withdraw and support the president's nomination before the campaign moved into Reagan's Sun Belt strongholds. As they had

done privately before the campaign had begun, Ford's supporters began publicly urging Reagan to pull out of the race in the name of party unity. It was at that point that the plan, as scheduled, began to bog down.

Reagan scored a series of important victories in the South and Southwest. By mid-May the Ford candidacy had fallen behind in the convention delegate count. Ford survived with a large victory in his home state of Michigan on May 18, breaking Reagan's momentum. Added to that victory were stepped-up efforts to cash in on Ford's incumbency with a flurry of patronage in key primary states and more effective usage of Ford's access to the press. The two candidates split the six May 25 primaries evenly, with Ford taking Kentucky, Tennessee and Oregon. The Border state wins were interpreted as a success for Ford, showing he could compete with Reagan for conservative votes.

The president finally regained the edge in the delegate count in late May by persuading his technically uncommitted supporters in New York and Pennsylvania to declare for him. Ford ended the primary season with an easy win in New Jersey and a hefty margin in Ohio. Reagan kept close with a landslide victory in California, ensuring that the nomination would turn on the status of the uncommitted delegates to the convention.

The Republican delegates arrived in Kansas City for their convention in August more evenly split than they had been since 1952. Both President Ford, breaking with tradition, and Ronald Reagan arrived in town three days before the balloting to continue their pursuit of delegates.

On the presidential roll call, Reagan, bolstered by the votes in California and some Deep South states, took a healthy lead. But Ford's strength in the big Northeastern states—New York, New Jersey, Pennsylvania, Connecticut, Ohio—and others such as Minnesota and Illinois pushed Ford ahead. There was a pause as the Virginia delegation was individually polled. And then West Virginia put the president over the top.

The final vote was 1,187 for Ford, 1,070 for Reagan, one vote from the New York delegation for Commerce Secretary Elliot L. Richardson and one abstention. On a voice vote the convention made the nomination unanimous.

Ford the next day selected Sen. Robert Dole of Kansas as his running mate after Reagan ruled out his acceptance of the second spot. Dole was seen as an effective gut fighter against the Carter forces who would allow Ford to keep his campaign style presidential.

Ford's basic campaign strategy was to portray himself as an experienced leader, a calm and reasonable man who had restored openness and respect to the presidency. Carter's strategy was to attack Ford as an inept leader who lacked the imagination and instincts to move the country forward.

Also campaigning was Eugene J. McCarthy, who ran as an Independent, unaffiliated with any party. The McCarthy campaign was aimed at people who had been frequent nonvoters in the past, a group making up nearly half the potential electorate. The Democrats, however, saw the McCarthy voter as a liberal Democrat who would choose Carter over Ford in a two-way race.

Results of the 1976 Elections

On Nov. 2 Jimmy Carter swept the South, took a majority in the East and did well enough in the Midwest to struggle home with a victory. But it was not easy. Carter's win in Ohio by 11,000 votes still left him with the smallest Electoral College margin since Woodrow Wilson won reelection in 1916. Without Ohio's 25 electoral votes, Carter's total would have dropped to 272, giving him the smallest edge in a hundred years.

In several states McCarthy's Independent candidacy appeared to have tipped the balance to Ford, although in the national popular vote count McCarthy made little impact, receiving less than 1 percent of the total.

Carter won by welding together varying proportions of Roosevelt's New Deal coalition: the South, the industrial Northeast, organized labor, minorities and the liberal community. Carter won majorities in each of these regions and voting groups and made a better than usual showing for a Democratic candidate in the rural Midwest.

Ford made his best showing in the West, winning 53 percent of the popular vote and carrying all but one state, Hawaii. Neither Ford nor Carter ran well in the region during the primaries, but the president benefited from traditional Republican strength and the absence of an intensive Carter effort in the region to score a series of one-sided victories.

An unusual number of new people were elected to the Senate in 1976, but it changed little in ideology and none at all in party lineup. Voters turned nine incumbent senators out of office, more than in any year since 1958. But they took care to treat both parties about the same way, and when the 95th Congress convened in January, there were 62 Senate Democrats and 38 Republicans, just as there were in the Senate that had left in October.

It was an extraordinarily large freshman class—18, including the replacement for Vice President-elect Mondale. Ten of the first-termers were Democrats; eight were Republicans. The large-scale rejection of incumbents had not been expected. The nine who lost represented more than one-third of all the incumbents seeking reelection. By some stroke of challengers' luck virtually every senator who found himself in a difficult race lost.

Three Democratic senators in the "class of 1958"—Vance Hartke of Indiana, Gale W. McGee of Wyoming and Frank E. Moss of Utah—lost decisively. The other four were easy winners. They were Robert C. Byrd of West Virginia, Harrison A. Williams Jr. of New Jersey, Howard W. Cannon of Nevada and Edmund S. Muskie of Maine.

But the group of senators that did worst in 1976 was the Republican "class of 1970," who had won their first terms six years earlier with Nixon administration help. All six senators ran for second terms in 1976, and four were beaten: J. Glenn Beall Jr. of Maryland, Bill Brock of Tennessee, James L. Buckley of New York (elected as a Conservative) and Robert Taft Jr. of Ohio.

The classes of 1958 and 1970 thus accounted for seven of the nine incumbent defeats on Nov. 2. The other two beaten incumbents were Democrats John V. Tunney of California and Joseph M. Montoya of New Mexico.

The ten new Democrats were Dennis DeConcini of Arizona, Spark M. Matsunaga of Hawaii, John Melcher of Montana, Howard M. Metzenbaum of Ohio, Daniel Patrick Moynihan of New York, Donald W. Riegle Jr. of Michigan, Paul S. Sarbanes of Maryland, Jim Sasser of Tennessee, Edward Zorinsky of Nebraska and Wendell R. Anderson, appointed from Minnesota.

The eight new Republicans were John H. Chafee of Rhode Island, John C. Danforth of Missouri, Orrin G. Hatch of Utah, S. I. "Sam" Hayakawa of California, John Heinz of Pennsylvania, Richard G. Lugar of Indiana, Harrison "Jack" Schmitt of New Mexico and Malcolm Wallop of Wyoming.

In the House the Democratic freshmen taught the Republicans a lesson in the power of incumbency, winning reelection almost unanimously to ensure a Democratic majority by the same 2-1 margin the party held in the 94th Congress. Democrats won 292 House seats, and the Republicans, 143.

The Democratic freshmen used the perquisites of office with consummate skill to build political strength and resist close identification with the rest of Congress and the federal bureaucracy. The nationwide Republican effort to brand them as big-spending radicals flopped and left the House GOP in the same minority status as before the elections.

Only 13 House incumbents—eight Democrats and five Republicans—lost their seats. This was far below the number retired by the voters in 1974, when 36 Republicans and four Democrats were defeated in the Watergate landslide that raised the Democrats to overwhelming dominance in the chamber.

The majority of the Democratic seats were safe, while most of the Republican ones were up for grabs, and many were won by the Democrats. The GOP held onto only nine of its 17 seats while winning three held by Democrats, for a net loss of five in this open category.

In gubernatorial races the Democrats gained one more governorship, defeating Republican candidates in 9 states out of the 14. The new lineup was 37 Democrats, 12 Republicans and one Independent, James B. Longley of Maine. Most of the races for governor ended as expected. Voters reelected five incumbents, defeated two others and elected nine new governors.

The one real upset was in Missouri, where Democrat Joseph P. Teasdale defeated Republican governor Christopher S. "Kit" Bond by 13,000 votes. Bond, Missouri's first GOP governor since World War II, was expected to win a second term.

Four states—Montana, North Dakota, Utah and Washington—chose Ford over Carter but elected Democratic governors. Delaware voted for Carter but elected a Republican as governor.

1977-79:
The 95th Congress

With a new and unknown president taking office in January 1977, Congress and the nation waited expectantly to see how Carter would tackle the intractable problems of energy and the economy. In addition, the new president would have to work out a constructive relationship with a Congress that had asserted its power after a long period of presidential dominance. It was also a Congress that had selected new Democratic leadership on both sides of the Capitol, caused by the retirement of Senate Majority Leader Mike Mansfield, D-Mont. and House Speaker Carl Albert, D-Okla.

In foreign affairs the country was at peace, but the administration had to plunge into the labyrinths of relations with the Soviet Union and China and wrestle with attempts to achieve peace in the Middle East.

Carter did not hesitate to get to work on these difficult problems, early proposing an economic stimulus package and an energy program. It soon became clear, however, that major roadblocks stood in the way of enacting significant legislation, especially in the energy area.

The lack of consensus on crucial issues, both in Congress and among the public, was one problem. Another was the continued rivalry between the legislative and executive branches, with congressional leaders accusing the new administration of ineptness and lack of leadership and the executive pointing to Congress' inherent inability to lead.

The partial deadlock reflected the malaise of a country that seemed to be ending its era of predominance in the world and continued economic expansion at home. How the country would cope with the new era remained unclear at the close of 1978.

The House installed Thomas P. O'Neill Jr., D-Mass., as Speaker. In a sharp contest for House majority leader, moderate representative Jim Wright of Texas won out. In the Senate, Democratic whip Robert C. Byrd of West Virginia was chosen unanimously as the new majority leader. Republicans also had a leadership contest for Senate minority leader, with Sen. Howard H. Baker Jr., R-Tenn., the victor.

In January 1978 President Carter presented Congress with his major tax cut and reform program. After working on taxes most of the year, Congress gave final approval Oct. 15 to an $18.7 billion tax cut for 1979 that included a substantial reduction in the tax on capital gains. The bill provided individual income tax reductions that were designed to offset Social Security and inflation-induced tax increases for 1979. In addition, it provided about 4.3 million taxpayers—mostly in the middle- and upper-income ranges—with generous capital gains tax reductions. For businesses, the bill included a reduction in corporate income tax rates and expanded investment tax credits.

In April 1977 Carter introduced his energy policy. For most of 1978 the measure was bogged down in the conference committee trying to resolve differences over the natural gas pricing section. Finally, on Oct. 15, 1978, Congress cleared the bill and sent it to the president.

In the summer of 1977 a political scandal hit the Carter administration that damaged the president's popularity. Questions were raised in the press about the propriety of a number of transactions that Bert Lance, Carter's director of the Office of Management and Budget, had engaged in during his banking career. The Lance matter preoccupied the White House until Lance's resignation in September 1977.

The Carter administration in 1977 laid the groundwork for two treaties with Panama, which were ratified by the Senate in April 1978. One would turn over the Panama Canal to Panama by the year 2000; the second guaranteed the United States' right to defend the canal after that date.

Carter's greatest foreign policy triumph came in September 1978 when he met at Camp David with Egyptian president Anwar Sadat and Israeli prime minister Menachem Begin to hammer out the outlines of a Middle East peace. The success of that effort gave Carter a major boost in prestige and in the polls. And it laid the groundwork for a possible solution to the 30-year-old Middle East conflict.

President Carter had one more big foreign policy surprise for 1978. In a joint communiqué issued Dec. 15, the United States and the People's Republic of China announced that they would formally recognize each other Jan. 1, 1979, and would exchange ambassadors and establish embassies March 1. This announcement ended another longstanding dispute: the 38-year refusal of the United States to recognize the Communists as the rulers of China.

The 1978 Midterm Elections

Republicans in the 1978 midterm campaign were curiously unable to capitalize on their own carefully developed issues in what ought to have been their kind of year.

Without a Republican president to have to defend, GOP congressional candidates were free to run against every branch of the federal government, a traffic that brought them enormous gains the last time they tried it, in 1966. Besides, the rise of tax resentment gave them a drum to beat, and they pounded on it in virtually every contested congressional district in the country.

Humiliated by their failure to gain any House or Senate seats at all in 1976, Republicans redesigned their strategy for the 1978 campaign. In the House they abandoned their attempts to defeat many of the Democrats first elected in 1974, switching to place their emphasis on older incumbents weak in constituent service and name identification. In both the House and Senate they involved themselves in primaries to see that promising candidates won.

But Republican leaders made one other decision that did not work as well as they had hoped: they chose to base congressional campaigns throughout the country on a plan, proposed by Rep. Jack F. Kemp of New York and Sen. William V. Roth Jr. of Delaware, to cut federal income taxes by one-third. It was difficult to find a Republican nominee in any contested state or district who did not talk about Kemp-Roth.

The Republican approach allowed Democratic opponents to seize the popular side of the issue by charging that a Kemp-Roth tax cut was inflationary. Democrats insisted that spending cuts were the proper course, co-opting normal Republican rhetoric.

Results of the 1978 Elections

The 1978 elections produced a Republican gain of three seats in the Senate, along with the second largest freshman Senate class in the history of popular elections. The new Senate lineup for the 96th Congress was 59 Democrats and 41 Republicans. The Democratic total included Harry F. Byrd Jr. of Virginia, elected as an Independent. While the GOP increase was not overwhelming, it was slightly greater than what GOP officials themselves expected a year before.

The GOP newcomers included Nancy Landon Kassebaum of Kansas, the first woman elected to the Senate without being preceded in Congress by her husband, and Thad Cochran, the first Republican senator elected in Mississippi since 1875. The only black in the Senate during the 95th Congress, Edward W. Brooke of Massachusetts, was defeated.

The large freshman classes of 1976 and 1978 differed markedly from their counterparts of the previous generation. The new freshman classes represented no distinct national trends. The 1976 class of 18 was composed of eight Republicans and 10 Democrats, and the 1978 newcomers included 11 Republicans and nine Democrats. The large Senate turnover in the 1970s meant that nearly half the members—48—were in their first terms as of January 1979.

The most notable conservative gains in the Senate occurred in Iowa, where Republican Roger Jepsen unseated incumbent Dick Clark, and in New Hampshire, where incumbent Democrat Thomas J. McIntyre lost to Gordon Humphrey.

The Democratic class of 1972 turned out to be somewhat more vulnerable than the Republican group. Democrats lost Clark, William D. Hathaway of Maine and Floyd K. Haskell of Colorado. In addition to their defeats, the seat of retiring Democratic senator James Abourezk of South Dakota was upturned by the Republicans.

Freshmen Democrats included Howell Heflin and Donald Stewart (both of Alabama), David Pryor (Arkansas),

Paul E. Tsongas (Massachusetts), Carl Levin (Michigan), Max Baucus (Montana), J. James Exon (Nebraska), Bill Bradley (New Jersey) and David L. Boren (Oklahoma). Republican newcomers were William L. Armstrong (Colorado), William S. Cohen (Maine), Rudy Boschwitz and David Durenberger (Minnesota), Larry Pressler (South Dakota), John Warner (Virginia) and Alan K. Simpson (Wyoming).

In the House, Republicans made modest inroads on the lopsided Democratic majority, making a net gain of 11 seats. But Democrats remained in firm control, winning 277 seats to 158 for the GOP. With a record 58 open seats in the House, Republicans hoped to make their biggest gains in the 39 open districts held by Democrats. But that strategy brought only a net gain of two, as Republicans captured eight Democratic-held open seats but lost six of their 19 vacant seats to the Democrats.

Campaigning against incumbents, usually a harder task, proved surprisingly successful for the GOP, as 14 Democratic House members were defeated, compared to five Republicans. It was the largest number of Democratic defeats since 1966, when 39 House Democrats, many of them brought in during the 1964 presidential landslide, lost their jobs.

In gubernatorial politics Republicans moved a step closer to respectability, increasing the number of statehouses under their control from 12 to 18. William Clements's upset election in Texas, Richard L. Thornburgh's come-from-behind triumph in Pennsylvania, and James A. Rhodes's narrow survival in Ohio guaranteed that the GOP would enter the 1980 election year with governors in five of the ten "megastates." That news diluted the Republican disappointment at failing to oust Democratic governor Hugh L. Carey in New York or even to come close against incumbent Democrat Edmund G. Brown in California.

1979-81:
The 96th Congress

The first session of the 96th Congress passed into history as a contradiction. Members came to Washington in 1979 spurred by a nationwide anti-government mood. Legislators, even some of the more liberal ones, talked bravely of the need to limit federal spending. Contrary to the rhetoric, which continued throughout the year, that session of Congress voted for massive new spending efforts and laid the groundwork for significant new federal involvement in the lives of American businesses and citizens.

The most massive expansion of the federal role was in the package of energy legislation, which was the focus of congressional debate most of the year. It called for spending billions of dollars on synthetic fuels development and imposing a major federal presence in the energy industry. It also was a year when advocates of more defense spending finally recouped from the travails of the Vietnam era and won a pledge of extra billions for the military from a president who initially opposed such increases.

Support for the energy package was grounded in troubled U.S. relations with oil-exporting nations and a continuing upward spiral in the cost of imported oil. Those trends were exacerbated by the crumbling of relations between the United States and Iran after militant Iranians seized the U.S. Embassy in Tehran and held 53 Americans hostage for the return of that nation's deposed shah, Mohammed Reza Pahlavi.

Advocates of higher defense spending, using the Iranian hostage situation as an example, argued more vigorously than ever before that America's strength and influence in the world were declining and that U.S. military strength was falling far behind that of the Soviet Union.

But if Congress acted with determination on energy and some other issues, it acted virtually not at all on the economic troubles of the nation. Faced with double-digit inflation and the threatened onset of a recession, Congress— much like the president—did not seem to know what to do. It appeared both were marking time until 1980 to decide whether federal action would help or worsen America's economic problems.

Congress showed little interest in social, consumer and environmental legislation. The realization was growing that the federal budget was not open-ended and that government spending decisions required some distasteful choices. Nevertheless, members approved Carter's request to create a separate Department of Education.

In 1980, facing an aggressive and unified Republican Party and worried by its own reputation for big spending, the Democratic-controlled Congress began the election year concentrating on trimming programs in order to balance the federal budget. A recession combined with spiraling inflation soon dashed the Democrats' balanced-budget hopes. But these new economic woes also did nothing to encourage the Democrats to resume pushing for some of their favorite programs. In addition, because of escalating campaign pressures, Democratic leaders delayed until after the election consideration of the budget and a number of other key bills.

By year's end, however, the Democrats found their scheme had backfired. Instead of rewarding them for their restraint, the elections had deprived them of their control of the White House and Senate and put them in a substantially weaker position in the House in 1981.

The 1980 Campaigns

President Carter won enough delegates at his party's primaries and caucuses to win the Democratic presidential nomination. But he faced significant opposition at the convention from Sen. Edward M. Kennedy of Massachusetts. Carter led Kennedy throughout the primary season, but as the convention neared, the momentum seemed to be with Kennedy. Although Carter continued to win more caucus delegates, Kennedy won five of the last eight primaries, which kept him in contention.

At the same time, the president's position in the popularity polls dropped, and Carter found himself in the midst of an embarrassing controversy over his brother Billy's connection with the Libyan government.

Alarmed by Carter's apparently diminishing reelection prospects, several party leaders grew concerned that a Carter defeat in November would drag down dozens of state and local candidates across the country. They called for an "open convention" that could nominate a compromise candidate. And they teamed up with Senator Kennedy to urge defeat of a proposed convention rule that would bind all delegates to vote on the first ballot for the candidate under whose banner they were elected.

When the convention opened, Carter could count 1,981.1 delegates pledged to him—315 more than he needed for the nomination. Kennedy had 1,225.8 delegates, and the only chance he had to gain the nomination was to defeat the rule. There were 122.1 uncommitted delegates and two for other candidates.

In the days before the convention opening Kennedy strategists claimed that there were continuing defections from the Carter camp. On Sunday they said they were within 50 to 100 votes of the majority needed to overturn the rule binding the delegates. But the Kennedy predictions and hopes proved to be exaggerated. The final tally on the rule showed 1,936.418 delegates favoring the binding rule and 1,390.580 opposing it. Passage of the rule ensured Carter's renomination. Shortly after the vote, Kennedy ended his nine-month challenge to the president by announcing that his name would not be placed in nomination on Aug. 13.

But Kennedy did not withdraw from the platform debate. The bitterly contested party platform pitted Carter against Kennedy and a coalition of special interest groups. The final document was filled with so many concessions to the Kennedy forces that it won only a halfhearted endorsement from the president.

Kennedy capped his platform victories with an Aug. 12 appearance before the delegates in which he presented a stunning speech to a tumultuous ovation. His speech created a sense of enormous energy within the hall and left the feeling that a significant political event had occurred.

By the following day Carter began to reassert control over the convention. In a statement issued just hours after the platform debate ended, the president refused to accept—as diplomatically as possible—many of the platform revisions. In his carefully worded statement, Carter did not flatly reject any of Kennedy's amendments, but he did not embrace them either. Carter concluded his statement with the unity refrain that had become the hallmark of every White House comment on the platform since the drafting process began: "The differences within our party on this platform are small in comparison with the differences between the Republican and Democratic party platforms."

Carter won his party's presidential nomination on the first ballot, and his vice president, Walter F. Mondale, easily won renomination. Kennedy pledged his support and even made a brief appearance on the platform with Carter and Mondale as the convention drew to a close. But it was uncertain whether the appeals for unity had succeeded.

On the Republican side Ronald Reagan had carefully cultivated an image as the presumed GOP front-runner for 1980 from the day Gerald Ford was defeated by Carter in 1976. During the primaries Reagan lost only four of the state preference primaries he entered. In states that chose their delegates in caucuses, Reagan was even more impressive, winning just under 400 of the 478 delegates picked by caucuses. But it was in the early primaries that Reagan was able to pare the field from a half-dozen major candidates to just two.

In South Carolina on March 8 Reagan knocked former Texas governor John B. Connally out of the race. Ten days later he deflated John B. Anderson's surging campaign with a victory in the representative's home state of Illinois. A similar result two weeks later in Wisconsin forced Anderson out of the GOP contest and into an unsuccessful Independent bid for the White House.

After four quick defeats Senate minority leader Howard H. Baker Jr. of Tennessee dropped out. Neither Rep. Philip M. Crane of Illinois nor Sen. Robert Dole of Kansas had ever caught the voters' attention. And on March 15 former president Gerald Ford put to rest growing speculation that he might jump into the race in an effort to stop Reagan. By April the GOP contest was reduced to former Texas representative George Bush's frantic efforts to catch Reagan in a few major states. It was too little, too late.

Having outdistanced all the competition, Reagan easily won his party's 1980 nomination at the Republican National Convention in Detroit. Reagan won on the first ballot, receiving 1,939 of the 1,994 delegate votes. His nomination was then made unanimous.

The unusual flap over the selection of the vice presidential nominee provided the only suspense at the convention. Rumors circulated that Ford was being tapped for the second spot. Ford himself had encouraged that speculation, although he declined to spell out his conditions. It became clear he wanted responsibilities that would have made him, in effect, co-president with Reagan. Late on July 16 the Reagan-Ford arrangement fell apart, and the two men agreed that it would be better for Ford to campaign for the GOP ticket than to be a member of it. The speculation prompted Reagan to make an unusual visit to the convention hall at 12:15 a.m. on July 17 to to announce his choice of George Bush as his running mate.

The American hostage crisis was injected into the campaign in the eleventh hour when Iranian leaders miscalculated that Carter would accept their demands in return for release of the hostages before election day. Although Carter tried to keep the negotiations—which reached a peak during the weekend before Nov. 4—out of the campaign, the publicity given them so close to the election worked against the president.

But what hurt Carter the most, in the opinion of many analysts, was his inability to improve the state of the economy. Throughout the fall campaign Reagan blamed Carter for almost tripling the inflation rate he had inherited from the Ford administration. During 1980 the rate averaged about 13 percent.

No one publicly forecast the rout that developed election night. Reagan's sweep was nationwide. In most of the states that were expected to be close or to go for Carter, Reagan won, frequently by comfortable margins. In states Reagan was expected to carry, he won overwhelmingly.

Reagan easily carried every region of the country, including the keystones of Carter's triumph four years before—the industrial Northeast and the president's native South.

Results of the 1980 Elections

The Republican victory did not stop with the presidency. The GOP rode the crest of a breathtaking sweep to take control of the Senate for the first time in a quarter-century. Although the Democrats retained their majority in the House, the national shift to the political right combined with a variety of scandals, complacency by some incumbents and unusually strong Reagan coattails cost the Democrats a net loss of 33 seats in the House. That made the Republicans 26 seats shy of controlling the House, although conservative Democrats were expected to give the GOP an ideological edge on many issues.

The 12 Senate seats won by Republicans represented the largest net gain in the Senate for any party since 1958, when the Democrats took control over 15 new seats. The new lineup was 53 Republicans and 47 Democrats. The 1980 GOP Senate victory was the first since 1952 and ended the longest one-party dominance of the Senate in American history.

In addition to their increases the Republicans held on to the 10 seats that were up in 1980. That included holding three open seats in Pennsylvania, Oklahoma and North Dakota and the New York seat of Republican senator Jacob K. Javits, who was defeated for renomination in the primary but ran for reelection on the Liberal Party ticket.

Democrats had 24 seats before the election and lost half of them. Not only would the Senate be more Republican; it would be noticeably more conservative. Several pillars of Democratic liberalism went down to defeat, including George McGovern of South Dakota, Warren G. Magnuson of Washington and John C. Culver of Iowa.

To replace the Democrats, Republicans elected a freshman Senate class made up largely of dedicated conservatives. Representatives Charles E. Grassley of Iowa, Steven D. Symms of Idaho, James Abdnor of South Dakota and Robert W. Kasten Jr. of Wisconsin had compiled distinctively conservative records in the House. John P. East of North Carolina, an expert in conservative political thought, was expected to carry out his beliefs in the Senate.

But there was a contingent of Republican moderates that could leaven some of the conservative impulses. Warren Rudman of New Hampshire, Arlen Specter of Pennsylvania and Slade Gorton of Washington all were from the moderate wing of their party.

Among the losing Democrats were four of the six prime targets of the National Conservative Political Action Committee, which prepared hard-hitting ads attacking the records of liberal senators. The targeted senators were Birch Bayh of Indiana, Culver of Iowa, McGovern of South Dakota, Thomas F. Eagleton of Missouri, Frank Church of Idaho and Alan Cranston of California. Bayh, Culver, McGovern and Church went down to defeat.

In the House the lineup going into the election was 273 Democrats to 159 Republicans. There also were three vacancies that had been held by Democrats. After the November vote, the new lineup was 243 Democrats to 192 Republicans. The Democratic total included one Independent.

The Republican net gain of 33 seats was the largest increase for the GOP since 1966. Most of the GOP gains came at the expense of incumbents. In all, 31 of the 392 incumbents running for reelection were turned out. Of those, 27 were Democrats who lost to Republicans. Only three incumbent Republicans were defeated.

There were 74 new faces in the new House, three fewer than in 1978. Republican freshmen had the edge with 52 seats, compared to 22 for the Democrats. Four new women—all Republicans—were elected, bringing the total number of women in the House to 19. There were four black freshmen, for a total of 17 black voting members. All were Democrats.

Republicans increased their hold on governorships by four states, bringing their nationwide total to 23. Democrats still maintained a lead, with 27 governors' chairs. The Republican additions came in states west of the Mississippi River: Arkansas, Missouri, North Dakota and Washington.

The Republican gain continued the party's gradual comeback on the gubernatorial level. After 1968, when the party won 31 governorships compared with the Democrats' 19, GOP gubernatorial fortunes slid to a low of 12 in 1977. The party began to make gains again in 1978, boosting its total by six. In 1979 the GOP added another governor in Louisiana.

Despite the party's success in gubernatorial races, Republicans advanced only negligibly in state legislatures, which were to redraw political boundaries in post-1980 census redistricting.

1981-83:
The 97th Congress

Dominated by Republicans for the first time in two and a half decades and guided by a forceful and popular president, Congress took bold steps in 1981 toward reducing the federal government's scope. Following the wishes of President Reagan, the 97th Congress slashed government spending, cut taxes for individuals and business and slimmed down federal regulatory activities.

The 1980 elections not only swept a conservative Republican into the White House but also floated the GOP into its first Senate majority since January 1955. The change in control meant that committee leadership shifted to the Republicans and that the Democrats were relegated to minority leadership. The new Senate majority leader was Howard H. Baker Jr. of Tennessee.

In the House the Democrats, under the leadership of Thomas P. O'Neill Jr. of Massachusetts, were still in the majority, though by a slimmer margin (243-192) than they enjoyed in the previous Congress. And the conservative leanings of many of their numbers made the Democratic leadership's grasp on House proceedings tentative at times.

When Reagan entered office in January 1981, he laid out what appeared to some to be contradictory goals for his presidency. To revitalize the economy and strengthen the nation, he would cut federal spending yet increase spending for defense, reduce taxes yet balance the budget. Many traditional Republicans in Congress were uneasy with this "supply-side" economic approach. But the GOP leaders in both houses proved to be effective and loyal lieutenants for their president.

Congress enacted $35.2 billion in fiscal 1982 program reductions, cut nearly $4 billion more from appropriations, approved a cut in individual and business taxes totaling $749 billion over a five-year period and added about $18 billion to the fiscal 1982 defense budget drafted by President Carter the year before. But the federal deficit for the year appeared to be heading over the $100 billion mark, and the economy was in recession. In the process of getting his program enacted, Reagan exhausted his winning coalition, stretched congressional procedures out of shape and bruised sensitive legislative egos.

Almost all the sweeping budget cuts Congress approved were made in one package, the budget "reconciliation" bill. The use of the reconciliation method in such a massive way was criticized by some members as an abuse of the budget process. The budget bill touched on virtually every federal activity except defense. Included in it were a multitude of changes in existing law, including provisions to tighten eligibility for public assistance, cut funds for subsidized housing programs, reduce school lunch subsidies and cut Medicaid payments to the states.

In September, when Reagan proposed a second package of $13 billion in further spending cuts and $3 billion in unspecified revenue increases for 1982, the president's coalition began to crumble. Even members who had worked hard for Reagan's first round of cuts had no stomach for a second in a single year. Moderate House Republicans threatened to desert him unless he shielded their pet programs. Conservative Democrats threatened to bail out over the growing deficit, and the Reagan team was split over the question of tax increases.

The president maintained symbolic pressure on Congress to make additional spending cuts, even bringing the government to a halt for a day in late November by vetoing a temporary funding resolution. But Congress was unwilling to make the cuts he demanded. The appropriations process ground to a halt, and the government limped through the end of the year on a series of temporary funding resolutions.

On defense, Congress granted Reagan's request for significant spending increases. The $200 billion fiscal 1982 defense appropriation was the largest peacetime appropriations bill ever approved.

Congress grew increasingly independent of the White House in 1982. The legislators adhered to President Reagan's general course of restraining domestic programs while increasing military spending, but they rejected many of the president's specific proposals. They substantially rewrote Reagan's fiscal 1983 budget and persuaded the president to support a large tax increase only a year after passing his three-year tax cut plan.

While modifying or rejecting many of Reagan's requests, Congress did not originate much of its own legislation in 1982. Faced with soaring federal deficits, members spent a lot of their time defending existing programs from budget cuts rather than trying to create new ones.

The 1982 Midterm Elections

The 1982 midterm elections produced major change in the House but left the Senate comparatively untouched. A combination of redistricting and recession produced a huge crop of 81 House freshmen, 57 of them Democrats. In the previous 30 years only three other elections had brought in that many new Democrats.

Redistricting played a major role in 1982. This was the election in which reapportionment, the rise of the Sun Belt and the decline of the Frost Belt were supposed to catch up with the Democrats, setting in motion a decade of conservative and Republican advance of power in the House. But it did not work out that way.

The Sun Belt proved the Republicans' greatest disappointment. The nationwide shift in population away from the industrial North gave Southern and Western states 17 new districts, and the GOP at one time hoped to take at least a dozen of them. But Democratic legislative cartography and unfriendly federal court action got in the way, and in the end Democrats won 10 of the 17.

Results of the 1982 Elections

The only thing remarkable about the 1982 Senate results was the sheer absence of change. Not only did the party ratio remain the same—54 Republicans and 46 Democrats—but 95 of the 100 senators returned to Washington. The class of five newcomers was the smallest in the 68-year history of popular Senate elections.

That stability was itself a dramatic reversal of recent election trends. During the previous decade a Senate seat had been one of the most difficult offices in U.S. politics to hold. While reelection rates for House incumbents regularly had run above 85 percent, senators struggled against well-financed challengers and effective special interest groups.

The Senate outcome was neither the "ratifying" election that Republicans had hoped for after their sweep of 1980 nor the "correcting" election that Democrats had wanted. But there were favorable results for both parties. Republicans kept their beachhead on Capitol Hill, ensuring that Ronald Reagan would be the first Republican president since Herbert Hoover to have a GOP Senate majority throughout his four-year term.

Democrats broke even in an election that could have relegated them to minority status in the Senate for a long time. Of the 33 seats that were contested in 1982, the Democrats were defending 19. They ended up winning 60.6 percent of the races.

In the House, Democrats scored a 26-seat gain, as voters expressed antipathy toward President Reagan's economic program but stopped short of repudiating it altogether. The outcome revealed an unusual degree of voter frustration with a party only two years into national power.

Democrats won 269 seats to 166 seats for the GOP, giving the Democrats a 103-seat advantage. Going into the election, Democrats held 241 seats and Republicans 192, with vacancies in two districts formerly occupied by Democrats. Twenty-six Republican incumbents and three sitting Democrats were beaten, nearly a mirror image of the 1980 election, in which the GOP lost three incumbents and unseated 28 Democratic members.

Hurt by losses in the economically distressed Midwest, Republicans saw their hold on the nation's governorships dwindle to 16 in the Nov. 2 elections. The Democrats controlled statehouses in 34 states. The GOP's net loss of seven statehouses—the party dropped nine and picked up two—ended a comeback in the party's gubernatorial fortunes. Republicans had been posting gains since 1977, when they hit a low point of 12 governors' chairs.

Of the Republican governors' seats that switched to the Democrats, five were in the Midwest, where the recession had been most acute, hitting both manufacturing and farming. Michigan, Minnesota, Nebraska, Ohio and Wisconsin opted for Democrats. Republican incumbents were retiring in all these states except Nebraska, where Gov. Charles Thone was turned out.

Republicans also encountered a setback in their progress in the South. They held four of the region's 13 governorships in 1982; in 1983 they had just two. Only Tennessee's Lamar Alexander won reelection.

In addition, Democrats took over GOP statehouses in Alaska and Nevada. Republicans assumed power in California, where George Deukmejian edged out Democrat Tom Bradley, and in New Hampshire, where GOP challenger John H. Sununu unseated Democratic incumbent Hugh Gallen. Each party had six open seats at stake. Democrats held all theirs except for California. Republicans managed to retain only Iowa.

Democrats also turned the tables on the GOP in state legislative elections, regaining most of the chambers taken by the Republicans in the previous two elections and ending a six-year decline in the number of legislatures under Democratic control.

1983-85:
The 98th Congress

Congress and President Reagan generally kept to their own turf in 1983, each going about business with little involvement from the other side. Unlike the first two years of the Reagan administration, when the president essentially wrote the economic script, Congress conducted its 1983 debate on deficits without Reagan's overt participation. And while Congress tried to assert itself on foreign policy, Reagan consistently called the global shots.

There were important bipartisan agreements in 1983 on Social Security, jobs legislation, the War Powers Resolution and fiscal 1984 appropriations bills. But these were rare commodities in a year in which political motivations ranked above policy considerations.

The prime example of this dilemma was the way Congress and Reagan reacted to massive federal deficits. No matter how many experts said soaring deficits hurt the economy, few people were willing to take the politically risky steps needed to cure the problem. Reagan made a calculated decision to stay out of the deficit debate, thereby ducking any responsibility for tax increases his advisers viewed as a

1984 election liability. Anti-deficit rhetoric was a constant refrain among legislators, but Congress took little decisive action on the issue.

Standing behind Reagan, House Speaker Thomas P. O'Neill Jr., D-Mass., in September helped push through a measure allowing the president to keep U.S. troops in Lebanon for up to eighteen months. In backing Reagan on Lebanon, Congress for the first time invoked major parts of the 1973 War Powers Resolution. On Oct. 23, 241 U.S. Marines, sailors and soldiers and 58 French paratroopers were killed by a terrorist truck bomb in Beirut. Subsequent efforts to revise or revoke the measure keeping troops in Lebanon failed in both houses. Under congressional pressure, Reagan announced in February 1984 that he had ordered the troop withdrawal.

Congress reluctantly continued to back Reagan's policy in Nicaragua. The House twice voted to force Reagan to stop backing rightist forces that were fighting to overthrow that country's leftist government. When the Senate refused to go along, a compromise was reached limiting aid to the rebels and requiring Reagan to seek explicit approval from Congress for additional aid.

Reagan won widespread approval in both chambers for the Oct. 25 invasion of the Caribbean island of Grenada. The president said the invasion was necessary to protect some one thousand Americans, mostly medical students, from civil strife that erupted following the murder of Marxist prime minister Maurice Bishop.

Reagan was victorious in most of his defense fights with Congress. He won the go-ahead for production of the MX missile, although the House came within a handful of votes of killing funding for the project.

On domestic issues Reagan met many disappointments on Capitol Hill in 1984. The president could not persuade Congress to approve his social agenda, which featured constitutional amendments to ban abortion and allow school prayer. Nor did Congress adopt his plan to give tuition tax credits to parents who sent their children to private schools, or his enterprise zone system to provide tax relief to businesses that created jobs in depressed areas.

One of the biggest problems remained the massive federal deficit. Although Congress took actions designed to reduce the deficit by $149 billion over three years, the tax increases and spending cuts were viewed as a mere "down payment" on a larger remedy. While legislators spent much of 1984 talking about the evils of the swelling federal deficit, they took only a first step toward a cure. Instead, many members figured they would deal with the problem in 1985, after the November elections.

The 1984 Campaigns

The focus in the early months of the presidential election was not on Reagan but on the Democratic candidates seeking their party's nomination. Sen. Alan Cranston of California was the first to toss his hat in the ring formally, announcing his candidacy Feb. 2, 1983. But Walter Mondale had informally started his campaign shortly after he and President Jimmy Carter lost to Reagan and George Bush in 1980.

Mondale was never particularly popular with the voters. His public personality and speaking style were bland, his traditional "New Deal" Democratic message seemed stale and, to many, ineffective, and his identification as a candidate of the special interests led voters to look closely and often approvingly at Mondale's competitors.

Before the primaries began, Mondale's main opponent seemed to be John Glenn, senator from Ohio and former astronaut. But the first delegate selection event of the season, the Iowa precinct caucuses of Feb. 20, was disastrous for Glenn as well as for two other conservative Democrats in the race, South Carolina senator Ernest F. Hollings and former Florida governor Reubin Askew. Together these three drew less than 10 percent of the vote. In New Hampshire a week later the results for Glenn, Hollings and Askew were just as discouraging. Hollings and Askew withdrew from the race.

Other challenges came from Colorado senator Gary Hart and from George McGovern, the former South Dakota senator whose losing 1972 presidential campaign Hart had managed. Glenn and McGovern withdrew from the race after Super Tuesday, leaving in contention Mondale, Hart and the Rev. Jesse Jackson, the first black to pursue seriously the presidential nomination of any major political party.

Hart's momentum was blunted almost as quickly as it began. In the week after Super Tuesday, he ran behind Mondale in six of seven delegate selection events. Then Mondale got a much-needed boost by winning the New York and Pennsylvania primaries. His chance to eliminate Hart evaporated when Hart won Ohio and Indiana. Mondale continued to lead in the number of delegates committed to him, and with his win in New Jersey June 5 he had enough delegates to win the nomination. But his campaign ended on the same lackluster note that had characterized most of the last four months; the same day Mondale claimed the nomination, Hart won three other primaries including California's.

Despite the difficult, sometimes bitter, primary season campaign, Democrats mustered a display of party unity at their convention and made a historic vice presidential choice. The Democratic National Convention picked Mondale to be the party standard bearer against President Reagan. As in much of his drive for the nomination, Mondale was almost overshadowed again, this time by the attention generated by his selection of New York representative Geraldine A. Ferraro to be his running mate. Ferraro was the first woman ever chosen for the national ticket by a major party.

President Reagan enjoyed the smoothest road to renomination that any presidential candidate could have. Brimming with confidence that President Reagan and Vice President Bush would be "the winning team" in November, a jubilant Republican Party held its convention in Dallas Aug. 20-23. With the ticket's renomination certain beforehand, the convention was more a celebration for GOP activists than a business meeting. Criticisms from the party's shrinking band of moderates, worried by the strongly conservative tone of the platform, did little to dispel the optimistic mood of delegates, who looked forward with confidence to Reagan's easy reelection victory.

Highlights of the fall campaign were the two presidential debates. The first, held Oct. 7, was focused on domestic issues. Mondale made a strong showing, which lessened his negative image. Equally important was the perception that Reagan turned in a poor performance; the 73-year-old president seemed tired and disorganized, leading journalists and Democrats to suggest that age was catching up with Reagan.

The second debate, on Oct. 21, focusing on foreign affairs, was a draw in the opinion of most analysts. The debate was not a significant boost to Mondale's campaign, and it allowed Reagan to ease concerns about his age and competence raised by his performance during the first debate. The vice presidential candidates also held a nationally televised debate, on Oct. 11. Most analysts viewed it as a draw or gave a slight edge to Bush.

Almost every thrust Mondale made was effectively parried by his Republican opponents. Mondale's efforts to draw attention to the massive budget deficits run up during Reagan's first term by promising a tax increase did not stand a chance against Reagan's promise not to raise taxes. Similarly Mondale's attempts to paint Reagan as a man who favored the rich over the poor, the majority over the minority, did not overcome charges that Mondale was a tool of the special interests.

In the end perhaps no Democrat could have defeated Ronald Reagan in 1984. For one thing most voters thought they were better off than they had been four years earlier. (Reagan first asked that question during his 1980 run against Carter and Mondale.) Perhaps more important, voters seemed to respond to Reagan's upbeat attitude and his promise of continued peace and prosperity.

Results of the 1984 Elections

There was never much doubt that Ronald Reagan, one of the most popular presidents in American history, would win reelection in 1984. And it would be hard to imagine a vote more decisive than the balloting that gave him his victory. Winning all but one state, he drew 59 percent of the popular vote, and he won a record 525 electoral votes.

Despite the size of Reagan's victory, its meaning remained unclear. The vote clearly exposed the Democrats' limited appeal in presidential elections. On the other hand, Democrats held their own in other elections. In the Senate, rather than gaining as most presidents do, Reagan lost two seats, reducing the Republican majority to 53-47. In the House of Representatives the president's party gained 14 seats, far short of the historical average for landslides. The GOP gained one governor for a lineup of 16 Republicans and 34 Democrats. Only in the state legislatures did the Republican Party make gains that could be considered significant.

Neither the Republicans nor the Democrats came away with quite what they wanted from the 1984 struggle for control of the Senate. Democrats had hoped to regain the majority they lost in 1980, when Republicans took control of the Senate for the first time since the 1954 elections. Republicans hoped that President Reagan's march to reelection would bring about a modest reprise of 1980, making the GOP hold on the Senate more secure.

But in this election Reagan was no trailblazer. Democrats retained 13 of the 14 seats they were defending, and a trio of Democratic House members captured Republican seats: Illinois representative Paul Simon edged out Sen. Charles H. Percy; Iowa representative Tom Harkin defeated Sen. Roger W. Jepsen; and Tennessee representative Albert Gore Jr. took the seat being vacated by Senate majority leader Howard H. Baker Jr. Countering the good news for the Democrats was an unexpected outcome in Kentucky: the defeat of Sen. Walter "Dee" Huddleston at the hands of Mitch McConnell.

Thus Democrats won a net gain of two Senate seats, shifting the party ratio to 53 Republicans and 47 Democrats. That standing was an improvement over the preelection ratio of 55-45 but a comedown from the Democrats' 1983 prediction that the party could recapture Senate control by picking up a number of Republican seats Democrats regarded as shaky.

As it turned out Democrats failed to win most of the GOP seats in the "at risk" category. The biggest Democratic disappointment came in North Carolina, where GOP incum-

bent Jesse Helms narrowly won his bitter battle with Democratic governor James B. Hunt Jr. It was the most expensive Senate contest ever, with the campaigns spending a total of about $22 million.

In four other key states where Democrats had hoped to pull upsets, Republicans prevailed easily: Mississippi senator Thad Cochran won against former governor William Winter; Sen. Gordon J. Humphrey won a second term in New Hampshire; Texas representative Phil Gramm, who switched parties in 1983, replaced retiring GOP senator John Tower; and Sen. Rudy Boschwitz took 58 percent in Minnesota, encountering no problems with Mondale's coattails because the Democratic presidential nominee barely carried his home state.

For the second time in a little over a decade, Republicans watched with disappointment as their presidential standard bearer swept triumphantly across the nation followed by a threadbare retinue of new U.S. House members. The Nov. 6 elections revealed considerable hesitation nationwide over an all-out endorsement of Republican policies, as voters in district after district stopped short of backing GOP challengers who campaigned on their loyalty to Ronald Reagan. After several closely contested battles were decided, Republicans had gained 14 seats, falling well short of making up the 26 seats they lost in the 1982 midterm elections. One seat, still undecided at year's end, eventually remained Democratic.

Not counting the undecided seat, Democrats retained control of the House with 252 members to the GOP's 182. Going into the election, Democrats held 266 seats and Republicans 167, with vacancies in a New Jersey district previously held by a Republican and in a Kentucky district held by a Democrat. Those seats stayed in their respective parties' hands and were filled for the remainder of the term in special elections. As a result of the election there were 43 House freshmen in 1985, a small class, due mostly to the relatively low number of open seats in 1984.

The gubernatorial elections did little to dent the Democratic Party's 2-1 advantage in governorships. Republicans notched victories in North Carolina, Rhode Island, Utah and West Virginia, where the statehouses were left vacant by departing Democratic incumbents. But the Democrats captured three seats, toppling Republican incumbents in North Dakota and Washington and picking up the seat left open by retiring GOP governor Richard A. Snelling in Vermont.

Republicans thus scored a net gain of one seat, boosting the total governorships under their control from 15 to 16 and reducing the number of states in the Democratic column from 35 to 34. The GOP's showing represented an improvement over 1982, when the party suffered a net loss of seven seats. Republicans still remained a long way, however, from capturing a majority of governorships, a feat they had last accomplished in 1969.

1985-87:
The 99th Congress

The 99th Congress compiled an extraordinary record. It revised the tax code more dramatically than at any time since World War II, rewrote immigration law, approved the most far-reaching environmental bills since the 1970s, boosted student aid, reversed President Reagan's policy toward South Africa and joined him in openly seeking to overthrow Nicaragua's leftist government.

Congress seized the legislative initiative from the White House in 1985 and dominated the Capitol Hill agenda to a degree unmatched since President Reagan took office in 1981. Although Reagan was able to rescue his top domestic priority—tax-overhaul legislation—with a last-minute personal lobbying campaign, the close call was a testament to the altered relationship between the White House and Capitol Hill.

On other issues ranging from deficit reduction to federal farm spending, from South Africa sanctions to Middle East arms sales, Congress called the shots, in stark contrast to the opening year of Reagan's first term.

Lawmakers made a historic year-end decision: passage of the Gramm-Rudman-Hollings legislation, which mandated paring of the federal deficit over the next five years until the budget was balanced in fiscal 1991. Although Congress embraced the budget reduction plan—offered by Republican senators Phil Gramm of Texas and Warren B. Rudman of New Hampshire and Democratic senator Ernest F. Hollings of South Carolina—as the best hope for future deficit control, many who shaped the measure were skeptical about its chances for working.

Deficit reduction had been the top priority of Senate majority leader Bob Dole, R-Kan., when the 99th Congress opened, but the expected deficit bequeathed to the next Congress remained about $180 billion.

In the two most important elections of 1985, moderation seemed to be the winning theme. Democrats retained the governorship in Virginia with Gerald L. Baliles, who mimicked the moderate philosophy of outgoing Democratic governor Charles S. Robb. Similarly, New Jersey Republican governor Thomas H. Kean thrived at the polls by positioning himself as more moderate than his party's national image. Because neither of the gubernatorial elections produced a partisan shift, the nationwide party lineup of governors remained at 34 Democrats and 16 Republicans—unchanged from 1984.

The 1986 Midterm Elections

The 1986 Senate campaigns deserve special notice for what they said about the state of electioneering in the latter half of the 1980s. Most spectacularly they laid to rest a theory that took hold in 1980—that the GOP's superior financial resources give it an infallible ability to win close contests. The notion gained widespread currency in 1982, when the GOP's high-tech campaign techniques and last-minute infusions of money saved several endangered Republican candidates. That year the GOP won five of the six contests in which the winner took 52 percent or less of the vote.

But in 1986 nine of the 11 races won by 52 percent or less went to Democrats. That achievement came in spite of daunting obstacles: the National Republican Senatorial Committee's nearly 8-1 funding advantage over its Democratic counterpart, a $10 million nationwide GOP get-out-the-vote effort, and an army of consultants, pollsters, media advisers and GOP field staff at the disposal of Republican candidates.

The difference lay in what each side did with the resources at its disposal. In many contests Democrats latched onto issues—of substance and of personality—that by election day were helping them frame the terms of the debate. Even more important, while the GOP was spending much of its money on television advertising and on a technology-driven voter mobilization effort, Democrats built on their strength at the grass roots. They developed extensive local organizations and, especially in the South, reawakened old party apparatuses and alliances.

In a year when there were so many close contests, the Republicans' lack of organizational depth hurt them, particularly in states where Democrats latched onto local issues that seemed more compelling to voters than national Republican pleas to keep the Senate in GOP hands.

The most striking examples of the Democrats' ability to outcampaign their opponents came in the South. All Democrats there used a variation on a single theme: that they were home-grown state patriots, while their opponents were national Republicans with little interest in local affairs. And all used their state's traditional Democratic base to surmount better-financed Republican efforts.

Results of the 1986 Elections

Democrats on Nov. 4, 1986, regained control of the Senate, which they had lost to the GOP in 1980. Six Republicans who won their seats that year were defeated in their bids for reelection, as Democrats captured nine GOP seats and lost only one of their own to take a 55-45 Senate majority. The results also gave Democrats the largest class of freshman senators since 1958. Of the 13 new senators, 11 were Democrats.

The party's most significant set of victories came in the South, where Democrats won six of seven Senate contests. Their gains elsewhere were scattered across the map. Farm unrest in the Midwest cost two GOP members of the class of 1980 their seats. In Washington State controversy over the possible situating of a high-level nuclear waste site in Hanford helped Brock Adams unseat Republican Slade Gorton.

The Democrats' other gains came in Maryland, where Rep. Barbara A. Mikulski easily won the seat of retiring GOP Sen. Charles McC. Mathias Jr., and in Nevada, where Rep. Harry Reid defeated former representative Jim Santini for the right to succeed retiring GOP senator Paul Laxalt.

The sole Republican pickup was in Missouri. There, former governor Christopher S. "Kit" Bond won the seat held by retiring Democratic veteran Thomas F. Eagleton.

Not every potentially close election broke the Democrats' way. In Oklahoma and Pennsylvania, Democratic representatives James R. Jones and Bob Edgar tried to turn local economic troubles to their advantage. Neither, however, could arouse the core Democratic constituency in the western half of their states. Oklahoma representative Don Nickles and Pennsylvania Republican Arlen Specter both won handily. And in Idaho, Democratic governor John V. Evans lost to conservative Republican Steven D. Symms.

In North Carolina, Democrat Terry Sanford stressed his longstanding ties to the state. At the same time, he painted incumbent James T. Broyhill as a captive of the Washington establishment. In Alabama, Rep. Richard C. Shelby attacked Republican senator Jeremiah Denton for being more interested in his personal agenda of "family" and social issues than in helping Alabama's economy.

Democratic representative John B. Breaux overcame an early lead by GOP representative W. Henson Moore to hold on to the Louisiana seat of retiring Democratic senator Russell B. Long. Breaux hammered away at Moore as a representative of GOP policies that were hurting Louisiana's farmers and its oil and gas industry.

In Georgia, Rep. Wyche Fowler Jr. ran an almost picture-perfect campaign against Republican incumbent Mack Mattingly. Fowler carried just under two-thirds of the state's 159 counties.

Florida's Democratic governor Bob Graham, a popular moderate, put Paula Hawkins on the defensive by portraying the first-term senator as a lightweight with a narrow focus. Hawkins won only 45 percent of the vote, the worst showing of any Senate incumbent.

Superior organization proved to be the key element in Democratic representative Timothy E. Wirth's victory over GOP representative Ken Kramer for the Senate seat left vacant by retiring Colorado Democrat Gary Hart. In California, where media ads played a crucial role, Democratic senator Alan Cranston ran a masterful campaign that kept Rep. Ed Zschau's legislative record in the spotlight for much of the campaign and prevented the Republicans from focusing on Cranston's performance.

House Republicans lost only five seats in 1986, giving the Democrats a 258-177 edge for the 100th Congress. It was an extraordinarily good election for incumbents of both parties. The five Republican incumbents who went down to defeat were Mike Strang of Colorado; Webb Franklin of Mississippi; Fred J. Eckert of New York; and Bill Cobey and Bill Hendon, both of North Carolina. The Democrats suffered only one incumbent casualty: Robert A. Young of Missouri. The number of incumbents defeated was the lowest in postwar history.

The freshman House class of 1986 included 23 Republicans and 27 Democrats. That was larger than the 43-member freshman class of 1984 but much smaller than the 74-member GOP-dominated class of 1980 and the Democrat-heavy, 80-member contingent elected in 1982.

The Republican Party made a strong showing in gubernatorial contests in 1986, winning a net gain of eight governorships. The Democrats, who entered the election holding 34 of the 50 governorships, saw their advantage drop to 26-24. The GOP count was the largest since 1970, when the party last held a majority of the governorships.

Republicans unseated Democratic incumbents in Texas and Wisconsin and won nine open seats that had been held by Democrats, including upset wins in Alabama and Arizona and a solid victory in Florida. Those victories were offset by the loss of three open Republican seats: in Oregon, Pennsylvania and Tennessee.

The base of the Republican success was a small core of popular incumbents: California's George Deukmejian, Rhode Island's Edward DiPrete and New Hampshire's John H. Sununu. The farm crisis that helped oust at least two Republican senators did not hurt most of the party's gubernatorial nominees. Iowa incumbent Terry E. Branstad won, as did three GOP candidates for open seats: Mike Hayden in Kansas, Kay A. Orr in Nebraska and George S. Michelson in South Dakota. Republicans also picked up the governorship in Maine.

Democratic ineptness aided the Republicans in several states, particularly in Alabama, where Guy Hunt became the state's first Republican governor since Reconstruction. In Illinois, incumbent GOP governor James R. Thompson was considered vulnerable to a challenge from Adlai E. Stevenson III, until two associates of Lyndon H. LaRouche Jr. won Democratic primaries for state office, causing Stevenson to renounce his own nomination and run as an Independent. A three-way race in Arizona helped elect conservative Republican Evan Mecham to succeed Democratic governor Bruce Babbitt in Arizona.

Despite the GOP's poor showing in Senate elections in the South, the party made its greatest gubernatorial gains in that region. In addition to picking up Texas and Alabama, the GOP elected Tampa mayor Bob Martinez in Florida, former governor and senator Henry L. Bellmon in Oklahoma and Carroll A. Campbell Jr. in South Carolina.

Democrats claimed three of the four seats being given up by Republican incumbents. Their largest catch was Pennsylvania, where Bob Casey defeated Lt. Gov. William W. Scranton III.

Republicans, however, were disappointed in their efforts to capture state legislatures. Nationwide, Democrats improved their lead in the number of legislative seats they controlled by 179 and won control of the legislatures in 28 states, two more than they dominated before the election. Republicans controlled both chambers in 10 legislatures, down from 11 before the election. Legislative control was split between the two parties in 11 states. (Nebraska has a nonpartisan, unicameral legislature.)

1987-89: The 100th Congress

The 100th Congress, by its number, had a historic resonance. It convened in the year that the United States was celebrating the bicentennial of its Constitution and the government of checks and balances created by that Constitution.

Fittingly enough, members commemorated the separation of powers that lay at the heart of the Constitution by challenging the president over the Iran-contra affair and by checking his attempt to reshape the judiciary through the appointment of a controversial justice to a pivotal Supreme Court vacancy. The budget deficit engendered partisan wrangling within Congress and between Congress and the president for much of 1987. After the Oct. 19, 1987, stock market crash, however, Congress and Reagan reached accord on a two-year deficit-reduction package.

For the first time since 1981 Democrats were in control of both chambers. Senate Democrats returned to power with a 55-45 margin; Robert C. Byrd of West Virginia was restored to his former position as majority leader. House Democrats, who increased their already formidable edge to 258-177, named Majority Leader Jim Wright of Texas to succeed Speaker Thomas P. O'Neill Jr. of Massachusetts, who had retired in 1986. Wright was unopposed.

Two issues consumed as much if not more congressional attention than the perennial budget battles. The Iran-contra affair rarely left the front pages from February 1987, when a White House commission said the president had all but lost control of his national security apparatus, to November, when the Senate and House select committees investigating the scandal published their report. Continual revelations about the White House plan to sell arms to Iran in exchange for U.S. hostages in the Middle East and the subsequent diversion of profits from the arms sale to the contra guerrillas in Nicaragua severely damaged Reagan's public standing.

Almost as soon as the Iran-contra hearings concluded, Reagan's nomination to fill a Supreme Court vacancy created an equally clamorous controversy. Reagan nominated Robert H. Bork, a federal appeals court judge who had gained notoriety when, as solicitor general in 1973, he fired Watergate special prosecutor Archibald Cox. After a bitter fight, Bork was rejected. Reagan's second nominee, Douglas H. Ginsburg, was forced to withdraw his nomination after he admitted that he had smoked marijuana when he was a law student and law professor. Reagan's third nominee, Anthony M. Kennedy, was confirmed unanimously in February 1988.

Despite these divisive battles and other flare-ups between the Republican White House and the Democratic Congress, the two sides managed to reconcile their differences on a number of major issues, including measures to bail out the Farm Credit System and the Federal Savings and Loan Insurance Corporation. For all its productivity, however, the 100th Congress left for its successor a pile of unfinished business, with the deficit-ridden federal budget teetering at the top.

The 1988 Campaigns

Vice President George Bush's nomination for the presidency was never in any real jeopardy. His candidacy, though, generated little enthusiasm, which encouraged several Republicans to enter the race. Two contenders, former Delaware governor Pierre S. du Pont IV and former secretary of state Alexander M. Haig Jr., left the race early.

The Iowa caucuses gave the Bush forces a momentary scare when their candidate came in third behind Sen. Bob Dole of Kansas and television evangelist Pat Robertson. A week later Bush trounced Dole in New Hampshire and then went on to sweep 16 states on Super Tuesday, shutting Dole out of the March 8 events altogether. New York representative Jack F. Kemp, who had hoped to win the backing of the party's conservative wing, did not fare well in the early primaries and decided to leave the race after Super Tuesday.

Bush confirmed his standing with Republican voters on March 15, decisively winning Illinois. Dole left the race two weeks later. On April 26 Bush won enough Pennsylvania delegates to clinch the Republican nomination.

On the Democratic side eight candidates entered the contest: former Arizona governor Bruce Babbitt; Delaware senator Joseph R. Biden Jr.; Gov. Michael Dukakis of Massachusetts; Rep. Richard A. Gephardt of Missouri; Sen. Albert Gore Jr. of Tennessee; former senator Gary Hart of Colorado; Jesse Jackson; and Sen. Paul Simon of Illinois. Dukakis did not emerge as the clear front-runner until well into the primary schedule.

By mid-March Jackson had accumulated more primary votes than any other Democrat and only four fewer delegates than Dukakis. Then came Wisconsin, where Dukakis beat Jackson by more than 200,000 votes. Dukakis followed his Wisconsin victory with a decisive win in New York. Dukakis went on to win all the remaining primaries except in the District of Columbia, which Jackson took. Even then, Dukakis was not assured of enough delegates until the last round of voting on June 7.

After years of internal warfare the Democrats staged a remarkable show of unity at their convention in Atlanta. The prospects for party peace were not at all guaranteed as the party gathered for its July 18-21 conclave. In the weeks before the convention Dukakis had two main tasks: to select a running mate and to find a way to involve Jackson in the fall campaign.

On July 12 Dukakis announced that he had chosen Texas senator Lloyd Bentsen to be his running mate. The decision angered Jackson supporters, who noted that Bentsen was both Southern and conservative and who believed that Jackson and his message had been slighted. Jackson then seemed to have scaled back his implicit demands that the vice presidential nomination be offered to him. At the same time Dukakis seemed to find ways to demonstrate his respect for Jackson without pandering to him. Both men seemed close to accommodation on platforms and rules issues.

Jackson's willingness to compromise on the platform contributed greatly to the bonhomie of Atlanta, signaling a victory of pragmatism over idealism. As a result the rest of the convention was tension-free, providing the backdrop for a Hollywood-style finale. Jackson himself kicked off the unity collaboration in an electrifying speech that unfurled his famous call for social justice and offered strong words of praise for Dukakis.

With the conclusion of Jackson's speech, his virtual domination of the convention gave way to the business at hand. On July 20 Democratic delegates nominated Dukakis, who won 2,876.25 votes to Jackson's 1,218.5. Jackson conceded by telephone, and the convention then ratified Dukakis's nomination by acclamation.

Running behind Michael Dukakis in the public opinion polls, George Bush came to the Republican National Convention in New Orleans in August with one main task: to convince delegates and the viewing public that he was not the "wimp" pictured by political cartoonists. His choice of Sen. Dan Quayle of Indiana as his running mate, however, heightened many of the doubts he had sought to dispel.

To maintain some suspense, Bush had not been expected to name his choice for vice president until the last day of the convention. But at a welcoming ceremony on Aug. 16, he announced his selection. Concern about Quayle's youth and government inexperience quickly surfaced. A major controversy erupted when reporters questioned Quayle about whether he had used family influence to get into the Indiana National Guard in 1969 to avoid service in the Vietnam War.

While controversy swirled around Quayle's selection, the convention business proceeded as if nothing unusual were happening. With no fights over the platform or party rules (both were approved without debate), the Republicans could concentrate on positioning themselves for the fall campaign.

Although Democrats began the fall campaign with high hopes for November, the campaign turned out to be a downhill slide for Dukakis. Dukakis left the Democratic convention as much as 17 points ahead of Bush in some polls. That lead evaporated under a withering Republican attack that began at the GOP convention. Despite continuing reservations among voters about the Quayle nomination, Bush surged ahead in the polls at the end of August. He maintained that advantage throughout the fall, emphasizing at every opportunity that Dukakis was a liberal out of step with the mainstream. Many scored Bush for his tactics, but few argued with their effectiveness.

Bush's ability to keep Dukakis on the defensive was reflected in the public opinion polls. A week before the election, they gave Bush as much as a 12-point lead.

Results of the 1988 Elections

George Bush was elected the nation's 41st president on Nov. 8, winning 54 percent of the popular vote. Bush's victory confirmed that, absent economic crisis or White House scandal, the burden of proof was on the Democrats to convince voters that their party could be trusted with the executive branch of the federal government.

Bush was the first candidate since John F. Kennedy to win the White House while his party lost seats in the House. And unlike Kennedy's, Bush's victory margin was substantial in a number of states. His inability to carry others into office may have been partly due to his message, which was essentially a call to "stay the course."

In reviewing the results of the 1988 Senate elections, both parties had cause for rue and relief. But it was the Republicans who felt the keener disappointment. Democrats won 19 of the 33 races, maintaining the 55-45 majority they had seized in the 1986 elections. They successfully defended 15 of their 18 seats and took over Republican seats in Connecticut, Virginia, Nebraska and Nevada.

GOP Senate leader Bob Dole conceded on election night that reclaiming the Senate had not been realistic in 1988. And the party could be pleased at capturing three historically Democratic seats as well as holding 11 of its own 15. Of the four the GOP lost, the only surprise came in Connecticut, where incumbent Lowell P. Weicker Jr. was edged out by Joseph I. Lieberman.

The GOP had all but conceded the other three seats to the Democrats a year before the election. In Virginia former governor Charles S. Robb succeeded Republican Paul S. Trible Jr., who retired after a single term. David K. Karnes of Nebraska lost to former Democratic governor Robert Kerry, and Chic Hecht of Nevada lost to sitting Democratic governor Richard H. Bryan.

The only Democratic incumbent the Republicans defeated was John Melcher of Montana. Conrad Burns became the state's first Republican senator elected in 42 years. The other two new Republican seats in the Senate were won by House minority whip Trent Lott of Mississippi and Rep. Connie Mack of Florida. The latest emblems of the GOP's new day in the Old South, they replaced retiring Democrats John C. Stennis and Lawton Chiles.

An important measure of a party's performance in any election year is its score in contests where no incumbent is running. In this category the GOP won four of six. The party held on to retiring Robert T. Stafford's seat in Vermont, where at-large representative James M. Jeffords had no trouble moving in. And former GOP senator Slade Gorton, whom the voters had turned out two years before, was elected to succeed retiring Republican senator Daniel J. Evans. Mack and Lott picked up the other two open seats.

The two Democrats winning open seats were Robb and Herbert Kohl of Wisconsin. Kohl succeeded Democrat William Proxmire, who retired.

In the House of Representatives election day was cause for celebration for more than 98 percent of the members seeking reelection. Only six of 408 incumbents on the ballot lost, four Republicans and two Democrats. The Democrats picked up a net of two seats, putting the partisan lineup in the House at 260 Democrats and 175 Republicans.

The most prominent member to fall was Fernand J. St Germain of Rhode Island, who was soundly rejected after being dogged by questions about his ethical conduct. And in Georgia the Democrats had little trouble knocking off Republican representative Pat Swindall, who was under indictment for allegedly lying to a grand jury about a money-laundering scheme.

Democratic representative Bill Chappell Jr. lost his Florida district after being battered by public questions about his links to a defense-procurement scandal. Democratic representative Roy Dyson of Maryland, also plagued by unfavorable stories about his links to the procurement scandal and his conduct in office, narrowly eked out a victory over a challenger he was expected to trounce.

Many victories in 1988 depended on more than political skills, personality and partisan appeal. The powers of incumbency—free mailing, press attention and fund-raising advantages—played a significant role in the election.

If the advantage of incumbency helped to explain why Republicans were having trouble reducing the Democratic advantages in the House, it did little to explain why they made no headway in the battle for open seats. In all, only three of the 27 open seats changed partisan hands, with the

Democrats winning two formerly GOP seats and the Republicans winning one seat held by the Democrats.

The 1988 results were unlikely to encourage challengers mulling the 1990 election. The 98 percent reelection rate from 1986 may well have played a role in discouraging competition in 1988, one of the quietest election years in recent memory.

There were 12 gubernatorial races on Nov. 8. Of the nine governors seeking reelection, eight won, all by stressing their managerial skill. The only incumbent to fail, West Virginia Republican Arch A. Moore Jr., was ousted because voters had lost confidence in his ability to steer the state's struggling economy toward better times. Democrat Gaston Caperton defeated Moore.

Two other GOP governors were as embattled as Moore—Edward DiPrete in Rhode Island and Norman H. Bangerter in Utah—but both eked out victories over stiff Democratic competition.

Those narrow GOP victories deflated the Democrats' high expectations of gubernatorial gains in 1988. Democrats were defending only four seats, compared with the GOP's eight. In addition, the three Democratic incumbents seeking reelection seemed solid, while Republicans looked to be struggling in at least four states. But on Nov. 8 the Democrats scored a net gain of just one governorship, bringing to 28 their number of chief executives. The GOP held 22 governorships.

The Post-Cold War Era

When the history of the early 1990s is written, the signal event will surely be the collapse of Soviet communism and the dissolution of the Union of Soviet Socialist Republics. The world watched as, one by one, the countries of the Warsaw Pact broke away from the Soviet Union to turn toward democracy and market economies and then as the Soviet Union itself broke apart. Seemingly overnight, the superpower rivalry that had dominated U.S. defense and foreign policy for nearly half a century was over.

For many Americans, however, these astounding events were overshadowed by economic recession. Faced with slow economic growth and high levels of unemployment, more and more people began to fear that they and their children would never be able to realize the American dream of a continually improving standard of living.

Those fears were to make Republican George Bush a one-term president. Bush, entering the White House on the popularity of his predecessor, Ronald Reagan, saw his own public approval ratings soar to record heights after the successful U.S.-led military action against Iraq in 1991. But Bush was never able to persuade voters that he had a credible plan for rejuvenating the economy or addressing other domestic problems, including a failing health insurance system and the huge budget deficits caused in part by the Reagan-Bush economic policies.

The Democratic-controlled Congress gave the president little quarter, although the two did cooperate to enact a far-reaching rewrite of the Clean Air Act. Other major achievements of the 101st and 102nd Congresses included measures making public and work places accessible to Americans with disabilities and a restructuring of the thrift industry. But severe image problems overshadowed these achievements. More often than not, the Democratic Congress clashed with the Republican White House, with legislative gridlock the result. This perceived ineptitude combined with numerous scandals to drive congressional approval ratings to record lows.

The military victory in Iraq was the crowning moment of George Bush's presidency. But the euphoria was fleeting. Almost as soon as the war had ended, Democrats succeeded in turning the nation's attention to the economy's miserable performance.

When Bush assumed office, the economy was still in what would become the longest peacetime expansion. Unemployment stood at 5.3 percent, and the inflation rate was 4.2 percent. But the expansion slowed during the first quarter of 1989, and the economy slid into recession.

The single action that may have dealt the biggest blow to Bush's political fortunes occurred in 1990 when Bush broke his 1988 campaign promise not to raise taxes. Concerned that a hemorrhaging deficit could severely damage the economy and his own re-election chances in 1992, Bush sought the help of Democrats to work out a bipartisan package deal that was expected to reduce the deficit by $500 billion over the next five years.

1989-91:
The 101st Congress

Despite the momentous events that rocked the world and nation in 1989-91, Congress' focus was on internal politics. Congress was consigned to a role that was, if not peripheral, at most reactive. Moreover, the 1988 elections had not given either the new Republican president, George Bush, or the Democratic-controlled Congress any clear mandate, and neither party had a compelling agenda of its own.

For much of the two years, congressional attention was focused inward, on events surrounding the resignations of House Speaker Jim Wright, D-Texas—the first time in history a Speaker had quit midterm—and House Majority Whip Tony Coelho, D-Calif. Questions about their personal ethics forced both men out of office. Thomas S. Foley of Washington was elected to succeed Wright as Speaker.

Ethics problems also surfaced for five senators who had intervened with federal regulators in behalf of an ailing savings and loan institution. The senators became known as the Keating Five, after the thrift's owner, Charles H. Keating Jr.

In the Senate, Democrat George J. Mitchell of Maine was serving his first years as majority leader, where he cautiously proceeded to impose order on the legislative schedule and to find consensus among Democrats. Most senators said Mitchell lived up to his promise to have an open, consultative leadership style. Relations with Republicans were easier than they had been under his predecessor, Robert C. Byrd, D-W.Va.

In Virginia in 1989, the state that billed itself as the "cradle of the Confederacy," Democratic Lt. Gov. L. Douglas Wilder became the nation's first elected black governor, succeeding another Democrat. In addition, the Democrats won the New Jersey statehouse from the Republicans in the only other governorship up that year.

The 1990 Midterm Elections

War and recession hovered ominously over the 1990 campaign, but neither figured prominently in its outcome. Instead, the election campaigns looked more like a series of hard-fought city council contests, shaped largely by personalities, local issues and a pronounced absence of clear-cut national themes.

While frustrated voters talked about "throwing the bums out," on Nov. 6 they returned incumbents to Washington en masse. Only one of the 32 Senate incumbents seeking re-election lost, while only 15 of the 406 House members who ran in the general election were defeated.

Altogether, the Republicans lost one Senate seat and eight House seats, weakening the administration's hand. Bush had come to depend upon a strategy of governing by veto in dealing with the heavily Democratic Congress. (As it turned out, a Bush veto was not overridden until the final days of the 102nd Congress.)

Colorado in 1990 became the first state to impose term limits on federal officeholders. (California, Colorado and Oklahoma voters also adopted ballot initiatives capping the service of state legislators.) But the broad anti-incumbent sentiment expressed toward Congress in pre-election polls did not materialize at the ballot box. *(Term limits, box, pp. 54-55)*

Only one Senate incumbent, Republican Rudy Boschwitz of Minnesota, was defeated. In the House, 96 percent of the incumbents seeking re-election were returned. Total turnover, including retirements, amounted to just 10 percent.

Despite winning more House seats (267) in 1990 than in any other election since the recession-year contest of 1982, the Democrats' share of the total, nationwide congressional vote was their lowest for any midterm election since 1966. In 1990 Democrats drew just 52.9 percent of all House votes. By comparison, when Democrats captured 269 seats in 1982, their share of the nationwide congressional vote was 55.2 percent, more than 2 percentage points higher than in 1990.

The statehouses proved to be the real workshop of democracy in 1990. Anti-incumbent sentiment overtook sitting Republican governors in four states and Democratic governors in two. Eight other statehouses also changed hands, with four going to Republicans, three to Democrats, and one (Alaska) to the Alaska Independence Party. All told, 14 governorships switched from one party to another and more incumbent governors were toppled than in any other year since 1970.

The GOP picked up Arizona's governorship in February 1991, when Republican candidate Fife Symington won a runoff election. And it gained another statehouse in March 1991 when Louisiana Gov. Buddy Roemer, elected as a Democrat in 1987, switched parties. That left the lineup at 27 Democrats, 21 Republicans and two independents.

Six of 23 gubernatorial incumbents who sought re-election lost their jobs. Two of the losses—Democrats James J. Blanchard of Michigan and Rudy Perpich of Minnesota—came as surprises.

In Connecticut, former GOP senator Lowell P. Weicker Jr. won the seat vacated by Democrat William A. O'Neill. Weicker, a maverick liberal Republican who lost a 1988 Senate re-election bid, chose to run on his own ticket instead of competing for the GOP nomination.

Alaska voters were similarly unfettered by convention, electing former Republican governor Walter J. Hickel. Hickel had thrown the race into disarray by jumping in on the Alaska Independence Party ticket only six weeks before the election. Republicans had nominated state senator Arliss Sturgulewski, but some were uncomfortable with her abortion rights stance, and even her running mate abandoned the ticket to run with Hickel.

1991-93:
The 102nd Congress

Hobbled by partisanship and purse strings, the 102nd Congress produced one of the shortest lists of legislative accomplishments in recent memory. Congress and the president enacted some notable measures, including the first overhaul of energy regulations in a decade, new regulation of the cable television industry and aid to the former Soviet republics. But the number of achievements paled in comparison with the number of bills that were considered but never enacted.

The 102nd Congress had hardly begun when its signal event arrived on Capitol Hill. After three days of somber but passionate debate, Congress on Jan. 12, 1991, gave President Bush authorization to go to war against Iraq. The vote represented the first time since Dec. 8, 1941, that Congress had exercised its constitutional authority to declare war.

Less than two months later, a triumphant Bush ascended the dais in the House of Representatives to tell the assembled Congress—and the nation—"Aggression is defeated; the war is over."

The end of the shooting war abroad, however, marked the beginning of a shouting war at home, as lawmakers turned their attention from the victory overseas to the sagging economy and other domestic concerns. But the budget deal that the White House and Congress wrote in 1990, combined with partisan politics in 1991, made significant progress on domestic issues nearly impossible. The Republican president used his veto, real and threatened, to stall Democratic measures he did not like, such as civil rights and extended unemployment benefits. Compromises were forged only after Bush's standing in the public opinion polls began to fall.

Once the war was successfully concluded, Operation Desert Storm receded from pre-eminence on the national agenda with startling speed. By late August, in what was likely to be a far more momentous development, the Soviet Union was falling apart.

While the war debate was Congress' finest hour in 1991, considerable competition existed for its low point. Two leading contenders were the confirmation hearings of Clarence Thomas to be an associate justice of the Supreme Court and the revelation that House members routinely wrote checks on the House bank without having the funds to cover them.

Thomas, a federal court of appeals judge, had been named to succeed Justice Thurgood Marshall, who was retiring. Thomas' conservative credentials had already made his confirmation as the second black to sit on the Court a subject of great controversy, but the hearings turned into a national soap opera in October after law school professor Anita F. Hill alleged that Thomas had sexually harassed her, and lurid details poured out of the hearing room. Thomas was confirmed, but the Senate's handling of the situation left women outraged and led many senators to call the confirmation process flawed.

The two-year Keating Five investigation also came to a conclusion in 1991. The Senate Ethics Committee reprimanded Alan Cranston, D-Calif., and it criticized in writing the four other senators—Democrats Dennis DeConcini of Arizona, John Glenn of Ohio, and Donald W. Riegle Jr. of Michigan, and Republican John McCain of Arizona—for their poor judgment in acting in behalf of Charles Keating, who owned a savings and loan that went bankrupt at a $2 billion cost to federal taxpayers.

Perhaps nothing symbolized the gridlock in Washington so much as the debate over urban aid in the wake of the Los Angeles riots in April 1992—the worst incident of domestic violence in 20 years. Congress and President Bush could not agree either on the amount and kind of aid or on how that aid should be funded. Democrats had to settle for $500 million in aid, a third of what they had proposed.

Congress's internal strife complicated matters. Along with the members' bank overdrafts problem, House leaders had to deal with a scandal at the House Post Office involving allegations that legislators had converted public funds into cash and that patronage employees sold drugs at the federal facility. Several employees pleaded guilty to various charges and a federal grand jury subpoenaed expense account records of three House members, including Ways and Means Chairman Dan Rostenkowski of Illinois.

The 1992 Campaigns

A year before the 1992 presidential campaign began, President Bush seemed poised for one of the smoothest re-elections in White House history. After he led the nation to victory in the brief Persian Gulf War, the president's popularity soared. Yet when he formally launched his candidacy in Washington on Feb. 12, 1992, Bush faced the prospect of spirited competition not only in the fall from the Democrats but also in the Republican primaries.

In the intervening 11 months, the economy had gone into what even the president called a "free fall." So, too, had Bush's popularity. The president had dropped from a peak of 89 percent approval in the Gallup Poll in March 1991 to 44 percent in February 1992. Not much that the White House did before or during the campaign helped revitalize either the economy or the president's political standing.

On the Democratic side, the nomination of Arkansas Gov. Bill Clinton seemed the most likely outcome as the campaign got under way. His campaign was well positioned on all major fronts—organization, message development, fund raising and endorsements. Clinton's early primary wins put him far ahead of the other Democratic contenders, but continuing doubts about Clinton's character raised questions about the governor's electability.

In addition to Clinton, just four other Democrats actively sought the nomination as the primary season began: former Massachusetts senator Paul E. Tsongas, former California governor Edmund G. "Jerry" Brown Jr. and senators Tom Harkin of Iowa and Bob Kerrey of Nebraska. None of the four had much following beyond their own regions, and all of them were long shots for the nomination. Brown, however, ran an innovative campaign, placing a $100 limit on contributions, which could be pledged by dialing a toll-free 800 number.

On the eve of the New Hampshire primary in February, renewed controversies surfaced about Clinton's draft status during the Vietnam War and allegations of marital infidelity. Calls went out for new candidates to enter the race. Some prominent Democrats considered but then dropped the idea because the nominating system seriously handicapped any late entry into the race.

As a result, voters in most states did not have a wide choice. In only five primaries could Democrats choose from a full field of active candidates. Clinton, Brown and Tsongas were the only candidates in another 10 primaries. As Harkin, Kerrey and then Tsongas dropped out, Clinton's main competition in the last two dozen primaries came from Brown.

Although he lost in New Hampshire, Clinton became the first Democrat to win primary victories in each of the 10 largest states. He scored more primary victories (32) than any other Democratic candidate ever had. And his nearly 10.5 million primary votes were more than any previous candidate, Democrat or Republican, had ever won in the history of the presidential primaries.

Bush's nomination for a second term was never in jeopardy, despite his sagging popularity. His only real challenge came from the party's conservative wing, which had been suspicious of Bush since at least 1980 when he ran for the nomination against Ronald Reagan, the conservatives' hero. Seizing what he saw as an opportunity, conservative commentator Patrick J. Buchanan, a former speechwriter for President Richard Nixon and one-time communications director for the Reagan White House, entered the race.

Although he collected fewer than 100 delegates, Buchanan found some support in his attacks on Bush. Bush won every primary, but he wound up with less than three-fourths of the Republican primary ballots, a far lower share than the last three elected Republican presidents (Reagan, Nixon and Dwight D. Eisenhower) had received on their road to re-election.

Former Louisiana state representative David Duke also ran a limited campaign for the presidency. But the former Ku Klux Klan member won little support among Republicans and ended his campaign on April 22.

After the conventions, Bush continued to try to focus voter attention on Clinton's character. But Clinton began the final phase of the campaign as the front runner, and nothing Bush did ever dislodged the Democrat from that position. By the time of the presidential debates in mid-October, the political community had reached virtually unanimous agreement that without a major news development or a Clinton misstep Bush was likely to lose his bid for a second term.

Results of the 1992 Elections

A plurality of American voters listened to Democratic presidential candidate Clinton's call for change in 1992 and turned President Bush out of office after only one term. Clinton, the governor of Arkansas, carried 32 states and the District of Columbia, won 370 of 538 electoral votes and outscored Bush by 5 percentage points—43 percent to 38 percent.

Clinton's was the most sweeping triumph for any Democrat since President Lyndon B. Johnson in 1964 and the best showing for any Democratic challenger since Franklin D. Roosevelt ousted Republican Herbert Hoover from the White House in 1932. In placing Clinton, 46, and Sen. Al Gore of Tennessee, 44, at the head of the government, Americans for the first time elected a president and vice president both born after World War II.

The widespread desire for a change in government also benefited independent candidate Ross Perot, the Texas billionaire who spoke bluntly of the need to reduce the federal budget deficit. Perot won 19 percent of the popular vote, the largest vote total for an independent candidate in presidential election history and the biggest vote share since 1912, when Theodore Roosevelt ran under the Progressive Party banner.

Change also reached Congress, where voters added record numbers of women, blacks and Hispanics. The new Senate would be the most diverse in history, with the addition of four women, including Carol Moseley-Braun, the first black woman ever elected to the body. More than one-fourth of the House members in 1993 would be freshmen, a result of retirements and redistricting as well as voter rejection of incumbents.

Overall, however, the partisan lineup in Congress was virtually the same, with the Democrats firmly in control of both chambers. The lineup in the Senate remained at 57 Democrats and 43 Republicans. At the beginning of the 103rd Congress, the House had 258 Democrats, 176 Republicans and one independent. The Republicans had gained 10 seats.

Anti-incumbency and "Year of the Woman" themes may have worked well in some Senate and House elections, but they had little effect in the 12 gubernatorial races in 1992. Voters seemed more concerned about economics and ethics. The four incumbent governors running for re-election—all Democrats—were returned to office. And a former Democratic governor won back his job after an eight-year absence. The three women running for governor in Montana, New Hampshire and Rhode Island all lost. Women held the governorships in Kansas, Oregon and Texas.

Altogether, Democrats won three seats formerly held by Republicans, while the GOP picked up one seat held by a Democrat, for a net gain of two seats for the Democrats. That gave the Democrats a total of 30 governorships; the Republicans held 18. Two governors were independents.

Voters in 14 states in 1992 approved limits on the number of terms their representatives and senators in Congress could serve.

End of an Era in the House

Almost from its beginning, the 103rd Congress was afflicted with a creeping case of paralysis. By the final days of the 1994 session, an end-of-era atmosphere had settled over the Capitol, especially in the House of Representatives.

The Democrats had held the House since the elections of 1954, when they regained a narrow majority midway through the first term of popular Republican president Dwight D. Eisenhower. In 1956 Eisenhower won re-election in a landslide, but it was not enough to recapture the House for his party. "Ike" was the first winning presidential candidate since Zachary Taylor in 1848 to fail to carry the House. Some political writers in 1956 interpreted the split decision to mean that Eisenhower had won not as a Republican but as a war hero (a personal distinction he shared with Taylor).

But in the years to come, American voters suggested they had other reasons for splitting their ballots, electing a Republican president and a Democratic House five more times in 1968, 1972, 1980, 1984 and 1988.

One theory offered to explain this pattern has emphasized the role of the Cold War, which seemed a permanent fact of life for nearly half a century. During these years, the electorate as a whole seemed more comfortable having Republican presidents handle the defense and foreign policy issues of the presidency. At the same time, the voters consistently elected Democratic majorities in Congress who could be counted on to create and sustain desirable domestic programs and perform various services for constituents.

When the Cold War ended in 1991, national security seemed less salient as an issue—as President George Bush was to learn when he lost to a former war protester named Bill Clinton in 1992. At the same time, Democrats were finding their 40-year-old formula for holding the House less reliable as well. They seemed beset by rising resentment of federal tax levels and increasing hostility toward government in general as expensive, overbearing and inefficient. Democrats struggled to respond to this challenge creatively or effectively, particularly in their failure to overhaul the health care system in the 103rd Congress.

1993-95: The 103rd Congress

The Democrats had won the presidency and retained Congress in 1992 with a promise of moderate, constructive change. Clinton ran as a "New Democrat" who would have government do fewer things but do them better. Clinton said he would restrain "big nanny" government and reduce the federal budget deficit—an issue forced to the top of the national agenda in part by the independent candidacy of billionaire H. Ross Perot (who received 19 percent of the popular vote). At the same time, the Clinton who campaigned in 1992 was brilliant in addressing the concerns of middle-class voters. He promised to get serious about public finances, but partly as a way to guarantee the financial future of such programs as health care, old-age pensions and education.

This broad mix of somewhat contradictory expectations went largely unmet. Congress waited for President Clinton to send a reform program with specific measures for it to pass. But when the new president—distracted, unfocused and inexperienced—had difficulty getting his program started, Congress failed to take the initiative in major areas until it was too late to build a record to defend in the 1994 elections.

When the 103rd adjourned in the fall of 1994, *The Washington Post* called it the worst Congress in living memory, and *The Baltimore Sun* called it simply "dysfunctional."

Clinton was distracted in the early going by symbolic issues of importance to certain Democratic constituencies: such as the acknowledgment of gays in the military and the promotion of more women to the highest ranks of government. Clinton also sacrificed much of his time, energy and political good to foreign crises in Somalia and Haiti, which were of little interest to most Americans.

These issues did little to build momentum for Clinton's legislative program. On the gay issue, he buckled under to opposition from Congress and the military establishment. He succeeded in finding a woman to be attorney general, but only after two highly publicized and embarrassing misfires.

And while he sent ideas to Congress on many issues, there was no effective follow-up. His cheerful ebullience and inability to get things done caused the influential British journal *The Economist*, to describe him in a cover story as "Mister Fizz" (and later to withdraw its 1992 endorsement in favor of his 1996 opponent).

Eventually, the Clinton administration and the Democratic leadership in Congress did agree to go to the voters in 1994 with accomplishments in three key areas—health care, crime and reducing the deficit. The goal was to lend plausibility to the idea that the Democrats could still deliver on the issues they had raised—and voters had responded to—in 1992.

The 103rd Congress managed to pass a deficit-reduction package in 1993, but without attracting a single Republican vote in either chamber. That left the majority open to the GOP's charge that the bill was more surely a tax-and-spend package than a reduction in the deficit or in unnecessary spending. During the 1994 and 1996 campaigns, Republicans would call the deficit reduction package "the largest peacetime tax increase in American history." The same could have been said of the last two tax increases enacted by Presidents Bush and Ronald Reagan in 1990 and 1982, respectively, which in constant dollars (adjusted for inflation) were even larger. But the charge stuck, in part because neither Clinton nor congressional Democrats did much to convince the nation that higher taxes were necessary. They argued that only the wealthiest Americans were really paying higher income taxes under the 1993 law, but Republicans replied by noting that the gasoline tax had been raised for everyone.

The Omnibus Crime Bill of 1994 was another disappointment in political terms. The Democratic leadership tried to cobble together three bills in one: a tough anti-crime

bill to please conservatives; a gun-control bill to please liberals; and a facilities construction and jobs creation bill to please voters in the communities affected. When the Republicans attacked the bill as bloated with pork and violative of 2nd Amendment rights, the House Democratic leaders had trouble keeping their troops in line (the Congressional Black Caucus defected, in part to protest the bill's provisions expanding use of the death penalty). The majority party could not muster the votes to bring the bill to the floor for official consideration in August 1994, a rare and humiliating event.

The leadership had to go humbly to the Republicans, led by then Minority Whip Newt Gingrich, R-Ga., and rewrite parts of the bill to get the votes for floor consideration. Some observers considered this a watershed in the 40-year history of Democratic control, and it took place less than three months before the midterm elections.

But an even greater debacle overtook the Democratic leadership in both chambers in their effort to enact an overhaul of the nation's health care system. Clinton placed First Lady Hillary Rodham Clinton at the head of a special panel on the issue. Her panel held hearings that were closed to the public before presenting a complex and unwieldy bill to Congress, where various individuals, committees and factions were already working on their versions. In the end, no bill had enough support to emerge from the pivotal House committee, and an eleventh-hour effort to fashion a viable bill in the Senate collapsed in the face of Republican opposition.

These major failures more than offset the 103rd Congress's legislative successes, which included enactment of the "Brady Bill" to require a waiting period for handgun purchases and ratification of the North American Free Trade Agreement (NAFTA)—and NAFTA was passed mostly with Republican votes.

The 1994 Midterm Elections

If the congressional Democrats ended the 103rd Congress in disarray, the House Republicans were on the march. A younger and more combative generation, led by Gingrich, completed their takeover of the party in the House when Minority Leader Robert Michel of Illinois announced he would retire. Gingrich and his cohort then drew up a 10-plank "Contract with America" that was signed by virtually every Republican running for the House in the fall of 1994—incumbents and challengers alike. It promised a more responsive institution in which issues would be debated in the light of day, and brought to an up-or-down vote. On substantive matters, the Republicans continued to promise lower taxes; a balanced budget; smaller, less intrusive government; and the promotion of morality, ethics and "family values" in society and government.

Gingrich accused the Democrats of breaking faith with the American people by promising a "New Democrat" administration but governing as free-spending and arrogant "Old Democrats" out of touch with the people. He predicted that the Republicans would regain the House after 40 years of Democratic rule.

Although that seemed a bold prediction, there had been signs that the voters were pulling back from the Democrats almost as soon as they had installed them in power. In December 1992, within weeks of Clinton's election, a special run-off election in Georgia brought the defeat of an incumbent Democrat, Sen. Wyche Fowler. The run-off had been forced by the state's majority-vote requirement, which was repealed in time to elect another Democrat to the state's other Senate seat by a plurality in 1996. In June, Kay Bailey

Term Limits for Members of Congress: . . .

The issue of term limits for members of Congress forces the gut instincts of the majority of the people into conflict with an articulate minority that has the law—as currently interpreted by the Supreme Court of the United States—on its side.

Popular resentment against Congress as an institution had been building up for some time before the term limits issue rose to importance in the 1990s. Its members were increasingly viewed as being primarily responsive to large donors whose contributions, combined with the other built-in advantages of incumbency, seemed to be making incumbents impossible to remove in an election. During the late 1980s, the incumbents' re-election rate was more than 90 percent.

The last straw was a series of nagging scandals in the 1980s. The decade began with "Abscam," the exposure of bribe-taking by several members of Congress. Most of the miscreants resigned, but one refused and became the first member to be expelled from Congress since the Civil War. The trend continued with the resignation of the Speaker of the House in 1989 under an ethics cloud and ended with the exposure of routine overdrafts by more than 100 representatives at the House's bank for members.

The Solution: Term Limits

A proposed solution—to end privileged and increasingly corrupt careerism by limiting tenure in Congress—sprang up in many states at once. The movement was coordinated by a volunteer national organization, Term Limits Inc. (TLI).

In 1990 Utah adopted term limits by legislation. That same year Colorado adopted them by referendum. And in November 1992, 14 more states adopted term limits for members of Congress by referendum. All 16 states limited Senate tenure to 12 years, while capping House service at 6, 8 or 12 years.

In most cases, the popular support for term limits was overwhelming. Nearly 21 million Americans—66 percent of those voting—supported term limits, a 200-year-old concept rejected by the Constitutional Convention of 1787 but rediscovered by modern-day voters disgusted by scandal and discontented with entrenched incumbents who appeared to tolerate scandal—and the decline of Congress as a respected institution.

Term Limits for Other Government Officials

Term limits are not new in U.S. politics. At the nation's beginning, the original states' suspicion of a strong executive caused several to limit their governors' tenure. Today, more than half the states have term limits for governors.

Presidents George Washington and Thomas Jefferson limited themselves to two terms voluntarily, and when that tradition was broken by Franklin Roosevelt in 1940, Congress proposed, and the states in 1951 ratified, the 22nd amendment to the Constitution, which made a two-term lifetime limit for presidents mandatory.

What is new in the 1990s is proposed term limits for other state and local officers, and for state and local legislators, as well as for members of Congress. There is no federal legal problem with citizens limiting tenure for state and local office. But there is a serious legal problem with term limits for members of Congress.

Constitutional Prohibitions

The movement for congressional term limits in the 1990s was soon derailed by the Supreme Court. In a 5-4 decision in *U.S. Term Limits Inc. v. Thornton*, the Court ruled in May 1995 that term limits were unconstitutional. The 1995 ruling was built upon an earlier decision. In 1969, the Court ruled 7-1 in *Powell v. McCormack* that the House had improperly denied Rep. Adam Clayton Powell Jr., D-N.Y. his seat. The House, rather than expel Powell for apparent misuse of public funds and other legal problems (Congress does have the constitutional power to expel its members) voted to exclude him instead by ordering the Speaker not to administer the oath to him. Powell's suit to invalidate the action (and recover two years lost pay) was upheld by the Court.

"The Constitution," Chief Justice Earl Warren wrote for the Court, "leaves the House without authority to exclude any person, duly elected by his constituents, who meets all the requirements for membership expressly required in the Constitution." These requirements are minimum age (25 for the House; 30 for the Senate); minimum length of citizenship (7 for the House; 9 for the Senate); and residence in the state choosing its representation in Congress.

Hutchison gained another Senate seat for the GOP in a special election to replace Sen. Lloyd Bentsen of Texas, who had resigned to become secretary of the Treasury. In November 1993 Republicans won both of the gubernatorial elections held (Christine Todd Whitman in New Jersey and George F. Allen in Virginia) and claimed the mayor's office in New York City as well.

But neither Gingrich's brash self-confidence, nor the election results leading up to November 1994, quite prepared Washington for what happened. The nation's verdict on the first two years of the Clinton administration—and on the 103rd Congress—could not have been clearer: The Republicans made a net gain of 52 House seats—their biggest gain since 1946—and seized gain control of that chamber for the first time in 40 years. They stormed into the majority in the Senate for the first time in eight years with a net gain of eight seats.

Six prominent national Democratic leaders were among the 34 incumbent representatives, two incumbent senators and four incumbent governors defeated for re-election. Rep. Thomas S. Foley of Washington was the first Speaker of the House to be unseated since the political turmoil leading into the Civil War. Rep. Dan Rostenkowski of Illinois, chairman of Ways and Means and an architect of the tax overhaul of 1986 and the budget agreements of 1990 and 1993, and Rep. Jack Brooks of Texas, chairman of the House Judiciary Committee and an author of the Omnibus Crime Bill, both lost. Sen. Jim Sasser of Tennessee, chairman of the Senate Budget Committee and another author of the 1990 and 1993 budget agreements, was defeated by a Republican doctor, Bill Frist.

... The People Versus the Law

Strengthening *Powell* in its *U.S. Term Limits Inc. v. Thornton* decision, the Court went further, ruling that states could not establish term limits for their members of Congress—either directly, or indirectly by hindering access to the ballot. The court said that former or current members' access had to be equal to that of every other constitutionally qualified person. (The case involved Arkansas, but applied to every state that had adopted term limits in 1990 and 1992.)

"Allowing individual states to adopt their own qualifications for congressional service would be inconsistent with the Framers' vision of a uniform National Legislature representing the people of the United States," Justice John Paul Stevens wrote for the Court.

TLI announced that it would try to find a constitutionally acceptable formula to make it more difficult for incumbents who had reached a state's desired limit of service to be re-elected. At the same time, supporters of term limits in Congress, almost all of them Republicans, were moving to amend the Constitution.

"The Scarlet Letter"

TLI's first effort to modify *Thornton* was to support state initiatives requiring members of Congress from those states to support a constitutional amendment limiting senators to 12 years and representatives to 6 years. Those incumbents who refused to support term limits would have a so-called "scarlet letter"—the phrase "disregarded voter instructions on term limits"—placed next to their names on the ballot the next time they ran.

TLI's "scarlet letter" initiative was placed on the ballots of 14 states in November 1996: it passed in nine of them. The Arkansas Supreme Court immediately disallowed the initiative, which passed with 61 percent approval in that state, as an unconstitutional effort to coerce legislators; to give legislative powers directly to the people; and to override the prerogative of Congress to propose amendments to the Constitution.

In February 1997, the U.S. Supreme Court let the Arkansas ruling stand without comment and without a vote (*Arkansas Term Limits v. Donovan*). TLI announced it would continue to devise new methods to limit terms in the hope of passing judicial scrutiny.

Amending the Constitution

In March 1995, two months before the *Thornton* decision, the House of Representatives—as part of the new Republican majority's "Contract with America"—voted on a proposed constitutional amendment to limit persons to 12 years of total service in each chamber of the Congress. The proposal obtained a 227-204 majority, but the vote was 61 short of the two-thirds required to propose an amendment to the states.

In February 1997, after nine states had passed "scarlet letter" instructions, the House Republican majority again tried to pass the amendment, but—reflecting the GOP's loss of nine seats in November 1996—the vote was closer: 217-211, or 69 short of two-thirds. The Senate leadership declined to take a position on the issue; it lacked the three-fifths support needed to end a threatened filibuster and bring the amendment to a vote.

TLI promised to raise the term limit issue in House and Senate elections in 1998 and thereafter—until term limits are enacted.

Term Limit Prospects

After the 1995 *Thornton* decision was announced, former House Speaker Tom Foley, D-Wash. said that "term limits are dead, but I don't believe for a minute that term-limit proponents are going to accept that."

Paul Jacob, the executive director of TLI, agreed with the second part of Foley's assessment. "The Court has struck down one avenue, but there are others," he said. TLI hopes to change the political dynamics of the issue by keeping the pressure on candidates for Congress to commit themselves in favor of a term limit amendment.

Jacob compared the issue to that of the popular election of U.S. senators, where public pressure finally forced a reluctant Senate to give in and to pass what in 1913 became the 17th amendment, mandating the population of senators (who had previously been elected by state legislatures).

TLI was encouraged by the defeat of Speaker Foley in 1994 after 30 years in the House, in large measure because of his outspoken opposition to term limits. And Rep. Ray Thornton, D-Ark., of the *Thornton* decision, retired from the House in 1996 after 12 years there, because of his state's vote for term limits.

Had Sasser won, he 'was expected to be elected the new Democratic leader of the Senate.

Governors Mario Cuomo of New York and Ann Richards of Texas, traditional liberals who had made stirring speeches to Democratic national conventions in 1984 and 1988 respectively, were also defeated. Their loss put GOP governors at the helm in all but one (Florida) of the nation's largest states. Republicans also unseated incumbent Democratic governors in Alabama and New Mexico and gained open gubernatorial offices in Connecticut, Idaho, Kansas, Oklahoma, Pennsylvania, Rhode Island, Tennessee and Wyoming. They lost open seats in Alaska and Maine (to an Independent), leaving themselves with a 30-19 lead in governors—their first such advantage since 1970. And they made substantial gains in state legislatures.

For the first time since 1920, not a single incumbent Republican representative, senator or governor was defeated for re-election. The Senate got its first freshman class with no Democrats since the Constitution was amended in 1913 to provide for popular election of senators. Democrats gained just four open seats in the House and the open governorship of Alaska.

The new Republicans in the Senate were Jon Kyl of Arizona, Olympia J. Snowe of Maine, Spencer Abraham of Michigan, Rod Grams of Minnesota, John Ashcroft of Missouri, Mike DeWine of Ohio, James Inhofe of Oklahoma, Rick Santorum of Pennsylvania, Bill Frist and Fred Thompson of Tennessee, and Craig Thomas oF Wyoming.

Several incumbent Democrats won closely contested Senate races: Diane Feinstein was re-elected in California,

Edward Kennedy in Massachusetts, Frank Lautenberg in New Jersey, Jeff Bingaman in New Mexico and Charles S. Robb in Viriginia. The Democrats also won close governorship races in Florida and Georgia. Otherwise the GOP victory was their most complete since the 1920 landslide that followed World War I.

1995-97:
The 104th Congress

But the Republicans, too, seemed to misread the nation almost as soon as the election celebrations were over. Just as the Democrats had spoiled their post-1992 opportunity to become the dominant party of the post-Cold War era, the GOP set itself up for a backlash in the 1996 elections that would give Clinton a second term and bring the Democrats back to life, if not to the majority, in the House.

But before the Republicans overreached themselves, and alienated the American voter by their combative style and uncompromising assault on government, they did succeed in restoring the House of Representatives as a functioning, open and responsive institution of government.

Elected Speaker without opposition in his party, Gingrich held his Republican majority to the "Contract with America" that virtually all had signed. And in the first 100 days of the 104th Congress, the GOP kept its promise of reform. The House voted on all elements of the Contract, passing all but the congressional term limit (which needed two-thirds to amend the Constitution).

Among other things, the Contract items would require Congress to appropriate money to pay for federally mandated programs and require that workplace regulations that Congress long ago imposed on private businesses also apply to Congress itself (including employee safety and equal employment opportunities). The Contract also gave the president a line-item veto with which to strike out "pork-barrel" spending. The House also passed a balanced-budget amendment to the Constitution, which failed the two-thirds majority test in the Senate by one vote.

Moreover, the new Republican majority streamlined the House, eliminating committees and sharply reducing staff and budget. It passed rules requiring open debate and public voting on issues. Sensing the public mood, the Democrats went along with most of these reforms, which enjoyed general approval. But the more important political question was to what ends these procedural reforms would be used. It was on these substantive issues that the GOP may have misinterpreted its mandate.

Speaker Gingrich, like President Clinton two years earlier, wanted to do everything he heard his voters calling for and do it right away. He called the GOP victory "a revolution."

The centerpiece of his revolution was a proposed budget he said would cut taxes and move toward a balanced budget while protecting Social Security and Medicare. The voters did not believe him, and the Democrats worked as hard to demonize the Republican budget as the GOP had worked to defeat health care and other initiatives in the 103rd Congress. There were warning signs of voter unease as early as the summer of 1995, but the new House Republicans were determined to push for their agenda.

GOP aggressiveness on the budget issue gave President Clinton a major opportunity to revive his fortunes. Gingrich and other Republican leaders were convinced Clinton would not dare veto their budget and appear to be blocking tax cuts

and a balanced budget on the eve of his re-election campaign.

But Clinton vetoed their budget, gambling that the public had turned suspicious of the GOP leadership. In the showdown that followed, the federal government went through two partial shutdowns in late 1995 and 1996. To the horror of congressional Republicans, polls showed the public siding with Clinton and blaming the shutdowns on Congress. It was the media-savy president who appeared reasonable and interested in serious negotiations. The Republicans lost much of their momentum, good will and sense of direction. They did not accomplish as much as they might have, and in 1998 they found themselves maneuvered into enacting a largely Democratic agenda that included raising the minimum wage.

Their strongly ideological approach to sensitive issues such as immigration, English-only language requirements and affirmative action cost them votes among Hispanic and Asian Americans while gaining few votes within their base. Similarly, they energized opposition by threatening to repeal a popular ban on semi-automatic assault weapons and by attacking popular restrictions on mining and logging on public lands.

Still the 104th Congress was able, with bipartisan support, to enact the most comprehensive social welfare legislation in 60 years. The 1996 welfare reform act ended the federal guarantee of a handout and attempted to move welfare recipients back into the job market. Congress also passed legislation extending a worker's right to retain current health insurance coverage after leaving a job.

The 1996 Campaigns

Starting in mid-1995, Clinton began a remarkable recovery that was the mirror of Bush's decline four years earlier. The 1994 election freed Clinton to ignore the Democratic left—except on such symbolic issues as race relations, equal opportunities for women, and improved educational opportunities. He moved quickly to the command positions at the center, promising to protect the American people from the "radical right."

Objections from the Democratic left were muted—even when Clinton signed the welfare reform bill—and Clinton ran unopposed for renomination in 1996. He was the first incumbent Democratic president to have a clear path to renomination since Franklin Roosevelt in the wartime election of 1944.

In the meantime, the Republicans were unable to rally behind a single champion who could unify the party, present a cogent alternative to Clinton and plausibly propose to govern the country.

The Republicans, dominated by Main Street economic conservatives, rallied behind Sen. Bob Dole of Kansas, the majority leader in the Senate. Dole was next in line in the GOP hierarchy, and he had many powerful friends. But he was also the choice of the establishment for want of a better candidate. Some supply-side Reagan Republicans, preaching tax cuts as the key to economic growth and a balanced budget, supported Sen. Phil Gramm of Texas. Others preferred Malcolm S. "Steve" Forbes, a political neophyte who was heir to a publishing fortune and willing to spend freely.

Most of the social conservatives and economic nationalists were led once again by Pat Buchanan, who had made an long-shot run for the nomination in 1992. After some rough early going (he lost in New Hampshire), Dole pulled ahead and clinched the Republican nomination by the end of March. But he fell behind Clinton in the polls early in 1996, and was never able to convince voters that he had a unifying view that would help him control his party and govern the country. Moreover, the quintessential "man of the Senate" did not appear to enjoy campaigning. Clinton, whose ebullient optimism and love of people are genuine, again proved himself a superb campaigner regardless of his limited success on the substantive issues.

Results of the 1996 Elections

On November 5, Bill Clinton became the first Democrat since Franklin Roosevelt to win more than one presidential election, The results were strikingly similar to the voting of 1992. Only five states voted differently from four years earlier: Florida and Arizona switched to Clinton, in part because Hispanics moved toward the Democrats and in part because older voters were distrustful of the GOP on Social Security and Medicare. Georgia, Montana and Colorado switched to the GOP. Clinton won with 49 percent of the vote to Dole's 41 percent. It was an improvement on the 43 percent Clinton had taken in 1992, but it fell shy of a majority. Perot, campaigning under the Reform Party banner, garnered less than half of the 19 percent he had won four years earlier as an independent. Clinton enjoyed a huge 16 percent margin among women voters and even larger majorities among single women and among blacks and Hispanics of both sexes.

Unlike 1992, Clinton claimed no broad mandate for reform. The total vote cast was eight million less than in 1992; and the percentage of eligible voters who turned out at the polls (49 percent) was the lowest since 1924.

Remarkably, the voters chose at the same time to return a Republican Congress, in a distant echo of the results of 1956 and 1848. Considering the presidential result, the congressional results were strikingly similar to 1994. The Republicans had a net loss of only nine seats in the House, and a net gain of two in the Senate, for a 227-207 edge in the House (with one Independent), and a 55-45 margin in the Senate.

The nine new Republican senators were Jeff Sessions of Alabama, Tim Hutchinson of Arkansas, Wayne Allard of Colorado, Sam Brownback and Pat Roberts of Kansas, Susan Collins of Maine, Chuck Hagel of Nebraska, Gordon Smith of Oregon and Michael Enzi of Wyoming. New Democratic senators were Max Cleland of Georgia, Richard J. Durbin of Illinois, Mary L. Landrieu of Louisiana, Robert G. Torricelli of New Jersey, Jack Reed of Rhode Island and Tim Johnson of South Dakota.

Unlike the blood bath of 1994, only three Democratic House incumbents were defeated in 1996, along with 18 Republicans. Only one incumbent senator (Larry Pressler, R-S.D.) and no incumbent governor was defeated. Democratic House gains in the Northeast and the West Coast were partly offset by GOP gains in the Mountain West, and by further Republican gains in the South.

Since the 1994 election, the GOP had gained the governorship of Louisiana in late 1995, and West Virginia in 1996, while losing New Hampshire. Clinton's successor as governor of Arkansas resigned after conviction of a felony and was succeeded by a Republican lieutenant-governor, leaving the nation with 32 Republican governors, 17 Democrats and 1 Independent (in Maine). The new governor of West Virginia, Cecil Underwood, had been the youngest in the nation when he was first elected in 1956. After winning a second term, 40 years later, he is now the oldest at 72.

The three elections held since the end of the Cold War gave the voters some of the constructive change they seemed to want. However, voters remained frustrated. The dominant impression left by the politics of 1992-96 was of an electorate standing ready to punish either of the two major parties if it comes to power and fails to fulfill expectations—or if it goes too far or too fast.

Senate Elections

The creation of the United States Senate was a result of the so-called "great compromise" at the Constitutional Convention in 1787. The small states wanted equal representation in Congress, fearing domination by the larger states under a population formula. The larger states, however, naturally wished for a legislature based on population, where their strength would prevail.

In compromising this dispute, delegates simply split the basis for representation between the two houses—population for the House of Representatives, equal representation by state for the Senate. By the terms of the compromise, each state was entitled to two senators. In a sense, they were conceived to be ambassadors from the states, representing the sovereign interests of the states to the federal government.

Election by State Legislatures

To elect these "ambassadors," the Founders chose the state legislatures instead of the people themselves. The argument was that legislatures would be able to give more sober and reflective thought than the people at large to the kind of persons needed to represent the states' interests to the federal government. The delegates also thought the state legislatures and thus the states would take a greater interest in the fledgling national government if they were involved in its operations this way. Furthermore, the state legislatures had chosen the members of the Continental Congress (the Congress under the Articles of Confederation), as well as the members of the Constitutional Convention itself, so the procedure was familiar to the delegates.

In choosing the state legislatures as the instruments of election for senators, the Constitutional Convention considered and abandoned several alternatives. Some delegates had suggested that the senators be elected by the House or appointed by the president from a list of nominees selected by the state legislatures. These ideas were discarded as making the Senate too dependent on another part of the federal government. Also turned down was a scheme for a system of electors, similar to presidential electors, to choose the senators in each state. And popular election was rejected as being too radical and inconvenient.

So deeply entrenched was the ambassadorial aspect of a senator's duty that state legislatures sometimes took it upon themselves to instruct senators on how to vote. This occasionally raised severe problems of conscience among senators and resulted in several resignations.

For example, in 1836 future president John Tyler was serving as a U.S. senator from Virginia. That year the Virginia legislature instructed him to vote for a resolution to expunge the Senate censure of President Andrew Jackson for his removal of the federal deposits from the Bank of the United States. Tyler, who had voted for the censure resolution, resigned from the Senate rather than comply.

In another instance, Sen. Hugh L. White of Tennessee, a Whig, resigned from the Senate in 1840 after being instructed by his state legislature to vote for the sub-treasury bill, an economic measure supported by the Democratic Van Buren administration.

Another problem for the Founders was the length of the senatorial term. The framers of the Constitution tried to balance two principles: the belief that relatively frequent elections were necessary to promote good behavior and the need for steadiness and continuity in government.

Delegates to the Constitutional Convention proposed terms of three, four, five, six, seven and nine years. They finally settled on six-year staggered terms, with one-third of the members coming up for election every two years. (*Classification of senators, terms, p. 61*)

Sources

Haynes, George H. *The Election of Senators.* New York: Henry Holt, 1906.

___. *The Senate of the United States, Its History and Practice.* Boston: Houghton Mifflin, 1938.

Hupman, Richard D. *Senate Election, Expulsion and Censure Cases from 1793 to 1972.* Compiled by the Senate library under the direction of Francis R. Valeo, secretary of the Senate. Washington, D.C.: Government Printing Office, 1972.

Riddick, Floyd M., Senate parliamentarian. *The Term of a Senator, When Does It Begin and End? Constitution, Laws and Precedents Pertaining to the Term of a Senator.* Prepared under the direction of Emery L. Frazier, secretary of the Senate. Washington, D.C.: Government Printing Office, 1966.

U.S. Senate. Committee on Rules and Administration. *Senate Manual.* 104th Cong., 1st sess. Washington, D.C.: Government Printing Office, 1995.

Changing Election Procedures

At first each state made its own arrangements for its state legislature to elect the senators. Many states required an election by the two chambers of the legislature sitting separately. That is, each chamber had to vote for the same candidate for him to be elected. Other states, however, provided for election by a joint ballot of the two chambers sitting together.

However, the Constitution specifically authorized Congress to regulate senatorial elections if it so chose. Article I, Section 4, Paragraph 1 states, "The times, places and manner of holding elections for Senators and Representatives shall be prescribed in each state by the legislature thereof; but the Congress may at any time by law make or alter such regulations, except as to the places of chusing Senators."

1866 Act of Congress

In 1866 Congress decided to exercise its authority. Procedures in some states, particularly those requiring concurrent majorities in both houses of the state legislature for election to the Senate, had resulted in numerous delays and vacancies.

The new federal law set up the following procedure: The first ballot for senator was to be taken by the two chambers of each state legislature voting separately. If no candidate received a majority of the vote in both houses, then the two chambers were to meet and ballot jointly until a majority choice emerged.

Also included in the 1866 law were provisions for roll-call votes in the state legislatures (secret ballots had been taken in several states) and for a definite timetable. The law directed that the first vote take place on the second Tuesday after the meeting and organization of the legislature, followed by a minimum of a single ballot on every legislative day thereafter until election of a senator resulted.

But the new uniform system did not have the desired effect. The requirement for a majority vote continued the frequency of deadlock. In fact one of the worst deadlocks in senatorial election history happened under the 1866 federal law.

The case occurred in Delaware at the end of the 19th century. In 1899, with the legislature divided between two factions of the Republican Party and the Democrats in the minority, no majority selection could be made for the senatorial term beginning March 4, 1899. So bitter was the Republican factional dispute that neither side would support a candidate acceptable to the other; nor would the Democrats play kingmaker by siding with one or the other Republican group. The dispute continued throughout the life of the 56th Congress (1899-1901), leaving a seat unfilled.

Furthermore, the term of Delaware's other Senate seat ended in 1901, necessitating another election. The same pattern continued, with the legislature unable to fill either seat, leaving Delaware totally unrepresented in the Senate from March 4, 1901, until March 1, 1903, when two senators were finally elected in the closing days of the 57th Congress (1901-03). The deadlock was broken when the two Republican factions split the state's two seats between them.

Abuses of Election by Legislatures

Besides the frequent deadlocks, critics pointed to what they saw as other faults in the system. They charged that the party caucuses in the state legislatures, as well as individual members, were subject to intense and unethical lobbying practices by supporters of various senatorial candidates. The relatively small size of the electing body and the high stakes involved—a seat in the Senate—often tempted the use of questionable methods in conducting the elections.

Allegations that such methods were used involved the Senate itself in election disputes. The Constitution makes Congress the judge of its own members. Article I, Section 5, Paragraph 1 states, "Each House shall be the judge of the elections, returns and qualifications of its own members. . . ."

One of the most sensational cases concerned the election of William Lorimer, R-Ill. Lorimer won on the 99th ballot taken by the Illinois legislature in 1909. A year after he had taken his seat, the Senate cleared Lorimer of charges that he had won election by bribery. But the revelation of new evidence prompted another investigation, and in 1912 the Senate voted that Lorimer's election was invalid and that he was not entitled to his seat.

Critics had still another grievance against the legislative method of choosing senators. They contended that elections to the state legislatures were often overshadowed by senatorial contests. Thus when voters went to the polls to choose their state legislators, they sometimes would be urged to disregard state and local issues and vote for a legislator who promised to support a certain candidate for the U.S. Senate. This, the critics said, led to neglect of state government and issues. Moreover, drawn-out Senate contests tended to hold up the consideration of state business.

Demands for Popular Elections

But the main criticism of legislative elections was that they distorted or even blocked the will of the people. Throughout the 19th century, the movement toward popular election had taken away from the legislatures the right to elect government and presidential electors in states that had such provisions. Now attention focused on the Senate.

Five times around the turn of the century the House passed constitutional amendments to provide for Senate elections by popular vote—in the 52nd Congress on Jan. 16, 1893; in the 53rd Congress on July 21, 1894; in the 55th Congress on May 11, 1898; in the 56th Congress on April 13, 1900, and in the 57th Congress on Feb. 13, 1902. But each time the Senate refused to act.

Frustrated in their desire for direct popular elections, reformers began implementing various formulas for pre-selecting Senate candidates, attempting to reduce the legislative balloting to something approaching a mere formality. In some cases party conventions endorsed nominees for the Senate, allowing the voters at least to know who the members of the legislature were likely to support. Southern states early in the century adopted the party primary to choose Senate nominees. However, legislators never could be legally bound to support anyone because the Constitution gave them the unfettered power of electing to the Senate whomever they chose.

Oregon took the lead in instituting non-binding popular elections. Under a 1901 law, voters expressed their choice for senator in popular ballots. While the election results had no legal force, the law required that the popular returns be formally announced to the state legislature before it elected a senator.

At first the law did not work—the winner of the informal popular vote in 1902 was not chosen senator by the legislature. But the reformers increased their pressure, demanding that candidates for the legislature sign a pledge to vote for the winner of the popular vote. By 1908 the plan was successful. The Republican legislature elected to the Senate

59

Senate Appointments and Special Elections

Governors were given specific authority in the Constitution to make temporary appointments to the Senate. Article I, Section 3, Paragraph 2 states: "If vacancies happen by resignation, or otherwise, during the recess of the legislature of any state, the executive thereof may make temporary appointments until the next meeting of the legislature, which shall then fill such vacancies."

The principle was established as early as 1794 that a vacancy created solely because a state legislature had failed to elect a new senator could not be filled by appointment, because the vacancy had not occurred "during the recess of the legislature."

For example, the term of Sen. Matthew Quay, R-Pa. (1887-99, 1901-04) expired March 3, 1899. The legislature was in session but had not re-elected him. Nor did it elect anyone before adjourning that April 20. Thereupon, the governor appointed Quay to the vacancy; but the Senate did not allow Quay to take the seat, because the vacancy had occurred during the meeting of the legislature. In 1901 the legislature elected Quay for the remainder of the term.

On the other hand, if a senator's term expired and the legislature was *not* in session, a governor was able to make an appointment—but only until the legislature either elected a successor or adjourned without electing one. For example, on March 3, 1809, the term of Sen. Samuel Smith, D-R-Md. (1803-15, 1822-33) expired. The legislature was not then in session and had not elected a successor. Therefore the governor appointed Smith to fill the vacancy until the next meeting of the legislature, which was scheduled for June 5, 1809. The Senate ruled that he was entitled to the seat. During the subsequent meeting of the state legislature that year, Smith was elected to a full term.

Whatever the condition under which an appointment had been made, it was to last only through the next state legislative session. Even if a legislature failed to elect a new senator, the appointed senator's service was to expire with the adjournment of the state legislature.

This principle was confirmed in the case of Sen. Samuel Phelps, Whig-Vt. (1839-51, 1853-54). Phelps was appointed in January 1853 to a vacancy caused by the death of Sen. William Upham, Whig-Vt. (1843-53), whose term was to run through March 3, 1855. As the legislature was in recess, Phelps continued to serve until the expiration of the 32nd Congress on March 3, 1853, and also during a special session of the 33rd Congress in March and April 1853. The Vermont legislature met during October and December without electing a senator to fill the unexpired term. Phelps then showed up for the regular session of the 33rd Congress in December, but the Senate in March 1854 decided he was not entitled to retain his seat, because the legislature had met and adjourned without electing a new senator.

17th Amendment and Special Elections

The adoption of the 17th Amendment in 1913, providing for popular election of senators, altered the provision for gubernatorial appointment of senators to fill vacancies. The amendment provided that, in case of a vacancy, "the executive authority of such state shall issue writs of election to fill such vacancies: *Provided*, that the legislature of any state may empower the executive thereof to make temporary appointments until the people fill the vacancies by election as the legislature may direct." Under this provision, state legislatures allowed governors to make temporary appointments until the vacancy could be filled by a special election. Special elections—elections held to fill unexpired terms—were usually held in November of an even-numbered year. Some states, however, provided for special elections to be held within just a few months after the vacancy occurred.

Before ratification of the 17th Amendment the term of an appointee generally ended when a successor was elected to fill the unexpired term or at the end of the six-year term, whichever occurred first. After the ratification of the 17th Amendment but before ratification of the 20th Amendment in 1933, senators who were elected to fill lengthy unexpired terms usually could take office immediately, displacing an appointee. If an appointee was serving near the close of a six-year term, most states would hold simultaneous elections to fill both the six-year term and the four-month "lame-duck" term. Sometimes different persons would be elected to each term.

To eliminate the lame-duck sessions that ran from December of an even-numbered year through March 3 of the next year, the 20th Amendment changed the March 3 beginning date of the terms for Congress and the president to Jan. 3. After the so-called lame-duck amendment took effect, senators elected to fill vacancies in terms that had several years to run would take office immediately, as before, but, if a vacancy occurred near the end of a six-year term, an appointee would often serve until the Jan. 3 expiration date, eliminating the necessity for a special election.

Some states, however, have held elections in November for the remaining two months of a term. Georgia voters in 1972, for example, found on the ballot two Senate elections, one for a six-year term and one for a two-month term to fill the unexpired term of Sen. Richard B. Russell, D (1933-71), who died in office.

Dates of Service

Title II, Section 36 of the U.S. Code sets the dates on which senators appointed or elected to fill unexpired terms formally begin service and go on the payroll. The service of an appointee commences the day of appointment and continues until a successor is elected and qualified. If the Senate is in sine die adjournment when a new senator is elected to succeed an appointee, he will take office and begin receiving his salary on the day after the election.

If the Senate is in session when a new senator is elected to succeed an appointee, the new senator may take office when he presents himself before the Senate to take the oath; the appointee may continue in office until this occurs or the Senate adjourns sine die, whichever happens first. The term of the newly elected senator would then begin at sine die adjournment.

Democrat George Chamberlain, the winner of the popular contest. Several other states—including Colorado, Kansas, Minnesota, Montana, Nevada and Oklahoma—adopted the Oregon method.

The 17th Amendment

Despite these palliatives, pressures continued to mount for a switch to straight popular elections. Frustrated at the failure of the Senate to act, proponents of change began pushing for a convention to propose this and perhaps other amendments to the Constitution. (Article V of the Constitution provides two methods of proposing amendments—either passage by two-thirds of both houses of Congress or through the calling of a special convention if requested by the legislatures of two-thirds of the states. In either case any amendment proposed by Congress or by a special convention must be ratified by three-fourths of the states.)

Conservatives began to fear a convention more than they did popular election of senators. There was no precedent for an amending convention and conservatives worried that it might be dominated by liberals and progressives who would propose numerous amendments and change the very nature of the government. Consequently, their opposition to popular election of senators diminished.

At the same time progressives of both parties made strong gains in the midterm elections of 1910. Some successful Senate candidates had made pledges to work for adoption of a constitutional amendment providing for popular election. In this atmosphere the Senate debated and finally passed the amendment on June 12, 1911, by a vote of 64-24. The House concurred in the Senate version on May 13, 1912, by a vote of 238-39. Ratification of the 17th Amendment was completed by the requisite number of states on April 8, 1913, and was proclaimed a part of the Constitution by Secretary of State William Jennings Bryan on May 31, 1913.

The first popularly elected senator was chosen in a special election in November 1913. He was Sen. Blair Lee, D-Md. (1914-17), elected for the remaining three years of the unexpired term of Sen. Isidor Rayner, D (1905-12), who had died in office.

There was no wholesale changeover in membership when the 17th Amendment became effective. In fact every one of the 23 senators elected by state legislatures for their previous terms, and running for re-election to full terms in November 1914, was successful. Seven had retired or died, and two had been defeated for renomination.

The changeover in method of electing senators ended the frequent legislative stalemates in choosing members of the Senate. Otherwise many things remained the same. There were still election disputes, including charges of corruption, as well as miscounting of votes.

Election Disputes

Election disputes continued to occupy the Senate. A bitter contest for a New Hampshire Senate seat in 1974 between Republican representative Louis C. Wyman and Democrat John A. Durkin wound up in the Senate after a seesaw battle between New Hampshire authorities over who had won. The state Ballot Law Commission had finally awarded the victory to Wyman by two votes, but Durkin took his case to the Senate. After wrestling with the problem for seven months, the Senate gave up and declared the seat vacant. A new election was held Sept. 16, 1975, which Durkin won decisively.

Senate's Three Classes

The Senate is divided into three classes or groups of members. A member's class depends on the year in which he or she is elected. Article I, Section 3, Paragraph 2 of the Constitution, relating to the classification of senators in the first and succeeding Congresses, provides that "Immediately after they shall be assembled in consequence of the first election, they shall be divided as equally as may be into three classes. The seats of the Senators of the first class shall be vacated at the expiration of the second year, of the second class at the expiration of the fourth year and of the third class at the expiration of the sixth year, so that one-third may be chosen every second year. . . ."

Thus senators belonging to class one began their regular terms in the years 1789, 1791, 1797, 1803, etc., continuing through the present day to 1983, 1989, 1995 and were to be up for re-election in 2000. Senators belonging to class two began their regular terms in 1789, 1793, 1799, 1805, etc., continuing through to the present day in 1985, 1991, 1997 and were to be up for re-election in 2002. And senators belonging to class three began their regular terms in 1789, 1795, 1801, 1807, etc., continuing through the present day to 1981, 1987, 1993 and coming up for re-election in 1998.

Sessions and Terms

In the fall of 1788, the expiring Continental Congress established a schedule for the incoming government under the new Constitution. The Congress decided that the new government was to commence on the first Wednesday in March 1789—March 4. Even though the House did not achieve a quorum until April 1 and the Senate April 6, and President Washington was not inaugurated until April 30, Senate, House and presidential terms were still considered to have begun March 4. The term of the first Congress continued through March 3, 1791. Because congressional and presidential terms were fixed at exactly two, four and six years, March 4 became the official date of transition from one administration to another every four years and from one Congress to another every two years.

'Long' and 'Short' Sessions

The Constitution did not mandate a regular congressional session to begin March 4. Instead, Article I, Section 4, Paragraph 2 called for at least one congressional session every year, to convene on the first Monday in December unless Congress by law set a different day. Consequently, except when called by the president for special sessions, or when Congress itself set a different day, Congress convened in regular session each December, until the passage of the 20th Amendment in 1933.

The December date resulted in a long and short session. The first (long) session would meet in December of an odd-numbered year and continue into the next year, usually adjourning some time the next summer. The second (short) session began in December of an even-numbered year and continued through March 3 of the next year, when its term ran out. It also became customary for the Senate to meet in brief special session on March 4 or March 5, especially in years when a new president was inaugurated, to act on presidential nominations.

To illustrate with an example of a typical Congress, the 29th (1845-47): President James K. Polk, D, was inaugurated on March 4, 1845. The Senate met in special session from March 4 to March 20 to confirm Polk's Cabinet and other appointments. Then the first regular session convened Dec. 1, 1845, working until Aug. 10, 1846, when it adjourned. The second, a short session, lasted from Dec. 7, 1846, through March 3, 1847.

Since it was not clear whether terms of members of Congress ended at midnight March 3 or noon March 4, the custom evolved of extending the legislative day of March 3, in odd-numbered years, to noon March 4.

The 20th Amendment

The political consequence of the short session was to encourage filibusters and other delaying tactics by members determined to block legislation that would die upon the automatic adjournment of Congress on March 3. Moreover, the Congresses that met in short session always included a substantial number of "lame-duck" members who had been defeated at the polls, yet were able quite often to determine the legislative outcome of the session.

Dissatisfaction with the short session began to mount after 1900. During the Wilson administration (1913-21), each of four such sessions ended with a Senate filibuster and the loss of important bills including several funding bills. Sen. George W. Norris, R-Neb. (1913-43), became the leading advocate of a constitutional amendment to abolish the short session by starting the terms of Congress and the president in January instead of March. The Senate approved the Norris amendment five times during the 1920s, only to see it blocked in the House each time. It was finally approved by both chambers in 1932 and became the 20th Amendment upon ratification by the 36th state in 1933.

The amendment provided that the terms of senators and representatives would begin and end at noon on the third day of January of the year following the election. However, according to the *Senate Manual* (1995 edition, p. 961), "In view of the impracticality of dealing with split days, . . . it has been the long established practice for payment of salaries, computation of allowances and recording of service to credit a Member for the full day of the third of January he takes office and consider his term as ended at the close of business on the second of January six years later." Congressional Quarterly has retained this convention in the list of senators in this volume, with dates of service shown as beginning on Jan. 3 and ending on Jan. 2.

The 20th Amendment also established noon Jan. 20 as the day on which the president and vice president take office. It provided also that Congress should meet annually on Jan. 3 "unless they shall by law appoint a different day." The second session of the 73rd Congress was the first to convene on the new date, Jan. 3, 1934. Franklin D. Roosevelt was the first president and John N. Garner the first vice president to be inaugurated on Jan. 20, at the start of their second terms in 1937.

The amendment was intended to permit Congress to extend its first session for as long as necessary and to complete the work of its second session before the next election, thereby obviating legislation by a lame-duck body.

The Historical Significance of Southern Primaries

Because of the overwhelming dominance of the Democratic Party in the South during the first half of the 20th century, the party's primaries became, in effect, the region's significant elections. The 11 states that constitute the South—all members of the Civil War Confederacy—are Alabama, Arkansas, Florida, Georgia, Louisiana, Mississippi, North Carolina, South Carolina, Tennessee, Texas and Virginia.

In his classic study *Southern Politics in State and Nation*, V. O. Key Jr. concluded, "In fact, the Democratic primary is no nominating method at all. The primary is the election. . . ." That was in 1949, shortly before Republicans began seriously challenging Democrats for hegemony in the region.

But Key's observation holds true for the 20th century up through the time of his study and for much of the period since, depending on the particular state and election involved. Of the 132 elections to the Senate held in the 11 former Confederate states in the period 1919-48, the Democratic nominee won 131 times. The only exception was a special election in Arkansas in 1937 when the Democratic nominee lost to an independent Democrat.

The Southern shift to the Republican Party began on the presidential level in 1964, when Barry Goldwater's criticisms of civil rights laws found a wide audience. In 1972 Republican presidential nominee Richard Nixon carried all 11 states of the Old South with at least 65 percent of the vote. In 1984 and 1988 Ronald Reagan and George Bush did almost as well, carrying every Southern state with at least 58 percent (Reagan) or 54 percent (Bush) of the vote. Although the Democrats regained the White House in 1992 and 1996, the party's all-Southern ticket of Bill Clinton of Arkansas and Al Gore of Tennessee carried only four Southern states in both elections. In 1992 Clinton and Gore won Arkansas, Georgia, Louisiana and Tennessee. In 1996 the ticket lost Georgia but picked up Florida—the first time the state had gone Democratic since 1976.

From the 1960s to the 1990s, the growth of the Republican Party in Southern congressional delegations was steady but slower than on the presidential level. The first popularly elected Republican U.S. senator from the South, John G. Tower of Texas, won a special election in 1961. Thereafter, Republicans won their first Senate seats in South Carolina (1966), Tennessee (1966), Florida (1968), North Carolina and Virginia (1972), Mississippi (1978), Alabama and Georgia (1980), and Arkansas (1996).

Thirty years of political realignment in the South culminated in the 1994 congressional elections when the Republican Party won majority status in the South. Not since Reconstruction had the GOP held a majority of the region's seats in the House or in the Senate. The historic election also ushered in Republican control of Congress with Southern GOP leadership: in 1995 Newt Gingrich of Georgia was elected Speaker of the House and in 1996 Trent Lott of Mississippi was elected Senate majority leader. The 1996 congressional elections solidified GOP gains. In the 11 Southern states, the Republicans outnumbered the Democrats 15 to 7 in Senate seats and 71 to 54 in U.S. House seats.

After the 1996 elections, Republican dominance in South looked secure for the foreseeable future. The dramatic population influx in the 1980s and 1990s had reshaped the Southern political landscape to the Republican advantage. Old-time Democratic voters were overwhelmed in many parts of the South by more independent or GOP-oriented newcomers. Younger voters found the region's historical Democratic roots irrelevant to their concerns. The GOP also aggressively fielded candidates where it once gave the Democrats a free ride. For their part, these candidates emphasized traditional values, an emphasis that resonated among the regions' white voters, who constituted a majority of the electorate in every Southern state. Although most of the Senate contests in the South were competitive in the 1990s, one sign of the swing to Republican power in the region came in 1990 when Republican senator Thad Cochran of Mississippi faced no Democratic opposition in the general election.

Runoff Primaries

The South along with the rest of the nation instituted primaries during the first two decades of the 20th century. By 1920 all 11 Southern states were choosing their Democratic senatorial nominees through the primary process.

Sources

Heard, Alexander, and Donald S. Strong. *Southern Primaries and Elections, 1920-1949.* 1950. Reprint. Salem, N.H.: Ayers, 1970.

Key, V. O. Jr. *Southern Politics in State and Nation.* New York: Alfred A. Knopf, 1949.

Secretaries of state and state handbooks of the 11 Southern states.

But because the primaries were, for all practical purposes, the deciding election, many legislators began to doubt the effectiveness of a system that frequently allowed a candidate in a multi-candidate race to win a plurality of the popular vote—and thus the Democratic nomination that ensured election—even though he received only a small percentage of the total primary vote.

So, most Southern states adopted the runoff primary—a second election following the first primary, usually by two to four weeks—that matched only the top two contenders from the first primary. The runoff system was adopted in Alabama in 1931, Arkansas in 1939, Florida in 1929, Georgia in 1917 (with the county unit system, *see p. 65*), Louisiana in 1922, Mississippi in 1902, North Carolina in 1915, South Carolina in 1915 and Texas in 1918. (Arkansas had adopted the runoff in 1933, abandoned it in 1935, then reinstituted it in 1939.) Virginia adopted the runoff in 1969 but repealed it in 1971.

After 1969 Tennessee remained the only Southern state to nominate by plurality. In that state's 1976 Senate race, James Sasser won the Democratic nomination with only 44.2 percent of the vote in a field of 5 candidates. Sasser went on to win his first election to the Senate in November.

Runoffs are not always obligatory. In most states, if the second-place finisher in the primary does not want a runoff, the first-place candidate is then the winner without a runoff. In the Virginia Democratic primary of 1970, for example, front-runner George C. Rawlings missed winning a majority of the vote in the first primary, winding up with 45.7 percent. However, Clive L. DuVal who placed a close second with 45.1 percent, declined a runoff. No runoff was held and Rawlings automatically became the Democratic nominee. (Rawlings lost the general election to former Democratic senator Harry F. Byrd Jr., who ran as an independent.)

Jackson's Anti-runoff Campaign

Jesse L. Jackson, contender for the 1984 Democratic presidential nomination, mounted an attack against the runoff feature in the spring of that year. Jackson hoped to persuade the 10 other Southern states to join Tennessee in avoiding the runoff.

Jackson argued that runoffs injured black candidates' chances of victory because in the second election whites, who comprised the majority of registered voters, usually voted on the basis of race.

Jackson carried his plea to the Democratic National Convention, which defeated his move to abolish runoffs, 2,500.8 to 1,253.2. Supporters argued that runoffs prevented the election of fringe candidates when more qualified candidates split the vote in hotly contested primaries. In addition, conservative Southerners opposed having a national convention decide their own state election procedures.

Preferential Primaries

Three Southern states—Alabama, Florida and Louisiana—tried to avoid the effort and expense of runoff elections by experimenting with a preferential system of primary voting. All three later switched to the runoff system—Alabama after the election of 1930, Florida after the election of 1928 and Louisiana (whose system was similar to Alabama's) after the election of 1920. Louisiana modified its system yet again in 1975, this time to a two-step process: an initial non-partisan primary followed by a general election runoff between the two top finishers.

Under the preferential system a voter, instead of simply marking an X opposite one candidate's name, writes the digits 1 *or* 2, beside the names of two candidates. This indicates the "preference" order the voter gives each of the candidates, the number one indicating his first choice, the number two his second choice. To determine the winner, without a runoff, second-choice votes are added to the first-choice votes and the candidate with the highest combined total wins.

Alabama. Under the Alabama system, each voter expressed a first and second choice. If no candidate received a majority of the first choices, all but the two leaders were eliminated. All second choices expressed for the two leaders were then added to their first-choice totals, the candidate with the highest combined total winning.

In the Democratic primary for U.S. senator on May 13, 1920, for a special four-year term to fill a vacancy, the candidates were J. Thomas Heflin and three persons whose first names are not available: White, O'Neal and Rushton. Heflin, with 49,554 first-choice votes, led the field but received only 37.9 percent of the total. White ran second with 34,854 first-choice votes, or 26.6 percent; O'Neal had 33,174 first-choice votes, or 25.4 percent, and Rushton was last with 13,232 first-choice votes, or 10.1 percent. Thus, in many Southern states a runoff would have been necessary. But instead of a runoff all second-choice votes cast for the two leaders—Heflin and White—were added to their first-choice ballots. A total of 11,062 second-choice votes were cast for Heflin by voters whose first choice had gone to one of the other three candidates. Added to his first-choice vote of 49,554, this gave Heflin a grand total of 60,016 votes. White received 12,699 second-choice votes—more than Heflin—but the second-choice votes were not enough to raise his grand total above Heflin's. White thus wound up with a grand total of 47,553 votes, and Heflin was the winner.

Florida. The Florida system of preference voting differed somewhat from the Alabama system. In Florida, as in Alabama, each voter expressed a first and second choice. Also as in Alabama, if no candidate received a majority of first choices, all candidates but the two highest first-choice candidates were eliminated. To determine the winner, the second choices expressed for the two highest *on the ballots of eliminated candidates only* were added to the first-choice totals. (In Alabama, the second choices for the two leaders expressed on ballots for *all* candidates, including the two leaders, were added to the first-choice totals.)

The preference system, however, did not prove useful. Apparently it was too confusing for voters, most of whom did not bother to cast second-choice votes. In the Alabama election discussed above, for example, there were 130,814 first-choice votes, but only 34,768 second-choice votes.

Louisiana. Not satisfied with either the partisan runoff or the preferential primary, Louisiana adopted a law in 1975 that allowed its voters to participate in an initial open primary followed by a runoff general election between the two top finishers. In the primary, all candidates of all parties were to be on the ballot, but party designations were optional and at the individual candidate's discretion. A candidate receiving more than 50 percent of the primary vote would be unopposed in the general election. If no candidate received more than 50 percent of the vote, the two candidates receiving the greatest number of votes—regardless of party—would oppose each other in the runoff general election.

Thus, in 1978, when the first Senate seat was chosen under this new system, two candidates, both Democrats, entered the initial open primary. There were no Republican, independent or minor party candidates. J. Bennett Johnston received 59.4 percent of the vote, and he was elected senator. (Louisiana in 1978 dispensed with the runoff general election if the primary winner received more than 50 percent of the vote.) If Johnston had placed first with less than 50 percent of the vote, the runoff general election would have been between him and the second-place finisher, even though the other candidate was also a Democrat.

Georgia: County Unit System

Another variant of the primary system was Georgia's county unit system. Each county in the state was apportioned a certain number of unit votes. The candidate who received the largest number of popular votes in the county was awarded all the county's unit votes, even if he won only a plurality and not a majority. A candidate had to have a majority of the state's county unit votes to win the primary; otherwise a runoff became necessary. The runoff also was held on the basis of the county unit system.

For example, as of 1946, there were 410 county unit votes. The eight most populous counties had six unit votes each, the next 30 most populous counties had four each, and the remaining 121 counties had two each. The system was weighted toward rural and sparsely populated areas, because every county, no matter how small, had at least two unit votes.

The county unit system sometimes produced winners who received less than a majority of popular votes. Although no senators were ever elected through the county unit system without also attaining a majority of the popular vote, political scientist Key found that in two of 16 gubernatorial races between 1915 and 1948 the winner of a majority of county units received less than a majority of the popular votes. In a third case, that of 1946, the winner of the county unit vote, Eugene Talmadge, actually received fewer popular votes than his chief opponent, James V. Carmichael.

The county unit system fell before the Supreme Court's "one-person, one-vote" doctrine. In the 1963 case, *Gray v. Sanders*, the court declared the Georgia county unit system unconstitutional because of the disparity in representation between the urban and rural areas.

Special Elections

As in other states, special elections in the South are held to fill vacancies for Senate seats when they occur. However, vacancies sometimes happen at times inconvenient for going through the lengthy runoff primary process prior to the special election. Either the filing deadline for the primaries has passed, or the vacancy occurs in a year when there is no regular primary scheduled. In such cases, the Democratic state committee sometimes selects the party nominee without holding a primary.

This process has led to unexpected results. In Arkansas in 1937, for example, a special election was held on Oct. 19 for the five years remaining in the term of Democratic senator Joseph T. Robinson, who had died in office. The Democratic state committee chose Gov. Carl E. Bailey as the party's official nominee. But Rep. John E. Miller of the 2nd District promptly jumped into the race as an independent Democrat, complaining that Democratic voters had not been given a choice of who their nominee should be. The result was a Miller victory, with 60.5 percent of the vote.

In an even more sensational case, this time in a regular election, the Democratic Party leadership in South Carolina found its wishes thwarted in 1954 when it nominated Edgar

---

Preference and Runoff Primaries

State	Preferential Primary	Runoff Primary Adopted
Alabama	Until 1931	1931
Arkansas	—	1939[1]
Florida	Until 1929	1929
Georgia	—	1917[2]
Louisiana[3]	Until 1922	1922
Mississippi	—	1902
North Carolina	—	1915
South Carolina	—	1915
Tennessee[4]	—	—
Texas	—	1918
Virginia[5]	—	—

1. Arkansas adopted the runoff in 1933, abandoned it in 1935 and reinstituted it in 1939.
2. Runoff held under county unit system; see text opposite.
3. Louisiana used the runoff "for a time prior to 1916," according to political scientist V. O. Key Jr.; in 1975 Louisiana adopted an initial non-partisan primary followed by a general election runoff.
4. Tennessee has never used the preferential or runoff primary. Candidates are nominated by winning a plurality; see text, p. 000.
5. Virginia adopted the runoff primary in 1969 and repealed it in 1971.

Sources: Heard, Alexander, and Donald S. Strong. *Southern Primaries and Elections.* 1950. Reprint. Salem, N.H.: Ayers, 1970. Key, V. O. Jr. *Southern Politics in State and Nation.* New York: Alfred A. Knopf, 1949. Virginia secretary of state.

A. Brown following the death of Sen. Burnet R. Maybank, who had won renomination in the June Democratic primary. Former governor Strom Thurmond, feeling aggrieved that he had been deprived of a chance for the Senate nomination, entered the November election as a write-in candidate. With the backing of the outgoing governor, James F. Byrnes, Thurmond won the race overwhelmingly, 143,444 to 83,525—making him the only senator ever elected on a write-in vote.

Texas' Runoff Special Elections

To avoid the pitfalls sometimes encountered when candidates are chosen without a primary, Texas adopted a unique method of holding special elections for U.S. House and Senate seats. All candidates, no matter which party they belong to, compete in a free-for-all first election. If no one receives a majority, a second election is held between the top two candidates, regardless of party. Thus, the second election could occur between two Democrats, between two Republicans, or between a Democrat and a Republican or even between third-party candidates. The system was used in the 1961 special Senate contest to fill the vacancy caused when Democratic senator Lyndon B. Johnson resigned to become vice president. In the first contest, there were 73 candidates competing, with Republican John G. Tower and Democrat William Blakley finishing first and second. The second election resulted in a Tower victory, 448,217 to 437,874. The same system prevails for Texas' special U.S. House elections.

White Primaries

Closely connected with the history of Southern Democratic primaries is the issue of race. In many Southern states, blacks were long barred from participation in the Democratic primary, either on a statewide basis or in various counties. To exclude blacks from the primaries, the Democratic Party was designated as a private association or club. The practice was defended as constitutional because the 15th Amendment, ratified in 1870, prohibited only *states*, not private associations, from denying the right to vote to persons on account of race or color. However, in 1944 the Supreme Court, in the case of *Smith v. Allwright,* declared the white primary unconstitutional, holding that it was an integral part of the election machinery for choosing state and federal officials.

Poll Tax. Another device used in limiting both black and white voters was the poll tax, which required the payment of a fee before voting. The amount of the poll tax ranged from one to two dollars, but in Alabama, Mississippi, Virginia and Georgia before 1945 the tax was cumulative. Thus, a new voter in Georgia could face up to $47 in fees. Various regulations as to the time and manner of payment of the tax also substantially reduced the number of voters. In Mississippi, for example, a person wanting to vote in the Democratic primary (usually held in August) had to pay his poll tax on or before the first day of the two preceding Februarys—long before most voters had even begun to think about the election.

The poll tax was barred in federal elections by ratification of the 24th Amendment in January 1964. The amendment simply stated that the "right of citizens of the United States to vote in any primary or other election .... shall not be denied or abridged by the United States or any other State by reason of failure to pay any poll tax or other tax."

Literacy Tests. The literacy test was another method used to limit the Southern franchise to whites. Voters were required to read and/or write correctly—usually a section of the state or federal Constitution. Sometimes, voters who could not pass the test could have the materials read to them, to see if they could "understand" or "interpret" it correctly. This provision allowed local voting officials, inevitably whites, to judge whether voters passed the tests; it usually resulted in whites passing and blacks failing.

However, in his study of Southern politics, Key concluded that informal pressures—including economic reprisals and other sanctions—were more important in limiting the black franchise than were the official suffrage limitations.

By the 1970s most formal bars to voting in the South, and many informal ones, had been lifted, either by constitutional amendment, federal laws, state action or protest movements.

United States Senators, 1947-1997

Sources: U.S. Senators, 1947-1997

This section (pages 69 to 78) contains a listing of United States senators who served from Jan. 3, 1947, through October 1997—from the 80th Congress to the first session of the 105th Congress. Arranged alphabetically by state, the lists provide the name, political affiliation and dates of service of each senator in chronological order within each class. *(Explanation of Senate classes, p. 61)* For those senators, who as of Jan. 3, 1947, were continuing terms begun earlier, the date upon which they began their Senate service is listed. This listing includes those senators who were appointed by their governors to vacant seats. Even in the modern era some senators served partial terms and were never elected by popular ballots.

The primary source for the names, classes and dates of service of senators is the *Senate Manual* (U.S. Government Printing Office, Washington, D.C., 1995). Congressional Quarterly obtained additional information in certain cases from the *Biographical Directory of the United States Congress, 1774-1989* (U.S. Government Printing Office, Washington, D.C., 1989). Congressional Quarterly editors updated the list from state secretaries of state after 1996 elections. Footnotes were derived from all sources.

Party Affiliation

Determinations of senators' party affiliations were based on three sources. From 1947 to 1972 party designations were taken from the Inter-University Consortium for Political and Social Research (ICPSR) popular vote returns (pages 81 to 100). However, if a senator was elected in any one election with the support of more than one political party, only the major party is indicated in the listing. For example, Sen. Robert F. Kennedy of New York, who in 1964 was the nominee of both the Democratic and Liberal parties, appears as a Democrat (D).

Also from 1947 on, whenever senators switched parties during their period of service, each party is listed even if the senator was not formally elected as a nominee of the new party. For example, Sen. Wayne Morse of Oregon (1945-69) is listed as a Republican, Independent and Democrat (R, I, D). He was elected twice as a Republican in 1944 and 1950, left that party in 1952 and called himself an Independent until 1955, and then became a Democrat. He was re-elected as a Democrat in 1956 and 1962.

The following party abbreviations are used in this section:

CR	Conservative Republican
D	Democrat
DFL	Democrat Farmer-Labor
I	Independent
I-R	Independent-Republican
R	Republican

Footnotes have been used to indicate the following circumstances:

• The appointment of a senator by the govenor of his state to fill an unexpired term. In such cases the service of an appointee ended at the expiration of the six-year term, or when a new senator was elected, or after the recess of the state legislature. *(For explanation of terms of appointees, see p. 60.)* In many cases, the appointee was elected to the Senate while serving there by appointment. In these cases, the footnote states that the senator was appointed and "subsequently elected."

• The death or resignation of a senator before the expiration of the term for which he was elected or appointed. In a number of instances, retiring or defeated senators resigned shortly before the start of a new congressional session. This enabled the succeeding senator to take office early by appointment, thereby giving him seniority over other newly elected senators. The practice has become less common due to changes in seniority rules. Resignations are footnoted but subsequent appointments are not. However, the dates of service shown in the main listing account for the complete period served.

• The expulsion of a senator by the Senate, and certain cases of disputed elections. Information on these was obtained from *Senate Election, Expulsion and Censure Cases* (S Doc 92-7), a publication prepared in 1972 by the Senate Rules and Administration Committee.

• A change in political party affiliation by a senator, if it could be determined that the senator was elected or appointed as a member of one political party but was subsequently re-elected as a nominee of a different party.

United States Senators, 1947-1997

ALABAMA

(Became a state Dec. 14, 1819)

Class 2

Senators	Dates of Service	
John Sparkman (D)	Nov. 6, 1946	Jan. 2, 1979
Howell Heflin (D)	Jan. 3, 1979	Jan. 2, 1997
Jeff Sessions (R)	Jan. 3, 1997	

Class 3

Lister Hill (D)[1]	Jan. 11, 1938	Jan. 2, 1969
James B. Allen (D)[2]	Jan. 3, 1969	June 1, 1978
Maryon Pittman Allen (D)[3]	June 8, 1978	Nov. 7, 1978
Donald W. Stewart (D)[4]	Nov. 8, 1978	Jan. 1, 1981
Jeremiah Denton (R)	Jan. 2, 1981	Jan. 2, 1987
Richard C. Shelby (D, R)[5]	Jan. 3, 1987	

Alabama
1. Appointed by governor to fill vacancy. Subsequently elected.
2. Died June 1, 1978.
3. Appointed by governor to fill vacancy.
4. Resigned Jan. 1, 1981.
5. Elected as a Democrat in 1986 and 1992. Shelby became a Republican on Nov. 9, 1994.

ALASKA

(Became a state Jan. 3, 1959)

Class 2

Senators	Dates of Service	
E. L. Bartlett (D)[1]	Jan. 3, 1959	Dec. 11, 1968
Ted Stevens (R)[2]	Dec. 24, 1968	

Class 3

Ernest Gruening (D)	Jan. 3, 1959	Jan. 2, 1969
Mike Gravel (D)	Jan. 3, 1969	Jan. 2, 1981
Frank H. Murkowski (R)	Jan. 3, 1981	

Alaska
1. Died Dec. 11, 1968.
2. Appointed by governor to fill vacancy. Subsequently elected.

ARIZONA

(Became a state Feb. 14, 1912)

Class 1

Senators	Dates of Service	
Ernest W. McFarland (D)	Jan. 3, 1941	Jan. 2, 1953
Barry Goldwater (R)	Jan. 3, 1953	Jan. 2, 1965
Paul J. Fannin (R)	Jan. 3, 1965	Jan. 2, 1977

Dennis DeConcini (D)	Jan. 3, 1977	Jan. 2, 1995
Jon Kyl (R)	Jan. 3, 1995	

Class 3

Carl Hayden (D)	March 4, 1927	Jan. 2, 1969
Barry Goldwater (R)	Jan. 3, 1969	Jan. 2, 1987
John McCain (R)	Jan. 3, 1987	

ARKANSAS

(Became a state June 15, 1836)

Class 2

Senators	Dates of Service	
John L. McClellan (D)[1]	Jan. 3, 1943	Nov. 28, 1977
Kaneaster Hodges Jr. (D)[2]	Dec. 10, 1977	Jan. 2, 1979
David Pryor (D)	Jan. 3, 1979	Jan. 2, 1997
Tim Hutchinson (R)	Jan. 3, 1997	

Class 3

J. William Fulbright (D)[3]	Jan. 3, 1945	Dec. 31, 1974
Dale Bumpers (D)	Jan. 3, 1975	

Arkansas
1. Died Nov. 28, 1977.
2. Appointed by governor to fill vacancy.
3. Resigned Dec. 31, 1974.

CALIFORNIA

(Became a state Sept. 9, 1850)

Class 1

Senators	Dates of Service	
William F. Knowland (R)[1]	Aug. 26, 1945	Jan. 2, 1959
Clair Engle (D)[2]	Jan. 3, 1959	July 30, 1964
Pierre Salinger (D)[3]	Aug. 4, 1964	Dec. 31, 1964
George Murphy (R)[4]	Jan. 1, 1965	Jan. 2, 1971
John V. Tunney (D)[5]	Jan. 2, 1971	Jan. 1, 1977
S. I. Hayakawa (R)	Jan. 2, 1977	Jan. 2, 1983
Pete Wilson (R)[6]	Jan. 3, 1983	Jan. 7, 1991
John Seymour (R)[7]	Jan. 10, 1991	Nov. 3, 1992
Dianne Feinstein (D)	Nov. 10, 1992	

Class 3

Sheridan Downey (D)[8]	Jan. 3, 1939	Nov. 30, 1950
Richard M. Nixon (R)[9]	Dec. 4, 1950	Jan. 1, 1953
Thomas H. Kuchel (R)[10]	Jan. 2, 1953	Jan. 2, 1969
Alan Cranston (D)	Jan. 3, 1969	Jan. 2, 1993
Barbara Boxer (D)	Jan. 3, 1993	

California
1. Appointed by governor to fill vacancy. Subsequently elected.
2. Died July 30, 1964.

3. *Appointed by governor to fill vacancy. Resigned Dec. 31, 1964.*
4. *Resigned Jan. 2, 1971.*
5. *Resigned Jan. 1, 1977.*
6. *Resigned Jan. 7, 1991, having been elected governor.*
7. *Appointed by governor to fill vacancy. Resigned Nov. 3, 1992.*
8. *Resigned Nov. 30, 1950.*
9. *Resigned Jan. 1, 1953, having been elected U.S. vice president.*
10. *Appointed by governor to fill vacancy. Subsequently elected.*

COLORADO

(Became a state Aug. 1, 1876)

Class 2

Senators	Dates of Service	
Edwin C. Johnson (D)	Jan. 3, 1937	Jan. 2, 1955
Gordon Allott (R)	Jan. 3, 1955	Jan. 2, 1973
Floyd K. Haskell (D)	Jan. 3, 1973	Jan. 2, 1979
William L. Armstrong (R)	Jan. 3, 1979	Jan. 2, 1991
Hank Brown (R)	Jan. 3, 1991	Jan. 2, 1997
Wayne Allard (R)	Jan. 3, 1997	

Class 3

Senators	Dates of Service	
Eugene D. Millikin (R)[1]	Dec. 20, 1941	Jan. 2, 1957
John A. Carroll (D)	Jan. 3, 1957	Jan. 2, 1963
Peter H. Dominick (R)	Jan. 3, 1963	Jan. 2, 1975
Gary Hart (D)	Jan. 3, 1975	Jan. 2, 1987
Timothy E. Wirth (D)	Jan. 3, 1987	Jan. 2, 1993
Ben Nighthorse Campbell (D, R)[2]	Jan. 3, 1993	

Colorado
1. *Appointed by governor to fill vacancy. Subsequently elected.*
2. *Elected as a Democrat in 1992. Campbell became a Republican on March 3, 1995.*

CONNECTICUT

(Ratified the Constitution Jan. 9, 1788)

Class 1

Senators	Dates of Service	
Raymond E. Baldwin (R)[1]	Dec. 27, 1946	Dec. 17, 1949
William Benton (D)[2]	Dec. 17, 1949	Jan. 2, 1953
William A. Purtell (R)	Jan. 3, 1953	Jan. 2, 1959
Thomas J. Dodd (D)	Jan. 3, 1959	Jan. 2, 1971
Lowell P. Weicker Jr. (R)	Jan. 3, 1971	Jan. 2, 1989
Joseph I. Lieberman (D)	Jan. 3, 1989	

Class 3

Senators	Dates of Service	
Brien McMahon (D)[3]	Jan. 3, 1945	July 28, 1952
William A. Purtell (R)[4]	Aug. 29, 1952	Nov. 4, 1952
Prescott Bush (R)	Nov. 5, 1952	Jan. 2, 1963
Abraham Ribicoff (D)	Jan. 3, 1963	Jan. 2, 1981
Christopher J. Dodd (D)	Jan. 3, 1981	

Connecticut
1. *Resigned Dec. 17, 1949.*
2. *Appointed by governor to fill vacancy. Subsequently elected.*
3. *Died July 28, 1952.*
4. *Appointed by governor to fill vacancy.*

DELAWARE

(Ratified the Constitution Dec. 7, 1787)

Class 1

Senators	Dates of Service	
John J. Williams (R)[1]	Jan. 3, 1947	Dec. 31, 1970
William V. Roth Jr. (R)	Jan. 1, 1971	

Class 2

Senators	Dates of Service	
C. Douglass Buck (R)	Jan. 3, 1943	Jan. 2, 1949
J. Allen Frear Jr. (D)	Jan. 3, 1949	Jan. 2, 1961
J. Caleb Boggs (R)	Jan. 3, 1961	Jan. 2, 1973
Joseph R. Biden Jr. (D)	Jan. 3, 1973	

Delaware
1. *Resigned Dec. 31, 1970.*

FLORIDA

(Became a state March 3, 1845)

Class 1

Senators	Dates of Service	
Spessard L. Holland (D)[1]	Sept. 25, 1946	Jan. 2, 1971
Lawton Chiles (D)	Jan. 3, 1971	Jan. 2, 1989
Connie Mack (R)	Jan. 3, 1989	

Class 3

Senators	Dates of Service	
Claude Pepper (D)	Nov. 4, 1936	Jan. 2, 1951
George A. Smathers (D)	Jan. 3, 1951	Jan. 2, 1969
Edward J. Gurney (R)[2]	Jan. 3, 1969	Dec. 31, 1974
Richard Stone (D)[3]	Jan. 2, 1975	Dec. 31, 1980
Paula Hawkins (R)	Jan. 1, 1981	Jan. 2, 1987
Bob Graham (D)	Jan. 3, 1987	

Florida
1. *Appointed by governor to fill vacancy. Subsequently elected.*
2. *Resigned Dec. 31, 1974.*
3. *Resigned Dec. 31, 1980.*

GEORGIA

(Ratified the Constitution Jan. 2, 1788)

Class 2

Senators	Dates of Service	
Richard B. Russell (D)[1]	Jan. 12, 1933	Jan. 21, 1971
David H. Gambrell (D)[2]	Feb. 1, 1971	Nov. 7, 1972
Sam Nunn (D)	Nov. 8, 1972	Jan. 2, 1997
Max Cleland (D)	Jan. 3, 1997	

Class 3

Senators	Dates of Service	
Walter F. George (D)	Nov. 22, 1922	Jan. 2, 1957
Herman E. Talmadge (D)	Jan. 3, 1957	Jan. 2, 1981
Mack Mattingly (R)	Jan. 3, 1981	Jan. 2, 1987
Wyche Fowler (D)	Jan. 3, 1987	Jan. 2, 1993
Paul Coverdell (R)	Jan. 3, 1993	

Georgia
1. *Died Jan. 21, 1971.*
2. *Appointed by governor to fill vacancy.*

HAWAII

(Became a state Aug. 21, 1959)

Class 1

Senators	Dates of Service	
Hiram L. Fong (R)	Aug. 21, 1959	Jan. 2, 1977
Spark M. Matsunaga (D)[1]	Jan. 3, 1977	April 15, 1990
Daniel K. Akaka (D)[2]	May 16, 1990	

Class 3

Oren E. Long (D)	Aug. 21, 1959	Jan. 2, 1963
Daniel K. Inouye (D)	Jan. 3, 1963	

Hawaii
1. *Died April 15, 1990.*
2. *Appointed by governor to fill vacancy. Subsequently elected.*

IDAHO

(Became a state July 3, 1890)

Class 2

Senators	Dates of Service	
Henry C. Dworshak (R)	Nov. 6, 1946	Jan. 2, 1949
Bert H. Miller (D)[1]	Jan. 3, 1949	Oct. 8, 1949
Henry C. Dworshak (R)[2]	Oct. 14, 1949	July 23, 1962
Len B. Jordan (R)[3]	Aug. 6, 1962	Jan. 2, 1973
James A. McClure (R)	Jan. 3, 1973	Jan. 2, 1991
Larry E. Craig (R)	Jan. 3, 1991	

Class 3

Glen H. Taylor (D)	Jan. 3, 1945	Jan. 2, 1951
Herman Welker (R)	Jan. 3, 1951	Jan. 2, 1957
Frank Church (D)	Jan. 3, 1957	Jan. 2, 1981
Steven D. Symms (R)	Jan. 3, 1981	Jan. 2, 1993
Dirk Kempthorne (R)	Jan. 3, 1993	

Idaho
1. *Died Oct. 8, 1949.*
2. *Appointed by governor to fill vacancy. Subsequently elected. Died July 23, 1962.*
3. *Appointed by governor to fill vacancy. Subsequently elected.*

ILLINOIS

(Became a state Dec. 3, 1818)

Class 2

Senators	Dates of Service	
C. Wayland Brooks (R)	Nov. 22, 1940	Jan. 2, 1949
Paul H. Douglas (D)	Jan. 3, 1949	Jan. 2, 1967
Charles H. Percy (R)	Jan. 3, 1967	Jan. 2, 1985
Paul Simon (D)	Jan. 3, 1985	Jan. 2, 1997
Richard J. Durbin (D)	Jan. 3, 1997	

Class 3

Scott W. Lucas (D)	Jan. 3, 1939	Jan. 2, 1951
Everett McKinley Dirksen (R)[1]	Jan. 3, 1951	Sept. 7, 1969
Ralph Tyler Smith (R)[2]	Sept. 17, 1969	Nov. 16, 1970
Adlai E. Stevenson III (D)	Nov. 17, 1970	Jan. 2, 1981
Alan J. Dixon (D)	Jan. 3, 1981	Jan. 2, 1993
Carol Moseley Braun (D)	Jan. 3, 1993	

Illinois
1. *Died Sept. 7, 1969.*
2. *Appointed by governor to fill vacancy.*

INDIANA

(Became a state Dec. 11, 1816)

Class 1

Senators	Dates of Service	
William E. Jenner (R)	Jan. 3, 1947	Jan. 2, 1959
Vance Hartke (D)	Jan. 3, 1959	Jan. 2, 1977
Richard G. Lugar (R)	Jan. 3, 1977	

Class 3

Homer E. Capehart (R)	Jan. 3, 1945	Jan. 2, 1963
Birch Bayh (D)	Jan. 3, 1963	Jan. 2, 1981
Dan Quayle (R)[1]	Jan. 3, 1981	Jan. 3, 1989
Daniel R. Coats (R)[2]	Jan. 3, 1989	

Indiana
1. *Resigned Jan. 3, 1989, having been elected vice president of the United States.*
2. *Appointed by governor to fill vacancy. Subsequently elected.*

IOWA

(Became a state Dec. 28, 1846)

Class 2

Senators	Dates of Service	
George A. Wilson (R)	Jan. 14, 1943	Jan. 2, 1949
Guy M. Gillette (D)	Jan. 3, 1949	Jan. 2, 1955
Thomas E. Martin (R)	Jan. 3, 1955	Jan. 2, 1961
Jack Miller (R)	Jan. 3, 1961	Jan. 2, 1973
Dick Clark (D)	Jan. 3, 1973	Jan. 2, 1979
Roger W. Jepsen (R)	Jan. 3, 1979	Jan. 2, 1985
Tom Harkin (D)	Jan. 3, 1985	

Class 3

Bourke B. Hickenlooper (R)	Jan. 3, 1945	Jan. 2, 1969
Harold E. Hughes (D)	Jan. 3, 1969	Jan. 2, 1975
John C. Culver (D)	Jan. 3, 1975	Jan. 2, 1981
Charles E. Grassley (R)	Jan. 3, 1981	

KANSAS

(Became a state Jan. 29, 1861)

Class 2

Senators	Dates of Service	
Arthur Capper (R)	March 4, 1919	Jan. 2, 1949
Andrew F. Schoeppel (R)[1]	Jan. 3, 1949	Jan. 21, 1962
James B. Pearson (R)[2]	Jan. 31, 1962	Dec. 23, 1978
Nancy Landon Kassebaum (R)	Dec. 23, 1978	Jan. 2, 1997
Pat Roberts (R)	Jan. 3, 1997	

Class 3

Clyde M. Reed (R)[3]	Jan. 3, 1939	Nov. 8, 1949
Harry Darby (R)[4]	Dec. 2, 1949	Nov. 28, 1950
Frank Carlson (R)	Nov. 29, 1950	Jan. 2, 1969

Robert Dole (R)[5]	Jan. 3, 1969	June 11, 1996
Sheila Frahm (R)[6]	June 11, 1996	Nov. 27, 1996
Sam Brownback (R)	Nov. 27, 1996	

Kansas
1. *Died Jan. 21, 1962.*
2. *Appointed by governor to fill vacancy. Subsequently elected. Resigned Dec. 23, 1978.*
3. *Died Nov. 8, 1949.*
4. *Appointed by governor to fill vacancy.*
5. *Resigned June 11, 1996.*
6. *Appointed by governor to fill vacancy. Resigned Nov. 27, 1996*

KENTUCKY

(Became a state June 1, 1792)

Class 2

Senators	Dates of Service	
John Sherman Cooper (R)	Nov. 6, 1946	Jan. 2, 1949
Virgil Chapman (D)[1]	Jan. 3, 1949	March 8, 1951
Thomas R. Underwood (D)[2]	March 19, 1951	Nov. 4, 1952
John Sherman Cooper (R)	Nov. 5, 1952	Jan. 2, 1955
Alben W. Barkley (D)[3]	Jan. 3, 1955	April 30, 1956
Robert Humphreys (D)[4]	June 21, 1956	Nov. 6, 1956
John Sherman Cooper (R)	Nov. 7, 1956	Jan. 2, 1973
Walter D. Huddleston (D)	Jan. 3, 1973	Jan. 2, 1985
Mitchell McConnell (R)	Jan. 3, 1985	

Class 3

Senators	Dates of Service	
Alben W. Barkley (D)[5]	March 4, 1927	Jan. 19, 1949
Garrett L. Withers (D)[6]	Jan. 20, 1949	Nov. 26, 1950
Earle C. Clements (D)	Nov. 27, 1950	Jan. 2, 1957
Thruston B. Morton (R)[7]	Jan. 3, 1957	Dec. 16, 1968
Marlow W. Cook (R)[8]	Dec. 17, 1968	Dec. 27, 1974
Wendell H. Ford (D)	Dec. 28, 1974	

Kentucky
1. *Died March 8, 1951.*
2. *Appointed by governor to fill vacancy.*
3. *Died April 30, 1956.*
4. *Appointed by governor to fill vacancy.*
5. *Resigned Jan. 19, 1949, to become vice president of the United States.*
6. *Appointed by governor to fill vacancy.*
7. *Resigned Dec. 16, 1968.*
8. *Resigned Dec. 27, 1974.*

LOUISIANA

(Became a state April 30, 1812)

Class 2

Senators	Dates of Service	
Allen J. Ellender (D)[1]	Jan. 3, 1937	July 27, 1972
Elaine S. Edwards (D)[2]	Aug. 1, 1972	Nov. 13, 1972
J. Bennett Johnston (D)	Nov. 14, 1972	Jan. 2, 1997
Mary L. Landrieu (D)	Jan. 3, 1997	

Class 3

Senators	Dates of Service	
John H. Overton (D)[3]	March 4, 1933	May 14, 1948
William C. Feazel (D)[4]	May 18, 1948	Dec. 30, 1948
Russell B. Long (D)	Dec. 31, 1948	Jan. 2, 1987
John B. Breaux (D)	Jan. 3, 1987	

Louisiana
1. *Died July 27, 1972.*
2. *Appointed by governor to fill vacancy. Resigned Nov. 13, 1972.*

3. *Died May 14, 1948.*
4. *Appointed by governor to fill vacancy.*

MAINE

(Became a state March 15, 1820)

Class 1

Senators	Dates of Service	
Ralph O. Brewster (R)	Jan. 3, 1941	Jan. 2, 1953
Frederick G. Payne (R)	Jan. 3, 1953	Jan. 2, 1959
Edmund S. Muskie (D)[1]	Jan. 3, 1959	May 7, 1980
George J. Mitchell (D)[2]	May 17, 1980	Jan. 2, 1995
Olympia J. Snowe (R)	Jan. 3, 1995	

Class 2

Senators	Dates of Service	
Wallace H. White Jr. (R)	March 4, 1931	Jan. 2, 1949
Margaret Chase Smith (R)	Jan. 3, 1949	Jan. 2, 1973
William D. Hathaway (D)	Jan. 3, 1973	Jan. 2, 1979
William S. Cohen (R)	Jan. 3, 1979	Jan. 2, 1997
Susan Collins (R)	Jan. 3, 1997	

Maine
1. *Resigned May 7, 1980, having been confirmed secretary of state.*
2. *Appointed by governor to fill vacancy. Subsequently elected.*

MARYLAND

(Ratified the Constitution April 28, 1788)

Class 1

Senators	Dates of Service	
Herbert R. O'Conor (D)	Jan. 3, 1947	Jan. 2, 1953
J. Glenn Beall (R)	Jan. 3, 1953	Jan. 2, 1965
Joseph D. Tydings (D)	Jan. 3, 1965	Jan. 2, 1971
J. Glenn Beall Jr. (R)	Jan. 3, 1971	Jan. 2, 1977
Paul S. Sarbanes (D)	Jan. 3, 1977	

Class 3

Senators	Dates of Service	
Millard E. Tydings (D)	March 4, 1927	Jan. 2, 1951
John Marshall Butler (R)	Jan. 3, 1951	Jan. 2, 1963
Daniel B. Brewster (D)	Jan. 3, 1963	Jan. 2, 1969
Charles Mathias Jr. (R)	Jan. 3, 1969	Jan. 2, 1987
Barbara A. Mikulski (D)	Jan. 3, 1987	

MASSACHUSETTS

(Ratified the Constitution Feb. 6, 1788)

Class 1

Senators	Dates of Service	
Henry Cabot Lodge Jr. (R)	Jan. 3, 1947	Jan. 2, 1953
John F. Kennedy (D)[1]	Jan. 3, 1953	Dec. 22, 1960
Benjamin A. Smith II (D)[2]	Dec. 27, 1960	Nov. 6, 1962
Edward M. Kennedy (D)	Nov. 7, 1962	

Class 2

Senators	Dates of Service	
Leverett Saltonstall (R)	Jan. 10, 1945	Jan. 2, 1967
Edward W. Brooke (R)	Jan. 3, 1967	Jan. 2, 1979
Paul E. Tsongas (D)[3]	Jan. 3, 1979	Jan. 2, 1985
John F. Kerry (D)	Jan. 3, 1985	

Massachusetts
1. *Resigned Dec. 22, 1960, having been elected president of the United States.*
2. *Appointed by governor to fill vacancy.*
3. *Resigned Jan. 2, 1985.*

MICHIGAN

(Became a state Jan. 26, 1837)

Class 1

Senators	Dates of Service	
Arthur H. Vandenberg (R)[1]	March 31, 1928	April 18, 1951
Blair Moody (D)[2]	April 22, 1951	Nov. 4, 1952
Charles E. Potter (R)	Nov. 5, 1952	Jan. 2, 1959
Philip A. Hart (D)[3]	Jan. 3, 1959	Dec. 26, 1976
Donald W. Riegle Jr. (D)	Dec. 30, 1976	Jan. 2, 1995
Spencer Abraham (R)	Jan. 3, 1995	

Class 2

Senators	Dates of Service	
Prentiss M. Brown (D)	Nov. 19, 1936	Jan. 2, 1943
Homer Ferguson (R)	Jan. 3, 1943	Jan. 2, 1955
Patrick V. McNamara (D)[4]	Jan. 3, 1955	April 30, 1966
Robert P. Griffin (R)[5]	May 11, 1966	Jan. 2, 1979
Carl Levin (D)	Jan. 3, 1979	

Michigan
1. *Appointed by governor to fill vacancy. Subsequently elected. Died April 18, 1951.*
2. *Appointed by governor to fill vacancy.*
3. *Died Dec. 26, 1976.*
4. *Died April 30, 1966.*
5. *Appointed by governor to fill vacancy. Subsequently elected.*

MINNESOTA

(Became a state May 11, 1858)

Class 1

Senators	Dates of Service	
Edward J. Thye (R)	Jan. 3, 1947	Jan. 2, 1959
Eugene J. McCarthy (DFL)	Jan. 3, 1959	Jan. 2, 1971
Hubert H. Humphrey (DFL)[1]	Jan. 3, 1971	Jan. 13, 1978
Muriel Humphrey (DFL)[2]	Jan. 25, 1978	Nov. 7, 1978
Dave Durenberger (I-R)	Nov. 8, 1978	Jan. 2, 1995
Rod Grams (R)	Jan. 3, 1995	

Class 2

Senators	Dates of Service	
Joseph H. Ball (R)	Jan. 3, 1943	Jan. 2, 1949
Hubert H. Humphrey (DFL)[3]	Jan. 3, 1949	Dec. 29, 1964
Walter F. Mondale (DFL)[4]	Dec. 30, 1964	Dec. 30, 1976
Wendell R. Anderson (DFL)[5]	Dec. 30, 1976	Dec. 29, 1978
Rudy Boschwitz (I-R)	Dec. 30, 1978	Jan. 2, 1991
Paul Wellstone (DFL)	Jan. 3, 1991	

Minnesota
1. *Died Jan. 13, 1978.*
2. *Appointed by governor to fill vacancy.*
3. *Resigned Dec. 29, 1964, having been elected vice president of the United States.*
4. *Appointed by governor to fill vacancy. Subsequently elected. Resigned Dec. 30, 1976, having been elected vice president of the United States.*
5. *Appointed by governor to fill vacancy. Resigned Dec. 29, 1978.*

MISSISSIPPI

(Became a state Dec. 10, 1817)

Class 1

Senators	Dates of Service	
Theodore G. Bilbo (D)[1]	Jan. 3, 1935	Jan. 2, 1947
John C. Stennis (D)	Nov. 5, 1947	Jan. 2, 1989
Trent Lott (R)	Jan. 3, 1989	

Class 2

Senators	Dates of Service	
James O. Eastland (D)[2]	Jan. 3, 1943	Dec. 27, 1978
Thad Cochran (R)	Dec. 27, 1978	

Mississippi
1. *Elected for term beginning Jan. 3, 1947, but was never sworn in. Died Aug. 21, 1947.*
2. *Resigned Dec. 27, 1978.*

MISSOURI

(Became a state Aug. 10, 1821)

Class 1

Senators	Dates of Service	
James P. Kem (R)	Jan. 3, 1947	Jan. 2, 1953
Stuart Symington (D)[1]	Jan. 3, 1953	Dec. 27, 1976
John C. Danforth (R)	Dec. 27, 1976	Jan. 2, 1995
John Ashcroft (R)	Jan. 3, 1995	

Class 3

Senators	Dates of Service	
Forrest C. Donnell (R)	Jan. 3, 1945	Jan. 2, 1951
Thomas C. Hennings Jr. (D)[2]	Jan. 3, 1951	Sept. 13, 1960
Edward V. Long (D)[3]	Sept. 23, 1960	Dec. 27, 1968
Thomas F. Eagleton (D)	Dec. 28, 1968	Jan. 2, 1987
Christopher S. Bond (R)	Jan. 3, 1987	

Missouri
1. *Resigned Dec. 27, 1976.*
2. *Died Sept. 13, 1960.*
3. *Appointed by governor to fill vacancy. Subsequently elected. Resigned Dec. 27, 1968.*

MONTANA

(Became a state Nov. 8, 1889)

Class 1

Senators	Dates of Service	
Zales N. Ecton (R)	Jan. 3, 1947	Jan. 2, 1953
Mike Mansfield (D)	Jan. 3, 1953	Jan. 2, 1977
John Melcher (D)	Jan. 3, 1977	Jan. 2, 1989
Conrad Burns (R)	Jan. 3, 1989	

Class 2

Senators	Dates of Service	
James E. Murray (D)	Nov. 7, 1934	Jan. 2, 1961
Lee Metcalf (D)[1]	Jan. 3, 1961	Jan. 12, 1978
Paul G. Hatfield (D)[2]	Jan. 22, 1978	Dec. 14, 1978
Max Baucus (D)	Dec. 15, 1978	

Montana
1. *Died Jan. 12, 1978.*
2. *Appointed by governor to fill vacancy. Resigned Dec. 14, 1978.*

NEBRASKA

(Became a state March 1, 1867)

Class 1

Senators	Dates of Service	
Hugh Butler (R)[1]	Jan. 3, 1941	July 1, 1954
Sam W. Reynolds (R)[2]	July 3, 1954	Nov. 7, 1954
Roman L. Hruska (R)[3]	Nov. 8, 1954	Dec. 27, 1976
Edward Zorinsky (D)[4]	Dec. 28, 1976	March 6, 1987
David Karnes (R)[5]	March 13, 1987	Jan. 2, 1989
Bob Kerrey (D)	Jan. 3, 1989	

Class 2

Senators	Dates of Service	
Kenneth S. Wherry (R)[6]	Jan. 3, 1943	Nov. 29, 1951
Fred A. Seaton (R)[7]	Dec. 10, 1951	Nov. 4, 1952
Dwight Griswold (R)[8]	Nov. 5, 1952	Apr. 12, 1954
Eva Bowring (R)[9]	April 16, 1954	Nov. 7, 1954
Hazel H. Abel (R)[10]	Nov. 8, 1954	Dec. 31, 1954
Carl T. Curtis (R)	Jan. 1, 1955	Jan. 2, 1979
J. James Exon (D)	Jan. 3, 1979	Jan. 2, 1997
Chuck Hagel (R)	Jan. 3, 1997	

Nebraska
1. *Died July 1, 1954.*
2. *Appointed by governor to fill vacancy.*
3. *Resigned Dec. 27, 1976.*
4. *Died March 6, 1987*
5. *Appointed by governor to fill vacancy.*
6. *Died Nov. 29, 1951.*
7. *Appointed by governor to fill vacancy.*
8. *Died April 12, 1954.*
9. *Appointed by governor to fill vacancy.*
10. *Resigned Dec. 31, 1954.*

NEVADA

(Became a state Oct. 31, 1864)

Class 1

Senators	Dates of Service	
George W. Malone (R)	Jan. 3, 1947	Jan. 2, 1959
Howard W. Cannon (D)	Jan. 3, 1959	Jan. 2, 1983
Chic Hecht (R)	Jan. 3, 1983	Jan. 2, 1989
Richard H. Bryan (D)	Jan. 3, 1989	

Class 3

Senators	Dates of Service	
Patrick A. McCarran (D)[1]	March 4, 1933	Sept. 28, 1954
Ernest S. Brown (R)[2]	Oct. 1, 1954	Dec. 1, 1954
Alan Bible (D)[3]	Dec. 2, 1954	Dec. 17, 1974
Paul Laxalt (R)	Dec. 18, 1974	Jan. 2, 1987
Harry Reid (D)	Jan. 3, 1987	

Nevada
1. *Died Sept. 28, 1954.*
2. *Appointed by governor to fill vacancy.*
3. *Resigned Dec. 17, 1974.*

NEW HAMPSHIRE

(Ratified the Constitution June 21, 1788)

Class 2

Senators	Dates of Service	
Styles Bridges (R)[1]	Jan. 3, 1937	Nov. 26, 1961
Maurice J. Murphy Jr. (R)[2]	Dec. 7, 1961	Nov. 6, 1962
Thomas J. McIntyre (D)	Nov. 7, 1962	Jan. 2, 1979
Gordon J. Humphrey (R)[3]	Jan. 3, 1979	Dec. 4, 1990
Robert C. Smith (R)	Dec. 7, 1990	

Class 3

Senators	Dates of Service	
Charles W. Tobey (R)[4]	Jan. 3, 1939	July 24, 1953
Robert W. Upton (R)[5]	Aug. 14, 1953	Nov. 7, 1954
Norris Cotton (R)[6]	Nov. 8, 1954	Dec. 31, 1974
Louis C. Wyman (R)[7]	Jan. 1, 1975	Jan. 2, 1975
Norris Cotton (R)[8]	Aug. 8, 1975	Sept. 18, 1975
John A. Durkin (D)[9]	Sept. 18, 1975	Dec. 29, 1980
Warren B. Rudman (R)	Dec. 29, 1980	Jan. 2, 1993
Judd Gregg (R)	Jan. 3, 1993	

New Hampshire
1. *Died Nov. 26, 1961.*
2. *Appointed by governor to fill vacancy.*
3. *Resigned Dec. 4, 1990.*
4. *Died July 24, 1953.*
5. *Appointed by governor to fill vacancy.*
6. *Resigned Dec. 31, 1974.*
7. *Appointed by governor to fill vacancy. Wyman and John A. Durkin (D) both claimed to have been elected to the seat for a six-year term beginning Jan. 3, 1975. Neither was seated. After unsuccessfully attempting for seven months to determine the winner, the Senate July 30, 1975, voted to declare the seat vacant effective Aug. 8, 1975.*
8. *Appointed by governor to fill vacancy.*
9. *Resigned Dec. 29, 1980.*

NEW JERSEY

(Ratified the Constitution Dec. 18, 1787)

Class 1

Senators	Dates of Service	
H. Alexander Smith (R)	Dec. 7, 1944	Jan. 2, 1959
Harrison A. Williams Jr. (D)[1]	Jan. 3, 1959	March 11, 1982
Nicholas F. Brady (R)[2]	April 12, 1982	Dec. 26, 1982
Frank R. Lautenberg (D)	Dec. 27, 1982	

Class 2

Senators	Dates of Service	
Albert W. Hawkes (R)	Jan. 3, 1943	Jan. 2, 1949
Robert C. Hendrickson (R)	Jan. 3, 1949	Jan. 2, 1955
Clifford P. Case (R)	Jan. 3, 1955	Jan. 2, 1979
Bill Bradley (D)	Jan. 3, 1979	Jan. 2, 1997
Robert G. Torricelli (D)	Jan. 3, 1997	

New Jersey
1. *Resigned March 11, 1982.*
2. *Appointed by governor to fill vacancy. Resigned Dec. 26, 1982.*

NEW MEXICO

(Became a state Jan. 6, 1912)

Class 1

Senators	Dates of Service	
Dennis Chavez (D)[1]	May 11, 1935	Nov. 18, 1962
Edwin L. Mechem (R)[2]	Nov. 30, 1962	Nov. 3, 1964
Joseph M. Montoya (D)	Nov. 4, 1964	Jan. 2, 1977
Harrison (Jack) Schmitt (R)	Jan. 3, 1977	Jan. 2, 1983
Jeff Bingaman (D)	Jan. 3, 1983	

Class 2

Senators	Dates of Service	
Carl A. Hatch (D)[3]	Oct. 10, 1933	Jan. 2, 1949
Clinton P. Anderson (D)	Jan. 3, 1949	Jan. 2, 1973
Pete V. Domenici (R)	Jan. 3, 1973	

1. Appointed by governor to fill vacancy. Subsequently elected. Died Nov. 18, 1962.
2. Appointed by governor to fill vacancy.
3. Appointed by governor to fill vacancy. Subsequently elected.

11. Appointed by governor to fill vacancy.
12. Officially sworn in on Dec. 10, 1986.

NEW YORK

(Ratified the Constitution July 26, 1788)

Class 1

Senators	Dates of Service	
Irving M. Ives (R)	Jan. 3, 1947	Jan. 2, 1959
Kenneth B. Keating (R)	Jan. 3, 1959	Jan. 2, 1965
Robert F. Kennedy (D)[1]	Jan. 3, 1965	June 6, 1968
Charles E. Goodell (R)[2]	Sept. 10, 1968	Jan. 2, 1971
James L. Buckley (C-R)	Jan. 3, 1971	Jan. 2, 1977
Daniel Patrick Moynihan (D)	Jan. 3, 1977	

Class 3

Senators	Dates of Service	
Robert F. Wagner (D)[3]	March 4, 1927	June 28, 1949
John Foster Dulles (R)[4]	July 7, 1949	Nov. 8, 1949
Herbert H. Lehman (D)	Nov. 9, 1949	Jan. 2, 1957
Jacob K. Javits (R)	Jan. 9, 1957	Jan. 2, 1981
Alfonse M. D'Amato (R)	Jan. 3, 1981	

New York
1. Died June 6, 1968.
2. Appointed by governor to fill vacancy.
3. Resigned June 28, 1949.
4. Appointed by governor to fill vacancy.

NORTH CAROLINA

(Ratified the Constitution Nov. 21, 1789)

Class 2

Senators	Dates of Service	
William B. Umstead (D)[1]	Dec. 18, 1946	Dec. 30, 1948
J. Melville Broughton (D)[2]	Dec. 31, 1948	March 6, 1949
Frank P. Graham (D)[3]	March 29, 1949	Nov. 26, 1950
Willis Smith (D)[4]	Nov. 27, 1950	June 23, 1953
Alton A. Lennon (D)[5]	July 10, 1953	Nov. 28, 1954
W. Kerr Scott (D)[6]	Nov. 29, 1954	April 16, 1958
B. Everett Jordan (D)[7]	April 19, 1958	Jan. 2, 1973
Jesse Helms (R)	Jan. 3, 1973	

Class 3

Senators	Dates of Service	
Clyde R. Hoey (D)[8]	Jan. 3, 1945	May 12, 1954
Sam J. Ervin Jr. (D)[9]	June 5, 1954	Dec. 31, 1974
Robert Morgan (D)	Jan. 3, 1975	Jan. 2, 1981
John P. East (R)[10]	Jan. 3, 1981	June 29, 1986
James T. Broyhill (R)[11]	July 14, 1986	Nov. 4, 1986
Terry Sanford (D)[12]	Nov. 5, 1986	Jan. 2, 1993
Lauch Faircloth (R)	Jan. 3, 1993	

North Carolina
1. Appointed by governor to fill vacancy.
2. Died March 6, 1949.
3. Appointed by governor to fill vacancy.
4. Died June 23, 1953.
5. Appointed by governor to fill vacancy.
6. Died April 16, 1958.
7. Appointed by governor to fill vacancy. Subsequently elected.
8. Died May 12, 1954.
9. Appointed by governor to fill vacancy. Subsequently elected. Resigned Dec. 31, 1974.
10. Died June 29, 1986.

NORTH DAKOTA

(Became a state Nov. 2, 1889)

Class 1

Senators	Dates of Service	
William Langer (R)[1]	Jan. 3, 1941	Nov. 8, 1959
C. Norman Brunsdale (R)[2]	Nov. 19, 1959	Aug. 7, 1960
Quentin N. Burdick (D)[3]	Aug. 8, 1960	Sept. 8, 1992
Jocelyn B. Burdick (D)[4]	Sept. 12, 1982	Dec. 4, 1992
Kent Conrad (D)	Dec. 5, 1992	

Class 3

Senators	Dates of Service	
Milton R. Young (R)[5]	March 12, 1945	Jan. 2, 1981
Mark Andrews (R)	Jan. 3, 1981	Jan. 2, 1987
Kent Conrad (D)[6]	Jan. 3, 1987	Dec. 4, 1992
Byron L. Dorgan (D)	Dec. 15, 1992	

North Dakota
1. Died Nov. 8, 1959.
2. Appointed by governor to fill vacancy.
3. Died Sept. 8, 1992.
4. Appointed by governor to fill vacancy.
5. Appointed by governor to fill vacancy. Subsequently elected.
6. Resigned Dec. 4, 1992.

OHIO

(Became a state March 1, 1803)

Class 1

Senators	Dates of Service	
John W. Bricker (R)	Jan. 3, 1947	Jan. 2, 1959
Stephen M. Young (D)	Jan. 3, 1959	Jan. 2, 1971
Robert Taft Jr. (R)[1]	Jan. 3, 1971	Dec. 28, 1976
Howard M. Metzenbaum (D)	Dec. 29, 1976	Jan. 2, 1995
Mike DeWine (R)	Jan. 3, 1995	

Class 3

Senators	Dates of Service	
Robert A. Taft (R)[2]	Jan. 3, 1939	July 31, 1953
Thomas A. Burke (D)[3]	Nov. 10, 1953	Dec. 2, 1954
George H. Bender (R)	Dec. 16, 1954	Jan. 2, 1957
Frank J. Lausche (D)	Jan. 3, 1957	Jan. 2, 1969
William B. Saxbe (R)[4]	Jan. 3, 1969	Jan. 4, 1974
Howard M. Metzenbaum (D)[5]	Jan. 4, 1974	Dec. 23, 1974
John Glenn (D)	Dec. 24, 1974	

Ohio
1. Resigned Dec. 28, 1976.
2. Died July 31, 1953.
3. Appointed by governor to fill vacancy.
4. Resigned Jan. 4, 1974.
5. Appointed by governor to fill vacancy. Resigned Dec. 23, 1974.

OKLAHOMA

(Became a state Nov. 16, 1907)

Class 2

Senators	Dates of Service	
Edward H. Moore (R)	Jan. 3, 1943	Jan. 2, 1949
Robert S. Kerr (D)[1]	Jan. 3, 1949	Jan. 1, 1963

J. Howard Edmondson (D)[2]	Jan. 7, 1963	Nov. 3, 1964
Fred R. Harris (D)	Nov. 4, 1964	Jan. 2, 1973
Dewey F. Bartlett (R)	Jan. 3, 1973	Jan. 2, 1979
David L. Boren (D)[3]	Jan. 3, 1979	Nov. 15, 1994
James M. Inhofe (R)	Nov. 17, 1994	

Class 3

Elmer Thomas (D)	March 4, 1927	Jan. 2, 1951
A. S. Mike Monroney (D)	Jan. 3, 1951	Jan. 2, 1969
Henry Bellmon (R)	Jan. 3, 1969	Jan. 2, 1981
Don Nickles (R)	Jan. 3, 1981	

Oklahoma
1. *Died Jan. 1, 1963.*
2. *Appointed by governor to fill vacancy.*
3. *Resigned Nov. 15, 1994.*

OREGON

(Became a state Feb. 14, 1859)

Class 2

Senators	Dates of Service	
Guy Cordon (R)[1]	March 4, 1944	Jan. 2, 1955
Richard L. Neuberger (D)[2]	Jan. 3, 1955	March 9, 1960
Hall S. Lusk (D)[3]	March 16, 1960	Nov. 8, 1960
Maurine B. Neuberger (D)	Nov. 9, 1960	Jan. 2, 1967
Mark O. Hatfield (R)	Jan. 10, 1967	Jan. 2, 1997
Gordon H. Smith (R)	Jan. 3, 1997	

Class 3

Wayne L. Morse (R, I, D)[4]	Jan. 3, 1945	Jan. 2, 1969
Bob Packwood (R)[5]	Jan. 3, 1969	Oct. 1, 1995
Ron Wyden (D)	Feb. 6, 1996	

Oregon
1. *Appointed by governor to fill vacancy. Subsequently elected.*
2. *Died March 9, 1960.*
3. *Appointed by governor to fill vacancy.*
4. *Elected as a Republican in 1944 and 1950, as a Democrat in 1956 and 1962. Morse was also an Independent from Oct. 24, 1952, to Feb. 17, 1955.*
5. *Resigned Oct. 1, 1995.*

PENNSYLVANIA

(Ratified the Constitution Dec. 12, 1787)

Class 1

Senators	Dates of Service	
Edward Martin (R)	Jan. 3, 1947	Jan. 2, 1959
Hugh Scott (R)	Jan. 3, 1959	Jan. 2, 1977
John Heinz (R)[1]	Jan. 3, 1977	April 4, 1991
Harris Wofford (D)[2]	May 9, 1991	Jan. 2, 1995
Rick Santorum (R)	Jan. 3, 1995	

Class 3

Francis J. Myers (D)	Jan. 3, 1945	Jan. 2, 1951
James H. Duff (R)	Jan. 16, 1951	Jan. 2, 1957
Joseph S. Clark (D)	Jan. 3, 1957	Jan. 2, 1969
Richard S. Schweiker (R)	Jan. 3, 1969	Jan. 2, 1981
Arlen Specter (R)	Jan. 3, 1981	

Pennsylvania
1. *Died April 4, 1991.*
2. *Appointed by governor to fill vacancy. Subsequently elected.*

RHODE ISLAND

(Ratified the Constitution May 29, 1790)

Class 1

Senators	Dates of Service	
J. Howard McGrath (D)[1]	Jan. 3, 1947	Aug. 23, 1949
Edward L. Leahy (D)[2]	Aug. 24, 1949	Dec. 18, 1950
John O. Pastore (D)[3]	Dec. 19, 1950	Dec. 28, 1976
John H. Chafee (R)	Dec. 29, 1976	

Class 2

Theodore F. Green (D)	Jan. 3, 1937	Jan. 2, 1961
Claiborne Pell (D)	Jan. 3, 1961	Jan. 2, 1997
Jack Reed (D)	Jan. 3, 1997	

Rhode Island
1. *Resigned Aug. 23, 1949.*
2. *Appointed by governor to fill vacancy.*
3. *Resigned Dec. 28, 1976.*

SOUTH CAROLINA

(Ratified the Constitution May 23, 1788)

Class 2

Senators	Dates of Service	
Burnet R. Maybank (D)[1]	Nov. 5, 1941	Sept. 1, 1954
Charles E. Daniel (D)[2]	Sept. 6, 1954	Dec. 23, 1954
Strom Thurmond (D)[3]	Dec. 24, 1954	April 4, 1956
Thomas A. Wofford (D)[4]	April 5, 1956	Nov. 6, 1956
Strom Thurmond (D, R)[5]	Nov. 7, 1956	

Class 3

Olin D. Johnston (D)[6]	Jan. 3, 1945	April 18, 1965
Donald Russell (D)[7]	April 22, 1965	Nov. 8, 1966
Ernest F. Hollings (D)	Nov. 9, 1966	

South Carolina
1. *Died Sept. 1, 1954.*
2. *Appointed by governor to fill vacancy. Resigned Dec. 23, 1954.*
3. *Resigned April 4, 1956.*
4. *Appointed by governor to fill vacancy.*
5. *Became a Republican on Sept. 16, 1964.*
6. *Died April 18, 1965.*
7. *Appointed by governor to fill vacancy.*

SOUTH DAKOTA

(Became a state Nov. 2, 1889)

Class 2

Senators	Dates of Service	
Harlan J. Bushfield (R)[1]	Jan. 3, 1943	Sept. 27, 1948
Vera C. Bushfield (R)[2]	Oct. 6, 1948	Dec. 26, 1948
Karl E. Mundt (R)	Dec. 31, 1948	Jan. 2, 1973
James Abourezk (D)	Jan. 3, 1973	Jan. 2, 1979
Larry Pressler (R)	Jan. 3, 1979	Jan. 2, 1997
Tim Johnson (D)	Jan. 3, 1997	

Class 3

J. Chandler Gurney (R)	Jan. 3, 1939	Jan. 2, 1951
Francis Case (R)[3]	Jan. 3, 1951	June 22, 1962
Joe H. Bottum (R)[4]	July 9, 1962	Jan. 2, 1963

George McGovern (D)	Jan. 3, 1963	Jan. 2, 1981
James Abdnor (R)	Jan. 3, 1981	Jan. 2, 1987
Thomas A. Daschle (D)	Jan. 3, 1987	

South Dakota
1. Died Sept. 27, 1948.
2. Appointed by governor to fill vacancy. Resigned Dec. 26, 1948.
3. Died June 22, 1962.
4. Appointed by governor to fill vacancy.

TENNESSEE

(Became a state June 1, 1796)

Class 1

Senators	Dates of Service	
Kenneth D. McKellar (D)	March 4, 1917	Jan. 2, 1953
Albert Gore (D)	Jan. 3, 1953	Jan. 2, 1971
Bill Brock (R)	Jan. 3, 1971	Jan. 2, 1977
Jim Sasser (D)	Jan. 3, 1977	Jan. 2, 1995
Bill Frist (R)	Jan. 3, 1995	

Class 2

Tom Stewart (D)	Jan. 16, 1939	Jan. 2, 1949
Estes Kefauver (D)[1]	Jan. 3, 1949	Aug. 10, 1963
Herbert S. Walters (D)[2]	Aug. 20, 1963	Nov. 3, 1964
Ross Bass (D)	Nov. 4, 1964	Jan. 2, 1967
Howard H. Baker Jr. (R)	Jan. 3, 1967	Jan. 2, 1985
Albert Gore Jr. (D)[3]	Jan. 3, 1985	Jan. 1, 1993
Harlan Mathews (D)[4]	Jan. 2, 1993	Dec. 2, 1994
Fred Thompson (R)	Dec. 9, 1994	

Tennessee
1. Died Aug. 10, 1963.
2. Appointed by governor to fill vacancy.
3. Resigned Jan. 1, 1993, having been elected vice president of the United States.
4. Appointed by governor to fill vacancy.

TEXAS

(Became a state Dec. 29, 1845)

Class 1

Senators	Dates of Service	
Tom Connally (D)	March 4, 1929	Jan. 2, 1953
Price Daniel (D)[1]	Jan. 3, 1953	Jan. 14, 1957
William A. Blakley (D)[2]	Jan. 15, 1957	April 28, 1957
Ralph Yarborough (D)	April 29, 1957	Jan. 2, 1971
Lloyd Bentsen (D)[3]	Jan. 3, 1971	Jan. 20, 1993
Bob Krueger (D)[4]	Jan. 21, 1993	June 14, 1993
Kay Bailey Hutchison (R)	June 14, 1993	

Class 2

W. Lee O'Daniel (D)	Aug. 4, 1941	Jan. 2, 1949
Lyndon B. Johnson (D)[5]	Jan. 3, 1949	Jan. 3, 1961
William A. Blakley (D)[6]	Jan. 3, 1961	June 14, 1961
John Tower (R)	June 15, 1961	Jan. 2, 1985
Phil Gramm (R)	Jan. 3, 1985	

Texas
1. Resigned Jan. 14, 1957.
2. Appointed by governor to fill vacancy.
3. Resigned Jan. 20, 1993, having been appointed secretary of the treasury.
4. Appointed by governor to fill vacancy.

5. Resigned Jan. 3, 1961, having been elected vice president of the United States.
6. Appointed by governor to fill vacancy.

UTAH

(Became a state Jan. 4, 1896)

Class 1

Senators	Dates of Service	
Arthur V. Watkins (R)	Jan. 3, 1947	Jan. 2, 1959
Frank E. Moss (D)	Jan. 3, 1959	Jan. 2, 1977
Orrin G. Hatch (R)	Jan. 3, 1977	

Class 3

Elbert D. Thomas (D)	March 4, 1933	Jan. 2, 1951
Wallace F. Bennett (R)[1]	Jan. 3, 1951	Dec. 20, 1974
Jake Garn (R)	Dec. 21, 1974	Jan. 2, 1993
Robert F. Bennett (R)	Jan. 3, 1993	

Utah
1. Resigned Dec. 20, 1974.

VERMONT

(Became a state March 4, 1791)

Class 1

Senators	Dates of Service	
Ralph E. Flanders (R)[1]	Nov. 1, 1946	Jan. 2, 1959
Winston L. Prouty (R)[2]	Jan. 3, 1959	Sept. 10, 1971
Robert T. Stafford (R)[3]	Sept. 16, 1971	Jan 2, 1989
James M. Jeffords (R)	Jan. 3, 1989	

Class 3

George D. Aiken (R)	Jan. 10, 1941	Jan. 2, 1975
Patrick J. Leahy (D)	Jan. 3, 1975	

Vermont
1. Appointed by governor to fill vacancy. Subsequently elected.
2. Died Sept. 10, 1971.
3. Appointed by governor to fill vacancy. Subsequently elected.

VIRGINIA

(Ratified the Constitution June 25, 1788)

Class 1

Senators	Dates of Service	
Harry Flood Byrd (D)[1]	March 4, 1933	Nov. 10, 1965
Harry F. Byrd Jr. (D, I)[2]	Nov. 12, 1965	Jan. 2, 1983
Paul S. Trible Jr. (R)	Jan. 3, 1983	Jan. 2, 1989
Charles S. Robb (D)	Jan. 3, 1989	

Class 2

A. Willis Robertson (D)[3]	Nov. 6, 1946	Dec. 30, 1966
William B. Spong Jr. (D)	Dec. 31, 1966	Jan. 2, 1973
William Lloyd Scott (R)[4]	Jan. 3, 1973	Jan. 1, 1979
John W. Warner (R)	Jan. 2, 1979	

Virginia
1. Appointed by governor to fill vacancy. Subsequently elected. Resigned Nov. 10, 1965.

2. Appointed by governor to fill vacancy. Subsequently elected as a Democrat in 1966, as an Independent in 1970.
3. Resigned Dec. 30, 1966.
4. Resigned Jan. 1, 1979.

WASHINGTON

(Became a state Nov. 11, 1889)

Class 1

Senators	Dates of Service	
Harry P. Cain (R)	Dec. 26, 1946	Jan. 2, 1953
Henry M. Jackson (D)[1]	Jan. 3, 1953	Sept. 1, 1983
Daniel J. Evans (R)[2]	Sept. 12, 1983	Jan. 2, 1989
Slade Gorton (R)	Jan. 3, 1989	

Class 3

Warren G. Magnuson (D)	Dec. 14, 1944	Jan. 2, 1981
Slade Gorton (R)	Jan. 3, 1981	Jan. 2, 1987
Brock Adams (D)	Jan. 3, 1987	Jan. 2, 1993
Patty Murray (D)	Jan. 3, 1993	

Washington
1. Died Sept. 1, 1983.
2. Appointed by governor to fill vacancy. Subsequently elected.

WEST VIRGINIA

(Became a state June 19, 1863)

Class 1

Senators	Dates of Service	
Harley M. Kilgore (D)[1]	Jan. 3, 1941	Feb. 28, 1956
William R. Laird III (D)[2]	March 13, 1956	Nov. 6, 1956
Chapman Revercomb (R)	Nov. 7, 1956	Jan. 2, 1959
Robert C. Byrd (D)	Jan. 3, 1959	

Class 2

Chapman Revercomb (R)	Jan. 3, 1943	Jan. 2, 1949
Matthew M. Neely (D)[3]	Jan. 3, 1949	Jan. 18, 1958
John D. Hoblitzell Jr. (R)[4]	Jan. 25, 1958	Nov. 4, 1958
Jennings Randolph (D)	Nov. 5, 1958	Jan. 2, 1985
John D. Rockefeller (D)	Jan. 15, 1985	

West Virginia
1. Died Feb. 28, 1956.
2. Appointed by governor to fill vacancy.
3. Died Jan. 18, 1958.
4. Appointed by governor to fill vacancy.

WISCONSIN

(Became a state May 29, 1848)

Class 1

Senators	Dates of Service	
Joseph R. McCarthy (R)[1]	Jan. 3, 1947	May 2, 1957
William Proxmire (D)	Aug. 28, 1957	Jan. 2, 1989
Herbert H. Kohl (D)	Jan. 3, 1989	

Class 3

Alexander Wiley (R)	Jan. 3, 1939	Jan. 2, 1963
Gaylord Nelson (D)	Jan. 3, 1963	Jan. 2, 1981
Bob Kasten (R)	Jan. 3, 1981	Jan. 2, 1993
Russell D. Feingold (D)	Jan. 3, 1993	

Wisconsin
1. Died May 2, 1957.

WYOMING

(Became a state July 10, 1890)

Class 1

Senators	Dates of Service	
Joseph C. O'Mahoney (D)[1]	Jan. 1, 1934	Jan. 2, 1953
Frank A. Barrett (R)	Jan. 3, 1953	Jan. 2, 1959
Gale W. McGee (D)	Jan. 3, 1959	Jan. 2, 1977
Malcolm Wallop (R)	Jan. 3, 1977	Jan. 2, 1995
Craig Thomas (R)	Jan. 3, 1995	

Class 2

E. V. Robertson (R)	Jan. 3, 1943	Jan. 2, 1949
Lester C. Hunt (D)[2]	Jan. 3, 1949	June 19, 1954
Edward D. Crippa (R)[3]	June 24, 1954	Nov. 28, 1954
Joseph C. O'Mahoney (D)	Nov. 29, 1954	Jan. 2, 1961
John Joseph Hickey (D)[4]	Jan. 3, 1961	Nov. 6, 1962
Milward L. Simpson (R)	Nov. 7, 1962	Jan. 2, 1967
Clifford P. Hansen (R)[5]	Jan. 3, 1967	Dec. 31, 1978
Alan K. Simpson (R)	Jan. 1, 1979	Jan. 2, 1997
Michael B. Enzi (R)	Jan. 3, 1997	

Wyoming
1. Appointed by governor to fill vacancy. Subsequently elected.
2. Died June 19, 1954.
3. Appointed by governor to fill vacancy.
4. Keith Thomson (R), who had been elected Nov. 8, 1960, to a full six-year term beginning Jan. 3, 1961, died Dec. 9, 1960. Hickey, the incumbent governor, resigned and was appointed by his successor to fill the vacancy.
5. Resigned Dec. 31, 1978.

Senate Popular Vote Returns, 1946-1996

Sources for Senate Popular Returns

The Senate popular election returns presented in this section *(pp. 81-100)* for the years 1946 through 1973 were obtained from the Inter-University Consortium for Political and Social Research (ICPSR) at the University of Michigan. For Senate elections from 1974 to 1996, returns were obtained from Richard M. Scammon and Alice V. McGillivray, *America Votes*, vols. 11-21 (Washington, D.C.: Congressional Quarterly, 1975-1995) and Rhodes Cook and Alice V. McGillivray *America Votes*, vol. 22 (Washington, D.C.: Congressional Quarterly, 1997). Returns for the 1975 special election in New Hampshire were obtained form the New Hampshire secretary of state.

The symbol # next to returns before 1974 indicates that Congressional Quarterly obtained the returns from a source other than the ICPSR. The most frequently used alternative source was *Statistics of the Congressional Elections of ___*, published by the Clerk of the House of Representatives for every general election year since 1920. The following are the alternative sources used in this section. For the 1950 special election in Kentucky: *Statistics of the Congressional Election of Nov. 7, 1950.* For the 1952 election in Maine: *Statistics of the Congressional and Presidential Election of Nov. 4, 1952.* For the 1946 election in Maryland: *Statistics of the Congressional Election of Nov. 5, 1946.* For the 1948 special election in North Carolina: *Statistics of the Congressional and Presidential Election of Nov. 2, 1948.* For the 1961 special primary in Texas: Richard M. Scammon (ed.), *America Votes 5*, (Pittsburgh: Univeristy of Pittsburgh, 1964), p. 401. For the 1972 special election in Vermont: Richard M. Scammon (ed.), *America Votes 10*, (Washington: Congressional Quarterly, 1973), p. 372.

While the complete source annotations for the ICPSR collection are too extensive to publish here, information on the sources for specific election returns can be obtained through the ICPSR.

Presentation of Returns

The Senate returns are arranged alphabetically by state and in chronological order by class of senator within each state listing. *(For an explanation of Senate classes, see p. 61.)* The candidates receiving the greatest number of popular votes is listed first with his or her vote total and percentage of the total vote cast, followed in descending order of votes received by all other candidates who received *at least 5 percent* of the total vote cast.

Special elections to fill vacancies are designated in the returns. *(For an explanation of special elections, see p. 60)*

When a state *simultaneously* held a special election to fill the remaining few months of an unexpired term and a general election for the next full six-year term, the special election is listed *before* the general election. For example, see page 82 where the 1946 California general and special election returns appear.

Vote Totals and Percentages

The ICPSR collection includes all candidates receiving popular votes. In the *Congressional Elections 1946-1996*, only Senate candidates receiving *at least 5 percent of the total vote* for that election are included. For example, the ICPSR data collection for the 1964 New York senatorial election, 7,151,686 votes were cast, with Robert F. Kennedy receiving 3,823,749 votes (53.47 percent), Kenneth B. Keating receiving 3,104,056 votes (43.40 percent) and other candidates receiving the remaining 223,881 votes (3.13 percent).

The returns for the 1964 New York Senate election appear on page 93. Returns for the other minor candidates not listed because they received less than 5 percent of the total vote. The percentage listed for Kennedy is 53.5 and for Keating is 43.4. The procedure used throughout this section was to calculate percentages to two decimal places on the basis of the total number of votes cast in the election and round each percentage to one decimal place. Due to rounding and scattered votes for other candidates, percentages do not add to 100 percent.

Party Designations

In the ICPSR returns, the distinct—and in many cases, *multiple*—party designations appearing in the original sources are preserved. In many cases party labels represent combinations of multi-party support received by individual candidates. If, for example, on the ballot and official returns more than one party name was listed next to a candidate's name, then the party designation appearing in the election returns for that candidate will be a unique abbreviation for that combination of parties. *(For a list of party abbreviations, see p. 100.)*

In the special case of a candidate's name listed separately on the original ballot under more than one party—where returns were reported *separately* for each party—Congressional Quarterly has summed the votes recorded under the several parties and that figure appears as the candidate's total vote. Whenever separate party totals have been summed, a *comma* separates the abbreviations of the parties contributing the largest and second largest share of the total vote.

Most cases of this special situation occurred in New York and Pennsylvania during this century. For example, in the 1964 New York election cited above, Kennedy's total vote of 3,823,749 was comprised of votes received as the Democratic Party nominee and as the Liberal Party nominee.

Congressional Quarterly has also included party abbreviations for the two parties that contributed the most votes to Kennedy's total—separated by a comma. Thus, immediately following his name appear the abbreviations—D, L—indicating that Kennedy was a candidate of two parties and that the greatest number of votes he received was as a Democrat.

Senate Popular Vote Returns, 1946-1996

ALABAMA

Candidates	Votes	%

Class 2

Special Election

1946	John Sparkman (D)	163,217	100.0

1948	John Sparkman (D)	185,534	84.0
	Paul G. Parsons (R)	35,341	16.0
1954	John Sparkman (D)	259,348	82.5
	J. Foy Guin Jr. (R)	55,110	17.5
1960	John Sparkman (D)	389,196	70.2
	Julian Elgin (R)	164,868	29.8
1966	John Sparkman (D)	482,138	60.1
	John Grenier (R)	313,018	39.0
1972	John Sparkman (D)	654,491	62.3
	Winton M. Blount (R)	347,523	33.1
1978	Howell Heflin (D)	547,054	94.0
	Jerome B. Couch (P)	34,951	6.0
1984	Howell Heflin (D)	860,535	62.8
	Albert Lee Smith Jr. (R)	498,508	36.3
1990	Howell Heflin (D)	717,814	60.6
	Bill Cabaniss (R)	467,190	39.4
1996	Jeff Sessions (R)	786,436	52.5
	Roger Bedford (D)	681,651	45.6

Class 3

1950	Lister Hill (D)	125,534	76.5
	John G. Crommelin Jr. (I)	38,477	23.5
1956	Lister Hill (D)	330,182	100.0
1962	Lister Hill (D)	201,937	50.9
	James D. Martin (R)	195,134	49.1
1968	Jim Allen (D)	638,774	70.0
	Perry Hooper (R)	201,227	22.1
	Robert Schwenn (NDPA)	72,699	8.0
1974	Jim Allen (D)	501,541	95.8

Special Election

1978	Donald W. Stewart (D)	401,852	54.9
	James D. Martin (R)	316,170	43.2

1980	Jeremiah Denton (R)	650,362	50.2
	James E. Folsom Jr. (D)	610,175	47.1
1986	Richard C. Shelby (D)	609,360	50.3
	Jeremiah Denton (R)	602,537	49.7
1992	Richard C. Shelby (D)	1,022,698	64.9
	Richard Sellers (R)	522,015	33.1

ALASKA

Candidates	Votes	%

Class 2

1958	E. L. Bartlett (D)	40,939	83.8
	R. E. Robertson (R)	7,299	15.0
1960	E. L. Bartlett (D)	38,041	63.4
	Lee L. McKinley (R)	21,937	36.6
1966	E. L. Bartlett (D)	49,289	75.5
	Lee L. McKinley (R)	15,961	24.5

Special Election

1970	Ted Stevens (R)	47,908	59.6
	Wendell P. Kay (D)	32,456	40.4

1972	Ted Stevens (R)	74,216	77.3
	Gene Guess (D)	21,791	22.7
1978	Ted Stevens (R)	92,783	75.6
	Donald W. Hobbs (D)	29,574	24.1
1984	Ted Stevens (R)	146,919	71.2
	John E. Havelock (D)	58,804	28.5
1990	Ted Stevens (R)	125,806	66.2
	Michael Beasley (D)	61,152	32.2
1996	Ted Stevens (R)	177,893	76.7
	Jed Whittaker (GREEN)	29,037	12.5
	Theresa Nangle Obermeyer (D)	23,977	10.3

Explanation of Symbols

In the returns for Senate elections *symbols* are used to denote special circumstances. In cases where no symbol is used, the candidate who received the most votes won the election to the Senate.

The following is a key to the symbols used:

✔ Elected to the Senate, but the number of votes and the percentage of the total vote received by the winner are not available.

* The symbol is used in two kinds of situations: (1) When the winner of the election died before the term of office was to begin; (2) When the apparent winner was not permitted to take office. *(For an explanation of specific cases, consult the appropriate state in the list of senators, pp. 69-78).*

Information was obtained from a source other than the Inter-University Consortium for Political and Social Research. *(For a listing of other sources, see p. 80)*

Class 3

1958	Ernest Gruening (D)	26,063	52.6
	Mike Stepovich (R)	23,462	47.4
1962	Ernest Gruening (D)	33,827	58.1
	Ted Stevens (R)	24,354	41.9
1968	Mike Gravel (D)	36,527	45.1
	Elmer Rasmuson (R)	30,286	37.4
	Ernest Gruening (I)	14,118	17.4
1974	Mike Gravel (D)	54,361	58.3
	C. R. Lewis (R)	38,914	41.7
1980	Frank H. Murkowski (R)	84,159	53.7
	Clark S. Gruening (D)	72,007	45.9
1986	Frank H. Murkowski (R)	97,674	54.0
	Glenn Olds (D)	79,727	44.1
1992	Frank H. Murkowski (R)	127,163	53.0
	Tony Smith (D)	92,065	38.4
	Mary E. Jordan (GREEN)	20,019	8.4

ARIZONA

	Candidates	Votes	%

Class 1

1946	Ernest W. McFarland (D)	80,415	69.2
	Ward S. Powers (R)	35,022	30.1
1952	Barry Goldwater (R)	132,063	51.3
	Ernest W. McFarland (D)	125,338	48.7
1958	Barry Goldwater (R)	164,593	56.1
	Ernest W. McFarland (D)	129,030	43.9
1964	Paul Fannin (R)	241,084	51.4
	Roy Elson (D)	227,704	48.6
1970	Paul Fannin (R)	228,284	56.0
	Sam Grossman (D)	179,512	44.0
1976	Dennis DeConcini (D)	400,334	54.0
	Sam Steiger (R)	321,236	43.3
1982	Dennis DeConcini (D)	411,970	56.9
	Pete Dunn (R)	291,749	40.3
1988	Dennis DeConcini (D)	660,403	56.7
	Keith DeGreen (R)	478,060	41.1
1994	Jon Kyl (R)	600,999	53.7
	Sam Coppersmith (D)	442,510	39.5
	Scott Grainger (LIBERT)	75,493	6.7

Class 3

1950	Carl Hayden (D)	116,246	62.8
	Bruce Brockett (R)	68,846	37.2
1956	Carl Hayden (D)	170,816	61.4
	Ross F. Jones (R)	107,447	38.6
1962	Carl Hayden (D)	199,217	54.9
	Evan Mecham (R)	163,388	45.1
1968	Barry Goldwater (R)	274,607	57.2
	Roy Elson (D)	205,338	42.8
1974	Barry Goldwater (R)	320,396	58.3
	Jonathan Marshall (D)	229,523	41.7
1980	Barry M. Goldwater (R)	432,371	49.5
	Bill Schulz (D)	422,972	48.4
1986	John McCain (R)	521,850	60.5
	Richard Kimball (D)	340,965	39.5
1992	John McCain (R)	771,395	55.8
	Claire Sargent (D)	436,321	31.6
	Evan Mecham (I)	145,361	10.5

ARKANSAS

	Candidates	Votes	%

Class 2

1948	John L. McClellan (D)	216,401	93.3
	R. Walter Tucker (I)	15,521	6.7
1954	John L. McClellan (D)	291,058	100.0
1960	John L. McClellan (D)	✔	
1966	John L. McClellan (D)	✔	
1972	John L. McClellan (D)	386,398	60.8
	Wayne H. Babbitt (R)	248,238	39.1
1978	David H. Pryor (D)	399,916	76.6
	Tom Kelly (R)	84,722	16.2
	John G. Black (I)	37,488	7.2
1984	David Pryor (D)	502,341	57.3
	Ed Bethune (R)	373,615	42.7
1990	David Pryor (D)	493,910	99.8
1996	Tim Hutchinson (R)	445,942	52.7
	Winston Bryant (D)	400,241	47.3

Class 3

1950	J. William Fulbright (D)	302,582	100.0
1956	J. William Fulbright (D)	331,679	83.0
	Ben C. Henley (R)	68,016	17.0
1962	J. William Fulbright (D)	214,867	68.7
	Kenneth Jones (R)	98,013	31.3
1968	J. William Fulbright (D)	349,965	59.2
	Charles Bernard (R)	241,739	40.9
1974	Dale Bumpers (D)	461,056	84.9
	John Harris Jones (R)	82,026	15.1
1980	Dale Bumpers (D)	477,905	59.1
	Bill Clark (R)	330,576	40.9
1986	Dale Bumpers (D)	433,092	62.3
	Asa Hutchinson (R)	262,300	37.7
1992	Dale Bumpers (D)	553,635	60.2
	Mike Huckabee (R)	366,373	39.8

CALIFORNIA

	Candidates	Votes	%

Class 1

Special Election

1946	William F. Knowland (R)	425,273	74.3
	Will Rogers Jr. (D)	90,723	15.9

1946	William F. Knowland (R)	1,428,067	54.1
	Will Rogers Jr. (D)	1,167,161	44.2
1952	William F. Knowland (R-D)	3,982,448	87.7
	Reuben W. Borough (I PROG)	542,270	11.9
1958	Clair Engle (D)	2,927,693	57.0
	Goodwin J. Knight (R)	2,204,337	42.9
1964	George Murphy (R)	3,628,555	51.5
	Pierre Salinger (D)	3,411,912	48.5
1970	John V. Tunney (D)	3,496,558	53.9
	George Murphy (R)	2,877,617	44.3
1976	S. I. Hayakawa (R)	3,748,973	50.2
	John V. Tunney (D)	3,502,862	46.9
1982	Pete Wilson (R)	4,022,565	51.5
	Edmund G. Brown Jr. (D)	3,494,968	44.8
1988	Pete Wilson (R)	5,143,409	52.8
	Leo T. McCarthy (D)	4,287,253	44.0

Special Election

1992	Dianne Feinstein (D)	5,853,651	*54.3*
	John Seymour (R)	4,093,501	*38.0*

1994	Diane Feinstein (D)	3,977,063	*46.8*
	Michael Huffington (R)	3,811,501	*44.8*

Class 3

1950	Richard M. Nixon (R)	2,183,454	*59.2*
	Helen Gahagan Douglas (D)	1,502,507	*40.8*

Special Election

1954	Thomas H. Kuchel (R)	2,090,836	*53.2*
	Samuel William Yorty (D)	1,788,071	*45.5*

1956	Thomas H. Kuchel (R)	2,892,918	*54.0*
	Richard Richards (D)	2,445,816	*45.6*
1962	Thomas H. Kuchel (R)	3,180,483	*56.3*
	Richard Richards (D)	2,452,839	*43.4*
1968	Alan Cranston (D)	3,680,352	*51.8*
	Max Rafferty (R)	3,329,148	*46.9*
1974	Alan Cranston (D)	3,693,160	*60.5*
	H. L. "Bill" Richardson (R)	2,210,267	*36.2*
1980	Alan Cranston (D)	4,705,399	*56.5*
	Paul Gann (R)	3,093,426	*37.1*
1986	Alan Cranston (D)	3,646,672	*49.3*
	Ed Zschau (R)	3,541,804	*47.9*
1992	Barbara Boxer (D)	5,173,467	*47.9*
	Bruce Herschensohn (R)	4,644,182	*43.0*

COLORADO

Candidates	Votes	%

Class 2

1948	Edwin C. Johnson (D)	340,719	*66.8*
	Will F. Nicholson (R)	165,069	*32.4*
1954	Gordon Allott (R)	248,502	*51.3*
	John A. Carroll (D)	235,686	*48.7*
1960	Gordon Allott (R)	389,428	*53.5*
	Robert L. Knous (D)	334,854	*46.0*
1966	Gordon Allott (R)	368,307	*58.0*
	Roy Romer (D)	266,198	*41.9*
1972	Floyd K. Haskell (D)	457,545	*49.4*
	Gordon Allott (R)	447,957	*48.4*
1978	William L. Armstrong (R)	480,596	*58.7*
	Floyd K. Haskell (D)	330,247	*40.3*
1984	Nancy Dick (D)	449,327	*34.6*
	William L. Armstrong (R)	833,821	*64.2*
1990	Hank Brown (R)	569,048	*55.7*
	Josie Heath (D)	425,746	*41.7*
1996	Wayne Allard (R)	750,325	*51.1*
	Tom Strickland (D)	677,600	*46.1*

Class 3

1950	Eugene D. Millikin (R)	239,734	*53.3*
	John A. Carroll (D)	210,442	*46.8*
1956	John A. Carroll (D)	319,872	*50.2*
	Dan Thornton (R)	317,102	*49.8*
1962	Peter H. Dominick (R)	328,655	*53.6*
	John A. Carroll (D)	279,586	*45.6*
1968	Peter H. Dominick (R)	459,952	*58.6*
	Stephen L. R. McNichols (D)	325,584	*41.5*
1974	Gary Hart (D)	471,691	*57.2*
	Peter H. Dominick (R)	325,508	*39.5*
1980	Gary Hart (D)	590,501	*50.3*

	Mary E. Buchanan (R)	571,295	*48.7*
1986	Timothy E. Wirth (D)	529,449	*49.9*
	Ken Kramer (R)	512,994	*48.4*
1992	Ben Nighthorse Campbell (D)	803,725	*51.8*
	Terry Considine (R)	662,893	*42.7*

CONNECTICUT

Candidates	Votes	%

Class 1

Special Election

1946	Raymond E. Baldwin (R)	378,707	*55.8*
	Wilbur L. Cross (D)	278,188	*41.0*

1946	Raymond E. Baldwin (R)	381,328	*56.1*
	Joseph M. Tone (D)	276,424	*40.7*

Special Election

1950	William Benton (D)	431,413	*49.2*
	Prescott S. Bush (R)	430,311	*49.1*

1952	William A. Purtell (R)	573,854	*52.5*
	William Benton (D)	485,066	*44.4*
1958	Thomas J. Dodd (D)	554,841	*57.5*
	William A. Purtell (R)	410,622	*42.5*
1964	Thomas J. Dodd (D)	781,008	*64.6*
	John Lodge (R)	426,939	*35.3*
1970	Lowell P. Weicker Jr. (R)	454,721	*41.7*
	Joseph D. Duffey (D)	368,111	*33.8*
	Thomas J. Dodd (DODD I)	266,497	*24.5*
1976	Lowell P. Weicker Jr. (R)	785,683	*57.7*
	Gloria Schaffer (D)	561,018	*41.2*
1982	Lowell P. Weicker Jr. (R)	545,987	*50.4*
	Anthony T. Moffett (D)	499,146	*46.1*
1988	Joseph I. Lieberman (D)	688,499	*49.8*
	Lowell P. Weicker Jr. (R)	678,454	*49.0*
1994	Joseph I. Lieberman (D, ACP)	723,842	*67.0*
	Jerry Labriola (R)	334,833	*31.0*

Class 3

1950	Brien McMahon (D)	453,646	*51.7*
	Joseph E. Talbot (R)	409,053	*46.6*

Special Election

1952	Prescott S. Bush (R)	559,465	*51.2*
	Abraham A. Ribicoff (D)	530,505	*48.5*

1956	Prescott S. Bush (R)	610,829	*54.8*
	Thomas J. Dodd (D)	479,460	*43.1*
1962	Abraham A. Ribicoff (D)	527,522	*51.3*
	Horace Seely-Brown (R)	501,694	*48.8*
1968	Abraham A. Ribicoff (D)	655,043	*54.3*
	Edwin H. May (R)	551,455	*45.7*
1974	Abraham A. Ribicoff (D)	690,820	*63.7*
	James H. Brannen III (R)	372,055	*34.3*
1980	Christopher J. Dodd (D)	763,969	*56.3*
	James L. Buckley (R)	581,884	*42.9*
1986	Christopher J. Dodd (D)	632,695	*64.8*
	Roger W. Eddy (R)	340,438	*34.8*
1992	Christopher J. Dodd (D, ACP)	882,569	*58.8*
	Brook Johnson (R)	572,036	*38.1*

DELAWARE

Candidates	Votes	%

Class 1

	Candidates	Votes	%
1946	John J. Williams (R)	62,603	55.2
	James M. Tunnell (D)	50,910	44.9
1952	John J. Williams (R)	93,020	54.5
	A. I. du Pont Bayard (D)	77,685	45.5
1958	John J. Williams (R)	82,280	53.3
	Elbert N. Carvel (D)	72,152	46.7
1964	John J. Williams (R)	103,782	51.7
	Elbert N. Carvel (D)	96,850	48.3
1970	William V. Roth Jr. (R)	94,979	58.8
	Jacob Zimmerman (D)	64,740	40.1
1976	William V. Roth Jr. (R)	125,502	55.8
	Thomas C. Maloney (D)	98,055	43.6
1982	William V. Roth Jr. (R)	105,357	55.2
	David N. Levinson (D)	84,413	44.2
1988	William V. Roth Jr. (R)	151,115	62.1
	S. B. Woo (D)	92,378	37.9
1994	William V. Roth Jr. (R)	111,088	55.8
	Charles M. Oberly (D)	84,554	42.5

Class 2

	Candidates	Votes	%
1948	J. Allen Frear Jr. (D)	71,888	50.9
	Clayton Douglass Buck (R)	68,246	48.3
1954	J. Allen Frear Jr. (D)	82,511	56.9
	Herbert B. Warburton (R)	62,389	43.1
1960	J. Caleb Boggs (R)	98,874	50.7
	J. Allen Frear Jr. (D)	96,090	49.3
1966	J. Caleb Boggs (R)	97,268	59.1
	James M. Tunnell Jr. (D)	67,263	40.9
1972	Joseph R. Biden Jr. (D)	116,006	50.5
	J. Caleb Boggs (R)	112,844	49.1
1978	Joseph R. Biden Jr. (D)	93,930	58.0
	James H. Baxter (R)	66,479	41.0
1984	Joseph R. Biden Jr. (D)	147,831	60.1
	John M. Burris (R)	98,101	39.1
1990	Joseph R. Biden Jr. (D)	112,918	62.7
	M. Jane Brady (R)	64,554	35.8
1996	Joseph R. Biden Jr. (D)	165,465	60.0
	Raymond J. Clatworthy (R)	105,088	38.1

FLORIDA

Candidates	Votes	%

Class 1

	Candidates	Votes	%
1946	Spessard L. Holland (D)	156,232	78.7
	J. Harry Schad (R)	42,413	21.4
1952	Spessard L. Holland (D)	616,665	99.8
1958	Spessard L. Holland (D)	386,113	71.2
	Leland Hyzer (R)	155,956	28.8
1964	Spessard L. Holland (D)	997,585	63.9
	Claude R. Kirk Jr. (R)	562,212	36.0
1970	Lawton Chiles (D)	902,438	53.9
	William C. Cramer (R)	772,817	46.1
1976	Lawton Chiles (D)	1,799,518	63.0
	John Grady (R)	1,057,886	37.0
1982	Lawton Chiles (D)	1,637,667	61.7
	Van B. Poole (R)	1,015,330	38.3
1988	Connie Mack (R)	2,051,071	50.4
	Buddy MacKay (D)	2,016,553	49.6
1994	Connie Mack (R)	2,894,726	70.5
	Hugh E. Rodham (D)	1,210,412	29.5

Class 3

	Candidates	Votes	%
1950	George A. Smathers (D)	238,987	76.2
	John P. Booth (R)	74,228	23.7
1956	George A. Smathers (D)	655,418	100.0
1962	George A. Smathers (D)	657,633	70.0
	Emerson Rupert (R)	281,381	30.0
1968	Edward J. Gurney (R)	1,131,499	55.9
	Leroy Collins (D)	892,637	44.1
1974	Richard Stone (D)	781,031	43.4
	Jack Eckerd (R)	736,674	40.9
	John Grady (AM)	282,659	15.7
1980	Paula Hawkins (R)	1,822,460	51.7
	Bill Gunter (D)	1,705,409	48.3
1986	Bob Graham (D)	1,877,231	54.7
	Paula Hawkins (R)	1,551,888	45.3
1992	Bob Graham (D)	3,244,299	65.4
	Bill Grant (R)	1,715,156	34.6

GEORGIA

Candidates	Votes	%

Class 2

	Candidates	Votes	%
1948	Richard B. Russell (D)	362,104	99.9
1954	Richard B. Russell (D)	333,917	100.0
1960	Richard B. Russell (D)	576,140	99.9
1966	Richard B. Russell (D)	631,002	100.0

Special Election

1972	Sam Nunn (D)	404,890	52.0
	Fletcher Thompson (R)	362,501	46.5

1972	Sam Nunn (D)	635,970	54.0
	Fletcher Thompson (R)	542,331	46.0
1978	Sam Nunn (D)	536,320	83.1
	John W. Stokes (R)	108,808	16.9
1984	Sam Nunn (D)	1,344,104	79.9
	Jon Michael Hicks (R)	337,196	20.1
1990	Sam Nunn (D)	1,033,439	100.0
1996	Max Cleland (D)	1,103,993	48.9
	Guy Millner (R)	1,073,969	47.5

Class 3

1950	Walter F. George (D)	261,290	100.0
1956	Herman E. Talmadge (D)	541,094	100.0
1962	Herman E. Talmadge (D)	306,250	100.0
1968	Herman E. Talmadge (D)	885,103	77.5
	E. Earl Patton (R)	256,796	22.5
1974	Herman E. Talmadge (D)	627,376	71.7
	Jerry Johnson (R)	246,866	28.2
1980	Mack Mattingly (R)	803,686	50.9
	Herman E. Talmadge (D)	776,143	49.1
1986	Wyche Fowler Jr. (D)	623,707	50.9
	Mack Mattingly (R)	601,241	49.1
1992[1]	Wyche Fowler Jr. (D)	1,108,416	49.2
	Paul Coverdell (R)	1,073,282	47.7

Runoff Election[1]

1992	Paul Coverdell (R)	635,114	50.6
	Wyche Fowler Jr. (D)	618,877	49.4

Georgia

1. Georgia law requires election by a majority of the popular vote and provides for a runoff between the two top finishers when neither gained a majority in the regular election.

HAWAII

Candidates	Votes	%

Class 1

1959	Hiram L. Fong (R)	87,161	52.9
	Frank F. Fasi (D)	77,647	47.1
1964	Hiram L. Fong (R)	110,747	53.0
	Thomas P. Gill (D)	96,789	46.4
1970	Hiram L. Fong (R)	124,163	51.6
	Cecil Heftel (D)	116,597	48.4
1976	Spark M. Matsunaga (D)	162,305	53.7
	William F. Quinn (R)	122,724	40.6
1982	Spark M. Matsunaga (D)	245,386	80.1
	Clarence J. Brown (R)	52,071	17.0
1988	Spark M. Matsunaga (D)	247,941	76.5
	Maria M. Hustace (R)	66,987	20.7

Special Election

1990	Daniel K. Akaka (D)	188,901	54.0
	Patricia Saiki (R)	155,978	44.6
1994	Daniel K. Akaka (D)	256,189	71.8
	Maria M. Hustace (R)	86,320	24.2

Class 3

1959	Oren E. Long (D)	83,700	51.1
	Wilfred C. Tsukiyama (R)	79,123	48.3
1962	Daniel K. Inouye (D)	136,294	69.4
	Ben Dillingham (R)	60,067	30.6
1968	Daniel K. Inouye (D)	189,248	83.4
	Wayne C. Thiessen (R)	34,008	15.0
1974	Daniel K. Inouye (D)	207,454	82.9
	James D. Kimmel (PP)	42,767	17.1
1980	Daniel K. Inouye (D)	224,485	77.9
	Cooper Brown (R)	53,068	18.4
1986	Daniel K. Inouye (D)	241,887	73.6
	Frank Hutchinson (R)	86,910	26.4
1992	Daniel K. Inouye (D)	208,266	57.3
	Rick Reed (R)	97,928	26.9
	Linda B. Martin (GREEN)	49,921	13.7

IDAHO

Candidates	Votes	%

Class 2

Special Election

1946	Henry C. Dworshak (R)	105,523	58.6
	George E. Donart (D)	74,629	41.4
1948	Bert C. Miller (D)	107,000	50.0
	Henry C. Dworshak (R)	103,868	48.5

Special Election

1950	Henry C. Dworshak (R)	104,608	51.9
	Claude J. Burtenshaw (D)	97,092	48.1
1954	Henry C. Dworshak (R)	142,269	62.8
	Glen H. Taylor (D)	84,139	37.2
1960	Henry C. Dworshak (R)	152,648	52.3
	R. F. "Bob" McLaughlin (D)	139,448	47.7

Special Election

1962	Len B. Jordan (R)	131,279	51.0
	Gracie Pfost (D)	126,398	49.1
1966	Len B. Jordan (R)	139,819	55.4
	Ralph R. Harding (D)	112,637	44.6
1972	James A. McClure (R)	161,804	52.3
	William E. "Bud" Davis (D)	140,913	45.5
1978	James A. McClure (R)	194,412	68.4
	Dwight Jensen (D)	89,635	31.6
1984	James A. McClure (R)	293,193	72.2
	Peter M. Busch (D)	105,591	26.0
1990	Larry E. Craig (R)	193,641	61.3
	Ron J. Twilegar (D)	122,295	38.7
1996	Larry E. Craig (R)	283,532	57.0
	Walt Minnick (D)	198,422	39.9

Class 3

1950	Herman Welker (R)	124,237	61.7
	D. Worth Clark (D)	77,180	38.3
1956	Frank Church (D)	149,096	56.2
	Herman Welker (R)	102,781	38.7
	Glen H. Taylor (WRITE IN)	13,415	5.1
1962	Frank Church (D)	141,657	54.7
	Jack Hawley (R)	117,129	45.3
1968	Frank Church (D)	173,482	60.3
	George V. Hansen (R)	114,394	39.7
1974	Frank Church (D)	145,140	56.1
	Robert L. Smith (R)	109,072	42.1
1980	Steven D. Symms (R)	218,701	49.7
	Frank Church (D)	214,439	48.8
1986	Steven D. Symms (R)	196,958	51.6
	John V. Evans (D)	185,066	48.4
1992	Dirk Kempthorne (R)	270,468	56.5
	Richard Stallings (D)	208,036	43.5

ILLINOIS

Candidates	Votes	%

Class 2

1948	Paul H. Douglas (D)	2,147,754	55.1
	C. Wayland Brooks (R)	1,740,026	44.6
1954	Paul H. Douglas (D)	1,804,338	53.6
	Joseph T. Meek (R)	1,563,683	46.4
1960	Paul H. Douglas (D)	2,530,943	54.6
	Samuel W. Witwer (R)	2,093,846	45.2
1966	Charles H. Percy (R)	2,100,449	55.0
	Paul H. Douglas (D)	1,678,147	43.9
1972	Charles H. Percy (R)	2,867,078	62.2
	Roman Pucinski (D)	1,721,031	37.4
1978	Charles H. Percy (R)	1,698,711	53.3
	Alex Seith (D)	1,448,187	45.5
1984	Paul Simon (D)	2,397,303	50.1
	Charles H. Percy (R)	2,308,039	48.2
1990	Paul Simon (D)	2,115,377	65.1
	Lynn Martin (R)	1,135,628	34.9
1996	Richard J. Durbin (D)	2,384,028	56.1
	Al Salvi (R)	1,728,824	40.7

Class 3

1950	Everett McKinley Dirksen (R)	1,951,984	53.9
	Scott W. Lucas (D)	1,657,630	45.8
1956	Everett McKinley Dirksen (R)	2,307,352	54.1
	Richard Stengel (D)	1,949,883	45.7
1962	Everett McKinley Dirksen (R)	1,961,202	52.9
	Sidney R. Yates (D)	1,748,007	47.1

1968	Everett McKinley Dirksen (R)	2,358,947	53.0
	William G. Clark (D)	2,073,242	46.6

Special Election

1970	Adlai E. Stevenson III (D)	2,065,054	57.4
	Ralph Tyler Smith (R)	1,519,718	42.2

1974	Adlai E. Stevenson III (D)	1,811,496	62.2
	George M. Burditt (R)	1,084,884	37.2
1980	Alan J. Dixon (D)	2,565,302	56.0
	David C. O'Neal (R)	1,946,296	42.5
1986	Alan J. Dixon (D)	2,033,926	65.1
	Judy Koehler (R)	1,053,793	33.7
1992	Carol Moseley-Braun (D)	2,631,229	53.3
	Richard S. Williamson (R)	2,126,833	43.1

INDIANA

Candidates	Votes	%

Class 1

1946	William E. Jenner (R)	739,809	54.9
	M. Clifford Townsend (D)	584,288	43.4
1952	William E. Jenner (R)	1,020,605	52.4
	Henry F. Schricker (D)	911,169	46.8
1958	R. Vance Hartke (D)	973,636	56.5
	Harold W. Handley (R)	731,635	42.4
1964	R. Vance Hartke (D)	1,128,505	54.3
	D. Russell Bontrager (R)	941,519	45.3
1970	R. Vance Hartke (D)	870,990	50.1
	Richard L. Roudebush (R)	866,707	49.9
1976	Richard G. Lugar (R)	1,275,833	58.8
	R. Vance Hartke (D)	878,522	40.5
1982	Richard G. Lugar (R)	978,301	53.8
	Floyd Fithian (D)	828,400	45.6
1988	Richard G. Lugar (R)	1,430,525	68.1
	Jack Wickes (D)	668,778	31.9
1994	Richard G. Lugar (R)	1,039,625	67.4
	Jim Jontz (D)	470,799	30.5

Class 3

1950	Homer E. Capehart (R)	844,303	52.8
	Alex M. Campbell (D)	741,025	46.4
1956	Homer E. Capehart (R)	1,084,262	55.2
	Claude R. Wickard (D)	871,781	44.4
1962	Birch Bayh (D)	905,491	50.3
	Homer E. Capehart (R)	894,547	49.7
1968	Birch Bayh (D)	1,060,456	51.7
	William D. Ruckelshaus (R)	988,571	48.2
1974	Birch Bayh (D)	889,269	50.7
	Richard G. Lugar (R)	814,117	46.4
1980	Dan Quayle (R)	1,182,414	53.8
	Birch Bayh (D)	1,015,962	46.2
1986	Dan Quayle (R)	936,143	60.6
	Jill Long (D)	595,192	38.5

Special Election

1990	Daniel R. Coats (R)	806,048	53.6
	Baron P. Hill (D)	696,639	46.4

1992	Daniel R. Coats (R)	1,267,972	57.3
	Joseph H. Hogsett (D)	900,148	40.7

IOWA

Candidates	Votes	%

Class 2

1948	Guy M. Gillette (D)	578,226	57.8
	George A. Wilson (R)	415,778	41.6
1954	Thomas E. Martin (R)	442,409	52.2
	Guy M. Gillette (D)	402,712	47.5
1960	Jack Miller (R)	642,463	51.9
	Herschel C. Loveless (D)	595,119	48.1
1966	Jack Miller (R)	522,339	60.9
	E. B. Smith (D)	324,114	37.8
1972	Dick Clark (D)	662,637	55.1
	Jack Miller (R)	530,525	44.1
1978	Roger W. Jepsen (R)	421,598	51.1
	Dick Clark (D)	395,066	47.9
1984	Tom Harkin (D)	716,883	55.5
	Roger W. Jepsen (R)	564,381	43.7
1990	Tom Harkin (D)	535,975	54.5
	Tom Tauke (R)	446,869	45.4
1996	Tom Harkin (D)	634,166	51.8
	Jim Ross Lightfoot (R)	571,807	46.7

Class 3

1950	Bourke B. Hickenlooper (R)	470,613	54.8
	Albert J. Loveland (D)	383,766	44.7
1956	Bourke B. Hickenlooper (R)	635,499	53.9
	R. M. Evans (D)	543,156	46.1
1962	Bourke B. Hickenlooper (R)	431,364	53.4
	E. B. Smith (D)	376,602	46.6
1968	Harold E. Hughes (D)	574,884	50.3
	David M. Stanley (R)	568,469	49.7
1974	John C. Culver (D)	462,947	52.0
	David M. Stanley (R)	420,546	47.3
1980	Charles E. Grassley (R)	683,014	53.5
	John C. Culver (D)	581,545	45.5
1986	Charles E. Grassley (R)	588,880	66.0
	John P. Roehrick (D)	299,406	33.6
1992	Charles E. Grassley (R)	899,761	69.6
	Jean Lloyd-Jones (D)	351,561	27.2

Iowa

1. Disputed election. See list of senators, Iowa, p. 000.

KANSAS

Candidates	Votes	%

Class 2

1948	Andrew F. Schoeppel (R)	393,412	54.9
	George McGill (D)	305,987	42.7
1954	Andrew F. Schoeppel (R)	348,144	56.3
	George McGill (D)	258,575	41.8
1960	Andrew F. Schoeppel (R)	485,499	54.6
	Frank Theis (D)	388,895	43.8

Special Election

1962	James B. Pearson (R)	344,689	56.2
	Paul L. Aylward (D)	260,756	42.5

1966	James B. Pearson (R)	350,077	52.2
	J. Floyd Breeding (D)	303,223	45.2
1972	James B. Pearson (R)	622,591	71.4
	Arch Tetzlaff (D)	200,764	23.0
1978	Nancy Landon Kassebaum (R)	403,354	53.9
	William R. Roy (D)	317,602	42.4

1984	Nancy Landon Kassebaum (R)	757,402	76.0
	James R. Maher (D)	211,664	21.2
1990	Nancy Landon Kassebaum (R)	578,605	73.6
	Dick Williams (D)	207,491	26.4
1996	Pat Roberts (R)	652,677	62.0
	Sally Thompson (D)	362,380	34.4

Class 3

Special Election

1950	Frank Carlson (R)	321,718	55.2
	Paul Aiken (D)	261,405	44.8

1950	Frank Carlson (R)	335,880	54.3
	Paul Aiken (D)	271,365	43.8
1956	Frank Carlson (R)	477,822	57.9
	George Hart (D)	333,939	40.5
1962	Frank Carlson (R)	388,500	62.4
	K. L. Smith (D)	223,630	35.9
1968	Robert Dole (R)	490,911	60.1
	William I. Robinson (D)	315,911	38.7
1974	Robert Dole (R)	403,983	50.9
	William R. Roy (D)	390,451	49.1
1980	Robert Dole (R)	598,686	63.8
	John Simpson (D)	340,271	36.2
1986	Robert Dole (R)	576,902	70.0
	Guy MacDonald (D)	246,664	30.0
1992	Robert Dole (R)	706,246	62.7
	Gloria O'Dell (D)	349,525	31.0

Special Election

1996	Sam Brownback (R)	574,021	53.9
	Jill Docking (D)	461,344	43.3

KENTUCKY

Candidates	Votes	%

Class 2

Special Election

1946	John Sherman Cooper (R)	327,652	53.3
	John Young Brown (D)	285,829	46.5

1948	Virgil Chapman (D)	408,256	51.4
	John Sherman Cooper (R)	383,776	48.3

Special Election

1952	John Sherman Cooper (R)	494,576	51.5
	Thomas R. Underwood (D)	465,652	48.5

1954	Alben W. Barkley (D)	434,109	54.5
	John Sherman Cooper (R)	362,948	45.5

Special Election

1956	John Sherman Cooper (R)	538,505	53.2
	Lawrence W. Wetherby (D)	473,140	46.8

1960	John Sherman Cooper (R)	644,087	59.2
	Keen Johnson (D)	444,290	40.8
1966	John Sherman Cooper (R)	483,805	64.5

	John Young Brown (D)	266,079	35.5
1972	Walter D. Huddleston (D)	528,550	50.9
	Louie B. Nunn (R)	494,337	47.6
1978	Walter D. Huddleston (D)	290,730	61.0
	Louie Guenthner (R)	175,766	36.9
1984	Mitch McConnell (R)	644,990	49.9
	Walter D. Huddleston (D)	639,721	49.5
1990	Mitch McConnell (R)	478,034	52.2
	Harvey Sloane (D)	437,976	47.8
1996	Mitch McConnell (R)	724,794	55.5
	Steven L. Beshear (D)	560,012	42.8

Class 3

Special Election

1950	Earle C. Clements (D)	317,320#	54.4
	Charles I. Dawson (R)	265,994#	45.6

1950	Earle C. Clements (D)	334,249	54.2
	Charles I. Dawson (R)	278,368	45.1
1956	Thruston B. Morton (R)	506,903	50.4
	Earle C. Clements (D)	499,922	49.7
1962	Thruston B. Morton (R)	432,648	52.8
	Wilson W. Wyatt (D)	387,440	47.2
1968	Marlow W. Cook (R)	484,260	51.4
	Katherine Peden (D)	448,960	47.6
1974	Wendell H. Ford (D)	399,406	53.5
	Marlow W. Cook (R)	328,982	44.1
1980	Wendell H. Ford (D)	720,861	65.1
	Mary Louise Foust (R)	386,029	34.9
1986	Wendell H. Ford (D)	503,775	74.4
	Jackson M. Andrews (R)	173,330	25.6
1992	Wendell H. Ford (D)	836,888	62.9
	David L. Williams (R)	476,604	35.8

LOUISIANA

Candidates	Votes	%

Class 2

1948	Allen J. Ellender (D)	330,315	100.0
1954	Allen J. Ellender (D)	207,115	100.0
1960	Allen J. Ellender (D)	432,228	79.8
	George W. Reese Jr. (R)	109,698	20.2
1966	Allen J. Ellender (D)	437,695	100.0
1972	J. Bennett Johnston (D)	598,987	55.2
	John J. McKeithen (I)	250,161	23.1
	Ben C. Toledano (R)	206,846	19.1
1978[1]	J. Bennett Johnston (D)	—	—
1984[1]	J. Bennett Johnston (D)	—	—
1990[1]	J. Bennett Johnston (D)	—	—
1996	Mary L. Landrieu (D)	852,945	50.2
	Louis "Woody" Jenkins (R)	847,157	49.8

Class 3

Special Election

1948	Russell B. Long (D)	305,346	74.9
	Clem S. Clarke (R)	102,339	25.1

1950	Russell B. Long (D)	220,907	87.7
	Charles S. Gerth (R)	30,931	12.3
1956	Russell B. Long (D)	335,564	100.0
1962	Russell B. Long (D)	318,838	75.6
	Taylor Walters O'Hearn (R)	103,066	24.4
1968	Russell B. Long (D)	518,586	100.0

1974	Russell B. Long (D)	434,643	100.0
1980[1]	Russell B. Long (D)	—	—
1986	John B. Breaux (D)	723,586	52.8
	W. Henson Moore (R)	646,311	47.2
1992[1]	John B. Breaux (D)	—	—

Louisiana

1. Dash (—) indicates candidate elected in primary. Since 1978, Louisiana has held an open-primary election with candidates from all parties running on the same ballot. Any candidate who receives a majority is elected; if no candidate receives 50 percent, there is a runoff election in November between the two top finishers.

MAINE

	Candidates	Votes	%

Class 1

1946	Ralph O. Brewster (R)	111,215	63.6
	Peter M. MacDonald (D)	63,799	36.5
1952	Frederick G. Payne (R)	139,205	58.7
	Roger P. Dube (D)	82,665	34.9
	Earl S. Grant (I)	15,294#	6.4
1958	Edmund S. Muskie (D)	172,842	60.8
	Frederick G. Payne (R)	111,522	39.2
1964	Edmund S. Muskie (D)	253,511	66.6
	Clifford G. McIntire (R)	127,040	33.4
1970	Edmund S. Muskie (D)	199,954	61.9
	Neil S. Bishop (R)	123,906	38.3
1976	Edmund S. Muskie (D)	292,704	60.2
	Robert A. G. Monks (R)	193,489	39.8
1982	George J. Mitchell (D)	279,819	60.9
	David F. Emery (R)	179,882	39.1
1988	George J. Mitchell (D)	452,590	81.2
	Jasper S. Wyman (R)	104,758	18.8
1994	Olympia J. Snowe (R)	308,244	60.3
	Thomas H. Andrews (D)	186,042	36.4

Class 2

1948	Margaret Chase Smith (R)	159,182	71.3
	Adrian H. Scolten (D)	64,074	28.7
1954	Margaret Chase Smith (R)	144,530	58.6
	Paul A. Fullam (D)	102,075	41.4
1960	Margaret Chase Smith (R)	256,890	61.7
	Lucia M. Cormier (D)	159,809	38.4
1966	Margaret Chase Smith (R)	188,291	59.0
	Elmer H. Violette (D)	131,136	41.1
1972	William D. Hathaway (D)	224,270	53.2
	Margaret Chase Smith (R)	197,040	46.8
1978	William S. Cohen (R)	212,294	56.6
	William D. Hathaway (D)	127,327	33.9
	Hayes E. Gahagan (I)	27,824	7.4
1984	William S. Cohen (R)	404,414	73.3
	Elizabeth H. Mitchell (D)	142,626	25.9
1990	William S. Cohen (R)	319,167	61.3
	Neil Rolde (D)	201,053	38.6
1996	Susan Collins (R)	298,422	49.2
	Joseph E. Brennan (D)	266,226	43.9

MARYLAND

	Candidates	Votes	%

Class 1

1946	Herbert R. O'Conor (D)	237,232#	50.2
	David John Markey (R)	235,000#	49.8
1952	J. Glenn Beall (R)	449,823	52.5

	George P. Mahoney (D)	406,370	47.5
1958	J. Glenn Beall (R)	382,021	51.0
	Thomas D'Alesandro Jr. (D)	367,270	49.0
1964	Joseph D. Tydings (D)	678,649	62.8
	J. Glenn Beall (R)	402,393	37.2
1970	J. Glenn Beall Jr. (R)	484,960	50.7
	Joseph D. Tydings (D)	460,442	48.1
1976	Paul S. Sarbanes (D)	772,101	56.5
	J. Glenn Beall Jr. (R)	530,439	38.8
1982	Paul S. Sarbanes (D)	707,356	63.5
	Lawrence J. Hogan (R)	407,334	36.5
1988	Paul S. Sarbanes (D)	999,166	61.8
	Alan L. Keyes (R)	617,537	38.2
1994	Paul S. Sarbanes (D)	809,125	59.1
	William Brock (R)	559,908	40.9

Class 3

1950	John Marshall Butler (R)	326,291	53.0
	Millard E. Tydings (D)	283,180	46.0
1956	John Marshall Butler (R)	473,059	53.0
	George P. Mahoney (D)	419,108	47.0
1962	Daniel B. Brewster (D)	439,723	62.0
	Edward T. Miller (R)	269,131	38.0
1968	Charles McC. Mathias Jr. (R)	541,893	47.8
	Daniel B. Brewster (D)	443,367	39.1
	George P. Mahoney (I)	148,467	13.1
1974	Charles McC. Mathias Jr. (R)	503,223	57.3
	Barbara A. Mikulski (D)	374,563	42.7
1980	Charles McC. Mathias Jr. (R)	850,970	66.2
	Edward T. Conroy (D)	435,118	33.8
1986	Barbara A. Mikulski (D)	675,229	60.7
	Linda Chavez (R)	437,419	39.3
1992	Barbara A. Mikulski (D)	1,307,610	71.0
	Alan L. Keyes (R)	533,688	29.0

MASSACHUSETTS

	Candidates	Votes	%

Class 1

1946	Henry Cabot Lodge Jr. (R)	989,736	59.6
	David I. Walsh (D)	660,200	39.7
1952	John F. Kennedy (D)	1,211,984	51.4
	Henry Cabot Lodge Jr. (R)	1,141,247	48.4
1958	John F. Kennedy (D)	1,362,926	73.2
	Vincent J. Celeste (R)	488,318	26.2

Special Election

1962	Edward M. Kennedy (D)	1,162,611	55.4
	George C. Lodge (R)	877,669	41.9

1964	Edward M. Kennedy (D)	1,716,907	74.3
	Howard Whitmore Jr. (R)	587,663	25.4
1970	Edward M. Kennedy (D)	1,202,856	62.1
	Josiah A. Spaulding (R)	715,978	37.0
1976	Edward M. Kennedy (D)	1,726,657	69.3
	Michael Robertson (R)	722,641	29.0
1982	Edward M. Kennedy (D)	1,247,084	60.8
	Raymond Shamie (R)	784,602	38.3
1988	Edward M. Kennedy (D)	1,693,344	65.0
	Joseph D. Malone (R)	884,267	33.9
1994	Edward M. Kennedy (D)	1,265,997	58.1
	W. Mitt Romney (R)	894,000	41.0

Class 2

1948	Leverett Saltonstall (R)	1,088,475	53.0
	John I. Fitzgerald (D)	954,398	46.4

		Votes	%
1954	Leverett Saltonstall (R)	956,605	50.5
	Foster Furcolo (D)	927,899	49.0
1960	Leverett Saltonstall (R)	1,358,556	56.2
	Thomas J. O'Connor Jr. (D)	1,050,725	43.5
1966	Edward W. Brooke (R)	1,213,473	60.7
	Endicott Peabody (D)	774,761	38.7
1972	Edward W. Brooke (R)	1,505,932	63.5
	John J. Droney (D)	823,278	34.7
1978	Paul E. Tsongas (D)	1,093,283	55.1
	Edward W. Brooke (R)	890,584	44.8
1984	John F. Kerry (D)	1,393,150	55.1
	Raymond Shamie (R)	1,136,913	44.9
1990	John F. Kerry (D)	1,321,712	57.1
	Jim Rappaport (R)	992,917	42.9
1996	John F. Kerry (D)	1,334,345	52.2
	William F. Weld (R)	1,142,837	44.7

MICHIGAN

	Candidates	Votes	%
	Class 1		
1946	Arthur H. Vandenberg (R)	1,085,570	67.1
	James H. Lee (D)	517,923	32.0

Special Election

1952	Charles E. Potter (R)	1,417,032	51.2
	Blair Moody (D)	1,347,705	48.7

1952	Charles E. Potter (R)	1,428,352	50.6
	Blair Moody (D)	1,383,416	49.0
1958	Philip A. Hart (D)	1,216,966	53.6
	Charles E. Potter (R)	1,046,963	46.1
1964	Philip A. Hart (D)	1,996,912	64.4
	Elly M. Peterson (R)	1,096,272	35.3
1970	Philip A. Hart (D)	1,744,672	66.8
	Lenore Romney (R)	858,438	32.9
1976	Donald W. Riegle Jr. (D)	1,831,031	52.5
	Marvin L. Esch (R)	1,635,087	46.8
1982	Donald W. Riegle Jr. (D)	1,728,793	57.7
	Philip E. Ruppe (R)	1,223,288	40.9
1988	Donald W. Riegle Jr. (D)	2,116,865	60.4
	Jim Dunn (R)	1,348,219	38.5
1994	Spencer Abraham (R)	1,578,770	51.9
	Bob Carr (D)	1,300,960	42.7

	Class 2		
1948	Homer Ferguson (R)	1,045,156	50.7
	Frank E. Hook (D)	1,000,329	48.5
1954	Patrick V. McNamara (D)	1,088,550	50.8
	Homer Ferguson (R)	1,049,420	48.9
1960	Patrick V. McNamara (D)	1,669,179	51.7
	Alvin M. Bentley (R)	1,548,873	48.0

Special Election

1966	Robert P. Griffin (R)	1,321,222	56.0
	G. Mennen Williams (D)	1,031,138	43.7

1966	Robert P. Griffin (R)	1,363,530	55.9
	G. Mennen Williams (D)	1,069,484	43.8
1972	Robert P. Griffin (R)	1,781,065	52.3
	Frank J. Kelley (D)	1,577,178	46.3
1978	Carl Levin (D)	1,484,193	52.1
	Robert P. Griffin (R)	1,362,165	47.9
1984	Carl Levin (D)	1,915,831	51.8
	Jack Lousma (R)	1,745,302	47.2

1990	Carl Levin (D)	1,471,753	57.5
	Bill Schuette (R)	1,055,695	41.2
1996	Carl Levin (D)	2,195,738	58.4
	Ronna Romney (R)	1,500,106	39.9

MINNESOTA

	Candidates	Votes	%
	Class 1		
1946	Edward J. Thye (R)	517,775	58.9
	Theodore Jorgenson (DFL)	349,520	39.8
1952	Edward J. Thye (R)	785,649	56.6
	William E. Carlson (DFL)	590,011	42.5
1958	Eugene J. McCarthy (DFL)	608,847	52.9
	Edward J. Thye (R)	536,629	46.6
1964	Eugene J. McCarthy (DFL)	931,363	60.3
	Wheelock Whitney (R)	605,933	39.3
1970	Hubert H. Humphrey (DFL)	788,256	57.8
	Clark MacGregor (R)	568,025	41.6
1976	Hubert H. Humphrey (DFL)	1,290,736	67.5
	Gerald W. Brekke (R)	478,611	25.0
	Paul Helm (AM)	125,612	6.6

Special Election

1978	Dave Durenberger (I-R)	957,908	61.4
	Robert E. Short (DFL)	538,675	34.5

1982	Dave Durenberger (I-R)	949,207	52.6
	Mark Dayton (DFL)	840,401	46.6
1988	Dave Durenberger (I-R)	1,176,210	56.2
	Hubert H. Humphrey III (DFL)	1,856,694	40.9
1994	Rod Grams (R)	869,653	49.1
	Ann Wynia (D)	781,860	44.1
	Dean M. Barkley (I)	95,400	5.4

	Class 2		
1948	Hubert H. Humphrey (DFL)	729,494	59.9
	Joseph H. Ball (R)	482,801	39.7
1954	Hubert H. Humphrey (DFL)	642,193	56.4
	Val Bjornson (R)	479,619	42.1
1960	Hubert H. Humphrey (DFL)	884,168	57.5
	P. Kenneth Peterson (R)	648,586	42.2
1966	Walter F. Mondale (DFL)	685,840	53.9
	Robert A. Forsythe (R)	574,868	45.2
1972	Walter F. Mondale (DFL)	981,320	56.7
	Phil Hansen (R)	742,121	42.9
1978	Rudy Boschwitz (I-R)	894,092	56.6
	Wendell R. Anderson (DFL)	638,375	40.4
1984	Rudy Boschwitz (I-R)	1,199,926	58.1
	Joan Anderson Growe (DFL)	852,844	41.3
1990	Paul Wellstone (DFL)	911,999	50.4
	Rudy Boschwitz (I-R)	864,375	47.8
1996	Paul Wellstone (D)	1,098,493	50.3
	Rudy Boschwitz (R)	901,282	41.3
	Dean Barkley (REF)	152,333	7.0

MISSISSIPPI

	Candidates	Votes	%
	Class 1		
1946	Theodore G. Bilbo (D)	46,747*	100.0

Special Election

1947	John C. Stennis (D)	52,068	26.9
	William M. Colmer (D)	45,725	23.6
	Forrest B. Jackson (D)	43,642	22.5
	Paul B. Johnson Jr. (D)	27,159	14.0
	John E. Rankin (D)	24,492	12.6

1952	John C. Stennis (D)	233,919	100.0
1958	John C. Stennis (D)	61,039	100.0
1964	John C. Stennis (D)	343,364	100.0
1970	John C. Stennis (D)	286,622	88.4
	William R. Thompson (I)	37,593	11.6
1976	John C. Stennis (D)	554,433	100.0
1982	John C. Stennis (D)	414,099	64.2
	Haley Barbour (R)	230,927	35.8
1988	Trent Lott (R)	510,380	53.9
	Wayne Dowdy (D)	436,339	46.1
1994	Trent Lott (R)	418,333	68.8
	Ken Harper (D)	189,752	31.2

Class 2

1948	James O. Eastland (D)	151,478	100.0
1954	James O. Eastland (D)	100,848	95.6
1960	James O. Eastland (D)	244,341	91.8
	Joe A. Moore (R)	21,807	8.2
1966	James O. Eastland (D)	258,248	65.5
	Prentiss Walker (R)	105,652	26.8
	Clifton R. Whitley (I)	30,641	7.8
1972	James O. Eastland (D)	375,102	58.1
	Gil Carmichael (R)	249,779	38.7
1978	Thad Cochran (R)	263,089	45.1
	Maurice Dantin (D)	185,454	31.8
	Charles Evers (I)	133,646	22.9
1984	Thad Cochran (R)	580,314	60.9
	William D. Winter (D)	371,926	39.1
1990	Thad Cochran (R)	274,244	100.0
1996	Thad Cochran (R)	624,154	71.0
	James W. Hunt (D)	240,647	27.4

MISSOURI

Candidates	Votes	%

Class 1

1946	James P. Kem (R)	572,556	52.7
	Frank Briggs (D)	511,544	47.1
1952	Stuart Symington (D)	1,008,523	54.0
	James P. Kem (R)	858,170	45.9
1958	Stuart Symington (D)	780,083	66.5
	Hazel Palmer (R)	393,847	33.6
1964	Stuart Symington (D)	1,186,666	66.6
	Jean Paul Bradshaw (R)	596,377	33.5
1970	Stuart Symington (D)	655,431	51.1
	John C. Danforth (R)	617,903	48.2
1976	John C. Danforth (R)	1,090,067	56.9
	Warren E. Hearnes (D)	813,571	42.5
1982	John C. Danforth (R)	784,876	50.8
	Harriett Woods (D)	758,629	49.1
1988	John C. Danforth (R)	1,407,416	67.7
	Jay Nixon (D)	660,045	31.8
1994	John Ashcroft (R)	1,060,149	59.7
	Alan Wheat (D)	633,697	35.7

Class 3

1950	Thomas C. Hennings Jr. (D)	685,732	53.6
	Forrest C. Donnell (R)	593,139	46.4
1956	Thomas C. Hennings Jr. (D)	1,015,936	56.4

	Herbert Douglas (R)	785,048	43.6

Special Election

1960	Edward V. Long (D)	999,656	53.2
	Lon Hocker (R)	880,576	46.8

1962	Edward V. Long (D)	666,929	54.6
	Crosby Kemper (R)	555,330	45.4
1968	Thomas F. Eagleton (D)	887,414	51.1
	Thomas B. Curtis (R)	850,544	48.9
1974	Thomas F. Eagleton (D)	735,433	60.1
	Thomas B. Curtis (R)	480,900	39.3
1980	Thomas F. Eagleton (D)	1,074,859	52.0
	Gene McNary (R)	985,399	47.7
1986	Christopher S. Bond (R)	777,612	52.6
	Harriett Woods (D)	699,624	47.4
1992	Christopher S. Bond (R)	1,221,901	51.9
	Geri Rothman-Serot (D)	1,057,967	44.9

MONTANA

Candidates	Votes	%

Class 1

1946	Zales N. Ecton (R)	101,901	53.5
	Leif Erickson (D)	86,476	45.4
1952	Mike Mansfield (D)	133,109	50.8
	Zales N. Ecton (R)	127,360	48.6
1958	Mike Mansfield (D)	174,910	76.2
	Lou W. Welch (R)	54,573	23.8
1964	Mike Mansfield (D)	180,643	64.5
	Alex Blewett (R)	99,367	35.5
1970	Mike Mansfield (D)	150,060	60.5
	Harold E. Wallace (R)	97,809	39.5
1976	John Melcher (D)	206,232	64.2
	Stanley C. Burger (R)	115,213	35.8
1982	John Melcher (D)	174,861	54.5
	Larry Williams (R)	133,789	41.7
1988	Conrad Burns (R)	189,445	51.9
	John Melcher (D)	175,809	48.1
1994	Conrad Burns (R)	218,542	62.4
	Jack Mudd (D)	131,845	37.6

Class 2

1948	James E. Murray (D)	125,193	56.7
	Tom J. Davis (R)	94,458	42.7
1954	James E. Murray (D)	114,591	50.4
	Wesley A. D'Ewart (R)	112,863	49.6
1960	Lee Metcalf (D)	140,331	50.7
	Orvin B. Fjare (R)	136,281	49.3
1966	Lee Metcalf (D)	138,166	53.2
	Tim Babcock (R)	121,697	46.8
1972	Lee Metcalf (D)	163,609	52.0
	Henry S. Hibbard (R)	151,316	48.1
1978	Max Baucus (D)	160,353	55.7
	Larry Williams (R)	127,589	44.3
1984	Max Baucus (D)	215,704	56.9
	Chuck Cozzens (R)	154,308	40.7
1990	Max Baucus (D)	217,563	68.1
	Allen C. Kolstad (R)	93,836	29.4
1996	Max Baucus (D)	201,935	49.6
	Dennis Rehberg (R)	182,111	44.7

NEBRASKA

Candidates	Votes	%

Class 1

	Candidates	Votes	%
1946	Hugh Butler (R)	271,208	70.8
	John E. Mekota (D)	111,751	29.2
1952	Hugh Butler (R)	408,971	69.1
	Stanley D. Long (D)	164,660	27.8

Special Election

1954	Roman L. Hruska (R)	250,341	60.9
	James F. Green (D)	160,881	39.1

1958	Roman L. Hruska (R)	232,227	55.6
	Frank B. Morrison (D)	185,152	44.4
1964	Roman L. Hruska (R)	345,772	61.4
	Raymond W. Arndt (D)	217,605	38.6
1970	Roman L. Hruska (R)	240,894	52.5
	Frank B. Morrison (D)	217,681	47.4
1976	Edward Zorinsky (D)	313,809	52.4
	John Y. McCollister (R)	284,284	47.5
1982	Edward Zorinsky (D)	363,350	66.6
	Jim Keck (R)	155,760	28.5
1988	Bob Kerrey (D)	378,717	56.7
	David Karnes (R)	278,250	41.7
1994	Bob Kerrey (D)	317,297	54.8
	Jan Stoney (R)	260,668	45.0

Class 2

1948	Kenneth S. Wherry (R)	267,575	56.7
	Terry Carpenter (D)	204,320	43.3

Special Election

1952	Dwight Griswold (R)	369,841	63.6
	William Ritchie (D)	211,898	36.4

Special Election

1954	Hazel H. Abel (R)	233,589	57.8
	William H. Meier (D)	170,828	42.2

1954	Carl T. Curtis (R)	255,695	61.1
	Keith Neville (D)	162,990	38.9
1960	Carl T. Curtis (R)	352,748	58.9
	Robert B. Conrad (D)	245,837	41.1
1966	Carl T. Curtis (R)	296,116	61.2
	Frank B. Morrison (D)	187,950	38.8
1972	Carl T. Curtis (R)	301,841	53.1
	Terry Carpenter (D)	265,922	46.8
1978	J. James Exon (D)	334,276	67.6
	Donald Shasteen (R)	159,806	32.3
1984	J. James Exon (D)	332,217	51.9
	Nancy Hoch (R)	307,147	48.0
1990	J. James Exon (D)	349,779	58.9
	Hal Daub (R)	243,013	40.9
1996	Chuck Hagel (R)	379,933	56.1
	Ben Nelson (D)	281,904	41.7

NEVADA

Candidates	Votes	%

Class 1

	Candidates	Votes	%
1946	George W. Malone (R)	27,801	55.2
	Berkeley L. Bunker (D)	22,553	44.8
1952	George W. Malone (R)	41,906	51.7
	Thomas B. Mechling (D)	39,184	48.3
1958	Howard W. Cannon (D)	48,732	57.7
	George W. Malone (R)	35,760	42.3
1964	Howard W. Cannon (D)	67,336	50.0
	Paul Laxalt (R)	67,288	50.0
1970	Howard W. Cannon (D)	85,187	57.7
	William J. Raggio (R)	60,838	41.2
1976	Howard W. Cannon (D)	127,295	63.0
	David Towell (R)	63,471	31.4
1982	Chic Hecht (R)	120,377	50.1
	Howard W. Cannon (D)	114,720	47.7
1988	Richard H. Bryan (D)	175,548	50.2
	Chic Hecht (R)	161,336	46.1
1994	Richard H. Bryan (D)	193,804	52.7
	Hal Furman (R)	156,020	42.4

Class 3

1950	Patrick A. McCarran (D)	35,829	58.0
	George E. Marshall (R)	25,933	42.0

Special Election

1954	Alan Bible (D)	45,043	58.1
	Ernest S. Brown (R)	32,470	41.9

1956	Alan Bible (D)	50,677	52.6
	Cliff Young (R)	45,712	47.4
1962	Alan Bible (D)	63,443	65.3
	William B. Wright (R)	33,749	34.7
1968	Alan Bible (D)	83,622	54.8
	Ed Fike (R)	69,068	45.2
1974	Paul Laxalt (R)	79,605	47.0
	Harry Reid (D)	78,981	46.6
1980	Paul Laxalt (R)	144,224	58.5
	Mary Gojack (D)	92,129	37.4
1986	Harry Reid (D)	130,955	50.0
	Jim Santini (R)	116,606	44.5
1992	Harry Reid (D)	253,150	51.0
	Demar Dahl (R)	199,413	40.2

NEW HAMPSHIRE

Candidates	Votes	%

Class 2

	Candidates	Votes	%
1948	Styles Bridges (R)	129,600	58.1
	Alfred E. Fortin (D)	91,760	41.2
1954	Styles Bridges (R)	117,150	60.2
	Gerard L. Morin (D)	77,386	39.8
1960	Styles Bridges (R)	173,521	60.4
	Herbert W. Hill (D)	114,024	39.7

Special Election

1962	Thomas J. McIntyre (D)	117,612	52.3
	Perkins Bass (R)	107,199	47.7

1966	Thomas J. McIntyre (D)	123,888	54.0
	Harrison R. Thyng (R)	105,241	45.9

1972	Thomas J. McIntyre (D)	184,495	56.9
	Wesley Powell (R)	139,852	43.1
1978	Gordon J. Humphrey (R)	133,745	50.7
	Thomas J. McIntyre (D)	127,945	48.5
1984	Gordon J. Humphrey (R)	225,828	58.7
	Norman E. D'Amours (D)	157,447	41.0
1990	Robert C. Smith (R)	189,792	65.1
	John A. Durkin (D)	91,299	31.3
1996	Robert C. Smith (R)	242,304	49.2
	Dick Swett (D)	227,397	46.2

Class 3

1950	Charles W. Tobey (R)	106,142	55.7
	Emmet J. Kelley (D)	72,473	38.0
	Wesley Powell (I)	11,958	6.3

Special Election

| 1954 | Norris Cotton (R) | 114,068 | 60.2 |
| | Stanley J. Betley (D) | 75,490 | 39.8 |

1956	Norris Cotton (R)	161,424	64.1
	Laurence M. Pickett (D)	90,519	35.9
1962	Norris Cotton (R)	134,035	59.7
	Alfred Catalfo Jr. (D)	90,444	40.3
1968	Norris Cotton (R)	170,163	59.3
	John W. King (D)	116,816	40.7
1974[1]	Louis C. Wyman (R)	110,926*	49.7
	John A. Durkin (D)	110,924	49.7

Special Election[1]

1975	John A. Durkin (D)	140,778	53.6
	Louis C. Wyman (R)	113,007	43.1
	Carmen C. Chimento (AM)	8,787	3.3

1980	Warren B. Rudman (R)	195,563	52.1
	John A. Durkin (D)	179,455	47.8
1986	Warren B. Rudman (R)	154,090	62.9
	Endicott Peabody (D)	79,222	32.4
1992	Judd Gregg (R)	249,591	48.1
	John Rauh (D)	234,982	45.3

New Hampshire
1. Wyman's two-vote margin was challenged by Durkin. The Senate refused to seat either candidate. After seven months of fruitless efforts to decide a winner, the Senate voted July 30, 1975, to declare the seat vacant effective Aug. 8, 1975. In a special election Sept. 16, 1975, Durkin defeated Wyman.

NEW JERSEY

Candidates		Votes	%
	Class 1		
1946	H. Alexander Smith (R)	799,808	58.5
	George E. Brunner (D)	548,458	40.1
1952	H. Alexander Smith (R)	1,286,782	55.5
	Archibald S. Alexander (D)	1,011,187	43.6
1958	Harrison A. Williams Jr. (D)	966,832	51.4
	Robert Winthrop Kean (R)	882,287	46.9
1964	Harrison A. Williams Jr. (D)	1,677,515	61.9
	Bernard M. Shanley (R)	1,011,280	37.3
1970	Harrison A. Williams Jr. (D)	1,157,074	54.0
	Nelson G. Gross (R)	903,026	42.2
1976	Harrison A. Williams Jr. (D)	1,681,140	60.7
	David F. Norcross (R)	1,054,508	38.0
1982	Frank R. Lautenberg (D)	1,117,549	50.9
	Millicent Fenwick (R)	1,047,626	47.8

1988	Frank R. Lautenberg (D)	1,599,905	53.5
	Pete Dawkins (R)	1,349,937	45.2
1994	Frank R. Lautenberg (D)	1,033,487	50.3
	Garabed "Chuck" Haytaian (R)	966,244	47.0

Class 2

1948	Robert C. Hendrickson (R)	934,720	50.0
	Archibald S. Alexander (D)	884,414	47.3
1954	Clifford P. Case (R)	861,528	48.7
	Charles R. Howell (D)	858,158	48.5
1960	Clifford P. Case (R)	1,483,832	55.7
	Thorn Lord (D)	1,151,385	43.2
1966	Clifford P. Case (R)	1,278,843	60.0
	Warren W. Wilentz (D)	788,021	37.0
1972	Clifford P. Case (R)	1,743,854	62.5
	Paul J. Krebs (D)	963,573	34.5
1978	Bill Bradley (D)	1,082,960	55.3
	Jeffrey Bell (R)	844,200	43.1
1984	Bill Bradley (D)	1,986,644	64.2
	Mary V. Mochary (R)	1,080,100	35.2
1990	Bill Bradley (D)	977,810	50.4
	Christine Todd Whitman (R)	918,874	47.4
1996	Robert G. Torricelli (D)	1,519,328	52.7
	Dick Zimmer (R)	1,227,817	42.6

NEW MEXICO

Candidates		Votes	%
	Class 1		
1946	Dennis Chavez (D)	68,650	51.5
	Patrick J. Hurley (R)	64,632	48.5
1952	Dennis Chavez (D)	122,543	51.1
	Patrick J. Hurley (R)	117,168	48.9
1958	Dennis Chavez (D)	127,496	62.7
	Forrest S. Atchley (R)	75,827	37.3
1964	Joseph M. Montoya (D)	178,209	54.7
	Edwin L. Mechem (R)	147,562	45.3
1970	Joseph M. Montoya (D)	151,486	52.3
	Anderson Carter (R)	135,004	46.6
1976	Harrison "Jack" Schmitt (R)	234,681	56.8
	Joseph M. Montoya (D)	176,382	42.7
1982	Jeff Bingaman (D)	217,682	53.8
	Harrison "Jack" Schmitt (R)	187,128	46.2
1988	Jeff Bingaman (D)	321,983	63.3
	Bill Valentine (R)	186,579	36.7
1994	Jeff Bingaman (D)	249,989	54.0
	Colin R. McMillan (R)	213,025	46.0

Class 2

1948	Clinton P. Anderson (D)	108,269	57.2
	Patrick J. Hurley (R)	80,226	42.4
1954	Clinton P. Anderson (D)	111,351	57.3
	Edwin L. Mechem (R)	83,071	42.7
1960	Clinton P. Anderson (D)	190,654	63.4
	William Colwes (R)	109,897	36.6
1966	Clinton P. Anderson (D)	137,205	53.1
	Anderson Carter (R)	120,988	46.9
1972	Pete V. Domenici (R)	204,253	54.0
	Jack Daniels (D)	173,815	46.0
1978	Pete V. Domenici (R)	183,442	53.4
	Toney Anaya (D)	160,045	46.6
1984	Pete V. Domenici (R)	361,371	71.9
	Judith A. Pratt (D)	141,253	28.1
1990	Pete V. Domenici (R)	296,712	72.9
	Tom R. Benavides (D)	110,033	27.1
1996	Pete V. Domenici (R)	357,171	64.7
	Art Trujillo (D)	164,356	29.8

NEW YORK

Candidates	Votes	%

Class 1

	Candidates	Votes	%
1946	Irving M. Ives (R)	2,559,365	52.6
	Herbert H. Lehman (D, AM LAB)	2,308,112	47.4
1952	Irving M. Ives (R)	3,853,934	55.2
	John Cashmore (D)	2,521,736	36.1
	George S. Counts (L)	489,775	7.0
1958	Kenneth B. Keating (R)	2,842,942	50.8
	Frank S. Hogan (D, L)	2,709,950	48.4
1964	Robert F. Kennedy (D, L)	3,823,749	53.5
	Kenneth B. Keating (R)	3,104,056	43.4
1970	James L. Buckley (C, I ALNC)	2,288,190	38.8
	Richard L. Ottinger (D)	2,171,232	36.8
	Charles E. Goodell (R, L)	1,434,472	24.3
1976	Daniel Patrick Moynihan (D, L)	3,422,594	54.2
	James L. Buckley (R, C)	2,836,633	44.9
1982	Daniel Patrick Moynihan (D, L)	3,232,146	65.1
	Florence M. Sullivan (R, C)	1,696,766	34.2
1988	Daniel Patrick Moynihan (D, L)	4,048,649	67.0
	Robert R. McMillan (R, C)	1,875,784	31.1
1994	Daniel Patrick Moynihan (D, L)	2,646,541	55.2
	Bernadette Castro (R, C, TCN)	1,988,308	41.5

Class 3

Special Election

	Candidates	Votes	%
1949	Herbert H. Lehman (D, L)	2,582,438	52.0
	John Foster Dulles (R)	2,384,381	48.0
1950	Herbert H. Lehman (D, L)	2,632,313	50.3
	Joe R. Hanley (R)	2,367,353	45.3
1956	Jacob K. Javits (R)	3,723,933	53.3
	Robert F. Wagner Jr. (D, L)	3,265,159	46.7
1962	Jacob K. Javits (R)	3,272,417	57.4
	James B. Donovan (D, L)	2,289,323	40.1
1968	Jacob K. Javits (R, L)	3,269,772	49.7
	Paul O'Dwyer (D)	2,150,695	32.7
	James L. Buckley (C)	1,139,402	17.3
1974	Jacob K. Javits (R, L)	2,340,188	45.3
	Ramsey Clark (D)	1,973,781	38.2
	Barbara A. Keating (C)	822,584	15.9
1980	Alfonse M. D'Amato (R, C)	2,699,652	44.9
	Elizabeth Holtzman (D)	2,618,661	43.5
	Jacob K. Javits (L)	664,544	11.0
1986	Alfonse M. D'Amato (R, C)	2,378,197	56.9
	Mark Green (D)	1,723,216	41.2
1992	Alfonse M. D'Amato (R, C)	3,166,994	49.0
	Robert Abrams (D, L)	3,086,200	47.8

NORTH CAROLINA

Candidates	Votes	%

Class 2

Special Election

	Candidates	Votes	%
1948	J. Melville Broughton (D)	534,917#	100.0
1948	J. Melville Broughton (D)	540,762	70.7
	John A. Wilkinson (R)	220,307	28.8

Special Election

	Candidates	Votes	%
1950	Willis Smith (D)	364,912	67.0
	E. L. Gavin (R)	177,753	32.6

Special Election

	Candidates	Votes	%
1954	W. Kerr Scott (D)	402,268	100.0
1954	W. Kerr Scott (D)	408,312	65.9
	Paul C. West (R)	211,322	34.1

Special Election

	Candidates	Votes	%
1958	B. Everett Jordan (D)	431,492	70.0
	Richard C. Clarke Jr. (R)	184,977	30.0
1960	B. Everett Jordan (D)	793,521	61.4
	Kyle Hayes (R)	497,964	38.6
1966	B. Everett Jordan (D)	501,440	55.6
	John S. Shallcross (R)	400,502	44.4
1972	Jesse Helms (R)	795,248	54.0
	Nick Galifianakis (D)	677,293	46.0
1978	Jesse Helms (R)	619,151	54.5
	John Ingram (D)	516,663	45.5
1984	Jesse Helms (R)	1,156,768	51.7
	James B. Hunt, Jr. (D)	1,070,488	47.8
1990	Jesse Helms (R)	1,087,331	52.5
	Harvey B. Gantt (D)	981,573	47.4
1996	Jesse Helms (R)	1,345,833	52.6
	Harvey B. Gantt (D)	1,173,875	45.9

Class 3

	Candidates	Votes	%
1950	Clyde R. Hoey (D)	376,473	68.7
	Halsey B. Leavitt (R)	171,804	31.3

Special Election

	Candidates	Votes	%
1954	Sam J. Ervin Jr. (D)	410,574	100.0
1956	Sam J. Ervin Jr. (D)	731,353	66.6
	Joel A. Johnson (R)	367,475	33.4
1962	Sam J. Ervin Jr. (D)	491,520	60.5
	Claude L. Greene Jr. (R)	321,635	39.6
1968	Sam J. Ervin Jr. (D)	870,406	60.6
	Robert Vance Somers (R)	566,934	39.4
1974	Robert B. Morgan (D)	633,775	62.1
	William E. Stevens (R)	377,618	37.0
1980	John P. East (R)	898,064	50.0
	Robert Morgan (D)	887,653	49.4
1986	Terry Sanford (D)	823,662	51.8
	James T. Broyhill (R)	767,668	48.2
1992	Lauch Faircloth (R)	1,297,892	50.3
	Terry Sanford (D)	1,194,015	46.3

NORTH DAKOTA

Candidates	Votes	%

Class 1

	Candidates	Votes	%
1946	William Langer (R)	88,210	53.3
	Arthur E. Thompson (I)	38,804	23.5
	Abner B. Larson (D)	38,368	23.2
1952	William Langer (R)	157,907	66.4
	Harold A. Morrison (D)	55,347	23.3
	Fred G. Aandahl (I)	24,741	10.4
1958	William Langer (R)	117,070	57.2
	Raymond Vendsel (D)	84,892	41.5

Special Election

1960	Quentin N. Burdick (D)	104,593	49.7
	John E. Davis (R)	103,475	49.2

1964	Quentin N. Burdick (D)	149,264	57.6
	Thomas S. Kleppe (R)	109,681	42.4
1970	Quentin N. Burdick (D)	134,519	61.3
	Thomas S. Kleppe (R)	82,996	37.8
1976	Quentin N. Burdick (D)	175,772	62.1
	Richard Stroup (R)	103,466	36.6
1982	Quentin N. Burdick (D)	164,873	62.8
	Gene Knorr (R)	89,304	34.0
1988	Quentin N. Burdick (D)	171,899	59.4
	Earl Strinden (R)	112,937	39.1

Special Election

1992	Kent Conrad (D)	102,887	63.3
	Jack Dalrymple (R)	54,726	33.7

1994	Kent Conrad (D)	137,157	58.0
	Ben Clayburgh (R)	99,390	42.0

Class 3

Special Election

1946	Milton R. Young (R)	75,998	55.5
	William Lanier (D)	37,507	27.4
	Gerald P. Nye (I)	20,848	15.2

1950	Milton R. Young (R)	126,209	67.6
	Harry O'Brien (D)	60,507	32.4
1956	Milton R. Young (R)	155,305	63.6
	Quentin N. Burdick (D)	87,919	36.0
1962	Milton R. Young (R)	135,705	60.7
	William Lanier (D)	88,032	39.4
1968	Milton R. Young (R)	154,968	64.6
	Herschel Lashkowitz (D)	80,815	33.7
1974	Milton R. Young (R)	114,117	48.4
	William L. Guy (D)	113,931	48.3
1980	Mark Andrews (R)	210,347	70.3
	Kent Johanneson (D)	86,658	29.0
1986	Kent Conrad (D)	143,932	49.8
	Mark Andrews (R)	141,797	49.1
1992	Byron L. Dorgan (D)	179,347	59.0
	Steve Sydness (R)	118,162	38.9

OHIO

Candidates	Votes	%

Class 1

Special Election

1946	Kingsley A. Taft (R)	1,193,942	56.2
	Henry P. Webber (D)	929,584	43.8

1946	John W. Bricker (R)	1,275,774	57.0
	James W. Huffman (D)	947,610	42.4
1952	John W. Bricker (R)	1,878,961	54.6
	Michael V. DiSalle (D)	1,563,330	45.4
1958	Stephen M. Young (D)	1,652,211	52.5
	John W. Bricker (R)	1,497,199	47.5
1964	Stephen M. Young (D)	1,923,608	50.2
	Robert Taft Jr. (R)	1,906,781	49.8

1970	Robert Taft Jr. (R)	1,565,682	49.7
	Howard M. Metzenbaum (D)	1,495,262	47.5
1976	Howard M. Metzenbaum (D)	1,941,113	49.5
	Robert A. Taft Jr. (R)	1,823,774	46.5
1982	Howard M. Metzenbaum (D)	1,923,767	56.7
	Paul E. Pfeifer (R)	1,396,790	41.1
1988	Howard M. Metzenbaum (D)	2,480,038	57.0
	George V. Voinovich (R)	1,872,716	43.0
1994	Mike DeWine (R)	1,836,556	53.4
	Joel Hyatt (D)	1,348,213	39.2
	Joseph J. Slovenec (I)	252,031	7.3

Class 3

1950	Robert A. Taft (R)	1,645,643	57.5
	Joseph T. Ferguson (D)	1,214,459	42.5

Special Election

1954	George H. Bender (R)	1,257,874	50.1
	Thomas A. Burke (D)	1,254,899	49.9

1956	Frank J. Lausche (D)	1,864,589	52.9
	George H. Bender (R)	1,660,910	47.1
1962	Frank J. Lausche (D)	1,843,813	61.6
	John Marshall Briley (R)	1,151,292	38.4
1968	William B. Saxbe (R)	1,928,964	51.5
	John J. Gilligan (D)	1,814,152	48.5
1974	John Glenn (D)	1,930,670	64.6
	Ralph J. Perk (R)	918,133	30.7
1980	John Glenn (D)	2,770,786	68.8
	James E. Betts (R)	1,137,695	28.2
1986	John Glenn (D)	1,949,208	62.5
	Thomas N. Kindness (R)	1,171,893	37.5
1992	John Glenn (D)	2,444,419	51.0
	Mike DeWine (R)	2,028,300	42.3
	Martha K. Grevatt (I)	321,234	6.7

OKLAHOMA

Candidates	Votes	%

Class 2

1948	Robert S. Kerr (D)	441,654	62.3
	Ross Rizley (R)	265,169	37.4
1954	Robert S. Kerr (D)	335,127	55.8
	Fred M. Mock (R)	262,013	43.7
1960	Robert S. Kerr (D)	474,116	54.8
	B. Hayden Crawford (R)	385,646	44.6

Special Election

1964	Fred R. Harris (D)	466,782	51.2
	Bud Wilkinson (R)	445,392	48.8

1966	Fred R. Harris (D)	343,157	53.7
	Pat J. Patterson (R)	295,585	46.3
1972	Dewey F. Bartlett (R)	516,934	51.4
	Ed Edmondson (D)	478,212	47.6
1978	David L. Boren (D)	493,953	65.5
	Robert B. Kamm (R)	247,857	32.9
1984	David L. Boren (D)	906,131	75.6
	Will E. Crozier (R)	280,638	23.4
1990	David L. Boren (D)	735,684	83.2
	Stephen Jones (R)	148,814	16.8

Special Election

1994	James M. Inhofe (R)	542,390	55.2
	Dave McCurdy (D)	392,488	40.0

| 1996 | James M. Inhofe (R) | 670,610 | 56.7 |
| | Jim Boren (D) | 474,162 | 40.1 |

Class 3

1950	A. S. Mike Monroney (D)	345,953	54.8
	W. H. "Bill" Alexander (R)	285,224	45.2
1956	A. S. Mike Monroney (D)	459,996	55.4
	Douglas McKeever (R)	371,146	44.7
1962	A. S. Mike Monroney (D)	353,890	53.2
	B. Hayden Crawford (R)	307,966	46.3
1968	Henry Bellmon (R)	470,120	51.7
	A. S. Mike Monroney (D)	419,658	46.2
1974	Henry Bellmon (R)	390,997	49.4
	Ed Edmondson (D)	387,162	48.9
1980	Don Nickles (R)	587,252	53.5
	Andrew Coats (D)	478,283	43.5
1986	Don Nickles (R)	493,436	55.2
	James R. Jones (D)	400,230	44.8
1992	Don Nickles (R)	757,876	58.5
	Steve Lewis (D)	494,350	38.2

OREGON

Candidates	Votes	%

Class 2

1948	Guy Cordon (R)	299,295	60.0
	Manley J. Wilson (D)	199,275	40.0
1954	Richard L. Neuberger (D)	285,775	50.2
	Guy Cordon (R)	283,313	49.8

Special Election

| 1960 | Maurine B. Neuberger (D) | 422,024 | 55.0 |
| | Elmo Smith (R) | 345,464 | 45.0 |

1960	Maurine B. Neuberger (D)	412,757	54.6
	Elmo Smith (R)	343,009	45.4
1966	Mark O. Hatfield (R)	354,391	51.7
	Robert B. Duncan (D)	330,374	48.2
1972	Mark O. Hatfield (R)	494,671	53.7
	Wayne Morse (D)	425,036	46.2
1978	Mark O. Hatfield (R)	550,165	61.6
	Vernon Cook (D)	341,616	38.3
1984	Mark O. Hatfield (R)	808,152	66.5
	Margie Hendricksen (D)	406,122	33.4
1990	Mark O. Hatfield (R)	590,095	53.7
	Harry Lonsdale (D)	507,743	46.2
1996	Gordon H. Smith (R)	677,336	49.8
	Tom Bruggere (D)	624,370	45.9

Class 3

1950	Wayne Morse (R)	376,510	74.8
	Howard Latourette (D)	116,780	23.2
1956	Wayne Morse (D)	396,849	54.2
	Douglas McKay (R)	335,405	45.8
1962	Wayne Morse (D)	344,716	54.2
	Sig Unander (R)	291,587	45.8
1968	Bob Packwood (R)	408,825	50.2
	Wayne Morse (D)	405,380	49.8
1974	Bob Packwood (R)	420,984	54.9
	Betty Roberts (D)	338,591	44.2
1980	Bob Packwood (R)	594,290	52.1
	Ted Kulongoski (D)	501,963	44.0
1986	Bob Packwood (R)	656,317	63.0
	Rick Bauman (D)	375,735	36.0
1992	Bob Packwood (R)	717,455	52.1
	Les AuCoin (D)	639,851	46.5

Special Election

| 1996 | Ron Wyden (D) | 571,739 | 48.4 |
| | Gordon H. Smith (R) | 553,519 | 46.8 |

PENNSYLVANIA

Candidates	Votes	%

Class 1

1946	Edward Martin (R)	1,853,458	59.3
	Joseph F. Guffey (D)	1,245,338	39.8
1952	Edward Martin (R)	2,331,034	51.6
	Guy Kurtz Bard (D)	2,168,546	48.0
1958	Hugh Scott (R)	2,042,586	51.2
	George M. Leader (D)	1,929,821	48.4
1964	Hugh Scott (R)	2,429,858	50.6
	Genevieve Blatt (D)	2,359,223	49.1
1970	Hugh Scott (R)	1,874,106	51.4
	William G. Sesler (D)	1,653,774	45.4
1976	John Heinz (R)	2,381,891	52.4
	William J. Green III (R)	2,126,977	46.8
1982	John Heinz (R)	2,136,418	59.3
	Cyril H. Wecht (D)	1,412,965	39.2
1988	John Heinz (R)	2,901,715	66.5
	Joseph C. Vignola (D)	1,416,764	32.4

Special Election

| 1991 | Harris Wofford (D) | 1,860,760 | 55.0 |
| | Dick Thornburgh (R) | 1,521,986 | 45.0 |

| 1994 | Rick Santorum (R) | 1,735,691 | 49.4 |
| | Harris Wofford (D) | 1,648,481 | 46.9 |

Class 3

1950	James H. Duff (R)	1,820,400	51.3
	Francis J. Myers (D)	1,694,076	47.7
1956	Joseph S. Clark (D)	2,268,641	50.1
	James H. Duff (R)	2,250,671	49.7
1962	Joseph S. Clark (D)	2,238,383	51.1
	James E. Van Zandt (R)	2,134,649	48.7
1968	Richard S. Schweiker (R)	2,399,762	51.9
	Joseph S. Clark (D)	2,117,662	45.8
1974	Richard S. Schweiker (R)	1,843,317	53.0
	Peter Flaherty (D)	1,596,121	45.9
1980	Arlen Specter (R)	2,230,404	50.5
	Peter Flaherty (D)	2,122,391	48.0
1986	Arlen Specter (R)	1,906,537	56.4
	Bob Edgar (D)	1,448,219	42.9
1992	Arlen Specter (R)	2,358,125	49.1
	Lynn Yeakel (D)	2,224,966	46.3

RHODE ISLAND

Candidates	Votes	%

Class 1

| 1946 | J. Howard McGrath (D) | 150,748 | 55.1 |
| | W. Gurnee Dyer (R) | 122,780 | 44.9 |

Special Election

| 1950 | John O. Pastore (D) | 184,520 | 61.6 |
| | Austin T. Levy (R) | 114,890 | 38.4 |

Year	Candidate	Votes	%
1952	John O. Pastore (D)	225,128	54.8
	Bayard Ewing (R, CLEAN GV)	185,850	45.2
1958	John O. Pastore (D)	222,166	64.5
	Bayard Ewing (R)	122,353	35.5
1964	John O. Pastore (D)	319,607	82.7
	Ronald R. Lagueux (R)	66,715	17.3
1970	John O. Pastore (D)	230,469	67.5
	John McLaughlin (R)	107,351	31.5
1976	John H. Chafee (R)	230,329	57.7
	Richard P. Lorber (D)	167,665	42.0
1982	John H. Chafee (R)	175,495	51.2
	Julius C. Michaelson (D)	167,283	48.8
1988	John H. Chafee (R)	217,273	54.6
	Richard A. Licht (D)	180,717	45.4
1994	John H. Chafee (R)	222,856	64.5
	Linda J. Kushner (D)	122,532	35.5

Class 2

Year	Candidate	Votes	%
1948	Theodore F. Green (D)	190,284	59.3
	Thomas P. Hazard (R)	130,668	40.7
1954	Theodore F. Green (D)	193,654	59.3
	Walter I. Sundlun (R)	132,970	40.7
1960	Claiborne Pell (D)	275,575	68.9
	Raoul Archambault (R)	124,408	31.1
1966	Claiborne Pell (D)	219,331	67.7
	Ruth M. Briggs (R)	104,838	32.3
1972	Claiborne Pell (D)	221,942	53.7
	John H. Chafee (R)	188,990	45.7
1978	Claiborne Pell (D)	229,557	75.1
	James G. Reynolds (R)	76,061	24.9
1984	Claiborne Pell (D)	286,780	72.6
	Barbara Leonard (R)	108,492	27.4
1990	Claiborne Pell (D)	225,105	61.8
	Claudine Schneider (R)	138,947	38.2
1996	Jack Reed (D)	230,676	63.5
	Nancy J. Mayer (R)	127,368	35.1

SOUTH CAROLINA

	Candidates	Votes	%

Class 2

Year	Candidate	Votes	%
1948	Burnet R. Maybank (D)	135,998	96.5
1954	Strom Thurmond (WRITE IN)	143,442	63.1
	Edgar A. Brown (D)	83,525	36.8

Special Election

Year	Candidate	Votes	%
1956	Strom Thurmond (D)	245,371	100.0

Year	Candidate	Votes	%
1960	Strom Thurmond (D)	330,164	100.0
1966	Strom Thurmond (R)	271,297	62.2
	Bradley Morrah (D)	164,955	37.8
1972	Strom Thurmond (R)	415,806	63.3
	Eugene N. Zeigler (D)	241,056	36.7
1978	Strom Thurmond (R)	351,733	55.6
	Charles D. Ravenel (D)	281,119	44.4
1984	Strom Thurmond (R)	644,815	66.8
	Melvin Purvis Jr. (R)	306,982	31.8
1990	Strom Thurmond (R)	482,032	64.2
	Bob Cunningham (D)	244,112	32.5
1996	Strom Thurmond (R)	619,859	53.4
	Elliott Close (D)	510,951	44.0

Class 3

Year	Candidate	Votes	%
1950	Olin D. Johnston (D)	50,240	99.9
1956	Olin D. Johnston (D)	230,150	82.2
	L. P. Crawford (R)	49,695	17.8
1962	Olin D. Johnston (D)	178,712	57.2
	W. D. Workman Jr. (R)	133,930	42.8

Special Election

Year	Candidate	Votes	%
1966	Ernest F. Hollings (D)	223,790	51.4
	Marshall Parker (R)	212,032	48.7

Year	Candidate	Votes	%
1968	Ernest F. Hollings (D)	404,060	61.9
	Marshall Parker (R)	248,780	38.1
1974	Ernest F. Hollings (D)	356,126	69.5
	Gwenyfred Bush (R)	146,645	28.6
1980	Ernest F. Hollings (D)	612,554	70.4
	Marshall T. Mays (R)	257,946	29.6
1986	Ernest F. Hollings (D)	465,500	63.1
	Henry D. McMaster (R)	262,886	35.6
1992	Ernest F. Hollings (D)	591,030	50.1
	Thomas F. Hartnett (R)	554,175	46.9

SOUTH DAKOTA

	Candidates	Votes	%

Class 2

Year	Candidate	Votes	%
1948	Karl E. Mundt (R)	144,084	59.3
	John A. Engel (D)	98,749	40.7
1954	Karl E. Mundt (R)	135,071	57.3
	Kenneth Holum (D)	100,674	42.7
1960	Karl E. Mundt (R)	160,181	52.4
	George McGovern (D)	145,261	47.6
1966	Karl E. Mundt (R)	150,517	66.3
	Donn H. Wright (D)	76,563	33.7
1972	James Abourezk (D)	174,773	57.0
	Robert W. Hirsch (R)	131,613	42.9
1978	Larry Pressler (R)	170,832	66.8
	Don Barnett (D)	84,767	33.2
1984	Larry Pressler (R)	235,176	74.5
	George V. Cunningham (D)	80,537	25.5
1990	Larry Pressler (R)	135,682	52.4
	Ted Muenster (D)	116,727	45.1
1996	Tim Johnson (D)	166,533	51.3
	Larry Pressler (R)	157,954	48.7

Class 3

Year	Candidate	Votes	%
1950	Francis Case (R)	160,670	63.9
	John A. Engel (D)	90,692	36.1
1956	Francis Case (R)	147,621	50.8
	Kenneth Holum (D)	143,001	49.2
1962	George McGovern (D)	127,458	50.1
	Joe Bottum (R)	126,861	49.9
1968	George McGovern (D)	158,961	56.8
	Archie Gubbrud (R)	120,951	43.2
1974	George McGovern (D)	147,929	53.0
	Leo K. Thorsness (R)	130,955	47.0
1980	James Abdnor (R)	190,594	58.2
	George McGovern (D)	129,018	39.4
1986	Thomas Daschle (D)	152,657	51.6
	James Abdnor (R)	143,173	48.4
1992	Thomas Daschle (D)	217,095	64.9
	Charlene Haar (R)	108,733	32.5

TENNESSEE

	Candidates	Votes	%
	Class 1		
1946	Kenneth D. McKellar (D)	145,654	66.6
	W. B. Ladd (R)	57,237	26.2
	John R. Neal (I)	11,516	5.3
1952	Albert Gore (D)	545,432	74.2
	Hobart F. Atkins (R)	153,479	20.9
1958	Albert Gore (D)	317,324	79.0
	Hobart F. Atkins (R)	76,371	19.0
1964	Albert Gore (D)	570,542	53.6
	Dan H. Kuykendall (R)	493,475	46.4
1970	Bill Brock (R)	562,645	51.3
	Albert Gore (D)	519,858	47.4
1976	Jim Sasser (D)	751,180	52.5
	Bill Brock (R)	673,231	47.0
1982	Jim Sasser (D)	780,113	61.9
	Robin L. Beard (D)	479,642	38.1
1988	Jim Sasser (D)	1,020,061	65.1
	Bill Andersen (R)	541,033	34.5
1994	Bill Frist (R)	834,226	56.4
	Jim Sasser (D)	623,164	42.1
	Class 2		
1948	Estes Kefauver (D)	326,062	65.3
	B. Carroll Reece (R)	166,947	33.5
1954	Estes Kefauver (D)	249,121	70.0
	Tom Wall (R)	106,971	30.0
1960	Estes Kefauver (D)	594,460	71.8
	A. Bradley Frazier (R)	234,053	28.3

Special Election

1964	Ross Bass (D)	568,905	52.1
	Howard H. Baker Jr. (R)	517,330	47.4

1966	Howard H. Baker Jr. (R)	483,063	55.7
	Frank G. Clement (D)	383,843	44.3
1972	Howard H. Baker Jr. (R)	716,539	61.6
	Ray Blanton (D)	440,599	37.9
1978	Howard H. Baker Jr. (R)	642,644	55.5
	Jane Eskind (D)	466,228	40.3
1984	Albert Gore Jr. (D)	1,000,607	60.7
	Victor Ashe (R)	557,016	33.8
	Ed McAteer (I)	87,234	5.3
1990	Albert Gore Jr. (D)	530,898	67.7
	William R. Hawkins (R)	233,703	29.8

Special Election

1994	Fred Thompson (R)	885,998	60.4
	Jim Cooper (D)	565,930	38.6

1996	Fred Thompson (R)	1,091,554	61.4
	Houston Gordon (D)	654,937	36.8

TEXAS

	Candidates	Votes	%
	Class 1		
1946	Tom Connally (D)	336,931	88.5
	Murray C. Sells (R)	43,619	11.5
1952	Price Daniel (D, R)	1,894,671	100.0

Special Election

1957	Ralph Yarborough (D)	364,878	38.1
	Martin Dies (D)	290,869	30.4
	Thad Hutcheson (R)	219,591	22.9
1958	Ralph Yarborough (D)	587,030	74.6
	Roy Whittenburg (R)	185,926	23.6
1964	Ralph Yarborough (D)	1,463,958	56.2
	George Bush (R)	1,134,337	43.6
1970	Lloyd Bentsen (D)	1,193,814	53.5
	George Bush (R)	1,036,045	46.4
1976	Lloyd Bentsen (D)	2,199,956	56.8
	Alan Steelman (R)	1,636,370	42.2
1982	Lloyd Bentsen (D)	1,818,223	58.6
	James M. Collins (R)	1,256,759	40.5
1988	Lloyd Bentsen (D)	3,149,806	59.2
	Beau Boulter (R)	2,129,228	40.0

Special Primary[1]

1993	Kay Bailey Hutchison (R)	593,338	29.0
	Bob Krueger (D)	593,239	29.0
	Joe L. Barton (R)	284,135	13.9
	Jack Fields (R)	277,560	13.6
	Richard Fisher (D)	165,564	8.1

Special Runoff Election[1]

1993	Kay Bailey Hutchison (R)	1,188,716	67.3
	Bob Krueger (D)	576,538	32.7

1994	Kay Bailey Hutchison (R)	2,604,218	60.8
	Richard Fisher (D)	1,639,615	38.3

	Class 2		
1948	Lyndon B. Johnson (D)	702,785	66.2
	Jack Porter (R)	349,665	32.9
1954	Lyndon B. Johnson (D)	539,319	84.7
	Carlos G. Watson (R)	94,131	14.8
1960	Lyndon B. Johnson (D)	1,306,605	58.0
	John G. Tower (R)	926,653	41.1

Special Primary[1]

1961	John G. Tower (R)	327,308#	30.9
	William A. Blakley (D)	190,818#	18.1
	Jim Wright (D)	171,328#	16.2
	Will Wilson (D)	121,961#	11.5
	Maury Maverick Jr. (D)	104,992#	9.9
	Henry B. Gonzalez (D)	97,659#	9.2

Special Runoff Election[1]

1961	John G. Tower (R)	448,217	50.6
	William A. Blakley (D)	437,874	49.4

1966	John G. Tower (R)	842,501	56.4
	Waggoner Carr (D)	643,855	43.1
1972	John G. Tower (R)	1,822,877	53.4
	Barefoot Sanders (D)	1,511,985	44.3
1978	John G. Tower (R)	1,151,376	49.8
	Bob Krueger (D)	1,139,149	49.3
1984	Phil Gramm (R)	3,111,348	58.5
	Lloyd Doggett (D)	2,202,557	41.4
1990	Phil Gramm (R)	2,302,357	60.2
	Hugh Parmer (D)	1,429,986	37.4
1996	Phil Gramm (R)	3,027,680	54.8
	Victor M. Morales (D)	2,428,776	43.9

Texas

1. Under Texas law passed after the 1957 special election, candidates in special elections for the Senate would all run together in a primary with party affiliation. If none received a majority of the vote in the first primary, a runoff would be held between the top two contenders.

UTAH

	Candidates	Votes	%
	Class 1		
1946	Arthur V. Watkins (R)	101,142	51.2
	Abe Murdock (D)	96,257	48.8
1952	Arthur V. Watkins (R)	177,435	54.3
	Walter K. Granger (D)	149,598	45.7
1958	Frank E. Moss (D)	112,827	38.7
	Arthur V. Watkins (R)	101,471	34.8
	J. Bracken Lee (I)	77,013	26.4
1964	Frank E. Moss (D)	227,822	57.3
	Ernest L. Wilkinson (R)	169,562	42.7
1970	Frank E. Moss (D)	210,207	56.2
	Laurence J. Burton (R)	159,004	42.5
1976	Orrin G. Hatch (R)	290,221	53.7
	Moss E. Frank (D)	241,948	44.8
1982	Orrin G. Hatch (R)	309,332	58.3
	Ted Wilson (D)	219,482	41.3
1988	Orrin G. Hatch (R)	430,089	67.1
	Brian H. Moss (D)	203,364	31.7
1994	Orrin G. Hatch (R)	357,297	68.8
	Patrick A. Shea (D)	146,938	28.3
	Class 3		
1950	Wallace F. Bennett (R)	142,427	53.9
	Elbert D. Thomas (D)	121,198	45.8
1956	Wallace F. Bennett (R)	178,261	54.0
	Alonzo F. Hopkin (D)	152,120	46.0
1962	Wallace F. Bennett (R)	166,755	52.4
	David S. King (D)	151,656	47.6
1968	Wallace F. Bennett (R)	225,075	53.7
	Milton L. Weilenmann (D)	192,168	45.8
1974	Jake Garn (R)	210,299	50.0
	Wayne Owens (D)	185,377	44.1
1980	Jake Garn (R)	437,675	73.6
	Dan Berman (D)	151,454	25.5
1986	Jake Garn (R)	314,608	72.3
	Craig Oliver (D)	115,523	26.6
1992	Robert F. Bennett (R)	420,069	55.4
	Wayne Owens (D)	301,228	39.7

VERMONT

	Candidates	Votes	%
	Class 1		
1946	Ralph E. Flanders (R)	54,729	74.6
	Charles P. McDevitt (D)	18,594	25.4
1952	Ralph E. Flanders (R)	111,406	72.3
	Allan R. Johnston (D)	42,630	27.7
1958	Winston L. Prouty (R)	64,900	52.2
	Frederick J. Fayette (D)	59,536	47.8
1964	Winston L. Prouty (R, I)	87,879	53.5
	Frederick J. Fayette (D)	76,457	46.5
1970	Winston L. Prouty (R)	91,198	58.9
	Philip H. Hoff (D)	62,271	40.2

Special Election

1972	Robert T. Stafford (R)	45,888#	64.3
	Randolph T. Major (D)	23,842#	33.4

1976	Robert T. Stafford (R)	94,481	50.0
	Thomas P. Salmon (D)	85,682	45.3
1982	Robert T. Stafford (R)	84,450	50.3
	James A. Guest (D)	79,340	47.2
1988	James M. Jeffords (R)	163,183	67.9
	William Gray (D)	71,460	29.8
1994	James M. Jeffords (R)	106,505	50.3
	Jan Backus (D)	85,868	40.6
	Gavin T. Mills (I)	12,465	5.9
	Class 3		
1950	George D. Aiken (R)	69,543	78.0
	James E. Bigelow (D)	19,608	22.0
1956	George D. Aiken (R)	103,101	66.4
	Bernard G. O'Shea (D)	52,184	33.6
1962	George D. Aiken (R)	81,241	66.9
	W. Robert Johnson (D)	40,134	33.1
1968	George D. Aiken (R, D)	157,154	99.9
1974	Patrick J. Leahy (D, I VT)	70,629	49.5
	Richard W. Mallary (R)	66,223	46.4
1980	Patrick J. Leahy (D)	104,176	49.8
	Stewart M. Ledbetter (R)	101,421	48.5
1986	Patrick J. Leahy (D)	124,123	63.2
	Richard A. Snelling (R)	67,798	34.5
1992	Patrick J. Leahy (D)	154,762	54.2
	James H. Douglas (R)	123,854	43.3

VIRGINIA

	Candidates	Votes	%
	Class 1		
1946	Harry F. Byrd (D)	163,960	64.9
	Lester S. Parsons (R)	77,005	30.5
1952	Harry F. Byrd (D)	398,677	73.4
	H. M. Vise Sr. (ID)	69,133	12.7
	Clarke T. Robb (SOCIAL D)	67,281	12.4
1958	Harry F. Byrd (D)	317,221	69.3
	Louise Wensel (I)	120,224	26.3
1964	Harry F. Byrd (D)	592,260	63.8
	Richard A. May (R)	176,624	19.0
	James W. Respess (I)	95,526	10.3

Special Election

1966	Harry F. Byrd Jr. (D)	389,028	53.3
	Lawrence M. Traylor (R)	272,804	37.4
	John W. Carter (C)	57,692	7.9

1970	Harry F. Byrd Jr. (I)	506,623	53.5
	George C. Rawlings Jr. (D)	295,057	31.2
	Ray Garland (R)	145,031	15.3
1976	Harry F. Byrd Jr. (I)	890,778	57.2
	Elmo R. Zumwalt (D)	596,009	38.3
1982	Paul S. Trible Jr. (R)	724,571	51.2
	Richard Davis (D)	690,839	48.8
1988	Charles S. Robb (D)	1,474,086	71.2
	Maurice A. Dawkins (R)	593,652	28.7
1994	Charles S. Robb (D)	938,376	45.6
	Oliver L. North (R)	882,213	42.9
	J. Marshall Coleman (I)	235,324	11.4

Class 2

Special Election

1946	A. Willis Robertson (D)	169,680	68.2
	Robert H. Woods (R)	72,253	29.0

1948	A. Willis Robertson (D)	253,865	65.6
	Robert H. Woods (R)	119,366	30.8
1954	A. Willis Robertson (D)	244,844	79.9
	Charles William Lewis Jr. (ID)	32,681	10.7
	Clarke T. Robb (SOCIAL D)	28,922	9.4
1960	A. Willis Robertson (D)	506,169	81.3
	Stuart D. Baker (ID)	88,718	14.2
1966	William B. Spong Jr. (D)	429,855	58.6
	James P. Ould Jr. (R)	245,681	33.5
	F. Lee Hawthorne (C)	58,251	7.9
1972	William Lloyd Scott (R)	718,337	51.5
	William B. Spong Jr. (D)	643,963	46.1
1978	John W. Warner (R)	613,232	50.2
	Andrew P. Miller (D)	608,511	49.8
1984	John W. Warner (R)	1,406,194	70.0
	Edythe C. Harrison (D)	601,142	29.9
1990	John W. Warner (R)	876,782	80.9
	Nancy B. Spannaus (I)	196,755	18.2
1996	John W. Warner (R)	1,235,744	52.5
	Mark Warner (D)	1,115,982	47.4

WASHINGTON

Candidates	Votes	%

Class 1

1946	Harry P. Cain (R)	358,847	54.3
	Hugh B. Mitchell (D)	298,683	45.2
1952	Henry M. Jackson (D)	595,288	56.2
	Harry P. Cain (R)	460,884	43.5
1958	Henry M. Jackson (D)	597,040	67.3
	William B. Bantz (R)	278,271	31.4
1964	Henry M. Jackson (D)	875,950	72.2
	Lloyd J. Andrews (R)	337,138	27.8
1970	Henry M. Jackson (D)	879,385	82.4
	Charles W. Elicker (R)	170,790	16.0
1976	Henry M. Jackson (D)	1,071,219	71.8
	George M. Brown (R)	361,546	24.2
1982	Henry M. Jackson (D)	943,655	69.0
	Doug Jewett (R)	332,273	24.3
	King Lysen (I)	72,297	5.3

Special Election

| 1983 | Daniel J. Evans (R) | 617,699 | 55.4 |
| | Mike Lowry (D) | 496,393 | 44.6 |

1988	Slade Gorton (R)	944,359	51.1
	Mike Lowry (D)	904,183	48.9
1994	Slade Gorton (R)	947,821	55.7
	Ron Sims (D)	752,352	44.3

Class 3

1950	Warren G. Magnuson (D)	397,719	53.4
	Walter Williams (R)	342,464	46.0
1956	Warren G. Magnuson (D)	685,565	61.1
	Arthur B. Langlie (R)	436,652	38.9
1962	Warren G. Magnuson (D)	491,365	52.1
	Richard G. Christensen (R)	446,204	47.3
1968	Warren G. Magnuson (D)	796,183	64.4
	Jack Metcalf (R)	435,894	35.3
1974	Warren G. Magnuson (D)	611,811	60.7
	Jack Metcalf (R)	363,626	36.1
1980	Slade Gorton (R)	936,317	54.2
	Warren G. Magnuson (D)	792,052	45.8
1986	Brock Adams (D)	677,471	50.6
	Slade Gorton (R)	650,931	48.7
1992	Patty Murray (D)	1,197,973	54.0
	Rod Chandler (R)	1,020,829	46.0

WEST VIRGINIA

Candidates	Votes	%

Class 1

1946	Harley M. Kilgore (D)	273,151	50.3
	Thomas Sweeney (R)	269,617	49.7
1952	Harley M. Kilgore (D)	470,019	53.6
	Chapman Revercomb (R)	406,554	46.4

Special Election

| 1956 | Chapman Revercomb (R) | 432,123 | 53.7 |
| | William C. Marland (D) | 373,051 | 46.3 |

1958	Robert C. Byrd (D)	381,745	59.2
	Chapman Revercomb (R)	263,172	40.8
1964	Robert C. Byrd (D)	515,015	67.7
	Cooper P. Benedict (R)	246,072	32.3
1970	Robert C. Byrd (D)	345,965	77.6
	Elmer H. Dodson (R)	99,658	22.4
1976	Robert C. Byrd (D)	566,423	99.9
1982	Robert C. Byrd (D)	387,170	68.5
	Cleve K. Benedict (R)	173,910	30.8
1988	Robert C. Byrd (D)	410,983	64.8
	M. Jay Wolfe (R)	223,564	35.2
1994	Robert C. Byrd (D)	290,495	69.0
	Stan Klos (R)	130,441	31.0

Class 2

1948	Matthew M. Neely (D)	435,354	57.0
	Chapman Revercomb (R)	328,534	43.0
1954	Matthew M. Neely (D)	325,263	54.8
	Thomas Sweeney (R)	268,066	45.2

Special Election

| 1958 | Jennings Randolph (D) | 374,167 | 59.3 |
| | John D. Hoblitzell Jr. (R) | 256,510 | 40.7 |

1960	Jennings Randolph (D)	458,355	55.3
	Cecil H. Underwood (R)	369,935	44.7
1966	Jennings Randolph (D)	292,325	59.5
	Francis J. Love (R)	198,891	40.5
1972	Jennings Randolph (D)	486,310	66.5
	Louise Leonard (R)	245,531	33.6
1978	Jennings Randolph (D)	249,034	50.5
	Arch A. Moore Jr. (R)	244,317	49.5
1984	John D. "Jay" Rockefeller IV (D)	374,233	51.8
	John R. Raese (R)	344,680	47.7
1990	John D. "Jay" Rockefeller IV (D)	276,234	68.3
	John Yoder (R)	128,071	31.7
1996	John D. "Jay" Rockefeller IV (D)	456,526	76.6
	Betty A. Burks (R)	139,088	23.4

WISCONSIN

Candidates	Votes	%

Class 1

1946	Joseph R. McCarthy (R)	620,430	61.3
	Howard J. McMurray (D)	378,772	37.4
1952	Joseph R. McCarthy (R)	870,444	54.2
	Thomas E. Fairchild (D)	731,402	45.6

Special Election

1957	William Proxmire (D)	435,985	56.4
	Walter J. Kohler Jr. (R)	312,931	40.5
1958	William Proxmire (D)	682,440	57.1
	Roland J. Steinle (R)	510,398	42.7
1964	William Proxmire (D)	892,013	53.3
	Wilbur N. Renk (R)	780,116	46.4
1970	William Proxmire (D)	948,445	70.8
	John E. Erickson (R)	381,297	28.5
1976	William Proxmire (D)	1,396,970	72.2
	Stanley York (R)	521,902	27.0
1982	William Proxmire (D)	983,311	63.6
	Scott McCallum (R)	527,355	34.1
1988	Herb Kohl (D)	1,128,625	52.1
	Susan Engeleiter (R)	1,030,440	47.5
1994	Herb Kohl (D)	912,662	58.3
	Robert T. Welch (R)	636,989	40.7

Class 3

1950	Alexander Wiley (R)	595,283	53.3
	Thomas E. Fairchild (D)	515,539	46.2
1956	Alexander Wiley (R)	892,473	58.6
	Henry W. Maier (D)	627,903	41.2
1962	Gaylord Nelson (D)	662,342	52.6
	Alexander Wiley (R)	594,846	47.2
1968	Gaylord Nelson (D)	1,020,931	61.7
	Jerris Leonard (R)	633,910	38.3
1974	Gaylord Nelson (D)	740,700	61.8
	Thomas E. Petri (R)	429,327	35.8
1980	Bob Kasten (R)	1,106,311	50.2
	Gaylord Nelson (D)	1,065,487	48.3
1986	Bob Kasten (R)	754,573	50.9
	Ed Garvey (D)	702,963	47.4
1992	Russell D. Feingold (D)	1,290,662	52.6
	Bob Kasten (R)	1,129,599	46.0

WYOMING

Candidates	Votes	%

Class 1

1946	Joseph C. O'Mahoney (D)	45,843	56.2
	Harry B. Henderson (R)	35,714	43.8
1952	Frank A. Barrett (R)	67,176	51.6

	Joseph C. O'Mahoney (D)	62,921	48.4
1958	Gale McGee (D)	58,035	50.8
	Frank A. Barrett (R)	56,122	49.2
1964	Gale McGee (D)	76,485	54.0
	John S. Wold (R)	65,185	46.0
1970	Gale McGee (D)	67,207	55.8
	John S. Wold (R)	53,279	44.2
1976	Malcolm Wallop (R)	84,810	54.6
	Gale McGee (D)	70,558	45.4
1982	Malcolm Wallop (R)	94,725	56.7
	Rodger McDaniel (D)	72,466	43.3
1988	Malcolm Wallop (R)	91,143	50.4
	John Vinich (D)	89,821	49.6
1994	Craig Thomas (R)	118,754	58.9
	Mike Sullivan (D)	79,287	39.3

Class 2

1948	Lester C. Hunt (D)	57,953	57.1
	Edward V. Robertson (R)	43,527	42.9

Special Election

1954	Joseph C. O'Mahoney (D)	57,163	51.6
	William Henry Harrison (R)	53,705	48.4

1954	Joseph C. O'Mahoney (D)	57,845	51.5
	William Henry Harrison (R)	54,407	48.5
1960	Keith Thomson (R)	78,103*	56.4
	Raymond B. Whitaker (D)	60,447	43.6

Special Election

1962	Milward L. Simpson (R)	69,043	57.8
	J. J. Hickey (D)	50,329	42.2

1966	Clifford P. Hansen (R)	63,548	51.8
	Teno Roncalio (D)	59,141	48.2
1972	Clifford P. Hansen (R)	101,314	71.3
	Mike Vinich (D)	40,753	28.7
1978	Alan K. Simpson (R)	82,908	62.2
	Raymond B. Whitaker (D)	50,456	37.8
1984	Alan K. Simpson (R)	146,373	78.3
	Victor A. Ryan (D)	40,525	21.7
1990	Alan K. Simpson (R)	100,784	63.9
	Kathy Helling (D)	56,848	36.1
1996	Michael B. Enzi (R)	114,116	54.1
	Kathy Karpan (D)	89,103	42.2

Political Party Abbreviations

The following political party abbreviations are used in the Senate popular vote returns section.

ACP	A Connecticut Party	I	Independent	LIBERT	Libertarian
AM	American	I ALNC	Independent Alliance	NDPA	National Democratic
AM LAB	American Labor	ID	Independent		Party of Alabama
C	Conservative		Democrat	P	Prohibition
CLEAN GV	Clean Government	I PROG	Independent	PP	People's
D	Democrat		Progressive	R	Republican
DFL	Democrat Farmer-	I-R	Independent Republican	REF	Reform
	Labor	I VT	Independent	SOCIAL D	Social Democrat
DODD I	Dodd Independent		Vermonters	TCN	Tax Cut Now
GREEN	Green	L	Liberal	WRITE IN	Write in

Senate Primary Vote
Returns, 1946-1996

Sources: Senate Primary Returns

Senatorial primary returns for all 50 states are presented in this section *(pp. 103-164)*. Returns for most states go back to 1956. Senatorial primary returns for 11 Southern states (Alabama, Arkansas, Florida, Georgia, Louisiana, Mississippi, North Carolina, South Carolina, Tennessee, Texas and Virginia) go back to 1946 where available *(for a discussion of the importance of Southern primaries, see pp. 63-66)*.

The major source for primary election returns for all non-Southern states from 1956 to 1994 was the *America Votes* series, compiled biennially by Richard M. Scammon and Alice V. McGillivray of the Elections Research Center, Washington, D.C., and published by Congressional Quarterly. For all 1996 returns, the source was Rhodes Cook and Alice V. McGillivray, *U.S. Primary Elections* (Washington, D.C.: Congressional Quarterly, 1997). Other sources were the returns obtained by Congressional Quarterly after each federal election from the state secretaries of state. In cases of discrepancies, *Congressional Elections 1946-1996*, accepted the *America Votes* figure. The first year for which *America Votes* reported primary returns, 1956, was chosen as the starting point for most states because senatorial primary votes for earlier years are not readily available.

For the 11 Southern states the primary election returns presented for the years 1946 through 1973 were obtained, except where indicted by a footnote, from the Inter-University Consortium for Political and Social Research (ICPSR) at the University of Michigan. Major sources for returns from 1973 to 1994 were Congressional Quarterly, which obtained them from the state secretaries of state and Scammon and McGillivray's *America Votes* series.

The vast majority of Southern primaries during the period of 1946 to 1973 were held to nominate candidates of the dominant Democratic Party. In most cases, the winner of the Democratic primary went into the general election facing no Republican opponent and almost certain of victory.

Compilation of ICPSR Data File

Statewide candidate totals for Southern primary elections for senator were prepared by the ICPSR staff from several sources. Election returns for the years prior to 1949 were obtained from *Southern Primaries and Elections* (University: University of Alabama Press, 1950), edited by Alexander Heard and Donald S. Strong. It should be noted that, although they transcribed their data from official returns, Professors Heard and Strong found that many of the returns contained errors and discrepancies between the sum of county totals and the state total, or returns published as final in newspapers and secretary of state reports. No attempt was made by Heard and Strong to correct these discrepancies because the source of the error could not be determined.

For the period from 1949 to 1972, candidate totals were acquired from two sources. The first was a collection of Southern primary electoral statistics prepared from official returns by Hugh Davis Graham, chairman, division of social sciences, University of Maryland (Balti-

more County), and Numan V. Bartley, department of history, University of Georgia (Athens). In addition, reference was made to official returns supplied to ICPSR by the various secretaries of state in conjunction with the ICPSR effort to maintain its continuing collection of election materials. The returns obtained from Bartley and Graham, and the secretary of state offices, were compared with published reports of the election outcomes (notably state manuals and the *America Votes* series) to verify the completeness and accuracy of the returns.

Presentation of Returns

The returns for Senate primaries are arranged alphabetically by state and in chronological order by class of senator within each state listing. *(For an explanation of Senate classes, see p. 61)* Candidates are listed in descending order, with the candidate receiving the greatest number of popular votes listed first. Percentage of the total vote is listed for each candidate who received *at least 5 percent* of the total vote cast. *(For political party abbreviations, see p. 164)*

Primaries for special elections to fill vacancies and runoff primaries are designated in the returns. For Southern states prior to 1974, Republican primary results have been included, whenever available.

Names, Vote Totals and Percentages

The names of senatorial primary candidates are listed as they appeared in the source materials. In a few cases, first names are not known. In some cases the full names of candidates (instead of shortened forms) have been used for consistency across elections.

Percentages of the total vote were calculated on the basis of each candidate's proportion of the *total number of votes cast* for all candidates. Percentages have been calculated to two decimal places and rounded to one place. Due to rounding and the scattered votes of minor candidates, percentages in individual primary races may not add up to 100.

If no vote is shown for a candidate but the percentage of total vote is listed as 100 percent, in most cases the candidates in question ran unopposed and state election officials either did not bother to put the candidate's name on the ballot or simply did not make an effort to record the total number of votes.

When Senate primary elections were held under a preferential voting system and the use of second choice votes was required to determine a winner, the symbol ✔ appears next to the winner's name. *(Explanation of preferential voting, p. 64)*

There were a number of unusual cases in the history of Southern Senate primaries in which the nominee of one or both major parties was chosen by a party committee rather than in a primary. In these cases, the names of the nominees will appear in the primary returns along with a footnote indicating the particular circumstances.

Where no primary is indicated for a year in which a state elected a senator, it generally means that party conventions chose the nominees. Notes at the end of a state's listing explain other unusual circumstances.

Senate Primary Returns, 1946-1996

ALABAMA

Candidates	Votes	%
Class 2		

1946 — **Democratic Special Primary**

Candidates	Votes	%
John Sparkman (D)	85,049	50.1
James A. Simpson (D)	46,762	27.6
Frank W. Boykin (D)	35,982	21.2

1948 — **Democratic Primary**

Candidates	Votes	%
John Sparkman (D)	235,464	75.7
Philip J. Hamm (D)	61,308	19.7

1954 — **Democratic Primary**

Candidates	Votes	%
John Sparkman (D)	323,877	58.3
Laurie C. Battle (D)	208,166	37.4

1960 — **Democratic Primary**

Candidates	Votes	%
John Sparkman (D)	335,722	83.1
John G. Crommelin Jr. (D)	51,571	12.8

1966 — **Democratic Primary**

Candidates	Votes	%
John Sparkman (D)	378,295	57.0
Frank E. Dixon (D)	133,139	20.1
John G. Crommelin Jr. (D)	114,622	17.3
Mrs. Frank R. Stewart (D)	37,889	5.7

1972 — **Republican Primary**

Candidates	Votes	%
Winton M. "Red" Blount (R)	27,736	54.2
James D. Martin (R)	16,800	32.8
Bert Nettles (R)	5,765	11.3

Democratic Primary

Candidates	Votes	%
John Sparkman (D)	331,818	50.3
Melba T. Allen (D)	194,690	29.5
Lambert C. Mims (D)	87,461	13.3

1978 — **Republican Primary**

Candidates	Votes	%
James D. Martin (R)[1]		100.0

Democratic Primary

Candidates	Votes	%
Howell Heflin (D)	369,270	43.3
Walter Flowers (D)	236,894	27.8
John Baker (D)	191,110	22.4

Democratic Runoff

Candidates	Votes	%
Howell Heflin (D)	556,685	64.9
Walter Flowers (D)	300,654	35.1

1984 — **Republican Primary**

Candidates	Votes	%
Albert Lee Smith Jr. (R)	27,304	61.8
Doug Carter (R)	8,067	18.3
Joseph Keith (R)	5,171	11.7
Clint Wilkes (R)	3,644	8.2

Democratic Primary

Candidates	Votes	%
Howell Heflin (D)	399,817	83.2
Charles Wayne Borden (D)	47,462	9.9
Mrs. Frank Ross Stewart (D)	33,114	6.9

1990 — **Republican Primary**

Candidates	Votes	%
Bill Cabaniss (R)		100.0

Democratic Primary

Candidates	Votes	%
Howell Heflin (D)	540,876	81.4
Mrs. Frank Ross Stewart (D)	123,508	18.6

1996 — **Republican Primary**

Candidates	Votes	%
Jeff Sessions (R)	82,373	37.8
Sid McDonald (R)	47,320	21.7
Charles Woods (R)	24,409	11.2
Frank McRight (R)	21,964	10.1
Walter D. Clark (R)	18,745	8.6
Jimmy Blake (R)	15,385	7.1

Republican Runoff

Candidates	Votes	%
Jeff Sessions (R)	81,622	59.3
Sid McDonald (R)	56,131	40.7

Democratic Primary

Candidates	Votes	%
Roger Bedford (D)	141,360	44.8
Glen Browder (D)	91,203	28.9
Natalie Davis (D)	71,588	22.7

Democratic Runoff

Candidates	Votes	%
Roger Bedford (D)	141,747	61.6
Glen Browder (D)	88,415	38.4

Class 3

1950 — **Democratic Primary**

Candidates	Votes	%
Lister Hill (D)		✔

	Candidates	Votes	%
1956	**Democratic Primary**		
	Lister Hill (D)	247,519	68.2
	John G. Crommelin Jr. (D)	115,440	31.8
1962	**Democratic Primary**		
	Lister Hill (D)	363,613	73.7
	Donald G. Hallmark (D)	72,855	14.8
	John G. Crommelin Jr. (D)	56,822	11.5
1968	**Democratic Primary**		
	James B. Allen (D)	224,483	41.9
	Armistead I. Selden (D)	190,283	35.5
	Bob Smith (D)	72,928	13.6
	James E. Folsom (D)	32,004	6.0
	Democratic Runoff		
	James B. Allen (D)	196,511	50.5
	Armistead I. Selden (D)	192,448	49.5
1974	**Democratic Primary**		
	James B. Allen (D)	572,584	82.8
	John Taylor (D)	118,848	17.2
1978[2]	**Republican Special Primary**		
	George Nichols (R)[3]	15,637	72.5
	Elvin McCary (R)	5,941	27.5
	Democratic Special Primary		
	Maryon Pittman Allen (D)	334,758	44.6
	Donald W. Stewart (D)	259,795	34.6
	Ted Taylor (D)	70,894	9.4
	Dan Wiley (D)	66,689	8.9
	Democratic Special Runoff		
	Donald W. Stewart (D)	502,346	57.2
	Maryon Pittman Allen (D)	375,894	42.8
1980	**Republican Primary**		
	Jeremiah Denton (R)	73,708	63.8
	Armistead Selden (R)	41,825	36.2
	Democratic Primary		
	Donald W. Stewart (D)	222,540	48.6
	Jim Folsom Jr. (D)	163,196	35.7
	Finis St. John (D)	51,260	11.2
	Democratic Runoff		
	Jim Folsom Jr. (D)	204,486	50.6
	Donald W. Stewart (D)	199,428	49.4
1986	**Republican Primary**		
	Jeremiah Denton (R)	29,805	88.5
	Richard W. Vickers (R)	3,854	11.5
	Democratic Primary		
	Richard C. Shelby (D)	420,155	51.3
	James B. Allen Jr. (D)	284,206	34.7
	Ted McLaughlin (D)	70,784	8.6

	Candidates	Votes	%
1992	**Republican Primary**		
	Richard Sellers (R)		100.0
	Democratic Primary		
	Richard C. Shelby (D)	304,957	61.5
	Chris McNair (D)	136,836	27.6
	Bob Miller (D)	28,432	5.7
	Mrs. Frank Ross Stewart (D)	25,956	5.2

Alabama
1. Martin withdrew after the primary to run for the short-term Senate seat. He was not replaced.
2. A special election was held to fill the remaining two years of the term of Sen. James B. Allen (D), who died June 1, 1978.
3. Nichols withdrew after the primary and James D. Martin was substituted by the state committee.

ALASKA[1]

	Candidates	Votes	%
	Class 2		
1958[2]	**Republican Primary**		
	R. E. Robertson (R)		100.0
	Democratic Primary		
	E. L. Bartlett (D)		100.0
1960	**Republican Primary**		
	Lee L. McKinley (R)	8,867	68.2
	Lawrence M. Brayton (R)	4,131	31.8
	Democratic Primary		
	E. L. Bartlett (D)		100.0
1966	**Republican Primary**		
	Lee L. McKinley (R)	9,310	55.8
	Lawrence M. Brayton (R)	5,492	32.9
	Maxine B. Whaley (R)	1,866	11.2
	Democratic Primary		
	E. L. Bartlett (D)	27,994	87.2
	T. J. Bichsel (D)	1,864	5.8
1970[3]	**Republican Special Primary**		
	Ted Stevens (R)	39,062	96.7
	Democratic Special Primary		
	Wendell P. Kay (R)	16,729	56.8
	Joe Josephson (R)	12,730	43.2
1972	**Republican Primary**		
	Ted Stevens (R)		100.0
	Democratic Primary		
	Gene Guess (D)		100.0

	Candidates	Votes	%
1978	**Republican Primary**		
	Ted Stevens (R)		100.0
	Democratic Primary		
	Donald W. Hobbs (D)	10,589	55.0
	Joe Sonneman (D)	8,662	45.0
1984	**Republican Primary**		
	Ted Stevens (R)	65,552	100.0
	Democratic Primary		
	John E. Havelock (D)	19,074	65.5
	Dave Carlson (D)	4,620	15.9
	Michael Beasley (D)	2,443	8.4
	Joe Tracanna (D)	1,661	5.7
1990	**Republican Primary**		
	Ted Stevens (R)	81,968	70.2
	Robert M. Bird (R)	34,824	29.8
	Democratic Primary		
	Michael Beasley (D)	12,371	57.0
	Tom Taggart (D)	9,329	43.0
1996	**Republican Primary**		
	Ted Stevens (R)	71,043	67.7
	Dave W. Cuddy (R)	32,994	31.5
	Democratic Primary		
	Theresa Obermeyer (D)	4,072	33.8
	Joseph A. Sonneman (D)	2,643	21.9
	Michael Beasley (D)	1,968	16.3
	Henry J. Blake Jr. (D)	1,157	9.6
	Lawrence Freiberger (D)	921	7.6
	Frank Vondersaar (D)	655	5.4
	Robert Alan Gigler (D)	631	5.2
	Green Primary		
	Jed Whittaker (GREEN)	3,751	100.0

Class 3

	Candidates	Votes	%
1958[2]	**Republican Primary**		
	Mike Stepovich (R)		100.0
	Democratic Primary		
	Ernest Gruening (D)		100.0
1962	**Republican Primary**		
	Ted Stevens (R)	11,000	72.5
	Frank Cook (R)	4,175	27.5
	Democratic Primary		
	Ernest Gruening (D)	18,525	86.3
	R. L. Veach (D)	2,946	13.7

	Candidates	Votes	%
1968	**Republican Primary**		
	Elmer Rasmuson (R)	10,320	53.1
	Ted Stevens (R)	9,111	46.9
	Democratic Primary		
	Mike Gravel (D)	17,971	52.9
	Ernest Gruening (D)	16,015	47.1
1974	**Republican Primary**		
	C. R. Lewis (R)	21,065	52.7
	Terry Miller (R)	16,336	40.8
	Red Stevens (R)	2,207	5.5
	Democratic Primary		
	Mike Gravel (D)	22,834	54.3
	Gene Guess (D)	15,090	35.9
	Richard J. Greuel (D)	3,367	8.0
1980	**Republican Primary**		
	Frank H. Murkowski (R)	16,292	59.0
	Arthur R. Kennedy (R)	5,527	20.0
	Morris Thompson (R)	3,635	13.2
	Democratic Primary		
	Clark S. Gruening (D)	39,719	54.9
	Mike Gravel (D)	31,504	43.5
1986	**Republican Primary**		
	Frank H. Murkowski (R)		100.0
	Democratic Primary		
	Glenn Olds (D)	36,995	75.0
	Bill Barnes (D)	4,871	9.9
	Dave Carlson (D)	4,211	8.5
	Libertarian Primary		
	Chuck House (LIBERT)		100.0
1992[4]	**Republican Primary**		
	Frank H. Murkowski (R)	37,486	80.5
	Jed Whittaker (R)	9,065	19.5
	Democratic Primary		
	Tony Smith (D)	33,162	48.8
	William L. Hensley (D)	29,586	43.5
	Green Primary		
	Mary E. Jodan (GREEN)	5,989	100.0

Alaska

1. In Alaska's so-called "jungle" primaries, all candidates for an office appeared together on the same ballot with their parties designated. Nominations went to the Republican and Democrat receiving the most votes for the office. Percentages were calculated here as if candidates had run in separate party primaries.

2. Alaska became a state Jan. 3, 1959. The first Senate elections for that state were for unspecified terms. The Senate later determined that Sen. Bartlett would serve two years (Class 2) and Sen. Gruening, four (Class 3).

3. A special election was held to fill the remaining two years of the term of Sen. E. L. Bartlett (D), who died Dec. 11, 1968. The first two years of the vacancy were filled by appointee Ted Stevens (R).

4. In 1992 the Republican primary was a closed primary with only candidates from that party on the ballot. All other parties ran on a multi-party ballot with nominations going to the candidate with the highest vote in each party.

ARIZONA

Candidates	Votes	%
Class 1		

1958   **Republican Primary**

Barry Goldwater (R)		100.0

Democratic Primary

Ernest W. McFarland (D)	111,429	72.5
Stephen W. Langmade (D)	42,199	27.5

1964   **Republican Primary**

Paul Fannin (R)		100.0

Democratic Primary

Roy L. Elson (D)	76,697	41.4
Renz L. Jennings (D)	64,331	34.7
Howard V. Peterson (D)	22,424	12.1
George Gavin (D)	10,291	5.6

1970   **Republican Primary**

Paul Fannin (R)		100.0

Democratic Primary

Sam Grossman (D)	78,006	65.2
John Kruglick (D)	27,324	22.8
H. L. Kelly (D)	14,238	11.9

1976   **Republican Primary**

Sam Steiger (R)	102,843	52.5
John B. Conlan (R)	93,033	47.5

Democratic Primary

Dennis DeConcini (D)	121,423	53.4
Carolyn Warner (D)	71,612	31.5
Wade Church (D)	34,266	15.1

Libertarian Primary

Allan Norwitz (LIBERT)		100.0

1982   **Republican Primary**

Pete Dunn (R)	97,391	55.1
Dean Sellers (R)	79,375	44.9

Democratic Primary

Dennis DeConcini (D)	140,328	84.4
Caroline P. Killeen (D)	25,909	15.6

Candidates	Votes	%
Libertarian Primary		

Randall Clamons (LIBERT)		100.0

1988   **Republican Primary**

Keith DeGreen (R)		100.0

Democratic Primary

Dennis DeConcini (D)		100.0

1994   **Republican Primary**

Jon Kyl (R)	231,275	99.0

Democratic Primary

Sam Coopersmith (D)	82,057	32.2
Richard Mahoney (D)	81,998	32.1
Cindy Resnick (D)	75, 563	29.6
Dave Moss (D)	15, 612	6.1

Libertarian Primary

Scott Grainger (LIBERT)	5,424	100.0

Class 3

1956   **Republican Primary**

Ross F. Jones (R)	31,246	79.3
Albert H. Mackenzie (R)	8,147	20.7

Democratic Primary

Carl Hayden (D)	99,859	82.4
Robert E. Miller (D)	21,370	17.6

1962   **Republican Primary**

Evan Mecham (R)	40,300	59.0
Stephen Shadegg (R)	27,965	41.0

Democratic Primary

Carl Hayden (D)	117,688	76.5
W. Lee McLane (D)	36,158	23.5

1968   **Republican Primary**

Barry Goldwater (R)		100.0

Democratic Primary

Roy L. Elson (D)	95,231	62.8
Bob Kennedy (D)	41,397	27.3
Dick Herbert (D)	15,061	9.9

1974   **Republican Primary**

Barry Goldwater (R)		100.0

Democratic Primary

Jonathan Marshall (D)	79,225	53.6
George Oglesby (D)	36,262	24.5
William M. Feighan (D)	32,449	21.9

	Candidates	Votes	%
1980	**Republican Primary**		
	Barry Goldwater (R)		100.0
	Democratic Primary		
	Bill Schulz (D)	97,520	55.4
	James F. McNulty Jr. (D)	58,894	33.4
	Frank DePaoli (D)	19,259	10.9
	Libertarian Primary		
	Fred Esser (LIBERT)		100.0
1986	**Republican Primary**		
	John McCain (R)		100.0
	Democratic Primary		
	Richard Kimball (D)		100.0
1992	**Republican Primary**		
	John McCain (R)		100.0
	Democratic Primary		
	Claire Sargent (D)	124,174	56.8
	Truman Spangrud (D)	94,326	43.2

ARKANSAS

	Candidates	Votes	%
	Class 2		
1948	**Democratic Primary**		
	John L. McClellan (D)		100.0
1954	**Democratic Primary**		
	John L. McClellan (D)		100.0
1960	**Democratic Primary**		
	John L. McClellan (D)		100.0
1966	**Democratic Primary**		
	John L. McClellan (D)	310,526	77.2
	Foster Johnson (D)	91,746	22.8
1972	**Republican Primary**		
	Wayne H. Babbitt (R)		100.0
	Democratic Primary		
	John L. McClellan (D)	220,588	44.7
	David Pryor (D)	204,058	41.4
	Ted Boswell (D)	62,496	12.7
	Democratic Runoff		
	John L. McClellan (D)	242,983	52.0
	David Pryor (D)	224,262	48.0

	Candidates	Votes	%
1978	**Republican Primary**		
	Tom Kelly (R)		100.0
	Democratic Primary		
	David Pryor (D)	198,039	34.3
	Jim Guy Tucker (D)	187,568	32.5
	Ray Thornton (D)	184,095	31.9
	Democratic Runoff		
	David Pryor (D)	265,525	54.9
	Jim Guy Tucker (D)	218,026	45.1
1984	**Republican Primary**		
	Ed Bethune (R)		100.0
	Democratic Primary		
	David Pryor (D)		100.0
1990	**Democratic Primary**		
	David Pryor (D)		100.0
1996	**Republican Primary**		
	Mike Huckabee (R)[1]		100.0
	Democratic Primary		
	Winston Bryant (D)	129,328	39.3
	Lu Hardin (D)	71,889	21.9
	Bill Bristow (D)	58,093	17.7
	Sandy McMath (D)	42,303	12.9
	Kevin Smith (D)	21,774	6.6
	Democratic Runoff		
	Winston Bryant (D)	123,273	54.7
	Lu Hardin (D)	101,901	45.3

	Candidates	Votes	%
	Class 3		
1950	**Democratic Primary**		
	J. William Fulbright (D)	189,200	100.0
1956	**Republican Primary**		
	Kenneth G. Jones (R)		100.0
	Democratic Primary		
	J. William Fulbright (D)		100.0
1962	**Democratic Primary**		
	J. William Fulbright (D)	253,751	66.1
	Winston G. Chandler (D)	129,987	33.9
1968	**Republican Primary**		
	Charles T. Bernard (R)		100.0

Candidates	Votes	%
Democratic Primary		
J. William Fulbright (D)	220,684	52.9
James Johnson (D)	132,038	31.7
Bobby K. Hayes (D)	52,906	12.7
1974 Republican Primary		
John H. Jones (R)		100.0
Democratic Primary		
Dale Bumpers (D)	380,748	65.0
J. William Fulbright (D)	204,630	35.0
1980 Republican Primary		
Bill Clark (R)		100.0
Democratic Primary		
Dale Bumpers (D)		100.0
1986 Republican Primary		
Asa Hutchinson (R)		100.0
Democratic Primary		
Dale Bumpers (D)		100.0
1992 Republican Primary		
Mike Huckabee (R)	41,346	79.1
David Busby (R)	10,892	20.9
Democratic Primary		
Dale Bumpers (D)	322,458	64.5
Julia H. Jones (D)	177,273	35.5

Arkansas

1. Huckabee withdrew from the Senate race May 30 to become governor. The state Republican Party selected Rep. Tim Hutchinson as the Republican nominee to run in the general election.

CALIFORNIA

Candidates	Votes	%
Class 1		
1958[1] Republican Primary		
Goodwin J. Knight (R)	790,939	49.1
George Christopher (R)	558,245	34.7
Clair Engle (D)	173,845	10.8
Democratic Primary		
Clair Engle (D)	1,558,622	70.8
Goodwin J. Knight (R)	385,170	17.5
George Christopher (R)	221,783	10.1
1964 Republican Primary		
George Murphy (R)	1,121,591	54.1
Leland M. Kaiser (R)	689,323	33.3
Fred Hall (R)	261,036	12.6

Candidates	Votes	%
Democratic Primary		
Pierre Salinger (D)	1,177,517	44.3
Alan Cranston (D)	1,037,748	39.0
George McLain (D)	180,405	6.8
1970 Republican Primary		
George Murphy (R)	1,325,271	64.3
Norton Simon (R)	670,702	32.5
Democratic Primary		
John V. Tunney (D)	1,010,812	41.6
George E. Brown (D)	812,463	33.4
Kenneth Hahn (D)	417,970	17.2
American Independent Primary		
Charles C. Ripley (AMI)	14,115	65.0
John Ortman (AMI)	7,600	34.9
Peace and Freedom Primary		
Robert Scheer (PFP)		100.0
1976 Republican Primary		
S. I. Hayakawa (R)	886,743	38.2
Robert H. Finch (R)	614,240	26.5
Alphonzo E. Bell (R)	532,969	23.0
John L. Harmer (R)	197,252	8.5
Democratic Primary		
John V. Tunney (D)	1,774,879	53.8
Tom Hayden (D)	1,210,637	36.7
American Independent Primary		
Jack McCoy (AMI)		100.0
Peace and Freedom Primary		
David Wald (PFP)		100.0
1982 Republican Primary		
Pete Wilson (R)	851,292	37.5
Paul N. McCloskey (R)	577,267	25.5
Barry M. Goldwater Jr. (R)	408,308	18.0
Robert K. Dornan (R)	181,970	8.0
Democratic Primary		
Edmund G. Brown Jr. (D)	1,392,660	50.7
Gore Vidal (D)	415,366	15.1
Paul B. Carpenter (D)	415,198	15.1
Daniel K. Whitehurst (D)	167,574	6.1
American Independent Primary		
Theresa Dietrich (AMI)		100.0
Peace and Freedom Primary		
David Wald (PFP)		100.0
Libertarian Primary		
Joseph Fuhrig (LIBERT)		100.0

	Candidates	Votes	%
1988	**Republican Primary**		
	Pete Wilson (R)		*100.0*
	Democratic Primary		
	Leo T. McCarthy (D)	2,367,067	*81.7*
	John H. Abbott (D)	220,331	*7.6*
	Robert J. Banuelos (D)	163,882	*5.7*
	Charles Greene (D)	146,307	*5.0*
	American Independent Primary		
	Merton D. Short (AMI)		*100.0*
	Libertarian Primary		
	Jack Dean (LIBERT)		*100.0*
	Peace and Freedom Primary		
	M. Elizabeth Munoz (PFP)	3,701	*58.5*
	Gloria Garcia (PFP)	2,623	*41.5*
1992[2]	**Republican Special Primary**		
	John Seymour (R)	1,216,096	*51.2*
	William E. Dannemeyer (R)	638,279	*26.9*
	Jim Trinity (R)	306,182	*12.9*
	William B. Allen (R)	216,177	*9.1*
	Democratic Special Primary		
	Dianne Feinstein (D)	1,775,730	*57.8*
	Gray Davis (D)	1,009,761	*32.8*
	American Independent Special Primary		
	Paul Meeuwenberg (AMI)		*100.0*
	Libertarian Special Primary		
	Richard B. Boddie (LIBERT)		*100.0*
	Peace and Freedom Special Primary		
	Gerald Horne (PFP)	5,681	*64.0*
	Jamie Mangia (PFP)	3,195	*36.0*
1994	**Republican Primary**		
	Michael Huffington (R)	1,072,558	*55.4*
	William E. Dannemeyer (R)	565,864	*29.3*
	Kate Squires (R)	202,387	*10.5*
	Democratic Primary		
	Dianne Feinstein (D)	1,635,837	*74.2*
	Ted J. Andromidas (D)	297,128	*13.5*
	Daniel D. O'Dowd (D)	271,615	*12.3*
	American Independent Primary		
	Paul Meeuwenberg (AMI)	17,747	*100.0*
	Libertarian Primary		
	Richard B. Boddie (LIBERT)	13,596	*100.0*
	Peace and Freedom Primary		
	Elizabeth Cervantes Barron (PFP)	3,487	*70.7*
	Larry D. Hampshire (PFP)	1,445	*29.3*

	Candidates	Votes	%
	Green Primary		
	Barbara Blong (GREEN)	9,006	*52.8*
	Kent W. Smith (GREEN)	3,846	*22.6*
	"None of the above"	4,203	*24.6*

Class 3

	Candidates	Votes	%
1956[1]	**Republican Primary**		
	Thomas H. Kuchel (R)	1,332,074	*90.4*
	Democratic Primary		
	Richard Richards (D)	1,004,336	*53.4*
	Thomas H. Kuchel (R)	494,066	*26.2*
	Samuel W. Yorty (D)	383,813	*20.4*
	Prohibition Party Primary		
	Ray Gourley (P)		*100.0*
1962	**Republican Primary**		
	Thomas H. Kuchel (R)	1,357,975	*75.0*
	Lloyd Wright (R)	247,300	*13.7*
	Howard Jarvis (R)	180,768	*10.0*
	Democratic Primary		
	Richard Richards (D)	1,674,563	*82.6*
	Gabriel Green (D)	171,379	*8.5*
	J. F. Coleman (D)	170,296	*8.4*
1968	**Republican Primary**		
	Max Rafferty (R)	1,112,947	*50.1*
	Thomas H. Kuchel (R)	1,043,315	*46.9*
	Democratic Primary		
	Alan Cranston (D)	1,681,825	*59.0*
	Anthony C. Beilenson (D)	644,844	*22.6*
	Walter R. Buchanan (D)	227,798	*8.0*
	William M. Bennett (D)	207,720	*7.3*
	Peace and Freedom Primary		
	Paul Jacobs (PFP)		*100.0*
1974	**Republican Primary**		
	H. L. "Bill" Richardson (R)	1,061,986	*64.6*
	Earl W. Brian (R)	273,636	*16.7*
	James E. Johnson (R)	118,715	*7.2*
	William H. Reinholz (R)	107,217	*6.5*
	Democratic Primary		
	Alan Cranston (D)	2,262,574	*83.5*
	Howard L. Gifford (D)	318,080	*11.7*
	American Independent Primary		
	Jack McCoy (AMI)		*100.0*
	Peace and Freedom Primary		
	Gayle M. Justice (PFP)		*100.0*

	Candidates	Votes	%
1980	**Republican Primary**		
	Paul Gann (R)	934,433	40.0
	Samuel W. Yorty (R)	668,583	28.6
	John G. Schmitz (R)	442,839	19.0
	Democratic Primary		
	Alan Cranston (D)	2,608,746	79.9
	Richard Morgan (D)	350,394	10.7
	American Independent Primary		
	James C. Griffin (AMI)		100.0
	Peace and Freedom Primary		
	David Wald (PFP)		100.0
	Libertarian Primary		
	David Bergland (LIBERT)		100.0
1986	**Republican Primary**		
	Ed Zschau (R)	737,384	37.1
	Bruce Herschensohn (R)	587,852	29.6
	Michael D. Antonovich (R)	180,010	9.1
	Bobbi Fiedler (R)	143,032	7.2
	Ed Davis (R)	130,309	6.6
	Democratic Primary		
	Alan Cranston (D)	1,807,242	80.7
	Charles Greene (D)	165,594	7.4
	John H. Abbott (D)	124,218	5.5
	American Independent Primary		
	Edward B. Vallen (AMI)		100.0
	Peace and Freedom Primary		
	Paul Kangas (PFP)	2,495	51.6
	Lenni Brenner (PFP)	2,344	48.4
	Libertarian Primary		
	Breck McKinley (LIBERT)		100.0
1992	**Republican Primary**		
	Bruce Herschensohn (R)	956,146	38.2
	Tom Campbell (R)	895,970	35.8
	Sonny Bono (R)	417,848	16.7
	Democratic Primary		
	Barbara Boxer (D)	1,339,126	43.7
	Leo T. McCarthy (D)	935,209	30.5
	Mel Levine (D)	667,359	21.8
	American Independent Primary		
	Jerome McCready (AMI)		100.0
	Libertarian Primary		
	June R. Genis (LIBERT)		100.0

Candidates	Votes	%
Peace and Freedom Primary		
Genevieve Torres (PFP)	5,492	60.3
Shirley Lee (PFP)	3,610	39.7

California

1. California's cross-filing law permitted a candidate to enter both the Democratic and Republican primaries. The law was repealed after 1958.

2. A special election was held to fill the remaining two years of the term of Sen. Pete Wilson (R), who resigned Jan. 7, 1991, after being elected governor. The first two years of the vacancy were filled by appointee John Seymour (R).

COLORADO

	Candidates	Votes	%
	Class 2		
1960	**Republican Primary**		
	Gordon Allott (R)		100.0
	Democratic Primary		
	Robert L. Knous (D)		100.0
1966	**Republican Primary**		
	Gordon Allott (R)		100.0
	Democratic Primary		
	Roy Romer (D)		100.0
1972	**Republican Primary**		
	Gordon Allott (R)		100.0
	Democratic Primary		
	Floyd K. Haskell (D)	77,574	58.8
	Anthony F. Vollack (D)	54,298	41.2
1978	**Republican Primary**		
	William L. Armstrong (R)	108,573	73.4
	Jack Swigert (R)	39,247	26.6
	Democratic Primary		
	Floyd K. Haskell (D)		100.0
1984	**Republican Primary**		
	William L. Armstrong (R)	105,870	100.0
	Democratic Primary		
	Nancy Dick (D)	78,248	51.0
	Carlos F. Lucero (D)	75,277	49.0
1990	**Republican Primary**		
	Hank Brown (R)		100.0
	Democratic Primary		
	Josie Heath (D)	116,099	58.6
	Carlos F. Lucero (D)	82,173	41.4

	Candidates	Votes	%
1996	**Republican Primary**		
	Wayne Allard (R)	115,064	*56.8*
	Gale Norton (R)	87,394	*43.2*
	Democratic Primary		
	Tom Strickland (D)	87,294	*66.1*
	Gene Nichol (D)	44,709	*33.9*

Class 3

	Candidates	Votes	%
1956	**Republican Primary**		
	Dan Thornton (R)		*100.0*
	Democratic Primary		
	John A. Carroll (D)	62,688	*50.8*
	Charles Brannan (D)	60,701	*49.2*
1962	**Republican Primary**		
	Peter H. Dominick (R)		*100.0*
	Democratic Primary		
	John A. Carroll (D)		*100.0*
1968	**Republican Primary**		
	Peter H. Dominick (R)		*100.0*
	Democratic Primary		
	Stephen McNichols (D)	92,250	*58.5*
	Kenneth Montfort (D)	65,347	*41.5*
1974	**Republican Primary**		
	Peter H. Dominick (R)		*100.0*
	Democratic Primary		
	Gary Hart (D)	81,161	*39.9*
	Herrick S. Roth (D)	66,819	*32.9*
	Martin P. Miller (D)	55,339	*27.2*
1980	**Republican Primary**		
	Mary E. Buchanan (R)	65,803	*30.8*
	Howard W. Callaway (R)	64,256	*30.1*
	Sam Zakhem (R)	42,629	*20.0*
	John M. Cogswell (R)	40,651	*19.0*
	Democratic Primary		
	Gary Hart (D)		*100.0*
1986	**Republican Primary**		
	Ken Kramer (R)		*100.0*
	Democratic Primary		
	Timothy E. Wirth (D)		*100.0*
1992	**Republican Primary**		
	Terry Considine (R)	122,427	*100.0*

	Candidates	Votes	%
	Democratic Primary		
	Ben Nighthorse Campbell (D)	117,634	*45.5*
	Richard D. Lamm (D)	93,599	*36.2*
	Josie Heath (D)	47,418	*18.3*

CONNECTICUT [1]

Class 1

	Candidates	Votes	%
1970	**Republican Primary**		
	Lowell P. Weicker Jr. (R)	77,057	*60.3*
	John M. Lupton (R)	50,657	*39.7*
	Democratic Primary		
	Joseph D. Duffey (D)	79,166	*43.7*
	Alphonsus J. Donahue (D)	66,916	*36.8*
	Edward L. Marcus (D)	35,715	*19.7*
1994	**Republican Primary**		
	Jerry Labriola (R)	69,972	*66.8*
	Joe Bentivegna (R)	34,733	*33.2*

Class 3

	Candidates	Votes	%
1980	**Republican Primary**		
	James L. Buckley (R)	64,962	*56.5*
	Richard C. Buzzuto (R)	50,096	*43.5*
1992	**Republican Primary**		
	Brook Johnson (R)	50,305	*59.4*
	Christopher Burnham (R)	40,542	*40.6*

Connecticut
1. In Connecticut, party conventions nominated candidates subject to a system of "challenge" primaries that allowed defeated candidates to petition for a popular vote if they received at least 20 percent of the convention vote.

DELAWARE

Class 1

	Candidates	Votes	%
1982	**Republican Primary**		
	William V. Roth Jr. (R)		*100.0*
	Democratic Primary		
	David N. Levinson (D)		*100.0*
1988	**Republican Primary**		
	William V. Roth Jr. (R)		*100.0*
	Democratic Primary[1]		
	S. B. Woo (D)	20,225	*50.0*
	Samuel S. Beard (D)	20,154	*50.0*

	Candidates	Votes	%
1994	**Republican Primary**		
	William V. Roth Jr. (R)		100.0
	Democratic Primary		
	Charles M. Oberly (D)		100.0

Class 2

	Candidates	Votes	%
1978 [2]	**Republican Primary**		
	James H. Baxter (R)	12,107	53.7
	James E. Venema (R)	10,422	46.3
1984	**Republican Primary**		
	John M. Burris (R)		100.0
	Democratic Primary		
	Joseph R. Biden (D)		100.0
1990	**Republican Primary**		
	M. Jane Brady (R)		100.0
	Democratic Primary		
	Joseph R. Biden (D)		100.0
1996	**Republican Primary**		
	Raymond J. Clatworthy (R)	18,638	82.2
	Vance Phillips (R)	3,307	14.6
	Democratic Primary		
	Joseph R. Biden (D)		100.0

Delaware

1. Data are given for the recount vote.
2. From 1972 through 1978 Delaware used a system of "challenge" primaries, in which a candidate for statewide office who received at least 35 percent of the convention vote could challenge the endorsed candidate in a primary. There was no Senate election in Delaware in 1980, the first year that the state used the direct primary system.

FLORIDA

	Candidates	Votes	%
	Class 1		
1946	**Democratic Primary**		
	Spessard L. Holland (D)	204,352	60.7
	Robert A. "Lex" Green (D)	109,040	32.4
1952	**Democratic Primary**		
	Spessard L. Holland (D)	485,515	84.2
	William A. Gaston (D)	91,011	15.8

	Candidates	Votes	%
1958	**Republican Primary**		
	Leland Hyzer (R)		100.0
	Democratic Primary		
	Spessard L. Holland (D)	408,084	55.9
	Claude Pepper (D)	321,377	44.1
1964	**Republican Primary**		
	Claude R. Kirk Jr. (R)		100.0
	Democratic Primary		
	Spessard L. Holland (D)	676,014	70.0
	Brailey Odham (D)	289,454	30.0
1970	**Republican Primary**		
	William C. Cramer (R)	220,553	62.5
	G. Harrold Carswell (R)	121,281	34.4
	Democratic Primary		
	Farris Bryant (D)	240,222	32.9
	Lawton Chiles (D)	188,300	25.8
	Fred Schultz (D)	175,745	24.1
	Al Hastings (D)	91,948	12.6
	Democratic Runoff		
	Lawton Chiles (D)	474,420	65.7
	Farris Bryant (D)	247,211	34.3
1976	**Republican Primary**		
	John Grady (R)	164,644	54.5
	Walter Sims (R)	74,684	24.7
	Helen S. Hansel (R)	62,718	20.8
	Democratic Primary		
	Lawton Chiles (D)		100.0
1982	**Republican Primary**		
	Van B. Poole	154,158	41.6
	David H. Bludworth	116,030	31.3
	George Snyder	100,607	27.1
	Republican Runoff		
	Van B. Poole	131,638	58.1
	David H. Bludworth	95,024	41.9
	Democratic Primary		
	Lawton Chiles (D)		100.0
1988	**Republican Primary**		
	Connie Mack (R)	405,296	61.8
	Robert W. Merkle (R)	250,730	38.2
	Democratic Primary		
	Bill Gunter (D)	383,721	38.0
	Buddy McKay (D)	263,946	26.1
	Dan Mica (D)	179,524	17.8

Candidates	Votes	%
Patricia Prank (D)	119,277	*11.8*
Claude R. Kirk Jr. (D)	51,387	*5.0*

Democratic Runoff

Buddy McKay (D)	369,266	*52.0*
Bill Gunter (D)	340,918	*48.0*

1994   **Republican Primary**

Connie Mack (R)		*100.0*

Democratic Primary

Hugh E. Rodham (D)	255,605	*33.8*
Mike Wiley (D)	188,551	*24.9*
Ellis Rubin (D)	161,386	*21.3*
Arturo Perez (D)	151,121	*20.0*

Class 3

1950   **Democratic Primary**

George A. Smathers (D)	387,215	*54.8*
Claude Pepper (D)	319,754	*45.2*

1956   **Democratic Primary**

George A. Smathers (D)	614,663	*87.5*
Erle Griffis (D)	87,525	*12.5*

1962   **Republican Primary**

Emerson H. Rupert (R)		*100.0*

Democratic Primary

George A. Smathers (D)	587,562	*84.2*
Roger L. Davis (D)	74,565	*10.7*
Douglas Randolph Voorhees (D)	35,832	*5.1*

1968   **Republican Primary**

Edward J. Gurney (R)	169,805	*80.0*
Herman W. Goldner (R)	42,347	*20.0*

Democratic Primary

Leroy Collins (D)	426,096	*49.5*
Earl Faircloth (D)	397,642	*46.2*

Democratic Runoff

Leroy Collins (D)	410,689	*50.2*
Earl Faircloth (D)	407,696	*49.8*

1974   **Republican Primary**

Jack M. Eckerd (R)	186,897	*67.5*
Paula Hawkins (R)	90,049	*32.5*

Democratic Primary

Bill Gunter (D)	236,185	*29.8*
Richard Stone (D)	157,301	*19.8*
Richard A. Pettigrew (D)	146,728	*18.5*
Mallory E. Horne (D)	90,684	*11.4*
Glenn W. Turner (D)	51,326	*6.5*

Candidates	Votes	%
Democratic Runoff		
Richard Stone (D)	321,683	*50.8*
Bill Gunter (D)	311,044	*49.2*

1980   **Republican Primary**

Paula Hawkins (R)	209,856	*48.1*
Louis Frey (R)	119,834	*27.5*
Ander Crenshaw (R)	54,767	*12.6*

Republican Runoff

Paula Hawkins (R)	293,600	*61.6*
Louis Frey (R)	182,911	*38.4*

Democratic Primary

Richard Stone (D)	355,287	*32.1*
Bill Gunter (D)	335,859	*30.3*
Buddy MacKay (D)	272,538	*24.6*
Richard A. Pettigrew (D)	108,154	*9.8*

Democratic Runoff

Bill Gunter (D)	594,676	*51.8*
Richard Stone (D)	554,268	*48.2*

1986   **Republican Primary**

Paula Hawkins (R)	491,953	*88.7*
Jon L. Shudlick (R)	62,474	*11.3*

Democratic Primary

Bob Graham (D)	851,586	*85.0*
Robert P. Kunst (D)	149,797	*15.0*

1992   **Republican Primary**

Bill Grant (R)	413,457	*56.1*
Rob Quartel (R)	196,524	*26.7*
Hugh Brotherton (R)	126,878	*17.2*

Democratic Primary

Bob Graham (D)	968,618	*84.3*
Jim Mahorner (D)	180,405	*15.7*

GEORGIA

Candidates	Votes	%
Class 2		

1948   **Democratic Primary**

Richard B. Russell (D)	703,048	*100.0*

1954   **Democratic Primary**

Richard B. Russell (D)	619,129	*100.0*

1960   **Democratic Primary**

Richard B. Russell (D)	560,256	*100.0*

1966   **Democratic Primary**

Richard B. Russell (D)	596,209	*90.6*
Harry L. Hyde (D)	61,922	*9.4*

Senate Elections

	Candidates	Votes	%
1972[1]	**Republican Special Primary**		
	Fletcher Thompson (R)	70,859	100.0
	Republican Primary		
	Fletcher Thompson (R)	71,464	91.1
	Democratic Special Primary		
	David H. Gambrell (D)	258,216	34.3
	Sam Nunn (D)	170,689	22.7
	S. Ernest Vandiver (D)	151,908	20.2
	Hosea Williams (D)	45,613	6.1
	J. B. Stoner (D)	38,261	5.1
	Democratic Special Runoff		
	Sam Nunn (D)	326,186	52.1
	David H. Gambrell (D)	299,919	47.9
	Democratic Primary		
	David H. Gambrell (D)	225,470	31.5
	Sam Nunn (D)	166,035	23.2
	S. Ernest Vandiver (D)	147,135	20.5
	Hosea Williams (D)	46,153	6.4
	J. B. Stoner (D)	40,675	5.7
	Democratic Runoff		
	Sam Nunn (D)	334,670	54.2
	David H. Gambrell (D)	283,414	45.9
1978	**Republican Primary**		
	John W. Stokes (R)	14,443	58.5
	Dean Parkison (R)	10,250	41.5
	Democratic Primary		
	Sam Nunn (D)	525,703	80.0
	Jack Dorsey (D)	71,223	10.8
1984	**Republican Primary**		
	Mike Hicks (R)	27,547	41.1
	Kelly Stratton Brown (R)	26,657	39.7
	J. W. Tibbs Jr. (R)	12,849	19.2
	Republican Runoff		
	Mike Hicks (R)	16,987	67.1
	J. W. Tibbs Jr. (R)	8,336	32.9
	Democratic Primary		
	Sam Nunn (D)	801,412	90.2
	Jim Boyd (D)	86,973	9.8
1990	**Democratic Primary**		
	Sam Nunn (D)		100.0
1996	**Republican Primary**		
	Guy Millner (R)	187,177	41.9
	Johnny Isakson (R)	155,141	34.7
	Clint Day (R)	83,610	18.7

	Candidates	Votes	%
	Republican Runoff		
	Guy Millner (R)	169,240	52.8
	Johnny Isakson (R)	151,560	47.2
	Democratic Primary		
	Max Cleland (D)	517,697	100.0

Class 3

	Candidates	Votes	%
1950	**Democratic Primary**		
	Walter F. George (D)	470,156	82.5
	Alex McLennan (D)	79,886	14.0
1956	**Democratic Primary**		
	Herman E. Talmadge (D)	498,327	80.3
	M. E. Thompson (D)	122,152	19.7
1962	**Democratic Primary**		
	Herman E. Talmadge (D)	673,782	88.0
	Henry M. Henderson (D)	91,664	12.0
1968	**Republican Primary**		
	E. Earl Patton (R)	20,316	59.5
	Jack Sells (R)	13,805	40.5
	Democratic Primary		
	Herman E. Talmadge (D)	697,915	77.1
	Maynard H. Jackson Jr. (D)	207,171	22.9
1974	**Republican Primary**		
	Jerry R. Johnson (R)		100.0
	Democratic Primary		
	Herman E. Talmadge (D)	523,133	81.5
	Carlton Myers (D)	119,011	18.5
1980	**Republican Primary**		
	Mack Mattingly (R)	28,191	59.8
	E. J. Bagley (R)	6,082	12.9
	Hulon M. Madeley (R)	3,999	8.5
	Dean Parkison (R)	3,219	6.8
	Nick M. Belluso (R)	2,947	6.3
	J. W. Tibbs Jr. (R)	2,700	5.7
	Democratic Primary		
	Herman E. Talmadge (D)	432,215	42.0
	Zell Miller (D)	247,766	24.1
	Norman Underwood (D)	183,683	17.8
	Dawson Mathis (D)	133,729	13.0
	Democratic Runoff		
	Herman E. Talmadge (D)	559,615	58.6
	Zell Miller (D)	395,773	41.4
1986	**Republican Primary**		
	Mack Mattingly (R)	74,743	95.0

Candidates	Votes	%
Democratic Primary		
Wyche Fowler (D)	314,787	50.2
Hamilton Jordan (D)	196,307	31.3
John D. Russell (D)	100,881	16.1
1992 **Republican Primary**		
Paul Coverdell (R)	100,016	37.1
Bob Barr (R)	65,471	24.3
John Knox (R)	64,514	23.9
Charles Tanksley (R)	32,590	12.1
Republican Runoff		
Paul Coverdell (R)	80,435	50.5
Bob Barr (R)	78,887	49.5
Democratic Primary		
Wyche Fowler (D)	683,274	100.0

Georgia

1. *Two Senate primaries were held simultaneously in 1972, a special primary for the remainder of the term of Richard B. Russell (D), who died Jan. 21, 1971, and a regular primary for the full term beginning in January 1973. Gambrell, who was appointed to the Senate seat in 1971, led candidates in both parties, but lost both primary runoffs to Nunn. Returns for the special primary from the Elections Research Center, Washington, D.C.*

HAWAII

Candidates	Votes	%
Class 1		
1959[1] **Republican Primary**		
Hiram L. Fong (R)		100.0
Democratic Primary		
Frank F. Fasi (D)	46,868	59.9
William H. Heen (D)	31,317	40.0
1964 **Republican Primary**		
Hiram L. Fong (R)	31,770	95.2
Democratic Primary		
Thomas P. Gill (D)	71,298	64.0
Nadao Yoshinaga (D)	37,253	33.4
1970 **Republican Primary**		
Hiram L. Fong (R)		100.0
Democratic Primary		
Cecil Heftel (D)	78,934	62.4
Tony N. Hodges (D)	30,430	24.1
Neil Abercrombie (D)	17,058	13.5
1976 **Republican Primary**		
William F. Quinn (R)	32,058	93.7
Spencer J. Cabral (R)	2,170	6.3

Candidates	Votes	%
Democratic Primary		
Spark M. Matsunaga (D)	105,731	51.0
Patsy Mink (D)	84,732	40.9
Libertarian Primary		
Rockne Johnson (LIBERT)		100.0
Non-Partisan Primary		
James D. Kimmel (NON PART)		100.0
People's Primary		
Anthony N. Hodges (PP)		100.0
1982 **Republican Primary**		
Clarence J. Brown (R)	6,142	65.2
Arbis D. Shipley (R)	3,279	34.8
Democratic Primary		
Spark M. Matsunaga (D)		100.0
Independent Democratic Primary		
E. F. Bernier-Nachtwey (ID)		100.0
1988 **Republican Primary**		
Maria M. Hustace (R)	18,124	48.7
Leonard Mednick (R)	13,590	36.4
Susanne Sydney (R)	5,526	14.8
Democratic Primary		
Spark M. Matsunaga (D)	180,853	86.9
Robert Zimmerman (D)	27,360	13.1
Libertarian Primary		
Ken Schoolland (LIBERT)		100.0
1990[2] **Republican Special Primary**		
Patricia Saiki (R)	39,847	85.8
Richard I. C. Sutton (R)	2,443	5.3
Democratic Special Primary		
Daniel K. Akaka (D)	180,235	90.7
Paul Snider (D)	18,427	9.3
Libertarian Special Primary		
Ken Schoolland (LIBERT)		100.0
1994 **Republican Primary**		
Maria M. Hustace (R)	16,647	40.9
Richard C. S. Ho (R)	9,069	22.3
Frances D. Bollinger (R)	7,869	19.3
Paul A. Manner (R)	2,640	6.5
Robert H. Harker (R)	2,454	6.0
James DeLuze (R)	2,046	5.0
Democratic Primary		
Daniel K. Akata (D)	168,877	100.0

Candidates	Votes	%
Libertarian Primary		
Richard Rowland (LIBERT)	351	100.0

Class 3

1959[1]

Candidates	Votes	%
Republican Primary		
Wilfred C. Tsukiyama (R)		100.0
Democratic Primary		
Oren E. Long (D)	61,345	83.9
Kenneth E. Young (D)	9,036	12.3
Commonwealth Primary		
Eugene Ressencourt (CP)		100.0

1962

Candidates	Votes	%
Republican Primary		
Ben F. Dillingham (R)		100.0
Democratic Primary		
Daniel K. Inouye (D)	80,707	93.6
Frank Troy (D)	5,476	6.3

1968

Candidates	Votes	%
Republican Primary		
Wayne C. Thiessen (R)		100.0
Democratic Primary		
Daniel K. Inouye (D)	111,135	87.5
William Lampard (D)	14,357	11.3
Peace and Freedom Primary		
Oliver Lee (PFP)		100.0

1974

Candidates	Votes	%
Democratic Primary		
Daniel K. Inouye (D)		100.0
Peoples Primary		
James D. Kimmel (PP)	61	64.9
Floyd Nachtwey (PP)	33	35.1

1980

Candidates	Votes	%
Republican Primary		
Cooper Brown (R)	3,219	39.0
Lawrence I. Weisman (R)	2,586	31.4
Dan Dew (R)	1,854	22.5
E. F. Bernier-Nachtwey (R)	584	7.1
Democratic Primary		
Daniel K. Inouye (D)	198,468	87.5
Kamuela Price (D)	15,361	6.8
John P. Fritz (D)	12,929	5.7
Libertarian Primary		
H. E. Shasteen (LIBERT)		100.0

1986

Candidates	Votes	%
Republican Primary		
Frank Hutchinson (R)	20,375	67.7
Marvin Franklin (R)	9,714	32.3
Democratic Primary		
Daniel K. Inouye (D)		100.0

116

1992

Candidates	Votes	%
Republican Primary		
Rick Reed (R)	33,250	74.1
Maria M. Hustace (R)	9,348	20.8
John James (R)	2,250	5.0
Democratic Primary		
Daniel K. Inouye (D)	141,273	76.1
Wayne K. Nishiki (D)	44,505	24.0
Green Primary		
Linda B. Martin (GREEN)		100.0
Libertarian Primary		
Richard O. Rowland (LIBERT)		100.0

Hawaii

1. Hawaii became a state Aug. 21, 1959. The first Senate elections for that state were for unspecified terms. The Senate later determined that Sen. Fong would serve the long term (Class 1) and Sen. Long, the short term (Class 3).

2. A special election was held to fill the remaining four years of the term of Sen. Spark Matsunaga (D), who died April 15, 1990.

IDAHO

Class 2

Candidates	Votes	%

1960

Candidates	Votes	%
Republican Primary		
Henry C. Dworshak (R)		100.0
Democratic Primary		
Gregg Potvin (D)	16,524	23.7
Bob McLaughlin (D)	14,694	21.1
Compton White (D)	14,515	20.8
A. W. Brunt (D)	13,015	18.7
Joseph R. Garry (D)	10,899	15.6
Democratic Runoff		
R. F. "Bob" McLaughlin	13,117	51.9
Gregg Potvin	12,174	48.1

1966

Candidates	Votes	%
Republican Primary		
Len B. Jordan (R)		100.0
Democratic Primary		
Ralph R. Harding (D)		100.0

1972

Candidates	Votes	%
Republican Primary		
James A. McClure (R)	46,522	36.1
George Hansen (R)	35,412	27.4
Glen Wegner (R)	24,582	19.1
Robert E. Smylie (R)	22,497	17.4
Democratic Primary		
William E. "Bud" Davis (D)	23,953	36.1
W. Anthony Park (D)	17,636	26.5
Byron Johnson (D)	15,526	23.4
Rose Bowman (D)	9,327	14.0

	Candidates	Votes	%
1978	**Republican Primary**		
	James A. McClure (R)		100.0
	Democratic Primary		
	Dwight Jensen (D)		100.0
1984	**Republican Primary**		
	James A. McClure (R)	102,125	100.0
	Democratic Primary		
	Peter M. Busch (D)	27,871	62.0
	Louis A. Hatheway (D)	17,065	38.0
1990	**Republican Primary**		
	Larry E. Craig (R)	65,830	59.0
	Jim Jones (R)	45,733	41.0
	Democratic Primary		
	Ron J. Twilegar (D)	30,154	64.5
	David C. Steed (D)	16,587	35.5
1996	**Republican Primary**		
	Larry E. Craig (R)	106,817	100.0
	Democratic Primary		
	Walt Minnick (D)	34,551	100.0

Class 3

	Candidates	Votes	%
1956	**Republican Primary**		
	Herman Welker (R)	31,399	42.5
	William S. Holden (R)	21,081	28.5
	Ray J. Davis (R)	12,349	16.7
	John C. Sanborn (R)	8,261	11.2
	Democratic Primary		
	Frank Church (D)	27,942	37.7
	Glen H. Taylor (D)	27,742	37.5
	Claude Burtenshaw (D)	11,738	15.9
	Alvin McCormack (D)	6,596	8.9
1962	**Republican Primary**		
	Jack Hawley (R)	38,210	60.2
	George Hansen (R)	25,223	39.8
	Democratic Primary		
	Frank Church (D)		100.0
1968	**Republican Primary**		
	George Hansen (R)		100.0
	Democratic Primary		
	Frank Church (D)		100.0

	Candidates	Votes	%
1974	**Republican Primary**		
	Robert L. Smith (R)	45,553	72.0
	Donald L. Winder (R)	13,406	21.2
	Charles Bolstridge (R)	4,331	6.8
	Democratic Primary		
	Frank Church (D)	53,659	85.8
	Leon R. Olson (D)	8,904	14.2
	American Primary		
	Jean L. Stoddard (AM)		100.0
1980	**Republican Primary**		
	Steven D. Symms (R)		100.0
	Democratic Primary		
	Frank Church (D)		100.0
	Libertarian Primary		
	Larry Fullmer (LIBERT)		100.0
1986	**Republican Primary**		
	Steven D. Symms (R)		100.0
	Democratic Primary		
	John V. Evans (D)		100.0
1992	**Republican Primary**		
	Dirk Kempthorne (R)	67,001	57.4
	Rodney W. Beck (R)	26,977	23.1
	Milton E. Erhart (R)	22,682	19.4
	Democratic Primary		
	Richard Stallings (D)	40,102	71.7
	Matt Schaffer (D)	8,976	16.0
	David W. Shepherd (D)	6,882	12.3

ILLINOIS

	Candidates	Votes	%
	Class 2		
1960	**Republican Primary**		
	Samuel W. Witwer (R)	249,849	31.5
	Warren E. Wright (R)	226,449	28.6
	William H. Rentschler (R)	202,600	25.6
	John W. Lewis (R)	48,989	6.2
	Democratic Primary		
	Paul H. Douglas (D)		100.0
1966	**Republican Primary**		
	Charles H. Percy (R)	605,815	90.6
	Howard J. Doyle (R)	38,636	5.8

Candidates	Votes	%
Democratic Primary		
Paul H. Douglas (D)		100.0
1972 **Republican Primary**		
Charles H. Percy (R)		100.0
Democratic Primary		
Roman C. Pucinski (D)	859,890	70.6
W. Dakin Williams (D)	357,744	29.4
1978 **Republican Primary**		
Charles H. Percy (R)	401,409	84.2
Lar Daly (R)	74,739	15.7
Democratic Primary		
Alex Seith (D)	483,196	69.5
Anthony R. Martin-Trigona (D)	212,105	30.5
1984 **Republican Primary**		
Charles H. Percy (R)	387,865	59.3
Tom Corcoran (R)	239,847	36.7
Democratic Primary		
Paul Simon (D)	556,757	35.6
Roland W. Burris (D)	360,182	23.0
Alex Seith (D)	327,125	20.9
Philip J. Rock (D)	303,397	19.4
1990 **Republican Primary**		
Lynn Martin (R)		100.0
Democratic Primary		
Paul Simon (D)		100.0
1996 **Republican Primary**		
Al Salvi (R)	377,141	47.6
Bob Kustra (R)	342,935	43.3
Robert Marshall (R)	43,937	5.6
Democratic Primary		
Richard J. Durbin (D)	512,520	64.9
Pat Quinn (D)	233,138	29.5
Libertarian Primary		
Robin J. Miller (LIBERT)	1,258	73.7
David F. Hoscheidt (LIBERT)	448	26.3

Class 3

Candidates	Votes	%
1956 **Republican Primary**		
Everett McKinley Dirksen (R)		100.0
Democratic Primary		
Richard Stengel (D)		100.0

Candidates	Votes	%
1962 **Republican Primary**		
Everett McKinley Dirksen (R)	742,973	87.1
Harley D. Jones (R)	109,574	12.8
Democratic Primary		
Sidney R. Yates (D)	744,128	77.2
Lar Daly (D)	219,169	22.7
1968 **Republican Primary**		
Everett McKinley Dirksen (R)	622,710	92.1
Roy C. Johnson (R)	53,069	7.8
Democratic Primary		
William G. Clark (D)		100.0
1970 **Republican Special Primary**		
Ralph Tyler Smith (R)	414,489	58.9
William H. Rentschler (R)	271,648	38.6
Democratic Special Primary		
Adlai E. Stevenson III (D)		100.0
1974 **Republican Primary**		
George M. Burditt (R)	432,796	84.7
Lar Daly (R)	78,146	15.3
Democratic Primary		
Adlai E. Stevenson III (D)	822,248	82.9
W. Dakin Williams (D)	169,662	17.1
1980 **Republican Primary**		
David C. O'Neal (R)	424,634	41.5
William J. Scott (R)	352,138	34.4
Richard E. Carver (R)	245,668	24.1
Democratic Primary		
Alan J. Dixon (D)	671,746	66.9
Alex Seith (D)	190,339	18.9
Robert A. Wallace (D)	64,037	6.4
1986 **Republican Primary**		
Judy Koehler (R)	266,214	55.0
George A. Ranney (R)	217,720	45.0
Democratic Primary		
Alan J. Dixon (D)	720,571	84.8
Sheila Jones (D)	129,474	15.2
1992 **Republican Primary**		
Richard S. Williamson (R)	608,079	100.0
Democratic Primary		
Carol Moseley-Braun (D)	557,694	38.3
Alan J. Dixon (D)	504,077	34.6
Albert F. Hofeld (D)	394,497	27.1

INDIANA

Candidates	Votes	%

Class 1

1976[1] Republican Primary

| Richard G. Lugar (R) | 393,064 | 65.5 |
| Edgar D. Whitcomb (R) | 179,203 | 29.8 |

Democratic Primary

| R. Vance Hartke (D) | 304,076 | 53.1 |
| Philip H. Hayes (D) | 268,790 | 46.9 |

1982 Republican Primary

| Richard G. Lugar (R) | | 100.0 |

Democratic Primary

| Floyd Fithian (D) | 262,644 | 59.5 |
| Michael Kendall (D) | 178,702 | 40.5 |

1988 Republican Primary

| Richard G. Lugar (R) | | 100.0 |

Democratic Primary

| Jack Wickes (D) | | 100.0 |

1994 Republican Primary

| Richard G. Lugar (R) | 398,111 | 100.0 |

Democratic Primary

| Jim Jontz (D) | 191,619 | 54.8 |
| John W. Taylor (D) | 158,159 | 45.2 |

Class 3

1980 Republican Primary

| Dan Quayle (R) | 397,273 | 77.1 |
| Roger F. Marsh (R) | 118,273 | 22.9 |

Democratic Primary

| Birch Bayh (D) | | 100.0 |

1986 Republican Primary

| Dan Quayle (R) | | 100.0 |

Democratic Primary

| Jill Long (D) | 258,085 | 73.5 |
| Georgia D. Irey (D) | 93,079 | 26.5 |

1990[2] Republican Special Primary

| Daniel R. Coats (R) | | 100.0 |

Democratic Special Primary

| Baron P. Hill (D) | | 100.0 |

1992 Republican Primary

| Daniel R. Coats (R) | 389,119 | 100.0 |

Democratic Primary

| Joseph H. Hogsett (D) | 320,732 | 100.0 |

Indiana

1. Before 1976, when Indiana adopted a primary system, party conventions nominated candidates for statewide office.

2. A special election was held to fill the remaining two years of the term of Sen. Dan Quayle (R), who resigned Jan. 3, 1989, after being elected vice president. The first two years of the vacancy were filled by appointee Daniel R. Coats (R).

IOWA

Candidates	Votes	%

Class 2

1960[1] Republican Primary

Jack Miller (R)	66,455	30.8
Dayton Countryman (R)	62,500	29.0
Rollo Bergeson (R)	31,559	14.6
Ken Stringer (R)	29,927	13.9
Oliver J. Reeve (R)	14,414	6.7
Ernest J. Seemann (R)	10,931	5.1

Democratic Primary

| Herschel C. Loveless (D) | | 100.0 |

1966 Republican Primary

| Jack Miller (R) | 141,141 | 83.9 |
| Herbert H. Hoover (R) | 27,007 | 16.1 |

Democratic Primary

E. B. Smith (D)	39,870	50.1
Gary L. Cameron (D)	22,650	28.5
Ernest J. Seeman (D)	8,646	10.9
Robert L. Nereim (D)	8,343	10.5

1972 Republican Primary

| Jack Miller (R) | 170,590 | 84.4 |
| Ralph Scott (R) | 31,607 | 15.6 |

Democratic Primary

| Dick Clark (D) | | 100.0 |

American Independent Primary

| William A. Rocap (AMI) | | 100.0 |

1978 Republican Primary

Roger W. Jepsen (R)	87,397	57.3
Maurie Van Nostrand (R)	54,189	35.5
Joe Bertroche (R)	10,860	7.1

Candidates	Votes	%
Democratic Primary		
Dick Clark (D)	87,880	80.5
Gerald Baker (D)	13,132	12.0
Robert L. Nereim (D)	8,176	7.5

1984   **Republican Primary**

Candidates	Votes	%
Roger W. Jepsen (R)	113,996	100.0
Democratic Primary		
Tom Harkin (D)	106,005	100.0

1990   **Republican Primary**

Candidates	Votes	%
Tom Tauke (R)		100.0
Democratic Primary		
Tom Harkin (D)		100.0

1996   **Republican Primary**

Candidates	Votes	%
Jim Ross Lightfoot (R)	101,608	61.5
Maggie Tinsman (R)	40,955	24.8
Steve Grubbs (R)	22,554	13.6
Democratic Primary		
Tom Harkin (D)	98,737	99.2

Class 3

1956   **Republican Primary**

Candidates	Votes	%
Bourke B. Hickenlooper (R)	157,652	67.7
Dayton Countryman (R)	75,264	32.3
Democratic Primary		
R. M. Evans (D)	64,195	63.1
Lumund Wilcox (D)	37,590	36.9

1962   **Republican Primary**

Candidates	Votes	%
Bourke B. Hickenlooper (R)	164,535	85.4
Herbert H. Hoover (R)	28,095	14.6
Democratic Primary		
E. B. Smith (D)		100.0

1968   **Republican Primary**

Candidates	Votes	%
David M. Stanley (R)	143,854	58.7
James E. Bromwell (R)	65,509	26.7
Dayton Countryman (R)	22,049	9.0
William N. Plymat (R)	13,485	5.5
Democratic Primary		
Harold E. Hughes (D)	103,936	86.8
Robert L. Nereim (D)	15,772	13.2

1974   **Republican Primary**

Candidates	Votes	%
David M. Stanley (R)	87,464	66.9
George F. Milligan (R)	43,206	33.1

Candidates	Votes	%
Democratic Primary		
John C. Culver (D)		100.0

1980   **Republican Primary**

Candidates	Votes	%
Charles E. Grassley (R)	170,120	66.7
Tom Stoner (R)	89,409	33.3
Democratic Primary		
John C. Culver (D)		100.0

1986   **Republican Primary**

Candidates	Votes	%
Charles E. Grassley (R)		100.0
Democratic Primary		
John P. Roehrick (D)	88,347	83.8
Juan Cortez (D)	16,987	16.1

1992   **Republican Primary**

Candidates	Votes	%
Charles E. Grassley (R)	109,273	99.7
Democratic Primary		
Jean Lloyd-Jones (D)	60,615	60.8
Rosanne Freeburg (D)	38,774	38.9

Iowa

1. Because no candidate in Iowa's 1960 Republican primary received the minimum percentage required for Senate nomination, a state convention was held, resulting in the nomination of Miller.

KANSAS

Candidates	Votes	%
Class 2		

1960   **Republican Primary**

Candidates	Votes	%
Andrew F. Schoeppel (R)	201,753	80.0
Henry P. Cleaver (R)	50,507	20.0
Democratic Primary		
Frank Theis (D)	88,194	59.1
Joseph W. Henkle (D)	60,942	40.9

1962[1]   **Republican Special Primary**

Candidates	Votes	%
James B. Pearson (R)	124,854	62.3
Edward F. Arn (R)	75,524	37.7
Democratic Special Primary		
Paul L. Aylward (D)		100.0

1966   **Republican Primary**

Candidates	Votes	%
James B. Pearson (R)	101,523	50.3
R. F. Ellsworth (R)	83,083	41.1
Ava A. Anderson (R)	10,095	5.0

Candidates	Votes	%
Democratic Primary		
J. Floyd Breeding (D)	51,860	*49.9*
K. L. Smith (D)	19,433	*18.7*
Harold S. Herd (D)	16,963	*16.3*
Leigh Warner (D)	15,625	*15.0*

1972 **Republican Primary**

Candidates	Votes	%
James B. Pearson (R)	229,908	*82.2*
Harlan D. House (R)	49,825	*17.8*
Democratic Primary		
Arch O. Tezlaff (D)		*100.0*

1978 **Republican Primary**

Candidates	Votes	%
Nancy Landon Kassebaum (R)	67,324	*30.6*
Wayne Angell (R)	54,161	*24.6*
Sam Hardage (R)	30,248	*13.7*
Jan Meyers (R)	20,933	*9.5*
Deryl K. Schuster (R)	18,568	*8.5*
Norman E. Gaar (R)	14,502	*6.6*
Democratic Primary		
William R. Roy (D)	100,508	*76.7*
Dorothy K. White (D)	13,865	*10.6*
James R. Maher (D)	11,556	*8.8*

1984 **Republican Primary**

Candidates	Votes	%
Nancy Landon Kassebaum (R)	214,429	*100.0*
Democratic Primary		
James R. Maher (D)	97,843	*100.0*

1990 **Republican Primary**

Candidates	Votes	%
Nancy Landon Kassebaum (R)	267,946	*87.2*
R. Gregory Walstrom (R)	39,379	*12.8*
Democratic Primary		
William R. Roy (D)[2]	86,174	*56.9*
Dick Williams (D)	65,395	*43.1*

1996 **Republican Primary**

Candidates	Votes	%
Pat Roberts (R)	245,411	*78.2*
Tom Little (R)	25,052	*8.0*
Thomas L. Oyler (R)	23,266	*7.4*
Richard L. Cooley (R)	20,060	*6.4*
Democratic Primary		
Sally Thompson (D)	121,476	*100.0*

Class 3

1956 **Republican Primary**

Candidates	Votes	%
Frank Carlson (R)	215,364	*77.9*
Walter I. Biddle (R)	61,053	*22.1*

Candidates	Votes	%
Democratic Primary		
George Hart (D)	54,553	*40.4*
Paul L. Aylward (D)	54,085	*40.0*
Fred Kilian (D)	16,384	*12.1*
Marlyn Korf (D)	10,176	*7.5*

1962 **Republican Primary**

Candidates	Votes	%
Frank Carlson (R)	167,498	*86.9*
Joe Corpstein (R)	25,168	*13.1*
Democratic Primary		
K. L. Smith (D)	65,876	*62.5*
Joseph J. Poizner (D)	39,458	*37.5*

1968 **Republican Primary**

Candidates	Votes	%
Robert Dole (R)	190,782	*68.5*
William H. Avery (R)	87,801	*31.5*
Democratic Primary		
William I. Robinson (D)	56,242	*40.9*
James K. Logan (D)	50,709	*36.9*
K. L. Smith (D)	13,698	*10.0*

1974 **Republican Primary**

Candidates	Votes	%
Robert Dole (R)		*100.0*
Democratic Primary		
William R. Roy (D)	125,634	*85.0*
George Hart (D)	22,109	*15.0*

1980 **Republican Primary**

Candidates	Votes	%
Robert Dole (R)	201,484	*81.9*
Jim H. Grainge (R)	44,674	*18.1*
Democratic Primary		
John Simpson (D)	52,004	*35.8*
James R. Maher (D)	46,322	*31.9*
John A. Barnes (D)	16,466	*11.3*
Ken North (D)	14,218	*9.8*
Ed Phillips (D)	8,838	*6.1*
Howard C. Lee (D)	7,461	*5.1*

1986 **Republican Primary**

Candidates	Votes	%
Robert Dole (R)	228,301	*84.4*
Shirley J. A. Landis (R)	42,237	*15.6*
Democratic Primary		
Guy MacDonald (D)	31,942	*27.7*
Darrell T. Ringer (D)	30,483	*26.4*
W. H. Addington (D)	21,082	*18.3*
Lionel Kunst (D)	18,795	*16.3*
Jim Oyler (D)	13,201	*11.4*

1992 **Republican Primary**

Candidates	Votes	%
Robert Dole (R)	244,480	*80.4*
Richard W. Rodewald (R)	59,589	*19.6*

Candidates	Votes	%
Democratic Primary		
Gloria O'Dell (D)	111,015	*69.2*
Fred Phelps (D)	49,416	*30.8*
1996[3] **Republican Special Primary**		
Sam Brownback (R)	187,914	*54.8*
Sheila Frahm (R)	142,487	*41.6*
Democratic Special Primary		
Jill Docking (D)	127,012	*74.4*
Joan Finney (D)	43,726	*25.6*

Kansas

1. A special election was held to fill the remaining four years of the term of Sen. Andrew Schoeppel (R), who died Jan. 21, 1962.

2. Roy withdrew after the primary and Williams was substituted by the state party committee.

3. A special election was held to fill the remaining two years of the term of Sen. Robert Dole (R), who resigned June 11, 1996, to run for president. Appointee Sheila Frahm filled the vacancy until the November election; she resigned Nov. 27, 1996.

KENTUCKY

Candidates	Votes	%
Class 2		
1960[1] **Republican Primary**		
John Sherman Cooper (R)	50,896	*96.3*
Democratic Primary		
Keen Johnson (D)	112,797	*58.0*
John Young Brown (D)	75,897	*39.0*
1966 **Republican Primary**		
John Sherman Cooper (R)	65,023	*92.8*
Democratic Primary		
John Young Brown (D)	71,759	*75.6*
Gaines P. Wilson (D)	12,921	*13.6*
James Ward Lentz (D)	5,399	*5.7*
J. N. R. Cecil (D)	4,861	*5.1*
1972 **Republican Primary**		
Louie B. Nunn (R)	57,348	*69.7*
Robert E. Gable (R)	18,107	*22.0*
Democratic Primary		
Walter D. Huddleston (D)	106,144	*71.6*
Sandy Hockensmith (D)	14,786	*10.0*
James E. Wallace (D)	11,290	*7.6*
Willis V. Johnson (D)	8,727	*5.9*
1978 **Republican Primary**		
Louie Guenthner (R)	14,218	*47.2*
Oline Carmical (R)	9,346	*31.0*
Thurman J. Hamlin (R)	6,550	*21.8*

Candidates	Votes	%
Democratic Primary		
Walter D. Huddleston (D)	89,333	*75.6*
Jack A. Watson (D)	13,177	*11.1*
William J. Taylor (D)	8,710	*7.4*
George W. Tolhurst (D)	6,921	*5.9*
1984 **Republican Primary**		
Mitchell McConnell (R)	39,465	*79.2*
C. Roger Harker (R)	3,798	*7.6*
T. William Klein (R)	3,352	*6.7*
Thurman Hamlin (R)	3,202	*6.4*
Democratic Primary		
Walter D. Huddleston (D)		*100.0*
1990 **Republican Primary**		
Mitchell McConnell (R)	64,063	*88.5*
Tommy Klein (R)	8,310	*11.5*
Democratic Primary		
Harvey Sloane (D)	183,789	*59.3*
John Brock (D)	126,318	*40.7*
1996 **Republican Primary**		
Mitchell McConnell (R)	88,620	*88.6*
Democratic Primary		
Steven L. Beshear (D)	177,859	*66.4*
Tom Barlow (D)	64,235	*24.0*
Shelby Lanier Jr. (D)	25,856	*9.6*
Class 3		
1956[1] **Republican Primary**		
Thruston B. Morton (R)	42,038	*70.6*
Julian H. Golden (R)	12,976	*21.8*
Granville Thomas (R)	4,495	*7.6*
Democratic Primary		
Earle C. Clements (D)	218,353	*60.8*
Joe B. Bates (D)	136,533	*38.0*
1962 **Republican Primary**		
Thruston B. Morton (R)	41,892	*91.2*
Thurman J. Hamlin (R)	4,048	*8.8*
Democratic Primary		
Wilson W. Wyatt (D)	127,403	*77.0*
Marion Vance (D)	28,513	*17.2*
James L. Delk (D)	9,483	*5.7*
1968 **Republican Primary**		
Marlow W. Cook (R)	73,171	*62.0*
Eugene Siler (R)	39,743	*33.7*

Candidates	Votes	%
Democratic Primary		
Katherine Peden (D)	86,317	43.8
John Young Brown (D)	51,509	26.2
Foster Ockerman (D)	25,602	13.0
Ted Osborn (D)	20,049	10.2

1974 Republican Primary

Marlow W. Cook (R)	35,904	87.6
Thurman J. Hamlin (R)	2,826	6.9
T. William Klein (R)	2,256	5.5

Democratic Primary

Wendell H. Ford (D)	136,458	84.8
Harvey E. Brazin (D)	24,436	15.2

American Primary

William E. Parker (AM)		100.0

1980 Republican Primary

Mary Louise Foust (R)	25,717	42.0
Granville Thomas (R)	10,246	16.7
Jackson M. Andrews (R)	8,382	13.7
T. William Klein (R)	6,418	10.5
Yale J. Lubkin (R)	5,669	9.2
DeSota Vaught (R)	4,848	7.9

Democratic Primary

Wendell H. Ford (D)	188,047	87.0
Flora T. Stuart (D)	28,202	13.0

1986 Republican Primary

Jackson M. Andrews (R)	16,211	39.0
Carl W. Brown (R)	9,724	23.3
Tommy Klein (R)	8,595	20.6
Thurman J. Hamlin (R)	7,062	17.0

Democratic Primary

Wendell H. Ford (D)		100.0

1992 Republican Primary

David L. Williams (R)	49,880	60.9
Philip Thompson (R)	25,026	30.5
Denny Ormerod (R)	7,066	8.6

Democratic Primary

Wendell H. Ford (D)		100.0

Kentucky

1. Candidates for the special election to fill the unexpired term of Sen. Alben W. Barkley (D), who died April 30, 1956, were nominated by the Democratic and Republican state committees, not by primaries. The 1956 Senate primary in Kentucky was for the Class 3 seat that was slated to be filled that year.

LOUISIANA[1]

Candidates	Votes	%
Class 2		

1948 Democratic Primary

Allen J. Ellender (D)	284,293	61.7
James Domengeaux (D)	119,459	25.9
Charles S. Gerth (D)	57,047	12.4

1954 Democratic Primary

Allen J. Ellender (D)	268,064	59.2
Frank B. Ellis (D)	162,775	35.9

1960 Republican Primary

George W. Reese Jr. (R)	726	72.3
William Dane (R)	278	27.7

Democratic Primary

Allen J. Ellender (D)		100.0

1966 Democratic Primary

Allen J. Ellender (D)	494,519	74.2
J. D. Deblieux (D)	94,154	14.1
Troyce E. Guice (D)	78,137	11.7

1972 Republican Primary

C. M. McLean (R)[2]		100.0

Democratic Primary

J. Bennett Johnston (D)	623,078	79.4
Frank Tunney Allen (D)	88,198	11.2
Allen J. Ellender (D)[3]	73,088	9.3

1978 Open Primary

J. Bennett Johnston (D)	498,773	59.4
Louis "Woody" Jenkins (D)	340,896	40.6

1984 Open Primary

J. Bennett Johnston (D)	838,181	85.7
Robert M. Ross (R)	86,546	8.9
Larry N. "Boo-ga-loo" Cooper (R)	52,746	5.4

1990 Open Primary

J. Bennett Johnston (D)	752,902	53.9
David E. Duke (R)	607,391	43.5

1996 Open Primary

Louis "Woody" Jenkins (R)	322,244	26.2
Mary L. Landrieu (D)	264,268	21.5
Richard P. Ieyoub (D)	250,682	20.4
David E. Duke (R)	141,489	11.5
Jimmy Hayes (R)	71,699	5.8

	Candidates	Votes	%
	Class 3		
1948	**Democratic Special Primary**		
	Russell B. Long (D)	264,143	*51.0*
	Robert F. Kennon (D)	253,668	*49.0*
1950	**Democratic Primary**		
	Russell B. Long (D)	359,330	*68.5*
	Malcolm E. LaFargue (D)	156,918	*29.9*
1956	**Democratic Primary**		
	Russell B. Long (D)		*100.0*
1962	**Republican Primary**		
	Taylor W. O'Hearn (R)		*100.0*
	Democratic Primary		
	Russell B. Long (D)	407,162	*80.2*
	Philemon A. Stamant (D)	100,843	*19.9*
1968	**Republican Primary**		
	Richard H. Kilbourne (R)[4]		*100.0*
	Democratic Primary		
	Russell B. Long (D)	494,467	*87.0*
	Maurice P. Blanche (D)	73,791	*13.0*
1974	**Democratic Primary**		
	Russell B. Long (D)	520,606	*74.7*
	Sherman A. Bernard (D)	131,540	*18.9*
	Annie Smart (D)	44,341	*6.4*
1980	**Open Primary**		
	Russell B. Long (D)	484,770	*57.6*
	Louis "Woody" Jenkins (D)	325,922	*38.8*
1986	**Open Primary**		
	W. Henson Moore (R)	529,433	*44.2*
	John B. Breaux (D)	447,328	*37.3*
	Samuel B. Nunez (D)	73,505	*6.1*
1992	**Open Primary**		
	John B. Breaux (D)	616,021	*73.1*
	John Khachturian (I)	74,785	*8.9*
	Lyle Stockstill (R)	69,986	*8.3*
	Nick J. Accardo (D)	45,839	*5.4*

Louisiana

1. In 1978 Louisiana eliminated the partisan primary for U.S. senator and instituted an open primary with candidates from all parties on the same ballot. Any candidate who receives a majority appears in the general election unopposed. If no candidate receives 50 percent of the vote, there is a runoff election, without regard to party affiliation, between the top two finishers.

2. McLean withdrew from the race after the primary. The Republican state central committee substituted Ben C. Toledano as the candidate for the general election.

3. Ellender died July 27, 1972, before the Aug. 19 primary in which he was a candidate for renomination to a seventh term. But Ellender's name remained on the ballot for the primary, which Johnston won without a runoff.

4. Kilbourne withdrew from the race after the primary. The Republicans did not choose any substitute candidate, thus allowing Long to run unopposed in the November election.

MAINE

	Candidates	Votes	%
	Class 1		
1958	**Republican Primary**		
	Frederick G. Payne (R)	82,448	*83.6*
	Herman D. Sahagian (R)	16,133	*16.4*
	Democratic Primary		
	Edmund S. Muskie (D)		*100.0*
1964	**Republican Primary**		
	Clifford McIntire (R)		*100.0*
	Democratic Primary		
	Edmund S. Muskie (D)		*100.0*
1970	**Republican Primary**		
	Neil S. Bishop (R)	45,216	*59.8*
	Abbott O. Greene (R)	30,201	*40.0*
	Democratic Primary		
	Edmund S. Muskie (D)		*100.0*
1976	**Republican Primary**		
	Robert A. G. Monks (R)	65,224	*83.9*
	Plato Truman (R)	12,552	*16.1*
	Democratic Primary		
	Edmund S. Muskie (D)		*100.0*
1982	**Republican Primary**		
	David F. Emery (R)		*100.0*
	Democratic Primary		
	George J. Mitchell (D)		*100.0*
1988	**Republican Primary**		
	Jaspar S. Wyman (R)		*100.0*
	Democratic Primary		
	George J. Mitchell (D)		*100.0*
1994	**Republican Primary**		
	Olympia J. Snowe (R)	80,686	*99.9*
	Democratic Primary		
	Thomas H. Andrews (D)	83,108	*99.8*
	Class 2		
1960	**Republican Primary**		
	Margaret Chase Smith (R)		*100.0*

Candidates	Votes	%
Democratic Primary		
Lucia M. Cormier (D)		100.0
1966 **Republican Primary**		
Margaret Chase Smith (R)		100.0
Democratic Primary		
Elmer H. Violette (D)	23,259	45.2
Plato Truman (D)	19,844	38.5
Jack L. Smith (D)	8,386	16.3
1972 **Republican Primary**		
Margaret Chase Smith (R)	76,964	66.7
Robert A. G. Monks (R)	38,345	33.3
Democratic Primary		
William D. Hathaway (D)	61,921	90.8
Jack L. Smith (D)	6,263	9.2
1978 **Republican Primary**		
William S. Cohen (R)		100.0
Democratic Primary		
William D. Hathaway (D)		100.0
1984 **Republican Primary**		
William S. Cohen (R)		100.0
Democratic Primary		
Elizabeth H. Mitchell (D)		100.0
1990 **Republican Primary**		
William S. Cohen (R)		100.0
Democratic Primary		
Neil Rolde (D)		100.0
1996 **Republican Primary**		
Susan M. Collins (R)	53,339	55.5
W. John Hathaway (R)	29,792	31.0
Robert A. G. Monks (R)	12,943	13.5
Democratic Primary		
Joseph E. Brennan (D)	48,335	56.7
Sean F. Faircloth (D)	21,204	24.9
Richard A. Spencer (D)	10,236	12.0
Jean Hay (D)	4,524	5.3

MARYLAND[1]

Candidates	Votes	%
Class 1		
1958 **Republican Primary**		
J. Glenn Beall (R)	67,580	89.6
Henry J. Laque (R)	7,826	10.4

Candidates	Votes	%
Democratic Primary		
Thomas D'Alesandro Jr. (D)	125,408	34.7
George P. Mahoney (D)	119,796	33.2
James Bruce (D)	53,365	14.8
Clarence D. Long (D)	47,290	13.1
1964 **Republican Primary**		
J. Glenn Beall (R)	68,930	59.8
James P. Gleason (R)	35,645	30.9
William A. Albaugh (R)	8,352	7.2
Democratic Primary		
Joseph D. Tydings (D)	279,564	64.5
Louis L. Goldstein (D)	155,086	26.6
John J. Harbaugh (D)	22,665	5.2
1970 **Republican Primary**		
J. Glenn Beall Jr. (R)	99,687	83.5
Harry L. Simms (R)	9,927	8.3
Wainwright Dawson (R)	9,786	8.2
Democratic Primary		
Joseph D. Tydings (D)	242,874	52.7
George P. Mahoney (D)	173,157	37.6
Walter G. Finch (D)	33,361	7.2
1976 **Republican Primary**		
J. Glenn Beall Jr. (R)		100.0
Democratic Primary		
Paul S. Sarbanes (D)	302,983	56.5
Joseph D. Tydings (D)	191,875	35.8
1982 **Republican Primary**		
Lawrence J. Hogan (R)	79,375	65.5
Donovan B. Finch (R)	25,290	20.8
William A. Albaugh (R)	16,599	13.7
Democratic Primary		
Paul S. Sarbanes (D)	432,931	81.1
1988 **Republican Primary**		
Thomas L. Blair (R)[2]	68,268	45.6
James G. Bennett (R)	19,720	13.2
Patrick L. McDonough (R)	16,305	10.9
E. Robert Zarwell (R)	10,725	7.2
Albert Ceccone (R)	9,601	6.4
John C. Webb (R)	8,405	5.6
Horace S. Rich (R)	8,031	5.4
Democratic Primary		
Paul S. Sarbanes (D)	309,919	85.8
B. Emerson Sweatt (D)	25,932	7.2
A. Robert Kaufman (D)	25,450	7.0

	Candidates	Votes	%
1994	**Republican Primary**		
	William E. Brock (R)	82,223	37.8
	Ruthann Aron (R)	56,369	25.9
	Ronald Franks (R)	38,213	17.6
	Ross Z. Pierpont (R)	17,306	8.0
	John C. Webb (R)	12,179	5.6
	Democratic Primary		
	Paul S. Sarbanes (D)	382,115	78.9
	John B. Liston (D)	52,031	10.7
	Dennard A. Gayle (D)	30,665	6.3

Class 3

	Candidates	Votes	%
1956	**Republican Primary**		
	John Marshall Butler (R)	58,642	86.6
	Earl E. Knepper (R)	5,376	7.9
	Henry J. Laque (R)	3,696	5.5
	Democratic Primary		
	Millard E. Tydings (D)[3]	142,238	47.5
	George P. Mahoney (D)	134,246	44.8
1962	**Republican Primary**		
	Edward T. Miller (R)	43,437	48.1
	James P. Gleason (R)	34,523	38.3
	Harry L. Simms (R)	7,689	8.5
	Henry J. Laque (R)	4,565	5.1
	Democratic Primary		
	Daniel B. Brewster (D)	182,272	52.2
	Blair Lee (D)	100,915	28.9
	Elbert M. Byrd (D)	32,147	9.2
	Herbert J. Hoover (D)	19,719	5.6
1968	**Republican Primary**		
	Charles McC. Mathias Jr. (R)	66,777	80.0
	Harry L. Simms (R)	11,927	14.3
	Paul F. Wattay (R)	4,790	5.7
	Democratic Primary		
	Daniel B. Brewster (D)	150,481	67.4
	Ross Z. Pierpont (D)	38,555	17.3
	Walter G. Finch (D)	19,829	8.9
	Richard R. Howes (D)	14,224	6.4
1974	**Republican Primary**		
	Charles McC. Mathias Jr. (R)	79,823	75.8
	Ross Z. Pierpont (R)	25,512	24.2
	Democratic Primary		
	Barbara A. Mikulski (D)	132,658	40.9
	Bernard L. Talley (D)	79,080	24.4
	Walter G. Finch (D)	32,068	9.9
	Xavier A. Aragona (D)	17,668	5.4
1980	**Republican Primary**		
	Charles McC. Mathias Jr. (R)	82,430	55.0
	John M. Brennan (R)	24,848	16.6

	Candidates	Votes	%
	V. Dallas Merrell (R)	23,073	15.4
	Roscoe G. Bartlett (R)	10,970	7.3
	Democratic Primary		
	Edward T. Conroy (D)	79,033	22.4
	Victor L. Crawford (D)	52,803	15.0
	Robert L. Douglass (D)	43,035	12.2
	Dennis C. McCoy (D)	40,510	11.5
	R. Spencer Oliver (D)	35,407	10.4
	John A. Kennedy (D)	20,255	5.7
	Frank J. Broschart (D)	19,455	5.5
1986	**Republican Primary**		
	Linda Chavez (R)	100,888	73.1
	Michael Schaefer (R)	16,902	12.2
	Democratic Primary		
	Barbara A. Mikulski (D)	307,876	49.5
	Michael D. Barnes (D)	195,086	31.4
	Harry Hughes (D)	88,908	14.3
1992	**Republican Primary**		
	Alan L. Keyes (R)	95,831	45.9
	Martha S. Klima (R)	20,758	10.0
	Joseph I. Cassilly (R)	16,091	7.7
	Ross Z. Pierpont (R)	12,658	6.1
	S. Rob Sobhani (R)	12,423	6.0
	Democratic Primary		
	Barbara A. Mikulski (D)	376,444	76.8
	Thomas M. Wheatley (D)	31,214	6.4
	Walter Boyd (D)	26,467	5.4

Maryland

1. *Until 1962 Maryland used a system of convention unit votes, with each county (and each of the six legislative districts into which Baltimore city was divided) being allocated as many unit votes as it had members of the state legislature, ranging from three to seven. These unit votes were automatically credited to the candidate carrying the county or legislative district.*

2. *Blair withdrew after the Republican primary. Alan L. Keyes was substituted by the party state central committee.*

3. *In 1956, because Tydings and Mahoney tied in unit votes at 76 each, Tydings won the nomination with the higher popular vote. But illness forced him to retire from the campaign and Mahoney was substituted by the party state committee.*

MASSACHUSETTS

	Candidates	Votes	%
	Class 1		
1958	**Republican Primary**		
	Vincent J. Celeste (R)		100.0
	Democratic Primary		
	John F. Kennedy (D)		100.0
1962[1]	**Republican Special Primary**		
	George C. Lodge (R)	244,921	55.5
	Laurence Curtis (R)	196,444	44.5

Candidates	Votes	%
Democratic Special Primary		
Edward M. Kennedy (D)	559,303	*72.9*
Edward J. McCormack (D)	247,403	*27.1*

1964 Republican Primary

Howard Whitmore (R)		*100.0*

Democratic Primary

Edward M. Kennedy (D)		*100.0*

1970 Republican Primary

Josiah A. Spaulding (R)	109,306	*57.3*
John J. McCarthy (R)	81,356	*42.7*

Democratic Primary

Edward M. Kennedy (D)		*100.0*

1976 Republican Primary

Michael Robertson (R)		*100.0*

Democratic Primary

Edward M. Kennedy (D)	534,725	*73.9*
Robert E. Dinsmore (D)	117,496	*16.2*
Frederick C. Langone (D)	59,315	*8.2*

1982 Republican Primary

Raymond Shamie (R)		*100.0*

Democratic Primary

Edward M. Kennedy (D)		*100.0*

1988 Republican Primary

Joseph Malone (R)		*100.0*

Democratic Primary

Edward M. Kennedy (D)		*100.0*

1994 Republican Primary

W. Mitt Romney (R)	188,280	*82.0*
John R. Lakian (R)	40,898	*17.8*

Democratic Primary

Edward M. Kennedy (D)	391,637	*98.9*

Class 2

1960 Republican Primary

Leverett Saltonstall (R)		*100.0*

Democratic Primary

Thomas J. O'Connor (D)	270,081	*48.3*
Foster Furcolo (D)	217,939	*39.0*
Edmund C. Buckley (D)	70,744	*12.7*

Candidates	Votes	%
1966 Republican Primary		
Edward W. Brooke (R)		*100.0*

Democratic Primary

Endicott Peabody (D)	320,967	*50.3*
John F. Collins (D)	265,016	*41.6*
Thomas B. Adams (D)	51,435	*8.1*

1972 Republican Primary

Edward W. Brooke (R)		*100.0*

Democratic Primary

John J. Droney (D)	215,523	*45.1*
Gerald O'Leary (D)	169,876	*35.5*
John P. Lynch (D)	92,979	*19.4*

1978 Republican Primary

Edward W. Brooke (R)	146,351	*53.3*
Avi Nelson (R)	128,388	*46.7*

Democratic Primary

Paul E. Tsongas (D)	296,915	*35.6*
Paul Guzzi (D)	258,960	*31.0*
Kathleen Sullivan Alioto (D)	161,036	*19.3*
Howard Phillips (D)	65,397	*7.8*
Elaine Noble (D)	52,464	*6.3*

1984 Republican Primary

Raymond Shamie (R)	173,851	*62.4*
Elliot L. Richardson (R)	104,761	*37.6*

Democratic Primary

John F. Kerry (D)	322,470	*40.8*
James M. Shannon (D)	297,941	*37.7*
David M. Bartley (D)	85,910	*10.9*
Michael Joseph Connolly (D)	82,999	*10.5*

1990 Republican Primary

Jim Rappaport (R)	265,093	*66.2*
Daniel W. Daly (R)	135,647	*33.8*

Democratic Primary

John F. Kerry (D)		*100.0*

1996 Republican Primary

William F. Weld (R)	72,600	*98.6*

Democratic Primary

John Kerry (D)	221,213	*98.6*

Massachusetts

1. A special election was held to fill the remaining two years of the term of Sen. John F. Kennedy (D), who resigned Dec. 22, 1960, after being elected president. The first two years of the vacancy were filled by appointee Benjamin A. Smith.

MICHIGAN

Candidates	Votes	%

Class 1

1958 Republican Primary

Charles E. Potter (R)		100.0

Democratic Primary

Philip A. Hart (D)	297,767	80.2
Homer Martin (D)	73,334	19.8

1964 Republican Primary

Elly M. Peterson (R)	219,883	39.0
James F. O'Neil (R)	192,825	34.2
Edward A. Meany (R)	151,498	26.8

Democratic Primary

Philip A. Hart (D)		100.0

1970 Republican Primary

Lenore Romney (R)	277,086	51.3
Robert J. Huber (R)	262,938	48.7

Democratic Primary

Philip A. Hart (D)		100.0

1976 Republican Primary

Marvin L. Esch (R)	209,250	44.2
Thomas E. Brennan (R)	129,917	27.5
Robert J. Huber (R)	82,092	17.3
Deane Baker (R)	51,852	11.0

Democratic Primary

Donald W. Riegle Jr. (D)	325,705	44.3
Richard H. Austin (D)	208,310	28.3
James G. O'Hara (D)	170,473	23.2

1982 Republican Primary

Philip E. Ruppe (R)	253,082	46.0
William S. Ballenger (R)	122,523	22.3
Robert J. Huber (R)	102,693	18.7
Deane Baker (R)	71,902	13.0

Democratic Primary

Donald W. Riegle Jr. (D)		100.0

1988 Republican Primary

Jim Dunn (R)	245,275	61.1
Robert J. Huber (R)	155,984	38.9

Democratic Primary

Donald W. Riegle (D)		100.0

1994 Republican Primary

Spencer Abraham (R)	292,399	51.9
Ronna E. Romney (R)	270,304	48.0

Candidates	Votes	%
Democratic Primary		

M. Robert Carr (D)	157,585	24.0
Lana Pollack (D)	151,323	23.1
Joel Ferguson (D)	130,125	19.8
William M. Brodhead (D)	94,601	14.4
John F. Kelley (D)	71,964	11.0
Carl J. Marlinga (D)	50,329	7.7

Class 2

1960 Republican Primary

Alvin M. Bentley (R)	344,043	72.0
Donald S. Leonard (R)	133,562	28.0

Democratic Primary

Patrick V. McNamara (D)		100.0

1966[1] Republican Special Primary

Robert P. Griffin (R)	356,700	100.0

Democratic Special Primary

G. Mennen Williams (D)	381,496	59.6
Jerome P. Cavanagh (D)	258,822	40.4

1966 Republican Primary

Robert P. Griffin (R)	387,892	100.0

Democratic Primary

G. Mennen Williams (D)	437,438	60.1
Jerome P. Cavanagh (D)	290,465	39.9

1972 Republican Primary

Robert P. Griffin (R)		100.0

Democratic Primary

Frank J. Kelley (D)		100.0

1978 Republican Primary

Robert P. Griffin (R)	322,530	78.3
L. Brooks Patterson (R)	89,383	21.7

Democratic Primary

Carl Levin (D)	226,584	38.9
Phil Power (D)	115,117	19.8
Richard F. Vander Veen (D)	89,257	15.3
Anthony Derezinski (D)	53,696	9.2
John Otterbacher (D)	50,860	8.7
Paul Rosenbaum (D)	46,892	8.1

1984 Republican Primary

Jack Lousma (R)	328,002	62.7
Jim Dunn (R)	194,657	37.2

Democratic Primary

Carl Levin (D)	376,873	100.0

	Candidates	Votes	%
1990	**Republican Primary**		
	Bill Schuette (R)	270,434	*59.7*
	Clark Durant (R)	182,592	*40.3*
	Democratic Primary		
	Carl Levin (D)		*100.0*
1996	**Republican Primary**		
	Ronna E. Romney (R)	355,583	*52.1*
	Jim Nicholson (R)	326,835	*47.9*
	Democratic Primary		
	Carl Levin (D)	405,580	*99.9*

Michigan

1. *Robert P. Griffin (R) was appointed in May 1966 to fill the vacancy caused by the death of Sen. Patrick V. McNamara (D) on April 30. On Aug. 2 two Senate primaries were held simultaneously, a special primary for the remainder of McNamara's term and a regular primary for the full term beginning in January 1967. Griffin, who was unopposed for the Republican nomination, and G. Mennen Williams (D) won both primaries. In the November general election Griffin defeated Williams for both the short and the full terms. Returns for the special primary from the Elections Research Center, Washington, D.C.*

MINNESOTA[1]

	Candidates	Votes	%
	Class 1		
1958	**Republican Primary**		
	Edward J. Thye (R)	202,241	*91.0*
	E. C. Slettedahl (R)	13,734	*6.2*
	Democratic Primary		
	Eugene J. McCarthy (DFL)	279,796	*75.7*
	Hjalmar Petersen (DFL)	76,340	*20.6*
1964	**Republican Primary**		
	Wheelock Whitney (R)		*100.0*
	Democratic Primary		
	Eugene J. McCarthy (DFL)	245,068	*90.5*
	R. H. Underdahl (DFL)	14,562	*5.4*
1970	**Republican Primary**		
	Clark MacGregor (R)	220,353	*93.3*
	John D. Baucom (R)	15,797	*6.7*
	Democratic Primary		
	Hubert H. Humphrey (DFL)	338,705	*79.2*
	Earl D. Craig (DFL)	88,709	*20.8*
1976	**Republican Primary**		
	Gerald W. Brekke (I-R)	76,183	*54.5*
	Richard Franson (I-R)	32,115	*23.0*
	John H. Glover (I-R)	13,014	*9.3*
	Roland Riemers (I-R)	9,307	*6.7*
	Bea Mooney (I-R)	9,150	*6.5*

	Candidates	Votes	%
	Democratic Primary		
	Hubert H. Humphrey (DFL)	317,632	*91.3*
	Dick Bullock (DFL)	30,262	*8.7*
1978[2]	**Republican Special Primary**		
	Dave Durenberger (I-R)	139,187	*67.3*
	Malcolm Moos (I-R)	32,314	*15.6*
	Ken Nordstrom (I-R)	14,635	*7.1*
	Will Lundquist (I-R)	12,261	*5.9*
	Democratic Special Primary		
	Robert E. Short (DFL)	257,269	*48.0*
	Donald M. Fraser (DFL)	253,818	*47.4*
	American Special Primary		
	Paul Helm (AM)		*100.0*
1982	**Republican Primary**		
	Dave Durenberger (I-R)	287,651	*93.4*
	Mary Jane Rachner (I-R)	20,401	*6.6*
	Democratic Primary		
	Mark Dayton (DFL)	359,014	*69.1*
	Eugene J. McCarthy (DFL)	125,229	*24.1*
1988	**Republican Primary**		
	Dave Durenberger (I-R)	112,413	*93.5*
	Democratic Primary		
	Hubert H. Humphrey III (DFL)	153,808	*90.6*
	Kent S. Herschbach (DFL)	15,994	*9.4*
1994	**Republican Primary**		
	Rod Grams (I-R)	269,931	*58.2*
	Joanell M. Dyrstad (I-R)	163,205	*35.2*
	Democratic Primary		
	Ann Wynia (DFL)	236,476	*61.6*
	Tom Foley (DFL)	126,756	*33.0*
	Class 2		
1960	**Republican Primary**		
	P. K. Peterson (R)	256,641	*89.5*
	James Malcolm Williams (R)	30,242	*10.5*
	Democratic Primary		
	Hubert H. Humphrey (D)		*100.0*
1966	**Republican Primary**		
	Robert A. Forsythe (R)	211,282	*81.2*
	Henry A. Johnsen (R)	48,941	*18.8*
	Democratic Primary		
	Walter F. Mondale (DFL)	410,841	*91.0*
	Ralph E. Franklin (DFL)	40,785	*9.0*

	Candidates	Votes	%
1972	**Republican Primary**		
	Philip Hansen (R)		100.0
	Democratic Primary		
	Walter F. Mondale (DFL)	230,679	89.9
1978	**Republican Primary**		
	Rudy Boschwitz (I-R)	185,393	86.8
	Harold E. Stassen (I-R)	28,170	13.2
	Democratic Primary		
	Wendell R. Anderson (DFL)	286,209	56.9
	John S. Connolly (DFL)	159,974	31.8
	American Primary		
	Sal Carlone (AM)		100.0
1984	**Republican Primary**		
	Rudy Boschwitz (I-R)	162,555	96.6
	Democratic Primary		
	Joan Anderson Growe (DFL)	238,190	75.9
	Robert W. "Bob" Mattson (DFL)	61,489	19.6
1990	**Republican Primary**		
	Rudy Boschwitz (I-R)	293,619	86.9
	John J. Zeleniak (I-R)	44,202	13.1
	Democratic Primary		
	Paul D. Wellstone (DFL)	226,306	60.4
	James W. Nichols (DFL)	129,302	34.5
	Gene Schenk (DFL)	19,379	5.2
1996	**Republican Primary**		
	Rudy Boschwitz (R)	158,678	80.6
	Stephen Young (R)	16,324	8.3
	Bert McKasy (R)	12,711	6.5
	Democratic Primary		
	Paul Wellstone (D)	194,699	86.4
	Dick Franson (D)	16,465	7.3
	Reform Primary		
	Dean Barkley (REF)	3,553	100.0

Minnesota

1. In Minnesota, the Democratic Party is known as the Democratic-Farmer-Labor Party (DFL) and the Republican Party is known as the Independent Republican Party (I-R).

2. A special election was held to fill the unexpired term of Sen. Hubert H. Humphrey (DFL), who died Jan. 13, 1978.

MISSISSIPPI

	Candidates	Votes	%
	Class 1		
1946	**Democratic Primary**		
	Theodore G. Bilbo (D)	97,820	51.0
	Ellis (D)	58,005	30.2
	Ross A. Collins (D)	18,875	9.8
	Levings (D)	15,720	8.2
1952	**Democratic Primary**		
	John C. Stennis (D)	191,380	89.4
	William P. Davis (D)	22,802	10.7
1958	**Democratic Primary**		
	John C. Stennis (D)		100.0
1964	**Democratic Primary**		
	John C. Stennis (D)	173,764	97.4
1970	**Democratic Primary**		
	John C. Stennis (D)		100.0
1976	**Democratic Primary**		
	John C. Stennis (D)	157,943	85.4
	E. Michael Marks (D)	27,016	14.6
1982	**Republican Primary**		
	Haley Barbour (R)	30,636	74.2
	Bobby Richard (R)	10,651	25.8
	Democratic Primary		
	John C. Stennis (D)	145,817	75.1
	Charles Pittman (D)	33,651	17.3
	Colon Johnston (D)	14,696	7.6
1988	**Republican Primary**		
	Trent Lott (R)		100.0
	Democratic Primary		
	Wayne Dowdy (D)	189,954	53.4
	Dick Molpus (D)	152,126	42.8
1994	**Republican Primary**		
	Trett Lott (R)	72,543	95.4
	Democratic Primary		
	Ken Harper (D)	62,963	46.7
	Hiram Eastland (D)	38,976	28.9
	Jorja P. Turnipseed (D)	17,873	13.3
	James W. Hunt (D)	7,843	5.8
	Shawn O'Hara (D)	7,189	5.3
	Class 2		
1948	**Democratic Primary**		
	James O. Eastland (D)		100.0

	Candidates	Votes	%
1954	**Democratic Primary**		
	James O. Eastland (D)	136,836	62.0
	Carroll Gartin (D)	83,761	38.0
1960	**Democratic Primary**		
	James O. Eastland (D)	136,735	94.2
	Ance Blakeney (D)	8,397	5.8
1966	**Republican Primary**		
	Prentiss Walker (R)		100.0
	Democratic Primary		
	James O. Eastland (D)	240,171	83.1
	Clifton Whitley (D)	34,323	11.9
	Charles P. Mosby (D)	14,591	5.1
1972	**Republican Primary**		
	Gil Carmichael (R)	18,369	79.1
	James H. Meredith (R)	4,859	20.9
	Democratic Primary		
	James O. Eastland (D)	203,847	70.2
	Taylor Webb (D)	67,656	23.3
	Louis Fondren (D)	18,753	6.5
1978	**Republican Primary**		
	Thad Cochran (R)	51,212	69.1
	Charles W. Pickering (R)	22,949	30.9
	Democratic Primary		
	Maurice Dantin (D)	102,968	27.2
	Cliff Finch (D)	98,751	26.1
	Charles Sullivan (D)	78,702	20.8
	William L. Waller (D)	74,465	19.7
	Democratic Runoff		
	Maurice Dantin (D)	235,904	65.3
	Cliff Finch (D)	125,109	34.7
1984	**Republican Primary**		
	Thad Cochran (R)		100.0
	Democratic Primary		
	William Winter (D)	88,883	69.5
	W. W. Easley III (D)	15,363	12.0
	William L. Gilbert (D)	13,843	10.8
	Billy Taylor (D)	9,786	7.6
1990	**Republican Primary**		
	Thad Cochran (R)		100.0
1996	**Republican Primary**		
	Thad Cochran (R)	138,813	95.4
	Democratic Primary		
	James W. Hunt (D)	47,483	58.8
	Shawn O'Hara (D)	33,336	41.2

MISSOURI

	Candidates	Votes	%
	Class 1		
1958	**Republican Primary**		
	Hazel Palmer (R)	61,481	44.6
	William M. Thomas (R)	36,438	26.5
	Homer S. Cotton (R)	27,023	19.6
	Hiram Grosby (R)	12,818	9.3
	Democratic Primary		
	Stuart Symington (D)	365,470	92.2
	Lawrence L. Hastings (D)	19,954	5.0
1964	**Republican Primary**		
	Jean P. Bradshaw (R)	165,048	78.2
	Morris D. Duncan (R)	46,030	21.8
	Democratic Primary		
	Stuart Symington (D)	563,313	92.0
	William M. Thomas (D)	35,509	5.8
1970	**Republican Primary**		
	John C. Danforth (R)	165,728	72.6
	Doris M. Bass (R)	45,049	19.7
	Morris D. Duncan (R)	17,670	7.7
	Democratic Primary		
	Stuart Symington (D)	392,670	89.3
	American Primary		
	Gene Chapman (AM)	684	47.1
	Lawrence Petty (AM)	400	27.5
	Ralph A. DePugh (AM)	368	25.4
1976	**Republican Primary**		
	John C. Danforth (R)	284,025	93.5
	Gregory Hansman (R)	19,796	6.5
	Democratic Primary		
	Jerry Litton (D)[1]	401,822	45.4
	Warren E. Hearnes (D)	233,544	26.4
	James W. Symington (D)	222,681	25.2
1982	**Republican Primary**		
	John C. Danforth (R)	217,162	73.9
	Mel Hancock (R)	61,378	20.9
	Democratic Primary		
	Harriett Woods (D)	263,259	44.8
	Burleigh Arnold (D)	140,446	23.9
	Tom Ryan (D)	75,599	12.9
	Thomas E. Zych (D)	35,876	6.1
1988	**Republican Primary**		
	John C. Danforth (R)		100.0

Candidates	Votes	%
Democratic Primary		
Jeremiah W. Nixon (D)		100.0

	Candidates	Votes	%
1994	**Republican Primary**		
	John Ashcroft (R)	260,065	83.2
	Democratic Primary		
	Alan Wheat (D)	215,171	41.0
	Marsha Murphy (D)	200,937	38.3
	Jim Thomas (D)	60,204	11.5
	Libertarian Primary		
	Bill Johnson	1,604	69.7
	Rickey Jamerson	698	30.3

Class 3

	Candidates	Votes	%
1956	**Republican Primary**		
	Herbert Douglas (R)	83,458	40.8
	Albert E. Schoenbeck (R)	78,747	38.5
	William M. Thomas (R)	28,924	14.1
	William E. Van Taay (R)	13,556	6.6
	Democratic Primary		
	Thomas C. Hennings Jr. (D)[2]	389,986	95.9
1962	**Republican Primary**		
	Crosby Kemper (R)	119,136	66.6
	Duane Cox (R)	23,606	13.2
	Morris D. Duncan (R)	15,109	8.5
	William M. Thomas (R)	14,131	7.9
	Democratic Primary		
	Edward V. Long (D)	370,826	86.5
	Lewis E. Morris (D)	37,507	8.8
1968	**Republican Primary**		
	Thomas B. Curtis (R)	192,028	84.5
	Morris D. Duncan (R)	24,418	10.8
	Democratic Primary		
	Thomas F. Eagleton (D)	224,017	36.6
	Edward V. Long (D)	198,901	32.5
	True Davis (D)	178,961	29.3
1974	**Republican Primary**		
	Thomas B. Curtis (R)	136,447	81.9
	Paul M. Robinett (R)	16,882	10.1
	Gregory Hansman (R)	13,285	8.0
	Democratic Primary		
	Thomas F. Eagleton (D)	420,681	87.5
	Pat O'Brien (D)	30,389	6.3
	Lee C. Sutton (D)	29,835	6.2

	Candidates	Votes	%
1980	**Republican Primary**		
	Gene McNary (R)	197,060	61.5
	David Doctorian (R)	82,332	25.7
	Morris D. Duncan (R)	21,959	6.9
	Gregory Hansman (R)	18,893	5.9
	Democratic Primary		
	Thomas F. Eagleton (D)	553,392	82.8
	Lee C. Sutton (D)	53,280	8.2
	Herb Fillmore (D)	38,677	6.0
1986	**Republican Primary**		
	Christopher Bond (R)	239,961	88.9
	Democratic Primary		
	Harriett Woods (D)	362,287	75.6
	James J. Askew (D)	44,292	9.2
	Oren L. Staley (D)	34,009	7.1
1992	**Republican Primary**		
	Christopher Bond (R)	337,795	82.7
	Wes Hummel (R)	70,626	17.3
	Democratic Primary		
	Geri Rothman-Serot (D)	224,984	35.6
	Bill Peacock (D)	67,723	10.7
	Mert Bernstein (D)	59,290	9.4
	George D. Weber (D)	57,254	9.1
	Barbara M. Manson (D)	50,091	7.9
	Carol A. Coe (D)	48,634	7.7
	David Westfall (D)	38,509	6.1

Missouri

1. Litton, the winner of the Democratic Senate primary on Aug. 3, 1976, died the same day and the Missouri Democratic central committee substituted Hearnes, the second-place finisher, as the party's nominee.

2. Candidates for the short-term Senate seat vacated by the death of Sen. Thomas C. Hennings Jr. (D) in September 1960 were nominated by the Democratic and Republican state committees of Missouri.

MONTANA

	Candidates	Votes	%
	Class 1		
1958	**Republican Primary**		
	Lou W. Welch (R)	19,860	50.8
	Blanche Anderson (R)	19,264	49.2
	Democratic Primary		
	Mike Mansfield (D)	97,207	91.7
1964	**Republican Primary**		
	Alex Blewett (R)	31,934	59.4
	Lyman Brewster (R)	12,375	23.0
	Antoinette Rosell (R)	9,480	17.6

Candidates	Votes	%
Democratic Primary		
Mike Mansfield (D)	109,904	*85.5*
Joseph P. Monaghan (D)	18,630	*14.5*

1970 Republican Primary

Harold E. Wallace (R)		*100.0*

Democratic Primary

Mike Mansfield (D)	68,146	*77.2*
Tom McDonald (D)	10,733	*12.2*
John W. Lawlor (D)	9,384	*10.6*

1976 Republican Primary

Stanley C. Burger (R)	32,313	*40.4*
Dave Drum (R)	27,257	*34.1*
John F. Tierney (R)	15,129	*18.9*
Larry L. Gilbert (R)	5,258	*6.6*

Democratic Primary

John Melcher (D)	84,413	*87.9*
Ray E. Gulick (D)	11,593	*12.1*

1982 Republican Primary

Larry Williams (R)	49,615	*88.1*
Willie D. Morris (R)	6,696	*11.9*

Democratic Primary

John Melcher (D)	83,539	*68.3*
Michael A. Bond (D)	33,565	*27.4*

1988 Republican Primary

Conrad Burns (R)	63,330	*84.7*
Tom Faranda (R)	11,427	*15.3*

Democratic Primary

John Melcher (D)	88,457	*74.5*
Robert C. Kelleher (D)	30,212	*25.5*

1994 Republican Primary

Conrad Burns (R)	82,827	*100.0*

Democratic Primary

Jack Mudd (D)	58,371	*47.2*
John Melcher (D)	39,607	*32.0*
Becky Shaw (D)	25,688	*20.8*

Class 2

1960 Republican Primary

Orvin B. Fjare (R)	25,899	*38.5*
Sumner Gerard (R)	17,932	*26.6*
Wayne Montgomery (R)	13,527	*20.1*
James H. Morrow (R)	5,261	*7.8*

Democratic Primary

Lee Metcalf (D)	45,339	*35.1*
John W. Bonner (D)	33,246	*25.8*

Candidates	Votes	%
Le Roy Anderson (D)	26,152	*20.3*
John W. Mahan (D)	24,208	*18.8*

1966 Republican Primary

Tim M. Babcock (R)		*100.0*

Democratic Primary

Lee Metcalf (D)		*100.0*

1972 Republican Primary

Henry S. Hibbard (R)	43,028	*49.7*
Harold E. Wallace (R)	26,463	*30.6*
Norman C. Wheeler (R)	13,826	*16.0*

Democratic Primary

Lee Metcalf (D)	106,491	*86.4*
Jerome Peters (D)	16,729	*13.6*

1978 Republican Primary

Larry Williams (R)	35,479	*61.6*
Bill Osborne (R)	16,436	*28.6*
Clancy Rich (R)	5,622	*9.8*

Democratic Primary

Max S. Baucus (D)	87,085	*65.3*
Paul Hatfield (D)	25,789	*19.3*
John Driscoll (D)	18,184	*13.6*

1984 Republican Primary

Chuck Cozzens (R)	33,661	*50.7*
Ralph Bouma (R)	17,900	*27.0*
Aubyn Curtiss (R)	14,729	*22.2*

Democratic Primary

Max S. Baucus (D)	80,726	*79.4*
Bob Ripley (D)	20,979	*20.6*

1990 Republican Primary

Allen C. Kolstad (R)	38,097	*43.6*
Bruce Vorhauer (R)	30,837	*35.3*
Bill Farrell (R)	11,833	*13.5*
John Domenech (R)	6,654	*7.6*

Democratic Primary

Max S. Baucus (D)	81,687	*82.8*
John Driscoll (D)	12,622	*12.8*

1996 Republican Primary

Dennis Rehberg (R)	82,158	*73.8*
Ed Borcherdt (R)	14,670	*13.2*
John K. McDonald (R)	14,485	*13.0*

Democratic Primary

Max S. Baucus (D)	85,976	*100.0*

Candidates	Votes	%
Reform Primary		
Becky Shaw (REF)	930	*68.0*
Webb Sullivan (REF)	437	*32.0*

NEBRASKA

Candidates	Votes	%
Class 1		

1958 | **Republican Primary**

Candidates	Votes	%
Roman L. Hruska (R)		*100.0*
Democratic Primary		
Frank B. Morrison (D)	35,482	*51.9*
Eugene O'Sullivan (D)	26,436	*38.6*
Mike F. Kracher (D)	6,500	*9.5*

1964 | **Republican Primary**

Candidates	Votes	%
Roman L. Hruska (R)		*100.0*
Democratic Primary		
Raymond W. Arndt (D)		*100.0*

1970 | **Republican Primary**

Candidates	Votes	%
Roman L. Hruska (R)	159,057	*85.6*
Otis Glebe (R)	26,627	*14.3*
Democratic Primary		
Frank B. Morrison (D)	85,293	*67.2*
Wallace C. Peterson (D)	34,856	*27.5*
David J. Thomas (D)	6,610	*5.2*

1976 | **Republican Primary**

Candidates	Votes	%
John Y. McCollister (R)	150,732	*78.3*
Richard F. Proud (R)	41,519	*21.6*
Democratic Primary		
Edward Zorinsky (D)	79,988	*48.6*
Hess Dyas (D)	77,384	*47.0*

1982 | **Republican Primary**

Candidates	Votes	%
Jim Keck (R)	104,550	*66.0*
Ken Cameron (R)	53,453	*33.8*
Democratic Primary		
Edward Zorinsky (D)		*100.0*

1988 | **Republican Primary**

Candidates	Votes	%
David Karnes (R)	117,439	*54.8*
Harold J. Daub (R)	96,436	*45.0*
Democratic Primary		
Bob Kerrey (D)	156,498	*91.4*
Ken L. Michaelis (D)	14,248	*8.3*

Candidates	Votes	%
New Alliance Primary		
Ernest Chambers (NA)		*100.0*

1994 | **Republican Primary**

Candidates	Votes	%
Gene Spence (R)	69,529	*38.1*
Ralph Knobel (R)	57,719	*31.6*
Alan Jacobsen (R)	27,374	*15.0*
John DeCamp (R)	24,414	*13.4*
Democratic Primary		
Bob Kerry (D)	107,137	*99.3*

Class 2

1960 | **Republican Primary**

Candidates	Votes	%
Carl T. Curtis (R)		*100.0*
Democratic Primary		
Ralph G. Brooks (D)[1]	41,777	*42.4*
Clair A. Callan (D)	34,052	*34.5*
Albert J. Baker (D)	14,355	*14.6*
Mike F. Kracher (D)	8,424	*8.5*

1966 | **Republican Primary**

Candidates	Votes	%
Carl T. Curtis (R)		*100.0*
Democratic Primary		
Frank B. Morrison (D)	91,178	*78.0*
Raymond W. Arndt (D)	25,657	*21.9*

1972 | **Republican Primary**

Candidates	Votes	%
Carl T. Curtis (R)	141,213	*74.0*
Ronald L. Blauvelt (R)	30,138	*15.8*
Christine M. Kneifl (R)	10,941	*5.7*
Democratic Primary		
Terry Carpenter (D)	52,779	*29.0*
Wallace C. Peterson (D)	49,569	*27.2*
Wayne W. Ziebarth (D)	42,181	*23.1*
Donald Searcy (D)	25,854	*14.2*

1978 | **Republican Primary**

Candidates	Votes	%
Donald Shasteen (R)	127,525	*78.4*
Lenore R. Etchison (R)	34,916	*21.5*
Democratic Primary		
J. James Exon (D)		*100.0*

1984 | **Republican Primary**

Candidates	Votes	%
Nancy Hoch (R)	61,009	*40.5*
John W. DeCamp (R)	24,730	*16.4*
Richard N. Thompson (R)	23,720	*15.7*
Fred A. Lockwood (R)	21,115	*14.0*
Ken Cameron (R)	16,123	*10.7*

Candidates	Votes	%
Democratic Primary		
J. James Exon (D)	135,242	100.0
1990 Republican Primary		
Harold J. Daub (R)	178,232	91.3
Otis Glebe (R)	16,367	8.4
Democratic Primary		
J. James Exon (D)		100.0
1996 Republican Primary		
Chuck Hagel (R)	112,953	62.2
Don Stenberg (R)	67,974	37.5
Democratic Primary		
Ben Nelson (D)	93,140	97.0

Nebraska

1. Brooks, winner of the Senate primary, died in September 1960 and the Nebraska Democratic state committee substituted Robert Conrad as the party's nominee. Conrad had been a candidate for the Democratic gubernatorial nomination.

NEVADA[1]

Candidates	Votes	%
Class 1		
1958 Republican Primary		
George W. Malone (R)		100.0
Democratic Primary		
Howard W. Cannon (D)	22,787	51.7
Fred Anderson (D)	21,319	48.3
1964 Republican Primary		
Paul Laxalt (R)	25,220	90.3
Wilford Owen Woodruff (R)	1,433	5.1
Democratic Primary		
Howard W. Cannon (D)	36,320	59.6
William A. Galt (D)	12,054	19.8
Harry Claiborne (D)	10,807	17.7
1970 Republican Primary		
William J. Raggio (R)	32,816	90.5
Wilford O. Woodruff (R)	3,456	9.5
Democratic Primary		
Howard W. Cannon (D)	54,320	89.3
Walter D. Duesenberg (D)	4,350	7.1
1976 Republican Primary		
David Towell (R)	25,960	67.4
S. M. Cavnar (R)	5,964	15.5
"None of these candidates"	5,164	13.4

Candidates	Votes	%
Democratic Primary		
Howard W. Cannon (D)	61,407	85.8
"None of these candidates"	4,817	6.7
1982 Republican Primary		
Chic Hecht (R)	26,940	39.1
Rick Fore (R)	17,065	24.8
Jack Kenney (R)	12,191	17.7
S. M. Cavnar (R)	6,327	9.2
"None of these candidates"	5,411	7.8
Democratic Primary		
Howard W. Cannon (D)	54,288	49.7
James Santini (D)	49,735	45.5
1988 Republican Primary		
Chic Hecht (R)	55,473	82.1
Larry Scheffler (R)	5,618	8.3
"None of these candidates"	6,460	9.6
Democratic Primary		
Richard H. Bryan (D)	62,278	79.5
Patrick M. Fitzpatrick (D)	4,721	6.0
"None of these candidates"	7,035	9.0
1994 Republican Primary		
Hal Furman (R)	58,521	50.5
Charles Woods (R)	29,601	25.5
Democratic Primary		
Richard H. Bryan (D)		100.0
Class 3		
1956 Republican Primary		
Clifton Young (R)		100.0
Democratic Primary		
Alan Bible (D)	26,784	68.2
Mahlon Brown (D)	8,043	20.5
Harvey Dickerson (D)	2,436	6.2
Jay Sourwine (D)	2,020	5.1
1962 Republican Primary		
William B. Wright (R)	17,478	69.7
Charles B. Grant (R)	6,811	27.1
Democratic Primary		
Alan Bible (D)	38,556	76.2
Jack Streeter (D)	10,703	21.1
1968 Republican Primary		
Ed Fike (R)	20,585	53.0
William J. Raggio (R)	17,634	45.4

Candidates	Votes	%
Democratic Primary		
Alan Bible (D)		100.0
1974 **Republican Primary**		
Paul Laxalt (R)	33,660	81.3
Jim Talbert (R)	3,984	9.6
S. M. Cavnar (R)	3,752	9.1
Democratic Primary		
Harry Reid (D)	44,768	58.6
Maya Miller (D)	25,738	33.7
Dan Miller (D)	5,869	7.7
1980 **Republican Primary**		
Paul Laxalt (R)	45,857	90.3
Richard A. Glister (R)	2,509	5.0
Democratic Primary		
Mary Gojack (D)		100.0
1986 **Republican Primary**		
James Santini (R)	55,947	80.3
Richard Gilster (R)	3,544	5.1
"None of these candidates"	8,214	11.8
Democratic Primary		
Harry Reid (D)	74,275	82.7
Manny Beals (D)	7,039	7.8
"None of these candidates"	8,486	9.4
1992 **Republican Primary**		
Demar Dahl (R)	37,667	36.9
Bob Gore (R)	31,963	31.3
"None of these candidates"	13,523	13.2
Andy Anderson (R)	8,351	8.2
Democratic Primary		
Harry Reid (D)	64,828	52.8
Charles Wood (D)	48,364	39.4

Nevada

1. In Nevada, primary voters may vote for "None of these candidates." The "None of these candidates" vote is given here only where it amounted to 5 percent or more of the total.

NEW HAMPSHIRE

Candidates	Votes	%
Class 2		
1960 **Republican Primary**		
Styles Bridges (R)	87,629	92.9
Albert Levitt (R)	6,681	7.1

Candidates	Votes	%
Democratic Primary		
Herbert W. Hill (D)	16,198	40.2
Alphonse Roy (D)	13,782	34.3
Frank L. Sullivan (D)	10,266	25.5
1962[1] **Republican Special Primary**		
Perkins Bass (R)	31,037	31.3
Doloris Bridges (R)	29,345	29.6
Maurice J. Murphy (R)	24,204	24.4
Chester E. Merrow (R)	14,417	14.6
Democratic Special Primary		
Thomas J. McIntyre (D)		100.0
1966 **Republican Primary**		
Harrison R. Thyng (R)	22,741	29.5
Wesley Powell (R)	18,145	23.5
William R. Johnson (R)	17,410	22.6
Lane Dwinell (R)	10,781	14.0
Doloris Bridges (R)	7,613	9.9
Democratic Primary		
Thomas J. McIntyre (D)		100.0
1972 **Republican Primary**		
Wesley Powell (R)	42,837	48.0
Peter J. Booras (R)	19,714	22.1
David A. Brock (R)	16,326	18.3
Marshall W. Cobleigh (R)	10,106	11.3
Democratic Primary		
Thomas J. McIntyre (D)		100.0
1978 **Republican Primary**		
Gordon J. Humphrey (R)	35,503	50.4
James A. Masiello (R)	18,371	26.1
Alf E. Jacobson (R)	13,619	19.4
Democratic Primary		
Thomas J. McIntyre (D)	31,796	80.7
Raymond J. Coughlan (D)	7,605	19.3
1984 **Republican Primary**		
Gordon J. Humphrey (R)	57,763	99.1
Democratic Primary		
Norman E. D'Amours (D)	42,371	99.3
1990 **Republican Primary**		
Robert C. Smith (R)	56,215	65.0
Tom Christo (R)	25,286	29.2
Democratic Primary		
John A. Durkin (D)	20,222	41.4
James W. Donchess (D)	15,205	31.1
John Rauh (D)	12,935	26.5

	Candidates	Votes	%
1996	**Republican Primary**		
	Robert C. Smith (R)	85,223	97.3
	Democratic Primary		
	Dick Swett (D)	32,461	52.0
	John Rauh (D)	29,395	47.1
	Libertarian Primary		
	Ken Blevens (LIBERT)	663	86.0

Class 3

	Candidates	Votes	%
1956	**Republican Primary**		
	Norris Cotton (R)	61,673	89.5
	Joseph Moore (R)	7,264	10.5
	Democratic Primary		
	Laurence M. Pickett (D)		100.0
1962	**Republican Primary**		
	Norris Cotton (R)	87,445	94.4
	Norman LePage (R)	5,167	5.6
	Democratic Primary		
	Alfred Catalfo (D)		100.0
1968	**Republican Primary**		
	Norris Cotton (R)	78,058	92.4
	John C. Mongan (R)	6,279	7.4
	Democratic Primary		
	John W. King (D)		100.0
1974	**Republican Primary**		
	Louis C. Wyman (R)	66,749	83.0
	Leslie R. Babb (R)	13,670	17.0
	Democratic Primary		
	John A. Durkin (D)	22,258	50.0
	Laurence I. Radway (D)	14,646	32.9
	Dennis J. Sullivan (D)	6,330	14.2
1980	**Republican Primary**		
	Warren B. Rudman (R)	20,206	20.3
	John H. Sununu (R)	16,885	16.9
	Wesley Powell (R)	14,861	14.9
	Edward B. Hager (R)	9,821	9.9
	Lawrence J. Brady (R)	9,426	9.5
	David H. Bradley (R)	9,361	9.4
	Anthony Campaigne (R)	8,495	8.6
	George B. Roberts (R)	7,397	7.4
	Democratic Primary		
	John A. Durkin (D)	36,933	79.6
	William F. Sullivan (D)	9,486	20.4

	Candidates	Votes	%
1986	**Republican Primary**		
	Warren B. Rudman (R)		100.0
	Democratic Primary		
	Endicott Peabody (D)	20,568	61.2
	Robert L. Dupay (D)	6,108	18.2
	Robert A. Patton (D)	3,721	11.1
	Andrew D. Tempelman (D)	2,601	7.8
1992	**Republican Primary**		
	Judd Gregg (R)	57,141	49.8
	Harold Eckman (R)	43,264	37.7
	Jean T. White (R)	10,642	9.3
	Democratic Primary		
	John Rauh (D)	41,923	50.5
	Brenda J. Elias (D)	15,943	19.2
	Terry Bennett (D)	11,699	14.1
	Jeanne Stapleton (D)	7,804	9.4

New Hampshire
1. *A special election was held to fill the remaining four years of the term of Sen. Styles Bridges (R), who died Nov. 26, 1961.*

NEW JERSEY

	Candidates	Votes	%
	Class 1		
1958	**Republican Primary**		
	Robert W. Kean (R)	152,884	43.0
	Bernard M. Shanley (R)	128,990	36.3
	Robert Morris (R)	73,658	20.7
	Democratic Primary		
	Harrison A. Williams Jr. (D)	152,413	43.1
	John J. Grogan (D)	139,605	39.5
	Joseph E. McLean (D)	61,478	17.4
1964	**Republican Primary**		
	Bernard M. Shanley (R)		100.0
	Democratic Primary		
	Harrison A. Williams Jr. (D)		100.0
1970	**Republican Primary**		
	Nelson G. Gross (R)	150,662	65.4
	James A. Quaremba (R)	43,547	18.9
	Joseph T. Gavin (R)	36,208	15.7
	Democratic Primary		
	Harrison A. Williams Jr. (D)	190,692	65.6
	Frank J. Guarini (D)	100,045	34.4
1976	**Republican Primary**		
	David F. Norcross (R)	196,457	68.3
	Martin E. Wendelken (R)	45,472	15.8

Candidates	Votes	%
James E. Parker (R)	27,672	9.6
N. Leonard Smith (R)	17,892	6.2

Democratic Primary

Harrison A. Williams Jr. (D)	378,553	85.1
Stephen J. Foley (D)	66,178	14.9

1982   **Republican Primary**

Millicent Fenwick (R)	193,683	54.3
Jeffrey Bell (R)	163,145	45.7

Democratic Primary

Frank R. Lautenberg (D)	104,666	26.0
Andrew Maguire (D)	92,878	23.0
Joseph A. LeFante (D)	81,440	20.2
Barbara B. Sigmund (D)	45,708	11.3
Howard Rosen (D)	28,427	7.0

1988   **Republican Primary**

Peter M. Dawkins (R)		100.0

Democratic Primary

Frank R. Lautenberg (D)	362,072	79.5
Elnardo J. Webster (D)	51,938	11.4
Harold J. Young (D)	41,303	9.1

1994   **Republican Primary**

Garabed Haytaian (R)	126,768	67.3
Brian T. Kennedy (R)	61,532	32.7

Democratic Primary

Frank R. Lautenberg (D)	151,416	81.0
Bill Campbell (D)	26,066	13.9
Lynne A. Speed (D)	9,563	5.1

Class 2

1960   **Republican Primary**

Clifford P. Case (R)	230,802	63.7
Robert Morris (R)	120,729	33.3

Democratic Primary

Thorn Lord (D)	177,429	81.6
Richard M. Glassner (D)	40,134	18.4

1966   **Republican Primary**

Clifford P. Case (R)		100.0

Democratic Primary

Warren W. Wilentz (D)	197,428	72.7
David Frost (D)	31,289	11.5
John J. Winberry (D)	19,745	7.3
Clarence Coggins (D)	16,775	6.2

1972   **Republican Primary**

Clifford P. Case (R)	187,268	70.1
James W. Ralph (R)	79,776	29.9

Candidates	Votes	%

Democratic Primary

Paul J. Krebs (D)	135,000	43.2
Daniel M. Gaby (D)	86,213	27.6
Joseph T. Karcher (D)	51,321	16.4
Henry Kielbasa (D)	40,235	12.9

1978   **Republican Primary**

Jeffrey Bell (R)	118,555	50.7
Clifford P. Case (R)	115,082	49.3

Democratic Primary

Bill Bradley (D)	217,502	58.9
Richard C. Leone (D)	97,667	26.4
Alexander J. Menza (D)	32,386	8.8

1984   **Republican Primary**

Mary V. Mochary (R)	111,851	61.4
Robert Morris (R)	70,418	38.6

Democratic Primary

Bill Bradley (D)	404,301	92.9
Elliot Greenspan (D)	30,680	7.0

1990   **Republican Primary**

Christine Todd Whitman (R)		100.0

Democratic Primary

Bill Bradley (D)	197,454	92.4
Daniel Z. Seyler (D)	16,287	7.6

1996   **Republican Primary**

Dick Zimmer (R)	144,121	68.0
Richard A. Du Haime (R)	42,155	19.9
Dick La Rossa (R)	25,608	12.1

Democratic Primary

Robert G. Torricelli (D)	223,444	100.0

NEW MEXICO

Candidates	Votes	%

Class 1

1958   **Republican Primary**

Forrest S. Atchley (R)	10,384	51.3
Reginaldo Espinoza (R)	9,861	48.7

Democratic Primary

Dennis Chavez (D)	68,689	65.7
E. S. Walker (D)	35,927	34.3

1964   **Republican Primary**

Edwin L. Mechem (R)		100.0

Candidates	Votes	%
Democratic Primary		
Joseph M. Montoya (D)		100.0
1970 Republican Primary		
Anderson Carter (R)	32,122	57.8
David F. Cargo (R)	17,951	32.3
Harold G. Thompson (R)	5,544	10.0
Democratic Primary		
Joseph M. Montoya (D)	85,285	73.1
Richard B. Edwards (D)	31,381	26.9
1976 Republican Primary		
Harrison "Jack" Schmitt (R)	34,074	71.7
Eugene W. Pierce (R)	10,965	23.1
Arthur A. Lavine (R)	2,481	5.2
Democratic Primary		
Joseph M. Montoya (D)	96,063	66.3
Robert R. Sims (D)	48,824	33.7
1982 Republican Primary		
Harrison "Jack" Schmitt (R)		100.0
Democratic Primary		
Jeff Bingaman (D)	91,780	54.4
Jerry Apodaca (D)	66,598	39.4
Virginia R. Keehan (D)	10,466	6.2
1988 Republican Primary		
William Valentine (R)	35,809	43.4
Rick Montoya (R)	23,162	28.1
Corky Morris (R)	16,539	20.1
Joseph J. Carraro (R)	6,928	8.4
Democratic Primary		
Jeff Bingaman (D)		100.0
1994 Republican Primary		
Colin R. McMillan (R)	65,119	72.6
Bill Turner (R)	13,178	14.7
Robin D. Otten (R)	11,439	12.7
Democratic Primary		
Jeff Bingaman (D)	165,148	100.0

Class 2

Candidates	Votes	%
1960 Republican Primary		
William F. Colwes (R)	18,884	53.0
Joseph Rendon (R)	11,866	33.3
Frederic W. Airy (R)	4,859	13.6

Candidates	Votes	%
Democratic Primary		
Clinton P. Anderson (D)	98,037	81.3
James P. Speer (D)	9,360	7.8
N. Tito Quintana (D)	8,981	7.4
1966 Republican Primary		
Anderson Carter (R)		100.0
Democratic Primary		
Clinton P. Anderson (D)		100.0
1972 Republican Primary		
Pete V. Domenici (R)	37,337	63.2
David F. Cargo (R)	12,522	21.2
E. Lee Francis (R)	4,583	7.8
Democratic Primary		
Jack Daniels (D)	45,648	29.7
Robert A. Mondragon (D)	29,603	19.3
David L. Norvell (D)	24,917	16.2
Thomas G. Morris (D)	22,849	14.9
1978 Republican Primary		
Pete V. Domenici (R)		100.0
Democratic Primary		
Toney Anaya (D)		100.0
1984 Republican Primary		
Pete V. Domenici (R)	42,760	100.0
Democratic Primary		
Judith A. Pratt (D)	67,722	45.5
Nick Franklin (D)	56,434	37.9
Anselmo A. Chavez (D)	24,694	16.6
1990 Republican Primary		
Pete V. Domenici (R)		100.0
Democratic Primary		
Tom R. Benavides (D)		100.0
1996 Republican Primary		
Pete V. Domenici (R)	69,394	100.0
Democratic Primary		
Art Trujillo (D)	84,721	70.6
Eric Treisman (D)	35,363	29.4
Green Primary		
Abraham J. Gutmann (GREEN)	952	61.5
Sam Hitt (GREEN)	597	38.6

NEW YORK[1]

Candidates	Votes	%

Class 1

1970

Republican Primary

Charles E. Goodell (R)		100.0

Democratic Primary

Richard L. Ottinger (D)	366,789	39.6
Paul O'Dwyer (D)	302,438	32.7
Theodore C. Sorensen (D)	154,434	16.7
Richard D. McCarthy (D)	102,224	11.0

Conservative Primary

James L. Buckley (C)		100.0

Liberal Primary

Charles E. Goodell (L)		100.0

1976

Republican Primary

James L. Buckley (R)	242,527	70.5
Peter A. Peyser (R)	101,629	29.5

Democratic Primary

Daniel Patrick Moynihan (D)	333,697	36.4
Bella S. Abzug (D)	323,705	35.3
Ramsey Clark (D)	94,191	10.3
Paul O'Dwyer (D)	82,689	9.0
Abraham J. Hirschfeld (D)	82,331	9.0

Conservative Primary

James L. Buckley (C)		100.0

Liberal Primary

Henry S. Stern (L)[2]		100.0

1982

Republican Primary

Florence M. Sullivan (R)	216,486	42.4
Muriel Siebert (R)	157,446	30.8
Whitney N. Seymour (R)	136,974	26.8

Democratic Primary

Daniel Patrick Moynihan (D)	922,059	85.1
Melvin Klenetsky (D)	161,012	14.9

Conservative Primary

Florence M. Sullivan (C)		100.0

Liberal Primary

Daniel Patrick Moynihan (L)		100.0

Right to Life Primary

Florence M. Sullivan (RTL)		100.0

1988

Republican Primary

Robert McMillan (R)		100.0

Candidates	Votes	%

Democratic Primary

Daniel Patrick Moynihan (D)		100.0

Conservative Primary

Robert McMillan (R)		100.0

Liberal Primary

Daniel Patrick Moynihan (L)		100.0

Right to Life Primary

Adelle R. Nathanson (RTL)		100.0

1994

Republican Primary

Bernadette Castro (R)		100.0

Democratic Primary

Daniel Patrick Moynihan (D)	526,766	74.7
Al Sharpton (D)	178,231	25.3

Conservative Primary

Bernadette Castro (C)	12,300	62.9
Henry F. Hewes (C)	7,251	37.1

Liberal Primary

Daniel Patrick Moynihan (L)		100.0

Right to Life Primary

Henry F. Hewes (RTL)		100.0

Class 3

1968

Republican Primary

Jacob K. Javits (R)		100.0

Democratic Primary

Paul O'Dwyer (D)	275,877	36.1
Eugene H. Nickerson (D)	257,639	33.7
Joseph Y. Resnick (D)	229,893	30.1

Conservative Primary

James L. Buckley (C)		100.0

Liberal Primary

Jacob K. Javits (L)	10,277	72.1
Murray Baron (L)	3,969	27.8

1974

Republican Primary

Jacob K. Javits (R)		100.0

Democratic Primary

Ramsey Clark (D)	414,327	48.0
Lee Alexander (D)	255,250	29.6
Abraham J. Hirschfeld (D)	194,076	22.5

Candidates	Votes	%
Conservative Primary		
Barbara A. Keating (C)		100.0
Liberal Primary		
Jacob K. Javits (L)		100.0

1980

Candidates	Votes	%
Republican Primary		
Alfonse M. D'Amato (R)	323,468	55.7
Jacob K. Javits (R)	257,433	44.3
Democratic Primary		
Elizabeth Holtzman (D)	378,567	40.7
Bess Myerson (D)	292,767	31.5
John V. Lindsay (D)	146,815	15.8
John Santucci (D)	111,129	12.0
Conservative Primary		
Alfonse M. D'Amato (C)		100.0
Liberal Primary		
Jacob K. Javits (R)		100.0
Right to Life Primary		
Alfonse M. D'Amato (RTL)		100.0

1986

Candidates	Votes	%
Republican Primary		
Alfonse M. D'Amato (R)		100.0
Democratic Primary		
John S. Dyson (D)		100.0
Right to Life Primary		
Alfonse M. D'Amato (RTL)		100.0

1992

Candidates	Votes	%
Republican Primary		
Alfonse M. D'Amato (R)		100.0
Democratic Primary		
Robert Abrams (D)	426,904	37.0
Geraldine A. Ferraro (D)	415,650	36.0
Al Sharpton (D)	166,665	14.5
Elizabeth Holtzman (D)	144,026	12.5
Conservative Primary		
Alfonse M. D'Amato (C)		100.0
Liberal Primary		
Robert Abrams (L)		100.0
Right to Life Primary		
Alfonse M. D'Amato (RTL)		100.0

New York
1. Until 1968, when New York adopted a primary system, party conventions or state central committees nominated candidates for statewide office.
2. Stern withdrew after the primary and the Liberal Party's state committee substituted Daniel Patrick Moynihan (D) as the Liberal nominee.

NORTH CAROLINA

Candidates	Votes	%
Class 2		

1948

Candidates	Votes	%
Democratic Primary		
J. Melville Broughton (D)	207,981	53.1
William B. Umstead (D)	183,865	46.9
Democratic Special Primary		
J. Melville Broughton (D)	206,605	52.3
William B. Umstead (D)	188,420	47.7

1950

Candidates	Votes	%
Democratic Special Primary		
Frank P. Graham (D)	303,605	49.1
Willis Smith (D)	250,222	40.5
Robert R. Reynolds (D)	58,752	9.5
Democratic Special Runoff		
Willis Smith (D)	281,114	51.8
Frank P. Graham (D)	261,789	48.2

1954

Candidates	Votes	%
Democratic Primary		
W. Kerr Scott (D)	312,053	50.8
Alton Lennon (D)	286,730	46.7
Democratic Special Primary		
W. Kerr Scott (D)	274,674	49.4
Alton Lennon (D)	264,265	47.5

1958

| B. Everett Jordan (D)[1] | | |
| Richard C. Clarke Jr. (R) | | |

1960

Candidates	Votes	%
Republican Primary		
Kyle Hayes (R)		100.0
Democratic Primary		
B. Everett Jordan (D)	324,188	54.3
Addison Hewlett (D)	217,899	36.5
Robert W. Gregory (D)	31,463	5.3

1966

Candidates	Votes	%
Republican Primary		
John S. Shallcross (R)		100.0
Democratic Primary		
B. Everett Jordan (D)	445,454	79.3
Hubert E. Seymour (D)	116,548	20.7

1972

Candidates	Votes	%
Republican Primary		
Jesse Helms (R)	92,496	60.1
James C. Johnson (R)	45,303	29.5
William H. Booe (R)	16,032	10.4
Democratic Primary		
Nick Galifianakis (D)	377,993	49.3
B. Everett Jordan (D)	340,391	44.4

141

Candidates	Votes	%
Democratic Runoff		
Nick Galifianakis (D)	333,558	*55.5*
B. Everett Jordan (D)	267,997	*44.6*

1978

Candidates	Votes	%
Republican Primary		
Jesse Helms (R)		*100.0*
Democratic Primary		
Luther H. Hodges Jr. (D)	260,868	*40.1*
John Ingram (D)	170,715	*26.2*
Lawrence Davis (D)	105,381	*16.2*
McNeill Smith (D)	82,703	*12.7*
Democratic Runoff		
John Ingram (D)	244,469	*54.2*
Luther H. Hodges Jr. (D)	206,223	*45.8*

1984

Candidates	Votes	%
Republican Primary		
Jesse Helms (R)	134,675	*90.6*
George Wimbish (R)	13,899	*9.4*
Democratic Primary		
James B. Hunt Jr. (D)	655,429	*77.5*
Thomas L. Allred (D)	126,841	*15.0*
Harrill Jones (D)	63,676	*7.5*

1990

Candidates	Votes	%
Republican Primary		
Jesse Helms (R)	157,345	*84.3*
L. C. Nixon (R)	15,355	*8.2*
George Wimbish (R)	13,895	*7.4*
Democratic Primary		
Harvey B. Gantt (D)	260,179	*37.5*
Mike Easley (D)	209,934	*30.3*
John Ingram (D)	120,990	*17.4*
R. P. Thomas (D)	82,883	*12.0*
Democratic Runoff		
Harvey B. Gantt (D)	273,567	*56.9*
Mike Easley (D)	207,283	*43.1*

1996

Candidates	Votes	%
Republican Primary		
Jesse Helms (R)		*100.0*
Democratic Primary		
Harvey B. Gantt (D)	308,837	*52.4*
Charlie Sanders (D)	245,297	*41.6*
Ralph M. McKinney Jr. (D)	34,829	*5.9*

Class 3

1950

Candidates	Votes	%
Democratic Primary		
Clyde R. Hoey (D)		*100.0*

	Candidates	Votes	%
1954	Sam J. Ervin Jr. (D)[2]		

1956

Candidates	Votes	%
Republican Primary		
Joel A. Johnson (R)		*100.0*
Democratic Primary		
Sam J. Ervin Jr. (D)	360,967	*84.6*
Marshall C. Kurfees (D)	65,512	*15.4*

1962

Candidates	Votes	%
Republican Primary		
Claude L. Greene Jr. (R)	31,756	*61.1*
C. H. Babcock (R)	20,246	*38.9*
Democratic Primary		
Sam J. Ervin Jr. (D)		*100.0*

1968

Candidates	Votes	%
Republican Primary		
Robert V. Somers (R)	48,351	*36.6*
J. L. Zimmerman (R)	43,644	*33.1*
Edwin W. Tenney (R)	40,023	*30.3*
Republican Runoff		
Robert V. Somers (R)	8,816	*60.0*
J. L. Zimmerman (R)	5,734	*39.4*
Democratic Primary		
Sam J. Ervin Jr. (D)	499,392	*78.3*
Charles A. Pratt (D)	60,362	*9.5*
John T. Gathings (D)	48,357	*7.6*

1974

Candidates	Votes	%
Republican Primary		
William E. Stevens (R)	62,419	*65.1*
Wood Hall Young (R)	26,918	*28.1*
B. E. "Bee" Sweatt (R)	6,520	*6.8*
Democratic Primary		
Robert Morgan (D)	294,986	*50.4*
Nick Galifianakis (D)	189,815	*32.4*
Henry Hall Wilson (D)	67,247	*11.5*

1980

Candidates	Votes	%
Republican Primary		
John P. East (R)		*100.0*
Democratic Primary		
Robert Morgan (D)		*100.0*

1986

Candidates	Votes	%
Republican Primary		
James T. Broyhill (R)	139,570	*66.5*
David B. Funderburk (R)	63,593	*30.3*
Democratic Primary		
Terry Sanford (D)	409,394	*60.2*
John Ingram (D)	111,557	*16.4*
Fountain Odom (D)	49,689	*7.3*
William I. Belk (D)	33,821	*5.0*

	Candidates	Votes	%
1992	**Republican Primary**		
	Lauch Faircloth (R)	129,159	47.7
	Sue Myrick (R)	81,801	30.2
	Eugene Johnston (R)	46,112	17.0
	Larry E. Harrington (R)	13,496	5.0
	Democratic Primary		
	Terry Sanford (D)		100.0

North Carolina

1. *Sen. W. Kerr Scott (D 1954-58) died April 16, 1958. Jordan was appointed to succeed him. Jordan and Clarke were designated by the state committee of their respective parties to run in the Nov. 4 special election for the remaining two years of Scott's term. Jordan won.*

2. *Sen. Clyde R. Hoey (D 1945-54) died May 12, 1954. Ervin was appointed to replace him and was also named by the Democratic state executive committee to run in a Nov. 2 special election for the remaining two years of the term.*

NORTH DAKOTA

	Candidates	Votes	%
	Class 1		
1958	**Republican Primary**		
	William Langer (R)[1]	68,541	65.5
	Clyde Duffy (R)	34,152	32.6
	Democratic Primary		
	Raymond Vendsel (D)	30,775	65.8
	Anson Anderson (D)	15,999	34.2
1964	**Republican Primary**		
	Tom Kleppe (R)		100.0
	Democratic Primary		
	Quentin N. Burdick (D)		100.0
1970	**Republican Primary**		
	Tom Kleppe (R)		100.0
	Democratic Primary		
	Quentin N. Burdick (D)		100.0
1976	**Republican Primary**		
	Richard Stroup (R)		100.0
	Democratic Primary		
	Quentin N. Burdick (D)		100.0
	American Primary		
	Clarence Haggard (AM)		100.0
1982	**Republican Primary**		
	Gene Knorr (R)		100.0

	Candidates	Votes	%
	Democratic Primary		
	Quentin N. Burdick (D)		100.0
1988	**Republican Primary**		
	Earl Strinden (R)		100.0
	Democratic Primary		
	Quentin N. Burdick (D)[2]		100.0
	Libertarian Primary		
	Kenneth C. Gardner (LIBERT)		100.0
1994	**Republican Primary**		
	Ben Clayburgh (R)	49,493	100.0
	Democratic Primary		
	Kent Conrad (D)	66,265	100.0
	Class 3		
1956	**Republican Primary**		
	Milton R. Young (R)	88,738	88.6
	Ray R. Lake (R)	11,398	11.4
	Democratic Primary		
	Quentin N. Burdick (D)		100.0
1962	**Republican Primary**		
	Milton R. Young (R)	67,938	92.2
	Roger Vorachek (R)	5,729	7.8
	Democratic Primary		
	William Lanier (D)		100.0
1968	**Republican Primary**		
	Milton R. Young (R)		100.0
	Democratic Primary		
	Herschel Lashkowitz (D)		100.0
1974	**Republican Primary**		
	Milton R. Young (R)		100.0
	Democratic Primary		
	William L. Guy (D)	55,269	83.0
	Robert P. McCarney (D)	11,286	17.0
1980	**Republican Primary**		
	Mark Andrews (R)		100.0
	Democratic Primary		
	Kent Johanneson (D)	30,789	77.4
	Michael P. Saba (D)	9,013	22.6

	Candidates	Votes	%
1986	**Republican Primary**		
	Mark Andrews (R)		*100.0*
	Democratic Primary		
	Kent Conrad (R)		*100.0*
1992[2]	**Republican Primary**		
	Steve Sydness (R)	45,611	*100.0*
	Democratic Primary		
	Byron L. Dorgan (D)	68,113	*100.0*

North Dakota

1. No primaries were held for the June 1960 special election in North Dakota to fill the vacancy caused by Langer's death. Nominees were selected by state conventions.

2. A special election was also held to fill the remaining two years of the term of Sen. Quentin N. Burdick (D), who died Sept. 8, 1992. Both major-party candidates were nominated by the state party committees and no primaries were held.

OHIO

	Candidates	Votes	%
	Class 1		
1958	**Republican Primary**		
	John W. Bricker (R)		*100.0*
	Democratic Primary		
	Stephen M. Young (D)		*100.0*
1964	**Republican Primary**		
	Robert A. Taft Jr. (R)	606,944	*79.1*
	Ted W. Brown (R)	160,263	*20.9*
	Democratic Primary		
	Stephen M. Young (D)	520,641	*66.5*
	John Glenn (D)	206,956	*26.4*
1970	**Republican Primary**		
	Robert A. Taft Jr. (R)	472,202	*50.3*
	James A. Rhodes (R)	466,932	*49.7*
	Democratic Primary		
	Howard M. Metzenbaum (D)	430,469	*46.3*
	John Glenn (D)	417,027	*44.9*
	Kenneth W. Clement (D)	50,375	*5.4*
	American Independent Primary		
	Richard B. Kay (AMI)		*100.0*
1976	**Republican Primary**		
	Robert A. Taft Jr. (R)		*100.0*

	Candidates	Votes	%
	Democratic Primary		
	Howard M. Metzenbaum (D)	576,124	*53.6*
	James V. Stanton (D)	400,552	*37.3*
	James D. Nolan (D)	62,979	*5.8*
1982	**Republican Primary**		
	Paul E. Pfeifer (R)	364,579	*60.0*
	Walter E. Beckjord (R)	180,198	*29.7*
	Bill Ress (WRITE IN)	62,446	*10.3*
	Democratic Primary		
	Howard M. Metzenbaum (D)	810,785	*82.9*
	Norbert G. Dennerll (D)	167,778	*17.1*
	Libertarian Primary		
	Philip Herzing (LIBERT)		*100.0*
1988	**Republican Primary**		
	George Voinovich (R)		*100.0*
	Democratic Primary		
	Howard Metzenbaum (D)	1,070,934	*83.6*
	Ralph A. Applegate (D)	210,508	*16.4*
1994	**Republican Primary**		
	Mike Dewine (R)	422,366	*52.0*
	Bernadine Healy (R)	263,559	*32.5*
	Gene Watts (R)	83,103	*10.2*
	George H. Rhodes (R)	42,633	*5.3*
	Democratic Primary		
	Joel Hyatt (D)	432,360	*46.2*
	Mary O. Boyle (D)	415,851	*44.5*
	Ralph A. Applegate (D)	86,677	*9.3*
	Class 3		
1956	**Republican Primary**		
	George H. Bender (R)		*100.0*
	Democratic Primary		
	Frank J. Lausche (D)		*100.0*
1962	**Republican Primary**		
	John M. Briley (R)	177,987	*35.3*
	Charles E. Fry (R)	143,320	*28.4*
	John S. Ballard (R)	132,924	*26.3*
	Ross Pepple (R)	50,221	*10.0*
	Democratic Primary		
	Frank J. Lausche (D)	437,902	*74.0*
	Albert T. Ball (D)	90,609	*15.3*
	Raymond Warren Beringer (D)	63,543	*10.7*

	Candidates	Votes	%
1968	**Republican Primary**		
	William B. Saxbe (R)	575,178	*82.3*
	William L. White (R)	71,191	*10.2*
	Albert E. Payne (R)	52,393	*7.5*
	Democratic Primary		
	John J. Gilligan (D)	544,814	*55.4*
	Frank J. Lausche (D)	438,588	*44.6*
1974	**Republican Primary**		
	Ralph J. Perk (R)	341,078	*64.8*
	Peter E. Voss (R)	185,342	*35.2*
	Democratic Primary		
	John Glenn (D)	571,871	*54.4*
	Howard M. Metzenbaum (D)	480,123	*45.6*
1980	**Republican Primary**		
	James E. Betts (R)		*100.0*
	Democratic Primary		
	John Glenn (D)	934,230	*85.9*
	Frances A. Waterman (D)	88,506	*8.1*
	Francis Hunstiger (D)	64,270	*5.9*
1986	**Republican Primary**		
	Thomas N. Kindness (R)		*100.0*
	Democratic Primary		
	John H. Glenn (D)	678,171	*87.6*
	Don Scott (D)	96,309	*12.4*
1992	**Republican Primary**		
	Mike DeWine (R)	583,805	*70.3*
	George H. Rhodes (R)	246,625	*29.7*
	Democratic Primary		
	John H. Glenn (D)	859,622	*100.0*

OKLAHOMA

	Candidates	Votes	%
	Class 2		
1960	**Republican Primary**		
	B. Hayden Crawford (R)	37,508	*70.4*
	Herbert K. Hyde (R)	15,743	*29.6*
	Democratic Primary		
	Robert S. Kerr (D)	300,061	*77.6*
	Thomas C. Dunn (D)	65,139	*16.8*
	D. R. Condo (D)	21,420	*5.5*

	Candidates	Votes	%
1964[1]	**Republican Special Primary**		
	Bud Wilkinson (R)	100,544	*79.2*
	Thomas J. Harris (R)	19,170	*15.1*
	Forest W. Beall (R)	7,211	*5.7*
	Democratic Special Primary		
	J. Howard Edmondson (D)	215,455	*36.4*
	Fred R. Harris (D)	190,868	*32.3*
	Raymond Gary (D)	170,869	*28.9*
	Democratic Special Runoff		
	Fred R. Harris (D)	277,362	*60.9*
	J. Howard Edmondson (D)	178,051	*39.1*
1966	**Republican Primary**		
	Pat J. Patterson (R)	36,036	*42.5*
	Don Kinkaid (R)	32,137	*37.9*
	Gustav K. Brandborg (R)	16,617	*19.6*
	Republican Runoff		
	Pat J. Patterson (R)	42,550	*58.3*
	Don Kinkaid (R)	30,452	*41.7*
	Democratic Primary		
	Fred R. Harris (D)	359,747	*83.6*
	W. R. Owens (D)	41,580	*9.7*
	Billy E. Brown (D)	29,184	*6.8*
1972	**Republican Primary**		
	Dewey F. Bartlett (R)	94,935	*93.1*
	C. W. Wood (R)	7,029	*6.9*
	Democratic Primary		
	Ed Edmondson (D)	249,729	*56.3*
	Charles Nesbitt (D)	92,101	*20.8*
	Al Terrill (D)	33,520	*7.6*
	Jed Johnson (D)	28,795	*6.5*
1978	**Republican Primary**		
	Robert B. Kamm (R)		*100.0*
	Democratic Primary		
	David L. Boren (D)	252,560	*45.8*
	Ed Edmondson (D)	155,626	*28.2*
	Gene Stipe (D)	114,423	*20.8*
	Democratic Runoff		
	David L. Boren (D)	281,587	*60.5*
	Ed Edmondson (D)	184,175	*39.5*
1984	**Republican Primary**		
	George L. Mothershed (R)	46,933	*39.3*
	Will E. "Bill" Crozier (R)	39,581	*33.1*
	Gar Graham (R)	32,901	*27.6*

Candidates	Votes	%
Democratic Primary		
David L. Boren (D)	432,534	*89.9*
Marshall Luse (D)	48,761	*10.1*

1990

Candidates	Votes	%
Republican Primary		
Stephen Jones (R)		*100.0*
Democratic Primary		
David L. Boren (D)	445,969	*84.3*
Virginia Jenner (D)	57,909	*10.9*

1994[2]

Candidates	Votes	%
Republican Special Primary		
James M. Inhofe (R)	159,001	*77.8*
Tony Caldwell (R)	45,359	*22.2*
Democratic Special Primary		
Dave McCurdy (D)	283,095	*64.9*
Cody L. Graves (D)	153,367	*35.1*

1996

Candidates	Votes	%
Republican Primary		
James M. Inhofe (R)	116,241	*75.3*
Dan Lowe (R)	38,044	*24.7*
Democratic Primary		
Jim Boren (D)	186,611	*55.5*
Don McCorkell (D)	122,635	*36.5*
David Louis Annanders (D)	26,794	*8.0*
Libertarian Primary		
Agnes Marie Regier (LIBERT)	1,511	*51.4*
Michael A. Clem (LIBERT)	1,429	*48.6*

Class 3

1956

Candidates	Votes	%
Republican Primary		
Douglas McKeever (R)	24,447	*55.5*
Paul V. Beck (R)	7,666	*17.4*
Ernest G. Albright (R)	6,539	*14.8*
Dan M. Madrano (R)	5,379	*12.2*
Democratic Primary		
A. S. Mike Monroney (D)	245,572	*71.1*
H. O. Doenges (D)	54,546	*15.8*
Ora J. Fox (D)	29,825	*8.6*

1962

Candidates	Votes	%
Republican Primary		
B. Hayden Crawford (R)		*100.0*
Democratic Primary		
A. S. Mike Monroney (D)	335,922	*74.3*
Wilson Wallace (D)	64,996	*14.4*
Billy E. Brown (D)	26,440	*5.8*
Woodrow W. Bussey (D)	24,725	*5.5*

1968

Candidates	Votes	%
Republican Primary		
Henry Bellmon (R)		*100.0*

Candidates	Votes	%
Democratic Primary		
A. S. Mike Monroney (D)	281,697	*76.3*
W. R. Owens (D)	32,823	*8.9*
Jesse L. Leeds (D)	22,843	*6.2*
Billy E. Brown (D)	20,681	*5.6*
American Primary		
George Washington (AM)	414	*57.6*
Landis B. Hiniker (AM)	305	*42.4*

1974

Candidates	Votes	%
Republican Primary		
Henry Bellmon (R)	132,888	*87.1*
Warner M. Hornbeck (R)	19,733	*12.9*
Democratic Primary		
Ed Edmondson (D)	288,665	*48.7*
Charles Nesbitt (D)	222,727	*37.5*
Wilburn Cartwright (D)	35,107	*5.9*
Democratic Runoff		
Ed Edmondson (D)	306,178	*58.7*
Charles Nesbitt (D)	215,685	*41.3*

1980

Candidates	Votes	%
Republican Primary		
Don Nickles (R)	47,879	*34.7*
John Zink (R)	45,914	*33.3*
Ed Noble (R)	39,839	*28.9*
Republican Runoff		
Don Nickles (R)	81,697	*65.6*
John Zink (R)	42,818	*34.4*
Democratic Primary		
Robert S. Kerr Jr. (D)	156,666	*34.0*
Andrew Coats (D)	154,762	*33.6*
Gene Howard (D)	55,503	*12.1*
James E. Hamilton (D)	49,369	*10.7*
Democratic Runoff		
Andrew Coats (D)	209,952	*53.0*
Robert S. Kerr Jr. (D)	185,814	*46.9*
Libertarian Primary		
Robert Murphy (LIBERT)		*100.0*

1986

Candidates	Votes	%
Republican Primary		
Don Nickles (R)		*100.0*
Democratic Primary		
James R. Jones (R)	324,907	*67.4*
George Gentry (R)	157,141	*32.6*

1992

Candidates	Votes	%
Republican Primary		
Don Nickles (R)		*100.0*
Democratic Primary		
Steve Lewis (D)		*100.0*

Oklahoma
1. A special election was held to fill the remaining two years of the term of Sen. Robert S. Kerr (D), who died Jan. 1, 1963.
2. A special election was held to fill the remaining two years of the term of Sen. David L. Boren (D), who resigned Nov. 15, 1994.

OREGON

Candidates	Votes	%
Class 2		

1960[1] Republican Special Primary

Candidates	Votes	%
Elmo E. Smith (R)	201,024	85.5
George Altvater (R)	33,022	14.0

Democratic Special Primary

Maurine B. Neuberger (D)	244,865	99.5

1960 Republican Primary

Elmo E. Smith (R)	179,575	76.5
George Altvater (R)	20,438	8.7
R. F. Cook (R)	19,443	8.3
Thomas Killam (R)	14,490	6.2

Democratic Primary

Maurine B. Neuberger (D)	211,961	77.9
Harry C. Fowler (D)	28,032	10.3
William B. Murphy (D)	16,245	6.0

1966 Republican Primary

Mark O. Hatfield (R)	178,782	75.9
Walter Huss (R)	30,906	13.1
James Bacaloff (R)	19,699	8.4

Democratic Primary

Robert B. Duncan (D)	161,189	62.2
Howard Morgan (D)	89,174	34.4

1972 Republican Primary

Mark O. Hatfield (R)	171,594	61.1
Lynn Engdahl (R)	63,859	22.8
Kenneth A. Brown (R)	30,826	11.0

Democratic Primary

Wayne L. Morse (D)	173,147	43.7
Robert B. Duncan (D)	130,845	33.0
Don Willner (D)	74,060	18.7

1978 Republican Primary

Mark O. Hatfield (R)	159,617	65.7
Bert W. Hawkins (R)	43,350	17.8
Robert D. Maxwell (R)	24,294	10.0
Richard L. Schnepel (R)	15,628	6.4

Democratic Primary

Vernon Cook (D)	151,754	58.3
John Sweeney (D)	41,599	16.0
Jack A. Brown (D)	35,211	13.5
Steve Anderson (D)	30,066	11.6

1984 Republican Primary

Candidates	Votes	%
Mark O. Hatfield (R)	214,114	78.6
John T. Schiess (R)	26,848	9.9
Sherry Reynolds (R)	18,590	6.8

Democratic Primary

Margie Hendriksen (D)	249,142	75.8
Sam Kahl (D)	79,317	24.1

1990 Republican Primary

Mark Hatfield (R)	220,449	78.3
Randy Prince (R)	59,970	21.3

Democratic Primary

Harry Lonsdale (D)	162,529	64.1
Steve Anderson (D)	34,305	13.5
Neale S. Hyatt (D)	20,684	8.2
Brooks Washburne (D)	13,766	5.4

1996 Republican Primary

Gordon Smith (R)	224,428	78.1
Lon Mabon (R)	23,479	8.2
Kirby Brumfield (R)	15,744	5.5

Democratic Primary

Tom Bruggere (D)	151,288	49.6
Harry Lonsdale (D)	76,059	24.9
Bill Dwyer (D)	30,871	10.1
Jerry Rust (D)	27,773	9.1
Anna Nevenich (D)	16,827	5.5

Class 3

1956 Republican Primary

Douglas McKay (R)	123,281	49.5
Phil Hitchcock (R)	99,296	39.8
Elmer Deetz (R)	23,170	9.3

Democratic Primary

Wayne L. Morse (D)	195,784	83.4
Woody Smith (D)	38,959	16.6

1962 Republican Primary

Sig Ulander (R)	106,821	50.1
Edwin R. Durno (R)	72,955	34.2
Harold M. Livingston (R)	16,880	7.9

Democratic Primary

Wayne L. Morse (D)	183,385	79.8
Charles E. Gilbert (D)	46,171	20.1

1968 Republican Primary

Bob Packwood (R)	241,464	88.0
John S. Boyd (R)	32,807	12.0

Democratic Primary

Wayne L. Morse (D)	185,091	49.0
Robert B. Duncan (D)	174,795	46.3

147

	Candidates	Votes	%
1974	**Republican Primary**		
	Bob Packwood (R)		100.0
	Democratic Primary		
	Wayne L. Morse (D)[2]	155,729	49.0
	Jason Boe (D)	125,055	39.3
	Robert T. Daly (D)	21,881	6.9
1980	**Republican Primary**		
	Bob Packwood (R)	191,127	62.4
	Brenda Jose (R)	45,973	15.0
	Kenneth A. Brown (R)	23,599	7.7
	Rosalie Huss (R)	22,929	7.5
	Willard D. Severn (R)	22,281	7.3
	Democratic Primary		
	Ted Kulongoski (D)	161,153	47.7
	Charles O. Porter (D)	69,649	20.6
	Jack Sumner (D)	46,107	13.6
	John Sweeney (D)	39,691	11.7
	Gene Arvidson (D)	20,548	6.1
1986	**Republican Primary**		
	Bob Packwood (R)	171,985	57.6
	Joe P. Lutz (R)	126,315	42.3
	Democratic Primary		
	James Weaver (D)[3]	183,334	61.6
	Rod Monroe (D)	44,553	15.0
	Rick Bauman (D)	41,939	14.1
	Steve Anderson (D)	26,130	8.8
1992	**Republican Primary**		
	Bob Packwood (R)	176,939	59.1
	John DeZell (R)	61,128	20.4
	Stephanie J. Salvey (R)	27,088	9.0
	Randy Prince (R)	20,358	6.8
	Democratic Primary		
	Les AuCoin (D)	153,029	42.2
	Harry Lonsdale (D)	152,699	42.1
	Joseph Wetzel (D)	32,183	8.9
	Bob Bell (D)	23,700	6.5
1995[4]	**Republican Special Primary**		
	Gordon Smith (R)	246,060	63.0
	Norma Paulus (R)	98,158	25.1
	Jack Roberts (R)	29,687	7.6
	Democratic Special Primary		
	Ron Wyden (D)	212,532	49.7
	Peter A. DeFazio (D)	187,411	43.8

Oregon

1. A special election to fill the unexpired term of Sen. Richard L. Neuberger (D), who died March 9, 1960, was held in conjunction with the election for the full term, beginning Jan. 3, 1961. His widow, Maurine B. Neuberger (D), and Elmo Smith (R), won both primaries and Maurine Neuberger went on to defeat Smith in the November general election for both the short and full terms. The short term had been filled until the election by Hall Lusk.

Returns for the special primary from the Elections Research Center, Washington, D.C.

2. Sen. Morse died after winning the primary and the Democratic state central committee substituted Betty Roberts as the party's nominee.

3. Weaver withdrew after the Democratic primary. Bauman was substituted by the party state central committee.

4. A special election was held to fill the remaining four years of the term of Sen. Bob Packwood (R), who resigned Oct. 1, 1995.

PENNSYLVANIA

Candidates	Votes	%
Class 1		
1958 **Republican Primary**		
Hugh Scott (R)	766,102	74.0
Weldon B. Heyburn (R)	160,857	15.5
Harrison A. Moyer (R)	108,179	10.4
Democratic Primary		
George M. Leader (D)	724,645	74.2
1964 **Republican Primary**		
Hugh Scott (R)	869,774	88.9
W. Henry McFarland (R)	106,376	10.9
Democratic Primary		
Genevieve Blatt (D)	461,111	45.4
Michael A. Musmanno (D)	460,620	45.4
David B. Roberts (D)	93,311	9.2
1970 **Republican Primary**		
Hugh Scott (R)		100.0
Democratic Primary		
William G. Sesler (D)	477,680	53.8
Norval D. Reece (D)	241,731	27.3
Frank Mesaros (D)	167,779	18.9
American Independent Primary		
W. Henry McFarland (AMI)		100.0
Constitution Primary		
Frank W. Gaydosh (CONST)		100.0
1976 **Republican Primary**		
John Heinz (R)	358,715	37.7
Arlen Specter (R)	332,513	35.0
George R. Packard (R)	160,379	16.9
Democratic Primary		
William J. Green III (D)	762,733	68.8
Jeanette Reibman (D)	345,264	31.1
Constitution Primary		
Andrew J. Watson (CONST)		100.0

	Candidates	Votes	%
1982	**Republican Primary**		
	John Heinz (R)		100.0
	Democratic Primary		
	Cyril H. Wecht (D)	426,625	57.2
	John J. Logue (D)	166,078	22.3
	Cyril E. Sagan (D)	152,631	20.5
1988	**Republican Primary**		
	H. John Heinz (R)[1]		100.0
	Democratic Primary		
	Joseph C. Vignola (D)	492,153	45.4
	Susan S. Kefover (D)	371,443	34.2
	Steve Douglas (D)	145,614	13.4
	John J. Logue (D)	76,020	7.0
1994	**Republican Primary**		
	Rick Santorum (R)	667,115	81.5
	Joe Watkins (R)	150,969	18.5
	Democratic Primary		
	Harris Wofford (D)	714,930	100.0

Class 3

	Candidates	Votes	%
1956	**Republican Primary**		
	James H. Duff (R)	803,971	85.0
	Paul E. Sanger (R)	141,820	15.0
	Democratic Primary		
	Joseph S. Clark (D)		100.0
1962	**Republican Primary**		
	James E. Van Zandt (R)		100.0
	Democratic Primary		
	Joseph S. Clark (D)		100.0
1968	**Republican Primary**		
	Richard S. Schweiker (R)		100.0
	Democratic Primary		
	Joseph S. Clark (D)	460,380	53.3
	John H. Dent (D)	402,799	46.7
1974	**Republican Primary**		
	Richard S. Schweiker (R)		100.0
	Democratic Primary		
	Peter Flaherty (D)	485,361	47.1
	Herbert S. Denenberg (D)	447,081	43.3
	Frank Mesaros (D)	64,070	6.2
	Constitution Primary		
	George W. Shankey (CONST)		100.0

	Candidates	Votes	%
1980	**Republican Primary**		
	Arlen Specter (R)	419,372	36.4
	Bud Haabestad (R)	382,281	33.2
	Edward L. Howard (R)	148,200	12.9
	Democratic Primary		
	Peter Flaherty (D)	771,119	53.2
	Joseph Rhodes (D)	179,107	12.4
	Peter Liacouras (D)	116,975	8.1
	C. Delores Tucker (D)	107,483	7.4
	Ed Mezvinsky (D)	100,841	7.0
	Tom Anderson (D)	89,656	6.2
1986	**Republican Primary**		
	Arlen Specter (R)	434,623	76.2
	Richard A. Stokes (R)	135,673	23.8
	Democratic Primary		
	Robert W. Edgar (D)	432,940	47.3
	Don Bailey (D)	408,460	44.7
	George R. H. Elder (D)	46,663	5.1
1992	**Republican Primary**		
	Arlen Specter (R)	683,118	65.1
	Stephen F. Freind (R)	366,608	34.9
	Democratic Primary		
	Lynn Yeakel (D)	556,372	44.8
	Mark S. Singel (D)	403,656	32.5
	Bob Colville (D)	172,845	13.9

Pennsylvania

1. *Heinz died April 4, 1991. A special election was held in 1991 to fill the vacancy. Candidates were nominated by state party committees, therefore no primaries were held.*

RHODE ISLAND

	Candidates	Votes	%
	Class 1		
1958	**Republican Primary**		
	Bayard Ewing (R)		100.0
	Democratic Primary		
	John O. Pastore (D)		100.0
1964	**Republican Primary**		
	Ronald R. Lagueux (R)		100.0
	Democratic Primary		
	John O. Pastore (D)		100.0
1970	**Republican Primary**		
	John McLaughlin (R)		100.0

	Candidates	Votes	%
	Democratic Primary		
	John O. Pastore (D)	54,090	*88.1*
	John Quattrocchi (D)	7,332	*11.9*
1976	**Republican Primary**		
	John H. Chafee (R)		*100.0*
	Democratic Primary		
	Richard P. Lorber (D)	60,118	*37.8*
	Philip W. Noel (D)	60,018	*37.7*
	John P. Hawkins (D)	25,456	*16.0*
1982	**Republican Primary**		
	John H. Chafee (R)		*100.0*
	Democratic Primary		
	Julius C. Michaelson (D)	56,800	*82.4*
	Helen E. Flynn (D)	12,159	*17.6*
1988	**Republican Primary**		
	John H. Chafee (R)		*100.0*
	Democratic Primary		
	Richard A. Licht (D)		*100.0*
1994	**Republican Primary**		
	John H. Chafee (R)	27,906	*69.0*
	Thomas R. Post Jr. (R)	12,517	*31.0*
	Democratic Primary		
	Linda J. Kushner (D)	45,718	*100.0*

Class 2

	Candidates	Votes	%
1960	**Republican Primary**		
	Raoul Archambault (R)		*100.0*
	Democratic Primary		
	Claiborne Pell (D)	83,184	*61.3*
	Dennis J. Roberts (D)	44,924	*33.1*
	Howard McGrath (D)	7,535	*5.6*
1966	**Republican Primary**		
	Ruth M. Briggs (R)	15,451	*82.1*
	Charles H. Eden (R)	3,363	*17.9*
	Democratic Primary		
	Claiborne Pell (D)		*100.0*
1972	**Republican Primary**		
	John H. Chafee (R)		*100.0*
	Democratic Primary		
	Claiborne Pell (D)		*100.0*

	Candidates	Votes	%
1978	**Republican Primary**		
	James G. Reynolds (R)		*100.0*
	Democratic Primary		
	Claiborne Pell (D)	69,729	*87.0*
	Raymond J. Greiner (D)	6,076	*7.6*
	Francis P. Kelley (D)	4,330	*5.4*
1984	**Republican Primary**		
	Barbara Leonard (R)	108,492	*100.0*
	Democratic Primary		
	Claiborne Pell (D)	82,394	*100.0*
1990	**Republican Primary**		
	Claudine Schneider (R)		*100.0*
	Democratic Primary		
	Claiborne Pell (D)		*100.0*
1996	**Republican Primary**		
	Nancy J. Mayer (R)	11,600	*77.5*
	Thomas R. Post Jr. (R)	2,302	*15.4*
	Theodore Leonard (R)	1,072	*7.2*
	Democratic Primary		
	Jack Reed (D)	59,336	*86.1*
	Don Gil (D)	9,554	*13.9*

SOUTH CAROLINA

	Candidates	Votes	%
	Class 2		
1948	**Democratic Primary**		
	Burnet R. Maybank (D)	172,611	*51.6*
	William Jennings Bryan Dorn (D)	83,068	*24.9*
	Bennett (D)	45,068	*13.5*
	Johnstone (D)	18,184	*5.4*
1954	**Democratic Primary**		
	Burnet R. Maybank (D)[1]		*100.0*
1956	**Democratic Special Primary**		
	Strom Thurmond (D)		*100.0*
1960	**Democratic Primary**		
	Strom Thurmond (D)	273,795	*89.5*
	R. B. Herbert (D)	32,136	*10.5*
1966	**Democratic Primary**		
	Bradley Morrah (D)	167,401	*55.9*
	John B. Culbertson (D)	131,870	*44.1*

	Candidates	Votes	%
1972	**Democratic Primary**		
	Eugene N. Ziegler (D)	201,170	*58.7*
	John B. Culbertson (D)	141,757	*41.3*
1978	**Republican Primary**		
	Strom Thurmond (R)		*100.0*
	Democratic Primary		
	Charles D. Ravenel (D)	205,348	*55.9*
	John B. Culbertson (D)	69,184	*18.8*
	James T. Triplett (D)	50,951	*13.9*
	William T. McElveen (D)	41,550	*11.3*
1984	**Republican Primary**		
	Strom Thurmond (R)	44,662	*94.3*
	R. H. Cunningham (R)	2,693	*5.7*
	Democratic Primary		
	Melvin Pervis Jr. (D)	149,730	*50.2*
	Cecil J. Williams (D)	148,586	*49.8*
1990	**Republican Primary**		
	Strom Thurmond (R)		*100.0*
	Democratic Primary		
	Bob Cunningham (D)		*100.0*
1996	**Republican Primary**		
	Strom Thurmond (R)	132,157	*60.6*
	Harold Worley (R)	65,670	*30.1*
	Charlie Thompson (R)	20,188	*9.3*
	Democratic Primary		
	Elliott Springs Close (D)	102,988	*62.1*
	Cecil J. Williams (D)	62,794	*37.9*

Class 3

	Candidates	Votes	%
1950	**Democratic Primary**		
	Olin D. Johnston (D)	186,180	*54.0*
	Strom Thurmond (D)	158,904	*46.1*
1956	**Democratic Primary**		
	Olin D. Johnston (D)		*100.0*
1962	**Democratic Primary**		
	Olin D. Johnston (D)	210,918	*65.7*
	Ernest F. Hollings (D)	110,023	*34.3*
1966	**Democratic Special Primary**		
	Ernest F. Hollings (D)	196,405	*60.8*
	Donald S. Russell (D)	126,595	*39.2*
1968	**Democratic Primary**		
	Ernest F. Hollings (D)	307,561	*78.3*
	John B. Culbertson (D)	85,219	*21.7*

	Candidates	Votes	%
1974	**Republican Primary**		
	Gwenyfred Bush (R)		*100.0*
	Democratic Primary		
	Ernest F. Hollings (D)		*100.0*
1980	**Republican Primary**		
	Marshall T. Mays (R)	14,075	*42.6*
	Charles F. Rhodes (R)	11,395	*34.5*
	Robert K. Carley (R)	7,575	*22.9*
	Republican Runoff		
	Marshall T. Mays (R)	6,853	*64.8*
	Charles F. Rhodes (R)	3,717	*35.2*
	Democratic Primary		
	Ernest F. Hollings (D)	266,796	*81.2*
	Nettie D. Dickerson (D)	34,720	*10.6*
	William P. Kreml (D)	27,049	*8.2*
1986	**Republican Primary**		
	Henry D. McMaster (R)	27,695	*53.4*
	Henry S. Jordan (R)	24,164	*46.6*
	Democratic Primary		
	Ernest F. Hollings (D)		*100.0*
1992	**Republican Primary**		
	Thomas F. Hartnett (R)	123,572	*76.8*
	Charlie E. Thompson (R)	37,352	*23.2*
	Democratic Primary		
	Ernest F. Hollings (D)		*100.0*

South Carolina

1. Maybank had been renominated July 13, 1954, but died Sept. 1. Officials of the South Carolina Democratic Party, charged with replacing him on the ballot for the November general election, declined to order a new primary and selected state Sen. Edgar A. Brown as their candidate. He was defeated in the election by former governor Strom Thurmond (D 1947-51), who waged a successful write-in campaign.

SOUTH DAKOTA

	Candidates	Votes	%
	Class 2		
1960	**Republican Primary**		
	Karl E. Mundt (R)		*100.0*

	Candidates	Votes	%
	Democratic Primary		
	George McGovern (D)		*100.0*
1966	**Republican Primary**		
	Karl E. Mundt (R)	66,758	*82.1*
	Richard R. Murphy (R)	14,593	*17.9*
	Democratic Primary		
	Donn H. Wright (D)		*100.0*
1972	**Republican Primary**[1]		
	Robert W. Hirsch (R)	27,322	*27.4*
	Gordon Mydland (R)	22,297	*22.3*
	Chuck Lien (R)	21,995	*22.0*
	Kenneth D. Stofferahn (R)	16,615	*16.6*
	Tom Reardon (R)	11,592	*11.6*
	Democratic Primary		
	James Abourezk (D)	46,931	*79.4*
	George Blue (D)	12,163	*20.6*
1978	**Republican Primary**		
	Larry Pressler (R)	66,893	*73.9*
	Ronald F. Williamson (R)	23,646	*26.1*
	Democratic Primary		
	Don Barnett (D)	37,319	*55.1*
	Kenneth D. Stofferahn (D)	30,384	*44.9*
1984	**Republican Primary**		
	Larry Pressler (R)		*100.0*
	Democratic Primary		
	George V. Cunningham (D)	31,376	*68.1*
	Dean L. Sinclair (D)	14,672	*31.8*
1990	**Republican Primary**		
	Larry Pressler (R)		*100.0*
	Democratic Primary		
	Ted Muenster (D)		*100.0*
1996	**Republican Primary**		
	Larry Pressler (R)		*100.0*
	Democratic Primary		
	Tim Johnson (D)		*100.0*

Class 3

	Candidates	Votes	%
1956	**Republican Primary**		
	Francis Case (R)		*100.0*
	Democratic Primary		
	Kenneth Holum (D)	23,464	*60.8*
	Merton B. Tice (D)	15,099	*39.1*

	Candidates	Votes	%
1962	**Republican Primary**		
	Francis Case (R)[2]	57,583	*83.5*
	A. C. Miller (R)	11,414	*16.5*
	Democratic Primary		
	George McGovern (D)		*100.0*
1968	**Republican Primary**		
	Archie M. Gubbrud (R)		*100.0*
	Democratic Primary		
	George McGovern (D)		*100.0*
1974	**Republican Primary**		
	Leo K. Thorsness (R)	49,716	*52.3*
	Al Schock (R)	35,406	*37.3*
	Barbara B. Gunderson (R)	9,852	*10.4*
	Democratic Primary		
	George McGovern (D)		*100.0*
1980	**Republican Primary**		
	James Abdnor (R)	68,196	*72.9*
	Dale Bell (R)	25,314	*27.1*
	Democratic Primary		
	George McGovern (D)	44,822	*62.4*
	Larry Schumaker (D)	26,958	*37.6*
1986	**Republican Primary**		
	James Abdnor (R)	63,414	*54.5*
	William J. Janklow (R)	52,924	*45.5*
	Democratic Primary		
	Thomas A. Daschle (D)		*100.0*
1992	**Republican Primary**		
	Charlene Haar (R)		*100.0*
	Democratic Primary		
	Thomas A. Daschle (D)		*100.0*

South Dakota

1. *A state Republican convention was held June 26 because no one received the 35 percent required for nomination under the South Dakota primary law. Hirsch was nominated at this convention.*

2. *Case died shortly after winning the primary and the Republican state committee substituted Joe H. Bottum as the party's nominee.*

TENNESSEE

	Candidates	Votes	%
	Class 1		
1946	**Republican Primary**		
	William B. Ladd (R)	30,954	*100.0*

Candidates	Votes	%
Democratic Primary		
Kenneth D. McKellar (D)	188,805	62.0
Edward W. Carmack (D)	107,363	35.2

1952   **Democratic Primary**

Candidates	Votes	%
Albert Gore (D)	334,957	56.5
Kenneth D. McKellar (D)	245,054	41.4

1958   **Republican Primary**

Candidates	Votes	%
Hobart F. Atkins (R)		100.0

Democratic Primary

Candidates	Votes	%
Albert Gore (D)	375,439	59.0
Prentice Cooper (D)	253,191	39.8

1964   **Republican Primary**

Candidates	Votes	%
Dan H. Kuykendall (R)		100.0

Democratic Primary

Candidates	Votes	%
Albert Gore (D)	401,163	84.7
Sam J. Galloway (D)	37,974	8.0

1970   **Republican Primary**

Candidates	Votes	%
Bill Brock (R)	176,703	74.9
Tex Ritter (R)	54,401	23.0

Democratic Primary

Candidates	Votes	%
Albert Gore (D)	269,770	51.0
Hudley Crockett (D)	238,767	45.2

1976   **Republican Primary**

Candidates	Votes	%
Bill Brock (R)		100.0

Democratic Primary

Candidates	Votes	%
James R. Sasser (D)	244,930	44.2
John J. Hooker (D)	171,716	31.0
Harry Sadler (D)	54,125	9.8
David Bolin (D)	44,056	8.0
Lester Kefauver (D)	29,864	5.4

1982   **Republican Primary**

Candidates	Votes	%
Robin L. Beard (R)	205,271	91.4
William B. Thompson (R)	19,277	8.6

Democratic Primary

Candidates	Votes	%
James R. Sasser (D)	511,059	88.9
Charles G. Vick (D)	13,488	11.1

1988   **Republican Primary**

Candidates	Votes	%
Bill Anderson (R)	115,341	72.9
Alice W. Algood (R)	34,413	21.8
Hubert D. Patty (R)	8,358	5.3

Democratic Primary

Candidates	Votes	%
James R. Sasser (D)		100.0

1994   **Republican Primary**

Candidates	Votes	%
Bill Frist (R)	197,734	44.4
Bob Corker (R)	143,808	32.3
Steve Wilson (R)	50,274	11.3
Harold Sterling (R)	28,425	6.4

Democratic Primary

Candidates	Votes	%
James R. Sasser (D)	402,610	100.0

Class 2

1948   **Republican Primary**

Candidates	Votes	%
B. Carroll Reece (R)	82,522	81.7
Allen J. Strawbridge (R)	18,526	18.3

Democratic Primary

Candidates	Votes	%
Estes Kefauver (D)	171,791	42.4
A. Tom Stewart (D)	129,873	32.1
John A. Mitchell (D)	96,192	23.7

1954   **Democratic Primary**

Candidates	Votes	%
Estes Kefauver (D)	440,497	68.2
Pat Sutton (D)	186,363	28.9

1960   **Republican Primary**

Candidates	Votes	%
A. Bradley Frazier (R)	16,633	58.8
Hansel Proffitt (R)	11,667	41.2

Democratic Primary

Candidates	Votes	%
Estes Kefauver (D)	463,848	64.6
Andrew T. Taylor (D)	249,336	34.7

1964[1]   **Republican Special Primary**

Candidates	Votes	%
Howard H. Baker Jr. (R)	93,301	85.0
Charles Moffett (R)	10,596	9.6
Hubert D. Patty (R)	5,947	5.4

Democratic Special Primary

Candidates	Votes	%
Ross Bass (D)	330,213	50.8
Frank G. Clement (D)	233,245	35.9
M. M. Bullard (D)	86,718	13.3

1966   **Republican Primary**

Candidates	Votes	%
Howard H. Baker Jr. (R)	112,617	75.7
Kenneth Roberts (R)	36,043	24.2

Democratic Primary

Candidates	Votes	%
Frank G. Clement (D)	384,322	51.2
Ross Bass (D)	366,079	48.8

1972   **Republican Primary**

Candidates	Votes	%
Howard H. Baker Jr. (R)	242,373	97.0

Democratic Primary

Candidates	Votes	%
Ray Blanton (D)	292,249	76.4
Don Palmer (D)	40,700	10.6

	Candidates	Votes	%
1978	**Republican Primary**		
	Howard H. Baker Jr. (R)	205,680	83.4
	Harvey D. Howard (R)	21,154	8.6
	Democratic Primary		
	Jane Eskind (D)	196,156	34.5
	Bill Bruce (D)	170,795	30.1
	J. D. Lee (D)	89,939	15.8
	James Boyd (D)	48,458	8.5
1984	**Republican Primary**		
	Victor Ashe (R)	145,774	86.5
	Jack McNeil (R)	17,970	10.7
	Democratic Primary		
	Albert Gore Jr. (D)	345,527	100.0
1990	**Republican Primary**		
	William R. Hawkins (R)	54,317	38.9
	Ralph Brown (R)	53,873	38.5
	Patrick K. Hales (R)	31,515	22.5
	Democratic Primary		
	Albert Gore Jr. (D)		100.0
1994[2]	**Republican Special Primary**		
	Fred Thompson (R)	235,386	64.2
	John Baker (R)	131,431	35.8
	Democratic Special Primary		
	Jim Cooper (D)	375,615	100.0
1996	**Republican Primary**		
	Fred Thompson (R)	266,549	94.1
	Jim F. Counts (R)	16,715	5.9
	Democratic Primary		
	Houston Gordon (D)	156,704	63.5
	Ashley M. King (D)	89,887	36.4

Tennessee

1. A special election was held to fill the remaining two years of the term of Sen. Estes Kefauver (D), who died Aug. 10, 1963. The first year of the vacancy was filled by appointee Herbert S. Walker (D).

2. A special election was held to fill the remaining two years of the term of Sen. Albert Gore Jr. (D), who resigned Jan 1, 1993, after being elected vice president. The first two years of the vacancy were filled by appointee Harlan Mathews (D).

TEXAS

	Candidates	Votes	%
	Class 1		
1946	**Democratic Primary**		
	Tom Connally (D)	823,818	75.4
	Floyd E. Ryan (D)	85,292	7.8

	Candidates	Votes	%
	Cyclone Davis (D)	74,252	6.8
	Terrell Sledge (D)	66,947	6.1
1952	**Democratic Primary**		
	Price Daniel (D)	940,770	72.6
	Lindley Beckworth (D)	285,842	22.0
	E. W. Napier (D)	70,132	5.4
1958	**Republican Primary**		
	Roy Whittenburg (R)		100.0
	Democratic Primary		
	Ralph Yarborough (D)	761,511	58.7
	William A. Blakley (D)	535,418	41.3
1964	**Republican Primary**		
	George Bush (R)	62,985	44.1
	Jack Cox (R)	45,561	31.9
	Robert Morris (R)	28,279	19.8
	Republican Runoff		
	George Bush (R)	49,751	62.1
	Jack Cox (R)	30,333	37.9
	Democratic Primary		
	Ralph Yarborough (D)	904,811	57.4
	Gordon McLendon (D)	672,573	42.6
1970	**Republican Primary**		
	George Bush (R)	96,806	87.6
	Robert Morris (R)	13,654	12.4
	Democratic Primary		
	Lloyd Bentsen (D)	816,641	53.0
	Ralph Yarborough (D)	724,122	47.0
1976	**Republican Primary**		
	Alan Steelman (R)	251,252	70.5
	Hugh Sweeney (R)	64,404	18.1
	Louis Leman (R)	40,651	11.4
	Democratic Primary		
	Lloyd Bentsen (D)	970,983	63.5
	Phil Gramm (D)	427,597	28.0
	Hugh Wilson (D)	10,715	7.2
1982	**Republican Primary**		
	James M. Collins (R)	152,469	58.0
	Walter H. Mengden (R)	91,780	34.9
	Don L. Richardson (R)	18,616	7.1
	Democratic Primary		
	Lloyd Bentsen (D)	987,153	78.1
	Joe Sullivan (D)	276,314	21.9

	Candidates	Votes	%
1988	**Republican Primary**		
	Wes Gilbreath (R)	275,080	*36.7*
	Beau Boulter (R)	228,676	*30.5*
	Milton E. Fox (R)	138,031	*18.4*
	Ned Snead (R)	107,560	*14.4*
	Republican Runoff		
	Beau Boulter (R)	111,134	*60.2*
	Wes Gilbreath (R)	73,573	*40.0*
	Democratic Primary		
	Lloyd Bentsen (D)	1,365,736	*84.8*
	Joe Sullivan (D)	244,805	*15.2*
1994	**Republican Primary**		
	Kay Bailey Hutchison (R)	467,975	*84.3*
	Stephen Hopkins (R)	34,703	*6.2*
	Democratic Primary		
	Jim Mattox (D)	416,503	*40.5*
	Richard Fisher (D)	388,090	*37.8*
	Michael A. Andrews (D)	159,793	*15.5*
	Evelyn K. Lantz (D)	63,523	*6.2*

Class 2

	Candidates	Votes	%
1948	**Democratic Primary**		
	Coke R. Stevenson (D)	477,077	*39.7*
	Lyndon B. Johnson (D)	405,617	*33.7*
	George Peddy (D)	237,195	*19.7*
	Democratic Runoff		
	Lyndon B. Johnson (D)	494,191	*50.0*
	Coke R. Stevenson (D)	494,104	*50.0*
1954	**Democratic Primary**		
	Lyndon B. Johnson (D)	883,264	*71.4*
	Dudley T. Dougherty (D)	354,188	*28.6*
1960	**Democratic Primary**		
	Lyndon B. Johnson (D)		*100.0*
1966	**Republican Primary**		
	John Tower (R)		*100.0*
	Democratic Primary		
	Waggoner Carr (D)	899,523	*79.9*
	John R. Willoughby (D)	226,598	*20.1*
1972	**Republican Primary**		
	John Tower (R)		*100.0*
	Democratic Primary		
	Ralph Yarborough (D)	1,032,606	*50.0*
	Barefoot Sanders (D)	787,504	*38.1*
	Hugh Wilson (D)	125,460	*6.1*

	Candidates	Votes	%
	Democratic Runoff		
	Barefoot Sanders (D)	1,008,499	*52.1*
	Ralph Yarborough (D)	928,132	*47.9*
1978	**Republican Primary**		
	John Tower (R)		*100.0*
	Democratic Primary		
	Robert Krueger (D)	853,460	*54.7*
	Joe Christie (D)	707,738	*45.3*
1984	**Republican Primary**		
	Phil Gramm (R)	246,716	*73.2*
	Ron Paul (R)	55,431	*16.4*
	Rob Mosbacher (R)	26,279	*7.8*
	Democratic Primary		
	Kent Hance (D)	456,446	*31.2*
	Lloyd Doggett (D)	456,173	*31.2*
	Robert Krueger (D)	454,886	*31.1*
	Democratic Runoff		
	Lloyd Doggett (D)	489,932	*50.0*
	Kent Hance (D)	489,834	*50.0*
	Democratic Runoff Recount		
	Lloyd Doggett (D)	491,251	*50.1*
	Kent Hance (D)	489,906	*50.0*
1990	**Republican Primary**		
	Phil Gramm (R)		*100.0*
	Democratic Primary		
	Hugh Parmer (D)	766,284	*75.4*
	Harley Schlanger (D)	249,445	*24.6*
1996	**Republican Primary**		
	Phil Gramm (R)	838,339	*85.0*
	David Young (R)	75,463	*7.7*
	Henry C. "Hank" Grover (R)	72,400	*7.3*
	Democratic Primary		
	Victor M. Morales (D)	322,218	*36.2*
	John Bryant (D)	267,545	*30.0*
	Jim Chapman (D)	239,427	*26.9*
	John Will Odam (D)	61,433	*6.9*
	Democratic Runoff		
	Victor M. Morales (D)	246,614	*51.2*
	John Bryant (D)	235,281	*48.8*

UTAH[1]

Candidates	Votes	%
Class 1		

1958

Republican Primary

Candidates	Votes	%
Arthur V. Watkins (R)	39,593	68.1
Carvel Mattsson (R)	18,563	31.9

Democratic Primary

Candidates	Votes	%
Frank E. Moss (D)	35,862	59.2
Brigham E. Roberts (D)	24,736	40.8

1964

Republican Primary

Candidates	Votes	%
Ernest L. Wilkinson (R)	61,167	50.7
Sherman P. Lloyd (R)	59,398	49.3

Democratic Primary

Candidates	Votes	%
Frank E. Moss (D)		100.0

1970

Republican Primary

Candidates	Votes	%
Laurence J. Burton (R)		100.0

Democratic Primary

Candidates	Votes	%
Frank E. Moss (D)		100.0

1976

Republican Primary

Candidates	Votes	%
Orrin G. Hatch (R)	104,490	64.6
Jack Carlson (R)	57,249	35.4

Democratic Primary

Candidates	Votes	%
Frank E. Moss (D)		100.0

1994

Independent Primary

Candidates	Votes	%
Craig Oliver (I)	818	56.9
Bill Rigley (I)	620	43.1

Class 3		

1956

Republican Primary

Candidates	Votes	%
Wallace F. Bennett (R)		100.0

Democratic Primary

Candidates	Votes	%
Alonzo F. Hopkin (D)	44,980	56.8
Herbert B. Maw (D)	34,246	43.2

1962

Republican Primary

Candidates	Votes	%
Wallace F. Bennett (R)	70,519	59.2
J. Bracken Lee (R)	48,606	40.8

Democratic Primary

Candidates	Votes	%
David S. King (D)	55,965	77.4
Calvin L. Rampton (D)	16,327	22.6

1968

Republican Primary

Candidates	Votes	%
Wallace F. Bennett (R)	81,945	60.9
Mark E. Anderson (R)	52,689	39.1

Democratic Primary

Candidates	Votes	%
Milton Weilenmann (D)	47,908	50.7
Phil L. Hansen (D)	46,579	49.3

1974

Republican Primary

Candidates	Votes	%
Jake Garn (R)		100.0

Democratic Primary

Candidates	Votes	%
Wayne Owens (D)		100.0

American Primary

Candidates	Votes	%
Bruce Bangerter (AM)	2,254	50.9
Kenneth R. Larsen (AM)	2,173	49.1

1980

Democratic Primary

Candidates	Votes	%
Dan Berman (D)	28,930	50.2
A. Stephen Dirks (D)	28,643	49.7

American Primary

Candidates	Votes	%
George M. Batchelor (AM)	675	54.5
Larry Topham (AM)	563	45.5

1986

Democratic Primary

Candidates	Votes	%
Craig Oliver (D)	14,654	50.5
Terry Williams (D)	14,379	49.5

1992

Republican Primary

Candidates	Votes	%
Robert F. Bennett (R)	135,514	51.4
Joe Cannon (R)	128,125	48.6

Democratic Primary

Candidates	Votes	%
Wayne Owens (D)	74,124	61.4
Doug Anderson (D)	46,622	38.6

Utah

1. *From 1980 to 1988, some Democratic and Republican candidates were nominated by convention.*

VERMONT

Candidates	Votes	%
Class 1		

1958

Republican Primary

Candidates	Votes	%
Winston L. Prouty (R)	31,866	64.6
Lee E. Emerson (R)	17,468	35.4

Democratic Primary

Candidates	Votes	%
Frederick J. Fayette (D)		100.0

	Candidates	Votes	%
1964	**Republican Primary**		
	Winston L. Prouty (R)		*100.0*
	Democratic Primary		
	Frederick J. Fayette (D)	12,388	*71.0*
	William H. Meyer (D)	4,913	*28.2*
1970	**Republican Primary**		
	Winston L. Prouty (R)		*100.0*
	Democratic Primary		
	Philip H. Hoff (D)	23,082	*69.7*
	Fiore L. Bove (D)	7,941	*24.0*
	William H. Meyer (D)	2,024	*6.1*
1972[1]	**Republican Special Primary**		
	Robert T. Stafford (R)		*100.0*
	Democratic Special Primary		
	Randolph T. Major (D)		*100.0*
1976	**Republican Primary**		
	Robert T. Stafford (R)	24,338	*68.7*
	John J. Welch (R)	10,911	*30.8*
	Democratic Primary		
	Thomas P. Salmon (D)	21,674	*52.7*
	Scott Skinner (D)	19,238	*46.8*
	Liberty Union Primary		
	Nancy Kaufman (LU)	362	*69.6*
	John Medeiros (LU)	146	*28.1*
1982	**Republican Primary**		
	Robert T. Stafford (R)	26,323	*46.2*
	Stewart M. Ledbetter (R)	19,743	*34.7*
	John M. McClaughry (R)	10,692	*18.8*
	Democratic Primary		
	James A. Guest (D)	11,352	*67.1*
	Thomas E. McGregor (D)	3,749	*22.1*
	Earl S. Gardner (D)	1,281	*7.6*
	Citizens Primary		
	Ion Laskaris (CIT)		*100.0*
	Liberty Union Primary		
	Jerry Levy (LU)		*100.0*
1988	**Republican Primary**		
	James M. Jeffords (R)	30,555	*60.8*
	Mike Griffes (R)	19,593	*39.0*
	Democratic Primary		
	William Gray (D)		*100.0*

	Candidates	Votes	%
	Liberty Union Primary		
	Jerry Levy (LU)		*100.0*
1994	**Republican Primary**		
	James M. Jeffords (R)	24,766	*91.6*
	Democratic Primary		
	Jan Backus (D)	16,217	*53.6*
	Doug Costle (D)	13,139	*43.5*
	Liberty Union Primary		
	Jerry Levy (LU)	289	*90.0*

Class 3

	Candidates	Votes	%
1956	**Republican Primary**		
	George D. Aiken (R)		*100.0*
	Democratic Primary		
	Bernard G. O'Shea (D)		*100.0*
1962	**Republican Primary**		
	George D. Aiken (R)		*100.0*
	Democratic Primary		
	W. Robert Johnson (D)	5,718	*54.7*
	William H. Meyer (D)	4,741	*45.3*
1968	**Republican Primary**		
	George D. Aiken (R)	42,248	*72.8*
	William K. Tufts (R)	15,786	*27.2*
	Democratic Primary		
	George D. Aiken (WRITE IN)	1,354	*61.8*
	Others (WRITE IN)	438	*20.0*
	Philip H. Hoff (WRITE IN)	400	*18.2*
1974	**Republican Primary**		
	Richard W. Mallary (R)	27,221	*59.1*
	Charles R. Ross (R)	16,479	*35.8*
	Democratic Primary		
	Patrick J. Leahy (D)	19,801	*83.9*
	Nathaniel Frothingham (D)	3,703	*15.7*
1980	**Republican Primary**		
	Stewart M. Ledbetter (R)	16,518	*35.3*
	James E. Mullin (R)	12,256	*26.2*
	Tom Evslin (R)	8,575	*18.3*
	T. Garry Buckley (R)	5,209	*11.1*
	Robert Schuettinger (R)	3,450	*7.4*
	Democratic Primary		
	Patrick J. Leahy (D)		*100.0*

Candidates	Votes	%
Liberty Union Primary		
Earl S. Gardner (LU)		100.0
1986 **Republican Primary**		
Richard A. Snelling (R)	21,477	75.1
Anthony N. Doria (R)	6,493	22.7
Democratic Primary		
Patrick J. Leahy (D)		100.0
Liberty Union Primary		
Jerry Levy (LU)		100.0
1992 **Republican Primary**		
James H. Douglas (R)	28,693	78.2
John L. Gropper (R)	7,395	20.2
Democratic Primary		
Patrick J. Leahy (D)	24,721	97.6
Liberty Union Primary		
Jerry Levy (LU)		100.0

Vermont

1. A special election was held to fill the remaining four years of the term of Sen. Winston L. Prouty (R), who died Sept. 10, 1971. The first year of the vacancy was filled by appointee Robert T. Stafford (R).

VIRGINIA[1]

Candidates	Votes	%
Class 1		
1946 **Democratic Primary**		
Harry F. Byrd (D)	141,923	63.5
Martin A. Hutchinson (D)	81,605	36.5
1952 **Democratic Primary**		
Harry F. Byrd (D)	216,438	62.7
Francis Pickens Miller (D)	128,869	37.3
1958 **Democratic Primary**		
Harry F. Byrd (D)		100.0
1964 **Democratic Primary**		
Harry F. Byrd (D)		100.0
1966[2] **Democratic Special Primary**		
Harry F. Byrd Jr. (D)	221,221	51.0
Armistead L. Boothe (D)	212,996	49.1
1970 **Democratic Primary[3]**		
George C. Rawlings (D)	58,874	45.7
Clive L. DuVal (D)	58,174	45.1
Milton Colvin (D)	11,911	9.2

Candidates	Votes	%
1976 **Democratic Primary**		
Elmo R. Zumwalt (D)		100.0
1994 **Republican Primary**		
Oliver L. North (R)		100.0
Democratic Primary		
Charles S. Robb (D)	154,561	57.9
Virgil H. Goode (D)	90,547	33.9
Sylvia L. Clute (D)	17,329	6.5
Class 2		
1946 **Democratic Special Primary**		
A. Willis Robertson (D)	✔	
1948 **Democratic Primary**		
A. Willis Robertson (D)	80,340	70.3
James P. Hart Jr. (D)	33,928	29.7
1954 **Democratic Primary**		
A. Willis Robertson (D)		100.0
1960 **Democratic Primary**		
A. Willis Robertson (D)		100.0
1966 **Democratic Primary**		
William B. Spong Jr. (D)	216,885	50.1
A. Willis Robertson (D)	216,274	49.9
1972 **Democratic Primary**		
William B. Spong Jr. (D)		100.0
1996 **Republican Primary**		
John W. Warner (R)	323,520	65.6
James C. "Jim" Miller (R)	170,015	34.4

Virginia

1. Following 1976, candidates were nominated by state party convention.
2. A special election was held in 1966 to fill the remaining four years of the term of Sen. Harry F. Byrd (D), who resigned Nov. 10, 1965. The first year of the vacancy was filled by Byrd's son and appointee Harry F. Byrd Jr. (D).
3. Rawlings became the Democratic nominee when DuVal did not request a runoff.

WASHINGTON

Candidates	Votes	%
Class 1		
1958 **Republican Primary**		
William B. Bantz (R)		100.0
Democratic Primary		
Henry M. Jackson (D)	334,862	85.8
Alice F. Bryant (D)	55,200	14.1

Candidates	Votes	%
1964 **Republican Primary**		
Lloyd J. Andrews (R)	216,616	*81.2*
David J. Williams (R)	37,450	*14.0*
Democratic Primary		
Henry M. Jackson (D)	478,892	*90.6*
Alice F. Bryant (D)	29,052	*5.5*
1970 **Republican Primary**		
Charles W. Elicker (R)	33,262	*37.1*
Howard S. Reed (R)	22,293	*24.9*
R. J. Odman (R)	14,856	*16.6*
William H. Davis (R)	11,207	*12.5*
Bill Patrick (R)	7,976	*8.9*
Democratic Primary		
Henry M. Jackson (D)	497,309	*84.3*
Carl Maxey (D)	79,201	*13.4*
1976 **Republican Primary**		
George M. Brown (R)	51,885	*29.5*
Warren Hanson (R)	43,905	*25.0*
Harry C. Nielsen (R)	28,030	*15.9*
Wilbur R. Parkin (R)	21,639	*12.3*
William H. Davis (R)	16,881	*9.6*
Clarice L. R. Privette (R)	13,526	*7.7*
Democratic Primary		
Henry M. Jackson (D)	549,974	*87.4*
Dennis Kelley (D)	54,470	*8.7*
1982 **Republican Primary**		
Doug Jewett (R)	73,616	*46.3*
Larry Penberthy (R)	46,037	*28.9*
Ken Talbott (R)	15,581	*9.8*
Patrick S. McGowan (R)	13,054	*8.2*
Democratic Primary		
Henry M. Jackson (D)	450,580	*94.9*
1983[1] **Republican Special Primary**		
Dan Evans (R)	250,046	*64.3*
Lloyd E. Cooney (R)	133,799	*34.4*
Democratic Special Primary		
Mike Lowry (D)	179,509	*61.5*
Charles Royer (D)	103,304	*35.4*
1988 **Republican Primary**		
Slade Gorton (R)	335,846	*85.3*
Doug Smith (R)	31,512	*8.0*
William C. Goodloe (R)	26,224	*6.7*
Democratic Primary		
Mike Lowry (D)	297,399	*55.2*
Don Bonker (D)	241,170	*44.8*

Candidates	Votes	%
1994 **Republican Primary**		
Slade Gorton (R)	492,251	*92.8*
Warren E. Hanson (R)	26,628	*5.0*
Democratic Primary		
Ron Sims (D)	162,382	*42.0*
Mike James (D)	138,005	*35.7*
Scott Hardman (D)	29,973	*7.7*
Jesse Wineberry (D)	24,698	*6.4*

Class 3

Candidates	Votes	%
1956 **Republican Primary**		
Arthur B. Langlie (R)		*100.0*
Democratic Primary		
Warren G. Magnuson (D)		*100.0*
1962 **Republican Primary**		
Richard G. Christensen (R)	178,616	*82.1*
Ben Larson (R)	38,759	*17.8*
Democratic Primary		
Warren G. Magnuson (D)	280,981	*93.7*
John Patric (D)	18,849	*6.3*
1968 **Republican Primary**		
Jack Metcalf (R)	210,981	*73.6*
Harvey L. Cole (R)	40,844	*14.2*
Ralph O. Westlake (R)	25,756	*9.0*
Democratic Primary		
Warren G. Magnuson (D)	373,303	*92.9*
Arthur DeWitt (D)	28,683	*7.1*
1974 **Republican Primary**		
Jack Metcalf (R)	103,616	*61.0*
Jesse Chiang (R)	31,193	*18.4*
Donald C. Knutson (R)	13,738	*8.1*
June Riggs (R)	8,491	*5.0*
Democratic Primary		
Warren G. Magnuson (D)	288,038	*92.5*
John Patric (D)	23,438	*7.5*
1980 **Republican Primary**		
Slade Gorton (R)	313,560	*55.6*
Lloyd E. Cooney (R)	229,178	*40.7*
Democratic Primary		
Warren G. Magnuson (D)	348,471	*92.4*
1986 **Republican Primary**		
Slade Gorton (R)	291,735	*93.0*

Candidates	Votes	%
Democratic Primary		
Brock Adams (D)	287,258	91.7
Socialist Workers Primary		
Jill Fein (SOC WORK)		100.0
1992 **Republican Primary**		
Rod Chandler (R)	228,083	42.1
Leo K. Thorsness (R)	185,498	34.2
Tim Hill (R)	128,232	23.7
Democratic Primary		
Patty Murray (D)	318,455	56.7
Don Bonker (D)	208,321	37.1

Washington

1. A special election was held to fill the remaining five years of the term of Sen. Henry M. Jackson (D), who died Sept. 1, 1983. Under Washington's so-called "jungle" primary, all 33 candidates appeared on the same Oct. 11 ballot with their party designations. The two highest vote getters, Dan Evans (R) and Mike Lowry (D), won ballot positions for the special election. Percentages are calculated here as if candidates had run in separate party primaries.

WEST VIRGINIA

Candidates	Votes	%
Class 1		
1956[1] **Republican Special Primary**		
Chapman Revercomb (R)	79,106	41.5
Tom Sweeney (R)	57,556	30.2
Philip H. Hill (R)	37,574	19.7
A. J. Carey (R)	11,268	5.9
Democratic Special Primary		
William C. Marland (D)	118,159	37.2
John G. Fox (D)	104,869	33.1
Byron B. Randolph (D)	56,945	17.9
Walter G. Crichton (D)	26,972	8.5
1958 **Republican Primary**		
Chapman Revercomb (R)		100.0
Democratic Primary		
Robert C. Byrd (D)	170,686	80.2
Fleming N. Alderson (D)	23,915	11.2
Jack R. Delligatti (D)	18,235	8.6
1964 **Republican Primary**		
Cooper P. Benedict (R)		100.0
Democratic Primary		
Robert C. Byrd (D)	268,368	85.4
William F. Champe (D)	45,738	14.6

Candidates	Votes	%
1970[2] **Democratic Primary**		
Robert C. Byrd (D)	195,725	89.0
John J. McOwen (D)	24,286	11.0
1976[2] **Democratic Primary**		
Robert C. Byrd (D)		100.0
1982 **Republican Primary**		
Cleveland K. Benedict (R)	73,638	80.9
James A. Washburn (R)	9,877	10.8
Frederick A. Weiland (R)	7,531	8.3
Democratic Primary		
Robert C. Byrd (D)		100.0
1988 **Republican Primary**		
M. Jay Wolfe (R)	81,286	70.3
Bernie Lumbert (R)	34,273	29.7
Democratic Primary		
Robert C. Byrd (D)	252,767	80.8
Bobbie E. Myers (D)	60,186	19.2
1994 **Republican Primary**		
Stan Klos (R)	46,709	60.2
Arthur Gindin (R)	30,824	39.8
Democratic Primary		
Robert C. Byrd (D)	190,061	85.4
James M. Fuller (D)	20,057	9.0
Paul Nuchims (D)	12,381	5.6
Class 2		
1958[3] **Republican Special Primary**		
John D. Hoblitzell (R)		100.0
Democratic Special Primary		
Jennings Randolph (D)	102,547	47.2
William C. Marland (D)	77,901	35.8
Arnold M. Vickers (D)	25,439	11.7
W. R. Wilson (D)	11,540	5.3
1960 **Republican Primary**		
Cecil H. Underwood (R)		100.0
Democratic Primary		
Jennings Randolph (R)		100.0
1966 **Republican Primary**		
Francis J. Love (R)	61,479	63.4
Harold G. Cutright (R)	35,530	36.6
Democratic Primary		
Jennings Randolph (D)		100.0

	Candidates	Votes	%
1972	**Republican Primary**		
	Louise Leonard (R)		*100.0*
	Democratic Primary		
	Jennings Randolph (D)		*100.0*
1978	**Republican Primary**		
	Arch A. Moore Jr. (R)	90,406	*90.6*
	Donald G. Michels (R)	9,414	*9.4*
	Democratic Primary		
	Jennings Randolph (D)	181,480	*80.5*
	Sharon Rogers (D)	43,991	*19.5*
1984	**Republican Primary**		
	John R. Raese (R)	61,389	*47.8*
	Samuel N. Kusic (R)	44,820	*34.9*
	J. Frank Deem (R)	13,707	*10.7*
	Democratic Primary		
	John D. "Jay" Rockefeller IV (D)	240,559	*66.3*
	Lacy Wright (D)	51,591	*14.2*
	Ken Auvil (D)	41,408	*11.4*
	Homer L. Harris (D)	29,138	*8.0*
1990	**Republican Primary**		
	John Yoder (R)		*100.0*
	Democratic Primary		
	John D. "Jay" Rockefeller IV (D)	200,161	*84.7*
	Ken B. Thompson (D)	21,669	*9.2*
1996	**Republican Primary**		
	Betty A. Burks (R)	90,446	*100.0*
	Democratic Primary		
	John D. "Jay" Rockefeller IV (D)	280,303	*88.4*
	Bruce Barilla (D)	36,637	*11.6*

West Virginia

1. *A special election was held to fill the remaining two years of the term of Sen. Harley M. Kilgore (D), who died Feb. 28, 1956.*

2. *No Republican candidates entered the 1970 and 1976 Senate primaries. After the primary date in 1970, the party designated Elmer H. Dodson as the Republican candidate. No Republican candidate was designated in 1976.*

3. *A special election was held to fill the remaining two years of the term of Sen. Matthew M. Neely (D), who died Jan. 18, 1958.*

WISCONSIN

	Candidates	Votes	%
	Class 1		
1957[1]	**Republican Special Primary**		
	Walter J. Kohler (R)	109,256	*34.4*
	Glenn R. Davis (R)	100,532	*31.7*

	Candidates	Votes	%
	Alvin E. O'Konski (R)	66,784	*21.0*
	Warren P. Knowles (R)	23,996	*7.6*
	Democratic Special Primary		
	William Proxmire (D)	86,341	*60.3*
	Clement J. Zablocki (D)	56,817	*39.7*
1958	**Republican Primary**		
	Roland J. Steinle (R)		*100.0*
	Democratic Primary		
	William Proxmire (D)	220,146	*85.6*
	Harry Halloway (D)	20,880	*8.1*
	Arthur J. McGurn (D)	16,014	*6.2*
1964	**Republican Primary**		
	Wilbur N. Renk (R)		*100.0*
	Democratic Primary		
	William Proxmire (D)	295,676	*88.8*
	Kenneth F. Klinkert (D)	20,022	*6.0*
	Arlyn F. Wollenburg (D)	17,333	*5.2*
1970	**Republican Primary**		
	John E. Erickson (R)		*100.0*
	Democratic Primary		
	William Proxmire (D)		*100.0*
	American Primary		
	Edmond E. Hou-Seye (AM)		*100.0*
1976	**Republican Primary**		
	Stanley York (R)		*100.0*
	Democratic Primary		
	William Proxmire (D)		*100.0*
1982	**Republican Primary**		
	Scott McCallum (R)	182,043	*67.7*
	Paul T. Brewer (R)	86,728	*32.3*
	Democratic Primary		
	William Proxmire (D)	467,214	*86.1*
	Marcel Dandeneau (D)	75,258	*13.9*
	Libertarian Primary		
	George Liljenfeldt (LIBERT)		*100.0*
	Constitution Primary		
	Sanford G. Knapp (CONST)		*100.0*
1988	**Republican Primary**		
	Susan Engeleiter (R)	209,025	*57.0*
	Stephen B. King (R)	148,601	*40.5*

Candidates	Votes	%
Democratic Primary		
Herbert H. Kohl (D)	249,226	46.8
Anthony S. Earl (D)	203,479	38.2
Edward R. Garvey (D)	55,225	10.4
1994 **Republican Primary**		
Robert T. Welch (R)	157,109	47.4
Matthew Gunderson (R)	74,460	22.4
Cate Zeuske (R)	56,248	17.0
Thomas M. Fitzpatrick (R)	43,695	13.2
Democratic Primary		
Herbert H. Kohl (D)	135,982	89.6
Edmond Hou-Seye (D)	15,579	10.3
1994 **Libertarian Primary**		
James Dean (LIBERT)	1,030	100.0

Class 3

Candidates	Votes	%
1956 **Republican Primary**		
Alexander Wiley (R)	221,042	48.9
Glenn R. Davis (R)	211,016	46.7
Democratic Primary		
Henry W. Maier (D)	169,999	66.9
Elliot N. Walstead (D)	83,801	33.0
1962 **Republican Primary**		
Alexander Wiley (R)	347,155	80.3
Arlyn F. Wollenburg (R)	85,044	19.7
Democratic Primary		
Gaylord Nelson (D)		100.0
1968 **Republican Primary**		
Jerris Leonard (R)	133,060	50.7
Robert I. Johnson (R)	73,344	28.0
James J. Donohue (R)	45,523	17.4
Democratic Primary		
Gaylord Nelson (D)		100.0
1974 **Republican Primary**		
Thomas E. Petri (R)	130,523	85.2
James A. Sigl (R)	22,714	14.8
Democratic Primary		
Gaylord Nelson (D)		100.0
American Primary		
Gerald L. McFarren (AM)		100.0

	Candidates	Votes	%
1980	**Republican Primary**		
	Robert W. Kasten (R)	134,586	36.8
	Terry J. Kohler (R)	106,270	29.0
	Douglass Cofrin (R)	84,355	23.0
	Russell A. Olson (R)	40,823	11.1
	Democratic Primary		
	Gaylord Nelson (D)		100.0
	Constitution Primary		
	James P. Wickstrom (CONST)		100.0
	Libertarian Primary		
	Bervin J. Larson (LIBERT)		100.0
1986	**Republican Primary**		
	Robert W. Kasten (R)		100.0
	Democratic Primary		
	Edward R. Garvey (D)	126,408	47.6
	Matthew J. Flynn (D)	101,777	38.3
	Gary R. George (D)	29,485	11.1
1992	**Republican Primary**		
	Robert W. Kasten (R)	197,488	80.5
	Roger W. Faulkner (R)	47,804	19.5
	Democratic Primary		
	Russell D. Feingold (D)	367,746	69.7
	Jim Moody (D)	74,472	14.1
	Joseph W. Checota (D)	71,570	13.6

Wisconsin

1. A special election was held to fill the remaining one and one-half years of the term of Sen. Joseph R. McCarthy (R), who died May 2, 1957.

WYOMING

	Candidates	Votes	%
	Class 1		
1958	**Republican Primary**		
	Frank A. Barrett (R)		100.0
	Democratic Primary		
	Gale McGee (D)	22,098	59.5
	Hepburn T. Armstrong (D)	15,024	40.5
1964	**Republican Primary**		
	John S. Wold (R)	23,278	52.0
	K. L. Sailors (R)	21,522	48.0
	Democratic Primary		
	Gale McGee (D)	39,140	89.6
	I. Wayne Kinney (D)	4,535	10.4

	Candidates	Votes	%
1970	**Republican Primary**		
	John S. Wold (R)	40,276	*88.0*
	Arthur E. Linde (R)	5,479	*12.0*
	Democratic Primary		
	Gale McGee (D)	32,956	*79.6*
	D. P. Svilar (D)	8,448	*20.4*
1976	**Republican Primary**		
	Malcolm Wallop (R)	41,445	*76.6*
	Nels T. Larson (R)	6,965	*12.9*
	Doyle W. Henry (R)	5,727	*10.6*
	Democratic Primary		
	Gale McGee (D)		*100.0*
1982	**Republican Primary**		
	Malcolm Wallop (R)	61,650	*80.9*
	Richard Redland (R)	14,543	*19.1*
	Democratic Primary		
	Rodger McDaniel (D)		*100.0*
1988	**Republican Primary**		
	Malcolm Wallop (R)	55,752	*83.2*
	Nora M. Lewis (R)	3,933	*5.9*
	I. W. Kinney (R)	3,716	*5.5*
	Democratic Primary		
	John P. Vinich (D)	23,214	*47.2*
	Pete Maxfield (D)	14,613	*29.7*
	Lynn Simons (D)	11,350	*23.1*
1994	**Republican Primary**		
	Craig Thomas (R)	81,381	*100.0*
	Democratic Primary		
	Mike Sullivan (D)	39,563	*100.0*

Class 2

	Candidates	Votes	%
1960	**Republican Primary**		
	E. Keith Thomson (R)	31,596	*69.1*
	Frank A. Barrett (R)	13,380	*29.2*
	Democratic Primary		
	Raymond B. Whitaker (D)	18,031	*44.1*
	Velma Linford (D)	13,792	*33.8*
	Carl A. Johnson (D)	5,370	*13.1*
	Charles B. Chittim (D)	3,653	*8.9*
1962[1]	**Republican Special Primary**		
	Milward L. Simpson (R)	30,124	*59.6*
	K. L. Sailors (R)	20,383	*40.4*

	Candidates	Votes	%
	Democratic Special Primary		
	J. J. Hickey (D)		*100.0*
1966	**Republican Primary**		
	Clifford P. Hansen (R)	40,102	*86.1*
	I. Wayne Kinney (R)	6,468	*13.9*
	Democratic Primary		
	Teno Roncalio (D)		*100.0*
1972	**Republican Primary**		
	Clifford P. Hansen (R)		*100.0*
	Democratic Primary		
	Mike Vinich (D)	16,148	*52.5*
	Doyle W. Henry (D)	5,642	*18.4*
	Patrick E. Shanklin (D)	4,665	*15.2*
	William E. Fritchell (D)	4,281	*13.9*
1978	**Republican Primary**		
	Alan K. Simpson (R)	37,332	*54.7*
	Hugh Binford (R)	20,768	*30.4*
	Gordon H. Barrows (R)	8,494	*12.4*
	Democratic Primary		
	Raymond B. Whitaker (D)	19,854	*47.6*
	Dean M. Larson (D)	11,039	*26.5*
	Charles Carroll (D)	10,797	*25.9*
1984	**Republican Primary**		
	Alan K. Simpson (R)	66,178	*87.9*
	Stephen Tarver (R)	9,137	*12.1*
	Democratic Primary		
	Victor A. Ryan (D)	17,608	*45.3*
	Al Hamburg (D)	12,088	*31.1*
	Michael J. Dee (D)	9,187	*23.6*
1990	**Republican Primary**		
	Alan K. Simpson (R)	69,142	*84.4*
	Nora M. Lewis (R)	6,577	*8.0*
	Douglas W. Crook (R)	6,201	*7.6*
	Democratic Primary		
	Kathy Helling (D)	12,103	*35.1*
	Howard O'Connor (D)	7,196	*20.9*
	Al Hamburg (D)	6,483	*18.8*
	Emmett Jones (D)	4,455	*12.9*
	Dale Bulman (D)	2,291	*6.6*
	Don C. Jolliffe (D)	1,983	*5.7*
1996	**Republican Primary**		
	Michael B. Enzi (R)	27,056	*32.5*
	John Barrasso (R)	24,918	*29.9*
	Curt Meier (R)	14,739	*17.7*
	Nimi McConigley (R)	6,005	*7.2*
	Kevin P. Meenan (R)	6,000	*7.2*

Candidates	Votes	%
Democratic Primary		
Kathy Karpan (D)	32,419	86.1
Mickey Kalinay (D)	5,245	13.9

Wyoming

1. *A special election was held to fill the unexpired term of E. Keith Thomson (R), who died after winning the Senate seat in 1960. J. J. Hickey (D), the incumbent governor, resigned in January 1961 and his successor appointed him to the seat, where he served until after the special election was held, in November 1962.*

Political Party Abbreviations

The following political party abbreviations are used in the Senate primary vote returns section.

AM	American	DFL	Democrat Farmer-Labor	LU	Liberty Union
AM I	American Independent	GREEN	Green	PFP	Peace and Freedom
C	Conservative	I	Independent	P	Prohibition
CIT	Citizens	ID	Independent Democrat	REF	Reform
CONST	Constitution	I-R	Independent Republican	R	Republican
CP	Commonwealth	L	Liberal	RTL	Right to Life
D	Democrat	LIBERT	Libertarian	SOC WORK	Socialist Workers

House Elections

The authors of the Constitution of the United States recognized that the new government needed a chief executive to carry out the laws and a judiciary to resolve conflicts arising from them. But it was Congress, the lawmaking body, that the Founders designed to be the heart of the new Republic.

There was little question that the new Congress should be bicameral, in accordance with the practice of the English Parliament, which was followed by most of the colonial governments and 10 of the 13 states. As George Mason put it during the Constitutional Convention in 1787, the minds of Americans were settled on two points: "an attachment to republican government [and] an attachment to more than one branch in the Legislature."

But little agreement existed over how the members of each of the chambers should be chosen. The nationalists insisted that the new government rest on the consent of the people rather than the state legislatures. So they held it essential that at least "the first branch," or House, be elected popularly. The government "ought to possess. . . the mind or sense of the people at large," said one of the Framers, James Wilson of Pennsylvania. Those who were suspicious of a national government preferred election to the House by the state legislatures. "The people immediately should have as little to do" with electing the government as possible, said Roger Sherman, because "they want information and are constantly liable to be misled." Election by the legislatures was twice defeated, however, and popular election for the House agreed to with only one state dissenting.

There was little support for the view that the people also should elect the Senate. Nor did the delegates to the Constitutional Convention think that the House should choose members of the Senate from among persons nominated by the state legislatures. Election of the Senate by the state legislatures was agreed to with only two states dissenting.

For the sake of convenience, the Senate is often referred to as the "upper body" of Congress, and the House as the "lower body." But those terms are not used in the Constitution, and in fact the two chambers are equal in stature and legislative power. No bill can become law unless it is passed by both chambers in identical form and signed by the president.

Representatives naturally naturally resent having the House called the "lower body." Yet, from the earliest days of the Republic, the House has been generally regarded as somehow less prestigious than the Senate. The French scholar Alexis de Tocqueville wrote in the 1830s of being struck by "the vulgar demeanor" of the House as compared with the Senate, and the same impression still widely exists. But in the public mind today, neither chamber is held in very high esteem. (*Congressional Characteristics and Public Opinion, box, p. 167*)

The People's Branch

The House of Representatives was to be the branch of government closest to the people. The members would be popularly elected; the terms of office would be two years so that the representatives would not lose touch with their homes; and the House would be a numerous branch, with members having relatively small constituencies.

The lower houses of the state legislatures served as models for the U.S. House. All the states had at least one chamber elected by popular vote. Ten states had two-house legislatures; Georgia, Pennsylvania and Vermont had popularly elected unicameral legislatures.

Article I, Section 2 of the Constitution set few requirements for election to the House: a representative had to be at least 25 years of age, have been a U.S. citizen for seven years and be an inhabitant of the state from which elected.

The Constitution left the qualification of voters to the states, with one overriding principle: the qualifications could be no more restrictive than for the most numerous branch of each of the states' own legislatures. At first, property qualifications for voting were general. Five states required ownership of real estate, five mandated either real estate or other property and three required personal wealth or payment of public taxes. But the democratic trend of the early 19th century swept away most property qualifications, producing practically universal white male suffrage by the 1830s.

Over the years several changes in the Constitution also broadened the franchise. The 15th Amendment (1870) extended the franchise to newly freed slaves; the 19th

---

Sources

Galloway, George B. *History of the House of Representatives.* 2nd ed. New York: Crowell, 1976.

Jones, Charles O. *Every Second Year.* Washington, D.C.: Brookings, 1967.

Amendment (1920) granted the right of suffrage to women; the 23rd Amendment (1961) extended the presidential vote to the District of Columbia; the 24th Amendment (1964) abolished the poll tax; and the 26th Amendment (1971) lowered the voting age to 18 from 21. In 1965 Congress passed the Voting Rights Act to remove barriers several states and localities had erected to keep blacks and other minorities from voting.

Two-Year Term

Many delegates to the Constitutional Convention preferred annual elections for the House, believing that the body should reflect the wishes of the people as closely as possible. James Madison, however, argued for a three-year term, to allow representatives to gain knowledge and experience in national affairs as well as the affairs of their own localities. The delegates compromised on two-year terms.

The two-year term has not been universally popular. From time to time proposals have been made to extend the term to four years. The movement to extend the House term to four years last gained momentum after President Lyndon B. Johnson urged the extension in his 1966 State of the Union address. His proposal received more applause than any other part of his speech.

However, the proposed amendment never emerged from committee. Opponents criticized the proposal's provision that the four-year term coincide with the presidential term. This would create a House of "coattail riders," critics said, and end the minority party's traditional gains in non-presidential election years. This fear of diminishing the independence of the House appeared to be the principal factor that killed the proposal. *(Results of House Elections, 1946-1996, table, p. 170)*

Size of the House

The size of the original House was written into Article I, Section 2 of the Constitution, along with directions to apportion the House according to population after the first census in 1790. Until the first census and apportionment, the 13 states were to have the following numbers of representatives: Connecticut, 5; Delaware, 1; Georgia, 3; Maryland, 6; Massachusetts, 8; New Hampshire, 3; New Jersey, 4; New York, 6; North Carolina, 5; Pennsylvania, 8; Rhode Island, 1; South Carolina, 5; Virginia, 10. This apportionment of seats —65 in all—thus mandated by the Constitution remained in effect during the first and second Congresses (1789-93). (Seats allotted to North Carolina and Rhode Island were not filled until 1790, after those states had ratified the Constitution.)

By act of Congress (April 14, 1792), an apportionment measure provided for a ratio of one member for every 33,000 inhabitants and fixed the exact number of representatives to which each state was entitled. Congress enacted a new apportionment measure, including the mathematical formula to be used, every 10 years (except 1920) until a permanent law became effective in 1929. In 1911 Congress set the maximum size of the House at 435 members, where it has remained since the 1912. *(Reapportionment, p. 174)*

In 1996, on average, each House member represented about 600,000 persons.

Majority Elections

Five New England states at one time or another had a requirement for majority victory in congressional elections. The requirement provided that, to win a seat in the U.S. House, a candidate had to achieve more than 50 percent of the popular vote. If no candidate gained such a majority, new elections were held until one contender succeeded.

The provision was last invoked in Maine in 1844, in New Hampshire in 1845, in Vermont in 1866, in Massachusetts in 1848 and in Rhode Island in 1892. Sometimes, multiple races were necessary because none of the candidates could achieve the required majority. In the 4th District of Massachusetts in 1848-49, for example, 12 successive elections were held to try to choose a representative. None of them was successful, and the district remained unrepresented in the House during the 31st Congress (1849-51).

Multi-Member Districts

In the early days of the House several states had districts that elected more than one representative. For example, in 1824 Maryland's 5th District chose two representatives, while the remaining seven districts chose one each. And in Pennsylvania two districts (the 4th and 9th) elected three representatives each, and four districts (the 7th, 8th, 11th and 17th) chose two representatives each.

As late as 1838, New York still had as many as five multi-member districts—one (the 3rd) electing four members and four (the 8th, 17th, 22nd and 23rd) choosing two each. But the practice ended in 1842 when Congress enacted a law that "no one district may elect more than one Representative." The provision was a part of the reapportionment legislation following the census of 1840.

Elections in Odd-Numbered Years

Another practice that has faded out over the years was general elections in odd-numbered years for the House. Prior to ratification of the 20th (lame-duck) Amendment in 1933, regular sessions of Congress began in December of odd-numbered years. There were, therefore, 11 months in the odd-numbered years to elect members before the beginning of the congressional session. For example, in 1841 the following states held general elections for representative for the 27th Congress, convening that year: Alabama, Connecticut, Illinois, Indiana, Kentucky, Maryland, Mississippi, New Hampshire, North Carolina, Rhode Island, Tennessee and Virginia.

The practice continued until late in the century. In 1875 four states still chose their representatives in regular odd-year elections: California, Connecticut, Mississippi and New Hampshire. But by 1880 all members of the House were being chosen in even-numbered years (except for special elections to fill vacancies). One major problem encountered by states choosing their representatives in odd-numbered years was the possibility of a special session of the new Congress being called before the states' elections were held. Depending on the date of the election, a state could be unrepresented in the House. For example, California elected its U.S. House delegation to the 40th Congress (1867-69) on Sept. 4, 1867, in plenty of time for the first regular session scheduled for Dec. 2. But the Congress already had met in two special sessions—March 4 to March 20 and July 3 to July 20—without any representation from California.

Southern Anomalies

Many of the anomalies in election of U.S. representatives occurred in the South. That region's experience with slavery, Civil War, Reconstruction and racial antagonisms created special problems for the regular electoral process.

Article I, Section 2 of the Constitution contained a formula for counting slaves for apportionment purposes: every five slaves would be counted as three persons. Thus, the total population of a state to be used in determining its congres-

Congressional Characteristics and Public Opinion

From the early days of the Republic until the present, the American public has criticized the abilities, ethical standards and performance of members of Congress. Through the years the House has received more criticism than the Senate, perhaps because senators were not elected by popular vote until 1914.

An early but still familiar critique of Congress was written in the 1830s by Alexis de Tocqueville, the French aristocrat, scholar and astute observer of America. After he had seen both chambers in session, Tocqueville wrote the following in his famous book of observations, *Democracy in America*:

> On entering the House of Representatives at Washington, one is struck by the vulgar demeanor of that great assembly. Often there is not a distinguished man in the whole number. Its members are almost all obscure individuals, whose names bring no associations to mind. They are mostly village lawyers, men in trade, or even persons belonging to the lower classes of society. In a country in which education is very general, it is said that the representatives of the people do not always know how to write correctly.
>
> At a few yards' distance is the door of the Senate, which contains within a small space a large proportion of the celebrated men of America. Scarcely an individual is to be seen in it who has not had an active and illustrious career: the Senate is composed of eloquent advocates, distinguished generals, wise magistrates, and statesmen of note, whose arguments would do honor to the most remarkable parliamentary debates of Europe.

Profile of 'Average' Member

A more modern—and charitable—description of the "average" member of Congress was presented in a popular textbook of the 1960s, *American Democracy*:

> He is a little over 50, has served in Congress for a number of years, and has had previous political experience before coming to Congress, such as membership in his state legislature. He has a college degree, is a lawyer by profession, a war veteran, and, before coming to Congress, was a well-known and popular member of the community. He has been reasonably successful in business or the practice of law, although not so successful that he is sacrificing a huge income in giving up his private occupation for a public job. Congress is clearly not an accurate cross section of the American people but neither is it a community of intellectuals and technicians.

The description was accurate, even to the exclusive use of "he." Although the composition had changed some by the 1990s, most members of Congress were male, Caucasian and Christian, especially Protestant. Of the 535 members of Congress at the beginning of 1997, 60 were women, 38 were African American (not including the non-voting delegate from the District of Columbia), 18 were Hispanic, and 6 were of Asian, Pacific Islander or Native American heritage. Among religious groups, Protestants have comprised nearly two-thirds of the membership of both houses in recent years, although Roman Catholic members have become more numerous than members belonging to any single Protestant denomination. Catholics took the lead from Methodists in 1965 and retained it 32 years later. At the beginning of 1997, there were 151 Catholics. More than two-thirds of the Protestant members were affiliated with four denominations: Baptists led with 67, followed by 59 Methodists, 53 Presbyterians and 42 Episcopalians. There were 34 Jewish members. The average age for senators was 58 while the average for representatives was 52.

It was likely that a senator was a former House member but rare that a representative had served earlier in the Senate. Although by 1997 the legal profession long had been dominant among members of both houses, most other occupations—including banking, business, public service, education, journalism, farming, law enforcement and medicine—had been represented. In 1997 in the House of Representatives for the first time there were more members from a business or banking background (181) than from a law one (172). There were still more lawyers (53) than any other profession in the Senate. The principal occupational groups underrepresented were the clergy, scientists and blue-collar workers.

Although many members came from established professions, that did little to enhance their public image. Polls indicated that contemporary Americans retained a certain skepticism about the character of their politicians. A Gallup Poll taken in June 1979 found that only 19 percent of Americans approved of the way Congress was doing its job, while 61 percent disapproved. Another Gallup survey released nine months later showed that 78 percent of Americans believed that some members of Congress won election by using "unethical and illegal methods in their campaigns." In addition, four out of 10 persons surveyed believed that at least 20 percent of the members of Congress employed questionable methods to get elected. This poll was taken after disclosure of what came to be known as the Abscam affair, in which a few members were alleged to have taken bribes from undercover FBI agents posing as wealthy Arabs in return for political and legislative favors. Subsequent to the poll, one senator and six members of the House were convicted for their parts in the scandal.

More recent polls offered further evidence of the poor public image of politicians in the United States. Harris surveys found that the percentage of people with a positive view of the job done by Congress dropped from 47 percent in mid-1985 to 40 percent at the end of 1989. By October 1991, according to a *New York Times* poll, Congress' general approval rating was 27 percent. The low approval rating of Congress was one factor that helped Republicans win control of Congress in the midterm 1994 elections. Although the Republican leadership initially received a high approval rating, public opinion quickly reverted to the modern trend of disapproval. A July 1997 Gallup Poll found that 61 percent thought that the GOP Congress was out of touch with the American people.

sional representation would be the free population plus three-fifths of the slave population.

After the Civil War and the emancipation of the slaves, blacks were fully counted for the purposes of apportionment. The 14th Amendment, required that apportionment be based on "the whole number of persons in each State. . . ." On this basis, several Southern states tried to claim immediate additional representation on readmission to the Union. Tennessee, for example, chose an extra U.S. representative, electing him at large in 1868, and claimed that inasmuch as its slaves were now free the state had added to its apportionment population a sufficient number to give it nine instead of eight representatives. Virginia took similar action in 1869 and 1870; South Carolina did it in both 1868 and 1870. But the House declined to seat the additional representatives, declaring that states would have to await the regular reapportionment following the 1870 census for any changes in their representation.

Part of the 14th Amendment affected—or was intended to affect—Southern representation in the House. The second paragraph of the amendment states, "When the right to vote at any election for the choice of electors for President and Vice President of the United States, Representatives in Congress, the executive and judicial officers of a State, or the members of the legislature thereof, is denied to any of the male inhabitants of such state, being twenty-one years of age, and citizens of the United States, or in any other way abridged, except for participation in rebellion, or other crime, the basis of representation [in the U.S. House] shall be reduced in the proportion which the number of such male citizens shall bear to the whole number of male citizens twenty-one years of age in such state."

Designed as a club to force the South to accept black voting participation, the provision was incorporated in the reapportionment legislation of 1872. According to the legislation, the number of representatives from any state interfering with the exercise of the right to vote was to be reduced in proportion to the number of inhabitants of voting age whose right to go to the polls was denied or abridged.

But the provision never was put into effect because of the difficulty of determining the exact number of persons whose right to vote was being abridged and also because of the decline of Northern enthusiasm for forcing Reconstruction policies on the South.

As an alternative to invoking the difficult 14th Amendment provision, Congress often considered election challenges filed against members from the South. When Republicans were in control of the House, several Democrats from the former Confederate states found themselves unseated, often on charges that black voting rights were abused in their districts.

During the 47th Congress (1881-83) five Democrats from former Confederate states were unseated; in the 51st Congress (1889-91), six; and in the 54th Congress (1895-97), seven.

Special Elections

When a vacancy occurs in the House, the usual procedure is for the governor of the affected state to call a special election. Such elections may be held at any time throughout the year, and there are usually several during each two-year Congress.

At times there are delays in the calling of special elections. One of the longest periods in recent years when a congressional district went unrepresented occurred in 1959-60.

On April 28, 1959, Rep. James G. Polk, D (1931-41, 1949-59), of the Ohio 6th District died. But not until November 1960 was there an election to replace him. It was held simultaneously with the general election, and the winner, Ward M. Miller, R, served only the two months remaining in the term. For the full term, both Republicans and Democrats nominated candidates different from those who ran for the short term.

In the days of the lame-duck sessions of Congress, elections for the remainder of a term quite often were held simultaneously with the general election, because the session following the election was an important working meeting that lasted until March 4.

However, since the passage of the 20th Amendment and the ending of most lame-duck sessions, elections for the remaining two months of a term have become less common. Miller, for example, never was sworn in because Congress was not in session during the period when he was waiting to serve as a representative.

Usually states are more prompt in holding special House elections than was Ohio in 1959-60. One of the most rapid instances of succession occurred in Texas' 10th District in 1963. Democratic representative Homer Thornberry (1949-63) submitted his resignation on Sept. 26, 1963, to take effect Dec. 20. On the strength of Thornberry's post-dated resignation, a special election was held in his district—the first election was held Nov. 9 and the runoff on Dec. 17. The winner, J. J. Pickle, D, was ready to take his seat as soon as Thornberry stepped down. He was sworn in the next day, Dec. 21, 1963.

Disputed House Elections

Perhaps the most dramatic election dispute settled by the House in recent years was that of the Mississippi Five in 1965. The governor of Mississippi certified the election to the House in 1964 of four Democrats and one Republican. The Democrats were Thomas G. Abernethy, William M. Colmer, Jamie L. Whitten and John Bell Williams; the Republican was Prentiss Walker.

Their right to be seated was contested by a biracial group, the Mississippi Freedom Democratic Party, formed originally to challenge the seating of an all-white delegation from the state to the 1964 Democratic National Convention. This group, when unsuccessful in getting its candidates on the 1964 congressional election ballot, conducted a rump election in which Annie Devine, Virginia Gray and Fannie L. Hamer were the winners.

The three women, when they sought entrance to the House floor, were barred. However, Speaker John W. McCormack, D-Mass., asked the regular Mississippi representatives-elect to stand aside while the other members of the House were sworn in. William F. Ryan, D-N.Y., sponsor of the challenge, contended that the regular congressional election in Mississippi was invalid because blacks had been systematically prevented from voting. A resolution to seat the regular Mississippi delegation was adopted on Jan. 4, 19
65, by a voice vote.

Later that year Congress enacted the Voting Rights Act of 1965, which contained strict sanctions against states that practiced discrimination against minority voters.

McCloskey-McIntyre Contest

Three 1984 House races were so close that the losers contested the results. One race, in Indiana, led to four months of acrimony between Democrats and Republicans over what appeared to be the closest House contest in the 20th century. Debate on the election took up far more time than almost any other issue the House considered in 1985.

After the Nov. 6 election, incumbent Democrat Frank McCloskey appeared to have won reelection to his Indiana 8th District seat by 72 votes. But correction of an arithmetical error (ballots in two precincts were counted twice) gave Republican challenger Richard D. McIntyre an apparent 34-vote victory. On that basis, the Indiana secretary of state Dec. 14 certified McIntyre the winner.

But when Congress convened Jan. 3, 1985, the Democratic-controlled House refused to seat McIntyre, voting instead to declare the seat vacant pending an investigation of alleged irregularities in the election. Three times after that—in February, March and April—Republicans pushed the seating of McIntrye to a vote, losing each time while picking up no more than a handful of votes from the Democrats.

A recount completed Jan. 22 showed McIntyre's lead had increased to 418 votes, after more than 4,800 ballots were thrown out for technical reasons. But a House Administration Committee task force, with auditors from the General Accounting Office, conducted its own recount and, on a 2-1 partisan split, found McCloskey the winner by four votes. Republicans then tried to get a new election by declaring the seat vacant. Their attempt lost, 200-229. Nineteen Democrats joined 181 Republicans in voting for a new election.

The next day, before the House Administration Committee's recommendation to seat McCloskey came to a vote, Republicans moved to send the issue back to the panel with orders to count 32 controversial absentee ballots that the task force had decided, on a 2-1 vote, not to count. That motion was rejected, 183-246.

The House then approved the resolution 236-190, with 10 Democrats joining the Republicans in voting against it. GOP members walked out of the House chamber in protest, accusing Democrats of stealing the election.

The Supreme Court May 28 refused to get involved in the dispute. Without a dissenting vote, it denied Indiana permission to sue the House in the Supreme Court.

A U.S. district court judge in Washington, D.C., dismissing a suit brought by McIntyre against House Democrats and House officers, ruled March 1 that the House had the constitutional right to judge its own membership.

On Feb. 7, a federal district court in Indiana had dismissed a separate suit filed by McIntyre challenging recount procedures in two of the district's counties and ruled that the House alone was responsible for determining the validity of contested ballots.

Other 1984 Contested Elections

Results in two other close House races also were contested, but those challenges, in Guam and Idaho, were unsuccessful. On July 24, the House agreed by voice vote to a resolution dismissing a challenge by Democrat Antonio Borja Won Pat, the former non-voting delegate from Guam, against Republican Ben Blaz. Won Pat, who had represented Guam in Congress since 1973, had lost the November 1984 election by about 350 votes. Won Pat had protested, among other things, that Blaz had not won an absolute majority of the votes cast, as required by law. On Oct. 2, the House threw out a challenge by former representative George Hansen, R-Idaho, against Democrat Richard H. Stallings. Hansen, who was convicted in 1984 of filing false financial disclosure forms, charged, among other things, vote fraud in his 170-vote loss to Stallings. The House dismissed the challenge by a 247-4 vote, with 169 members, mostly Republicans, voting "present."

Results of House Elections . . .

	1946	1948	1950	1952	1954	1956	1958	1960	1962	1964	1966	1968	1970
National Totals													
Democrats	188	263	235	213	232	234	283	263	259	295	248	243	255
Republicans	246	171	199	221	203	201	153	174	176	140	187	192	180
Alabama													
Democrats	9	9	9	9	9	9	9	9	8[1]	3	5	5	5
Republicans	0	0	0	0	0	0	0	0	0	5	3	3	3
Alaska													
Democrats	—	—	—	—	—	—	1	1	1	1	0	0	1
Republicans	—	—	—	—	—	—	0	0	0	0	1	1	0
Arizona													
Democrats	2	2	2	1	1	1	1	1	2[2]	2	1	1	1
Republicans	0	0	0	1	1	1	1	1	1	1	2	2	2
Arkansas													
Democrats	7	7	7	6[1]	6	6	6	6	4[1]	4	3	3	3
Republicans	0	0	0	0	0	0	0	0	0	0	1	1	1
California													
Democrats	9	10	10	11[2]	11	13	16	16	25[2, 4]	23	21	21	20
Republicans	14	13	13	19	19	17	14	14	13	15	17	17	18
Colorado													
Democrats	1	3	2	2	2	2	3	2	2	4	3	3	2
Republicans	3	1	2	2	2	2	1	2	2	0	1	1	2
Connecticut													
Democrats	0	3	2	1	1	0	6	4	5	6	5	4	3
Republicans	6	3	4	5	5	6	0	2	1	0	1	2	2
Delaware													
Democrats	0	0	0	0	1	0	1	1	1	1	0	0	0
Republicans	1	1	0	1	0	0	0	0	0	0	1	1	1
Florida													
Democrats	6	6	6	8[2]	7	7	7	7	10[2]	10	9	9	9
Republicans	0	0	0	0	1	1	1	1	2	2	3	3	3
Georgia													
Democrats	10	10	10	10	10	10	10	10	10	9	8	8	8
Republicans	0	0	0	0	0	0	0	0	0	1	2	2	2
Hawaii													
Democrats	—	—	—	—	—	—	—	1	2[2]	2	2	2	2
Republicans	—	—	—	—	—	—	—	0	0	0	0	0	0
Idaho													
Democrats	0	1	0	1	1	1	1	2	2	1	0	0	0
Republicans	2	1	2	1	1	1	1	0	0	1	2	2	2
Illinois													
Democrats	6	12	8	9[1]	12	11	14	14	12[1]	13	12	12	12
Republicans	20	14	18	16	13	14	11	11	12	11	12	12	12
Indiana													
Democrats	2	7	2	1	2	2	8	4[3]	4	6	5	4	5
Republicans	9	4	9	10	9	9	3	7	7	5	6	7	6
Iowa													
Democrats	0	0	0	0	0	1	4	2	1[1]	6	2	2	2
Republicans	8	8	8	8	8	7	4	6	6	1	5	5	5
Kansas													
Democrats	0	0	0	1	0	1	3	1	0[1]	0	0	0	1
Republicans	6	6	6	5	6	5	3	5	5	5	5	5	4
Kentucky													
Democrats	6	7	7	6[1]	6	6	7	7	5[1]	6	4	4	5
Republicans	3	2	2	2	2	2	1	1	2	1	3	3	2
Louisiana													
Democrats	8	8	8	8	8	8	8	8	8	8	8	8	8
Republicans	0	0	0	0	0	0	0	0	0	0	0	0	0
Maine													
Democrats	0	0	0	0	0	1	2	0	0[1]	1	2	2	2
Republicans	3	3	3	3	3	2	1	3	2	1	0	0	0
Maryland													
Democrats	4	4	3	3[2]	4	4	7	6	6[2]	6	5	4	5
Republicans	2	2	3	4	3	3	0	1	2	2	3	4	3
Massachusetts													
Democrats	5	4	6	6	7	7	8	8	7[1]	7	7	7	8
Republicans	9	8	8	8	7	7	6	6	5	5	5	5	4
Michigan													
Democrats	3	5	5	5[2]	7	6	7	7	8[2]	12	7	7	7
Republicans	14	12	12	13	11	12	11	11	11	7	12	12	12
Minnesota													
Democrats	1	4	4	4	5	5	4	3	4[1]	4	3	3	4
Republicans	8	5	5	5	4	4	5	6	4	4	5	5	4
Mississippi													
Democrats	7	7	7	6[1]	6	6	6	6	5[1]	4	5	5	5
Republicans	0	0	0	0	0	0	0	0	0	1	0	0	0
Missouri													
Democrats	4	12	10	7	9	10	10	9	8[1]	8	8	9	9
Republicans	9	1	3	4	2	1	1	2	2	2	2	1	1
Montana													
Democrats	1	1	1	1	1	2	2	1	1	1	1	1	1
Republicans	1	1	1	1	1	0	0	1	1	1	1	1	1

...1946-1996

	1946	1948	1950	1952	1954	1956	1958	1960	1962	1964	1966	1968	1970
Nebraska													
Democrats	0	1	0	0	0	0	2	0	0[1]	1	0	0	0
Republicans	4	3	4	4	4	4	2	4	3	2	3	3	3
Nevada													
Democrats	0	1	1	0	0	1	1	1	1	1	1	1	1
Republicans	1	0	0	1	1	0	0	0	0	0	0	0	0
New Hampshire													
Democrats	0	0	0	0	0	0	0	0	0	1	0	0	0
Republicans	2	2	2	2	2	2	2	2	2	1	2	2	2
New Jersey													
Democrats	2	5	5	5	6	4	5	6	7[2]	11	9	9	9
Republicans	12	9	9	9	8	10	9	8	8	4	6	6	6
New Mexico													
Democrats	2	2	2	2	2	2	2	2	2	2	2	0	1
Republicans	0	0	0	0	0	0	0	0	0	0	0	2	1
New York													
Democrat	16	24	23	16[1]	17	17	19	22	20[1]	27	26	26	24
Republicans	28	20	22	27	26	26	24	21	21	14	15	15	17
North Carolina													
Democrats	12	12	12	11	11	11	11	11	9[1]	9	8	7	7
Republicans	0	0	0	1	1	1	1	1	2	2	3	4	4
North Dakota													
Democrat	0	0	0	0	0	0	1	0	0	1	0	0	1
Republicans	2	2	2	2	2	2	1	2	2	1	2	2	1
Ohio													
Democrats	4	12	7	6	6	6	9	7	6[2]	10	5	6	7
Republicans	19	11	15	16	17	17	14	16	18	14	19	18	17
Oklahoma													
Democrats	6	8	6	5[1]	5	5	5	5	5	5	4	4	4
Republicans	2	0	2	1	1	1	1	1	1	1	2	2	2
Oregon													
Democrats	0	0	0	0	1	3	3	2	3	3	2	2	2
Republicans	4	4	4	4	3	1	1	2	1	1	2	2	2
Pennsylvania													
Democrats	5	16	13	11[1]	14	13	16	14	13[1]	15	14	14	14
Republicans	28	19	20	19	16	17	14	16	14	12	13	13	13
Rhode Island													
Democrats	2	2	2	2	2	2	2	2	2	2	2	2	2
Republicans	0	0	0	0	0	0	0	0	0	0	0	0	0
South Carolina													
Democrats	6	6	6	6	6	6	6	6	6	6	5	5	5
Republicans	0	0	0	0	0	0	0	0	0	0	1	1	1
South Dakota													
Democrats	0	0	0	0	0	1	1	0	0	0	0	0	2
Republicans	2	2	2	2	2	1	1	2	2	2	2	2	0
Tennessee													
Democrats	8	8	8	7[1]	7	7	7	7	6	6	5	5	5
Republicans	2	2	2	2	2	2	2	2	3	3	4	4	4
Texas													
Democrats	21	21	21	22[2]	21	21	21	21	21[2]	23	21	20	20
Republicans	0	0	0	0	1	1	1	1	2	0	2	3	3
Utah													
Democrats	1	2	2	0	0	0	1	2	0	1	0	0	1
Republicans	1	0	0	2	2	2	1	0	2	1	2	2	1
Vermont													
Democrats	0	0	0	0	0	0	1	0	0	0	0	0	0
Republicans	1	1	1	1	1	1	0	1	1	1	1	1	1
Virginia													
Democrats	9	9	9	7[2]	8	8	8	8	8	8	6	5	4
Republicans	0	0	0	3	2	2	2	2	2	2	4	5	6
Washington													
Democrats	1	2	2	1[2]	1	1	1	2	1	5	5	5	6
Republicans	5	4	4	6	6	6	6	5	6	2	2	2	1
West Virginia													
Democrats	2	6	6	5	6	4	5	5	4[1]	4	4	5	5
Republicans	4	0	0	1	0	2	1	1	1	1	1	0	0
Wisconsin													
Democrats	0	2	1	1	3	3	5	4	4	5	3	3	5
Republicans	10	8	9	9	7	7	5	6	6	5	7	7	5
Wyoming													
Democrats	0	0	0	0	0	0	0	0	1	0	0	1	1
Republicans	1	1	1	1	1	1	1	1	1	0	1	1	0

1. State lost seats due to reapportionment.
2. State gained seats due to reapportionment.
3. Indiana 1960 and Indiana 1984: National and state totals reflect the final outcome of a contested election in which a Republican was first certified the winner, but the House decided to seat the Democrat.
4. California 1962, Alaska 1972 and Louisiana 1972: National and state totals reflect the re-election of a Democrat who died before the election but whose name remained on the ballot.

Results of House Elections . . .

	1972	1974	1976	1978	1980	1982	1984	1986	1988	1990	1992	1994	1996
National Totals													
Democrats	243	291	292	277	243	269	253	258	260	267	258	204	207
Republicans	192	144	143	158	192	166	182	177	175	167	176	230	227
Alabama													
Democrats	4[1]	4	4	4	4	5	5	5	5	5	4	4	2
Republicans	3	3	3	3	3	2	2	2	2	2	3	3	5
Alaska													
Democrats	1[4]	0	0	0	0	0	0	0	0	0	0	0	0
Republicans	0	1	1	1	1	1	1	1	1	1	1	1	1
Arizona													
Democrats	1[2]	1	2	2	2	2[2]	1	1	1	1	3[2]	1	1
Republicans	3	3	2	2	2	3	4	4	4	4	3	5	5
Arkansas													
Democrats	3	3	3	2	2	2	3	3	3	3	2	2	2
Republicans	1	1	1	2	2	2	1	1	1	1	2	2	2
California													
Democrats	23[2]	28	29	26	22	28[2]	27	27	27	26	30[2]	27	29
Republicans	20	15	14	17	21	17	18	18	18	19	22	25	23
Colorado													
Democrats	2[2]	3	3	3	3	3[2]	2	3	3	3	2	2	2
Republicans	3	2	2	2	2	3	4	3	3	3	4	4	4
Connecticut													
Democrats	3	4	4	5	4	4	3	3	3	3	3	3	4
Republicans	3	2	2	1	2	2	3	3	3	3	3	3	2
Delaware													
Democrats	0	0	0	0	0	1	1	1	1	1	0	0	0
Republicans	1	1	1	1	1	0	0	0	0	0	1	1	1
Florida													
Democrats	11[2]	10	10	12	11	13[2]	12	12	10	9	10[2]	8	8
Republicans	4	5	5	3	4	6	7	7	9	10	13	15	15
Georgia													
Democrats	9	10	10	9	9	9	8	8	9	9	7[2]	4	3
Republicans	1	0	0	1	1	1	2	2	1	1	4	7	8
Hawaii													
Democrats	2	2	2	2	2	2	2	1	1	2	2	2	2
Republicans	0	0	0	0	0	0	0	1	1	0	0	0	0
Idaho													
Democrats	0	0	0	0	0	0	1	1	1	2	1	0	0
Republicans	2	2	2	2	2	2	1	1	1	0	1	2	2
Illinois													
Democrats	10	13	12	11	10	12[1]	13	13	14	15	12[1]	10	10
Republicans	14	11	12	13	14	10	9	9	8	7	8	10	10
Indiana													
Democrats	4	9	8	7	6	5[1]	5[3]	6	6	8	7	4	4
Republicans	7	2	3	4	5	5	5	4	4	2	3	6	6
Iowa													
Democrats	3[1]	5	4	3	3	3	2	2	2	2	1[1]	0	1
Republicans	3	1	2	3	3	3	4	4	4	4	4	5	4
Kansas													
Democrats	1	1	2	1	1	2	2	2	2	2	2[1]	0	0
Republicans	4	4	3	4	4	3	3	3	3	3	2	4	4
Kentucky													
Democrats	5	5	5	4	4	4	4	4	4	4	4[1]	2	1
Republicans	2	2	2	3	3	3	3	3	3	3	2	4	5
Louisiana													
Democrats	7[4]	6[5]	6	5	6	6	6	5	4	4	4[1]	4	2
Republicans	1	2	2	3	2	2	2	3	4	4	3	3	5
Maine													
Democrats	1	0	0	0	0	0	0	1	1	1	1	1	2
Republicans	1	2	2	2	2	2	2	1	1	1	1	1	0
Maryland													
Democrats	4	5	5	6	7	7	6	6	6	5	4	4	4
Republicans	4	3	3	2	1	1	2	2	2	3	4	4	4
Massachusetts													
Democrats	9[6]	10	10	10	10	10[1]	10	10	10	10	8[1]	8	10
Republicans	3	2	2	2	2	1	1	1	1	1	2	2	0
Michigan													
Democrats	7	12	11	13	12	12[1]	11	11	11	11	10[1]	9	10
Republicans	12	7	8	6	7	6	7	7	7	7	6	7	6
Minnesota													
Democrats	4	5	5	4	3	5	5	5	5	6	6	6	6
Republicans	4	3	3	4	5	3	3	3	3	2	2	2	2
Mississippi													
Democrats	3	3	3	3	3	3	3	4	4	5	5	4	2
Republicans	2	2	2	2	2	2	2	1	1	0	0	1	3
Missouri													
Democrats	9	9	8	8	6	6[1]	6	5	5	6	6	6	5
Republicans	1	1	2	2	4	3	3	4	4	3	3	3	4
Montana													
Democrats	1	2	1	1	1	1	1	1	1	1	1[1]	1	1
Republicans	1	0	1	1	1	1	1	1	1	1	1	0	0
Nebraska													
Democrats	0	0	1	1	0	0	0	0	1	1	1	0	0
Republicans	3	3	2	2	3	3	3	3	2	2	2	3	3

. . . 1946-1996 (continued)

	1972	1974	1976	1978	1980	1982	1984	1986	1988	1990	1992	1994	1996
Nevada													
Democrats	0	1	1	1	1	1[2]	1	1	1	1	1	0	0
Republicans	1	0	0	0	0	1	1	1	1	1	1	2	2
New Hampshire													
Democrats	0	1	1	1	1	1	0	0	0	1	1	0	0
Republicans	2	1	1	1	1	1	2	2	2	1	1	2	2
New Jersey													
Democrats	8	12	11	10	8	9[1]	8	8	8	8	7[1]	5	6
Republicans	7	3	4	5	7	5	6	6	6	6	6	8	7
New Mexico													
Democrats	1	1	1	1	0	1[2]	1	1	1	1	1	1	1
Republicans	1	1	1	1	2	2	2	2	2	2	2	2	2
New York													
Democrats	22[1]	27	28	26	22	20[1]	19	20	21	21	18[1]	17	18
Republicans	17	12	11	13	17	14	15	14	13	13	13	14	13
North Carolina													
Democrats	7	9	9	9	7	9	6	8	8	7	8[2]	4	6
Republicans	4	2	2	2	4	2	5	3	3	4	4	8	6
North Dakota													
Democrats	0[1]	0	0	0	1	1	1	1	1	1	1	1	1
Republicans	1	1	1	1	0	0	0	0	0	0	0	0	0
Ohio													
Democrats	7[1]	8	10	10	11	10[1]	11	11	11	11	10[1]	6	8
Republicans	16	15	13	13	12	11	10	10	10	10	9	13	11
Oklahoma													
Democrats	5	6	5	5	5	5	5	4	4	4	4	1	0
Republicans	1	0	1	1	1	1	1	2	2	2	2	5	6
Oregon													
Democrats	2	4	4	4	3	3[2]	3	3	3	4	4	3	4
Republicans	2	0	0	0	1	2	2	2	2	1	1	2	1
Pennsylvania													
Democrats	13[1]	14	17	15	13[6]	13[1]	13	12	12	11	11[1]	11	11
Republicans	12	11	8	10	12	10	10	11	11	12	10	10	10
Rhode Island													
Democrats	2	2	2	2	1	1	1	1	0	1	1	2	2
Republicans	0	0	0	0	1	1	1	1	2	1	1	0	0
South Carolina													
Democrats	4	5	5	4	2	3	3	4	4	4	3	2	2
Republicans	2	1	1	2	4	3	3	2	2	2	3	4	4
South Dakota													
Democrats	1	0	0	1	1	1[1]	1	1	1	1	1	1	0
Republicans	1	2	2	1	1	0	0	0	0	0	0	0	1
Tennessee													
Democrats	3[1]	5	5	5	5	6[2]	6	6	6	6	6	4	4
Republicans	5	3	3	3	3	3	3	3	3	3	3	5	5
Texas													
Democrats	20[2]	21	22	20	19	22[2]	17	17	19	19	21[2]	19	17
Republicans	4	3	2	4	5	5	10	10	8	8	9	11	13
Utah													
Democrats	2	2	1	1	0	0[2]	0	1	1	2	2	1	0
Republicans	0	0	1	1	2	3	3	2	2	1	1	2	3
Vermont													
Democrats	0	0	0	0	0	0	0	0	0	0	0	0	0
Republicans	1	1	1	1	1	1	1	1	1	0	0	0	0
Virginia													
Democrats	3	5	4	4	1	4	4	5	5	6	7[2]	6	6
Republicans	7	5	6	6	9	6	6	5	5	4	4	5	5
Washington													
Democrats	6	6	6	6	5	5[2]	5	5	5	5	8[2]	2	3
Republicans	1	1	1	1	2	3	3	3	3	3	1	7	6
West Virginia													
Democrats	4[1]	4	4	4	2	4	4	4	4	4	3[1]	3	3
Republicans	0	0	0	0	2	0	0	0	0	0	0	0	0
Wisconsin													
Democrats	5[1]	7	7	6	5	5	5	5	5	4	4	3	5
Republicans	4	2	2	3	4	4	4	4	4	5	5	6	4
Wyoming													
Democrats	1	1	0	0	0	0	0	0	0	0	0	0	0
Republicans	0	0	0	1	1	1	1	1	1	1	1	1	1

5. *Louisiana 1974: National and state totals reflect the final outcome of a contested election in which no winner was declared, followed by a special election won by the Republican.*

6. *Massachusetts 1972 and Pennsylvania 1980: National and state Democratic totals reflect the election of an Independent candidate who previously announced he would serve as a Democrats.*

Note: The above totals do not include "other" representatives elected as independent or third party candidates. Those numbers are California: Progressive 1936 (1). (No formal party. The representative became a Democrat in 1938.) Minnesota: Farmer-Labor 1928 (1), 1930 (1), 1932 (5), 1934 (3), 1936 (5), 1938 (1), 1940 (1) and 1942 (1). (Merged with Democrats in 1944.) New York: American Labor 1938 through 1948 (1). (Party disbanded after 1954.) Ohio: Independent 1950 and 1952 (1). (Defeated by Democrat in 1954.) Wisconsin: Progressive 1934 (7), 1936 (7), 1938 (2), 1940 (3), 1942 (2) and 1944 (1). (Disbanded after 1944. The last Progressive became a Republican in 1946.) And Vermont: Independent 1990, 1992, 1994 and 1996 (1). National totals: 1928 (1), 1930 (1), 1932 (5), 1934 (10), 1936 (13), 1938 (4), 1940 (5), 1942 (4), 1944 (2), 1946 through 1952 (1), and 1990 through 1996 (1).

Reapportionment and Redistricting

Reapportionment—the redistribution of the 435 House seats among the states to reflect shifts in population—and redistricting—the redrawing of congressional district boundaries within the states—are among the most important processes in the U.S. political system. They help to determine whether the House will be dominated by Democrats or Republicans, liberals or conservatives, and whether racial or ethnic minorities receive what the American people view as fair representation.

Reapportionment occurs every 10 years on the basis of the decennial population census. States where populations grew quickly during the previous 10 years gain congressional seats, while those that lost population or grew much more slowly than the national average lose seats. The number of seats for the rest of the states remains the same.

The states that gain or lose seats must usually make extensive changes in their congressional maps. Even those states with stable delegations must make modifications that account for population shifts within their boundaries, in accordance with Supreme Court's "one-person, one-vote" rulings.

In most states, the state legislatures are responsible for drawing up and enacting the new district map. The majority party in each state legislature is thus often in a position to draw a congressional district map that enhances the fortunes of its incumbents and candidates at the expense of the opposing party. "Some members may find their old district no longer recognizable, or their home located in someone else's district. Others will find the music has stopped and they are, quite literally, without a seat. Or they will find themselves thrown together in a single district with another incumbent—often from the same party," wrote one reporter. "The scramble to prevent or minimize such political problems involves some of the most brutal combat in American politics, for the power to draw district lines is the power not only to end one politician's career but often to enfranchise or disenfranchise a neighborhood, a city, a party, a social or economic group or even a race by concentrating or diluting their votes within a given district."[1]

Among the many unique features to emerge in the remarkable nation-creating endeavor of 1787 was a national legislative body whose membership was to be elected by the people and apportioned on the basis of population. In keeping with the nature of the Constitution, however, only fundamental rules and regulations were provided. The interpretation and implementation of the instructions contained in the document were left to future generations.

Within this flexible framework many questions soon arose. How large was the House of Representatives to be? What mathematical formula was to be used in calculating the distribution of seats among the various states? Were the representatives to be elected at large or by districts? If by districts, what standards should be used in fixing their boundaries? Congress and the courts have been wrestling with these questions for 200 years.

Until the mid-20th century such questions generally remained in the hands of the legislators. But with the population increasingly concentrated in urban areas, variations in populations among rural and urban districts in a single state grew more and more pronounced. Efforts to persuade Congress to address the issue of heavily populated but underrepresented areas proved unsuccessful. Legislators from rural areas were so intent on preventing power from slipping from their hands that they managed to block reapportionment of the House after the 1920 census.

Not long afterward litigants tried, repeatedly and unsuccessfully, to persuade the Supreme Court to order the states to revise congressional district boundaries in line with population shifts. A breakthrough finally occurred in 1964 in the case of *Wesberry v. Sanders*, when the Court declared that the Constitution required that "as nearly as practicable, one man's vote in a congressional election is to be worth as much as another's."

In the years that followed the Court repeatedly reaffirmed its one-person, one-vote requirement. Following the 1980 and 1990 censuses, several states adopted new maps that had districts of nearly equal population but that disregarded other traditional factors—such as the compactness of the district or the integrity of county and city lines. So long as they are equal in population; and so long as they do not dilute the representation of blacks, Hispanics and Asian Americans; these partisan gerrymanders, designed to benefit one party at the expense of the other, have not been disallowed by the Supreme Court. But gerrymanders designed primarily to increase minority membership in the House are now being scrutinized closely.

Early History

Modern legislative bodies are descended from the councils of feudal lords and gentry that medieval kings summoned for the purpose of raising revenues and armies. The councils represented only certain groups of people, such as the nobility, the clergy, the landed gentry and town merchants; the notion of equal representation for equal numbers of people or even for all groups of people had not yet begun to develop.

Beginning as little more than administrative and advisory arms of the throne, royal councils in time developed into lawmaking bodies and acquired powers that eventually eclipsed those of the monarchs they served. In England the king's council became Parliament, with the higher nobility and clergy making up the House of Lords and representatives of the gentry and merchants making up the House of Commons. The power struggle between king and council climaxed in the mid-1600s, when the king was executed and a "benevolent" dictatorship was set up under Oliver Cromwell. Although the monarchy was soon restored, by 1800 Parliament was clearly the more powerful branch of the English government.

The growth of the powers of Parliament, as well as the development of English ideas of representation during the 17th and 18th centuries, had a profound effect on the colonists in America. Representative assemblies were unifying forces behind the breakaway of the colonies from England and the establishment of the newly independent nation.

Colonists in America generally modeled their legislatures after England's, using both population and land units as bases for apportionment. Patterns of early representation varied. "Nowhere did representation bear any uniform relation to the number of electors. Here and there the factor of size had been crudely recognized," Robert Luce noted in his book *Legislative Principles.2*

The Continental Congress, with representation from every colony, proclaimed in the Declaration of Independence in 1776 that governments derive "their just powers from the consent of the governed" and that "the right of representation in the legislature" is an "inestimable right" of the people. The Constitutional Convention of 1787 included representatives from all the states. However, in neither of these bodies were the state delegations or voting powers proportional to population.

In New England the town was usually the basis for representation. In the Middle Atlantic region the county frequently was used. Virginia used the county with additional representation for specified cities. In many areas, towns and counties were fairly equal in population, and territorial representation afforded roughly equal representation for equal numbers of people. Delaware's three counties, for example, were of almost equal population and had the same representation in the legislature. But in Virginia the disparity was enormous (from 951 people in one county to 22,015 in another). Thomas Jefferson criticized the state's constitution on the ground that "among those who share the representation, the shares are unequal."[3]

The Framers' Intentions

What, then, did the Framers of the Constitution have in mind about who would be represented in the House of Representatives and how?

The Constitution declares only that each state is to be allotted a certain number of representatives. It does not state specifically that congressional districts must be equal or nearly equal in population. Nor does it explicitly require that a state create districts at all. However, it seems clear that the first clause of Article I, Section 2, providing that House members should be chosen "by the people of the several states," indicates that the House of Representatives, in contrast to the Senate, was to represent people rather than states.

The third clause of Article I, Section 2 provided that congressional apportionment among the states must be according to population. "There is little point in giving the states congressmen 'according to their respective numbers' if the states do not redistribute the members of their delegations on the same principle," Andrew Hacker argued in his book *Congressional Districting.* "For representatives are not the property of the states, as are the senators, but rather belong to the people who happen to reside within the boundaries of those states. Thus, each citizen has a claim to be regarded as a political unit equal in value to his neighbors."[4]

Hacker also examined the Constitutional Convention, *The Federalist* papers (essays written by Alexander Hamilton, John Jay and James Madison in defense of the Constitution), and the state conventions ratifying the Constitution for evidence of the Framers' intentions with regard to representation. He found that the issue of unequal representation arose only once during debate in the Constitutional Convention. The occasion was Madison's defense of Article I, Section 4, of the proposed Constitution, giving Congress the power to override state regulations on "the times. . . . and manner" of holding elections for members of Congress. Madison's argument related to the fact that many state legislatures of the time were badly malapportioned: "The inequality of the representation in the legislatures of particular states would produce a like inequality in their representation in the national legislature, as it was presumable that the counties having the power in the former case would secure it to themselves in the latter."[5]

The implication was that states would create congressional districts and that unequal districting was undesirable and should be prevented.

Madison made this interpretation even more clear in his contributions to *The Federalist* papers. Arguing in favor of the relatively small size of the projected House of Representatives, he wrote in No. 56: "Divide the largest state into ten or twelve districts and it will be found that there will be no peculiar local interests. . . . which will not be within the knowledge of the Representative of the district."

In the same paper Madison said, "The Representatives of each state will not only bring with them a considerable knowledge of its laws, and a local knowledge of their respective districts, but will probably in all cases have been members, and may even at the very time be members, of the state legislature, where all the local information and interests of the state are assembled, and from whence they may easily be conveyed by a very few hands into the legislature of the United States." And, finally, in the *Federalist* No. 57 Madison stated that "each Representative of the United States will be elected by five or six thousand citizens." In making these arguments, Madison seems to have assumed that all or most representatives would be elected by districts rather than at large.[6]

In the states' ratifying conventions, the grant to Congress by Article I, Section 4, of ultimate jurisdiction over the "times, places and manner of holding elections" (except the places of choosing senators) held the attention of many delegates. There were differences over the merits of this section, but no justification of unequal districts was prominently used to attack the grant of power. Further evidence that individual districts were the intention of the Founding Fathers was given in the New York ratifying convention, when Alexander Hamilton said, "The natural and proper mode of holding elections will be to divide the state into districts in proportion to the number to be elected. This state will consequently be divided at first into six."[7]

From his study of the sources relating to the question of congressional districting, Hacker concluded,

---

Constitutional Provisions

Article I, Section 2: The House of Representatives shall be composed of Members chosen every second Year by the People of the several States, and the Electors in each State shall have the Qualifications requisite for Electors of the most numerous Branch of the State Legislature....

Representatives and direct Taxes shall be apportioned among the several States which may be included within this Union, according to their respective Numbers, which shall be determined by adding to the whole Number of free Persons, including those bound to Service for a Term of Years, and excluding Indians not taxed, three fifths of all other Persons. The actual Enumeration shall be made within three Years after the first Meeting of the Congress of the United States, and within every subsequent Term of ten Years, in such Manner as they shall by Law direct. The Number of Representatives shall not exceed one for every thirty thousand, but each State shall have at least one Representative....

Article I, Section 4: The Times, Places and Manner of holding Elections for Senators and Representatives, shall be prescribed in each State by the Legislature thereof; but the Congress may at any time by Law make or alter such Regulations, except as to the Place of Chusing Senators....

Amendment XIV, Section 2 to Article I: Representatives shall be apportioned among the several States according to their respective numbers, counting the whole number of persons in each State, excluding Indians not taxed. But when the right to vote at any election for the choice of electors for President and Vice President of the United States, Representatives in Congress, the Executive and Judicial officers of a State, or the members of the Legislature thereof, is denied to any of the male inhabitants of such State, being twenty-one years of age, and citizens of the United States, or in any way abridged, except for participation in rebellion, or other crime, the basis of representation therein shall be reduced in the proportion which the number of such male citizens shall bear to the whole number of male citizens twenty-one years of age in such State.

There is, then, a good deal of evidence that those who framed and ratified the Constitution intended that the House of Representatives have as its constituency a public in which the votes of all citizens were of equal weight.... The House of Representatives was designed to be a popular chamber, giving the same electoral power to all who had the vote. And the concern of Madison ... that districts be equal in size was an institutional step in the direction of securing this democratic principle.[8]

Reapportionment: The Number of Seats

The Constitution made the first apportionment, which was to remain in effect until the first census was taken. No reliable figures on the population were available at the time.

The Constitution's apportionment yielded a 65-member House. The seats were allotted among the 13 states as follows: New Hampshire, three; Massachusetts, eight; Rhode Island and Providence Plantations, one; Connecticut, five; New York, six; New Jersey, four; Pennsylvania, eight; Delaware, one; Maryland, six; Virginia, ten; North Carolina, five; South Carolina, five; and Georgia, three. This apportionment remained in effect during the First and Second Congresses (1789-93).

Apparently realizing that apportionment of the House was likely to become a major bone of contention, the First Congress submitted to the states a proposed constitutional amendment containing a formula to be used in future reapportionments. The amendment provided that following the taking of a decennial census one representative would be allotted for every 30,000 people until the House membership reached 100. Once that level was reached, there would be one representative for every 40,000 people until the House membership reached 200, when there would be one representative for every 50,000 people.

First Apportionment by Congress

The states, however, refused to ratify the reapportionment-formula amendment, which forced Congress to enact apportionment legislation after the first census was taken in 1790. The first apportionment bill was sent to the president in March 1792. President George Washington sent the bill back to Congress without his signature—the first presidential veto.

The bill had incorporated the constitutional minimum of 30,000 as the size of each district. But the population of each state was not a simple multiple of 30,000; significant fractions were left over. For example, Vermont was found to be entitled to 2.851 representatives, New Jersey to 5.98 and Virginia to 21.018. A formula had to be found that would deal in the fairest possible manner with unavoidable variations from exact equality.

Accordingly, Congress proposed in the first apportionment bill to distribute the members on a fixed ratio of one representative for each 30,000 inhabitants and give an additional member to each state with a fraction exceeding one-half. Washington's veto was based on the belief that eight states would receive more than one representative for each 30,000 people under this formula.

A motion to override the veto was unsuccessful. A new bill meeting the president's objections, approved in April 1792, provided for a ratio of one member for every 33,000 inhabitants and fixed the exact number of representatives to which each state was entitled. The total membership of the House was to be 105. In dividing the population of the various states by 33,000, all remainders were to be disregarded. Thomas Jefferson devised the solution, known as the method of rejected fractions.

Jefferson's Method

Jefferson's method of reapportionment resulted in great inequalities among districts. A Vermont district would contain 42,766 inhabitants, a New Jersey district 35,911 and a Virginia district only 33,187. Jefferson's method emphasized what was considered to be the ideal size of a congressional district rather than what the size of the House ought to be.

The reapportionment act based on the census of 1800 continued the ratio of 33,000, which provided a House of 141 members. The third apportionment bill, enacted in 1811, fixed the ratio at 35,000, yielding a House of 181 members. Following the 1820 census Congress set the ratio at 40,000 inhabitants per district, which produced a House of 213 members. The act of May 22, 1832, fixed the ratio at 47,700, resulting in a House of 240 members.

Dissatisfaction with inequalities produced by the method of rejected fractions grew. Launching a vigorous attack against it, Daniel Webster urged adoption of a method that would assign an additional representative to each state with a large fraction. Webster outlined his reasoning in a report he submitted to Congress in 1832:

> The Constitution, therefore, must be understood not as enjoining an absolute relative equality—because that would be demanding an impossibility—but as requiring of Congress to make the apportionment of Representatives among the several states according to their respective numbers, *as near as may be*. That which cannot be done perfectly must be done in a manner as near perfection as can be. . . . In such a case approximation becomes a rule.[9]

Following the 1840 census Congress adopted a reapportionment method similar to that advocated by Webster. The method fixed a ratio of one representative for every 70,680 people. This figure was reached by deciding on a fixed size of the House in advance (223), dividing that figure into the total national "representative population," and using the result (70,680) as the fixed ratio. The population of each state was then divided by this ratio to find the number of its representatives and the states were assigned an additional representative for each fraction over one-half. Under this method the actual size of the House dropped. *(Congressional apportionment, table, p. 180)*

The modified reapportionment formula adopted by Congress in 1842 was more satisfactory than the previous method, but another change was made following the census of 1850. Proposed by Rep. Samuel F. Vinton of Ohio, the new system became known as the Vinton method.

Vinton Apportionment Formula

Under the Vinton formula Congress first fixed the size of the House and then distributed the seats. The total qualifying population of the country was divided by the desired number of representatives, and the resulting number became the ratio of population to each representative. The population of each state was divided by this ratio, and each state received the number of representatives equal to the whole number in the quotient for that state. Then, to reach the required size of the House, additional representatives were assigned based on the remaining fractions, beginning with the state having the largest fraction. This procedure differed from the 1842 method only in the last step, which assigned one representative to every state having a fraction larger than one-half.

Proponents of the Vinton method pointed out that it had the distinct advantage of fixing the size of the House in advance and taking into account at least the largest fractions. The concern of the House turned from the ideal size of a congressional district to the ideal size of the House itself.

Under the 1842 reapportionment formula, the exact size of the House could not be fixed in advance. If every state with a fraction over one-half were given an additional representative, the House might wind up with a few more or a few less than the desired number. However, under the Vinton method, only states with the largest fractions were given additional House members and only up to the desired total size of the House.

Vinton Apportionments

Six reapportionments were carried out under the Vinton method. The 1850 census act contained three provisions not included in any previous law. First, it required reapportionment not only after the census of 1850 but also after all the subsequent censuses; second, it purported to fix the size of the House permanently at 233 members; and third, it provided in advance for an automatic apportionment by the secretary of the interior under the method prescribed in the act.

Following the census of 1860 an automatic reapportionment was to be carried out by the Interior Department. However, because the size of the House was to remain at the 1850 level, some states faced loss of representation and others were to gain fewer seats than they expected. To avert that possibility, an act was approved in 1862 increasing the size of the House to 241 and giving an extra representative to eight states—Illinois, Iowa, Kentucky, Minnesota, Ohio, Pennsylvania, Rhode Island and Vermont.

Apportionment legislation following the 1870 census contained several new provisions. The act fixed the size of the House at 283, with the proviso that the number should be increased if new states were admitted. A supplemental act assigned one additional representative each to Alabama, Florida, Indiana, Louisiana, New Hampshire, New York, Pennsylvania, Tennessee and Vermont.

With the Reconstruction era at its height in the South, the reapportionment legislation of 1872 reflected the desire of Congress to enforce Section 2 of the new 14th Amendment. That section attempted to protect the right of blacks to vote by providing for reduction of representation in the House of a state that interfered with the exercise of that right. The number of representatives of such a state was to be reduced in proportion to the number of inhabitants of voting age whose right to go to the polls was denied or abridged. The reapportionment bill repeated the language of Section 2, but the provision never was put into effect because of the difficulty of determining the exact number of people whose right to vote was being abridged.

The reapportionment act of 1882 provided for a House of 325 members, with additional members for any new states admitted to the Union. No new apportionment provisions were added. The acts of 1891 and 1901 were routine as far as apportionment was concerned. The 1891 measure provided for a House of 356 members, and the 1901 statute increased the number to 386.

Problems with Vinton Method

Despite the apparent advantages of the Vinton method, certain difficulties revealed themselves as the formula was applied. Zechariah Chafee Jr., of the Harvard Law School summarized these problems in an article in the *Harvard Law Review* in 1929. The method, he pointed out, suffered from what he called the "Alabama paradox." Under that aberration, an increase in the total size of the House might be accompanied by an actual loss of a seat by some states, even though there had been no corresponding change in population. This phenomenon first appeared in tables prepared for Congress in 1881, which gave Alabama eight members in a House of 299 but only seven members in a House of 300. It could even happen that the state that lost a seat was the one state that had expanded in population, while all the others had fewer people.

Chafee concluded from his study of the Vinton method:

> Thus, it is unsatisfactory to fix the ratio of population per Representative before seats are distributed. Either the size of the House comes out haphazard, or, if this be determined in advance, the absurdities of the "Alabama paradox" vitiate the apportionment. Under present conditions, it is essential to determine the size of the House in advance; the problem thereafter is to distribute the

required number of seats among the several states as nearly as possible in proportion to their respective populations so that no state is treated unfairly in comparison with any other state.[10]

Maximum Membership of House

In 1911 the membership of the House was fixed at 433. Provision was made for the addition of one representative each from Arizona and New Mexico, which were expected to become states in the near future. Thus, the size of the House reached 435, where it has remained with the exception of a brief period, 1959-63, when the admission of Alaska and Hawaii raised the total temporarily to 437.

Limiting the size of the House amounted to recognition that the body soon would expand to unmanageable proportions if Congress continued the practice of adding new seats every 10 years to match population gains without depriving any state of its existing representation. Agreement on a fixed number made the task of reapportionment all the more difficult when the population not only increased but became much more mobile. Population shifts brought Congress up hard against the politically painful necessity of taking seats away from slow-growing states to give the fast-growing states adequate representation.

A new mathematical calculation was adopted for the reapportionment following the 1910 census. Devised by W. F. Willcox of Cornell University, the new system established a priority list that assigned seats progressively, beginning with the first seat above the constitutional minimum of at least one seat for each state. When there were 48 states, this method was used to assign the forty-ninth member, the fiftieth member, and so on, until the agreed upon size of the House was reached. The method was called major fractions and was used after the censuses of 1910, 1930 and 1940. There was no reapportionment after the 1920 census.

1920s Struggle

The results of the 14th decennial census were announced in December 1920, just after the short session of the 66th Congress convened. The 1920 census showed that for the first time in history most Americans were urban residents. This came as a profound shock to people accustomed to emphasizing the nation's rural traditions and the virtues of life on farms and in small towns as Thomas Jefferson had. Jefferson once wrote:

> Those who labor in the earth are the chosen people of God, if ever He had a chosen people, whose breasts He had made His peculiar deposit for substantial and genuine virtue. . . . The mobs of great cities add just as much to the support of pure government as sores do to the strength of the human body. . . . I think our governments will remain virtuous for many centuries as long as they are chiefly agricultural: and this shall be as long as there shall be vacant lands in any part of America. When they get piled up upon one another in large cities as in Europe, they will become corrupt as in Europe.[11]

As their power waned throughout the latter part of the nineteenth century and the early part of the twentieth, farmers clung to the Jeffersonian belief that somehow they were more pure and virtuous than the growing number of urban residents. When finally faced with the fact that they were in the minority, these country residents put up a strong rearguard action to prevent the inevitable shift of congressional districts to the cities. They succeeded in postponing reapportionment legislation for almost a decade.

Rural representatives insisted that, because the 1920 census was taken as of Jan. 1, the farm population had been undercounted. In support of this contention, they argued that many farm laborers were seasonally employed in the cities at that time of year. Furthermore, midwinter road conditions probably had prevented enumerators from visiting many farms, they said, and other farmers were said to have been uncounted because they were absent on winter vacation trips. The change of the census date to Jan. 1 in 1920 had been made to conform to recommendations of the U.S. Department of Agriculture, which had asserted that the census should be taken early in the year if an accurate statistical picture of farming conditions was to be obtained. (From 1790 through 1990, except for 1920, every census date has been in April, June or August. Since 1930, it has been April 1.)

Another point raised by rural legislators was that large numbers of unnaturalized aliens were congregated in northern cities, with the result that these cities gained at the expense of constituencies made up mostly of citizens of the United States. Rep. Homer Hoch, R-Kan., submitted a table showing that in a House of 435 representatives, exclusion from the census count of people not naturalized would have altered the allocation of seats in 16 states. Southern and Western farming states would have retained the number of seats allocated to them in 1911 or would have gained, while Northern industrial states and California would have lost or at least would have gained fewer seats.

A constitutional amendment to exclude all aliens from the enumeration for purposes of reapportionment was proposed during the 70th Congress (1927-29) by Hoch, Sen. Arthur Capper, R-Kan., and others. But nothing further came of the proposals.

Reapportionment Bills Opposed

The first bill to reapportion the House according to the 1920 census was drafted by the House Census Committee early in 1921. Proceeding on the principle that no state should have its representation reduced, the committee proposed to increase the total number of representatives from 435 to 483. But the House voted 267-76 to keep its membership at 435. The bill then was blocked by a Senate committee, where it died when the 66th Congress expired March 4, 1921.

Early in the 67th Congress, the House Census Committee again reported a bill, this time fixing the total membership at 460, an increase of 25. Two states—Maine and Massachusetts—would have lost one representative each and 16 states would have gained. On the House floor an unsuccessful attempt was made to fix the number at the existing 435, and the House sent the bill back to committee.

During the 68th Congress (1923-25), the House Census Committee failed to report any reapportionment bill. In April 1926, midway through the 69th Congress (1925-27), it became apparent that the committee would not produce a reapportionment measure. A motion to discharge a reapportionment bill from the committee failed, however, and the matter once again put aside.

Coolidge Intervention

President Calvin Coolidge, who previously had made no reference to reapportionment in his communications to Congress, announced in January 1927 that he favored passage of a new apportionment bill during the short session of the 69th Congress, which would end in less than two months. The House Census Committee refused to act. Its chairman, Rep. E. Hart Fenn, R-Conn., therefore moved in the House to suspend the rules and pass a bill he had introduced authorizing the secretary of commerce to reapportion the House immediately after the 1930 census. The motion was voted down 183-197.

The Fenn bill was rewritten early in the 70th Congress (1927-29) to give Congress itself a chance to act before the proposed reapportionment by the secretary of commerce should go into effect. The House passed an amended version of the Fenn bill in January 1929, and it was quickly reported by the Senate Commerce Committee. Repeated efforts to bring it up for floor action ahead of other bills failed. Its supporters gave up the fight when it became evident that senators from states slated to lose representation were ready to carry on a filibuster that would have blocked not only reapportionment but all other measures.

Hoover Intervention

President Herbert Hoover listed provision for the 1930 census and reapportionment as "matters of emergency legislation" that should be acted upon in the special session of the 71st Congress, which was convened on April 15, 1929. In response to this urgent request, the Senate June 13 passed, 48-37, a combined census-reapportionment bill that had been approved by voice vote of the House two days earlier.

The 1929 law established a permanent system of reapportioning the 435 House seats following each census. It provided that immediately after the convening of the 71st Congress for its short session in December 1930, the president was to transmit to Congress a statement showing the population of each state together with an apportionment of representatives to each state based on the existing size of the House. Failing enactment of new apportionment legislation, that apportionment would go into effect without further action and would remain in effect for ensuing elections to the House of Representatives until another census had been taken and another reapportionment made.

Because two decades had passed between reapportionments, a greater shift than usual took place following the 1930 census. California's House delegation was almost doubled, rising from 11 to 20. Michigan gained four seats, Texas three, and New Jersey, New York and Ohio two each. Twenty-one states lost a total of 27 seats; Missouri lost three, and Georgia, Iowa, Kentucky and Pennsylvania each lost two.

To test the fairness of two allocation methods—the familiar major fractions and the new equal proportions system—the 1929 act required the president to report the distribution of seats by both methods. But, pending legislation to the contrary, the method of major fractions was to be used.

The two methods gave an identical distribution of seats based on 1930 census figures. However, in 1940 the two methods gave different results: under major fractions, Michigan would gain a seat lost by Arkansas; under equal proportions, no change would occur in either state. The automatic reapportionment provisions of the 1929 act went into effect in January 1941. But the House Census Committee moved to reverse the result, favoring the method of equal proportions and the certain Democratic seat in Arkansas over a possible Republican gain if the seat were shifted to Michigan. The Democratic-controlled Congress went along, adopting equal proportions as the method to be used in reapportionment calculations after the 1950 and subsequent censuses, and making this action retroactive to January 1941 to save Arkansas its seat.

While politics doubtless played a part in the timing of the action taken in 1941, the method of equal proportions had come to be accepted as the best available: It had been worked out by Edward V. Huntington of Harvard in 1921. At the request of the Speaker of the House, all known methods

of apportionment were considered in 1929 by the National Academy of Sciences Committee on Apportionment. The committee expressed its preference for equal proportions.

Method of Equal Proportions

The method of equal proportions involves complicated mathematical calculations. In brief, each of the 50 states is initially assigned the one seat to which it is entitled by the Constitution. Then "priority numbers" for states to receive second seats, third seats and so on are calculated by dividing the state's population by the square root of $n(n-1)$, where "n" is the number of seats for that state. The priority numbers are then lined up in order and the seats given to the states with priority numbers until 435 are awarded.

The method is designed to make the proportional difference in the average district size in any two states as small as possible. After the 1981 reapportionment, for example, South Dakota's single district was the most populous, with 690,768 residents, while Montana's two districts, each with slightly fewer than 400,000 people, were the least populous. Under the 1990 apportionment, Montana lost a seat; its remaining district was the most populous, with 803,655 residents. With 455,975 people, Wyoming's single district was the least populous. The mean population per district nationwide was about 572,500 in 1990. By 1996 the mean population had topped 600,000.

The 1990 Apportionment

Concern about the accuracy of the 1990 census, which is the basis for reapportionment and redistricting, led to calls for a statistical adjustment of the census count to compensate for a population undercount. An undercount was not a new problem. In 1980 the Census Bureau estimated that it counted about 99 percent of the white population but only about 94 percent of the blacks. In addition to determining the number of House seats each state has, the census is also the basis for distributing funding for many federal aid programs. Democrats, especially those representing inner-city districts where the undercount is believed to be comparatively high, have long argued for a statistical adjustment to compensate for undercounting. Several cities with large minority populations sought but failed to win adjustment of the 1980 census count.

Given the disappointing response to the census questionnaire and other problems encountered in conducting the 1990 census, many observers estimated that the undercount would be higher than the 1980 undercount. But the controversy over the 1990 count began even before the census was taken, when the Commerce Department, the parent agency to the Census Bureau, announced in 1987 that it would not statistically adjust the 1990 data. That fueled charges that the Republican administration was undercounting a Democratic constituency. New York City, along with other cities, states and civil rights organizations, quickly brought a lawsuit to force the Census Bureau to make a statistical adjustment to account for people who were missed. But in April 1993 a federal judge in New York upheld the Commerce Department's decision not to adjust the head count. That settled the matter for the decade, but the issue of how best to conduct an accurate census—an issue fundamental to the perceived fairness of the American political system—has yet to be resolved for the 2000 census.

Redistricting: Drawing the Lines

Although the Constitution contained provisions for the apportionment of U.S. House seats among the states, it was silent about how the members should be elected. In the

Congressional Apportionment, 1789-1990

	Constitution[2]	Year of Census[1]																		
	(1789)	1790	1800	1810	1820	1830	1840	1850	1860	1870	1880	1890	1900	1910	1930[3]	1940	1950	1960	1970	1980	1990
Ala.				1[4]	3	5	7	7	6	8	8	9	9	10	9	9	9	8	7	7	7
Alaska																	1[4]	1	1	1	1
Ariz.														1[4]	1	2	2	3	4	5	6
Ark.						1[4]	1	2	3	4	5	6	7	7	7	7	6	4	4	4	4
Calif.							2[4]	2	3	4	6	7	8	11	20	23	30	38	43	45	52
Colo.										1[4]	1	2	3	4	4	4	4	4	5	6	6
Conn.	5	7	7	7	6	6	4	4	4	4	4	4	5	5	6	6	6	6	6	6	6
Del.	1	1	1	2	1	1	1	1	1	1	1	1	1	1	1	1	1	1	1	1	1
Fla.							1[4]	1	1	2	2	2	3	4	5	6	8	12	15	19	23
Ga.	3	2	4	6	7	9	8	8	7	9	10	11	11	12	10	10	10	10	10	10	11
Hawaii																	1[4]	2	2	2	2
Idaho											1[4]	1	1	2	2	2	2	2	2	2	2
Ill.				1[4]	1	3	7	9	14	19	20	22	25	27	27	26	25	24	24	22	20
Ind.				1[4]	3	7	10	11	11	13	13	13	13	13	12	11	11	11	11	10	10
Iowa							2[4]	2	6	9	11	11	11	11	9	8	8	7	6	6	5
Kan.									1	3	7	8	8	8	7	6	6	5	5	5	4
Ky.		2	6	10	12	13	10	10	9	10	11	11	11	11	9	9	8	7	7	7	6
La.				1[4]	3	3	4	4	5	6	6	6	7	8	8	8	8	8	8	8	7
Maine				7[4]	7	8	7	6	5	5	4	4	4	4	3	3	3	2	2	2	2
Md.	6	8	9	9	9	8	6	6	5	6	6	6	6	6	6	6	7	8	8	8	8
Mass.	8	14	17	13[5]	13	12	10	11	10	11	12	13	14	16	15	14	14	12	12	11	10
Mich.						1[4]	3	4	6	9	11	12	12	13	17	17	18	19	19	18	16
Minn.								2[4]	2	3	5	7	9	10	9	9	9	8	8	8	8
Miss.				1[4]	1	2	4	5	5	6	7	7	8	8	7	7	6	5	5	5	5
Mo.					1	2	5	7	9	13	14	15	16	16	13	13	11	10	10	9	9
Mont.											1[4]	1	1	2	2	2	2	2	2	2	1
Neb.									1[4]	1	3	6	6	6	5	4	4	3	3	3	3
Nev.									1[4]	1	1	1	1	1	1	1	1	1	1	2	2
N.H.	3	4	5	6	6	5	4	3	3	3	2	2	2	2	2	2	2	2	2	2	2
N.J.	4	5	6	6	6	6	5	5	5	7	7	8	10	12	14	14	14	15	15	14	13
N.M.														1[4]	1	2	2	2	2	3	3
N.Y.	6	10	17	27	34	40	34	33	31	33	34	34	37	43	45	45	43	41	39	34	31
N.C.	5	10	12	13	13	13	9	8	7	8	9	9	10	10	11	12	12	11	11	11	12
N.D.											1[4]	1	2	3	2	2	2	2	1	1	1
Ohio			1[4]	6	14	19	21	21	19	20	21	21	21	22	24	23	23	24	23	21	19
Okla.													5[4]	8	9	8	6	6	6	6	6
Ore.								1[4]	1	1	1	2	2	3	3	4	4	4	4	5	5
Pa.	8	13	18	23	26	28	24	25	24	27	28	30	32	36	34	33	30	27	25	23	21
R.I.	1	2	2	2	2	2	2	2	2	2	2	2	2	3	2	2	2	2	2	2	2
S.C.	5	6	8	9	9	9	7	6	4	5	7	7	7	7	6	6	6	6	6	6	6
S.D.											2[4]	2	2	3	2	2	2	2	2	1	1
Tenn.		1[4]	3	6	9	13	11	10	8	10	10	10	10	10	9	10	9	9	8	9	9
Texas							2[4]	2	4	6	11	13	16	18	21	21	22	23	24	27	30
Utah												1[4]	1	2	2	2	2	2	2	3	3
Vt.		2	4	6	5	5	4	3	3	3	2	2	2	2	1	1	1	1	1	1	1
Va.	10	19	22	23	22	21	15	13	11	9	10	10	10	10	9	9	10	10	10	10	11
Wash.											1[4]	2	3	5	6	6	7	7	7	8	9
W.Va.										3	4	4	5	6	6	6	6	5	4	4	3
Wis.							2[4]	3	6	8	9	10	11	11	10	10	10	10	9	9	9
Wyo.											1[4]	1	1	1	1	1	1	1	1	1	1
Total	65	106	142	186	213	242	232	237	243	293	332	357	391	435	435	435	437[6]	435	435	435	435

1. Apportionment effective with congressional election two years after census.
2. Original apportionment made in Constitution, pending first census.
3. No apportionment was made in 1920.
4. These figures are not based on any census, but indicate the provisional representation accorded newly admitted states by Congress, pending the next census.
5. Twenty members were assigned to Massachusetts, but seven of these were credited to Maine when that area became a state.
6. Normally 435, but temporarily increased two seats by Congress when Alaska and Hawaii became states.

Sources: *Biographical Directory of the United States Congress 1774-1989;* Bureau of the Census.

beginning some states divided their territory into geographic districts, permitting only one member of Congress to be elected from each district.

But others allowed would-be House members to run at large, with voters able to cast as many votes as there were seats to be filled. Still other states created what were known as multimember districts, in which a single geographic unit would elect two or more members of the House. At various times, some states used combinations of these methods. For example, a state might elect 10 representatives from 10 individual districts and two at large.

In the first few elections to the House, New Hampshire, Pennsylvania, New Jersey and Georgia elected their representatives at large, as did Rhode Island and Delaware, the two states with only a single representative. Districts were used in Massachusetts, New York, Maryland, Virginia and South Carolina. In Connecticut a preliminary election was held to nominate three times as many people as the number of representatives to be chosen at large in the subsequent election. But a prevailing trend developed toward election of representatives by single-member districts. By 1840, 22 of the 31 states elected their representatives by districts. New Hampshire, New Jersey, Georgia, Alabama, Mississippi and Missouri, with a combined representation of 33 House seats, elected their representatives at large. Three states, Arkansas, Delaware and Florida, had only one representative each.

Those states that used congressional districts quickly developed what came to be known as the gerrymander. The term refers to the practice of drawing district lines so as to maximize the advantage of a political party or interest group. The name originated from a salamander-shaped congressional district created by the Massachusetts legislature in 1812 when Elbridge Gerry was governor. *(Origins of the Gerrymander, box, this page)*

Constant efforts were made during the early 1800s to lay down national rules, by means of a constitutional amendment, for congressional districting. The first resolution proposing a mandatory division of each state into districts was introduced in Congress in 1800. In 1802 the legislatures of Vermont and North Carolina adopted resolutions in support of such action. From 1816 to 1826, 22 states adopted resolutions proposing the election of representatives by districts.

In Congress Sen. Mahlon Dickerson, R-N. J., proposed such an amendment regularly almost every year from 1817 to 1826. It was adopted by the Senate three times, in 1819, 1820 and 1822, but each time it failed to reach a vote in the House. Although the constitutional amendment was unsuccessful, a law passed in 1842 required contiguous single-member congressional districts. That law required representatives to be "elected by districts composed of contiguous territory equal in number to the representatives to which said state may be entitled, no one district electing more than one Representative."

The districting provisions of the 1842 act were not repeated in the legislation that followed the 1850 census. But in 1862 an act separate from the reapportionment act revived the provisions of the act of 1842 requiring districts to be composed of contiguous territory.

The 1872 reapportionment act again repeated the districting provisions and went even further by adding that districts should contain "as nearly as practicable an equal number of inhabitants." Similar provisions were included in the acts of 1881 and 1891. In the act of 1901, the words "compact territory" were added, and the clause then read "contiguous

Origins of the Gerrymander

The practice of "gerrymandering" — the excessive manipulation of the shape of a legislative district to benefit a certain incumbent or party — is probably as old as the Republic, but the name originated in 1812.

In that year the Massachusetts Legislature carved out of Essex County a district which historian John Fiske said had a "dragonlike contour." When the painter Gilbert Stuart saw the misshapen district, he penciled in a head, wings, and claws and exclaimed: "That will do for a salamander!" — to which editor Benjamin Russell replied: "Better say a Gerrymander" — after Elbridge Gerry, then governor of Massachusetts.

and compact territory and containing as nearly as practicable an equal number of inhabitants." This requirement appeared also in the legislation of 1911. The "contiguous and compact" provisions of the act subsequently lapsed, and Congress has never replaced them.

Several unsuccessful attempts were made to enforce redistricting provisions. Despite the districting requirements enacted in 1842, New Hampshire, Georgia, Mississippi and Missouri elected their representatives at large that autumn. When the new House convened for its first session, on December 4, 1843, objection was made to seating the representatives of the four states.

The House debated the matter in February 1844. With the Democratic party holding a majority of more than 60, and with 18 of the 21 challenged members being Democrats, the House decided to seat the members. However, by 1848 all four states had come around to electing their representatives by districts.

The next challenge a representative encountered over federal districting laws occurred in 1901. A charge was leveled that the existing Kentucky redistricting law did not comply with the reapportionment law of 1901; the charge aimed at preventing the seating of Rep. George G. Gilbert, D, of Kentucky's 8th District. The committee assigned to investigate the matter turned aside the challenge, asserting that the federal act was not binding on the states. The reasons given were practical and political:

> Your committee are therefore of opinion that a proper construction of the Constitution does not warrant the conclusion that by that instrument Congress is clothed with power to determine the boundaries of Congressional districts, or to revise the acts of a State Legislature in fixing such boundaries; and your committee is further of opinion that even if such power is to be implied from the language of the Constitution, it would be in the last degree unwise and intolerable that it should exercise it. To do so would be to put into the hands of Congress the ability to disfranchise, in effect, a large body of the electors. It would give Congress the power to apply to all the States, in favor of one party, a general system of gerrymandering. It is true that the same method is to a large degree resorted to by the several states, but the division of political power is so general and diverse that notwithstanding the inherent vice of the system of gerrymandering, some kind of equality of distribution results.[12]

In 1908 the Virginia legislature transferred Floyd County from the 5th District to the 6th District. As a result, the population of the 5th was reduced from 175,579 to 160,191 and that of the 6th was increased from 181,571 to 196,959. The average for the state was 185,418. The newly elected representative from the 5th District, Edward W. Saunders, D, was challenged by his opponent in the election on the ground that the Virginia law of 1908 was null and void because it did not conform with the federal reapportionment law of 1901, or with the constitution of Virginia. Had the district included the counties that were a part of it before enactment of the 1908 state legislation, Saunders's opponent would have had a majority of the votes.

The majority of the congressional investigating committee upheld the challenge and recommended that Saunders's opponent be seated. For the first time, it appeared that the districting legislation would be enforced, but the House did not take action on the committee's report and Saunders was seated.

Court Action on Redistricting

After the long and desultory battle over reapportionment in the 1920s, those who were unhappy over the inaction of Congress and the state legislatures began taking their cases to court. At first, the protesters had no luck. But as the population disparities grew in both federal and state legislative districts and the Supreme Court began to show a tendency to intervene, the objectors were more successful.

Finally, in a series of decisions beginning in 1962 with *Baker v. Carr* (369 U.S. 186), the Court exerted great influence over the redistricting process, ordering that congressional districts as well as state and local legislative districts be drawn so that their populations would be as nearly equal as possible.[13]

Supreme Court's 1932 Decision

Baker v. Carr essentially reversed the direction the Court had taken in 1932. *Wood v. Broom* (287 U.S. 1) was a case challenging the constitutionality of a Mississippi redistricting law because it violated the standards of the 1911 federal redistricting act. The question was whether the federal act was still in effect. That law, which required that districts be separate, compact, contiguous and equally populated, had been neither specifically repealed nor reaffirmed in the 1929 reapportionment act.

Speaking for the Court, Chief Justice Charles Evans Hughes ruled that the 1911 act, in effect, had expired with the approval of the 1929 apportionment act and that the standards of the 1911 act therefore were no longer applicable. The Court reversed the decision of a lower federal court, which had permanently enjoined elections under the new Mississippi redistricting act.

'Political Thicket'

Not until 1946, in *Colegrove v. Green* (328 U.S. 549), did the Court again rule in a significant case dealing with congressional redistricting. The case was brought by Kenneth Colegrove, a political science professor at Northwestern University, who alleged that congressional districts in Illinois, which varied between 112,116 and 914,053 in population, were so unequal that they violated the 14th Amendment's guarantee of equal protection of the laws. A seven-member Supreme Court divided 4-3 in dismissing the suit.

Justice Felix Frankfurter gave the opinion of the Court, speaking for himself and Justices Stanley F. Reed and Harold H. Burton. Frankfurter's opinion cited *Wood v. Broom* to indicate that Congress had deliberately removed the standard set by the 1911 act. He also said that he, Reed, and Burton agreed with the minority that the Court should have dismissed the case. The issue, Frankfurter said, was

> of a peculiarly political nature and therefore not meant for judicial interpretation.... The short of it is that the Constitution has conferred upon Congress exclusive authority to secure fair representation by the states in the popular House and has left to that House determination whether states have fulfilled their responsibility. If Congress failed in exercising its powers, whereby standards of fairness are offended, the remedy lies ultimately with the people.... To sustain this action would cut very deep into the very being of Congress. Courts ought not to enter this political thicket. The remedy for unfairness in districting is to secure state legislatures that will apportion properly, or to invoke the ample powers of Congress.

Frankfurter also said that the Court could not affirmatively remap congressional districts and that elections at large would be politically undesirable.

In a dissenting opinion Justice Hugo L. Black, joined by Justices William O. Douglas and Frank Murphy, maintained that the district court did have jurisdiction over congressional redistricting. The three justices cited as evidence a section of the U.S. Code that allowed district courts to redress deprivations of constitutional rights occurring through action of the states. Black's opinion also rested on an earlier case in which the Court had indicated that federal constitutional questions, unless "frivolous," fall under the jurisdiction of the federal courts. Black asserted that the appellants had standing to sue and that the population disparities violated the equal protection clause of the 14th Amendment.

Changing Views

In the ensuing years, law professors, political scientists and other commentators increasingly criticized the *Colegrove* doctrine and grew impatient with the Supreme Court's reluctance to intervene in redistricting disputes. At the same time, the membership of the Court was changing, and the new members were more inclined toward judicial action on redistricting.

In the 1950s the Court decided two cases that laid some groundwork for its subsequent reapportionment decisions. The first was *Brown v. Board of Education* (347 U.S. 483, 1954), the historic school desegregation case, in which the Court decided that an individual citizen could assert a right to equal protection of the laws under the 14th Amendment, contrary to the "separate but equal" doctrine of public facilities for white and black citizens. Six years later, in *Gomillion v. Lightfoot* (364 U.S. 339, 1960), the Court held that the Alabama legislature could not draw the city limits of Tuskegee so as to exclude nearly every black vote. In his opinion Justice Frankfurter drew a clear line between redistricting challenges based on the 14th Amendment, such as *Colegrove*, and challenges to discriminatory redistricting based on the 15th Amendment's voting rights protections, as in *Gomillion*. But Justice Charles E. Whittaker said that the equal protection clause was the proper constitutional basis for the decision. One commentator later remarked that *Gomillion* amounted to a "dragon" in the "political thicket" of *Colegrove*.

By 1962 only three members of the *Colegrove* Court remained: Justices Black and Douglas, dissenters in that case, and Justice Frankfurter, aging spokesman for restraint in the exercise of judicial power.

By then it was clear that malapportionment within the states no longer could be ignored. By 1960 not a single state legislative body existed in which there was not at least a 2-to-1 population disparity between the most and the least heavily populated districts. For example, the disparity was 242-1 in the Connecticut House, 223-1 in the Nevada Senate 141-1 in the Rhode Island Senate and 9-1 in the Georgia Senate. Studies of the effective vote of large and small counties in state legislatures between 1910 and 1960 showed that the effective vote of the most populous counties had slipped while their percentage of the national population had more than doubled. The most lightly populated counties, on the other hand, advanced from a position of slight overrepresentation to one of extreme overrepresentation, holding almost twice as many seats as they would be entitled to by population size alone. Predictably, the rural-dominated state legislatures resisted every move toward reapportioning state legislative districts to reflect new population patterns.

Population imbalance among congressional districts was substantially lopsided but by no means so gross. In Texas the 1960 census showed the most heavily populated district had four times as many inhabitants as the most lightly populated. Arizona, Maryland and Ohio each had at least one district with three times as many inhabitants as the least populated. In most cases rural areas benefited from the population imbalance in congressional districts. As a result of the postwar population movement out of central cities to the surrounding areas, the suburbs were the most underrepresented.

Baker v. Carr

Against this background a group of Tennessee city dwellers successfully broke the longstanding precedent against federal court involvement in legislative apportionment problems. For more than half a century, since 1901, the Tennessee legislature had refused to reapportion itself, even though a decennial reapportionment based on population was specifically required by the state's constitution. In the meantime, Tennessee's population had grown and shifted dramatically to urban areas. By 1960 the House legislative districts ranged from 3,454 to 36,031 in population, while the Senate districts ranged from 39,727 to 108,094. Appeals by urban residents to the rural-controlled Tennessee legislature proved fruitless. A suit brought in the state courts to force reapportionment was rejected on grounds that the courts should stay out of legislative matters.

City dwellers then appealed to the federal courts, stating that they had no redress: the legislature had refused to act for more than half a century, the state courts had refused to intervene and Tennessee had no referendum or initiative laws. They charged that there was "a debasement of their votes by virtue of the incorrect, obsolete and unconstitutional apportionment" to such an extent that they were being deprived of their right to equal protection of the laws under the 14th Amendment.

The Supreme Court on March 26, 1962, handed down its historic decision in *Baker v. Carr*, ruling in favor of the Tennessee city dwellers by a 6-2 margin. In the majority opinion, Justice William J. Brennan Jr., emphasized that the federal judiciary had the power to review the apportionment of state legislatures under the 14th Amendment's equal protection clause. "The mere fact that a suit seeks protection as a political right," Brennan wrote, "does not mean that it presents a political question" that the courts should avoid.

In a vigorous dissent, Justice Frankfurter said the majority decision constituted "a massive repudiation of the experience of our whole past" and was an assertion of "destructively novel judicial power." He contended that the lack of any clear basis for relief "catapults the lower courts" into a "mathematical quagmire." Frankfurter insisted that "there is not under our Constitution a judicial remedy for every political mischief." Appeal for relief, Frankfurter maintained, should not be made in the courts, but "to an informed civically militant electorate."

The Court had abandoned the view that malapportionment questions were outside its competence. But it stopped there and in *Baker v. Carr* did not address the merits of the challenge to the legislative districts.

Gray v. Sanders

The one-person, one-vote rule was set out by the Court almost exactly one year after its decision in *Baker v. Carr*. But the case in which the announcement came did not involve congressional districts.

In *Gray v. Sanders* (372 U.S. 368, 1963) the Court found that Georgia's county-unit primary system for electing state officials—a system that weighted votes to give advantage to rural districts in statewide primary elections—denied voters equal protection of the laws. All votes in a statewide election must have equal weight, the Court held:

> How then can one person be given twice or 10 times the voting power of another person in a statewide election merely because he lives in a rural area or because he lives in the smallest rural county? Once the geographical unit for which a representative is to be chosen is designated, all who participate in the election are to have an equal vote— whatever their race, whatever their sex, whatever their occupation, whatever their income, and wherever their home may be in that geographical unit. This is required by the Equal Protection Clause of the Fourteenth Amendment. The concept of "we the people" under the Constitution visualizes no preferred class of voters but equality among those who meet the basic qualification. The idea that every voter is equal to every other voter in his State, when he casts his ballot in favor of one of several competing candidates, underlies many of our decisions.... The conception of political equality from the Declaration of Independence to Lincoln's Gettysburg Address, to the Fif-

Gerrymandering:
The Shape of the House

Traditionally, there are two types of gerrymanders. One is the partisan gerrymander, where a single party draws the lines to its advantage. The other is the proincumbent (sometimes called the "bipartisan" or "sweetheart") gerrymander, where the lines are drawn to protect incumbents, with any gains or losses in the number of seats shared between the two parties. In states where control of the state government is divided, proincumbent gerrymanders are common.

In the eyes of some Republicans, either species of gerrymander was likely to ensure their continued minority status in the House. Democrats, who have controlled the House since 1955, countered that the GOP suffered from unattractive candidates, not gerrymandered districts. The 1990 reapportionment saw widespread examples of a third type of gerrymander: drawing lines to preserve or create minority districts.

Indeed, some academics maintain that the extent of gerrymandering and its impact on the composition of the House are exaggerated. "To a large extent," said Everett C. Ladd, the director of the Roper Center for Public Opinion at the University of Connecticut, "the population is voting without regard to party. So the precise location of the congressional district lines is not so important as it was in an earlier era."

Partisan gerrymanders do not always achieve their goals. Republican legislators in Indiana redrew their map in 1981 with the hope that it would turn the Democrats' congressional majority into a 7-3 GOP edge. Instead, by the end of the decade Democrats held a 7-3 advantage.

Given the extremely high incumbent reelection rates that have prevailed since the end of World War II, redistricting does increase the possibility of turnover, because most states must redraw their districts to accommodate population shifts within the state as well as the gain or loss of any seats. Typically, some members of the House of Representatives choose to retire rather than stand for election in redesigned districts. But with rare exceptions a proincumbent spin in much of the line drawing diminishes the prospects for dramatic partisan turnover.

Sweetheart gerrymandering rarely attracts much attention. But this method of mapping has a powerful effect on the House. "Districts get more Democratic for Democrats and more Republican for Republicans. Competition is minimized," said Bernard Grofman, a political scientist at the University of California at Irvine. "Because the majority of House seats are controlled by Democrats, proincumbent line drawing helps perpetuate the Democratic House majority."

---

teenth, Seventeenth, and Nineteenth Amendments can mean only one thing—one person, one vote.

The Rule Applied

The Court's rulings in *Baker* and *Gray* concerned the equal weighting and counting of votes cast in state elections. In 1964, deciding the case of *Wesberry v. Sanders*, the Court applied the one-person, one-vote principle to congressional districts and set equality as the standard for congressional redistricting.

Shortly after the *Baker* decision was handed down, James P. Wesberry Jr., an Atlanta resident and a member of the Georgia Senate, filed suit in federal court in Atlanta claiming that gross disparity in the population of Georgia's congressional districts violated 14th Amendment rights of equal protection of the laws. At the time, Georgia districts ranged in population from 272,154 in the rural 9th District in the northeastern part of the state to 823,860 in the 5th District in Atlanta and its suburbs. District lines had not been changed since 1931. The state's number of House seats remained the same in the interim, but Atlanta's district population—already high in 1931 compared with the others—had more than doubled in 30 years, making a 5th District vote worth about one-third that of a vote in the 9th District.

In June 1962 the three-judge federal court divided 2-1 in dismissing Wesberry's suit. The majority reasoned that the precedent of *Colegrove* still controlled in congressional district cases. The judges cautioned against federal judicial interference with Congress and against "depriving others of

the right to vote" if the suit should result in at-large elections. They suggested that the Georgia legislature (under court order to reapportion itself) or the U.S. Congress might better provide relief. Wesberry then appealed to the Supreme Court.

On Feb. 17, 1964, the Supreme Court ruled in *Wesberry v. Sanders* (376 U.S. 1) that congressional districts must be substantially equal in population. The Court, which upheld Wesberry's challenge by a 6-3 decision, based its ruling on the history and wording of Article I, Section 2, of the Constitution, which states that representatives shall be apportioned among the states according to their respective numbers and be chosen by the people of the several states. This language, the Court stated, meant that "as nearly as is practicable, one man's vote in a congressional election is to be worth as much as another's."

The majority opinion, written by Justice Black and supported by Chief Justice Earl Warren and Justices Brennan, Douglas, Arthur J. Goldberg and Byron R. White, said: "While it may not be possible to draw congressional districts with mathematical precision, that is no excuse for ignoring our Constitution's plain objective of making equal representation for equal numbers of people the fundamental goal for the House of Representatives."

In a strongly worded dissent, Justice John M. Harlan asserted that the Constitution did not establish population as the only criterion of congressional districting but left the subject to the discretion of the states, subject only to the supervisory power of Congress. "The constitutional right which the Court creates is manufactured out of whole cloth," Harlan concluded.

The *Wesberry* opinion established no precise standards for districting beyond declaring that districts must be as nearly equal in population "as is practicable." In his dissent Harlan suggested that a disparity of more than 100,000 between a state's largest and smallest districts would "presumably" violate the equality standard enunciated by the majority. On that basis, Harlan estimated, the districts of 37 states with 398 representatives would be unconstitutional, "leaving a constitutional House of 37 members now sitting."

Neither did the Court's decision make any reference to gerrymandering, since it discussed only the population, not the shape of districts. In a separate opinion handed down the same day as *Wesberry*, the Court dismissed a challenge to congressional districts in New York City, which had been brought by voters who charged that Manhattan's "silk-stocking" 17th District had been gerrymandered to exclude blacks and Puerto Ricans.

Strict Equality

Five years elapsed between *Wesberry v. Sanders* and the Court's next application of constitutional standards to congressional districting. In 1967 the Court hinted at the strict stance it would adopt two years later. With two unsigned opinions, the Court sent back to Indiana and Missouri for revision those two states' congressional redistricting plans because they allowed variations of as much as 20 percent from the average district population.

Two years later Missouri's revised plan returned to the Court for full review. By a 6-3 vote, the Court rejected the plan. It was unacceptable, the Court held in *Kirkpatrick v. Preisler* (385 U.S. 450, 1969), because it allowed a variation of as much as 3.1 percent from perfectly equal population districts. Thus the Court made clear its stringent application of the one-person, one-vote rule to congressional districts.

There was no "fixed numerical or percentage population variance small enough to be considered *de minimis* and to satisfy without question the 'as nearly as practicable' standard," Justice Brennan wrote for the Court in 1969. "Equal representation for equal numbers of people is a principle designed to prevent debasement of voting power and diminution of access to elected Representatives. Toleration of even small deviations detracts from these purposes."

The only permissible variances in population, the Court ruled, were those that were unavoidable despite the effort to achieve absolute equality or those that could be legally justified. The variances in Missouri could have been avoided, the Court said.

None of Missouri's arguments for the plan qualified as "legally acceptable" justifications. The Court rejected the argument that population variance was necessary to allow representation of distinct interest groups. It said that acceptance of such variances to produce districts with specific interests was "antithetical" to the basic purpose of equal representation.

Justice White dissented from the majority opinion, which he characterized as "an unduly rigid and unwarranted application of the Equal Protection Clause which will unnecessarily involve the courts in the abrasive task of drawing district lines." White added that some "acceptably small" population variance could be established. He indicated that considerations of existing political boundaries and geographical compactness could justify to him some variation from "absolute equality" of population.

Justice Harlan, joined by Justice Potter Stewart, dissented, saying that "whatever room remained under this Court's prior decisions for the free play of the political process in matters of reapportionment is now all but eliminated by today's Draconian judgments."

Practical Results

As a result of the Court's decisions of the 1960s, nearly every state was forced to redraw its congressional district lines—sometimes more than once. By the end of the decade, 39 of the 45 states with more than one representative had made the necessary adjustments.

Furthermore, redistricting based on the 1970 census resulted in districts that differed only slightly in population from the state average. Among House members elected in 1972, 385 of 435 represented districts that varied by less than 1 percent from the state average district population.

By contrast, only nine of the districts in the Congress elected in 1962 deviated less than 1 percent from the state average; 81 were between 1 and 5 percent; 87 from 5 to 10 percent; and in 236 districts the deviation was 10 percent or greater. Twenty-two House members were elected at large.

The Supreme Court made only one major ruling concerning congressional districts during the 1970s. In 1973 the Court declared the Texas congressional districts, as redrawn in 1971, unconstitutional because of excessive population variance among districts. The variance between the largest and smallest districts was 4.9872 percent. The Court returned the case to a three-judge federal panel, which adopted a new congressional district plan.

Precise Equality

Following the 1980 census, the Supreme Court went further and ruled that one person, one vote meant precise equality. In a 5-4 decision in 1983, the Court ruled in *Karcher v. Daggett* (462 U.S. 725) that states must adhere as closely as possible to the one-person, one-vote standard and bear the burden of proving that deviations from precise population equality were made in pursuit of a legitimate goal. The decision overturned New Jersey's congressional map because the variation between the most populated and the least populated districts was 0.69 percent.

Brennan, who wrote the Court's opinion in *Baker* and *Kirkpatrick*, also wrote the opinion in *Karcher*, contending that population differences between districts "could have been avoided or significantly reduced with a good-faith effort to achieve population equality."

"Adopting any standard other than population equality, using the best census data available, would subtly erode the Constitution's ideal of equal representation," Brennan wrote. "In this case, appellants argue that a maximum deviation of approximately 0.7 percent should be considered *de minimis*. If we accept that argument, how are we to regard deviations of 0.8 percent, 0.95 percent, 1.0 percent or 1.1 percent? . . . To accept the legitimacy of unjustified, though small population deviations in this case would mean to reject the basic premise of *Kirkpatrick* and *Wesberry*."

Brennan said that "any number of consistently applied legislative policies might justify" some population variation. These included "making districts compact, respecting municipal boundaries, preserving the cores of prior districts, and avoiding contests between incumbent Representatives." However, he cautioned, the state must show "with some specificity that a particular objective required the specific deviations in its plan, rather than simply relying on general assertions."

In his dissent Justice White criticized the majority for its "unreasonable insistence on an unattainable perfection in the equalizing of congressional districts." He warned that the decision would invite "further litigation of virtually every congressional redistricting plan in the nation."

As a result of the *Karcher* decision, most states came very close to precise equality after the 1990 census. Texas, for example, gave all 30 of its districts the exact same population: 566,217. But this Texas plan became involved in another redistricting issue of the 1990s: it tortured the shape of its districts, dividing communities, in order to maximize the number of black and Hispanic representatives. (*"Minority Representation," below*)

Partisan Gerrymandering

In *Karcher* the Court did not address the underlying political issue in the New Jersey case, which was that its map had been drawn to serve Democratic partisan interests.

Following the 1980 census, House Democratic leaders, led by Rep. Philip Burton of California, realized that they could gerrymander districts for partisan advantage so long as they created new districts with precisely equal population. Burton helped Democratic legislators to redistrict in several states.

In Missouri, a federal court accepted the Democrats' proposal over the Republican plan because its districts were more equal in population. The Democrats succeeded in dismantling a Republican district in a part of the state where population was growing, while preserving an inner-city Democratic district in St. Louis that was losing population. The plan cost a Republican incumbent his seat.

The Democrats gave the disallowed New Jersey plan some of the most oddly shaped districts in the country. One constituency, known as the "fishhook" by its detractors, twisted through central New Jersey's industrial landscape, picking up Democratic voters along the way. Another stretched from the suburbs of New York to the fringes of Trenton. The revised plan, which met the Court's new standard of precise equality, was almost as blatantly partisan.

But Burton's masterpiece was drawn in his home state of California. Widely recognized as a classic example of a partisan gerrymander, the map featured a number of oddly shaped districts, drawn neither compactly nor with respect to community boundaries, but all with nearly equal populations. As one commentator described it, "Burton carefully stretched districts from one Democratic enclave to another—sometimes joining them with nothing but a bridge, a stretch of harbor, or a spit of land. . . .—avoiding Republicans block for block and household for household."[14] Before the 1982 elections, Democrats held 22 congressional districts, Republicans 21. With the Burton map in place for the 1982 elections, Democrats won 28 seats, Republicans only 17 (reapportionment had given California two additional seats after the 1980 census). Political analysts estimated that gerrymandering accounted for 9 or 10 of the 26 House seats the Democrats gained nationally that year.

Republican Rep. Robert E. Badham filed a lawsuit against the Burton plan in federal district court in 1983. In the wake of statements by Supreme Court Justices that they would hear challenges to gerrymandering, the district court held a hearing on *Badham v. Eu* but dismissed the Republican complaint by a 2-1 vote. The court in essence ruled that a party seeking to overturn a gerrymandered map must show a general pattern of exclusion from the political process, which the California Republican party, in control of the governorship, a Senate seat, and 40 percent of the House

seats, could not do. The Republicans appealed to the Supreme Court, but the Court refused to become involved, voting 6-3 in 1989 to reaffirm the lower court's decision without comment.

And, in what appears to be its current definitive word on the constitutionality of partisan gerrymandering, the Court in December 1996 let stand a lower court ruling that redistricting is a political process, and that legislatures may draw districts to protect incumbents, or to give one party an advantage (*Miller v. Ohio*).

Minority Representation

There is, however, one form of gerrymandering expressly forbidden by law: redistricting for the purpose of racial discrimination. The Voting Rights Act of 1965, extended in 1970, 1975 and 1982, banned redistricting that diluted the voting strength of black communities. Other minorities, including Hispanics, Asian Americans, Native Americans and native Alaskans, subsequently were brought under the protection of the law.

In 1980 the Supreme Court for the first time narrowed the reach of the Voting Rights Act in the case of *Mobile v. Bolden*, a challenge to the at-large system of electing city commissioners used in Mobile, Alabama.[15] By a vote of 6-3, the Court ruled that proof of discriminatory intent by the commissioners was necessary before a violation could be found; the fact that no black had ever been elected under the challenged system was not proof enough.

The *Mobile* decision set off an immediate reaction on Capitol Hill. In extending the Voting Rights Act in 1982, Congress amended it to outlaw any practice that has the effect of discriminating against blacks or other minorities—regardless of the lawmakers' intent.

Based on the 1982 amendments, the Justice Department later adopted a "results test" for another part of the act (Section 5), which requires certain states and localities with a history of discrimination to have their electoral plans "precleared" by the department. In 1986 the Supreme Court applied this test in *Thornburg v. Gingles* (478 U.S. 30), ruling that six of North Carolina's multimember legislative districts impermissibly diluted black voting strength. Sharply departing from *Mobile*, the Court held that since very few blacks had been elected from these districts, the system must be in violation of the law.

Thus, within a period of six years, the burden of proof was shifted from minorities, who had been required to show that lines were being drawn to dilute their voting strength, to lawmakers, who had to show that they had done all they could to maximize minority voting strength.

Another important ruling came in 1989, when a special three-judge federal panel ordered Arkansas to redraw its state legislative districts to create almost as many black majority districts as was mathematically possible. The *Jeffers v. Clinton* decision was left intact by the Supreme Court, which declined to hear the case.

Further, in 1990, a federal district judge ruled in *Garza v. County of Los Angeles* that the Los Angeles County Board of Supervisors had violated the Voting Rights Act by gerrymandering its districts to dilute the Hispanic vote. The judge ordered the creation of a majority-Hispanic district.

In the 1990s round of redistricting, for the first time, states operated under federal legal mandates to draw lines that maximized the number of "majority-minority" districts—constituencies where blacks and Hispanics made up a majority of the population. Redistricting experts also argued about how to draw lines in areas where the minority population was sizable but not large or compact enough to make up a majority in a new district.

In the first lower court ruling on this matter, a three-judge panel in *Armour v. Ohio* ordered the pooling of blacks in the Youngstown area into a state House district whose population would be one-third black. The court said that minority voters then would have "the ability to elect the candidate of their choice"—though not necessarily a black candidate. In *Turner v. Arkansas*, a three-judge panel ruled against black and Republican plaintiffs who wanted Arkansas to create a 42 percent black minority-influenced district, maintaining that the criteria established in *Thornburg* required only the creation of majority-minority districts. After the 1990 census, Republicans joined with black groups and worked with the Justice Department to concentrate black voters in racially gerrymandered districts so that more blacks—and more Republicans—could be elected to Congress in the 1990s.

Redistricting efforts in the 1990s that went too far in expanding the Voting Rights Act's 1982 amendments came quickly under scrutiny by the Supreme Court. On June 28, 1993, the Court in *Shaw v. Reno*, invited a new round of lawsuits challenging the constitutionality of districts drawn to ensure the election of minorities. Its 5-4 ruling, the Court reinstated a suit by five white North Carolinians who contended that the state's congressional district map, which created in 1992 two sinuous majority-black districts, violated their 14th Amendment right to "equal protection under law." While the Court did not immediately invalidate North Carolina's map or rule in favor of the plaintiffs' complaint, it did give legal standing to challenges to any congressional map with an oddly shaped majority-minority district that may not be defensible on grounds other than race.

In her majority opinion, Justice Sandra Day O'Connor decried the creation of districts based solely on racial composition. She wrote, "[W]e believe that reapportionment is one area in which appearances do matter. A reapportionment plan that includes in one district individuals . . . who may have little in common with one another but the color of their skin bears an uncomfortable resemblance to political apartheid." O'Connor's opinion was regarded as signaling dissatisfaction with the broad interpretation of the Voting Rights Act's mandate, as expressed in *Thornburg*, for states to create minority districts wherever possible.

Two years after *Shaw*, in June 1995, the Supreme Court reinforced and more clearly defined its earlier ruling. In another 5-4 decision, the Court in *Miller v. Johnson* struck down a Georgia redistricting plan that created three black-majority districts, including one that joined two black communities 260 miles apart.

In his majority opinion for the Court, Justice Anthony M. Kennedy agreed with Justice O'Connor in *Shaw*, saying that government "may not separate its citizens into different voting districts on the basis of race." The use of race as "the predominant factor" in drawing voting districts is presumed to be unconstitutional, he wrote, unless it serves a compelling government interest and is narrowly tailored to further that goal. Georgia's plan did not serve such an interest, Kennedy wrote, because the Justice Department had abused its authority, had misinterpreted the Voting Rights Act, and thus had improperly forced Georgia to maximize the number of its minority-dominant districts.[16]

As a result of *Miller v. Johnson*, the tide of affirmative U.S. government action to maximize minority representation in the House receded for the moment. (The logical impossibility of trying to achieve proportional results with single-member districts was never prominently discussed.) In fact, the pendulum swung quickly in the opposite direction as the constitutionality of majority-minority districts was challenged in many states. Federal courts, using the criteria established by the Supreme Court, ordered several states to redraw unconstitutional districts that were racially gerrymandered.

Florida, Louisiana, Texas and Georgia redrew their majority-minority districts in time for the 1996 elections. Although the proportion of minorities dropped below a majority in these districts, the black and Hispanic incumbents were reelected, thus showing that they could survive without a majority constituency. (Georgia had become the most striking example of what blacks and Republicans wanted to accomplish: Georgia had three black Democrats and eight white Republicans—all of whom were re-elected in 1996.)

In February 1997 Virginia was ordered to redraw a black-dominated district in Richmond for the 1998 elections. In March 1997 North Carolina redistricted (after the Supreme Court reheard *Shaw* and finally struck down the state's redistricting plan in June 1996). In August 1997 New York redrew its convoluted Hispanic-majority 12th district that had joined widely separated Hispanic neighborhoods in New York City. With the new map—that necessitated also redrawing five neighboring congressional districts—the Hispanic population of the 12th district dropped from 58 percent to 45 percent. By September 1997 there were also pending challenges to majority-minority districts in South Carolina and Illinois. (The state of Illinois, admitting that ethnicity was the predominant factor in drawing its Hispanic-dominated district in Chicago, asserted its belief in a legitimate "compelling state interest" in giving its large Hispanic population the opportunity to elect one representative of its own.)

It is too early to say whether the issue of race and redistricting will linger beyond the 2000 census, or will decline in importance, as the issue of precise equality of population seems to have done.

Congress and Redistricting

Critics of judicial activism in forcing redistricting forget that Congress could have re-established guidelines for creating districts that are relatively equal in population, relatively compact in shape, and respectful of communities and neighborhoods, but chose not to do so despite growing public restiveness after World War II.

In January 1951 President Harry S. Truman asked for a ban on gerrymandering, an end to at-large seats in states having more than one representative, and a sharp reduction in the huge differences in size among congressional districts within most states. On behalf of the administration, Emanuel Celler, D-N. Y., chairman of the House Judiciary Committee, introduced a bill reflecting these requests, but the committee took no action.

Celler regularly introduced his bill throughout the 1950s and early 1960s, but it made no headway until the Supreme Court handed down the *Wesberry* decision in 1964. The House passed a version of the Celler bill in 1965, largely to discourage the Supreme Court from imposing even more rigid criteria. The Senate, however, took no action, citing the lateness of the hour, and the measure died. It was later, after this repeated failure to act, that the Supreme Court required precise equality of population.

In 1967, after defeating a conference report that would have prevented the courts from ordering a state to redistrict or to hold at-large elections until after the 1970 census, Congress finally approved a measure to ban at-large elections in all states entitled to more than one representative. It was the only redistricting measure passed by Congress since 1940. Exceptions were made for New Mexico and Hawaii, which had a tradition of electing their representatives at large—without any ethnic or racial implications. Both states, however, soon passed districting laws, New Mexico for the 1968 elections and Hawaii for 1970. Thus 1970 marks the first time that every member of the House was elected from a single-member district (including those states with only one member).

Bills to increase the size of the House to prevent states from losing seats as a result of population shifts have been introduced after most censuses, but Congress has given little consideration to any of them since the reapportionment stalemate of the 1920s. Except for temporary increases after Alaska and Hawaii became states, the number of representatives has remained 435 since the election of 1912.

Notes

1. Ronald D. Elving, "Redistricting: Drawing Power with a Map," *Editorial Research Reports*, February 15, 1991, 99.

2. Robert Luce, *Legislative Principles* (New York: Houghton Mifflin, 1930; New York: DaCapo Press, 1971), 342.

3. Thomas Jefferson, *The Portable Thomas Jefferson*, ed. Merrill D. Peterson, part 3, *Notes on the State of Virginia* (New York: Viking, 1965), 163.

4. Andrew Hacker, *Congressional Districting: The Issue of Equal Representation*, rev. ed. (Washington, D. C.: Brookings, 1964), 6-7.

5. Max Farrand, ed., *The Records of the Federal Convention of 1787*, vol. 2 (New Haven, Conn.: Yale University Press, 1911, 1966), 241.

6. *The Federalist Papers*, with an introduction by Clinton Rossiter (New York: New American Library, 1961), 347-348, 354.

7. Quoted in Laurence F. Schmeckebier, *Congressional Apportionment* (Washington, D. C.: Brookings, 1941), 131.

8. Hacker, *Congressional Districting*, 14.

9. Quoted in Schmeckebier, *Congressional Apportionment*, 113.

10. Zechariah Chafee Jr., "Congressional Reapportionment," *Harvard Law Review* (1929): 1015-1047.

11. Jefferson, *Notes on the State of Virginia*, 217.

12. Quoted in Schmeckebier, *Congressional Apportionment*, 137.

13. The following summary is based on *Congressional Quarterly's Guide to the U.S. Supreme Court*, 3rd ed. Vol. I. (Washington, D. C.: Congressional Quarterly, 1996), 519-531.

14. Elving, "Redistricting," 107.

15. The discussion of minority representation is based on Rhodes Cook, "Map-Drawers Must Toe the Line in Upcoming Redistricting," *Congressional Quarterly Weekly Report*, September 1, 1990, 2786-2793.

16. Holly Idelson, "Court Takes a Harder Line on Minority Voting Blocs," *Congressional Quarterly Weekly Report*, July 1, 1995, 1944-1946.

House Popular Vote Returns, 1946-1996

Sources for House Popular Returns

The popular election returns for the House of Representatives presented in this section *(pp. 192-324)* for the years 1946-1972 were obtained from the Inter-University Consortium for Political and Social Research (ICPSR) at the University of Michigan. Major sources for returns since 1973 were Congressional Quarterly, which obtained them from the state secretaries of state, and the *America Votes* series: Richard M. Scammon and Alice V. McGillivray, vols. 11-21 (Washington, D.C.: Congressional Quarterly, 1975-1995) and Rhodes Cook and Alice V. McGillivray, vol. 22 (Washington, D.C.: Congressional Quarterly, 1997).

The symbol # next to returns before 1974 indicates that Congressional Quarterly obtained the returns from a source other than the ICPSR. A complete set of other sources used appears on page 325. A "House Candidates Index" is located on pages 340-371.

Presentation of Returns

The House returns are arranged chronologically by year and alphabetically by state for each year. Within each state, single-member districts are listed first in numerical order. At-large seats appear at the end of the single-member districts with "AL" in the district identification column.

Special election results appear after all general election returns for each state under a separate "Special Elections" heading. Returns for special off-year elections are listed at the end of the preceding year's general election returns.

Names and Party Designations

Candidate names appear to the right of the district number, with the candidate receiving the highest number of votes listed first. Other candidates who received *at least 5 percent* of the total votes cast are listed in descending order.

In the ICPSR returns, the distinct—and in many cases, *multiple*—party designations appearing in the original sources are preserved. In many cases party labels represent combinations of multi-party support received by individual candidates. If, for example, on the ballot and official returns more than one party name was listed next to a candidate's name, then the party designation appearing in the election returns for that candidate will be a unique abbreviation for that combination of parties. *(For a list of party abbreviations, see p. 191.)*

In the special case of a candidate's name listed separately on the original ballot under more than one party—where returns were reported *separately* for each party—Congressional Quarterly has summed the votes recorded under the several parties and that figure appears as the candidate's total vote. Whenever separate party totals have been summed, a *comma* separates the abbreviations of the parties contributing the largest and second largest share of the total vote.

Most cases of this special situation occurred in New York and Pennsylvania during this century. For example, in the original ICPSR returns for the House election in New York's 25th District in 1972, Hamilton Fish Jr. received votes from being the Republican Party candidate and from being the Conservative Party candidate. Congressional Quarterly summed all votes (144,386) received by Fish from these two parties *(p. 264)*.

Congressional Quarterly indicated the two parties that contributed the votes to Fish's total—separated by a comma. Thus, immediately following his name appear the abbreviations (R, C), indicating that Fish was a candidate of two or more parties and that he received most votes as a Republican.

Vote Totals and Percentages

Each candidate's total vote and percentage of the total vote cast for all candidates appear in columns to the right of the candidate's name and party designation. Percentages have been calculated to two decimal places and rounded to one place. For example, in the 1972 New York election cited above, the percentage listed for Fish is 71.6 and for his opponent, John M. Burns III, is 26.9. Returns for the other minor candidates are not listed because they received less than 5 percent of the total vote. Due to rounding and the scattered votes of minor candidates, percentages in individual House races may not add up to 100.

If no vote total is shown for a candidate but the percentage listed is 100 percent, in most cases the candidate ran unopposed. State election officials either did not put the candidate's name on the ballot or simply did not make an effort to record the total number of votes.

In some cases, percentages do not appear next to candidates in single-member districts because vote totals for all the candidates who ran in the district were not available even though the names of all candidates may appear. In such cases, the symbol appears in the vote column of the winning candidate.

Explanation of Symbols in House Returns

In the returns for House elections *symbols* are used to denote special circumstances. In cases where no symbol is used, the candidate who received the most votes won the election to the House. The following is a key to the symbols used:

✔ Elected to the House. The symbol is used to identify winning candidates in three types of situations: (1) When candidates ran for two or more at-large seats in states which chose all of their at-large representatives in a single election; (2) when the vote total and percentage of one or more of the candidates are unavailable; and (3) when a candidate who did not receive the highest vote total was seated by the House.

‡ The symbol is used when an election dispute resulted in the unseating of a representative *after* he was sworn in. (*For discussion of specific cases, consult* the Biographical Directory of the United States Congress, 1774-1989, *U.S. Government Printing Office, Washington, D.C., 1989; hereafter referred to as the* Biographical Directory.)

* The symbol is used for three types of situations: (1) When a representative-elect died or declined his seat before the constitutionally set date for the beginning of his term—Jan. 3 for all elections from 1946 to 1996; (2) when the House refused to seat any candidate claiming election to a seat; and (3) when state law required a candidate to obtain a popular vote majority for election to the House, but the candidate receiving the most votes failed to receive a majority. (*For discussion of specific cases, consult the* Biographical Directory.)

Information for 1946-1973 returns was obtained from a source other than the Inter-University Consortium for Political and Social Research. (*For a listing of other sources, see p. 325.*)

Footnotes. Numbered footnotes are used to explain unusual situations, such as a series of elections in the same year in the same House district, anomalies resulting from reapportionment and special procedures for conducting House elections in certain states.

Political Party Abbreviations

The following political party abbreviations are used in the House popular vote returns.

AC	Anti-corruption	FTP	For the People	NON PART	Non Partisan
ACP	A Connecticut Party	GOOD GOV	Good Government	NP	National Prohibition
AGA	American Grassroots Alternative	GREEN	Green	PEROT CHOICE	Perot Choice
AIP	American Independent	I	Independent	PF, PFP	Peace and Freedom
ALI	Alaskan Independent	IA	Independent American	POP	Populist
ALL PP	All Peoples	IFC	Independents for Change	PROG	Progressive
AM	American	IFP	Independents for Perot	PS	Protect Seniors
AM I	American Independent	IND	Independent	R	Republican
AM LAB	American Labor	INDC	Independence	R-D	Republican-Democrat
C	Conservative	INS	Independent Neighbors	REF	Reform
CC	Change Congress	IPP CH	Independent People's Choice	RP	Rate Payers Against LILCO
CIT	Citizens	I PROG	Independent Progressive		
CLUNEY	Cluney Taxpayers Good Government	IR, I-R	Independent Republican	RPI	Ross Perot Independent
		IV	Independent Voters	RTL	Right to Life
COM	Communist	I VT	Independent Vermonters	SILENT	Silent Majority
CONST	Constitution	KTAX	Taxpayers Party of Kentucky	SIS	Staten Island Secession
CR	Conservative Republican			SM	Save Medicare
CS	Common Sense	L	Liberal	SOC	Socialist
CST	Constitutional	LIBERT	Libertarian	SOCIAL D	Social Democrat
D	Democrat	LIF	Long Island First	SOC WORK	Socialist Workers
DFL	Democrat Farmer-Labor	LLJ	Life-Liberty-Justice	TCP-LI	Tax Cut Party-Long Island
D-IP	Democrat-Independent Progressive	LRU	La Raza Unida		
		LU	Liberty Union	U CIT	United Citizen
D & P	Democrat and Prohibition	MINN TAX	Minnesota Taxpayers	USLP	U.S. Labor Party
		MSTAX	Mississippi Taxpayers	UT	Unity
D & PROG	Democrat and Progressive	NA	New Alliance	U TAX	United Taxpayers
		NDPA	National Democratic Party of Alabama	VETS F	Veterans Farmer
D-R	Democratic-Republican			VETS V	Veterans Victory
ECR	Economic Recovery	NEIGH	Neighborhood	VR	Voter Rights
EJ	Economic Justice	NEW I	New Independent	WRITE IN	Write in
ENVIRON	Environment	NF	Nuclear Freeze	WTP	We The People
FDM	Freedom	NL	Natural Law	YOUNGMAN	Youngman
FF	Four Freedoms				

1946 House Elections

ALABAMA

Candidates	Votes	%
1 Frank W. Boykin (D)	12,448	100.0
2 George M. Grant (D)	17,711	100.0
3 George W. Andrews (D)	13,397	100.0
4 Sam Hobbs (D)	16,299	88.1
Roger S. Bingham (R)	2,207	11.9
5 Albert Rains (D)	21,560	100.0
6 Pete Jarman (D)	13,551	100.0
7 Carter Manasco (D)	22,853	72.7
M. H. Woodward (R)	8,565	27.3
8 John J. Sparkman (D)	17,624*	92.4
Arthur South (R)	1,453	7.6
9 Laurie C. Battle (D)	29,940	94.1
J. G. Bass (R)	1,880	5.9

ARIZONA

	Votes	
AL John R. Murdock (D)	74,948✓	
Richard F. Harless (D)	71,836✓	
Denver C. Henson (R)	37,033	
John H. Curnutte (R)	36,185	
Karl M. Wilson (COM)	831	

ARKANSAS

Candidates	Votes	%
1 Ezekiel C. Gathings (D)	20,250	100.0
2 Wilbur D. Mills (D)	22,955	100.0
3 James W. Trimble (D)	24,950	100.0
4 Fadjo Cravens (D)	13,844	100.0
5 Brooks Hays (D)	21,777	85.2
James R. Harris (R)	2,881	11.3
6 William F. Norrell (D)	23,892	84.7
M. O. Evans (I)	4,305	15.3
7 Oren Harris (D)	15,584	100.0

CALIFORNIA

Candidates	Votes	%
1 Clarence F. Lea (D-R)	77,653	99.8
2 Clair Engle (D-R)	57,895	100.0
3 Leroy Johnson (R-D)	116,792	100.0
4 Franck R. Havenner (D)	60,655	52.9
Truman R. Young (R)	54,113	47.2
5 Richard J. Welch (R-D)	94,293	100.0
6 George P. Miller (D-R)	118,548	99.9
7 John J. Allen Jr. (R)	61,508	56.2
Patrick W. McDonough (D)	47,988	43.8
8 John Z. Anderson (R-D)	113,325	99.9
9 Bertrand W. Gearhart (R)	50,171	53.7
Hubert Phillips (D)	43,244	46.3
10 Alfred J. Elliott (D-R)	51,843	99.8
11 Ernest K. Bramblett (R)	41,902	53.1
George E. Outland (D)	36,996	46.9
12 Richard M. Nixon (R)	65,586	56.0
H. Jerry Voorhis (D)	49,994	42.7
13 Norris Poulson (R)	48,071	51.8
Ned R. Healy (D)	44,712	48.2
14 Helen Gahagan Douglas (D)	53,536	54.3
Frederick M. Roberts (R)	44,914	45.6
15 Gordon L. McDonough (R-D)	106,020	99.4
16 Donald L. Jackson (R)	78,264	53.9
Harold Harby (D)	45,951	31.6
Ellis E. Patterson	20,945	14.4
17 Cecil R. King (D-R)	110,654	99.4
18 Willis W. Bradley (R)	67,363	52.8
Clyde Doyle (D)	60,218	47.2
19 Chet Holifield (D-R)	50,666	97.2
20 Carl Hinshaw (R)	98,283	59.3
Everett G. Burkhalter (D)	67,317	40.6
21 Harry R. Sheppard (D)	37,229	52.7
Lowell E. Lathrop (R)	33,395	47.3
22 John Phillips (R)	59,935	62.1
Ray Adkinson (D)	36,649	37.9
23 Charles K. Fletcher (R)	69,411	56.3
Ed V. Izac (D)	53,898	43.7

COLORADO

Candidates	Votes	%
1 John A. Carroll (D)	60,513	51.8
Dean M. Gillespie (R)	55,724	47.7
2 William S. Hill (R)	54,768	65.7
Frank A. Safranek (D)	27,393	32.9
3 J. Edgar Chenoweth (R)	45,043	54.6
Walter W. Johnson (D)	37,496	45.4
4 Robert F. Rockwell (R)	28,894	58.8
Thomas Matthews (D)	20,290	41.3

CONNECTICUT

Candidates	Votes	%
1 William J. Miller (R)	93,006	53.1
Herman P. Kopplemann (D)	82,231	46.9
2 Horace Seely-Brown Jr. (R)	59,828	55.3
Chase Going Woodhouse (D)	48,376	44.7
3 Ellsworth B. Foote (R)	76,408	58.9
James P. Geelan (D)	53,404	41.1
4 John Davis Lodge (R)	93,513	57.1
Henry A. Mucci (D)	57,913	35.4
Stanley W. Mayhew (SOC)	9,427	5.8
5 James T. Patterson (R)	51,790	53.1
Thomas Radzevich (D)	39,785	40.8
John C. Cluney (SOC, CLUNEY)	5,984	6.1
AL Antoni N. Sadlak (R)	377,972	55.6
Joseph F. Ryter (D)	277,872	40.9

DELAWARE

	Votes	%
AL J. Caleb Boggs (R)	63,516	56.4
Philip A. Traynor (D)	49,105	43.6

FLORIDA

Candidates	Votes	%
1 J. Hardin Peterson (D)	31,145	100.0
2 Emory H. Price (D)	26,093	100.0
3 Robert L. F. Sikes (D)	18,455	100.0
4 George A. Smathers (D)	37,002	71.9
Norman N. Curtis (R)	14,458	28.1
5 Joe Hendricks (D)	24,695	61.3
M. J. Moss Jr. (R)	15,591	38.7
6 Dwight L. Rogers (D)	13,733	71.1
Joseph P. Moe (R)	5,591	28.9

GEORGIA

Candidates	Votes	%
1 Prince H. Preston (D)	20,937	99.8
2 E. E. Cox (D)	10,805	100.0
3 Stephen Pace (D)	8,961	100.0
4 A. Sidney Camp (D)	8,476	100.0
5 James C. Davis (D)	31,444	61.6
Helen Douglas Mankin (I)	19,527#	38.3
6 Carl Vinson (D)	13,566	100.0
7 Henderson Lanham (D)	7,573	100.0
8 W. M. Wheeler (D)	8,986	100.0
9 John Wood (D)	14,815	100.0
10 Paul Brown (D)	16,398	100.0

Special Election

	Votes	%
5 Helen Douglas Mankin (D)	11,067	36.5
Thomas L. Camp	10,275	33.9
Ben T. Huiet	2,724	9.0
J. E. B. Stewart	2,363	7.8

IDAHO

Candidates	Votes	%
1 Abe McGregor Goff (R)	37,326	50.6
Compton I. White (D)	36,509	49.5
2 John Sanborn (R)	63,692	60.7
Pete Leguineche (D)	41,231	39.3

ILLINOIS

Candidates	Votes	%
1 William L. Dawson (D)	38,040	56.8
William E. King (R)	28,945	43.2
2 Richard B. Vail (R)	156,697	51.3
William A. Rowan (D)	148,995	48.7
3 Fred E. Busbey (R)	169,543	57.2
Edward A. Kelly (D)	126,638	42.8
4 Martin Gorski (D)	68,113	70.7
John T. Parsons (R)	28,251	29.3
5 Adolph J. Sabath (D)	34,904	71.6
Michael A. Francisco (R)	13,859	28.4
6 Thomas J. O'Brien (D)	171,778	52.0
Harold C. Woodward (R)	158,702	48.0
7 Thomas L. Owens (R)	252,981	55.0
William W. Link (D)	206,963	45.0
8 Thomas S. Gordon (D)	38,317	77.3
Scott John Vitell (R)	11,266	22.7
9 Robert J. Twyman (R)	54,615	51.3
Alexander J. Resa (D)	51,788	48.7
10 Ralph E. Church (R)	201,010	64.7
Harold H. Kolbe (D)	109,712	35.3
11 Chauncey W. Reed (R)	120,640	74.9
Louis William Oswald (D)	40,355	25.1
12 Noah M. Mason (R)	73,431	69.1
Richard G. Myrland (D)	32,816	30.9
13 Leo E. Allen (R)	48,238	77.8
Michael M. Kinney (D)	13,767	22.2
14 Anton J. Johnson (R)	45,723	62.1
Carl E. Wright Jr. (D)	27,877	37.9
15 Robert B. Chiperfield (R)	49,895	64.3
Henry D. Sullivan (D)	27,667	35.7
16 Everett M. Dirksen (R)	64,534	67.5
Hans A. Spading (D)	31,091	32.5
17 Leslie C. Arends (R)	45,969	71.2
Carl Vrooman (D)	18,617	28.8
18 Edward H. Jenison (R)	56,537	65.1
C. E. Spang (D)	30,305	34.9
19 Rolla C. McMillen (R)	64,063	62.5
Olive Remington Goldman (D)	38,485	37.5
20 Sidney E. Simpson (R)	34,923	58.8
Don Irving (D)	24,508	41.2
21 Evan Howell (R)	55,609	55.1
Roscoe Bonjean (D)	45,293	44.9
22 Melvin Price (D)	69,669	50.7
Calvin D. Johnson (R)	67,665	49.3
23 Charles W. Vursell (R)	51,440	54.9
Homer Kasserman (D)	42,237	45.1
24 Roy Clippinger (R)	37,909	58.9
Edward Hines (D)	26,483	41.1
25 C. W. Bishop (R)	53,831	59.8
Sherman S. Carr (D)	36,217	40.2
AL William G. Stratton (R)	1,906,717	55.1
Emily Taft Douglas (D)	1,539,248	44.5

INDIANA

Candidates	Votes	%
1 Ray J. Madden (D)	51,809	51.9
Charles W. Gannon (R)	46,677	46.8
2 Charles A. Halleck (R)	66,423	61.3
Margaret A. Afflis (D)	40,847	37.7
3 Robert A. Grant (R)	73,239	55.6
John S. Gonas (D)	57,425	43.6
4 George W. Gillie (R)	59,790	59.4
Walter E. Frederick (D)	39,766	39.5
5 Forest A. Harness (R)	79,752	55.0
William W. Welsh (D)	61,364	42.3
6 Noble J. Johnson (R)	65,926	57.4
Thomas A. Sigler (D)	47,972	41.7
7 Gerald W. Landis (R)	63,667	50.7
James E. Noland (D)	59,908	47.7
8 Edward A. Mitchell (R)	66,050	51.8
Winfield K. Denton (D)	60,385	47.3
9 Earl Wilson (R)	58,384	55.8
Oliver O. Dixon (D)	45,316	43.3

INDIANA

	Candidates	Votes	%
10	Raymond S. Springer (R)	70,969	59.3
	Frank C. Unger (D)	44,807	37.4
11	Louis Ludlow (D)	79,040	51.1
	Albert J. Beveridge (R)	74,745	48.3

IOWA

	Candidates	Votes	%
1	Thomas E. Martin (R)	52,488	61.5
	Clair A. Williams (D)	32,849	38.5
2	Henry O. Talle (R)	60,111	59.1
	Richard V. Bernhart (D)	41,544	40.9
3	John W. Gwynne (R)	48,346	62.0
	Dan J. P. Ryan (D)	29,661	38.0
4	Karl M. LeCompte (R)	43,753	58.4
	A. E. Augustine (D)	31,203	41.6
5	Paul Cunningham (R)	41,679	59.4
	Vince L. Browner (D)	28,490	40.6
6	James I. Dolliver (R)	40,595	63.4
	Oscar E. Johnson (D)	23,422	36.6
7	Ben F. Jensen (R)	40,152	63.0
	Philip A. Allen (D)	23,567	37.0
8	Charles B. Hoeven (R)	37,868	68.6
	George A. Heikens (D)	17,303	31.4

KANSAS

	Candidates	Votes	%
1	Albert M. Cole (R)	63,076	64.3
	James W. Lowry (D)	35,045	35.7
2	Errett P. Scrivner (R)	56,363	58.8
	Murray H. Hodges (D)	39,484	41.2
3	Herbert A. Meyer (R)	41,624	55.4
	Jo E. Gaitskill (D)	33,578	44.7
4	Edward H. Rees (R)	68,658	56.2
	William P. Warren (D)	53,617	43.9
5	Clifford R. Hope (R)	54,578	62.7
	Arthur L. Sparks (D)	32,538	37.4
6	Wint Smith (R)	44,343	58.1
	G. E. Bengtson (D)	28,911	37.9

KENTUCKY

	Candidates	Votes	%
1	Noble J. Gregory (D)	32,121	66.2
	William E. Porter (R)	16,064	33.1
2	Earle C. Clements (D)	38,020	56.6
	Thomas W. Hines (R)	29,124	43.4
3	Thruston B. Morton (R)	61,899	58.1
	Emmet O'Neal (D)	44,599	41.9
4	Frank L. Chelf (D)	33,116	53.1
	Don Victor Drye Sr. (R)	29,304	47.0
5	Brent Spence (D)	26,444	51.2
	Marion W. Moore (R)	25,240	48.8
6	Virgil Chapman (D)	43,176	55.0
	W. D. Rogers (R)	35,368	45.0
7	W. Howes Meade (R)	30,070	59.4
	A. J. May (D)	20,596	40.7
8	Joe B. Bates (D)	33,408	52.6
	Ray Schmauch (R)	30,127	47.4
9	John M. Robsion (R)	54,306	100.0

LOUISIANA

	Candidates	Votes	%
1	F. Edward Hebert (D)	29,329	91.8
	Dennison Suarez (R)	2,614	8.2
2	Hale Boggs (D)	29,457	90.7
	Harold M. Herbst (R)	3,037	9.4
3	James Domengeaux (D)	4,595	100.0
4	Overton Brooks (D)	8,499	100.0
5	Otto E. Passman (D)	6,049	100.0
6	James H. Morrison (D)	8,781	100.0
7	Henry D. Larcade Jr. (D)	5,907	100.0
8	A. Leonard Allen (D)	7,740	100.0

MAINE

	Candidates	Votes	%
1	Robert Hale (R)	38,975	59.6
	John C. Fitzgerald (D)	26,378	40.4
2	Margaret Chase Smith (R)	39,791	60.7
	Edward J. Beauchamp (D)	25,739	39.3
3	Frank Fellows (R)	31,622	72.9
	John M. Coghill (D)	11,743	27.1

MARYLAND

	Candidates	Votes	%
1	Edward T. Miller (R)	27,364	50.9
	Dudley George Roe (D)	26,360	49.1
2	Hugh A. Meade (D)	69,211	52.4
	David G. Harry (R)	62,760	47.6
3	Thomas D'Alesandro Jr. (D)	24,347	63.9
	Edward N. Kowzan (R)	13,761	36.1
4	George H. Fallon (D)	31,453	57.2
	Paul Robertson (R)	23,499	42.8
5	Lansdale G. Sasscer (D)	40,929	58.2
	Edwin A. Glenn (R)	29,406	41.8
6	J. Glenn Beall (R)	55,667	58.1
	Arch McDonald (D)	40,198	41.9

MASSACHUSETTS

	Candidates	Votes	%
1	John W. Heselton (R)	59,222	58.0
	John J. Falvey (D)	40,549	39.7
2	Charles R. Clason (R)	59,754	51.4
	Foster Furcolo (D)	56,459	48.6
3	Philip J. Philbin (D)	69,038	62.2
	Carroll H. Balcom (R)	42,033	37.8
4	Harold D. Donohue (D)	59,847	49.5
	Pehr G. Holmes (R)	58,663	48.5
5	Edith Nourse Rogers (R)	98,488	71.6
	Oliver S. Allen (D)	38,575	28.0
6	George J. Bates (R)	79,709	70.2
	Richard B. O'Keefe (D)	33,823	29.8
7	Thomas J. Lane (D)	59,871	60.8
	Ernest Bentley (R)	37,250	37.8
8	Angier L. Goodwin (R)	76,305	63.5
	Anthony M. Roche (D)	43,827	36.5
9	Charles L. Gifford (R)	69,831	60.8
	William McAuliffe (D)	43,367	37.8
10	Christian A. Herter (R)	96,607	64.0
	Paul J. McCarty (D)	54,421	36.0
11	John F. Kennedy (D)	69,093	71.9
	Lester W. Bowen (R)	26,007	27.1
12	John W. McCormack (D)	92,622	100.0
13	Richard B. Wigglesworth (R)	87,839	67.5
	James J. Goode Jr. (D)	42,274	32.5
14	Joseph W. Martin Jr. (R)	71,566	63.6
	Martha Sharp (D)	40,999	36.4

MICHIGAN

	Candidates	Votes	%
1	George G. Sadowski (D)	57,753	65.9
	John B. Sosnowski (R)	29,293	33.4
2	Earl C. Michener (R)	66,486	71.2
	William R. Kelley (D)	26,141	28.0
3	Paul W. Shafer (R)	59,823	68.9
	Herschel W. Carney (D)	25,914	29.9
4	Clare E. Hoffman (R)	58,798	72.5
	Harvey Hope Jarvis (D)	21,514	26.5
5	Bartel J. Jonkman (R)	63,093	71.6
	Earle W. Reynolds (D)	25,022	28.4
6	William W. Blackney (R)	69,203	57.3
	Arthur Elliott (D)	50,684	42.0
7	Jesse P. Wolcott (R)	64,404	74.2
	Earl J. Tallman (D)	21,708	25.0
8	Fred L. Crawford (R)	58,725	72.6
	J. Charles Mottashed (D)	21,375	26.4
9	Albert J. Engel (R)	49,017	71.8
	J. Willard Krause (D)	18,828	27.6
10	Roy O. Woodruff (R)	44,853	71.1
	Herman N. Butler (D)	17,737	28.1
11	Fred Bradley (R)	41,436	65.9
	Cecil W. Bailey (D)	21,340	33.9
12	John B. Bennett (R)	40,717	54.4
	Frank E. Hook (D)	33,799	45.2
13	Howard A. Coffin (R)	50,539	52.8
	George D. O'Brien (D)	44,883	46.9
14	Harold F. Youngblood (R)	69,968	53.3
	Louis C. Rabaut (D)	60,808	46.3
15	John D. Dingell (D)	59,111	51.9
	Harry Henderson (R)	54,296	47.7
16	John Lesinski (D)	57,773	51.9
	Albert A. Riddering (R)	52,376	47.1
17	George A. Dondero (R)	102,336	64.7
	John W. L. Hicks (D)	54,928	34.7

MINNESOTA

	Candidates	Votes	%
1	August H. Andresen (R)	65,906	68.4
	Karl F. Rolvaag (DFL)	30,439	31.6
2	Joseph P. O'Hara (R)	69,487	76.0
	L. J. Kilbride (DFL)	21,947	24.0
3	George MacKinnon (R)	57,397	51.5
	Roy W. Wier (DFL)	52,797	47.3
4	Edward J. Devitt (R)	45,667	51.5
	Frank T. Starkey (DFL)	41,897	47.2
5	Walter H. Judd (R)	66,837	58.3
	Douglas Hall (DFL)	47,777	41.7
6	Harold Knutson (R)	55,401	57.4
	J. Edward Anderson (DFL)	41,147	42.6
7	H. Carl Andersen (R)	57,869	65.4
	Donald M. Lawson (DFL)	30,667	34.6
8	John A. Blatnik (DFL)	62,876	57.7
	William A. Pittenger (R)	46,189	42.4
9	Harold C. Hagen (R)	50,031	63.9
	Verner Nelson (DFL)	28,211	36.1

MISSISSIPPI

	Candidates	Votes	%
1	John E. Rankin (D)	5,429	100.0
2	Jamie L. Whitten (D)	6,411	100.0
3	William M. Whittington (D)	4,265	100.0
4	Thomas G. Abernethy (D)	10,017	100.0
5	W. Arthur Winstead (D)	7,122	100.0
6	William M. Colmer (D)	6,448	100.0
7	John Bell Williams (D)	10,345	100.0

MISSOURI

	Candidates	Votes	%
1	Samuel W. Arnold (R)	37,584	50.3
	Walter G. Stillwell (D)	37,105	49.7
2	Max Schwabe (R)	44,292	51.1
	Will L. Nelson Jr. (D)	42,437	48.9
3	William C. Cole (R)	38,828	52.8
	William Orr Sawyers (D)	34,730	47.2
4	C. Jasper Bell (D)	41,843	55.1
	Vernon D. Fulcrut (R)	34,066	44.9
5	Albert L. Reeves Jr. (R)	42,065	53.7
	Enos A. Axtell (D)	36,324	46.3
6	Marion T. Bennett (R)	54,034	58.6
	Tom B. Hembree (D)	38,113	41.4
7	Dewey Short (R)	50,588	65.4
	Don Ervin (D)	26,712	34.6
8	Parke M. Banta (R)	42,076	51.1
	A. S. J. Carnahan (D)	40,241	48.9
9	Clarence Cannon (D)	35,253	53.9
	William Barton (R)	30,199	46.1
10	Orville Zimmerman (D)	37,236	60.6
	Walter K. Dillon (R)	24,164	39.4
11	Claude I. Bakewell (R)	41,220	50.8
	John B. Sullivan (D)	39,879	49.2
12	Walter C. Ploeser (R)	93,136	58.2
	Henry W. Simpson (D)	66,878	41.8
13	Frank M. Karsten (D)	41,229	54.8
	Alfred L. Grattendick (R)	34,062	45.2

MONTANA

	Candidates	Votes	%
1	Mike Mansfield (D)	47,418	57.6
	W. R. Rankin (R)	34,958	42.4
2	Wesley A. D'Ewart (R)	58,307	54.1
	John J. Holmes (D)	48,564	45.1

NEBRASKA

	Candidates	Votes	%
1	Carl T. Curtis (R)	73,602	66.4
	William H. Meier (D)	37,280	33.6
2	Howard Buffett (R)	53,398	58.3
	Frank A. Jelen (D)	38,125	41.7
3	Karl Stefan (R)	64,016	72.2
	Hans O. Jensen (D)	20,161	22.7
	Paul Burke (I)	4,516#	5.1
4	Arthur L. Miller (R)	57,708	71.3
	Stanley D. Long (D)	23,234	28.7

NEVADA

	Candidates	Votes	%
AL	Charles H. Russell (R)	28,859	58.8
	Malcolm McEachin (D)	20,187	41.2

NEW HAMPSHIRE

	Candidates	Votes	%
1	Chester E. Merrow (R)	53,909	59.8
	Josaphet T. Benoit (D)	36,316	40.3
2	Norris Cotton (R)	45,963	64.9
	Patrick J. Hinchey (D)	24,904	35.1

NEW JERSEY

	Candidates	Votes	%
1	Charles A. Wolverton (R)	82,919	63.5
	George F. Neutze (D)	47,631	36.5
2	T. Millet Hand (R)	54,511	67.1
	Edward T. Keeley (D)	26,740	32.9
3	James C. Auchincloss (R)	70,302	64.9
	John W. Zimmermann (D)	36,177	33.4
4	Frank A. Mathews Jr. (R)	50,221	52.6
	Charles R. Howell (D)	45,225	47.4
5	Charles A. Eaton (R)	69,338	61.3
	John J. George (D)	43,593	38.6
6	Clifford P. Case (R)	69,395	64.7
	Walter H. Van Hoesen (D)	35,378	33.0
7	J. Parnell Thomas (R)	65,426	69.0
	Robert B. Meyner (D)	29,418	31.0
8	Gordon Canfield (R)	57,616	70.5
	John V. Breslin (D)	23,007	28.2
9	Harry L. Towe (R)	74,870	69.1
	John M. Mehler (D)	33,553	31.0
10	Fred A. Hartley Jr. (R)	44,619	52.5
	Peter W. Rodino Jr. (D)	38,889	45.7
11	Frank L. Sundstrom (R)	46,034	60.4
	Robert F. J. McGarry (D)	28,545	37.5
12	Robert W. Kean (R)	55,732	63.6
	Raymond C. Connell (D)	30,389	34.7
13	Mary T. Norton (D)	69,440	64.4
	John A. Jones (R)	36,270	33.7
14	Edward J. Hart (D)	65,979	63.2
	Edward P. Nicolay (R)	38,008	36.4

NEW MEXICO

	Candidates	Votes	%
AL	Georgia L. Lusk (D)	66,420✓	
	Antonio M. Fernandez (D)	65,242✓	
	Earl Douglas (R)	60,519	
	Herman G. Baca (R)	58,937	

NEW YORK

	Candidates	Votes	%
1	W. Kingsland Macy (R)	83,877	77.3
	Eugene T. O'Neill (D)	22,855	21.1
2	Leonard W. Hall (R)	123,873	78.4
	Josephine U. Mayes (D, AM LAB)	34,217	21.6
3	Henry J. Latham (R)	98,722	69.7
	Aloysius J. Maickel (D)	32,002	22.6
4	Gregory McMahon (R)	57,176	53.3
	Emily B. Barry (D)	38,227	35.6
	George H. Rooney (AM LAB)	7,439	6.9
5	Robert Tripp Ross (R)	66,754	53.0
	James A. Phillips (D, AM LAB)	59,092	47.0
6	Robert J. Nodar Jr. (R)	59,438	53.9

	Candidates	Votes	%
	James J. Delaney (D, AM LAB)	50,944	46.1
7	John J. Delaney (D, AM LAB)	49,449	57.5
	Roy M. D. Richardson (R)	36,510	42.5
8	Joseph L. Pfeifer (D, AM LAB)	34,876	53.9
	Paul W. Williams (R)	29,851	46.1
9	Eugene J. Keogh (D, L)	41,304	48.6
	Samuel R. Scialabba (R)	27,289	32.1
	Anthony Scimeca (AM LAB)	16,359	19.3
10	Andrew L. Somers (D, AM LAB)	57,658	57.9
	Victor Wichum (R)	33,642	33.8
	August Claessens (L)	8,314	8.4
11	James J. Heffernan (D, AM LAB)	69,089	60.4
	Alfred C. McKenzie (R)	45,279	39.6
12	John J. Rooney (D)	36,399	54.0
	Vincent J. Longhi (R, AM LAB)	31,052	46.0
13	Donald L. O'Toole (D, AM LAB)	51,406	53.5
	Charles H. Weadon (R)	44,674	46.5
14	Leo F. Rayfiel (D, AM LAB)	79,336	75.0
	Robert H. Thayer (R)	26,450	25.0
15	Emanuel Celler (D, AM LAB)	78,543	78.7
	Lauri T. Laisi (R)	21,094	21.1
16	Ellsworth B. Buck (R, VETS V)	49,758	61.2
	John Burry (D, AM LAB)	31,583	38.8
17	Frederic R. Coudert Jr. (R)	66,063	57.5
	Myron Sulzberger (D)	39,216	34.2
	Joseph Clark Baldwin (AM LAB)	9,527	8.3
18	Vito Marcantonio (D, AM LAB)	42,229	54.2
	Frederick V. P. Bryan (R)	35,693	45.8
19	Arthur G. Klein (D, AM LAB)	48,437	71.4
	William I. Lehrfeld (R)	19,410	28.6
20	Sol Bloom (D, AM LAB)	57,208	61.1
	Jules J. Justin (R)	36,450	38.9
21	Jacob K. Javits (R, L)	46,897	46.0
	Daniel Flynn (D)	40,652	39.9
	Eugene P. Connolly (AM LAB)	14,359	14.1
22	Adam Clayton Powell Jr. (D, AM LAB)	32,573	62.5
	Grant Reynolds (R)	19,514	37.5
23	Walter A. Lynch (D)	52,616	43.4
	Peter Wynne (R)	30,534	25.2
	David A. Schlossberg (AM LAB)	25,229	20.8
	William Wacks (L)	12,803	10.6
24	Benjamin J. Rabin (D)	39,316	44.2
	Roy Soden (AM LAB)	24,249	27.3
	David Scher (R)	16,931	19.0
	Bernice Benedick (L)	8,504	9.6
25	Charles A. Buckley (D)	47,142	32.5
	Charles Garside (R)	46,853	32.3
	Edward V. Morand (AM LAB)	25,353	17.5
	Ira J. Palestine (L)	15,814	10.9
	John A. Devany (VETS V)	9,791	6.8
26	David Potts (R)	58,061	44.1
	Peter A. Quinn (D)	49,067	37.3
	Gerald O'Reilly (AM LAB)	17,379	13.2
	Augustus Batten (L)	7,140	5.4
27	Ralph W. Gwinn (R)	84,882	68.6
	Francis X. Nulty (D, AM LAB)	38,950	31.5
28	Ralph A. Gamble (R)	83,533	75.4
	Morris Karnes (D, AM LAB)	27,236	24.6
29	Katharine St. George (R)	60,769	58.2
	James K. Welsh (D, VETS F)	40,174	38.4
30	Jay LeFevre (R)	80,469	69.5
	John F. Killgrew (D, AM LAB)	35,240	30.5

	Candidates	Votes	%
31	Bernard W. Kearney (R)	66,395	59.2
	Carroll A. Gardner (D, AM LAB)	45,777	40.8
32	William T. Byrne (D, AM LAB)	79,042	55.1
	William K. Sanford (R)	64,325	44.9
33	Dean P. Taylor (R)	89,778	69.9
	David J. Fitzgerald (D, AM LAB)	38,666	30.1
34	Clarence E. Kilburn (R)	64,217	73.0
	William G. Houk (D)	22,368	25.4
35	Hadwen C. Fuller (R)	58,040	54.3
	Frank A. Emma (D, AM LAB)	48,854	45.7
36	R. Walter Riehlman (R)	76,372	63.3
	Lawson Barnes (D, AM LAB)	44,371	36.7
37	Edwin Arthur Hall (R)	59,920	71.7
	Charles R. Wilson (D, AM LAB)	23,687	28.3
38	John Taber (R)	63,382	72.1
	George T. Franklin (D)	24,576	27.9
39	W. Sterling Cole (R)	61,330	72.6
	William Heidt Jr. (D, AM LAB)	23,205	27.4
40	Kenneth B. Keating (R)	84,852	60.5
	George F. Rogers (D, AM LAB)	55,321	39.5
41	James W. Wadsworth (R)	65,975	71.5
	Charles J. Reap (D, AM LAB)	26,332	28.5
42	Walter Gresham Andrews (R)	71,862	62.6
	William R. Lupton (D, AM LAB)	43,028	37.4
43	Edward J. Elsaesser (R)	71,758	62.6
	Charles P. McCabe (D)	38,108	33.2
44	John C. Butler (R)	67,495	57.5
	James B. Downey (D, AM LAB)	49,798	42.5
45	Daniel A. Reed (R)	53,327	70.4
	Joseph E. Proudman (D, AM LAB)	20,205	26.7

Special Election

	Candidates	Votes	%
19	Arthur G. Klein (D)	17,360	49.5
	Johannes Stell (AM LAB)	13,415	38.2
	William S. Shea (R)	4,314	12.3

NORTH CAROLINA

	Candidates	Votes	%
1	Herbert C. Bonner (D)	9,993	89.2
	Zeno O. Ratcliff (R)	1,208	10.8
2	John H. Kerr (D)	9,426	100.0
3	Graham A. Barden (D)	14,798	66.7
	H. B. Kornegay (R)	7,385	33.3
4	Harold D. Cooley (D)	22,977	65.7
	Ben L. Spence (R)	12,005	34.3
5	John H. Folger (D)	26,316	62.9
	S. Evan Hall (R)	15,521	37.1
6	Carl T. Durham (D)	18,564	63.4
	A. A. McDonald (R)	10,721	36.6
7	J. Bayard Clark (D)	15,428	73.9
	H. Edmund Rodgers (R)	5,445	26.1
8	Charles B. Deane (D)	29,920	54.2
	Joseph H. Whicker Sr. (R)	25,305	45.8
9	Robert L. Doughton (D)	36,007	54.9
	Clyde R. Greene (R)	29,585	45.1
10	Hamilton C. Jones (D)	24,614	53.9
	P. C. Burkholder (R)	21,096	46.2
11	Alfred L. Bulwinkle (D)	25,544	58.5
	C. Y. Nanney Jr. (R)	18,143	41.5
12	Monroe M. Redden (D)	43,690	60.5
	Guy Weaver (R)	28,531	39.5

Special Elections

	Candidates	Votes	%
8	Jane Pratt (D)	31,058	79.5
	H. Frank Hulin (R)	8,017	20.5
10	Sam J. Ervin Jr. (D)	2,303	99.7

NORTH DAKOTA

Candidates	Votes	%
AL William Lemke (R)	103,205✔	
Charles R. Robertson (R)	102,087✔	
James M. Hanley (D)	41,189	
Edwin Cooper (D)	29,865	

OHIO

	Candidates	Votes	%
1	Charles H. Elston (R)	72,909	64.2
	G. Andrews Espy (D)	40,594	35.8
2	William E. Hess (R)	67,067	63.2
	Francis G. Davis (D)	39,112	36.8
3	Raymond H. Burke (R)	71,171	52.0
	Edward J. Gardner (D)	65,749	48.0
4	Robert F. Jones (R)	46,718	59.2
	Merl J. Bragg (D)	32,160	40.8
5	Cliff Clevenger (R)	30,623	60.3
	Willard Thomas (D)	20,163	39.7
6	Edward O. McCowen (R)	39,992	54.8
	Franklin E. Smith (D)	33,013	45.2
7	Clarence J. Brown (R)	63,390	68.0
	Carl H. Ehl (D)	29,824	32.0
8	Frederick C. Smith (R)	40,755	64.0
	John T. Siemon (D)	22,945	36.0
9	Homer A. Ramey (R)	59,394	50.1
	Michael V. DiSalle (D)	59,057	49.9
10	Thomas A. Jenkins (R)	35,406	66.7
	H. A. McCown (D)	17,719	33.4
11	Walter E. Brehm (R)	31,576	60.6
	Lester S. Reid (D)	20,543	39.4
12	John M. Vorys (R)	74,691	62.0
	Arthur P. Lamneck (D)	45,779	38.0
13	Alvin F. Weichel (R)	49,725	72.1
	Frank W. Thomas (D)	19,237	27.9
14	Walter B. Huber (D)	88,178	52.6
	Fred W. Danner (R)	77,674	46.4
15	Percy W. Griffiths (R)	36,564	53.2
	Robert T. Secrest (D)	32,159	46.8
16	Henderson H. Carson (R)	65,639	55.8
	William R. Thom (D)	51,931	44.2
17	J. Harry McGregor (R)	57,167	65.3
	Wesley W. Purdy (D)	30,406	34.7
18	Earl R. Lewis (R)	55,140	58.8
	Eugene A. Blum (D)	38,606	41.2
19	Michael J. Kirwan (D)	88,872	59.9
	Norman W. Adams (R)	59,607	40.2
20	Michael A. Feighan (D)	49,670	67.0
	Walter E. Obert (R)	24,476	33.0
21	Robert Crosser (D)	49,111	64.0
	James S. Hudec (R)	27,657	36.0
22	Frances P. Bolton (R)	174,823	69.1
	Earl Heffley (D)	69,050	27.3
AL	George H. Bender (R)	1,281,864	59.5
	William M. Boyd (D)	871,660	40.5

OKLAHOMA

		Votes	%
1	George B. Schwabe (R)	61,205	54.5
	Oras A. Shaw (D)	51,041	45.5
2	William G. Stigler (D)	32,559	63.1
	Ferd P. Snider (R)	19,029	36.9
3	Carl Albert (D)	38,699	85.0
	Eleanor L. Watson (R)	6,835	15.0
4	Glen D. Johnson (D)	36,559	64.4
	Pliney S. Frye (R)	20,230	35.6
5	A. S. Mike Monroney (D)	47,173	52.0
	Carmon C. Harris (R)	43,508	48.0
6	Toby Morris (D)	30,408	65.7
	Joe Hart Jr. (R)	15,912	34.4
7	Preston E. Peden (D)	26,585	78.7
	J. Warren White (R)	7,204	21.3
8	Ross Rizley (R)	30,240	54.8
	Tom Hieronymus (D)	24,954	45.2

OREGON

		Votes	%
1	Walter Norblad (R)	67,535	72.0
	Lyman Ross (D)	26,278	28.0

		Votes	%
2	Lowell Stockman (R)	32,541	67.4
	Lamar Townsend (D)	15,744	32.6
3	Homer D. Angell (R)	74,061	56.7
	Lew Wallace (D)	56,525	43.3
4	Harris Ellsworth (R)	42,868	69.2
	Louis A. Wood (D)	19,118	30.8

PENNSYLVANIA

		Votes	%
1	James Gallagher (R)	70,680	57.3
	William Barrett (D)	52,593	42.7
2	Robert N. McGarvey (R)	70,474	51.4
	William T. Granahan (D)	66,674	48.6
3	Hardie Scott (R)	83,618	62.1
	Albert S. Townsend (D)	50,962	37.9
4	Franklin J. Maloney (R)	55,239	50.2
	John Edward Sheridan (D)	49,025	44.6
	John K. Rice (U CIT)	5,688	5.2
5	George W. Sarbacher Jr. (R)	73,946	56.9
	William J. Green Jr. (D)	56,086	43.1
6	Hugh Scott (R)	82,671	58.5
	Herbert J. McGlinchey (D)	58,557	41.5
7	E. Wallace Chadwick (R)	76,021	66.5
	Vernon A. O'Rourke (D)	38,253	33.5
8	Charles L. Gerlach (R)	49,196	59.0
	Henry Chapin (D)	34,260	41.1
9	Paul B. Dague (R)	64,311	72.7
	Edgar Campbell (D)	24,175	27.3
10	James P. Scoblick (R)	47,704	51.0
	Frank X. Murray (D)	45,843	49.0
11	Mitchell Jenkins (R)	58,413	50.8
	Daniel J. Flood (D)	56,570	49.2
12	Ivor D. Fenton (R)	62,151	62.7
	Ralph M. Bashore (D)	36,954	37.3
13	Frederick A. Muhlenberg (R)	33,409	54.6
	Daniel K. Hoch (D)	25,073	41.0
14	Wilson D. Gillette (R)	43,142	67.4
	James S. Fields (D)	20,842	32.6
15	Robert F. Rich (R)	44,264	68.5
	Richard F. Hartzell (D)	20,376	31.5
16	Samuel K. McConnell Jr. (R)	76,314	74.4
	William L. Batt Jr. (D)	26,305	25.6
17	Richard M. Simpson (R)	37,194	66.2
	Lowell H. Alexander (D)	18,972	33.8
18	John C. Kunkel (R)	77,349	69.0
	William B. Freeland (D)	34,708	31.0
19	Leon H. Gavin (R)	41,500	68.0
	Lloyd N. Huth (D)	18,199	29.8
20	Francis E. Walter (D)	39,751	52.5
	Norman A. Peil (R)	36,008	47.5
21	Chester H. Gross (R)	45,559	52.0
	John W. Brehm (D)	42,118	48.0
22	James E. Van Zandt (R)	42,217	65.9
	John A. Shartle (D)	21,853	34.1
23	William J. Crow (R)	34,194	52.9
	John W. Rankin (D)	30,493	47.1
24	Thomas E. Morgan (D)	39,749	56.8
	Roy A. Purviance (R)	30,231	43.2
25	Louis E. Graham (R)	53,932	58.8
	Samuel G. Neff (D)	37,723	41.2
26	Harve Tibbott (R)	49,573	54.6
	Thomas A. Owens (D)	41,224	45.4
27	Augustine B. Kelley (D)	46,137	52.9
	Roy C. McKenna (R)	41,030	47.1
28	Carroll D. Kearns (R)	56,835	63.9
	Charles W. Webb (D)	32,166	36.1
29	John McDowell (R)	55,329	53.5
	Harry J. Davenport (D)	48,091	46.5
30	Robert J. Corbett (R)	57,827	60.1
	James W. Knox (D)	38,362	39.9
31	James G. Fulton (R)	70,419	63.8
	Edward A. Schultz (D)	40,010	36.2
32	Herman P. Eberharter (D)	62,963	62.8
	Ignatius J. Pillart (D)	37,247	37.2
33	Frank Buchanan (D)	51,656	57.9
	John Robert Brown Jr. (R)	37,555	42.1

RHODE ISLAND

	Candidates	Votes	%
1	Aime J. Forand (D)	74,324	56.7
	Raymond A. Mailloux (R)	55,900	42.6
2	John E. Fogarty (D)	74,349	52.6
	John J. Kelly Jr. (R)	66,987	47.4

SOUTH CAROLINA

		Votes	%
1	L. Mendel Rivers (D)	5,354	99.5
2	John J. Riley (D)	4,795	98.6
3	W. J. Bryan Dorn (D)	3,527	99.9
4	Joseph R. Bryson (D)	3,363	99.6
5	James P. Richards (D)	3,357	100.0
6	John L. McMillan (D)	5,671	96.9

SOUTH DAKOTA

		Votes	%
1	Karl E. Mundt (R)	76,720	61.5
	Merton B. Tice (D)	48,065	38.5
2	Francis H. Case (R)	28,011	73.7
	John B. Reinhard (D)	10,008	26.3

TENNESSEE

		Votes	%
1	Dayton E. Phillips (R)	24,144	100.0
2	John Jennings Jr. (R)	28,752	84.0
	James Douglas Wyrick (I)	5,485	16.0
3	Estes Kefauver (D)	26,779	90.8
	George Bagwell (I)	2,725	9.2
4	Albert A. Gore (D)	7,624	67.5
	H. E. McLean (R)	3,673	32.5
5	Joe L. Evins (D)	11,646	100.0
6	J. Percy Priest (D)	7,178	77.1
	Will T. Perry (R)	2,135	22.9
7	Wirt Courtney (D)	11,658	100.0
8	Thomas J. Murray (D)	11,891	100.0
9	Jere Cooper (D)	12,685	100.0
10	Clifford Davis (D)	37,069	100.0

TEXAS

		Votes	%
1	Wright Patman (D)	11,929	100.0
2	Jesse M. Combs (D)	19,909	96.2
3	Lindley Beckworth (D)	10,686	100.0
4	Sam Rayburn (D)	11,957	93.7
	Floyd Harry (R)	800	6.3
5	J. Frank Wilson (D)	12,267	75.8
	L. W. Stayart (R)	3,921	24.2
6	Olin E. Teague (D)	11,421	100.0
7	Tom Pickett (D)	14,810	100.0
8	Albert Thomas (D)	42,163	90.8
	R. F. Burns (R)	4,253	9.2
9	Joseph J. Mansfield (D)	16,712	100.0
10	Lyndon B. Johnson (D)	16,947	100.0
11	W. R. Poage (D)	9,178	100.0
12	Wingate H. Lucas (D)	15,266	87.7
	E. M. Hyder (R)	2,146	12.3
13	Ed Gossett (D)	17,714	100.0
14	John E. Lyle (D)	30,064	100.0
15	Milton H. West (D)	16,674	100.0
16	R. Ewing Thomason (D)	8,114	100.0
17	Omar Burleson (D)	14,874	100.0
18	Eugene Worley (D)	12,475	74.1
	F. T. O'Brien (R)	4,357	25.9
19	George H. Mahon (D)	15,791	94.6
	M. D. Temple (R)	905	5.4
20	Paul J. Kilday (D)	10,543	100.0
21	O. Clark Fisher (D)	15,943	100.0

UTAH

		Votes	%
1	Walter K. Granger (D)	44,888	50.1
	David J. Wilson (R)	44,784	49.9
2	William A. Dawson (R)	56,402	52.7
	J. Will Robinson (D)	50,598	47.3

VERMONT

Candidates	Votes	%
AL Charles A. Plumley (R)	46,985	64.3
Matthew J. Caldbeck (D)	26,056	35.7

VIRGINIA

Candidates	Votes	%
1 S. Otis Bland (D)	13,863	75.0
Walter Johnson (R)	4,628	25.0
2 Porter Hardy Jr. (D)	19,267	65.7
Sidney H. Kelsey (R)	10,078	34.3
3 J. Vaughan Gary (D)	21,947	73.3
Earle Lutz (R)	7,974	26.7
4 Patrick Henry Drewry (D)	13,636	87.1
Andrew S. Condrey (P)	2,012	12.9
5 Thomas B. Stanley (D)	17,741	73.5
William L. Creasy (R)	6,390	26.5
6 J. Lindsay Almond Jr. (D)	20,068	64.8
Frank R. Angell (R)	10,641	34.4
7 Burr P. Harrison (D)	19,535	62.3
Karl Jenkins (R)	11,813	37.7
8 Howard Worth Smith (D)	21,252	62.1
Lawrence Michael (R)	12,950	37.9
9 John W. Flannagan Jr. (D)	20,610	51.8
S. H. Sutherland (R)	17,152	43.1
John Albert Goodpasture Jr. (I)	2,026	5.1

Special Elections

	Votes	%
5 Thomas B. Stanley (D)	17,862	75.4
William L. Creasy (R)	5,829	24.6

Candidates	Votes	%
7 Burr P. Harrison (D)	19,711	62.5
Karl Jenkins (R)	11,809	37.5

WASHINGTON

	Votes	%
1 Homer R. Jones (R)	113,289	63.8
Hugh De Lacy (D)	64,155	36.2
2 Henry M. Jackson (D)	54,089	53.1
Payson Peterson (R)	47,838	46.9
3 Fred Norman (R)	47,875	53.9
Charles R. Savage (D)	40,980	46.1
4 Hal Holmes (R)	51,476	67.6
Earl S. Coe (D)	24,662	32.4
5 Walt Horan (R)	58,535	61.3
John T. Little (D)	34,870	36.5
6 Thor C. Tollefson (R)	56,702	53.9
John M. Coffee (D)	48,431	46.1

WEST VIRGINIA

	Votes	%
1 Francis J. Love (R)	45,691	53.1
Matthew M. Neely (D)	40,370	46.9
2 Melvin C. Snyder (R)	41,224	51.4
Jennings Randolph (D)	39,041	48.6
3 Edward G. Rohrbough (R)	42,386	51.5
Cleveland M. Bailey (D)	39,872	48.5
4 Hubert S. Ellis (R)	54,932	52.7
M. G. Burnside (D)	49,408	47.4

Candidates	Votes	%
5 John Kee (D)	43,154	56.9
Hartley Sanders (R)	32,754	43.2
6 Erland H. Hedrick (D)	57,461	53.0
Harold H. Neff (R)	51,064	47.1

WISCONSIN

	Votes	%
1 Lawrence H. Smith (R)	58,344	56.5
John R. Redstrom (D)	44,188	42.8
2 Robert K. Henry (R)	68,794*	62.9
William G. Rice (D)	39,657	36.3
3 William H. Stevenson (R)	65,177	96.1
4 John C. Brophy (R)	49,144	36.5
Edmund V. Bobrowicz (D)	44,398	33.0
Thaddeus F. B. Wasielewski (I)	38,502	28.6
5 Charles J. Kersten (R)	76,364	54.1
Andrew J. Biemiller (D)	59,764	42.3
6 Frank B. Keefe (R)	58,444	64.2
Edwin W. Webster (D)	31,550	34.7
7 Reid F. Murray (R)	60,390	71.6
Elmer E. Fraley (D)	23,481	27.8
8 John W. Byrnes (R)	67,840	64.7
Martin J. Young (D)	37,013	35.3
9 Merlin Hull (R)	70,527	99.0
10 Alvin E. O'Konski (R)	40,263	53.0
Henry J. Berquist (D)	32,238	42.4

WYOMING

	Votes	%
AL Frank A. Barrett (R)	44,512	56.0
John J. McIntyre (D)	34,946	44.0

1947 House Elections

NEW YORK

Special Election

	Votes	%
14 Abraham J. Multer (D, L)	47,849	58.2
Victor J. Rabinowitz (AM LAB)	20,800	25.3
Jacob P. Fefkowitz (R)	13,597	16.5

WISCONSIN

Special Election

	Votes	%
2 Glenn R. Davis (R)	24,023	50.6
Thompson (D)	23,181	48.8

1948 House Elections

ALABAMA

Candidates	Votes	%
1 Frank W. Boykin (D)	19,778	100.0
2 George M. Grant (D)	21,271	100.0
3 George W. Andrews (D)	16,279	100.0
4 Sam Hobbs (D)	17,282	85.0
B. Hogan Stewart (R)	3,054	15.0
5 Albert Rains (D)	20,548	100.0
6 Edward deGraffenried (D)	13,968	82.4
W. P. Ivey (R)	2,994	17.7
7 Carl A. Elliott (D)	21,552	100.0
8 Robert E. Jones Jr. (D)	19,060	88.4
Harry J. Frahn (R)	2,510	11.6
9 Laurie C. Battle (D)	33,781	87.1
Hiram Dodd (R)	5,006	12.9

ARIZONA

Candidates	Votes	%
1 John R. Murdock (D)	42,565	58.4
John H. Udall (R)	29,864	41.0
2 Harold A. Patten (D)	54,066	62.8
Albert R. Buehman (R)	30,140	35.0

ARKANSAS

Candidates	Votes	%
1 Ezekiel C. Gathings (D)	34,676	100.0
2 Wilbur D. Mills (D)	29,922	100.0
3 James W. Trimble (D)	27,278	68.6
Dalton Dotson (R)	12,462	31.4
4 Boyd Tackett (D)	29,338	87.8
C. R. Starbird (R)	4,094	12.3
5 Brooks Hays (D)	36,440	87.0
Thad Tisdale (R)	5,471	13.1
6 William F. Norrell (D)	40,291	100.0
7 Oren Harris (D)	32,982	100.0

CALIFORNIA

Candidates	Votes	%
1 Hubert B. Scudder (R)	82,947	54.5
Sterling J. Norgard (D-IP)	68,951	45.3
2 Clair Engle (D-R)	78,555	100.0
3 Leroy Johnson (R-D)	166,571	84.4
James B. Willard (I PROG)	30,878	15.6
4 Franck R. Havenner (D)	73,704	51.0
William S. Mailliard (R)	68,875	47.7
5 Richard J. Welch (R-D)	116,347	100.0
6 George P. Miller (D-R)	194,985	99.9
7 John J. Allen Jr. (R)	78,534	51.4
Buel G. Gallagher (D-IP)	74,318	48.6
8 Jack Z. Anderson (R-D)	161,743	79.9
Paul Taylor (I PROG)	40,670	20.1
9 Cecil F. White (D)	72,826	51.3
Bertrand W. Gearhart (R)	66,563	46.9
10 Thomas H. Werdel (R-D)	67,448	71.3
Sam James Miller (I PROG)	27,168	28.7
11 Ernest K. Bramblett (R-D)	87,143	80.7
Cole Weston (I PROG)	14,582	13.5
George E. Outland	6,157	5.7
12 Richard M. Nixon (R-D)	141,509	86.9
Una W. Rice (I PROG)	19,631	12.1
13 Norris Poulson (R)	62,951	52.6
Ned R. Healy (D-IP)	56,624	47.3
14 Helen Gahagan Douglas (D)	89,581	65.3
W. Wallace Braden (R)	44,611	32.5
15 Gordon L. McDonough (R-D)	131,933	83.0
Maynard J. Omerberg (I PROG)	27,007	17.0
16 Donald L. Jackson (R)	121,198	57.0
Ellis E. Patterson (D-IP)	91,268	42.9
17 Cecil R. King (D-R)	194,782	99.9
18 Clyde Doyle (D)	105,687	51.1
Willis W. Bradley (R)	92,721	44.9
19 Chet Holifield (D)	72,900	69.7
Joseph Francis Quigley (R)	28,698	27.5

Candidates	Votes	%
20 Carl Hinshaw (R-D)	204,710	81.5
William B. Esterman (I PROG)	46,232	18.4
21 Harry R. Sheppard (D)	61,383	55.2
Lowell E. Lathrop (R)	47,411	42.6
22 John Phillips (R-D)	115,697	99.9
23 Clinton D. McKinnon (D)	112,534	55.8
Charles K. Fletcher (R)	87,138	43.2

COLORADO

Candidates	Votes	%
1 John A. Carroll (D)	106,096	64.8
Christopher F. Cusack (R)	57,541	35.2
2 William S. Hill (R)	71,868	51.9
George L. Bickel (D)	66,579	48.1
3 John H. Marsalis (D)	65,114	50.7
J. Edgar Chenoweth (R)	63,312	49.3
4 Wayne N. Aspinall (D)	34,695	51.9
Robert F. Rockwell (R)	32,206	48.1

CONNECTICUT

Candidates	Votes	%
1 Abraham A. Ribicoff (D)	127,802	54.7
William J. Miller (R)	103,294	44.2
2 Chase Going Woodhouse (D)	69,339	51.7
Horace Seely-Brown Jr. (R)	64,916	48.4
3 John A. McGuire (D)	84,449	49.7
Ellsworth B. Foote (R)	83,310	49.1
4 John Davis Lodge (R)	117,727	55.2
William Gaston (D)	92,618	43.4
5 James T. Patterson (R)	62,804	51.1
Vincent P. Kiernan (D)	58,300	47.4
AL Antoni N. Sadlak (R)	433,311	49.3
Fred Trotta (D)	429,348	48.8

DELAWARE

Candidates	Votes	%
AL J. Caleb Boggs (R)	71,127	50.6
J. Carl McGuigan (D)	68,909	49.0

FLORIDA

Candidates	Votes	%
1 J. Hardin Peterson (D)	66,348	100.0
2 Charles E. Bennett (D)	55,715	91.1
Camille Geneau (R)	5,413	8.9
3 Robert L. F. Sikes (D)	30,730	100.0
4 George A. Smathers (D)	63,665	81.0
J. L. Wambaugh (R)	14,912	19.0
5 A. S. Herlong Jr. (D)	46,939	70.7
M. J. Moss Jr. (R)	19,501	29.4
6 Dwight L. Rogers (D)	31,933	66.7
Rolf Kaltenborn (R)	15,977	33.4

GEORGIA

Candidates	Votes	%
1 Prince H. Preston (D)	42,677	100.0
2 E. E. Cox (D)	26,815	100.0
3 Stephen Pace (D)	32,098	100.0
4 A. Sidney Camp (D)	33,522	100.0
5 James C. Davis (D)	54,637	99.6
6 Carl Vinson (D)	29,446	100.0
7 Henderson Lanham (D)	45,195	100.0
8 W. M. Wheeler (D)	35,608	100.0
9 John S. Wood (D)	29,699	100.0
10 Paul Brown (D)	35,479	100.0

IDAHO

Candidates	Votes	%
1 Compton I. White (D)	46,846	51.8
Abe McGregor Goff (R)	41,404	45.7
2 John C. Sanborn (R)	61,690	50.7
Asael Lyman (D)	59,006	48.5

ILLINOIS

Candidates	Votes	%
1 William L. Dawson (D)	98,690	67.0
William E. King (R)	43,034	29.2
2 Barratt O'Hara (D)	91,648	50.5
Richard B. Vail (R)	85,119	46.9
3 Neil J. Linehan (D)	91,204	52.9
Fred E. Busbey (R)	81,175	47.1
4 James V. Buckley (D)	89,557	52.1
Leslie E. Salter (R)	82,310	47.9
5 Martin Gorski (D)	114,660	72.5
John L. Waner (R)	43,610	27.6
6 Thomas J. O'Brien (D)	127,918	68.4
John M. Coan (R)	53,548	28.6
7 Adolph J. Sabath (D)	133,199	73.7
Francis C. Sperry (R)	47,602	26.3
8 Thomas S. Gordon (D)	101,098	65.1
Herbert F. Geisler (R)	54,316	35.0
9 Sidney R. Yates (D)	91,271	54.5
Robert J. Twyman (R)	73,301	43.8
10 Richard W. Hoffman (R)	109,031	58.1
Marvin J. Peters (D)	78,533	41.9
11 Chester A. Chesney (D)	80,750	50.8
James C. Moreland (R)	78,269	49.2
12 Edgar A. Jonas (R)	98,956	51.4
Blair L. Varnes (D)	88,795	46.1
13 Ralph E. Church (R)	123,978	68.0
Willard C. Walters (D)	58,340	32.0
14 Chauncey W. Reed (R)	94,962	68.3
Richard Plum (D)	44,050	31.7
15 Noah M. Mason (R)	74,213	56.4
G. M. Wells (D)	57,296	43.6
16 Leo E. Allen (R)	76,840	58.5
Albert H. Manus Jr. (D)	54,481	41.5
17 Leslie C. Arends (R)	71,220	62.8
Carl Vrooman (D)	42,226	37.2
18 Harold H. Velde (R)	61,652	52.1
Dale E. Sutton (D)	56,688	47.9
19 Robert B. Chiperfield (R)	69,733	54.0
Fred J. Brown (D)	59,397	46.0
20 Sid Simpson (R)	59,067	53.1
Henry D. Sullivan (D)	52,235	46.9
21 Peter F. Mack Jr. (D)	69,619	53.1
Joseph L. Moore (R)	61,452	46.9
22 Rolla C. McMillen (R)	64,625	53.2
Olive Remington Goldman (D)	56,893	46.8
23 Edward H. Jenison (R)	57,800	51.8
Wayne R. Cook (D)	53,885	48.3
24 Charles W. Vursell (R)	57,732	50.6
John David Upchurch (D)	56,262	49.4
25 Melvin Price (D)	101,927	69.5
Russell H. Classen (R)	44,728	30.5
26 C. W. Bishop (R)	54,993	51.9
Kent E. Keller (D)	51,028	48.1

INDIANA

Candidates	Votes	%
1 Ray J. Madden (D)	78,898	60.7
Theodore L. Sendak (R)	50,194	38.6
2 Charles A. Halleck (R)	71,907	55.2
Theodore J. Smith (D)	57,245	44.0
3 Thurman C. Crook (D)	86,382	51.9
Robert A. Grant (R)	78,935	47.5
4 Edward H. Kruse Jr. (D)	66,689	50.8
George W. Gillie (R)	63,403	48.3
5 John R. Walsh (D)	91,861	51.9
Forest A. Harness (R)	82,730	46.8
6 Cecil M. Harden (R)	66,414	49.9
Jack J. O'Grady (D)	65,931	49.5
7 James E. Noland (D)	74,396	53.7
Gerald W. Landis (R)	62,855	45.4
8 Winfield K. Denton (D)	89,990	55.4
Edward A. Mitchell (R)	71,634	44.1
9 Earl Wilson (R)	59,787	51.6
Christopher D. Moritz (D)	55,333	47.7

INDIANA

Candidates	Votes	%
10 Ralph Harvey (R)	76,036	52.5
Robert C. Oliver (D)	67,081	46.3
11 Andrew Jacobs Sr. (D)	103,046	50.6
George L. Denny (R)	98,451	48.4

IOWA

Candidates	Votes	%
1 Thomas E. Martin (R)	70,959	53.6
James D. France (D)	60,860	45.9
2 Henry O. Talle (R)	82,139	53.6
T. W. Mullaney (D)	70,272	45.9
3 H. R. Gross (R)	78,838	58.3
Dan J. P. Ryan (D)	56,002	41.4
4 Karl LeCompte (R)	53,384	51.5
Steven V. Carter (D)	49,894	48.2
5 Paul Cunningham (R)	60,103	50.8
Vincent L. Browner (D)	57,370	48.5
6 James I. Dolliver (R)	55,641	55.8
James E. Irwin (D)	43,997	44.2
7 Ben F. Jensen (R)	59,173	56.9
W. A. Byers (D)	44,857	43.1
8 Charles B. Hoeven (R)	56,970	55.2
L. J. McGivern (D)	45,796	44.4

KANSAS

Candidates	Votes	%
1 Albert M. Cole (R)	68,395	60.5
James L. Quinn (D)	44,711	39.5
2 Errett P. Scrivner (R)	68,324	51.9
Philip A. Dergance (D)	63,431	48.1
3 Herbert A. Meyer (R)	46,935	55.0
Marcus C. Black (D)	38,391	45.0
4 Edward H. Rees (R)	88,605	55.6
William J. Kropp (D)	70,778	44.4
5 Clifford R. Hope (R)	77,160	65.0
Henry D. Parkinson (D)	41,614	35.0
6 Wint Smith (R)	55,013	57.6
Leslie E. Davis (D)	40,553	42.4

KENTUCKY

Candidates	Votes	%
1 Noble J. Gregory (D)	50,720	100.0
2 John Whitaker (D)	54,586	63.4
Mallam Lake (R)	31,527	36.6
3 Thruston B. Morton (R)	74,168	53.0
Ralph H. Logan (D)	64,877	46.3
4 Frank L. Chelf (D)	45,538	59.5
Stanley Jaggers (R)	31,062	40.6
5 Brent Spence (D)	47,518	66.2
George T. Smith (R)	24,240	33.8
6 Thomas R. Underwood (D)	60,659	60.7
John N. Menefee (R)	39,251	39.3
7 Carl D. Perkins (D)	39,788	60.5
W. Howes Meade (R)	26,007	39.5
8 Joe B. Bates (D)	52,328	58.6
Hubert Counts (R)	34,127	38.2
9 James S. Golden (R)	60,309	100.0

LOUISIANA

Candidates	Votes	%
1 F. Edward Hebert (D)	36,748	100.0
2 Hale Boggs (D)	61,316	100.0
3 Edwin E. Willis (D)	26,587	66.4
J. Paulin Duhe (R)	13,437	33.6
4 Overton Brooks (D)	32,045	100.0
5 Otto E. Passman (D)	34,362	100.0
6 James H. Morrison (D)	47,515	100.0
7 Henry D. Larcade Jr. (D)	36,053	100.0
8 A. Leonard Allen (D)	33,613	100.0

MAINE

Candidates	Votes	%
1 Robert Hale (R)	52,536	62.5
James A. McVicar (D)	31,528	37.5
2 Charles P. Nelson (R)	50,552	67.2
Benjamin J. Arena (D)	24,698	32.8

Candidates	Votes	%
3 Frank Fellows (R)	38,692	70.9
F. Davis Clark (D)	15,888	29.1

MARYLAND

Candidates	Votes	%
1 Edward T. Miller (R)	29,700	52.4
S. Scott Beck Jr. (D)	27,024	47.6
2 William P. Bolton (D)	99,157	55.2
A. Earl Shipley (R)	76,235	42.5
3 Edward A. Garmatz (D)	32,138	68.8
John A. Janetzke Jr. (R)	13,131	28.1
4 George H. Fallon (D)	38,486	58.2
James W. Miller (R)	21,084	31.9
John E. T. Camper (PROG)	6,552	9.9
5 Lansdale G. Sasscer (D)	45,902	59.7
C. Maurice Weidemeyer (R)	30,997	40.3
6 J. Glenn Beall (R)	59,856	55.3
F. Byrne Austin (D)	48,304	44.7

MASSACHUSETTS

Candidates	Votes	%
1 John W. Heselton (R)	75,582	57.2
Patrick J. O'Malley (D)	56,604	42.8
2 Foster Furcolo (D)	81,775	54.9
Charles R. Clason (R)	67,267	45.1
3 Philip J. Philbin (D)	104,601	73.9
Carroll H. Balcom (R)	36,855	26.1
4 Harold D. Donohue (D)	89,064	59.2
John J. Maginnis (R)	61,448	40.8
5 Edith Nourse Rogers (R)	139,288	100.0
6 George J. Bates (R)	108,179	100.0
7 Thomas J. Lane (D)	100,333	79.2
A. Prescott Barker (R)	26,339	20.8
8 Angier L. Goodwin (R)	75,844	51.0
Anthony M. Roche (D)	72,767	49.0
9 Donald W. Nicholson (R)	82,750	56.7
Jacinto F. Diniz (D)	63,275	43.3
10 Christian A. Herter (R)	118,741	69.5
Walter A. O'Brien Jr. (D)	52,022	30.5
11 John F. Kennedy (D)	106,366	100.0
12 John W. McCormack (D)	125,015	100.0
13 Richard B. Wigglesworth (R)	89,913	56.6
David J. Concannon (D)	69,050	43.4
14 Joseph W. Martin Jr. (R)	87,973	61.4
Joseph M. Mendonca (D)	55,369	38.6

MICHIGAN

Candidates	Votes	%
1 George G. Sadowski (D)	101,954	83.5
Rudolph G. Tenerowicz (R)	19,609	16.1
2 Earl C. Michener (R)	65,006	55.8
Preston W. Slosson (D)	50,148	43.0
3 Paul W. Shafer (R)	64,637	59.4
Leeman J. McCarty (D)	42,146	38.7
4 Clare E. Hoffman (R)	61,059	64.9
Tom Surprise (D)	31,429	33.4
5 Gerald R. Ford Jr. (R)	74,191	60.5
Fred J. Barr Jr. (D)	46,972	38.3
6 William W. Blackney (R)	73,465	49.8
George D. Stevens (D)	72,681	49.3
7 Jesse P. Wolcott (R)	68,903	59.0
Harvey C. Whetzel (D)	47,040	40.3
8 Fred L. Crawford (R)	61,394	61.3
Louis C. Schwinger (D)	37,125	37.1
9 Albert J. Engel (R)	51,771	58.5
John George Hosko (D)	35,805	40.5
10 Roy O. Woodruff (R)	49,206	63.3
Edward J. Daugherty (D)	27,742	35.7
11 Charles E. Potter (R)	48,633	63.6
Violet L. Patterson (D)	27,265	35.6
12 John B. Bennett (R)	42,955	56.6
Gene A. Saari (D)	32,485	42.8
13 George D. O'Brien (D)	76,947	62.5
Howard A. Coffin (R)	45,761	37.1
14 Louis C. Rabaut (D)	99,227	57.0
Harold F. Youngblood (R)	74,474	42.7
15 John D. Dingell (D)	92,579	65.0
Charles G. Burns (R)	49,286	34.6

Candidates	Votes	%
16 John Lesinski (D)	97,826	62.5
Kirby L. Wilson Jr. (R)	57,730	36.9
17 George A. Dondero (R)	116,427	52.7
John J. Brown (D)	103,390	46.8

MINNESOTA

Candidates	Votes	%
1 August H. Andresen (R)	80,345	61.4
Karl F. Rolvaag (DFL)	50,533	38.6
2 Joseph P. O'Hara (R)	82,886	63.9
Milton F. Maxwell (DFL)	46,894	36.1
3 Roy W. Wier (DFL)	87,171	54.6
George MacKinnon (R)	72,402	45.4
4 Eugene J. McCarthy (DFL)	78,476	59.4
Edward J. Devitt (R)	53,574	40.6
5 Walter H. Judd (R)	76,313	54.0
Marcella F. Killen (DFL)	65,113	46.0
6 Fred Marshall (DFL)	66,601	51.7
Harold Knutson (R)	62,194	48.3
7 H. Carl Andersen (R)	63,879	52.5
James M. Youngdale (DFL)	57,863	47.5
8 John A. Blatnik (DFL)	88,501	66.6
William A. Berlin (R)	44,306	33.4
9 Harold C. Hagen (R)	57,189	54.6
Oscar A. Johnson (DFL)	47,476	45.4

MISSISSIPPI

Candidates	Votes	%
1 John E. Rankin (D)	16,800	100.0
2 Jamie L. Whitten (D)	13,771	100.0
3 William M. Whittington (D)	17,369	100.0
4 Thomas G. Abernethy (D)	15,290	98.4
5 W. Arthur Winstead (D)	22,641	100.0
6 William M. Colmer (D)	29,751	100.0
7 John Bell Williams (D)	36,663	100.0

MISSOURI

Candidates	Votes	%
1 Clare Magee (D)	56,226	57.6
Wat Arnold (R)	41,365	42.4
2 Morgan M. Moulder (D)	66,062	56.7
Max Schwabe (R)	50,372	43.2
3 Philip J. Welch (D)	69,599	57.1
William C. Cole (R)	52,290	42.9
4 Theodore Leonard Irving (D)	74,752	64.1
Richard A. Erickson (R)	41,576	35.7
5 Richard W. Bolling (D)	59,961	55.9
Albert L. Reeves Jr. (R)	47,371	44.1
6 George H. Christopher (D)	63,390	51.4
Marion T. Bennett (R)	59,959	48.6
7 Dewey Short (R)	61,242	54.0
Thomas A. Johnson (D)	52,255	46.0
8 S. J. Carnahan (D)	60,081	57.2
Parke M. Banta (R)	44,887	42.8
9 Clarence Cannon (D)	56,669	61.7
Robert V. Niedner (R)	35,232	38.3
10 Paul C. Jones (D)	67,564	71.6
W. K. Dillon (R)	26,760	28.4
11 John B. Sullivan (D)	78,162	64.7
Claude I. Bakewell (R)	40,719	33.7
12 Raymond W. Karst (D)	132,920	55.0
Walter C. Ploeser (R)	107,861	44.6
13 Frank M. Karsten (D)	77,245	70.6
Charles P. McBride (R)	32,217	29.4

MONTANA

Candidates	Votes	%
1 Mike Mansfield (D)	64,276	67.9
Albert H. Angstman (R)	29,937	31.6
2 Wesley A. D'Ewart (R)	61,124	51.0
Willard E. Fraser (D)	58,711	49.0

NEBRASKA

Candidates	Votes	%
1 Carl T. Curtis (R)	76,359	57.2
Frank B. Morrison (D)	57,031	42.8

NEBRASKA

Candidates	Votes	%
2 Eugene D. O'Sullivan (D)	58,443	51.4
Howard Buffett (R)	55,199	48.6
3 Karl Stefan (R)	71,513	64.8
Duane K. Peterson (D)	38,846	35.2
4 Arthur L. Miller (R)	65,549	63.6
C. Edgar Leafdale (D)	37,511	36.4

NEVADA

Candidates	Votes	%
AL Walter S. Baring (D)	29,733	50.7
Charles H. Russell (R)	28,972	49.4

NEW HAMPSHIRE

Candidates	Votes	%
1 Chester E. Merrow (R)	64,794	55.5
Peter R. Poirier (D)	51,262	43.9
2 Norris Cotton (R)	59,505	57.4
Richard W. Leonard (D)	43,289	41.8

NEW JERSEY

Candidates	Votes	%
1 Charles A. Wolverton (R)	89,211	53.0
John W. Donges (D)	77,012	45.8
2 T. Millet Hand (R)	62,804	61.7
William E. Stringer (D)	38,194	37.5
3 James C. Auchincloss (R)	87,538	58.5
Charles F. Sullivan (D)	59,810	40.0
4 Charles R. Howell (D)	77,018	61.5
Albert C. Jones (R)	48,204	38.5
5 Charles A. Eaton (R)	92,286	57.4
George C. Miller (D)	66,387	41.3
6 Clifford P. Case (R)	83,285	55.3
H. Frank Pettit (D)	61,465	40.8
7 J. Parnell Thomas (R)	72,873	56.2
John J. Carlin (D)	56,095	43.2
8 Gordon Canfield (R)	59,191	47.5
Charles S. Joelson (D)	59,043	47.4
9 Harry L. Towe (R)	90,153	62.3
James S. Brown (D)	54,682	37.8
10 Peter W. Rodino Jr. (D)	58,668	50.7
Anthony Guiliano (R)	52,898	45.7
11 Hugh J. Addonizio (D)	52,644	47.7
Frank L. Sundstrom (R)	50,920	46.2
12 Robert W. Kean (R)	63,232	48.6
Harry Dudkin (D)	58,495	44.9
13 Mary T. Norton (D)	84,487	68.1
Leon Banach (R)	39,661	32.0
14 Edward J. Hart (D)	76,881	62.8
Michael Bongiovanni (R)	45,564	37.2

NEW MEXICO

Candidates	Votes	%
AL John E. Miles (D)	108,529 ✔	
Antonio M. Fernandez (D)	105,300 ✔	
Ben F. Meyer (R)	76,695	
Herman G. Baca (R)	73,661	
Clinton E. Jencks (PROG)	805	

NEW YORK

Candidates	Votes	%
1 W. Kingsland Macy (R)	101,924	66.0
Harold W. Worzel (D)	48,816	31.6
2 Leonard W. Hall (R)	144,052	68.1
Richard T. Mayes (D, L)	62,142	29.4
3 Henry J. Latham (R)	104,476	56.5
George J. Gross (D)	65,247	35.3
4 L. Gary Clemente (D)	62,190	46.9
Gregory McMahon (R)	58,192	43.8
Thomas J. McCabe (AM LAB)	7,681	5.8
5 T. Vincent Quinn (D, L)	83,213	49.8
Robert Tripp Ross (R)	72,012	43.1
Morris Pottish (AM LAB)	11,994	7.2
6 James J. Delaney (D, L)	76,828	54.2
Robert Nodar Jr. (R)	55,844	39.4
Irma Lindheim (AM LAB)	9,092	6.4
7 John J. Delaney (D, AM LAB)	65,162*	60.0

Candidates	Votes	%
Francis E. Dorn (R, L)	43,483	40.0
8 Joseph L. Pfeifer (D, AM LAB)	61,037	67.7
Benjamin F. Westervelt Jr (R)	25,773	28.6
9 Eugene J. Keogh (D, L)	59,711	56.2
Philip Hodes (R)	26,700	25.1
Murray Rosof (AM LAB)	19,803	18.6
10 Andrew L. Somers (D, L)	69,502	56.1
Arthur S. Hirsch (R)	32,290	26.1
Ada B. Jackson (AM LAB)	22,067	17.8
11 James J. Heffernan (D, L)	74,974	54.9
Alfred C. McKenzie (R)	41,289	30.2
Frank Serri (AM LAB)	20,340	14.9
12 John J. Rooney (D, L)	55,021	60.4
John J. Miller (R)	29,061	31.9
Vincent J. Longhi (AM LAB)	6,968	7.7
13 Donald L. O'Toole (D, L)	66,111	52.8
Charles A. Fisher (R)	44,718	35.7
James Griesi (AM LAB)	14,440	11.5
14 Abraham J. Multer (D, R)	103,676	77.8
Lee Pressman (AM LAB)	29,502	22.2
15 Emanuel Celler (D, AM LAB)	94,828	81.4
Henry D. Dorfman (R)	21,703	18.6
16 James J. Murphy (D, L)	51,185	49.3
Frank A. Pavis (R)	45,623	44.0
Frank Cremonesi (AM LAB)	6,991	6.7
17 Frederic R. Coudert Jr. (R)	74,581	53.2
Arthur T. Sawyer (D, L)	52,101	37.2
Alvin Udell (AM LAB)	13,401	9.6
18 Vito Marcantonio (AM LAB)	36,278	36.9
John P. Morrissey (D)	31,211	31.7
John Ellis (R, L)	30,899	31.4
19 Arthur G. Klein (D, AM LAB)	77,426	74.4
Herbert Lasky (R)	20,697	19.9
Stephen C. Vladeck (L)	5,886	5.7
20 Sol Bloom (D, L)	73,866	59.4
Jules J. Justin (R)	34,819	28.0
Eugene P. Connolly (AM LAB)	15,727	12.6
21 Jacob K. Javits (R, L)	66,527	50.7
Paul O'Dwyer (D, AM LAB)	64,654	49.3
22 Adam Clayton Powell Jr. (D, AM LAB)	63,523	76.4
Harold C. Burton (R)	14,012	16.9
Edna D. Moseley (L)	5,583	6.7
23 Walter A. Lynch (D, R)	121,523	83.0
Leon Straus (AM LAB)	24,903	17.0
24 Isidore Dollinger (D, R)	74,971	63.1
Leo Isacson (AM LAB)	43,933	37.0
25 Charles A. Buckley (D, R)	138,706	82.2
Albert E. Kahn (AM LAB)	30,112	17.8
26 Christopher C. McGrath (D, L)	91,456	54.8
David M. Potts (R)	57,061	34.2
Nicholas Carnes (AM LAB)	18,379	11.0
27 Ralph W. Gwinn (R)	81,144	52.1
Richard W. McSpedon (D, L)	67,541	43.4
28 Ralph A. Gamble (R)	88,822	62.7
Charles J. Nager (D, L)	46,335	32.7
29 Katharine St.George (R)	79,229	60.1
William G. Pendergast (D, L)	48,063	36.5
30 Jay LeFevre (R)	91,649	64.8
Robert R. Decormier (D, AM LAB)	49,691	35.2
31 Bernard W. Kearney (R)	77,725	55.3
William M. Murphy (D, L)	58,215	41.4
32 William T. Byrne (D, L)	88,476	55.6
Lawrence J. Collins (R)	65,341	41.1
33 Dean P. Taylor (R)	98,618	63.7
Joseph T. Hammer (D, L)	52,059	33.6
34 Clarence E. Kilburn (R)	70,715	60.7
Francis K. Purcell (D)	43,777	37.6
35 John C. Davies (D, L)	62,855	48.9
Hadwen C. Fuller (R)	62,717	48.8
36 R. Walter Riehlman (R)	78,409	50.5
Richard T. Mosher (D, L)	71,847	46.3

Candidates	Votes	%
37 Edwin Arthur Hall (R)	65,848	63.4
Myron C. Sloat (D)	35,503	34.2
38 John Taber (R)	66,695	58.0
Francis J. Souhan (D)	48,222	42.0
39 W. Sterling Cole (R)	70,659	64.3
Donald J. O'Connor (D, L)	37,272	33.9
40 Kenneth B. Keating (R)	90,305	51.4
George F. Rogers (D, AM LAB)	85,505	48.6
41 James W. Wadsworth Jr. (R)	67,882	59.1
Bernard E. Hart (D)	45,155	39.3
42 William L. Pfeiffer (R)	75,842	51.1
Mary Louise Nice (D, L)	69,290	46.6
43 Anthony F. Tauriello (D, L)	72,388	50.8
Edward J. Elsaesser (R)	66,729	46.9
44 Chester C. Gorski (D, L)	79,795	51.8
John C. Butler (R)	71,275	46.2
45 Daniel A. Reed (R)	58,340	60.1
Hubert D. Bliss (D)	35,406	36.5

Special Election

Candidates	Votes	%
24 Leo Isacson (AM LAB)	22,697	55.9
Karl Propper (D)	12,598	31.0
Dean Alfange (L)	3,843	9.5

NORTH CAROLINA

Candidates	Votes	%
1 Herbert C. Bonner (D)	31,850	92.7
Zeno O. Ratcliff (R)	2,507	7.3
2 John H. Kerr (D)	36,227	96.0
3 Graham A. Barden (D)	34,997	78.8
Perry G. Crumpler (R)	9,407	21.2
4 Harold D. Cooley (D)	57,658	78.1
Joel A. Johnson (R)	15,866	21.5
5 Richard Thurmond Chatham (D)	47,575	72.7
John Tucker Day (R)	17,041	26.1
6 Carl T. Durham (D)	50,659	72.1
Ralph O. Smith (R)	17,906	25.5
7 F. Ertel Carlyle (D)	43,292	84.3
J. O. West (R)	7,839	15.3
8 Charles B. Deane (D)	46,941	62.7
Lafayette Williams (R)	27,924	37.3
9 Robert L. Doughton (D)	51,586	59.6
Clyde R. Greene (R)	35,008	40.4
10 Hamilton C. Jones (D)	48,043	59.6
Roy A. Harmon (R)	32,321	40.1
11 Alfred L. Bulwinkle (D)	40,009	64.9
Calvin R. Edney (R)	21,614	35.1
12 Monroe M. Redden (D)	52,036	63.1
W. W. Candler (R)	30,456	36.9

NORTH DAKOTA

Candidates	Votes	%
AL William Lemke (R)	132,343 ✔	
Usher L. Burdick (R)	128,454 ✔	
Alfred Dale (D)	56,702	
John M. Weiler	1,758	

OHIO

Candidates	Votes	%
1 Charles H. Elston (R)	73,952	51.7
Morse Johnson (D)	69,240	48.4
2 Earl T. Wagner (D)	75,062	52.9
William E. Hess (R)	66,968	47.2
3 Edward Breen (D)	110,204	58.2
Raymond H. Burke (R)	79,162	41.8
4 William M. McCulloch (R)	57,321	55.7
Earl Ludwig (D)	45,534	44.3
5 Cliff Clevenger (R)	34,950	52.1
Dan Batt (D)	32,076	47.9
6 James G. Polk (D)	46,944	53.1
Edward O. McCowen (R)	41,492	46.9
7 Clarence J. Brown (R)	71,737	100.0
8 Frederick C. Smith (R)	43,929	54.5
Andrew T. Durbin (D)	36,685	45.5

OHIO

	Candidates	Votes	%
9	Thomas H. Burke (D)	85,409	53.8
	Homer A. Ramey (R)	73,394	46.2
10	Thomas A. Jenkins (R)	38,330	57.9
	Delmar A. Canaday (D)	27,913	42.1
11	Walter E. Brehm (R)	33,796	50.9
	Joseph C. Allen (D)	32,667	49.2
12	John M. Vorys (R)	95,575	52.1
	Robert M. Draper (D)	87,770	47.9
13	Alvin F. Weichel (R)	55,408	59.2
	Dwight A. Blackmore (D)	38,264	40.9
14	Walter B. Huber (D)	125,346	57.2
	Ed Rowe (R)	92,535	42.2
15	Robert T. Secrest (D)	45,575	56.4
	P. W. Griffiths (R)	35,294	43.6
16	John McSweeney (D)	79.859	52.6
	Henderson H. Carson (R)	71,871	47.4
17	J. Harry McGregor (R)	60,234	52.9
	Robert W. Levering (D)	53,651	47.1
18	Wayne L. Hays (D)	65,475	54.1
	Earl R. Lewis (R)	55,455	45.9
19	Michael J. Kirwan (D)	134,444	68.1
	William Bacon (R)	63,079	31.9
20	Michael A. Feighan (D)	64,241	100.0
21	Robert Crosser (D)	72,417	76.0
	Harry W. Mitchell (R)	22,932	24.1
22	Frances P. Bolton (R)	170,085	54.7
	Jack G. Day (D)	141,018	45.3
AL	Stephen M. Young (D)	1,455,972	52.0
	George H. Bender (R)	1,342,409	48.0

OKLAHOMA

	Candidates	Votes	%
1	William Franklin Gilmer (D)	77,949	53.3
	George B. Schwabe (R)	68,423	46.8
2	William G. Stigler (D)	43,801	70.6
	George T. Balch (R)	18,236	29.4
3	Carl Albert (D)	57,300	83.9
	Russell Overstreet (R)	11,007	16.1
4	Tom Steed (D)	53,419	72.1
	Clyde T. Patrick (R)	20,716	27.9
5	A. S. Mike Monroney (D)	95,248	67.4
	Carmon C. Harris (R)	45,985	32.6
6	Toby Morris (D)	47,857	73.7
	George E. Young (R)	17,100	26.3
7	Victor E. Wickersham (D)	39,380	79.4
	J. Warren White (R)	10,236	20.6
8	George H. Wilson (D)	42,417	58.0
	Martin Garber (R)	30,687	42.0

OREGON

	Candidates	Votes	%
1	Walter Norblad (R)	88,587	63.3
	Edward E. Gideon (D)	45,904	32.8
2	Lowell Stockman (R)	42,730	58.2
	C. J. Shorb (D)	30,743	41.8
3	Homer D. Angell (R)	99,464	55.5
	Roland C. Bartlett (D)	66,436	37.1
	Peggy T. Carlson (PROG)	13,171	7.4
4	Harris Ellsworth (R)	65,606	66.6
	William F. Tanton (D & PROG)	32,931	33.4

PENNSYLVANIA

	Candidates	Votes	%
1	William A. Barrett (D)	70,165	53.4
	John De Nero (R)	61,165	46.6
2	William T. Granahan (D)	82,863	54.4
	Robert N. McGarvey (R)	69,604	45.7
3	Hardie Scott (R)	76,009	52.0
	Maurice S. Osser (D)	70,075	48.0
4	Earl Chudoff (D)	70,129	55.7
	Franklin J. Maloney (R)	50,236	39.9
5	William J. Green Jr. (D)	77,221	50.7
	George W. Sarbacher Jr. (R)	75,007	49.3
6	Hugh Scott (R)	86,755	57.0
	Herbert J. McGlinchey (D)	65,535	43.0

	Candidates	Votes	%
7	Benjamin F. James (R)	91,394	61.3
	Arnold M. Snyder (D)	56,263	37.8
8	Franklin H. Lichtenwalter (R)	62,229	59.2
	Wynne James Jr. (D)	42,878	40.8
9	Paul B. Dague (R)	74,726	67.1
	W. Roger Simpson (D)	36,677	32.9
10	Harry P. O'Neill (D)	64,289	58.5
	Nelson Nichols (R)	45,587	41.5
11	Daniel J. Flood (D)	68,628	51.8
	Robert H. Stroh (R)	63,797	48.2
12	Ivor D. Fenton (R)	68,089	60.6
	John Oshinskie (D)	44,345	39.4
13	George M. Rhodes (D)	40,415	50.3
	Frederick A. Muhlenberg (R)	37,261	46.4
14	Wilson D. Gillette (R)	47,715	65.2
	David Burchell (D)	25,484	34.8
15	Robert F. Rich (R, P)	48,760	61.6
	Patrick A. McGowan (D)	30,457	38.5
16	Samuel K. McConnell Jr. (R)	84,997	66.9
	Harry Hellar Kelly (D)	42,118	33.1
17	Richard M. Simpson (R)	38,735	64.5
	Ira Garman (D)	21,339	35.5
18	John C. Kunkel (R)	81,704	63.7
	Theodore C. Frederick Jr. (D)	46,586	36.3
19	Leon H. Gavin (R)	43,520	63.7
	Francis J. Manno (D)	24,800	36.3
20	Francis E. Walter (D)	54,041	58.8
	Roy E. James (R)	37,904	41.2
21	James F. Lind (D)	54,152	53.7
	Chester H. Gross (R)	46,701	46.3
22	James E. Van Zandt (R)	46,451	60.4
	Julia Luigia Maietta (D)	30,454	39.6
23	Anthony Cavalcante (D)	42,084	54.3
	William J. Crow (R)	35,384	45.7
24	Thomas E. Morgan (D)	56,282	65.4
	Roy A. Purviance (R)	29,768	34.6
25	Louis E. Graham (R)	56,966	52.6
	Andrew G. Katcher (D)	51,391	47.4
26	Robert L. Coffey Jr. (D)	62,061	55.4
	Harve Tibbott (R)	50,005	44.6
27	Augustine B. Kelley (D)	64,943	62.2
	W. Urban Gillespie (R)	39,517	37.8
28	Carroll D. Kearns (R)	65,276	54.5
	James A. Kennedy (D)	54,402	45.5
29	Harry J. Davenport (D)	63,454	54.2
	John McDowell (R)	53,609	45.8
30	Robert J. Corbett (R)	56,932	50.3
	J. R. Montgomery (D)	56,233	49.7
31	James G. Fulton (R)	75,147	56.4
	John J. Kane Jr. (D)	58,113	43.6
32	Herman P. Eberharter (D)	80,600	72.7
	Albert J. Weilersbacher (R)	30,328	27.3
33	Frank Buchanan (D)	74,508	69.2
	Albert G. Brown (R)	33,107	30.8

RHODE ISLAND

	Candidates	Votes	%
1	Aime J. Forand (D)	95,045	62.0
	Oscar J. V. Hurteau (R)	58,209	38.0
2	John E. Fogarty (D)	98,586	59.7
	Thomas J. Paolino (R)	66,672	40.3

SOUTH CAROLINA

	Candidates	Votes	%
1	L. Mendel Rivers (D)	24,529	89.1
	W. T. Baggott (R)	2,989	10.9
2	Hugo S. Sims Jr. (D)	27,677	96.5
3	James B. Hare (D)	19,181	97.8
4	Joseph R. Bryson (D)	26,098	94.9
	James B. Gaston (R)	1,410	5.1
5	James P. Richards (D)	14,544	97.1
6	John L. McMillan (D)	21,703	97.1

SOUTH DAKOTA

	Candidates	Votes	%
1	Harold O. Lovre (R)	99,062	53.5
	Merton B. Tice (D)	85,957	46.5

	Candidates	Votes	%
2	Francis H. Case (R)	36,713	65.9
	Jessie E. Sanders (D)	18,988	34.1

TENNESSEE

	Candidates	Votes	%
1	Dayton E. Phillips (R)	54,439	84.7
	Arthur W. Bright (D)	9,806	15.3
2	John Jennings Jr. (R)	43,849	58.0
	Thomas P. Fowler (IR)	31,743	42.0
3	James B. Frazier Jr. (D)	44,683	67.3
	W. E. Michael (R)	20,740	31.3
4	Albert Gore (D)	21,445	64.3
	Tom T. Tucker Jr. (R)	11,910	35.7
5	Joe L. Evins (D)	27,777	100.0
6	J. Percy Priest (D)	28,951	81.4
	Jesse L. Perry (R)	6,056	17.0
7	James P. Sutton (D)	28,058	100.0
8	Thomas J. Murray (D)	25,170	69.2
	J. Sam Johnson Jr. (R)	11,229	30.9
9	Jere Cooper (D)	26,033	91.1
	S. Homer Tatum (R)	2,555	8.9
10	Clifford Davis (D)	49,371	93.1
	Dwight V. Kyle (R)	3,670	6.9

TEXAS

	Candidates	Votes	%
1	Wright Patman (D)	40,162	100.0
2	Jesse M. Combs (D)	55,072	93.3
	Don Parker (R)	3,978	6.7
3	Lindley Beckworth (D)	36,361	88.7
	R. E. Kennedy (R)	4,642	11.3
4	Sam Rayburn (D)	38,211	100.0
5	J. Frank Wilson (D)	66,484	98.4
6	Olin E. Teague (D)	18,731	99.8
7	Tom Pickett (D)	27,945	100.0
8	Albert Thomas (D)	100,721	85.5
	Joe Ingraham (R)	17,124	14.5
9	Clark W. Thompson (D)	55,606	100.0
10	Homer Thornberry (D)	45,007	100.0
11	W. R. Poage (D)	39,795	96.2
12	Wingate H. Lucas (D)	61,206	89.1
	Elton M. Hyder (R)	7,480	10.9
13	Ed Gossett (D)	44,274	100.0
14	John E. Lyle Jr. (D)	59,163	88.9
	J. M. Swafford (R)	7,202	10.8
15	Lloyd M. Bentsen Jr. (D)	27,402	100.0
16	Ken Regan (D)	37,173	99.5
17	Omar Burleson (D)	34,078	100.0
18	Eugene Worley (D)	48,985	88.7
	J. Evetts Haley (R)	6,266	11.3
19	George Mahon (D)	58,585	95.6
20	Paul J. Kilday (D)	43,709	75.3
	J. P. Ledvina (R)	14,376	24.8
21	O. Clark Fisher (D)	45,274	100.0

UTAH

	Candidates	Votes	%
1	Walter K. Granger (D)	66,641	59.0
	David J. Wilson (R)	46,229	41.0
2	Reva Beck Bosone (D)	92,770	57.5
	William A. Dawson (R)	68,693	42.5

VERMONT

	Candidates	Votes	%
AL	Charles A. Plumley (R)	74,076	60.7
	Robert W. Ready (D)	47,767	39.2

VIRGINIA

	Candidates	Votes	%
1	S. Otis Bland (D)	24,746	80.0
	Stanley G. Adams (R)	5,753	18.6
2	Porter Hardy Jr. (D)	28,071	61.2
	Walter E. Hoffman (R)	15,800	34.4
3	J. Vaughan Gary (D)	33,950	72.9
	Richard C. Poage (R)	11,291	24.3
4	Watkins M. Abbitt (D)	22,029	100.0

VIRGINIA

Candidates	Votes	%
5 Thomas B. Stanley (D)	23,879	99.5
6 Clarence G. Burton (D)	29,589	64.7
John Strickler (R)	15,854	34.7
7 Burr P. Harrison (D)	25,799	60.4
Stephen D. Timberlake (R)	16,890	39.6
8 Howard W. Smith (D)	33,563	54.8
Tyrrell Krum (R)	25,420	41.5
9 Thomas B. Fugate (D)	33,550	52.4
T. Eugene Worrell (R)	30,466	47.6

Special Election

	Votes	%
6 Clarence G. Burton (D)	30,841	65.2
John Strickler (R)	16,435	34.8

WASHINGTON

	Votes	%
1 Hugh B. Mitchell (D)	100,030	50.8
Homer R. Jones (R)	92,215	46.8
2 Henry M. Jackson (D)	83,824	61.6
Payson Peterson (R)	48,413	35.6
3 Russell V. Mack (R)	61,856	52.1
Charles R. Savage (D)	56,947	47.9

Candidates	Votes	%
4 Hal Holmes (R)	58,105	53.2
John F. Eubank (D)	51,195	46.8
5 Walt Horan (R)	67,757	54.6
John F. McKay (D)	56,343	45.4
6 Thor C. Tollefson (R)	72,988	55.1
Jack E. Knudsen (D)	54,166	40.9

WEST VIRGINIA

	Votes	%
1 Robert L. Ramsay (D)	68,829	57.3
Francis J. Love (R)	51,381	42.7
2 Harley O. Staggers (D)	61,786	54.7
Melvin C. Snyder (R)	51,226	45.3
3 Cleveland M. Bailey (D)	68,055	57.1
Edward G. Rohrbough (R)	51,123	42.9
4 Maurice G. Burnside (D)	72,378	53.1
Hubert S. Ellis (R)	64,001	46.9
5 John Kee (D)	71,664	65.1
Hartley Sanders (R)	38,446	34.9
6 Erland H. Hedrick (D)	99,842	62.5
D. L. Salisbury (R)	59,900	37.5

WISCONSIN

Candidates	Votes	%
1 Lawrence H. Smith (R)	67,387	51.9
Jack Harvey (D)	61,791	47.6
2 Glenn R. Davis (R)	74,306	53.9
Horace W. Wilkie (D)	62,953	45.6
3 Gardner R. Withrow (R)	69,727	69.2
Frank J. Antoine (D)	30,650	30.4
4 Clement J. Zablocki (D)	89,391	55.9
John C. Brophy (R)	63,161	39.5
5 Andrew J. Biemiller (D)	91,072	53.1
Charles J. Kersten (R)	76,782	44.8
6 Frank B. Keefe (R)	60,675	55.5
Kenneth Kunde (D)	47,844	43.8
7 Reid F. Murray (R)	64,531	62.5
Ralph E. Kronenwetter (D)	37,307	36.1
8 John W. Byrnes (R)	70,905	56.7
Martin J. Young (D)	53,287	42.6
9 Merlin Hull (R)	76,903	98.1
10 Alvin E. O'Konski (R)	52,124	54.8
Daniel W. Hoan (D)	39,523	41.6

WYOMING

	Votes	%
AL Frank A. Barrett (R)	50,218	51.5
L. G. Flannery (D)	47,246	48.5

1949 House Elections

NEW YORK

Special Election

Candidates	Votes	%
7 Louis B. Heller (D, L)	22,939	54.8
Francis E. Dorn (R)	16,179	38.7
Minneola Ingersoll (AM LAB)	2,712	6.5
10 Edna F. Kelly (D)	48,945	55.1
Jules Cohen (L)	24,419	27.5
George H. Fankuchen (R)	15,514	17.5

Candidates	Votes	%
20 Franklin D. Roosevelt Jr (L, FF)	40,822	50.7
Benjamin Shalleck (D)	24,352	30.2
William H. McIntyre (R)	10,026	12.5
Annette T. Rubinstein (AM LAB)	5,348	6.6

House Candidates Index

For an index of all House candidates listed in this section (pages 192-324), see pages 340-371. Instructions for use of the House Candidates Index appear on page 340.

1950 House Elections

ALABAMA

Candidates	Votes	%
1 Frank W. Boykin (D)	14,206	100.0
2 George M. Grant (D)	17,441	100.0
3 George W. Andrews (D)	10,914	100.0
4 Kenneth A. Roberts (D)	14,608	93.7
J. P. Carter (R)	980	6.3
5 Albert Rains (D)	17,269	100.0
6 Edward deGraffenried (D)	11,709	100.0
7 Carl A. Elliott (D)	20,580	100.0
8 Robert E. Jones Jr. (D)	13,742	100.0
9 Laurie C. Battle (D)	30,743	100.0

ARIZONA

Candidates	Votes	%
1 John R. Murdock (D)	51,526	60.6
Carl W. Divelbiss (R)	33,528	39.4
2 Harold A. Patten (D)	63,991	69.1
John H. Curnutte (R)	28,622	30.9

ARKANSAS

Candidates	Votes	%
1 Ezekiel C. Gathings (D)	47,238	100.0
2 Wilbur D. Mills (D)	31,048	100.0
3 James W. Trimble (D)	34,434	100.0
4 Boyd Tackett (D)	43,156	100.0
5 Brooks Hays (D)	54,338	100.0
6 William F. Norrell (D)	46,467	100.0
7 Oren Harris (D)	39,121	100.0

CALIFORNIA

Candidates	Votes	%
1 Hubert B. Scudder (R)	85,122	54.0
Roger Kent (D)	72,584	46.0
2 Clair Engle (D-R)	85,103	100.0
3 Leroy Johnson (R-D)	177,269	100.0
4 Franck R. Havenner (D)	83,078	67.2
Raymond D. Smith (R)	40,569	32.8
5 John F. Shelley (D-R)	117,988	100.0
6 George P. Miller (D-R)	192,342	100.0
7 John J. Allen Jr. (R)	74,069	55.3
Lyle E. Cook (D)	59,976	44.7
8 Jack Z. Anderson (R-D)	168,510	83.1
John A. Peterson (I PROG)	34,176	16.9
9 Allan Oakley Hunter (R)	76,015	52.0
Cecil F. White (D)	70,201	48.0
10 Thomas H. Werdel (R)	59,313	53.6
Ardis M. Walker (D)	51,409	46.4
11 Ernest K. Bramblett (R)	59,780	52.1
Marion R. Walker (D)	55,020	47.9
12 Patrick J. Hillings (R)	107,933	60.1
Steve Zetterberg (D)	71,682	39.9
13 Norris Poulson (R-D)	83,296	84.8
Ellen P. Davidson (I PROG)	14,789	15.1
14 Samuel William Yorty (D)	47,653	49.4
Jack W. Hardy (R)	35,543	36.8
Charlotta A. Bass (I PROG)	13,364	13.8
15 Gordon L. McDonough (R-D)	112,704	87.1
Jeanne Cole (I PROG)	16,559	12.8
16 Donald L. Jackson (R)	115,970	59.2
Esther Murray (D)	79,744	40.7
17 Cecil R. King (D-R)	166,334	99.9
18 Clyde Doyle (D)	97,177	50.5
Craig Hosmer (R)	95,308	49.5
19 Chet Holifield (D-R)	73,317	90.9
Myra Tanner Weiss (I)	7,329	9.1
20 Carl Hinshaw (R-D)	211,012	85.1
William B. Esterman (I PROG)	26,508	10.7
21 Harry R. Sheppard (D)	62,994	57.4
R. E. Reynolds (R)	46,693	42.6
22 John Phillips (R-D)	114,497	99.9
23 Clinton D. McKinnon (D)	94,137	51.0
Leslie E. Gehres (R)	90,398	49.0

COLORADO

Candidates	Votes	%
1 Byron Rogers (D)	70,165	50.3
Richard Luxford (R)	67,436	48.4
2 William S. Hill (R)	73,045	57.5
George L. Bickel (D)	53,313	42.0
3 J. Edgar Chenoweth (R)	58,831	51.6
John H. Marsalis (D)	55,110	48.4
4 Wayne N. Aspinall (D)	35,797	57.3
Jack Evans (R)	26,674	42.7

CONNECTICUT

Candidates	Votes	%
1 Abraham A. Ribicoff (D)	134,258	58.1
Harry Schwolsky (R)	96,251	41.7
2 Horace Seely-Brown Jr. (R)	68,747	50.8
Chase Going Woodhouse (D)	66,523	49.2
3 John A. McGuire (D)	89,391	51.9
Ellsworth B. Foote (R)	82,304	47.8
4 Albert P. Morano (R)	111,939	53.1
Dennis M. Carroll (D)	88,682	42.1
5 James T. Patterson (R)	65,915	53.0
J. Gregory Lynch (D)	56,752	45.7
AL Antoni N. Sadlak (R)	433,912	49.4
Joseph W. Bogdanski (D)	426,485	48.6

DELAWARE

Candidates	Votes	%
AL J. Caleb Boggs (R)	73,313	56.7
Henry M. Winchester (D)	56,091	43.4

FLORIDA

Candidates	Votes	%
1 Chester B. McMullen (D)	40,466	100.0
2 Charles E. Bennett (D)	34,334	100.0
3 Robert L. F. Sikes (D)	24,548	100.0
4 Bill Lantaff (D)	65,758	82.1
Joseph Edward Worton (R)	14,305	17.9
5 A. S. Herlong Jr. (D)	32,475	76.5
Carl K. Landes (R)	9,958	23.5
6 Dwight L. Rogers (D)	31,205	100.0

GEORGIA

Candidates	Votes	%
1 Prince H. Preston (D)	29,716	100.0
2 E. E. Cox (D)	18,920	100.0
3 E. L. Forrester (D)	24,221	100.0
4 A. Sidney Camp (D)	21,900	100.0
5 James C. Davis (D)	49,317	100.0
6 Carl Vinson (D)	22,402	100.0
7 Henderson Lanham (D)	23,595	100.0
8 W. M. Wheeler (D)	21,573	100.0
9 John S. Wood (D)	20,943	100.0
10 Paul Brown (D)	27,568	100.0

IDAHO

Candidates	Votes	%
1 John T. Wood (R)	41,823	50.5
Gracie Pfost (D)	41,040	49.5
2 Hamer Budge (R)	66,966	57.1
James H. Hawley Jr. (D)	50,255	42.9

ILLINOIS

Candidates	Votes	%
1 William L. Dawson (D)	69,056	61.6
Archibald James Carey Jr. (R)	41,944	37.4
2 Richard B. Vail (R)	83,023	53.6
Barratt O'Hara (D)	71,945	46.4
3 Fred E. Busbey (R)	87,241	54.5
Neil J. Linehan (D)	72,676	45.4
4 William E. McVey (R)	73,542	55.8
James V. Buckley (D)	58,190	44.2
5 John C. Kluczynski (D)	91,589	65.6
Edward M. Gaynor (R)	48,052	34.4
6 Thomas J. O'Brien (D)	106,701	64.5
John M. Fay (R)	58,534	35.4
7 Adolph J. Sabath (D)	109,841	71.8
Henry E. Hayes (R)	43,211	28.2
8 Thomas S. Gordon (D)	77,736	59.3
Philip Grontkowski (R)	53,305	40.7
9 Sidney R. Yates (D)	74,699	51.8
Maxwell A. Goodwin (R)	69,552	48.2
10 Richard W. Hoffman (R)	117,498	66.5
Charles J. Michal (D)	59,127	33.5
11 Timothy P. Sheehan (R)	81,358	56.7
Chester A. Chesney (D)	62,050	43.3
12 Edgar A. Jonas (R)	96,489	56.2
Charles J. Komaiko (D)	75,226	43.8
13 Marguerite Stitt Church (R)	140,750	74.1
Thomas F. Dolan (D)	49,187	25.9
14 Chauncey W. Reed (R)	103,312	74.2
Homer R. McElroy (D)	35,856	25.8
15 Noah M. Mason (R)	82,155	63.3
Wayne F. Caskey (D)	47,633	36.7
16 Leo E. Allen (R)	82,190	67.3
Russell J. Goldman (D)	39,944	32.7
17 Leslie C. Arends (R)	74,643	66.8
Joe W. Russell (D)	37,096	33.2
18 Harold H. Velde (R)	72,499	61.6
Walter Durley Boyle (D)	45,214	38.4
19 Robert B. Chiperfield (R)	69,379	59.0
John Michael Kerwin Jr. (D)	48,286	41.0
20 Sid Simpson (R)	62,138	59.3
Howard Manning (D)	42,647	40.7
21 Peter F. Mack Jr. (D)	67,704	52.8
Benjamin S. Deboice (R)	60,530	47.2
22 William L. Springer (R)	67,668	60.7
Robert B. Borchers (D)	43,795	39.3
23 Edward H. Jenison (R)	63,669	55.9
Laurence F. Arnold (D)	50,143	44.1
24 Charles W. Vursell (R)	62,692	55.3
John David Upchurch (D)	50,638	44.7
25 Melvin Price (D)	78,812	64.9
Rogers D. Jones (R)	42,696	35.1
26 C. W. Bishop (R)	53,207	51.2
Kent E. Keller (D)	50,759	48.8

INDIANA

Candidates	Votes	%
1 Ray J. Madden (D)	62,666	52.6
Paul Cyr (R)	56,063	47.0
2 Charles A. Halleck (R)	74,872	57.2
Dale E. Beck (D)	55,153	42.2
3 Shepard J. Crumpacker Jr. (R)	83,816	52.8
Thurman C. Crook (D)	73,646	46.4
4 E. Ross Adair (R)	69,741	56.2
Edward H. Kruse Jr. (D)	53,550	43.1
5 John V. Beamer (R)	91,929	54.1
John R. Walsh (D)	76,878	45.3
6 Cecil M. Harden (R)	69,789	52.4
Jack H. Mankin (D)	62,915	47.2
7 William G. Bray (R)	68,885	50.0
James E. Noland (D)	67,992	49.3
8 Winfield K. Denton (D)	78,750	51.1
Herman L. McCray (R)	74,573	48.3
9 Earl Wilson (R)	63,229	54.9
Charles W. Long (D)	51,350	44.6
10 Ralph Harvey (R)	81,392	58.7
Vernon J. Dwyer (D)	56,149	40.5
11 Charles B. Brownson (R)	116,068	56.5
Andrew Jacobs Sr. (D)	88,418	43.0

IOWA

Candidates	Votes	%
1 Thomas E. Martin (R)	70,058	61.7
James D. France (D)	43,140	38.0

IOWA

Candidates	Votes	%
2 Henry O. Talle (R)	79,066	58.8
Eugene J. Kean (D)	55,359	41.2
3 Harold R. Gross (R)	73,490	64.0
James O. Babcock (D)	40,786	35.5
4 Karl M. LeCompte (R)	51,168	56.7
Steven V. Carter (D)	38,649	42.8
5 Paul Cunningham (R)	57,429	56.9
Gibson C. Holliday (D)	43,105	42.7
6 James I. Dolliver (R)	56,982	64.6
Maurice O'Reilly (D)	30,877	35.0
7 Ben F. Jensen (R)	55,291	62.1
James A. Hart (D)	33,617	37.7
8 Charles B. Hoeven (R)	56,942	64.1
L. J. McGivern (D)	31,689	35.7

KANSAS

	Votes	%
1 Albert M. Cole (R)	66,607	66.5
Ewell Steward (D)	33,562	33.5
2 Errett P. Scrivner (R)	56,862	52.2
Milton Sullivant (D)	52,015	47.8
3 Myron V. George (R)	42,263	54.7
Barnes Griffith (D)	35,028	45.3
4 Edward H. Rees (R)	77,856	58.9
Louis A. Donnell (D)	54,438	41.2
5 Clifford R. Hope (R)	60,608	61.0
Robert L. Bock (D)	38,767	39.0
6 Wint Smith (R)	51,653	59.6
F. F. Wasinger (D)	35,087	40.5

Special Election

	Votes	%
3 Myron V. George (R)	41,676	54.5
Barnes Griffith (D)	34,845	45.5

KENTUCKY

	Votes	%
1 Noble J. Gregory (D)	34,970	100.0
2 John A. Whitaker (D)	41,226	100.0
3 Thruston B. Morton (R)	62,363	55.5
Alex P. Humphrey (D)	49,935	44.5
4 Frank L. Chelf (D)	35,529	100.0
5 Brent Spence (D)	33,920	63.3
Thomas W. Hardesty (R)	19,670	36.7
6 Thomas R. Underwood (D)	39,762	100.0
7 Carl D. Perkins (D)	34,767	56.1
O. W. Thompson (R)	27,190	43.9
8 Joe B. Bates (D)	37,727	60.5
Elmer C. Roberts (R)	24,627	39.5
9 James S. Golden (R)	46,928	100.0

LOUISIANA

	Votes	%
1 F. Edward Hebert (D)	35,456	100.0
2 Hale Boggs (D)	39,232	100.0
3 Edwin E. Willis (D)	21,591	100.0
4 Overton Brooks (D)	25,529	100.0
5 Otto E. Passman (D)	22,478	100.0
6 James H. Morrison (D)	34,718	100.0
7 Henry D. Larcade Jr. (D)	22,931	100.0
8 A. Leonard Allen (D)	25,140	100.0

MAINE

	Votes	%
1 Robert Hale (R)	48,869	54.0
Lucia M. Cormier (D)	41,620	46.0
2 Charles P. Nelson (R)	49,743	57.7
John J. Maloney Jr. (D)	36,506	42.3
3 Frank Fellows (R)	38,289	62.9
John V. Keenan (D)	22,605	37.1

MARYLAND

	Votes	%
1 Edward T. Miller (R)	36,005	57.0
Thomas F. Johnson (D)	27,122	43.0
2 James P. S. Devereux (R)	99,497	50.2
William P. Bolton (D)	96,498	48.7

Candidates	Votes	%
3 Edward A. Garmatz (D)	27,646	65.7
Louis R. Milio (R)	14,430	34.3
4 George H. Fallon (D)	34,769	56.8
James W. Miller (R)	25,287	41.3
5 Lansdale G. Sasscer (D)	54,152	57.5
Thomas S. Carr (R)	40,031	42.5
6 J. Glenn Beall (R)	70,707	61.9
Russell Peter Hartle (D)	43,540	38.1

MASSACHUSETTS

	Votes	%
1 John W. Heselton (R)	88,018	68.9
Anna Sullivan (D)	39,717	31.1
2 Foster Furcolo (D)	76,494	54.6
Chester T. Skibinski (R)	63,493	45.4
3 Philip J. Philbin (D)	93,591	71.5
John F. Fuller (R)	37,258	28.5
4 Harold D. Donohue (D)	76,881	56.9
John Winslow (R)	57,483	42.6
5 Edith Nourse Rogers (R)	116,474	76.1
Clement Gregory McDonough (D)	36,530	23.9
6 William H. Bates (R)	94,162	73.7
Richard M. Russell (D)	33,578	26.3
7 Thomas J. Lane (D)	91,854	78.5
Laurence A. Doyle (R)	24,307	20.8
8 Angier L. Goodwin (R)	71,938	53.9
John B. Carr (D)	61,559	46.1
9 Donald W. Nicholson (R)	78,655	58.1
August J. Cormier (D)	55,949	41.3
10 Christian A. Herter (R)	88,549	57.8
Francis X. Hurley (D)	63,618	41.5
11 John F. Kennedy (D)	87,699	82.3
Vincent J. Celeste (R)	18,302	17.2
12 John W. McCormack (D)	102,940	84.0
John J. Biggins (R)	16,746	13.7
13 Richard B. Wigglesworth (R)	90,387	62.2
David J. Concannon (D)	54,243	37.3
14 Joseph W. Martin Jr. (R)	84,508	64.3
Edward P. Grace (D)	46,332	35.3

MICHIGAN

	Votes	%
1 Thaddeus M. Machrowicz (D)	75,478	82.2
Rudolph G. Tenerowicz (R)	14,619	15.9
2 George Meader (R)	61,574	60.4
John P. Dawson (D)	39,771	39.0
3 Paul W. Shafer (R)	58,489	61.4
Thomas B. Woodworth (D)	35,877	37.6
4 Clare E. Hoffman (R)	58,625	68.6
Forest A. Schoonard (D)	26,301	30.8
5 Gerald R. Ford Jr. (R)	72,829	66.7
James H. McLaughlin (D)	35,927	32.9
6 William W. Blackney (R)	70,100	52.8
Herbert W. Devine (D)	61,435	46.3
7 Jesse P. Wolcott (R)	66,951	63.0
Roy E. Visnaw (D)	38,953	36.6
8 Fred L. Crawford (R)	55,001	60.5
Leland S. Jennings (D)	35,164	38.7
9 Ruth Thompson (R)	43,910	54.5
Noel P. Fox (D)	36,222	45.0
10 Roy O. Woodruff (R)	47,489	66.2
William J. Kelly (D)	24,198	33.8
11 Charles E. Potter (R)	50,523	66.5
Fred L. Hanscom (D)	25,254	33.2
12 John B. Bennett (R)	43,010	61.7
John Sabol (D)	26,667	38.3
13 George D. O'Brien (D)	56,388	61.4
Clarence J. McLeod (R)	35,178	38.3
14 Louis C. Rabaut (D)	76,938	51.5
Richard Durant (R)	72,137	48.3
15 John D. Dingell (D)	73,238	64.1
Robert L. Berry (R)	40,865	35.7
16 John Lesinski Jr. (D)	80,229	60.7
Kirby L. Wilson Jr. (R)	50,873	38.5
17 George A. Dondero (R)	114,274	55.6
Eugene G. Donohoe (D)	90,712	44.1

MINNESOTA

Candidates	Votes	%
1 August H. Andresen (R)	75,016	67.1
Burton Chambers (DFL)	36,839	32.9
2 Joseph P. O'Hara (R)	69,304	59.9
Harry Sieben (DFL)	46,452	40.1
3 Roy W. Wier (DFL)	73,786	51.7
Alfred D. Lindley (R)	68,947	48.3
4 Eugene J. McCarthy (DFL)	59,930	60.4
Ward Fleming (R)	39,307	39.6
5 Walter H. Judd (R)	71,243	58.7
Marcella F. Killen (DFL)	48,759	40.2
6 Fred Marshall (DFL)	63,911	56.2
Robert F. Lee (R)	49,879	43.8
7 H. Carl Andersen (R)	65,644	61.7
Carl J. Eastvold (DFL)	40,785	38.3
8 John A. Blatnik (DFL)	72,440	62.9
William A. Pittenger (R)	42,705	37.1
9 Harold C. Hagen (R)	56,928	61.9
Curtiss Olson (DFL)	30,808	33.5

MISSISSIPPI

	Votes	%
1 John E. Rankin (D)	8,994	92.5
Glenn Haynes (R)	730	7.5
2 Jamie L. Whitten (D)	5,891	100.0
3 Frank E. Smith (D)	6,529	92.5
Nelson E. Taylor (R)	529	7.5
4 Thomas G. Abernethy (D)	12,602	95.8
5 W. Arthur Winstead (D)	13,395	97.6
6 William M. Colmer (D)	15,964	87.9
Frank H. Harper (I)	2,199	12.1
7 John Bell Williams (D)	19,321	96.4

MISSOURI

	Votes	%
1 Clare Magee (D)	43,384	54.4
Wat Arnold (R)	36,403	45.6
2 Morgan M. Moulder (D)	49,408	53.0
Max Schwabe (R)	43,816	47.0
3 Philip J. Welch (D)	48,244	51.1
William C. Cole (R)	46,154	48.9
4 Theodore Leonard Irving (D)	53,424	61.6
Vernon D. Fulcrut (R)	33,367	38.5
5 Richard W. Bolling (D)	45,762	54.5
Richard C. Jensen (R)	38,276	45.6
6 Orland K. Armstrong (R)	55,176	50.7
George H. Christopher (D)	53,593	49.3
7 Dewey Short (R)	60,557	58.7
Daniel J. Leary (D)	42,629	41.3
8 Albert S. J. Carnahan (D)	49,894	54.7
Parke M. Banta (R)	41,406	45.4
9 Clarence Cannon (D)	43,950	61.5
John H. Fahien (R)	27,573	38.6
10 Paul C. Jones (D)	44,469	100.0
11 John B. Sullivan (D)	57,225	64.5
Sidney J. Redman (R)	31,163	35.2
12 Thomas B. Curtis (R)	110,757	50.9
Raymond W. Karst (D)	106,728	49.0
13 Frank M. Karsten (D)	58,832	68.2
Hal A. Hamilton (R)	27,366	31.7

MONTANA

	Votes	%
1 Mike Mansfield (D)	54,394	60.3
Ralph Y. McGinnis (R)	34,945	38.7
2 Wesley A. D'Ewart (R)	65,003	54.1
John J. Holmes (D)	53,854	44.8

NEBRASKA

	Votes	%
1 Carl T. Curtis (R)	67,164	54.5
Clarence G. Miles (D)	55,972	45.5
2 Howard Buffett (R)	71,126	63.5
Eugene D. O'Sullivan (D)	40,939	36.5
3 Karl Stefan (R)	68,889	66.9
Duane K. Peterson (D)	34,017	33.1
4 Arthur L. Miller (R)	64,661	65.8
Hans J. Holtorf Jr. (D)	33,562	34.2

NEVADA

Candidates	Votes	%
AL Walter S. Baring (D)	31,843	52.8
A. E. MacKenzie (R)	28,485	47.2

NEW HAMPSHIRE

	Votes	%
1 Chester E. Merrow (R)	57,371	57.5
Frank L. Sullivan (D)	42,371	42.5
2 Norris Cotton (R)	55.116	64.5
George Brummer (D)	30,389	35.5

NEW JERSEY

	Votes	%
1 Charles A. Wolverton (R)	85,100	56.8
John J. Crean (D)	64,868	43.3
2 T. Millet Hand (R)	54,897	54.3
Elmer H. Wene (D)	46,121	45.7
3 James C. Auchincloss (R)	79,374	62.4
John C. Applegate (D)	47,055	37.0
4 Charles R. Howell (D)	60,364	52.2
Gill Robb Wilson (R)	55,364	47.8
5 Charles A. Eaton (R)	80,678	61.6
Thomas Chabrak (D)	50,220	38.4
6 Clifford P. Case (R)	74,739	62.2
Harry Mopsick (D)	45,376	37.8
7 William B. Widnall (R)	79,421	69.7
Emil M. Wulster (D)	34,578	30.3
8 Gordon Canfield (R)	60,420	63.6
Charles H. Roemer (D)	34,194	36.0
9 Harry L. Towe (R)	67,712	57.8
Karl D. Van Wagner (D)	38,421	32.8
Carl E. Ring (I)	10,932	9.3
10 Peter W. Rodino Jr. (D)	60,432	61.0
William H. Rawson (R)	38,613	39.0
11 Hugh J. Addonizio (D)	46,242	51.6
Albert L. Vreeland (R)	42,581	47.5
12 Robert Winthrop Kean (R)	54,123	53.1
Harry Dudkin (D)	45,525	44.7
13 Alfred D. Sieminski (D)	55,008	51.9
Edward S. Binkowski (R)	43,851	41.4
Michael A. Fiore (IPP CH)	7,072	6.7
14 Edward J. Hart (D)	61,410	59.2
Michael Bongiovanni (R)	42,272	40.8

NEW MEXICO

	Votes	%
AL John J. Dempsey (D)	97,187✔	
Antonio M. Fernandez (D)	96,291✔	
Steiner Mason (R)	75,447	
Jose E. Armijo (R)	68,762	

NEW YORK

	Votes	%
1 Ernest Greenwood (D, L)	76,375	49.2
W. Kingsland Macy (R)	76,240	49.1
2 Leonard W. Hall (R)	129,291	67.1
Lawrence W. McKeown (D, L)	60,152	31.2
3 Henry J. Latham (R)	92,466	56.3
James Pasta (D)	55,285	33.6
Mark Starr (L)	11,122	6.8
4 L. Gary Clemente (D, L)	55,793	54.2
Gregory McMahon (R)	43,055	41.8
5 T. Vincent Quinn (D)	63,620	48.4
Robert Tripp Ross (R)	54,061	41.1
Bernard Brown (L)	7,857	6.0
6 James J. Delaney (D, L)	60,725	56.8
Herbert Suppan (R)	41,615	38.9
7 Louis B. Heller (D, L)	47,466	57.0
Francis E. Dorn (R)	30,379	36.5
Lester Zirin (AM LAB)	5,454	6.6
8 Victor L. Anfuso (D)	42,305	61.9
Joseph R. Fontanetta (R)	18,551	27.2
Antonio Iandiorio (AM LAB)	4,119	6.0
9 Eugene J. Keogh (D, R)	73,280	91.0
Helen Wishnofsky (AM LAB)	7,267	9.0

Candidates	Votes	%
10 Edna F. Kelly (D, L)	66,847	67.1
David L. Samuels (R)	25,485	25.6
Gerald Root (AM LAB)	7,327	7.4
11 James J. Heffernan (D, L)	67,560	62.9
Alfred C. McKenzie (R)	31,558	29.4
Blanche Katz (AM LAB)	8,270	7.7
12 John J. Rooney (D, L)	42,396	61.6
Joseph J. Petito (R)	22,796	33.1
Vincent J. Longhi (AM LAB)	3,628	5.3
13 Donald L. O'Toole (D, L)	54,919	59.6
James F. O'Hara (R)	35,418	36.7
Ralph Shapiro (AM LAB)	6,247	6.5
14 Abraham J. Multer (D, L)	75,020	70.6
P. Vincent Landi (R)	21,350	20.1
Helen Phillips (AM LAB)	9,859	9.3
15 Emanuel Celler (D, L)	72,396	72.8
Louis H. Heiger (R)	17,144	17.2
William Podell (AM LAB)	9,916	10.0
16 James J. Murphy (D, L)	42,516	50.5
Edward J. McCormick (R)	37,363	44.4
Frank Cremonesi (AM LAB)	4,340	5.2
17 Frederic R. Coudert Jr. (R)	57,247	53.4
Irving M. Engel (D, L)	44,502	41.5
Robert T. Leicester (AM LAB)	5,492	5.1
18 James G. Donovan (D, R)	49,448	57.8
Vito Marcantonio (AM LAB)	36,095	42.2
19 Arthur G. Klein (D, L)	58,616	66.4
Edward I. Goldberg (R)	21,034	23.8
Bernard Harkavy (AM LAB)	8,597	9.7
20 Franklin D. Roosevelt Jr. (D, L)	57,432	62.1
Henry V. Poor (R)	29,305	31.7
John W. Darr Jr. (AM LAB)	5,717	6.2
21 Jacob K. Javits (R, L)	62,604	61.7
Bennett I. Schlessel (D)	33,349	32.9
William M. Mandel (AM LAB)	5,419	5.4
22 Adam Clayton Powell Jr. (D)	35,233	63.5
Elmer A. Carter (R, L)	15,208	27.4
John Quillian (AM LAB)	5,050	9.1
23 Sidney A. Fine (D)	64,270	56.3
William J. Waterman (R)	22,103	19.4
Harold Bauman (L)	17,882	15.7
Robert Diamond (AM LAB)	9,847	8.6
24 Isidore Dollinger (D)	54,628	62.5
Barnett Levy (R)	11,303	12.9
Herman Woskow (L)	10,774	12.3
Stephen J. White (AM LAB)	10,755	12.3
25 Charles A. Buckley (D)	64,353	46.8
Solon S. Kane (R)	40,552	29.5
Max Bloom (L)	20,929	15.2
Charles J. Hendley (AM LAB)	11,707	8.5
26 Christopher C. McGrath (D)	69,152	51.4
Fred E. Schiemann (R)	44,598	33.1
Ernest Doerfler (L)	11,518	8.6
August Buhr (AM LAB)	9,333	6.9
27 Ralph W. Gwinn (R)	78,221	55.9
George A. Brenner (D, L)	59,759	42.7
28 Ralph A. Gamble (R)	79,440	67.5
Morris E. Lasker (D)	35,059	29.8
29 Katharine St. George (R)	72,721	61.8
Harry O. Prince (D, L)	43,315	36.8
30 James Ernest Wharton (R)	86,053	65.8
James R. Bourne (D)	41,833	32.0
31 Bernard W. Kearney (R)	79,007	64.1
John H. Peterson (D)	41,680	33.8
32 William T. Byrne (D)	90,420	58.8
John T. Casey (R)	60,087	39.1
33 Dean P. Taylor (R)	100,425	69.0
Joseph T. Hammer (D)	42,680	29.3
34 Clarence E. Kilburn (R)	67,739	66.4
Mildred McGill (D)	32,446	31.8
35 William R. Williams (R)	60,657	51.6
John C. Davies (D, L)	54,284	46.2
36 R. Walter Riehlman (R)	81,508	61.9
Alfred W. Haight (D, L)	50,107	38.9

Candidates	Votes	%
37 Edwin Arthur Hall (R)	60,278	64.6
John J. Burns (D, L)	33,018	35.4
38 John Taber (R)	68,474	68.8
Robert G. Gordon (D, L)	31,115	31.2
39 W. Sterling Cole (R)	64,377	66.3
Donald J. O'Connor (D, L)	31,639	32.6
40 Kenneth B. Keating (R)	103,710	65.8
A. Roger Clarke (D, L)	52,363	33.2
41 Harold C. Ostertag (R)	64,801	64.1
Bernard E. Hart (D, L)	35,370	35.0
42 William E. Miller (R)	75,377	58.6
Mary Louise Nice (D, L)	53,310	41.4
43 Edmund P. Radwan (R)	61,781	50.8
Anthony F. Tauriello (D, L)	58,327	48.0
44 John C. Butler (R)	69,260	50.3
Chester C. Gorski (D, L)	66,541	48.3
45 Daniel A. Reed (R)	54,490	66.0
Frederick S. Buck (D)	27,317	33.1

NORTH CAROLINA

	Votes	%
1 Herbert C. Bonner (D)	14,698	92.8
Zeno O. Ratcliff (R)	1,147	7.2
2 John H. Kerr (D)	15,602	100.0
3 Graham A. Barden (D)	21,287	100.0
4 Harold D. Cooley (D)	34,580	72.8
Ray F. Swain (R)	12,945	27.2
5 Richard Thurmond Chatham (D)	29,598	100.0
6 Carl T. Durham (D)	27,751	75.4
A. A. McDonald (R)	9,075	24.6
7 F. Ertel Carlyle (D)	21,911	84.0
Irvin B. Tucker Jr. (R)	4,171	16.0
8 Charles B. Deane (D)	40,834	59.6
T. E. Story (R)	27,688	40.4
9 Robert L. Doughton (D)	47,183	61.2
Fate J. Beal (R)	29,982	38.9
10 Hamilton C. Jones (D)	33,591	52.3
Louis G. Rogers (R)	30,591	47.7
11 Woodrow W. Jones (D)	31,712	68.9
A. W. Whitehurst (R)	14,293	31.1
12 Monroe M. Redden (D)	46,851	63.7
John A. Wagner (R)	26,710	36.3

Special Election

	Votes	%
11 Woodrow W. Jones (D)	31,460	67.3
A. W. Whitehurst (R)	15,295	32.7

NORTH DAKOTA

	Votes	%
AL Fred G. Aandahl (R)	119,047✔	
Usher L. Burdick (R)	110,534✔	
Ervin Schumacher (D)	62,322	
E. A. Johansson (D)	32,946	

OHIO

	Votes	%
1 Charles H. Elston (R)	77,507	59.1
Rollin H. Everett (D)	53,760	41.0
2 William E. Hess (R)	69,543	52.7
Earl T. Wagner (D)	62,542	47.4
3 Edward Breen (D)	92,840	54.5
Paul F. Schenck (R)	77,634	45.5
4 William M. McCulloch (R)	65,640	66.8
Carleton Carl Reiser (D)	32,686	33.2
5 Cliff Clevenger (R)	36,096	57.5
Dan Batt (D)	26,689	42.5
6 James G. Polk (D)	40,335	50.8
Edward O. McCowen (R)	38,996	49.2
7 Clarence J. Brown (R)	77,660	68.4
Ben J. Goldman (D)	35,818	31.6
8 Jackson E. Betts (R)	47,761	62.7
W. Dexter Hazen (D)	28,379	37.3
9 Frazier Reams (I)	51,024	36.6
Thomas H. Burke (D)	45,268	32.4
Homer A. Ramey (R)	43,301	31.0

OHIO

	Candidates	Votes	%
10	Thomas A. Jenkins (R)	39,584	65.2
	William J. Curry (D)	21,117	34.8
11	Walter E. Brehm (R)	33,648	53.1
	Mell G. Underwood Jr. (D)	29,687	46.9
12	John M. Vorys (R)	117,396	64.1
	John W. Guy (D)	65,860	35.9
13	Alvin F. Weichel (R)	58,484	70.9
	Dwight A. Blackmore (D)	24,042	29.1
14	William H. Ayres (R)	102,868	48.7
	Walter B. Huber (D)	100,947	47.8
15	Robert T. Secrest (D)	47,448	61.6
	Holland M. Gary (R)	29,573	38.4
16	Frank T. Bow (R)	77,306	50.7
	John McSweeney (D)	75,255	49.3
17	J. Harry McGregor (R)	71,382	64.3
	Robert W. Levering (D)	39,726	35.8
18	Wayne L. Hays (D)	58,295	50.8
	Robert L. Quinn (R)	56,508	49.2
19	Michael J. Kirwan (D)	119,245	63.8
	Henry P. Kosling (R)	67,661	36.2
20	Michael A. Feighan (D)	60,565	74.2
	Paul W. Cassidy (R)	21,044	25.8
21	Robert Crosser (D)	66,341	75.5
	William Hodge (R)	21,588	24.6
22	Frances P. Bolton (R)	219,788	62.7
	Chat Paterson (D)	130,623	37.3
AL	George H. Bender (R)	1,447,154	53.9
	Stephen M. Young (D)	1,237,409	46.1

OKLAHOMA

		Votes	%
1	George B. Schwabe (R)	72,367	52.9
	Dixie Gilmer (D)	64,481	47.1
2	William G. Stigler (D)	36,552	66.2
	Cleo Crain (R)	18,687	33.8
3	Carl Albert (D)	46,404	82.8
	Charles Powell (R)	9,639	17.2
4	Tom Steed (D)	43,838	68.1
	Glenn O. Young (R)	20,527	31.9
5	John Jarman (D)	72,877	58.8
	C. E. Barnes (R)	51,008	41.2
6	Toby Morris (D)	38,166	67.1
	George Campbell (R)	18,743	32.9
7	Victor Wickersham (D)	28,733	67.1
	K. B. Cornell (R)	14,078	32.9
8	Page H. Belcher (R)	38,285	54.2
	George H. Wilson (D)	32,401	45.8

OREGON

		Votes	%
1	Walter Norblad (R)	93,547	66.5
	Roy R. Hewitt (D)	47,155	33.5
2	Lowell Stockman (R)	41,365	55.4
	Vernon Bull (D)	33,282	44.6
3	Homer D. Angell (R)	90,232	50.7
	Carl C. Donaugh (D)	77,606	43.6
4	Harris Ellsworth (R)	63,211	59.5
	David C. Shaw (D)	43,053	40.5

PENNSYLVANIA

		Votes	%
1	William A. Barrett (D)	69,300	53.8
	Robert M. Sebastian (R)	59,593	46.2
2	William T. Granahan (D)	83,344	57.0
	Max Slepin (R)	62,970	43.0
3	Hardie Scott (R)	68,217	50.3
	Maurice S. Osser (D)	67,286	49.7
4	Earl Chudoff (D)	65,255	57.5
	Theodore O. Spaulding (R)	48,280	42.5
5	William J. Green Jr. (D)	84,177	55.5
	George W. Sarbacher Jr. (R)	67,525	44.5
6	Hugh Scott (R)	74,316	50.0
	Ethan Allen Doty (D)	73,913	49.7
7	Benjamin F. James (R)	91,387	62.7
	Hubert P. Earle (D)	54,425	37.3
8	Albert C. Vaughn (R)	56,300	58.2
	George F. Kane (D)	40,502	41.8

	Candidates	Votes	%
9	Paul B. Dague (R)	70,368	67.2
	Philip Ragan (D)	34,317	32.8
10	Harry P. O'Neill (D)	56,158	51.5
	Fraser P. Donlan (R)	52,859	48.5
11	Daniel J. Flood (D)	77,466	54.4
	Elwood H. Jones (R)	65,015	45.6
12	Ivor D. Fenton (R)	67,135	56.8
	James H. Gildea (D)	51,028	43.2
13	George M. Rhodes (D)	36,335	49.8
	James W. Bertolet (R)	34,640	47.5
14	Wilson D. Gillette (R)	45,986	60.9
	John E. Snedeker (D)	29,538	39.1
15	Alvin R. Bush (R)	47,697	60.7
	Paul A. Rothfuss (D)	28,759	36.6
16	Samuel K. McConnell Jr (R)	81,366	66.2
	Leon C. MacMullen (D)	41,642	33.9
17	Richard M. Simpson (R)	40,029	62.8
	James L. Gatins (D)	23,762	37.3
18	Walter M. Mumma (R)	78,577	63.7
	James M. Quigley (D)	44,871	36.4
19	Leon H. Gavin (R)	42,719	62.8
	Fred C. Barr (D)	25,348	37.2
20	Francis E. Walter (D)	49,660	58.3
	George M. Berg (R)	35,487	41.7
21	James F. Lind (D)	48,550	52.2
	Francis Worley (D)	44,465	47.8
22	James E. Van Zandt (R)	42,701	59.5
	Arthur H. Reede (D)	29,080	40.5
23	Edward L. Sittler Jr. (R)	39,431	51.8
	Anthony Cavalcante (D)	36,740	48.2
24	Thomas E. Morgan (D)	46,875	59.1
	John J. Cairns Jr. (R)	32,470	40.9
25	Louis E. Graham (R)	55,866	52.4
	Samuel Gunnett Neff (D)	50,686	47.6
26	John P. Saylor (R)	63,445	52.5
	Lewis E. Evans (D)	57,396	47.5
27	Augustine B. Kelley (D)	53,229	57.1
	George E. Berry Jr. (R)	40,037	42.9
28	Carroll D. Kearns (R)	67,604	57.0
	Steve Filipkowski (D)	51,060	43.0
29	Harmar D. Denny Jr. (R)	54,076	52.6
	Harry J. Davenport (D)	48,198	46.9
30	Robert J. Corbett (R)	58,096	56.5
	J. R. Montgomery (D)	44,778	43.5
31	James G. Fulton (R)	82,525	67.5
	Wilber I. Newstetter Jr. (D)	39,776	32.5
32	Herman P. Eberharter (D)	66,077	68.7
	James E. Dougherty (R)	30,088	31.3
33	Frank Buchanan (D)	63,257	65.8
	Cornelius McLaughlin Sr. (R)	32,858	34.2

RHODE ISLAND

		Votes	%
1	Aime J. Forand (D)	90,065	63.2
	Francis R. Foley (R)	52,553	36.9
2	John E. Fogarty (D)	93,039	60.8
	Wilford S. Budlong (R)	60,036	39.2

SOUTH CAROLINA

		Votes	%
1	L. Mendel Rivers (D)	6,753	100.0
2	John J. Riley (D)	9,747	100.0
3	W. J. Bryan Dorn (D)	8,126	100.0
4	Joseph R. Bryson (D)	7,976	99.9
5	James P. Richards (D)	10,648	100.0
6	John L. McMillan (D)	7,131	100.0

SOUTH DAKOTA

		Votes	%
1	Harold O. Lovre (R)	116,173	60.8
	Merton B. Tice (D)	74,983	39.2
2	E. Y. Berry (R)	34,533	60.3
	Sam H. Bober (D)	22,737	39.7

TENNESSEE

		Votes	%
1	B. Carroll Reece (R)	33,308	46.5
	Dayton Phillips (IR)	20,121	28.1

	Candidates	Votes	%
	Kyle K. King (D)	18,260	25.5
2	Howard H. Baker (R)	38,585	52.2
	Frank W. Wilson (D)	35,349	47.8
3	James B. Frazier Jr. (D)	23,807	100.0
4	Albert Gore (D)	11,112	100.0
5	Joe L. Evins (D)	15,283	100.0
6	J. Percy Priest (D)	10,047	65.9
	James W. Perkins (I)	5,189	34.1
7	James P. Sutton (D)	13,520	100.0
8	Thomas J. Murray (D)	13,623	100.0
9	Jere Cooper (D)	9,276	100.0
10	Clifford Davis (D)	15,128	100.0

TEXAS

		Votes	%
1	Wright Patman (D)	12,444	100.0
2	Jesse M. Combs (D)	16,900	100.0
3	Lindley Beckworth (D)	11,784	91.1
	R. E. Kennedy (R)	1,145	8.9
4	Sam Rayburn (D)	11,546	100.0
5	J. Frank Wilson (D)	23,568	100.0
6	Olin Teague (D)	8,118	98.1
7	Tom Pickett (D)	12,537	100.0
8	Albert Thomas (D)	19,068	77.8
	B. F. Hanna (R)	5,427	22.2
9	Clark W. Thompson (D)	20,200	100.0
10	Homer Thornberry (D)	13,703	100.0
11	W. R. Poage (D)	10,576	100.0
12	Wingate H. Lucas (D)	13,179	80.7
	H. G. Neely (R)	3,162	19.4
13	Ed Gossett (D)	14,761	100.0
14	John E. Lyle Jr. (D)	31,201	100.0
15	Lloyd M. Bentsen Jr. (D)	18,524	100.0
16	Ken Regan (D)	8,928	100.0
17	Omar Burleson (D)	10,228	100.0
18	Walter Rogers (D)	25,666	52.5
	B. H. Guill (R)	23,259	47.5
19	George Mahon (D)	17,828	93.9
	M. D. Temple (R)	1,162	6.1
20	Paul J. Kilday (D)	9,138	100.0
21	O. Clark Fisher (D)	16,334	100.0

Special Election

		Votes	%
18	Ben H. Guill (R)	✔	#

UTAH

		Votes	%
1	Walter K. Granger (D)	54,161	51.1
	Preston L. Jones (R)	51,868	48.9
2	Reva B. Bosone (D)	84,283	53.4
	Ivy B. Priest (R)	73,535	46.6

VERMONT

		Votes	%
AL	Winston L. Prouty (R)	65,248	73.4
	Herbert B. Comings (D)	22,709	25.6

VIRGINIA

		Votes	%
1	Edward J. Robeson Jr. (D)	18,741	81.0
	Nile Straughan (R)	2,518	10.9
	Stanley S. Garner (I)	1,878	8.1
2	Porter Hardy Jr. (D)	14,846	99.9
3	J. Vaughan Gary (D)	15,300	89.6
	Phronia A. McNeill (PROG)	1,095	6.4
4	Watkins M. Abbitt (D)	8,325	99.9
5	Thomas B. Stanley (D)	9,433	99.9
6	Clarence G. Burton (D)	12,287	99.3
7	Burr P. Harrison (D)	19,932	69.4
	J. A. Garber (R)	8,786	30.6
8	Howard W. Smith (D)	29,730	57.2
	Tyrrell Krum (R)	21,071	40.6
9	Thomas B. Fugate (D)	26,802	58.4
	George C. Sutherland (R)	19,118	41.6

Special Election

		Votes	%
1	Edward J. Robeson Jr (D)	10,988	42.5
	William A. Wright	7,667	29.6
	Blake T. Newton	5,425	21.0
	Nile Straughan (R)	1,792	6.9

Footnote, see p. 206.

WASHINGTON

	Candidates	Votes	%
1	Hugh B. Mitchell (D)	90,053	51.4
	F. F. Powell (R)	84,024	47.9
2	Henry M. Jackson (D)	73,296	61.2
	Herb Wilson (R)	45,737	38.2
3	Russell V. Mack (R)	55,056	52.9
	Gordon M. Quarnstrom (D)	48,623	46.8
4	Hal Holmes (R)	61,544	64.3
	Ted Little (D)	34,174	35.7
5	Walt Horan (R)	60,273	54.8
	Robert Dellwo (D)	49,767	45.2
6	Thor C. Tollefson (R)	71,785	60.5
	John M. Coffee (D)	46,249	39.0

WEST VIRGINIA

		Votes	%
1	Robert L. Ramsay (D)	53,584	51.7
	Francis J. Love (R)	49,987	48.3

	Candidates	Votes	%
2	Harley O. Staggers (D)	53,485	54.4
	Melvin C. Snyder (R)	44,925	45.7
3	Cleveland M. Bailey (D)	56,794	54.4
	Rush D. Holt (R)	47,589	45.6
4	Maurice G. Burnside (D)	64,265	51.7
	Hubert S. Ellis (R)	60,171	48.4
5	John Kee (D)	61,000	65.8
	Arnold G. Porterfield (R)	31,777	34.3
6	Erland H. Hedrick (D)	85,793	61.6
	Latelle M. LaFollette Jr. (R)	53,466	38.4

WISCONSIN

		Votes	%
1	Lawrence H. Smith (R)	70,883	57.2
	Jack Harvey (D)	53,071	42.8
2	Glenn R. Davis (R)	75,281	57.6
	Horace W. Wilkie (D)	55,117	42.2
3	Gardner R. Withrow (R)	54,783	58.8
	Patrick J. Lucey (D)	38,265	41.0

	Candidates	Votes	%
4	Clement J. Zablocki (D)	83,564	60.9
	John C. Brophy (R)	53,702	39.1
5	Charles J. Kersten (R)	75,955	51.6
	Andrew J. Biemiller (D)	71,203	48.4
6	William K. Van Pelt (R)	66,289	65.1
	Kenneth Kunde (D)	35,618	35.0
7	Reid F. Murray (R)	63,433	68.3
	Edward G. Gilbertson (D)	29,408	31.7
8	John W. Byrnes (R)	71,908	62.1
	John W. Reynolds Jr. (D)	43,877	37.9
9	Merlin Hull (R)	60,337	70.8
	Arthur L. Henning (D)	24,871	29.2
10	Alvin E. O'Konski (R)	46,722	57.0
	Rodney J. Edwards (D)	35,281	43.0

WYOMING

		Votes	%
AL	William Henry Harrison (R)	50,865	54.5
	John B. Clark (D)	42,483	45.5

1. Guill received 7,717 votes (23.2 percent) for a plurality victory over a field of 11 candidates. The election is significant as he became the first Republican elected from the South (not including the two easternmost Tennessee districts that had been Republican since the Civil War) since 1930.

1951 House Elections

KENTUCKY

Special Election

		Votes	%
6	John C. Watts (D)	28,599	55.3
	Otis C. Thomas (R)	23,108	44.7

MISSOURI

Special Election

		Votes	%
11	Claude I. Bakewell (R)	25,849#	57.3
	Harry Schendel (D)	19,275#	42.7

NEW YORK

Special Election

		Votes	%
5	Robert Tripp Ross (R)	17,300	53.1
	Hugh Quinn (D)	11,438	35.1
	George Cranmore (L)	2,641	8.1

TEXAS

Special Election

		Votes	%
13	Frank Ikard (D)	8,970	31.0
	Jenkins	5,363	18.5
	Jackson	5,101	17.6
	Wagonseller	4,225	14.6
	McFarland	2,786	9.6
	Crouch	2,423	8.4

1952 House Elections

ALABAMA

	Candidates	Votes	%
1	Frank W. Boykin (D)	30,758	100.0
2	George Grant (D)	38,421	100.0
3	George W. Andrews (D)	29,321	100.0
4	Kenneth A. Roberts (D)	31,389	100.0
5	Albert Rains (D)	43,843	100.0
6	Armistead I. Selden Jr. (D)	24,058	100.0
7	Carl Elliott (D)	33,533	72.6
	Cyrus Kitchens (R)	12,689	27.5
8	Robert E. Jones Jr. (D)	41,293	87.3
	H. G. Williams (R)	5,984	12.7
9	Laurie C. Battle (D)	51,537	100.0

ARIZONA

1	John J. Rhodes (R)	66,512	54.0
	John R. Murdock (D)	56,622	46.0
2	Harold A. Patten (D)	71,245	56.9
	William C. Frey (R)	54,021	43.1

ARKANSAS

1	Ezekiel C. Gathings (D)	42,494	100.0
2	Wilbur D. Mills (D)	36,252	100.0
3	James W. Trimble (D)	49,284	56.0
	Jack Joyce (R)	38,784	44.0
4	Oren Harris (D)	65,374	100.0
5	Brooks Hays (D)	53,056	78.8
	Alonzo A. Ross (R)	13,105	19.5
6	William F. Norrell (D)	62,378	100.0

CALIFORNIA

1	Hubert B. Scudder (R-D)	137,801	86.3
	Carl Sullivan (I PROG)	21,734	13.6
2	Clair Engle (D-R)	124,179	100.0
3	John E. Moss Jr. (D)	87,335	50.8
	Leslie E. Wood (R)	82,133	47.8
4	William S. Mailliard (R)	102,359	55.0
	Franck R. Havenner (D)	83,748	45.0
5	John F. Shelley (D-R)	107,542	100.0
6	Robert L. Condon (D)	87,768	50.6
	John F. Baldwin Jr. (R)	85,756	49.4
7	John J. Allen Jr. (R-D)	120,666	84.2
	John Allen Johnson (I PROG)	22,408	15.6
8	George P. Miller (D-R)	156,445	99.9
9	J. Arthur Younger (R)	71,426	53.1
	Harold F. Taggart (D)	61,028	45.3
10	Charles S. Gubser (R)	106,375	59.2
	Arthur L. Johnson (D)	70,271	39.1
11	Leroy Johnson (R-D)	101,052	87.1
	Leslie B. Schlingheyde (I PROG)	14,999	12.9
12	A. Oakley Hunter (R-D)	103,587	99.3
13	Ernest K. Bramblett (R)	79,496	51.0
	Will Hayes (D)	76,516	49.0
14	Harlan Hagen (D)	70,809	51.0
	Thomas H. Werdel (R)	68,011	49.0
15	Gordon L. McDonough (R-D)	142,545	99.7
16	Donald L. Jackson (R)	79,121	59.7
	Jerry K. Harter (D)	53,337	40.2
17	Cecil R. King (D)	114,650	54.6
	Robert H. Finch (R)	92,587	44.1
18	Craig Hosmer (R)	90,438	55.5
	Joseph M. Kennick (D)	72,457	44.5
19	Chet Holifield (D-R)	126,606	87.0
	Ida Alvarez (I PROG)	13,724	9.4
20	Carl Hinshaw (R-D)	109,509	99.7
21	Edgar W. Hiestand (R)	112,100	53.6
	Everett G. Burkhalter (D)	97,007	46.4
22	Joseph F. Holt (R)	85,039	60.5
	Dean E. McHenry (D)	55,534	39.5

	Candidates	Votes	%
23	Clyde Doyle (D-R)	138,356	87.3
	Olive T. Thompson (I PROG)	17,501	11.1
24	Norris Poulson (R-D)	119,799	87.2
	Bertram L. Sharp (I PROG)	17,307	12.6
25	Patrick J. Hillings (R)	135,465	64.3
	Woodrow Wilson Sayre (D)	75,125	35.7
26	Samuel William Yorty (D-R)	157,973	88.0
	Horace V. Alexander (I PROG)	21,465	12.0
27	Harry R. Sheppard (D)	68,773	55.0
	Carl B. Hilliard (R)	56,202	45.0
28	James B. Utt (R)	106,972	63.0
	Lionel Van Deerlin (D)	62,779	37.0
29	John Phillips (R-D)	73,144	99.7
30	Bob Wilson (R)	121,332	59.6
	Degraff Austin (D)	82,311	40.4

COLORADO

1	Byron G. Rogers (D)	101,864	50.8
	Mason Knuckles (R)	97,442	48.6
2	William S. Hill (R)	113,566	63.1
	Ralph L. Williams (D)	66,300	36.9
3	J. Edgar Chenoweth (R)	84,739	57.7
	John H. Marsalis (D)	62,025	42.3
4	Wayne N. Aspinall (D)	39,676	50.0
	Howard M. Shults (R)	39,647	50.0

CONNECTICUT

1	Thomas J. Dodd (D)	160,080	54.0
	John Ashmead (R)	136,540	46.0
2	Horace Seely-Brown Jr. (R)	90,827	55.5
	William M. Citron (D)	72,868	44.5
3	Albert W. Cretella (R)	111,018	52.8
	John A. McGuire (D)	99,408	47.2
4	Albert P. Morano (R)	164,689	60.1
	Joseph P. Lyford (D)	107,881	39.4
5	James T. Patterson (R)	83,848	56.7
	John A. Speziale (D)	64,020	43.3
AL	Antoni N. Sadlak (R)	601,238	55.0
	Stanley J. Pribyson (D)	489,645	44.8

DELAWARE

AL	Herbert B. Warburton (R)	88,285	51.9
	Joseph J. Scannel (D)	81,730	48.1

FLORIDA

1	Courtney Campbell (D)	69,149	50.7
	William C. Cramer (R)	67,286	49.3
2	Charles E. Bennett (D)	64,080	100.0
3	Robert L. F. Sikes (D)	74,909	100.0
4	Bill Lantaff (D)	115,611	66.0
	Dorothea M. B. Vermorel (R)	59,458	34.0
5	A. S. Herlong Jr. (D)	89,943	100.0
6	Dwight L. Rogers (D)	55,901	60.8
	Janet H. Fitzgerald (R)	36,113	39.3
7	James A. Haley (D)	36,973	56.3
	Kent S. McKinley (R)	28,725	43.7
8	D. R. Matthews (D)	43,447	100.0

GEORGIA

1	Prince H. Preston (D)	57,088	100.0
2	E. E. Cox (D)	42,226*	100.0
3	E. L. Forrester (D)	53,161	100.0
4	A. Sidney Camp (D)	52,327	100.0
5	James C. Davis (D)	83,920	100.0

	Candidates	Votes	%
6	Carl Vinson (D)	49,635	100.0
7	Henderson Lanham (D)	65,416	99.9
8	W. M. Wheeler (D)	51,349	99.9
9	Phil M. Landrum (D)	47,327	100.0
10	Paul Brown (D)	44,646	100.0

IDAHO

1	Gracie Pfost (D)	54,725	50.3
	John T. Wood (R)	54,134	49.7
2	Hamer H. Budge (R)	103,047	66.2
	W. H. Jensen (D)	52,692	33.8

ILLINOIS

1	William L. Dawson (D)	95,899	73.5
	Edgar G. Brown (R)	34,571	26.5
2	Barratt O'Hara (D)	94,253	51.4
	Richard B. Vail (R)	89,080	48.6
3	Fred E. Busbey (R)	102,328	54.5
	Neil J. Linehan (D)	85,539	45.5
4	William E. McVey (R)	131,215	56.6
	Arthur E. Dillner (D)	100,809	43.5
5	John C. Kluczynski (D)	104,900	64.5
	Ernest L. Kaysen (R)	57,775	35.5
6	Thomas J. O'Brien (D)	112,121	63.1
	John L. Roach (R)	65,537	36.9
7	Adolph J. Sabath (D)	111,960*	70.0
	Louis F. Capuzi (R)	48,000	30.0
8	Thomas S. Gordon (D)	87,871	59.0
	William F. Cooper (R)	61,048	41.0
9	Sidney R. Yates (D)	87,285	52.4
	Robert R. Siegrist (R)	79,429	47.6
10	Richard W. Hoffman (R)	138,560	65.0
	John Schaffenegger (D)	74,467	35.0
11	Timothy P. Sheehan (R)	103,265	59.4
	Stanley W. Morten (D)	70,691	40.6
12	Edgar A. Jonas (R)	113,762	55.7
	Philip A. Fleischman (D)	90,444	44.3
13	Marguerite Stitt Church (R)	184,696	70.6
	Lawrence J. Hayes (D)	77,068	29.4
14	Chauncey W. Reed (R)	137,881	71.5
	William E. Hartnett (D)	54,953	28.5
15	Noah M. Mason (R)	103,398	63.7
	Stanley Hubbs (D)	59,050	36.4
16	Leo E. Allen (R)	110,182	66.5
	John P. Barton (D)	55,399	33.5
17	Leslie C. Arends (R)	105,042	63.6
	John A. Kinneman (D)	60,112	36.4
18	Harold H. Velde (R)	83,706	55.2
	John T. McNaughton (D)	67,905	44.8
19	Robert B. Chiperfield (R)	94,141	60.8
	Ray Simkins (D)	60,619	39.2
20	Sidney E. Simpson (R)	84,994	61.8
	John R. Roy (D)	52,586	38.2
21	Peter F. Mack Jr. (D)	94,026	52.5
	Edward H. Jenison (R)	85,248	47.6
22	William L. Springer (R)	92,851	63.0
	David W. Beggs Jr. (D)	54,576	37.0
23	Charles Vursell (R)	89,428	57.7
	W. Carl Johnston (D)	65,442	42.3
24	Melvin Price (D)	117,408	64.8
	Phyllis Stewart Schlafly (R)	63,778	35.2
25	C. W. Bishop (R)	88,810	56.2
	C. Edwin Hair (D)	69,245	43.8

INDIANA

1	Ray J. Madden (D)	93,187	56.4
	Elliott Belshaw (R)	71,617	43.3
2	Charles A. Halleck (R)	94,795	63.3
	L. Dewey Burham (D)	54,025	36.1
3	Shepard J. Crumpacker Jr. (R)	107,839	54.5
	Charles C. Price (D)	88,776	44.9

INDIANA

Candidates	Votes	%
4 E. Ross Adair (R)	95,613	63.7
Howard L. Morrison (D)	53,154	35.4
5 John V. Beamer (R)	114,081	56.9
Philip C. Dermond (D)	84,825	42.3
6 Cecil M. Harden (R)	86,899	55.7
Jack H. Mankin (D)	68,709	44.0
7 William G. Bray (R)	85,601	56.1
Thomas J. Courtney (D)	66,218	43.4
8 D. Bailey Merrill (R)	98,226	52.6
Winfield K. Denton (D)	87,770	47.0
9 Earl Wilson (R)	74,052	56.4
Edward Lewis (D)	56,759	43.2
10 Ralph Harvey (R)	103,937	59.9
Fred V. Culp (D)	67,932	39.1
11 Charles B. Brownson (R)	160,929	59.4
John C. Carvey (D)	109,403	40.4

IOWA

Candidates	Votes	%
1 Thomas E. Martin (R)	105,526	62.9
Clair A. Williams (D)	62,011	36.9
2 Henry O. Talle (R)	114,553	62.2
T. W. Mullaney (D)	69,421	37.7
3 H. R. Gross (R)	109,992	65.8
George R. Laub (D)	56,871	34.0
4 Karl M. LeCompte (R)	73,317	61.9
Earl E. Glassburner (D)	44,900	37.9
5 Paul Cunningham (R)	95,057	58.8
Alvin P. Meyer (D)	66,303	41.0
6 James I. Dolliver (R)	86,842	68.7
Francis G. Cutler (D)	39,245	31.1
7 Ben F. Jensen (R)	82,462	67.3
Thomas J. Keleher (D)	39,999	32.6
8 Charles B. Hoeven (R)	94,561	99.7

KANSAS

Candidates	Votes	%
1 Howard S. Miller (D)	68,909	51.5
Albert M. Cole (R)	64,963	48.5
2 Errett P. Scrivner (R)	91,676	57.3
Claude L. Rice (D)	68,396	42.7
3 Myron V. George (R)	57,126	59.5
Fred L. Hedges (D)	38,960	40.6
4 Edward H. Rees (R)	118,206	59.4
Bill Porter (D)	80,697	40.6
5 Clifford R. Hope (R)	90,967	70.9
Art McAnarney (D)	37,361	29.1
6 Wint Smith (R)	66,723	62.6
Horace A. Santry (D)	39,955	37.5

KENTUCKY

Candidates	Votes	%
1 Noble J. Gregory (D)	66,106	65.8
W. Mallam Lake (R)	34,360	34.2
2 Garrett L. Withers (D)	57,518	54.4
David C. Brodie (R)	48,191	45.6
3 John M. Robsion Jr. (R)	95,041	54.0
B. L. Shamburger (D)	80,347	45.7
4 Frank L. Chelf (D)	55,670	55.9
R. H. Hutchison Jr. (R)	43,981	44.1
5 Brent Spence (D)	78,431	55.4
William D. Cochran (R)	63,058	44.6
6 John C. Watts (D)	68,554	56.3
Leslie A. Henderson (R)	53,297	43.7
7 Carl D. Perkins (D)	53,238	58.2
Curtis Clark (R)	38,290	41.8
8 James S. Golden (R)	78,584	68.9
W. D. Scalf (D)	35,556	31.2

LOUISIANA

Candidates	Votes	%
1 F. Edward Hebert (D)	71,448	66.4
George W. Reese Jr. (R)	36,161	33.6
2 Hale Boggs (D)	68,112	100.0
3 Edwin E. Willis (D)	33,184	100.0
4 Overton Brooks (D)	40,724	100.0
5 Otto E. Passman (D)	32,743	100.0

Candidates	Votes	%
6 James H. Morrison (D)	61,744	100.0
7 T. A. Thompson (D)	40,811	100.0
8 George S. Long (D)	31,476	100.0

MAINE

Candidates	Votes	%
1 Robert Hale (R)	56,239	61.6
James A. McVicar (D)	35,078	38.4
2 Charles P. Nelson (R)	55,393	66.8
Leland B. Currier (D)	27,527	33.2
3 Clifford G. McIntire (R)	45,095	76.2
Philip R. Sharpe (D)	14,103	23.8

MARYLAND

Candidates	Votes	%
1 Edward T. Miller (R)	47,164	61.0
Dudley George Roe (D)	30,162	39.0
2 James P. S. Devereux (R)	95,811	61.4
A. Gordon Boone (D)	60,121	38.6
3 Edward A. Garmatz (D)	60,659	70.9
Jerry Toula (R)	24,879	29.1
4 George H. Fallon (D)	54,215	54.7
Samuel Hopkins (R)	44,974	45.3
5 Frank Small Jr. (R)	68,405	50.4
Richard E. Lankford (D)	67,366	49.6
6 DeWitt S. Hyde (R)	94,603	57.8
Stella B. Werner (D)	69,050	42.2
7 Samuel N. Friedel (D)	63,652	51.4
William F. Laukaitis (R)	60,277	48.6

MASSACHUSETTS

Candidates	Votes	%
1 John W. Heselton (R)	101,512	67.1
William H. Burns (D)	49,379	32.7
2 Edward P. Boland (D)	88,424	51.8
Troy T. Murray (R)	81,847	48.0
3 Philip J. Philbin (D)	108,743	67.3
Frank M. Walker (R)	52,348	32.4
4 Harold D. Donohue (D)	93,530	54.4
Carl A. Sheridan (R)	77,536	45.1
5 Edith Nourse Rogers (R)	146,269	75.9
Helen M. Fitzgerald (D)	45,650	23.7
6 William H. Bates (R)	139,567	95.1
7 Thomas J. Lane (D)	105,662	74.7
John L. Southwick Jr. (R)	34,663	24.5
8 Angier L. Goodwin (R)	85,918	50.9
John C. Carr Jr. (D)	82,114	48.7
9 Donald W. Nicholson (R)	103,708	59.2
James F. O'Neill (D)	71,129	40.6
10 Laurence Curtis (R)	101,221	54.3
Frederick C. Hailer Jr. (D)	84,021	45.1
11 Thomas P. O'Neill (D)	86,532	69.3
Jesse A. Rogers (R)	37,816	30.3
12 John W. McCormack (D)	111,986	82.2
James S. Tremblay (R)	24,271	17.8
13 Richard B. Wigglesworth (R)	114,761	60.6
David J. Crowley (D)	74,730	39.4
14 Joseph W. Martin Jr. (R)	108,215	63.2
Edward F. Doolan (D)	62,554	36.5

MICHIGAN

Candidates	Votes	%
1 Thaddeus M. Machrowicz (D)	118,695	84.2
Rudolph S. Tenerowicz (R)	21,442	15.2
2 George Meader (R)	101,341	63.4
John P. Dawson (D)	58,024	36.3
3 Paul W. Shafer (R)	95,061	62.0
Kenneth G. Brown (D)	57,666	37.6
4 Clare E. Hoffman (R)	87,703	66.6
Murle E. Gorton (D)	43,450	33.0
5 Gerald R. Ford Jr. (R)	109,807	66.3
Vincent E. O'Neill (D)	55,147	33.3
6 Kit Clardy (R)	108,263	52.6
Donald Hayworth (D)	96,682	47.0
7 Jesse P. Wolcott (R)	101,936	60.3
Ira D. McCoy (D)	66,699	39.5

Candidates	Votes	%
8 Alvin M. Bentley (R)	91,731	66.6
Clarence V. Smazel (D)	45,431	33.0
9 Ruth Thompson (R)	70,456	59.5
John H. Piercey (D)	47,456	40.1
10 Elford A. Cederberg (R)	69,727	67.5
William J. Kelly (D)	33,602	32.5
11 Victor A. Knox (R)	54,883	59.3
Prentiss M. Brown Jr. (D)	37,701	40.7
12 John B. Bennett (R)	47,160	58.2
E. Burr Sherwood (D)	33,892	41.8
13 George D. O'Brien (D)	88,473	64.8
Clarence J. McLeod (R)	47,881	35.1
14 Louis C. Rabaut (D)	117,027	53.1
Richard Durant (R)	103,366	46.9
15 John D. Dingell (D)	109,109	66.7
Gregory M. Pillon (R)	54,236	33.2
16 John Lesinski Jr. (D)	139,011	60.6
Harold J. Smith (R)	89,159	38.9
17 Charles G. Oakman (R)	94,517	52.9
Martha W. Griffiths (D)	84,001	47.0
18 George A. Dondero (R)	108,673	56.2
Arthur J. Law (D)	84,308	43.6

MINNESOTA

Candidates	Votes	%
1 August H. Andresen (R)	103,218	69.4
George Alfson (DFL)	45,496	30.6
2 Joseph P. O'Hara (R)	101,641	67.7
Richard T. Malone (DFL)	48,404	32.3
3 Roy W. Wier (DFL)	115,008	52.2
Ed Willow (R)	105,320	47.8
4 Eugene J. McCarthy (DFL)	98,015	61.7
Roger G. Kennedy (R)	60,827	38.3
5 Walter H. Judd (R)	99,027	59.2
Karl F. Rolvaag (DFL)	68,326	40.8
6 Fred Marshall (DFL)	74,041	52.6
J. Arthur Bensen (R)	66,764	47.4
7 H. Carl Andersen (R)	87,460	62.7
James M. Youngdale (DFL)	52,144	37.4
8 John A. Blatnik (DFL)	91,465	62.6
Ernest R. Orchard (R)	54,756	37.5
9 Harold C. Hagen (R)	70,402	60.6
Curtiss T. Olson (DFL)	45,874	39.5

MISSISSIPPI

Candidates	Votes	%
1 Thomas G. Abernethy (D)	40,333	100.0
2 Jamie L. Whitten (D)	29,025	100.0
3 Frank E. Smith (D)	23,906	87.2
Paul Clark (R)	3,523	12.8
4 John Bell Williams (D)	50,318	100.0
5 Arthur Winstead (D)	39,919	94.1
Henry J. Maddox (R)	2,501	5.9
6 William M. Colmer (D)	51,227	100.0

MISSOURI

Candidates	Votes	%
1 Frank M. Karsten (D)	126,583	64.2
Eugene A. Miller (R)	70,479	35.8
2 Thomas B. Curtis (R)	125,625	56.9
Donald McClanahan (D)	95,208	43.1
3 Leonor K. Sullivan (D)	107,428	64.8
Claude I. Bakewell (R)	58,413	35.2
4 Jeffrey P. Hillelson (R)	96,988	53.3
Leonard Irving (D)	84,899	46.7
5 Richard Bolling (D)	90,357	56.0
Frank C. Rayburn (R)	70,898	44.0
6 William C. Cole (R)	89,428	52.4
Robert O. Richardson (D)	81,237	47.6
7 Dewey Short (R)	115,842	61.7
John Hosmer (D)	71,936	38.3
8 A. S. J. Carnahan (D)	69,068	52.9
Francis E. Howard (R)	61,621	47.2
9 Clarence Cannon (D)	98,965	54.8
S. W. (Wat) Arnold (R)	81,806	45.3
10 Paul C. Jones (D)	71,156	60.7
Andrew Sandegren (R)	46,033	39.3
11 Morgan M. Moulder (D)	74,362	50.4
Max Schwabe (R)	73,104	49.6

MONTANA

	Candidates	Votes	%
1	Lee Metcalf (D)	55,679	50.3
	Wellington D. Rankin (R)	54,086	48.9
2	Wesley A. D'Ewart (R)	90,210	62.0
	Willard E. Fraser (D)	55,203	38.0

NEBRASKA

1	Carl T. Curtis (R)	117,336	72.1
	Samuel Freeman (D)	45,523	28.0
2	Roman L. Hruska (R)	81,185	56.1
	James A. Hart (D)	63,485	43.9
3	Robert D. Harrison (R)	89,879	71.9
	Alan A. Dusatko (D)	35,213	28.2
4	Arthur L. Miller (R)	98,032	73.3
	Francis D. Lee (D)	35,628	26.7

NEVADA

AL	Clifton Young (R)	40,683	50.5
	Walter S. Baring (D)	39,912	49.5

NEW HAMPSHIRE

1	Chester E. Merrow (R)	82,689	60.2
	Peter R. Poirier (D)	54,746	39.8
2	Norris Cotton (R)	80,061	66.5
	John Guay (D)	40,373	33.5

NEW JERSEY

1	Charles A. Wolverton (R)	118,367	55.0
	Alfred R. Pierce (D)	96,162	44.7
2	T. Millet Hand (R)	79,955	63.4
	Charles Edward Rupp (D)	46,174	36.6
3	James C. Auchincloss (R)	124,292	64.4
	John W. Zimmermann (D)	67,642	35.0
4	Charles R. Howell (D)	84,733	54.7
	John J. Inglesby (R)	70,076	45.3
5	Peter H. B. Frelinghuysen Jr. (R)	133,276	62.2
	Aldona L. Appleton (D)	80,922	37.8
6	Clifford P. Case (R)	121,252	63.9
	H. Frank Pettit (D)	67,159	35.4
7	William B. Widnall (R)	130,603	68.3
	Vito A. Concilio (D)	60,553	31.7
8	Gordon Canfield (R)	97,338	62.6
	John J. Winberry (D)	54,367	35.0
9	Frank C. Osmers Jr. (R)	125,402	66.2
	William H. McNulty (D)	63,175	33.4
10	Peter W. Rodino Jr. (D)	78,612	56.9
	Alexander J. Matturri (R)	57,740	41.8
11	Hugh J. Addonizio (D)	68,273	52.2
	William O. Barnes Jr. (R)	60,461	46.3
12	Robert Winthrop Kean (R)	84,949	54.8
	Martin S. Fox (D)	70,046	45.2
13	Alfred D. Sieminski (D)	72,987	55.2
	Julius D. Canter (R)	54,581	41.2
14	Edward J. Hart (D)	67,109	51.5
	William J. Bozzuffi (R)	59,112	45.4

NEW MEXICO

AL	John J. Dempsey (D)	121,477	
	Antonio M. Fernandez (D)	119,925	
	Homer J. Berkshire (R)	112,297	
	Ed Guthmann (R)	109,595	

NEW YORK

1	Stuyvesant Wainwright (R)	114,135	60.4
	Ernest Greenwood (D, L)	74,174	39.3
2	Steven B. Derounian (R)	132,512	68.8
	Joseph Liff (D)	54,725	28.4
3	Frank J. Becker (R)	128,007	65.4
	Richard A. O'Leary (D)	60,800	31.0

	Candidates	Votes	%
4	Henry J. Latham (R)	123,132	62.6
	Joseph J. Perrini (D, L)	70,755	36.0
5	Albert H. Bosch (R)	86,168	53.5
	L. Gary Clemente (D, L)	73,083	45.3
6	Lester Holtzman (D, L)	105,261	49.2
	Robert Tripp Ross (R)	104,720	48.9
7	James J. Delaney (D, L)	87,204	51.0
	William Adam Schulz (R)	80,896	47.3
8	Louis B. Heller (D, L)	75,772	65.3
	Benjamin F. Westervelt Jr. (R)	37,884	32.6
9	Eugene J. Keogh (D, L)	83,841	61.1
	Joseph M. Soviero (R)	48,998	35.7
10	Edna F. Kelly (D, L)	105,302	71.2
	George W. Thomas (R)	42,498	28.8
11	Emanuel Celler (D, L)	127,091	73.8
	Henry D. Dorfman (R)	37,244	21.6
12	Francis E. Dorn (R)	75,895	52.7
	Donald L. O'Toole (D, L)	65,650	45.6
13	Abraham J. Multer (D, L)	112,152	68.3
	P. Vincent Landi (R)	45,664	27.8
14	John J. Rooney (D, L)	86,952	64.2
	Jacob P. Lefkowitz (R)	45,004	33.2
15	John H. Ray (R)	97,023	57.9
	James J. Murphy (D, L)	69,538	41.5
16	Adam Clayton Powell Jr. (D)	72,562	73.9
	Richard L. Baltimore Jr. (R)	15,937	16.2
	Clarence Francis (L)	7,125	7.3
17	Frederic R. Coudert Jr. (R)	84,821	57.0
	Harry Grossman (D, L)	60,624	40.7
18	James G. Donovan (D, R)	88,629	92.6
	Vito Magli (AM LAB)	7,047	7.4
19	Arthur G. Klein (D, L)	77,267	66.0
	Edward I. Goldberg (R)	34,795	29.7
20	Franklin D. Roosevelt Jr. (D, L)	81,591	60.2
	Clarence C. Vambell (R)	49,905	36.8
21	Jacob K. Javits (R, L)	89,866	63.4
	John C. Hart (D)	47,637	33.6
22	Sidney A. Fine (D)	90,474	58.0
	Martin Greene (R)	38,681	24.8
	David Wells (L)	21,606	13.9
23	Isidore Dollinger (D)	78,350	63.8
	Sidney S. Flaum (R)	23,238	18.9
	Harry Kavesh (L)	14,393	11.7
	Howard Fast (AM LAB)	6,834	5.6
24	Charles A. Buckley (D)	82,343	46.5
	Solon S. Kane (R)	58,096	32.8
	Herman Woskow (L)	29,425	16.6
25	Paul A. Fino (R)	85,308	50.1
	Bernard J. O'Connell (D)	68,862	40.4
	Louis Schifrin (L)	13,325	7.8
26	Ralph A. Gamble (R)	116,091	67.3
	Flora Chudson (D, L)	55,184	32.0
27	Ralph W. Gwinn (R)	108,575	58.5
	George A. Brenner (D, L)	75,781	40.9
28	Katharine St. George (R)	102,476	65.6
	Marion K. Sanders (D, L)	52,994	33.9
29	J. Ernest Wharton (R)	115,502	69.8
	Walter Donnaruma (D)	46,727	28.2
30	Leo W. O'Brien (D, L)	101,178	53.7
	John F. Forner Jr. (R)	86,651	46.0
31	Dean P. Taylor (R)	114,656	70.6
	Helen Nolan Neil (D)	44,367	27.3
32	Bernard W. Kearney (R)	111,025	67.4
33	Clarence E. Kilburn (R)	98,653	69.0
	Maurice N. McGrath (D)	41,803	29.2
34	William R. Williams (R)	97,488	58.8
	Charles Ray Wilson (D)	65,080	39.3
35	R. Walter Riehlman (R)	113,778	63.2
	Arthur B. McGuire (D, L)	65,763	36.5
36	John Taber (R)	110,304	69.9
	Donald J. O'Connor (D, L)	47,189	29.9
37	W. Sterling Cole (R)	131,172	69.4
	Jean Ivory (D)	57,474	30.4
38	Kenneth B. Keating (R)	128,566	69.3
	Victor Kruppenbacher (D, L)	56,177	30.3
39	Harold C. Ostertag (R)	107,501	65.8
	O. Richard Judson (D, L)	55,483	34.0

	Candidates	Votes	%
40	William E. Miller (R)	102,565	59.6
	E. Dent Lackey (D, L)	69,087	40.2
41	Edmund P. Radwan (R)	95,755	55.9
	Anthony F. Tauriello (D, L)	75,552	44.1
42	John R. Pillion (R)	100,434	55.2
	Chester C. Gorski (D, L)	81,201	44.6
43	Daniel A. Reed (R)	91,534	66.2
	Harry D. Johnson (D)	44,276	32.0

Special Election

32	Leo W. O'Brien (D, L)	66,849	70.8
	John F. Forner Jr. (R)	27,276	28.9

NORTH CAROLINA

1	Herbert C. Bonner (D)	43,104	100.0
2	L. H. Fountain (D)	51,213	94.8
	W. B. White (R)	2,822	5.2
3	Graham A. Barden (D)	45,458	76.2
	Everette L. Peterson (R)	14,239	23.9
4	Harold D. Cooley (D)	79,520	75.3
	Paul C. West (R)	26,039	24.7
5	Thurmond Chatham (D)	74,884	98.2
6	Carl T. Durham (D)	84,203	69.5
	Louis F. Ferree (R)	36,912	30.5
7	F. Ertel Carlyle (D)	62,884	98.5
8	Charles B. Deane (D)	67,764	59.9
	Walter B. Love (R)	45,451	40.2
9	Hugh Q. Alexander (D)	68,624	51.5
	Walter P. Johnson (R)	64,662	48.5
10	Charles Raper Jonas (R)	82,428	57.4
	Hamilton C. Jones (D)	61,149	42.6
11	Woodrow W. Jones (D)	61,540	63.0
	George M. Pritchard (R)	36,157	37.0
12	George A. Shuford (D)	63,045	56.9
	Hugh Montieth (R)	47,752	43.1

NORTH DAKOTA

AL	Usher L. Burdick (R)	181,218	
	Otto Krueger (R)	156,829	
	Edward Nesemeier (D)	49,829	

OHIO

1	Gordon H. Scherer (R)	96,385	61.6
	Walter A. Kelly (D)	60,015	38.4
2	William E. Hess (R)	90,417	56.6
	Earl T. Wagner (D)	69,341	43.4
3	Paul F. Schenck (R)	112,325	51.1
	Thomas B. Talbot (D)	107,551	48.9
4	William M. McCulloch (R)	93,442	68.3
	Carleton Carl Reiser (D)	43,426	31.7
5	Cliff Clevenger (R)	72,168	63.2
	Dan Batt (D)	42,104	36.9
6	James G. Polk (D)	67,220	50.1
	Leo Blackburn (R)	66,896	49.9
7	Clarence J. Brown (R)	98,354	100.0
8	Jackson E. Betts (R)	75,768	68.7
	Henry P. Drake (D)	34,474	31.3
9	Frazier Reams (I)	74,821	40.9
	Thomas H. Burke (D)	61,047	33.4
	Gilmore Flues (R)	46,989	25.7
10	Thomas A. Jenkins (R)	63,339	64.0
	Delmar A. Canaday (D)	35,666	36.0
11	Oliver P. Bolton (R)	91,204	58.8
	Robert J. Kilpatrick (D)	63,930	41.2
12	John M. Vorys (R)	134,693	62.3
	George T. Tarbutton (D)	81,665	37.8
13	Alvin F. Weichel (R)	63,344	58.8
	George C. Steinemann (D)	44,467	41.3
14	William H. Ayres (R)	117,745	58.5
	Walter B. Huber (D)	83,463	41.5
15	Robert T. Secrest (D)	62,913	64.3
	P. W. Griffiths (R)	34,966	35.7
16	Frank T. Bow (R)	98,447	54.4
	John McSweeney (D)	82,522	45.6

OHIO

	Candidates	Votes	%
17	J. Harry McGregor (R)	94,624	68.2
	James J. Mayer (D)	44,117	31.8
18	Wayne L. Hays (D)	78,277	55.8
	Clarence L. Wetzel (R)	62,081	44.2
19	Michael J. Kirwan (D)	91,074	66.3
	Allen Russell (R)	46,202	33.7
20	Michael A. Feighan (D)	109,211	65.2
	John H. Ferguson (R)	58,271	34.8
21	Robert Crosser (D)	100,340	68.6
	Lawrence O. Payne (R)	45,896	31.4
22	Frances P. Bolton (R)	87,316	58.8
	Chat Paterson (D)	61,197	41.2
23	George H. Bender (R)	85,752	64.6
	Michael P. O'Brien (D)	47,090	35.5

OKLAHOMA

	Candidates	Votes	%
1	Page Belcher (R)	121,442	58.6
	H. G. Dickey (D)	85,647	41.4
2	Ed Edmondson (D)	92,407	59.2
	Edward E. Easton (R)	60,550	38.8
3	Carl Albert (D)	73,185	77.9
	Frank D. McSherry (R)	20,735	22.1
4	Tom Steed (D)	67,024	58.7
	John L. Goode (R)	46,446	40.7
5	John Jarman (D)	128,627	62.4
	Edwin Whitney Burch (R)	77,425	37.6
6	Victor E. Wickersham (D)	98,823	63.3
	K. B. Cornell (R)	57,261	36.7

OREGON

	Candidates	Votes	%
1	Walter Norblad (R)	124,720	68.0
	Robert B. Jones (D)	58,796	32.0
2	Sam Coon (R)	57,155	58.5
	John G. Jones (D)	40,550	41.5
3	Homer D. Angell (R)	125,504	54.0
	Alfred H. Corbett (D)	107,099	46.0
4	Harris Ellsworth (R)	100,970	66.3
	Walter A. Swanson (D)	51,298	33.7

PENNSYLVANIA

	Candidates	Votes	%
1	William A. Barrett (D)	89,879	68.2
	James Iannucci (R)	41,948	31.8
2	William T. Granahan (D)	105,553	61.8
	Daniel J. McCauley Jr. (R)	65,159	38.2
3	James A. Byrne (D)	81,837	58.4
	Morton Witkin (R)	58,191	41.6
4	Earl Chudoff (D)	90,077	69.9
	Joseph R. Burns (R)	38,228	29.7
5	William J. Green Jr (D)	104,112	54.2
	Philip Richman (R)	88,040	45.8
6	Hugh Scott (R)	93,368	51.7
	Harrington Herr (D)	87,124	48.2
7	Benjamin F. James (R)	127,918	61.7
	Murray P. Zealor (D)	79,423	38.3
8	Karl C. King (R)	83,966	59.3
	Wilson H. Stephenson (D)	57,723	40.7
9	Paul B. Dague (R)	100,578	66.2
	Philip E. Ragan (D)	51,268	33.8
10	Joseph L. Carrigg (R)	89,820	53.6
	Harry P. O'Neill (D)	77,758	46.4
11	Edward J. Bonin (R)	80,310	50.2
	Daniel J. Flood (D)	79,722	49.8
12	Ivor D. Fenton (R)	79,859	60.7
	Peter Krehel (D)	51,736	39.3
13	Samuel K. McConnell Jr. (R)	114,672	66.4
	Frank A. Keegan (D)	57,974	33.6
14	George M. Rhodes (D)	48,427	49.7
	James W. Bertolet (R)	48,019	49.2
15	Francis E. Walter (D)	61,566	54.8
	John Russell Craig (R)	50,871	45.2
16	Walter M. Mumma (R)	83,493	61.7
	David V. Randall (D)	51,825	38.3
17	Alvin R. Bush (R)	82,058	64.2
	Patrick A. McGowan (D)	44,376	34.7

	Candidates	Votes	%
18	Richard M. Simpson (R)	75,723	63.5
	Philip R. Shoemaker (D)	43,555	36.5
19	S. Walter Stauffer (R)	72,466	52.3
	James F. Lind (D)	66,165	47.7
20	James E. Van Zandt (R)	62,804	62.8
	Joseph A. Moran (D)	37,152	37.2
21	Augustine B. Kelley (D)	73,223	52.9
	J. Cleveland McKenna (R)	65,252	47.1
22	John P. Saylor (R)	77,391	52.4
	William D. Shettig (D)	70,218	47.6
23	Leon H. Gavin (R)	73,001	67.8
	Fred C. Barr (D)	34,633	32.2
24	Carroll D. Kearns (R)	90,276	57.1
	Clinton J. Bebell (D)	67,790	42.9
25	Louis E. Graham (R)	77,577	50.4
	Frank M. Clark (D)	76,214	49.6
26	Thomas E. Morgan (D)	105,581	59.1
	Edward J. Sittler Jr. (R)	72,981	40.9
27	James C. Fulton (R)	118,915	62.6
	Thomas J. O'Toole (D)	71,039	37.4
28	Herman P. Eberharter (D)	98,432	58.7
	Harmar D. Denny (R)	69,288	41.3
29	Robert J. Corbett (R)	115,069	61.7
	Lee T. Sellars (D)	71,573	38.4
30	Vera Buchanan (D)	115,292	63.6
	Peter F. Bender (R)	65,926	36.4

RHODE ISLAND

	Candidates	Votes	%
1	Aime J. Forand (D)	105,404	54.9
	Berthelot Leclaire (R)	86,523	45.1
2	John E. Fogarty (D)	115,057	53.4
	James O. Watts (R)	100,305	46.6

SOUTH CAROLINA

	Candidates	Votes	%
1	L. Mendel Rivers (D)	30,483	100.0
2	John J. Riley (D)	42,201	100.0
3	W. J. Bryan Dorn (D)	44,237	93.8
	David Dows (R)	2,849	6.0
4	Joseph R. Bryson (D)	77,850	100.0
5	James P. Richards (D)	42,081	93.9
	Herbert L. Crosland (R)	2,722	6.1
6	John L. McMillan (D)	41,328	100.0

SOUTH DAKOTA

	Candidates	Votes	%
1	Harold O. Lovre (R)	151,449	68.5
	Goldie Wells (D)	69,777	31.5
2	E. Y. Berry (R)	45,688	69.0
	George A. Bangs (D)	20,561	31.0

TENNESSEE

	Candidates	Votes	%
1	B. Carroll Reece (R)	70,556	65.9
	Arthur W. Bright (D)	36,477	34.1
2	Howard H. Baker (R)	84,977	69.0
	Boyd W. Cox (D)	38,268	31.1
3	James B. Frazier Jr. (D)	56,473	70.0
	Joseph M. Parker (R)	24,177	30.0
4	Joe L. Evins (D)	65,787	100.0
5	J. Percy Priest (D)	49,925	67.5
	Homer P. Wall (R)	24,056	32.5
6	Pat Sutton (D)	56,878	100.0
7	Tom Murray (D)	39,529	100.0
8	Jere Cooper (D)	34,877	100.0
9	Clifford Davis (D)	101,427	85.7
	William P. Chenault (I)	16,972	14.3

TEXAS

	Candidates	Votes	%
1	Wright Patman (D)	56,491	100.0
2	Jack Brooks (D)	83,267	79.0
	R. C. Reed (R)	22,108	21.0
3	Brady Gentry (D)	57,033	100.0
4	Sam Rayburn (D)	47,888	100.0
5	J. Frank Wilson (D)	172,539	100.0
6	Olin E. Teague (D)	49,461	100.0

	Candidates	Votes	%
7	John Dowdy (D)	52,420	100.0
8	Albert Thomas (D)	200,608	100.0
9	Clark W. Thompson (D)	96,214	100.0
10	Homer Thornberry (D)	65,924	100.0
11	W. R. Poage (D)	59,088	100.0
12	Wingate Lucas (D)	101,964	100.0
13	Frank Ikard (D)	72,373	100.0
14	John E. Lyle Jr. (D)	94,866	100.0
15	Lloyd M. Bentsen Jr. (D)	63,753	99.9
16	Ken Regan (D)	67,782	100.0
17	Omar Burleson (D)	59,386	100.0
18	Walter Rogers (D)	77,661	100.0
19	George Mahon (D)	87,894	100.0
20	Paul J. Kilday (D)	64,841	100.0
21	O. C. Fisher (D)	65,762	100.0
AL	Martin Dies (D, R)	1,979,811	100.0

UTAH

	Candidates	Votes	%
1	Douglas R. Stringfellow (R)	76,545	60.5
	Ernest R. McKay (D)	49,898	39.5
2	William A. Dawson (R)	105,296	52.6
	Reva Beck Bosone (D)	95,084	47.5

VERMONT

	Candidates	Votes	%
AL	Winston L. Prouty (R)	109,871	71.8
	Herbert B. Comings (D)	43,187	28.2

VIRGINIA

	Candidates	Votes	%
1	Edward J. Robeson Jr. (D)	24,836	99.6
2	Porter Hardy Jr. (D)	28,948	99.9
3	J. Vaughan Gary (D)	36,085	57.5
	Walter R. Gambill (R)	26,488	42.2
4	Watkins M. Abbitt (D)	23,806	99.8
5	Thomas B. Stanley (D)	19,971	99.9
6	Richard H. Poff (R)	34,041	51.5
	Clarence G. Burton (D)	31,997	48.4
7	Burr P. Harrison (D)	37,360	79.1
	Glenn W. Ruebush (R)	9,876	20.9
8	Howard W. Smith (D)	29,670	75.7
	Homer G. Richey (I)	9,495	24.2
9	William C. Wampler (R)	35,047	51.7
	M. M. Long (D)	32,735	48.3
10	Joel T. Broyhill (R)	33,152	50.2
	Edmund D. Campbell (D)	32,830	49.7

WASHINGTON

	Candidates	Votes	%
1	Thomas M. Pelly (R)	121,926	51.4
	Stimson Bullitt (D)	114,617	48.3
2	Jack Westland (R)	91,853	54.2
	Harry F. Henson (D)	77,179	45.6
3	Russell V. Mack (R)	75,165	53.3
	Gordon M. Quarnstrom (D)	65,715	46.6
4	Hal Holmes (R)	92,551	67.6
	William Bryan (D)	44,464	32.5
5	Walter F. Horan (R)	82,530	56.0
	Robert D. Dellwo (D)	64,820	44.0
6	Thor C. Tollefson (R)	110,169	59.8
	John J. O'Connell (D)	74,143	40.2
AL	Don Magnuson (D)	515,213	50.5
	Al Canwell (R)	504,783	49.5

WEST VIRGINIA

	Candidates	Votes	%
1	Robert H. Mollohan (D)	72,218	52.9
	Francis J. Love (R)	64,216	47.1
2	Harley O. Staggers (D)	67,172	51.5
	Kermit R. Mason (R)	63,320	48.5
3	Cleveland M. Bailey (D)	71,926	53.4
	Frank Love (R)	62,839	46.6
4	Will E. Neal (R)	82,104	53.3
	M. G. Burnside (D)	71,819	46.7

WEST VIRGINIA

Candidates	Votes	%
5 Elizabeth Kee (D)	83,653	*63.8*
Cyrus H. Gadd (R)	47,519	*36.2*
6 Robert C. Byrd (D)	104,387	*55.6*
Latelle M. LaFollette (R)	83,429	*44.4*

WISCONSIN

Candidates	Votes	%
1 Lawrence H. Smith (R)	99,742	*59.4*
Arnie W. Agnew (D)	68,269	*40.6*
2 Glenn R. Davis (R)	116,542	*62.9*
Horace W. Wilkie (D)	68,665	*37.1*

Candidates	Votes	%
3 Gardner R. Withrow (R)	96,908	*75.1*
Edna Bowen (D)	32,165	*24.9*
4 Clement J. Zablocki (D)	131,098	*64.3*
John C. Schafer (R)	72,869	*35.7*
5 Charles J. Kersten (R)	112,048	*51.6*
Andrew J. Biemiller (D)	105,013	*48.4*
6 William K. Van Pelt (R)	103,464	*71.7*
Ralph A. Norem (D)	40,910	*28.3*
7 Melvin R. Laird (R)	95,049	*72.3*
Ernest Kluck (D)	36,387	*27.7*
8 John W. Byrnes (R)	114,183	*73.6*
Robert C. Schultz (D)	40,980	*26.4*

Candidates	Votes	%
9 Merlin Hull (R)	81,258	*65.2*
Kent L. Pillsbury (D)	43,437	*34.8*
10 Alvin E. O'Konski (R)	73,527	*67.4*
Roland Kannenberg (D)	35,597	*32.6*

WYOMING

Candidates	Votes	%
AL William Henry Harrison (R)	76,161	*60.1*
Robert R. Ross Jr. (D)	50,559	*39.9*

1953 House Elections

GEORGIA

Special Election

Candidates	Votes	%
2 J. L. Pilcher (D)	10,936	*35.5*
H. Grady Rawls	9,764	*31.7*
H. L. Wingate Jr.	6,073	*19.7*
John E. Sheffield Jr.	3,130	*10.2*

ILLINOIS

Special Election

Candidates	Votes	%
7 James B. Bowler (D)	31,600	*83.5*
Philip J. Boffa (R)	6,239	*16.5*

NEW JERSEY

Special Election

Candidates	Votes	%
6 Harrison A. Williams Jr. (D)	68,871	*50.8*
George F. Hetfield (R)	66,796	*49.2*

VIRGINIA

Special Election

Candidates	Votes	%
5 William M. Tuck (D)	16,693	*57.8*
Lorne R. Campbell	12,182	*42.2*

WISCONSIN

Special Election

Candidates	Votes	%
9 Lester R. Johnson (D)	27,852	*56.9*
Arthur L. Padrutt (R)	21,127	*43.1*

1954 House Elections

ALABAMA

Candidates	Votes	%
1 Frank W. Boykin (D)	27,462	100.0
2 George Grant (D)	30,661	100.0
3 George Andrews (D)	22,371	100.0
4 Kenneth A. Roberts (D)	28,660	100.0
5 Albert Rains (D)	38,257	100.0
6 Armistead I. Selden Jr. (D)	18,753	100.0
7 Carl Elliott (D)	31,988	78.9
W. B. Engle (R)	8,547	21.1
8 Robert E. Jones Jr. (D)	29,414	91.6
Adin Batson (R)	2,689	8.4
9 George Huddleston Jr. (D)	40,986	100.0

ARIZONA

Candidates	Votes	%
1 John J. Rhodes (R)	60,423	53.1
L. S. Adams (D)	53,307	46.9
2 Stewart L. Udall (D)	68,085	62.1
Henry Zipf (R)	41,587	37.9

ARKANSAS

Candidates	Votes	%
1 Ezekiel C. Gathings (D)	38,951	100.0
2 Wilbur D. Mills (D)	33,038	100.0
3 James W. Trimble (D)	60,035	100.0
4 Oren Harris (D)	51,579	100.0
5 Brooks Hays (D)	51,828	100.0
6 William F. Norrell (D)	44,833	100.0

CALIFORNIA

Candidates	Votes	%
1 Hubert B. Scudder (R)	83,762	59.1
Max Kortum (D)	58,004	40.9
2 Clair Engle (D-R)	113,104	100.0
3 John E. Moss Jr. (D)	96,238	65.3
James H. Phillips (R)	51,111	34.7
4 William S. Mailliard (R)	88,439	61.2
Philip A. O'Rourke (D)	52,980	36.7
5 John F. Shelley (D-R)	86,428	100.0
6 John F. Baldwin Jr. (R)	72,336	50.9
Robert L. Condon (D)	69,776	49.1
7 John J. Allen Jr. (R)	64,083	53.0
Stanley K. Crook (D)	56,807	47.0
8 George P. Miller (D)	101,803	65.4
Jess M. Ritchie (R)	53,869	34.6
9 J. Arthur Younger (R)	60,648	54.5
Harold F. Taggart (D)	50,619	45.5
10 Charles S. Gubser (R)	94,418	61.2
Paul V. Birmingham (D)	59,843	38.8
11 Leroy Johnson (R)	54,716	52.6
Carl Sugar (D)	49,388	47.4
12 B. F. Sisk (D)	63,911	53.8
Oakley Hunter (R)	54,903	46.2
13 Charles M. Teague (R)	69,287	52.5
Timothy I. O'Reilly (D)	62,786	47.5
14 Harlan Hagen (D)	75,194	65.1
Al Blain (R)	40,270	34.9
15 Gordon L. McDonough (R)	77,651	56.9
Frank P. O'Sullivan (D)	58,785	43.1
16 Donald L. Jackson (R)	63,124	60.8
S. Mark Hogue (D)	40,659	39.2
17 Cecil R. King (D)	97,828	60.1
Robert H. Finch (R)	64,967	39.9
18 Craig Hosmer (R)	71,731	55.0
Joseph M. Kennick (D)	58,647	45.0
19 Chet Holifield (D)	90,269	74.8
Raymond R. Pritchard (R)	30,404	25.2
20 Carl Hinshaw (R)	71,213	71.2
Eugene Radding (D)	28,838	28.8
21 Edgar W. Hiestand (R)	100,258	58.7
William E. Roskam (D)	70,486	41.3
22 Joe Holt (R)	65,165	58.2
William M. Costley (D)	46,875	41.8

Candidates	Votes	%
23 Clyde Doyle (D)	90,729	70.9
Frank G. Bussing (R)	34,911	27.3
24 Glenard P. Lipscomb (R)	65,431	56.9
George Arnold (D)	49,592	43.1
25 Patrick J. Hillings (R)	113,027	65.2
John G. Sobieski (D)	60,370	34.8
26 James Roosevelt (D)	94,261	60.1
Theodore R. Owings (R)	62,585	39.9
27 Harry R. Sheppard (D)	65,389	64.8
Martin K. Barrett (R)	35,594	35.3
28 James B. Utt (R)	95,680	66.2
Harriet Enderle (D)	48,785	33.8
29 John Phillips (R)	42,420	57.9
Bruce Shangle (D)	30,781	42.1
30 Bob Wilson (R)	94,623	60.4
Ross T. McIntire (D)	61,994	39.6

COLORADO

Candidates	Votes	%
1 Byron G. Rogers (D)	84,745	55.6
Ellen G. Harris (R)	67,210	44.1
2 William S. Hill (R)	80,162	55.3
Lacy L. Wilkinson (D)	64,776	44.7
3 J. Edgar Chenoweth (R)	62,884	53.0
Alva B. Adams (D)	55,750	47.0
4 Wayne N. Aspinall (D)	34,294	53.5
Charles E. Wilson (R)	29,818	46.5

CONNECTICUT

Candidates	Votes	%
1 Thomas J. Dodd (D)	148,935	57.0
Wallace Barnes (R)	112,526	43.0
2 Horace Seely-Brown Jr. (R)	72,833	50.7
Henry H. Pierce Jr. (D)	70,853	49.3
3 Albert W. Cretella (R)	94,977	52.7
James F. Gartland (D)	85,369	47.3
4 Albert P. Morano (R)	123,890	56.2
Edward R. Fay Jr. (D)	91,184	41.4
5 James T. Patterson (R)	68,451	52.8
David Brady (D)	61,313	47.3
AL Antoni N. Sadlak (R)	474,585	51.0
Joseph P. Lyford (D)	455,887	49.0

DELAWARE

Candidates	Votes	%
AL Harris B. McDowell Jr. (D)	79,201	54.9
Lillian I. Martin (R)	65,035	45.1

FLORIDA

Candidates	Votes	%
1 William C. Cramer (R)	52,287	50.8
Courtney Campbell (D)	50,744	49.3
2 Charles E. Bennett (D)	14,376	100.0
3 Robert L. F. Sikes (D)	27,013	100.0
4 Dante B. Fascell (D)	47,697	100.0
5 A. S. Herlong Jr. (D)	35,971	100.0
6 Dwight L. Rogers (D)	39,148	100.0
7 James A. Haley (D)	23,469	55.5
E. B. Sutton (R)	18,850	44.5
8 D. R. Matthews (D)	16,732	100.0

GEORGIA

Candidates	Votes	%
1 Prince H. Preston (D)	26,205	83.7
Frank Downing	5,100	16.3
2 J. L. Pilcher (D)	26,705	99.9
3 E. L. Forrester (D)	34,973	100.0
4 John J. Flynt Jr. (D)	32,400	100.0
5 James C. Davis (D)	54,069	64.4
Charles A. Moye Jr. (R)	29,911	35.6
6 Carl Vinson (D)	26,250	100.0
7 Henderson L. Lanham (D)	35,147	100.0

Candidates	Votes	%
8 Iris Faircloth Blitch (D)	27,037	100.0
9 Phil M. Landrum (D)	26,849	100.0
10 Paul Brown (D)	28,068	100.0

IDAHO

Candidates	Votes	%
1 Gracie B. Pfost (D)	50,214	54.9
Erwin H. Schwiebert (R)	41,293	45.1
2 Hamer H. Budge (R)	81,824	60.8
William P. Whitaker (D)	52,681	39.2

ILLINOIS

Candidates	Votes	%
1 William L. Dawson (D)	71,472	75.3
Genoa S. Washington (R)	23,470	24.7
2 Barratt O'Hara (D)	80,016	61.6
Richard B. Vail (R)	49,970	38.4
3 James C. Murray (D)	77,675	53.8
Fred E. Busbey (R)	66,767	46.2
4 William E. McVey (R)	94,125	52.2
William A. Rowan (D)	86,372	47.9
5 John C. Kluczynski (D)	92,780	73.2
S. Charles Bubacz (R)	33,987	26.8
6 Thomas J. O'Brien (D)	99,590	71.7
Orville F. Corbin (R)	39,289	28.3
7 James B. Bowler (D)	97,398	78.4
Charles M. Barrett (R)	26,763	21.6
8 Thomas S. Gordon (D)	74,837	68.4
James L. Doherty (R)	34,535	31.6
9 Sidney R. Yates (D)	73,187	60.3
Ralph Lee Goodman (R)	48,130	39.7
10 Richard W. Hoffman (R)	90,961	57.3
Helen J. Kelleher (D)	67,903	42.7
11 Timothy P. Sheehan (R)	67,141	50.9
Harry H. Semrow (D)	64,788	49.1
12 Charles A. Boyle (D)	82,518	54.1
Edgar A. Jonas (R)	69,999	45.9
13 Marguerite Stitt Church (R)	146,184	69.6
Richard A. Griffin (D)	63,852	30.4
14 Chauncey W. Reed (R)	100,024	72.4
Richard Plum (D)	38,161	27.6
15 Noah M. Mason (R)	72,576	62.8
Richard A. Mohan (D)	42,934	37.2
16 Leo E. Allen (R)	77,557	100.0
17 Leslie C. Arends (R)	79,044	65.0
Branson Wright (D)	42,600	35.0
18 Harold H. Velde (R)	59,963	57.5
Howard S. Beeney (D)	44,408	42.6
19 Robert B. Chiperfield (R)	64,772	56.5
John M. Kerwin Jr. (D)	49,876	43.5
20 Sidney E. Simpson (R)	68,104	62.9
James A. Barry (D)	40,165	37.1
21 Peter F. Mack Jr. (D)	83,501	54.8
Edward H. Jenison (R)	68,924	45.2
22 William L. Springer (R)	66,797	62.0
Robert W. Martin (D)	40,873	38.0
23 Charles W. Vursell (R)	69,179	52.9
Albert R. Imle (D)	61,493	47.1
24 Melvin Price (D)	90,482	69.2
John T. Thomas (R)	40,358	30.9
25 Kenneth J. Gray (D)	69,562	52.6
C. W. Bishop (R)	62,659	47.4

INDIANA

Candidates	Votes	%
1 Ray J. Madden (D)	81,217	61.4
Robert H. Moore (R)	50,439	38.2
2 Charles A. Halleck (R)	73,717	59.6
James H. Berg (D)	49,996	40.4
3 Shepard J. Crumpacker Jr. (R)	85,884	50.4
John Brademas (D)	83,851	49.2
4 E. Ross Adair (R)	71,436	59.8
Fred W. Greene (D)	47,384	39.7

INDIANA

	Candidates	Votes	%
5	John V. Beamer (R)	88,428	53.1
	John R. Walsh (D)	76,972	46.2
6	Cecil M. Harden (R)	67,371	52.5
	John W. King (D)	60,896	47.5
7	William G. Bray (R)	75,608	55.4
	George D. Gettinger (D)	60,594	44.4
8	Winfield K. Denton (D)	82,264	52.1
	D. Bailey Merrill (R)	74,960	47.5
9	Earl Wilson (R)	61,285	51.7
	Wilfrid J. Ullrich (D)	57,350	48.3
10	Ralph Harvey (R)	76,132	55.9
	Inez M. Scholl (D)	59,103	43.4
11	Charles B. Brownson (R)	108,044	54.9
	Charles H. Boswell (D)	88,173	44.8

IOWA

	Candidates	Votes	%
1	Fred Schwengel (R)	67,128	57.0
	John O'Connor (D)	50,577	43.0
2	Henry O. Talle (R)	72,231	55.4
	Ruben V. Austin (D)	58,092	44.6
3	H. R. Gross (R)	68,307	62.1
	George R. Laub (D)	41,622	37.9
4	Karl M. LeCompte (R)	49,608	55.6
	Herschel C. Loveless (D)	39,652	44.4
5	Paul Cunningham (R)	61,355	55.6
	James A. McLaughlin (D)	49,063	44.4
6	James I. Dolliver (R)	53,457	60.3
	Lumund F. Wilcox (D)	35,137	39.7
7	Ben F. Jensen (R)	51,022	60.4
	Elmer G. Carlson (D)	33,492	39.6
8	Charles B. Hoeven (R)	55,214	63.8
	Roy B. Holland (D)	31,296	36.2

KANSAS

	Candidates	Votes	%
1	William H. Avery (R)	56,079	54.3
	Howard S. Miller (D)	47,165	45.7
2	Errett P. Scrivner (R)	64,263	54.7
	Newell A. George (D)	53,302	45.3
3	Myron V. George (R)	41,342	55.4
	William M. Monypeny (D)	33,307	44.6
4	Ed H. Rees (R)	77,920	56.2
	Robert M. Green (D)	60,697	43.8
5	Clifford R. Hope (R)	64,023	64.9
	Robert L. Bock (D)	34,691	35.1
6	Wint Smith (R)	43,831	53.3
	Elmo J. Mahoney (D)	38,369	46.7

KENTUCKY

	Candidates	Votes	%
1	Noble J. Gregory (D)	62,210	100.0
2	William H. Natcher (D)	49,231	100.0
3	John M. Robsion Jr. (R)	72,073	50.2
	Harrison M. Robertson (D)	71,500	49.8
4	Frank Chelf (D)	49,496	100.0
5	Brent Spence (D)	63,640	61.0
	M. J. See (R)	40,679	39.0
6	John C. Watts (D)	59,434	60.9
	Robert L. Milby (R)	38,145	39.1
7	Carl D. Perkins (D)	44,353	60.4
	Curtis Clark (R)	29,115	39.6
8	Eugene T. Siler (R)	56,182	63.4
	Mitchel S. Fannin (D)	32,128	36.3

LOUISIANA

	Candidates	Votes	%
1	F. Edward Hebert (D)	38,213	82.3
	George W. Reese Jr. (R)	8,212	17.7
2	Hale Boggs (D)	37,583	100.0
3	Edwin E. Willis (D)	15,808	100.0
4	Overton Brooks (D)	24,587	100.0
5	Otto E. Passman (D)	21,831	100.0
6	James H. Morrison (D)	30,082	100.0
7	T. Ashton Thompson (D)	21,525	100.0
8	George S. Long (D)	18,482	100.0

MAINE

	Candidates	Votes	%
1	Robert Hale (R)	47,327	52.1
	James C. Oliver (D)	43,561	47.9
2	Charles P. Nelson (R)	45,819	54.0
	Thomas E. Delahanty (D)	39,075	46.0
3	Clifford G. McIntire (R)	39,749	60.5
	Kenneth B. Colbath (D)	25,912	39.5

MARYLAND

	Candidates	Votes	%
1	Edward T. Miller (R)	35,221	55.6
	Edward Turner (D)	28,184	44.5
2	James P. S. Devereux (R)	67,179	56.1
	William P. Bolton (D)	52,540	43.9
3	Edward A. Garmatz (D)	45,531	97.2
4	George H. Fallon (D)	40,029	57.2
	Arthur W. Sherwood (R)	29,921	42.8
5	Richard E. Lankford (D)	60,850	53.7
	Frank Small Jr. (R)	52,420	46.3
6	DeWitt S. Hyde (R)	69,658	51.4
	Edward J. Ryan (D)	65,760	48.6
7	Samuel N. Friedel (D)	49,221	54.5
	Edward C. Dukehart (R)	41,027	45.5

MASSACHUSETTS

	Candidates	Votes	%
1	John W. Heselton (R)	68,420	55.6
	John J. Dwyer (D)	54,675	44.4
2	Edward P. Boland (D)	77,899	59.6
	Vernon E. Bradley (R)	52,725	40.4
3	Philip J. Philbin (D)	110,013	100.0
4	Harold D. Donohue (D)	83,053	57.1
	Andrew B. Holmstrom (R)	62,318	42.9
5	Edith Nourse Rogers (R)	139,989	100.0
6	William H. Bates (R)	91,916	71.2
	Andrew J. Gillis (D)	37,216	28.8
7	Thomas J. Lane (D, R)	102,659	100.0
8	Torbert H. Macdonald (D)	74,568	53.2
	Angier L. Goodwin (R)	65,614	46.8
9	Donald W. Nicholson (R)	81,378	56.6
	James F. O'Neill (D)	62,445	43.4
10	Laurence Curtis (R)	72,502	50.7
	Jackson J. Holtz (D)	70,608	49.3
11	Thomas P. O'Neill Jr. (D)	75,613	78.2
	Charles S. Bolster (R)	21,039	21.8
12	John W. McCormack (D)	79,073	100.0
13	Richard B. Wigglesworth (R)	90,924	58.0
	James F. Gardner (D)	65,854	42.0
14	Joseph W. Martin Jr. (R)	87,840	62.0
	Edward F. Doolan (D)	53,818	38.0

MICHIGAN

	Candidates	Votes	%
1	Thaddeus M. Machrowicz (D)	91,435	88.3
	Rudolph G. Tenerowicz (R)	11,731	11.3
2	George Meader (R)	69,825	59.8
	J. Henry Owens (D)	46,817	40.1
3	August E. Johansen (R)	65,942	59.4
	Charles C. Wickett (D)	44,574	40.2
4	Clare E. Hoffman (R)	62,025	62.3
	Gordon A. Elferdink (D)	37,500	37.7
5	Gerald R. Ford Jr. (R)	81,702	63.3
	Robert S. McAllister (D)	47,453	36.7
6	Don Hayworth (D)	80,325	51.1
	Kit Clardy (R)	76,335	48.6
7	Jesse P. Wolcott (R)	71,651	52.8
	Ira D. McCoy (D)	63,797	47.0
8	Alvin M. Bentley (R)	65,813	62.7
	Clarence V. Smazel (D)	38,828	37.0
9	Ruth Thompson (R)	50,659	55.7
	Theodore E. A. Engstrom (D)	39,966	44.0
10	Elford A. Cederberg (R)	50,570	61.4
	William J. Kelly (D)	31,794	38.6
11	Victor A. Knox (R)	41,665	54.9
	Harold Beaton (D)	34,204	45.1

	Candidates	Votes	%
12	John B. Bennett (R)	39,531	55.9
	Frank E. Hook (D)	31,187	44.1
13	Charles C. Diggs Jr. (D)	64,716	65.8
	Landon Knight (R)	33,127	33.7
14	Louis C. Rabaut (D)	97,297	58.2
	Joseph A. Moynihan Jr. (R)	69,503	41.6
15	John D. Dingell (D)	85,100	72.7
	Gregory M. Pillon (R)	31,815	27.2
16	John Lesinski (D)	121,557	67.9
	Stanley A. Grendel (R)	56,815	31.7
17	Martha W. Griffiths (D)	75,258	52.2
	Charles G. Oakman (R)	68,613	47.6
18	George A. Dondero (R)	80,771	53.9
	Paul Sutton (D)	69,131	46.1

MINNESOTA

	Candidates	Votes	%
1	August H. Andresen (R)	72,686	60.9
	Robert C. Olson (DFL)	46,678	39.1
2	Joseph P. O'Hara (R)	71,592	57.9
	Harry Sieben (DFL)	52,089	42.1
3	Roy W. Wier (DFL)	98,467	54.4
	Edward Willow (R)	82,389	45.6
4	Eugene J. McCarthy (DFL)	81,651	63.0
	Richard C. Hansen (R)	47,933	37.0
5	Walter H. Judd (R)	69,901	55.8
	Anders Thompson (DFL)	55,452	44.2
6	Fred Marshall (DFL)	72,922	61.9
	Oscar J. Jerde (R)	44,850	38.1
7	H. Carl Andersen (R)	60,120	52.6
	Douglas P. Hunt (DFL)	54,140	47.4
8	John A. Blatnik (DFL)	89,778	71.8
	Ernie Orchard (R)	35,241	28.2
9	Coya Knutson (DFL)	48,999	51.2
	Harold C. Hagen (R)	46,664	48.8

MISSISSIPPI

	Candidates	Votes	%
1	Thomas G. Abernethy (D)	15,944	100.0
2	Jamie L. Whitten (D)	13,516	100.0
3	Frank E. Smith (D)	13,468	100.0
4	John Bell Williams (D)	19,164	100.0
5	Arthur Winstead (D)	17,400	100.0
6	William M. Colmer (D)	21,806	100.0

MISSOURI

	Candidates	Votes	%
1	Frank M. Karsten (D)	89,649	66.3
	Bill Bangert (R)	45,653	33.7
2	Thomas B. Curtis (R)	83,861	54.7
	Eugene H. Buder (D)	69,450	45.3
3	Leonor K. Sullivan (D)	67,715	71.0
	George W. Curran (R)	27,598	29.0
4	George H. Christopher (D)	62,012	51.6
	Jeffrey P. Hillelson (R)	58,152	48.4
5	Richard Bolling (D)	50,874	58.9
	Samuel Lee Chaney (R)	35,477	41.1
6	W. R. Hull Jr. (D)	60,380	53.6
	William C. Cole (R)	52,203	46.4
7	Dewey Short (R)	67,918	53.6
	J. M. Lowry (D)	58,729	46.4
8	A. S. J. Carnahan (D)	52,658	57.3
	Dorman L. Steelman (R)	39,326	42.8
9	Clarence Cannon (D)	65,862	59.0
	Noel Carpenter (R)	45,765	41.0
10	Paul C. Jones (D)	34,009	63.9
	Clyde Whaley (R)	19,179	36.1
11	Morgan M. Moulder (D)	54,384	55.3
	L. C. Davis (R)	43,959	44.7

MONTANA

	Candidates	Votes	%
1	Lee Metcalf (D)	52,614	56.0
	Winfield E. Page (R)	41,375	44.0
2	Orvin B. Fjare (R)	66,103	50.6
	LeRoy H. Anderson (D)	64,495	49.4

NEBRASKA

Candidates	Votes	%
1 Phil Weaver (R)	68,563	58.6
Frank B. Morrison (D)	48,457	41.4
2 Jackson B. Chase (R)	52,471	53.0
James A. Hart (D)	46,629	47.1
3 Robert D. Harrison (R)	61,124	65.2
Ernest M. Luther (D)	32,562	34.8
4 Arthur L. Miller (R)	68,189	70.4
Carlton W. Laird (D)	28,695	29.6

NEVADA

Candidates	Votes	%
AL Clifton Young (R)	42,321	54.5
Walter S. Baring (D)	35,318	45.5

NEW HAMPSHIRE

Candidates	Votes	%
1 Chester E. Merrow (R)	54,052	50.2
Thomas J. McIntyre (D)	53,584	49.8
2 Perkins Bass (R)	51,010	60.4
George F. Brown (D)	33,415	39.6

NEW JERSEY

Candidates	Votes	%
1 Charles A. Wolverton (R)	92,070	54.4
J. Frank Crawford (D)	77,100	45.5
2 T. Millet Hand (R)	65,551	63.6
Clayton E. Burdick (D)	37,541	36.4
3 James C. Auchincloss (R)	89,085	57.6
Charles F. Sullivan (D)	65,685	42.4
4 Frank Thompson Jr. (D)	72,884	58.4
William G. Freeman (R)	51,998	41.6
5 Peter H. B. Frelinghuysen (R)	99,946	59.3
Luther H. Martin (D)	68,702	40.7
6 Harrison A. Williams Jr. (D)	85,784	56.1
Fred E. Shepard (R)	64,164	41.9
7 William B. Widnall (R)	99,977	63.2
Eugene E. Demarest (D)	58,211	36.8
8 Gordon Canfield (R)	65,359	54.8
Charles S. Joelson (D)	53,844	45.1
9 Frank C. Osmers Jr. (R)	87,008	60.2
Walter J. O'Connell (D)	57,445	39.8
10 Peter W. Rodino Jr. (D)	62,384	63.4
William E. McGlynn (R)	36,056	36.6
11 Hugh J. Addonizio (D)	52,311	56.3
Philip Insabella (R)	38,351	41.2
12 Robert Winthrop Kean (R)	59,151	53.1
Martin S. Fox (D)	52,314	46.9
13 Alfred D. Sieminski (D)	60,108	60.8
Norman Roth (R)	26,638	26.9
Jeremiah J. O'Callaghan (I)	12,174	12.3
14 T. James Tumulty (D)	58,069	62.4
Vincent J. Dellay (R)	32,485	34.9

NEW MEXICO

Candidates	Votes	%
AL John J. Dempsey (D)	111,713✔	
Antonio M. Fernandez (D)	109,837✔	
Thomas H. Childers (R)	77,151	
Warren R. Cobean (R)	76,528	

NEW YORK

Candidates	Votes	%
1 Stuyvesant Wainwright (R)	108,130	63.1
Ernest Greenwood (D, L)	62,853	36.7
2 Steven B. Derounian (R)	98,610	63.7
William R. Brennan Jr. (D, L)	55,477	35.8
3 Frank J. Becker (R)	93,396	58.3
John T. Cogley (D, L)	66,703	41.7
4 Henry J. Latham (R)	74,621	54.2
Thomas A. Dent (D)	55,479	40.3
Robert A. Rose (L)	7,526	5.5
5 Albert H. Bosch (R)	50,778	51.7
William Kerwick (D)	43,086	43.9
6 Lester Holtzman (D, L)	81,033	54.4
Seymour Halpern (R)	67,681	45.5
7 James J. Delaney (D, L)	62,541	59.0
Joseph Stockinger (R)	43,525	41.0
8 Victor L. Anfuso (D, L)	51,993	77.7
Eugene J. Renne (R)	14,948	22.3
9 Eugene J. Keogh (D, L)	59,392	71.1
Harry Keller (R)	22,808	27.3
10 Edna F. Kelly (D, L)	80,541	76.8
Abraham Sher (R)	22,479	21.4
11 Emanuel Celler (D, L)	103,788	83.5
Henry D. Dorfman (R)	20,452	16.5
12 Francis E. Dorn (R)	49,449	51.3
Donald L. O'Toole (D, L)	46,926	48.7
13 Abraham J. Multer (D, L)	89,907	78.8
Joseph Moriber (R)	21,881	19.2
14 John J. Rooney (D, L)	61,879	73.1
Alfred A. Manti (R)	21,598	25.5
15 John H. Ray (R)	56,020	51.6
Vincent R. Fitzpatrick (D, L)	52,292	48.1
16 Adam Clayton Powell Jr. (D)	43,545	77.6
Harold C. Burton (R)	8,904	15.9
Formington Taylor (L)	3,701	6.6
17 Frederic R. Coudert Jr. (R)	48,999	50.2
Anthony B. Akers (D, L)	48,685	49.8
18 James G. Donovan (D, R)	49,850	86.8
Amos Basel (L)	6,219	10.8
19 Arthur G. Klein (D, L)	56,634	74.6
Henry E. Delrosso (R)	19,310	25.4
20 Irwin D. Davidson (D, L)	58,030	67.2
Warren L. Schnur (R)	26,462	30.7
21 Herbert Zelenko (D, L)	63,284	67.8
Floyd Cramer (R)	29,995	32.2
22 Sidney A. Fine (D)	72,091	67.9
Henry Rose (R)	18,952	17.8
Louis Schifrin (L)	13,249	12.5
23 Isidore Dollinger (D)	58,490	75.6
Philip Myer (R)	9,976	12.9
Bernice Benedick (L)	8,869	11.5
24 Charles A. Buckley (D)	69,552	58.3
Charles V. Scanlan (R)	31,670	26.6
Elias Rosenblatt (L)	18,067	15.2
25 Paul A. Fino (R)	59,409	50.4
Salvatore J. Milano (D)	50,818	43.1
Ernest Doerfler (L)	7,624	6.5
26 Ralph A. Gamble (R)	81,608	64.0
Julia L. Crews (D, L)	45,892	36.0
27 Ralph W. Gwinn (R)	83,866	57.2
John R. Harold (D, L)	62,797	42.8
28 Katharine St. George (R)	79,587	64.9
Paul G. Reilly (D, L)	40,109	32.7
29 J. Ernest Wharton (R)	88,227	66.5
Robert D. Byron (D)	42,084	31.7
30 Leo W. O'Brien (D, L)	104,585	61.2
James W. Smith (R)	66,319	38.8
31 Dean P. Taylor (R)	86,768	66.3
Joseph R. MacLaren (D, L)	44,212	33.8
32 Bernard W. Kearney (R)	77,891	61.5
David C. Prince (D)	48,808	38.5
33 Clarence E. Kilburn (R)	70,708	68.1
Harold Blake (D)	31,279	30.1
34 William R. Williams (R)	77,659	59.3
Vernon E. Olin (D, L)	53,112	40.6
35 R. Walter Riehlman (R)	90,002	63.5
James H. O'Connor (D, L)	51,358	36.3
36 John Taber (R)	79,850	68.4
Daniel J. Carey (D, L)	36,910	31.6
37 W. Sterling Cole (R)	94,840	71.7
John E. Bloomer (D, L)	37,525	28.3
38 Kenneth B. Keating (R)	103,293	71.9
Rubin Brodsky (D, L)	40,400	28.1
39 Harold C. Ostertag (R)	82,769	64.8
George W. Cooke (D, L)	45,000	35.2
40 William E. Miller (R)	77,016	60.9
Mariano A. Lucca (D)	46,956	37.1
41 Edmund P. Radwan (R)	77,259	63.1
Bernard J. Wojtkowiak (D, L)	45,144	36.9
42 John R. Pillion (R)	82,707	57.6
John J. Zablotny (D, L)	60,880	42.4
43 Daniel A. Reed (R)	66,852	64.8
James F. Crowley (D)	34,590	33.5

NORTH CAROLINA

Candidates	Votes	%
1 Herbert C. Bonner (D)	20,650	92.5
W. T. Love (R)	1,685	7.5
2 L. H. Fountain (D)	14,471	100.0
3 Graham A. Barden (D)	24,837	77.3
Christine P. Odom (R)	7,301	22.7
4 Harold D. Cooley (D)	34,406	100.0
5 Thurmond Chatham (D)	31,781	66.2
Joe New (R)	16,194	33.8
6 Carl T. Durham (D)	30,118	74.3
Rufus K. Haworth Jr. (R)	10,446	25.8
7 F. Ertel Carlyle (D)	21,669	81.3
J. O. West (R)	5,001	18.8
8 Charles B. Deane (D)	39,028	59.1
Harold W. Gavin (R)	26,966	40.9
9 Hugh Q. Alexander (D)	54,103	52.2
William E. Stevens Jr. (R)	49,555	47.8
10 Charles Raper Jonas (R)	51,492	57.5
J. C. Sedberry (D)	38,080	42.5
11 Woodrow W. Jones (D)	36,766	67.5
R. R. Ramsey (R)	17,721	32.5
12 George A. Shuford (D)	44,258	61.6
Charles Cunningham (R)	27,651	38.5

NORTH DAKOTA

Candidates	Votes	%
AL Usher L. Burdick (R)	124,845✔	
Otto Krueger (R)	106,341✔	
P. W. Lanier (D)	64,089	
Raymond G. Vendsel (D)	49,183	

OHIO

Candidates	Votes	%
1 Gordon H. Scherer (R)	71,042	64.3
Mrs. Warwick B. Hobart (D)	39,421	35.7
2 William E. Hess (R)	69,695	58.4
Earl T. Wagner (D)	49,690	41.6
3 Paul F. Schenck (R)	82,701	52.6
Thomas B. Talbot (D)	74,585	47.4
4 William M. McCulloch (R)	67,762	67.6
Forrest L. Blankenship (D)	32,474	32.4
5 Cliff Clevenger (R)	49,265	59.5
Martin W. Feigert (D)	33,483	40.5
6 James G. Polk (D)	54,044	52.2
Leo Blackburn (R)	49,531	47.8
7 Clarence J. Brown (R)	62,821	63.9
G. Louie Wren (D)	35,504	36.1
8 Jackson E. Betts (R)	52,196	63.1
Thomas M. Dowd (D)	30,592	37.0
9 Thomas L. Ashley (D)	48,471	36.4
Frazier Reams (I)	44,656	33.6
Irving C. Reynolds (R)	39,933	30.0
10 Thomas A. Jenkins (R)	45,277	61.7
Truman A. Morris (D)	28,150	38.3
11 Oliver P. Bolton (R)	74,065	65.3
Edward C. Kaley (D)	39,404	34.7
12 John M. Vorys (R)	94,585	61.5
Jacob F. Myers (D)	59,210	38.5
13 A. D. Baumhart Jr. (R)	46,524	59.1
George C. Steinemann (D)	32,177	40.9
14 William H. Ayres (R)	82,086	54.6
John L. Smith (D)	68,204	45.4
15 John E. Henderson (R)	38,524	54.0
Max Lewis Underwood (D)	32,795	46.0
16 Frank T. Bow (R)	79,371	58.3
Thomas H. Nichols (D)	56,787	41.7
17 J. Harry McGregor (R)	63,301	64.6
Robert W. Levering (D)	34,638	35.4
18 Wayne L. Hays (D)	59,165	57.3
Walter J. Hunston (D)	44,143	42.7
19 Michael J. Kirwan (D)	69,324	67.5
David S. Edwards (R)	33,352	32.5

OHIO

Candidates	Votes	%
20 Michael A. Feighan (D)	81,304	67.7
John H. Ferguson (R)	38,865	32.3
21 Charles A. Vanik (D)	76,201	76.0
Francis E. Young (R)	24,076	24.0
22 Frances P. Bolton (R)	61,738	58.4
Chat Paterson (D)	44,072	41.7
23 William E. Minshall Jr. (R)	69,994	67.5
Bernice S. Pyke (D)	33,639	32.5

OKLAHOMA

Candidates	Votes	%
1 Page Belcher (R)	79,151	58.8
Ben Crowley (D)	55,391	41.2
2 Ed Edmondson (D)	67,872	64.7
Percy Butler (R)	37,030	35.3
3 Carl Albert (D)	52,662	83.3
Jasper N. Butler (R)	10,554	16.7
4 Tom Steed (D)	43,915	100.0
5 John Jarman (D)	72,380	66.0
George E. Young (R)	37,223	34.0
6 Victor E. Wickersham (D)	62,119	69.3
Reece L. Russell (R)	27,492	30.7

OREGON

Candidates	Votes	%
1 Walter Norblad (R)	98,592	63.0
Donnell Mitchell (D)	57,882	37.0
2 Sam Coon (R)	43,731	52.6
Al Ullman (D)	39,475	47.4
3 Edith Green (D)	103,976	52.4
Tom McCall (R)	94,368	47.6
4 Harris Ellsworth (R)	70,695	55.9
Charles O. Porter (D)	55,775	44.1

PENNSYLVANIA

Candidates	Votes	%
1 William A. Barrett (D)	68,531	61.5
Joseph A. Graham Jr. (R)	42,893	38.5
2 William T. Granahan (D)	80,377	61.3
Albert A. Ciardi (R)	50,857	38.8
3 James A. Byrne (D)	61,639	55.4
Charles H. Sporkin (R)	49,702	44.6
4 Earl Chudoff (D)	60,564	65.7
W. Beverly Carter Jr. (R)	31,551	34.2
5 William J. Green Jr. (D)	87,435	55.0
Francis P. McCusker (R)	71,462	45.0
6 Hugh Scott (R)	74,328	50.6
Alexander Hemphill (D)	72,587	49.4
7 Benjamin F. James (R)	101,282	60.9
O. Arthur Cappiello (D)	65,086	39.1
8 Karl C. King (R)	62,897	51.2
John P. Fullam (D)	59,848	48.8
9 Paul B. Dague (R)	76,163	62.7
Edward G. Wilson (D)	45,402	37.4
10 Joseph L. Carrigg (R)	74,515	50.5
Robert H. Jones (D)	73,046	49.5
11 Daniel J. Flood (D)	70,254	50.9
Edward J. Bonin (R)	67,682	49.1
12 Ivor D. Fenton (R)	62,779	55.5
Charles E. Lotz (D)	50,373	44.5
13 Samuel K. McConnell Jr. (R)	91,639	64.3
Joseph C. Mansfield (D)	50,796	35.7
14 George M. Rhodes (D)	50,765	62.0
Donald F. Spang (R)	31,136	38.0
15 Francis E. Walter (D)	56,871	61.6
LeRoy Mikels (R)	35,464	38.4
16 Walter M. Mumma (R)	69,240	59.8
Richard A. Swank (D)	46,619	40.2
17 Alvin R. Bush (R)	57,928	56.5
William T. Longe (D)	44,543	43.5
18 Richard M. Simpson (R)	58,959	55.9
Robert M. Meyers (D)	46,463	44.1
19 James M. Quigley (D)	62,108	51.0
S. Walter Stauffer (R)	59,594	49.0
20 James E. Van Zandt (R)	48,561	56.3
John R. Stewart (D)	37,725	43.7

Candidates	Votes	%
21 Augustine B. Kelley (D)	70,224	61.1
Herbert O. Morrison (R)	44,789	38.9
22 John P. Saylor (R)	66,270	51.9
Robert S. Glass (D)	61,474	48.1
23 Leon H. Gavin (R)	53,616	61.9
Fred C. Barr (D)	33,044	38.1
24 Carroll D. Kearns (R)	66,005	52.0
Edmund T. Rogers (D)	60,842	48.0
25 Frank M. Clark (D)	66,223	53.5
Louis E. Graham (R)	57,657	46.5
26 Thomas E. Morgan (D)	95,531	65.3
Branko Stupar (R)	50,768	34.7
27 James G. Fulton (R)	92,533	62.8
Charles J. Chamberlin (D)	54,876	37.2
28 Herman P. Eberharter (D)	85,550	65.1
Guy C. Read (R)	45,913	34.9
29 Robert J. Corbett (R)	83,846	60.6
William G. Foley (D)	54,511	39.4
30 Vera D. Buchanan (D)	98,318	69.0
David J. Smith (R)	44,157	31.0

RHODE ISLAND

Candidates	Votes	%
1 Aime J. Forand (D)	89,678	59.1
Arthur Carrelas (R)	61,990	40.9
2 John E. Fogarty (D)	105,522	60.5
James O. Watts (R)	68,869	39.5

SOUTH CAROLINA

Candidates	Votes	%
1 L. Mendel Rivers (D)	33,402	97.8
2 John J. Riley (D)	44,484	97.7
3 W. J. Bryan Dorn (D)	30,790	99.3
4 Robert T. Ashmore (D)	43,857	99.2
5 James P. Richards (D)	26,950	100.0
6 John L. McMillan (D)	31,141	98.9

SOUTH DAKOTA

Candidates	Votes	%
1 Harold O. Lovre (R)	102,797	58.0
Francis G. Dunn (D)	74,450	42.0
2 E. Y. Berry (R)	34,476	63.9
Ray Satterlee (D)	19,444	36.1

TENNESSEE

Candidates	Votes	%
1 B. Carroll Reece (R)	32,991	62.5
Arthur Bright (D)	19,828	37.5
2 Howard H. Baker (R)	47,989	58.0
C. Howard Bozeman (D)	34,688	42.0
3 James B. Frazier Jr. (D)	30,558	59.2
O. M. Spence (R)	21,081	40.8
4 Joe L. Evins (D)	27,613	100.0
5 J. Percy Priest (D)	20,849	90.8
Robert M. Donihi (R)	2,123	9.2
6 Ross Bass (D)	26,081	99.4
7 Tom Murray (D)	17,708	100.0
8 Jere Cooper (D)	15,078	100.0
9 Clifford Davis (D)	40,121	83.5
W. A. Danielson (R)	7,926	16.5

TEXAS

Candidates	Votes	%
1 Wright Patman (D)	18,104	100.0
2 Jack Brooks (D)	25,008	100.0
3 Brady Gentry (D)	20,767	100.0
4 Sam Rayburn (D)	15,177	100.0
5 Bruce Alger (R)	27,982	52.9
Wallace Savage (D)	24,904	47.1
6 Olin E. Teague (D)	15,161	100.0
7 John Dowdy (D)	18,361	100.0
8 Albert Thomas (D)	60,374	62.1
W. B. Butler (R)	36,405	37.4
9 Clark W. Thompson (D)	29,972	100.0
10 Homer Thornberry (D)	23,752	100.0
11 W. R. Poage (D)	17,739	100.0
12 Jim Wright (D)	35,611	98.8

Candidates	Votes	%
13 Frank Ikard (D)	25,085	100.0
14 John J. Bell (D)	36,284	93.8
D. C. DeWitt (R)	2,384	6.2
15 Joe M. Kilgore (D)	29,113	100.0
16 J. T. Rutherford (D)	25,122	100.0
17 Omar Burleson (D)	18,484	100.0
18 Walter Rogers (D)	25,430	64.9
Leroy LaMaster (R)	13,756	35.1
19 George Mahon (D)	26,829	100.0
20 Paul J. Kilday (D)	23,533	100.0
21 O. C. Fisher (D)	25,381	100.0
AL Martin Dies (D)	555,446	88.0
Tom Nolan (R)	75,472	12.0

UTAH

Candidates	Votes	%
1 Henry Aldous Dixon (R)	55,542	53.4
Walter K. Granger (D)	48,535	46.6
2 William A. Dawson (R)	90,864	57.2
Reva Beck Bosone (D)	68,090	42.8

VERMONT

Candidates	Votes	%
AL Winston L. Prouty (R)	70,143	61.4
John J. Boylan Jr. (D)	44,141	38.6

VIRGINIA

Candidates	Votes	%
1 Edward J. Robeson Jr. (D)	16,029	99.8
2 Porter Hardy Jr. (D)	18,190	74.4
George V. Credle Jr. (R)	6,243	25.6
3 J. Vaughan Gary (D)	19,466	58.0
J. Calvitt Clarke Jr. (R)	14,088	42.0
4 Watkins M. Abbitt (D)	14,728	99.9
5 William M. Tuck (D)	13,042	99.9
6 Richard H. Poff (R)	32,855	62.3
Ernest Robertson (D)	19,727	37.4
7 Burr P. Harrison (D)	22,025	74.2
John Paul Ruddick (R)	7,669	25.8
8 Howard W. Smith (D)	17,321	66.6
C. S. Lenhart (I)	8,679	33.4
9 W. Pat Jennings (D)	39,238	50.5
William C. Wampler (R)	38,239	49.2
10 Joel T. Broyhill (R)	29,221	53.8
John C. Webb (D)	24,667	45.4

WASHINGTON

Candidates	Votes	%
1 Thomas M. Pelly (R)	101,913	52.6
Hugh B. Mitchell (D)	91,721	47.4
2 Jack Westland (R)	73,264	52.2
Harry F. Henson (D)	67,232	47.9
3 Russell V. Mack (R)	70,844	64.9
Clyde V. Tisdale (D)	38,344	35.1
4 Hal Holmes (R)	67,171	61.0
Fred Yoder (D)	42,911	39.0
5 Walt Horan (R)	68,628	58.6
Art Garton (D)	48,542	41.4
6 Thor C. Tollefson (R)	80,241	55.2
John T. McCutcheon (D)	65,011	44.8
AL Don Magnuson (D)	464,045	57.3
Al Canwell (R)	342,089	42.2

WEST VIRGINIA

Candidates	Votes	%
1 Robert H. Mollohan (D)	52,609	52.7
Arch A. Moore Jr. (R)	47,199	47.3
2 Harley O. Staggers (D)	50,283	55.0
Albert M. Morgan (R)	41,171	45.0
3 Cleveland M. Bailey (D)	54,684	58.9
Joseph B. Lightburn (R)	38,218	41.1
4 M. G. Burnside (D)	56,498	50.2
Will E. Neal (R)	55,994	49.8
5 Elizabeth Kee (D)	52,349	67.5
Fred O. Blue (R)	25,267	32.6
6 Robert C. Byrd (D)	73,535	62.7
Pat B. Withrow Jr. (R)	43,685	37.3

WISCONSIN

	Candidates	Votes	%
1	Lawrence H. Smith (R)	65,562	54.4
	Edward A. Krenzke (D)	54,864	45.6
2	Glenn R. Davis (R)	74,460	54.0
	Gaylord A. Nelson (D)	63,449	46.0
3	Gardner R. Withrow (R)	56,228	62.1
	Joseph A. Seep (D)	34,375	37.9

	Candidates	Votes	%
4	Clement J. Zablocki (D)	100,120	71.1
	John C. Schafer (R)	40,723	28.9
5	Henry S. Reuss (D)	77,208	52.3
	Charles J. Kersten (R)	70,565	47.8
6	William K. Van Pelt (R)	68,653	62.5
	Russell S. Johnson (D)	41,191	37.5
7	Melvin R. Laird (R)	57,581	59.1
	Kenneth E. Anderson (D)	39,828	40.9
8	John W. Byrnes (R)	73,588	62.0
	Jerome J. Reinke (D)	45,037	38.0

	Candidates	Votes	%
9	Lester R. Johnson (D)	52,485	55.4
	William E. Owen (R)	42,234	44.6
10	Alvin E. O'Konski (R)	49,325	59.8
	Basil G. Kennedy (D)	33,219	40.2

WYOMING

	Candidates	Votes	%
AL	E. Keith Thomson (R)	61,111	56.2
	Sam Tully (D)	47,660	43.8

1956 House Elections

ALABAMA

	Candidates	Votes	%
1	Frank W. Boykin (D)	31,469	100.0
2	George Grant (D)	36,613	100.0
3	George W. Andrews (D)	29,547	100.0
4	Kenneth A. Roberts (D)	33,591	73.4
	Roy Banks (R)	12,166	26.6
5	Albert Rains (D)	45,281	100.0
6	Armistead I. Selden Jr. (D)	22,513	100.0
7	Carl Elliott (D)	31,988	100.0
8	Robert E. Jones Jr. (D)	46,730	80.1
	Mrs. James G. Fortney (R)	11,634	19.9
9	George Huddleston Jr. (D)	56,414	65.9
	W. L. Longshore Jr. (R)	29,222	34.1

ARIZONA

	Candidates	Votes	%
1	John J. Rhodes (R)	78,998	54.9
	William P. Mahoney Jr. (D)	64,805	45.1
2	Stewart L. Udall (D)	82,110	60.1
	John G. Speiden (R)	54,596	39.9

ARKANSAS

	Candidates	Votes	%
1	Ezekiel C. Gathings (D)	25,622	100.0
2	Wilbur D. Mills (D)	19,540	100.0
3	James W. Trimble (D)	54,481	61.4
	William S. Spicer (R)	34,318	38.7
4	Oren Harris (D)	37,284	100.0
5	Brooks Hays (D)	56,271	100.0
6	William F. Norrell (D)	42,447	100.0

CALIFORNIA

	Candidates	Votes	%
1	Hubert B. Scudder (R)	102,604	53.6
	Clement W. Miller (D)	88,962	46.4
2	Clair Engle (D-R)	136,544	100.0
3	John E. Moss Jr. (D)	132,930	68.6
	Noel C. Stevenson (R)	60,889	31.4
4	William S. Mailliard (R)	109,188	61.9
	James L. Quigley (D)	67,132	38.1
5	John F. Shelley (D-R)	104,358	100.0
6	John F. Baldwin Jr. (R)	98,683	53.7
	H. Roberts Quinney (D)	84,965	46.3
7	John J. Allen Jr. (R)	75,932	52.8
	Laurence L. Cross (D)	67,931	47.2
8	George P. Miller (D)	136,720	65.6
	Robert Lee Watkins (R)	71,700	34.4
9	J. Arthur Younger (R)	96,388	60.3
	James T. McKay (D)	63,504	39.7
10	Charles S. Gubser (R)	128,891	60.7
	William H. Vatcher Jr. (D)	83,586	39.3
11	John J. McFall (D)	70,630	53.1
	Leroy Johnson (R)	62,448	46.9
12	B. F. Sisk (D)	109,920	73.0
	Robert B. Moore (R)	40,663	27.0
13	Charles M. Teague (R)	104,009	59.6
	William Kirk Stewart (D)	70,567	40.4
14	Harlan Hagan (D)	94,461	63.0
	Myron D. Tisdel (R)	55,509	37.0
15	Gordon L. McDonough (R)	97,182	57.9
	Emery S. Petty (D)	70,681	42.1
16	Donald L. Jackson (R)	83,050	60.8
	G. Robert Fleming (D)	53,624	39.2
17	Cecil R. King (D)	157,270	64.9
	Charles A. Franklin (R)	84,900	35.1
18	Craig Hosmer (R)	103,108	59.3
	Raymond C. Simpson (D)	70,911	40.8
19	Chet Holifield (D)	116,287	73.8
	Roy E. Reynolds (R)	41,269	26.2
20	H. Allen Smith (R)	85,459	70.8
	Eugene Radding (D)	35,249	29.2
21	Edgar W. Hiestand (R)	153,679	62.6
	W. C. Stethem (D)	91,683	37.4
22	Joe Holt (R)	97,317	59.8
	Irving Glasband (D)	65,314	40.2
23	Clyde Doyle (D & P)	120,109	70.9
	E. Elgie Calvin (R)	49,198	29.1
24	Glenard P. Lipscomb (R)	84,120	61.9
	Fay Porter (D)	51,692	38.1
25	Patrick J. Hillings (R)	166,305	63.8
	John G. Sobieski (D)	94,180	36.2
26	James Roosevelt (D)	133,036	68.8
	Edward H. Gibbons (R)	60,230	31.2
27	Harry R. Sheppard (D-R)	124,662	99.8
28	James B. Utt (R)	159,456	64.5
	Gordon T. Shepard (D)	87,691	35.5
29	Dalip S. Saund (D)	54,989	51.5
	Jacqueline Cochran Odlum (R)	51,690	48.4
30	Bob Wilson (R)	142,753	66.8
	George A. Cheney (D)	71,112	33.3

COLORADO

	Candidates	Votes	%
1	Byron G. Rogers (D)	116,487	57.8
	Robert S. McCollum (R)	85,127	42.2
2	William S. Hill (R)	107,153	53.4
	Byron L. Johnson (D)	93,572	46.6
3	J. Edgar Chenoweth (R)	74,196	50.2
	Alva B. Adams (D)	73,503	49.8
4	Wayne N. Aspinall (D)	48,489	61.8
	Hugh L. Caldwell (R)	30,026	38.2

CONNECTICUT

	Candidates	Votes	%
1	Edwin H. May Jr. (R)	161,360	53.5
	Patrick J. Ward (D)	139,147	46.1
2	Horace Seely-Brown Jr. (R)	99,274	59.1
	Douglas J. Bennet (D)	68,847	41.0
3	Albert W. Cretella (R)	126,850	60.0
	Robert N. Giaimo (D)	84,568	40.0
4	Albert P. Morano (R)	194,333	68.4
	Jack Stock (D)	88,487	31.1
5	James T. Patterson (R)	91,690	61.9
	Luke F. Martin (D)	56,375	38.1
AL	Antoni N. Sadlak (R)	683,387	61.5
	Matthew P. Kuta (D)	428,709	38.6

DELAWARE

	Candidates	Votes	%
AL	Harry G. Haskell Jr. (R)	91,538	52.0
	Harris B. Mcdowell Jr. (D)	84,644	48.0

FLORIDA

	Candidates	Votes	%
1	William C. Cramer (R)	105,958	56.4
	Winton H. King (D)	82,075	43.7
2	Charles E. Bennett (D)	66,614	100.0
3	Robert L. F. Sikes (D)	86,272	89.6
	Arthur Barker Sr. (R)	10,042	10.4
4	Dante B. Fascell (D)	120,509	60.9
	Leland Hyzer (R)	77,301	39.1
5	A. S. Herlong Jr. (D)	73,498	51.4
	Arnold L. Lund (R)	69,378	48.6
6	Paul G. Rogers (D)	73,259	54.7
	Dorothy A. Smith (R)	60,570	45.3
7	James A. Haley (D)	47,985	62.4
	G. M. Nelson (R)	28,900	37.6
8	Donald R. Matthews (D)	39,362	100.0

GEORGIA

	Candidates	Votes	%
1	Prince H. Preston (D)	40,360	78.3
	Harry P. Anestos (I)	10,931	21.2
2	J. L. Pilcher (D)	41,270	100.0
3	E. L. Forrester (D)	51,703	100.0
4	John J. Flynt Jr. (D)	51,568	100.0
5	James C. Davis (D)	85,292	59.2
	Randolph W. Thrower (R)	58,777	40.8
6	Carl Vinson (D)	42,766	100.0
7	Henderson Lanham (D)	69,873	99.5
8	Iris Faircloth Blitch (D)	50,068	100.0
9	Phil M. Landrum (D)	47,360	100.0
10	Paul Brown (D)	41,812	99.8

IDAHO

	Candidates	Votes	%
1	Gracie B. Pfost (D)	60,170	55.1
	Louise Shadduck (R)	48,974	44.9
2	Hamer H. Budge (R)	90,738	60.0
	J. W. Reynolds (D)	60,552	40.0

ILLINOIS

	Candidates	Votes	%
1	William L. Dawson (D)	66,704	64.4
	George W. Lawrence (R)	36,847	35.6
2	Barratt O'Hara (D)	86,386	55.3
	George B. McKibbin (R)	69,892	44.7
3	Emmet F. Byrne (R)	92,967	51.5
	James C. Murray (D)	87,677	48.6
4	William E. McVey (R)	155,447	60.0
	Michael Hinko (D)	103,494	40.0
5	John C. Kluczynski (D)	96,399	61.8
	Lawrence Welnowski (R)	59,608	38.2
6	Thomas J. O'Brien (D)	94,281	62.0
	John J. Dillon (R)	57,750	38.0
7	James B. Bowler (D)	93,732	71.7
	Gabriel L. Grimaldi (R)	37,068	28.3
8	Thomas S. Gordon (D)	73,628	59.5
	Victor O. Wright (R)	50,055	40.5
9	Sidney R. Yates (D)	75,511	54.0
	Johann S. Ackerman (R)	64,237	46.0
10	Harold R. Collier (R)	132,928	64.5
	Marvin E. Lore (D)	73,331	35.6
11	Timothy P. Sheehan (R)	95,140	55.5
	Roman C. Pucinski (D)	76,400	44.5
12	Charles A. Boyle (D)	100,273	53.2
	Edgar A. Jonas (R)	88,315	46.8
13	Marguerite Stitt Church (R)	229,358	71.6
	Helen Benson Leys (D)	91,059	28.4
14	Russell W. Keeney (R)	151,236	70.6
	Harold J. Spelman (D)	63,067	29.4
15	Noah M. Mason (R)	103,557	64.6
	Stanley Hubbs (D)	56,802	35.4
16	Leo E. Allen (R)	106,734	63.7
	Glen F. Kunkle (D)	60,748	36.3
17	Leslie C. Arends (R)	106,463	64.9
	C. E. Spang (D)	57,467	35.1
18	Robert H. Michel (R)	87,187	58.8
	Fred Allen (D)	61,099	41.2
19	Robert B. Chiperfield (R)	85,497	55.8
	Martin P. Sutor (D)	67,691	44.2
20	Sidney E. Simpson (R)	79,641	59.7
	Henry W. Pollock (D)	53,882	40.4
21	Peter F. Mack Jr. (D)	94,565	53.5
	Frederic S. O'Hara (R)	82,251	46.5
22	William L. Springer (R)	93,399	62.3
	E. H. Winegarner (D)	56,612	37.7
23	Charles W. Vursell (R)	79,862	52.6
	Albert R. Imle (D)	72,070	47.4
24	Melvin Price (D)	121,381	68.2
	Waldo E. Schellenger (R)	56,568	31.8
25	Kenneth J. Gray (D)	82,845	53.8
	Samuel J. Scott (R)	71,048	46.2

INDIANA

	Candidates	Votes	%
1	Ray J. Madden (D)	93,658	52.6
	Donald K. Stimson Jr. (R)	84,125	47.2
2	Charles A. Halleck (R)	94,852	62.2
	Thurman C. Crook (D)	57,049	37.4

INDIANA

	Candidates	Votes	%
3	F. Jay Nimtz (R)	109,907	53.1
	John Brademas (D)	97,196	46.9
4	E. Ross Adair (R)	96,531	63.5
	F. Dean Bechtol (D)	55,284	36.3
5	John V. Beamer (R)	113,586	56.4
	William C. Whitehead (D)	86,797	43.1
6	Cecil M. Harden (R)	86,020	55.0
	John W. King (D)	70,035	44.8
7	William G. Bray (R)	87,635	57.2
	Vernon R. Hill (D)	65,482	42.8
8	Winfield K. Denton (D)	95,699	50.1
	D. Bailey Merrill (R)	95,003	49.7
9	Earl Wilson (R)	70,926	53.4
	Wilfrid J. Ullrich (D)	61,465	46.3
10	Ralph Harvey (R)	98,301	56.3
	Gerald C. Carmony (D)	75,665	43.3
11	Charles B. Brownson (R)	155,541	59.4
	John C. Carvey (D)	106,021	40.5

IOWA

	Candidates	Votes	%
1	Fred D. Schwengel (R)	94,223	58.0
	Ronald O. Bramhall (D)	68,287	42.0
2	Henry O. Talle (R)	95,999	51.4
	Leonard G. Wolf (D)	90,843	48.6
3	H. R. Gross (R)	97,590	58.6
	Michael Micich (D)	69,076	41.5
4	Karl M. LeCompte (R)	58,024	50.7
	Steven V. Carter (D)	56,406	49.3
5	Paul Cunningham (R)	85,178	51.1
	William F. Denman (D)	81,418	48.9
6	Merwin Coad (D)	64,625	50.1
	James I. Dolliver (R)	64,427	49.9
7	Ben F. Jensen (R)	64,967	55.4
	John L. Jensen (D)	52,389	44.6
8	Charles B. Hoeven (R)	76,165	60.1
	Robert J. Salem (D)	50,597	39.9

KANSAS

	Candidates	Votes	%
1	William H. Avery (R)	69,841	53.1
	Howard S. Miller (D)	60,313	45.8
2	Errett P. Scrivner (R)	93,609	54.9
	Newell A. George (D)	77,049	45.2
3	Myron V. George (R)	48,246	55.0
	Denver D. Hargis (D)	39,407	45.0
4	Edward H. Rees (R)	111,970	53.8
	John D. Montgomery (D)	96,002	46.2
5	J. Floyd Breeding (D)	64,392	50.5
	John W. Crutcher (R)	63,057	49.5
6	Wint Smith (R)	52,145	51.1
	Elmo J. Mahoney (D)	49,933	48.9

KENTUCKY

	Candidates	Votes	%
1	Noble J. Gregory (D)	75,726	100.0
2	William H. Natcher (D)	55,103	52.3
	R. B. Blankenship (R)	50,266	47.7
3	John M. Robsion Jr. (R)	111,598	56.8
	Philip Ardery (D)	84,912	43.2
4	Frank Chelf (D)	51,675	56.3
	John B. Preston (D)	40,129	43.7
5	Brent Spence (D)	59,402	55.9
	Jule Appel (R)	46,821	44.1
6	John C. Watts (D)	69,468	52.7
	Wallace Jones (R)	62,313	47.3
7	Carl D. Perkins (D)	77,564	52.4
	Scott Craft (R)	70,450	47.6
8	Eugene Siler (R)	80,067	71.7
	W. D. Scalf (D)	31,632	28.3

LOUISIANA

	Candidates	Votes	%
1	F. Edward Hebert (D)	69,500	100.0
2	Hale Boggs (D)	69,715	64.5
	George R. Blue (R)	38,344	35.5
3	Edwin E. Willis (D)	19,075	100.0
4	Overton Brooks (D)	40,583	68.1
	Calhoun Allen Jr. (R)	19,041	31.9
5	Otto E. Passman (D)	18,210	100.0
6	James H. Morrison (D)	58,414	100.0
7	T. A. Thompson (D)	36,432	100.0
8	George S. Long (D)	18,341	100.0

MAINE

	Candidates	Votes	%
1	Robert Hale (R)	58,028	50.0
	James C. Oliver (D)	57,999	50.0
2	Frank M. Coffin (D)	55,430	53.4
	James L. Reid (R)	48,292	46.6
3	Clifford G. McIntire (R)	44,095	60.7
	Kenneth B. Colbath (D)	28,612	39.4

MARYLAND

	Candidates	Votes	%
1	Edward T. Miller (R)	42,731	55.7
	Hamilton P. Fox (D)	33,961	44.3
2	James P. S. Devereux (R)	103,103	58.1
	A. Gordon Boone (D)	74,224	41.9
3	Edward A. Garmatz (D)	48,397	69.8
	Harry Kemper (R)	20,990	30.3
4	George H. Fallon (D)	44,260	53.8
	George Denys Hubbard (R)	37,957	46.2
5	Richard E. Lankford (D)	88,227	56.8
	William B. Prendergast (R)	67,072	43.2
6	Dewitt S. Hyde (R)	100,580	54.3
	John R. Foley (D)	84,837	45.8
7	Samuel N. Friedel (D)	70,512	59.0
	David A. Halley (R)	48,949	41.0

MASSACHUSETTS

	Candidates	Votes	%
1	John W. Heselton (R)	92,269	63.6
	Howard W. Shea (D)	52,213	36.0
2	Edward P. Boland (D)	103,563	61.2
	Foster W. Doty (R)	65,598	38.8
3	Philip J. Philbin (D)	114,848	70.9
	Robert A. Parker (R)	47,041	29.1
4	Harold D. Donohue (D)	104,653	59.4
	Mary R. Wheeler (R)	71,437	40.6
5	Edith Nourse Rogers (R)	150,957	73.3
	Lawrence E. Corcoran (D)	55,038	26.7
6	William H. Bates (R)	131,310	100.0
7	Thomas J. Lane (D)	87,415	64.5
	Robert T. Breed (R)	48,173	35.5
8	Torbert H. Macdonald (D)	92,463	54.8
	C. Eugene Farnam (R)	76,312	45.2
9	Donald W. Nicholson (R)	111,860	61.1
	William McAuliffe (D)	71,245	38.9
10	Laurence Curtis (R)	93,327	53.0
	Jackson J. Holtz (D)	82,882	47.0
11	Thomas P. O'Neill Jr. (D)	83,532	75.3
	Rudolph E. Mottola (R)	27,384	24.7
12	John W. McCormack (D)	89,943	82.5
	James S. Tremblay (D)	19,099	17.5
13	Richard B. Wigglesworth (R)	109,950	55.6
	Richard E. McCormack (D)	87,719	44.4
14	Joseph W. Martin Jr. (R)	111,420	62.4
	Edward F. Doolan (D)	67,183	37.6

MICHIGAN

	Candidates	Votes	%
1	Thaddeus M. Machrowicz (D)	112,290	86.1
	Walter Czarnecki (R)	18,137	13.9
2	George Meader (R)	105,940	63.1
	Franklin J. Shepherd (D)	61,456	36.6
3	August E. Johansen (R)	100,056	63.8
	Truman Barkhuff (D)	56,119	35.8
4	Clare E. Hoffman (R)	83,876	62.0
	Samuel I. Clark (D)	51,491	38.0
5	Gerald R. Ford Jr. (R)	120,349	67.1
	George E. Clay (D)	58,899	32.9
6	Charles E. Chamberlain (R)	116,570	50.8
	Don Hayworth (D)	112,603	49.0
7	Robert J. McIntosh (R)	114,674	53.7
	Ira D. McCoy (D)	98,928	46.3
8	Alvin M. Bentley (R)	93,357	64.1
	William R. Hart (D)	51,897	35.6
9	Robert P. Griffin (R)	68,166	56.0
	William E. Baker (D)	53,609	44.0
10	Elford A. Cederberg (R)	72,781	65.6
	William J. Kelly (D)	38,166	34.4
11	Victor A. Knox (R)	53,117	56.1
	Prentiss M. Brown Jr. (D)	41,600	43.9
12	John B. Bennett (R)	45,721	56.3
	Joseph S. Mack (D)	35,434	43.7
13	Charles C. Diggs Jr. (D)	87,353	69.8
	Willis F. Ward (R)	37,860	30.2
14	Louis C. Rabaut (D)	122,079	56.8
	Harold F. Youngblood (R)	92,933	43.2
15	John D. Dingell (D)	111,827	74.1
	Larry Middleton (R)	38,973	25.8
16	John Lesinski (D)	176,663	64.1
	Arthur Kurtz (R)	98,172	35.6
17	Martha W. Griffiths (D)	112,811	53.3
	George E. Smith (R)	98,432	46.5
18	William S. Broomfield (R)	141,058	56.7
	Paul Sutton (D)	107,609	43.3

MINNESOTA

	Candidates	Votes	%
1	August H. Andresen (R)	92,092	61.5
	Arnold L. Fredriksen (DFL)	57,747	38.5
2	Joseph P. O'Hara (R)	97,520	63.8
	Harold Zupp (DFL)	55,336	36.2
3	Roy W. Wier (DFL)	127,356	52.0
	George Mikan (R)	117,716	48.0
4	Eugene J. McCarthy (DFL)	103,320	64.1
	Edward C. Slettedahl (R)	57,947	35.9
5	Walter H. Judd (R)	82,258	56.0
	Joseph Robbie (DFL)	64,602	44.0
6	Fred Marshall (DFL)	76,396	56.2
	Joseph L. Kaczmarek (R)	59,568	43.8
7	H. Carl Andersen (R)	76,271	55.9
	Clint Haroldson (DFL)	60,168	44.1
8	John A. Blatnik (DFL)	108,565	73.2
	Alfred J. Weinberg (R)	39,795	26.8
9	Coya Knutson (DFL)	58,916	52.7
	Harold C. Hagen (R)	52,937	47.3

MISSISSIPPI

	Candidates	Votes	%
1	Thomas G. Abernethy (D)	38,021	100.0
2	Jamie L. Whitten (D)	23,513	100.0
3	Frank E. Smith (D)	19,369	100.0
4	John Bell Williams (D)	42,085	100.0
5	Arthur Winstead (D)	35,461	100.0
6	William M. Colmer (D)	47,083	100.0

MISSOURI

	Candidates	Votes	%
1	Frank M. Karsten (D)	136,873	66.3
	Bill Bangert (R)	69,661	33.7
2	Thomas B. Curtis (R)	123,596	51.8
	James L. Sullivan (D)	114,837	48.2
3	Leonor K. Sullivan (D)	96,416	69.7
	Sidney R. Redmond (R)	42,023	30.4
4	George H. Christopher (D)	98,106	51.8
	Jeffrey P. Hillelson (R)	91,392	48.2
5	Richard Bolling (D)	77,287	57.2
	Lemot Jones Jr. (R)	57,778	42.8
6	W. R. Hull Jr. (D)	85,021	52.0
	Stanley I. Dale (R)	78,637	48.1
7	Charles H. Brown (D)	90,986	50.3
	Dewey Short (R)	89,926	49.7
8	A. S. J. Carnahan (D)	69,336	54.3
	Frank W. May (R)	58,425	45.7
9	Clarence Cannon (D)	100,065	100.0
10	Paul C. Jones (D)	69,536	100.0

MISSOURI

	Candidates	Votes	%
11	Morgan M. Moulder (D)	72,594	50.8
	George H. Miller (R)	70,286	49.2

MONTANA

	Candidates	Votes	%
1	Lee Metcalf (D)	69,644	62.1
	W. D. McDonald (R)	42,591	38.0
2	Leroy H. Anderson (D)	76,805	50.9
	Orvin B. Fjare (R)	74,164	49.1

NEBRASKA

	Candidates	Votes	%
1	Phil Weaver (R)	102,012	67.0
	Samuel Freeman (D)	50,351	33.1
2	Glenn Cunningham (R)	77,253	53.4
	Joseph V. Benesch (D)	65,039	45.0
3	Robert D. Harrison (R)	62,645	50.1
	Lawrence Brock (D)	62,399	49.9
4	Arthur L. Miller (R)	81,731	65.8
	Carlton W. Laird (D)	42,583	34.3

NEVADA

	Candidates	Votes	%
AL	Walter S. Baring (D)	51,100	54.2
	Richard W. Horton (R)	43,154	45.8

NEW HAMPSHIRE

	Candidates	Votes	%
1	Chester E. Merrow (R)	78,296	57.4
	James B. Sullivan (D)	58,104	42.6
2	Perkins Bass (R)	77,019	66.0
	George F. Brown (D)	39,726	34.0

NEW JERSEY

	Candidates	Votes	%
1	Charles A. Wolverton (R)	133,153	58.3
	J. Frank Crawford (D)	94,758	41.5
2	T. Millet Hand (R)	83,433*	67.9
	Thomas C. Stewart (D)	39,383	32.0
3	James C. Auchincloss (R)	136,780	65.3
	Sidney Shiff (D)	72,617	34.7
4	Frank Thompson Jr. (D)	89,646	54.5
	William H. Wells (R)	74,737	45.5
5	Peter H. B. Frelinghuysen Jr. (R)	153,829	64.5
	Francis C. Foley Jr. (D)	84,374	35.4
6	Florence P. Dwyer (R)	106,414	50.6
	Harrison A. Williams Jr. (D)	102,015	48.5
7	William B. Widnall (R)	151,573	70.7
	Daniel Amster (D)	62,924	29.3
8	Gordon Canfield (R)	96,484	60.8
	Walter H. Gardner (D)	61,464	38.7
9	Frank C. Osmers Jr. (R)	135,498	67.8
	Robert D. Gruen (D)	63,728	31.9
10	Peter W. Rodino Jr. (D)	71,311	56.1
	G. George Addonizio (R)	55,761	43.9
11	Hugh J. Addonizio (D)	63,482	51.7
	Chester K. Ligham (R)	57,447	46.8
12	Robert Winthrop Kean (R)	90,032	59.7
	Irving L. Hodes (D)	58,364	38.7
13	Alfred D. Sieminski (D)	54,841	45.0
	Norman H. Roth (R)	54,784	44.9
14	Vincent J. Dellay (R)	61,600	52.3
	T. James Tumulty (D)	53,713	45.6

NEW MEXICO

	Candidates	Votes	%
AL	John J. Dempsey (D)	129,625✔	
	Antonio M. Fernandez (D)	128,330*	
	Dudley Cornell (R)	114,719	
	Forrest Atchley (R)	112,531	

NEW YORK

	Candidates	Votes	%
1	Stuyvesant Wainwright (R)	191,356	65.8
	T. Bronson O'Reilly (D, L)	99,304	34.2
2	Steven B. Derounian (R)	148,098	67.5
	Julius J. Damato (D, L)	71,422	32.5
3	Frank J. Becker (R)	143,559	61.9
	Francis X. Hardiman (D, L)	88,245	38.1
4	Henry J. Latham (R)	116,670	55.8
	Joseph J. Perrini (D, L)	92,217	44.2
5	Albert H. Bosch (R)	87,154	58.6
	John J. Quinn (D, L)	61,678	41.4
6	Lester Holtzman (D)	128,545	56.9
	Albert H. Buschmann (R)	97,558	43.2
7	James J. Delaney (D, L)	78,030	50.0
	Joseph Stockinger (R)	77,928	50.0
8	Victor L. Anfuso (D, L)	59,998	65.6
	Julius Reinlieb (R)	31,399	34.4
9	Eugene J. Keogh (D, L)	75,814	62.8
	Benjamin W. Feldman (R)	44,916	37.2
10	Edna F. Kelly (D, L)	100,808	73.2
	Abraham Sher (R)	36,878	26.8
11	Emanuel Celler (D, L)	131,508	77.7
	Henry D. Dorfman (R)	37,651	22.3
12	Francis E. Dorn (R)	76,137	57.6
	Donald L. O'Toole (D, L)	56,035	42.4
13	Abraham J. Multer (D, L)	110,469	71.2
	Joseph Moriber (R)	44,771	28.8
14	John J. Rooney (D, L)	77,706	64.2
	Jacob P. Lefkowitz (R)	43,343	35.8
15	John H. Ray (R)	98,093	61.4
	Ralph Di Iorio (D, L)	60,989	38.2
16	Adam Clayton Powell Jr. (D)	59,339	69.7
	Joseph A. Bailey (R)	16,960	19.9
	Formington Taylor (L)	8,801	10.3
17	Frederic R. Coudert Jr. (R)	68,874	50.9
	Anthony B. Akers (D, L)	66,396	49.1
18	Alfred E. Santangelo (D, L)	47,953	58.0
	James G. Donovan (R)	34,748	42.0
19	Leonard Farbstein (D, L)	68,411	68.4
	Maurice G. Henry Jr. (R)	31,546	31.6
20	Ludwig Teller (D, L)	70,726	63.8
	Milton H. Adler (R)	40,191	36.2
21	Herbert Zelenko (D, L)	81,464	66.5
	Dalton J. Shapo (R)	41,070	33.5
22	James C. Healey (D)	88,441	64.1
	Henry Rose (R)	34,084	24.7
	David I. Wells (L)	15,524	11.3
23	Isidore Dollinger (D)	70,238	68.5
	Philip Myer (R)	22,414	21.9
	Hyman Fromowitz (L)	9,880	9.6
24	Charles A. Buckley (D)	90,076	54.7
	Harold Grosberg (R)	53,172	32.3
	Elias Rosenblatt (L)	21,444	13.0
25	Paul A. Fino (R)	104,771	59.4
	Edward A. Cunningham (D)	62,729	35.5
	Bernard Tobacman (L)	8,989	5.1
26	Edwin B. Dooley (R)	123,996	67.5
	Julia L. Crews (D, L)	59,842	32.6
27	Ralph W. Gwinn (R)	117,100	58.1
	William D. Carlebach (D, L)	84,568	41.9
28	Katharine St. George (R)	103,114	62.2
	William H. Mauldin (D, L)	62,770	37.8
29	J. Ernest Wharton (R)	124,211	71.4
	Vincent di Gennaro (D, L)	49,725	28.6
30	Leo W. O'Brien (D, L)	104,022	55.8
	Robert E. Gray (R)	82,429	44.2
31	Dean P. Taylor (R)	116,682	71.8
	Theodore A. Knapp (D, L)	45,767	28.2
32	Bernard W. Kearney (R)	107,959	67.5
	R. Joseph Giblin (D, L)	52,064	32.5
33	Clarence E. Kilburn (R)	103,419	72.7
	Louis J. Britton (D, L)	38,793	27.3
34	William R. Williams (R)	95,681	57.5
	Edwin L. Slusarczyk (D, L)	70,837	42.5
35	R. Walter Riehlman (R)	124,108	67.1
	Thomas J. Lowery (D)	59,534	32.2
36	John Taber (R)	109,101	69.6
	Lewis S. Bell (D, L)	47,764	30.4
37	Sterling Cole (R)	136,044	71.7
	Francis P. Hogan (D, L)	53,830	28.4
38	Kenneth B. Keating (R)	135,572	71.7
	Reed Harding (D, L)	53,477	28.3
39	Harold C. Ostertag (R)	116,043	70.5
	William H. Mostyn (D, L)	48,634	29.5
40	William E. Miller (R)	117,051	64.3
	A. Thorne Hills (D, L)	64,872	35.7
41	Edmund P. Radwan (R)	99,151	64.4
	Edward P. Jehle (D, L)	54,776	35.6
42	John R. Pillion (R)	117,178	58.7
	James Kane Jr. (D)	80,568	40.3
43	Daniel A. Reed (R)	93,079	68.7
	T. Joseph Lynch (D, L)	42,476	31.3

Special Election

	Candidates	Votes	%
22	James C. Healey (D)	9,473	72.3
	Sidney Burnstein (L)	1,943	14.8
	Barnett Davis (R)	1,691	12.9

NORTH CAROLINA

	Candidates	Votes	%
1	Herbert C. Bonner (D)	44,271	88.6
	Zeno O. Ratcliff (R)	5,693	11.4
2	L. H. Fountain (D)	49,812	100.0
3	Graham A. Barden (D)	47,251	78.8
	Joe Reynolds (R)	12,698	21.2
4	Harold D. Cooley (D)	76,560	100.0
5	Ralph J. Scott (D)	58,552	59.7
	Joe New (R)	39,561	40.3
6	Carl T. Durham (D)	73,111	100.0
7	Alton Lennon (D)	65,424	84.0
	C. Dana Malpass (R)	12,477	16.0
8	A. Paul Kitchin (D)	64,220	59.5
	Fred Myers (R)	43,732	40.5
9	Hugh Q. Alexander (D)	68,181	53.9
	A. M. Miller (R)	58,407	46.1
10	Charles Raper Jonas (R)	89,743	62.7
	Ben E. Douglas (D)	53,475	37.3
11	Basil L. Whitener (D)	59,417	100.0
12	George A. Shuford (D)	55,927	54.5
	Richard C. Clarke Jr. (R)	46,760	45.5

NORTH DAKOTA

	Candidates	Votes	%
AL	Usher L. Burdick (R)	143,514✔	
	Otto Krueger (R)	136,003✔	
	Agnes Geelan (D)	85,743	
	S. B. Hocking (D)	83,284	

OHIO

	Candidates	Votes	%
1	Gordon H. Scherer (R)	91,181	64.7
	Leonard D. Slutz (D)	49,701	35.3
2	William E. Hess (R)	109,099	65.5
	James T. Dewan (D)	57,554	34.5
3	Paul F. Schenck (R)	135,152	59.0
	R. William Patterson (D)	93,782	41.0
4	William M. McCulloch (R)	93,607	68.8
	Ortha C. Barr Jr. (D)	42,416	31.2
5	Cliff Clevenger (R)	69,774	62.3
	George E. Rafferty (D)	42,181	37.7
6	James G. Polk (D)	72,229	54.5
	Albert L. Daniels (R)	60,300	45.5
7	Clarence J. Brown (R)	91,439	66.0
	Joseph A. Sullivan (D)	47,220	34.1
8	Jackson E. Betts (R)	70,690	63.5
	Robert M. Corry (D)	40,716	36.6
9	Thomas L. Ashley (D)	100,696	55.3
	Harvey G. Straub (R)	81,562	44.8
10	Thomas A. Jenkins (R)	71,295	100.0
11	David S. Dennison Jr. (R)	96,707	58.4
	James P. Bennett (D)	68,831	41.6
12	John M. Vorys (R)	128,682	61.8
	Walter J. Shapter Jr. (D)	79,597	38.2
13	A. D. Baumhart Jr. (R)	79,324	70.7
	J. P. Henderson (D)	32,900	29.3
14	William H. Ayres (R)	123,105	58.9
	Bernard Rosen (D)	85,946	41.1
15	John E. Henderson (R)	55,126	60.5
	Herbert U. Smith (D)	35,954	39.5

OHIO

	Candidates	Votes	%
16	Frank T. Bow (R)	101,324	55.2
	John McSweeney (D)	82,206	44.8
17	J. Harry McGregor (R)	88,931	66.5
	Robert W. Levering (D)	44,806	33.5
18	Wayne L. Hays (D)	78,962	59.6
	Joseph Miller (R)	53,627	40.5
19	Michael J. Kirwan (D)	92,924	68.7
	Ralph E. Turner (R)	42,293	31.3
20	Michael A. Feighan (D)	105,562	65.3
	John H. Ferguson (R)	56,209	34.8
21	Charles A. Vanik (D)	96,106	71.6
	Charles H. Loeb (R)	38,060	28.4
22	Frances P. Bolton (R)	96,468	66.7
	Harry A. Blachman (D)	48,169	33.3
23	William E. Minshall Jr. (R)	102,707	69.0
	George A. Hurley (D)	46,247	31.1

OKLAHOMA

	Candidates	Votes	%
1	Page Belcher (R)	114,896	57.2
	Harry B. Moreland (D)	86,123	42.8
2	Ed Edmondson (D)	83,976	60.2
	Percy Butler (R)	55,416	39.8
3	Carl Albert (D)	60,620	76.5
	Chapin Wallace (R)	18,182	23.0
4	Tom Steed (D)	57,416	61.1
	Harold H. Potter (R)	36,534	38.9
5	John Jarman (D)	110,416	63.7
	Hobart H. Hobbs (R)	62,812	36.3
6	Toby Morris (D)	86,770	68.9
	Fred L. Coogan (R)	39,153	31.1

OREGON

	Candidates	Votes	%
1	Walter Norblad (R)	109,360	54.7
	Jason Lee (D)	90,567	45.3
2	Al Ullman (D)	53,219	50.7
	Sam Coon (R)	51,844	49.4
3	Edith Green (D)	146,250	61.6
	Phil J. Roth (R)	91,239	38.4
4	Charles O. Porter (D)	90,355	51.3
	Harris Ellsworth (R)	85,860	48.7

PENNSYLVANIA

	Candidates	Votes	%
1	William A. Barrett (D)	74,511	62.7
	A. J. Cammarota (R)	44,333	37.3
2	Kathryn E. Granahan (D)	95,567	62.3
	Robert F. Frankenfield (R)	57,773	37.7
3	James A. Byrne (D)	71,161	59.9
	Charles H. Sporkin (R)	47,550	40.1
4	Earl Chudoff (D)	75,374	69.1
	Horace C. Scott (R)	33,672	30.9
5	William J. Green Jr. (D)	107,021	53.3
	James J. Schissler (R)	93,612	46.7
6	Hugh Scott (R)	90,966	51.5
	Herbert J. McGlinchey (D)	85,541	48.5
7	Benjamin F. James (R)	137,764	61.9
	William A. Welsh (D)	84,764	38.1
8	Willard S. Curtin (R)	98,023	55.9
	John P. Fullam (D)	77,229	44.1
9	Paul B. Dague (R)	110,230	68.4
	Edward G. Wilson (D)	50,947	31.6
10	Joseph L. Carrigg (R)	91,103	55.8
	Jerome P. Casey (D)	72,178	44.2
11	Daniel J. Flood (D)	83,178	53.1
	Enoch H. Thomas Jr. (R)	73,606	47.0
12	Ivor D. Fenton (R)	72,125	56.5
	George G. Lindsay (D)	55,642	43.6
13	Samuel K. McConnell Jr. (R)	127,627	66.7
	Alfred M. Klein (D)	63,610	33.3
14	George M. Rhodes (D)	51,088	51.3
	Thomas K. Leinbach (R)	48,129	48.4
15	Francis E. Walter (D)	63,204	55.6
	George M. Berg (R)	50,491	44.4

	Candidates	Votes	%
16	Walter M. Mumma (R)	84,617	60.5
	Guy J. Swope (D)	55,260	39.5
17	Alvin R. Bush (R)	74,748	58.6
	Dean R. Fisher (D)	52,900	41.4
18	Richard M. Simpson (R)	77,833	59.9
	Ross E. Hershberger (D)	52,180	40.1
19	S. Walter Stauffer (R)	79,448	53.8
	James M. Quigley (D)	68,171	46.2
20	James E. Van Zandt (R)	65,457	63.0
	John R. Stewart (D)	38,483	37.0
21	Augustine B. Kelley (D)	78,744	56.8
	Herbert O. Morrison (R)	59,786	43.2
22	John P. Saylor (R)	85,540	56.9
	Joseph C. Dolan (D)	64,689	43.1
23	Leon H. Gavin (R)	72,365	66.1
	Grace M. Sloan (D)	37,122	33.9
24	Carroll D. Kearns (R)	93,824	57.8
	William D. Thomas (D)	68,625	42.2
25	Frank M. Clark (D)	81,339	51.3
	Sidney L. Lockley (R)	77,150	48.7
26	Thomas E. Morgan (D)	104,049	61.9
	I. Willits McCaskey (R)	64,129	38.1
27	James G. Fulton (R)	126,247	66.0
	Kenneth L. Stilley (D)	64,917	34.0
28	Herman P. Eberharter (D)	88,725	57.8
	Richard C. Witt (R)	64,905	42.3
29	Robert J. Corbett (R)	114,109	64.7
	Joseph A. Guerrier (D)	62,225	35.3
30	Elmer J. Holland (D)	103,389	59.8
	Ross V. Walker (R)	69,495	40.2

RHODE ISLAND

	Candidates	Votes	%
1	Aime J. Forand (D)	96,732	55.8
	Samuel H. Ramsay (R)	76,714	44.2
2	John E. Fogarty (D)	105,496	52.2
	Thomas H. Needham (R)	96,568	47.8

SOUTH CAROLINA

	Candidates	Votes	%
1	L. Mendel Rivers (D)	31,112	100.0
2	John J. Riley (D)	49,284	100.0
3	W. J. Bryan Dorn (D)	39,270	92.9
	Mrs. Maka Knox (R)	2,885	6.8
4	Robert T. Ashmore (D)	53,722	85.1
	Dan H. Wallace Jr (R)	9,393	14.9
5	Robert Hemphill (D)	36,454	100.0
6	John L. McMillan (D)	39,749	100.0

SOUTH DAKOTA

	Candidates	Votes	%
1	George McGovern (D)	116,516	52.4
	Harold O. Lovre (R)	105,835	47.6
2	E. Y. Berry (R)	36,681	55.9
	Tom Eastman Jr. (D)	28,984	44.1

TENNESSEE

	Candidates	Votes	%
1	B. Carroll Reece (R)	86,531	72.1
	Arthur Bright (D)	33,403	27.9
2	Howard H. Baker (R)	90,127	100.0
3	James B. Frazier Jr. (D)	55,715	53.7
	P. H. Wood (R)	47,954	46.3
4	Joe L. Evins (D)	56,191	98.4
5	J. Carlton Loser (D)	54,318	74.5
	George S. Spence (R)	18,585	25.5
6	Ross Bass (D)	47,098	100.0
7	Tom Murray (D)	36,301	100.0
8	Jere Cooper (D)	27,485	100.0
9	Clifford Davis (D)	90,874	71.8
	Herbert Harper (R)	35,783	28.3

TEXAS

	Candidates	Votes	%
1	Wright Patman (D)	54,837	100.0
2	Jack Brooks (D)	81,343	100.0
3	Lindley Beckworth (D)	47,570	83.5
	R. E. Kennedy (R)	9,402	16.5
4	Sam Rayburn (D)	41,867	100.0
5	Bruce Alger (R)	102,380	55.6
	Henry Wade (D)	81,705	44.4
6	Olin Teague (D)	42,383	100.0
7	John Dowdy (D)	44,456	100.0
8	Albert Thomas (D)	137,950	60.5
	C. A. Friloux Jr. (R)	86,640	38.0
9	Clark W. Thompson (D)	88,487	100.0
10	Homer Thornberry (D)	68,697	100.0
11	W. R. Poage (D)	56,990	100.0
12	Jim Wright (D)	110,196	100.0
13	Frank Ikard (D)	66,108	100.0
14	John Young (D)	85,922	87.3
	Olive B. Stichter (R)	12,517	12.7
15	Joe M. Kilgore (D)	64,011	100.0
16	J. T. Rutherford (D)	50,704	64.6
	Charles H. Gibson (R)	27,821	35.4
17	Omar Burleson (D)	53,000	100.0
18	Walter Rogers (D)	75,243	100.0
19	George Mahon (D)	85,566	100.0
20	Paul J. Kilday (D)	67,707	100.0
21	O. C. Fisher (D)	60,344	100.0
AL	Martin Dies (D)	1,436,831	98.5

UTAH

	Candidates	Votes	%
1	Henry Aldous Dixon (R)	74,107	60.9
	Carlyle F. Gronning (D)	47,533	39.1
2	William A. Dawson (R)	119,683	57.6
	Oscar W. McConkie Jr. (D)	87,970	42.4

VERMONT

	Candidates	Votes	%
AL	Winston L. Prouty (R)	103,736	67.1
	Camille E. St. Amour (D)	50,797	32.9

VIRGINIA

	Candidates	Votes	%
1	Edward J. Robeson Jr. (D)	31,839	50.8
	Horace E. Henderson (R)	30,799	49.2
2	Porter Hardy Jr. (D)	46,958	76.4
	William R. Burns (R)	14,483	23.6
3	J. Vaughan Gary (D)	46,109	59.1
	Roy E. Cabell Jr. (R)	31,947	40.9
4	Watkins M. Abbitt (D)	51,434	99.9
5	William M. Tuck (D)	39,771	67.4
	Jackson L. Kiser (R)	19,263	32.6
6	Richard H. Poff (R)	51,279	62.1
	John L. Whitehead (D)	31,043	37.6
7	Burr P. Harrison (D)	40,069	69.0
	A. R. Dunning (R)	17,970	31.0
8	Howard W. Smith (D)	38,648	67.3
	Horace B. Clay (R)	18,813	32.7
9	W. Pat Jennings (D)	49,448	54.1
	William C. Wampler (R)	41,957	45.9
10	Joel T. Broyhill (R)	53,149	56.2
	Warren D. Quenstedt (D)	40,553	42.9

WASHINGTON

	Candidates	Votes	%
1	Thomas M. Pelly (R)	129,768	58.1
	James B. Wilson (D)	93,492	41.9
2	Jack Westland (R)	105,975	56.0
	Payson Peterson (D)	83,195	44.0
3	Russell V. Mack (R)	80,520	56.5
	Al McCoy (D)	61,962	43.5
4	Hal Holmes (R)	76,769	50.4
	Frank LeRoux (D)	75,519	49.6
5	Walt Horan (R)	83,230	53.8
	Tom Delaney (D)	71,571	46.2
6	Thor C. Tollefson (R)	108,014	54.0
	John T. McCutcheon (D)	91,878	46.0
AL	Don Magnuson (D)	621,118	58.5
	Philip Evans (R)	439,896	41.5

WEST VIRGINIA

Candidates	Votes	%
1 Arch A. Moore Jr. (R)	65,096	50.3
C. Lee Spillers (D)	64,334	49.7
2 Harley O. Staggers (D)	63,327	52.4
Mary Elkins (R)	57,597	47.6
3 Cleveland M. Bailey (D)	62,240	51.5
Daniel L. Louchery (R)	58,623	48.5
4 Will E. Neal (R)	78,225	52.8
M. G. Burnside (D)	69,871	47.2
5 Elizabeth Kee (D)	68,638	60.7
William H. Sanders (R)	44,479	39.3
6 Robert C. Byrd (D)	99,854	57.4
Cleo S. Jones (R)	74,110	42.6

WISCONSIN

Candidates	Votes	%
1 Lawrence H. Smith (R)	94,882	57.1
Gerald T. Flynn (D)	71,379	42.9
2 Donald E. Tewes (R)	101,444	55.3
Robert W. Kastenmeier (D)	81,922	44.7
3 Gardner R. Withrow (R)	74,000	61.2
Norman M. Clapp (D)	46,911	38.8
4 Clement J. Zablocki (D)	128,213	65.7
William J. Burke (R)	67,063	34.3
5 Henry S. Reuss (D)	118,603	57.8
Russell Wirth Jr. (R)	86,764	42.3
6 William K. Van Pelt (R)	96,783	67.2
Rudolph J. Ploetz (D)	47,277	32.8

Candidates	Votes	%
7 Melvin R. Laird (R)	80,143	61.9
Margaret Anderson (D)	49,442	38.2
8 John W. Byrnes (R)	97,952	64.7
Milo Singler (D)	53,567	35.4
9 Lester R. Johnson (D)	62,476	51.4
Arthur L. Peterson (R)	59,024	48.6
10 Alvin E. O'Konski (R)	67,250	64.5
Carl E. Lauri (D)	36,941	35.5

WYOMING

	Votes	%
AL Keith Thomson (R)	69,903	58.2
Jerry A. O'Callaghan (D)	50,225	41.8

1957 House Elections

ILLINOIS

Special Election

	Votes	%
7 Roland V. Libonati (D)	32,221	88.1
Anthony C. Catena (R)	4,353	11.9

NEW JERSEY

Special Election

	Votes	%
2 Milton W. Glenn (R)	58,129	54.8
Joseph G. Hancock (D)	47,647	44.9

House Candidates Index

For an index of all House candidates listed in this section (pages 192-324), see pages 340-371. Instructions for use of the House Candidates Index appear on page 340.

1958 House Elections

ALABAMA

Candidates	Votes	%
1 Frank W. Boykin (D)	19,499	100.0
2 George Grant (D)	27,972	100.0
3 George W. Andrews (D)	17,389	100.0
4 Kenneth A. Roberts (D)	25,133	100.0
5 Albert Rains (D)	31,687	100.0
6 Armistead I. Selden Jr. (D)	18,557	100.0
7 Carl Elliott (D)	29,936	100.0
8 Robert E. Jones (D)	22,710	100.0
9 George Huddleston Jr. (D)	38,229	86.3
Frank L. Mason (R)	6,050	13.7

ALASKA

(Became a state Jan. 3, 1959)

	Votes	%
AL Ralph J. Rivers (D)	27,945	57.5
Henry A. Benson (R)	20,699	42.6

ARIZONA

	Votes	%
1 John J. Rhodes (R)	86,959	59.3
Joe Haldiman Jr. (D)	59,816	40.8
2 Stewart L. Udall (D)	79,651	60.9
John G. Speiden (R)	51,140	39.1

ARKANSAS

	Votes	%
1 Ezekiel C. Gathings (D)		100.0
2 Wilbur D. Mills (D)		100.0
3 James W. Trimble (D)		100.0
4 Oren Harris (D)		100.0
5 Dale Alford (WRITE IN)	30,739	51.0
Brooks Hays (D)	29,483	49.0
6 William F. Norrell (D)		100.0

CALIFORNIA

	Votes	%
1 Clem W. Miller (D)	102,096	54.9
Frederick G. Dupuis (R)	83,807	45.1
2 Harold T. Johnson (D)	90,850	61.0
Curtis W. Tarr (R)	58,199	39.1
3 John E. Moss Jr. (D-R)	169,727	100.0
4 William S. Mailliard (R)	98,574	60.0
George D. Collins Jr. (D)	65,798	40.0
5 John F. Shelley (D-R)	99,171	100.0
6 John F. Baldwin Jr. (R)	92,669	51.0
Howard H. Jewel (D)	89,192	49.0
7 Jeffery Cohelan (D)	65,699	50.9
John J. Allen Jr. (R)	63,270	49.1
8 George P. Miller (D-R)	181,437	100.0
9 J. Arthur Younger (R)	90,735	58.8
Elma D. Oddstad (R)	63,597	41.2
10 Charles S. Gubser (R)	118,715	54.6
Russell B. Bryan (D)	98,894	45.4
11 John J. McFall (D)	86,924	69.3
Fredrick S. Van Dyke (R)	38,427	30.7
12 B. F. Sisk (D)	112,702	81.1
Daniel K. Halpin (R)	26,228	18.9
13 Charles M. Teague (R)	98,381	57.0
William Kirk Stewart (D)	74,160	43.0
14 Harlan Hagen (D-R)	120,347	99.9
15 Gordon L. McDonough (R)	77,267	52.0
Emery S. Petty (D)	71,192	48.0
16 Donald L. Jackson (R)	70,724	57.8
Melvin Lennard (D)	51,616	42.2
17 Cecil R. King (D)	182,965	75.3
Leonard Di Miceli (R)	59,973	24.7
18 Craig Hosmer (R)	95,682	60.0
Harry S. May (D)	63,684	40.0
19 Chet Holifield (D)	131,421	83.4
Harry Vincent Leppek (R)	26,092	16.6
20 H. Allen Smith (R)	72,311	66.0
Raymond Robert Farrell (D)	37,331	34.1

Candidates	Votes	%
21 Edgar W. Hiestand (R)	127,238	51.9
Mrs. Rudd Brown (D)	118,141	48.1
22 Joe Holt (R)	87,785	55.4
Irving Glasband (D)	70,777	44.6
23 Clyde Doyle (D-R)	140,817	100.0
24 Glenard P. Lipscomb (R)	68,184	56.4
William H. Ware Jr. (D)	52,804	43.6
25 George A. Kasem (D)	135,009	50.1
Prescott O. Lieberg (R)	134,406	49.9
26 James Roosevelt (D)	125,495	72.2
Crispus Wright (R)	48,248	27.8
27 Harry R. Sheppard (D)	105,062	72.3
Robert M. Castle (R)	40,317	27.7
28 James B. Utt (R)	152,855	58.2
T. R. Boyett (D)	109,794	41.8
29 Dalip S. Saund (D)	64,518	62.4
John Babbage (R)	38,899	37.6
30 Bob Wilson (R)	112,290	55.3
Lionel Van Deerlin (D)	90,641	44.7

COLORADO

	Votes	%
1 Byron G. Rogers (D)	107,567	66.7
John L. Harpel (R)	53,801	33.3
2 Byron L. Johnson (D)	95,409	53.9
John G. Mackie (R)	80,467	45.5
3 J. Edgar Chenoweth (R)	63,655	50.2
Fred M. Betz (D)	63,112	49.8
4 Wayne N. Aspinall (D)	43,785	63.6
J. R. (Dick) Wells (R)	25,048	36.4

CONNECTICUT

	Votes	%
1 Emilio Q. Daddario (D)	146,115	54.3
Edwin H. May Jr. (R)	122,770	45.7
2 Chester Bowles (D)	79,672	53.3
Horace Seely-Brown Jr. (R)	69,837	46.7
3 Robert N. Giaimo (D)	101,028	56.2
Albert W. Cretella (R)	78,665	43.8
4 Donald J. Irwin (D)	119,766	50.9
Albert P. Morano (R)	115,505	49.1
5 John S. Monagan (D)	72,604	53.8
James T. Patterson (R)	62,353	46.2
AL Frank Kowalski (D)	542,315	56.0
Antoni N. Sadlak (R)	425,452	44.0

DELAWARE

	Votes	%
AL Harris B. McDowell Jr. (D)	76,797	50.2
Harry G. Haskell Jr. (R)	76,099	49.8

FLORIDA

	Votes	%
1 William C. Cramer (R)	79,876	58.8
Winton H. King (D)	56,005	41.2
2 Charles E. Bennett (D)	32,975	100.0
3 Robert L. F. Sikes (D)	27,855	100.0
4 Dante B. Fascell (D)	56,051	100.0
5 A. Sydney Herlong Jr. (D)	63,245	67.0
William C. Coleman (R)	31,188	33.0
6 Paul G. Rogers (D)	71,189	71.5
Charles P. Ware (R)	28,355	28.5
7 James A. Haley (D)	28,953	100.0
8 D. R. Matthews (D)	18,669	100.0

GEORGIA

	Votes	%
1 Prince H. Preston (D)	13,488	100.0
2 John L. Pilcher (D)	8,712	100.0
3 E. L. Forrester (D)	16,703	100.0
4 John J. Flynt Jr. (D)	17,054	100.0
5 James C. Davis (D)	32,135	100.0

Candidates	Votes	%
6 Carl Vinson (D)	15,569	100.0
7 Harlan Erwin Mitchell (D)	13,913	100.0
8 Iris Faircloth Blitch (D)	12,940	100.0
9 Phil M. Landrum (D)	14,019	100.0
10 Paul Brown (D)	14,103	100.0

Special Election

	Votes	%
7 Harlan Erwin Mitchell (D)	16,426	95.5

IDAHO

	Votes	%
1 Gracie B. Pfost (D)	60,083	62.4
A. B. Curtis (R)	36,178	37.6
2 Hamer H. Budge (R)	78,553	55.0
Tim Brennan (D)	64,214	45.0

ILLINOIS

	Votes	%
1 William L. Dawson (D)	60,778	72.2
Theodore R. M. Howard (R)	23,384	27.8
2 Barratt O'Hara (D)	75,691	68.3
Harold E. Marks (R)	34,203	30.9
3 William T. Murphy (D)	79,886	56.5
Emmet F. Byrne (R)	55,513	39.2
4 Edward J. Derwinski (R)	106,691	52.0
Leland H. Rayson (D)	98,657	48.0
5 John C. Kluczynski (D)	96,591	76.1
Theodore Wozniak (R)	30,374	23.9
6 Thomas J. O'Brien (D)	90,796	73.1
Frank S. Estes (R)	33,392	26.9
7 Roland V. Libonati (D)	90,974	83.0
Anthony A. Catena (R)	18,595	17.0
8 Daniel D. Rostenkowski (D)	73,413	74.6
William F. H. Schmidt (R)	25,011	25.4
9 Sidney R. Yates (D)	70,989	67.0
Homer P. Hargraves Jr. (R)	34,909	33.0
10 Harold R. Collier (R)	84,045	54.3
William J. McGah Jr. (D)	70,621	45.7
11 Roman C. Pucinski (D)	79,167	56.7
Timothy P. Sheehan (R)	60,347	43.3
12 Charles A. Boyle (D)	85,129	60.8
Allen A. Freeman (R)	54,967	39.2
13 Marguerite Stitt Church (R)	165,910	67.1
Laurence A. Kusek (D)	81,326	32.9
14 Elmer J. Hoffman (R)	96,381	64.3
Peter J. Fiefer (D)	53,449	35.7
15 Noah M. Mason (R)	58,829	52.5
Dorothy G. O'Brien (D)	53,196	47.5
16 Leo E. Allen (R)	71,049	61.4
Milton A. Lundstrom (D)	44,723	38.6
17 Leslie C. Arends (R)	70,125	61.0
William T. Larkin (D)	44,821	39.0
18 Robert H. Michel (R)	57,929	59.5
James W. McGee (D)	39,464	40.5
19 Robert B. Chiperfield (R)	52,049	50.5
John C. Watson (D)	51,104	49.5
20 Edna Simpson (R)	57,412	55.3
Henry W. Pollock (D)	46,076	44.4
21 Peter F. Mack Jr. (D)	87,134	58.8
Norma Eaton (R)	61,137	41.2
22 William L. Springer (R)	65,080	60.5
Carlton H. Myers (D)	42,533	39.5
23 George E. Shipley (D)	65,114	50.1
Charles W. Vursell (R)	64,927	49.9
24 Melvin Price (D)	94,231	76.1
Alex Chouinard (R)	29,670	24.0
25 Kenneth J. Gray (D)	78,385	58.2
Carl D. Sneed (R)	56,257	41.8

INDIANA

	Votes	%
1 Ray J. Madden (D)	95,801	66.4
Edward P. Keck (R)	47,588	33.0
2 Charles A. Halleck (R)	71,933	52.2
George H. Bowers (D)	65,792	47.8

INDIANA

	Candidates	Votes	%
3	John Brademas (D)	101,802	56.9
	F. Jay Nimtz (R)	77,014	43.1
4	E. Ross Adair (R)	69,745	50.1
	W. Robert Fleming (D)	69,478	49.9
5	J. Edward Roush (D)	97,184	53.7
	John V. Beamer (R)	83,852	46.3
6	Fred Wampler (D)	71,669	51.5
	Cecil M. Harden (R)	67,549	48.5
7	William G. Bray (R)	77,045	53.8
	Thomas L. Lemon (D)	66,217	46.2
8	Winfield K. Denton (D)	100,611	61.5
	Franklin E. Katterjohn (R)	63,005	38.5
9	Earl Hogan (D)	62,810	50.3
	Earl Wilson (R)	62,064	49.7
10	Randall S. Harmon (D)	76,757	50.8
	Ralph Harvey (R)	74,500	49.3
11	Joseph W. Barr (D)	113,674	52.1
	Charles B. Brownson (R)	104,555	47.9

IOWA

	Candidates	Votes	%
1	Fred Schwengel (R)	59,577	53.4
	Thomas J. Dailey (D)	51,996	46.6
2	Leonard G. Wolf (D)	67,022	51.1
	Henry O. Talle (R)	64,073	48.9
3	H. R. Gross (R)	61,920	53.7
	Michael Micich (D)	53,467	46.3
4	Steven V. Carter (D)	42,479	52.0
	John Kyl (R)	39,233	48.0
5	Neal Smith (D)	61,693	52.3
	Paul Cunningham (R)	56,320	47.7
6	Merwin Coad (D)	57,491	58.3
	Robert E. Waggoner (R)	41,204	41.8
7	Ben F. Jensen (R)	41,053	51.5
	Ellsworth O. Hays (D)	38,660	48.5
8	Charles B. Hoeven (R)	49,418	52.7
	Donald E. O'Brien (D)	44,310	47.3

KANSAS

	Candidates	Votes	%
1	William H. Avery (R)	60,198	51.2
	Robert W. Domme (D)	55,749	47.4
2	Newell A. George (D)	69,954	50.8
	Errett P. Scrivner (R)	67,882	49.3
3	Denver D. Hargis (D)	42,718	51.7
	Myron V. George (R)	39,872	48.3
4	Edward H. Rees (R)	89,611	50.7
	Warner Moore (D)	87,244	49.3
5	J. Floyd Breeding (D)	60,549	53.1
	Clifford R. Hope Jr. (R)	53,387	46.9
6	Wint Smith (R)	43,782	49.2
	Elmo J. Mahoney (D)	43,549	49.0

KENTUCKY

	Candidates	Votes	%
1	Frank Stubblefield (D)	41,214	85.0
	James G. Bondy (R)	7,263	15.0
2	William H. Natcher (D)	38,941	76.1
	Wayland Render (R)	12,239	23.9
3	Frank W. Burke (D)	73,121	52.2
	John M. Robsion Jr. (R)	67,059	47.8
4	Frank Chelf (D)	19,310	100.0
5	Brent Spence (D)	34,919	71.9
	Jule Appel (R)	13,631	28.1
6	John C. Watts (D)	29,199	94.7
	Wallace Jones	1,622	5.3
7	Carl D. Perkins (D)	56,756	65.8
	E. L. Raybourn (R)	29,505	34.2
8	Eugene Siler (R)	34,728	68.0
	W. D. Scalf (D)	16,311	32.0

LOUISIANA

	Candidates	Votes	%
1	F. Edward Hebert (D)	41,861	100.0
2	Hale Boggs (D)	46,614	91.8
	John Patrick Conway (R)	4,160	8.2
3	Edwin E. Willis (D)	8,692	100.0
4	Overton Brooks (D)	23,844	100.0
5	Otto E. Passman (D)	14,900	100.0
6	James H. Morrison (D)	20,599	100.0
7	T. A. Thompson (D)	10,328	100.0
8	Harold B. McSween (D)	11,125	100.0

MAINE

	Candidates	Votes	%
1	James C. Oliver (D)	55,686	52.1
	Robert Hale (R)	51,231	47.9
2	Frank M. Coffin (D)	59,054	61.3
	Neil Bishop (R)	37,219	38.7
3	Clifford G. McIntire (R)	40,156	56.0
	Gerald J. Grady (D)	31,616	44.1

MARYLAND

	Candidates	Votes	%
1	Thomas F. Johnson (D)	32,328	50.6
	Edward T. Miller (R)	31,610	49.4
2	Daniel B. Brewster (D)	87,667	61.0
	Fife Symington (R)	56,165	39.1
3	Edward A. Garmatz (D)	49,649	84.0
	Harry Kemper (R)	9,470	16.0
4	George H. Fallon (D)	45,646	71.6
	Louis W. Collier (R)	18,094	28.4
5	Richard E. Lankford (D)	96,919	75.1
	Robert E. Ennis (R)	32,072	24.9
6	John R. Foley (D)	78,987	51.4
	DeWitt S. Hyde (R)	74,683	48.6
7	Samuel N. Friedel (D)	72,692	73.6
	Elizabeth P. Brown (R)	26,144	26.5

MASSACHUSETTS

	Candidates	Votes	%
1	Silvio O. Conte (R)	66,067	55.3
	James M. Burns (D)	52,853	44.2
2	Edward P. Boland (D)	103,079	100.0
3	Phillip J. Philbin (D)	114,483	100.0
4	Harold D. Donohue (D)	93,993	63.8
	Charles D. Briggs Jr. (R)	53,359	36.2
5	Edith Nourse Rogers (R)	116,072	66.0
	William H. Sullivan (D)	59,746	34.0
6	William H. Bates (R)	106,807	100.0
7	Thomas J. Lane (D)	84,243	75.6
	Robert T. Breed (R)	27,215	24.4
8	Torbert H. Macdonald (D)	91,263	66.4
	Gordon F. Hughes (R)	46,274	33.6
9	Hastings Keith (R)	82,659	54.7
	John Almeida Jr. (D)	68,486	45.3
10	Laurence Curtis (R)	71,100	52.2
	John L. Saltonstall Jr. (D)	65,159	47.8
11	Thomas P. O'Neill Jr. (D)	68,353	80.4
	Elliott H. Stone (R)	16,669	19.6
12	John W. McCormack (D)	72,523	100.0
13	James A. Burke (D)	89,073	53.5
	William W. Jenness (R)	77,400	46.5
14	Joseph W. Martin Jr. (R)	90,751	61.0
	Edward F. Doolan (D)	57,920	39.0

MICHIGAN

	Candidates	Votes	%
1	Thaddeus M. Machrowicz (D)	82,288	90.4
	Walter Czarnecki (R)	8,502	9.3
2	George Meader (R)	73,954	58.8
	Robert G. Hall (D)	51,323	40.8
3	August E. Johansen (R)	68,144	60.4
	John R. O'Meara (D)	44,189	39.2
4	Clare E. Hoffman (R)	59,780	59.9
	Gordon A. Elferdink (D)	39,765	39.8
5	Gerald R. Ford Jr. (R)	88,156	63.6
	Richard F. Vander Veen (D)	50,203	36.2
6	Charles E. Chamberlain (R)	92,313	52.1
	Don Hayworth (D)	84,418	47.7
7	James G. O'Hara (D)	87,299	50.7
	Robert J. McIntosh (R)	84,531	49.1
8	Alvin M. Bentley (R)	69,858	62.2
	James O. Pino (D)	42,467	37.8
9	Robert P. Griffin (R)	56,780	56.7
	Jan B. Vanderploeg (D)	43,196	43.1
10	Elford A. Cederberg (R)	54,316	61.1
	Daniel B. Reed (D)	34,390	38.7
11	Victor A. Knox (R)	41,689	52.3
	Prentiss M. Brown Jr. (D)	37,995	47.6
12	John B. Bennett (R)	39,239	57.0
	Joseph S. Mack (D)	29,506	42.9
13	Charles C. Diggs Jr. (D)	57,354	72.7
	Charles P. White (R)	21,280	27.0
14	Louis C. Rabaut (D)	97,236	64.2
	Lois V. Nair (R)	53,987	35.7
15	John D. Dingell (D)	79,216	78.5
	Austin W. Curtis Jr. (R)	21,414	21.2
16	John Lesinski (D)	145,665	71.8
	Ralph B. Guy (R)	56,488	27.8
17	Martha W. Griffiths (D)	96,660	60.3
	Lucas S. Miel (R)	63,323	39.5
18	William S. Broomfield (R)	101,100	52.6
	Leslie H. Hudson (D)	90,526	47.1

MINNESOTA

	Candidates	Votes	%
1	Albert H. Quie (R)	73,345	57.0
	Eugene P. Foley (DFL)	55,445	43.1
2	Ancher Nelsen (R)	71,623	57.1
	Conrad H. Hammar (DFL)	53,869	42.9
3	Roy W. Wier (DFL)	98,449	51.6
	Leonard E. Lindquist (R)	92,190	48.4
4	Joseph E. Karth (DFL)	72,952	56.4
	Frank S. Farrell (R)	56,484	43.6
5	Walter H. Judd (R)	59,739	57.3
	Joseph Robbie (DFL)	44,453	42.7
6	Fred Marshall (DFL)	73,881	64.3
	Hugo Holmstrom (R)	41,018	35.7
7	H. Carl Andersen (R)	61,265	53.3
	A. I. Johnson (DFL)	53,689	46.7
8	John A. Blatnik (DFL)	97,046	75.6
	Roy W. Ranum (R)	31,343	24.4
9	Odin Langen (R)	47,863	50.7
	Coya Knutson (DFL)	46,473	49.3

Special Election

		Votes	%
1	Albert H. Quie (R)	44,276	50.3
	Eugene P. Foley (DFL)	43,674	49.7

MISSISSIPPI

		Votes	%
1	Thomas G. Abernethy (D)	12,413	100.0
2	Jamie L. Whitten (D)	7,982	100.0
3	Frank E. Smith (D)	4,644	100.0
4	John Bell Williams (D)	8,665	100.0
5	Arthur Winstead (D)	14,517	100.0
6	William M. Colmer (D)	13,243	100.0

MISSOURI

		Votes	%
1	Frank M. Karsten (D)	99,368	75.8
	Paul E. Corning Jr. (R)	31,804	24.3
2	Thomas B. Curtis (R)	88,321	51.9
	James L. Sullivan (D)	81,811	48.1
3	Leonor K. Sullivan (D)	63,679	79.2
	Josiah C. Thomas (R)	16,753	20.8
4	George H. Christopher (D)	72,792	64.0
	James A. Rahm (R)	40,912	36.0
5	Richard Bolling (D)	53,622	70.0
	Richard W. Byrne (R)	22,953	30.0
6	W. R. Hull Jr. (D)	64,277	64.9
	Clyde M. Kirk (R)	34,758	35.1
7	Charles H. Brown (D)	76,239	53.7
	Noel Cox (R)	65,666	46.3
8	A. S. J. Carnahan (D)	58,628	64.3
	Francis Howard (R)	32,543	35.7
9	Clarence Cannon (D)	67,555	64.8
	Anthony Schroeder (R)	36,758	35.2

MISSOURI

	Candidates	Votes	%
10	Paul C. Jones	44,892	70.7
	Gilbert Degenhardt (R)	18,633	29.3
11	Morgan M. Moulder (D)	54,014	56.9
	Don W. Owensby (R)	40,839	43.1

MONTANA

	Candidates	Votes	%
	Lee Metcalf (D)	68,586	69.5
	Jean Walterskirschen (R)	30,111	30.5
2	LeRoy H. Anderson (D)	79,140	61.0
	Ashton Jones (R)	50,633	39.0

NEBRASKA

	Candidates	Votes	%
1	Phil Weaver (R)	62,770	53.4
	Clair A. Callan (D)	54,705	46.6
2	Glenn Cunningham (R)	67,660	64.8
	Francis M. Casey (D)	36,842	35.3
3	Lawrence Brock (D)	53,033	55.1
	Robert D. Harrison (R)	43,236	44.9
4	Donald F. McGinley (D)	50,870	52.3
	Arthur L. Miller (R)	46,474	47.7

NEVADA

	Candidates	Votes	%
AL	Walter S. Baring (D)	55,053	66.9
	Robert C. Horton (R)	27,275	33.1

NEW HAMPSHIRE

	Candidates	Votes	%
1	Chester E. Merrow (R)	62,734	58.5
	Alphonse Roy (D)	44,051	41.0
2	Perkins Bass (R)	52,636	58.4
	Stuart V. Nims (D)	37,212	41.3

NEW JERSEY

	Candidates	Votes	%
1	William T. Cahill (R)	96,619	50.3
	Alexander Feinberg (D)	94,790	49.3
2	Milton W. Glenn (R)	58,621	53.4
	Joseph G. Hancock (D)	50,558	46.1
3	James C. Auchincloss (R)	98,826	56.1
	Thomas F. Guthrie Jr. (D)	77,423	43.9
4	Frank Thompson Jr. (D)	83,388	63.0
	A. Jerome Moore (R)	48,990	37.0
5	Peter H. B. Frelinghuysen Jr. (R)	111,250	55.7
	David S. North (D)	87,966	44.0
6	Florence P. Dwyer (R)	88,084	51.1
	Jack B. Dunn (D)	80,779	46.9
7	William B. Widnall (R)	103,169	59.6
	J. Emmet Cassidy (D)	69,250	40.0
8	Gordon Canfield (R)	68,385	58.1
	Joseph R. Brumale (D)	48,481	41.2
9	Frank C. Osmers Jr. (R)	92,513	57.4
	Daniel W. Allen (D)	67,633	42.0
10	Peter W. Rodino Jr. (D)	60,482	63.9
	G. George Addonizio (R)	32,946	34.8
11	Hugh J. Addonizio (D)	50,821	59.3
	John P. Langan (R)	34,821	40.7
12	George M. Wallhauser (R)	57,510	52.7
	Thomas J. Holleran (D)	49,463	45.3
13	Cornelius E. Gallagher (D)	61,094	66.1
	Samuel F. Kanis (R)	23,001	24.9
14	Dominick V. Daniels (D)	56,475	62.9
	Frank A. Musto (R)	29,614	33.0

NEW MEXICO

	Candidates	Votes	%
AL	Joseph M. Montoya (D)	124,924✓	
	Thomas G. Morris (D)	115,928✓	
	William A. Thompson (R)	72,922	
	George W. McKim (R)	70,925	

NEW YORK

	Candidates	Votes	%
1	Stuyvesant Wainwright (R)	155,387	57.5
	Otis G. Pike (D, L)	115,019	42.5
2	Steven B. Derounian (R)	113,820	60.5
	Walter A. Lynch Jr. (D, L)	74,194	39.5
3	Frank J. Becker (R)	109,245	54.4
	A. William Larson (D, L)	91,514	45.6
4	Seymour Halpern (R)	78,054	52.6
	Joseph J. Perrini (D, L)	70,437	47.4
5	Albert A. Bosch (R)	56,839	52.1
	William Kerwick (D)	47,661	43.7
6	Lester Holtzman (D, L)	106,762	63.6
	George T. Reilly (R)	61,204	36.4
7	James J. Delaney (D, L)	71,007	61.1
	Edward V. Lisoski (R)	45,135	38.9
8	Victor L. Anfuso (D, L)	43,656	71.7
	Leon F. Nadrowski (R)	17,271	28.4
9	Eugene J. Keogh (D, L)	61,816	72.1
	Anton Eyring (R)	23,957	27.9
10	Edna F. Kelly (D, L)	77,351	76.1
	Jerome P. Schneider (R)	24,286	23.9
11	Emanuel Celler (D, L)	105,011	81.4
	Jesse M. Browser (R)	24,034	18.6
12	Francis E. Dorn (R)	51,861	52.7
	Thomas J. Cuite (D)	39,275	39.9
	Leroy Bowman (L)	7,322	7.4
13	Abraham J. Multer (D, L)	88,406	76.1
	Hyman D. Siegel (R)	27,701	23.9
14	John J. Rooney (D, L)	60,703	70.6
	Anthony D'Allessandro (R)	25,319	29.4
15	John H. Ray (R, U TAX)	65,318	52.8
	Vincent R. Fitzpatrick (D, L)	58,351	47.2
16	Adam Clayton Powell Jr. (D, R)	56,383	90.8
	Earl Brown (L)	5,705	9.2
17	John V. Lindsay (R)	54,459	53.9
	Anthony B. Akers (D, L)	46,570	46.1
18	Alfred E. Santangelo (D)	36,601	59.4
	George A. Eyer Jr. (R)	20,848	33.8
	Manuel Velazquez (L)	4,201	6.8
19	Leonard Farbstein (D, L)	55,069	73.1
	Gonzales Suarez (R)	20,232	26.9
20	Ludwig Teller (D, L)	50,735	67.0
	Milton H. Adler (R)	24,933	33.0
21	Herbert Zelenko (D, L)	67,743	72.5
	Carl Medonick (R)	25,699	27.5
22	James C. Healey (D)	65,996	65.2
	Alex J. Soled (R)	20,777	20.5
	David I. Wells (L)	14,391	14.2
23	Isidore Dollinger (D)	49,452	71.5
	Simon M. Koenig (R)	12,278	17.7
	Hector Mathew (L)	7,469	10.8
24	Charles A. Buckley (D)	71,616	56.2
	Charles V. Scanlan (R)	35,993	28.3
	Murray Koenig (L)	19,759	15.5
25	Paul A. Fino (R)	79,857	57.8
	Neal P. Bottiglieri (D, L)	58,396	42.2
26	Edwin B. Dooley (R)	98,677	63.2
	Phil E. Gilbert Jr. (D, L)	57,465	36.8
27	Robert R. Barry (R)	104,240	58.2
	Richard W. McSpedon (D, L)	74,883	41.8
28	Katharine St.George (R)	84,536	59.7
	David Sive (D)	53,981	38.1
29	J. Ernest Wharton (R)	93,647	63.4
	Christopher D. Morris (D, L)	54,153	36.6
30	Leo W. O'Brien (D, L)	109,744	64.7
	George H. Witbeck Jr. (R)	59,958	35.3
31	Dean P. Taylor (R)	87,704	63.8
	John R. Cummins (D, L)	49,777	36.2
32	Samuel S. Stratton (D, L)	73,384	54.0
	Walter C. Shaw (R)	62,443	46.0
33	Clarence E. Kilburn (R)	73,698	64.8
	Robert P. McDonald (D, L)	40,010	35.2
34	Alexander Pirnie (R)	70,482	50.8
	Edwin L. Slusarczyk (D, L)	68,271	49.2

	Candidates	Votes	%
35	R. Walter Riehlman (R)	90,285	53.8
	Caryl M. Kline (D, L)	77,449	46.2
36	John Taber (R)	84,019	64.7
	Frank B. Lent (D, L)	45,822	35.3
37	Howard W. Robison (R)	101,279	65.8
	Francis P. Hogan (D, L)	52,636	34.2
38	Jessica McC Weis (R)	92,944	58.2
	Alphonse L. Cassetti (D, L)	66,806	41.8
39	Harold C. Ostertag (R)	90,004	65.2
	Harold L. Rakov (D, L)	48,144	34.8
40	William E. Miller (R)	90,066	60.8
	Mariano A. Lucca (D)	54,728	36.9
41	Thaddeus J. Dulski (D, L)	60,360	50.3
	James O. Moore Jr. (R)	59,634	49.7
42	John R. Pillion (R)	99,799	58.9
	Joseph R. Stiglmeier (D, L)	69,747	41.1
43	Daniel A. Reed (R)	68,896	63.8
	T. Joseph Lynch (D)	36,799	34.1

Special Election

		Votes	%
37	Howard W. Robison (R)	45,920	59.8
	Francis P. Hogan (D, L)	30,891	40.2

NORTH CAROLINA

	Candidates	Votes	%
1	Herbert C. Bonner (D)	12,743	100.0
2	L. H. Fountain (D)	17,061	100.0
3	Graham A. Barden (D)	22,426	79.1
	Joe A. Dunn (R)	5,927	20.9
4	Harold D. Cooley (D)	30,505	75.6
	L. T. Dark Jr. (R)	9,863	24.4
5	Ralph J. Scott (D)	40,544	71.6
	William E. Morrow (R)	16,048	28.4
6	Carl T. Durham (D)	35,715	100.0
7	Alton Lennon (D)	27,902	89.0
	C. Dana Malpass (R)	3,461	11.0
8	A. Paul Kitchin (D)	43,793	63.4
	F. D. B. Harding (R)	25,276	36.6
9	Hugh Q. Alexander (D)	57,672	66.5
	William White (R)	29,065	33.5
10	Charles Raper Jonas (R)	56,487	51.9
	David Clark (D)	52,306	48.1
11	Basil L. Whitener (D)	37,926	100.0
12	David M. Hall (D)	52,609	62.5
	W. Harold Sams (R)	31,524	37.5

NORTH DAKOTA

	Candidates	Votes	%
AL	Quentin N. Burdick (D)	99,562✓	
	Don L. Short (R)	97,862✓	
	Orris G. Nordhougen (R)	92,124	
	S. B. Hocking (D)	78,889	

OHIO

	Candidates	Votes	%
1	Gordon H. Scherer (R)	70,686	56.6
	W. Ted Osborne (D)	54,119	43.4
2	William E. Hess (R)	86,656	54.7
	James O. Bradley (D)	71,674	45.3
3	Paul F. Schenck (R)	102,806	52.4
	Thomas B. Talbot (D)	93,401	47.6
4	William M. McCulloch (R)	73,448	61.0
	Marjorie Conrad Struna (D)	46,933	39.0
5	Delbert L. Latta (R)	52,612	53.9
	George Rafferty (D)	44,971	46.1
6	James G. Polk (D)	76,566	62.0
	Elmer S. Barrett (R)	46,924	38.0
7	Clarence J. Brown (R)	75,085	60.5
	Joseph A. Sullivan (D)	48,994	39.5
8	Jackson E. Betts (R)	62,232	61.3
	Virgil M. Gase (D)	39,343	38.7
9	Thomas L. Ashley (D)	102,115	61.6
	William K. Gernheuser (R)	63,660	38.4
10	Walter H. Moeller (D)	47,939	52.9
	Homer E. Abele (R)	42,607	47.1

OHIO

Candidates	Votes	%
11 Robert E. Cook (D)	79,468	50.3
David Dennison Jr. (R)	78,501	49.7
12 Samuel L. Devine (R)	100,684	54.4
Walter J. Shapter Jr. (D)	84,470	45.6
13 Albert D. Baumhart Jr. (R)	65,169	58.9
J. William McCray (D)	45,390	41.1
14 William H. Ayres (R)	114,827	60.1
Jack B. Arnold (D)	76,138	39.9
15 John E. Henderson (R)	48,316	57.3
Herbert U. Smith (D)	36,062	42.7
16 Frank T. Bow (R)	100,678	57.4
John G. Freedom (D)	74,660	42.6
17 Robert W. Levering (D)	63,650	51.7
Lawrence Burns (R)	59,490	48.3
18 Wayne L. Hays (D)	88,813	71.6
Francis Wallace (R)	35,322	28.5
19 Michael J. Kirwan (D)	93,660	75.0
Loren E. Van Brocklin (R)	31,192	25.0
20 Michael A. Feighan (D)	113,200	79.4
Malvern E. Schultz (R)	29,308	20.6
21 Charles A. Vanik (D)	93,987	80.4
Ermer L. Watson (R)	22,956	19.6
22 Frances P. Bolton (R)	71,139	55.3
Chat Paterson (D)	57,508	44.7
23 William E. Minshall Jr. (R)	95,267	66.5
Daniel Winston (D)	47,953	33.5

OKLAHOMA

Candidates	Votes	%
1 Page H. Belcher (R)	74,853	50.8
Herbert William Wright Jr. (D)	71,190	48.3
2 Ed Edmondson (D)	75,492	79.1
Milo Ritter (R)	19,996	20.9
3 Carl Albert (D)	43,868	90.9
Chapin Wallace (R)	4,398	9.1
4 Tom Steed (D)	43,837	74.1
Rolla C. Calkins (R)	15,359	26.0
5 John Jarman (D)	79,917	82.3
Hobart H. Hobbs (R)	17,137	17.7
6 Toby Morris (D)	54,967	66.7
Fred L. Coogan (R)	27,425	33.3

OREGON

Candidates	Votes	%
1 Walter Norblad (R)	95,420	54.9
Robert Y. Thornton (D)	78,362	45.1
2 Al Ullman (D)	50,166	61.1
Marion T. Weatherford (R)	31,987	38.9
3 Edith Green (D)	131,164	65.8
John Johnston (R)	68,235	34.2
4 Charles O. Porter (D)	79,166	56.3
Paul Geddes (R)	61,386	43.7

PENNSYLVANIA

Candidates	Votes	%
1 William A. Barrett (D)	67,531	64.7
Gerard Iannelli (R)	36,854	35.3
2 Kathryn E. Granahan (D)	84,058	66.3
Maurice M. Green (R)	42,759	33.7
3 James A. Byrne (D)	65,201	63.5
James Thomas McDermott (R)	37,420	36.5
4 Robert N. C. Nix (D)	63,031	72.6
Cecil B. Moore (R)	23,845	27.5
5 William J. Green Jr. (D)	100,680	55.3
D. Donald Jamieson (R)	81,530	44.8
6 Herman Toll (D)	83,491	55.4
Fred C. Gartner (R)	67,205	44.6
7 William H. Milliken Jr. (R)	114,275	59.2
Hubert P. Earle (D)	78,747	40.8
8 Willard S. Curtin (R)	85,010	54.3
Harold Lefcourt (D)	71,583	45.7
9 Paul B. Dague (R)	88,193	61.9
James C. N. Paul (D)	54,220	38.1
10 Stanley A. Prokop (D)	74,890	50.4
Joseph L. Carrigg (R)	73,601	49.6

Candidates	Votes	%
11 Daniel J. Flood (D)	89,167	61.7
Herman C. Kersteen (R)	55,349	38.3
12 Ivor D. Fenton (R)	64,960	54.9
Charles E. Lotz (D)	53,402	45.1
13 John A. Lafore Jr. (R)	104,156	62.9
John T. Synnestvedt (D)	61,475	37.1
14 George M. Rhodes (D)	51,281	58.3
Thomas C. Anthony Jr. (R)	36,170	41.1
15 Francis E. Walter (D)	60,742	61.1
Luther H. Ackerman (R)	38,726	38.9
16 Walter M. Mumma (R)	70,810	56.6
John H. Bream (D)	54,245	43.4
17 Alvin Bush (R)	65,071	56.0
C. Max Hess (D)	51,053	44.0
18 Richard M. Simpson (R)	67,719	56.3
Ross E. Hershberger (D)	52,514	43.7
19 James M. Quigley (D)	67,603	51.5
S. Walter Stauffer (R)	63,749	48.5
20 James E. Van Zandt (R)	61,010	64.9
Julia L. Maietta (D)	33,060	35.1
21 John H. Dent (D)	70,828	59.2
Edward S. Stiteler (R)	48,925	40.9
22 John P. Saylor (R)	77,407	57.0
Robert S. Glass (D)	58,434	43.0
23 Leon H. Gavin (R)	60,080	61.1
Thomas P. Kennedy (D)	38,179	38.9
24 Carroll D. Kearns (R)	76,870	53.8
James P. O'Brien (D)	65,937	46.2
25 Frank M. Clark (D)	80,704	58.9
Thomas W. King Jr. (R)	56,375	41.1
26 Thomas E. Morgan (D)	92,755	64.8
Harry T. Zimmer Jr. (R)	50,403	35.2
27 James G. Fulton (R)	105,998	64.1
Emery F. Bacon (D)	59,283	35.9
28 William S. Moorhead (D)	82,081	67.3
Harry L. Verbofsky (R)	39,900	32.7
29 Robert J. Corbett (R)	97,203	63.6
Lee T. Sellars (D)	55,575	36.4
30 Elmer J. Holland (D)	98,244	66.7
Harold E. Morgan (R)	49,093	33.3

RHODE ISLAND

Candidates	Votes	%
1 Aime J. Forand (D)	97,425	62.9
Francis E. Martineau (R)	57,581	37.2
2 John E. Fogarty (D)	117,506	63.3
Robert L. Gammell (R)	67,942	36.6

SOUTH CAROLINA

Candidates	Votes	%
1 L. Mendel Rivers (D)	13,538	100.0
2 John J. Riley (D)	13,677	100.0
3 W. J. Bryan Dorn (D)	9,528	99.9
4 Robert T. Ashmore (D)	17,247	100.0
5 Robert W. Hemphill (D)	9,780	100.0
6 John L. McMillan (D)	12,862	100.0

SOUTH DAKOTA

Candidates	Votes	%
1 George McGovern (D)	107,202	53.4
Joe Foss (R)	93,388	46.6
2 E. Y. Berry (R)	31,908	55.6
J. T. McCullen (D)	25,491	44.4

TENNESSEE

Candidates	Votes	%
1 B. Carroll Reece (D)	42,615	58.7
Mayne W. Miller (D)	29,999	41.3
2 Howard H. Baker (R)	49,420	67.7
John Grady O'Hara Sr. (D)	23,470	32.2
3 James B. Frazier Jr. (D)	31,267	100.0
4 Joe L. Evins (D)	38,062	100.0
5 J. Carlton Loser (D)	30,879	94.4
Porter Freeman (R)	1,824#	5.6
6 Ross Bass (D)	33,445	97.2
7 Tom Murray (D)	24,053	100.0
8 Robert A. Everett (D)	19,145	100.0
9 Clifford Davis (D)	46,550	100.0

TEXAS

Candidates	Votes	%
1 Wright Patman (D)	19,203	100.0
2 Jack Brooks (D)	47,092	100.0
3 Lindley Beckworth (D)	22,751	100.0
4 Sam Rayburn (D)	15,942	100.0
5 Bruce Alger (R)	62,722	52.6
Barefoot Sanders (D)	56,566	47.4
6 Olin Teague (D)	25,827	100.0
7 John Dowdy (D)	22,733	96.7
8 Albert Thomas (D)	33,393	88.2
R. E. Nesmith (R)	4,477	11.8
9 Clark W. Thompson (D)	36,012	100.0
10 Homer Thornberry (D)	28,990	100.0
11 W. R. Poage (D)	21,900	100.0
12 Jim Wright (D)	38,180	100.0
13 Frank Ikard (D)	27,671	100.0
14 John Young (D)	37,861	100.0
15 Joe M. Kilgore (D)	28,404	100.0
16 J. T. Rutherford (D)	28,744	100.0
17 Omar Burleson (D)	25,123	100.0
18 Walter Rogers (D)	34,617	100.0
19 George Mahon (D)	29,068	100.0
20 Paul J. Kilday (D)	23,539	100.0
21 O. C. Fisher (D)	26,497	100.0
22 Bob Casey (D)	43,660	61.7
T. Everton Kennerly (R)	23,317	33.0
Jack Gardner	3,789	5.4

UTAH

Candidates	Votes	%
1 Henry Aldous Dixon (R)	58,141	53.9
M. Blaine Peterson (D)	49,735	46.1
2 David S. King (D)	91,213	51.1
William A. Dawson (R)	87,234	48.9

VERMONT

Candidates	Votes	%
AL William H. Meyer (D)	63,131	51.5
Harold J. Arthur (R)	59,536	48.5

VIRGINIA

Candidates	Votes	%
1 Thomas N. Downing (D)	31,765	99.9
2 Porter Hardy Jr. (D)	32,758	100.0
3 J. Vaughan Gary (D)	34,040	76.1
Richard R. Ryder (R)	10,668	23.9
4 Watkins M. Abbitt (D)	37,679	87.1
Frank M. McCann (I)	5,556	12.9
5 William M. Tuck (D)	26,322	100.0
6 Richard H. Poff (R)	37,779	56.7
Richard F. Pence (R)	28,530	42.9
7 Burr P. Harrison (D)	30,486	76.6
Henry A. Oder Jr. (I)	9,294	23.4
8 Howard W. Smith (D)	28,815	99.7
9 W. Pat Jennings (D)	34,685	76.6
T. L. Maness (I)	10,615	23.4
10 Joel T. Broyhill (R)	37,764	52.3
Joseph H. Freehill (D)	33,553	46.5

WASHINGTON

Candidates	Votes	%
1 Thomas M. Pelly (R)	98,897	70.1
Robert Odman (D)	42,128	29.9
2 Jack Westland (R)	62,152	53.6
Hugh B. Mitchell (D)	53,436	46.1
3 Russell V. Mack (R)	69,745	60.9
Victor A. Meyers (D)	44,515	38.9
4 Catherine May (R)	66,544	54.0
Frank LeRoux (D)	56,308	45.7
5 Walt Horan (R)	67,072	53.2
Tom Delaney (D)	58,431	46.3
6 Thor C. Tollefson (R)	63,560	53.5
John M. Coffee (D)	54,536	45.9
7 Don Magnuson (D)	96,841	70.9
Bob Jones (R)	39,708	29.1

WEST VIRGINIA

	Candidates	Votes	%
1	Arch A. Moore Jr. (R)	55,613	54.6
	Robert H. Mollohan (D)	46,262	45.4
2	Harley O. Staggers (D)	57,761	62.7
	Ward W. Keesecker (R)	34,436	37.4
3	Cleveland M. Bailey (D)	59,084	59.9
	Rex Keith Bumgardner (R)	39,507	40.1
4	Ken Hechler (D)	60,794	51.5
	Will E. Neal (R)	57,291	48.5
5	Elizabeth Kee (D)	63,873	99.8
6	John M. Slack Jr. (D)	93,209	66.1
	F. O'Dair Duff (R)	47,852	33.9

WISCONSIN

	Candidates	Votes	%
1	Gerald T. Flynn (D)	63,065	50.6
	Eleanor J. Smith (R)	61,615	49.4
2	Robert W. Kastenmeier (D)	78,009	52.1
	Donald E. Tewes (R)	71,748	47.9
3	Gardner R. Withrow (R)	47,858	51.2
	Norman M. Clapp (D)	45,608	48.8
4	Clement J. Zablocki (D)	112,226	74.1
	James J. Arnold (R)	39,167	25.9
5	Henry S. Reuss (D)	104,374	69.5
	Otto R. Werkmeister (R)	45,901	30.5
6	William K. Van Pelt (R)	61,490	52.8
	James Megellas (D)	55,031	47.2

	Candidates	Votes	%
7	Melvin R. Laird (R)	59,186	60.5
	Kenneth Traeger (D)	38,702	39.5
8	John W. Byrnes (R)	69,682	57.3
	Milo Singler (D)	51,887	42.7
9	Lester R. Johnson (D)	55,420	63.1
	Charles A. Hornbeck (R)	32,425	36.9
10	Alvin E. O'Konski (R)	58,801	67.1
	Basil G. Kennedy (D)	28,830	32.9

WYOMING

	Candidates	Votes	%
AL	Keith Thomson (R)	59,894	53.6
	Ray Whitaker (D)	51,886	46.4

1959 House Elections

HAWAII

(Became a state Aug. 21, 1959)

	Candidates	Votes	%
AL	Daniel K. Inouye (D)	111,727	68.2
	Charles H. Silva (R)	51,058	31.2

IOWA

Special Election

		Votes	%
4	John Henry Kyl (R)#	28,326	52.3
	C. Edwin Gilmour (D)	25,809	47.7

NEW YORK

Special Election

		Votes	%
43	Charles E. Goodell (R)	27,454	65.0
	Robert E. McCaffery (D)	14,250	33.8

House Candidates Index

For an index of all House candidates listed in this section (pages 192-324), see pages 340-371. Instructions for use of the House Candidates Index appear on page 340.

1960 House Elections

ALABAMA

	Candidates	Votes	%
1	Frank W. Boykin (D)	45,225	100.0
2	George Grant (D)	44,487	100.0
3	George Andrews (D)	33,881	100.0
4	Kenneth A. Roberts (D)	34,855	99.9
5	Albert Rains (D)	48,772	100.0
6	Armistead I. Selden Jr. (D)	23,245	100.0
7	Carl Elliott (D)	36,124	100.0
8	Robert E. Jones (D)	52,411	79.2
	H. G. Williams (R)	13,800	20.8
9	George Huddleston Jr. (D)	70,567	67.3
	William P. Ivey (R)	34,317	32.7

ALASKA

	Candidates	Votes	%
AL	Ralph J. Rivers (D)	33,546	56.8
	R. L. (Ron) Rettig (R)	25,517	43.2

ARIZONA

	Candidates	Votes	%
1	John J. Rhodes (R)	121,563	59.2
	Richard F. Harless (D)	83,676	40.8
2	Stewart L. Udall (D)	95,512	55.8
	Mac C. Matheson (R)	75,811	44.3

ARKANSAS

	Candidates	Votes	%
1	Ezekiel C. Gathings (D)		100.0
2	Wilbur D. Mills (D)		100.0
3	James W. Trimble (D)		100.0
4	Oren Harris (D)		100.0
5	Dale Alford (D)	57,617	82.7
	L. J. Churchill (R)	12,054	17.3
6	William F. Norrell (D)		100.0

CALIFORNIA

	Candidates	Votes	%
1	Clem Miller (D)	115,829	51.6
	Fred G. Dupuis (R)	108,505	48.4
2	Harold T. Johnson (D)	109,565	62.7
	Fredric H. Nagel Jr. (R)	65,198	37.3
3	John E. Moss Jr. (D)	200,439	100.0
4	William S. Mailliard (R)	118,249	65.3
	Phillips D. Davies (D)	62,814	34.7
5	John F. Shelley (D)	104,507	83.7
	Nick Verreos (R)	20,305	16.3
6	John F. Baldwin (R)	128,418	58.7
	Douglas R. Page (D)	90,260	41.3
7	Jeffery Cohelan (D)	79,776	57.0
	Lewis F. Sherman (R)	60,065	43.0
8	George P. Miller (D)	152,476	62.0
	Robert E. Hannon (R)	93,403	38.0
9	J. Arthur Younger (R)	116,589	59.2
	John D. Kaster (D)	80,227	40.8
10	Charles S. Gubser (R)	170,063	58.9
	Russell B. Bryan (D)	118,520	41.1
11	John J. McFall (D)	97,368	65.4
	Clifford B. Bull (R)	51,473	34.6
12	B. F. Sisk (D-R)	141,974	99.9
13	Charles M. Teague (R)	146,072	65.0
	L. Boyd Finch (D)	78,597	35.0
14	Harlen Hagen (D)	97,026	56.5
	G. Ray Arnett (R)	74,800	43.5
15	Gordon L. McDonough (R)	89,234	51.3
	Norman H. Martell (D)	84,650	48.6
16	Alphonzo Bell (R)	83,601	55.4
	Jerry Pacht (D)	67,318	44.6
17	Cecil R. King (D)	206,620	67.7
	Tom Coffee (R)	98,510	32.3
18	Craig Hosmer (R)	129,851	70.0
	D. Patrick Ahern (D)	55,735	30.0
19	Chet Holifield (D)	145,479	78.2
	Gordon S. McWilliams (R)	40,491	21.8

	Candidates	Votes	%
20	H. Allen Smith (R)	90,214	70.1
	Gareth W. Sadler (D)	38,497	29.9
21	Edgar W. Hiestand (R)	179,376	58.4
	Mrs. Rudd Brown (D)	127,591	41.6
22	James C. Corman (D)	104,919	51.1
	Lemoine Blanchard (R)	100,321	48.9
23	Clyde Doyle (D)	148,415	74.2
	Emmett A. Schwartz (R)	51,548	25.8
24	Glenard P. Lipscomb (R)	82,497	59.7
	Norman Hass (D)	55,613	40.3
25	John H. Rousselot (R)	182,545	53.6
	George A. Kasem (D)	158,289	46.4
26	James Roosevelt (D)	150,318	73.4
	William E. McIntyre (R)	54,540	26.6
27	Harry R. Sheppard (D)	123,645	66.8
	Robert M. Castle (R)	61,484	33.2
28	James B. Utt (R)	241,765	60.9
	Max E. Woods (D)	155,221	39.1
29	D. S. Saund (D)	76,139	57.1
	Charles H. Jameson (R)	57,319	43.0
30	Bob Wilson (R)	158,679	59.3
	Walter Wencke (D)	108,882	40.7

COLORADO

	Candidates	Votes	%
1	Byron G. Rogers (D)	121,610	60.0
	Robert D. Rolander (R)	81,042	40.0
2	Peter H. Dominick (R)	150,964	57.6
	Byron L. Johnson (D)	111,077	42.4
3	J. Edgar Chenoweth (R)	85,825	52.1
	Franklin R. Stewart (D)	79,069	48.0
4	Wayne N. Aspinall (D)	58,731	68.5
	Charles P. Casteel (R)	26,961	31.5

CONNECTICUT

	Candidates	Votes	%
1	Emilio Q. Daddario (D)	193,330	58.5
	Thomas F. Brennan (R)	137,386	41.5
2	Horace Seely-Brown Jr. (R)	93,971	50.1
	William L. St. Onge (D)	93,515	49.9
3	Robert N. Giaimo (D)	124,547	54.9
	Albert W. Cretella (R)	102,271	45.1
4	Abner W. Sibal (R)	160,654	51.3
	Donald J. Irwin (D)	150,205	48.0
5	John S. Monagan (D)	88,310	55.1
	James T. Patterson (R)	71,964	44.9
AL	Frank Kowalski (D)	657,680	54.0
	Antoni N. Sadlak (R)	560,803	46.0

DELAWARE

	Candidates	Votes	%
AL	Harris B. McDowell Jr. (D)	98,227	50.5
	James T. McKinstry (R)	96,337	49.5

FLORIDA

	Candidates	Votes	%
1	William C. Cramer (R)	159,515	58.4
	James M. McEwen (D)	113,504	41.6
2	Charles E. Bennett (D)	94,570	82.5
	J. Edward Musser (R)	20,090	17.5
3	Robert L. F. Sikes (D)	95,062	100.0
4	Dante B. Fascell (D)	194,023	70.5
	Hugh M. Tartaglia (R)	81,209	29.5
5	A. Sydney Herlong Jr. (D)	113,938	100.0
6	Paul G. Rogers (D)	138,226	62.0
	John D. Kruse (R)	84,776	38.0
7	James A. Haley (D)	65,144	61.4
	Henry S. Bartholomew (R)	40,923	38.6
8	D. R. Matthews (D)	46,794	100.0

GEORGIA

	Candidates	Votes	%
1	G. Elliott Hagan (D)	53,749	100.0
2	J. L. Pilcher (D)	43,596	100.0
3	E. L. Forrester (D)	55,005	99.7
4	John J. Flynt Jr. (D)	53,394	100.0
5	James C. Davis (D)	80,023	99.7
6	Carl Vinson (D)	44,237	100.0
7	John W. Davis (D)	69,717	74.2
	E. Ralph Ivey (R)	24,285	25.8
8	Iris Faircloth Blitch (D)	50,456	99.8
9	Phil M. Landrum (D)	57,549	100.0
10	Robert G. Stephens Jr. (D)	41,679	99.9

HAWAII

	Candidates	Votes	%
AL	Daniel K. Inouye (D)	135,827	74.4
	Fred Titcomb (R)	46,812	25.6

IDAHO

	Candidates	Votes	%
1	Gracie B. Pfost (D)	68,863	60.4
	Thomas A. Leupp (R)	45,166	39.6
2	Ralph R. Harding (D)	90,161	51.2
	Hamer H. Budge (R)	86,100	49.9

ILLINOIS

	Candidates	Votes	%
1	William L. Dawson (D)	75,938	77.8
	Genoa S. Washington (R)	21,660	22.2
2	Barratt O'Hara (D)	103,535	66.6
	Bernard E. Epton (R)	52,028	33.4
3	William T. Murphy (D)	114,523	59.1
	Emmet F. Byrne (R)	79,307	40.9
4	Edward J. Derwinski (R)	179,480	55.7
	Frank G. Sulewski (D)	142,772	44.3
5	John C. Kluczynski (D)	121,240	71.2
	Edward J. Tomek (R)	49,030	28.8
6	Thomas J. O'Brien (D)	107,474	71.7
	Frank Estes (R)	42,361	28.3
7	Roland Victor Libonati (D)	28,494	54.5
	Lawrence J. Blasi (R)	23,840	45.6
8	Dan Rostenkowski (D)	81,092	67.2
	Henry Klinger Jr. (R)	39,651	32.8
9	Sidney R. Yates (D)	80,681	60.1
	Chester E. Emanuelson (R)	53,686	40.0
10	Harold R. Collier (R)	126,671	57.1
	Edward V. Hanrahan (D)	95,214	42.9
11	Roman C. Pucinski (D)	101,224	54.0
	Timothy P. Sheehan (R)	86,305	46.0
12	Edward R. Finnegan (D)	94,907	50.8
	Theodore P. Fields (R)	91,978	49.2
13	Marguerite Stitt Church (R)	268,647	66.0
	Tyler Thompson (D)	138,348	34.0
14	Elmer J. Hoffman (R)	167,128	63.8
	Hayes Beall (D)	94,945	36.2
15	Noah M. Mason (R)	93,986	50.5
	Dorothy G. O'Brien (D)	92,301	49.6
16	John B. Anderson (R)	115,693	62.3
	Edwin M. Nelson (D)	69,944	37.7
17	Leslie C. Arends (R)	107,896	61.3
	William T. Larkin (D)	68,020	38.7
18	Robert H. Michel (R)	94,388	59.3
	Richard A. Estep (D)	64,885	40.7
19	Robert B. Chiperfield (R)	82,622	50.6
	John C. Watson (D)	80,700	49.4
20	Paul Findley (R)	77,286	55.6
	Montgomery B. Carrott (D)	61,790	44.4
21	Peter F. Mack Jr. (D)	102,154	54.7
	J. Waldo Ackerman Jr. (R)	84,471	45.3
22	William L. Springer (R)	98,438	61.4
	James T. Nally (D)	61,837	38.6
23	George E. Shipley (D)	80,718	51.6
	Frank H. Walker (R)	75,809	48.4
24	Melvin Price (D)	144,560	72.2
	Phyllis Schlafly (R)	55,620	27.8
25	Kenneth J. Gray (D)	92,227	57.9
	Gordon E. Kerr (R)	67,067	42.1

INDIANA

	Candidates	Votes	%
1	Ray J. Madden (D)	136,443	64.7
	Philip P. Parker (R)	73,984	35.1
2	Charles A. Halleck (R)	95,920	57.5
	George H. Bowers (D)	70,464	42.2
3	John Brademas (D)	115,070	52.4
	F. Jay Nimtz (R)	104,430	47.6
4	E. Ross Adair (R)	100,419	58.2
	Byron McCammon (D)	72,251	41.8
5	J. Edward Roush (D)	107,357#	50.0
	George O. Chambers (R)	107,258#	50.0
6	Richard L. Roudebush (R)	84,662	52.0
	Fred Wampler (D)	78,247	48.0
7	William G. Bray (R)	95,998	60.1
	Thomas C. Cravens (D)	63,646	39.9
8	Winfield K. Denton (D)	108,058	53.2
	Alvan V. Burch (R)	94,694	46.6
9	Earl Wilson (R)	71,402	50.6
	Earl Hogan (D)	69,761	49.4
10	Ralph Harvey (R)	104,885	57.1
	Randall S. Harmon (D)	78,716	42.9
11	Donald Cogley Bruce (R)	154,676	53.7
	Joseph W. Barr (D)	133,153	46.2

IOWA

	Candidates	Votes	%
1	Fred Schwengel (R)	104,737	60.9
	Walter J. Guenther (D)	67,287	39.1
2	James E. Bromwell (R)	108,137	52.6
	Leonard G. Wolf (D)	97,608	47.4
3	H. R. Gross (R)	99,046	56.3
	Edward J. Gallagher Jr. (D)	76,837	43.7
4	John Kyl (R)	65,016	56.6
	C. Edwin Gilmour (D)	49,918	43.4
5	Neal Smith (D)	91,808	53.0
	Floyd M. Burgeson (R)	81,474	47.0
6	Merwin Coad (D)	70,353	53.6
	Curtis G. Riehm (R)	60,834	46.4
7	Ben F. Jensen (R)	66,037	55.8
	Duane Orton (D)	52,214	44.2
8	Charles B. Hoeven (R)	77,583	57.5
	Donald E. O'Brien (D)	57,333	42.5

KANSAS

	Candidates	Votes	%
1	William H. Avery (R)	84,816	63.1
	Marshall G. Gardiner (D)	49,598	36.9
2	Robert F. Ellsworth (R)	95,346	52.3
	Newell A. George (D)	86,905	47.7
3	Walter L. McVey (R)	49,429	51.2
	Denver D. Hargis (D)	47,127	48.8
4	Garner E. Shriver (R)	119,275	55.2
	William I. Robinson (D)	96,706	44.8
5	J. Floyd Breeding (D)	75,687	55.5
	Joe W. Hunter (R)	60,794	44.5
6	Bob Dole (R)	62,335	59.3
	William A. Davis (D)	42,869	40.8

KENTUCKY

	Candidates	Votes	%
1	Frank A. Stubblefield (D)	66,248	100.0
2	William H. Natcher (D)	55,877	100.0
3	Frank W. Burke (D)	115,421	50.3
	Henry R. Heyburn (R)	114,263	49.8
4	Frank Chelf (D)	48,743	100.0
5	Brent Spence (D)	63,555	55.4
	Jule Appel (R)	51,125	44.6
6	John C. Watts (D)	74,500	54.7
	Howard A. Dickey (R)	61,795	45.3
7	Carl D. Perkins (D)	82,746	56.1
	Herbert Rowland (R)	64,687	43.9
8	Eugene Siler (R)	81,903	71.8
	Donald R. Shepherd (D)	32,163	28.2

LOUISIANA

	Candidates	Votes	%
1	F. Edward Hebert (D)	70,465	82.2
	Norman W. Prendergast (R)	15,314	17.9
2	Hale Boggs (D)	81,034	78.0
	Elliot Ross Buckley (R)	22,818	22.0
3	Edwin E. Willis (D)	52,428	83.6
	Floyd J. Duplantis (R)	10,286	16.4
4	Overton Brooks (D)	48,286	74.2
	Fred C. McClanahan (R)	16,827	25.8
5	Otto E. Passman (D)	22,181	100.0
6	James H. Morrison (D)	78,640	85.6
	Charles H. Dillemuth (R)	13,233	14.4
7	T. A. Thompson (D)	60,007	100.0
8	Harold B. McSween (D)	28,492	100.0

MAINE

	Candidates	Votes	%
1	Peter Garland (R)	85,821	53.8
	James C. Oliver (D)	73,826	46.2
2	Stanley R. Tupper (R)	71,271	53.2
	John C. Donovan (D)	62,309	46.5
3	Clifford G. McIntire (R)	73,742	64.1
	David G. Roberts (D)	41,307	35.9

MARYLAND

	Candidates	Votes	%
1	Thomas F. Johnson (D)	42,219	53.6
	Edward T. Miller (R)	36,508	46.4
2	Daniel B. Brewster (D)	126,452	58.6
	Fife Symington (R)	89,262	41.4
3	Edward A. Garmatz (D)	57,154	80.3
	Robert J. Gerstung (R)	14,026	19.7
4	George H. Fallon (D)	48,145	65.5
	Melvin R. Kenney (R)	25,394	34.5
5	Richard E. Lankford (D)	120,773	62.2
	Carlyle J. Lancaster (R)	73,433	37.8
6	Charles McC. Mathias Jr. (R)	115,088	52.0
	John R. Foley (D)	106,098	48.0
7	Samuel N. Friedel (D)	81,474	64.5
	David M. Blum (R)	44,779	35.5

MASSACHUSETTS

	Candidates	Votes	%
1	Silvio O. Conte (R)	102,921	68.5
	William H. Burns (D)	46,863	31.2
2	Edward P. Boland (D)	135,815	100.0
3	Philip J. Philbin (D)	145,237	100.0
4	Harold D. Donohue (D)	122,364	64.5
	Robert N. Scola (R)	67,270	35.5
5	F. Bradford Morse (R)	123,161	54.5
	William C. Madden (D)	102,765	45.5
6	William H. Bates (R)	112,835	65.9
	Mary Kennedy (D)	58,312	34.1
7	Thomas J. Lane (D)	117,237	100.0
8	Torbert H. Macdonald (D)	114,333	65.8
	Ward Collins Cramer (R)	59,550	34.3
9	Hastings Keith (R)	110,955	55.7
	Edward F. Harrington (D)	88,222	44.3
10	Laurence Curtis (R)	98,257	58.2
	Joseph J. Mulhern (D)	70,510	41.8
11	Thomas P. O'Neill Jr. (D)	87,866	100.0
12	John W. McCormack (D)	86,057	100.0
13	James A. Burke (D)	126,936	58.5
	Charles J. Gabriel (R)	89,921	41.5
14	Joseph W. Martin Jr. (R)	115,209	60.3
	Edward F. Doolan (D)	75,815	39.7

MICHIGAN

	Candidates	Votes	%
1	Thaddeus M. Machrowicz (D)	102,948	88.4
	Walter Czarnecki (R)	13,157	11.3
2	George Meader (R)	110,124	59.6
	Thomas P. Payne (D)	74,276	40.2
3	August E. Johansen (R)	100,918	60.6
	Samuel I. Clark (D)	65,402	39.2
4	Clare E. Hoffman (R)	90,831	62.3
	Edward Burns (D)	54,655	37.5
5	Gerald R. Ford Jr. (R)	131,461	66.8
	William S. Reamon (D)	65,064	33.1
6	Charles E. Chamberlain (R)	138,355	56.6
	Jerome F. O'Rourke (D)	105,864	43.3
7	James G. O'Hara (D)	142,795	53.3
	Robert J. McIntosh (R)	124,750	46.6
8	James Harvey (R)	94,405	62.2
	Mary M. Harden (D)	57,126	37.6
9	Robert P. Griffin (R)	77,541	59.6
	Donald G. Jennings (D)	52,375	40.3
10	Elford A. Cederberg (R)	75,846	62.1
	Daniel E. Reed (D)	46,140	37.8
11	Victor A. Knox (R)	54,300	54.9
	Prentiss M. Brown Jr. (D)	44,650	45.1
12	John B. Bennett (R)	48,422	60.8
	Robert C. McCarthy (D)	31,137	39.1
13	Charles C. Diggs Jr. (D)	76,812	71.4
	Robert B. Blackwell (R)	30,369	28.2
14	Louis C. Rabaut (D)	132,602	62.7
	Lois V. Nair (R)	78,548	37.1
15	John D. Dingell (D)	111,761	79.4
	Robert J. Robbins (R)	28,532	20.3
16	John Lesinski (D)	211,733	66.0
	Lee H. Clark (R)	108,332	33.8
17	Martha W. Griffiths (D)	134,660	57.6
	Richard E. Morell (R)	98,721	42.2
18	William S. Broomfield (R)	163,233	55.9
	James Kellis (D)	128,678	44.0

MINNESOTA

	Candidates	Votes	%
1	Albert H. Quie (R)	100,381	60.5
	George Shepherd (DFL)	65,422	39.5
2	Ancher Nelsen (R)	96,471	57.2
	Russel Schwandt (DFL)	72,239	42.8
3	Clark MacGregor (R)	154,847	51.6
	Roy W. Wier (DFL)	139,908	46.6
4	Joseph E. Karth (DFL)	108,738	61.0
	Joseph J. Mitchell (R)	69,635	39.0
5	Walter H. Judd (R)	86,223	60.9
	George W. Matthews (DFL)	55,377	39.1
6	Fred Marshall (DFL)	87,332	59.6
	Frank L. King (R)	59,305	40.4
7	H. Carl Andersen (R)	73,487	52.5
	Gordon E. Duenow (DFL)	66,609	47.6
8	John A. Blatnik (DFL)	107,154	69.5
	Jerry H. Ketola (R)	47,099	30.5
9	Odin Langen (R)	62,322	52.2
	Coya Knutson (DFL)	57,114	47.8

MISSISSIPPI

	Candidates	Votes	%
1	Thomas G. Abernethy (D)	44,381	93.6
	Edward W. Scott (R)	3,018	6.4
2	Jamie L. Whitten (D)	23,942	100.0
3	Frank E. Smith (D)	25,592	92.7
	W. A. Clark (R)	2,018	7.3
4	John Bell Williams (D)	58,974	100.0
5	Arthur Winstead (D)	40,480	100.0
6	William M. Colmer (D)	59,372	100.0

MISSOURI

	Candidates	Votes	%
1	Frank M. Karsten (D)	161,394	70.8
	Sam J. Kallaos (R)	66,640	29.2
2	Thomas B. Curtis (R)	150,327	56.7
	Richard L. Carp (D)	114,803	43.3
3	Leonor K. Sullivan (D)	87,637	73.3
	Morton L. Schwartz (R)	31,902	26.7
4	William J. Randall (D)	111,557	54.0
	Kenneth K. Lowe (R)	95,070	46.0
5	Richard Bolling (D)	74,834	61.0
	Clinton H. Gates (R)	47,810	39.0
6	W. R. Hull Jr. (D)	93,285	54.6
	Ethan H. Campbell (R)	77,638	45.4
7	Durward G. Hall (R)	107,208	54.9
	Charles H. Brown (D)	88,162	45.1
8	Richard Ichord (D)	79,020	58.0
	Curtis J. Tindel (R)	57,234	42.0
9	Clarence Cannon (D)	107,384	59.8
	Anthony C. Schroeder (R)	72,098	40.2
10	Paul C. Jones (D)	69,997	100.0
11	Morgan M. Moulder (D)	74,866	50.1
	Robert A. Bartel (R)	74,505	49.9

MONTANA

	Candidates	Votes	%
1	Arnold Olsen (D)	63,081	53.3
	George P. Sarsfield (R)	55,347	46.7
2	James F. Battin (R)	78,277	50.9
	Leo Graybill Jr. (D)	75,507	49.1

NEBRASKA

1	Phil Weaver (R)	89,016	55.8
	Gerald T. Whelan (D)	70,626	44.2
2	Glenn Cunningham (R)	101,347	66.6
	Joseph V. Benesch (D)	50,768	33.4
3	Ralph F. Beermann (R)	67,129	51.3
	Lawrence Brock (D)	63,838	48.7
4	Dave Martin (R)	69,754	51.1
	Donald F. McGinley (D)	66,699	48.9

NEVADA

AL	Walter S. Baring (D)	59,616	57.5
	George W. Malone (R)	43,986	42.5

NEW HAMPSHIRE

1	Chester E. Merrow (R)	88,118	56.6
	Romeo J. Champagne (D)	67,717	43.5
2	Perkins Bass (R)	77,701	60.3
	Stuart V. Nims (D)	51,145	39.7

NEW JERSEY

1	William T. Cahill (R)	153,817	57.6
	John A. Healey (D)	112,802	42.2
2	Milton W. Glenn (R)	77,894	56.6
	John A. Miller (D)	59,520	43.2
3	James C. Auchincloss (R)	139,590	53.1
	Katharine E. White (D)	123,280	46.9
4	Frank Thompson Jr. (D)	115,761	60.2
	A. Jerome Moore (R)	76,067	39.6
5	Peter H. B. Frelinghuysen Jr. (R)	170,859	58.6
	Jerome H. Taub (D)	120,302	41.3
6	Florence P. Dwyer (R)	136,723	57.7
	Jack B. Dunn (D)	98,043	41.4
7	William B. Widnall (R)	156,758	63.7
	James Dobbins (D)	88,649	36.0
8	Charles S. Joelson (D)	88,100	52.0
	Walter F. Kennedy (R)	74,165	43.8
9	Frank C. Osmers Jr. (R)	127,088	58.1
	Vincent T. McKenna (D)	91,065	41.6
10	Peter W. Rodino Jr. (D)	84,859	65.3
	Alphonse A. Miele (R)	43,238	33.3
11	Hugh J. Addonizio (D)	75,533	61.4
	Frank A. Palmieri (R)	44,580	36.2
12	George M. Wallhauser (R)	76,945	50.2
	Robert R. Peacock (D)	73,119	47.7
13	Cornelius E. Gallagher (D)	80,490	68.3
	Samuel F. Kanis (R)	37,350	31.7
14	Dominick V. Daniels (D)	64,359	57.4
	Frank A. Musto (R)	46,770	41.7

NEW MEXICO

AL	Thomas C. Morris (D)	172,577	58.0
	John D. Robb (R)	124,101	41.7
AL	Joseph M. Montoya (D)	176,514	58.6
	Edward W. Balcomb (R)	123,683	41.1

NEW YORK

1	Otis G. Pike (D, L)	187,286	50.4
	Stuyvesant Wainwright (R)	184,549	49.6
2	Steven B. Derounian (R)	139,423	61.0
	John J. Drury (D, L)	89,176	39.0
3	Frank J. Becker (R)	133,416	54.1
	Julius J. Rosen (D, L)	113,143	45.9

	Candidates	Votes	%
4	Seymour Halpern (R)	115,736	55.1
	Bernard A. Helfat (D, L)	94,390	44.9
5	Joseph P. Addabbo (D, L)	60,453	54.2
	George Archinal (R)	51,129	45.8
6	Lester Holtzman (D, L)	155,904	65.6
	Vincent L. Pitaro (R)	81,694	34.4
7	James J. Delaney (D, L)	92,424	60.7
	Edward V. Lisoski (R)	59,882	39.3
8	Victor L. Anfuso (D, L)	60,030	72.9
	Leon F. Nadrowski (R)	22,318	27.1
9	Eugene J. Keogh (D, L)	84,941	72.3
	Herman Sanders (R)	32,538	27.7
10	Edna F. Kelly (D, L)	98,938	76.6
	Jerome P. Schneider (R)	30,243	23.4
11	Emanuel Celler (D, L)	139,397	81.6
	Seymour Besunder (R)	31,378	18.4
12	Hugh L. Carey (D, L)	65,996	50.4
	Francis E. Dorn (R)	64,899	49.6
13	Abraham J. Multer (D, L)	117,087	75.4
	Joseph A. DeMarco (R)	38,189	24.6
14	John J. Rooney (D, L)	80,972	70.6
	Carlo G. Colavito (R)	33,769	29.4
15	John H. Ray (R)	80,218	48.7
	John M. Murphy (D)	77,812	47.2
16	Adam Clayton Powell Jr. (D)	59,957	71.6
	Joseph A. Bailey (R)	14,706	17.6
	Arthur O. Boyer (L)	9,093	10.9
17	John V. Lindsay (R)	81,006	60.2
	William J. Vanden Heuvel (D, L)	53,574	39.8
18	Alfred E. Santangelo (D)	47,749	58.3
	Charles Muzzicato (R)	27,419	33.5
	Faustino Louis Garcia (L)	6,680	8.2
19	Leonard Farbstein (D, L)	68,445	72.4
	Thomas P. O'Callaghan (R)	26,054	27.6
20	William F. Ryan (D)	55,272	55.7
	Morris Aarons (R)	30,046	30.3
	Ludwig Teller (L)	13,884	14.0
21	Herbert Zelenko (D, L)	87,775	74.6
	Thomas H. Bartzos (R)	29,835	25.4
22	James C. Healey (D)	78,717	65.0
	Dominick A. Fusco (R)	24,958	20.6
	David I. Wells (L)	17,438	14.4
23	Jacob H. Gilbert (D)	61,474	70.6
	Benjamin Thornley (R)	15,208	17.5
	Nicholas B. Gyory (L)	10,420	12.0
24	Charles A. Buckley (D)	89,140	56.6
	Michael R. Cappelli (R)	43,110	27.4
	Murray Koenig (L)	25,283	16.1
25	Paul A. Fino (R)	112,187	59.8
	Eugene L. Sugarman (D)	66,539	35.5
26	Edwin B. Dooley (R)	98,506	52.6
	Phil E. Gilbert Jr. (D, L)	88,879	47.4
27	Robert R. Barry (R)	121,533	56.3
	John R. Harold (D)	86,997	40.3
28	Katharine St.George (R)	107,179	58.7
	James E. Truex (D, L)	75,448	41.3
29	J. Ernest Wharton (R)	103,966	56.7
	Gore Vidal (D, L)	79,252	43.3
30	Leo W. O'Brien (D, L)	117,692	62.9
	Irving I. Waxman (R)	69,549	37.1
31	Carleton J. King (R)	99,604	60.4
	Louis E. Wolfe (D, L)	65,305	39.6
32	Samuel S. Stratton (D, L)	98,990	62.3
	W. Clyde Wright (R)	59,890	37.7
33	Clarence E. Kilburn (R)	91,710	61.9
	Edward J. Gosier (D)	53,130	35.9
34	Alexander Pirnie (R)	98,063	55.3
	Edwin L. Slusarczyk (D, L)	79,153	44.7
35	R. Walter Riehlman (R)	105,241	53.8
	Jerome M. Wilson (D)	87,347	44.6
36	John Taber (R)	84,441	52.6
	Francis J. Souhan (D, L)	76,120	47.4
37	Howard W. Robison (R)	123,782	63.4
	Joseph V. Julian (D, L)	71,354	36.6
38	Jessica McC. Weis (R)	114,871	57.6
	Arthur B. Curran Jr. (D, L)	84,716	42.4
39	Harold C. Ostertag (R)	103,162	59.7
	Henry R. Dutcher Jr. (D, L)	69,704	40.3

	Candidates	Votes	%
40	William E. Miller (R)	104,752	53.6
	Mariano A. Lucca (D)	85,005	43.5
41	Thaddeus J. Dulski (D, L)	82,114	56.2
	Ralph J. Radwan (R)	63,889	43.8
42	John R. Pillion (R)	122,073	55.4
	Charles J. McCabe (D)	93,492	42.4
43	Charles E. Goodell (R)	87,585	62.8
	T. Joseph Lynch (D)	48,423	34.7

Special Election

23	Jacob H. Gilbert (D)	4,594	82.3
	Simon M. Koenig (R)	574	10.3
	Hector Mathew (L)	411	7.4

NORTH CAROLINA

1	Herbert C. Bonner (D)	48,809	86.6
	Zeno O. Ratcliff (R)	7,587	13.5
2	L. H. Fountain (D)	51,156	87.8
	L. Paul Gooding (R)	7,135	12.2
3	David N. Henderson (D)	51,193	71.2
	Jack D. Brinson (R)	20,674	28.8
4	Harold D. Cooley (D)	75,464	66.6
	Elam Reamuel Temple Jr. (R)	37,821	33.4
5	Ralph J. Scott (D)	66,079	57.6
	Russell F. Biggam (R)	48,572	42.4
6	Horace R. Kornegay (D)	79,809	59.6
	Holland L. Robb (R)	54,028	40.4
7	Alton Lennon (D)	71,726	76.5
	Joel C. Clifton (R)	21,997	23.5
8	A. Paul Kitchin (D)	71,429	56.3
	A. M. Snipes (R)	55,372	43.7
9	Hugh Q. Alexander (D)	75,909	53.1
	W. S. Bogle (R)	67,033	46.9
10	Charles Raper Jonas (R)	97,138	58.6
	David Clark (D)	68,761	41.5
11	Basil L. Whitener (D)	65,478	61.1
	Kelly Dixon (R)	41,763	38.9
12	Roy A. Taylor (D)	61,170	52.0
	Heinz Rollman (R)	56,368	48.0

Special Election

12	Roy A. Taylor (D)	28,744	98.6

NORTH DAKOTA

AL	Don L. Short (R)	135,579✔	
	Hjalmar Nygaard (R)	127,118✔	
	Raymond Vendsel (D)	120,773	
	Anson J. Anderson (D)	109,207	

OHIO

1	Gordon H. Scherer (R)	88,899	58.9
	W. Ted Osborne (D)	62,043	41.1
2	Donald D. Clancy (R)	118,046	57.4
	H. A. Sand (D)	87,531	42.6
3	Paul F. Schenck (R)	167,117	62.0
	R. William Patterson (D)	102,237	38.0
4	William M. McCulloch (R)	99,683	65.4
	Joseph J. Murphy (D)	52,797	34.6
5	Delbert L. Latta (R)	85,175	67.3
	Tom P. McRitchie (D)	41,375	32.7
6	William H. Harsha Jr. (R)	80,124	55.2
	Franklin E. Smith (D)	65,045	44.8
7	Clarence J. Brown (R)	105,026	65.5
	Joseph A. Sullivan (D)	55,451	34.6
8	Jackson E. Betts (R)	81,373	67.7
	Virgil M. Gase (D)	38,871	32.3
9	Thomas Ludlow Ashley (D)	108,688	56.9
	Howard C. Cook (R)	82,433	43.1
10	Walter H. Moeller (D)	58,085	52.5
	Oakley C. Collins (R)	52,479	47.5
11	Robert E. Cook (D)	104,183	51.0
	David S. Dennison Jr. (R)	99,991	49.0
12	Samuel L. Devine (R)	140,236	60.7
	Richard E. Liming (D)	90,894	39.3

OHIO

	Candidates	Votes	%
13	Charles A. Mosher (R)	73,110	51.4
	J. William McCray (D)	69,033	48.6
14	William H. Ayres (R)	145,526	61.5
	John H. Mihaly (D)	91,103	38.5
15	Tom V. Moorehead (R)	49,742	51.2
	Herbert U. Smith (D)	47,366	48.8
16	Frank T. Bow (R)	130,542	62.5
	John G. Freedom (D)	78,257	37.5
17	John M. Ashbrook (R)	79,609	53.0
	Robert W. Levering (D)	70,470	47.0
18	Wayne L. Hays (D)	96,474	65.6
	Walter Jay Hunston (R)	50,698	34.5
19	Michael J. Kirwan (D)	102,874	68.9
	Paul E. Stevens (R)	46,537	31.2
20	Michael A. Feighan (D)	113,302	67.8
	Leonard G. Richter (R)	53,845	32.2
21	Charles A. Vanik (D)	103,460	73.0
	William O. Walker (R)	38,326	27.0
22	Frances P. Bolton (R)	88,389	56.9
	Chat Paterson (D)	66,930	43.1
23	William E. Minshall (R)	123,364	67.3
	Daniel Winston (D)	59,893	32.7

Special Election

6	Ward M. Miller (R)	76,520	55.4
	Gladys E. Davis (D)	61,713	44.6

OKLAHOMA

1	Page Belcher (R)	133,964	63.8
	Yates Land (D)	75,934	36.2
2	Ed Edmondson (D)	79,732	57.0
	Bill Sharp (R)	60,253	43.0
3	Carl Albert (D)	56,138	74.9
	George B. Sherritt (R)	18,799	25.1
4	Tom Steed (D)	54,181	60.7
	Don H. Crall (R)	35,028	39.3
5	John Jarman (D)	125,286	66.6
	Hobart H. Hobbs (R)	62,971	33.5
6[1]	Victor Wickersham (D)	68,192	50.4
	Clyde Wheeler Jr. (R)	67,116	49.6

OREGON

1	Walter Norblad (R)	144,743	65.1
	Marv Owens (D)	77,689	34.9
2	Al Ullman (D)	62,690	59.6
	Ronald E. Phair (R)	42,516	40.4
3	Edith Green (D)	157,243	63.9
	Wallace L. Lee (R)	88,906	36.1
4	Edwin R. Durno (R)	96,022	51.1
	Charles O. Porter (D)	91,947	48.9

PENNSYLVANIA

1	William A. Barrett (D)	88,805	77.0
	Michael Grasso Jr. (R)	26,601	23.1
2	Kathryn E. Granahan (D)	109,452	72.3
	Joseph C. Bruno (R)	42,019	27.7
3	James A. Byrne (D)	80,258	69.7
	Joseph Patrick Gorham (R)	34,956	30.3
4	Robert N. C. Nix (D)	84,053	78.4
	Clarence M. Smith (R)	23,146	21.6
5	William J. Green Jr. (D)	140,658	61.0
	James W. Gilmour (R)	90,087	39.0
6	Herman Toll (D)	109,275	59.6
	David O. Maxwell (R)	74,132	40.4
7	William H. Milliken Jr.(R)	136,021	53.0
	Henry Gouley (D)	120,839	47.0
8	Willard S. Curtin (R)	121,564	56.1
	Donald V. Hock (D)	95,140	43.9
9	Paul B. Dague (R)	128,917	66.6
	Howard H. Halsey (D)	64,659	33.4
10	William W. Scranton (R)	97,012	54.8
	Stanley A. Prokop (D)	80,097	45.2
11	Daniel J. Flood (D)	115,042	67.1
	Donald B. Ayers (R)	56,428	32.9

	Candidates	Votes	%
12	Ivor D. Fenton (R)	72,061	52.4
	William H. Deitman (D)	65,585	47.7
13	Richard S. Schweiker (R)	142,966	61.8
	Warren M. Ballard (D)	88,486	38.2
14	George M. Rhodes (D)	60,211	53.8
	James H. Mantis (R)	51,746	46.2
15	Francis E. Walter (D)	67,830	55.2
	Woodrow A. Horn (R)	55,125	44.8
16	Walter M. Mumma (R)	93,831	62.5
	Miles Albright (D)	56,267	37.5
17	Herman T. Schneebeli (R)	82,040	56.7
	Dean R. Fisher (D)	62,695	43.3
18	J. Irving Whalley (R)	88,397	62.3
	Robert M. Meyers (D)	53,453	37.7
19	George A. Goodling (R)	88,776	53.2
	James M. Quigley (D)	78,043	46.8
20	James E. Van Zandt (R)	77,776	67.8
	Robert N. Hendershot (D)	36,997	32.2
21	John H. Dent (D)	85,853	56.0
	William L. Batten (R)	65,551	42.8
22	John P. Saylor (R)	89,261	57.4
	William D. Patton (D)	66,383	42.7
23	Leon H. Gavin (R)	74,542	62.4
	John H. Cartwright (D)	43,927	36.8
24	Carroll D. Kearns (R)	95,149	51.0
	Chester C. Hampton (D)	91,498	49.0
25	Frank M. Clark (D)	102,750	58.1
	Fred A. Obley (R)	74,217	41.9
26	Thomas E. Morgan (D)	111,362	63.6
	Bartley P. Osborne (R)	63,702	36.4
27	James G. Fulton (R)	127,995	59.1
	Margaret Lee Walgren (D)	88,660	40.9
28	William S. Moorhead (D)	99,491	67.8
	Arthur O. Sharron (R)	47,232	32.2
29	Robert J. Corbett (R)	117,009	59.2
	Russell M. Douthett (D)	80,497	40.8
30	Elmer J. Holland (D)	126,619	68.6
	Jerome M. Meyers (R)	58,063	31.4

Special Election

18	J. Irving Whalley (R)	86,527	62.3
	Robert M. Meyers (D)	52,324	37.7

RHODE ISLAND

1	Fernard J. St.Germain (D)	117,162	66.2
	Theophile Martin (R)	59,737	33.8
2	John E. Fogarty (D)	151,544	70.4
	Robert L. Gammell (R)	63,795	29.6

SOUTH CAROLINA

1	L. Mendel Rivers (D)	47,153	100.0
2	John J. Riley (D)	63,207	100.0
3	William J. Bryan Dorn (D)	52,398	100.0
4	Robert T. Ashmore (D)	68,973	100.0
5	Robert W. Hemphill (D)	46,815	99.8
6	John L. McMillan (D)	49,780	100.0

SOUTH DAKOTA

1	Ben Reifel (R)	126,033	54.9
	Ray Fitzgerald (D)	103,755	45.2
2	E. Y. Berry (R)	42,550	59.8
	W. H. Raff (D)	28,666	40.3

TENNESSEE

1	B. Carroll Reece (R)	103,872	75.4
	Arthur Bright (D)	33,873	24.6
2	Howard H. Baker (R)	98,839	100.0
3	James B. Frazier Jr. (D)	62,827	100.0
4	Joe L. Evins (D)	60,730	100.0
5	J. Carlton Loser (D)	42,524	100.0
6	Ross Bass (D)	55,736	100.0
7	Tom Murray (D)	34,130	100.0
8	Robert A. Everett (D)	30,124	100.0
9	Clifford Davis (D)	120,159	100.0

TEXAS

	Candidates	Votes	%
1	Wright Patman (D)	58,674	100.0
2	Jack Brooks (D)	75,657	69.7
	F. S. Newmann (R)	32,473	29.9
3	Lindley Beckworth (D)	59,386	100.0
4	Sam Rayburn (D)	44,902	100.0
5	Bruce Alger (R)	129,886	57.3
	Joe Pool (D)	96,709	42.7
6	Olin Teague (D)	56,603	100.0
7	John Dowdy (D)	61,586	100.0
8	Albert Thomas (D)	76,767	68.6
	Anthony J. P. Farris (R)	24,486	21.9
	Robert Nesmith (CST)	10,684	9.5
9	Clark Thompson (D)	98,586	94.3
	P. D. Rogers (CST)	5,981	5.7
10	Homer Thornberry (D)	75,165	98.1
11	W. R. Poage (D)	64,351	100.0
12	Jim Wright (D)	115,797	100.0
13	Frank Ikard (D)	75,972	100.0
14	John Young (D)	105,792	100.0
15	Joe Kilgore (D)	76,421	100.0
16	J. T. Rutherford (D)	63,634	58.9
	Dorothy Wynell (CST)	24,996	23.1
	Ford Chapman (R)	19,491	18.0
17	Omar Burleson (D)	60,401	77.6
	Max Mossholder (CST)	17,400	22.4
18	Walter Rogers (D)	79,675	100.0
19	George Mahon (D)	77,415	85.7
	J. R. Anderson (CST)	12,953	14.3
20	Paul J. Kilday (D)	84,487	100.0
21	O. C. Fisher (D)	63,277	100.0
22	Bob Casey (D)	109,418	58.3
	J. C. Noonan (R)	73,503	39.2

UTAH

1	M. Blaine Peterson (D)	65,939	50.0
	A. Walter Stevenson (R)	65,871	50.0
2	David S. King (D)	120,771	50.8
	Sherman P. Lloyd (R)	116,881	49.2

VERMONT

AL	Robert T. Stafford (R)	94,905	57.2
	William H. Meyer (D)	71,111	42.8

VIRGINIA

1	Thomas N. Downing (D)	53,768	82.4
	Richard A. May (R)	11,429	17.5
2	Porter Hardy Jr. (D)	49,750	75.8
	Louis B. Fine (R)	15,758	24.0
3	J. Vaughan Gary (D)	52,908	77.8
	T. Coleman Andrews	14,907	21.9
4	Watkins M. Abbitt (D)	39,408	99.5
5	William M. Tuck (D)	30,154	98.9
6	Richard H. Poff (R)	60,371	82.4
	J. B. Brayman (SOCIAL D)	12,700	17.3
7	Burr P. Harrison (D)	42,199	99.6
8	Howard W. Smith (D)	42,809	75.7
	Lawrence M. Traylor (R)	13,410	23.7
9	W. Pat Jennings (D)	47,372	58.0
	E. Summers Sheffey (R)	34,280	42.0
10	Joel T. Broyhill (R)	64,408	55.0
	Ralph Kaul (D)	52,647	45.0

WASHINGTON

1	Thomas M. Pelly (R)	124,721	70.2
	Carl Viking Holman (D)	53,009	29.8
2	Jack Westland (R)	87,802	60.2
	Payson Peterson (D)	58,154	39.8
3	Julia Butler Hansen (D)	76,930	53.4
	Dale M. Nordquist (R)	67,060	46.6
4	Catherine May (R)	94,210	58.8
	Roy Mundy (D)	65,964	41.2
5	Walt Horan (R)	94,042	59.4
	Bernard J. Gallagher (D)	64,321	40.6

1. Figures are for December recount. Election was contested after initial vote tally had Wheeler winning by 188 votes.

WASHINGTON

Candidates	Votes	%
6 Thor C. Tollefson (R)	83,158	56.5
John G. McCutcheon (D)	64,167	43.6
7 Don Magnuson (D)	95,663	50.0
John Stender (R)	95,524	50.0

Special Election

3 Julia Butler Hansen (D)	71,416	53.1
Dale M. Nordquist (R)	63,058	46.9

WEST VIRGINIA

1 Arch A. Moore Jr. (R)	81,018	60.3
Steven D. Narick (D)	53,318	39.7
2 Harley O. Staggers (D)	74,184	60.3
Charles J. Whiston (R)	48,903	39.7

Candidates	Votes	%
3 Cleveland M. Bailey (D)	71,718	59.8
James M. Knowles Jr. (R)	48,258	40.2
4 Ken Hechler (D)	82,931	53.2
Clyde Pinson (R)	73,052	46.8
5 Elizabeth Kee (D)	77,524	69.5
L. M. LaFollette (R)	34,052	30.5
6 John M. Slack Jr. (D)	108,452	61.8
George W. King (R)	67,070	38.2

WISCONSIN

1 Henry C. Schadeberg (R)	97,662	52.7
Gerald T. Flynn (D)	87,646	47.3
2 Robert W. Kastenmeier (D)	119,885	53.4
Donald E. Tewes (R)	104,744	46.6
3 Vernon W. Thomson (R)	71,677	54.6
Norman M. Clapp (D)	59,527	45.4

Candidates	Votes	%
4 Clement J. Zablocki (D)	155,789	71.7
Samuel P. Murray (R)	61,468	28.3
5 Henry S. Reuss (D)	126,314	57.7
Kirby Hendee (R)	92,526	42.3
6 William K. Van Pelt (R)	91,450	55.8
James Megellas (D)	72,442	44.2
7 Melvin R. Laird (R)	95,152	67.1
Kenneth Traeger (D)	46,606	32.9
8 John W. Byrnes (R)	101,132	58.8
Milo Singler (D)	70,740	41.2
9 Lester R. Johnson (D)	74,268	56.6
Perry M. Hull (R)	57,069	43.5
10 Alvin E. O'Konski (R)	73,114	95.0

WYOMING

AL William Henry Harrison (R)	70,241	52.3
Hepburn T. Armstrong (D)	64,090	47.7

1961 House Elections

ARIZONA

Special Election

2 Morris K. Udall (D)	51,304#	51.0
Mac C. Matheson (R)	49,297#	49.0

ARKANSAS

Special Election

6 Catherine D. Norrell (D)	10,209#	43.1
John Harris Jones (D)	5,955#	25.1
M. C. Lewis Jr. (D)	5,499#	23.2
James F. Cross (D)	1,727#	7.3

LOUISIANA

Special Election

4 Joe D. Waggonner Jr. (D)	33,892	54.5
Charlton H. Lyons (R)	28,250	45.5

MICHIGAN

Special Election

1 Lucien N. Nedzi (D)	33,690#	85.5
Walter Czarnecki (R)	5,729#	14.5

PENNSYLVANIA

Special Election

16 John C. Kunkel (R)	43,220	65.6
Kathryn Z. Vanderslice (D)	22,698	34.4

TENNESSEE

Special Election

1 Louise G. Reece (R)	29,819#	62.9
William W. Faw (D)	15,718#	33.2

TEXAS [1]

Special Elections

4 Ray Roberts (D)	8,154	36.9
R. C. Slagle (D)	5,945	26.9
David Brown (D)	2,393	10.8
Conner Harrington (R)	2,353	10.6
Jack Finney (D)	2,211	10.0
13 Graham B. Purcell Jr. (D)	8,960	33.6
Joe Meissner (R)	6,740	25.3
Jack Hightower (D)	6,157	23.1
Vernon Stewart (D)	2,706	10.2
Jimmy P. Horany (D)	2,076	7.8
20 Henry B. Gonzalez (D)	52,696	54.6
John Goode	42,511	44.0

1. In Texas special elections for the House held prior to 1961, all candidates ran against each other in one election regardless of party; the candidate receiving the most votes was the winner. Thus Lyndon B. Johnson won a 1937 special election with 27.7 percent of the vote (see p. 1183).

The Texas law was changed in 1961 to require that in a special election, if no candidate received a majority, a special election runoff would be held between the top two candidates.

Thus, in the three House special elections held in Texas in 1961, only the election in the 20th district produced a majority vote winner. In the 4th and 13th districts, no candidate received a majority. Runoff special elections between the top two candidates in each district were held in 1962; see page 1247.

1962 House Elections

ALABAMA

Candidates	Votes	%
AL George Huddleston Jr. (D)	304,210✓	
Armistead I. Selden Jr. (D)	295,882✓	
George Andrews (D)	293,182✓	
George Grant (D)	288,074✓	
Albert Rains (D)	271,075✓	
Kenneth A. Roberts (D)	269,410✓	
Robert E. Jones (D)	258,674✓	
Carl Elliott (D)	257,299✓	
John H. Buchanan Jr. (R)	141,202	
Tom Abernethy (R)	138,963	
Evan Foreman Jr. (R)	136,339	
J. Chester Robinson (N SR)	32,446	

ALASKA

Candidates	Votes	%
AL Ralph J. Rivers (D)	31,953	54.5
Lowell Thomas Jr. (R)	26,638	45.5

ARIZONA

Candidates	Votes	%
1 John J. Rhodes (R)	113,240	58.7
Howard V. Peterson (D)	79,763	41.3
2 Morris K. Udall (D)	64,510	58.3
Richard K. Burke (R)	46,219	41.7
3 George F. Senner Jr. (D)	25,359	56.0
John P. Clark (R)	19,933	44.0

ARKANSAS

Candidates	Votes	%
1 Ezekiel C. Gathings (D)		100.0
2 Wilbur D. Mills (D)		100.0
3 James W. Trimble (D)	58,786	69.4
Cy Carney Jr. (R)	25,987	30.7
4 Oren Harris (D)	74,972	77.4
Warren Lieblong (R)	21,818	22.5

CALIFORNIA

Candidates	Votes	%
1 Clem Miller (D)	100,962*	50.8
Don H. Clausen (R)	97,949	49.2
2 Harold T. Johnson (D)	106,239	64.6
Fredric H. Nagel Jr. (R)	58,150	35.4
3 John E. Moss Jr (D)	138,257	74.8
George W. G. Smith (R)	46,510	25.2
4 Robert L. Leggett (D)	55,563	56.5
L. V. Honsinger (R)	42,762	43.5
5 John F. Shelley (D)	64,493	80.4
Roland S. Charles (R)	15,670	19.5
6 William S. Mailliard (R)	105,762	58.7
John A. O'Connell (D)	74,429	41.3
7 Jeffery Cohelan (D)	86,215	64.5
Leonard L. Cantando (R)	47,409	35.5
8 George P. Miller (D)	97,014	72.5
Harold Petersen (R)	36,810	27.5
9 Don Edwards (D)	79,616	65.9
Joseph Francis Donovan (R)	41,104	34.0
10 Charles S. Gubser (R)	106,419	60.7
James P. Thurber Jr. (D)	68,885	39.3
11 J. Arthur Younger (R)	101,963	62.3
William J. Keller (D)	61,623	37.7
12 Burt L. Talcott (R)	75,424	61.3
William K. Stewart (D)	47,576	38.7
13 Charles M. Teague (R)	84,743	64.9
George J. Holgate (D)	45,746	35.1
14 John F. Baldwin (R)	99,040	62.9
Charles R. Weidner (D)	58,369	37.1
15 John J. McFall (D)	97,322	70.0
Arthur L. Young (R)	41,726	30.0
16 B. F. Sisk (D)	108,339	71.9
Arthur L. Selland (R)	42,401	28.1

Candidates	Votes	%
17 Cecil R. King (D)	74,964	67.2
Ted Bruinsma (R)	36,663	32.8
18 Harlan Hagen (D)	91,684	58.9
Ray Arnett (R)	64,037	41.1
19 Chet Holifield (D)	78,436	61.6
Robert T. Ramsay (R)	48,976	38.4
20 H. Allen Smith (R)	119,938	70.6
Leon Mayer (D)	49,850	29.4
21 Augustus F. Hawkins (D)	73,465	84.5
Herman Smith (R)	13,371	15.4
22 James C. Corman (D)	75,294	53.6
Charles S. Foote (R)	65,087	46.4
23 Clyde Doyle (D)	83,269	64.2
Del Clawson (R)	46,488	35.8
24 Glenard P. Lipscomb (R)	120,884	70.3
Knox Mellon (D)	50,970	29.7
25 Ronald Brooks Cameron (D)	62,371	53.1
John H. Rousselot (R)	53,961	45.9
26 James Roosevelt (D)	112,162	68.3
Daniel Beltz (R)	52,063	31.7
27 Everett G. Burkhalter (D)	66,979	52.1
Edgar W. Hiestand (R)	61,538	47.9
28 Alphonzo Bell (R)	162,233	64.0
Robert J. Felixson (D)	91,305	36.0
29 George E. Brown Jr. (D)	73,740	55.6
H. L. Richardson (R)	58,760	44.3
30 Edward R. Roybal (D)	69,008	56.5
Gordon L. McDonough (R)	53,104	43.5
31 Charles H. Wilson (D)	76,631	52.2
Gordon Hahn (R)	70,154	47.8
32 Craig Hosmer (R)	115,915	70.7
J. J. Johovich (D)	47,917	29.2
33 Harry R. Sheppard (D)	96,192	59.0
William R. Thomas (R)	66,764	41.0
34 Richard T. Hanna (D)	90,758	55.9
Robert A. Geier (R)	71,478	44.1
35 James B. Utt (R)	133,737	68.5
Burton Shamsky (D)	61,395	31.5
36 Bob Wilson (R)	91,626	61.8
William C. Godfrey (D)	56,637	38.2
37 Lionel Van Deerlin (D)	63,821	51.3
Dick Wilson (R)	60,460	48.6
38 Patrick Minor Martin (R)	68,583	55.9
Dalip S. Saund (D)	54,022	44.1

COLORADO

Candidates	Votes	%
1 Byron G. Rogers (D)	94,680	56.0
William B. Chenoweth (R)	74,392	44.0
2 Donald G. Brotzman (R)	134,939	61.9
Conrad L. McBride (D)	83,235	38.2
3 J. Edgar Chenoweth (R)	74,848	54.7
Albert J. Tomsic (D)	62,097	45.3
4 Wayne N. Aspinall (D)	42,462	58.7
Leo R. Sommerville (R)	29,943	41.4

CONNECTICUT

Candidates	Votes	%
1 Emilio Q. Daddario (D)	162,844	57.5
James F. Collins (R)	118,767	41.9
2 William L. St.Onge (D)	83,652	50.8
Moses A. Savin (R)	81,010	49.2
3 Robert Giaimo (D)	104,728	56.0
Daniel Reinhardsen Jr. (R)	82,215	44.0
4 Abner W. Sibal (R)	132,595	52.0
Francis X. Lennon Jr. (D)	122,362	48.0
5 John S. Monagan (D)	83,321	58.5
John A. Rand (R)	59,072	41.5
AL Bernard F. Grabowski (D)	543,424	52.7
John M. Lupton (R)	487,575	47.3

DELAWARE

Candidates	Votes	%
AL Harris B. McDowell Jr. (D)	81,166	52.9
Wilmer F. Williams (R)	71,934	46.9

FLORIDA

Candidates	Votes	%
1 Robert L. F. Sikes (D)	35,781	81.9
M. M. Woolley (R)	7,902	18.1
2 Charles E. Bennett (D)	41,378	99.7
3 Claude Pepper (D)	59,985	57.6
Bob Peterson (R)	44,164	42.4
4 Dante B. Fascell (D)	67,136	64.5
J. C. McGlon Jr. (R)	36,981	35.5
5 A. Sydney Herlong Jr. (D)	54,383	65.2
Hubert H. Hevey Jr. (R)	29,008	34.8
6 Paul G. Rogers (D)	102,396	64.2
Frederick A. Kibbe (R)	57,112	35.8
7 James A. Haley (D)	52,417	66.8
F. Onell Rogells (R)	26,042	33.2
8 D. R. Matthews (D)	23,387	100.0
9 Don Fuqua (D)	23,651	75.3
Wilfred C. Varn (R)	7,735	24.6
10 Sam M. Gibbons (D)	41,426	70.6
Victor A. Rule (R)	17,214	29.4
11 Edward J. Gurney (R)	46,814	51.9
John A. Sutton (D)	43,348	48.1
12 William C. Cramer (R)	78,982	64.5
Grover C. Criswell Jr. (D)	43,431	35.5

GEORGIA

Candidates	Votes	%
1 G. Elliott Hagan (D)	25,229	97.6
2 John L. Pilcher (D)	18,967	96.3
3 E. L. Forrester (D)	25,001	100.0
4 John J. Flynt Jr. (D)	21,214	100.0
5 Charles L. Weltner (D)	60,583	55.6
L. J. O'Callaghan (R)	48,466	44.4
6 Carl Vinson (D)	19,701	100.0
7 John W. Davis (D)	28,994	72.4
Ralph Ivey (R)	11,048	27.6
8 J. Russell Tuten (D)	19,694	100.0
9 Phil M. Landrum (D)	25,942	100.0
10 Robert G. Stephens Jr. (D)	27,169	100.0

HAWAII

Candidates	Votes	%
AL Thomas P. Gill (D)	123,649✓	
Spark M. Matsunaga (D)	123,599✓	
Albert W. Evensen (R)	70,880	
Richard Ike Sutton (R)	46,292	

IDAHO

Candidates	Votes	%
1 Compton I. White Jr. (D)	51,422	53.0
Erwin H. Schwiebert (R)	45,552	47.0
2 Ralph R. Harding (D)	83,152	52.8
Orval Hansen (R)	74,203	47.2

ILLINOIS

Candidates	Votes	%
1 William L. Dawson (D)	98,305	74.1
Benjamin C. Duster (R)	34,379	25.9
2 Barratt O'Hara (D)	78,119	62.3
Philip G. Bixler (R)	47,336	37.7
3 William T. Murphy (D)	82,866	51.6
Ernest E. Michaels (R)	77,814	48.4
4 Edward J. Derwinski (R)	114,954	64.9
Richard E. Friedman (R)	62,189	35.1
5 John C. Kluczynski (D)	84,455	63.4
Joseph Potempa (R)	48,825	36.6
6 Thomas J. O'Brien (D)	72,183	77.7
Adolph Herda (R)	20,690	22.3
7 Roland Victor Libonati (D)	86,677	78.8
Joseph D. Day (R)	23,285	21.2
8 Dan Rostenkowski (D)	112,778	60.8
Irvin R. Tchon (R)	72,726	39.2

ILLINOIS

	Candidates	Votes	%
9	Edward R. Finnegan (D)	80,378	54.8
	Thomas E. Ward (R)	66,196	45.2
10	Harold R. Collier (R)	149,761	66.6
	Joseph A. Salerno (D)	74,986	33.4
11	Roman C. Pucinski (D)	103,677	52.7
	Henry J. Hyde (R)	92,910	47.3
12	Robert McClory (R)	76,335	63.9
	John Clark Kimball (D)	43,200	36.1
13	Donald Rumsfeld (R)	139,230	63.5
	John A. Kennedy (D)	79,419	36.2
14	Elmer J. Hoffman (R)	107,285	59.7
	Jerome M. Ziegler (D)	72,390	40.3
15	Charlotte T. Reid (R)	77,718	60.3
	Stanley H. Cowan (D)	49,444	38.3
16	John B. Anderson (R)	78,594	66.9
	Walter S. Busky (D)	38,853	33.1
17	Leslie C. Arends (R)	87,612	62.5
	Donald M. Laughlin (D)	52,592	37.5
18	Robert H. Michel (R)	75,957	61.2
	Francis D. Nash (D)	48,177	38.8
19	Robert T. McLoskey (R)	66,547	55.9
	David Dedoncker (D)	52,482	44.1
20	Paul Findley (R)	100,558	52.9
	Peter F. Mack Jr. (D)	89,522	47.1
21	Kenneth J. Gray (D)	96,971	60.0
	Frank H. Walker (R)	64,687	40.0
22	William L. Springer (R)	70,870	59.8
	Bob Wilson (D)	47,745	40.3
23	George E. Shipley (D)	99,133	51.7
	Edward H. Jenison (R)	92,562	48.3
24	Melvin Price (D)	95,522	73.8
	Kurt Glaser (R)	33,993	26.3

INDIANA

	Candidates	Votes	%
1	Ray J. Madden (D)	104,212	60.5
	Harold Moody (R)	67,230	39.0
2	Charles A. Halleck (R)	82,971	57.6
	John J. Murray (D)	61,076	42.4
3	John Brademas (D)	92,609	51.9
	Charles W. Ainlay (R)	85,845	48.1
4	E. Ross Adair (R)	80,693	55.6
	Ronald R. Ross (D)	64,553	44.4
5	J. Edward Roush (D)	92,264	51.6
	George O. Chambers (R)	86,403	48.4
6	Richard L. Roudebush (R)	76,506	52.7
	Fred Wampler (D)	68,777	47.3
7	William G. Bray (R)	82,160	57.8
	Elden C. Tipton (D)	59,953	42.2
8	Winfield K. Denton (D)	95,126	55.7
	Earl J. Heseman (R)	75,731	44.3
9	Earl Wilson (R)	65,287	52.1
	John Pritchard (D)	59,985	47.9
10	Ralph Harvey (R)	81,007	52.9
	John E. Mitchell (D)	72,009	47.1
11	Donald Cogley Bruce (R)	127,763	54.3
	Andrew Jacobs Jr. (D)	107,747	45.8

IOWA

	Candidates	Votes	%
1	Fred Schwengel (R)	65,975	61.1
	Harold Stephens (D)	42,000	38.9
2	James E. Bromwell (R)	67,475	52.8
	Frank W. Less (D)	60,296	47.2
3	H. R. Gross (R)	66,337	56.7
	Neel F. Hill (D)	50,580	43.3
4	John Kyl (R)	65,538	55.9
	Gene W. Glenn (D)	51,810	44.2
5	Neal Smith (D)	73,963	62.8
	Sonja C. Egenes (R)	43,877	37.2
6	Charles B. Hoeven (R)	66,940	58.5
	Donald W. Murray (D)	47,542	41.5
7	Ben F. Jensen (R)	56,341	56.1
	Edward J. Peters (D)	44,171	44.0

KANSAS

	Candidates	Votes	%
1	Bob Dole (R)	102,499	55.8
	J. Floyd Breeding (D)	81,092	44.2
2	William H. Avery (R)	72,945	65.2
	Harry F. Kehoe (D)	38,923	34.8
3	Robert F. Ellsworth (R)	60,865	63.4
	Bill Sparks (D)	35,166	36.6
4	Garner E. Shriver (R)	72,712	66.9
	Lawrence J. Wetzel (D)	35,922	33.1
5	Joe Skubitz (R)	66,705	53.3
	Wade A. Myers (D)	58,453	46.7

KENTUCKY

	Candidates	Votes	%
1	Frank A. Stubblefield (D)	53,240	100.0
2	William H. Natcher (D)	45,999	100.0
3	M. G. (Gene) Snyder (R)	94,579	50.8
	Frank W. Burke (D)	91,544	49.2
4	Frank Chelf (D)	57,956	52.9
	Clyde Middleton (R)	51,637	47.1
5	Eugene Siler (R)	59,326	100.0
6	John C. Watts (D)	53,454	100.0
7	Carl D. Perkins (D)	70,195	56.8
	C. Alex Parker Jr. (R)	52,640	42.6

LOUISIANA

	Candidates	Votes	%
1	F. Edward Hebert (D)	57,326	100.0
2	Hale Boggs (D)	57,395	67.2
	David C. Treen (R)	27,971	32.8
3	Edwin E. Willis (D)	26,170	100.0
4	Joe D. Waggonner Jr. (D)	29,754	100.0
5	Otto E. Passman (D)	24,609	100.0
6	James H. Morrison (D)	48,894	100.0
7	T. Ashton Thompson (D)	33,983	100.0
8	Gillis W. Long (D)	25,682	64.0
	John W. Lewis Jr. (R)	14,448	36.0

MAINE

	Candidates	Votes	%
1	Stanley R. Tupper (R)	85,864	59.6
	Ronald Kellam (D)	58,129	40.4
2	Clifford G. McIntire (R)	72,349	51.1
	William D. Hathaway (D)	69,159	48.9

MARYLAND

	Candidates	Votes	%
1	Rogers C. B. Morton (R)	33,674	53.2
	Thomas F. Johnson (D)	29,653	46.8
2	Clarence D. Long (D)	85,383	51.9
	Fife Symington (R)	79,075	48.1
3	Edward A. Garmatz (D)	41,446	100.0
4	George H. Fallon (D)	35,077	72.3
	John E. Brondau (R)	13,425	27.7
5	Richard E. Lankford (D)	85,612	59.5
	Joseph M. Baker Jr. (R)	58,332	40.5
6	Charles McC. Mathias Jr. (R)	106,212	60.9
	John Foley (D)	68,116	39.1
7	Samuel N. Friedel (D)	57,958	70.0
	Caroline R. Ramsay (R)	24,825	30.0
AL	Carlton R. Sickles (D)	388,107	55.7
	Newton Steers (R)	308,792	44.3

MASSACHUSETTS

	Candidates	Votes	%
1	Silvio O. Conte (R)	106,498	74.4
	William K. Hefner (D)	36,711	25.6
2	Edward P. Boland (D)	92,340	67.8
	Samuel S. Rodman (R)	43,873	32.2
3	Philip J. Philbin (D)	129,326	72.4
	Frank Anthony (R)	49,418	27.7
4	Harold D. Donohue (D)	145,166	90.4
	Stanley Shogren (P)	15,310	9.5
5	F. Bradford Morse (R)	112,455	57.4
	Thomas J. Lane (D)	83,504	42.6
6	William H. Bates (R)	113,104	56.2
	George J. O'Shea (D)	88,187	43.8
7	Torbert H. Macdonald (D)	119,117	71.6
	Gordon F. Hughes (R)	47,289	28.4
8	Thomas P. O'Neill Jr. (D)	100,814	73.0
	Howard Greyber (R)	37,374	27.1
9	John W. McCormack (D)	105,565	100.0
10	Joseph W. Martin Jr. (R)	124,091	65.5
	Edward F. Doolan (D)	65,443	34.5
11	James A. Burke (D)	121,030	64.3
	Harry F. Stimpson (R)	67,138	35.7
12	Hastings Keith (R)	107,000	64.2
	Alexander Byron (D)	59,681	35.8

MICHIGAN

	Candidates	Votes	%
1	Lucien N. Nedzi (D)	82,321	89.3
	Walter Czarnecki (R)	9,916	10.8
2	George Meader (R)	88,427	58.4
	Thomas P. Payne (D)	63,036	41.6
3	August E. Johansen (R)	77,316	59.5
	Paul H. Todd Jr. (D)	52,667	40.5
4	Edward Hutchinson (R)	73,308	63.8
	Leland D. Mitchell (D)	41,620	36.2
5	Gerald R. Ford Jr. (R)	110,043	67.0
	William G. Reamon (D)	54,112	33.0
6	Charles E. Chamberlain (R)	112,861	54.5
	Don Hayworth (D)	94,157	45.5
7	James G. O'Hara (D)	127,067	56.3
	H. Charles Knill (R)	98,742	43.7
8	James Harvey (R)	77,022	60.5
	Jerome T. Hart (D)	50,376	39.5
9	Robert P. Griffin (R)	66,645	59.4
	Donald G. Jennings (D)	45,536	40.6
10	Elford A. Cederberg (R)	63,452	61.5
	Hubert C. Evans (D)	39,771	38.5
11	Victor A. Knox (R)	48,244	56.7
	Warren P. Cleary (D)	36,886	43.3
12	John B. Bennett (R)	41,784	63.3
	William J. Bolognesi (D)	24,240	36.7
13	Charles C. Diggs Jr. (D)	59,688	71.2
	Robert B. Blackwell (R)	24,134	28.8
14	Harold M. Ryan (D)	108,025	61.8
	Lois V. Nair (R)	66,889	38.2
15	John D. Dingell (D)	94,197	83.0
	Ernest Richards (R)	19,258	17.0
16	John Lesinski Jr. (D)	180,626	67.9
	Laverne O. Elliott (R)	85,485	32.1
17	Martha W. Griffiths (D)	122,021	59.3
	James F. O'Neil (R)	83,870	40.7
18	William S. Broomfield (R)	149,863	59.6
	George J. Fulkerson (D)	101,468	40.4
AL	Neil Staebler (D)	1,392,221	52.0
	Alvin M. Bentley (R)	1,282,082	47.9

Special Election

		Votes	%
14	Harold M. Ryan (D)	30,367#	50.5
	Robert E. Waldron (R)	29,600#	49.2

MINNESOTA

	Candidates	Votes	%
1	Albert H. Quie (R)	90,632	57.5
	David L. Graven (DFL)	66,956	42.5
2	Ancher Nelsen (R)	81,557	62.2
	Conrad H. Hammar (DFL)	49,543	37.8
3	Clark MacGregor (R)	87,730	60.2
	Irving R. Keldsen (DFL)	58,066	39.8
4	Joseph E. Karth (DFL)	93,519	59.5
	Harry Strong (R)	63,766	40.5
5	Donald M. Fraser (DFL)	87,002	51.8
	Walter H. Judd (R)	80,865	48.2
6	Alec G. Olson (DFL)	77,310	50.1
	Robert J. Odegard (R)	76,962	49.9
7	Odin Langen (R)	70,546	52.0
	Harding C. Noblitt (DFL)	65,161	48.0
8	John A. Blatnik (DFL)	101,567	65.7
	Jerry H. Ketola (R)	52,996	34.3

MISSISSIPPI

	Candidates	Votes	%
1	Thomas G. Abernathy (D)	26,251	100.0
2	Jamie L. Whitten (D)	31,344	100.0
3	John Bell Williams (D)	38,093	100.0

MISSISSIPPI

	Candidates	Votes	%
4	Arthur Winstead (D)	21,730	83.0
	Sterling P. Davis (I)	4,461	17.0
5	William M. Colmer (D)	39,735	100.0

MISSOURI

	Candidates	Votes	%
1	Frank M. Karsten (D)	82,216	70.7
	Charles F. Cherry (R)	34,089	29.3
2	Thomas B. Curtis (R)	102,861	56.3
	Philip V. Maher (D)	79,732	43.7
3	Leonor K. Sullivan (D)	81,346	70.5
	J. Marvin Krause (R)	34,031	29.5
4	William J. Randall (D)	59,599	53.9
	John D. Fox (R)	50,945	46.1
5	Richard Bolling (D)	54,166	58.9
	Walter McCarty (R)	37,835	41.1
6	W. R. Hull Jr. (D)	62,366	55.3
	Ethan H. Campbell (R)	50,339	44.7
7	Durward G. Hall (R)	84,651	57.7
	Jim Thomas (D)	62,082	42.3
8	Richard Ichord (D)	77,535	59.0
	David W. Bernhardt (R)	53,862	41.0
9	Clarence Cannon (D)	74,254	61.2
	Anthony C. Schroeder (R)	47,026	38.8
10	Paul C. Jones (D)	50,581	60.6
	Truman Farrow (R)	32,828	39.4

MONTANA

	Candidates	Votes	%
1	Arnold Olsen (D)	55,611	52.8
	Wayne Montgomery (R)	49,760	47.2
2	James F. Battin (R)	79,315	55.4
	Leo Graybill Jr. (D)	63,755	44.6

NEBRASKA

	Candidates	Votes	%
1	Ralph F. Beermann (R)	85,559	50.9
	Clair A. Callan (D)	73,768	43.9
	George C. Menkens	8,794	5.2
2	Glenn Cunningham (R)	83,139	69.5
	Thomas N. Bonner (D)	36,577	30.6
3	Dave Martin (R)	103,079	65.6
	John A. Hoffman (D)	54,058	34.4

NEVADA

	Candidates	Votes	%
AL	Walter S. Baring (D)	66,866	71.7
	J. Carlton Adair (R)	26,458	28.4

NEW HAMPSHIRE

	Candidates	Votes	%
1	Louis C. Wyman (R)	65,651	53.1
	J. Oliva Huot (D)	57,910	46.9
2	James C. Cleveland (R)	56,152	57.5
	Eugene S. Daniell (D)	41,539	42.5

NEW JERSEY

	Candidates	Votes	%
1	William T. Cahill (R)	119,633	58.8
	Neil F. Deighan Jr. (D)	83,405	41.0
2	Milton W. Glenn (R)	61,285	52.7
	Paul R. Porreca (D)	54,317	46.7
3	James C. Auchincloss (R)	82,220	56.9
	Peter J. Gannon (D)	62,258	43.1
4	Frank Thompson Jr. (D)	88,668	63.8
	Ephraim Tomlinson (R)	49,952	35.9
5	Peter H. B. Frelinghuysen Jr. (R)	86,133	66.0
	Eugene M. Friedman (D)	43,347	33.2
6	Florence P. Dwyer (R)	110,143	59.6
	Lillian Walsh Egolf (D)	73,436	39.8
7	William B. Widnall (R)	110,926	61.4
	J. Emmet Cassidy (D)	68,330	37.8
8	Charles S. Joelson (D)	75,820	65.0
	Walter W. Porter Jr. (R)	39,903	34.2

	Candidates	Votes	%
9	Frank C. Osmers Jr. (R)	89,345	56.9
	Donald R. Sorkow (D)	66,140	42.2
10	Peter W. Rodino Jr. (D)	62,616	72.8
	Charles Allan Baretski (R)	22,819	26.5
11	Joseph G. Minish (D)	48,102	59.5
	Frank A. Palmieri (R)	30,244	37.4
12	George M. Wallhauser (R)	57,169	52.5
	Robert R. Peacock (D)	50,783	46.6
13	Cornelius E. Gallagher (D)	62,636	77.1
	Eugene P. Kenny (R)	17,063	21.0
14	Dominick V. Daniels (D)	54,000	70.6
	Michael J. Bell (R)	21,303	27.9
15	Edward J. Patten (D)	86,651	56.7
	Bernard F. Rodgers (R)	66,142	43.3

NEW MEXICO

	Candidates	Votes	%
AL	Thomas G. Morris (D)	152,684	64.4
	Junio Lopez (R)	84,457	35.6
AL	Joseph M. Montoya (D)	128,651	52.5
	Jack C. Redman (R)	116,262	47.5

NEW YORK

	Candidates	Votes	%
1	Otis G. Pike (D, L)	85,619	61.7
	Walter M. Ormsby (R)	53,133	38.3
2	James R. Grover Jr. (R)	70,352	55.7
	Robert J. Flynn (D, L)	55,963	44.3
3	Steven B. Derounian (R)	86,430	59.2
	George Soll (D, L)	59,635	40.8
4	John W. Wydler (R)	74,508	56.4
	Joseph A. Daley (D, L)	56,438	42.7
5	Frank J. Becker (R)	89,964	57.5
	Franklin Bear (D, L)	66,502	42.5
6	Seymour Halpern (R)	96,475	63.3
	Leonard L. Finz (D, L)	55,883	36.7
7	Joseph P. Addabbo (D, L)	80,983	59.3
	George Archinal (R)	55,654	40.7
8	Benjamin S. Rosenthal (D, L)	104,895	66.4
	Arthur McCrossen (R)	53,122	33.6
9	James J. Delaney (D)	85,987	58.8
	Charles H. Cohen (R)	51,325	35.1
	Mark Starr (L)	9,051	6.2
10	Emanuel Celler (D, L)	90,216	80.0
	Seymour Besunder (R)	21,210	19.0
11	Eugene J. Keogh (D, L)	60,082	71.6
	Abraham L. Banner (R)	23,844	28.4
12	Edna F. Kelly (D, L)	106,375	70.0
	Louis London Goldberg (R)	45,492	30.0
13	Abraham J. Multer (D, L)	116,753	74.6
	Melvyn M. Rothman (R)	39,765	25.4
14	John J. Rooney (D, L)	54,298	70.9
	Leon F. Nadrowski (R)	22,287	29.1
15	Hugh L. Carey (D, L)	55,602	50.2
	Francis E. Dorn (R)	55,219	49.8
16	John M. Murphy (D)	57,666	47.5
	Robert T. Connor (R)	55,821	45.9
	George B. Murphy (L)	8,043	6.6
17	John V. Lindsay (R)	98,024	68.7
	Martin B. Dworkis (D, L)	44,728	31.3
18	Adam Clayton Powell Jr. (D)	59,125	69.6
	Ramon A. Martinez (R)	18,313	21.6
	Mae P. Watts (L)	7,457	8.8
19	Leonard Farbstein (D)	59,880	58.5
	Richard S. Aldrich (R, OP)	31,244	30.5
	Bentley Kassal (L)	11,233	11.0
20	William F. Ryan (D, L)	94,425	72.6
	Gilbert A. Robinson (R)	35,664	27.4
21	James C. Healey (D)	65,242	67.4
	Stanley L. Slater (R)	20,354	21.0
	Lillian Gulker (L)	11,187	11.6
22	Jacob H. Gilbert (D)	51,241	70.4
	Oscar Gonzalez-Suarez (R)	14,901	20.5
	David Grand (L)	6,629	9.1

	Candidates	Votes	%
23	Charles A. Buckley (D)	69,836	54.4
	John J. Parker (R)	39,692	30.9
	John P. Hagan (L)	18,749	14.6
24	Paul A. Fino (R)	77,785	60.1
	Alfred E. Santangelo (D)	46,455	35.9
25	Robert R. Barry (R)	109,989	61.5
	A. Frank Reel (D, L)	68,859	38.5
26	Ogden R. Reid (R)	93,064	60.9
	Stanley W. Church (D, L)	59,725	39.1
27	Katharine St. George (R)	86,958	57.9
	William F. Ward Jr. (D, L)	63,306	42.1
28	J. Ernest Wharton (R)	94,531	64.1
	Morton E. Gilday (D, L)	52,994	35.9
29	Leo W. O'Brien (D, L)	126,313	60.1
	Wolfgang J. Riemer (R)	83,719	39.9
30	Carleton J. King (R)	108,860	63.8
	William W. Egan (D)	57,822	33.9
31	Clarence E. Kilburn (R)	66,283	60.0
	Francis G. Healey (D, L)	44,171	40.0
32	Alexander Pirnie (R)	77,875	57.6
	Virgil C. Crisafulli (D, L)	57,414	42.4
33	Howard W. Robison (R)	92,460	66.8
	Theodore W. Maurer (D)	41,412	29.9
34	R. Walter Riehlman (R)	84,780	54.8
	Lee Alexander (D)	67,149	43.4
35	Samuel S. Stratton (D, L)	78,560	54.5
	Janet Hill Gordon (R)	65,697	45.5
36	Frank J. Horton (R)	96,581	59.3
	Robert R. Bickal (D, L)	66,371	40.7
37	Harold C. Ostertag (R)	101,821	64.3
	Norman C. Katner (D, L)	56,428	35.7
38	Charles E. Goodell (R)	83,361	68.4
	T. Joseph Lynch (D)	36,992	30.3
39	John R. Pillion (R)	99,527	62.6
	Angelo S. Deloia (D)	55,774	35.1
40	William E. Miller (R)	72,706	52.0
	E. Dent Lackey (D, L)	67,004	48.0
41	Thaddeus J. Dulski (D, L)	93,982	71.5
	Daniel J. Kij (R)	37,544	28.5

Special Election

	Candidates	Votes	%
6	Benjamin S. Rosenthal (D, L)	16,115#	44.5
	Thomas F. Galvin (R)	15,851#	43.8
	Emil Levin (I)	4,245#	11.7

NORTH CAROLINA

	Candidates	Votes	%
1	Herbert C. Bonner (D)	17,898	100.0
2	L. H. Fountain (D)	21,050	100.0
3	David N. Henderson (D)	34,056	100.0
4	Harold D. Cooley (D)	45,249	58.1
	George E. Ward (R)	32,593	41.9
5	Ralph J. Scott (D)	47,009	59.2
	A. M. Snipes (R)	32,427	40.8
6	Horace R. Kornegay (D)	43,021	59.9
	Blackwell P. Robinson (R)	28,827	40.1
7	Alton Lennon (D)	33,173	77.0
	James E. Walsh Jr. (R)	9,895	23.0
8	Charles R. Jonas (R)	64,703	56.0
	A. Paul Kitchin (D)	50,926	44.0
9	James T. Broyhill (R)	67,608	50.5
	Hugh Q. Alexander (D)	66,332	49.5
10	Basil L. Whitener (D)	52,641	55.1
	Carrol M. Barringer (R)	42,908	44.9
11	Roy A. Taylor (D)	70,791	55.2
	Robert Brown (R)	57,422	44.8

NORTH DAKOTA

	Candidates	Votes	%
1	Hjalmar C. Nygaard (R)	61,330	54.6
	Scott Anderson (D)	50,924	45.4
2	Don L. Short (R)	56,203	54.0
	Robert Vogel (D)	47,825	46.0

OHIO

	Candidates	Votes	%
1	Carl W. Rich (R)	74,320	62.7
	Monica Nolan (D)	44,264	37.3
2	Donald D. Clancy (R)	105,750	62.8
	H. A. Sand (D)	62,733	37.2
3	Paul F. Schenck (R)	113,584	57.0
	Martin A. Evers (D)	85,573	43.0
4	William M. McCulloch (R)	77,790	70.3
	Marjorie Conrad Struna (D)	32,866	29.7
5	Delbert L. Latta (R)	69,272	70.4
	William T. Hunt (D)	29,114	29.6
6	William H. Harsha (R)	72,743	60.4
	Jerry C. Rasor (D)	47,737	39.6
7	Clarence J. Brown (R)	83,680	67.7
	Robert A. Riley (D)	39,908	32.3
8	Jackson E. Betts (R)	66,458	70.1
	Morris Laderman (D)	28,400	29.9
9	Thomas L. Ashley (D)	86,443	57.4
	Martin A. Janis (R)	64,279	42.7
10	Homer E. Abele (R)	46,158	52.3
	Walter H. Moeller (D)	42,131	47.7
11	Oliver P. Bolton (R)	74,573	50.6
	Robert E. Cook (D)	72,936	49.5
12	Samuel L. Devine (R)	130,316	68.3
	Paul D. Cassidy (D)	60,563	31.7
13	Charles A. Mosher (R)	63,858	55.1
	J. Grant Keys (D)	52,030	44.9
14	William H. Ayres (R)	100,909	53.7
	Oliver Ocasek (D)	86,947	46.3
15	Robert T. Secrest (D)	41,856	52.4
	Tom V. Moorehead (R)	38,095	47.7
16	Frank T. Bow (R)	96,512	60.1
	Ed Witmer (D)	64,213	40.0
17	John M. Ashbrook (R)	69,976	58.6
	Robert W. Levering (D)	49,415	41.4
18	Wayne L. Hays (D)	66,327	61.0
	John J. Carrigg (R)	42,336	39.0
19	Michael J. Kirwan (D)	75,967	62.2
	William Vincent Williams (R)	46,200	37.8
20	Michael A. Feighan (D)	91,544	71.0
	Leonard G. Richter (R)	37,325	29.0
21	Charles A. Vanik (D)	79,514	79.9
	Leodis Harris (R)	20,027	20.1
22	Frances P. Bolton (R)	74,603	64.6
	Edward Corrigan (D)	35,353	30.6
23	William E. Minshall (R)	107,510	71.5
	Emil C. Weber (D)	42,907	28.5
AL	Robert Taft Jr. (R)	1,786,018	60.5
	Richard D. Kennedy (D)	1,164,776	39.5

OKLAHOMA

1	Page Belcher (R)	102,585	68.6
	Herbert W. Wright Jr. (D)	46,949	31.4
2	Ed Edmondson (D)	65,968	56.7
	Bill Sharp (R)	50,481	43.4
3	Carl Albert (D)	56,010	100.0
4	Tom Steed (D)	66,000	100.0
5	John Jarman (D)	90,392	68.9
	William P. Pointon Jr. (R)	40,825	31.1
6	Victor Wickersham (D)	56,508	53.6
	Glenn L. Gibson (R)	48,985	46.4

OREGON

1	Walter Norblad (R)	119,263	61.8
	R. Blaine Whipple (D)	73,641	38.2
2	Al Ullman (D)	53,335	64.0
	Robert W. Chandler (R)	29,995	36.0
3	Edith Green (D)	131,573	66.0
	Stanley E. Hartman (R)	67,830	34.0
4	Robert B. Duncan (D)	83,660	53.9
	Carl Fisher (R)	71,483	46.1

PENNSYLVANIA

1	William A. Barrett (D)	102,722	63.5
	Winifred H. Malinowsky (R)	58,953	36.5

	Candidates	Votes	%
2	Robert N. C. Nix (D)	86,812	67.1
	Arthur C. Thomas (R)	42,607	32.9
3	James A. Byrne (D)	81,405	59.3
	Joseph R. Burns (R)	55,827	40.7
4	Herman Toll (D)	104,300	56.0
	Frank J. Barbera (R)	82,014	44.0
5	William J. Green Jr. (D)	94,501	55.9
	Michael J. Bednarek (R)	74,557	44.1
6	George M. Rhodes (D)	112,959	51.2
	Ivor D. Fenton (R)	107,724	48.8
7	William H. Milliken (R)	136,955	60.8
	John A. Reilly (D)	88,482	39.3
8	Willard S. Curtin (R)	101,853	54.8
	James A. Michener (D)	84,043	45.2
9	Paul B. Dague (R)	113,880	67.2
	Richard C. Keller (D)	55,565	32.8
10	Joseph M. McDade (R)	95,754	52.5
	William D. Combar (D)	86,680	47.5
11	Daniel J. Flood (D)	101,754	66.5
	Donald B. Ayers (R)	51,263	33.5
12	J. Irving Whalley (R)	98,190	60.5
	A. Reed Hayes (D)	64,227	39.5
13	Richard S. Schweiker (R)	135,847	66.6
	Lee F. Driscoll Jr. (D)	68,234	33.4
14	William S. Moorhead (D)	93,130	65.7
	Joseph M. Beatty (R)	48,726	34.4
15	Francis E. Walter (D)	63,574	57.5
	Woodrow A. Horn (R)	46,928	42.5
16	John C. Kunkel (R)	90,113	66.7
	John A. Walter (D)	44,932	33.3
17	Herman T. Schneebeli (R)	96,088	62.9
	William W. Litke (D)	56,692	37.1
18	Robert J. Corbett (R)	108,433	64.3
	Edward F. Cook (D)	60,260	35.7
19	George A. Goodling (R)	82,924	56.8
	Earl D. Warner (D)	62,995	43.2
20	Elmer J. Holland (D)	106,971	67.4
	Budd Edward Sheppard (R)	51,688	32.6
21	John H. Dent (D)	80,410	59.6
	Charles E. Scalf (R)	54,543	40.4
22	John P. Saylor (R)	82,584	57.5
	Donald J. Perry (D)	61,054	42.5
23	Leon H. Gavin (R)	79,158	58.6
	Frank M. O'Neil (D)	54,798	40.6
24	James D. Weaver (R)	82,213	51.4
	Peter J. Joyce (D)	77,749	48.6
25	Frank M. Clark (D)	87,552	56.4
	Harvey R. Robinson (R)	67,603	43.6
26	Thomas E. Morgan (D)	94,932	61.7
	Jerome Hahn (R)	58,945	38.3
27	James G. Fulton (R)	112,034	65.5
	Margaret Lee Walgren (D)	58,984	34.5

RHODE ISLAND

1	Fernard J. St.Germain (D)	80,333	56.8
	R. Gordon Butler (R)	61,186	43.2
2	John E. Fogarty (D)	127,184	71.8
	John F. Kennedy (R)	49,955	28.2

SOUTH CAROLINA

1	L. Mendel Rivers (D)	39,176	100.0
2	Albert W. Watson (D)	39,149	52.8
	Floyd D. Spence (R)	34,947	47.2
3	W. J. Bryan Dorn (D)	34,545	100.0
4	Robert T. Ashmore (D)	47,044	100.0
5	Robert W. Hemphill (D)	28,989	93.9
	Robert M. Doster (R)	1,861	6.0
6	John L. McMillan (D)	36,811	100.0

Special Election

2	Corinne B. Riley (D)	3,626#	100.0

SOUTH DAKOTA

1	Ben Reifel (R)	113,975	59.2
	Ralph A. Nauman (D)	78,421	40.8

	Candidates	Votes	%
2	E. Y. Berry (R)	37,092	61.5
	M. W. Morrie Clarkson (D)	23,243	38.5

TENNESSEE [1]

1	James Quillen (R)	49,320	53.9
	Herbert Silvers (D)	40,113	43.8
2	Howard H. Baker (R)	61,306	70.6
	Tally R. Livingston (D)	25,579	29.4
3	Bill Brock (R)	47,604	51.1
	Wilkes T. Thrasher Jr. (D)	45,597	48.9
4	Joe L. Evins (D)	46,005	87.9
	Arch M. Eaton Sr. (I)	6,310	12.1
5	Richard Fulton	47,756	60.4
	J. Carleton Loser	30,182	38.2
6	Ross Bass (D)	36,404	81.8
	J. J. Underwood Jr. (I)	8,120	18.2
7	Tom Murray (D)	24,746	100.0
8	Robert A. Everett (D)	23,521	97.3
9	Clifford Davis (D)	55,345	50.6
	Robert B. James (R)	54,132	49.5

TEXAS

1	Wright Patman (D)	26,669	67.3
	James Timberlake (R)	12,938	32.7
2	Jack Brooks (D)	47,137	68.8
	Roy James Jr. (R)	21,385	31.2
3	Lindley Beckworth (D)	26,915	52.0
	William Steger (R)	24,803	48.0
4	Ray Roberts (D)	23,757	72.0
	Conner Harrington (R)	9,165	28.0
5	Bruce Alger (R)	89,938	56.3
	Bill Jones (D)	69,813	43.7
6	Olin E. Teague (D)	33,617	100.0
7	John Dowdy (D)	37,756	88.2
	Raymond Ramage (R)	5,045	11.8
8	Albert Thomas (D)	51,285	71.5
	Anthony Farris (R)	20,475	28.5
9	Clark W. Thompson (D)	56,179	66.3
	Dave Oaks (R)	28,594	33.7
10	Homer Thornberry (D)	43,396	63.3
	Jim Dobbs (R)	25,165	36.7
11	W. R. Poage (D)	41,698	100.0
12	Jim Wright (D)	53,705	60.6
	Del Barron (R)	34,879	39.4
13	Graham B. Purcell (D)	37,941	67.1
	Joe Meissner (R)	18,578	32.9
14	John Young (D)	60,803	70.4
	Lawrence E. Hoover (R)	25,623	29.7
15	Joe Kilgore (D)	53,552	100.0
16	Ed Foreman (R)	44,095	53.8
	J. T. Rutherford (D)	37,821	46.2
17	Omar Burleson (D)	46,895	100.0
18	Walter Rogers (D)	43,389	58.8
	Jack Seale (R)	30,393	41.2
19	George Mahon (D)	46,925	67.1
	Dennis Taylor (R)	23,022	32.9
20	Henry B. Gonzalez (D)	62,776	100.0
21	O. C. Fisher (D)	39,261	76.1
	E. S. Mayer Jr. (R)	12,310	23.9
22	Bob Casey (D)	73,141	53.6
	Ross Baker (R)	63,452	46.5
AL	Joe Pool (D)	870,860	56.1
	Desmond A. Barry (R)	680,569	43.9

Special Runoff Elections [2]

4	Ray Roberts (D)	16,109	54.3
	R. C. Slagle Jr. (R)	13,572	45.7
13	Graham B. Purcell Jr. (D)	23,905	62.9
	Joe Meissner (R)	14,098	37.1

UTAH

1	Laurence J. Burton (R)	59,032	50.9
	Morris Blaine Peterson (D)	56,989	49.1

Footnotes, see p. 236.

UTAH

Candidates	Votes	%
2 Sherman P. Lloyd (R)	108,355	53.9
Bruce S. Jenkins (D)	92,631	46.1

VERMONT

	Votes	%
AL Robert T. Stafford (R)	68,822	56.7
Harold Raynolds (D)	52,535	43.3

VIRGINIA

Candidates	Votes	%
1 Thomas N. Downing (D)	21,664	99.7
2 Porter Hardy Jr. (D)	30,306	75.0
Louis B. Fine (R)	10,121	25.0
3 J. Vaughan Gary (D)	28,914	49.8
Louis H. Williams (R)	28,566	49.2
4 Watkins M. Abbitt (D)	30,642	99.5
5 William M. Tuck (D)	13,827	99.8
6 Richard H. Poff (R)	44,060	65.2
John P. Wheeler (D)	23,280	34.5
7 John O. Marsh Jr. (D)	26,302	50.6
J. Kenneth Robinson (R)	25,704	49.4
8 Howard W. Smith (D)	20,931	98.7
9 W. Pat Jennings (D)	32,893	61.2
Leon Owens (D)	20,851	38.8
10 Joel T. Broyhill (R)	49,611	55.4
Augustus C. Johnson (D)	39,940	44.6

WASHINGTON

Candidates	Votes	%
1 Thomas M. Pelly (R)	108,561	73.7
Alice Franklin Bryant (D)	38,669	26.3
2 Jack Westland (R)	70,498	59.8
Milo Moore (D)	47,333	40.2
3 Julia Butler Hansen (D)	69,045	65.3
Edwin J. Alexander (R)	36,629	34.7
4 Catherine May (R)	83,182	67.0
David A. Gallant (D)	40,887	33.0
5 Walt Horan (R)	78,504	64.4
Bernard J. Gallagher (D)	43,333	35.6
6 Thor C. Tollefson (R)	79,838	71.1
Dawn Olson (D)	32,513	28.9
7 K. W. Stinson (R)	86,106	56.6
Don Magnuson (D)	66,052	43.4

WEST VIRGINIA

	Votes	%
1 Arch A. Moore Jr. (R)	97,556	59.9
Cleveland M. Bailey (D)	65,328	40.1
2 Harley O. Staggers (D)	62,291	58.7
Cooper P. Benedict (R)	43,769	41.3
3 John M. Slack Jr. (D)	74,743	61.7
M. G. Guthrie (R)	46,344	38.3
4 Ken Hechler (D)	83,507	57.8
Clyde B. Pinson (R)	60,931	42.2
5 Elizabeth Kee (D)	57,405	73.1
James Strother Crockett (R)	21,144	26.9

WISCONSIN

Candidates	Votes	%
1 Henry C. Schadeberg (R)	71,657	53.3
Gerald T. Flynn (D)	62,800	46.7
2 Robert W. Kastenmeier (D)	89,740	52.5
Ivan H. Kindschi (R)	81,274	47.5
3 Vernon W. Thomson (R)	54,237	61.3
Walter P. Thoresen (D)	34,240	38.7
4 Clement J. Zablocki (D)	117,029	72.5
David F. Tillotson (R)	44,368	27.5
5 Henry S. Reuss (D)	103,705	63.6
Thomas F. Nelson (R)	59,441	36.4
6 William K. Van Pelt (R)	71,298	59.2
John A. Race (D)	49,238	40.9
7 Melvin R. Laird (R)	68,418	66.1
John E. Evans (D)	35,151	33.9
8 John W. Byrnes (R)	80,808	62.8
Owen F. Monfils (D)	47,833	37.2
9 Lester R. Johnson (D)	50,025	55.6
Dennis B. Danielson (R)	39,955	44.4
10 Alvin E. O'Konski (R)	52,451	63.2
J. Louis Hanson (D)	30,556	36.8

WYOMING

	Votes	%
AL William Henry Harrison (R)	71,489	61.4
Louis A. Mankus (D)	44,985	38.6

1963 House Elections

CALIFORNIA

Special Elections

	Votes	%
1 Don Clausen (R)	79,292	54.2
William F. Grader (D)	65,339	44.7
23 Del Clawson (R)	33,042	53.2
Carley V. Porter (D)	21,969	35.4

NORTH DAKOTA

Special Election

	Votes	%
1 Mark Andrews (R)	47,062#	49.1
John Hove (D)	42,470#	44.3
John W. Scott (CR)	5,995#	6.3

PENNSYLVANIA

Special Elections

	Votes	%
15 Fred B. Rooney (D)	48,846#	53.5
Robert G. Bartlett (R)	42,374#	46.5
23 Albert W. Johnson (R)	64,137#	58.4
William T. Hagerty (D)	45,677#	41.6

TEXAS [1]

Special Election

	Votes	%
10 J. J. Pickle (D)	14,389#	35.0
Jim Dobbs (R)	13,702#	33.3
Jack Ritter (D)	13,027#	31.7

Special Runoff Election

	Votes	%
10 J. J. Pickle (D)	27,228#	62.9
Jim Dobbs (R)	16,052#	37.1

1962 Elections

1. The race in Tennessee's 5th district was held without party affiliation. It was an out-growth of a disputed Democratic primary between Fulton and Loser. Neither was given the Democratic nomination and the general election was conducted on a non-partisan basis.

2. These elections were runoffs between the two candidates who finished with the most votes in special primaries held in 1961, but failed to win a majority. (See Texas 1961, p. 1243.)

1963 Elections

1. Under Texas's special election law, a majority was required to win the House seat. Since no candidate had a majority in the initial special election, a runoff special election was held between the top two finishers. (See Texas 1961 for explanation of Texas special election law, p. 1243.)

1964 House Elections

ALABAMA

	Candidates	Votes	%
1	Jack Edwards (R)	54,522	59.9
	John Tyson (D)	36,482	40.1
2	William L. Dickinson (R)	49,936	61.7
	George M. Grant (D)	29,628	36.6
3	George Andrews (D)	27,939	100.0
4	Glenn Andrews (R)	40,143	58.6
	Kenneth A. Roberts (D)	27,800	40.6
5	Armistead I. Selden Jr. (D)	42,784	53.0
	Robert French (R)	37,960	47.0
6	John Buchanan (R)	69,246	60.6
	George Huddleston Jr. (D)	45,090	39.4
7	James D. Martin (R)	65,353	59.6
	George C. Hawkins (D)	44,386	40.5
8	Robert E. Jones (D)	43,842	100.0

ALASKA

	Candidates	Votes	%
AL	Ralph J. Rivers (D)	34,605	51.5
	Lowell Thomas Jr. (R)	32,566	48.5

ARIZONA

	Candidates	Votes	%
1	John J. Rhodes (R)	140,507	55.3
	John Ahearn (D)	113,669	44.7
2	Morris K. Udall (D)	86,499	58.7
	William E. Kimble (R)	60,782	41.3
3	George F. Senner Jr. (D)	30,565	51.5
	Sam Steiger (R)	28,802	48.5

ARKANSAS

	Candidates	Votes	%
1	E. C. Gathings (D)		100.0
2	Wilbur D. Mills (D)		100.0
3	James W. Trimble (D)	71,228	54.7
	J. E. Hinshaw (R)	58,884	45.3
4	Oren Harris (D)		100.0

CALIFORNIA

	Candidates	Votes	%
1	Don H. Clausen (R)	141,018	59.1
	George McCabe (D)	97,651	40.9
2	Harold T. Johnson (D)	125,774	64.6
	Chester C. Merriam (R)	68,835	35.4
3	John E. Moss (D)	166,688	74.3
	Einar B. Gjelsteen (R)	57,630	25.7
4	Robert L. Leggett (D)	84,949	71.9
	Ivan Norris (R)	33,160	28.1
5	Phillip Burton (D)	71,638	100.0
6	William S. Mailliard (R)	125,869	63.7
	Thomas P. O'Toole (D)	71,894	36.4
7	Jeffery Cohelan (D)	100,901	66.1
	Lawrence E. McNutt (R)	51,675	33.9
8	George P. Miller (D)	108,771	70.3
	Donald E. McKay (R)	46,063	29.8
9	Don Edwards (D)	115,954	69.8
	William P. Hyde (R)	50,261	30.2
10	Charles S. Gubser (R)	151,027	63.1
	E. Day Carman (D)	88,240	36.9
11	J. Arthur Younger (R)	116,022	54.8
	W. Mark Sullivan (D)	95,747	45.2
12	Burt L. Talcott (R)	93,112	61.9
	Sanford Bolz (D)	57,243	38.1
13	Charles M. Teague (R)	104,744	57.4
	George E. Taylor (D)	77,763	42.6
14	John F. Baldwin (R)	117,272	64.9
	Russell M. Koch (D)	63,469	35.1
15	John J. McFall (D)	109,560	70.9
	Kenneth B. Gibson (R)	44,977	29.1
16	B. F. Sisk (D)	117,727	66.8
	David T. Harris (R)	58,604	33.2
17	Cecil R. King (D)	95,640	67.7
	Robert Muncaster (R)	45,688	32.3
18	Harlan Hagen (D)	121,304	66.7
	James E. Williams Jr. (R)	60,523	33.3

	Candidates	Votes	%
19	Chet Holifield (D)	97,934	65.4
	C. Everett Hunt (R)	51,747	34.6
20	H. Allen Smith (R)	132,402	67.9
	C. Bernard Kaufman (D)	62,645	32.1
21	Augustus F. Hawkins (D)	106,231	90.3
	Rayfield Lundy (R)	11,374	9.7
22	James C. Corman (D)	94,141	50.5
	Robert C. Cline (R)	92,133	49.5
23	Del Clawson (R)	90,721	55.4
	H. O. Van Petten (D)	72,903	44.5
24	Glenard P. Lipscomb (R)	139,784	67.9
	Bryan W. Stevens (D)	65,967	32.1
25	Ronald Brooks Cameron (D)	81,320	55.4
	Frank J. Walton (R)	65,344	44.6
26	James Roosevelt (D)	136,025	70.4
	Gil Seton (R)	57,209	29.6
27	Ed Reinecke (R)	83,141	51.7
	Tom Bane (D)	77,587	48.3
28	Alphonzo Bell (R)	205,347	65.6
	Gerald H. Gottlieb (D)	107,852	34.4
29	George E. Brown Jr. (D)	90,208	58.6
	Charles J. Farrington Jr. (R)	63,836	41.4
30	Edward R. Roybal (D)	90,329	66.3
	Alfred J. Feder (R)	45,912	33.7
31	Charles H. Wilson (D)	114,246	64.0
	Norman G. Shanahan (R)	64,256	36.0
32	Craig Hosmer (R)	132,603	68.9
	Michael Cullen (D)	59,765	31.1
33	Kenneth W. Dyal (D)	109,047	51.7
	Jerry L. Pettis (R)	101,742	48.3
34	Richard T. Hanna (D)	137,588	58.3
	Robert A. Geier (R)	98,606	41.8
35	James B. Utt (R)	167,791	65.0
	Paul B. Carpenter (D)	90,295	35.0
36	Bob Wilson (R)	105,346	59.1
	Quinton Whelan (D)	73,034	40.9
37	Lionel Van Deerlin (D)	85,624	58.2
	Dick Wilson (R)	61,373	41.8
38	John V. Tunney (D)	85,661	52.8
	Patrick Minor Martin (R)	76,525	47.2

Special Election

	Candidates	Votes	%
5	Phillip Burton (D)	26,698	53.6
	Nick A. Verreos (R)	12,777	25.7
	Tom Flowers (D)	3,841	7.7
	Joe Bortin (D)	3,327	6.7

COLORADO

	Candidates	Votes	%
1	Byron G. Rogers (D)	138,475	67.5
	Glenn R. Jones (R)	65,423	31.9
2	Roy H. McVicker (D)	109,526	50.6
	Donald G. Brotzman (R)	106,738	49.4
3	Frank E. Evans (D)	85,404	51.2
	J. Edgar Chenoweth (R)	81,544	48.8
4	Wayne N. Aspinall (D)	106,685	63.0
	Edwin S. Lamm (R)	62,617	37.0

CONNECTICUT

	Candidates	Votes	%
1	Emilio Q. Daddario (D)	141,310	70.0
	James F. Collins (R)	60,654	30.0
2	William L. St.Onge (D)	119,530	63.3
	Belton A. Copp (R)	69,403	36.7
3	Robert N. Giaimo (D)	126,353	63.9
	Bernard J. Burns (R)	71,393	36.1
4	Donald J. Irwin (D)	117,220	51.8
	Abner W. Sibal (R)	109,027	48.2
5	John S. Monagan (D)	133,072	67.3
	Charles W. Terrell Jr. (R)	64,651	32.7
6	Bernard F. Grabowski (D)	115,498	58.7
	Thomas J. Meskill Jr. (R)	81,105	41.2

DELAWARE

	Candidates	Votes	%
AL	Harris B. McDowell Jr. (D)	112,361	56.6
	James H. Snowden (R)	86,254	43.4

FLORIDA

	Candidates	Votes	%
1	Robert L. F. Sikes (D)	74,615	98.0
2	Charles E. Bennett (D)	99,191	72.7
	William T. Stockton Jr. (R)	37,283	27.3
3	Claude Pepper (D)	101,162	65.7
	Paul J. O'Neil (R)	52,758	34.3
4	Dante B. Fascell (D)	94,726	63.9
	Jay McGlon (R)	53,468	36.1
5	A. Sydney Herlong Jr. (D)	85,851	100.0
6	Paul G. Rogers (D)	168,573	66.1
	John D. Steele (R)	86,657	34.0
7	James A. Haley (D)	79,504	100.0
8	D. R. Matthews (D)	49,374	99.9
9	Don Fuqua (D)	44,917	98.8
10	Sam M. Gibbons (D)	69,860	99.6
11	Edward J. Gurney (R)	91,731	60.6
	Thomas S. Kenney (D)	59,746	39.4
12	William C. Cramer (R)	98,959	60.6
	F. Marion Harrelson (D)	64,378	39.4

GEORGIA

	Candidates	Votes	%
1	G. Elliott Hagan (D)	65,146	72.3
	J. Milton Lent (I)	25,006	27.7
2	Maston O'Neal (D)	37,634	99.9
3	Howard H. Callaway (R)	45,545	57.4
	Garland T. Byrd (D)	33,733	42.5
4	James A. Mackay (D)	66,488	56.9
	Roscoe Pickett (R)	50,326	43.1
5	Charles L. Weltner (D)	65,803	54.0
	L. J. O'Callaghan (R)	55,983	46.0
6	John J. Flynt Jr. (D)	69,712	100.0
7	John W. Davis (D)	69,575	54.7
	Ed Chapin (R)	57,562	45.3
8	J. Russell Tuten (D)	49,727	100.0
9	Phil M. Landrum (D)	59,186	60.5
	Jack Prince (R)	38,608	39.5
10	Robert G. Stephens Jr. (D)	45,418	100.0

HAWAII

	Candidates	Votes	%
AL	Spark M. Matsunaga (D)	140,224✔	
	Patsy Takemoto Mink (D)	106,909✔	
	John E. Milligan (R)	89,425	
	Richard Ike Sutton (R)	56,147	

IDAHO

	Candidates	Votes	%
1	Compton I. White Jr. (D)	56,203	51.7
	John N. Mattmiller (R)	52,468	48.3
2	George V. Hansen (R)	91,838	52.2
	Ralph R. Harding (D)	84,022	47.8

ILLINOIS

	Candidates	Votes	%
1	William L. Dawson (D)	150,953	84.9
	Wilbur N. Daniel (R)	26,823	15.1
2	Barratt O'Hara (D)	107,795	67.3
	William F. Scannell (R)	52,416	32.7
3	William T. Murphy (D)	120,711	59.1
	Emmet F. Byrne (R)	83,404	40.9
4	Edward J. Derwinski (R)	144,762	58.9
	Ray J. Rybacki (D)	100,895	41.1
5	John C. Kluczynski (D)	101,626	63.7
	Robert V. Kotowski (R)	57,871	36.3

ILLINOIS

	Candidates	Votes	%
6	Daniel J. Ronan (D)	89,850	83.4
	Joseph W. Halac (R)	17,918	16.6
7	Frank Annunzio (D)	106,708	85.9
	Ray Wolfram (R)	17,471	14.1
8	Dan Rostenkowski (D)	137,715	66.1
	Eugene L. Ebrom (R)	70,624	33.9
9	Sidney R. Yates (D)	113,851	63.9
	Robert S. Decker (R)	64,428	36.1
10	Harold R. Collier (R)	172,499	60.8
	Thomas E. Gause (D)	111,029	39.2
11	Roman C. Pucinski (D)	129,337	56.9
	Chester T. Podgorski (R)	98,132	43.1
12	Robert McClory (R)	97,003	58.6
	John Clark Kimball (D)	68,555	41.4
13	Donald Rumsfeld (R)	165,129	57.8
	Lynn A. Williams (D)	120,449	42.2
14	John N. Erlenborn (R)	145,830	59.0
	Jerome M. Ziegler (D)	101,432	41.0
15	Charlotte T. Reid (R)	103,709	58.4
	Poppy X. Mitchell (D)	73,741	41.6
16	John B. Anderson (R)	93,051	56.4
	Robert E. Brinkmeier (D)	71,992	43.6
17	Leslie C. Arends (R)	96,209	56.4
	Bernard J. Hughes (D)	74,261	43.6
18	Robert H. Michel (R)	91,173	54.0
	Edward P. Kohlbacher (D)	77,711	46.0
19	Gale Schisler (D)	81,800	52.4
	Robert T. McLoskey (R)	74,290	47.6
20	Paul Findley (R)	119,184	54.8
	Lester E. Collins (D)	98,256	45.2
21	Kenneth J. Gray (D)	117,701	65.0
	Mrs. Stillman J. Stanard (R)	63,431	35.0
22	William L. Springer (R)	80,895	53.0
	John J. Desmond (D)	71,875	47.1
23	George E. Shipley (D)	119,447	54.6
	Wayne S. Jones (R)	99,496	45.4
24	Melvin Price (D)	144,743	75.7
	G. S. Mirza (R)	46,419	24.3

INDIANA

	Candidates	Votes	%
1	Ray J. Madden (D)	133,089	63.7
	Arthur F. Endres (R)	75,226	36.0
2	Charles A. Halleck (R)	88,204	52.9
	John C. Raber (D)	78,566	47.1
3	John Brademas (D)	121,209	60.7
	Robert Lowell Miller (R)	78,642	39.4
4	E. Ross Adair (R)	89,437	52.1
	Max E. Hobbs (D)	82,284	47.9
5	J. Edward Roush (D)	114,252	55.2
	John R. Feighner (R)	92,802	44.8
6	Richard L. Roudebush (R)	86,168	54.1
	Karl O'Lessker (D)	73,002	45.9
7	William G. Bray (R)	84,427	54.2
	Elden C. Tipton (D)	71,461	45.8
8	Winfield K. Denton (D)	109,134	56.5
	Roger H. Zion (R)	84,135	43.5
9	Lee H. Hamilton (D)	74,939	54.4
	Earl Wilson (R)	62,780	45.6
10	Ralph Harvey (R)	89,303	50.5
	Russell E. Davis (D)	87,721	49.6
11	Andrew Jacobs Jr. (D)	149,342	50.5
	Don A. Tabbert (R)	146,424	49.5

IOWA

	Candidates	Votes	%
1	John R. Schmidhauser (D)	84,042	51.0
	Fred Schwengel (R)	80,697	48.9
2	John C. Culver (D)	97,470	52.2
	James E. Bromwell (R)	89,294	47.8
3	H. R. Gross (R)	83,455	50.1
	Stephen M. Peterson (D)	83,036	49.9
4	Bert Bandstra (D)	85,518	53.6
	John Kyl (R)	73,898	46.4
5	Neal Smith (D)	108,212	69.6
	Benjamin J. Gibson Jr. (R)	46,160	29.7
6	Stanley L. Greigg (D)	86,323	53.2
	Howard N. Sokol (R)	75,478	46.5

	Candidates	Votes	%
7	John R. Hansen (D)	78,243	53.5
	Ben F. Jensen (R)	67,942	46.5

KANSAS

	Candidates	Votes	%
1	Bob Dole (R)	113,212	51.2
	Bill Bork (D)	108,086	48.8
2	Chester L. Mize (R)	80,806	51.1
	John Montgomery (D)	77,189	48.9
3	Robert F. Ellsworth (R)	89,588	62.2
	A. Clayton Dial (D)	54,522	37.8
4	Garner Shriver (R)	84,800	59.4
	Jack Glaves (D)	58,057	40.6
5	Joe Skubitz (R)	83,120	56.4
	Reb Russell (D)	64,308	43.6

KENTUCKY

	Candidates	Votes	%
1	Frank Stubblefield (D)	84,574	100.0
2	William H. Natcher (D)	79,519	68.4
	Rhodes Bratcher (R)	36,664	31.6
3	Charles P. Farnsley (D)	117,892	53.8
	M. G. (Gene) Snyder (R)	101,168	46.2
4	Frank Chelf (D)	88,337	61.7
	Clyde Middleton (R)	54,937	38.3
5	Tim Lee Carter (R)	61,137	53.1
	Francis Jones Mills (D)	53,916	46.9
6	John C. Watts (D)	93,322	70.6
	John W. Swope (R)	38,869	29.4
7	Carl D. Perkins (D)	100,929	69.7
	Walter Clay Van Hoose (R)	43,921	30.3

LOUISIANA

	Candidates	Votes	%
1	F. Edward Hebert (D)	76,455	100.0
2	Hale Boggs (D)	77,009	55.1
	David C. Treen (R)	62,881	45.0
3	Edwin E. Willis (D)	52,532	62.3
	Robert J. Angers Jr. (R)	31,806	37.7
4	Joe D. Waggonner Jr. (D)	44,599	100.0
5	Otto E. Passman (D)	24,544	100.0
6	James H. Morrison (D)	82,686	62.9
	Floyd O. Crawford (R)	48,715	37.1
7	T. A. Thompson (D)	38,492	100.0
8	Speedy O. Long (D)	33,250	54.5
	William S. Walker (R)	27,735	45.5

MAINE

	Candidates	Votes	%
1	Stanley R. Tupper (R)	95,398	50.1
	Kenneth M. Curtis (D)	95,195	50.0
2	William D. Hathaway (D)	110,931	62.0
	Kenneth P. MacLeod (R)	67,978	38.0

MARYLAND

	Candidates	Votes	%
1	Rogers C. B. Morton (R)	40,762	53.1
	Harry R. Hughes (D)	36,013	46.9
2	Clarence D. Long (D)	143,132	65.9
	George A. Price (R)	74,067	34.1
3	Edward A. Garmatz (D)	56,295	100.0
4	George H. Fallon (D)	57,229	77.8
	Charles O'D. Evans (R)	16,372	22.2
5	Hervey G. Machen (D)	131,712	61.0
	Edward A. Potts (R)	84,318	39.0
6	Charles McC. Mathias Jr. (R)	134,521	54.5
	Royce Hanson (D)	112,410	45.5
7	Samuel N. Friedel (D)	99,654	79.5
	Thomas C. Hofstetter (R)	25,706	20.5
AL	Carlton R. Sickles (D)	683,143	69.4
	David Scull (R)	301,250	30.6

MASSACHUSETTS

	Candidates	Votes	%
1	Silvio O. Conte (R)	139,503	100.0
2	Edward P. Boland (D)	125,894	100.0
3	Philip J. Philbin (D)	177,917	100.0
4	Harold D. Donohue (D)	142,339	71.8
	Dudley B. Dumaine (R)	56,034	28.3
5	F. Bradford Morse (R)	137,735	65.0
	George W. Arvanitis (D)	74,133	35.0
6	William H. Bates (R)	141,733	64.6
	James G. Zafris Jr. (D)	77,646	35.4
7	Torbert H. Macdonald (D)	139,095	77.0
	Gordon F. Hughes (R)	41,671	23.1
8	Thomas P. O'Neill Jr. (D)	122,050	100.0
9	John W. McCormack (D)	118,385	80.3
	Jack E. Molesworth (R)	21,557	14.6
	Noel A. Day (I)	7,440	5.1
10	Joseph W. Martin Jr. (R)	133,403	63.0
	Edward F. Doolan (D)	78,415	37.0
11	James A. Burke (D)	179,261	100.0
12	Hastings Keith (R)	115,656	59.6
	Alexander Byron (D)	78,313	40.4

MICHIGAN

	Candidates	Votes	%
1	John Conyers Jr. (D)	138,589	83.6
	Robert B. Blackwell (R)	25,735	15.5
2	Weston E. Vivian (D)	77,806	50.4
	George Meader (R)	76,280	49.4
3	Paul H. Todd (D)	85,001	52.7
	August E. Johansen (R)	76,350	47.3
4	Edward Hutchinson (R)	83,391	54.3
	Russell W. Holcomb (D)	70,212	45.7
5	Gerald R. Ford (R)	101,810	61.2
	William G. Reamon (D)	64,488	38.8
6	Charles E. Chamberlain (R)	88,882	56.6
	Boyd K. Benedict (D)	68,265	43.4
7	John C. Mackie (D)	104,115	65.7
	Claude E. Sadler (R)	54,307	34.3
8	James Harvey (R)	84,588	54.7
	Sanford A. Brown (D)	69,931	45.3
9	Robert P. Griffin (R)	95,376	57.4
	Daniel Griffen (D)	70,693	42.6
10	Elford A. Cederberg (R)	87,232	56.6
	Hubert C. Evans (D)	66,835	43.4
11	Raymond F. Clevenger (D)	86,557	53.3
	Victor A. Knox (R)	75,955	46.7
12	James G. O'Hara (D)	126,769	74.8
	Robert G. Powell (R)	42,615	25.2
13	Charles C. Diggs Jr. (D)	102,413	85.8
	Bruce Watson (R)	16,585	13.9
14	Lucien N. Nedzi (D)	120,308	66.9
	George Bashara (R)	59,487	33.1
15	William D. Ford (D)	103,724	71.0
	John F. Fellrath Jr. (R)	42,464	29.1
16	John D. Dingell (D)	112,763	73.4
	Raymond B. Leonard (R)	40,673	26.5
17	Martha W. Griffiths (D)	136,230	72.8
	William P. Harrington (R)	50,580	27.0
18	William S. Broomfield (R)	109,777	59.5
	Frank J. Sierawski (D)	74,576	40.4
19	Billie S. Farnum (D)	88,441	53.4
	Richard D. Kuhn (R)	77,204	46.6

MINNESOTA

	Candidates	Votes	%
1	Albert H. Quie (R)	108,639	55.3
	George Daley (DFL)	87,789	44.7
2	Ancher Nelsen (R)	97,804	58.4
	Charles V. Simpson (DFL)	69,801	41.7
3	Clark MacGregor (R)	125,464	57.0
	Richard J. Parish (DFL)	94,682	43.0
4	Joseph E. Karth (DFL)	144,801	73.0
	John M. Drexler (R)	52,221	26.3
5	Donald M. Fraser (DFL)	127,963	61.9
	John W. Johnson (R)	78,767	38.1
6	Alec G. Olson (DFL)	95,848	51.8
	Robert J. Odegard (R)	89,228	48.2
7	Odin Langen (R)	84,304	50.8
	Ben M. Wichterman (DFL)	81,718	49.2
8	John A. Blatnik (DFL)	124,277	69.4
	David W. Glossbrenner (R)	54,691	30.6

MISSISSIPPI

Candidates	Votes	%
1 Thomas G. Abernethy (D)	60,052	100.0
2 Jamie L. Whitten (D)	70,218	100.0
3 John Bell Williams (D)	84,503	100.0
4 Prentiss Walker (R)	35,277	55.7
Arthur Winstead (D)	28,057	44.3
5 William M. Colmer (D)	83,120	100.0

MISSOURI

Candidates	Votes	%
1 Frank M. Karsten (D)	140,848	76.9
Theodore J. Fischer (R)	42,351	23.1
2 Thomas B. Curtis (R)	130,894	53.1
Sidney B. McClanahan (D)	115,446	46.9
3 Leonor K. Sullivan (D)	123,193	71.7
Howard C. Ohlendorf (R)	48,709	28.3
4 William J. Randall (D)	109,375	63.9
James M. Taylor (R)	61,854	36.1
5 Richard Bolling (D)	91,721	67.9
Robert B. Langworthy (R)	43,314	32.1
6 W. R. Hull Jr. (D)	110,532	64.7
Henry E. Wurst (R)	60,356	35.3
7 Durward G. Hall (R)	102,926	51.7
Jim Thomas (D)	96,120	48.3
8 Richard Ichord (D)	117,672	65.2
Ben A. Rogers (R)	62,823	34.8
9 William L. Hungate (D)	112,907	62.3
Anthony C. Schroeder (R)	68,032	37.6
10 Paul C. Jones (D)	89,698	67.4
Carl F. Painter (R)	43,304	32.6

Special Election

Candidates	Votes	%
9 William L. Hungate (D)	102,422	62.5
Anthony C. Schroeder (R)	61,439	37.5

MONTANA

Candidates	Votes	%
1 Arnold Olsen (D)	64,847	53.6
Wayne Montgomery (R)	55,417	45.8
2 James F. Battin (R)	84,241	54.1
Jack C. Toole (D)	71,461	45.9

NEBRASKA

Candidates	Votes	%
1 Clair A. Callan (D)	107,683	51.3
Ralph F. Beermann (R)	102,113	48.7
2 Glenn Cunningham (R)	81,660	53.1
John Richard Swenson (D)	72,003	46.9
3 Dave Martin (R)	104,380	52.8
William E. Colwell (D)	93,236	47.2

NEVADA

Candidates	Votes	%
AL Walter S. Baring (D)	82,748	63.3
George Von Tobel (R)	47,989	36.7

NEW HAMPSHIRE

Candidates	Votes	%
1 J. Oliva Huot (D)	79,097	51.4
Louis C. Wyman (R)	74,939	48.7
2 James C. Cleveland (R)	62,680	50.1
Charles B. Officer (D)	62,382	49.9

NEW JERSEY

Candidates	Votes	%
1 William T. Cahill (R)	150,805	56.2
William J. Procacci (D)	117,227	43.7
2 Thomas C. McGrath Jr. (D)	73,264	50.8
Milton W. Glenn (R)	70,997	49.2
3 James J. Howard (D)	105,803	50.4
Marcus Daly (R)	104,063	49.6
4 Frank Thompson Jr. (D)	134,747	67.5
Ephraim Tomlinson (R)	64,447	32.3
5 Peter H. B. Frelinghuysen (R)	122,168	63.6
Eugene M. Friedman (D)	70,001	36.4

Candidates	Votes	%
6 Florence P. Dwyer (R)	140,999	59.7
Richard J. Traynor (D)	95,021	40.3
7 William B. Widnall (R)	144,585	56.5
Edward H. Ihnen (D)	110,328	43.1
8 Charles S. Joelson (D)	112,483	67.5
J. Palmer Murphy (R)	53,732	32.3
9 Henry Helstoski (D)	111,741	50.1
Frank C. Osmers Jr. (R)	109,313	49.0
10 Peter W. Rodino Jr. (D)	92,488	74.0
Raymond W. Schroeder (R)	31,306	25.1
11 Joseph G. Minish (D)	82,457	69.6
William L. Stubbs (R)	35,956	30.4
12 Paul J. Krebs (D)	82,726	52.4
David H. Wiener (R)	72,601	46.0
13 Cornelius E. Gallagher (D)	89,360	77.1
Cresenzi W. Castaldo (R)	24,874	21.5
14 Dominick V. Daniels (D)	73,635	74.6
Cecil T. Woolsey (R)	25,068	25.4
15 Edward J. Patten (D)	131,393	63.2
Bernard F. Rodgers (R)	76,686	36.9

NEW MEXICO

Candidates	Votes	%
AL Thomas G. Morris (D)	194,407	61.8
Mike Sims (R)	120,349	38.2
AL E. S. Johnny Walker (D)	164,863	51.6
Jack C. Redman (R)	154,780	48.4

NEW YORK

Candidates	Votes	%
1 Otis G. Pike (D, L)	126,529	64.9
John J. Hart Jr. (R)	68,362	35.1
2 James R. Grover Jr. (R)	88,390	51.7
Edwyn Silberling (D, L)	82,757	48.4
3 Lester L. Wolff (D, L)	96,503	50.7
Steven B. Derounian (R)	93,883	49.3
4 John W. Wydler (R)	89,971	53.2
Joseph L. Marino (D)	73,148	43.2
5 Herbert Tenzer (D, L)	112,899	55.8
Ralph J. Edsell Jr. (R)	89,455	44.2
6 Seymour Halpern (R)	100,069	57.1
Emil Levin (D)	75,327	43.0
7 Joseph P. Addabbo (D, L)	121,091	69.8
Robert L. Nelson (R)	49,151	28.3
8 Benjamin S. Rosenthal (D, L)	148,696	75.0
Vincent P. Brevetti (R)	44,398	22.4
9 James J. Delaney (D)	109,973	65.9
Charles H. Cohen (R)	48,878	29.3
10 Emanuel Celler (D, L)	118,941	87.5
Samuel W. Held (R)	16,941	12.5
11 Eugene J. Keogh (D, L)	75,073	78.8
Herman Sanders (R)	17,732	18.6
12 Edna F. Kelly (D, L)	141,570	81.7
Carlo G. Colavito (R)	31,737	18.3
13 Abraham J. Multer (D)	129,414	69.1
Gerald S. Held (R)	34,809	18.6
Gerard M. Weisberg (L)	23,148	12.4
14 John J. Rooney (D, L)	68,165	77.4
Victor J. Tirabasso Jr. (R)	19,861	22.6
15 Hugh L. Carey (D, L)	66,567	53.6
Luigi R. Marano (R, C)	57,626	46.4
16 John M. Murphy (D, L)	89,438	61.4
David D. Smith (R, C)	56,238	38.6
17 John V. Lindsay (R)	135,807	71.5
Eleanor C. French (D, L)	44,533	23.5
Kieran O'Doherty (C)	9,491	5.0
18 Adam Clayton Powell Jr. (D)	94,222	84.6
Joseph A. Bailey (R)	11,621	10.4
19 Leonard Farbstein (D)	84,781	68.9
Henry E. Delrosso (R)	24,829	20.2
Edward A. Morrison (L)	12,129	9.9
20 William F. Ryan (D, L)	124,128	82.5
Ronald N. Gottlieb (R)	23,409	15.6
21 James H. Scheuer (D, L)	91,898	84.3
Henry Rose (R)	15,380	14.1
22 Jacob H. Gilbert (D)	70,147	81.6
Manuel R. Roque (R)	10,134	11.8

Candidates	Votes	%
Joseph A. Mazar (L)	5,026	5.8
23 Jonathan B. Bingham (D)	108,205	71.3
Patrick J. Foley (R)	30,476	20.1
John P. Hagan (L)	10,602	7.0
24 Paul A. Fino (R)	89,814	61.2
Robert J. Malang (D)	51,740	35.3
25 Richard Ottinger (D, L)	122,260	56.2
Robert R. Barry (R)	95,214	43.8
26 Ogden R. Reid (R)	102,064	54.9
Frank Conniff (D, L)	78,546	42.2
27 John G. Dow (D, L)	97,337	51.6
Katherine St. George (R)	91,172	48.4
28 Joseph Y. Resnick (D)	95,820	51.7
J. Ernest Wharton (R, C)	84,008	45.3
29 Leo W. O'Brien (D, L)	158,797	69.2
John D. Meader (R, C)	70,518	30.8
30 Carleton J. King (R)	100,950	50.3
Joseph J. Martin (D, L)	99,841	49.7
31 Robert C. McEwen (R, C)	74,380	54.6
Raymond E. Bishop (D, L)	61,726	45.4
32 Alexander Pirnie (R)	86,717	53.4
Robert Castle (D)	75,660	46.6
33 Howard W. Robison (R)	97,213	58.4
John L. Joy (D, L)	69,277	41.6
34 James M. Hanley (D, L)	96,219	51.2
R. Walter Riehlman (R, C)	91,697	48.8
35 Samuel S. Stratton (D, L)	110,948	64.0
Robert M. Quigley (R, C)	62,463	36.0
36 Frank J. Horton (R)	107,406	56.0
John C. Williams (D)	81,509	42.5
37 Barber B. Conable Jr. (R)	98,923	54.2
Neil F. Bubel (D)	80,411	44.0
38 Charles E. Goodell (R)	90,201	58.4
Robert V. Kelley (D, L)	64,179	41.6
39 Richard D. McCarthy (D, L)	108,235	52.8
John R. Pillion (R)	96,934	47.3
40 Henry P. Smith III (R)	90,745	51.5
Wesley J. Hilts (D)	81,531	46.3
41 Thaddeus J. Dulski (D, L)	130,961	82.1
Joseph A. Klawon (R)	28,578	17.9

NORTH CAROLINA

Candidates	Votes	%
1 Herbert C. Bonner (D)	52,567	82.6
Zeno O. Ratcliff (R)	11,108	17.4
2 L. H. Fountain (D)	62,406	100.0
3 David N. Henderson (D)	63,235	67.4
Sherman T. Rock (R)	30,557	32.6
4 Harold D. Cooley (D)	73,470	51.8
James C. Gardner (R)	68,387	48.2
5 Ralph J. Scott (D)	72,254	51.6
W. A. Armfield (R)	67,781	48.4
6 Horace R. Kornegay (D)	84,151	61.4
Walter G. Green (R)	52,964	38.6
7 Alton Lennon (D)	71,357	100.0
8 Charles R. Jonas (R)	85,869	54.3
W. D. James (D)	72,269	45.7
9 James T. Broyhill (R)	88,195	55.2
Robert M. Davis (D)	71,629	44.8
10 Basil L. Whitener (D)	78,684	58.7
W. Hall Young (R)	55,483	41.4
11 Roy A. Taylor (D)	85,880	60.5
Clyde M. Roberts (R)	55,996	39.5

NORTH DAKOTA

Candidates	Votes	%
1 Mark Andrews (R)	69,575	52.1
George A. Sinner (D)	63,208	47.4
2 Rolland Redlin (D)	60,751	52.5
Don L. Short (R)	54,878	47.5

OHIO

Candidates	Votes	%
1 John J. Gilligan (D)	74,525	51.9
Carl W. Rich (R)	69,114	48.1
2 Donald D. Clancy (R)	122,487	60.5
H. A. Sand (D)	79,824	39.5
3 Rodney M. Love (D)	129,469	52.0
Paul F. Schenck (R)	119,400	48.0

OHIO

	Candidates	Votes	%
4	William M. McCulloch (R)	81,204	55.7
	Robert H. Mihlbaugh (D)	64,667	44.3
5	Delbert L. Latta (R)	80,394	65.9
	Milford Landis (D)	41,621	34.1
6	William H. Harsha (R)	86,015	60.1
	Frank E. Smith (D)	57,223	40.0
7	Clarence J. Brown (R)	93,022	56.8
	Jerry R. Graham (D)	70,857	43.2
8	Jackson E. Betts (R)	73,395	61.8
	Frank Bennett (D)	45,445	38.2
9	Thomas L. Ashley (D)	109,167	62.9
	John O. Celusta (R)	64,401	37.1
10	Walter H. Moeller (D)	54,729	52.4
	Homer E. Abele (R)	49,744	47.6
11	J. William Stanton (R)	102,619	55.4
	C. D. Lambros (D)	82,728	44.6
12	Samuel L. Devine (R)	146,971	55.4
	Robert L. Van Heyde (D)	118,299	44.6
13	Charles A. Mosher (R)	75,945	54.7
	Louis G. Frey (D)	62,780	45.3
14	William H. Ayres (R)	126,088	54.7
	Frances McGovern (D)	104,547	45.3
15	Robert T. Secrest (D)	62,438	66.1
	Randall Metcalf (R)	31,983	33.9
16	Frank T. Bow (R)	101,802	52.2
	Robert D. Freeman (D)	93,255	47.8
17	John M. Ashbrook (R)	75,674	51.5
	Robert W. Levering (D)	71,291	48.5
18	Wayne L. Hays (D)	94,768	68.8
	Allen J. Dalrymple (R)	42,960	31.2
19	Michael J. Kirwan (D)	111,682	76.3
	Albert H. James (R)	34,654	23.7
20	Michael A. Feighan (D)	115,675	74.4
	Joseph A. Cipollone (R)	39,747	25.6
21	Charles A. Vanik (D)	113,157	90.1
	Eugene E. Smith (R)	12,416	9.9
22	Frances P. Bolton (R)	84,183	56.6
	Chat Paterson (D)	64,454	43.4
23	William E. Minshall (R)	131,554	67.2
	Norbert G. Dennerll Jr. (D)	64,162	32.8
AL	Robert E. Sweeney (D)	1,872,351	52.2
	Oliver P. Bolton (R)	1,716,480	47.8

OKLAHOMA

1	Page Belcher (R)	125,377	63.5
	Doug Martin (D)	71,998	36.5
2	Ed Edmondson (D)	90,466	61.4
	George L. Lange (R)	56,843	38.6
3	Carl Albert (D)	62,952	79.0
	Frank D. McSherry (R)	16,706	21.0
4	Tom Steed (D)	98,419	100.0
5	John Jarman (D)	130,014	70.8
	Homer Cowan (R)	53,596	29.2
6	Jed Johnson Jr. (D)	75,879	56.7
	Bayard C. Auchincloss (R)	58,041	43.3

OREGON

1	Wendell Wyatt (R)	122,010	53.1
	R. Blaine Whipple (D)	107,920	46.9
2	Al Ullman (D)	70,136	68.1
	Everett J. Thoren (R)	32,916	31.9
3	Edith Green (D)	157,882	65.6
	Lyle Dean (R)	82,468	34.3
4	Robert B. Duncan (D)	125,752	64.8
	Paul Jaffarian (R)	68,288	35.2

Special Election

1	Wendell Wyatt (R)	125,473	52.8
	R. Blaine Whipple (D)	112,112	47.2

PENNSYLVANIA

1	William A. Barrett (D)	129,471	71.8
	Alvin J. Bello (R)	50,780	28.2

	Candidates	Votes	%
2	Robert N. C. Nix (D)	125,100	80.2
	Melvin C. Howell (R)	30,801	19.8
3	James A. Byrne (D)	111,885	72.0
	John J. Poserina Jr. (R)	43,471	28.0
4	Herman Toll (D)	135,681	64.1
	James R. Cavanaugh (R)	75,901	35.9
5	William J. Green III (D)	117,049	65.2
	Edward H. Rovner (R)	62,446	34.8
6	George M. Rhodes (D)	144,697#	62.1
	James B. Bamford (R)	88,495#	37.9
7	G. Robert Watkins (R)	129,572	51.2
	Leonard Bachman (D)	123,750	48.9
8	Willard S. Curtin (R)	112,472	51.1
	Ralph O. Samuel (D)	107,670	48.9
9	Paul B. Dague (R)	111,545	57.7
	John A. O'Brien (D)	81,823	42.3
10	Joseph M. McDade (R)	90,903	50.8
	James J. Haggerty (D)	88,082	49.2
11	Daniel J. Flood (D)	116,875	77.4
	Charles R. Thomas (R)	34,057	22.6
12	J. Irving Whalley (R)	97,114	58.6
	Paul A. Stephens (D)	68,703	41.4
13	Richard S. Schweiker (R)	139,817	59.1
	William D. Searle (D)	96,849	40.9
14	William S. Moorhead (D)	117,525	74.8
	Alvin D. Capozzi (R)	39,513	25.2
15	Fred B. Rooney (D)	81,062	66.1
	Leo W. McCormick (R)	41,656	33.9
16	John C. Kunkel (R)	90,331	64.1
	William F. Stefanic (D)	50,509	35.9
17	Herman T. Schneebeli (R)	91,504	58.0
	William F. Plankenhorn (D)	66,266	42.0
18	Robert J. Corbett (R)	119,938	62.6
	Frank J. Reed (D)	71,621	37.4
19	N. Neiman Craley Jr. (D)	82,498	50.8
	George A. Goodling (R)	79,809	49.2
20	Elmer J. Holland (D)	126,846	74.4
	Ronald Bryan (R)	43,591	25.6
21	John H. Dent (D)	97,379	65.8
	Thomas M. Schooley Jr. (R)	50,513	34.2
22	John P. Saylor (R)	81,400	57.0
	James E. McCaffery (D)	61,482	43.0
23	Albert W. Johnson (R)	76,575	54.9
	John Still (D)	62,932	45.1
24	Joseph P. Vigorito (D)	92,612	50.8
	James D. Weaver (R)	89,828	49.2
25	Frank M. Clark (D)	121,140	70.3
	John Loth (R)	51,071	29.7
26	Thomas E. Morgan (D)	109,532	68.1
	Paul B. Riggle (R)	51,219	31.9
27	James G. Fulton (R)	120,395	62.7
	John A. Young (D)	71,519	37.3

Special Election

5	William J. Green III (D)	30,904#	58.6
	Edward H. Rovner (R)	21,832#	41.4

RHODE ISLAND

1	Fernard J. St.Germain (D)	110,056	66.3
	Roland H. Blanchette (R)	56,056	33.8
2	John E. Fogarty (D)	168,374	81.4
	Guy J. Wells (R)	38,601	18.7

SOUTH CAROLINA

1	L. Mendel Rivers (D)	64,804	99.6
2	Albert W. Watson (D)	88,682	97.6
3	W. J. Bryan Dorn (D)	65,920	99.9
4	Robert T. Ashmore (D)	81,727	100.0
5	Tom S. Gettys (D)	44,859	66.7
	Robert M. Doster (R)	22,384	33.3
6	John L. McMillan (D)	49,398	65.0
	E. R. Kirkland (R)	26,586	35.0

Special Election

5	Tom S. Gettys (D)	44,241	66.8
	Robert M. Doster (R)	22,031	33.2

SOUTH DAKOTA

	Candidates	Votes	%
1	Ben Reifel (R)	124,791	57.6
	George May (D)	92,057	42.5
2	E. Y. Berry (R)	39,657	56.0
	Byron T. Brown (D)	31,208	44.0

TENNESSEE

1	James H. Quillen (R)	94,535	71.7
	Arthur Bright (D)	37,252	28.3
2	John J. Duncan (R)	84,868	53.8
	Willard V. Yarbrough (D)	70,119	44.5
3	Bill Brock (R)	71,005	54.6
	Robert M. Summitt (D)	59,027	45.4
4	Joe L. Evins (D)	85,286	100.0
5	Richard Fulton (D)	74,597	59.8
	William R. Wills (R)	50,210	40.2
6	William R. Anderson (D)	66,817	78.2
	Cecil R. Hill (R)	18,595	21.8
7	Tom Murray (D)	35,612	53.6
	Julius Hurst (IR)	24,496	36.8
	Earl Maclin (I)	6,382	9.6
8	Robert A. Everett (D)	43,876	93.9
	Sarah Flannary (I)	2,865	6.1
9	George W. Grider (D)	108,425	52.5
	Robert James (R)	97,537	47.2

Special Election

2	Irene Baker (R)	40,708#	55.5
	Willard V. Yarbrough (D)	31,763#	43.3

TEXAS

1	Wright Patman (D)	52,698	74.6
	Mrs. William E. Jones (R)	17,967	25.4
2	Jack Brooks (D)	75,226	62.7
	John Greco (R)	44,772	37.3
3	Lindley Beckworth (D)	53,331	59.3
	James Warren (R)	36,566	40.7
4	Ray Roberts (D)	46,782	81.4
	Fred Banfield (R)	10,707	18.6
5	Earle Cabell (D)	172,287	57.5
	Bruce Alger (R)	127,568	42.5
6	Olin Teague (D)	55,155	82.2
	William Van Winkle (R)	11,967	17.8
7	John Dowdy (D)	64,456	83.6
	James W. Orr (R)	12,606	16.4
8	Albert Thomas (D)	103,595	76.8
	Bob Gilbert (R)	31,351	23.2
9	Clark Thompson (D)	105,631	75.3
	Dave Oakes (R)	34,692	24.7
10	Jake Pickle (D)	80,045	75.8
	Billie Pratt (R)	25,594	24.2
11	W. R. Poage (D)	62,175	81.5
	Charles M. Isenhower (R)	14,094	18.5
12	Jim Wright (D)	107,896	68.5
	Fred Dielman (R)	49,633	31.5
13	Graham Purcell (D)	67,947	75.2
	George Corse (R)	22,429	24.8
14	John Young (D)	105,352	77.5
	Billy Patton (R)	30,522	22.5
15	Eligio de la Garza (D)	66,897	69.4
	Joe Coulter (R)	29,551	30.6
16	Richard C. White (D)	70,262	55.7
	Ed Foreman (R)	55,951	44.3
17	Omar Burleson (D)	59,769	76.4
	Phil M. Bridges (R)	18,440	23.6
18	Walter Rogers (D)	58,701	55.0
	Robert Price (R)	48,054	45.0
19	George Mahon (D)	87,555	77.6
	Joe B. Phillips (R)	25,243	22.4
20	Henry B. Gonzalez (D)	103,464	64.6
	John M. O'Connell (R)	56,601	35.4
21	O. C. Fisher (D)	61,785	78.1
	Harry Claypool (R)	17,295	21.9
22	Bob Casey (D)	136,289	58.1
	Desmond Barry (R)	98,287	41.9
AL	Joe Pool (D)	1,690,674	66.9
	Bill Hayes (R)	826,991	32.7

UTAH

Candidates	Votes	%
1 Laurence J. Burton (R)	75,986	56.0
William G. Bruhn (D)	59,768	44.0
2 David S. King (D)	149,754	57.5
Thomas G. Judd (R)	110,512	42.5

VERMONT

	Votes	%
AL Robert T. Stafford (R, I)	92,252	56.4
Bernard G. O'Shea (D)	71,193	43.6

VIRGINIA

Candidates	Votes	%
1 Thomas N. Downing (D)	72,819	78.7
Wayne C. Thiessen (R)	19,698	21.3
2 Porter Hardy Jr. (D)	54,315	68.7
Wayne Lustig (R)	17,082	21.6
H. W. Grady Speers Jr. (I)	7,635	9.7
3 David E. Satterfield III (D)	43,880	34.5
Richard D. Obenshain (R)	43,226	34.0
Edward E. Haddock (I)	39,223	30.8
4 Watkins M. Abbitt (D)	53,857	69.5
S. W. Tucker (R)	23,682	30.5
5 William M. Tuck (D)	39,867	63.5
Robert L. Gilliam (R)	22,946	36.5
6 Richard H. Poff (R)	57,987	56.2
William B. Hopkins (D)	45,113	43.8
7 John O. Marsh Jr. (D)	47,888	69.6
Roy Erickson (R)	20,911	30.4

Candidates	Votes	%
8 Howard W. Smith (D)	49,440	69.4
Floyd Caldwell Bagley (I)	21,813	30.6
9 W. Pat Jennings (D)	51,106	58.2
Glen M. Williams (R)	36,668	41.8
10 Joel T. Broyhill (R)	80,370	50.7
Augustus C. Johnson (D)	78,242	49.3

WASHINGTON

	Votes	%
1 Thomas M. Pelly (R)	117,851	59.9
Edward Palmason (D)	78,876	40.1
2 Lloyd Meeds (D)	88,551	54.9
Jack Westland (R)	72,830	45.1
3 Julia Butler Hansen (D)	102,080	70.2
Harold L. Anderson (R)	43,415	29.8
4 Catherine May (R)	102,964	65.3
Stephen H. Huza (D)	54,819	34.7
5 Thomas S. Foley (D)	84,830	53.5
Walt Horan (R)	73,884	46.6
6 Floyd V. Hicks (D)	79,042	52.1
Thor C. Tollefson (R)	72,702	47.9
7 Brock Adams (D)	125,222	55.5
William Stinson (R)	100,119	44.4

WEST VIRGINIA

	Votes	%
1 Arch A. Moore Jr. (R)	115,799	61.4
John L. Bailey (D)	72,714	38.6
2 Harley O. Staggers (D)	87,928	65.0
Stanley R. Cox Jr. (R)	47,457	35.1
3 John M. Slack Jr. (D)	103,117	65.4
Jim Comstock (R)	54,566	34.6

Candidates	Votes	%
4 Ken Hechler (D)	109,287	61.2
Jack L. Miller (R)	69,253	38.8
5 James Kee (D)	77,156	70.0
Wade Hampton Ballard III (R)	33,108	30.0

WISCONSIN

	Votes	%
1 Lynn E. Stalbaum (D)	90,450	51.5
Henry C. Schadeberg (R)	85,117	48.5
2 Robert W. Kastenmeier (D)	108,148	63.6
Carl V. Kolata (R)	61,865	36.4
3 Vernon W. Thomson (R)	91,092	60.6
Harold C. Ristow (D)	59,173	39.4
4 Clement J. Zablocki (D)	125,683	74.2
Edward E. Estkowski (R)	43,773	25.8
5 Henry S. Reuss (D)	107,610	75.9
Robert Taylor (R)	34,059	24.0
6 John A. Race (D)	84,690	50.8
William K. Van Pelt (R)	82,103	49.2
7 Melvin R. Laird (R)	98,110	61.8
Thomas E. Martin (D)	60,758	38.2
8 John W. Byrnes (R)	96,160	59.6
Cletus J. Johnson (D)	65,292	40.4
9 Glenn R. Davis (R)	105,332	55.3
James P. Buckley (D)	85,071	44.7
10 Alvin E. O'Konski (R)	92,198	56.2
Edmund A. Nix (D)	71,983	43.8

WYOMING

	Votes	%
AL Teno Roncalio (D)	70,693	50.8
William Henry Harrison (R)	68,482	49.2

1965 House Elections

CALIFORNIA

Special Election

	Votes	%
26 Thomas M. Rees (D)	40,430	59.4
Edward M. Marshall (R)	27,579	40.5

LOUISIANA
Special Election

7 Edwin W. Edwards (D)

OHIO
Special Election

	Votes	%
7 Clarence J. Brown Jr. (R)	70,573	59.6
James A. Berry (D)	47,830	40.4

SOUTH CAROLINA

Special Election

	Votes	%
2 Albert W. Watson (R)	55,977#	69.3
Preston H. Callison (D)	24,761#	30.7

House Candidates Index

For an index of all House candidates listed in this section (pages 192-324), see pages 340-371. Instructions for use of the House Candidates Index appear on page 340.

1966 House Elections

ALABAMA

	Candidates	Votes	%
1	Jack Edwards (R)	58,515	65.8
	Warren L. Finch (D)	30,474	34.2
2	William L. Dickinson (R)	49,203	54.7
	Robert F. Whaley (D)	40,832	45.4
3	George Andrews (D)	61,015	100.0
4	Bill Nichols (D)	54,515	58.7
	Glenn Andrews (R)	38,402	41.3
5	Armistead I. Selden Jr. (D)	68,486	100.0
6	John Buchanan (R)	64,435	63.4
	Walter Emmett Perry (D)	37,131	36.6
7	Tom Bevill (D)	73,987	64.4
	Wayman Sherrer (R)	40,972	35.6
8	Robert E. Jones (D)	65,982	71.3
	Don Mayhall (R)	26,561	28.7

ALASKA

	Candidates	Votes	%
AL	Howard W. Pollock (R)	34,040	51.7
	Ralph J. Rivers (D)	31,867	48.4

ARIZONA

	Candidates	Votes	%
1	John J. Rhodes (R)	102,007	67.2
	L. Alton Riggs (D)	49,913	32.9
2	Morris K. Udall (D)	66,813	59.6
	G. Alfred McGinnis (R)	45,326	40.4
3	Sam Steiger (R)	57,145	56.9
	George F. Senner Jr. (D)	43,219	43.1

ARKANSAS

	Candidates	Votes	%
1	E. C. Gathings (D)		100.0
2	Wilbur Mills (D)		100.0
3	John P. Hammerschmidt (R)	83,938	53.1
	James W. Trimble (D)	74,009	46.9
4	David Pryor (D)	86,887	65.0
	Lynn Lowe (R)	46,804	35.0

Special Election

		Votes	%
4	David Pryor (D)	85,125	64.5
	Lynn Lowe (R)	46,764	35.0

CALIFORNIA

	Candidates	Votes	%
1	Don H. Clausen (R)	143,755	64.9
	Thomas T. Storer (D)	77,000	34.7
2	Harold T. Johnson (D)	131,145	70.9
	William H. Romack (R)	53,753	29.1
3	John E. Moss Jr. (D)	143,177	67.5
	Terry G. Feil (R)	69,057	32.5
4	Robert L. Leggett (D)	67,942	59.5
	Tom McHatton (R)	46,337	40.5
5	Phillip Burton (D)	56,476	71.3
	Terry R. Macken (R)	22,778	28.7
6	William S. Mailliard (R)	132,506	76.6
	Lerue Grim (D)	40,514	23.4
7	Jeffery Cohelan (D)	84,644	63.9
	Malcolm M. Champlin (R)	46,763	35.3
8	George P. Miller (D)	92,263	65.4
	Raymond P. Britton (R)	48,727	34.6
9	Don Edwards (D)	97,311	63.1
	Wilbur G. Durkee (R)	56,784	36.9
10	Charles S. Gubser (R)	156,549	69.1
	George Leppert (D)	70,013	30.9
11	J. Arthur Younger (R)	113,679	59.4
	Mark Sullivan (D)	77,605	40.6
12	Burt L. Talcott (R)	108,070	77.2
	Gerald V. Barron (D)	31,787	22.7
13	Charles M. Teague (R)	116,701	67.5
	Charles A. Storke (D)	56,240	32.5

	Candidates	Votes	%
14	Jerome R. Waldie (D)	108,668	56.4
	Frank J. Newman (R)	83,878	43.5
15	John J. McFall (D)	81,733	57.0
	Sam Van Dyken (R)	61,550	43.0
16	B. F. Sisk (D)	118,063	71.3
	Cecil F. White (R)	47,329	28.6
17	Cecil R. King (D)	76,962	60.8
	Don Cortum (R)	49,615	39.2
18	Robert B. Mathias (R)	96,699	55.9
	Harlan Hagen (D)	76,346	44.1
19	Chet Holifield (D)	82,592	62.2
	William R. Sutton (R)	50,068	37.7
20	H. Allen Smith (R)	128,896	73.4
	Raymond Freschi (D)	46,730	26.6
21	Augustus F. Hawkins (D)	74,216	84.8
	Norman A. Hodges (R)	13,294	15.2
22	James C. Corman (D)	94,420	53.5
	Robert C. Cline (R)	82,207	46.5
23	Del Clawson (R)	93,320	67.4
	Ed O'Connor (D)	45,141	32.6
24	Glenard P. Lipscomb (R)	148,190	76.2
	Earl G. McNall (D)	46,115	23.7
25	Charles E. Wiggins (R)	70,154	52.6
	Ronald Brooks Cameron (D)	63,345	47.5
26	Thomas M. Rees (D)	103,289	62.3
	Irving Teichner (R)	62,441	37.7
27	Ed Reinecke (R)	93,890	65.3
	John A. Howard (D)	49,785	34.6
28	Alphonzo Bell (R)	211,404	72.3
	Lawrence Sherman (D)	81,007	27.7
29	George E. Brown Jr. (D)	69,115	51.1
	Bill Orozco (R)	66,079	48.9
30	Edward R. Roybal (D)	72,173	66.4
	Henri O'Bryant Jr. (R)	36,506	33.6
31	Charles H. Wilson (D)	92,875	63.4
	Theodore Smith (R)	53,708	36.6
32	Craig Hosmer (R)	139,328	80.1
	Tracy Odell (D)	34,609	19.9
33	Jerry L. Pettis (R)	102,401	53.5
	Kenneth W. Dyal (D)	89,071	46.5
34	Richard T. Hanna (D)	127,976	55.8
	Frank La Magna (R)	101,410	44.2
35	James B. Utt (R)	189,582	73.1
	Thomas B. Lenhart (D)	69,873	26.9
36	Bob Wilson (R)	119,274	72.7
	William C. Godfrey (D)	44,365	27.1
37	Lionel Van Deerlin (D)	80,060	61.1
	Samuel S. Vener (R)	50,817	38.8
38	John V. Tunney (D)	83,216	54.5
	Robert R. Barry (R)	69,444	45.5

Special Election

		Votes	%
14	Jerome R. Waldie (D)	71,501#	51.2
	Frank J. Newman (R)	43,539#	31.2
	John A. Richardson (R)	14,693#	10.5

COLORADO

		Votes	%
1	Byron G. Rogers (D)	92,688	56.0
	Greg Pearson (R)	72,732	44.0
2	Donald G. Brotzman (R)	95,123	51.7
	Roy H. McVicker (D)	86,685	47.1
3	Frank E. Evans (D)	76,270	51.7
	David W. Enoch (R)	71,213	48.3
4	Wayne N. Aspinall (D)	84,107	58.6
	James P. Johnson (R)	59,404	41.4

CONNECTICUT

		Votes	%
1	Emilio Q. Daddario (D)	100,447	58.0
	John L. Bonee (R)	71,353	41.2
2	William L. St.Onge (D)	90,298	56.2
	Joseph H. Goldberg (R)	69,402	43.2
3	Robert Giaimo (D)	86,029	53.1
	Stelio Salmona (R)	67,226	41.5

	Candidates	Votes	%
	Robert M. Cook (AM I)	8,730	5.4
4	Donald J. Irwin (D)	89,709	50.9
	Abner W. Sibal (R)	86,337	49.0
5	John S. Monagan (D)	96,801	59.1
	Romeo G. Petroni (R)	67,094	40.9
6	Thomas J. Meskill Jr. (R)	81,907	48.9
	Bernard F. Grabowski (D)	79,865	47.7

DELAWARE

		Votes	%
AL	William V. Roth (R)	90,961	55.8
	Harris B. McDowell Jr. (D)	72,132	44.2

FLORIDA

		Votes	%
1	Robert L. F. Sikes (D)	55,547	95.1
2	Don Fuqua (D)	71,565	76.3
	Harold Hill (R)	22,281	23.7
3	Charles E. Bennett (D)	72,038	99.9
4	A. Sydney Herlong Jr. (D)	70,155	100.0
5	Edward J. Gurney (R)	75,875	99.7
6	Sam M. Gibbons (D)	50,772	99.8
7	James A. Haley (D)	64,498	63.2
	Joe Z. Lovingood (R)	37,586	36.8
8	William C. Cramer (R)	105,019	70.8
	Roy L. Reynolds (D)	43,275	29.2
9	Paul G. Rogers (D)	76,328	100.0
10	J. Herbert Burke (R)	80,989	60.6
	Joe Varon (D)	51,636	38.7
11	Claude Pepper (D)	62,195	99.9
12	Dante B. Fascell (D)	62,457	56.9
	Mike Thompson (R)	47,226	43.1

GEORGIA

		Votes	%
1	G. Elliott Hagan (D)	53,413	58.0
	Porter W. Carswell (R)	38,619	41.9
2	Maston O'Neal (D)	54,487	100.0
3	Jack Brinkley (D)	42,424	61.2
	Billy Mixon (R)	26,255	37.9
4	Ben B. Blackburn (R)	55,249	50.2
	James A. Mackay (D)	54,889	49.8
5	Fletcher Thompson (R)	55,423	60.1
	Archie Lindsey (D)	36,751	39.9
6	John J. Flynt Jr. (D)	74,175	67.9
	G. Paul Jones Jr. (R)	35,048	32.1
7	John W. Davis (D)	65,614	65.0
	E. Y. Chapin III (R)	35,383	35.0
8	W. S. Stuckey Jr. (D)	60,059	77.0
	Mack F. Mattingly (R)	17,926	23.0
9	Phil M. Landrum (D)	61,930	100.0
10	Robert G. Stephens Jr. (D)	54,141	65.7
	Leroy H. Simkins Jr. (R)	28,247	34.3

HAWAII

		Votes	%
AL	Patsy T. Mink (D)	140,880✔	
	Spark M. Matsunaga (D)	140,110✔	
	John S. Carroll (R)	67,281	
	James K. Kealoha (R)	62,473	

IDAHO

		Votes	%
1	James A. McClure (R)	70,410	51.8
	Compton I. White Jr. (D)	65,446	48.2
2	George V. Hansen (R)	79,024	70.3
	A. W. Brunt (D)	33,348	29.7

ILLINOIS

		Votes	%
1	William L. Dawson (D)	91,119	72.6
	David R. Reed (R)	34,421	27.4

ILLINOIS

	Candidates	Votes	%
2	Barratt O'Hara (D)	83,471	59.2
	Philip G. Bixler (R)	57,629	40.8
3	William T. Murphy (D)	83,857	52.0
	Albert F. Manion (R)	77,442	48.0
4	Edward J. Derwinski (R)	125,365	72.0
	Ray J. Rybacki (D)	48,673	28.0
5	John C. Kluczynski (D)	85,770	56.2
	Walter K. Kiltz (R)	66,735	43.8
6	Daniel J. Ronan (D)	84,126	57.0
	Samuel A. Decaro (R)	63,374	43.0
7	Frank Annunzio (D)	82,962	80.9
	Joseph D. Day (R)	19,650	19.2
8	Daniel D. Rostenkowski (D)	94,631	59.9
	John H. Leszynski (R)	63,377	40.1
9	Sydney R. Yates (D)	96,746	59.9
	Richard C. Storey Jr. (R)	64,875	40.1
10	Harold R. Collier (R)	132,650	69.4
	Frank J. Jirka Jr. (D)	58,376	30.6
11	Roman C. Pucinski (D)	105,996	50.9
	John J. Hoellen (R)	102,244	49.1
12	Robert McClory (R)	90,483	69.1
	Herbert L. Stern (D)	40,502	30.9
13	Donald Rumsfeld (R)	158,769	76.0
	James L. McCabe (D)	50,107	24.0
14	John N. Erlenborn (R)	130,442	71.7
	Kenneth McCleary (D)	51,385	28.3
15	Charlotte T. Reid (R)	102,018	72.3
	Selwyn L. Boyer (D)	39,123	27.7
16	John B. Anderson (R)	89,990	73.0
	Robert M. Whiteford (D)	33,274	27.0
17	Leslie C. Arends (R)	104,240	67.4
	Bernard J. Hughes (D)	50,350	32.6
18	Robert H. Michel (R)	80,293	58.4
	Thomas V. Cassidy (D)	57,100	41.6
19	Tom Railsback (R)	77,895	52.3
	Gale Schisler (D)	71,050	47.7
20	Paul Findley (R)	102,609	62.2
	Richard R. Wolfe (D)	62,343	37.8
21	Kenneth J. Gray (D)	103,128	56.2
	Bob Beckmeyer (R)	80,382	43.8
22	William L. Springer (R)	96,453	63.3
	Cameron B. Satterthwaite (D)	55,818	36.7
23	George E. Shipley (D)	95,156	56.4
	Leslie N. Jones (R)	73,463	43.6
24	Melvin Price (D)	82,513	71.5
	John S. Guthrie (R)	32,915	28.5

INDIANA

	Candidates	Votes	%
1	Ray J. Madden (D)	71,040	58.3
	Albert F. Harrigan (R)	50,804	41.7
2	Charles A. Halleck (R)	97,161	57.5
	Ralph G. McFadden (D)	71,825	42.5
3	John Brademas (D)	75,321	55.8
	Robert A. Ehlers (R)	59,731	44.2
4	E. Ross Adair (R)	94,457	63.5
	J. Byron Hayes (D)	54,331	36.5
5	J. Edward Roush (D)	76,176	51.1
	Kenneth Bowman (R)	72,873	48.9
6	William G. Bray (R)	124,087	65.7
	James M. Nicholson (D)	63,342	33.6
7	John T. Myers (R)	79,864	54.3
	Elden C. Tipton (D)	67,135	45.7
8	Roger H. Zion (R)	94,924	51.1
	Winfield K. Denton (D)	90,887	48.9
9	Lee H. Hamilton (D)	89,392	53.8
	John W. Lewis (R)	76,661	46.2
10	Richard L. Roudebush (R)	94,428	63.4
	Robert H. Staton (D)	54,515	36.6
11	Andrew Jacobs Jr. (D)	65,624	55.8
	Paul R. Oakes (R)	52,096	44.3

IOWA

	Candidates	Votes	%
1	Fred Schwengel (R)	64,795	51.3
	John R. Schmidhauser (D)	60,534	47.9
2	John C. Culver (D)	76,281	54.0
	Robert M. L. Johnson (R)	65,079	46.0

	Candidates	Votes	%
3	H. R. Gross (R)	79,343	62.1
	L. A. Touchae (D)	48,530	38.0
4	John Kyl (R)	65,259	51.7
	Bert Bandstra (D)	61,074	48.3
5	Neal Smith (D)	72,875	60.4
	Don Mahon (R)	46,981	39.0
6	Wiley Mayne (R)	73,274	57.4
	Stanley L. Greigg (D)	53,917	42.3
7	William J. Scherle (R)	64,217	59.0
	John R. Hansen (D)	44,529	40.9

KANSAS

	Candidates	Votes	%
1	Bob Dole (R)	97,487	68.6
	Berniece Henkle (D)	44,569	31.4
2	Chester L. Mize (R)	85,128	62.8
	Harry Wiles (D)	50,336	37.2
3	Larry Winn Jr. (R)	60,107	52.9
	Marvin E. Rainey (D)	51,108	45.0
4	Garner E. Shriver (R)	86,944	68.7
	Paul H. Gerling (D)	39,625	31.3
5	Joe Skubitz (R)	86,944	60.9
	Delno E. Bass (D)	55,933	39.2

KENTUCKY

	Candidates	Votes	%
1	Frank A. Stubblefield (D)	57,736	70.6
	Richard Nicholson (R)	24,085	29.4
2	William H. Natcher (D)	51,311	58.9
	R. Douglas Ford (R)	35,770	41.1
3	William O. Cowger (R)	66,577	59.0
	Norbert Blume (D)	46,240	41.0
4	M. G. (Gene) Snyder (R)	66,801	53.9
	Frank Chelf (D)	56,902	46.0
5	Tim Lee Carter (R)	65,596	75.4
	Eugene C. Harter (D)	21,452	24.6
6	John C. Watts (D)	58,182	65.1
	William McKinley Hendren (R)	31,266	35.0
7	Carl D. Perkins (D)	65,522	68.9
	C. F. See (R)	29,541	31.1

LOUISIANA

	Candidates	Votes	%
1	F. Edward Hebert (D)	68,523	100.0
2	Hale Boggs (D)	90,149	68.6
	Leonard L. Limes (R)	41,209	31.4
3	Edwin E. Willis (D)	46,533	59.7
	Hall M. Lyons (R)	31,444	40.3
4	Joe D. Waggonner Jr. (D)	48,345	100.0
5	Otto E. Passman (D)	38,660	100.0
6	John R. Rarick (D)	86,958	76.6
	Crayton G. Hall (R)	26,599	23.4
7	Edwin W. Edwards (D)	34,655	100.0
8	Speedy O. Long (D)	33,183	100.0

MAINE

	Candidates	Votes	%
1	Peter N. Kyros (D)	81,302	50.4
	Peter A. Garland (R)	72,984	45.2
2	William D. Hathaway (D)	85,956	56.8
	Howard M. Foley (R)	65,476	43.2

MARYLAND

	Candidates	Votes	%
1	Rogers C. B. Morton (R)	69,940	71.4
	H. C. Byrd (D)	28,025	28.6
2	Clarence D. Long (D)	79,963	69.3
	Paul T. McHenry Jr. (R)	35,476	30.7
3	Edward A. Garmatz (D)	56,980	100.0
4	George H. Fallon (D)	57,572	74.3
	G. Neilson Sigler (R)	19,930	25.7
5	Hervey G. Machen (D)	55,676	53.9
	Lawrence J. Hogan (R)	47,703	46.1
6	Charles McC. Mathias Jr. (R)	72,360	70.9
	Walter G. Finch (D)	29,637	29.1
7	Samuel N. Friedel (D)	61,959	76.0
	Stephen L. Rosenstein (R)	19,584	24.0

	Candidates	Votes	%
8	Gilbert Gude (R)	71,050	54.4
	Royce Hanson (D)	59,568	45.6

MASSACHUSETTS

	Candidates	Votes	%
1	Silvio O. Conte (R)	109,370	100.0
2	Edward P. Boland (D)	95,985	100.0
3	Philip J. Philbin (D)	126,664	71.0
	Howard A. Miller (R)	51,646	29.0
4	Harold D. Donohue (D)	137,681	100.0
5	F. Bradford Morse (R)	140,702	74.8
	Charles N. Tsapatsaris (D)	47,377	25.2
6	William H. Bates (R)	127,744	65.7
	Daniel L. Parent (D)	66,675	34.3
7	Torbert H. Macdonald (D)	119,543	74.5
	Gordon F. Hughes (R)	40,930	25.5
8	Thomas P. O'Neill Jr. (D)	102,104	100.0
9	John W. McCormack (D)	87,879	100.0
10	Margaret M. Heckler (R)	96,675	51.1
	Patrick H. Harrington Jr. (D)	92,516	48.9
11	James A. Burke (D)	141,465	74.8
	James L. Hofford (R)	47,705	25.2
12	Hastings Keith (R)	98,372	55.0
	Edward F. Harrington (D)	80,473	45.0

MICHIGAN

	Candidates	Votes	%
1	John Conyers (D)	89,908	84.2
	Rhecha R. Ross (R)	16,853	15.8
2	Marvin L. Esch (R)	65,205	51.0
	Weston E. Vivian (D)	62,536	49.0
3	Garry Brown (R)	68,912	52.3
	Paul H. Todd Jr. (D)	62,984	47.8
4	Edward Hutchinson (R)	78,190	67.8
	John V. Martin (D)	37,177	32.2
5	Gerald R. Ford (R)	88,108	68.5
	James Mathew Catchick (D)	40,435	31.5
6	Charles E. Chamberlain (R)	85,669	67.3
	Lee H. Wenke (D)	41,695	32.7
7	Donald W. Riegle Jr. (R)	71,166	54.1
	John C. Mackie (D)	60,408	45.9
8	James Harvey (R)	85,657	69.9
	Wager F. Clunis (D)	36,967	30.2
9	Guy Vander Jagt (R)	92,710	66.7
	Henry J. Dongvillo (D)	46,266	33.3
10	Elford A. Cederberg (R)	85,754	67.4
	Hubert C. Evans (D)	41,410	32.6
11	Phillip E. Ruppe (R)	70,820	51.8
	Raymond F. Clevenger (D)	65,875	48.2
12	James G. O'Hara (D)	84,379	65.1
	Patrick J. Driscoll (R)	45,199	34.9
13	Charles C. Diggs Jr. (D)	60,660	83.0
	Frank Daniels (R)	12,393	17.0
14	Lucien N. Nedzi (D)	77,851	59.7
	William J. Kennedy (R)	52,490	40.3
15	William D. Ford (D)	72,987	67.8
	Arpo Yemen (R)	34,619	32.2
16	John D. Dingell Jr. (D)	71,787	62.7
	John T. Dempsey (R)	42,738	37.3
17	Martha W. Griffiths (D)	90,541	69.2
	William P. Harrington (R)	40,334	30.8
18	William S. Broomfield (R)	102,501	67.8
	William H. Merrill (D)	48,627	32.2
19	Jack H. McDonald (R)	76,884	57.0
	Billie S. Farnum (D)	57,907	43.0

Special Election

	Candidates	Votes	%
9	Guy Vander Jagt (R)	91,056	66.6
	Henry J. Dongvillo (D)	45,699	33.4

MINNESOTA

	Candidates	Votes	%
1	Albert H. Quie (R)	109,312	65.9
	George Daley (DFL)	56,547	34.1
2	Ancher Nelson (R)	93,855	66.2
	Charles M. Christensen (DFL)	47,899	33.8

MINNESOTA

Candidates	Votes	%
3 Clark MacGregor (R)	122,775	65.4
Elva D. Walker (DFL)	64,861	34.6
4 Joseph Karth (DFL)	91,271	53.4
Stephan Maxwell (R)	79,667	46.6
5 Donald M. Fraser (DFL)	86,953	59.7
William Hathaway (R)	58,816	40.4
6 John M. Zwach (R)	80,710	51.4
Alec G. Olson (DFL)	76,439	48.6
7 Odin Langen (R)	84,914	63.2
Keith C. Davison (DFL)	49,388	36.8
8 John A. Blatnik (DFL)	116,969	100.0

MISSISSIPPI

Candidates	Votes	%
1 Thomas G. Abernethy (D)	47,359	68.8
W. B. Alexander (I)	14,700	21.4
Dock Drummond (I)	6,805	9.9
2 Jamie L. Whitten (D)	53,620	83.5
S. B. Wise (R)	10,622	16.5
3 John Bell Williams (D)	71,377	82.4
Emma Sanders (I)	15,218	17.6
4 G. V. (Sonny) Montgomery (D)	52,138	65.3
L. L. McAllister Jr. (R)	26,027	32.6
5 William M. Colmer (D)	58,080	70.0
James M. Moye (R)	24,865	30.0

MISSOURI

Candidates	Votes	%
1 Frank M. Karsten (D)	62,143	63.9
Robert L. Sharp (R)	35,053	36.1
2 Thomas B. Curtis (R)	102,985	66.2
William B. Milius (D)	52,527	33.8
3 Leonor K. Sullivan (D)	59,014	71.1
Homer McCracken (R)	23,953	28.9
4 William J. Randall (D)	54,330	60.9
Forest Nave Jr. (R)	34,952	39.2
5 Richard Bolling (D)	46,674	61.2
Willis Earl Salyers (R)	29,641	38.8
6 W. R. Hull Jr. (D)	55,418	58.0
John L. Leims (R)	40,185	42.0
7 Durward G. Hall (R)	86,626	62.3
Arch M. Skelton (D)	52,421	37.7
8 Richard Ichord (D)	61,128	58.1
Ben Rogers (R)	44,035	41.9
9 William L. Hungate (D)	68,472	55.3
Anthony C. Schroeder (R)	55,405	44.7
10 Paul C. Jones (D)	48,985	61.0
William Bruckerhoff (R)	31,263	39.0

MONTANA

Candidates	Votes	%
1 Arnold Olsen (D)	67,123	50.8
Richard Smiley (R)	64,925	49.2
2 James F. Battin (R)	76,015	60.2
John Melcher (D)	50,308	39.8

NEBRASKA

Candidates	Votes	%
1 Robert V. Denney (R)	93,628	51.2
Clair A. Callan (D)	89,363	48.8
2 Glenn Cunningham (R)	83,082	64.3
Richard Fellman (D)	46,235	35.8
3 David Martin (R)	115,893	73.0
John Homan (D)	42,920	27.0

NEVADA

Candidates	Votes	%
AL Walter S. Baring (D)	86,467	67.6
Ralph L. Kraemer (R)	41,383	32.4

NEW HAMPSHIRE

Candidates	Votes	%
1 Louis C. Wyman (R)	72,909	56.2
J. Oliva Huot (D)	56,750	43.8
2 James C. Cleveland (R)	66,176	66.7
William H. Barry Jr. (D)	32,838	33.1

NEW JERSEY

Candidates	Votes	%
1 John E. Hunt (R)	68,248	51.4
Michael J. Piarulli (D)	61,469	46.3
2 Charles W. Sandman Jr. (R)	72,014	51.5
Thomas C. McGrath Jr. (D)	65,494	46.9
3 James J. Howard (D)	81,382	52.7
James M. Coleman (R)	72,043	46.6
4 Frank Thompson Jr. (D)	82,271	56.2
Ralph Clark Chandler (R)	63,730	43.5
5 Peter H. B. Frelinghuysen (R)	108,375	70.8
Carter Jefferson (D)	41,476	27.1
6 William T. Cahill (R)	106,406	66.9
Walter Dubrow (D)	48,738	30.7
7 William B. Widnall (R)	101,253	66.4
Robert E. Hamer (D)	51,204	33.6
8 Charles S. Joelson (D)	80,725	59.6
Richard M. DeMarco (R)	51,784	38.2
9 Henry Helstoski (D)	74,320	50.9
Frank C. Osmers Jr. (R)	71,756	49.1
10 Peter W. Rodino Jr. (D)	71,699	64.3
Earl Harris (R)	36,508	32.7
11 Joseph G. Minish (D)	64,023	58.3
Leonard J. Felzenberg (R)	44,803	40.8
12 Florence P. Dwyer (R)	116,701	73.9
Robert F. Allen (D)	37,790	23.9
13 Cornelius E. Gallagher (D)	90,488	71.8
Ruth Swayze (R)	35,486	28.2
14 Dominick V. Daniels (D)	87,741	68.0
Thomas R. McSherry (R)	36,828	28.5
15 Edward J. Patten (D)	81,959	57.0
C. John Stroumtsos (R)	59,706	41.5

NEW MEXICO

Candidates	Votes	%
AL Thomas G. Morris (D)	140,057	55.9
Schuble C. Cook (R)	110,441	44.1
AL E. S. Johnny Walker (D)	126,984	50.5
Robert C. Davidson (R)	124,536	49.5

NEW YORK

Candidates	Votes	%
1 Otis G. Pike (D, L)	101,963	58.9
James M. Catterson Jr. (R)	58,296	33.7
Domenico Crachi Jr. (C)	12,731	7.4
2 James R. Grover Jr. (R)	79,649	54.7
Frank M. Corso (D, L)	49,743	34.1
Edward Campbell (C)	14,820	10.2
3 Lester L. Wolff (D, L)	81,959	50.3
Steven D. Derounian (R)	81,122	49.7
4 John W. Wydler (R)	86,677	59.7
Martin J. Steadman (D, L)	46,555	32.0
Donald H. Serrell (C)	10,035	6.9
5 Herbert Tenzer (D, L)	88,602	49.9
Thomas M. Brennan (R, C)	86,356	48.6
6 Seymour Halpern (R, L)	91,526	59.0
Gilbert T. Redleaf (D)	45,621	29.4
Ronald E. Weiss (C)	17,863	11.5
7 Joseph P. Addabbo (D, L)	93,758	64.9
Louis R. Mercogliano (R)	34,644	24.0
Raymond G. Carpenter (C)	16,070	11.1
8 Benjamin S. Rosenthal (D, L)	115,310	69.6
Thomas C. Gowlan (R)	36,573	22.1
Cyrus S. Julien (C)	13,726	8.3
9 James J. Delaney (D)	75,915	53.5
John F. Haggerty (R, C)	56,754	40.0
David Green (L)	9,182	6.5
10 Emanuel Celler (D, L)	76,439	82.1
Irwin A. Rosenberg (R)	16,702	17.9
11 Frank J. Brasco (D)	39,386	70.6
Benjamin W. Feldman (R)	12,200	21.9
Edward L. Johnson (L)	4,174	7.5
12 Edna F. Kelley (D, L)	87,651	72.7
Alfred Grant Walton (R)	29,390	24.4

Candidates	Votes	%
13 Abraham J. Multer (D)	95,511	61.9
Mary Gravina (R)	28,750	18.6
Herschell Chanin (L)	20,557	13.3
Michael J. Spadaro (C)	9,463	6.1
14 John J. Rooney (D, L)	43,142	76.2
Leon F. Nadrowski (R)	13,482	23.8
15 Hugh L. Carey (D, U TAX)	52,919	56.8
Herbert F. Ryan (R, C)	40,181	43.2
16 John M. Murphy (D, L)	71,889	57.4
Frank J. Biondolillo (R, C)	53,346	42.6
17 Theodore R. Kupferman (R)	69,492	47.7
Jerome L. Wilson (D, L)	67,334	46.2
Richard J. Callahan (C)	8,818	6.1
18 Adam C. Powell (D)	45,308*	74.1
Lassen L. Walsh (R)	10,711	17.5
Richard Prideaux (L)	3,954	6.5
19 Leonard Farbstein (D)	53,581	57.8
Henry E. Del Rosso (R, C)	24,340	26.2
Elaine M. Morrison (L)	11,349	12.2
20 William F. Ryan (D, L)	74,215	74.8
Norman C. Harlowe (R)	20,560	20.7
21 James H. Scheuer (D, L)	63,173	83.6
Burton Siegel (R)	12,414	16.4
22 Jacob H. Gilbert (D)	40,787	74.2
Pedro Luis Rodriguez (R, ALL PP)	10,603	19.3
Carlos Rosario (L)	3,552	6.5
23 Jonathan B. Bingham (D, L)	84,540	73.4
Harold Grosberg (R)	21,735	18.9
Walter A. Quinn Jr. (C)	8,949	7.8
24 Paul A. Fino (R, C)	80,882	63.9
Aileen B. Ryan (D)	42,291	33.4
25 Richard L. Ottinger (D, L)	106,952	54.6
Frederick J. Martin Jr. (R)	88,769	45.4
26 Ogden R. Reid (R)	107,031	69.3
Joseph L. Hutner (D)	39,203	25.4
Albert M. Gants (C)	8,159	5.3
27 John G. Dow (D, L)	79,424	47.2
Louis V. Mills (R)	74,816	44.5
Frederick P. Roland (C)	13,946	8.3
28 Joseph Y. Resnick (D, L)	84,940	50.3
Hamilton Fish Jr. (R)	78,258	46.3
29 Daniel E. Button (R, L)	107,671	53.3
Richard J. Conners (D)	91,174	45.1
30 Carleton J. King (R)	113,759	65.0
John S. Hall (D, L)	61,216	35.0
31 Robert C. McEwen (R)	75,680	67.6
Raymond E. Bishop (D, L)	36,273	32.4
32 Alexander Pirnie (R, L)	94,331	72.3
Robert Castle (D)	36,195	27.7
33 Howard W. Robison (R)	88,378	65.7
Blair G. Ewing (D, L)	45,761	34.0
34 James M. Hanley (D)	90,044	55.1
Stewart F. Hancock Jr. (R)	62,559	38.3
35 Samuel S. Stratton (D, L)	93,746	65.8
Frederick D. Dugan (R)	48,668	34.2
36 Frank J. Horton (R)	110,514	67.3
Milo Thomas (D)	37,129	22.6
Robert H. Detig (C)	10,493	6.4
37 Barber B. Conable Jr (R)	104,342	67.7
Kenneth Hed (D)	46,201	30.0
38 Charles E. Goodell (R)	82,137	67.2
Edison Leroy Jr (D)	35,785	29.3
39 Richard D. McCarthy (D, L)	95,671	52.3
John R. Pillion (R, C)	87,230	47.7
40 Henry P. Smith III (R)	85,801	61.2
William Levitt (D, L)	54,303	38.8
41 Thaddeus J. Dulski (D, L)	92,222	76.4
Frank X. Schwab (R, C)	28,491	23.6

Special Election

	Votes	%
17 Theodore R. Kupferman (R)	44,125	46.4
Orin Lehman (D)	43,206	45.4
Jeffrey St.John (C)	7,796	8.2

NORTH CAROLINA

	Candidates	Votes	%
1	Walter B. Jones (D)	43,539	61.4
	John P. East (R)	27,434	38.7
2	L. H. Fountain (D)	36,849	65.0
	Reece B. Gardiner (R)	19,888	35.1
3	David N. Henderson (D)	33,809	100.0
4	James C. Gardner (R)	60,686	56.5
	Harold D. Cooley (D)	46,673	43.5
5	Nick Galifianakis (D)	46,035	53.1
	G. Fred Steele Jr. (R)	40,729	46.9
6	Horace R. Kornegay (D)	42,677	51.6
	Richard B. Barnwell (R)	40,000	48.4
7	Alton Lennon (D)	40,512	100.0
8	Charles Raper Jonas (R)	56,382	71.5
	John G. Plumides (D)	22,465	28.5
9	James T. Broyhill (R)	80,989	63.3
	Robert Bingham (D)	46,882	36.7
10	Basil L. Whitener (D)	52,117	56.1
	W. Hall Young (R)	40,741	43.9
11	Roy A. Taylor (D)	72,855	52.8
	W. Scott Harvey (R)	65,187	47.2

Special Election

		Votes	%
1	Walter B. Jones (D)	21,773	60.3
	John P. East (R)	14,308	39.7

NORTH DAKOTA

		Votes	%
1	Mark Andrews (R)	66,011	66.2
	S. F. (Buckshot) Hoffner (D)	33,694	33.8
2	Thomas S. Kleppe (R)	50,801	52.0
	Rolland Redlin (D)	46,993	48.1

OHIO

		Votes	%
1	Robert Taft Jr. (R)	70,366	52.9
	John J. Gilligan (D)	62,580	47.1
2	Donald D. Clancy (R)	102,313	70.7
	Thomas E. Anderson (D)	42,367	29.3
3	Charles W. Whalen Jr. (R)	62,471	53.8
	Rodney M. Love (D)	53,658	46.2
4	William M. McCulloch (R)	66,142	63.6
	Robert H. Mihlbaugh (D)	37,855	36.4
5	Delbert L. Latta (R)	80,906	75.3
	John H. Shock (D)	26,503	24.7
6	William H. Harsha (R)	74,847	67.9
	Ottie W. Reno (D)	35,345	32.1
7	Clarence J. Brown Jr. (R)	81,225	100.0
8	Jackson E. Betts (R)	78,933	67.1
	Frank B. Bennett (D)	38,787	33.0
9	Thomas L. Ashley (D)	83,261	60.8
	Jane M. Kuebbeler (R)	53,777	39.2
10	Clarence E. Miller (R)	56,659	52.0
	Walter H. Moeller (D)	52,258	48.0
11	J. William Stanton (R)	86,273	69.3
	James F. Henderson (D)	38,206	30.7
12	Samuel L. Devine (R)	70,102	64.2
	Robert N. Shamansky (D)	39,140	35.8
13	Charles A. Mosher (R)	69,862	65.5
	Thomas E. Wolfe (D)	36,751	34.5
14	William H. Ayres (R)	77,819	59.7
	Charles F. Madden Jr. (D)	52,646	40.4
15	Chalmers P. Wylie (R)	57,993	59.9
	Robert L. Van Heyde (D)	38,805	40.1
16	Frank T. Bow (R)	87,597	61.1
	Robert D. Freeman (D)	55,775	38.9
17	John M. Ashbrook (R)	73,132	55.3
	Robert T. Secrest (D)	59,031	44.7
18	Wayne L. Hays (D)	73,657	64.2
	William H. Weir (R)	41,165	35.9
19	Michael J. Kirwan (D)	86,975	71.9
	Donald J. Lewis (R)	34,037	28.1
20	Michael A. Feighan (D)	63,629	76.1
	Clarence E. McLeod (R)	20,034	24.0
21	Charles A. Vanik (D)	81,210	81.7
	Frederick M. Coleman (R)	18,205	18.3

	Candidates	Votes	%
22	Frances P. Bolton (R)	71,927	55.9
	Anthony O. Calabrese Jr. (D)	56,803	44.1
23	William E. Minshall (R)	102,513	73.2
	Sheldon D. Clark (D)	37,489	26.8
24	Donald E. Lukens (R)	61,194	58.5
	James H. Pelley (D)	43,418	41.5

OKLAHOMA

		Votes	%
1	Page Belcher (R)	106,259	69.7
	Ed Cadenhead (D)	46,286	30.3
2	Ed Edmondson (D)	62,324	53.6
	Denzil D. Garrison (R)	53,919	46.4
3	Carl Albert (D)	43,049	77.2
	Whit Pate (R)	12,697	22.8
4	Tom Steed (D)	36,719	50.3
	Truman T. Branscum (R)	36,355	49.8
5	John Jarman (D)	96,464	69.6
	Melvin H. Gragg (R)	42,088	30.4
6	James V. Smith (R)	51,474	51.4
	Jed Johnson Jr. (D)	48,755	48.6

OREGON

		Votes	%
1	Wendell Wyatt (R)	144,361	74.3
	Malcolm H. Cross (D)	49,841	25.7
2	Al Ullman (D)	94,346	63.3
	Everett J. Thoren (R)	54,789	36.7
3	Edith Green (D)	114,687	66.9
	Lyle Dean (R)	56,598	33.0
4	John R. Dellenback (R)	94,154	62.7
	Charles O. Porter (D)	56,007	37.3

PENNSYLVANIA

		Votes	%
1	William A. Barrett (D)	90,100	66.1
	Beatrice K. Chernock (R)	46,280	33.9
2	Robert N. C. Nix (D)	76,372	59.9
	Herbert R. Cain Jr. (R)	51,079	40.1
3	James A. Byrne (D)	64,575	56.6
	Walter T. Darmopray (R)	49,434	43.4
4	Joshua Eilberg (D)	98,793	51.9
	Robert Baer Cohen (R)	91,620	48.1
5	William J. Green III (D)	86,128	59.1
	Michael J. Bednarek (R)	59,515	40.9
6	George M. Rhodes (D)	91,538	56.1
	Daniel B. Boyer Jr. (R)	71,508	43.9
7	Lawrence G. Williams (R)	101,042	63.2
	John J. Logue (D)	58,766	36.8
8	Edward G. Biester Jr. (R)	70,435	59.6
	Walter S. Farley Jr. (D)	47,845	40.5
9	G. Robert Watkins (R)	81,516	62.6
	Louis F. Waldmann (D)	48,656	37.4
10	Joseph M. McDade (R)	115,765	66.8
	Neil Trama (D)	57,615	33.2
11	Daniel J. Flood (D)	110,877	67.2
	Gerald C. Broadt (R)	54,032	32.8
12	J. Irving Whalley (R)	107,374	66.9
	J. Robert Rohm (D)	53,044	33.1
13	Richard S. Schweiker (R)	134,414	72.5
	William D. Searle (D)	51,024	27.5
14	William S. Moorhead (D)	83,967	68.3
	Richard L. Thornburgh (R)	39,024	31.7
15	Fred B. Rooney (D)	80,407	52.3
	George J. Joseph (R)	73,404	47.7
16	Edwin D. Eshleman (R)	82,527	69.2
	Richard F. Charles (D)	36,721	30.8
17	Herman T. Schneebeli (R)	109,169	66.2
	William Conrad Reuter (D)	55,761	33.8
18	Robert J. Corbett (R)	107,677	67.1
	John R. Wohlfarth (D)	52,714	32.9
19	George A. Goodling (R)	70,445	51.7
	N. Neiman Craley Jr. (D)	65,907	48.3
20	Elmer J. Holland (D)	93,068	65.9
	Joseph Sabol Jr. (R)	48,229	34.1
21	John H. Dent (D)	80,472	64.2
	Edward B. Byrne (R)	44,800	35.8

	Candidates	Votes	%
22	John P. Saylor (R)	103,808	67.5
	Frank H. Buck (D)	50,017	32.5
23	Albert W. Johnson (R)	81,658	62.8
	Robert W. Mitchell (D)	48,373	37.2
24	Joseph P. Vigorito (D)	85,193	55.3
	James D. Weaver (R)	68,955	44.7
25	Frank M. Clark (D)	92,073	64.5
	John F. Heath (R)	50,639	35.5
26	Thomas E. Morgan (D)	83,687	64.1
	Paul P. Riggle (R)	46,957	35.9
27	James G. Fulton (R)	108,731	67.7
	Stephen J. Arnold (D)	51,928	32.3

RHODE ISLAND

		Votes	%
1	Fernand J. St.Germain (D)	79,046	56.6
	Raymond W. Houghton (R)	60,093	43.0
2	John E. Fogarty (D)	117,911	64.7
	Everett C. Sammartino (R)	64,438	35.3

SOUTH CAROLINA

		Votes	%
1	L. Mendel Rivers (D)	59,055	100.0
2	Albert W. Watson (R)	48,742	64.3
	Fred Leclercq (D)	27,013	35.7
3	William J. Bryan Dorn (D)	42,834	57.8
	John Grisso (R)	31,331	42.2
4	Robert T. Ashmore (D)	43,611	100.0
5	Thomas S. Gettys (D)	41,550	99.2
6	John L. McMillan (D)	43,090	61.7
	Archie C. Odom (R)	26,702	38.3

SOUTH DAKOTA

		Votes	%
1	Ben Reifel (R)	80,592	66.7
	Francis C. Richter (D)	40,236	33.3
2	E. Y. Berry (R)	63,063	60.5
	Jack Allmon (D)	41,155	39.5

TENNESSEE

		Votes	%
1	James A. Quillen (R)	86,421	87.1
	Temus Bright (I)	12,819	12.9
2	John J. Duncan (R)	87,777	78.9
	Jake Armstrong (D)	23,538	21.2
3	Bill Brock (R)	67,705	64.2
	Franklin Haney (D)	37,720	35.8
4	Joe L. Evins (D)	72,621	90.0
	William Bean (I)	8,061	10.0
5	Richard H. Fulton (D)	55,685	63.0
	George Kelly (R)	32,706	37.0
6	William R. Anderson (D)	50,758	79.6
	Cecil Hill (I)	12,987	20.4
7	Ray Blanton (D)	45,083	50.6
	Julius Hurst (R)	43,118	48.4
8	Robert A. Everett (D)	53,338	75.2
	Jim Boyd (R)	17,608	24.8
9	Dan H. Kuykendall (R)	47,489	52.2
	George W. Grider (D)	43,553	47.8

TEXAS

		Votes	%
1	Wright Patman (D)	50,072	100.0
2	John Dowdy (D)	55,134	99.9
3	Joe Pool (D)	35,081	53.4
	James M. Collins (R)	30,588	46.6
4	Ray Roberts (D)	51,895	100.0
5	Earle Cabell (D)	39,977	61.0
	Duke Burgess (R)	25,563	39.0
6	Olin Teague (D)	42,017	100.0
7	George Bush (R)	53,756	57.1
	Frank Briscoe (D)	39,958	42.4
8	Bob Eckhardt (D)	38,497	92.3
	W. D. Spayne (CONST)	3,207	7.7
9	Jack Brooks (D)	47,604	100.0
10	J. J. Pickle (D)	55,424	74.3
	Jane Sumner (R)	18,343	24.6

TEXAS

Candidates	Votes	%
11 W. R. Poage (D)	39,140	94.9
Laurel N. Dunn (C)	2,102	5.1
12 Jim Wright (D)	27,070	100.0
13 Graham Purcell (D)	43,820	57.1
D. C. Norwood (R)	32,960	42.9
14 John Young (D)	52,861	100.0
15 Eligio de la Garza (D)	33,129	100.0
16 Richard C. White (D)	33,179	100.0
17 Omar Burleson (D)	52,169	100.0
18 Bob Price (R)	45,209	59.5
Dee D. Miller (D)	30,822	40.5
19 George Mahon (D)	56,792	100.0
20 Henry Gonzalez (D)	41,067	87.1
Robert C. Moore (C)	3,671	7.8
Bert Ellis (CONST)	2,390	5.1
21 O. C. Fisher (D)	60,497	100.0
22 Bob Casey (D)	60,817	100.0
23 Abraham Kazen (D)	50,322	96.4

Special Election

	Votes	%
8 Lera M. Thomas (D)	6,120#	74.0
Louis Leman (R)	2,147#	26.0

UTAH

	Votes	%
1 Laurence J. Burton (R)	99,750	66.5
J. Keith Melville (D)	50,260	33.5
2 Sherman P. Lloyd (R)	96,426	61.3
David S. King (D)	61,001	38.8

VERMONT

	Votes	%
AL Robert T. Stafford (R)	89,097	65.6
William J. Ryan (D)	46,643	34.4

VIRGINIA

Candidates	Votes	%
1 Thomas N. Downing (D)	51,016	99.8
2 Porter Hardy Jr. (D)	33,761	100.0
3 David E. Satterfield III (D)	51,576	99.6
4 Watkins M. Abbitt (D)	45,226	66.6
Edward J. Silverman (C)	14,827	21.8
5 William M. Tuck (D)	32,312	56.2
Robert L. Gilliam (R)	25,203	43.8
6 Richard H. Poff (R)	55,342	80.8
Murray A. Stoller (D)	13,113	19.2
7 John O. Marsh Jr. (D)	42,532	59.2
Edward O. McCue (R)	29,249	40.7
8 William Lloyd Scott (R)	50,782	57.2
George C. Rawlings Jr (D)	37,929	42.8
9 William C. Wampler (R)	49,413	53.7
W. Pat Jennings (D)	42,571	46.3
10 Joel T. Broyhill (R)	58,105	58.3
Clive L. Duval II (D)	41,502	41.7

WASHINGTON

	Votes	%
1 Thomas M. Pelly (R)	120,747	80.3
Alice Franklin Bryant (D)	29,686	19.7
2 Lloyd Meeds (D)	75,357	60.7
Eugene M. Smith (R)	44,727	36.0
3 Julia Butler Hansen (D)	78,601	65.8
Keith Kisor (R)	40,946	34.3
4 Catherine May (R)	77,929	62.1
Gustav Bansmer (D)	38,029	30.3
Floyd Paxton (C)	9,585	7.6
5 Thomas S. Foley (D)	74,571	56.5
Dorothy R. Powers (R)	57,310	43.5
6 Floyd V. Hicks (D)	73,164	60.4
George Mahler (R)	48,041	39.6
7 Brock Adams (D)	104,613	62.8
James Munn (R)	60,065	36.0

WEST VIRGINIA

Candidates	Votes	%
1 Arch A. Moore Jr. (R)	88,364	70.9
William M. Kidd (D)	36,242	29.1
2 Harley O. Staggers (D)	51,235	60.3
George L. Strader (R)	33,676	39.7
3 John M. Slack (D)	60,073	61.6
Mal Guthrie (R)	37,416	38.4
4 Ken Hechler (D)	71,751	59.7
Harry D. Humphreys (R)	48,396	40.3
5 James Kee (D)	42,722	63.6
Elizabeth Ann Bowen (R)	24,470	36.4

WISCONSIN

	Votes	%
1 Henry C. Schadeberg (R)	65,041	51.0
Lynn E. Stalbaum (D)	62,398	49.0
2 Robert W. Kastenmeier (D)	70,311	58.0
William B. Smith (R)	50,850	42.0
3 Vernon W. Thomson (R)	72,586	68.8
John D. Rice (D)	32,849	31.2
4 Clement J. Zablocki (D)	77,690	74.3
James E. Laessig (R)	26,863	25.7
5 Henry S. Reuss (D)	52,332	70.0
Curtis T. Pechtel (R)	22,167	29.7
6 William A. Steiger (R)	67,941	52.4
John A. Race (D)	61,761	47.6
7 Melvin R. Laird (R)	74,942	65.2
Norman L. Myhra (D)	40,093	34.9
8 John W. Byrnes (R)	75,817	61.3
Marvin S. Kagen (D)	47,926	38.7
9 Glenn R. Davis (R)	85,297	64.1
James P. Buckley (D)	47,674	35.9
10 Alvin E. O'Konski (R)	79,282	66.5
Carl E. Lauri (D)	39,863	33.5

WYOMING

	Votes	%
AL William Henry Harrison (R)	62,984	52.3
Al Christian (D)	57,442	47.7

1967 House Elections

CALIFORNIA

Special Primary Election [1]

11 Paul N. McCloskey Jr. (R)	52,882	34.3
Shirley Temple Black (R)	34,521	22.4
William H. Draper III (R)	19,566	12.7
Roy Archibald (D)	15,069	9.8
Earl B. Whitmore (R)	12,823	8.3
Edward M. Keating (D)	8,813	5.7

Special Election

11 Paul N. McCloskey Jr. (R)	66,385#	57.8
Roy Archibald (D)	44,319#	38.6

NEW YORK

Special Election [2]

18 Adam C. Powell (D)	27,963#	86.3
Lucille P. Williams (R)	3,999#	12.3

RHODE ISLAND

Special Election

2 Robert O. Tiernan (D)	56,051#	48.8
James DiPrete (R)	55,748#	48.5

1. Under California's special election law, a majority of the total vote cast was required for election. If no candidate achieved it, another election would be held with the top candidates from each party competing. In the 11th District, McCloskey had more votes than any other Republican, but not a majority of the total vote, so he became the Republican nominee against Archibald, the top Democrat, in the special election.

2. Following his re-election to the 90th Congress (1967-69) in 1966, Powell was not allowed to take the oath of office in January 1967 and was subsequently excluded by vote of the House March 1, 1967. A special election was held April 11, 1967, to fill the vacancy. Powell was again a candidate and won easily, but he never attempted to claim the seat and it remained vacant for the remainder of the Congress.

1968 House Elections

ALABAMA

	Candidates	Votes	%
1	Jack Edwards (R)	60,318	57.1
	Arnold Debrow (D)	40,593	38.4
2	William L. Dickinson (R)	60,743	55.4
	Robert Whaley (D)	37,533	34.2
	Richard Boone (NDPA)	11,446	10.4
3	George Andrews (D)	86,796	90.8
	Wilbur Johnston (NDPA)	8,031	8.4
4	Bill Nichols (D)	94,726	81.4
	Robert Kerr (R)	12,427	10.7
	T. Clemons (NDPA)	9,248	7.9
5	Walter Flowers (D)	69,110	56.2
	William McKinley Branch (NDPA)	28,040	22.8
	Frank Donaldson (R)	14,582	11.9
	Mike Simpson (I)	9,429	7.7
6	John Buchanan (R)	69,445	59.3
	Quinton Bowers (D)	34,608	29.6
	Thomas Wrenn (NDPA)	12,976	11.1
7	Tom Bevill (D)	106,132	76.1
	Jodie Connell (R)	29,923	21.5
8	Robert E. Jones (D)	85,528	76.1
	Ken Hearn (C)	16,900	15.0
	Charlie Burgess (NDPA)	7,140	6.4

ALASKA

	Candidates	Votes	%
AL	Howard W. Pollock (R)	43,577	54.2
	Nick Begich (D)	36,785	45.8

ARIZONA

	Candidates	Votes	%
1	John J. Rhodes (R)	137,761	71.6
	Robert E. Miller (D)	54,594	28.4
2	Morris K. Udall (D)	102,301	70.3
	G. Alfred McGinnis (R)	43,235	29.7
3	Sam Steiger (R)	79,667	63.4
	Ralph Watkins Jr. (D)	46,072	36.6

ARKANSAS

	Candidates	Votes	%
1	Bill Alexander (D)	80,293	68.9
	Guy Newcomb (R)	36,284	31.1
2	Wilbur D. Mills (D)		100.0
3	John Paul Hammerschmidt (R)	121,771	67.1
	Hardy Croxton (D)	59,642	32.9
4	David Pryor (D)		100.0

CALIFORNIA

	Candidates	Votes	%
1	Don H. Clausen (R)	133,597	75.2
	Donald W. Graham (D)	37,756	21.3
2	Harold T. Johnson (D)	127,744	60.7
	Osmer E. Dunaway (R)	78,986	37.6
3	John E. Moss (D)	107,446	56.0
	Elmore J. Duffy (R)	80,193	41.8
4	Robert L. Leggett (D)	90,126	55.6
	James M. Shumway (R)	67,225	41.5
5	Phillip Burton (D)	95,630	72.8
	Waldo Velasquez (R)	31,157	23.7
	Huey P. Newton (PFP)	12,279	7.5
6	William S. Mailliard (R)	151,336	73.4
	Phillip Drath (D)	54,928	26.6
7	Jeffery Cohelan (D)	102,689	62.9
	Barney E. Hilburn (R)	48,397	29.6
8	George P. Miller (D)	104,768	64.0
	Raymond P. Britton (R)	58,887	36.0
9	Don Edwards (D)	101,329	56.6
	Larry Fargher (R)	77,847	43.5
10	Charles S. Gubser (R)	160,563	67.3
	Grayson S. Taketa (D)	73,720	30.9
11	Paul N. McCloskey Jr. (R)	166,252	79.4
	Urban G. Whitaker (D)	40,957	19.6
12	Burt L. Talcott (R)	143,222	92.6
13	Charles M. Teague (R)	151,608	65.9
	Stanley K. Sheinbaum (D)	78,628	34.2
14	Jerome R. Waldie (D)	152,847	71.6
	David W. Schuh (R)	56,730	26.6
15	John J. McFall (D)	86,386	53.8
	Sam Van Dyken (R)	74,058	46.2
16	B. F. Sisk (D)	97,476	62.5
	Dave Harris (R)	55,188	35.4
17	Glenn M. Anderson (D)	77,250	50.7
	Joe Blatchford (R)	73,351	48.1
18	Robert B. Mathias (R)	100,115	65.2
	Harlan Hagen (D)	51,373	33.5
19	Chet Holifield (D)	99,069	63.1
	Bill Jones (R)	53,842	34.3
20	H. Allen Smith (R)	136,238	69.4
	Don White (D)	57,064	29.1
21	Augustus F. Hawkins (D)	89,536	91.6
	Rayfield Lundy (R)	8,244	8.4
22	James C. Corman (D)	103,695	56.9
	Joe Holt (R)	75,457	41.4
23	Del Clawson (R)	97,232	65.1
	Jim Sperrazzo (D)	52,202	34.9
24	Glenard P. Lipscomb (R)	155,443	72.8
	Fred W. Neal (D)	57,972	27.2
25	Charles E. Wiggins (R)	145,245	68.7
	Keith F. Shirey (D)	66,263	31.3
26	Thomas M. Rees (D)	134,642	65.4
	Irving Teichner (R)	64,505	31.4
27	Ed Reinecke (R)	162,854	72.2
	John T. Butchko (D)	62,824	27.8
28	Alphonzo Bell (R)	173,680	71.3
	John M. Pratt (D)	65,233	26.8
29	George E. Brown Jr. (D)	76,091	52.3
	Bill Orozco (R)	69,485	47.7
30	Edward R. Roybal (D)	76,967	67.4
	Samuel M. Cavnar (R)	37,234	32.6
31	Charles H. Wilson (D)	97,855	58.9
	James R. Dunn (R)	65,004	39.1
32	Craig Hosmer (R)	142,401	73.9
	Arthur J. Gottlieb (D)	46,404	24.1
33	Jerry L. Pettis (R)	123,507	66.3
	Al C. Ballard (D)	59,649	32.0
34	Richard T. Hanna (D)	107,113	50.9
	William J. Teague (R)	103,470	49.1
35	James B. Utt (R)	216,093	72.5
	Thomas B. Lenhart (D)	74,798	25.1
36	Bob Wilson (R)	148,854	71.6
	Don Lindgren (D)	59,011	28.4
37	Lionel Van Deerlin (D)	96,130	64.7
	Mike Schaefer (R)	52,547	35.3
38	John V. Tunney (D)	121,749	62.7
	Robert O. Hunter (R)	68,887	35.5

COLORADO

	Candidates	Votes	%
1	Byron G. Rogers (D)	91,199	45.7
	Frank A. Kemp (R)	82,677	41.5
	Gordon G. Barnewall (DENVER I)	25,499	12.8
2	Donald G. Brotzman (R)	152,153	62.9
	Roy H. McVicker (D)	89,917	37.2
3	Frank E. Evans (D)	88,368	52.1
	Paul Bradley (R)	81,173	47.9
4	Wayne N. Aspinall (D)	92,680	54.7
	Fred E. Anderson (R)	76,776	45.3

CONNECTICUT

	Candidates	Votes	%
1	Emilio Q. Daddario (D)	124,966	62.4
	Roger B. Ladd (R)	74,615	37.3
2	William L. St.Onge (D)	106,203	54.1
	Peter P. Mariani (R)	89,098	45.4
3	Robert Giaimo (D)	102,636	54.0
	Stelio Salmona (R)	80,696	42.5
4	Lowell P. Weicker Jr. (R)	113,749	51.4
	Donald J. Irwin (D)	104,723	47.3
5	John S. Monagan (D)	110,337	56.3
	Gaetano A. Russo Jr. (R)	85,591	43.7
6	Thomas J. Meskill (R)	126,208	62.3
	Robert M. Sharaf (D)	76,413	37.7

DELAWARE

	Candidates	Votes	%
AL	William V. Roth (R)	117,827	58.7
	Harris B. McDowell Jr. (D)	82,993	41.3

FLORIDA

	Candidates	Votes	%
1	Robert L. F. Sikes (D)	116,215	84.7
	John Drzazga (R)	21,063	15.3
2	Don Fuqua (D)	87,313	100.0
3	Charles E. Bennett (D)	103,540	78.9
	Bill Parsons (R)	27,696	21.1
4	Bill Chappell Jr. (D)	86,251	52.8
	William F. Herlong Jr. (R)	76,974	47.2
5	Louis Frey (R)	108,620	61.7
	James C. Robinson (D)	67,505	38.3
6	Sam M. Gibbons (D)	84,193	62.0
	Paul A. Saad (R)	51,637	38.0
7	James A. Haley (D)	91,539	55.0
	Joe Z. Lovingood (R)	74,896	45.0
8	William C. Cramer (R)	117,747	100.0
9	Paul G. Rogers (D)	111,539	56.2
	Robert W. Rust (R)	87,074	43.8
10	J. Herbert Burke (R)	99,844	54.9
	Elton J. Gissendanner (D)	82,138	45.1
11	Claude Pepper (D)	99,154	76.6
	Ronald I. Strauss (R)	30,324	23.4
12	Dante B. Fascell (D)	82,362	57.0
	Mike Thompson (R)	62,032	43.0

GEORGIA

	Candidates	Votes	%
1	G. Elliott Hagan (D)	77,403	68.2
	Joseph J. Tribble (R)	36,118	31.8
2	Maston O'Neal (D)	72,830	100.0
3	Jack Brinkley (D)	55,759	100.0
4	Ben B. Blackburn (R)	78,753	57.5
	James A. Mackay (D)	58,154	42.5
5	Fletcher Thompson (R)	79,258	55.6
	Charles L. Weltner (D)	63,183	44.4
6	John J. Flynt Jr. (D)	97,289	100.0
7	John W. Davis (D)	96,505	99.8
8	W. S. Stuckey Jr. (D)	64,912	100.0
9	Phil M. Landrum (D)	83,829	100.0
10	Robert G. Stephens (D)	80,674	100.0

HAWAII

	Candidates	Votes	%
AL	Spark M. Matsunaga (D)	161,954✔	
	Patsy T. Mink (D)	149,207✔	
	Neal S. Blaisdell (R)	78,733	
	George Dubois (R)	39,233	
	Jon D. Olsen (PFP)	2,432	
	Peter O. Lombardi (PFP)	2,026	

IDAHO

	Candidates	Votes	%
1	James A. McClure (R)	90,870	59.4
	Compton I. White (D)	62,002	40.6
2	Orval Hansen (R)	65,029	52.6
	Darrell Manning (D)	54,256	43.9

ILLINOIS

	Candidates	Votes	%
1	William L. Dawson (D)	119,207	84.6
	Janet Roberts Jenning (R)	21,758	15.4
2	Abner J. Mikva (D)	106,642	65.4
	Thomas R. Ireland (R)	56,513	34.6
3	William T. Murphy (D)	101,729	54.0
	Robert A. Podesta (R)	86,535	46.0
4	Edward J. Derwinski (R)	151,216	68.3
	Robert E. Creighton (D)	70,145	31.7
5	John C. Kluczynski (D)	96,584	55.4
	Joseph J. Krasowski (R)	77,887	44.6
6	Daniel J. Ronan (D)	94,779	59.7
	Gerald Dolezal (R)	63,999	40.3
7	Frank Annunzio (D)	86,769	83.1
	Thomas J. Lento (R)	17,594	16.9
8	Daniel Rostenkowski (D)	105,003	62.8
	Henry S. Kaplinski (R)	62,254	37.2
9	Sidney R. Yates (D)	119,032	64.4
	Edward V. Notz (R)	65,687	35.6
10	Harold R. Collier (R)	148,398	66.8
	Seymour C. Axelrood (D)	73,766	33.2
11	Roman C. Pucinski (D)	128,152	55.8
	John J. Hoellen (R)	101,665	44.2
12	Robert McClory (R)	120,370	70.4
	Albert S. Salvi (D)	50,525	29.6
13	Donald Rumsfeld (R)	186,714	72.7
	David C. Baylor (D)	69,987	27.3
14	John N. Erlenborn (R)	163,332	71.1
	Marc Karson (D)	66,293	28.9
15	Charlotte T. Reid (R)	121,432	68.7
	Benjamin P. Alschuler (D)	55,291	31.3
16	John B. Anderson (R)	111,037	67.4
	Stan Major (D)	53,838	32.7
17	Leslie C. Arends (R)	122,513	65.3
	Lester A. Hawthorne (D)	65,192	34.7
18	Robert H. Michel (R)	106,122	60.9
	James G. Hatcher (D)	68,173	39.1
19	Tom Railsback (R)	114,948	63.5
	Craig Lovitt (D)	66,135	36.5
20	Paul Findley (R)	124,121	66.2
	Donald L. Schilson (D)	63,412	33.8
21	Kenneth J. Gray (D)	111,425	54.2
	Val Oshel (R)	94,363	45.9
22	William L. Springer (R)	115,258	64.3
	Carl F. Firley (D)	63,957	35.7
23	George E. Shipley (D)	104,349	54.0
	Bert Hopper (R)	88,945	46.0
24	Melvin Price (D)	113,507	71.3
	John S. Guthrie (R)	45,649	28.7

INDIANA

		Votes	%
1	Ray J. Madden (D)	90,055	56.7
	Donald E. Taylor (R)	68,318	43.0
2	Earl F. Landgrebe (R)	104,238	55.1
	Edward F. Kelly (D)	85,084	44.9
3	John Brademas (D)	94,452	52.2
	William W. Erwin (R)	86,354	47.8
4	E. Ross Adair (R)	98,977	51.4
	J. Edward Roush (D)	93,515	48.6
5	Richard L. Roudebush (R)	114,537	63.0
	Robert C. Ford (D)	67,370	37.0
6	William G. Bray (R)	142,207	64.9
	Phillip L. Bayt (D)	76,940	35.1
7	John T. Myers (R)	115,921	59.8
	Elden C. Tipton (D)	78,045	40.2
8	Roger H. Zion (R)	109,585	54.5
	K. Wayne Kent (D)	91,642	45.5
9	Lee H. Hamilton (D)	102,707	54.4
	Robert D. Garton (R)	86,012	45.6
10	David W. Dennis (R)	98,090	53.9
	William J. Norton (D)	83,981	46.1
11	Andrew Jacobs Jr. (D)	80,015	53.1
	W. W. Hill Jr. (R)	70,725	46.9

IOWA

		Votes	%
1	Fred Schwengel (R)	91,419	53.0
	John R. Schmidhauser (D)	81,049	47.0

	Candidates	Votes	%
2	John C. Culver (D)	103,651	55.1
	Tom Riley (R)	84,634	45.0
3	H. R. Gross (R)	101,839	64.1
	John E. Van Eschen (D)	57,164	36.0
4	John Kyl (R)	83,259	53.9
	Bert Bandstra (D)	71,134	46.1
5	Neal Smith (D)	99,586	62.1
	Don Mahon (R)	60,710	37.9
6	Wiley Mayne (R)	100,802	65.0
	Jerry O'Sullivan (D)	54,171	35.0
7	William Scherle (R)	86,212	64.8
	Richard Oshlo (D)	46,774	35.2

KANSAS

		Votes	%
1	Keith G. Sebelius (R)	87,012	51.5
	George W. Meeker (D)	82,102	48.6
2	Chester L. Mize (R)	110,768	67.6
	Robert A. Swan (D)	53,151	32.4
3	Larry Winn (R)	100,877	62.8
	Newell A. George (D)	59,672	37.2
4	Garner E. Shriver (R)	101,991	64.7
	Patrick F. Kelly (D)	55,621	35.3
5	Joe Skubitz (R)	107,085	64.5
	A. F. Bramble (D)	59,005	35.5

KENTUCKY

		Votes	%
1	Frank A. Stubblefield (D)	72,072	100.0
2	William H. Natcher (D)	65,860	56.4
	Robert D. Simmons (R)	50,904	43.6
3	William O. Cowger (R)	70,318	56.0
	Tom Ray (D)	55,366	44.1
4	M. G. (Gene) Snyder (R)	103,793	65.0
	Gus Sheehan (D)	55,971	35.0
5	Tim Lee Carter (R)	86,391	72.8
	Thomas J. Roberts (D)	30,575	25.8
6	John C. Watts (D)	78,536	56.5
	Russell G. Mobley (R)	58,905	42.4
7	Carl D. Perkins (D)	82,594	62.0
	James D. Nickell (R)	50,699	38.0

LOUISIANA

		Votes	%
1	F. Edward Hebert (D)	70,658	100.0
2	Hale Boggs (D)	81,537	51.2
	David C. Treen (R)	77,633	48.8
3	Patrick T. Caffery (D)	39,215	100.0
4	Joe D. Waggonner Jr. (D)	63,788	100.0
5	Otto E. Passman (D)	34,901	100.0
6	John R. Rarick (D)	100,461	79.5
	Loyd J. Rockhold (R)	25,867	20.5
7	Edwin W. Edwards (D)	79,709	85.0
	Vance W. Plauche (R)	14,126	15.1
8	Speedy O. Long (D)	41,086	100.0

MAINE

		Votes	%
1	Peter N. Kyros (D)	113,501	56.6
	Horace A. Hildreth Jr. (R)	86,949	43.4
2	William D. Hathaway (D)	102,369	55.7
	Elden H. Shute (R)	81,398	44.3

MARYLAND

		Votes	%
1	Rogers C. B. Morton (R)	87,078	73.6
	E. Homer White Jr. (D)	31,250	26.4
2	Clarence D. Long (D)	86,025	59.1
	John E. Mudd (R)	59,635	40.9
3	Edward A. Garmatz (D)	63,269	81.3
	James E. Chew (R)	14,604	18.8
4	George H. Fallon (D)	60,651	65.6
	Thomas Paul Raimondi (R)	31,813	34.4
5	Lawrence J. Hogan (R)	89,073	52.7
	Hervey G. Machen (D)	79,870	47.3
6	J. Glenn Beall Jr. (R)	71,714	53.0
	Goodloe E. Byron (D)	63,597	47.0

	Candidates	Votes	%
7	Samuel N. Friedel (D)	81,048	79.6
	Arthur W. Downs (R)	20,745	20.4
8	Gilbert Gude (R)	109,167	60.9
	Margaret C. Schweinhaut (D)	70,109	39.1

MASSACHUSETTS

		Votes	%
1	Silvio O. Conte (R)	140,419	99.8
2	Edward P. Boland (D)	126,485	73.7
	Frederick M. Whitney Jr. (R)	45,262	26.4
3	Philip J. Philbin (D)	91,587	47.8
	Chandler Harrison Stevens (I)	53,047	27.7
	Laurence Curtis (R)	46,860	24.5
4	Harold D. Donohue (D)	121,211	61.0
	Howard A. Miller Jr. (R)	77,658	39.1
5	F. Bradford Morse (R)	124,930	60.4
	Robert C. Maguire (D)	81,875	39.6
6	William H. Bates (R)	136,951	66.1
	Deirdre Henderson (D)	70,304	33.9
7	Torbert H. Macdonald (D)	119,562	62.5
	William S. Abbot (R)	71,689	34.8
8	Thomas P. O'Neill Jr. (D)	107,645	100.0
	John W. McCormack (D)	77,347	89.2
	Allan C. Freeman (D)	15,906	17.1
10	Margaret M. Heckler (R)	138,220	67.4
	Edmund Dinis (D)	66,949	32.6
11	James A. Burke (D)	169,766	100.0
12	Hastings Keith (R)	173,295	99.9

MICHIGAN

		Votes	%
1	John Conyers Jr. (D)	127,847	100.0
2	Marvin L. Esch (R)	90,804	54.4
	Weston E. Vivian (D)	75,009	44.9
3	Garry Brown (R)	109,754	65.2
	Thomas L. Keenan (D)	58,692	34.8
4	Edward Hutchinson (R)	100,128	65.6
	John V. Martin (D)	52,441	34.4
5	Gerald R. Ford (R)	105,085	62.8
	Laurence E. Howard (D)	62,219	37.2
6	Charles E. Chamberlain (R)	103,423	64.1
	James A. Harrison (D)	57,839	35.9
7	Donald W. Riegle Jr. (R)	104,502	60.7
	William R. Blue (D)	67,779	39.3
8	James Harvey (R)	105,238	68.8
	Richard E. Davies (D)	47,639	31.2
9	Guy Vander Jagt (R)	111,754	67.5
	Jay A. Wabeke (D)	53,886	32.5
10	Elford A. Cederberg (R)	104,791	65.9
	Wayne Miller (D)	54,152	34.1
11	Philip E. Ruppe (R)	94,515	58.8
	Raymond F. Clevenger (D)	66,251	41.2
12	James G. O'Hara (D)	131,517	70.3
	Max B. Harris Jr. (R)	54,760	29.3
13	Charles C. Diggs Jr. (D)	81,951	86.4
	Eugene Beauregard (R)	12,873	13.6
14	Lucien N. Nedzi (D)	101,961	63.1
	Peter O'Rourke (R)	59,757	37.0
15	William D. Ford (D)	106,960	71.1
	John F. Boyle (R)	43,582	29.0
16	John D. Dingell Jr. (D)	105,690	73.9
	Monte R. Bona (R)	37,000	25.9
17	Martha W. Griffiths (D)	123,376	74.8
	John M. Siviter (R)	40,906	24.8
18	William S. Broomfield (R)	124,025	59.9
	Allen Zemmol (D)	82,234	39.7
19	Jack McDonald (R)	104,057	58.0
	Garry F. Frink (D)	75,250	42.0

MINNESOTA

		Votes	%
1	Albert H. Quie (R)	138,400	68.8
	George Daley (DFL)	62,916	31.3
2	Ancher Nelsen (R)	100,623	59.5
	Jon Wefald (DFL)	68,528	40.5

MINNESOTA

	Candidates	Votes	%
3	Clark MacGregor (R)	158,989	64.8
	Eugene E. Stokowski (DFL)	86,434	35.2
4	Joseph E. Karth (DFL)	129,082	61.3
	Emery Barrette (R)	81,392	38.7
5	Donald M. Fraser (DFL)	108,588	57.5
	Harmon T. Ogdahl (R)	78,819	41.8
6	John M. Zwach (R)	104,664	56.2
	J. Buford Johnson (DFL)	81,578	43.8
7	Odin Langen (R)	83,113	51.3
	Bob Bergland (DFL)	79,067	48.8
8	John A. Blatnik (DFL)	115,343	67.6
	James A. Hennen (R)	55,209	32.4

MISSISSIPPI

	Candidates	Votes	%
1	Thomas G. Abernethy (D)	73,800	100.0
2	Jamie L. Whitten (D)	71,260	100.0
3	Charles H. Griffin (D)	82,896	100.0
4	G. V. (Sonny) Montgomery (D)	78,768	70.1
	Prentiss Walker (R)	33,683	30.0
5	William M. Colmer (D)	108,297	100.0

Special Runoff Election[1]

		Votes	%
3	Charles H. Griffin (D)	87,713#	66.9
	Charles Evers (D)	43,303#	33.1

MISSOURI

	Candidates	Votes	%
1	William Clay (D)	79,295	64.2
	Curtis C. Crawford (R)	44,316	35.9
2	James W. Symington (D)	115,476	53.2
	Hugh Scott (R)	101,500	46.8
3	Leonor K. Sullivan (D)	106,150	73.4
	Homer McCracken (R)	38,439	26.6
4	William B. Randall (D)	104,056	57.9
	Leslie O. Olson (R)	75,790	42.1
5	Richard Bolling (D)	86,681	65.4
	Harold Masters (R)	45,951	34.7
6	W. R. Hull Jr. (D)	102,315	54.6
	James E. Austin (R)	85,237	45.5
7	Durward G. Hall (R)	123,958	63.8
	Edward J. Bonitt (D)	70,455	36.2
8	Richard Ichord (D)	108,416	57.5
	Eugene E. Northern (R)	79,179	42.0
9	William L. Hungate (D)	108,184	52.2
	Christopher S. Bond (R)	98,923	47.8
10	Bill D. Burlison (D)	78,326	54.0
	Vernon H. Landgraf (R)	66,830	46.0

MONTANA

	Candidates	Votes	%
1	Arnold Olsen (D)	74,974	53.6
	Richard Smiley (R)	64,862	46.4
2	James F. Battin (R)	83,888	67.9
	Robert L. Kelleher (D)	39,752	32.2

NEBRASKA

	Candidates	Votes	%
1	Robert V. Denney (R)	97,697	54.1
	Clair A. Callan (D)	78,374	43.4
2	Glenn Cunningham (R)	87,683	55.2
	Mrs. Frank B. Morrison (D)	71,254	44.8
3	Dave Martin (R)	123,838	67.8
	J. B. Dean (D)	58,728	32.2

NEVADA

	Candidates	Votes	%
AL	Walter S. Baring (D)	104,136	72.1
	James Michael Slattery (R)	40,209	27.9

NEW HAMPSHIRE

	Candidates	Votes	%
1	Louis C. Wyman (R)	100,269	63.4
	James T. Keefe (D)	57,959	36.6

	Candidates	Votes	%
2	James C. Cleveland (R)	88,609	71.1
	David C. Hoeh (D)	35,942	28.9

NEW JERSEY

	Candidates	Votes	%
1	John E. Hunt (R)	105,856	58.0
	Thomas S. Higgins (D)	74,703	41.0
2	Charles W. Sandman Jr. (R)	91,218	55.3
	David Dichter (D)	73,361	44.4
3	James J. Howard (D)	113,587	57.8
	Richard R. Stout (R)	82,441	41.9
4	Frank Thompson Jr. (R)	106,504	53.4
	Sydney S. Souter (D)	92,710	46.4
5	Peter H. B. Frelinghuysen Jr. (R)	143,963	68.2
	Robert F. Allen (D)	63,208	29.9
6	William T. Cahill (R)	138,060	65.7
	Robert A. Gasser (D)	71,338	34.0
7	William B. Widnall (R)	120,523	62.2
	Charles S. Gregg (D)	71,123	36.7
8	Charles S. Joelson (D)	100,653	61.4
	Richard M. DeMarco (R)	62,661	38.2
9	Henry Helstoski (D)	97,599	49.8
	Peter Moraites (R)	95,267	48.7
10	Peter W. Rodino Jr. (D)	89,109	63.8
	Celestino Clemente (R)	47,989	34.4
11	Joseph G. Minish (D)	91,496	65.5
	George M. Wallhauser Jr. (R)	46,426	33.2
12	Florence P. Dwyer (R)	146,264	71.6
	John B. Duff (D)	58,112	28.4
13	Cornelius E. Gallagher (D)	83,151	55.5
	Marion D. Dwyer (R)	52,159	34.8
	Jeremiah J. O'Callaghan (VI)	9,399	6.3
14	Dominick V. Daniels (D)	87,187	58.5
	Joseph Bartletta (R)	50,829	34.1
	Mervin Murray (C)	7,634	5.1
15	Edward J. Patten (D)	107,316	54.6
	George W. Luke (R)	88,043	44.8

NEW MEXICO

	Candidates	Votes	%
1	Manuel Lujan Jr. (R)	88,517	52.9
	Thomas G. Morris (D)	78,117	46.6
2	Ed Foreman (R)	71,857	50.5
	E. S. Johnny Walker (D)	69,858	49.1

NEW YORK

	Candidates	Votes	%
1	Otis G. Pike (D)	118,913	53.9
	James M. Catterson Jr. (R)	79,208	35.9
	Harold Haar (C)	19,470	8.8
2	James R. Grover Jr. (R, C)	129,731	69.0
	Charles A. Heeg (D)	53,552	28.5
3	Lester L. Wolff (D, L)	98,226	52.1
	Abe Seldin (R)	75,910	40.2
	Daniel L. Rice (C)	14,556	7.7
4	John W. Wydler (R, C)	116,190	70.1
	Michael J. Delguidice (D)	45,130	27.2
5	Allard K. Lowenstein (D, L)	99,193	50.7
	Mason L. Hampton Jr. (R, C)	96,427	49.3
6	Seymour Halpern (R, L)	95,016	57.5
	Franklin Miller (D)	49,676	30.1
	Thomas J. Adams (C)	20,511	12.4
7	Joseph P. Addabbo (D, L)	90,204#	66.3
	Louis R. Mercogliano (R, C)	45,813#	33.7
8	Benjamin S. Rosenthal (D, L)	120,257	69.8
	Jack M. Weinstein (R)	37,314	21.7
	Charles Witteck Jr. (C)	14,714	8.5
9	James J. Delaney (D)	69,462	49.7
	John F. Haggerty (R, C)	59,690	42.7
	Rose L. Rubin (L)	8,935	6.4

	Candidates	Votes	%
10	Emanuel Celler (D, L)	106,622	70.5
	Frank L. Martano (R, C)	44,551	29.5
11	Frank J. Brasco (D)	40,460	69.7
	Robert J. Hower (R)	10,708	18.4
	Basil E. Reynolds (C)	3,807	6.6
	Edward L. Johnson (L)	3,101	5.3
12	Shirley Chisholm (D)	34,885	66.5
	James Farmer (R, L)	13,777	26.3
	Ralph J. Carrano (C)	3,771	7.2
13	Bertram L. Podell (D)	107,960	68.2
	Jack Sterngass (R)	25,499	16.1
	Kenneth Haber (L)	15,392	9.7
	Robert C. Laborde (C)	9,504	6.0
14	John J. Rooney (D, L)	42,149	63.9
	Victor J. Tirabasso (R)	18,396	27.9
	Alice A. Capatosto (C)	5,422	8.2
15	Hugh L. Carey (D)	59,707	57.6
	Frank C. Spinner (R)	31,802	30.7
	Stephen P. Marion (C)	7,920	7.6
16	John M. Murphy (D)	73,253	48.8
	Frank J. Biondolillo (R, C)	69,126	46.0
	Joseph Kottler (L)	7,883	5.3
17	Edward I. Koch (D, L)	84,627	51.7
	Whitney North Seymour Jr. (R)	70,086	42.8
	Richard J. Callahan (C)	9,030	5.5
18	Adam Clayton Powell Jr. (D)	37,146	80.8
	Henry L. Hall (R)	7,215	15.7
19	Leonard Farbstein (D)	44,843	53.3
	Donald E. Weeden (R)	27,959	33.2
20	William F. Ryan (D, L)	66,192	78.8
	John G. Proudfit (R)	13,968	16.6
21	James H. Sheuer (D, L)	55,129	82.6
	Stanley L. Shapiro (R)	8,778	13.2
22	Jacob H. Gilbert (D)	45,144	76.2
	James N. Harris (R)	7,087	12.0
	Sergio S. Pena (L)	4,402	7.4
23	Jonathan B. Bingham (D, L)	94,108	71.9
	Alexander Sacks (R, C)	36,823	28.1
24	Mario Biaggi (D, C)	83,234	60.5
	Andrew Mantovani (R)	46,510	33.8
	John Patrick Hagan (L)	7,758	5.6
25	Richard L. Ottinger (D, L)	125,415	58.6
	Samuel Nakasian (R)	74,275	34.7
	Anthony J. DeVito (C)	14,463	6.8
26	Ogden R. Reid (R, L)	130,229	68.1
	Paul Davidoff (D)	44,084	23.1
	A. Lining Burnet (C)	16,877	8.8
27	Martin B. McKneally (R)	94,689	47.9
	John G. Dow (D, L)	88,894	44.9
	Frederick P. Roland (C)	14,239	7.2
28	Hamilton Fish Jr. (R)	91,590	48.2
	John S. Dyson (D)	86,827	45.6
29	Daniel E. Button (R, CIT)	119,039	56.9
	Jacob H. Herzog (D, C)	87,896	42.0
30	Carleton J. King (R, C)	124,995	66.5
	Orlando B. Potter (D, L)	62,897	33.5
31	Robert C. McEwen (R, C)	88,562	58.4
	K. Daniel Haley (D)	61,947	40.9
32	Alexander Pirnie (R, L)	95,793	64.1
	Anthony J. Montoya (D)	43,254	28.9
	Albert J. Bushong (C)	10,393	7.0
33	Howard W. Robison (R)	110,080	68.5
	Benjamin Nichols (D, L)	50,549	31.5
34	James M. Hanley (D)	96,520	51.3
	David V. O'Brien (R)	82,333	43.8
35	Samuel S. Stratton (D)	112,640	69.4
	George R. Metcalf (R)	47,849	29.5
36	Frank J. Horton (R)	138,400	70.4
	Augustine J. Marvin (D)	46,008	23.4
	Leo J. Kesselring (C)	9,916	5.0
37	Barber B. Conable Jr (R)	129,697	71.1
	Norman M. Gerhard (D)	50,930	27.9
38	James F. Hastings (R)	90,281	63.4
	Wilbur White Jr (D)	47,093	33.1
39	Richard D. McCarthy (D)	120,509	54.6
	Daniel E. Weber (R, L)	92,589	42.0

Footnote, see p. 251.

NEW YORK

Candidates	Votes	%
40 Henry P. Smith III (R, C)	106,984	64.8
Eugene O'Connor (D)	56,201	34.0
41 Thaddeus J. Dulski (D, L)	96,703	77.6
Edward P. Matter (R)	27,920	22.4

Special Election

13 Bertram L. Podell (D)	36,093#	49.7
Melvin Dubin (NEW LEAD)	27,856#	38.4
Gerald S. Held (R)	4,848#	6.7
Michael V. Ajello (C)	3,806#	5.2

NORTH CAROLINA

1 Walter B. Jones (D)	75,796	66.2
Reece B. Gardner (R)	38,660	33.8
2 L. H. Fountain (D)	92,542	100.0
3 David N. Henderson (D)	57,244	54.0
Herbert H. Howell (R)	48,815	46.0
4 Nick Galifianakis (D)	77,871	51.5
G. Fred Steele Jr. (R)	73,471	48.6
5 Wilmer Mizell (R)	84,905	52.4
Smith Bagley (D)	77,112	47.6
6 Richardson Preyer (D)	76,028	53.6
William L. Osteen (R)	65,703	46.4
7 Alton A. Lennon (D)	77,419	100.0
8 Earl B. Ruth (R)	70,480	51.2
Voit Gilmore (D)	67,281	48.8
9 Charles Raper Jonas (R)	94,510	100.0
10 James T. Broyhill (R)	87,811	54.9
Basil L. Whitener (D)	72,295	45.2
11 Roy A. Taylor (D)	91,477	56.3
W. Scott Harvey (R)	71,041	43.7

NORTH DAKOTA

1 Mark Andrews (R)	84,114	66.8
Bruce Hagen (D)	39,692	31.5
2 Thomas S. Kleppe (R)	55,962	49.9
Rolland Redlin (D)	54,655	48.7

OHIO

1 Robert Taft Jr. (R)	102,219	67.2
Karl F. Heiser (D)	49,830	32.8
2 Donald D. Clancy (R)	108,157	67.4
Don Driehaus (D)	52,327	32.6
3 Charles W. Whalen Jr. (R)	114,549	78.2
Paul Tipps (D)	32,012	21.8
4 William M. McCulloch (R)	129,435	99.9
5 Delbert L. Latta (R)	113,381	71.2
Louis Richard Batzler (D)	45,884	28.8
6 William H. Harsha (R)	107,289	72.4
Kenneth L. Kirby (D)	40,964	27.6
7 Clarence J. Brown Jr. (R)	97,581	63.8
Robert E. Cecile (R)	55,386	36.2
8 Jackson E. Betts (R)	101,974	71.4
Marie Baker (D)	40,898	28.6
9 Thomas L. Ashley (D)	85,280	57.4
Ben Marsh (R)	63,290	42.6
10 Clarence E. Miller (R)	102,890	69.3
Harry B. Crewson (D)	45,686	30.8
11 J. William Stanton (R)	116,323	75.4
Alan D. Wright (D)	38,063	24.7
12 Samuel L. Devine (R)	106,664	67.6
Herbert J. Pfeifer (D)	51,202	32.4
13 Charles A. Mosher (R)	97,158	61.9
Adrian F. Betleski (D)	59,864	38.1
14 William H. Ayres (R)	84,561	55.1
Oliver Ocasek (D)	68,889	44.9
15 Chalmers P. Wylie (R)	98,499	73.1
Russell H. Volkema (D)	35,861	26.6
16 Frank T. Bow (R)	101,495	59.6
Virgil L. Musser (D)	68,916	40.4
17 John M. Ashbrook (R)	100,148	64.9
Robert W. Levering (D)	54,127	35.1
18 Wayne L. Hays (D)	96,711	60.3
James F. Sutherland (R)	63,747	39.7

Candidates	Votes	%
19 Michael J. Kirwan (D)	101,813	69.7
Donald J. Lewis (R)	44,363	30.4
20 Michael A. Feighan (D)	72,918	72.4
J. William Petro (R)	27,827	27.6
21 Louis Stokes (D)	85,509	74.7
Charles P. Lucas (R)	28,931	25.3
22 Charles A. Vanik (D)	102,656	54.7
Frances P. Bolton (R)	84,975	45.3
23 William E. Minshall (R)	106,852	52.0
James V. Stanton (D)	98,825	48.1
24 Donald E. Lukens (R)	105,350	70.4
Lloyd D. Miller (D)	44,400	29.7

OKLAHOMA

1 Page Belcher (R)	92,513	59.3
John B. Jarboe (D)	63,451	40.7
2 Ed Edmondson (D)	77,192	54.9
Robert G. Smith (R)	63,437	45.1
3 Carl Albert (D)	85,981	68.4
Gerald L. Beasley Jr. (R)	39,740	31.6
4 Tom Steed (D)	67,352	53.6
James V. Smith (R)	58,253	46.4
5 John Jarman (D)	86,420	73.6
Bob Leeper (D)	30,931	26.4
6 John N. Happy Camp (R)	79,992	55.3
John W. Goodwin (D)	64,599	44.7

OREGON

1 Wendell Wyatt (R)	189,023	80.6
Thomas M. Baggs (D)	45,479	19.4
2 Al Ullman (D)	114,232	63.9
Marv Root (R)	64,478	36.1
3 Edith Green (D)	137,746	69.8
Douglas S. Warren (R)	59,447	30.1
4 John Dellenback (R)	104,159	58.9
Edward N. Fadely (D)	72,579	41.1

PENNSYLVANIA

1 William A. Barrett (D)	113,696	74.7
Leslie J. Carson Jr. (R)	38,432	25.3
2 Robert N. C. Nix (D)	102,869	70.0
Herbert R. McMaster (R)	44,041	30.0
3 James A. Byrne (D)	75,728	61.3
Richard R. Block (R)	47,813	38.7
4 Joshua Eilberg (D)	131,810	59.3
Alexander Kaptik Jr. (R)	88,229	39.7
5 William J. Green III (D)	108,243	69.1
Gregory J. Meade (R)	48,455	30.9
6 Gus Yatron (D)	94,247	51.4
Peter Yonavick (R)	87,090	47.5
7 Lawrence G. Williams (R)	105,699	56.5
Edward J. O'Halloran (D)	79,782	42.7
8 Edward G. Biester Jr. (R)	94,254	58.0
Richard M. Hepburn (D)	60,324	37.1
9 G. Robert Watkins (R)	100,399	62.9
Philip L. Harding (D)	56,532	35.4
10 Joseph M. McDade (R)	125,916	66.6
Robert J. Landy (D)	61,960	32.8
11 Daniel J. Flood (D)	128,794	70.0
Stanley Bunn (R)	52,475	28.5
12 J. Irving Whalley (R)	119,522	67.5
H. Richard Hostetler (D)	55,838	31.5
13 R. Lawrence Coughlin (R)	141,764	62.0
Robert D. Gates (D)	84,137	36.8
14 William S. Moorhead (D)	96,117	69.4
Algia Gary (R)	39,671	28.7
15 Fred B. Rooney (D)	106,877	58.8
Paul E. Henderson (R)	70,333	38.7
16 Edwin D. Eshleman (R)	98,877	68.9
Robert M. Going (D)	39,507	27.5
17 Herman T. Schneebeli (R, YOUNGMAN)	119,003	66.2
Donald J. Rippon (D)	57,093	31.7
18 Robert J. Corbett (R)	121,664	62.7
William T. Sherman (D)	68,434	35.3

Candidates	Votes	%
19 George A. Goodling (R)	93,352	57.7
Robert L. Myers (D)	65,903	40.8
20 Joseph M. Gaydos (D)	109,236	70.2
Joseph Sabol Jr. (R)	44,037	28.3
21 John H. Dent (D)	93,033	62.8
Thomas H. Young (R, CONST)	55,099	37.2
22 John P. Saylor (R)	98,576	58.0
John P. Murtha (D)	71,297	42.0
23 Albert W. Johnson (R)	87,968	61.5
Alan R. Cleeton (D)	54,453	38.0
24 Joseph P. Vigorito (D)	106,869	61.1
John V. Edwards (R)	66,429	38.0
25 Frank M. Clark (D)	105,048	63.1
Richard L. Doolittle (R)	59,576	35.8
26 Thomas E. Morgan (D)	95,898	63.6
Paul P. Riggle (R)	50,594	33.6
27 James G. Fulton (R)	130,784	66.7
Joseph L. Cosetti (D)	62,638	31.9

RHODE ISLAND

1 Fernand J. St.Germain (D)	97,945	60.4
Lincoln C. Almond (R)	62,394	38.5
2 Robert O. Tiernan (D)	124,044	61.2
Howard E. Russell Jr. (R)	78,502	38.8

SOUTH CAROLINA

1 L. Mendel Rivers (D)	95,428	100.0
2 Albert W. Watson (R)	63,877	57.6
Frank K. Sloan (D)	47,053	42.4
3 William J. Bryan Dorn (D)	74,104	66.1
John K. Grisso (R)	35,463	31.7
4 James R. Mann (D)	68,437	61.2
Charles Bradshaw (R)	43,440	38.8
5 Thomas S. Gettys (D)	72,805	74.7
Hugh J. Boyd (R)	21,246	21.8
6 John L. McMillan (D)	58,304	58.3
Ray Harris (R)	39,876	39.9

SOUTH DAKOTA

1 Ben Reifel (R)	85,232	58.0
Frank E. Denholm (D)	61,738	42.0
2 E. Y. Berry (R)	73,987	59.4
David Garner (D)	50,683	40.7

TENNESSEE

1 James H. Quillen (R)	100,712	85.2
Arthur Bright (D)	17,441	14.8
2 John J. Duncan (R)	97,832	82.4
Jake Armstrong (D)	17,547	14.8
3 Bill Brock (R)	76,390	57.0
J. William Pope Jr. (D)	57,565	43.0
4 Joe L. Evins (D)	74,041	75.9
J. D. Boles (R)	23,553	24.1
5 Richard Fulton (D)	61,045	48.7
George Kelley (R)	52,836	42.2
William F. Burton Jr. (I)	11,412	9.1
6 William Anderson (D)	61,223	59.4
Ronnie Page (R)	41,923	40.6
7 Ray Blanton (D)	80,893	66.1
John T. Williams (R)	41,457	33.9
8 Robert A. Everett (D)	70,644	100.0
9 Dan Kuykendall (R)	73,293	59.4
James E. Irwin (D)	45,434	36.8

TEXAS

1 Wright Patman (D)	87,038	100.0
2 John Dowdy (D)	87,565	100.0
3 James M. Collins (R)	81,696	59.4
Robert H. Hughes (D)	55,939	46.0
4 Ray Roberts (D)	95,413	100.0
5 Earle Cabell (D)	79,317	61.4
Roy Wagoner (R)	49,821	38.6

TEXAS

Candidates	Votes	%
6 Olin E. Teague (D)	90,889	100.0
7 George Bush (R)	110,455	100.0
8 Bob Eckhardt (D)	63,256	70.6
Joe Stevens (R)	26,402	29.5
9 Jack Brooks (D)	71,937	60.6
Henry Pressler (R)	46,829	39.4
10 J. J. (Jake) Pickle (D)	85,037	62.1
Ray Gabler (R)	51,933	37.9
11 W. R. Poage (D)	78,127	96.5
12 Jim Wright (D)	86,069	100.0
13 Graham Purcell (D)	83,839	55.8
Frank Crowley (R)	66,477	44.2
14 John Young (D)	89,868	100.0
15 Eligio de la Garza (D)	57,618	100.0
16 Richard C. White (D)	62,491	73.5
Donald Slaughter (R)	22,510	26.5
17 Omar Burleson (D)	90,856	100.0
18 Bob Price (R)	81,715	65.2
J. R. Brown (D)	43,568	34.8
19 George Mahon (D)	79,161	100.0
20 Henry B. Gonzalez (D)	64,112	81.5
Robert Schneider (R)	14,569	18.5
21 O. C. Fisher (D)	91,784	60.8
W. J. Alexander (R)	59,082	39.2
22 Bob Casey (D)	101,498	62.4
Walter Blaney (R)	61,278	37.7
23 Abraham Kazen Jr. (D)	75,026	100.0

Special Election

	Votes	%
3 James M. Collins (R)	13,828#	60.0
Mrs. Joe Pool (D)	9,209#	40.0

UTAH

	Votes	%
1 Laurence J. Burton (R)	139,456	68.1
Richard J. Maughan (D)	65,265	31.9
2 Sherman P. Lloyd (R)	130,127	61.7
Galen J. Ross (D)	80,948	38.4

VERMONT

	Votes	%
AL Robert T. Stafford (R, D)	156,956	99.9

VIRGINIA

Candidates	Votes	%
1 Thomas N. Downing (D)	96,265	72.9
J. Cornelius Fauntleroy Jr. (I)	19,229	14.6
James S. Stafford (R)	16,456	12.5
2 G. William Whitehurst (R)	51,184	54.2
Frederick T. Stant Jr. (D)	43,229	45.8
3 David E. Satterfield III (D)	94,118	60.3
John S. Hansen (R)	62,082	39.7
4 Watkins M. Abbitt (D)	81,723	71.5
S. W. Tucker (R)	32,548	28.5
5 W. C. (Dan) Daniel (D)	70,681	54.6
Weldon W. Tuck (R)	34,608	26.7
Ruth L. Harvey (I)	24,196	18.7
6 Richard H. Poff (R)	91,549	92.2
Tom Hufford (D)	7,221	7.3
7 John O. Marsh Jr. (D)	64,717	54.4
A. R. (Pete) Giesen Jr. (R)	51,349	43.2
8 William L. Scott (R)	92,121	64.9
Andrew H. McCutcheon (D)	49,731	35.1
9 William C. Wampler (R)	71,531	59.9
Joseph P. Johnson Jr. (D)	47,906	40.1
10 Joel T. Broyhill (R)	97,465	59.8
David Kinney (D)	65,474	40.2

WASHINGTON

	Votes	%
1 Thomas M. Pelly (R)	124,513	61.4
Don Cole (D)	76,456	37.7
2 Lloyd Meeds (D)	102,522	56.2
Wally Turner (R)	79,800	43.8
3 Julia Butler Hansen (D)	89,777	56.8
Wayne N. Adams (R)	68,387	43.2
4 Catherine May (R)	99,840	66.8
Lee Lukson (D)	49,601	33.2
5 Thomas S. Foley (D)	88,446	56.8
Richard M. Bond (R)	67,304	43.2
6 Floyd V. Hicks (D)	93,399	55.8
Anthony Chase (R)	72,177	43.1
7 Brock Adams (D)	123,429	65.6
Robert Eberle (R)	64,051	34.0

WEST VIRGINIA

Candidates	Votes	%
1 Robert H. Mollohan (D)	85,436	53.9
Tom Sweeney (R)	73,176	46.1
2 Harley O. Staggers (D)	91,022	61.5
George L. Strader (R)	56,911	38.5
3 John Slack (D)	82,911	60.5
Neal A. Kinsolving (R)	54,164	39.5
4 Ken Hechler (D)	94,507	64.2
Ralph Lewis Shannon (R)	52,636	35.8
5 James Kee (D)	80,204	66.2
J. Donald Clark (R)	41,038	33.9

WISCONSIN

	Votes	%
1 Henry C. Schadeberg (R)	89,182	50.9
Lynn E. Stalbaum (D)	86,067	49.1
2 Robert W. Kastenmeier (D)	107,804	59.9
Richard D. Murray (R)	72,229	40.1
3 Vernon W. Thomson (R)	95,606	63.7
Gunnar A. Gundersen (D)	54,517	36.3
4 Clement J. Zablocki (D)	118,203	72.6
Walter McCullough (R)	44,558	27.4
5 Henry S. Reuss (D)	76,607	67.8
Robert J. Dwyer (R)	35,536	31.4
6 William A. Steiger (R)	111,934	64.0
John A. Race (D)	60,059	34.3
7 Melvin R. Laird (R)	101,808	64.1
Lawrence Dahl (D)	56,964	35.9
8 John W. Byrnes (R)	111,859	68.0
John E. Nixon (D)	52,660	32.0
9 Glenn R. Davis (R)	126,392	63.1
Carol E. Baumann (D)	73,891	36.9
10 Alvin E. O'Konski (R)	106,266	65.9
Timothy J. Hirsch (D)	54,889	34.1

WYOMING

	Votes	%
AL John Wold (R)	77,363	62.7
Velma Linford (D)	45,950	37.3

1969 House Elections

CALIFORNIA[1]

Special Primary

	Votes	%
27 Barry Goldwater Jr. (R)	39,580#	31.3
John K. Van de Kamp (D)	17,356#	13.7
James B. Potter Jr. (R)	16,908#	13.4
Jack B. Lindsey (R)	13,818#	10.9
Gary Schlessinger (D)	12,278#	9.7
Patrick D. McGee (R)	8,532#	6.7

Special Election

	Votes	%
27 Barry M. Goldwater Jr. (R)	64,734	56.9
John K. Van de Kamp (D)	48,983	43.1

ILLINOIS

Special Election

	Votes	%
13 Philip M. Crane (R)	68,418	58.4
Edward A. Warman (D)	48,759	41.6

MASSACHUSETTS

Special Election

	Votes	%
6 Michael J. Harrington (D)	72,092#	52.4
William Saltonstall (R)	65,452#	47.6

MONTANA

Special Election

	Votes	%
2 John Melcher (D)	45,473#	50.8
W. S. Mather (R)	43,441#	48.6

NEW JERSEY

Special Election

	Votes	%
8 Robert A. Roe (D)	67,188	49.2
Eugene Boyle Jr. (R)	66,228	48.5

TENNESSEE

Special Election

	Votes	%
8 Ed Jones (D)	33,028#	47.6
W. J. Davis (AM)	16,375#	23.6
Leonard Dunavant (R)	15,773#	22.7

WISCONSIN

Special Election

	Votes	%
7 David R. Obey (D)	63,567	51.6
Walter J. Chilsen (R)	59,512	48.4

1968 Elections

1. The election returns shown from Mississippi's 3rd District were from a special runoff between Griffin and Evers, who had finished with the highest number of votes in an earlier special election. Both elections were held under a provision of Mississippi law requiring that all candidates in a special election for the House run against each other, regardless of party affiliations, with a majority required for election. Since neither Evers nor Griffin had a majority, the runoff was required.

The returns from the first special election were as follows: *Charles Evers (D), 33,706, 29.3%; Charles H. Griffin (D), 28,927, 25.2; Ellis Bodron (D), 22,842, 19.9; Troy Watkins (D), 10,476, 9.1; Joe Pigott (D), 8,314, 7.2; Hagan Thompson (R), 7,978, 6.9. Source: Mississippi Secretary of State.*

1969 Elections

1. No candidate received a majority of the vote, which was required to win in the first special election. Under California's special election law, the highest vote recipients from the first election from each party then faced each other in another election. In this case, Goldwater became the Republican nominee against Van de Kamp, the Democratic nominee.

1970 House Elections

ALABAMA

	Candidates	Votes	%
1	Jack Edwards (R)	63,457	60.6
	John Tyson (D)	27,457	26.2
	Noble Beasley (NDPA)	13,798	13.2
2	William L. Dickinson (R)	62,316	61.4
	Jack Winfield (D)	25,966	25.6
	Percy Smith Jr. (NDPA)	13,281	13.1
3	George Andrews (D)	70,015	89.1
	Detroit Lee (NDPA)	8,537	10.9
4	Bill Nichols (D)	77,701	83.7
	Glenn Andrews (R)	13,217	14.2
5	Walter Flowers (D)	78,368	75.9
	T. Y. Rogers (NDPA)	24,863	24.1
6	John Buchanan (R)	50,060	60.1
	John C. Schmarkey (D)	31,378	37.7
7	Tom Bevill (D)	87,797	100.0
8	Robert E. Jones (D)	76,413	84.9
	Ken Hearn (C)	7,599	8.4
	Thornton Stanley (NDPA)	4,846	5.4

ALASKA

		Votes	%
AL	Nick Begich (D)	44,137	55.1
	Frank H. Murkowski (R)	35,947	44.9

ARIZONA

		Votes	%
1	John J. Rhodes (R)	99,706	68.5
	Gerald A. Pollock (D)	45,870	31.5
2	Morris K. Udall (D)	86,760	69.0
	Morris Herring (R)	37,561	29.9
3	Sam Steiger (R)	81,239	62.1
	Orren Beaty (D)	49,626	37.9

ARKANSAS

		Votes	%
1	Bill Alexander (D)		100.0
2	Wilbur D. Mills (D)		100.0
3	John Paul Hammerschmidt (R)	115,532	66.7
	Donald Poe (D)	57,679	33.3
4	David Pryor (D)		100.0

CALIFORNIA

		Votes	%
1	Don H. Clausen (R)	108,358	63.4
	William M. Kortum (D)	62,688	36.7
2	Harold T. Johnson (D)	151,070	77.9
	Lloyd E. Gilbert (R)	37,223	19.2
3	John E. Moss (D)	117,496	61.6
	Elmore H. Duffy (R)	69,811	36.6
4	Robert L. Leggett (D)	103,485	68.0
	Andrew Gyorke (R)	48,783	32.0
5	Phillip Burton (D)	76,567	70.8
	John E. Parks (R)	31,570	29.2
6	William S. Mailliard (R)	96,393	53.4
	Russell R. Miller (D)	84,255	46.6
7	Ronald V. Dellums (D)	89,784	57.3
	John E. Healy (R)	64,691	41.3
8	George P. Miller (D)	104,311	69.0
	Michael A. Crane (R)	46,872	31.0
9	Don Edwards (D)	120,041	69.2
	Mark Guerra (R)	49,556	28.6
10	Charles S. Gubser (R)	135,864	62.0
	Stuart D. McLean (D)	80,530	36.8
11	Paul N. McCloskey Jr. (R)	144,500	77.5
	Robert E. Gomperts (D)	39,188	21.0
12	Burt L. Talcott (R)	95,549	63.6
	O'Brien Riordan (D)	50,942	33.9
13	Charles M. Teague (R)	127,507	59.1
	Gary K. Hart (D)	87,980	40.8
14	Jerome R. Waldie (D)	148,655	74.6
	Byron D. Athan (R)	50,750	25.5

	Candidates	Votes	%
15	John J. McFall (D)	98,442	63.1
	Sam Van Dyken (R)	55,546	35.6
16	B. F. Sisk (D)	95,118	66.4
	Phillip V. Sanchez (R)	43,843	30.6
17	Glenn M. Anderson (D)	83,739	62.2
	Michael C. Donaldson (R)	47,778	35.5
18	Robert B. Mathias (R)	86,071	63.2
	Milton S. Miller (D)	48,415	35.6
19	Chet Holifield (D)	98,578	70.4
	Bill Jones (R)	41,462	29.6
20	H. Allen Smith (R)	116,437	69.1
	Michael M. Stolzberg (D)	50,033	29.7
21	Augustus F. Hawkins (D)	75,127	94.5
	Southey M. Johnson (R)	4,349	5.5
22	James C. Corman (D)	95,256	59.4
	Tom Hayden (R)	63,297	39.5
23	Del Clawson (R)	77,346	63.3
	G. L. Chapman (D)	44,767	36.7
24	John H. Rousselot (R)	124,071	65.1
	Myrlie B. Evers (D)	61,777	32.4
25	Charles E. Wiggins (R)	116,169	63.3
	Leslie W. Craven (D)	64,386	35.1
26	Thomas M. Rees (D)	130,499	71.3
	Nathaniel Jay Friedman (R)	47,260	25.8
27	Barry M. Goldwater Jr. (R)	139,326	66.7
	N. (Toni) Kimmel (D)	63,652	30.5
28	Alphonzo Bell (R)	154,691	69.3
	Don McLaughlin (D)	57,882	25.9
29	George E. Danielson (D)	71,308	62.6
	Tom McMann (R)	42,620	37.4
30	Edward R. Roybal (D)	63,903	68.3
	Samuel M. Cavnar (R)	28,038	30.0
31	Charles H. Wilson (D)	102,071	73.2
	Fred L. Casmir (R)	37,416	26.8
32	Craig Hosmer (R)	119,340	71.5
	Walter L. Mallonee (D)	44,278	26.5
33	Jerry L. Pettis (R)	116,093	72.2
	Chester M. Wright (D)	44,764	27.8
34	Richard T. Hanna (D)	101,664	54.5
	William J. Teague (R)	82,167	44.0
35	John G. Schmitz (R)	192,765	67.0
	Thomas B. Lenhart (D)	87,019	30.3
36	Bob Wilson (R)	132,446	71.5
	Daniel K. Hostetter (D)	44,841	24.2
37	Lionel Van Deerlin (D)	93,952	72.1
	James B. Kuhn (R)	31,968	24.5
38	Victor V. Veysey (R)	87,479	49.8
	David A. Tunno (D)	85,684	48.8

Special Elections[1]

		Votes	%
24	John H. Rousselot (R)	62,749	68.2
	Myrlie B. Evers (D)	29,248	31.8
35	John G. Schmitz (R)	67,209	72.4
	David N. Hartman (D)	25,655	27.6

COLORADO

		Votes	%
1	James D. McKevitt (R)	84,843	51.6
	Craig S. Barnes (D)	74,444	45.3
2	Donald G. Brotzman (R)	125,274	63.4
	Richard G. Gebhardt (D)	72,339	36.6
3	Frank E. Evans (D)	87,090	63.7
	John C. Mitchell Jr. (R)	45,610	33.4
4	Wayne N. Aspinall (D)	76,244	55.1
	Bill Gossard (R)	62,169	44.9

CONNECTICUT

		Votes	%
1	William R. Cotter (D)	88,374	48.7
	Antonina P. Uccello (R)	87,209	48.1
2	Robert H. Steele (R)	92,846	53.3
	John F. Pickett (D)	81,492	46.7

	Candidates	Votes	%
3	Robert Giaimo (D)	89,042	52.9
	Robert J. Dunn (R)	69,084	41.1
4	Stewart B. McKinney (R)	104,494	56.6
	T. F. Gilroy Daly (D)	78,699	42.6
5	John S. Monagan (D)	96,947	54.8
	James T. Patterson (R)	78,414	44.3
6	Ella T. Grasso (D)	96,969	51.1
	Richard C. Kilbourne (R)	92,906	48.9

Special Election

		Votes	%
2	Robert H. Steele (R)	92,816	53.3
	John F. Pickett (D)	81,333	46.7

DELAWARE

		Votes	%
AL	Pierre S. duPont IV (R)	86,125	53.7
	John Daniello (D)	71,429	44.6

FLORIDA

		Votes	%
1	Robert L. F. Sikes (D)	88,744	80.2
	H. D. Shuemake (R)	21,951	19.8
2	Don Fuqua (D)		100.0
3	Charles E. Bennett (D)		100.0
4	Bill Chappell (D)	75,673	57.8
	Leonard V. Wood (R)	55,311	42.2
5	Louis Frey Jr. (R)	110,841	75.8
	Roy Girod (D)	35,398	24.2
6	Sam M. Gibbons (D)	78,832	72.3
	Robert A. Carter (R)	30,252	27.7
7	James A. Haley (D)	78,535	53.4
	Joe Z. Lovingood (R)	68,646	46.6
8	C. W. Bill Young (R)	120,466	67.2
	Ted A. Bailey (D)	58,904	32.8
9	Paul G. Rogers (D)	120,565	70.6
	Emil F. Danciu (R)	50,146	29.4
10	J. Herbert Burke (R)	81,170	54.1
	James J. Ward Jr. (D)	68,847	45.9
11	Claude Pepper (D)		100.0
12	Dante B. Fascell (D)	75,895	71.7
	Robert A. Zinzell (R)	29,935	28.3

GEORGIA

		Votes	%
1	G. Elliot Hagan (D)	70,856	100.0
2	Dawson Mathis (D)	59,994	91.8
	Thomas Ragsdale (R)	5,376	8.2
3	Jack Brinkley (D)	54,588	99.5
4	Ben B. Blackburn (R)	85,884	65.2
	Franklin Shumake (D)	45,908	34.8
5	Fletcher Thompson (R)	78,540	57.4
	Andrew Young (D)	58,394	42.6
6	John J. Flynt Jr. (D)	92,500	100.0
7	John W. Davis (D)	80,149	72.5
	Dick Fullerton (R)	30,392	27.5
8	W. S. Stuckey Jr. (D)	52,446	100.0
9	Phil M. Landrum (D)	64,603	71.7
	Bob Cooper (R)	25,476	28.3
10	Robert G. Stephens Jr. (D)	74,075	100.0

HAWAII

		Votes	%
1	Spark M. Matsunaga (D)	85,411	72.9
	Richard K. Cockey (R)	31,764	27.1
2	Patsy T. Mink (D)	91,038	100.0

IDAHO

		Votes	%
1	James A. McClure (R)	77,515	58.2
	William J. Brauner (D)	55,743	41.8
2	Orval Hansen (R)	66,428	65.7
	Marden E. Wells (D)	31,872	31.5

Footnote, see p. 256.

ILLINOIS

Candidates	Votes	%
1 Ralph H. Metcalfe (D)	93,272	91.0
Janet Roberts Jennings (R)	9,267	9.0
2 Abner J. Mikva (D)	88,252	74.7
Harold E. Marks (R)	29,853	25.3
3 Morgan F. Murphy (D)	97,693	68.9
Robert P. Rowan (R)	44,013	31.1
4 Edward J. Derwinski (R)	117,590	68.0
Melvin W. Morgan (D)	55,328	32.0
5 John C. Kluczynski (D)	97,278	68.8
Edmund P. Ochenkowski (R)	44,049	31.2
6 George W. Collins (D)	68,182	56.2
Alex J. Zabrosky (R)	53,240	43.9
7 Frank Annunzio (D)	70,112	87.3
Thomas J. Lento (R)	10,235	12.7
8 Dan Rostenkowski (D)	98,453	73.9
Henry S. Kaplinski (R)	34,841	26.1
9 Sidney R. Yates (D)	111,955	75.8
Edward Wolbank (R)	35,795	24.2
10 Harold R. Collier (R)	107,416	62.2
R. G. Logan (D)	65,170	37.8
11 Roman C. Pucinski (D)	137,090	71.9
James R. Mason (R)	53,461	28.1
12 Robert McClory (R)	84,356	62.1
James J. Cone (D)	51,499	37.9
13 Philip M. Crane (R)	124,649	58.0
Edward A. Warman (D)	90,364	42.0
14 John N. Erlenborn (R)	122,115	65.5
William J. Adelman (D)	64,231	34.5
15 Charlotte T. Reid (R)	95,222	68.9
James E. Todd (D)	43,014	31.1
16 John B. Anderson (R)	83,296	66.8
John E. Devine Jr. (D)	41,459	33.2
17 Leslie C. Arends (R)	92,917	62.3
Lester A. Hawthorne (D)	56,340	37.8
18 Robert H. Michel (R)	84,864	66.1
Rosa Lee Fox (D)	43,601	33.9
19 Tom Railsback (R)	92,247	68.2
James L. Shaw (D)	43,094	31.8
20 Paul Findley (R)	103,485	67.5
Billie M. Cox (D)	49,727	32.5
21 Kenneth J. Gray (D)	110,374	62.5
Fred Evans (R)	66,273	37.5
22 William L. Springer (R)	83,131	59.0
Robert C. Miller (D)	57,781	41.0
23 George E. Shipley (D)	91,158	54.0
Phyllis Schlafly (R)	77,762	46.0
24 Melvin Price (D)	88,637	74.2
Scott R. Randolph (R)	30,784	25.8

Special Election

6 George W. Collins (D)	68,949	55.7
Alex J. Zabrosky (R)	54,746	44.3

INDIANA

1 Ray J. Madden (D)	73,145	65.6
Eugene M. Kirtland (R)	38,294	34.4
2 Earl F. Landgrebe (R)	79,163	50.4
Philip A. Sprague (D)	77,959	49.6
3 John Brademas (D)	87,064	57.5
Don M. Newman (R)	64,249	42.5
4 J. Edward Roush (D)	86,582	51.9
E. Ross Adair (R)	80,326	48.1
5 Elwood H. Hillis (R)	86,199	56.0
Kathleen Z. Williams (D)	67,740	44.0
6 William G. Bray (R)	115,113	60.7
Terrence D. Straub (D)	74,599	39.3
7 John T. Myers (R)	97,152	57.1
William D. Roach (D)	73,042	42.9
8 Roger H. Zion (R)	93,088	52.6
J. David Huber (D)	83,911	47.4
9 Lee H. Hamilton (D)	104,599	62.5
Richard B. Wathen (R)	62,772	37.5
10 David W. Dennis (R)	81,439	50.8
Philip R. Sharp (D)	78,871	49.2
11 Andrew Jacobs Jr. (D)	71,329	58.3
Danny L. Burton (R)	50,990	41.7

IOWA

Candidates	Votes	%
1 Fred Schwengel (R)	60,270	49.8
Edward Mezvinsky (D)	59,505	49.2
2 John C. Culver (D)	84,049	60.5
Cole McMartin (R)	54,932	39.5
3 H. R. Gross (R)	66,087	59.0
Lyle D. Taylor (D)	45,958	41.0
4 John Kyl (R)	59,396	54.6
Roger Blobaum (D)	49,369	45.4
5 Neal Smith (D)	73,820	64.9
Don Mahon (R)	37,374	32.9
6 Wiley Mayne (R)	57,285	57.0
Fred H. Moore (D)	43,257	43.0
7 William J. Scherle (R)	53,084	62.7
Lou Galetich (D)	31,552	37.3

KANSAS

1 Keith G. Sebelius (R)	83,923	56.8
Billy D. Jellison (D)	63,791	43.2
2 William R. Roy (D)	80,161	52.3
Chester L. Mize (R)	68,843	45.0
3 Larry Winn Jr. (R)	74,603	53.0
James H. DeCoursey Jr. (D)	64,344	45.7
4 Garner E. Shriver (R)	85,058	63.2
James C. Junhke (D)	47,004	34.9
5 Joe Skubitz (R)	94,837	66.1
T. D. Saar Jr. (D)	48,688	33.9

KENTUCKY

1 Frank A. Stubblefield (D)	27,829	100.0
2 William H. Natcher (D)	21,024	100.0
3 Romano L. Mazzoli (D)	50,102	48.5
William O. Cowger (R)	49,891	48.3
4 M. G. (Gene) Snyder (R)	83,037	66.6
Charles W. Webster (D)	41,659	33.4
5 Tim Lee Carter (R)	49,266	80.4
Lyle Leonard Willis (D)	11,977	19.6
6 John C. Watts (D)	44,322	64.9
Gerald G. Gregory (R)	23,971	35.1
7 Carl D. Perkins (D)	50,672	75.3
Herbert E. Myers (R)	16,648	24.7

LOUISIANA

1 F. Edward Hebert (D)	66,284	87.4
Luke J. Fontana (I)	9,602	12.7
2 Hale Boggs (D)	51,812	69.3
Robert E. Lee (R)	19,703	26.3
3 Patrick T. Caffery (D)	48,677	100.0
4 Joe D. Waggonner Jr. (D)	44,848	100.0
5 Otto E. Passman (D)	31,087	100.0
6 John R. Rarick (D)	36,632	100.0
7 Edwin W. Edwards (D)	24,517	100.0
8 Speedy O. Long (D)	26,607	100.0

MAINE

1 Peter N. Kyros (D)	99,483	59.2
Ronald T. Speers (R)	68,671	40.8
2 William D. Hathaway (D)	96,235	64.2
Maynard G. Conners (R)	53,642	35.8

MARYLAND

1 Rogers C. B. Morton (R)	79,594	75.6
David S. Aland (D)	24,923	23.7
2 Clarence D. Long (D)	87,224	68.5
Ross Z. Pierpont (R)	40,177	31.5
3 Edward A. Garmatz (D)	52,374	100.0
4 Paul S. Sarbanes (D)	54,936	70.1
David Fentress (R)	23,491	30.0
5 Lawrence J. Hogan (R)	84,314	61.4
Royal Hart (D)	52,979	38.6

Candidates	Votes	%
6 Goodloe E. Byron (D)	59,267	50.8
George R. Hughes Jr. (R)	55,511	47.6
7 Parren J. Mitchell (D)	60,390	58.7
Peter Parker (R)	42,566	41.3
8 Gilbert Gude (R)	104,647	63.4
Thomas Hale Boggs Jr. (D)	60,453	36.6

MASSACHUSETTS

1 Silvio O. Conte (R)	117,045	100.0
2 Edward P. Boland (D)	111,430	100.0
3 Robert F. Drinan (D)	63,942	37.7
John McGlennon (R)	60,575	35.7
Philip J. Philbin (WRITE IN)	45,278	26.7
4 Harold D. Donohue (D)	95,016	54.3
Howard A. Miller Jr. (R)	79,870	45.7
5 F. Bradford Morse (R)	116,666	63.3
Richard Williams (D)	67,646	36.7
6 Michael J. Harrington (D)	114,276	61.7
Howard Phillips (R)	70,955	38.3
7 Torbert H. Macdonald (D)	115,597	72.2
Gordon F. Hughes (R)	44,463	27.8
8 Thomas P. O'Neill Jr. (D)	89,875	100.0
9 Louise Day Hicks (D)	50,269	59.2
Daniel J. Houton (I)	17,395	20.5
Laurence Curtis (R)	17,324	20.4
10 Margaret M. Heckler (R)	102,895	57.0
Bertram A. Yaffe (D)	77,497	43.0
11 James A. Burke (D)	143,026	100.0
12 Hastings Keith (R)	100,432	50.4
Gerry E. Studds (D)	98,910	49.6

MICHIGAN

1 John Conyers Jr. (D)	93,075	88.2
Howard L. Johnson (R)	11,876	11.3
2 Marvin L. Esch (R)	88,071	62.5
R. Michael Stillwagon (D)	52,782	37.5
3 Garry Brown (R)	80,447	56.3
Richard A. Enslen (D)	62,530	43.7
4 Edward Hutchinson (R)	74,471	61.9
David R. McCormack (D)	45,838	38.1
5 Gerald R. Ford Jr (R)	88,208	61.4
Jean McKee (D)	55,337	38.5
6 Charles E. Chamberlain (R)	84,276	60.3
John A. Cihon (D)	55,591	39.8
7 Donald W. Riegle Jr. (R)	97,683	69.2
Richard J. Ruhala (D)	41,235	29.2
8 James Harvey (R)	85,634	65.9
Richard E. Davies (D)	44,400	34.1
9 Guy A. Vander Jagt (R)	94,027	64.4
Charles Arthur Rogers (D)	51,223	35.1
10 Elford A. Cederberg (R)	82,528	59.1
Gerald J. Parent (D)	57,031	40.9
11 Philip E. Ruppe (R)	85,323	61.6
Nino Green (D)	53,146	38.4
12 James G. O'Hara (D)	129,287	76.1
Patrick Driscoll (R)	38,946	22.9
13 Charles C. Diggs Jr. (D)	56,872	86.2
Fred Engel (R)	9,141	13.9
14 Lucien N. Nedzi (D)	91,111	70.1
John L. Owen (R)	38,956	30.0
15 William D. Ford (D)	101,018	80.0
Ernest C. Fackler (R)	25,340	20.1
16 John D. Dingell (D)	90,540	79.1
William E. Rostron (R)	23,867	20.9
17 Martha W. Griffiths (D)	108,176	79.7
Thomas E. Klunzinger (R)	27,608	20.3
18 William S. Broomfield (R)	113,309	64.6
August Scholle (D)	62,081	35.4
19 Jack McDonald (R)	91,763	58.9
Fred L. Harris (D)	63,175	40.5

MINNESOTA

1 Albert H. Quie (R)	121,802	69.3
B. A. Lundeen (DFL)	53,995	30.7
2 Ancher Nelsen (R)	94,080	63.3
Clifford R. Adams (DFL)	54,498	36.7

MINNESOTA

	Candidates	Votes	%
3	Bill Frenzel (R)	110,921	50.6
	George Rice (DFL)	108,141	49.4
4	Joseph E. Karth (DFL)	131,263	74.2
	Frank L. Loss (R)	45,680	25.8
5	Donald M. Fraser (DFL)	83,207	57.1
	Dick Enroth (R)	61,682	42.3
6	John M. Zwach (R)	88,753	51.8
	Terry Montgomery (DFL)	81,004	47.3
7	Bob Bergland (DFL)	79,378	54.1
	Odin Langen (R)	67,296	45.9
8	John A. Blatnik (DFL)	118,149	78.0
	Paul Reed (R)	38,369	25.3

MISSISSIPPI

		Votes	%
1	Thomas G. Abernethy (D)	42,367	100.0
2	Jamie L. Whitten (D)	51,689	86.5
	Eugene Carter (I)	8,092	13.5
3	Charles H. Griffin (D)	50,527	63.7
	Ray Lee (R)	28,847	36.3
4	G. V. (Sonny) Montgomery (D)	66,064	100.0
5	William M. Colmer (D)	58,546	90.4
	Earnest J. Creel (I)	6,225	9.6

MISSOURI

		Votes	%
1	William Clay (D)	58,082	90.5
	Gerald G. Frischer (AM MO)	6,078	9.5
2	James W. Symington (D)	93,294	57.6
	Philip R. Hoffman (R)	66,503	41.1
3	Leonor K. Sullivan (D)	73,021	74.8
	Dale F. Troske (R)	24,651	25.2
4	William J. Randall (D)	80,153	60.1
	Leslie O. Olsen (R)	53,204	39.9
5	Richard Bolling (D)	51,668	61.3
	Randall Vanet (R)	31,806	37.8
6	W. R. Hull Jr. (D)	74,496	53.6
	Hugh A. Sprague (R)	63,789	45.9
7	Durward G. Hall (R)	92,965	100.0
8	Richard Ichord (D)	97,560	64.4
	John L. Caskanett (R)	53,181	35.1
9	William L. Hungate (D)	100,988	63.0
	Anthony C. Schroeder (R)	58,103	36.3
10	Bill D. Burlison (D)	62,764	56.0
	Gary Rust (R)	49,355	44.0

MONTANA

		Votes	%
1	Richard G. Shoup (R)	64,388	50.5
	Arnold Olsen (D)	63,175	49.5
2	John Melcher (D)	78,082	64.1
	Jack Rehberg (R)	43,752	35.9

NEBRASKA

		Votes	%
1	Charles Thone (R)	79,131	50.6
	Clair A. Callan (I)	40,919	26.2
	George Burrows (D)	36,240	23.2
2	John Y. McCollister (R)	69,671	51.8
	John Hlavacek (D)	64,520	48.0
3	Dave Martin (R)	93,705	59.5
	Donald Searcy (D)	63,698	40.5

NEVADA

		Votes	%
AL	Walter S. Baring (D)	113,496	82.5
	J. Robert Charles (R)	24,147	17.5

NEW HAMPSHIRE

		Votes	%
1	Louis C. Wyman (R)	72,170	67.4
	Chester E. Merrow (R)	34,882	32.6
2	James C. Cleveland (R)	74,219	69.6
	Eugene S. Daniell Jr. (D)	32,374	30.4

NEW JERSEY

	Candidates	Votes	%
1	John E. Hunt (R)	83,726	61.2
	Salvatore T. Mansi (D)	52,567	38.4
2	Charles W. Sandman Jr. (R)	69,392	51.7
	William J. Hughes (D)	64,882	48.3
3	James J. Howard (D)	87,973	55.2
	William F. Dowd (R)	68,675	43.1
4	Frank Thompson Jr. (D)	91,670	58.4
	Edward A. Costigan (R)	65,030	41.4
5	Peter H. B. Frelinghuysen (R)	111,553	66.4
	Ronald C. Eisele (D)	53,436	31.8
6	Edwin B. Forsythe (R)	88,051	53.6
	Charles B. Yates (D)	72,347	44.1
7	William B. Widnall (R)	90,410	58.6
	Arthur J. Lesemann (D)	63,928	41.4
8	Robert A. Roe (D)	75,056	61.0
	Alfred E. Fontanella (R)	48,011	39.0
9	Henry Helstoski (D)	91,589	56.6
	Henry L. Hoebel (R)	68,974	42.6
10	Peter W. Rodino Jr. (D)	71,003	70.0
	Griffith H. Jones (R)	30,460	30.0
11	Joseph G. Minish (D)	68,075	68.5
	James W. Shue (R)	31,369	31.5
12	Florence P. Dwyer (R)	109,537	66.2
	Daniel F. Lundy (D)	55,930	33.8
13	Cornelius E. Gallagher (D)	77,789	71.1
	Raul E. L. Comesanas (R)	27,929	25.5
14	Dominick V. Daniels (D)	77,771	69.7
	Carlo N. DeGennaro (R)	31,161	27.9
15	Edward J. Patten (D)	94,772	61.1
	Peter P. Garibaldi (R)	60,450	38.9

Special Election

		Votes	%
6	Edwin B. Forsythe (R)	89,565	54.8
	Charles B. Yates (D)	73,821	45.2

NEW MEXICO

		Votes	%
1	Manuel Lujan Jr. (R)	91,187	57.6
	Fabian Chavez Jr. (D)	64,598	40.8
2	Harold Runnels (D)	64,518	50.8
	Ed Foreman (R)	61,074	48.1

NEW YORK

		Votes	%
1	Otis G. Pike (D, L)	108,746	52.2
	Malcolm E. Smith Jr. (R, C)	99,503	47.8
2	James R. Grover Jr. (R, C)	107,443	66.1
	Harvey W. Sherman (D, L)	54,996	33.9
3	Lester L. Wolff (D, L)	94,414	54.4
	Raymond J. Rice (R, ENVIRON)	66,196	38.1
	Lola Camardi (C)	12,925	7.5
4	John W. Wydler (R)	91,787	57.1
	Karen S. Burstein (D, L)	56,411	35.1
	Donald A. Derham (C)	12,701	7.9
5	Norman F. Lent (R, C)	93,824	51.0
	Allard K. Lowenstein (D, L)	84,738	46.1
6	Seymour Halpern (R, L)	89,250	77.3
	John J. Flynn (C)	26,244	22.7
7	Joseph P. Addabbo (D, R)	112,983	90.8
	Christopher T. Acer (C)	11,515	9.3
8	Benjamin S. Rosenthal (D, L)	93,666	62.8
	Cosmo J. DiTucci (R, C)	55,406	37.2
9	James J. Delaney (D, R)	102,205	91.9
	Rose L. Rubin (L)	9,025	8.1
10	Emanuel Celler (D, L)	78,324	73.0
	Frank J. Occhiogrosso (R, C)	29,012	27.0
11	Frank J. Brasco (D)	60,919	78.6
	William Sampol (C)	9,462	12.2
	Paul Myrowitz (L)	7,156	9.2

	Candidates	Votes	%
12	Shirley Chisholm (D, L)	31,500	81.8
	John Coleman (R)	5,816	15.1
13	Bertram L. Podell (D)	102,247	77.0
	George W. McKenzie (R)	20,550	15.5
	Herbert Dicker (L)	9,925	7.5
14	John J. Rooney (D)	31,586	55.2
	John F. Jacobs (R, C)	15,222	26.6
	Peter E. Eikenberry (L)	10,452	18.3
15	Hugh L. Carey (D)	50,767	64.7
	Frank C. Spinner (R)	17,931	22.8
	Stephen P. Marion (C)	5,307	6.8
	Carl Saks (L)	4,506	5.7
16	John M. Murphy (D, CSI)	71,553	51.6
	David D. Smith (R, C)	62,597	45.2
17	Edward I. Koch (D, L)	98,300	62.0
	Peter J. Sprague (R)	50,647	32.0
	Richard J. Callahan (C)	9,586	6.1
18	Charles B. Rangel (D, R)	52,651	86.8
	Charles Taylor (C)	6,385	10.5
19	Bella S. Abzug (D)	46,947	52.3
	Barry Farber (R, L)	38,460	42.8
20	William F. Ryan (D, L)	73,509	78.7
	William Goldstein (R)	13,527	14.5
	Francis C. Saunders (C)	6,315	6.8
21	Herman Badillo (D, L)	38,866	83.7
	George B. Smaragdas (C)	7,561	16.3
22	James H. Scheuer (D, L)	50,372	71.6
	Robert M. Schneck (R, C)	19,994	28.4
23	Jonathan B. Bingham (D, L)	78,723	76.2
	George E. Sweeney (R)	16,172	15.7
	Nora M. Kardian (C)	8,456	8.2
24	Mario Biaggi (D, C)	106,942	69.9
	Joseph F. Periconi (R, SILENT)	38,173	24.9
	John Patrick Hagan (L)	7,970	5.2
25	Peter A. Peyser (R)	76,611	42.5
	William Dretzin (D)	66,688	37.0
	Anthony J. DeVito (C)	31,250	17.3
26	Ogden R. Reid (R, L)	109,783	66.4
	Michael A. Coffey (C)	29,702	18.0
	G. Russell James (D)	25,909	15.7
27	John G. Dow (D, L)	89,787	52.2
	Martin B. McKneally (R, C)	82,191	47.8
28	Hamilton Fish Jr. (R)	119,954	70.8
	John J. Greaney (D)	41,908	24.7
29	Samuel S. Stratton (D)	128,017	66.2
	Daniel E. Button (R, L)	65,339	33.8
30	Carleton J. King (R, C)	95,470	57.1
	Edward W. Pattison (D, L)	71,832	42.9
31	Robert C. McEwen (R, C)	90,585	72.4
	Erwin L. Bornstein (D)	34,568	27.6
32	Alexander Pirnie (R, L)	90,884	65.8
	Joseph Simmons (D)	47,306	34.2
33	Howard W. Robison (R)	90,196	66.5
	David Bernstein (D, L)	45,373	33.5
34	John H. Terry (R, C)	88,786	59.5
	Neal P. McCurn (D)	60,452	40.5
35	James M. Hanley (D)	82,425	51.9
	John F. O'Connor (R, C)	76,381	48.1
36	Frank J. Horton (R)	123,209	70.5
	Jordan E. Pappas (D)	38,898	22.3
	David F. Hampson (C)	10,442	6.0
37	Barber B. Conable Jr. (R)	107,677	65.9
	Richard N. Anderson (D, L)	48,061	29.4
38	James F. Hastings (R, C)	94,906	71.4
	James G. Cretekos (D)	37,961	28.6
39	Jack F. Kemp (R, C)	96,989	51.6
	Thomas P. Flaherty (D, L)	90,949	48.4
40	Henry P. Smith III (R, C)	87,183	63.4
	Edward Cuddy (D, L)	50,418	36.6
41	Thaddeus J. Dulski (D, L)	79,151	79.7
	William M. Johns (R, C)	20,108	20.3

NORTH CAROLINA

		Votes	%
1	Walter B. Jones (D)	41,674	70.2
	R. Frank Everett (R)	16,217	27.3

NORTH CAROLINA

	Candidates	Votes	%
2	L. H. Fountain (D)	38,891	100.0
3	David N. Henderson (D)	41,065	60.1
	Herbert H. Howell (R)	27,224	39.9
4	Nick Galifianakis (D)	49,866	52.4
	R. Jack Hawke (R)	45,386	47.7
5	Wilmer D. Mizell (R)	68,937	58.1
	James G. White (D)	49,663	41.9
6	Richardson Preyer (D)	47,693	66.0
	Clifton B. Barham Jr. (R)	20,739	28.7
	Lynwood Bullock (AM)	3,849	5.3
7	Alton A. Lennon (D)	37,377	72.0
	Frederick R. Weber (R)	14,529	28.0
8	Earl B. Ruth (R)	51,873	56.1
	H. Clifton Blue (D)	40,563	43.9
9	Charles Raper Jonas (R)	57,525	66.6
	Cy N. Bahakel (D)	28,801	33.4
10	James T. Broyhill (R)	63,936	57.1
	Basil L. Whitener (D)	48,113	42.9
11	Roy A. Taylor (D)	90,199	67.0
	Luke Atkinson (R)	44,376	33.0

NORTH DAKOTA

		Votes	%
1	Mark Andrews (R)	72,168	65.7
	James E. Brooks (D)	37,688	34.3
2	Arthur A. Link (D)	50,416	50.3
	Robert P. McCarney (R)	49,888	49.7

OHIO

		Votes	%
1	William J. Keating (R)	89,169	69.1
	Bailey W. Turner (D)	39,820	30.9
2	Donald D. Clancy (R)	77,071	55.9
	Gerald N. Springer (D)	60,860	44.1
3	Charles W. Whalen Jr. (R)	86,973	74.2
	Dempsey A. Kerr (D)	26,735	22.8
4	William M. McCulloch (R)	82,521	64.4
	Donald B. Laws (D)	45,619	35.6
5	Delbert L. Latta (R)	92,577	71.2
	Carl G. Sherer (D)	37,545	28.9
6	William H. Harsha (R)	82,772	67.8
	Raymond H. Stevens (D)	39,265	32.2
7	Clarence J. Brown Jr. (R)	84,448	69.4
	Joseph D. Lewis (D)	37,294	30.6
8	Jackson E. Betts (R)	90,916	100.0
9	Thomas L. Ashley (D)	82,777	70.9
	Allen H. Shapiro (R)	33,947	29.1
10	Clarence E. Miller (R)	80,838	66.5
	Doug Arnett (D)	40,669	33.5
11	J. William Stanton (R)	91,437	68.3
	Ralph Rudd (D)	42,542	31.8
12	Samuel L. Devine (R)	82,486	57.7
	James W. Goodrich (D)	60,538	42.3
13	Charles A. Mosher (R)	85,858	61.7
	Joseph J. Bartolomeo (D)	53,271	38.3
14	John F. Seiberling Jr. (D)	71,282	56.4
	William H. Ayres (R)	55,038	43.6
15	Chalmers P. Wylie (R)	81,536	70.6
	Manley L. McGee (D)	34,018	29.4
16	Frank T. Bow (R)	81,208	56.2
	Virgil L. Musser (D)	63,187	43.8
17	John M. Ashbrook (R)	79,472	62.2
	James C. Hood (D)	44,066	34.5
18	Wayne L. Hays (D)	82,071	68.3
	Robert Stewart (R)	38,104	31.7
19	Charles J. Carney (D)	73,222	58.5
	Margaret Dennison (R)	52,057	41.6
20	James V. Stanton (D)	70,140	81.3
	J. William Petro (R)	16,118	18.7
21	Louis Stokes (D)	74,340	77.6
	Bill Mack (R)	21,440	22.4
22	Charles A. Vanik (D)	114,790	71.5
	Adrian Fink (R)	45,657	28.5
23	William E. Minshall (R)	111,218	60.0
	Ronald M. Mottl (D)	73,765	39.8
24	Walter E. Powell (R)	63,344	51.5
	James D. Ruppert (D)	55,455	45.1

Special Election

	Candidates	Votes	%
19	Charles J. Carney (D)	70,161	58.4
	Margaret Dennison (R)	50,005	41.6

OKLAHOMA

		Votes	%
1	Page Belcher (R)	67,386	55.7
	James R. Jones (D)	53,598	44.3
2	Ed Edmondson (D)	87,131	70.8
	Gene Humphries (R)	35,989	29.2
3	Carl Albert (D)	112,458	100.0
4	Tom Steed (D)	67,743	63.7
	Jay G. Wilkinson (R)	37,081	34.9
5	John Jarman (D)	62,034	73.1
	Terry L. Campbell (R)	22,801	26.9
6	John N. Happy Camp (R)	81,959	64.2
	R. O. Cassity Jr. (D)	45,742	35.8

OREGON

		Votes	%
1	Wendell Wyatt (R)	147,239	71.8
	Vern Cook (D)	57,837	28.2
2	Al Ullman (D)	100,943	71.2
	Everett Thoren (R)	40,620	28.7
3	Edith Green (D)	118,919	73.7
	Robert E. Dugdale (R)	42,391	26.3
4	John Dellenback (R)	84,474	58.3
	James Weaver (D)	60,299	41.7

PENNSYLVANIA

		Votes	%
1	William A. Barrett (D)	79,425	69.2
	Joseph S. Ziccardi (R)	34,649	30.2
2	Robert N. C. Nix (D)	70,530	68.2
	Edward L. Taylor (R)	32,858	31.8
3	James A. Byrne (D)	54,755	56.4
	Gustine J. Pelagatti (R)	42,393	43.6
4	Joshua Eilberg (D)	113,920	59.4
	Charles F. Dougherty (R)	77,817	40.6
5	William J. Green III (D)	80,142	66.9
	James H. Ring (R)	38,955	32.5
6	Gus Yatron (D)	96,453	65.0
	Michael Kitsock (R)	48,397	32.6
7	Lawrence G. Williams (R)	91,042	59.3
	Joseph R. Breslin (D)	62,722	40.8
8	Edward G. Biester Jr. (R)	73,041	56.4
	Arthur Leo Hennessy Jr. (D)	51,464	39.7
9	John H. Ware III (R)	76,535	59.2
	Louis F. Waldman (D)	52,852	40.9
10	Joseph M. McDade (R)	102,716	65.4
	Edward J. Smith (D)	51,506	32.8
11	Daniel J. Flood (D)	146,789	96.6
12	J. Irving Whalley (R)	93,385	64.0
	Victor J. Karycki Jr. (D)	48,738	33.4
13	R. Lawrence Coughlin (R)	101,953	58.3
	Frank R. Romano (D)	68,743	39.3
14	William S. Moorhead (D)	72,509	76.5
	Barry Levine (R)	21,572	22.8
15	Fred B. Rooney (D)	93,169	66.9
	Charles H. Roberts (R)	44,103	31.7
16	Edwin D. Eshleman (R)	74,006	66.5
	John E. Pflum (D)	33,986	30.5
17	Herman T. Schneebeli (R)	88,173	57.9
	William P. Zurick (D)	60,714	39.9
18	Robert J. Corbett (R)	87,246	60.2
	Ronald E. Leslie (D)	54,639	37.7
19	George A. Goodling (R)	71,497	53.9
	Arthur L. Berger (D)	58,399	44.0
20	Joseph M. Gaydos (D)	84,911	77.0
	Joseph Honeygosky (R)	22,553	20.5
21	John H. Dent (D)	76,915	68.5
	Glenn G. Anderson (R)	33,396	29.7
22	John P. Saylor (R)	81,675	57.7
	Joseph F. O'Kicki (D)	58,720	41.5
23	Albert W. Johnson (R)	70,074	57.9
	Cecil R. Harrington (D)	50,908	42.1
24	Joseph P. Vigorito (D)	94,029	66.8
	Wayne R. Merrick (R)	44,395	31.5

	Candidates	Votes	%
25	Frank M. Clark (D)	92,638	69.7
	John Loth (R)	37,355	28.1
26	Thomas E. Morgan (D)	80,734	68.4
	Domenick A. Cupelli (R)	35,083	29.7
27	James G. Fulton (R)	86,932	60.5
	Douglas Walgren (D)	55,050	38.3

Special Election

		Votes	%
9	John H. Ware III (R)	44,077	57.0
	Louis F. Waldman (D)	31,353	40.5

RHODE ISLAND

		Votes	%
1	Fernand J. St.Germain (D)	86,283	61.0
	Walter J. Miska (R)	52,962	37.4
2	Robert O. Tiernan (D)	121,704	67.2
	William A. Dimitri Jr. (R)	61,819	34.2

SOUTH CAROLINA

		Votes	%
1	L. Mendel Rivers (D)	63,891*	100.0
2	Floyd Spence (R)	48,093	53.1
	Heyward McDonald (D)	42,005	46.4
3	William Jennings Bryan Dorn (D)	60,708	75.2
	H. Grady Ballard (R)	19,981	24.8
4	James R. Mann (D)	52,175	100.0
5	Thomas S. Gettys (D)	43,742	65.9
	B. Leonard Phillips (R)	21,911	33.0
6	John L. McMillan (D)	46,966	64.1
	Edward B. Baskin (R)	25,546	34.9

SOUTH DAKOTA

		Votes	%
1	Frank E. Denholm (D)	71,636	56.0
	Dexter H. Gunderson (R)	56,330	44.0
2	James Abourezk (D)	55,925	52.3
	Fred D. Brady (R)	51,092	47.7

TENNESSEE

		Votes	%
1	James H. Quillen (R)	78,896	67.9
	David Bruce Shine (D)	37,348	32.1
2	John J. Duncan (R)	85,849	73.3
	Roger Cowan (D)	30,146	25.7
3	LaMar Baker (R)	61,527	51.3
	Richard Winningham (D)	54,662	45.6
4	Joe L. Evins (D)	86,437	82.6
	J. Durelle Boles (R)	18,180	17.4
5	Richard Fulton (D)	89,900	70.6
	George Kelly (R)	37,522	29.5
6	William R. Anderson (D)	87,517	81.7
	Elmer Davies Jr. (R)	19,622	18.3
7	Ray Blanton (D)	83,904	74.2
	W. G. Doss (R)	29,139	25.8
8	Ed Jones (D)	66,590	100.0
9	Dan Kuykendall (R)	72,498	62.6
	Michael Osborn (D)	43,279	37.4

TEXAS

		Votes	%
1	Wright Patman (D)	67,883	78.9
	James Hogan (R)	18,614	21.6
2	John Dowdy (D)	52,634	73.6
	Eugene Hoyt (WRITE IN)	11,987#	17.2
	Joe Runnels (WRITE IN)	4,693#	6.8
3	James M. Collins (R)	63,690	60.6
	John Mead (D)	41,425	39.4
4	Ray Roberts (D)	70,103	100.0
5	Earle Cabell (D)	57,058	59.7
	Frank Crowley (R)	38,481	40.3
6	Olin E. Teague (D)	74,038	100.0
7	Bill Archer (R)	93,457	64.8
	Jim Greenwood (D)	50,750	35.2
8	Bob Eckhardt (D)	26,294	100.0

TEXAS

Candidates	Votes	%
9 Jack Brooks (D)	57,180	64.5
Henry Pressler (R)	31,483	35.5
10 J. J. Pickle (D)	78,872	100.0
11 W. R. Poage (D)	59,641	99.9
12 Jim Wright (D)	62,057	100.0
13 Graham B. Purcell (D)	80,070	64.9
Joe Staley (R)	43,319	35.1
14 John Young (D)	62,560	100.0
15 Eligio de la Garza (D)	54,498	76.2
Ben A. Martinez (R)	17,049	23.8
16 Richard C. White (D)	54,617	82.7
J. R. Provencio (R)	11,420	17.3
17 Omar Burleson (D)	70,040	100.0
18 Bob Price (R)	52,845	99.9
19 George Mahon (D)	59,996	100.0
20 Henry B. Gonzalez (D)	48,710	100.0
21 O. C. Fisher (D)	76,004	61.4
Richardson B. Gill (R)	47,868	38.6
22 Bob Casey (D)	73,514	55.7
A. W. Busch (R)	58,598	44.4
23 Abraham Kazen Jr. (D)	61,068	100.0

UTAH

Candidates	Votes	%
1 K. Gunn McKay (D)	95,499	51.3
Richard Richards (R)	89,269	47.9
2 Sherman P. Lloyd (R)	97,549	52.3
A. H. (Bob) Nance (D)	87,000	46.6

VERMONT

Candidates	Votes	%
AL Robert T. Stafford (R)	103,806	68.0
Bernard O'Shea (D)	44,415	29.1

VIRGINIA

Candidates	Votes	%
1 Thomas N. Downing (D)	71,465	100.0
2 G. William Whitehurst (R)	44,108	61.7
Joseph T. Fitzpatrick (D)	27,367	38.3
3 David E. Satterfield III (D)	73,123	65.2
J. Harvie Wilkinson III (R)	35,258	31.5
4 Watkins M. Abbitt (D)	55,246	61.0
Ben Ragsdale (I)	25,403	28.1
James M. Helms (R)	9,883	10.9
5 W. C. (Dan) Daniel (D)	54,274	73.0
Allen T. St.Clair Jr. (R)	20,039	27.0
6 Richard H. Poff (R)	62,350	74.6
Roy R. White (D)	21,241	25.4
7 J. Kenneth Robinson (R)	52,716	61.8
Murat Williams (D)	32,642	38.2
8 William L. Scott (R)	68,311	63.7
Darrel H. Stearns (D)	38,848	36.3
9 William C. Wampler (R)	53,960	60.9
Tate C. Buchanan (D)	34,609	39.1
10 Joel T. Broyhill (R)	67,650	54.5
Harold O. Miller (D)	56,603	45.6

WASHINGTON

Candidates	Votes	%
1 Thomas M. Pelly (R)	107,072	64.4
David A. Hughes (D)	53,156	32.0
2 Lloyd Meeds (D)	117,562	72.7
Edward A. McBride (R)	44,049	27.3
3 Julia Butler Hansen (D)	81,892	59.2
R. C. (Skip) McConkey (R)	56,566	40.9
4 Mike McCormack (D)	70,119	52.6
Catherine May (R)	63,244	47.4
5 Thomas S. Foley (D)	88,189	67.0
George Gamble (R)	43,376	33.0
6 Floyd V. Hicks (D)	98,282	69.4
John Jarstad (R)	42,213	29.8
7 Brock Adams (D)	99,308	66.6
Brian Lewis (R)	47,426	31.8

WEST VIRGINIA

Candidates	Votes	%
1 Robert H. Mollohan (D)	61,296	61.5
Ken Doll (R)	38,327	38.5
2 Harvey O. Staggers (D)	56,263	62.7
Richard M. Reddecliff (R)	33,509	37.3
3 John Slack (D)	57,630	65.4
Neal A. Kinsolving (R)	30,525	34.6
4 Ken Hechler (D)	62,531	67.4
Ralph Shannon (R)	30,255	32.6
5 James Kee (D)	48,286	70.4
Marian McQuade (R)	20,261	29.6

WISCONSIN

Candidates	Votes	%
1 Les Aspin (D)	87,428	60.9
Henry C. Schadeberg (R)	56,067	39.1
2 Robert W. Kastenmeier (D)	102,879	68.5
Norman Anderson (R)	46,620	31.0
3 Vernon W. Thomson (R)	64,891	55.5
Ray Short (D)	52,085	44.5
4 Clement J. Zablocki (D)	102,464	81.6
Phillip D. Mrozinski (R)	23,081	18.4
5 Henry S. Reuss (D)	60,630	75.9
Robert J. Dwyer (R)	18,360	23.0
6 William A. Steiger (R)	98,587	67.7
Franklin R. Utech (D)	44,794	30.8
7 David R. Obey (D)	88,746	67.6
Andre E. Le Tendre (R)	41,330	31.5
8 John W. Byrnes (R)	76,893	55.5
Robert J. Cornell (D)	60,345	43.6
9 Glenn R. Davis (R)	84,732	52.0
Fred N. Tabak (D)	78,123	48.0
10 Alvin E. O'Konski (R)	66,014	50.9
Walter Thoresen (D)	62,991	48.6

WYOMING

Candidates	Votes	%
AL Teno Roncalio (D)	58,456	50.3
Harry Roberts (R)	57,848	49.7

1971 House Elections

KENTUCKY

Special Election

Candidates	Votes	%
6 William P. Curlin (D)	29,778#	52.6
Raymond Nutter (R)	21,584#	38.1
Edgar A. Wallace	4,070#	7.2

MARYLAND

Special Election

Candidates	Votes	%
1 William O. Mills (R)	31,165	53.4
Elroy G. Boyer (D)	27,234	46.6

PENNSYLVANIA

Special Election

	Votes	%
18 H. John Heinz III (R)	103,543	66.6
John E. Connelly (D)	49,269	31.7

SOUTH CAROLINA

Special Election

Candidates	Votes	%
1 Mendel J. Davis (D)	38,012	48.6
James B. Edwards (R)	32,227	41.2
Victoria DeLee (I)	7,965	10.2

1970 Elections

[1] These two California special elections were held to fill unexpired terms in the 91st Congress (1969-71).

The returns for special House elections in the 24th and 35th Districts are from elections held after no candidate received a majority of the vote in the initial special primary elections. (California special primary law, see p. 1258)

Special Primary Election returns, 24th District: John H. Rousselot (R), 37,348, 29.0; Bill McColl (R), 35,682, 27.7; Myrlie B. Evers (D), 23,688, 18.4; Patrick J. Hillings (R), 22,394, 17.4; Jack Alex (R), 8,230, 6.4. Rousselot, the top Republican, and Evers, the top Democrat, thus qualified to meet in the special election. Source: California Secretary of State.

Special Primary Election returns, 35th District: Congressional Quarterly was unable to obtain complete official returns. Seven candidates competed for the seat, five Republicans and two Democrats. Schmitz, the Republican receiving the highest number of votes, and Hartman, the top Democrat, qualified to meet in the special election.

1972 House Elections

ALABAMA

	Candidates	Votes	%
1	Jack Edwards (R)	104,606	76.5
	O. W. McCrory (D)	24,357	17.8
	Thomas McAboy Jr. (NDPA)	7,747	5.7
2	William L. Dickinson (R)	80,362	54.9
	Ben C. Reeves (D)	60,769	41.5
3	Bill Nichols (D)	100,045	75.6
	Robert M. Kerr (R)	27,253	20.6
4	Tom Bevill (D)	108,039	69.6
	Ed Nelson (R)	46,551	30.0
5	Robert E. Jones (D)	101,303	74.2
	Digter J. Schrader (R)	33,352	24.4
6	John H. Buchanan Jr. (R)	91,499	59.8
	Ben Erdreich (D)	54,497	35.6
7	Walter Flowers (D)	95,060	84.8
	Lewis Black (NDPA)	15,703	14.0

Special Election

3	Elizabeth Andrews (D)	✔	

ALASKA

		Votes	%
AL	Nick Begich (D)	53,651*	56.2
	Don Young (R)	41,750	43.8

ARIZONA

		Votes	%
1	John J. Rhodes (R)	80,453	57.3
	Gerald A. Pollock (D)	59,900	42.7
2	Morris K. Udall (D)	97,616	63.5
	Gene Savoie (R)	56,188	36.5
3	Sam Steiger (R)	90,710	63.0
	Ted Wyckoff (D)	53,220	37.0
4	John B. Conlan (R)	82,511	53.0
	Jack E. Brown (D)	73,309	47.1

ARKANSAS

		Votes	%
1	Bill Alexander (D)	✔	
2	Wilbur D. Mills (D)	✔	
3	John Paul Hammerschmidt (R)	144,571	77.3
	Guy W. Hatfield (D)	42,481	22.7
4	Ray Thornton (D)	✔	

CALIFORNIA

		Votes	%
1	Don H. Clausen (R)	141,226	62.3
	William A. Nighswonger (D)	77,610	34.2
2	Harold T. Johnson (D)	149,590	68.4
	Frances X. Callahan (R)	62,727	28.7
3	John E. Moss (D)	151,706	69.9
	John Rakus (R)	65,298	30.1
4	Robert L. Leggett (D)	115,038	67.4
	Benjamin Chang (R)	55,540	32.6
5	Phillip Burton (D)	124,164	81.8
	Edlo E. Powell (R)	27,474	18.1
6	William S. Mailliard (R)	119,704	52.1
	Roger Boas (D)	110,144	47.9
7	Ronald V. Dellums (D)	126,913	55.9
	Peter Hannaford (R)	86,587	38.1
	Frank V. Cortese (AM I)	13,550	6.0
8	Fortney H. (Pete) Stark Jr. (D)	102,153	52.9
	Lew M. Warden Jr. (R)	90,970	47.1
9	Don Edwards (D)	123,994	72.3
	Herb Smith (R)	43,140	25.2
10	Charles S. Gubser (R)	140,342	64.6
	B. Frank Gillette (D)	76,839	35.4
11	Leo J. Ryan (D)	114,134	60.5
	Charles E. Chase (R)	69,632	36.9
12	Burt L. Talcott (R)	105,556	51.4
	Julian Camacho (D)	84,174	41.0

	Candidates	Votes	%
13	Charles M. Teague (R)	153,877	73.9
	Lester D. Cleveland (D)	54,299	26.1
14	Jerome R. Waldie (D)	159,335	77.6
	Floyd E. Sims (R)	46,082	22.4
15	John J. McFall (D)	146,358	100.0
16	B. F. Sisk (D)	134,132	79.1
	Carol O. Harner (R)	35,385	20.9
17	Paul N. McCloskey Jr. (R)	110,988	54.5
	James Stewart (D)	73,123	35.9
	James Gordon Knapp (WRITE IN)	19,377	9.5
18	Bob Mathias (R)	110,153	66.4
	Vincent J. Lavery (D)	55,829	33.6
19	Chet Holifield (D)	105,699	67.2
	Kenneth M. Fisher (R)	43,792	27.9
20	Carlos J. Moorhead (R)	122,309	57.4
	John Binkley (D)	90,842	42.6
21	Augustus F. Hawkins (D)	95,050	82.9
	Rayfield Lundy (R)	19,569	17.1
22	James C. Corman (D)	123,863	67.6
	Bruce P. Wolfe (R)	53,603	29.3
23	Del Clawson (R)	120,313	61.4
	Conrad G. Tuohey (D)	75,546	38.6
24	John H. Rousselot (R)	144,057	70.1
	Luther Mandell (D)	61,326	29.9
25	Charles E. Wiggins (R)	118,631	65.0
	Leslie W. Craven (D)	58,323	31.9
26	Thomas M. Rees (D)	164,351	68.7
	Philip Robert Rutta (R)	66,731	27.9
27	Barry Goldwater Jr. (R)	119,475	57.4
	Mark S. Novak (D)	88,548	42.6
28	Alphonzo Bell (R)	144,815	60.7
	Michael Shapiro (D)	89,517	37.5
29	George E. Danielson (D)	92,856	62.7
	Richard E. Ferraro (R)	49,590	33.5
30	Edward R. Roybal (D)	78,193	68.4
	Bill Brophy (R)	32,717	28.6
31	Charles H. Wilson (D)	87,975	52.3
	Ben Valentine (R)	71,395	42.5
	Roberta Lynn Wood (PFP)	8,788	5.2
32	Craig Hosmer (R)	149,514	65.9
	Dennis Murray (D)	72,481	32.0
33	Jerry L. Pettis (R)	140,868	75.0
	Ken Thompson (D)	46,911	25.0
34	Richard T. Hanna (D)	115,880	67.1
	John D. Ratterree (R)	49,971	29.0
35	Glenn M. Anderson (D)	105,667	74.8
	Vernon E. Brown (R)	35,614	25.2
36	William M. Ketchum (R)	88,071	52.7
	Timothy Lemucchi (D)	72,623	43.5
37	Yvonne Brathwaite Burke (D)	123,468	60.2
	Gregg Tria (R)	41,562	20.3
38	George E. Brown Jr. (D)	77,922	55.9
	Howard J. Snider (R)	60,459	43.4
39	Andrew J. Hinshaw (R)	149,081	65.7
	John W. Black (D)	77,817	34.3
40	Bob Wilson (R)	155,269	67.8
	Frank Caprio (D)	69,377	30.3
41	Lionel Van Deerlin (D)	116,980	74.1
	D. Richard Kau (R)	40,997	26.0
42	Clair W. Burgener (R)	158,475	67.5
	Bob Lowe (D)	68,381	29.1
43	Victor V. Veysey (R)	118,536	62.7
	Ernest Z. Robles (D)	70,455	37.3

COLORADO

		Votes	%
1	Patricia Schroeder (D)	101,832	52.0
	James D. McKevitt (R)	93,733	47.9
2	Donald G. Brotzman (R)	132,562	66.3
	Francis W. Brush (D)	66,817	33.4
3	Frank E. Evans (D)	107,511	66.3
	Chuck Brady (R)	54,556	33.7
4	James P. Johnson (R)	94,994	51.0
	Alan Merson (D)	91,151	49.0
5	William L. Armstrong (R)	104,214	62.3
	Byron L. Johnson (D)	60,948	36.5

CONNECTICUT

	Candidates	Votes	%
1	William R. Cotter (D)	130,701	56.9
	Richard M. Rittenband (R)	96,188	41.9
2	Robert H. Steele (R)	142,094	65.9
	Roger Hilsman (D)	73,400	34.1
3	Robert N. Giaimo (D)	121,217	53.3
	Henry A. Povinelli (R)	106,313	46.7
4	Stewart B. McKinney (R)	135,883	63.1
	James P. McLoughlin (D)	79,515	36.9
5	Ronald A. Sarasin (R)	117,578	51.2
	John S. Monagan (D)	112,142	48.8
6	Ella T. Grasso (D)	140,290	60.2
	John F. Walsh (R)	92,783	39.8

DELAWARE

		Votes	%
AL	Pierre S. duPont IV (R)	141,237	62.5
	Norma Handloff (D)	83,230	36.9

FLORIDA

		Votes	%
1	Robert L. F. Sikes (D)	✔	
2	Don Fuqua (D)	✔	
3	Charles E. Bennett (D)	101,441	82.0
	John F. Bowen (R)	22,219	18.0
4	Bill Chappell (D)	92,541	55.9
	P. T. Fleuchaus (R)	72,960	44.1
5	William D. Gunter Jr. (D)	97,902	55.5
	Jack P. Insco (R)	78,463	44.5
6	C. W. Bill Young (R)	156,150	76.0
	Michael O. Plunkett (D)	49,399	24.0
7	Sam Gibbons (D)	91,931	68.0
	Robert A. Carter (R)	43,343	32.0
8	James A. Haley (D)	89,068	57.8
	Roy Thompson Jr. (R)	64,920	42.2
9	Louis Frey Jr. (R)	✔	
10	L. A. (Skip) Bafalis (R)	113,461	62.0
	Bill Sikes (D)	69,502	38.0
11	Paul G. Rogers (D)	116,157	60.2
	Joel Karl Gustafson (R)	76,739	39.8
12	J. Herbert Burke (R)	110,750	62.8
	James T. Stephanis (D)	65,526	37.2
13	William Lehman (D)	92,258	61.6
	Paul D. Bethel (R)	57,418	38.4
14	Claude Pepper (D)	75,131	67.7
	Evelio S. Estrella (R)	35,935	32.4
15	Dante B. Fascell (D)	89,961	56.8
	Ellis S. Rubin (R)	68,320	43.2

GEORGIA

		Votes	%
1	Ronald B. (Bo) Ginn (D)	55,256	100.0
2	Dawson Mathis (D)	65,997	100.0
3	Jack Brinkley (D)	71,756	100.0
4	Ben B. Blackburn (R)	103,155	75.9
	F. Odell Welborn (D)	32,731	24.1
5	Andrew Young (D)	72,289	52.8
	Rodney M. Cook (R)	64,495	47.1
6	John J. Flynt Jr. (D)	70,586	100.0
7	John W. Davis (D)	59,031	58.3
	Charles B. Sherrill (R)	42,265	41.7
8	W. S. Stuckey Jr. (D)	71,283	62.4
	Ronnie Thompson (R)	42,986	37.6
9	Phil M. Landrum (D)	71,801	100.0
10	Robert G. Stephens Jr. (D)	68,096	100.0

HAWAII

		Votes	%
1	Spark M. Matsunaga (D)	73,826	54.7
	Fred W. Rohlfing (R)	61,138	45.3
2	Patsy T. Mink (D)	79,856	57.1
	Diana Hansen (R)	60,043	42.9

IDAHO

	Candidates	Votes	%
1	Steven D. Symms (R)	85,270	55.6
	Edward Williams (D)	68,106	44.4
2	Orval Hansen (R)	102,537	69.2
	Willis H. Ludlow (D)	40,081	27.1

ILLINOIS

	Candidates	Votes	%
1	Ralph H. Metcalfe (D)	136,755	91.4
	Louis H. Coggs (R)	12,877	8.6
2	Morgan F. Murphy (D)	115,306	75.0
	James E. Doyle (R)	38,391	25.0
3	Robert P. Hanrahan (R)	128,329	62.3
	Daniel P. Coman (D)	77,814	37.8
4	Edward J. Derwinski (R)	141,402	70.5
	C. F. Dore (D)	59,057	29.5
5	John C. Kluczynski (D)	121,278	72.8
	Leonard C. Jarzab (R)	45,264	27.2
6	Harold R. Collier (R)	124,486	61.2
	Michael R. Galasso (D)	79,002	38.8
7	George W. Collins (D)	95,018*	82.8
	Thomas J. Lento (R)	19,758	17.2
8	Daniel D. Rostenkowski (D)	110,457	74.0
	Edward L. Stepnowski (R)	38,758	26.0
9	Sidney R. Yates (D)	131,777	68.3
	Clark W. Fetridge (R)	61,083	31.7
10	Samuel H. Young (R)	120,681	51.6
	Abner J. Mikva (D)	113,222	48.4
11	Frank Annunzio (D)	118,637	53.3
	John J. Hoellen (R)	103,773	46.7
12	Philip M. Crane (R)	152,938	74.2
	E. L. Frank (D)	53,055	25.8
13	Robert McClory (R)	98,201	61.5
	Stanley W. Beetham (D)	61,537	38.5
14	John N. Erlenborn (R)	154,794	72.8
	James M. Wall (D)	57,874	27.2
15	Leslie C. Arends (R)	111,022	57.2
	Tim L. Hall (D)	82,925	42.8
16	John B. Anderson (R)	129,640	71.9
	John E. Devine Jr. (D)	50,649	28.1
17	George M. O'Brien (R)	100,175	55.7
	John J. Houlihan (D)	79,840	44.4
18	Robert H. Michel (R)	124,407	64.8
	Stephen N. Nordvall (D)	67,514	35.2
19	Thomas F. Railsback (R)	138,123	100.0
20	Paul Findley (R)	148,419	68.8
	Robert S. O'Shea (D)	67,445	31.2
21	Edward R. Madigan (R)	99,966	54.8
	Lawrence E. Johnson (D)	82,523	45.2
22	George E. Shipley (D)	124,589	56.5
	Robert B. Lamkin (R)	90,390	41.0
23	Melvin Price (D)	121,682	75.1
	Robert Mays (R)	40,428	24.9
24	Kenneth J. Gray (D)	138,867	93.7
	Hugh Muldoon (I)	9,398	6.3

Special Election

		Votes	%
15	Clifford D. Carlson (R)	31,543	54.8
	Tim L. Hall (D)	26,030	45.2

INDIANA

	Candidates	Votes	%
1	Ray J. Madden (D)	95,873	56.9
	Bruce R. Haller (R)	72,662	43.1
2	Earl F. Landgrebe (R)	110,406	54.7
	Floyd Fithian (D)	91,533	45.3
3	John Brademas (D)	103,949	55.2
	Don M. Newman (R)	81,369	43.2
4	J. Edward Roush (D)	100,327	51.5
	Allan Bloom (R)	94,492	48.5
5	Elwood Hillis (R)	124,692	64.1
	Kathleen Z. Williams (D)	69,746	35.9
6	William G. Bray (R)	112,525	64.8
	David W. Evans (D)	61,070	35.2
7	John T. Myers (R)	128,688	61.6
	Warren Henegar (D)	80,145	38.4

	Candidates	Votes	%
8	Roger H. Zion (R)	133,850	63.3
	Richard L. Deen (D)	77,371	36.6
9	Lee Hamilton (D)	122,698	62.9
	William A. Johnson (R)	72,325	37.1
10	David W. Dennis (R)	106,798	57.3
	Philip R. Sharp (D)	79,756	42.8
11	William H. Hudnut III (R)	95,839	51.2
	Andrew Jacobs Jr. (D)	91,238	48.8

IOWA

	Candidates	Votes	%
1	Edward Mezvinsky (D)	107,099	53.4
	Fred Schwengel (R)	91,609	45.7
2	John C. Culver (D)	115,489	59.2
	Theodore R. Ellsworth (R)	79,667	40.8
3	H. R. Gross (R)	109,113	55.7
	Lyle Taylor (D)	86,848	44.3
4	Neal Smith (D)	125,431	59.6
	John Kyl (R)	85,156	40.4
5	William J. Scherle (R)	108,596	55.3
	Tom Harkin (D)	87,937	44.7
6	Wiley Mayne (R)	103,284	52.5
	Berkley Bedell (D)	93,574	47.5

KANSAS

	Candidates	Votes	%
1	Keith G. Sebelius (R)	145,712	77.2
	Morris Coover (D)	40,678	21.6
2	William R. Roy (D)	106,276	60.6
	Charles D. McAtee (R)	65,071	37.1
3	Larry Winn Jr. (R)	122,358	71.0
	Charles Barsotti (D)	43,777	25.4
4	Garner E. Shriver (R)	120,120	73.2
	John S. Stevens (D)	40,753	24.8
5	Joe Skubitz (R)	128,639	72.3
	Lloyd L. Kitch (D)	49,169	27.7

KENTUCKY

	Candidates	Votes	%
1	Frank A. Stubblefield (D)	81,456	64.8
	Charles T. Banken (R)	42,286	33.7
2	William H. Natcher (D)	75,871	61.5
	J. C. Carter (R)	47,436	38.5
3	Romano L. Mazzoli (D)	86,810	62.2
	Phil Kaelin Jr. (R)	51,634	37.0
4	M. G. (Gene) Snyder (R)	110,902	73.8
	James W. Rogers (D)	39,332	26.2
5	Tim Lee Carter (R)	109,264	73.6
	Lyle L. Willis (D)	39,301	26.5
6	John Breckinridge (D)	76,185	52.4
	Laban P. Jackson (R)	68,012	46.8
7	Carl D. Perkins (D)	94,840	61.9
	Robert Holcomb (R)	58,286	38.1

LOUISIANA

	Candidates	Votes	%
1	F. Edward Hebert (D)	78,156	100.0
2	Hale Boggs (D)	68,093*	100.0
3	David C. Treen (R)	71,090	54.0
	J. Louis Watkins Jr. (D)	60,521	46.0
4	Joe D. Waggonner Jr. (D)	74,397	100.0
5	Otto E. Passman (D)	64,027	100.0
6	John R. Rarick (D)	84,275	100.0
7	John B. Breaux (D)	71,901	100.0
8	Gillis W. Long (D)	72,607	68.5
	R. S. Abramson (AM)	17,844	16.8
	Roy C. Strickland (R)	15,517	14.6

Special Election

		Votes	%
7	John B. Breaux (D)	✓	

MAINE

	Candidates	Votes	%
1	Peter N. Kyros (D)	129,408	59.4
	L. Robert Porteous Jr. (R)	88,588	40.6
2	William S. Cohen (R)	106,280	54.4
	Elmer H. Violette (D)	89,135	45.6

MARYLAND

	Candidates	Votes	%
1	William O. Mills (R)	86,326	70.5
	John R. Hargreaves (D)	36,139	29.5
2	Clarence D. Long (D)	123,346	65.8
	John J. Bishop Jr. (R)	64,119	34.2
3	Paul S. Sarbanes (D)	93,093	69.7
	Robert D. Morrow (R)	40,442	30.3
4	Marjorie S. Holt (R)	87,534	59.4
	Werner Fornos (D)	59,877	40.6
5	Lawrence J. Hogan (R)	90,016	62.9
	Edward T. Conroy (D)	53,049	37.1
6	Goodloe E. Byron (D)	107,283	64.8
	Edward J. Mason (R)	58,259	35.2
7	Parren J. Mitchell (D)	83,749	80.1
	Verdell Adair (R)	20,876	20.0
8	Gilbert Gude (R)	137,287	63.9
	Joseph G. Anastasi (D)	77,551	36.1

MASSACHUSETTS

	Candidates	Votes	%
1	Silvio O. Conte (R)	159,282	99.9
2	Edward P. Boland (D)	137,616	100.0
3	Harold D. Donohue (D)	156,703	99.9
4	Robert F. Drinan (D)	101,714	49.5
	Martin A. Linsky (R)	92,250	44.9
	John T. Collins (IC)	11,141	5.4
5	Paul W. Cronin (R)	110,970	53.5
	John F. Kerry (D)	92,847	44.7
6	Michael J. Harrington (D)	139,697	64.1
	James Brady Moseley (R)	78,381	35.9
7	Torbert H. Macdonald (D)	135,193	67.7
	Joan M. Aliberti (R)	64,357	32.3
8	Thomas P. O'Neill Jr. (D)	142,470	88.7
	John E. Powers Jr. (SOC WORK)	18,169	11.3
9	John Joseph Moakley (I)	70,571	43.2
	Louise Day Hicks (D)	67,143	41.1
	Howard M. Miller (R)	23,177	14.2
10	Margaret M. Heckler (R)	161,708	100.0
11	James A. Burke (D)	154,397	100.0
12	Gerry E. Studds (D)	117,710	50.2
	William D. Weeks (R)	116,592	49.8

MICHIGAN

	Candidates	Votes	%
1	John Conyers Jr. (D)	131,353	88.4
	Walter F. Girardot (R)	16,096	10.8
2	Marvin L. Esch (R)	103,321	56.0
	Marvin R. Stempien (D)	79,762	43.3
3	Garry Brown (R)	110,082	59.2
	James T. Brignall (D)	74,114	39.9
4	Edward Hutchinson (R)	111,185	67.3
	Charles W. Jameson (D)	54,141	32.8
5	Gerald Ford (R)	118,027	61.1
	Jean McKee (D)	72,782	37.7
6	Charles E. Chamberlain (R)	97,666	50.6
	Bob Carr (D)	95,209	49.4
7	Donald W. Riegle Jr. (R)	114,656	71.4
	Eugene L. Mattison (D)	48,883	30.5
8	James Harvey (R)	100,597	59.3
	Jerome Hart (D)	66,873	39.4
9	Guy A. Vander Jagt (R)	132,268	69.4
	Larry H. Olson (D)	56,236	29.5
10	Elford A. Cederberg (R)	121,368	66.7
	Bennie D. Graves (D)	56,149	30.9
11	Philip E. Ruppe (R)	135,786	69.4
	James Edward McNamara (D)	58,334	29.8
12	James G. O'Hara (D)	83,351	50.7
	David M. Serotkin (R)	80,667	49.0
13	Charles C. Diggs Jr. (D)	97,562	85.6
	Leonard F. Edwards (R)	15,180	13.3
14	Lucien N. Nedzi (D)	93,923	54.9
	Robert V. McGrath (R)	77,273	45.1
15	William D. Ford (D)	97,054	65.8
	Ernest C. Fackler (R)	48,504	32.9
16	John D. Dingell Jr. (D)	110,715	68.1
	William E. Rostron (R)	48,414	29.8
17	Martha W. Griffiths (D)	123,331	66.4
	Ralph E. Judd (R)	60,337	32.5

MICHIGAN

Candidates	Votes	%
18 Robert J. Huber (R)	95,053	52.6
Daniel S. Cooper (D)	85,580	47.4
19 William S. Broomfield (R)	123,697	70.4
George F. Montgomery (D)	50,355	28.6

MINNESOTA

Candidates	Votes	%
1 Albert H. Quie (R)	142,698	70.7
Charles S. Thompson (DFL)	59,106	29.3
2 Ancher Nelsen (R)	124,350	57.1
Charles V. Turnbull (DFL)	93,433	42.9
3 Bill Frenzel (R)	132,638	62.9
Jim Bell (DFL)	66,070	31.3
Donald Wright (MINN TAX)	12,234	5.8
4 Joseph E. Karth (DFL)	138,292	72.4
Steve Thompson (R)	52,786	27.6
5 Donald M. Fraser (DFL)	135,108	65.8
Allan Davisson (R)	50,014	24.4
Norm Selby (MINN TAX)	15,845	7.7
6 John M. Zwach (R)	114,537	51.0
Richard M. Nolan (DFL)	109,955	49.0
7 Bob Bergland (DFL)	133,067	59.1
Jon O. Haaven (R)	92,283	41.0
8 John A. Blatnik (DFL)	161,823	75.9
Edward Johnson (R)	51,314	24.1

MISSISSIPPI

Candidates	Votes	%
1 Jamie L. Whitten (D)	87,526	100.0
2 David R. Bowen (D)	69,892	61.9
Carl Butler (R)	39,117	34.7
3 G. V. (Sonny) Montgomery (D)	105,722	100.0
4 Thad Cochran (R)	67,655	47.9
Ellis B. Bodron (D)	62,148	44.0
Eddie L. McBride (I)	11,571	8.2
5 Trent Lott (R)	77,826	55.4
Ben Stone (D)	62,101	44.2

MISSOURI

Candidates	Votes	%
1 William Clay (D)	95,098	64.0
Richard O. Funsch (R)	53,596	36.0
2 James W. Symington (D)	134,332	63.5
John W. Cooper Jr. (R)	77,192	36.5
3 Leonor K. Sullivan (D)	124,365	69.3
Albert Holst (R)	54,523	30.4
4 William J. Randall (D)	108,131	57.4
Raymond E. Barrows (R)	80,228	42.6
5 Richard Bolling (D)	93,812	62.8
Vernon E. Rice (R)	53,257	35.6
6 Jerry Litton (D)	110,047	52.2
Russell Sloan (R)	91,610	43.5
7 Gene Taylor (R)	132,780	63.7
William Thomas (D)	75,613	36.3
8 Richard Ichord (D)	112,556	62.1
David R. Countie (R)	68,580	37.9
9 William L. Hungate (D)	132,150	66.5
Robert L. Prange (R)	66,528	33.5
10 Bill D. Burlison (D)	106,301	64.3
M. Francis Svendrowski (R)	59,083	35.7

MONTANA

Candidates	Votes	%
1 Richard G. Shoup (R)	88,373	53.7
Arnold Olsen (D)	76,073	46.3
2 John Melcher (D)	114,524	76.1
Richard L. Forester (R)	36,063	24.0

NEBRASKA

Candidates	Votes	%
1 Charles Thone (R)	126,789	64.2
Darrel E. Berg (D)	70,570	35.8
2 John Y. McCollister (R)	114,669	63.9
Patrick L. Cooney (D)	64,696	36.1
3 Dave Martin (R)	133,607	69.6
Warren Fitzgerald (D)	58,378	30.4

NEVADA

Candidates	Votes	%
AL David Towell (R)	94,113	52.2
James H. Bilbray (D)	86,349	47.9

NEW HAMPSHIRE

Candidates	Votes	%
1 Louis C. Wyman (R)	115,732	72.9
Chester E. Merrow (D)	42,996	27.1
2 James C. Cleveland (R)	107,021	67.6
Charles B. Officer (D)	51,259	32.4

NEW JERSEY

Candidates	Votes	%
1 John E. Hunt (R)	97,650	52.5
James J. Florio (D)	87,492	47.0
2 Charles W. Sandman Jr. (R)	133,096	65.7
John D. Rose (D)	69,374	34.3
3 James J. Howard (D)	103,893	53.0
William F. Dowd (R)	92,285	47.0
4 Frank Thompson Jr (D)	98,206	58.0
Peter P. Garibaldi (R)	71,030	42.0
5 Peter H. B. Frelinghuysen Jr. (R)	127,310	62.0
Frederick M. Bohen (D)	78,076	38.0
6 Edwin B. Forsythe (R)	123,610	62.8
Francis P. Brennen (D)	71,113	36.1
7 William B. Widnall (R)	124,365	57.9
Arthur J. Lesemann (D)	85,712	39.9
8 Robert A. Roe (D)	104,381	63.1
Walter E. Johnson (R)	61,073	36.9
9 Henry Helstoski (D)	119,543	55.8
Alfred D. Schiaffo (R)	94,747	44.2
10 Peter W. Rodino Jr. (D)	94,308	79.8
Kenneth C. Miller (R)	23,949	20.3
11 Joseph G. Minish (D)	120,227	57.5
Milton A. Waldor (R)	82,957	39.7
12 Matthew J. Rinaldo (R)	127,690	63.5
Jerry Fitzgerald English (D)	72,758	36.2
13 Joseph J. Maraziti (R)	109,640	55.7
Helen S. Meyner (D)	84,492	42.9
14 Dominick V. Daniels (D)	103,089	61.2
Richard T. Bozzone (R)	57,683	34.3
15 Edward J. Patten (D)	98,155	52.3
Fuller H. Brooks (R)	89,400	47.7

NEW MEXICO

Candidates	Votes	%
1 Manuel Lujan Jr. (R)	118,403	55.7
Eugene Gallegos (D)	94,239	44.3
2 Harold Runnels (D)	116,152	72.2
George E. Presson (R)	44,784	27.8

NEW YORK

Candidates	Votes	%
1 Otis G. Pike (D)	102,628	52.5
Joseph H. Boyd (R)	72,133	36.9
Robert D. L. Gardiner (C)	18,627	9.5
2 James R. Grover Jr. (R)	99,348	65.8
Fern Coste Dennison (D)	49,454	32.8
3 Angelo D. Roncallo (R)	103,620	57.0
Carter Bales (D)	73,429	40.4
Lawrence P. Russo (C)	14,768	8.1
4 Norman F. Lent (R)	125,422	62.4
Elaine B. Horowitz (D)	72,280	36.0
5 John W. Wydler (R)	133,332	62.4
Ferne M. Steckler (D)	67,709	31.7
6 Lester L. Wolff (D, L)	109,620	51.5
John T. Gallagher (R, C)	103,038	48.5
7 Joseph P. Addabbo (D, L)	103,110	75.0
John E. Hall (R)	28,296	20.6
8 Benjamin S. Rosenthal (D, L)	110,293	64.7
Frank A. La Pina (R, C)	60,166	35.3
9 James J. Delaney (D, R)	141,323	93.4
Loretta E. Gressey (L)	9,965	6.6
10 Mario Biaggi (D, R)	130,200	93.9
Michael S. Bank (L)	8,397	6.1
11 Frank J. Brasco (D)	87,869	63.9
Melvin Solomon (R, C)	43,105	31.3
12 Shirley Chisholm (D, L)	57,821	87.9
John M. Coleman (R)	6,373	9.7
13 Bertram L. Podell (D)	113,294	65.2
Joseph F. Marcucci (R)	44,293	25.5
Leonard M. Simon (L)	9,173	5.3
14 John J. Rooney (D, C)	45,515	53.9
Allard K. Lowenstein (L)	23,732	28.1
Francis J. Voyticky (R)	14,813	17.5
15 Hugh L. Carey (D)	77,019	52.2
John F. Gangemi (R)	63,446	43.0
16 Elizabeth Holtzman (D)	96,984	65.6
Nicholas R. Macchio (R)	33,828	22.9
Emanuel Celler (L)	10,337	7.0
17 John N. Murphy (D)	92,252	60.3
Mario D. Belardino (R, C)	60,812	39.7
18 Edward I. Koch (D, L)	125,117	69.9
Jane P. Langley (R)	52,379	29.3
19 Charles Rangel (D, R)	104,427	96.0
20 Bella S. Abzug (D)	85,558	55.7
Priscilla M. Ryan (L)	43,045	28.0
Annette Flatto Levy (R)	18,024	11.7
21 Herman Badillo (D, L)	48,441	86.9
Manuel A. Ramos (R)	6,366	11.4
22 Jonathan B. Bingham (D, L)	107,448	76.5
Charles A. Avarello (R, C)	33,045	23.5
23 Peter A. Peyser (R, C)	99,737	50.4
Richard L. Ottinger (D, L)	98,335	49.6
24 Ogden R. Reid (D, L)	107,979	52.2
Carl A. Vergari (R, C)	98,818	47.8
25 Hamilton Fish Jr. (R, C)	144,386	71.6
John M. Burns III (D)	54,271	26.9
26 Benjamin A. Gilman (R)	90,922	47.8
John G. Dow (D)	74,906	39.3
Yale Rapkin (C, NEW I)	24,569	12.9
27 Howard W. Robison (R)	114,902	62.2
David H. Blazer (D)	55,076	29.8
Patrick M. O'Neil (C)	9,521	5.2
28 Samuel S. Stratton (D)	182,395	80.0
John F. Ryan Jr. (R, C)	45,623	20.0
29 Carleton J. King (R, C)	148,170	69.9
Harold B. Gordon (D, L)	63,920	30.1
30 Robert C. McEwen (R, C)	114,193	66.0
Ernest J. Labaff (D, L)	58,788	34.0
31 Donald J. Mitchell (R, C)	98,454	51.0
Robert Castle (D)	75,513	39.1
Franklin Nichols (AP)	12,075	6.3
32 James M. Hanley (D)	111,481	57.2
Leonard C. Koldin (R, C)	83,451	42.8
33 William F. Walsh (R, C)	132,139	71.4
Clarence Kadys (D)	53,039	28.6
34 Frank Horton (R)	142,803	72.1
Jack Rubens (D)	46,509	23.5
35 Barber B. Conable (R)	127,298	67.9
Terence J. Spencer (D)	53,321	28.4
36 Henry P. Smith III (R, C)	110,238	57.3
Richard D. (Max) McCarthy (D, L)	82,095	42.7
37 Thaddeus J. Dulski (D, L)	114,603	72.2
William F. McLaughlin (R, C)	44,103	27.8
38 Jack F. Kemp (R, C)	156,967	73.2
Anthony P. Lo Russo (D, L)	57,585	26.8
39 James F. Hastings (R, C)	126,147	71.9
Wilbur White Jr (D)	49,253	28.1

NORTH CAROLINA

Candidates	Votes	%
1 Walter, B. Jones (D)	77,438	68.8
J. Jordan Bonner (R)	35,063	31.2
2 L. H. Fountain (D)	88,798	71.6
Erick P. Little (R)	35,193	28.4
3 David N. Henderson (D)	56,968	100.0

NORTH CAROLINA

Candidates	Votes	%
4 Ike F. Andrews (D)	72,972	50.3
R. Jack Hawke (R)	71,972	49.7
5 Wilmer D. Mizell (R)	101,375	64.8
Brooks Hays (D)	54,986	35.2
6 L. Richardson Preyer (D)	82,158	93.9
Lynwood Bullock (AM)	5,331	6.1
7 Charles Rose (D)	57,348	60.4
Jerry C. Scott (R)	36,726	38.7
8 Earl B. Ruth (R)	82,060	60.2
Richard Clark (D)	54,198	39.8
9 James G. Martin (R)	80,356	58.9
James Beatty (D)	56,171	41.1
10 James T. Broyhill (R)	103,119	72.6
Paul L. Beck (D)	39,025	27.5
11 Roy A. Taylor (D)	94,465	59.6
Jesse I. Ledbetter (R)	64,062	40.4

NORTH DAKOTA

	Candidates	Votes	%
AL	Mark Andrews (R)	195,360	72.7
	Richard Ista (D)	72,850	27.1

OHIO

Candidates	Votes	%
1 William J. Keating (R)	119,469	70.3
Karl F. Heiser (D)	50,575	29.7
2 Donald D. Clancy (R)	109,961	62.8
Penny Manes (D)	65,237	37.2
3 Charles W. Whalen Jr. (R)	111,253	76.2
John W. Lelack Jr. (D)	34,819	23.8
4 Tennyson Guyer (R)	109,612	62.7
Dimitri Nicholas (D)	65,216	37.3
5 Delbert L. Latta (R)	132,032	72.8
Bruce Edwards (D)	49,465	27.3
6 William H. Harsha (R)	128,394	100.0
7 Clarence J. Brown (R)	112,350	73.3
Dorothy Franke (I)	40,945	26.7
8 Walter E. Powell (R)	80,050	52.2
James D. Ruppert (D)	73,344	47.8
9 Thomas L. Ashley (D)	110,450	69.1
Joseph C. Richards (R)	49,388	30.9
10 Clarence E. Miller (R)	129,683	73.2
Robert H. Wheatley (D)	47,456	26.8
11 J. William Stanton (R)	106,841	68.2
Dennis M. Callahan (D)	49,891	31.8
12 Samuel L. Devine (R)	103,655	56.1
James W. Goodrich (D)	81,074	43.9
13 Charles A. Mosher (R)	111,242	68.2
John Michael Ryan (D)	51,991	31.9
14 John F. Seiberling (D)	135,068	74.4
Norman M. Holt (R)	46,490	25.6
15 Chalmers P. Wylie (R)	115,779	65.8
M. L. McGee (D)	55,314	31.4
16 Ralph S. Regula (R)	102,013	57.3
Virgil L. Musser (D)	75,929	42.7
17 John M. Ashbrook (R)	92,666	57.4
Raymond C. Beck (D)	62,512	38.7
18 Wayne L. Hays (D)	128,663	70.2
Robert Stewart (R)	54,572	29.8
19 Charles J. Carney (D)	109,979	64.0
Norman M. Parr (R)	61,934	36.0
20 James V. Stanton (D)	117,302	84.3
Thomas E. Vilt (R)	16,624	11.9
21 Louis Stokes (D)	99,190	81.1
James D. Johnson (R)	13,861	11.3
22 Charles A. Vanik (D)	126,462	63.9
Donald W. Gropp (R)	64,577	32.6
23 William E. Minshall (R)	98,594	49.4
Dennis J. Kucinich (D)	94,366	47.3

OKLAHOMA

Candidates	Votes	%
1 James R. Jones (D)	91,684	54.4
J. M. Hewgley (R)	73,786	43.8
2 Clem Rogers McSpadden (D)	105,110	71.1
Emery H. Toliver (R)	42,632	28.9
3 Carl Albert (D)	101,732	93.4
Harold J. Marshall (I)	7,242	6.7
4 Tom Steed (D)	85,578	71.3
William E. Crozier (R)	34,484	28.7
5 John Jarman (D)	69,710	60.4
Llewllyn L. Keller (R)	45,711	39.6
6 John N. Happy Camp (R)	113,567	72.7
William Patrick Schmitt (D)	42,663	27.3

OREGON

Candidates	Votes	%
1 Wendell Wyatt (R)	166,476	68.6
Ralph E. Bunch (D)	76,307	31.4
2 Al Ullman (D)	178,537	99.9
3 Edith Green (D)	141,086	62.4
Mike Walsh (R)	84,697	37.5
4 John Dellenback (R)	138,965	62.0
Charles O. Porter (D)	83,134	37.1

PENNSYLVANIA

Candidates	Votes	%
1 William A. Barrett (D)	118,953	66.1
Gus A. Pedicone (R)	59,807	33.2
2 Robert N. C. Nix (D)	107,509	70.2
Frederick D. Bryant (R)	45,753	29.9
3 William J. Green III (D)	101,144	63.3
Alfred Marroletti (R)	57,787	36.2
4 Joshua Eilberg (D)	129,105	55.9
William Pfender (R)	102,013	44.1
5 John H. Ware III (R)	121,346	64.7
Brower B. Yerger (D)	66,329	35.3
6 Gus Yatron (D)	119,557	64.5
Eugene W. Hubler (R)	64,076	34.6
7 Lawrence G. Williams (R)	122,622	60.6
Stuart S. Bowie (D)	79,578	39.4
8 Edward G. Biester (R)	115,799	64.4
Alan Williams (D)	64,069	35.6
9 E. G. Shuster (R)	95,913	61.7
Earl D. Collins (D)	59,386	38.2
10 Joseph M. McDade (R)	143,670	73.6
Stanley R. Coveleskie (D)	51,550	26.4
11 Daniel J. Flood (D)	124,336	68.3
Donald B. Ayers (R)	57,809	31.7
12 John P. Saylor (R)	122,628	68.2
Joseph Murphy (D)	57,314	31.9
13 R. Lawrence Coughlin (R)	139,085	66.6
Katherine L. Camp (D)	69,728	33.4
14 William S. Moorhead (D)	106,158	59.3
Roland S. Catarinella (R)	72,275	40.4
15 Fred B. Rooney (D)	99,937	60.8
Wardell F. Steigerwalt (R)	64,560	39.3
16 Edwin D. Eshleman (R)	112,292	73.5
Shirley S. Garrett (D)	40,534	26.5
17 Herman T. Schneebeli (R)	120,214	72.2
Donald J. Rippon (D)	44,202	26.6
18 H. John Heinz III (R)	144,521	72.8
Douglas Walgren (D)	53,929	27.2
19 George A. Goodling (R)	93,536	57.5
Richard P. Noll (D)	67,018	41.2
20 Joseph M. Gaydos (D)	117,933	61.5
William R. Hunt (R)	73,817	38.5
21 John H. Dent (D)	104,203	62.0
Thomas H. Young (R)	63,812	38.0
22 Thomas E. Morgan (D)	100,918	60.8
James R. Montgomery (R)	65,005	39.2
23 Albert W. Johnson (R)	90,615	56.5
Ernest A. Kassab (D)	69,813	43.5
24 Joseph P. Vigorito (D)	122,092	68.8
Alvin W. Levenhagen (R)	55,406	31.2
25 Frank M. Clark (D)	97,549	55.8
Gary A. Myers (R)	77,123	44.2

Special Election[1]

Candidates	Votes	%
27 William S. Conover (R)	28,647#	51.1
Douglas Walgren (D)	25,956#	46.3

RHODE ISLAND

Candidates	Votes	%
1 Fernand J. St.Germain (D)	120,705	62.4
John M. Feeley (R)	67,125	34.7
2 Robert O. Tiernan (D)	122,739	63.1
Donald P. Ryan (R)	77,661	40.0

SOUTH CAROLINA

Candidates	Votes	%
1 Mendel J. Davis (D)	61,625	54.5
J. Sidi Limehouse (R)	51,469	45.5
2 Floyd Spence (R)	83,543	99.9
3 William Jennings Bryan Dorn (D)	82,579	75.2
Roy Ethridge (R)	27,173	24.8
4 James R. Mann (D)	64,989	66.1
Wayne N. Whatley (R)	33,363	33.9
5 Tom S. Gettys (D)	66,343	60.9
B. Leonard Phillips (R)	42,620	39.1
6 Edward L. Young (R)	63,527	54.4
John W. Jenrette Jr (D)	53,324	45.6

SOUTH DAKOTA

Candidates	Votes	%
1 Frank E. Denholm (D)	94,442	60.5
John Vickerman (R)	61,589	39.5
2 James Abdnor (R)	79,546	54.9
Pat McKeever (D)	65,415	45.1

TENNESSEE

Candidates	Votes	%
1 James H. Quillen (R)	110,868	79.4
Bernard Cantor (D)	28,736	20.6
2 John J. Duncan (R)	109,925	100.0
3 LaMar Baker (R)	82,561	55.3
Howard Sompayrac (D)	62,536	41.9
4 Joe L. Evins (D)	93,042	81.1
Billy Joe Finney (R)	21,689	18.9
5 Richard Fulton (D)	93,555	62.6
Alfred Adams (R)	55,067	36.8
6 Robin L. Beard (R)	77,263	55.3
William R. Anderson (D)	60,254	43.1
7 Ed Jones (D)	92,419	70.5
Stockton Adkins (R)	38,726	29.5
8 Dan Kuykendall (R)	93,173	55.4
J. O. Patterson Jr. (D)	74,240	44.1

TEXAS

Candidates	Votes	%
1 Wright Patman (D)	93,891	100.0
2 Charles Wilson (D)	100,345	73.8
Charles O. Brightwell (R)	35,600	26.2
3 James Collins (R)	122,984	73.3
George A. Hughes (D)	44,708	26.7
4 Ray Roberts (D)	95,674	70.2
James Russell (R)	40,548	29.8
5 Alan Steelman (R)	74,932	55.7
Earle Cabell (D)	59,601	44.3
6 Olin E. Teague (D)	100,917	72.6
Carl Nigliazzo (R)	38,086	27.4
7 Bill Archer (R)	171,121	82.3
Jim Brady (D)	36,899	17.7
8 Bob Eckhardt (D)	73,909	64.6
Lewis Emerich (R)	39,686	34.7
9 Jack Brooks (D)	89,113	66.2
Randolph Reed (R)	45,462	33.8
10 J. J. Pickle (D)	130,973	91.2
Melissa Singler (SOC WORK)	12,682	8.8
11 W. R. Poage (D)	88,861	100.0
12 Jim Wright (D)	84,356	100.0
13 Bob Price (R)	87,084	54.8
Graham Purcell (D)	71,730	45.2
14 John Young (D)	89,725	100.0
15 Eligio de la Garza (D)	73,994	100.0
16 Richard C. White (D)	81,347	100.0
17 Omar Burleson (D)	95,122	100.0

1. Pennsylvania lost two House seats between the 1970 and 1972 general elections due to redistricting. The special election in the 27th District, held April 25, 1972, was for a partial term expiring Jan. 3, 1973, after which the district ceased to exist.

TEXAS

Candidates	Votes	%
18 Barbara C. Jordan (D)	85,672	80.6
Paul Merritt (R)	19,355	18.2
19 George Mahon (D)	97,084	100.0
20 Henry B. Gonzalez (D)	81,443	96.9
21 O. C. Fisher (D)	91,180	56.8
Douglas S. Harlan (R)	69,374	43.2
22 Bob Casey (D)	101,786	70.2
James Griffin (R)	42,094	29.0
23 Abraham Kazen (D)	72,799	100.0
24 Dale Milford (D)	91,054	65.1
Courtney Roberts (R)	48,853	34.9

UTAH

Candidates	Votes	%
1 K. Gunn McKay (D)	127,027	55.4
Robert K. Wolthuis (R)	96,296	42.0
2 Wayne Owens (D)	132,832	54.5
Sherman P. Lloyd (R)	107,185	44.0

VERMONT

Candidates	Votes	%
AL Richard W. Mallary (R)	120,924	65.0
William H. Meyer (D)	65,062	35.0

Special Election

Candidates	Votes	%
AL Richard W. Mallary (R)	39,903#	55.8
J. William O'Brien (D)	26,889#	37.6

VIRGINIA

Candidates	Votes	%
1 Thomas N. Downing (D)	100,901	78.1
Kenneth D. Wells (R)	28,310	21.9
2 G. William Whitehurst (R)	79,672	73.4
L. Charles Burlage (D)	28,803	26.6
3 David E. Satterfield III (D)	102,523	99.9

Candidates	Votes	%
4 Robert W. Daniel Jr. (R)	57,520	47.1
Robert E. Gibson (D)	45,776	37.5
Robert R. Hardy (I)	8,668	7.1
William E. Ward	6,172	5.1
5 W. C. (Dan) Daniel (D)	83,772	99.9
6 M. Caldwell Butler (R)	75,189	54.6
Willis N. Anderson (D)	53,928	39.2
Roy R. White (I)	8,531	6.2
7 J. Kenneth Robinson (R)	89,120	66.2
Murat Wills Williams (D)	45,513	33.8
8 Stanford E. Parris (R)	60,446	44.4
Robert F. Horan (D)	51,444	37.8
William R. Durland (I)	18,654	13.7
9 William C. Wampler (R)	98,178	71.9
Zane Dale Christian (D)	36,000	26.4
10 Joel T. Broyhill (R)	101,138	56.3
Harold O. Miller (D)	78,638	43.7

Special Election

Candidates	Votes	%
6 M. Caldwell Butler (R)	61,898	51.8
Willis M. Anderson (D)	47,588	39.8
Roy R. White (I)	10,098	8.4

WASHINGTON

Candidates	Votes	%
1 Joel Pritchard (R)	107,581	50.9
John Hempelmann (D)	104,959	49.7
2 Lloyd Meeds (D)	114,900	60.5
Bill Reams (R)	75,181	39.6
3 Julia Butler Hansen (D)	122,933	66.3
R. C. (Skip) McConkey (R)	62,564	33.7
4 Mike McCormack (D)	97,593	52.1
Stewart Bledsoe (R)	89,812	47.9
5 Thomas Foley (D)	150,580	81.3
Clarice L. R. Privette (R)	34,742	18.8
6 Floyd V. Hicks (D)	126,349	72.1
Thomas C. Lowry (R)	48,914	27.9

Candidates	Votes	%
7 Brock Adams (D)	140,307	85.4
J. J. (Tiny) Freeman (R)	19,889	12.1

WEST VIRGINIA

Candidates	Votes	%
1 Robert H. Mollohan (D)	130,062	69.4
George E. Kapnicky (R)	57,724	30.8
2 Harley O. Staggers (D)	128,286	70.0
David Dix (R)	54,949	30.0
3 John M. Slack (D)	118,346	63.7
T. David Higgins (R)	67,441	36.3
4 Ken Hechler (D)	100,600	61.0
Joe Neal (R)	64,242	39.0

WISCONSIN

Candidates	Votes	%
1 Les Aspin (D)	122,973	64.4
Merrill E. Stalbaum (R)	66,665	34.9
2 Robert W. Kastenmeier (D)	148,136	68.2
J. Michael Kelly (R)	68,167	31.4
3 Vernon W. Thomson (R)	112,905	54.7
Walter Thoresen (D)	91,953	44.6
4 Clement J. Zablocki (D)	149,078	75.7
Phillip D. Mrozinski (R)	45,003	22.8
5 Henry S. Reuss (D)	127,273	77.3
Frederick Van Hecke (R)	33,627	20.4
6 William A. Steiger (R)	130,701	65.8
James A. Adams (D)	63,643	32.0
7 David R. Obey (D)	135,385	62.8
Alvin E. O'Konski (R)	80,207	37.2
8 Harold V. Froehlich (R)	101,634	50.4
Robert J. Cornell (D)	97,795	48.5
9 Glenn R. Davis (R)	128,230	61.4
Ralph A. Fine (D)	76,585	36.7

WYOMING

Candidates	Votes	%
AL Teno Roncalio (D)	75,632	51.7
Bill Kidd (R)	70,667	48.3

1973 House Elections

ALASKA

Special Election

Candidates	Votes	%
AL Don Young (R)	35,044	51.4
Emil Notti (D)	33,123	48.6

ILLINOIS

Special Election

Candidates	Votes	%
7 Cardiss Collins (D)	33,875#	92.5

LOUISIANA

Special Election

Candidates	Votes	%
2 Corinne (Lindy) Boggs (D)	42,583	80.4
Robert E. Lee (R)	10,352	19.6

MARYLAND

Special Election

Candidates	Votes	%
1 Robert E. Bauman (R)	27,248	51.2
Frederick C. Malkus (D)	26,001	48.8

House Candidates Index

For an index of all House candidates listed in this section (pages 192-324), see pages 340-371. Instructions for use of the House Candidates Index appear on page 340.

1974 House Elections

ALABAMA

	Candidates	Votes	%
1	Jack Edwards (R)	60,710	59.5
	Augusta E. Wilson (D)	37,718	37.0
2	William L. Dickinson (R)	54,089	66.1
	Clair Chisler (D)	27,729	33.9
3	Bill Nichols (D)	63,582	95.9
4	Tom Bevill (D)	77,925	99.8
5	Robert E. Jones (D)	56,375	100.0
6	John Buchanan (R)	54,505	56.6
	Nina Miglionico (D)	39,444	41.0
7	Walter Flowers (D)	73,203	91.0
	Frank P. Walls (C)	5,175	6.4

ALASKA

		Votes	%
AL	Donald E. Young (R)	51,641	53.8
	William L. Hensley (D)	44,280	46.2

ARIZONA[1]

		Votes	%
1	John J. Rhodes (R)	63,847	51.1
	Patricia M. Fullinwider (D)	52,897	42.3
	J. M. Sanders (LLJ)	8,199	6.6
2	Morris K. Udall (D)	84,491	62.0
	Keith Dolgaard (R)	51,886	38.0
3	Sam Steiger (R)	71,497	51.1
	Pat Bosch (D)	68,424	48.9
4	John B. Conlan (R)	78,887	55.3
	Byron T. Brown (D)	63,677	44.7

ARKANSAS

		Votes	%
1	Bill Alexander (D)	104,247	90.6
	James Lawrence Dauer (R)	10,821	9.4
2	Wilbur D. Mills (D)	80,296	58.9
	Judy Petty (R)	56,038	41.1
3	John Paul Hammerschmidt (R)	89,324	51.8
	Bill Clinton (D)	83,030	48.2
4	Ray Thornton (D)		100.0

CALIFORNIA

		Votes	%
1	Harold T. Johnson (D)	138,082	85.8
	Dorothy D. Paradis (AIP)	22,881	14.2
2	Don H. Clausen (R)	95,929	53.0
	Oscar H. Klee (D)	77,232	42.7
3	John E. Moss (D)	122,134	72.3
	Ivaldo Lenci (R)	46,712	27.7
4	Robert L. Leggett (D)	101,152	100.0
5	John L. Burton (D)	88,909	59.6
	Thomas Caylor (R)	56,274	37.7
6	Phillip Burton (D)	85,712	71.3
	Tom Spinosa (R)	26,260	21.8
7	George Miller (D)	83,054	55.6
	Gary Fernandez (R)	66,325	44.4
8	Ronald V. Dellums (D)	95,041	56.6
	Jack Redden (R)	66,386	39.6
9	Fortney H. (Pete) Stark Jr. (D)	92,436	70.6
	Edson Adams (R)	38,521	29.4
10	Don Edwards (D)	87,978	77.0
	John M. Enright (R)	26,288	23.0
11	Leo J. Ryan (D)	106,429	75.8
	Brainard G. Merdinger (R)	29,861	21.3
12	Paul N. McCloskey Jr. (R)	103,692	69.1
	Gary G. Gillmor (D)	46,383	30.9
13	Norman Y. Mineta (D)	78,858	52.6
	George W. Milias (R)	63,573	42.4
14	John J. McFall (D)	102,180	70.9
	Charles M. Gibson (R)	34,775	24.1
15	B. F. Sisk (D)	80,897	72.0
	Carol O. Harner (R)	31,439	28.0
16	Burt L. Talcott (R)	76,356	49.2
	Julian Camacho (D)	74,168	47.8

	Candidates	Votes	%
17	John Krebs (D)	66,675	51.9
	Robert B. Mathias (R)	61,812	48.1
18	William M. Ketchum (R)	67,650	52.7
	George A. Seielstad (D)	60,733	47.3
19	Robert J. Lagomarsino (R)	84,249	56.3
	James D. Loebl (D)	65,469	43.7
20	Barry M. Goldwater Jr. (R)	98,410	61.2
	Arline Mathews (D)	62,326	38.8
21	James C. Corman (D)	88,915	73.5
	Mel Nadell (R)	32,038	26.5
22	Carlos J. Moorhead (R)	81,641	55.8
	Richard Hallin (D)	64,691	44.2
23	Thomas M. Rees (D)	122,076	71.4
	Jack E. Roberts (R)	48,826	28.6
24	Henry A. Waxman (D)	87,521	64.0
	Elliott Stone Graham (R)	45,128	33.0
25	Edward R. Roybal (D)	45,059	100.0
26	John H. Rousselot (R)	82,735	58.9
	Paul A. Conforti (D)	57,685	41.1
27	Alphonzo Bell (R)	102,663	63.9
	John Dalessio (D)	52,236	32.5
28	Yvonne Burke (D)	88,655	80.1
	Tom Neddy (R)	21,957	19.9
29	Augustus F. Hawkins (D)	47,204	100.0
30	George E. Danielson (D)	67,328	74.2
	John J. Perez (R)	23,383	25.8
31	Charles H. Wilson (D)	61,322	70.4
	Norman A. Hodges (R)	23,359	26.8
32	Glenn M. Anderson (D)	84,428	87.7
	Virgil V. Badalich (AIP)	8,874	9.2
33	Del Clawson (R)	72,471	53.4
	Robert E. White (D)	58,492	43.1
34	Mark W. Hannaford (D)	81,151	49.8
	Bill Bond (R)	75,426	46.3
35	Jim Lloyd (D)	61,903	50.3
	Victor V. Veysey (R)	61,168	49.7
36	George E. Brown Jr. (D)	69,766	62.6
	Jim Osgood (R)	35,938	32.3
	William E. Pasley (AIP)	5,711	5.1
37	Jerry L. Pettis (R)	89,849	63.2
	Bobby Ray Vincent (D)	46,783	32.9
38	Jerry M. Patterson (D)	68,335	54.0
	David Rehmann (R)	52,207	41.3
39	Charles E. Wiggins (R)	89,220	55.3
	William E. Farris (D)	65,170	40.4
40	Andrew J. Hinshaw (R)	116,449	63.4
	Roderick J. Wilson (D)	56,850	30.9
	Grayson L. Watkins (AIP)	10,498	5.7
41	Bob Wilson (R)	94,709	54.5
	Colleen M. O'Connor (D)	74,823	43.0
42	Lionel Van Deerlin (D)	70,579	69.9
	Wes Marden (R)	30,435	30.1
43	Clair W. Burgener (R)	115,275	60.4
	Bill Bandes (D)	75,629	39.6

Special Elections[2]

		Votes	%
6	John L. Burton (D)	73,114	50.0
	Thomas Caylor (R)	30,908	21.2
	Terence McGuire (D)	12,777	8.7
	Jean Wall (D)	8,501	5.8
	Sean McCarthy (R)	7,783	5.3
13	Robert J. Lagomarsino (R)	52,140	53.6
	James D. Loebl (D)	18,223	18.8
	James A. Browning (D)	7,536	7.8
	Roger I. Ikola (R)	6,155	6.3
	E.T. Jolicoeur (D)	5,786	6.0

COLORADO

		Votes	%
1	Patricia Schroeder (D)	94,583	58.5
	Frank K. Southworth (R)	66,046	40.8
2	Timothy W. Wirth (D)	93,728	51.9
	Donald G. Brotzman (R)	86,720	48.0
3	Frank E. Evans (D)	91,783	67.9
	E. Keith Records (R)	43,298	32.1

	Candidates	Votes	%
4	James P. Johnson (R)	82,982	52.0
	John S. Carroll (D)	76,452	48.0
5	William L. Armstrong (R)	85,326	57.7
	Ben Galloway (D)	56,888	38.5

CONNECTICUT

		Votes	%
1	William R. Cotter (D)	117,038	62.7
	F. Mac Buckley (R)	67,080	35.9
2	Christopher J. Dodd (D)	104,436	59.0
	Samuel B. Hellier (R)	69,380	39.2
3	Robert N. Giaimo (D)	114,316	65.1
	James F. Altham Jr. (R)	55,177	31.4
4	Stewart B. McKinney (R)	83,630	53.2
	James G. Kellis (D)	71,047	45.2
5	Ronald A. Sarasin (R)	94,998	50.4
	William R. Ratchford (D)	90,407	48.0
6	Anthony J. Moffett (D)	122,785	63.4
	Patsy J. Piscopo (R)	69,942	36.1

DELAWARE

		Votes	%
AL	Pierre S. duPont IV (R)	93,826	58.5
	James R. Soles (D)	63,490	39.6

FLORIDA

		Votes	%
1	Robert L. F. Sikes (D)		100.0
2	Don Fuqua (D)		100.0
3	Charles E. Bennett (D)		100.0
4	Bill Chappell Jr. (D)	74,720	68.2
	Warren A. Hauser (R)	34,867	31.8
5	Richard Kelly (R)	74,954	52.8
	JoAnn Saunders (D)	63,610	44.8
6	C. W. Bill Young (R)	109,302	75.8
	Herbert M. Monrose (D)	34,886	24.2
7	Sam Gibbons (D)		100.0
8	James A. Haley (D)	63,283	56.7
	Joe Z. Lovingood (R)	48,240	43.3
9	Louis Frey Jr. (R)	86,226	76.7
	William D. Rowland (D)	26,255	23.3
10	L. A. (Skip) Bafalis (R)	117,368	73.7
	Evelyn Tucker (D)	41,925	26.3
11	Paul G. Rogers (D)		100.0
12	J. Herbert Burke (R)	61,191	51.0
	Charles Friedman (D)	58,899	49.0
13	William Lehman (D)		100.0
14	Claude Pepper (D)	45,479	69.1
	Michael A. Carricarte (R)	20,383	30.9
15	Dante B. Fascell (D)	68,064	70.5
	S. Peter Capua (R)	28,444	29.5

GEORGIA

		Votes	%
1	Ronald B. (Bo) Ginn (D)	64,958	86.1
	Bill Gowan (R)	10,485	13.9
2	Dawson Mathis (D)	59,514	100.0
3	Jack Brinkley (D)	67,438	87.7
	Carl Savage (R)	9,453	12.3
4	Elliott H. Levitas (D)	61,211	55.1
	Ben B. Blackburn (R)	49,922	44.9
5	Andrew Young (D)	69,221	71.6
	Wyman C. Lowe (R)	27,397	28.3
6	John J. Flynt Jr. (D)	49,082	51.5
	Newt Gingrich (R)	46,308	48.5
7	Lawrence P. McDonald (D)	47,993	50.3
	Quincy Collins (R)	47,450	49.7
8	W. S. (Bill) Stuckey Jr. (D)	59,182	100.0
9	Phil M. Landrum (D)	64,096	74.8
	Ronald D. Reeves (R)	21,540	25.2
10	Robert G. Stephens Jr. (D)	45,843	68.4
	Gary Pleger (R)	21,214	31.6

Footnotes, see p. 266.

HAWAII

	Candidates	Votes	%
1	Spark M. Matsunaga (D)	71,552	59.3
	William B. Paul (R)	49,065	40.7
2	Patsy T. Mink (D)	86,916	62.6
	Carla W. Coray (R)	51,894	37.4

IDAHO

	Candidates	Votes	%
1	Steven D. Symms (R)	75,414	58.3
	J. Ray Cox (D)	54,001	41.7
2	George V. Hansen (R)	67,274	55.7
	Max Hanson (D)	53,599	44.3

ILLINOIS

	Candidates	Votes	%
1	Ralph H. Metcalfe (D)	75,206	93.7
	Oscar H. Haynes (R)	4,399	5.5
2	Morgan F. Murphy (D)	65,812	87.5
	James Ginderske (R)	9,386	12.5
3	Martin A. Russo (D)	65,336	52.6
	Robert P. Hanrahan (R)	58,891	47.4
4	Edward J. Derwinski (R)	68,428	59.2
	Ronald A. Rodger (D)	47,096	40.8
5	John C. Kluczynski (D)	93,069	86.0
	William H. G. Toms (R)	15,108	14.0
6	Henry J. Hyde (R)	66,027	53.4
	Edward V. Hanrahan (D)	57,654	46.6
7	Cardiss Collins (D)	63,962	87.9
	Donald L. Metzger (R)	8,800	12.1
8	Dan Rostenkowski (D)	75,011	86.5
	Salvatore E. Oddo (R)	11,664	13.5
9	Sidney R. Yates (D)	93,864	100.0
10	Abner J. Mikva (D)	83,457	50.9
	Samuel H. Young (R)	80,597	49.1
11	Frank Annunzio (D)	102,541	72.4
	Mitchell G. Zadrozny (R)	39,182	27.6
12	Philip M. Crane (R)	70,731	61.1
	Betty C. Spence (D)	45,049	38.9
13	Robert McClory (R)	51,405	54.5
	Stanley W. Beetham (D)	42,903	45.5
14	John N. Erlenborn (R)	77,718	66.6
	Robert H. Renshaw (D)	38,981	33.4
15	Tim L. Hall (D)	61,912	52.0
	Clifford D. Carlson (R)	54,278	45.6
16	John B. Anderson (R)	65,175	55.5
	Marshall Hungness (D)	33,724	28.7
	W. John Schade Jr. (IND)	18,580	15.8
17	George M. O'Brien (R)	59,984	51.5
	John J. Houlihan (D)	56,541	48.5
18	Robert H. Michel (R)	71,681	54.8
	Stephen L. Nordvall (D)	59,225	45.2
19	Tom Railsback (R)	84,049	65.3
	Jim Gende (D)	44,677	34.7
20	Paul Findley (R)	84,426	54.8
	Peter F. Mack (D)	69,551	45.2
21	Edward R. Madigan (R)	78,640	65.8
	Richard N. Small (D)	40,896	34.2
22	George E. Shipley (D)	97,921	59.8
	William A. Young (R)	65,731	40.2
23	Melvin Price (D)	78,347	80.5
	Scott R. Randolph (R)	18,987	19.5
24	Paul Simon (D)	108,417	59.6
	Val Oshel (R)	73,634	40.4

INDIANA

	Candidates	Votes	%
1	Ray J. Madden (D)	71,759	68.6
	Joseph D. Harkin (R)	32,793	31.4
2	Floyd J. Fithian (D)	101,856	61.1
	Earl F. Landgrebe (R)	64,950	38.9
3	John Brademas (D)	89,306	64.1
	Virginia R. Black (R)	50,116	35.9
4	J. Edward Roush (D)	83,604	51.9
	Walter P. Helmke (R)	75,031	46.5
5	Elwood Hillis (R)	95,331	56.6
	William T. Sebree (D)	73,239	43.4
6	David W. Evans (D)	78,414	52.4
	William G. Bray (R)	71,134	47.6

	Candidates	Votes	%
7	John T. Myers (R)	100,128	57.1
	Elden C. Tipton (D)	73,802	42.1
8	Philip H. Hayes (D)	100,121	53.4
	Roger H. Zion (R)	87,296	46.6
9	Lee H. Hamilton (D)	117,648	71.1
	Delson Cox Jr. (R)	47,881	28.9
10	Philip R. Sharp (D)	85,418	54.4
	David W. Dennis (R)	71,701	45.6
11	Andrew Jacobs Jr. (D)	81,508	52.5
	William H. Hudnut III (R)	73,793	47.5

IOWA

	Candidates	Votes	%
1	Edward Mezvinsky (D)	75,687	54.4
	James A. S. Leach (R)	63,540	45.6
2	Michael T. Blouin (D)	73,416	51.1
	Tom Riley (R)	69,088	48.1
3	Charles E. Grassley (R)	77,468	50.8
	Stephen J. Rapp (D)	74,895	49.2
4	Neal Smith (D)	96,755	63.9
	Chuck Dick (R)	53,756	35.5
5	Tom Harkin (D)	81,186	51.1
	William J. Scherle (R)	77,683	48.9
6	Berkley Bedell (D)	86,315	54.6
	Wiley Mayne (R)	71,695	45.4

KANSAS

	Candidates	Votes	%
1	Keith G. Sebelius (R)	101,565	58.4
	Donald C. Smith (D)	57,326	33.0
	Thelma Morgan (A)	13,009	7.5
2	Martha E. Keys (D)	84,864	55.0
	John C. Peterson (R)	67,650	43.9
3	Larry Winn Jr. (R)	89,664	62.9
	Samuel J. Wells (D)	49,976	35.0
4	Garner E. Shriver (R)	70,401	48.8
	Bert Chaney (D)	61,210	42.5
	John S. Stevens (A)	12,520	8.7
5	Joe Skubitz (R)	88,646	55.2
	Franklin D. Gaines (D)	72,024	44.8

KENTUCKY

	Candidates	Votes	%
1	Carroll Hubbard Jr. (D)	70,723	78.2
	Charles T. Banken Jr. (R)	16,937	18.7
2	William H. Natcher (D)	56,502	73.0
	Art Eddleman (R)	18,312	23.7
3	Romano L. Mazzoli (D)	75,571	69.7
	Vincent N. Barclay (R)	28,813	26.6
4	M. G. (Gene) Snyder (R)	63,845	51.7
	Kyle Hubbard (D)	59,539	48.3
5	Tim Lee Carter (R)	66,709	68.2
	Lyle L. Willis (D)	28,706	29.3
6	John B. Breckinridge (D)	63,010	72.1
	Thomas F. Rogers III (R)	21,039	24.1
7	Carl D. Perkins (D)	71,221	75.6
	Granville Thomas (R)	22,982	24.4

LOUISIANA [3]

	Candidates	Votes	%
1	F. Edward Hebert (D)	48,452	100.0
2	Corinne C. Boggs (D)	58,802	81.8
	Diane Morphos (R)	9,632	14.6
3	David C. Treen (R)	55,574	58.5
	Charles Grisbaum Jr. (D)	39,412	41.5
4	Joe D. Waggonner Jr. (D)	47,371	100.0
5	Otto E. Passman (D)	43,068	100.0
6	W. Henson Moore (R)		
	Jeff LaCaze (D)		
7	John B. Breaux (D)	59,406	89.3
	Jeremy J. Millett (IND)	7,131	10.7
8	Gillis W. Long (D)	41,704	100.0

MAINE [4]

	Candidates	Votes	%
1	David F. Emery (R)	94,203	50.2
	Peter N. Kyros (D)	93,524	49.8

	Candidates	Votes	%
2	William S. Cohen (R)	118,154	71.4
	Markham L. Gartley (D)	47,399	28.6

MARYLAND

	Candidates	Votes	%
1	Robert E. Bauman (R)	59,570	53.0
	Thomas J. Hatem (D)	52,853	47.0
2	Clarence D. Long (D)	103,222	77.1
	John M. Seney (R)	30,639	22.9
3	Paul S. Sarbanes (D)	93,218	83.8
	William H. Mathews (R)	17,967	16.2
4	Marjorie S. Holt (R)	61,208	58.1
	Fred L. Wineland (D)	44,059	41.9
5	Gladys N. Spellman (D)	45,211	52.6
	John B. Burcham Jr. (R)	40,805	47.4
6	Goodloe E. Byron (D)	90,882	73.7
	Elton R. Wampler (R)	32,416	26.3
7	Parren J. Mitchell (D)	43,252	100.0
8	Gilbert Gude (R)	104,675	65.9
	Sidney Kramer (D)	54,112	34.1

MASSACHUSETTS

	Candidates	Votes	%
1	Silvio O. Conte (R)	107,285	71.1
	Thomas R. Manning (D)	43,524	28.9
2	Edward P. Boland (D)	105,763	100.0
3	Joseph D. Early (D)	78,244	49.5
	David J. Lionett (R)	60,717	38.4
	Douglas J. Rowe (IND)	19,018	12.0
4	Robert F. Drinan (D)	77,286	50.8
	Jon Rotenberg (IND)	52,785	34.7
	Alvin Mandell (R)	21,922	14.4
5	Paul E. Tsongas (D)	99,518	60.6
	Paul W. Cronin (R)	64,596	39.4
6	Michael J. Harrington (D)	119,278	100.0
7	Torbert H. Macdonald (D)	122,165	79.8
	James J. Murphy (IND)	30,959	20.2
8	Thomas P. O'Neill Jr. (D)	107,042	87.9
	James Kiggin (USLP)	8,363	6.9
	Laura Ross (COM)	6,421	5.3
9	John Joseph Moakley (D)	94,804	89.3
	L. R. Sherman (USLP)	11,344	10.7
10	Margaret M. Heckler (R)	99,993	64.2
	Barry F. Monahan (D)	55,871	35.8
11	James A. Burke (D)	125,978	100.0
12	Gerry E. Studds (D)	138,779	74.8
	J. Alan MacKay (R)	46,787	25.2

MICHIGAN

	Candidates	Votes	%
1	John Conyers Jr. (D)	97,620	90.7
	Walter F. Girardot (R)	9,358	8.7
2	Marvin L. Esch (R)	72,245	52.3
	John S. Reuther (D)	62,755	45.4
3	Garry Brown (R)	70,151	51.2
	Paul H. Todd Jr. (D)	65,212	47.6
4	Edward Hutchinson (R)	64,731	53.1
	Richard E. Daugherty (D)	55,469	45.5
5	Richard F. Vander Veen (D)	80,778	52.6
	Paul G. Goebel Jr. (R)	66,659	43.4
6	Bob Carr (D)	73,956	49.3
	Clifford W. Taylor (R)	73,309	48.9
7	Donald W. Riegle Jr. (D)	81,014	64.7
	Robert E. Eastman (R)	41,603	33.2
8	Bob Traxler (D)	77,795	54.8
	James M. Sparling Jr. (R)	61,578	43.4
9	Guy A. Vander Jagt (R)	87,551	56.6
	Norman C. Halbower (R)	65,235	42.1
10	Elford A. Cederberg (R)	78,897	53.4
	Samuel D. Marble (D)	67,467	45.9
11	Philip E. Ruppe (R)	83,293	50.9
	Francis D. Brouillette (D)	79,793	48.8
12	James G. O'Hara (D)	89,822	72.2
	Eugene J. Tyza (R)	34,293	27.6
13	Charles C. Diggs Jr. (D)	63,246	87.4
	George E. McCall (R)	8,036	11.1
14	Lucien N. Nedzi (D)	93,973	71.2
	Herbert O. Steiger (R)	35,723	27.1
15	William D. Ford (D)	86,601	78.1
	Jack A. Underwood (R)	23,028	20.8

Footnotes, see p. 266.

MICHIGAN

Candidates	Votes	%
16 John D. Dingell (D)	95,834	77.7
Wallace D. English (R)	25,248	20.5
17 William M. Brodhead (D)	94,242	69.5
Kenneth C. Gallagher (R)	39,856	29.4
18 James J. Blanchard (D)	83,523	58.7
Robert J. Huber (R)	57,133	40.2
19 William S. Broomfield (R)	86,846	62.9
George F. Montgomery (D)	50,924	36.9

Special Elections

	Votes	%
5 Richard F. Vander Veen (D)	53,083	50.9
Robert Vander Laan (R)	46,160	44.3
8 Bob Traxler (D)	59,993	51.5
James M. Sparling Jr. (R)	56,548	48.5

MINNESOTA

	Votes	%
1 Albert H. Quie (R)	95,138	62.6
Uric Scott (D)	56,868	37.4
2 Tom Hagedorn (R)	88,071	53.1
Steve Babcock (D)	77,780	46.9
3 Bill Frenzel (R)	83,325	60.4
Bob Riggs (D)	54,630	39.6
4 Joseph E. Karth (D)	95,437	76.0
Joseph A. Rheinberger (R)	30,083	24.0
5 Donald M. Fraser (D)	90,012	73.8
Phil Ratte (R)	30,146	24.7
6 Richard Nolan (D)	96,465	55.4
Jon Grunseth (R)	77,797	44.6
7 Bob Bergland (D)	129,207	75.0
Dan Reber (R)	43,045	25.0
8 James L. Oberstar (D)	104,740	62.0
Jerome Arnold (R)	44,298	26.2
William R. Ojala (EJ)	16,932	10.0

MISSISSIPPI

	Votes	%
1 Jamie L. Whitten (D)	39,158	88.2
Jack Benney (IND)	5,250	11.8
2 David R. Bowen (D)	37,909	66.1
Ben F. Hilbun Jr. (R)	15,876	27.7
H. B. Wells (IND)	3,573	6.2
3 G. V. (Sonny) Montgomery (D)	43,020	100.0
4 Thad Cochran (R)	62,634	70.2
Kenneth L. Dean (D)	25,699	28.8
5 Trent Lott (R)	52,489	73.0
Walter W. Murphey (D)	10,333	14.4
Claudia Mertz (IND)	6,404	8.9

MISSOURI

	Votes	%
1 William (Bill) Clay (D)	61,933	68.3
Arthur O. Martin (R)	28,707	31.7
2 James W. Symington (D)	85,977	61.0
Howard C. Ohlendorf (R)	55,026	39.0
3 Leonor K. Sullivan (D)	96,201	74.3
Jo Ann P. Raisch (R)	31,489	24.3
4 William J. Randall (D)	82,447	67.9
Claude Patterson (R)	39,055	32.1
5 Richard Bolling (D)	57,081	69.1
John J. McDonough (R)	24,669	29.9
6 Jerry Litton (D)	101,609	78.9
Grover H. Speers (R)	27,147	21.1
7 Gene Taylor (R)	79,787	52.3
Richard L. Franks (D)	72,653	47.7
8 Richard H. Ichord (D)	86,595	69.9
James A. Noland Jr. (R)	37,369	30.1
9 William L. Hungate (D)	87,546	66.4
Milton Bischof Jr. (R)	44,318	33.6
10 Bill D. Burlison (D)	77,677	72.8
Truman Farrow (R)	29,050	27.2

MONTANA

Candidates	Votes	%
1 Max S. Baucus (D)	74,304	54.8
Richard G. Shoup (R)	61,309	45.2
2 John Melcher (D)	74,680	63.0
John K. McDonald (R)	43,853	37.0

NEBRASKA

	Votes	%
1 Charles Thone (R)	82,353	53.3
Hess Dyas (D)	72,099	46.7
2 John Y. McCollister (R)	72,731	55.2
Daniel C. Lynch (D)	59,142	44.8
3 Virginia Smith (R)	80,992	50.2
Wayne W. Ziebarth (D)	80,255	49.8

NEVADA

	Votes	%
AL James Santini (D)	93,665	55.8
David Towell (R)	61,182	36.4
Joel F. Hansen (IA)	13,119	7.8

NEW HAMPSHIRE

	Votes	%
1 Norman E. D'Amours (D)	58,388	52.1
David A. Banks (R)	53,610	47.9
2 James C. Cleveland (R)	69,068	64.2
Helen L. Bliss (D)	38,463	35.8

NEW JERSEY

	Votes	%
1 James J. Florio (D)	80,768	57.5
John E. Hunt (R)	54,069	38.5
2 William J. Hughes (D)	109,763	57.3
Charles W. Sandman Jr. (R)	79,064	41.3
3 James J. Howard (D)	105,979	68.9
Kenneth W. Clark (R)	45,932	29.8
4 Frank Thompson Jr. (D)	82,195	66.8
Henry J. Keller (R)	40,797	33.2
5 Millicent Fenwick (R)	81,498	53.4
Frederick M. Bohen (D)	66,380	43.5
6 Edwin B. Forsythe (R)	81,190	52.5
Charles B. Yates (D)	70,353	45.5
7 Andrew Maguire (D)	79,808	49.7
William B. Widnall (R)	71,377	44.4
Milton Gralla (IND)	9,520	5.9
8 Robert A. Roe (D)	83,724	73.9
Herman Schmidt (R)	27,839	24.6
9 Henry Helstoski (D)	99,592	64.5
Harold A. Pareti (R)	50,859	32.9
10 Peter W. Rodino Jr. (D)	53,094	81.0
John R. Taliaferro (R)	9,936	15.2
11 Joseph G. Minish (D)	98,957	69.2
William B. Grant (R)	42,036	29.4
12 Matthew J. Rinaldo (R)	92,829	65.0
Adam K. Levin (D)	46,246	32.4
13 Helen S. Meyner (D)	86,043	57.3
Joseph J. Maraziti (R)	64,166	42.7
14 Dominick V. Daniels (D)	85,438	79.9
Claire J. Sheridan (R)	17,231	16.1
15 Edward J. Patten (D)	92,593	71.0
E. J. Hammesfahr (R)	35,875	27.5

NEW MEXICO

	Votes	%
1 Manuel Lujan Jr. (R)	106,268	58.6
Robert A. Mondragon (D)	71,968	39.7
2 Harold Runnels (D)	90,127	66.7
Donald W. Trubey (R)	43,045	31.9

NEW YORK

	Votes	%
1 Otis G. Pike (D-L)	101,130	65.0
Donald R. Sallah (R)	44,513	28.6
Seth C. Morgan (C)	10,038	6.4
2 Thomas J. Downey (D)	58,289	48.8
James R. Grover Jr. (R)	53,344	44.7
Neil Greene (C)	7,818	6.5
3 Jerome A. Ambro Jr. (D)	76,383	51.8
Angelo D. Roncalio (R-C)	67,986	46.1
4 Norman F. Lent (R-C)	85,382	53.6
Franklin Ornstein (D-L)	73,822	46.4
5 John W. Wydler (R-C)	91,677	54.2
Allard K. Lowenstein (D-L)	77,356	45.8
6 Lester L. Wolff (D-L)	101,237	66.7
Edythe Layne (R-C)	50,528	33.3
7 Joseph P. Addabbo (D-R-L)	83,972	100.0
8 Benjamin S. Rosenthal (D-L)	90,200	79.0
Albert Lemishow (R-C)	23,980	21.0
9 James J. Delaney (D-R-C)	92,231	93.0
Theodore E. Garrison (L)	6,924	7.0
10 Mario Biaggi (D-R)	75,375	82.4
Francis L. McHugh (C)	10,250	11.2
John P. Hagan (L)	5,797	6.3
11 James H. Scheuer (D)	62,388	72.2
E. G. Desborough (R)	12,297	14.2
Christopher Acer (C)	7,181	8.3
Tibby Blum (L)	4,485	5.2
12 Shirley Chisholm (D-L)	26,468	80.2
Francis J. Voyticky (R)	4,577	13.9
13 Stephen J. Solarz (D-L)	91,008	81.8
Jack N. Dobosh (R)	20,229	18.2
14 Frederick W. Richmond (D)	33,195	71.3
Michael Carbajal Jr. (R)	5,360	11.5
Donald H. Elliott (L)	6,186	13.3
15 Leo C. Zeferetti (D-C)	53,733	58.4
Austen D. Canade (R)	34,814	37.9
16 Elizabeth Holtzman (D-L)	74,010	78.9
Joseph L. Gentili (R-C)	19,806	21.1
17 John M. Murphy (D)	63,805	57.7
Frank J. Biondolillo (R)	28,266	25.6
Jerome Kretchmer (L)	10,622	9.6
Michael Ajello (C)	7,808	7.1
18 Edward I. Koch (D-L)	91,985	76.7
John Boogaerts Jr. (R)	22,560	18.8
19 Charles B. Rangel (D-R-L)	63,146	96.9
20 Bella S. Abzug (D-L)	76,074	78.7
Stephen Posner (R)	15,053	15.6
21 Herman Badillo (D-L)	28,025	96.7
22 Jonathan B. Bingham (D-L)	77,157	85.1
Robert Black (R)	8,142	9.0
John DiGiovanni (C)	5,333	5.9
23 Peter A. Peyser (R-C)	80,361	57.6
W. S. Greenawalt (D-L)	59,108	42.4
24 Richard L. Ottinger (D)	82,542	57.8
Charles J. Stephens (R-C)	60,180	42.2
25 Hamilton Fish Jr. (R-C)	103,796	65.3
Nicholas B. Angell (D)	53,357	33.6
26 Benjamin A. Gilman (R)	81,562	54.0
John G. Dow (D-L)	58,161	38.5
Thomas Moore (C)	11,345	7.5
27 Matthew F. McHugh (D-L)	83,562	52.8
Alfred J. Libous (R)	68,273	43.1
28 Samuel S. Stratton (D)	156,439	80.6
Wayne E. Wagner (R)	33,493	17.3
29 Edward W. Pattison (D-L)	100,324	54.5
Carleton J. King (R-C)	83,768	45.5
30 Robert C. McEwen (R-C)	78,117	55.0
Roger W. Tubby (D-L)	63,893	45.0
31 Donald J. Mitchell (R-C)	94,319	59.6
Donald J. Reile (D)	59,639	37.7
32 James M. Hanley (D)	88,660	59.1
William E. Bush (R-C)	61,379	40.9
33 William F. Walsh (R)	97,380	65.3
Robert H. Bockman (D)	45,043	30.2
34 Frank Horton (R)	105,585	67.5
Irene Gossin (D)	45,408	29.0
35 Barber B. Conable Jr. (R)	90,269	56.8
Margaret Costanza (D)	63,012	39.6
36 John J. LaFalce (D-L)	90,498	59.6
Russell A. Rourke (R-C)	61,442	40.4
37 Henry J. Nowak (D-L)	84,064	75.0
Joseph R. Bala (R-C)	27,531	24.6
38 Jack F. Kemp (R-C)	126,687	72.1
Barbara C. Wicks (D-L)	48,929	27.9
39 James F. Hastings (R)	87,321	60.2
W. L. Parment (D-L)	53,866	37.1

NORTH CAROLINA

Candidates	Votes	%
1 Walter B. Jones (D)	55,323	77.5
Harry McMullan (R)	16,097	22.5
2 L. H. Fountain (D)	52,786	100.0
3 David N. Henderson (D)	50,931	100.0
4 Ike F. Andrews (D)	62,600	64.7
Ward Purrington (R)	33,521	34.6
5 Stephen L. Neal (D)	64,634	52.0
Wilmer Mizell (R)	59,182	47.6
6 Richardson Preyer (D)	56,507	63.7
R. S. Ritchie (R)	31,906	35.9
7 Charles G. Rose III (D)	49,780	100.0
8 W. G. (Bill) Hefner (D)	61,591	57.0
Earl B. Ruth (R)	46,500	43.0
9 James G. Martin (R)	51,032	54.4
Milton Short (D)	41,387	44.1
10 James T. Broyhill (R)	63,382	54.4
Jack L. Rhyne (D)	53,131	45.6
11 Roy A. Taylor (D)	89,163	66.0
Albert F. Gilman (R)	45,983	34.0

NORTH DAKOTA

Candidates	Votes	%
AL Mark Andrews (R)	130,184	55.7
Byron Dorgan (D)	103,504	44.3

OHIO

Candidates	Votes	%
1 Willis D. Gradison Jr. (R)	70,284	50.9
Thomas A. Luken (D)	67,685	49.1
2 Donald D. Clancy (R)	71,512	53.4
Edward W. Wolterman (D)	62,530	46.6
3 Charles W. Whalen Jr. (R)	82,159	100.0
4 Tennyson Guyer (R)	81,674	61.5
James L. Gehrlich (D)	51,065	38.5
5 Delbert L. Latta (R)	89,161	62.5
Bruce Edwards (D)	53,391	37.5
7 William H. Harsha (R)	93,400	68.2
Lloyd Allen Wood (D)	42,316	31.2
6 Clarence J. Brown (R)	73,503	60.5
Patrick L. Nelson (D)	34,828	28.7
Dorothy Franke (IND)	13,088	10.8
8 Thomas N. Kindness (R)	51,097	42.4
T. Edward Strinko (D)	45,701	38.0
Don Gingerich (IND)	23,616	19.6
9 Thomas L. Ashley (D)	64,831	52.8
C. S. Finkbeiner Jr. (R)	57,892	47.2
10 Clarence E. Miller (R)	100,521	70.4
H. Kent Bumpass (D)	42,333	29.6
11 J. William Stanton (R)	79,756	60.5
Michael D. Coffey (D)	52,017	39.5
12 Samuel L. Devine (R)	73,303	50.9
Fran Ryan (D)	70,818	49.1
13 Charles A. Mosher (R)	72,881	57.5
Fred M. Ritenauer (D)	53,766	42.5
14 John F. Seiberling (D)	93,931	75.4
Mark Figetakis (R)	30,603	24.6
15 Chalmers P. Wylie (R)	79,376	61.5
Mike McGee (D)	49,683	38.5
16 Ralph S. Regula (R)	92,986	65.6
John G. Freedom (D)	48,754	34.4
17 John M. Ashbrook (R)	70,708	52.7
David D. Noble (D)	63,342	47.3
18 Wayne L. Hays (D)	90,447	65.6
Ralph H. Romig (R)	47,385	34.4
19 Charles J. Carney (D)	97,709	72.7
James L. Ripple (R)	36,649	27.3
20 James V. Stanton (D)	86,405	86.9
Robert A. Frantz (R)	12,991	13.1
21 Louis Stokes (D)	58,969	82.0
Bill Mack (R)	12,986	18.0
22 Charles A. Vanik (D)	112,671	78.7
William J. Franz (R)	30,585	21.3
23 Ronald M. Mottl (D)	53,338	34.8
George E. Mastics (R)	46,810	30.5
Dennis J. Kucinich (IND)	45,186	29.4

Special Election

Candidates	Votes	%
1 Thomas A. Luken (D)	55,134	51.9
Willis D. Gradison Jr. (R)	51,063	48.1

OKLAHOMA

Candidates	Votes	%
1 James R. Jones (D)	88,159	67.9
George Alfred Mizer Jr. (R)	41,697	32.1
2 Theodore Risenhoover (D)	78,046	59.1
Ralph F. Keen (R)	54,110	40.9
3 Carl Albert (D)		100.0
4 Tom Steed (D)		100.0
5 John Jarman (D)	52,107	51.7
M. H. Edwards (R)	48,705	48.3
6 Glenn English (D)	76,392	53.2
John N. Happy Camp (R)	63,731	44.4

OREGON

Candidates	Votes	%
1 Les AuCoin (D)	114,629	56.0
Diarmuid O'Scannlain (R)	89,848	43.9
2 Al Ullman (D)	140,963	78.1
Kenneth Brown (R)	39,441	21.9
3 Robert Duncan (D)	129,290	70.4
John Piacentini (R)	54,080	29.5
4 James Weaver (D)	97,580	52.9
John Dellenback (R)	86,950	47.1

PENNSYLVANIA

Candidates	Votes	%
1 William A. Barrett (D)	96,988	75.8
Russell M. Nigro (R)	29,772	23.3
2 Robert N. C. Nix (D)	75,033	74.0
Jesse W. Woods Jr. (R)	26,353	26.0
3 William J. Green III (D)	84,675	75.4
Richard P. Colbert (R)	27,692	24.6
4 Joshua Eilberg (D)	123,952	71.0
Isadore Einhorn (R)	50,688	29.0
5 Richard T. Schulze (R)	83,526	59.6
Leo D. McDermott (D)	56,626	40.4
6 Gus Yatron (D)	111,127	74.6
Stephen Postupack (R)	35,805	24.0
7 Robert W. Edgar (D)	89,680	55.3
Stephen J. McEwen Jr. (R)	70,894	43.7
8 Edward G. Biester Jr. (R)	75,313	56.3
William B. Moyer (D)	54,815	40.9
9 E. G. Shuster (R)	73,881	56.5
Robert D. Ford (D)	56,844	43.5
10 Joseph M. McDade (R)	100,793	64.9
Thomas J. Hanlon (D)	54,401	35.1
11 Daniel J. Flood (D)	111,572	74.5
Richard A. Muzyka (R)	38,106	25.5
12 John P. Murtha (D)	89,193	58.1
Harry M. Fox (R)	64,414	41.9
13 R. Lawrence Coughlin (R)	98,985	62.5
Lawrence H. Curry (D)	59,433	37.5
14 William S. Moorhead (D)	93,169	77.4
Zachary Taylor Davis (R)	27,116	22.5
15 Fred B. Rooney (D)	85,905	100.0
16 Edwin D. Eshleman (R)	73,130	63.5
Michael J. Minney (D)	40,273	35.0
17 Herman T. Schneebeli (R)	70,274	52.1
Peter C. Wambach (D)	64,576	47.9
18 H. John Heinz III (R)	107,723	72.1
Francis J. McArdle (D)	41,706	27.9
19 William F. Goodling (R)	66,417	51.4
Arthur L. Berger (D)	61,414	47.6
20 Joseph M. Gaydos (D)	112,237	81.7
Joseph J. Anderko (R)	25,129	18.3
21 John H. Dent (D)	88,701	69.9
C. L. Sconing (R)	38,111	30.1
22 Thomas E. Morgan (D)	83,654	63.6
J. R. Montgomery (R)	41,706	31.7
23 Albert W. Johnson (R)	67,192	52.7
Yates Mast (D)	60,211	47.3
24 Joseph P. Vigorito (D)	76,920	58.6
Clement R. Scalzitti (R)	54,277	41.4
25 Gary A. Myers (R)	74,645	53.8
Frank M. Clark (D)	64,049	46.2

Special Election

Candidates	Votes	%
12 John P. Murtha (D)	60,538	49.9
Harry M. Fox (R)	60,416	49.8

RHODE ISLAND

Candidates	Votes	%
1 Fernand J. St Germain (D)	105,288	72.9
Ernest Barone (R)	39,096	27.1
2 Edward P. Beard (D)	124,759	78.2
Vincent J. Rotondo (R)	34,728	21.8

SOUTH CAROLINA

Candidates	Votes	%
1 Mendel J. Davis (D)	63,111	72.7
George B. Rast (R)	22,450	25.9
2 Floyd Spence (R)	58,936	56.1
Matthew J. Perry (D)	45,205	43.0
3 Butler C. Derrick Jr. (D)	55,120	61.8
Marshall J. Parker (R)	34,046	38.2
4 James R. Mann (D)	45,070	63.3
Robert L. Watkins (R)	26,185	36.7
5 Kenneth L. Holland (D)	47,614	61.4
Len Phillips (R)	29,294	37.8
6 John W. Jenrette Jr. (D)	45,396	52.0
Edward L. Young (R)	41,982	48.0

SOUTH DAKOTA

Candidates	Votes	%
1 Larry Pressler (R)	78,266	55.3
Frank E. Denholm (D)	63,339	44.7
2 James Abdnor (R)	88,746	67.8
Jack M. Weiland (D)	42,119	32.2

TENNESSEE

Candidates	Votes	%
1 James H. Quillen (R)	76,394	64.2
Lloyd Blevins (D)	42,523	35.8
2 John J. Duncan (R)	87,419	70.9
Jesse James Brown (D)	35,920	29.1
3 Marilyn Lloyd (D)	61,926	51.1
LaMar Baker (R)	55,580	45.9
4 Joe L. Evins (D)	94,847	99.9
5 Richard Fulton (D)	88,206	99.8
6 Robin L. Beard Jr. (R)	76,928	56.7
Tim Schaeffer (D)	58,824	43.3
7 Ed Jones (D)	83,231	100.0
8 Harold E. Ford (D)	67,925	49.9
Dan Kuykendall (R)	67,181	49.4

TEXAS

Candidates	Votes	%
1 Wright Patman (D)	49,426	68.6
James W. Farris (R)	22,619	31.4
2 Charles Wilson (D)	57,096	100.0
3 James M. Collins (R)	63,489	64.7
Harold Collum (D)	34,623	35.3
4 Ray Roberts (D)	48,209	74.9
Dick LeTourneau (R)	16,113	25.1
5 Alan Steelman (R)	28,446	52.1
Mike McKool (D)	26,190	47.9
6 Olin E. Teague (D)	53,345	83.0
Carl A. Nigliazzo (R)	10,908	17.0
7 Bill Archer (R)	70,363	79.2
Jim Brady (D)	18,524	20.8
8 Bob Eckhardt (D)	30,158	72.2
Donald D. Whitefield (R)	11,605	27.8
9 Jack Brooks (D)	37,275	61.9
Coleman R. Ferguson (R)	22,935	38.1
10 J. J. Pickle (D)	76,240	80.4
Paul A. Weiss (R)	18,560	19.6
11 W. R. Poage (D)	46,828	81.6
Don Clements (R)	9,883	17.2
12 Jim Wright (D)	42,632	78.7
James S. Garvey (R)	11,543	21.3

VIRGINIA

Candidates	Votes	%
1 Thomas N. Downing (D)	58,338	99.8
2 G. William Whitehurst (R)	49,369	60.0
Robert R. Richards (D)	32,923	40.0
3 David E. Satterfield III (D)	64,627	88.5
A. R. Ogden (IND)	7,574	10.4
4 Robert W. Daniel Jr. (R)	48,032	47.2
Lester E. Schlitz (D)	36,489	35.9
Curtis W. Harris (IND)	17,224	16.9
5 W. C. (Dan) Daniel (D)	52,459	99.4
6 M. Caldwell Butler (R)	45,805	45.1
Paul J. Puckett (D)	27,350	27.0
Warren D. Saunders (IND)	26,466	26.1
7 J. Kenneth Robinson (R)	54,267	52.6
George H. Gilliam (D)	48,611	47.1
8 Herbert E. Harris (D)	53,074	57.6
Stanford E. Parris (R)	38,997	42.4
9 William C. Wampler (R)	68,183	50.9
Charles J. Horne (D)	65,783	49.1
10 Joseph L. Fisher (D)	67,184	53.6
Joel T. Broyhill (R)	56,649	45.2

WEST VIRGINIA

Candidates	Votes	%
1 Robert H. Mollohan (D)	72,457	59.7
Joe Laurita Jr. (R)	48,966	40.3
2 Harley O. Staggers (D)	73,683	64.4
William H. Loy (R)	40,779	35.6
3 John M. Slack (D)	77,586	68.5
William L. Larcamp (R)	35,623	31.5
4 Ken Hechler (D)	66,420	100.0

WISCONSIN

	Votes	%
1 Les Aspin (D)	81,902	70.5
Leonard W. Smith (R)	34,288	29.5
2 Robert W. Kastenmeier (D)	93,561	64.8
Elizabeth T. Miller (R)	50,890	35.2
3 Alvin J. Baldus (D)	76,668	51.1
Vernon W. Thomson (R)	71,171	47.4
4 Clement J. Zablocki (D)	84,768	72.5
Lewis H. Collison (R)	27,818	23.8
5 Henry S. Reuss (D)	65,060	80.0
Mildred A. Morries (R)	16,293	20.0
6 William A. Steiger (R)	86,652	59.5
Nancy J. Simenz (D)	51,571	35.4
Harvey C. LeRoy (A)	7,432	5.1
7 David R. Obey (D)	104,648	70.5
Josef Burger (R)	43,558	29.4
8 Robert J. Cornell (D)	79,923	54.4
Howard V. Froehlich (R)	66,889	45.6
9 Robert W. Kasten Jr. (R)	77,733	52.9
Lynn S. Adelman (D)	66,071	45.0

Candidates (continued)

Candidates	Votes	%
13 Jack Hightower (D)	53,094	57.6
Robert Price (R)	39,087	42.4
14 John Young (D)	41,066	100.0
15 Eligio de la Garza (D)	42,567	100.0
16 Richard C. White (D)	42,880	100.0
17 Omar Burleson (D)	64,595	100.0
18 Barbara C. Jordan (D)	36,597	84.8
Robbins Mitchell (R)	6,053	14.0
19 George Mahon (D)	49,610	100.0
20 Henry B. Gonzalez (D)	39,358	100.0
21 Robert Krueger (D)	53,543	52.6
Douglas S. Harlan (R)	45,959	45.2
22 Bob Casey (D)	47,783	69.5
Ron Paul (R)	19,483	28.4
23 Abraham Kazen Jr. (D)	47,249	100.0
24 Dale Milford (D)	36,085	76.1
Joseph Beaman Jr. (R)	9,698	20.4

UTAH

	Votes	%
1 K. Gunn McKay (D)	124,793	62.6
Ronald W. Inkley (R)	62,807	31.5
L. S. Brown (A)	11,664	5.9
2 Allan T. Howe (D)	105,739	49.5
Stephen M. Harmsen (R)	100,259	46.9

VERMONT

	Votes	%
AL James M. Jeffords (R)	74,561	52.9
Francis J. Cain (D I VT)	56,342	40.0
Michael Parenti (LU)	9,961	7.1

WASHINGTON

	Votes	%
1 Joel Pritchard (R)	108,391	69.5
W. R. Knedlik (D)	44,655	28.6
2 Lloyd Meeds (D)	81,565	59.7
Ronald C. Reed (R)	53,157	38.9
3 Don Bonker (D)	93,980	60.9
A. Ludlow Kramer (R)	58,774	38.1
4 Mike McCormack (D)	84,949	58.9
Floyd Paxton (R)	59,249	41.1
5 Thomas S. Foley (D)	87,959	64.3
Gary G. Gage (R)	48,739	35.7
6 Floyd V. Hicks (D)	95,354	71.8
George M. Nalley (R)	37,400	28.2
7 Brock Adams (D)	85,593	71.1
Raymond Pritchard (R)	34,847	28.9

WYOMING

	Votes	%
AL Teno Roncalio (D)	69,434	54.7
Tom Stroock (R)	57,499	45.3

1975 House Elections

CALIFORNIA

Special Election

Candidates	Votes	%
37 Shirley N. Pettis (R)	53,165	60.5
Ron Pettis (D)	12,940	14.7
James L. Mayfield (D)	11,140	12.7
Frank M. Bogert (R)	4,773	5.4

ILLINOIS

Special Election

	Votes	%
5 John G. Fary (D)	55,036	71.9
Francis X. Lawlor (R)	21,491	28.1

LOUISIANA

Special Election [1]

	Votes	%
6 W. Henson Moore (R)	74,802	54.1
Jeff LaCaze (D)	63,366	45.9

TENNESSEE

Special Election

	Votes	%
5 Clifford Allen (D)	46,593	64.6
Bob Olsen (R)	24,901	34.5

1974 Election

1. LLJ, the party affiliation of the 1st District candidate, J. M. Sanders, stands for "Life, Liberty, Justice."

2. In the 6th District special election, 146,147 votes were were cast. To win outright without a second election, a candidate needed 73,074 votes. John L. Burton received 73,114 votes, 40 more than needed.

California was redistricted in 1974 for the November general election, changing the numbers of many of the districts. Burton was re-elected to the 94th Congress (1975-77) from the 5th District and Robert J. Lagomarsino from the 19th.

3. There are no reliable final returns for the House race in the 6th District. Post-election results showed Moore leading LaCaze by a handful of votes, but the outcome could not be determined because one voting machine had malfunctioned and did not record votes for LaCaze.

The case went to the Louisiana courts for resolution. LaCaze asked that persons who voted on the malfunctioning machine be polled again in court under oath and their votes added to the total, but the Louisiana Supreme Court rejected this plan and ordered a new election. Moore won easily. (See Louisiana 1975.)

4. The returns from the 1st District House race are not final. Kyros challenged Emery's election before the House Administration Committee, which conducted a partial recount of the returns until Kyros conceded defeat. The recount changed the total votes received by each candidate, but not the result.

1975 Election

1. This election, Jan. 7, 1975, was a court-ordered rerun held after it was found impossible to determine who won the November 1974 House race between the same two candidates. (See Louisiana 1974.)

1976 House Elections

ALABAMA

Candidates	Votes	%
1 Jack Edwards (R)	98,257	62.5
Bill Davenport (D)	58,906	37.5
2 William L. Dickinson (R)	90,069	57.6
J. Carole Keahey (D)	66,288	42.4
3 Bill Nichols (D)	106,935	99.0
4 Tom Bevill (D)	141,490	80.4
Leonard Wilson (R)	34,531	19.6
5 Ronnie G. Flippo (D)	113,553	100.0
6 John Buchanan (R)	92,113	56.7
Mel Bailey (D)	69,384	42.7
7 Walter Flowers (D)	110,496	100.0

ALASKA

Candidates	Votes	%
AL Donald E. Young (R)	83,722	70.8
Eben Hopson (D)	34,194	28.9

ARIZONA

Candidates	Votes	%
1 John J. Rhodes (R)	96,397	57.3
Patricia Fullinwider (D)	68,404	40.7
2 Morris K. Udall (D)	106,054	58.2
Laird Guttersen (R)	71,765	39.4
3 Bob Stump (R)	88,854	47.5
Fred Koory Jr. (R)	79,162	42.3
Bill McCune (NON PART I)	19,149	10.2
4 Eldon Rudd (R)	93,154	48.6
Tony Mason (D)	92,435	48.2

ARKANSAS

Candidates	Votes	%
1 Bill Alexander (D)	116,217	68.9
Harlan (Bo) Holleman (R)	52,565	31.1
2 Jim Guy Tucker (D)	144,780	86.4
James J. Kelly (R)	22,819	13.6
3 John Paul Hammerschmidt (R) [1]		100.0
4 Ray Thornton (D) [1]		100.0

CALIFORNIA

Candidates	Votes	%
1 Harold T. (Bizz) Johnson (D)	160,477	73.9
James E. Taylor (R)	56,539	26.1
2 Don H. Clausen (R)	121,290	56.0
Oscar H. Klee (D)	88,829	41.0
3 John E. Moss (D)	139,779	72.9
George R. Marsh Jr. (R)	52,075	27.1
4 Robert L. Leggett (D)	75,844	46.7
Albert Dehr (R)	75,193	46.3
Joseph E. (Ted) Sheedy (WRITE IN)	11,279	6.9
5 John L. Burton (D)	103,746	61.8
Branwell Fanning (R)	64,008	38.2
6 Phillip Burton (D)	86,493	66.1
Tom Spinosa (R)	35,359	27.0
Emily Siegel (PFP)	6,570	5.0
7 George Miller (D)	147,064	74.7
Robert L. Vickers (R)	45,863	23.3
8 Ronald V. Dellums (D)	122,342	62.1
Philip S. Breck Jr. (R)	68,374	34.7
9 Fortney H. Stark Jr. (D)	116,398	70.8
James K. Mills (R)	44,607	27.1
10 Don Edwards (D)	111,992	72.0
Herb Smith (R)	38,088	24.5
11 Leo J. Ryan (D)	107,618	61.1
Bob Jones (R)	62,435	35.4
12 Paul N. McCloskey Jr. (R)	130,332	66.2
David Harris (D)	61,526	31.3
13 Norman Y. Mineta (D)	135,291	66.8
Ernest L. Konnyu (R)	63,130	31.2
14 John J. McFall (D)	123,285	72.5
Roger A. Blain (R)	46,674	27.5
15 B. F. Sisk (D)	92,735	72.2
Carol O. Harner (R)	35,700	27.8

Candidates	Votes	%
16 Leon E. Panetta (D)	104,545	53.4
Burt L. Talcott (R)	91,160	46.6
17 John Krebs (D)	103,898	65.7
Henry J. Andreas (R)	54,270	34.3
18 William M. Ketchum (R)	101,658	64.2
Dean Close (D)	56,683	35.8
19 Robert J. Lagomarsino (R)	124,201	64.4
Dan Sisson (D)	68,722	35.6
20 Barry M. Goldwater Jr. (R)	146,158	67.2
Patti Lear Corman (D)	71,193	32.8
21 James C. Corman (D)	101,837	66.5
Erwin G. (Ed) Hogan (R)	44,094	28.8
22 Carlos J. Moorhead (R)	114,769	62.6
Robert L. Salley (D)	68,543	37.4
32 Anthony C. (Tony) Beilenson (D)	130,619	60.2
Thomas F. Bartman (R)	86,434	39.8
24 Henry A. Waxman (D)	108,296	67.8
David I. Simmons (R)	51,478	32.2
25 Edward R. Roybal (D)	57,966	71.9
Jim Madrid (R)	17,737	22.0
Marilyn Seals (PFP)	4,922	6.1
26 John H. Rousselot (R)	112,619	65.6
Bruce Latta (D)	59,093	34.4
27 Robert K. Dornan (R)	114,623	54.7
Gary Familian (D)	94,988	45.3
28 Yvonne Brathwaite Burke (D)	114,612	80.2
Edward S. Skinner (R)	28,303	19.8
29 Augustus F. Hawkins (D)	82,515	85.4
Michael D. Germonprez (R)	10,852	11.2
30 George E. Danielson (D)	82,767	74.4
Harry Couch (R)	28,503	25.6
31 Charles H. Wilson (D)	83,155	100.0
32 Glenn M. Anderson (D)	92,034	72.2
Clifford O. Young (R)	35,394	27.8
33 Del Clawson (R)	95,398	55.1
Ted Snyder (D)	77,807	44.9
34 Mark W. Hannaford (D)	100,988	50.7
Daniel E. Lungren (R)	98,147	49.3
35 Jim Lloyd (D)	87,472	53.3
Louis Brutocao (R)	76,765	46.7
36 George E. Brown Jr. (D)	90,830	61.6
Grant C. Carner (R)	49,368	33.5
William E. Pasley (AMI)	7,358	5.0
37 Shirley N. Pettis (R)	133,634	71.1
Douglas C. Nilson Jr. (D)	49,021	26.1
38 Jerry M. Patterson (D)	103,317	63.6
James Combs (R)	59,092	36.4
39 Charles E. Wiggins (R)	122,657	58.6
William E. Farris (D)	86,745	41.4
40 Robert E. Badham (R)	148,512	59.3
Vivian Hall (D)	102,132	40.7
41 Bob Wilson (R)	128,784	57.7
King Golden Jr. (D)	94,590	42.3
42 Lionel Van Deerlin (D)	103,062	76.0
Wes Marden (R)	32,565	24.0
43 Clair W. Burgener (R)	173,576	65.0
Pat Kelly (D)	93,475	35.0

COLORADO

Candidates	Votes	%
1 Patricia Schroeder (D)	103,037	53.2
Don Friedman (R)	89,384	46.2
2 Timothy E. Wirth (D)	121,336	50.5
Ed Scott (R)	118,936	49.5
3 Frank E. Evans (D)	89,308	51.0
Melvin H. Takaki (R)	82,269	47.0
4 James P. Johnson (R)	119,408	53.7
Dan Ogden (D)	78,355	35.2
Dick Davis (I)	20,398	9.2
5 William L. Armstrong (R)	126,784	66.4
Dorothy Hores (D)	64,067	33.6

CONNECTICUT

Candidates	Votes	%
1 William R. Cotter (D)	128,479	57.1
Lucien P. DiFazio Jr. (R)	94,106	41.8

Candidates	Votes	%
2 Christopher J. Dodd (D)	142,684	65.1
Richard M. Jackson (R)	74,743	34.1
3 Robert N. Giaimo (D)	121,623	54.6
John G. Pucciano (R)	96,714	43.4
4 Stewart B. McKinney (R)	126,314	61.0
Geoffrey G. Peterson (D)	76,722	37.1
5 Ronald A. Sarasin (R)	157,009	66.5
Michael J. Adanti (D)	77,308	32.7
6 Anthony J. Moffett (D)	134,914	56.6
Thomas F. Upson (R)	102,364	43.0

DELAWARE

Candidates	Votes	%
AL Thomas B. Evans Jr. (R)	110,677	51.5
Samuel L. Shipley (D)	102,431	47.7

FLORIDA

Candidates	Votes	%
1 Robert L. F. Sikes (D) [1]		100.0
2 Don Fuqua (D) [1]		100.0
3 Charles E. Bennett (D) [1]		100.0
4 Bill Chappell Jr. (D) [1]		100.0
5 Richard Kelly (R)	138,371	59.0
Jo Ann Saunders (D)	96,260	41.0
6 C. W. Bill Young (R)	151,371	65.2
Gabriel Cazares (D)	80,821	34.8
7 Sam M. Gibbons (D)	102,739	65.7
Dusty Owens (R)	53,599	34.3
8 Andy Ireland (D)	103,360	58.0
Robert Johnson (R)	74,794	42.0
9 Louis Frey Jr. (R)	130,509	78.1
Joseph A. Rosier (D)	36,630	21.9
10 L. A. (Skip) Bafalis (R)	164,273	66.3
Bill Sikes (D)	83,413	33.7
11 Paul G. Rogers (D)	199,031	91.1
Clyde Adams (AM)	19,406	8.9
12 J. Herbert Burke (R)	107,268	53.9
Charles Friedman (D)	91,749	46.1
13 William Lehman (D)	127,822	78.3
Lee Arnold Spiegelman (R)	35,357	21.7
14 Claude Pepper (D)	82,665	72.9
Evelio S. Estrella (R)	30,774	27.1
15 Dante B. Fascell (D)	121,292	70.4
Paul R. Cobb (R)	50,941	29.6

GEORGIA

Candidates	Votes	%
1 Ronald B. Ginn (D)	73,826	99.9
2 Dawson Mathis (D)	95,807	99.8
3 Jack Brinkley (D)	93,174	88.7
Steve Dugan (R)	11,829	11.3
4 Elliott H. Levitas (D)	110,261	68.3
George Warren (R)	51,140	31.7
5 Andrew Young (D)	96,056	66.7
Ed Gadrix (R)	47,998	33.3
6 John J. Flynt Jr. (D)	77,532	51.7
Newt Gingrich (R)	72,400	48.3
7 Lawrence P. McDonald (D)	84,587	55.1
Quincy Collins (R)	68,947	44.9
8 Billy Lee Evans (D)	91,351	69.7
Billy Adams (R)	39,623	30.3
9 Ed Jenkins (D)	113,245	79.0
Louise Wofford (R)	29,954	20.9
10 Doug Barnard (D)	94,782	99.9

HAWAII

Candidates	Votes	%
1 Cecil (Cec) Heftel (D)	60,050	43.6
Fred W. Rohlfing (R)	53,745	39.1
Kathy Hoshijo (I GOD GOV)	23,807	17.3
2 Daniel K. Akaka (D)	124,116	79.5
Hank Inouye (R)	23,917	15.3

IDAHO

Candidates	Votes	%
1 Steven D. Symms (R)	95,833	54.6
Ken Pursley (D)	79,662	45.4

267

Candidates	Votes	%
2 George V. Hansen (R)	84,175	*50.6*
Stan Kress (D)	82,237	*49.4*

ILLINOIS

Candidates	Votes	%
1 Ralph H. Metcalfe (D)	126,632	*92.3*
A. A. Rayner (R)	10,147	*7.4*
2 Morgan F. Murphy (D)	127,297	*84.7*
Spencer Leak (R)	23,037	*15.3*
3 Martin A. Russo (D)	115,591	*58.9*
Ronald Buikema (R)	79,434	*40.5*
4 Edward J. Derwinski (R)	124,847	*65.8*
Ronald A. Rodger (D)	64,924	*34.2*
5 John G. Fary (D)	119,336	*76.9*
Vincent Krok (R)	35,756	*23.1*
6 Henry J. Hyde (R)	106,667	*60.6*
Marilyn D. Clancy (D)	69,359	*39.4*
7 Cardiss Collins (D)	88,239	*84.8*
Newell Ward (R)	15,854	*15.2*
8 Dan Rostenkowski (D)	105,595	*80.5*
John F. Urbaszewski (R)	25,512	*19.5*
9 Sidney R. Yates (D)	121,915	*72.1*
Thomas J. Wajerski (R)	47,054	*27.8*
10 Abner J. Mikva (D)	106,804	*50.0*
Samuel H. Young (R)	106,603	*50.0*
11 Frank Annunzio (D)	135,755	*67.4*
Daniel C. Reber (R)	65,680	*32.6*
12 Philip M. Crane (R)	151,899	*72.8*
E. L. Frank (D)	56,644	*27.2*
13 Robert McClory (R)	109,726	*66.8*
James J. Cummings (D)	49,777	*30.3*
14 John N. Erlenborn (R)	176,076	*74.4*
Marie Agnes Fese (D)	60,505	*25.6*
15 Tom Corcoran (R)	102,555	*53.9*
Tim L. Hall (D)	87,676	*46.1*
16 John B. Anderson (R)	114,324	*67.9*
Stephen Eytalis (D)	54,002	*32.1*
17 George M. O'Brien (R)	113,145	*58.2*
Merlin E. Karlock (D)	81,220	*41.8*
18 Robert H. Michel (R)	108,028	*57.7*
Matthew Ryan (D)	79,102	*42.3*
19 Thomas F. Railsback (R)	132,571	*68.5*
John Craver (D)	60,967	*31.5*
20 Paul Findley (R)	137,223	*63.6*
Peter F. Mack Jr. (D)	78,634	*36.4*
21 Edward R. Madigan (R)	137,037	*74.5*
Anna Wall Scott (D)	46,996	*25.5*
22 George E. Shipley (D)	129,187	*61.4*
Ralph Y. McGinnis (R)	81,102	*38.6*
23 Melvin Price (D)	128,113	*78.6*
Sam P. Drenovac (R)	34,825	*21.4*
24 Paul Simon (D)	152,344	*67.4*
Peter G. Prineas (R)	73,766	*32.6*

INDIANA

Candidates	Votes	%
1 Adam Benjamin Jr. (D)	121,155	*71.3*
Robert J. Billings (R)	48,756	*28.7*
2 Floyd Fithian (D)	117,617	*54.8*
William W. Erwin (R)	95,505	*44.5*
3 John Brademas (D)	101,757	*56.9*
Thomas L. Thorson (R)	77,094	*43.1*
4 Dan Quayle (R)	107,762	*54.4*
J. Edward Roush (D)	88,361	*44.6*
5 Elwood H. Hillis (R)	127,194	*61.7*
William C. Stout (D)	78,807	*38.3*
6 David W. Evans (D)	105,773	*54.9*
David G. Crane (R)	86,854	*45.1*
7 John T. Myers (R)	130,005	*62.7*
John Elden Tipton (D)	77,355	*37.3*
8 David L. Cornwell (D)	109,013	*50.5*
Belden Bell (R)	107,013	*49.5*
9 Lee H. Hamilton (D)	136,056	*100.0*
10 Philip R. Sharp (D)	114,559	*59.8*
William G. Frazier (R)	76,890	*40.2*
11 Andrew Jacobs Jr. (D)	115,895	*60.4*
Lawrence L. Buell (R)	74,829	*39.0*

IOWA

Candidates	Votes	%
1 James A. S. Leach (R)	109,694	*51.9*
Edward Mezvinsky (D)	101,024	*47.8*

Candidates	Votes	%
2 Michael T. Blouin (D)	102,980	*50.3*
Tom Riley (R)	100,344	*49.1*
3 Charles E. Grassley (R)	117,957	*56.5*
Stephen J. Rapp (D)	90,981	*43.5*
4 Neal Smith (D)	145,343	*69.1*
Charles E. Minor (R)	65,013	*30.9*
5 Tom Harkin (D)	135,600	*64.9*
Kenneth R. Fulk (R)	71,377	*34.1*
6 Berkley Bedell (D)	133,507	*67.4*
Joanne D. Soper (R)	62,292	*31.5*

KANSAS

Candidates	Votes	%
1 Keith G. Sebelius (R)	142,311	*73.1*
Randy D. Yowell (D)	52,459	*26.9*
2 Martha E. Keys (D)	88,645	*50.7*
Ross R. Freeman (R)	82,946	*47.4*
3 Larry Winn Jr. (R)	123,578	*68.7*
Philip S. Rhoads (D)	52,110	*29.0*
4 Dan Glickman (D)	90,067	*50.3*
Garner E. Shriver (R)	86,832	*48.5*
5 Joe Skubitz (R)	109,573	*60.7*
Virgil L. Olson (D)	65,340	*36.2*

KENTUCKY

Candidates	Votes	%
1 Carroll Hubbard Jr. (D)	118,886	*82.0*
Bob Bersky (R)	26,089	*18.0*
2 William H. Natcher (D)	79,016	*60.4*
Walter A. Baker (R)	51,900	*39.6*
3 Romano L. Mazzoli (D)	80,496	*57.2*
Denzil J. Ramsey (R)	58,019	*41.2*
4 M. G. (Gene) Snyder (R)	97,493	*55.9*
Edward J. Winterberg (D)	77,009	*44.1*
5 Tim Lee Carter (R)	100,204	*66.6*
Charles C. Smith (D)	49,128	*32.6*
6 John Breckinridge (D)	90,695	*94.0*
Anthony A. McCord (AM)	5,795	*6.0*
7 Carl D. Perkins (D)	110,450	*73.2*
Granville Thomas (R)	40,381	*26.8*

LOUISIANA

Candidates	Votes	%
1 Richard A. Tonry (D)	61,652	*47.2*
Bob Livingston (R)	56,679	*43.4*
John R. Rarick (I)	12,227	*9.4*
2 Corinne (Lindy) (Mrs. Hale) Boggs (D)	85,923	*92.6*
Jules W. Hillery (I)	6,904	*7.4*
3 David C. Treen (R)	109,135	*73.3*
David H. Scheuermann Sr. (D)	39,728	*26.7*
4 Joe D. Waggonner Jr. (D)	76,406	*100.0*
5 Jerry Huckaby (D)	83,696	*52.5*
Frank Spooner (R)	75,574	*47.5*
6 W. Henson Moore III (R)	99,780	*65.2*
J. D. DeBlieux (D)	53,212	*34.8*
7 John B. Breaux (D)	117,196	*83.3*
Charles F. Huff (R)	23,414	*16.7*
8 Gillis W. Long (D)	106,285	*94.2*
Kent Courtney (I)	6,526	*5.8*

MAINE

Candidates	Votes	%
1 David F. Emery (R)	145,523	*57.4*
Frederick D. Barton (D)	108,105	*42.6*
2 William S. Cohen (R)	169,292	*77.1*
Leighton Cooney (D)	43,150	*19.7*

MARYLAND

Candidates	Votes	%
1 Robert E. Bauman (R)	85,919	*54.1*
Roy Dyson (D)	72,993	*45.9*
2 Clarence D. Long (D)	139,196	*70.9*
John M. Seney (R)	35,258	*18.0*
Ronald A. Meroney (I)	21,849	*11.1*
3 Barbara Mikulski (D)	107,014	*74.6*
Samuel A. Culotta (R)	36,447	*25.4*
4 Marjorie S. Holt (R)	95,158	*57.7*
Werner Fornos (D)	69,855	*42.3*

Candidates	Votes	%
5 Gladys N. Spellman (D)	77,836	*57.7*
John B. Burcham Jr. (R)	57,057	*42.3*
6 Goodloe E. Byron (D)	126,801	*70.8*
Arthur T. Bond (R)	52,203	*29.2*
7 Parren J. Mitchell (D)	94,991	*94.4*
William Salisbury (I)	5,642	*5.6*
8 Newton Steers (R)	111,274	*46.8*
Lanny Davis (D)	100,343	*42.2*
Robin Ficker (I)	26,035	*11.0*

MASSACHUSETTS

Candidates	Votes	%
1 Silvio O. Conte (R)	137,652	*63.8*
Edward A. McColgan (D)	78,181	*36.2*
2 Edward P. Boland (D)	134,408	*72.4*
Thomas P. Swank (R)	41,563	*22.4*
John D. McCarthy (USLP)	9,776	*5.3*
3 Joseph D. Early (D)	168,520	*100.0*
4 Robert F. Drinan (D)	109,268	*52.1*
Arthur D. Mason (R)	100,562	*47.9*
5 Paul E. Tsongas (D)	144,217	*67.3*
Roger P. Durkin (R)	70,036	*32.7*
6 Michael J. Harrington (D)	121,562	*54.8*
William E. Bronson (R)	91,655	*41.3*
7 Edward J. Markey (D)	162,126	*76.9*
Richard W. Daly (R)	37,063	*17.6*
8 Thomas P. O'Neill Jr. (D)	133,131	*74.4*
William A. Barnstead (R)	33,437	*18.7*
9 John Joseph Moakley (D)	103,901	*69.6*
Robert G. Cunningham (R)	34,547	*23.1*
Joseph M. O'Loughlin (I)	7,862	*5.3*
10 Margaret M. Heckler (R)	176,604	*100.0*
11 James A. Burke (D)	131,789	*69.0*
Danielle DeBenedictis (I)	59,240	*31.0*
12 Gerry E. Studds (D)	222,418	*100.0*

MICHIGAN

Candidates	Votes	%
1 John Conyers Jr. (D)	126,161	*92.4*
Isaac Hood (R)	8,927	*6.5*
2 Carl D. Pursell (R)	95,397	*49.8*
Edward C. Pierce (D)	95,053	*49.6*
3 Garry Brown (R)	99,231	*50.6*
Howard Wolpe (D)	95,261	*48.6*
4 Dave Stockman (R)	107,881	*60.0*
Richard E. Daugherty (D)	69,655	*38.8*
5 Harold S. Sawyer (R)	109,589	*53.3*
Richard F. Vander Veen (D)	94,973	*46.2*
6 Bob Carr (D)	108,909	*52.7*
Clifford W. Taylor (R)	96,008	*46.5*
7 Dale E. Kildee (D)	124,260	*70.0*
Robin Widgery (R)	50,301	*28.3*
8 Bob Traxler (D)	110,127	*59.0*
E. Brady Denton (R)	75,323	*40.4*
9 Guy A. Vander Jagt (R)	146,712	*70.0*
Stephen Fawley (D)	61,641	*29.4*
10 Elford A. Cederberg (R)	118,726	*56.5*
Donald J. Albosta (D)	89,980	*42.8*
11 Philip E. Ruppe (R)	118,871	*54.7*
Francis D. Brouillette (D)	97,325	*44.8*
12 David E. Bonior (D)	94,815	*52.4*
David M. Serotkin (R)	85,326	*47.2*
13 Charles C. Diggs Jr. (D)	83,387	*89.0*
Richard A. Golden (R)	9,002	*9.6*
14 Lucien N. Nedzi (D)	107,503	*66.5*
John Edward Getz (R)	52,995	*32.8*
15 William D. Ford (D)	117,313	*74.0*
James D. Walaskay (R)	39,157	*24.7*
16 John D. Dingell Jr. (D)	121,682	*75.9*
William E. Rostron (R)	36,378	*22.7*
17 William M. Brodhead (D)	112,746	*64.3*
James W. Burdick (R)	60,476	*34.5*
18 James J. Blanchard (D)	123,113	*66.1*
John E. Olsen (R)	60,995	*32.8*
19 William S. Broomfield (R)	131,799	*66.7*
Dorothea Becker (D)	64,337	*32.6*

MINNESOTA

Candidates	Votes	%
1 Albert H. Quie (I-R)	158,177	*68.2*
Robert C. Olson Jr. (DFL)	70,630	*30.5*

Candidates	Votes	%
2 Tom Hagedorn (I-R)	148,322	60.3
Gloria Griffin (DFL)	97,488	39.7
3 Bill Frenzel (I-R)	149,013	66.1
Jerome W. Coughlin (DFL)	72,044	32.0
4 Bruce F. Vento (DFL)	133,282	66.4
Andrew Engebretson (I-R)	59,767	29.8
5 Donald M. Fraser (DFL)	138,213	70.7
Richard M. Erdall (I-R)	50,764	26.0
6 Richard M. Nolan (DFL)	147,507	59.8
James Anderson (I-R)	99,201	40.2
7 Bob Bergland (DFL)	174,080	72.0
Bob Leiseth (I-R)	64,333	26.6
8 James L. Oberstar (DFL)	206,755	100.0

MISSISSIPPI

Candidates	Votes	%
1 Jamie L. Whitten (D)	93,687	100.0
2 David R. Bowen (D)	75,092	63.0
Roland Byrd (R)	42,601	35.7
3 G. V. (Sonny) Montgomery (D)	129,088	93.9
Dorothy Colby Cleveland (R)	8,321	6.1
4 Thad Cochran (R)	101,132	76.0
Sterling P. Davis (D)	28,737	21.6
5 Trent Lott (R)	104,554	68.2
Gerald Blessey (D)	48,724	31.8

MISSOURI

Candidates	Votes	%
1 William Clay (D)	87,310	65.5
Robert L. Witherspoon (R)	45,874	34.4
2 Robert A. Young (D)	111,568	51.1
Robert O. Snyder (R)	106,811	48.9
3 Richard A. Gephardt (D)	115,109	63.7
Joseph L. Badaracco (R)	65,623	36.3
4 Ike Skelton (D)	115,955	55.9
Richard A. King (R)	91,605	44.1
5 Richard Bolling (D)	100,876	68.0
Joanne M. Collins (R)	41,681	28.1
6 E. Thomas Coleman (R)	120,969	58.5
Morgan Maxfield (D)	83,755	40.5
7 Gene Taylor (R)	133,656	62.0
Dolan G. Hawkins (D)	81,848	38.0
8 Richard Ichord (D)	132,386	67.3
Charles R. Leick(R)	60,179	30.6
9 Harold L. Volkmer (D)	120,325	55.9
J. H. Frappier (R)	94,816	44.1
10 Bill D. Burlison (D)	131,675	72.1
Joe Carron (R)	51,024	27.9

MONTANA

Candidates	Votes	%
1 Max S. Baucus (D)	111,487	66.4
W. D. (Bill) Diehl (R)	56,297	33.6
2 Ron Marlenee (R)	84,149	55.0
Thomas E. Towe (D)	68,972	45.0

NEBRASKA

Candidates	Votes	%
1 Charles Thone (R)	146,558	73.2
Pauline F. Anderson (D)	53,703	26.8
2 John J. Cavanaugh (D)	106,296	54.6
Lee Terry (R)	88,352	45.4
3 Virginia Smith (R)	150,720	72.9
James T. Hansen (D)	51,012	24.7

NEVADA

Candidates	Votes	%
AL James Santini (D)	153,996	77.1
Walden Charles Earhart (R)	24,124	12.1
Janine M. Hansen.(IA)	12,038	6.0

NEW HAMPSHIRE

Candidates	Votes	%
1 Norman E. D'Amours (D)	107,806	68.0
John Adams (R)	48,087	30.3
2 James C. Cleveland (R)	100,911	60.5
J. Joseph Grandmaison (D)	65,792	39.5

NEW JERSEY

Candidates	Votes	%
1 James J. Florio (D)	136,624	70.1
Joseph I. McCullough Jr. (R)	56,363	28.9
2 William J. Hughes (D)	141,753	61.7
James R. Hurley (R)	87,915	38.3
3 James J. Howard (D)	127,164	62.1
Ralph A. Siciliano(R)	75,934	37.1
4 Frank Thompson Jr. (D)	113,281	66.3
Joseph S. Indyk (R)	54,789	32.1
5 Millicent Fenwick (R)	137,803	66.9
Frank R. Nero (D)	64,598	31.3
6 Edwin B. Forsythe (R)	125,920	58.8
Catherine A. Costa (D)	85,053	39.7
7 Andrew Maguire (D)	120,526	56.5
James J. Sheehan (R)	92,624	43.5
8 Robert A. Roe (D)	108,841	70.6
Bessie Doty (R)	44,775	29.0
9 Harold C. Hollenbeck (R)	107,454	53.1
Henry Helstoski (D)	89,723	44.3
10 Peter W. Rodino Jr. (D)	88,245	82.6
Tony Grandison (R)	17,129	16.0
11 Joseph G. Minish (D)	129,026	67.6
Charles A. Poekel Jr. (R)	59,397	31.1
12 Matthew J. Rinaldo (R)	136,973	73.1
Richard A. Buggelli (D)	49,189	26.3
13 Helen S. Meyner (D)	105,291	50.4
William E. Schluter (R)	100,050	47.9
14 Joseph A. LeFante (D)	73,174	49.9
Anthony L. Campenni (R)	66,319	45.2
15 Edward J. Patten (D)	106,170	59.0
Charles W. Wiley (R)	54,487	30.3
Dennis Adams Sr. (I)	14,543	8.1

NEW MEXICO

Candidates	Votes	%
1 Manuel Lujan Jr. (R)	162,587	72.1
Raymond Garcia (D)	61,800	27.4
2 Harold Runnels (D)	123,563	70.3
Donald W. Trubey (R)	52,131	29.7

NEW YORK

Candidates	Votes	%
1 Otis G. Pike (D,L)	135,528	65.3
Salvatore Nicosia (R)	61,671	29.7
2 Thomas J. Downey (D,I)	91,241	57.1
Peter Cohalan (R,C)	67,755	42.4
3 Jerome A. Ambro Jr. (D)	94,265	52.0
Howard T. Hogan Jr. (R,C)	84,824	46.8
4 Norman F. Lent (R,C)	106,058	55.8
Gerald P. Halpern (D,L)	83,971	44.2
5 John W. Wydler (R,C)	110,366	55.7
Allard K. Lowenstein (D,L)	87,868	44.3
6 Lester L. Wolff (D,L)	112,422	61.8
Vincent R. Balletta Jr. (R)	60,567	33.3
7 Joseph P. Addabbo (D,R,L)	107,312	94.7
8 Benjamin S. Rosenthal (D,L)	107,295	77.8
Albert Lemishow (R,C)	30,191	21.9
9 James J. Delaney (D,R,C)	109,552	95.1
10 Mario Biaggi (D,R)	106,222	91.6
Joanne S. Fuchs (C)	5,868	5.1
11 James H. Scheuer (D,L)	84,770	74.1
Arthur Cuccia (R)	19,203	16.8
Bryan F. Levinson (C)	6,316	5.5
12 Shirley Chisholm (D,L)	43,203	87.0
Horace Morancie (R)	5,336	10.8
13 Stephen J. Solarz (D,L)	110,624	83.7
Jack N. Dobosh (R,C)	21,600	16.3
14 Frederick W. Richmond (D,L)	55,723	85.0
Frank X. Gargiulo (R,C)	8,977	13.7
15 Leo C. Zeferetti (D,C)	69,242	63.2
Ronald J. D'Angelo (R)	33,641	30.7
Arthur J. Paone (L)	6,604	6.0
16 Elizabeth Holtzman (D,L)	93,995	82.9
Gladys Pemberton (R,C)	19,423	17.1
17 John M. Murphy (D)	89,126	65.6
Kenneth J. Grossberger (R)	27,734	20.4
John M. Peters (C)	10,399	7.7
Ned Schneir (L)	8,656	6.4
18 Edward I. Koch (D,L)	112,187	75.1
Sonia Landau (R)	29,728	19.9

Candidates	Votes	%
19 Charles B. Rangel (D,R,L)	91,672	97.0
20 Theodore S. Weiss (D,L)	91,977	83.2
Denise Weiseman (R)	14,114	12.8
21 Herman Badillo (D,R,L)	41,285	98.6
22 Jonathan B. Bingham (D,L)	92,044	86.4
Paul Slotkin (R)	11,130	10.4
23 Bruce F. Caputo (R,C)	93,006	53.6
J. Edward Meyer (D,L)	80,424	46.4
24 Richard L. Ottinger (D)	99,761	54.5
David V. Hicks (R,C)	81,111	44.3
25 Hamilton Fish Jr. (R,C)	139,434	70.5
Minna Post Peyser (D)	58,216	29.5
26 Benjamin A. Gilman (R)	120,049	65.3
John R. Maloney (D)	60,511	32.9
27 Matthew F. McHugh (D,L)	127,048	66.6
William H. Harter (R,C)	63,626	33.4
28 Samuel S. Stratton (D)	170,034	79.0
Mary A. Bradt (R,C)	44,053	20.5
29 Edward W. Pattison (D,L)	100,663	47.0
Joseph A. Martino (R)	96,476	45.0
James E. DeYoung (C)	15,337	7.2
30 Robert C. McEwen (R,C)	95,564	55.7
Norma A. Bartle (D)	75,951	44.3
31 Donald J. Mitchell (R,C)	123,143	66.5
Anita Maxwell (D)	62,032	33.5
32 James M. Hanley (D)	101,419	54.8
George C. Wortley (R,C)	81,597	44.1
33 William F. Walsh (R)	125,163	68.5
Charles R. Welch (D)	48,855	26.7
34 Frank J. Horton (R)	126,566	65.9
William C. Larsen (D)	58,247	30.3
35 Barber B. Conable Jr. (R)	120,738	64.3
Michael Macaluso (D,C)	67,177	35.7
36 John J. LaFalce (D,L)	123,246	66.6
Ralph J. Argen (R,C)	61,701	33.4
37 Henry J. Nowak (D,L)	100,042	78.2
Calvin Kimbrough (R)	23,660	18.5
38 Jack F. Kemp (R,C)	165,702	78.2
Peter J. Geraci (D,L)	46,307	21.8
39 Stanley N. Lundine (D)	109,986	61.8
Richard A. Snowden (R,C)	68,018	38.2

Special Election

	Votes	%
39 Stanley N. Lundine (D)	55,402	61.2
John T. Calkins (R)	35,107	38.8

NORTH CAROLINA

Candidates	Votes	%
1 Walter B. Jones (D)	98,611	75.9
Joseph M. Ward (R)	29,295	22.5
2 L. H. Fountain (D)	113,368	99.8
3 Charlie Whitley (D)	77,193	68.7
Willard J. Blanchard (R)	35,089	31.2
4 Ike F. Andrews (D)	92,165	60.6
Johnnie L. Gallemore Jr. (R)	59,917	39.4
5 Stephen L. Neal (D)	98,789	54.2
Wilmer D. Mizell (R)	83,129	45.6
6 Richardson Preyer (D)	103,851	96.3
7 Charles Rose (D)	95,463	81.3
M.H. (Mike) Vaughan (R)	21,955	18.7
8 W. G. (Bill) Hefner (D)	99,296	65.7
Carl Eagle (R)	49,094	32.5
9 James G. Martin (R)	82,297	53.5
Arthur Goodman Jr. (D)	70,847	46.1
10 James T. Broyhill (R)	99,882	59.8
John J. Hunt (D)	67,190	40.2
11 Lamar Gudger (D)	93,857	50.9
Bruce B. Briggs (R)	88,752	48.1

NORTH DAKOTA

Candidates	Votes	%
AL Mark Andrews (R)	181,018	62.4
Lloyd Omdahl (D)	104,263	36.0

OHIO

Candidates	Votes	%
1 Willis D. Gradison Jr. (R)	109,789	64.8
William F. Bowen (D)	56,995	33.6
2 Thomas A. Luken (D)	88,178	51.4
Donald D. Clancy (R)	83,459	48.6

Candidates	Votes	%
3 Charles W. Whalen Jr. (R)	100,871	69.4
Leonard Stubbs (D)	33,873	23.3
4 Tennyson Guyer (R)	121,173	70.1
Clinton G. Dorsey (D)	51,784	29.9
5 Delbert L. Latta (R)	124,910	67.4
Bruce Edwards (D)	60,304	32.6
6 William H. Harsha (R)	107,064	61.5
Ted Strickland (D)	67,067	38.5
7 Clarence J. Brown Jr. (R)	101,027	64.9
Dorothy Franke (D)	54,755	35.1
8 Thomas N. Kindness (R)	110,775	68.7
John W. Griffin (D)	46,424	28.8
9 Thomas L. Ashley (D)	91,040	54.2
C. S. Finkbeiner (R)	73,919	44.0
10 Clarence E. Miller (R)	127,147	68.8
James A. Plummer (D)	57,757	31.2
11 J. William Stanton (R)	120,716	71.7
Thomas R. West Jr. (D)	47,548	28.3
12 Samuel L. Devine (R)	90,987	46.5
Fran Ryan (D)	89,424	45.7
William R. Moss (I)	15,429	7.9
13 Don J. Pease (D)	108,061	66.0
Woodrow W. Mathna (R)	49,828	30.4
14 John F. Seiberling Jr. (D)	121,652	74.1
James E. Houston (R)	39,917	24.3
15 Chalmers P. Wylie (R)	109,630	65.5
Mike McGee (D)	57,741	34.5
16 Ralph S. Regula (R)	116,374	66.8
John G. Freedom (D)	55,671	32.0
17 John M. Ashbrook (R)	94,874	56.8
John C. McDonald (D)	72,168	43.2
18 Douglas Applegate (D)	116,901	62.9
Ralph R. McCoy (R)	45,735	24.6
William Crabbe (I)	21,537	11.6
19 Charles J. Carney (D)	90,386	50.2
Jack C. Hunter (R)	86,162	47.9
20 Mary Rose Oakar (D)	98,785	81.0
Raymond J. Grabow (I)	20,553	16.9
21 Louis Stokes (D)	91,903	83.8
Barbara Sparks (R)	12,434	11.3
22 Charles A. Vanik (D)	128,535	72.7
Harry A. Hanna (R)	42,727	24.2
32 Ronald M. Mottl (D)	130,576	73.2
Michael T. Scanlon (R)	47,804	26.8

OKLAHOMA

Candidates	Votes	%
1 James R. Jones (D)	100,945	54.0
James M. Inhofe (R)	84,374	45.1
2 Theodore Risenhoover (D)	102,402	54.0
E. L. (Bud) Stewart (R)	87,341	46.0
3 Wes Watkins (D)	151,271	82.0
Gerald L. Beasley Jr. (R)	31,732	17.2
4 Tom Steed (D)	116,425	74.9
M. C. Stanley (R)	34,170	22.0
5 M. H. Edwards (R)	78,651	49.9
Tom Dunlap (D)	74,752	47.4
6 Glenn English (D)	137,498	71.1
Carol McCurley (R)	55,953	28.9

OREGON

Candidates	Votes	%
1 Les AuCoin (D)	154,844	58.7
Philip N. Bladine (R)	109,140	41.3
2 Al Ullman (D)	173,313	72.0
Thomas H. Mercer (R)	67,431	28.0
3 Robert Duncan (D)	148,503	83.9
Martin Simon (I)	28,245	16.0
4 James Weaver (D)	122,475	50.0
Jerry Lausmann (R)	85,943	35.1
Jim Howard (I)	22,104	9.0
Theodora Nathan (I)	14,307	5.8

PENNSYLVANIA

Candidates	Votes	%
1 Michael (Ozzie) Myers (D)	117,087	73.5
Samuel N. Fanelli (R)	40,191	25.2
2 Robert N. C. Nix (D)	109,855	73.5
Jesse W. Woods Jr. (R)	37,907	25.4

Candidates	Votes	%
3 Raymond F. Lederer (D)	98,627	73.2
Terrence J. Schade (R)	35,491	26.3
4 Joshua Eilberg (D)	144,890	67.5
James E. Mugford (R)	69,700	32.5
5 Richard T. Schulze (R)	119,682	59.5
Anthony Campolo (D)	81,299	40.5
6 Gus Yatron (D)	133,624	73.8
Stephen Postupack (R)	46,103	25.5
7 Robert W. Edgar (D)	109,436	54.1
John N. Kenney (R)	92,788	45.9
8 Peter H. Kostmayer (D)	93,855	49.5
John S. Renninger (R)	92,543	48.8
9 E. G. Shuster (R,D)	154,359	100.0
10 Joseph M. McDade (R)	125,218	62.6
Edward Mitchell (D)	74,925	37.4
11 Daniel J. Flood (D)	130,175	70.8
Howard G. Williams (R)	53,621	29.2
12 John P. Murtha (D)	122,504	67.7
Ted Humes (R)	58,489	32.3
13 R. Lawrence Coughlin (R)	130,705	63.4
Gertrude Strick (D)	75,435	36.6
14 William S. Moorhead (D)	114,472	71.7
John F. Bradley (R)	43,308	27.1
15 Fred B. Rooney (D)	108,844	65.2
Alice Sivulich (R)	57,616	34.5
16 Robert S. Walker (R)	97,527	62.3
Michael J. Minney (D)	57,836	37.0
17 Allen E. Ertel (D)	86,158	50.7
H. Joseph Hepford (R)	82,370	48.5
18 Douglas Walgren (D)	113,787	59.5
Robert J. Casey (R)	77,594	40.5
19 William F. Goodling (R)	124,098	70.6
Richard P. Noll (D)	51,686	29.4
20 Joseph M. Gaydos (D)	134,961	75.0
John P. Kostelac (R)	44,432	24.7
21 John H. Dent (D)	99,160	59.4
Robert H. Miller (R)	67,763	40.6
22 Austin J. Murphy (D)	97,036	55.3
Roger Fischer (R)	77,030	43.9
23 Joseph S. Ammerman (D)	95,821	56.5
Albert W. Johnson (R)	73,641	43.5
24 Marc L. Marks (R)	101,048	55.4
Joseph P. Vigorito (D)	79,937	43.8
25 Gary A. Myers (R)	103,632	56.8
Eugene V. Atkinson (D)	78,857	43.2

RHODE ISLAND

Candidates	Votes	%
1 Fernand J. St Germain (D)	116,674	62.4
John J. Slocum Jr. (R)	68,080	36.4
2 Edward P. Beard (D)	154,453	76.5
Thomas V. Iannitti (R)	45,438	22.5

SOUTH CAROLINA

Candidates	Votes	%
1 Mendel J. Davis (D)	89,891	68.9
Lonnie Rowell (R)	40,598	31.1
2 Floyd D. Spence (R)	83,426	57.5
Clyde B. Livingston (D)	60,602	41.8
3 Butler C. Derrick (D)	117,740	99.9
4 James R. Mann (D)	91,721	73.5
Robert L. Watkins (R)	32,983	26.4
5 Kenneth L. Holland (D)	66,073	51.4
Bobby Richardson (R)	62,095	48.3
6 John W. Jenrette Jr. (D)	75,916	55.5
Edward L. Young (R)	60,288	44.0

SOUTH DAKOTA

Candidates	Votes	%
1 Larry Pressler (R)	121,587	79.8
James V. Guffey (D)	29,533	19.4
2 James Abdnor (R)	99,601	69.9
Grace Mickelson (D)	42,968	30.1

TENNESSEE

Candidates	Votes	%
1 James H. (Jimmy) Quillen (R)	97,781	57.9
Lloyd Blevins (D)	69,507	41.2

Candidates	Votes	%
2 John J. Duncan (R)	117,256	62.8
Mike Rowland (D)	69,449	37.2
3 Marilyn Lloyd (D)	123,872	67.5
LaMar Baker (R)	57,116	31.1
4 Albert Gore Jr. (D)	115,392	94.0
William H. McGlamery (I)	7,320	6.0
5 Clifford R. Allen (D)	125,830	92.4
Roger E. Bissell (I)	10,292	7.6
6 Robin L. Beard (R)	116,905	64.5
Ross Bass (D)	64,462	35.5
7 Ed Jones (D)	105,832	100.0
8 Harold E. Ford (D)	100,683	60.7
A. D. Alissandratos (R)	63,819	38.5

TEXAS

Candidates	Votes	%
1 Sam B. Hall Jr. (D)	135,384	83.7
James Hogan (R)	26,334	16.3
2 Charles Wilson (D)	133,910	95.0
James William Doyle III (AM)	6,992	5.0
3 James M. Collins (D)	171,343	74.0
Les E. Shackelford Jr. (D)	60,070	26.0
4 Ray Roberts (D)	105,394	62.7
Frank S. Glenn (R)	62,641	37.3
5 Jim Mattox (D)	67,871	54.0
Nancy Judy (R)	56,056	44.6
6 Olin E. Teague (D)	119,025	65.9
Wes Mowery (R)	60,316	33.4
7 Bill Archer (R)	193,127	100.0
8 Bob Eckhardt (D)	84,404	60.7
Nick Gearhart (R)	54,566	39.2
9 Jack Brooks (D)	112,945	99.9
10 J. J. (Jake) Pickle (D)	160,683	76.8
Paul McClure (R)	48,482	23.2
11 W. R. Poage (D)	92,142	57.4
Jack Burgess (R)	68,373	42.6
12 Jim Wright (D)	101,814	75.8
W. R. Durham (R)	31,941	23.8
13 Jack Hightower (D)	101,798	59.3
Bob Price (R)	69,328	40.4
14 John Young (D)	93,589	61.4
L. Dean Holford (R)	58,788	38.6
15 Eligio de la Garza (D)	102,837	74.4
R. L. (Lendy) McDonald (R)	35,446	25.6
16 Richard C. White (D)	71,876	57.8
Vic Shackelford (R)	52,499	42.2
17 Omar Burleson (D)	127,613	99.9
18 Barbara C. Jordan (D)	93,953	85.5
Sam H. Wright (R)	15,381	14.0
19 George Mahon (D)	87,908	54.6
Jim Reese (R)	72,991	45.4
20 Henry B. Gonzalez (D)	90,173	100.0
21 Robert Krueger (D)	149,395	71.0
Bobby A. Locke (R)	56,211	26.7
22 Bob Gammage (D)	96,535	50.1
Ron Paul (R)	96,267	49.9
23 Abraham Kazen Jr. (D)	96,481	100.0
24 Dale Milford (D)	82,743	63.4
Leo Berman (R)	47,075	36.1

Special Elections [2]

Candidates	Votes	%
1 Sam B. Hall Jr. (D)	20,556	72.0
Glen Jones (D)	6,327	22.2
22 Bob Gammage (D)	15,287	42.1
Ron Paul (R)	14,386	39.6
John S. Brunson (D)	3,670	10.1

Special Runoff Election

Candidates	Votes	%
22 Ron Paul (R)	39,041	56.2
Bob Gammage (D)	30,483	43.8

UTAH

Candidates	Votes	%
1 K. Gunn McKay (D)	155,631	58.2
Joe H. Ferguson (R)	106,542	39.8
2 Dan Marriott (R)	144,861	52.4
Allan T. Howe (D)	110,931	40.1
D. J. McCarty (WRITE IN)	20,508	7.4

VERMONT

Candidates	Votes	%
AL James M. Jeffords (R)	124,458	67.4
John A. Burgess (D,I VT)	60,202	32.6

VIRGINIA

Candidates	Votes	%
1 Paul S. Trible Jr. (R)	71,789	48.6
Robert E. Quinn (D)	70,159	47.5
2 G. William Whitehurst (R)	79,381	65.7
Robert E. Washington (D)	41,464	34.3
3 David E. Satterfield III (D)	129,066	87.9
A. R. Ogden (I)	17,503	11.9
4 Robert W. Daniel Jr. (R)	74,495	53.0
J. W. (Billy) O'Brien (D)	65,982	47.0
5 W. C. (Dan) Daniel (D)	101,038	100.0
6 M. Caldwell Butler (R)	90,830	62.2
Warren D. Saunders (I)	55.115	37.8
7 J. Kenneth Robinson (R)	115,508	81.6
James B. Hutt Jr. (I)	25,731	18.2
8 Herbert E. Harris (D)	83,245	51.6
James R. Tate (R)	68,729	42.6
Michael D. Cannon (I)	9,292	5.8
9 William C. Wampler (R)	96,052	57.3
Charles J. Horne (D)	71,439	42.6
10 Joseph L. Fisher (D)	103,689	54.7
Vincent F. Callahan Jr. (R)	73,616	38.8
E. Stanley Rittenhouse (I)	12,124	6.4

WASHINGTON

Candidates	Votes	%
1 Joel Pritchard (R)	161,354	71.9
Dave Wood (D)	58,006	25.8
2 Lloyd Meeds (D)	107,328	49.3
John Nance Garner (R)	106,786	49.0
3 Don Bonker (D)	145,198	70.8
Chuck Elhart (R)	57,517	28.0
4 Mike McCormack (D)	115,364	57.8
Dick Granger (R)	81,813	41.0
5 Thomas S. Foley (D)	120,415	58.0
Duane Alton (R)	84,262	40.6
6 Norman D. Dicks (D)	137,964	73.5
Robert M. Reynolds (R)	47,539	25.3
7 Brock Adams (D)	133,673	73.0
Raymond Pritchard (R)	46,448	25.4

WEST VIRGINIA

Candidates	Votes	%
1 Robert H. Mollohan (D)	108,103	58.0
John F. McCuskey (R)	78,159	42.0
2 Harley O. Staggers (D)	136,749	73.2
Jim Sloan (R)	50,079	26.8
3 John M. Slack (D)	128,086	99.7
4 Nick J. Rahall (D)	73,626	45.6
Ken Hechler (WRITE IN)	59,067	36.6
E. S. (Steve) Goodman (R)	28,825	17.8

WISCONSIN

Candidates	Votes	%
1 Les Aspin (D)	136,162	64.9
William W. Petrie (R)	71,427	34.0
2 Robert W. Kastenmeier (D)	155,158	65.6
Elizabeth T. Miller (R)	81,350	34.4
3 Alvin J. Baldus (D)	139,083	58.1
Adolf L. Gundersen (R)	100,218	41.9
4 Clement J. Zablocki (D)	172,166	100.0
5 Henry S. Reuss (D)	134,935	77.8
Robert L. Hicks (R)	36,413	21.0
6 William A. Steiger (R)	139,541	63.3
Joseph C. Smith (D)	80,715	36.6
7 David R. Obey (D)	171,366	73.3
Frank A. Savino (R)	60,952	26.1
8 Robert J. Cornell (D)	115,996	50.9
Harold V. Froehlich (R)	107,048	46.9
9 Robert W. Kasten Jr. (R)	163,791	65.9
Lynn M. McDonald (D)	84,706	34.1

WYOMING

	Votes	%
AL Teno Roncalio (D)	85,721	56.4
Larry Joe Hart (R)	66,147	43.6

1976 Election
1. Arkansas and Florida did not record the votes for unopposed candidates.
2. Texas election law required all candidates in special elections to run against each other, regardless of party. If no candidate received a majority, a special election runoff was held between the two candidates receiving the most votes in the special election.

1977 House Elections

GEORGIA

Special Election [1]

Candidates	Votes	%
5 Wyche Fowler Jr. (D)	29,898	39.6
John Lewis (D)	21,531	28.6
Paul D. Coverdell (R)	16,509	21.9

Special Runoff Election

	Votes	%
5 Wyche Fowler Jr. (D)	54,378	62.4
John Lewis (D)	32,732	37.6

LOUISIANA

Special Election

Candidates	Votes	%
1 Robert L. Livingston (R)	56,121	51.2
Ron Faucheux (D)	40,802	37.2
Sanford Krasnoff (I)	12,665	11.6

MINNESOTA

Special Election

	Votes	%
7 Arlan Stangeland (I-R)	71,340	57.6
Michael J. Sullivan (DFL)	45,490	36.7

WASHINGTON

Special Election

Candidates	Votes	%
7 John E. Cunningham (R)	42,650	54.0
Marvin Durning (D)	35,525	45.0

1977 Election
1. Georgia election law required all candidates in special elections to run against each other, regardless of party. If no candidate received a majority, a special election runoff was held between the two candidates receiving the most votes in the special election.

1978 House Elections

ALABAMA

Candidates	Votes	%
1 Jack Edwards (R)	71,711	63.9
L. W. (Red) Noonan (D)	40,450	36.1
2 William L. Dickinson (R)	57,924	54.0
Wendell Mitchell (D)	49,341	46.0
3 Bill Nichols (D)	74,895	100.0
4 Tom Bevill (D)	87,380	100.0
5 Ronnie G. Flippo (D)	68,985	96.8
6 John Buchanan (R)	65,700	61.7
Don Hawkins (D)	40,771	38.3
7 Richard C. Shelby (D)	77,742	93.8

ALASKA

Candidates	Votes	%
AL Don Young (R)	68,811	55.4
Patrick Rodey (D)	55,176	44.4

ARIZONA

Candidates	Votes	%
1 John J. Rhodes (R)	81,108	71.0
Ken Graves (D)	33,178	29.0
2 Morris K. Udall (D)	67,878	52.5
Tom Richey (R)	58,697	45.4
3 Bob Stump (D)	111,850	85.0
Kathleen Cooke (LIBERT)	19,813	15.0
4 Eldon Rudd (R)	90,768	63.1
Michael L. McCormick (D)	48,661	33.8

ARKANSAS

Candidates	Votes	%
1 Bill Alexander (D)		100.0
2 Ed Bethune (R)	65,285	51.2
Doug Brandon (D)	62,140	48.8
3 John Paul Hammerschmidt (R)	130,086	78.4
William C. Mears (D)	35,748	21.6
4 Beryl F. Anthony Jr. (D)		100.0

CALIFORNIA

Candidates	Votes	%
1 Harold T. Johnson (D)	125,122	59.4
James E. Taylor (R)	85,690	40.6
2 Don H. Clausen (R)	114,451	52.0
Norma Bork (D)	99,712	45.3
3 Robert T. Matsui (D)	105,537	53.4
Sandy Smoley (R)	91,966	46.6
4 Vic Fazio (D)	87,764	55.4
Rex Hime (R)	70,733	44.6
5 John L. Burton (D)	106,046	66.8
Dolores Skore (R)	52,603	33.2
6 Phillip Burton (D)	81,801	68.3
Tom Spinosa (R)	33,515	27.9
7 George Miller (D)	109,676	63.4
Paula Gordon (R)	58,332	33.7
8 Ronald V. Dellums (D)	94,824	57.4
Charles V. Hughes (R)	70,481	42.6
9 Fortney H. (Pete) Stark (D)	88,179	65.4
Robert S. Allen (R)	41,138	30.5
10 Don Edwards (D)	84,488	67.1
Rudy Hansen (R)	41,374	32.9
11 Leo J. Ryan (D)	92,882	60.5
David Welch (R)	54,621	35.6
12 Paul N. McCloskey Jr. (R)	116,982	73.1
Kirsten Olsen (D)	34,472	21.5
13 Norman Y. Mineta (D)	100,809	57.5
Dan O'Keefe (R)	69,306	39.5
14 Norman D. Shumway (R)	95,962	53.4
John J. McFall (D)	76,602	42.6
15 Tony Coelho (D)	75,212	60.1
Chris Patterakis (R)	49,914	39.9
16 Leon E. Panetta (D)	104,550	61.4
Eric Seastrand (R)	65,808	38.6
17 Charles (Chip) Pashayan Jr. (R)	81,296	54.5
John Krebs (D)	67,885	45.5
18 William Thomas (R)	85,663	59.2
Bob Sogge (D)	58,900	40.7

Candidates	Votes	%
19 Robert J. Lagomarsino (R)	123,192	71.7
Jerome Zamos (D)	41,672	24.3
20 Barry M. Goldwater Jr. (R)	129,714	66.4
Pat Lear (D)	65,695	33.6
21 James C. Corman (D)	73,869	59.5
G. (Rod) Walsh (R)	44,519	35.9
22 Carlos J. Moorehead (R)	99,502	64.6
Robert S. Henry (D)	54,442	35.4
23 Anthony C. (Tony) Beilenson (D)	117,498	65.6
Joseph Barbara (R)	61,496	34.4
24 Henry A. Waxman (D)	85,075	62.7
Howard G. Schaefer (R)	44,243	32.6
25 Edward R. Roybal (D)	45,881	67.4
Robert K. Watson (R)	22,205	32.6
26 John H. Rousselot (R)	113,059	100.0
27 Robert K. Dornan (R)	89,392	51.0
Carey Peck (D)	85,880	49.0
28 Julian C. Dixon (D)	97,592	100.0
29 Augustus F. Hawkins (D)	65,214	85.0
Uriah J. Fields (R)	11,512	15.0
30 George E. Danielson (D)	66,241	71.4
Henry Ares (R)	26,511	28.6
31 Charles H. Wilson (D)	55,667	67.7
Don Grimshaw (R)	26,490	32.2
32 Glenn M. Anderson (D)	74,004	71.4
Sonya (Sonny) Mathison (R)	23,242	22.4
Ida Bader (AM I)	6,363	6.1
33 Wayne Grisham (R)	79,533	56.0
Dennis S. Kazarian (D)	62,540	44.0
34 Daniel E. Lungren (R)	90,554	53.7
Mark W. Hannaford (D)	73,608	43.7
35 Jim Lloyd (D)	80,388	54.0
David Dreier (R)	68,442	46.0
36 George E. Brown Jr. (D)	80,448	62.9
Dana Warren Carmody (R)	47,417	37.1
37 Jerry Lewis (R)	106,581	61.4
Dan Corcoran (D)	60,463	34.8
38 Jerry M. Patterson (D)	75,471	58.6
Don Goedeke (R)	53,298	41.4
39 William E. Dannemeyer (R)	112,160	63.7
William E. Farris (D)	63,891	36.3
40 Robert E. Badham (R)	147,882	65.9
Jim McGuy (D)	76,358	34.1
41 Bob Wilson (R)	107,685	58.1
King Golden Jr. (D)	77,540	41.9
42 Lionel Van Deerlin (D)	85,126	73.7
Lawrence C. Mattera (R)	30,319	26.3
43 Clair W. Burgener (R)	167,150	68.7
Ruben B. Brooks (D)	76,308	31.3

COLORADO

Candidates	Votes	%
1 Patricia Schroeder (D)	82,742	61.5
Gene Hutcheson (R)	49,845	37.0
2 Timothy E. Wirth (D)	98,889	52.9
Ed Scott (R)	88,072	47.1
3 Ray Kogovsek (D)	69,669	49.3
Harold L. McCormick (R)	69,303	49.0
4 James P. (Jim) Johnson (R)	103,121	61.2
Morgan Smith (D)	65,241	38.8
5 Ken Kramer (R)	91,933	59.8
Gerry Frank (D)	52,914	34.4
L. W. Dan Bridges (I)	8,933	5.8

CONNECTICUT

Candidates	Votes	%
1 William R. Cotter (D)	102,749	59.5
Ben F. Andrews Jr. (R)	67,828	39.3
2 Christopher J. Dodd (D)	116,624	69.9
Thomas H. Connell (R)	50,167	30.1
3 Robert N. Giaimo (D)	96,830	58.1
John G. Pucciano (R)	66,663	40.0
4 Stewart B. McKinney (R)	83,990	58.4
Michael W. Morgan (D)	59,918	41.6
5 William R. Ratchford (D)	96,738	52.3
George C. Guidera (R)	88,162	47.7

Candidates	Votes	%
6 Toby Moffett (D)	119,537	64.2
Daniel F. MacKinnon (R)	66,664	35.8

DELAWARE

Candidates	Votes	%
AL Thomas B. Evans Jr. (R)	91,689	58.2
Gary E. Hindes (D)	64,863	41.2

FLORIDA

Candidates	Votes	%
1 Earl D. Hutto (D)	85,608	63.3
Warren Briggs (R)	49,715	36.7
2 Don Fuqua (D)	112,649	81.7
Peter L. W. Brathwaite (R)	25,148	18.3
3 Charles E. Bennett (D)		100.0
4 Bill Chappell Jr. (D)	113,302	73.1
Tom Boney (R)	41,647	26.9
5 Richard Kelly (R)	106,319	51.1
David R. Best (D)	101,867	48.9
6 C. W. Bill Young (R)	150,694	78.8
James A. Christison (D)	40,654	21.2
7 Sam Gibbons (D)		100.0
8 Andy Ireland (D)		100.0
9 Bill Nelson (D)	89,543	61.5
Edward J. Gurney (R)	56,074	38.5
10 L. A. (Skip) Bafalis (R)		100.0
11 Dan Mica (D)	123,346	55.3
Bill James (R)	99,757	44.7
12 Edward J. Stack (D)	107,037	61.6
J. Herbert Burke (R)	66,610	38.4
13 William Lehman (D)		100.0
14 Claude Pepper (D)	65,202	63.1
Al Cardenas (R)	38,081	36.9
15 Dante B. Fascell (D)	108,837	74.2
Herbert J. Hoodwin (R)	37,897	25.8

GEORGIA

Candidates	Votes	%
1 Bo Ginn (D)	36,961	100.0
2 Dawson Mathis (D)	42,234	100.0
3 Jack Brinkley (D)	54,881	100.0
4 Elliott H. Levitas (D)	60,284	80.9
Homer Cheung (R)	14,221	19.1
5 Wyche Fowler Jr. (D)	52,739	75.5
Thomas P. Bowles Jr. (R)	17,132	24.5
6 Newt Gingrich (R)	47,078	54.4
Virginia Shapard (D)	39,451	45.6
7 Larry P. McDonald (D)	47,090	66.5
Ernie Norsworthy (R)	23,698	33.5
8 Billy Lee Evans (D)	41,184	100.0
9 Ed Jenkins (D)	47,264	76.9
David G. Ashworth (R)	14,172	23.1
10 Doug Barnard (D)	50,122	100.0

HAWAII

Candidates	Votes	%
1 Cecil (Cec) Heftel (D)	84,552	73.3
William D. Spillane (R)	24,470	21.2
2 Daniel K. Akaka (D)	118,272	85.7
Charles Isaak (R)	15,697	11.4

IDAHO

Candidates	Votes	%
1 Steven D. Symms (R)	86,680	59.9
Roy Truby (D)	57,972	40.1
2 George Hansen (R)	80,591	57.3
Stan Kress (D)	60,040	42.7

ILLINOIS

Candidates	Votes	%
1 Bennett Stewart (D)	47,581	58.5
A. A. Rayner (R)	33,540	41.3
2 Morgan F. Murphy (D)	80,906	86.0
James Wognum (R)	11,104	11.8

Candidates	Votes	%
3 Marty Russo (D)	95,701	65.2
Robert L. Dunne (R)	51,098	34.8
4 Edward J. Derwinski (R)	94,435	66.9
Andrew D. Thomas (D)	46,788	33.1
5 John G. Fary (D)	98,702	84.0
Joseph A. Barracca (R)	18,802	16.0
6 Henry J. Hyde (R)	87,193	66.2
Jeanne P. Quinn (D)	44,543	33.8
7 Cardiss Collins (D)	64,716	86.3
James C. Holt (R)	10,273	13.7
8 Dan Rostenkowski (D)	81,457	86.0
Carl C. LoDico (R)	13,302	14.0
9 Sidney R. Yates (D)	87,543	75.3
John M. Collins (R)	28,673	24.7
10 Abner J. Mikva (R)	89,479	50.2
John E. Porter (R)	88,829	49.8
11 Frank Annunzio (D)	112,365	73.7
John Hoeger (R)	40,044	26.3
12 Philip M. Crane (R)	110,503	79.5
Gilbert Bogen (D)	28,424	20.5
13 Robert McClory (R)	64,060	61.2
Frederick J. Steffen (D)	40,675	38.8
14 John N. Erlenborn (R)	118,741	75.1
James A. Romanyak (D)	39,438	24.9
15 Tom Corcoran (R)	80,856	62.4
Tim L. Hall (D)	48,756	37.6
16 John B. Anderson (R)	76,752	65.4
Ernest W. Dahlin (D)	40,471	34.5
17 George M. O'Brien (R)	94,375	70.6
Clifford J. Sinclair (D)	39,260	29.4
18 Robert H. Michel (R)	85,973	65.9
Virgil R. Grunkemeyer (D)	44,527	34.1
19 Tom Railsback (R)	89,770	100.0
20 Paul Findley (R)	111,054	69.6
Victor W. Roberts (D)	48,426	30.4
21 Edward R. Madigan (R)	97,473	78.3
Kenneth E. Baughman (D)	27,054	21.7
22 Daniel B. Crane (R)	86,051	54.0
Terry L. Bruce (D)	73,331	46.0
23 Melvin Price (D)	74,247	74.2
Daniel J. Stack (R)	25,858	25.8
24 Paul Simon (D)	110,298	65.6
John T. Anderson (R)	57,763	34.4

INDIANA

Candidates	Votes	%
1 Adam Benjamin Jr. (D)	72,367	80.3
Owen W. Crumpacker (R)	17,419	19.3
2 Floyd Fithian (D)	82,402	56.5
J. Philip Oppenheim (R)	52,842	36.2
William Costas (I)	9,368	6.4
3 John Brademas (D)	64,336	55.5
Thomas L. Thorson (R)	50,145	43.3
4 Dan Quayle (R)	80,527	64.4
John D. Walda (D)	42,238	33.8
5 Elwood Hillis (R)	94,950	67.6
Max E. Heiss (D)	45,479	32.4
6 David W. Evans (D)	66,421	52.2
David G. Crane (R)	60,630	47.6
7 John T. Myers (R)	86,955	56.3
Charlotte Zietlow (D)	67,469	43.7
8 H. Joel Deckard (R)	83,019	52.0
David L. Cornwell (D)	76,654	48.0
9 Lee H. Hamilton Jr. (D)	99,727	65.6
Frank I. Hamilton Jr. (R)	52,218	34.4
10 Phil Sharp (D)	73,343	56.1
William G. Frazier (R)	55,999	42.8
11 Andy Jacobs Jr. (D)	61,504	57.2
Charles F. Bosma (R)	45,809	42.6

IOWA

Candidates	Votes	%
1 Jim Leach (R)	79,940	63.5
Dick Myers (D)	45,037	35.8
2 Tom Tauke (R)	72,644	52.3
Michael T. Blouin (D)	65,450	47.1
3 Charles E. Grassley (R)	103,659	74.8
John Knudson (D)	34,880	25.2
4 Neal Smith (D)	88,526	64.7
Charles E. Minor (R)	48,308	35.3

Candidates	Votes	%
5 Tom Harkin (D)	82,333	58.9
Julian B. Garrett (R)	57,377	41.1
6 Berkley Bedell (D)	87,139	66.3
Willis E. Junker (R)	44,320	33.7

KANSAS

Candidates	Votes	%
1 Keith G. Sebelius (R)	131,037	100.0
2 Jim Jeffries (R)	76,419	52.0
Martha Keys (D)	70,460	48.0
3 Larry Winn Jr. (R)	103,265	100.0
4 Dan Glickman (D)	100,139	69.5
James P. Litsey (R)	43,854	30.5
5 Robert Whittaker (R)	86,011	57.0
Donald L. Allegrucci (D)	62,402	41.4

KENTUCKY

Candidates	Votes	%
1 Carroll Hubbard Jr. (D)	44,090	100.0
2 William H. Natcher (D)	36,441	100.0
3 Romano L. Mazzoli (D)	37,346	65.7
Norbert D. Leveronne (R)	17,785	31.3
4 Gene Snyder (R)	62,087	65.8
George C. Martin (D)	32,212	34.2
5 Tim Lee Carter (R)	59,743	79.2
Jesse M. Ramey (D)	15,714	20.8
6 Larry J. Hopkins (R)	52,092	50.6
Tom Easterly (D)	47,436	46.1
7 Carl D. Perkins (D)	51,559	76.5
Granville Thomas (R)	15,861	23.5

LOUISIANA [1]

Candidates	Votes	%
1 Robert L. Livingston (R)		100.0
2 Lindy Boggs (D)		100.0
3 David C. Treen (R)		100.0
4 Claude (Buddy) Leach (D)	65,583	50.1
Jimmy Wilson (R)	65,317	49.9
5 Jerry Huckaby (D)		100.0
6 W. Henson Moore (R)		100.0
7 John B. Breaux (D)		100.0
8 Gillis W. Long (D)		100.0

MAINE

Candidates	Votes	%
1 David F. Emery (R)	120,791	61.5
John Quinn (D)	70,348	35.8
2 Olympia J. Snowe (R)	87,939	50.8
Markham L. Gartley (D)	70,691	40.8

MARYLAND

Candidates	Votes	%
1 Robert E. Bauman (R)	80,202	63.5
Joseph D. Quinn (D)	46,093	36.5
2 Clarence D. Long (D)	98,601	66.4
Malcolm M. McKnight (R)	49,886	33.6
3 Barbara A. Mikulski (D)	91,189	100.0
4 Marjorie S. Holt (R)	71,374	62.0
Sue F. Ward (D)	43,663	38.0
5 Gladys Noon Spellman (D)	64,868	77.2
Saul J. Harris (R)	19,160	22.8
6 Beverly Byron (D)	126,196	89.7
Melvin Perkins (R)	14,545	10.3
7 Parren J. Mitchell (D)	51,996	88.7
Debra Hanania Freeman (I)	6,626	11.3
8 Michael D. Barnes (D)	81,851	51.3
Newton I. Steers Jr. (R)	77,807	48.7

MASSACHUSETTS

Candidates	Votes	%
1 Silvio O. Conte (R)	131,773	100.0
2 Edward P. Boland (D)	101,570	72.8
Thomas P. Swank (R)	37,881	27.2
3 Joseph D. Early (D)	119,337	75.2
Charles Kevin MacLeod (R)	39,259	24.7
4 Robert F. Drinan (D)	111,353	100.0
5 James M. Shannon (D)	90,156	52.2

Candidates	Votes	%
John J. Buckley (R)	48,685	28.2
James J. Gaffney III (I)	33,835	19.6
6 Nicholas Mavroules (D)	97,099	53.8
William E. Bronson (R)	83,511	46.2
7 Edward J. Markey (D)	145,615	84.8
James J. Murphy (I)	26,017	15.2
8 Thomas P. O'Neill Jr. (D)	102,160	74.6
William A. Barnstead (R)	28,566	20.9
9 Joe Moakley (D)	106,805	91.8
Brenda Lee Franklin (SOC WORK)	6,794	5.8
10 Margaret M. Heckler (R)	102,080	61.1
John J. Marino (D)	64,868	38.9
11 Brian J. Donnelly (D)	133,644	91.7
H. Graham Lowry (USLP)	12,044	8.3
12 Gerry E. Studds (D)	176,704	99.9

MICHIGAN

Candidates	Votes	%
1 John Conyers Jr. (D)	89,646	92.9
Robert S. Arnold (R)	6,878	7.1
2 Carl D. Pursell (R)	97,503	67.6
Earl Greene (D)	45,631	31.6
3 Howard Wolpe (D)	83,932	51.3
Garry Brown (R)	79,572	48.7
4 Dave Stockman (R)	95,440	70.6
Morgan L. Hager Jr. (D)	38,204	28.3
5 Harold S. Sawyer (R)	81,794	49.4
Dale R. Sprik (D)	80,622	48.7
6 Bob Carr (D)	97,971	56.7
Mike Conlin (R)	74,718	43.3
7 Dale E. Kildee (D)	105,402	76.6
Gale N. Cronk (R)	29,958	21.8
8 Bob Traxler (D)	103,346	66.6
Norman R. Hughes (R)	51,900	33.4
9 Guy Vander Jagt (R)	122,363	69.6
Howard M. Leroux (D)	53,450	30.4
10 Donald J. Albosta (D)	94,913	51.5
Elford A. Cederberg (R)	89,451	48.5
11 Robert W. Davis (R)	96,351	54.9
Keith McLeod (D)	79,081	45.1
12 David E. Bonior (D)	82,892	54.9
Kirby Holmes (R)	68,063	45.1
13 Charles C. Diggs Jr. (D)	44,771	79.2
Dovie T. Pickett (R)	11,749	20.8
14 Lucien N. Nedzi (D)	84,032	67.4
John Edward Getz (R)	40,716	32.6
15 William D. Ford (D)	95,137	79.6
Edgar Nieten (R)	23,177	19.4
16 John D. Dingell (D)	93,387	76.5
Melvin E. Heuer (R)	26,827	22.0
17 William M. Brodhead (D)	106,303	95.2
18 James J. Blanchard (D)	113,037	74.5
Robert J. Salloum (R)	36,913	24.3
19 William S. Broomfield (R)	117,122	71.3
Betty F. Collier (D)	47,165	28.7

MINNESOTA

Candidates	Votes	%
1 Arlen Erdahl (I-R)	110,090	56.2
Gerry Sikorski (DFL)	83,271	42.5
2 Tom Hagedorn (I-R)	145,415	70.4
John F. Considine (DFL)	61,173	29.6
3 Bill Frenzel (I-R)	128,759	65.7
Michael O. Freeman (DFL)	67,120	34.3
4 Bruce F. Vento (DFL)	95,989	58.0
John R. Berg (I-R)	69,396	42.0
5 Martin Olav Sabo (DFL)	91,673	62.3
Michael Till (I-R)	55,412	37.7
6 Richard Nolan (DFL)	115,880	55.3
Russ Bjorhus (I-R)	93,742	44.7
7 Arlan Stangeland (I-R)	109,456	52.4
Gene R. Wenstrom (DFL)	93,055	44.5
8 James L. Oberstar (DFL)	171,125	87.2
John W. Hull (AM)	25,015	12.7

MISSISSIPPI

Candidates	Votes	%
1 Jamie L. Whitten (D)	57,358	66.6
T. K. Moffett (R)	26,734	31.0

Candidates	Votes	%
2 David R. Bowen (D)	57,678	61.7
Roland Byrd (R)	35,730	38.2
3 G. V. (Sonny) Montgomery (D)	101,685	92.3
Dorothy Cleveland (R)	8,408	7.6
4 Jon C. Hinson (R)	68,225	51.6
John Hampton Stennis (D)	34,837	26.4
Evan Doss (I)	25,134	19.0
5 Trent Lott (R)	97,177	100.0

MISSOURI

Candidates	Votes	%
1 William (Bill) Clay (D)	65,950	66.6
William E. White (R)	30,995	31.3
2 Robert A. Young (D)	102,911	56.4
Robert C. Chase (R)	79,495	43.6
3 Richard A. Gephardt (D)	121,565	81.9
Lee Buchschacher (R)	26,881	18.1
4 Ike Skelton (D)	120,748	72.8
William D. Baker (R)	45,116	27.2
5 Richard Bolling (D)	82,140	72.0
Steven L. Walter (R)	30,360	26.6
6 E. Thomas Coleman (R)	96,574	55.9
Phil Snowden (D)	76,061	44.1
7 Gene Taylor (R)	104,566	61.2
Jim Thomas (D)	66,351	38.8
8 Richard H. Ichord (D)	96,509	60.5
Donald D. Meyer (R)	63,109	39.5
9 Harold L. Volkmer (D)	135,170	74.7
Jerry A. Dent (R)	45,795	25.3
10 Bill D. Burlison (D)	99,148	65.3
James A. Weir (R)	52,687	34.7

MONTANA

Candidates	Votes	%
1 Pat Williams (D)	86,016	57.3
Jim Waltermire (R)	64,093	42.7
2 Ron Marlenee (R)	75,766	56.9
Thomas G. Monahan (D)	57,480	43.1

NEBRASKA

Candidates	Votes	%
1 Douglas K. Bereuter (R)	99,013	58.1
Hess Dyas (D)	71,311	41.9
2 John J. Cavanaugh (D)	77,135	52.3
Harold J. Daub Jr. (R)	70,309	47.7
3 Virginia Smith (R)	141,597	80.0
Marilyn Fowler (D)	35,371	20.0

NEVADA

Candidates	Votes	%
AL Jim Santini (D)	132,513	69.5
Bill O'Mara (R)	44,425	23.3

NEW HAMPSHIRE

Candidates	Votes	%
1 Norman E. D'Amours (D)	82,697	61.6
Daniel M. Hughes (R)	49,131	36.6
2 James C. Cleveland (R)	84,535	68.1
Edgar J. Helms (D)	39,546	31.9

NEW JERSEY

Candidates	Votes	%
1 James J. Florio (D)	106,096	79.4
Robert M. Deitch (R)	26,853	20.1
2 William J. Hughes (D)	112,768	66.4
James H. Biggs (R)	56,997	33.6
3 James J. Howard (D)	83,349	56.0
Bruce G. Coe (R)	64,730	43.5
4 Frank Thompson Jr. (D)	69,259	61.1
Christopher H. Smith (R)	41,833	36.9
5 Millicent Fenwick (R)	100,739	72.6
John T. Fahy (D)	38,108	27.4
6 Edwin B. Forsythe (R)	89,446	60.4
W. Thomas McGann (D)	56,874	38.4
7 Andrew Maguire (D)	78,358	52.5
Margaret S. Roukema (R)	69,543	46.6

Candidates	Votes	%
8 Robert A. Roe (D)	69,496	74.5
Thomas Melani (R)	23,842	25.5
9 Harold C. Hollenback (R)	73,478	48.9
Nicholas S. Mastorelli (R)	56,888	37.9
Henry Helstoski (I)	19,126	12.7
10 Peter W. Rodino Jr. (D)	55,074	86.4
John L. Pelt (R)	8,066	12.6
11 Joseph G. Minish (D)	88,294	70.5
Julius George Feld (R)	35,642	28.5
12 Matthew J. Rinaldo (R)	94,850	73.4
Richard McCormack (D)	34,423	26.6
13 James A. Courter (R)	77,301	51.8
Helen Meyner (D)	71,808	48.2
14 Frank J. Guarini (D)	67,008	63.6
Henry J. Hill (R)	21,355	20.3
Thomas E. McDonough (I)	15,015	14.3
15 Edward J. Patten (D)	55,944	48.3
Charles W. Wiley (R)	53,108	45.8

NEW MEXICO

Candidates	Votes	%
1 Manuel Lujan Jr. (R)	118,075	62.5
Robert Hawk (D)	70,761	37.5
2 Harold Runnels (D)	95,710	100.0

NEW YORK

Candidates	Votes	%
1 William Carney (R, C)	90,115	56.3
John F. Randolph (D)	67,180	41.9
2 Thomas J. Downey (D)	64,807	54.9
Harold J. Withers Jr. (R, C)	53,322	45.1
3 Jerome A. Ambro (D)	70,526	50.9
Gregory W. Carman (R, C)	66,458	47.9
4 Norman F. Lent (R, C)	94,711	66.1
Everett A. Rosenblum (D)	46,508	32.5
5 John W. Wydler (R, C)	84,864	58.4
John W. Matthews (D, L)	60,519	41.6
6 Lester L. Wolff (D, L)	80,799	60.0
Stuart L. Ain (R)	44,304	32.9
Howard Horowitz (C)	9,503	7.1
7 Joseph P. Addabbo (D, R, L)	73,066	94.9
Mark Elliott Scott (C)	3,935	5.1
8 Benjamin S. Rosenthal (D, L)	74,872	78.6
Albert Lemishow (R)	15,165	15.9
Paul C. Ruebenacker (C)	5,165	5.4
9 Geraldine A. Ferraro (D)	51,350	54.2
Alfred A. DelliBovi (R, C)	42,108	44.4
10 Mario Biaggi (D, R, L)	77,979	95.0
Carmen Ricciardi (C)	4,082	5.0
11 James H. Scheuer (D, L)	58,997	78.5
Kenneth Huhn (R, C)	16,206	21.5
12 Shirley Chisholm (D, L)	25,697	87.8
Charles Gibb (R)	3,580	12.2
13 Stephen J. Solarz (D, L)	68,837	81.1
Max Carasso (R, C)	16,002	18.9
14 Frederick Richmond (D. L)	31,339	76.9
Arthur Bramwell (R)	7,516	18.4
15 Leo C. Zeferetti (D, C)	49,272	68.1
Robert P. Whelan (R)	20,508	28.4
16 Elizabeth Holtzman (D, L)	59,703	81.9
Larry Penner (R, UT)	9,405	12.9
John H. Fox (C)	3,782	5.2
17 John M. Murphy (D)	54,228	54.2
John Michael Peters (R, C)	33,071	33.1
Thomas H. Stokes (L)	12,662	12.7
18 S. William Green (R)	60,867	53.3
Carter Burden (D, L)	53,434	46.7
19 Charles B. Rangel (D, R, L)	59,731	96.4
20 Ted Weiss (D. L)	64,275	84.6
Harry Torczyner (R)	11,661	15.4
21 Robert Garcia (D, R, L)	23,950	98.0
22 Jonathan B. Bingham (D, L)	58,727	84.1
Anthony J. Geidel Jr. (R, C)	11,110	15.9
23 Peter A. Peyser (D)	66,354	51.6
Angelo R. Martinelli (R, C)	59,455	46.2
24 Richard L. Ottinger (D)	75,397	56.1
Michael R. Edelman (R, C)	57,451	42.7
25 Hamilton Fish Jr. (R)	114,641	78.2
Gunars M. Ozols (D)	31,213	21.3
26 Benjamin A. Gilman (R)	87,059	62.3

Candidates	Votes	%
Charles E. Holbrook (D, L)	41,870	30.0
William R. Schaeffer Jr. (C)	10,708	7.7
27 Matthew F. McHugh (D)	83,413	55.8
Neil Tyler Wallace (R, C)	66,117	44.2
28 Samuel S. Stratton (D)	139,575	76.3
Paul H. Tocker (R, C)	36,017	19.7
29 Gerald B. Solomon (R, C)	99,518	54.0
Edward W. Pattison (D, L)	84,705	46.0
30 Robert C. McEwen (R)	85,478	60.5
Norma A. Bartle (D, L)	55,785	39.5
31 Donald J. Mitchell (R, C)	107,791	100.0
32 James M. Hanley (D)	76,251	52.4
Peter J. Del Giorno (R, C)	67,071	46.1
33 Gary A. Lee (R)	82,501	56.0
Roy A. Bernardi (D)	58,286	39.5
34 Frank Horton (R, D)	122,785	87.1
Leo J. Kesselring (C)	18,127	12.9
35 Barber B. Conable Jr. (R)	96,119	69.4
Francis C. Repicci (D)	36,428	26.3
36 John J. LaFalce (D, L)	99,497	74.1
Francina J. Cartonia (R)	31,527	23.5
37 Henry J. Nowak (D, L)	70,911	78.6
Charles Roth III (R)	17,585	19.5
38 Jack F. Kemp (R, C)	113,928	94.8
James A. Peck (L)	6,204	5.2
39 Stanley N. Lundine (D)	79,385	58.5
Crispin M. Maguire (R, C)	56,431	41.5

Special Elections

Candidates	Votes	%
18 S. William Green (R)	30,332	50.5
Bella S. Abzug (D, L)	29,189	48.5
21 Robert Garcia (R, L)	7,959	55.4
Louis Nine (D, C)	3,514	24.5
Ramon S. Valez (I)	2,280	15.9

NORTH CAROLINA

Candidates	Votes	%
1 Walter B. Jones (D)	67,716	80.1
James Newcomb (R)	16,814	19.9
2 L. H. Fountain (D)	61,851	78.2
Barry L. Gardner (R)	15,988	20.2
3 Charlie Whitley (D)	54,452	71.1
Willard J. Blanchard (R)	22,150	28.9
4 Ike F. Andrews (D)	74,249	94.4
Naudeen Beek (LIBERT)	4,436	5.6
5 Stephen L. Neal (D)	68,778	54.2
Hamilton C. Horton Jr. (R)	58,161	45.8
6 Richardson Preyer (D)	58,193	68.4
George Bemus (R)	26,882	31.6
7 Charlie Rose (D)	53,696	69.9
Raymond C. Schrump (R)	23,146	30.1
8 W. G. (Bill) Hefner (D)	63,168	59.0
Roger Austin (R)	43,942	41.0
9 James G. Martin (R)	66,157	68.3
Charles Maxwell (D)	29,761	30.7
10 James T. Broyhill (R)	67,004	100.0
11 Lamar Gudger (D)	75,460	53.4
R. Curtis Ratcliff (R)	65,832	46.6

NORTH DAKOTA

Candidates	Votes	%
AL Mark Andrews (R)	147,746	67.1
Bruce Hagen (D)	68,016	30.9

OHIO

Candidates	Votes	%
1 Bill Gradison (R)	73,593	64.5
Timothy M. Burke (D)	38,669	33.9
2 Thomas A. Luken (D)	64,522	52.4
Stanley J. Aronoff (R)	58,716	47.6
3 Tony P. Hall (D)	62,849	53.8
Dudley P. Kircher (R)	51,833	44.4
4 Tennyson Guyer (R)	85,575	68.5
John W. Griffin (D)	39,360	31.5
5 Delbert L. Latta (R)	85,547	62.6
James R. Sherck (D)	51,071	37.4
6 William H. Harsha (R)	85,592	64.9
Ted Strickland (D)	46,318	35.1

Candidates	Votes	%
7 Clarence J. Brown (R)	92,507	100.0
8 Thomas N. Kindness (R)	81,156	71.4
Lou Schroeder (D)	32,493	28.6
9 Thomas L. Ashley (D)	71,709	63.4
John C. Hoyt (R)	34,326	30.3
10 Clarence E. Miller (R)	99,329	73.9
James A. Plummer (D)	35,039	26.1
11 J. William Stanton (R)	89,327	68.1
Patrick J. Donlin (D)	37,131	28.3
12 Samuel L. Devine (R)	81,573	56.9
James L. Baumann (D)	61,698	43.1
13 Don J. Pease (D)	80,875	65.1
Mark W. Whitfield (R)	43,269	34.9
14 John F. Seiberling (D)	82,356	72.5
Walter J. Vogel (R)	31,311	27.5
15 Chalmers P. Wylie (R)	91,023	71.1
Henry W. Eckhart (D)	37,000	28.9
16 Ralph S. Regula (R)	105,152	78.0
Owen S. Hand Jr. (D)	29,640	22.0
17 John M. Ashbrook (R)	87,010	67.4
Kenneth R. Grier (D)	42,117	32.6
18 Douglas Applegate (D)	71,894	59.5
Bill Ress (R)	48,931	40.5
19 Lyle Williams (R)	71,890	50.7
Charles J. Carney (D)	69,977	49.3
20 Mary Rose Oakar (D)	76,973	100.0
21 Louis Stokes (D)	58,934	86.1
Bill Mack (R)	9,533	13.9
22 Charles A. Vanik (D)	87,551	66.0
Richard W. Sander (R)	30,935	23.3
James F. Sexton (I)	7,126	5.4
Robert E. Lehman (I)	6,960	5.2
23 Ronald M. Mottl (D)	99,975	74.8
Homes S. Taft (R)	33,732	25.2

OKLAHOMA

Candidates	Votes	%
1 James R. Jones (D)	73,886	59.9
Paula Unruh (R)	49,404	40.1
2 Mike Synar (D)	72,583	54.8
Gary L. Richardson (R)	59,853	45.2
3 Wes Watkins (D)		100.0
4 Tom Steed (D)	62,993	60.3
Scotty Robb (R)	41,421	39.7
5 Mickey Edwards (R)	71,451	79.9
Jesse D. Knipp (D)	17,978	20.1
6 Glenn English (D)	103,512	74.2
Harold Hunter (R)	36,031	25.8

OREGON

Candidates	Votes	%
1 Les AuCoin (D)	158,706	62.9
Nick Bunick (R)	93,640	37.1
2 Al Ullman (D)	152,099	69.1
Terry L. Hicks (R)	67,547	30.7
3 Robert Duncan (D)	151,895	84.6
Martin Simon (USLP)	27,120	15.1
4 James Weaver (D)	124,745	56.3
Jerry L. Lausmann (R)	96,953	43.7

PENNSYLVANIA

Candidates	Votes	%
1 Michael (Ozzie) Myers (D)	104,412	71.9
Samuel N. Fanelli (R)	37,913	26.1
2 William H. Gray III (D)	132,594	82.0
Roland J. Atkins (R)	25,785	15.9
3 Raymond F. Lederer (D)	86,915	71.8
Raymond S. Kauffman (R)	33,750	28.2
4 Charles F. Dougherty (R)	119,445	55.8
Joshua Eilberg (D)	87,555	44.2
5 Richard T. Schulze (R)	119,565	75.1
Murray P. Zealor (D)	36,704	24.9
6 Gus Yatron (D)	196,432	73.8
Stephen Mazur (R)	37,746	26.2
7 Robert W. Edgar (D)	79,771	50.3
Eugene D. Kane (R)	78,403	49.4
8 Peter H. Kostmayer (D)	89,276	61.1
G. Roger Bowers (R)	56,776	38.9
9 Bud Shuster (R)	101,151	74.9
Blaine L. Havice Jr. (D)	33,882	25.1
10 Joseph M. McDade (R)	116,003	76.5
Gene Basalyga (D)	35,721	23.5
11 Daniel J. Flood (D)	61,433	57.5
Robert P. Hudock (R)	45,335	42.5
12 John P. Murtha (D)	194,216	68.7
Luther V. Elkins (R)	47,442	31.3
13 Lawrence Coughlin (R)	112,711	70.5
Alan B. Rubenstein (D)	47,151	29.5
14 William S. Moorhead (D)	68,004	57.0
Stan Thomas (R)	49,992	41.9
15 Donald L. Ritter (R)	65,986	53.2
Fred B. Rooney (D)	58,077	46.8
16 Robert S. Walker (R)	91,910	77.0
Charles W. Boohar (D)	27,386	23.0
17 Allen E. Ertel (D)	79,234	59.6
Thomas R. Rippon (R)	53,613	40.4
18 Doug Walgren (D)	88,299	57.1
Ted Jacob (R)	65,088	42.1
19 Bill Goodling (R)	105,424	78.7
Rajeshwar Kumar (D)	28,577	21.3
20 Joseph M. Gaydos (D)	97,745	72.1
Kathleen M. Meyer (R)	37,745	27.9
21 Don Bailey (D)	73,712	52.9
Robert H. Miller (R)	65,622	47.1
22 Austin J. Murphy (D)	99,559	71.6
Marilyn C. Ecoff (R)	39,518	28.4
23 William F. Clinger Jr. (R)	73,194	54.3
Joseph S. Ammerman (D)	61,657	45.7
24 Marc L. Marks (R)	87,041	64.0
Joseph F. Vigorito (D)	48,894	36.0
25 Eugene V. Atkinson (D)	68,293	46.5
Tim Shaffer (R)	62,160	42.3
Robert Morris (I)	10,588	7.2

RHODE ISLAND

Candidates	Votes	%
1 Fernand J. St Germain (D)	86,768	61.2
John J. Slocum Jr. (R)	54,912	38.8
2 Edward P. Beard (D)	87,397	52.6
Claudine Schneider (R)	78,725	47.4

SOUTH CAROLINA

Candidates	Votes	%
1 Mendel J. Davis (D)	65,835	60.6
C. C. Wannamaker (R)	42,811	39.4
2 Floyd Spence (R)	71,208	57.3
Jack Bass (D)	53,021	42.7
3 Butler Derrick (D)	81,638	82.0
Anthony Panuccio (R)	17,973	18.0
4 Carroll A. Campbell Jr. (R)	51,377	52.1
Max M. Heller (D)	45,484	46.2
5 Ken Holland (D)	63,538	82.7
Harold Hough (I)	13,251	17.3
6 John W. Jenrette Jr. (D)	69,372	100.0

SOUTH DAKOTA

Candidates	Votes	%
1 Thomas A. Daschle (D)	64,683	50.1
Leo K. Thorsness (R)	64,544	49.9
2 James Abdnor (R)	70,780	56.0
Bob Samuelson (D)	55,516	44.0

TENNESSEE

Candidates	Votes	%
1 James H. (Jimmy) Quillen (R)	92,143	64.5
Gordon Ball (D)	50,694	35.5
2 John J. Duncan (R)	125,082	81.8
Margaret Francis (D)	27,745	18.2
3 Marilyn Lloyd (D)	108,282	88.9
Dan East (I)	13,535	11.1
4 Albert Gore Jr. (D)	108,695	100.0
5 Bill Boner (D)	68,608	51.4
Bill Goodwin (R)	47,288	35.4
Henry Haile (I)	17,674	13.2
6 Robin L. Beard Jr. (R)	114,630	74.6
Ron Arline (D)	38,954	25.4
7 Ed Jones (D)	96,863	72.9
Ross Cook (R)	36,003	27.1
8 Harold E. Ford (D)	80,776	69.7
Duncan Ragsdale (R)	33,679	29.1

TEXAS

Candidates	Votes	%
1 Sam B. Hall Jr. (D)	73,708	78.1
Fred Hudson (R)	20,700	21.9
2 Charles Wilson (D)	66,986	70.1
Jim (Matt) Dillon (R)	28,584	29.9
3 James M. Collins (R)	96,406	100.0
4 Ray Roberts (D)	58,336	61.5
Frank S. Glenn (R)	36,582	38.5
5 Jim Mattox (D)	35,524	50.3
Tom Pauken (R)	34,672	49.1
6 Phil Gramm (D)	66,025	65.1
Wesley H. Mowrey (R)	35,393	34.9
7 Bill Archer (R)	128,214	85.1
Robert L. Hutchings (D)	22,415	14.9
8 Bob Eckhardt (D)	39,429	61.5
Nick Gearhart (R)	24,673	38.5
9 Jack Brooks (D)	50,792	63.3
Randy Evans (R)	29,473	36.7
10 J. J. Pickle (D)	94,529	76.3
Emmett L. Hudspeth (R)	29,328	23.7
11 J. Marvin Leath (D)	53,354	51.6
Jack Burgess (R)	49,965	48.4
12 Jim Wright (D)	46,456	68.5
Claude K. Brown (R)	21,364	31.5
13 Jack Hightower (D)	75,271	74.9
Clifford A. Jones (D)	25,275	25.1
14 Joe Wyatt (D)	63,953	72.4
Joy Yates (R)	24,325	27.6
15 E. (Kika) de la Garza (D)	54,560	66.2
Robert L. McDonald (R)	27,853	33.8
16 Richard C. White (D)	53,090	70.0
Michael Giere (R)	22,743	30.0
17 Charles W. Stenholm (D)	69,030	68.1
Billy Lee Fisher (R)	32,302	31.9
18 Mickey Leland (D)	36,783	96.8
19 Kent Hance (D)	54,729	53.2
George W. Bush (R)	48,070	46.8
20 Henry B. Gonzalez (D)	51,584	100.0
21 Tom Loeffler (R)	84,336	57.0
Nelson W. Wolff (R)	63,501	43.0
22 Ron Paul (R)	54,643	50.6
Bob Gammage (D)	53,443	49.4
23 Abraham Kazen Jr. (D)	62,649	89.7
Augustin Mata (LRU)	7,185	10.3
24 Martin Frost (D)	39,201	54.1
Leo Berman (R)	33,314	45.9

UTAH

Candidates	Votes	%
1 Gunn McKay (D)	93,892	51.0
Jed J. Richardson (R)	85,028	46.2
2 Dan Marriott (R)	121,492	62.3
Edwin B. Firmage (D)	68,899	35.3

VERMONT

Candidates	Votes	%
AL James M. Jeffords (R)	90,688	75.3
S. Marie Dietz (D)	23,228	19.3
Peter Diamondstone (LU)	6,505	5.4

VIRGINIA

Candidates	Votes	%
1 Paul S. Trible Jr. (R)	89,158	72.1
Lew Puller (D)	34,578	27.9
2 G. William Whitehurst (R)	63,512	100.0
3 David E. Satterfield III (D)	104,550	87.7
Alan R. Ogden (I)	14,453	12.1
4 Robert W. Daniel Jr. (R)	77,827	99.9
5 Dan Daniel (D)	83,575	99.9
6 M. Caldwell Butler (R)	88,647	99.8
7 J. Kenneth Robinson (R)	84,517	64.3
Lewis Fickett (D)	46,950	35.7
8 Herbert E. Harris II (D)	56,137	50.5
John F. Herrity (R)	52,396	47.1
9 William C. Wampler (R)	76,877	61.9
Champ Clark (D)	47,367	38.1
10 Joseph L. Fisher (D)	70,892	53.3
Frank Wolf (R)	61,981	46.6

WASHINGTON

Candidates	Votes	%
1 Joel Pritchard (R)	99,942	*64.0*
Janice Niemi (D)	52,706	*33.7*
2 Al Swift (D)	70,620	*51.4*
John Nance Garner (R)	66,793	*48.6*
3 Don Bonker (D)	82,616	*58.6*
Rick Bennett (R)	58,270	*41.4*
4 Mike McCormack (D)	85,602	*61.1*
Susan Roylance (R)	54,389	*38.9*
5 Thomas S. Foley (D)	77,201	*48.0*
Duane Alton (R)	68,761	*42.7*
Mel Tonasket (I)	14,887	*9.3*
6 Norman D. Dicks (D)	71,057	*60.9*
James E. Beaver (R)	43,640	*37.4*
7 Mike Lowry (D)	67,450	*53.3*
John E. Cunningham (R)	59,052	*46.7*

WEST VIRGINIA

Candidates	Votes	%
1 Robert H. Mollohan (D)	76,372	*63.4*
Gene A. Haynes (R)	44,062	*36.6*

Candidates	Votes	%
2 Harley O. Staggers (D)	69,683	*55.3*
Cleveland K. Benedict (R)	56,272	*44.7*
3 John M. Slack (D)	74,837	*59.2*
David M. Staton (R)	51,584	*40.8*
4 Nick J. Rahall (D)	70,035	*100.0*

WISCONSIN

Candidates	Votes	%
1 Les Aspin (D)	77,146	*54.5*
William W. Petrie (R)	64,437	*45.5*
2 Robert W. Kastenmeier (D)	99,631	*57.7*
James A. Wright (R)	71,412	*41.3*
3 Alvin Baldus (D)	96,326	*62.8*
Michael S. Ellis (R)	57.060	*37.2*
4 Clement J. Zablocki (D)	101,575	*66.1*
Elroy G. Honadel (R)	52,125	*33.9*
5 Henry S. Reuss (D)	85,067	*73.1*
James R. Medina (R)	30,185	*25.9*

Candidates	Votes	%
6 William A. Steiger (R)	114,742	*69.6*
Robert J. Steffes (D)	48,785	*29.6*
7 David R. Obey (D)	110,874	*62.2*
Vinton A. Vesta (R)	65,750	*36.9*
8 Tobias A. Roth (R)	101,856	*57.9*
Robert J. Cornell (D)	73,925	*42.1*
9 F. James Sansenbrenner Jr. (R)	118,386	*61.1*
Matthew J. Flynn (D)	75,207	*38.8*

WYOMING

	Votes	%
AL Richard Cheney (R)	75,855	*58.6*
Bill Bagley (D)	53,522	*41.4*

1. For the 1978 House elections in Louisiana, an open primary was held with candidates from all parties running on the same ballot. Any candidate who received a majority was elected unopposed without any further appearance on the general election ballot. Where no candidate received 50 percent, there was a general election runoff between the top two finishers regardless of party. This condition prevailed only in Congressional District 4.

1979 House Elections

CALIFORNIA

Special Election

Candidates	Votes	%
11 Bill Royer (R)	52,585	*57.3*
G. W. Holsinger (D)	37,685	*41.1*

WISCONSIN

Special Election

	Votes	%
6 Thomas E. Petri (R)	71,715	*50.0*
Gary R. Goyke (D)	70,492	*49.5*

1980 House Elections

ALABAMA

Candidates	Votes	%
1 Jack Edwards (R)	111,089	94.8
Steve Smith (LIBERT)	6,130	5.2
2 William L. Dickinson (R)	104,796	60.6
Cecil Wyatt (D)	63,447	36.7
3 Bill Nichols (D)	107,654	100.0
4 Tom Bevill (D)	129,365	97.9
5 Ronnie G. Flippo (D)	117,626	94.1
Betty T. Benson (LIBERT)	7,341	5.9
6 Albert Lee Smith Jr. (R)	95,019	50.5
W.B. (Pete) Clifford (D)	87,536	46.6
7 Richard C. Shelby (D)	122,505	72.6
James E. Bacon (R)	43,320	25.7

ALASKA

Candidates	Votes	%
AL Don Young (R)	114,089	73.8
Kevin (Pat) Parnell (D)	39,922	25.8

ARIZONA

Candidates	Votes	%
1 John J. Rhodes (R)	136,961	73.3
Steve Jancek (D)	40,045	21.4
2 Morris K. Udall (D)	127,736	58.1
Richard H. Huff (R)	88,653	40.4
3 Bob Stump (D)	141,448	64.3
Bob Croft (R)	65,845	30.0
Sharon Hayse (LIBERT)	12,529	5.7
4 Eldon Rudd (R)	142,565	62.6
Les Miller (D)	85,046	37.4

ARKANSAS

Candidates	Votes	%
1 Bill Alexander (D)		100.0
2 Ed Bethune (R)	159,148	78.9
James G. Reid (D)	42,278	21.0
3 John Paul Hammerschmidt (R)		100.0
4 Beryl Anthony Jr. (D)		100.0

CALIFORNIA

Candidates	Votes	%
1 Eugene A. Chappie (R)	145,585	53.7
Harold T. Johnson (D)	107,993	39.8
Jim McClarin (LIBERT)	17,497	6.5
2 Don H. Clausen (R)	141,698	54.2
Norma K. Bork (D)	109,789	42.0
3 Robert T. Matsui (D)	170,670	70.6
Joseph Murphy (R)	64,215	26.5
4 Vic Fazio (D)	133,853	65.1
Albert Dehr (R)	60,935	29.6
Robert J. Burnside (LIBERT)	10,267	5.0
5 John L. Burton (D)	101,105	51.1
Dennis McQuaid (R)	89,624	45.3
6 Phillip Burton (D)	93,400	69.4
Tom Spinosa (R)	34,500	25.6
Roy Childs (LIBERT)	6,750	5.0
7 George Miller (D)	142,044	63.3
Giles St. Clair (R)	70,479	31.4
8 Ronald V. Dellums (D)	108,380	55.5
Charles V. Hughes (R)	76,580	39.2
Tom Mikuriya (LIBERT)	10,465	5.3
9 Fortney H. (Pete) Stark (D)	90,504	55.3
William J. Kennedy (R)	67,265	41.1
10 Don Edwards (D)	102,231	62.1
John M. Lutton (R)	45,987	27.9
Joseph Fuhrig (LIBERT)	11,904	7.2
11 Tom Lantos (D)	85,823	46.4
Bill Royer (R)	80,100	43.3
Wilson Branch (PFP)	13,723	7.4
12 Paul N. McCloskey Jr. (R)	143,817	72.2
Kirsten Olsen (D)	37,009	18.6
Bill Evers (LIBERT)	15,073	7.6
13 Norman Y. Mineta (D)	132,246	58.9
W.E. (Ted) Gagne (R)	79,766	35.5
14 Norman D. Shumway (R)	133,979	60.7
Ann Cerney (D)	79,883	36.2

Candidates	Votes	%
15 Tony Coelho (D)	108,072	71.8
Ron Schwartz (R)	37,895	25.2
16 Leon E. Panetta (D)	158,360	71.0
W.A. (Jack) Roth (R)	54,675	24.5
17 Charles Pashayan Jr. (R)	129,159	70.6
Willard H. Johnson (D)	53,780	29.4
18 William M. Thomas (R)	126,046	71.0
Mary (Pat) Timmermans (D)	51,415	29.0
19 Robert J. Lagomarsino (R)	162,854	77.7
Carmen Lodise (D)	36,990	17.6
20 Barry Goldwater Jr. (R)	199,681	78.8
Matt Miller (D)	43,025	17.0
21 Bobbi Fiedler (R)	74,843	48.7
James C. Corman (D)	74,091	48.2
22 Carlos J. Moorhead (R)	115,241	63.9
Pierce O'Donnell (D)	57,477	31.9
23 Anthony C. Beilenson (D)	126,020	63.2
Robert Winckler (R)	62,742	31.5
Jeffrey P. Lieb (LIBERT)	10,623	5.3
24 Henry A. Waxman (D)	93,569	63.8
Roland Cayard (R)	39,744	27.1
25 Edward R. Roybal (D)	49,080	66.0
Richard L. Ferraro Jr. (R)	21,116	28.4
William D. Mitchell (LIBERT)	4,169	5.6
26 Joseph L. Lisoni (D)	40,099	24.4
John H. Rousselot (R)	116,715	70.9
27 Robert K. Dornan (R)	109,807	51.0
Carey Peck (D)	100,061	46.5
28 Julian C. Dixon (D)	108,725	79.2
Robert Reid (R)	23,179	16.9
29 Augustus F. Hawkins (D)	80,095	86.1
Michael A. Hirt (R)	10,282	11.1
30 George E. Danielson (D)	74,119	72.1
J. Arthur Platten (R)	24,136	23.5
31 Mervyn M. Dymally (D)	69,146	64.4
Don Grimshaw (R)	38,203	35.6
32 Glenn M. Anderson (D)	84,057	65.9
John R. Adler (R)	39,260	30.8
33 Wayne Grisham (R)	122,439	70.9
Fred L. Anderson (D)	50,365	29.1
34 Dan Lungren (R)	138,024	71.8
Simone (D)	46,351	24.1
35 David Dreier (R)	100,743	51.8
Jim Lloyd (D)	88,279	45.4
36 George E. Brown Jr. (D)	88,634	52.5
John Paul Stark (R)	73,252	43.4
37 Jerry Lewis (R)	166,640	71.6
Donald M. Rusk (D)	58,462	25.1
38 Jerry M. Patterson (D)	91,880	55.5
Art Jacobson (R)	66,256	40.0
39 William Dannemeyer (R)	175,228	76.3
Leonard V. Lahtinen (D)	54,504	23.7
40 Robert E. Badham (R)	213,999	70.2
Michael F. Dow (D)	66,512	21.8
Dan Mahaffey (LIBERT)	24,486	8.0
41 Bill Lowery (R)	123,187	52.7
Bob Wilson (D)	101,101	43.2
42 Duncan L. Hunter (R)	79,713	53.3
Lionel Van Deerlin (D)	69,936	46.7
43 Clair W. Burgener (R)	299,037	86.5
Tom Metzger (D)	46,383	13.4

COLORADO

Candidates	Votes	%
1 Patricia Schroeder (D)	107,364	59.8
Naomi Bradford (R)	67,804	37.7
2 Timothy E. Wirth (D)	153,618	56.4
John McElderry (R)	111,825	41.1
3 Ray Kogovsek (D)	105,820	54.9
Harold McCormick (R)	84,292	43.7
4 Hank Brown (R)	178,221	68.4
Polly Baca Barragan (D)	76,849	29.5
5 Ken Kramer (R)	177,319	72.4
Ed Schreiber (D)	62,003	25.3

CONNECTICUT

Candidates	Votes	%
1 William R. Cotter (D)	137,849	63.0
Marjorie D. Anderson (R)	80,816	37.0
2 Samuel Gejdenson (D)	119,176	53.4
Tony Guglielmo (R)	104,107	46.6
3 Lawrence J. DeNardis (R)	117,024	52.3
Joseph I. Lieberman (D)	103,903	46.5
4 Stewart B. McKinney (R)	124,285	62.6
John A. Phillips (D)	74,326	37.4
5 William R. Ratchford (D)	117,316	50.4
Edward M. Donahue (R)	115,614	49.6
6 Toby Moffett (D)	142,685	59.0
Nicholas Schaus (R)	98,331	40.6

DELAWARE

Candidates	Votes	%
AL Thomas B. Evans Jr. (R)	133,842	61.8
Robert L. Maxwell (D)	81,227	37.5

FLORIDA

Candidates	Votes	%
1 Earl Hutto (D)	119,829	61.2
Warren Briggs (R)	75,939	38.8
2 Don Fuqua (D)	138,252	70.6
John R. LaCapra (R)	57,588	29.4
3 Charles E. Bennett (D)	104,672	77.0
Harry Radcliffe (R)	31,208	23.0
4 Bill Chappell Jr. (D)	147,775	65.8
Barney E. Dillard Jr. (R)	76,924	34.2
5 Bill McCollum (R)	177,603	55.8
David Best (D)	140,903	44.2
6 C.W. Bill Young (R)		100.0
7 Sam Gibbons (D)	132,529	71.8
Charles P. Jones (R)	52,138	28.2
8 Andy Ireland (D)	151,613	69.3
Scott Nicholson (R)	61,820	28.2
9 Bill Nelson (D)	139,468	70.4
Stan Dowiat (R)	58,734	29.6
10 L.A. (Skip) Bafalis (R)	272,393	78.9
Richard D. Sparkman (D)	72,646	21.1
11 Dan Mica (D)	201,713	59.5
Al Coogler (R)	137,520	40.5
12 Clay Shaw (R)	128,561	54.5
Alan S. Becker (D)	107,164	45.5
13 William Lehman (D)	127,828	74.9
Alvin E. Entin (R)	42,830	25.1
14 Claude Pepper (D)	95,820	74.9
Evelio S. Estrella (R)	32,027	25.1
15 Dante B. Fascell (D)	132,952	65.4
Herbert J. Hoodwin (R)	70,433	34.6

GEORGIA

Candidates	Votes	%
1 Bo Ginn (D)	82,145	100.0
2 Charles F. Hatcher (D)	92,264	73.6
Jack E. Harrell Jr. (R)	33,107	26.4
3 Jack Brinkley (D)	89,040	100.0
4 Elliott H. Levitas (D)	117,091	69.4
Barry E. Billington (R)	51,546	30.6
5 Wyche Fowler Jr. (D)	101,646	74.0
F. William Dowda (R)	35,640	26.0
6 Newt Gingrich (R)	96,071	59.1
Dock H. Davis (D)	66,606	40.9
7 Larry P. McDonald (D)	115,892	68.1
Richard L. Castellucis (R)	54,242	31.9
8 Billy Lee Evans (D)	91,103	74.6
Darwin Carter (R)	31,033	25.4
9 Ed Jenkins (D)	115,576	68.0
David G. Ashworth (R)	54,341	32.0
10 Doug Barnard (D)	102,177	80.2
Bruce J. Neubauer (R)	25,194	19.8

HAWAII

Candidates	Votes	%
1 Cecil Heftel (D)	98,256	79.8
Aloma Keen Noble (R)	19,819	16.1
2 Daniel K. Akaka (D)	141,477	89.9
Don G. Smith (LIBERT)	15,903	10.1

IDAHO

Candidates	Votes	%
1 Larry Craig (R)	116,845	53.7
Glenn W. Nichols (D)	100,697	46.3
2 George Hansen (R)	116,196	58.8
Diane Bilyeu (D)	81,364	41.2

ILLINOIS

1 Harold Washington (D)	119,562	95.5
2 Gus Savage (D)	129,771	88.1
Marsha A. Harris (R)	17,428	11.8
3 Marty Russo (D)	137,283	68.9
Lawrence C. Sarsoun (R)	61,955	31.1
4 Edward J. Derwinski (R)	152,377	68.0
Richard S. Jalovec (D)	71,814	32.0
5 John G. Fary (D)	106,142	79.6
Robert V. Kotowski (R)	27,136	20.4
6 Henry J. Hyde (R)	123,593	67.0
Mario Raymond Reda (D)	60,951	33.0
7 Cardiss Collins (D)	80,056	85.1
Ruth R. Hooper (R)	14,041	14.9
8 Dan Rostenkowski (D)	98,524	84.7
Walter F. Zilke (R)	17,845	15.3
9 Sidney R. Yates (D)	106,543	73.1
John D. Andrica (R)	39,244	26.9
10 John E. Porter (R)	137,707	60.7
Robert A. Weinberger (D)	89,008	39.3
11 Frank Annunzio (D)	121,166	69.8
Michael R. Zanillo (R)	52,417	30.2
12 Philip M. Crane (R)	185,080	74.1
David McCartney (D)	64,729	25.9
13 Robert McClory (R)	131,448	71.7
Michael Reese (D)	52,000	28.3
14 John N. Erlenborn (R)	202,583	76.8
LeRoy E. Kennel (D)	61,224	23.2
15 Tom Corcoran (R)	150,898	76.7
John P. Quillin (D)	45,721	23.3
16 Lynn M. Martin (R)	132,905	67.4
Douglas B. Aurand (D)	64,224	32.6
17 George M. O'Brien (R)	125,806	65.8
Michael A. Murer (D)	65,305	34.2
18 Robert H. Michel (R)	125,561	62.1
John L. Knuppel (D)	76,471	37.9
19 Tom Railsback (R)	142,616	73.4
Thomas J. Hand (D)	51,753	26.6
20 Paul Findley (R)	123,427	56.0
David L. Robinson (D)	96,950	44.0
21 Edward R. Madigan (R)	132,186	67.6
Penny L. Severns (D)	63,476	32.4
22 Daniel B. Crane (R)	146,014	68.8
Peter M. Voelz (D)	66,065	31.2
23 Melvin Price (D)	107,786	64.4
Ronald L. Davinroy (R)	59,644	35.6
24 Paul Simon (D)	112,134	49.1
John T. Anderson (R)	110,176	48.3

Special Election

10 John E. Porter (R)	36,981	54.0
Robert Weinberger (D)	30,929	46.0

INDIANA

1 Adam Benjamin Jr. (D)	112,016	72.0
Joseph D. Harkin (R)	43,537	28.0
2 Floyd Fithian (D)	122,326	54.1
Ernest Niemeyer (R)	103,957	45.9
3 John P. Hiler (R)	103,972	55.0
John Brademas (D)	85,136	45.0
4 Daniel R. Coats (R)	120,055	60.5
John D. Walda (D)	77,542	39.1
5 Elwood Hillis (R)	129,474	61.7
Nels J. Ackerson (D)	80,378	38.3
6 David W. Evans (D)	98,482	50.2
David G. Crane (R)	97,582	49.8
7 John T. Myers (R)	137,604	66.1
Patrick D. Carroll (D)	69,051	33.2
8 H. Joel Deckard (R)	119,415	55.2
Kenneth C. Snider (D)	97,059	44.8
9 Lee H. Hamilton (D)	136,574	64.4
George Meyers Jr. (R)	75,601	35.6
10 Phil Sharp (D)	103,083	53.4

Candidates	Votes	%
William G. Frazier (R)	90,051	46.6
11 Andy Jacobs Jr. (D)	105,468	57.3
Sheila Suess (R)	78,743	42.7

IOWA

1 Jim Leach (R)	133,349	64.1
Jim Larew (D)	72,602	34.9
2 Tom Tauke (R)	111,587	54.0
Steve Sovern (D)	93,175	45.1
3 Cooper Evans (R)	107,869	51.4
Lynn G. Cutler (D)	101,735	48.4
4 Neal Smith (D)	117,896	53.9
Donald C. Young (R)	100,335	45.9
5 Tom Harkin (D)	127,895	60.2
Cal Hultman (R)	84,472	39.8
6 Berkley Bedell (D)	129,460	64.3
Clarence S. Carney (R)	71,866	35.7

KANSAS

1 Pat Roberts (R)	121,545	62.3
Phil Martin (D)	73,586	37.7
2 Jim Jeffries (R)	92,107	53.9
Sam Keys (D)	78,859	46.1
3 Larry Winn Jr. (R)	109,294	55.5
Dan Watkins (D)	82,414	41.8
4 Dan Glickman (D)	124,014	68.9
Clay Hunter (R)	55,899	31.1
5 Bob Whittaker (R)	141,029	74.2
David L. Miller (D)	45,676	24.0

KENTUCKY

1 Carroll Hubbard Jr. (D)	118,565	100.0
2 William H. Natcher (D)	99,670	65.7
Mark T. Watson (R)	52,110	34.3
3 Romano L. Mazzoli (D)	85,873	63.7
Richard Cesler (R)	46,681	34.6
4 Gene Snyder (R)	126,049	67.0
Phil M. McGary (D)	62,138	33.0
5 Harold Rogers (R)	112,093	67.5
Ted R. Marcum (D)	54,027	32.5
6 Larry J. Hopkins (R)	105,376	58.9
Tom Easterly (D)	72,473	40.5
7 Carl D. Perkins (D)	117,665	100.0

LOUISIANA[1]

1 Robert L. Livingston (R)		100.0
2 Lindy Boggs (D)		100.0
3 W. J. (Billy) Tauzin (D)		100.0
4 Buddy Roemer (D)	103,625	63.8
Claude (Buddy) Leach (D)	58,705	36.2
5 Jerry Huckaby (D)		100.0
6 W. Henson Moore (R)		100.0
7 John B. Breaux (D)		100.0
8 Gillis W. Long (D)		100.0

Special Election

3. W. J. (Billy) Tauzin (D)	62,108	53.0
James Donelon (R)	54,815	47.0

MAINE

1 David F. Emery (R)	188,667	68.5
Harold C. Pachios (D)	86,819	31.5
2 Olympia J. Snowe (R)	186,406	78.5
Harold L. Silverman (D)	51,026	21.5

MARYLAND

1 Roy Dyson (D)	97,743	51.7
Robert E. Bauman (R)	91,143	48.3
2 Clarence D. Long (D)	121,017	57.4
Helen D. Bentley (R)	89,961	42.6
3 Barbara A. Mikulski (D)	102,293	76.1
Russell T. Schaffer (R)	32,074	23.9
4 Marjorie S. Holt (R)	120,985	71.9
James J. Riley (D)	47,375	28.1
5 Gladys Noon Spellman (D)	106,035	80.5

Candidates	Votes	%
Kevin R. Igoe (R)	25,693	19.5
6 Beverly B. Byron (D)	146,101	69.9
Raymond E. Beck (R)	62,913	30.1
7 Parren J. Mitchell (D)	97,104	88.5
Victor Clark Jr. (R)	12,650	11.5
8 Michael D. Barnes (D)	148,301	59.3
Newton I. Steers Jr. (R)	101,659	40.7

MASSACHUSETTS

1 Silvio O. Conte (R)	156,415	74.9
Helen Poppy Doyle (D)	52,457	25.1
2 Edward P. Boland (D)	120,711	67.2
Thomas P. Swank (R)	38,672	21.5
John B. Aubuchon (I)	20,247	11.3
3 Joseph D. Early (D)	141,560	72.3
David G. Skehan (R)	54,123	27.7
4 Barney Frank (D)	103,466	51.9
Richard A. Jones (R)	95,898	48.1
5 James M. Shannon (D)	136,758	66.0
William C. Sawyer (R)	70,547	34.0
6 Nicholas Mavroules (D)	111,393	50.8
Thomas H. Trimarco (R)	103,192	47.1
7 Edward J. Markey (D)	155,759	100.0
8 Thomas P. O'Neill Jr. (D)	128,689	78.4
William A. Barnstead (R)	35,477	21.6
9 Joe Moakley (D)	104,010	100.0
10 Margaret M. Heckler (R)	131,794	60.6
Robert E. McCarthy (D)	85,629	39.4
11 Brian J. Donnelly (D)	137,066	100.0
12 Gerry E. Studds (D)	195,791	73.2
Paul V. Doane (R)	71,620	26.8

MICHIGAN

1 John Conyers Jr. (D)	123,286	94.7
2 Carl D. Pursell (R)	115,562	57.3
Kathleen F. O'Reilly (D)	83,550	41.4
3 Howard Wolpe (D)	113,080	52.0
James S. Gilmore (R)	102,591	47.2
4 Dave Stockman (R)	148,950	74.7
Lyndon G. Furst (D)	47,777	24.0
5 Harold S. Sawyer (R)	118,061	53.1
Dale R. Sprik (D)	101,737	45.8
6 Jim Dunn (R)	111,272	50.6
Bob Carr (D)	108,548	49.4
7 Dale E. Kildee (D)	147,280	92.7
Dennis L. Berry (LIBERT)	11,507	7.2
8 Bob Traxler (D)	124,155	60.7
Norman R. Hughes (R)	77,009	37.7
9 Guy Vander Jagt (R)	168,713	96.5
10 Don Albosta (D)	126,962	52.4
Richard J. Allen (R)	111,496	46.0
11 Robert W. Davis (R)	146,205	65.5
Dan Dorrity (D)	75,515	33.8
12 David E. Bonior (D)	112,698	55.3
Kirk Walsh (R)	90,931	44.7
13 George W. Crockett Jr. (D)	79,719	91.5
M. Michael Hurd (R)	6,473	7.4
14 Dennis M. Hertel (D)	90,362	53.3
Vic Caputo (R)	78,395	46.2
15 William D. Ford (D)	113,492	67.6
Gerald R. Carlson (R)	53,046	31.6
16 John D. Dingell (D)	105,844	69.9
Pamella A. Seay (R)	42,735	28.2
17 William M. Brodhead (D)	127,525	73.1
Alfred L. Patterson (R)	44,313	25.4
18 James J. Blanchard (D)	135,705	65.3
Betty J. Suida (R)	68,575	33.0
19 William S. Broomfield (R)	168,530	72.7
Wayne E. Daniels (D)	60,100	25.9

MINNESOTA[2]

1 Arlen Erdahl (I-R)	171,099	71.8
Russell V. Smith (DFL)	67,279	28.2
2 Tom Hagedorn (I-R)	158,082	60.6
Harold J. Bergquist (DFL)	102,586	39.4
3 Bill Frenzel (I-R)	179,393	75.6
Joel Alexander Saliterman (DFL)	57,868	24.4
4 Bruce F. Vento (DFL)	119,182	58.5

Footnotes, see p. 281.

Candidates	Votes	%
John Berg (I-R)	82,537	40.5
5 Martin Olav Sabo (DFL)	126,451	70.1
John Doherty (I-R)	48,200	26.7
6 Vin Weber (I-R)	140,402	52.7
Archie Baumann (DFL)	126,173	47.3
7 Arlan Stangeland (I-R)	135,084	52.1
Gene Wenstrom (DFL)	124,026	47.9
8 James L. Oberstar (DFL)	182,228	70.4
Edward Fiore (I-R)	72,350	28.0

MISSISSIPPI

Candidates	Votes	%
1 Jamie L. Whitten (D)	104,269	63.0
T.K. Moffett (R)	61,292	37.0
2 David R. Bowen (D)	96,750	69.6
Frank Drake (R)	42,300	30.4
3 G.V. Montgomery (D)	128,035	100.0
4 Jon C. Hinson (R)	69,321	39.0
Leslie Burl McLemore (I)	52,959	29.8
Britt R. Singletary (D)	52,303	29.4
5 Trent Lott (R)	131,559	73.9
Jimmy McVeay (D)	46,416	26.1

MISSOURI

Candidates	Votes	%
1 William Clay (D)	91,272	70.2
Bill White (R)	38,667	29.8
2 Robert A. Young (D)	148,227	64.4
John O. Shields (R)	81,762	35.6
3 Richard A. Gephardt (D)	143,132	77.6
Robert A. Cedarburg (R)	41,277	22.4
4 Ike Skelton (D)	151,459	67.8
Bill Baker (R)	71,869	32.2
5 Richard Bolling (D)	110,957	70.1
Vincent E. Baker (R)	47,309	29.9
6 E. Thomas Coleman (R)	149,281	70.6
Vernon King (D)	62,048	29.4
7 Gene Taylor (R)	161,668	67.8
Ken Young (D)	76,844	32.2
8 Wendell Bailey (R)	127,675	57.1
Steve Gardner (D)	95,751	42.9
9 Harold L. Volkmer (D)	135,905	56.5
John W. Turner (R)	104,835	43.5
10 Bill Emerson (R)	116,167	55.2
Bill D. Burlison (D)	94,465	44.8

MONTANA

Candidates	Votes	%
1 Pat Williams (D)	112,866	61.4
John K. McDonald (R)	70,874	38.6
2 Ron Marlenee (R)	91,431	59.1
Tom Monahan (D)	63,370	40.9

NEBRASKA

Candidates	Votes	%
1 Douglas K. Bereuter (R)	160,705	78.6
Rex S. Story (D)	43,605	21.3
2 Hal Daub (R)	107,736	53.1
Richard M. Fellman (D)	88,843	43.8
3 Virginia Smith (R)	182,887	83.9
Stan Ditus (D)	34,967	16.0

NEVADA

Candidates	Votes	%
AL Jim Santini (D)	165,107	67.5
Vince Saunders (R)	63,163	25.8

NEW HAMPSHIRE

Candidates	Votes	%
1 Norman E. D'Amours (D)	114,061	60.8
Marshall W. Cobleigh (R)	73,565	39.2
2 Judd Gregg (R)	113,304	64.1
Maurice L. Arel (D)	63,350	35.9

NEW JERSEY

Candidates	Votes	%
1 James J. Florio (D)	147,352	76.7
Scott L. Sibert (R)	42,154	21.9
2 William J. Hughes (D)	135,437	57.5
Beech N. Fox (R)	97,072	41.2
3 James J. Howard (D)	106,269	49.9
Marie Sheehan Muhler (R)	104,184	49.0

Candidates	Votes	%
4 Christopher H. Smith (R)	95,447	56.6
Frank Thompson Jr. (D)	68,480	40.6
5 Millicent Fenwick (R)	156,016	77.5
Kieran E. Pillion Jr. (D)	41,269	20.5
6 Edwin B. Forsythe (R)	125,792	56.3
Lewis M. Weinstein (D)	92,227	41.3
7 Marge Roukema (R)	108,760	50.7
Andrew Maguire (D)	99,737	46.5
8 Robert A. Roe (D)	95,493	67.2
William R. Cleveland (R)	44,625	31.4
9 Harold C. Hollenbeck (R)	116,128	59.1
Gabriel Ambrosio (D)	75,321	38.3
10 Peter W. Rodino Jr. (D)	76,154	85.3
Everett J. Jennings (R)	11,778	13.2
11 Joseph G. Minish (D)	106,155	63.0
Robert A. Davis (R)	57,772	34.3
12 Matthew J. Rinaldo (R)	134,973	77.1
Rose Zeidwerg Monyek (D)	36,577	20.9
13 Jim Courter (R)	152,862	71.6
Dave Stickle (D)	56,251	26.4
14 Frank J. Guarini (D)	86,921	64.2
Dennis E. Teti (R)	45,606	33.7
15 Bernard J. Dwyer (D)	92,457	53.4
William O'Sullivan Jr. (R)	75,812	43.8

NEW MEXICO

Candidates	Votes	%
1 Manuel Lujan Jr. (R)	125,910	51.0
Bill Richardson (D)	120,903	49.0
2 Joe Skeen (WRITE IN)	61,564	38.0
David King (D)	55,085	34.0
Dorothy Runnels (WRITE IN)	45,343	28.0

NEW YORK

Candidates	Votes	%
1 William Carney (R,C,RTL)	115,213	56.3
Thomas A. Twomey (D)	85,629	41.9
2 Thomas J. Downey (D)	84,035	56.3
Louis J. Modica (R,RTL)	65,106	43.7
3 Gregory W. Carman (R,C)	87,952	50.1
Jerome A. Ambro (D,RTL)	83,389	47.5
4 Norman F. Lent (R,C,RTL)	117,455	66.8
Charles F. Brennan (D,L)	58,270	33.2
5 Raymond McGrath (R,C,RTL)	105,140	57.7
Karen S. Burstein (D,L)	77,228	42.3
6 John LeBoutillier (R,C,RTL)	89,762	52.8
Lester L. Wolff (D,L)	80,209	47.2
7 Joseph Addabbo (D,R,L)	96,137	95.3
8 Benjamin Rosenthal (D,L)	84,273	75.6
Albert Lemishow (R,C,RTL)	27,156	24.4
9 Geraldine A. Ferraro (D)	63,796	58.3
Vito P. Battista (R,C,RTL)	44,473	40.7
10 Mario Biaggi (D,R,L)	95,322	94.5
11 James H. Scheuer (D,L)	72,798	74.1
Andrew E. Carlan (R,C,RTL)	25,424	25.9
12 Shirley Chisholm (D,L)	35,446	87.1
Charles Gibbs (R)	3,372	8.3
13 Stephen J. Solarz (D,L)	81,954	79.4
Harry DeMell (R,C)	19,536	18.9
14 Fred Richmond (D,L)	45,029	76.1
Christopher Lovell (R,C)	8,257	14.0
Moses S. Harris (I)	4,151	7.0
15 Leo C. Zeferetti (D)	49,684	50.2
Paul M. Atanasio (R,C,RTL)	46,467	46.9
16 Charles E. Schumer (D,L)	67,343	77.5
Theodore Silverman (R,C)	17,050	19.6
17 Guy V. Molinari (R,C)	69,573	47.8
John M. Murphy (D,RTL)	50,954	35.0
Mary T. Codd (L)	25,118	17.2
18 S. William Green (R)	91,341	56.7
Mark J. Green (D,L)	68,786	42.7
19 Charles B. Rangel (D,R,L)	84,062	96.2
20 Ted Weiss (D,L)	86,454	82.4
James E. Greene (R)	15,350	14.6
21 Robert Garcia (D,R,L)	32,173	98.2
22 Jonathan B. Bingham (D,L)	66,301	83.9
Robert S. Black (R)	9,943	12.6
23 Peter A. Peyser (D)	85,749	56.2
Andrew Albanese (R,C)	66,771	43.8
24 Richard L. Ottinger (D)	100,182	59.4

Candidates	Votes	%
Joseph Christiana (R,C,RTL)	66,689	39.6
25 Hamilton Fish Jr. (R,C)	158,936	81.0
Gunars Ozols (D)	37,369	19.0
26 Benjamin A. Gilman (R)	137,159	74.3
Eugene Victor (D)	37,475	20.3
27 Matthew F. McHugh (D)	103,863	55.0
Neil T. Wallace (R,C)	83,096	44.0
28 Samuel S. Stratton (D)	164,088	77.9
Frank Wicks (R)	37,504	17.8
29 Gerald Solomon (R,C,RTL)	141,631	66.7
Rodger L. Hurley (D,L)	70,697	33.3
30 David O'B. Martin (R,C)	111,008	63.8
Mary Anne Krupsak (D,L)	54,896	31.6
31 Donald J. Mitchell (R,RTL)	135,976	77.5
Irving A. Schwartz (D,L)	39,589	22.5
32 George Wortley (R,C)	108,128	60.4
Jeffery S. Brooks (D, L)	56,535	31.6
Peter J. Del Giorno (RTL)	11,978	6.7
33 Gary A. Lee (R,C)	132,831	75.8
Dolores M. Reed (D,L)	39,542	22.6
34 Frank Horton (R)	133,278	72.9
James Toole (D)	37,883	20.7
35 Barber B. Conable Jr. (R)	127,623	72.2
John M. Owens (D,C)	44,754	25.3
36 John J. LaFalce (D,L)	122,929	71.7
H. William Feder (R,C,RTL)	48,428	28.3
37 Henry J. Nowak (D,L)	94,890	83.0
Roger Heymanowski (R,C)	16,560	14.5
38 Jack F. Kemp (R,C,RTL)	167,434	81.6
Gale A. Denn (D,L)	37,875	18.4
39 Stanley N. Lundine (D)	93,839	54.7
James Abdella (R,C)	75,039	43.8

NORTH CAROLINA

Candidates	Votes	%
1 Walter B. Jones (D)	108,738	100.0
2 L. H. Fountain (D)	99,297	73.4
Barry L. Gardner (R)	35,946	26.6
3 Charles Whitley (D)	84,862	68.3
Larry J. Parker (R)	39,393	31.7
4 Ike F. Andrews (D)	97,167	52.6
Thurman Hogan (R)	84,631	45.8
5 Stephen L. Neal (D)	99,117	51.0
Anne Bagnal (R)	94,894	48.8
6 Eugene Johnston (R)	80,275	51.1
Richardson Preyer (D)	76,957	48.9
7 Charlie Rose (D)	88,564	68.5
Vivian S. Wright (R)	40,270	31.3
8 W.G. (Bill) Hefner (D)	95,013	58.5
L.E. (Larry) Harris (R)	67,317	41.5
9 James G. Martin (R)	101,156	58.6
Randall R. Kincaid (D)	71,504	41.4
10 James T. Broyhill (R)	120,777	69.7
James O. Icenhour (D)	52,485	30.3
11 William M. Hendon (R)	104,485	53.5
Lamar Gudger (D)	90,789	46.5

NORTH DAKOTA

Candidates	Votes	%
AL Byron L. Dorgan (D)	166,437	56.8
Jim Smykowski (R)	124,707	42.6

OHIO

Candidates	Votes	%
1 Bill Gradison (R)	124,080	74.7
Donald J. Zwick (D)	38,529	23.2
2 Thomas A. Luken (D)	103,423	58.7
Tom Atkins (R)	72,693	41.3
3 Tony P. Hall (D)	95,558	57.3
Albert H. Sealy (R)	66,698	40.0
4 Tennyson Guyer (R)	133,795	72.3
Geraldine Tebben (D)	51,150	27.7
5 Delbert L. Latta (R)	137,003	70.4
James R. Sherck (D)	57,704	29.6
6 Bob McEwen (R)	101,288	54.6
Ted Strickland (D)	84,235	45.4
7 Clarence J. Brown (R)	124,137	76.1
Donald Hollister (D)	38,952	23.9
8 Thomas N. Kindness (R)	139,590	76.0
John W. Griffin (D)	44,162	24.0

Candidates	Votes	%
9 Ed Weber (R)	96,927	56.2
Thomas L. Ashley (D)	68,728	39.9
10 Clarence E. Miller (R)	143,403	74.4
Jack E. Stecher (D)	49,433	25.6
11 J. William Stanton (R)	128,507	69.3
Patrick J. Donlin (D)	51,224	27.6
12 Robert N. Shamansky (D)	108,690	52.6
Samuel L. Devine (R)	98,110	47.4
13 Don J. Pease (D)	113,439	63.8
David E. Armstrong (R)	64,296	36.2
14 John F. Seiberling (D)	103,336	64.9
Louis A. Mangels (R)	55,962	35.1
15 Chalmers P. Wylie (R)	129,025	72.6
Terry Freeman (D)	48,708	27.4
16 Ralph S. Regula (R)	149,960	79.3
Larry V. Slagle (D)	39,219	20.7
17 John M. Ashbrook (R)	128,870	72.9
Donald E. Yunker (D)	47,900	27.1
18 Douglas Applegate (D)	134,835	76.1
Gary L. Hammersley (R)	42,354	23.9
19 Lyle Williams (R)	107,032	58.1
Harry Meshel (D)	77,272	41.9
20 Mary Rose Oakar (D)	96,217	100.0
21 Louis Stokes (D)	83,188	88.2
Robert L. Woodall (R)	11,103	11.8
22 Dennis E. Eckart (D)	108,137	55.2
Joseph J. Nahra (R)	80,836	41.3
23 Ronald M. Mottl (D)	144,317	100.0

OKLAHOMA

Candidates	Votes	%
1 James R. Jones (D)	115,381	58.4
Richard C. Freeman (R)	82,293	41.6
2 Mike Synar (D)	101,516	54.0
Gary Richardson (R)	86,544	46.0
3 Wes Watkins (D)		100.0
4 Dave McCurdy (D)	74,245	51.0
Howard Rutledge (R)	71,339	49.0
5 Mickey Edwards (R)	90,053	68.4
David C. Hood (D)	36,815	28.0
6 Glenn English (D)	111,694	64.7
Carol McCurley (R)	60,980	35.3

OREGON

Candidates	Votes	%
1 Les AuCoin (D)	203,532	65.9
Lynn Engdahl (R)	105,083	34.0
2 Denny Smith (R)	141,854	48.8
Al Ullman (D)	138,089	47.5
3 Ron Wyden (D)	156,371	71.9
Darrell R. Conger (R)	60,940	28.0
4 James Weaver (D)	158,745	54.8
Michael Fitzgerald (R)	130,861	45.2

PENNSYLVANIA

Candidates	Votes	%
1 Thomas M. Foglietta (I)	58,737	37.8
Michael (Ozzie) Myers (D)	52,956	34.1
Robert R. Burke (R)	37,893	24.4
2 William H. Gray III (D)	127,106	96.4
3 Raymond F. Lederer (D)	67,942	54.5
William J. Phillips (R)	40,866	32.8
Max Weiner (CONSU)	11,849	9.5
4 Charles F. Dougherty (R)	127,475	63.3
Thomas J. Magrann (D)	73,895	36.7
5 Richard T. Schulze (R)	148,898	75.1
Grady G. Brickhouse (D)	47,092	23.8
6 Gus Yatron (D)	117,965	67.1
George Hulshart (R)	57,844	32.9
7 Robert W. Edgar (D)	99,381	53.1
Dennis J. Rochford (R)	87,643	46.9
8 James K. Coyne (R)	103,585	50.7
Peter H. Kostmayer (D)	99,593	48.7
9 Bud Shuster (R,D)	157,241	100.0
10 Joseph M. McDade (R)	145,703	76.6
Gene Basalyga (D)	43,152	22.7
11 James L. Nelligan (R)	93,621	51.9
Raphael Musto (D)	86,703	48.1
12 John P. Murtha (D)	106,750	59.4
Charles A. Getty (R)	72,999	40.6
13 Lawrence Coughlin (R)	138,212	70.0
Pete Slawek (D)	57,745	29.2

Candidates	Votes	%
14 William J. Coyne (D)	102,545	68.5
Stan Thomas (R)	44,071	29.5
15 Don Ritter (R)	99,874	59.6
Jeanette Reibman (D)	66,626	39.7
16 James A. Woodcock (D)	38,891	23.1
Robert S. Walker (R)	129,765	76.9
17 Allen E. Ertel (D)	97,995	60.6
Daniel S. Seiverling (R)	63,790	39.4
18 Doug Walgren (D)	127,641	68.5
Steven R. Snyder (R)	58,821	31.5
19 Bill Goodling (R)	136,873	76.0
Richard P. Noll (D)	41,584	23.1
20 Joseph M. Gaydos (D)	122,100	72.5
Kathleen M. Meyer (R)	46,313	27.5
21 Don Bailey (D)	112,427	68.4
Dirk Matson (R)	51,821	31.6
22 Austin J. Murphy (D)	118,084	69.5
Marilyn C. Ecoff (R)	50,020	29.5
23 William F. Clinger Jr. (R)	122,855	73.5
Peter Atigan (D)	41,033	24.6
24 Marc L. Marks (R)	86,687	49.7
David C. DiCarlo (D)	86,567	49.6
25 Eugene V. Atkinson (D)	119,817	67.1
Robert H. Morris (R)	58,768	32.9

Special Election

Candidates	Votes	%
11 Raphael Musto (D)	32,073	27.3
James Nelligan (R)	27,496	23.4
Frank Harrison (I)	20,475	17.4
Paul Kanjorski (I)	18,241	15.5
Ted Mitchell (I)	12,009	10.2

RHODE ISLAND

Candidates	Votes	%
1 Fernand J. St Germain (D)	120,756	67.6
William P. Montgomery (R)	57,844	32.4
2 Claudine Schneider (R)	115,051	55.3
Edward P. Beard (D)	92,970	44.7

SOUTH CAROLINA

Candidates	Votes	%
1 Thomas F. Hartnett (R)	81,988	51.6
Charles D. Ravenel (D)	76,743	48.3
2 Floyd Spence (R)	92,306	55.7
Tom Turnipseed (D)	73,353	44.3
3 Butler Derrick (D)	87,680	59.8
Marshall Parker (R)	57,840	39.4
4 Carroll Campbell Jr. (R)	90,941	92.6
Thomas Waldenfels (LIBERT)	6,984	7.1
5 Ken Holland (D)	99,773	87.5
Thomas Campbell (LIBERT)	14,252	12.5
6 John L. Napier (R)	75,964	51.7
John W. Jenrette Jr. (D)	70,747	48.2

SOUTH DAKOTA

Candidates	Votes	%
1 Thomas A. Daschle (D)	109,910	65.8
Bart Kull (R)	57,155	34.2
2 Clint Roberts (R)	88,991	58.4
Kenneth D. Stofferahn (D)	63,447	41.6

TENNESSEE

Candidates	Votes	%
1 James H. Quillen (R)	130,296	86.2
John Curtis (I)	20,816	13.8
2 John J. Duncan (R)	147,947	76.1
Dave Dunaway (D)	46,578	23.9
3 Marilyn Lloyd Bouquard (D)	117,355	61.1
Glen M. Byers (R)	74,761	38.9
4 Albert Gore Jr. (D)	137,612	79.3
James Beau Seigneur (R)	35,954	20.7
5 Bill Boner (D)	118,506	65.4
Mike Adams (R)	62,746	34.6
6 Robin L. Beard Jr. (R)	127,945	99.6
7 Ed Jones (D)	133,606	77.3
Daniel Campbell (R)	39,227	22.7
8 Harold E. Ford (D)	110,139	99.9

TEXAS

Candidates	Votes	%
1 Sam B. Hall Jr. (D)	137,665	100.0

Candidates	Votes	%
2 Charles Wilson (D)	142,496	69.3
F. H. Pannill Sr. (R)	60,742	29.5
3 James M. Collins (R)	218,228	79.3
Earle S. Porter (D)	49,667	18.0
4 Ralph M. Hall (D)	102,787	52.3
John H. Wright (R)	93,915	47.7
5 Jim Mattox (D)	70,892	51.0
Tom Pauken (R)	67,848	48.8
6 Phil Gramm (D)	144,816	70.9
Dave (Buster) Haskins (R)	59,503	29.1
7 Bill Archer (R)	242,810	82.1
Robert L. Hutchings (D)	48,594	16.4
8 Jack Fields (R)	72,856	51.8
Bob Eckhardt (D)	67,921	48.2
9 Jack Brooks (D)	103,225	99.7
10 J. J. Pickle (D)	135,618	59.1
John Biggar (R)	88,940	38.8
11 Marvin Leath (D)	128,520	100.0
12 Jim Wright (D)	99,104	59.9
Jim Bradshaw (R)	65,005	39.3
13 Jack Hightower (D)	98,779	55.0
Ron Slover (R)	80,819	45.0
14 William N. Patman (D)	93,884	56.8
Charles L. Concklin (R)	71,495	43.2
15 E. (Kika) de la Garza (D)	105,325	70.0
Lendy McDonald (R)	45,090	30.0
16 Richard C. White (D)	104,734	84.6
Catherine McDivitt (LIBERT)	19,010	15.4
17 Charles W. Stenholm (D)	130,465	100.0
18 Mickey Leland (D)	71,985	79.9
C. L. Kennedy (R)	16,128	17.9
19 Kent Hance (D)	126,632	93.5
J. D. Webster (LIBERT)	8,792	6.5
20 Henry B. Gonzalez (D)	84,113	81.9
Merle W. Nash (R)	17,725	17.3
21 Tom Loeffler (R)	196,424	76.5
Joe Sullivan (D)	58,425	22.8
22 Ron Paul (R)	106,797	51.0
Mike Andrews (D)	101,094	48.3
23 Abraham Kazen Jr. (D)	104,595	69.8
Bobby Locke (R)	45,139	30.1
24 Martin Frost (D)	93,690	61.3
Clay Smothers (R)	59,172	38.7

UTAH

Candidates	Votes	%
1 James V. Hansen (R)	157,111	52.1
Gunn McKay (D)	144,459	47.9
2 Dan Marriott (R)	194,885	67.0
Arthur L. Monson (D)	87,967	30.3

VERMONT

Candidates	Votes	%
AL James M. Jeffords (R)	154,274	79.2
Robin Lloyd (CIT)	24,758	12.7
Peter Diamondstone (LU)	15,218	7.8

VIRGINIA

Candidates	Votes	%
1 Paul S. Trible Jr. (R)	130,130	90.5
Sharon D. Grant (I)	13,688	9.5
2 G. William Whitehurst (R)	97,319	89.8
Kenneth Morrison (LIBERT)	11,003	10.2
3 Thomas J. Bliley Jr. (R)	96,524	51.6
John A. Mapp (D)	60,962	32.6
Howard H. Carwile (I)	19,549	10.5
James B. Turney (LIBERT)	9,852	5.3
4 Robert W. Daniel Jr. (R)	92,557	60.7
Cecil Y. Jenkins (D)	59,930	39.3
5 Dan Daniel (D)	112,143	99.9
6 M. Caldwell Butler (R)	123,125	99.2
7 J. Kenneth Robinson (R)	139,957	99.7
8 Stanford E. Parris (R)	95,624	48.8
Herbert E. Harris II (D)	94,530	48.3
9 William C. Wampler (R)	119,196	69.4
Roosevelt Ferguson (D)	52,636	30.6
10 Frank R. Wolf (R)	110,840	51.1
Joseph L. Fisher (D)	105,883	48.9

WASHINGTON

Candidates	Votes	%
1 Joel Pritchard (R)	180,475	78.3
Robin Drake (D)	41,830	18.1

Candidates	Votes	%	Candidates	Votes	%	Candidates	Votes	%
2 Al Swift (D)	162,002	63.9	Pat R. Hamilton (D)	80,940	44.1	Alvin Baldus (D)	126,859	49.0
Neal Snider (R)	82,639	32.6	3 Mick Staton (R)	94,583	52.7	4 Clement J. Zablocki (D)	146,437	70.0
3 Don Bonker (D)	155,906	62.7	John G. Hutchinson (D)	84,980	47.3	Elroy C. Honadel (R)	61,027	29.2
Rod Culp (R)	92,872	37.3	4 Nick J. Rahall (D)	117,595	76.6	5 Henry S. Reuss (D)	129,574	77.0
4 Sid Morrison (R)	134,691	57.4	Winton G. Covey Jr. (R)	36,020	23.4	David Bathke (R)	37,267	22.2
Mike McCormack (D)	100,114	42.6				6 Thomas E. Petri (R)	143,980	59.3
5 Thomas S. Foley (D)	120,530	51.9	**Special Election**			Gary R. Goyke (D)	98,628	40.7
John Sonneland (R)	111,705	48.1				7 David R. Obey (D)	164,340	64.7
6 Norman D. Dicks (D)	122,903	53.6	3 John G. Hutchinson (D)	51,169	53.8	Vinton A. Vesta (R)	89,745	35.3
Jim Beaver (R)	106,236	46.4	David Staton (R)	43,950	46.2	8 Toby Roth (R)	169,664	67.7
7 Mike Lowry (D)	112,848	57.3				Michael R. Monfils (D)	81,043	32.3
Ron Dunlap (R)	84,218	42.7				9 F. James Sensenbrenner (R)	206,227	78.4
			WISCONSIN			Gary C. Benedict (D)	56,838	21.6
WEST VIRGINIA			1 Les Aspin (D)	126,222	56.2			
			Kathryn H. Canary (R)	96,047	42.8	**WYOMING**		
1 Robert H. Mollohan (D)	107,471	63.6	2 Robert W. Kastenmeier (D)	142,037	54.0	AL Richard B. Cheney (R)	116,361	68.6
Joe Bartlett (R)	61,438	36.4	James A. Wright (R)	119,514	45.4	Jim Rogers (D)	53,338	31.4
2 Cleve Benedict (R)	102,805	55.9	3 Steven Gunderson (R)	132,001	51.0	David G. Glancy (D)	24,390	42.8

1981 House Elections

MARYLAND

Special Election

Candidates	Votes	%
5 Steny H. Hoyer (D)	42,573	55.2
Audrey Scott (R)	33,708	43.5

MICHIGAN

Special Election

Candidates	Votes	%
4 Mark Siljander (R)	36,046	72.6
Johnie Rodebush (D)	12,461	25.1

MISSISSIPPI

Special Election

	Votes	%
4 Wayne Dowdy (D)	55,656	50.4
Liles Williams (R)	54,744	49.6

OHIO

Special Election

Candidates	Votes	%
4 Michael Oxley (R)	41,987	50.2
Dale Locker (D)	41,646	49.8

PENNSYLVANIA

Special Election

	Votes	%
3 Joseph F. Smith (R, I)	29,907	52.5
David G. Glancy (D)	24,390	42.8

1980 Elections

1. For the 1980 House elections in Louisiana, an open primary election was held with candidates from all parties running on the same ballot. Any candidate who received a majority was elected unopposed, with no further appearance on the general election ballot. If no candidate received 50 percent, a runoff was held between the two top finishers.

2. In Minnesota the Democratic Party is known as the Democratic-Farmer-Labor Party and the Republican Party as the Independent-Republican Party; candidates appear on the ballot with these designations.

1982 House Elections

ALABAMA

Candidates	Votes	%
1 Jack Edwards (R)	87,901	61.0
Steve Gudac (D)	54,315	37.7
2 William L. Dickinson (R)	83,290	50.4
Billy Joe Camp (D)	81,904	49.6
3 Bill Nichols (D)	100,864	96.3
4 Tom Bevill (D)	118,595	100.0
5 Ronnie G. Flippo (D)	108,807	80.7
Leopold Yambrek (R)	24,593	18.2
6 Ben Erdreich (D)	88,029	53.2
Albert Lee Smith Jr. (R)	76,726	46.4
7 Richard C. Shelby (D)	124,070	96.8

ALASKA

Candidates	Votes	%
AL Don Young (R)	128,274	70.8
Dave Carlson (D)	52,001	28.7

ARIZONA

Candidates	Votes	%
1 John McCain (R)	89,116	65.9
William E. Hegarty (D)	41,261	30.5
2 Morris K. Udall (D)	73,468	70.9
Roy B. Laos (R)	28,407	27.4
3 Bob Stump (R)	101,198	63.3
Pat Bosch (D)	58,644	36.7
4 Eldon Rudd (R)	95,620	65.7
Wayne O. Earley (D)	44,182	30.4
5 Jim McNulty (D)	82,938	49.7
Jim Kolbe (R)	80,531	48.3

ARKANSAS

Candidates	Votes	%
1 Bill Alexander (D)	124,208	64.8
Chuck Banks (R)	67,427	35.2
2 Ed Bethune (R)	96,775	53.9
Charles L. George (D)	82,913	46.1
3 John Paul Hammerschmidt (R)	133,909	66.0
Jim McDougal (D)	69,089	34.0
4 Beryl Anthony Jr. (D)	121,256	65.6
Bob Leslie (R)	63,661	34.4

CALIFORNIA

Candidates	Votes	%
1 Douglas H. Bosco (D)	107,749	49.8
Don H. Clausen (R)	102,043	47.2
2 Gene Chappie (R)	116,172	57.9
John A. Newmeyer (D)	81,314	40.5
3 Robert T. Matsui (D)	194,680	89.6
Bruce A. Daniel (LIBERT)	16,222	7.5
4 Vic Fazio (D)	118,476	63.9
Roger B. Canfield (R)	67,047	36.1
5 Phillip Burton (D)	103,268	57.9
Milton Marks (R)	72,139	40.5
6 Barbara Boxer (D)	96,379	52.4
Dennis McQuaid (R)	82,128	44.6
7 George Miller (D)	126,952	67.2
Paul E. Vallely (R)	56,960	30.2
8 Ronald V. Dellums (D)	121,537	55.9
Claude B. Hutchison Jr. (R)	95,694	44.0
9 Fortney H. (Pete) Stark (D)	104,393	60.7
Bill J. Kennedy (R)	67,702	39.3
10 Don Edwards (D)	77,263	62.7
Bob Herriott (R)	41,506	33.7
11 Tom Lantos (D)	109,812	57.1
Bill Royer (R)	76,462	39.7
12 Ed Zschau (R)	115,365	62.9
Emmett Lynch (D)	61,372	33.5
13 Norman Y. Mineta (D)	110,805	65.9
Tom Kelly (R)	52,806	31.4
14 Norman D. Shumway (R)	134,225	63.4
Baron Reed (D)	77,400	36.6
15 Tony Coelho (D)	86,022	63.7

Candidates	Votes	%
Ed Bates (R)	45,948	34.0
16 Leon E. Panetta (D)	142,630	83.5
G. Richard Arnold (R)	24,448	14.3
17 Charles Pashayan Jr. (R)	80,271	54.0
Gene Tackett (D)	68,364	46.0
18 Richard Lehman (D)	92,762	59.5
Adrian C. Fondse (R)	59,664	38.3
19 Robert J. Lagomarsino (R)	112,486	61.1
Frank Frost (D)	66,042	35.8
20 William M. Thomas (R)	123,312	68.1
Robert J. Bethea (D)	57,769	31.9
21 Bobbi Fiedler (R)	138,474	71.8
George Henry Margolis (D)	46,412	24.1
22 Carlos J. Moorhead (R)	145,831	73.6
Harvey L. Goldhammer (D)	46,521	23.5
23 Anthony C. Beilenson (D)	120,788	59.6
David Armor (R)	82,031	40.4
24 Henry A. Waxman (D)	88,516	65.1
Jerry Zerg (R)	42,133	31.0
25 Edward R. Roybal (D)	71,106	85.5
Daniel John Gorham (LIBERT)	12,060	14.5
26 Howard L. Berman (D)	97,383	59.6
Hal Phillips (R)	66,072	40.4
27 Mel Levine (D)	108,347	59.5
Bart W. Christensen (R)	67,479	37.0
28 Julian C. Dixon (D)	103,469	78.9
David Goerz (R)	24,473	18.7
29 Augustus F. Hawkins (D)	97,028	79.8
Milton R. MacKaig (R)	24,568	20.2
30 Matthew G. (Marty) Martinez (D)	60,905	53.9
John H. Rousselot (R)	52,177	46.1
31 Mervyn M. Dymally (D)	86,718	72.4
Henry C. Minturn (R)	33,043	27.6
32 Glenn M. Anderson (D)	84,663	58.0
Brian Lungren (R)	57,863	39.6
33 David Dreier (R)	112,362	65.2
Paul Servelle (D)	55,514	32.2
34 Esteban Torres (D)	68,316	57.2
Paul R. Jackson (R)	51,026	42.8
35 Jerry Lewis (R)	112,786	68.3
Robert E. Erwin (D)	52,349	31.7
36 George E. Brown Jr. (D)	76,546	54.3
John Paul Stark (R)	64,361	45.7
37 Al McCandless (R)	105,065	59.1
Curtis P. (Sam) Cross (D)	68,510	38.5
38 Jerry M. Patterson (D)	73,914	52.4
William F. Dohr (R)	61,279	43.4
39 William E. Dannemeyer (R)	129,539	72.2
Frank G. Verges (D)	46,681	26.0
40 Robert E. Badham (R)	144,228	71.5
Paul Haseman (D)	52,546	26.1
41 Bill Lowery (R)	140,130	68.9
Tony Brandenburg (D)	58,677	28.8
42 Dan Lungren (R)	142,845	69.0
James P. Spellman (D)	58,690	28.3
43 Ron Packard (R WRITE-IN)	66,444	36.8
Roy (Pat) Archer (D)	57,995	32.1
Johnnie R. Crean (R)	56,297	31.1
44 Jim Bates (D)	78,474	64.9
Shirley M. Gissendanner (R)	38,447	31.8
45 Duncan L. Hunter (R)	117,771	68.6
Richard Hill (D)	50,148	29.2

Special Election

	Votes	%
30 Matthew G. (Marty) Martinez (D)	22,572	32.0
Dennis S. Kazarian (D)	20,313	29.0
Ralph Ramirez (R)	11,033	16.0

Special Runoff Election

	Votes	%
30 Matthew G. (Marty) Martinez (D)	14,593	51.0
Ralph Ramirez (R)	14,043	49.0

COLORADO

Candidates	Votes	%
1 Patricia Schroeder (D)	94,969	60.3
Arch Decker (R)	59,009	37.4
2 Timothy E. Wirth (D)	101,202	61.8
John C. Buechner (R)	59,590	36.4
3 Ray Kogovsek (D)	92,384	53.4
Tom Wiens (R)	77,410	44.8
4 Hank Brown (R)	105,550	69.8
Charles L. (Bud) Bishopp (D)	45,750	30.2
5 Ken Kramer (R)	84,479	59.5
Tom Cronin (D)	57,392	40.5
6 Jack Swigert (R)	98,909	62.2
Steve Hogan (D)	56,598	35.6

CONNECTICUT

Candidates	Votes	%
1 Barbara B. Kennelly (D)	126,798	68.1
Herschel A. Klein (R)	58,075	31.2
2 Sam Gejdenson (D)	95,254	55.8
Tony Guglielmo (R)	74,294	43.5
3 Bruce A. Morrison (D)	90,638	49.9
Lawrence J. DeNardis (R)	88,951	49.0
4 Stewart B. McKinney (R)	93,660	56.5
John A. Phillips (D)	71,110	42.9
5 William R. Ratchford (D)	101,362	58.5
Neal B. Hanlon (R)	70,808	40.8
6 Nancy L. Johnson (R)	99,703	51.7
William E. Curry Jr. (D)	92,178	47.8

Special Election

	Votes	%
1 Barbara B. Kennelly (D)	51,431	58.8
Ann P. Uccello (R)	36,085	41.2

DELAWARE

Candidates	Votes	%
AL Thomas R. Carper (D)	98,533	52.4
Thomas B. Evans Jr. (R)	87,153	46.3

FLORIDA

Candidates	Votes	%
1 Earl Hutto (D)	82,569	74.4
J. Terry Bechtol (R)	28,373	25.6
2 Don Fuqua (D)	79,143	61.7
Ron McNeil (R)	49,101	38.3
3 Charles E. Bennett (D)	73,802	84.1
George Grimsley (R)	13,972	15.9
4 Bill Chappell Jr. (D)	83,895	66.9
Larry Gaudet (R)	41,457	33.1
5 Bill McCollum (R)	69,993	58.8
Dick Batchelor (D)	49,070	41.2
6 Kenneth H. (Buddy) MacKay (D)	85,825	61.3
Ed Havill (R)	54,059	38.6
7 Sam Gibbons (D)	85,331	74.2
Ken Ayers (R)	29,632	25.8
8 C. W. Bill Young (R)		100.0
9 Michael Bilirakis (R)	95,009	51.2
George H. Sheldon (D)	90,697	48.8
10 Andy Ireland (D)		100.0
11 Bill Nelson (D)	101,746	70.6
Joel Robinson (R)	42,422	29.4
12 Tom Lewis (R)	81,893	52.6
Brad Culverhouse (D)	73,913	47.4
13 Connie Mack III (R)	132,951	65.1
Dana N. Stevens (D)	71,239	34.9
14 Daniel A. Mica (D)	128,646	73.0
Steve Mitchell (R)	47,560	27.0
15 E. Clay Shaw Jr. (R)	89,158	57.1
Edward J. Stack (D)	67,083	42.9
16 Larry Smith (D)	91,888	67.9
Maurice Berkowitz (R)	43,458	32.1
17 William Lehman (D)		100.0
18 Claude Pepper (D)	72,183	71.2
Ricardo Nunez (R)	29,196	28.8

Candidates	Votes	%
19 Dante B. Fascell (D)	74,312	58.8
Glenn Rinker (R)	51,969	41.2

GEORGIA

Candidates	Votes	%
1 Lindsay Thomas (D)	65,625	64.1
Herb Jones (R)	36,799	35.9
2 Charles Hatcher (D)	73,897	100.0
3 Richard Ray (D)	74,626	71.0
Tyron Elliott (R)	30,537	29.0
4 Elliott H. Levitas (D)	38,758	65.5
Dick Winder (R)	20,418	34.5
5 Wyche Fowler Jr. (D)	53,264	80.8
J. E. (Billy) McKinney (I)	9,049	13.7
Paul Jones (R)	3,633	5.5
6 Newt Gingrich (R)	62,352	55.3
Jim Wood (D)	50,459	44.7
7 Larry P. McDonald (D)	71,647	61.1
Dave Sellers (R)	45,569	38.9
8 J. Roy Rowland (D)	75,009	100.0
9 Ed Jenkins (D)	86,514	77.0
Charles Sherwood (R)	25,907	23.0
10 Doug Barnard Jr. (D)	80,311	100.0

HAWAII

Candidates	Votes	%
1 Cecil Heftel (D)	134,779	89.9
Rockne H. Johnson (LIBERT)	15,128	10.1
2 Daniel K. Akaka (D)	132,072	89.2
Gregory B. Mills (NP)	9,080	6.2

IDAHO

Candidates	Votes	%
1 Larry E. Craig (R)	86,277	53.7
Larry LaRocco (D)	74,388	46.3
2 George Hansen (R)	83,873	52.3
Richard Stallings (D)	76,608	47.7

ILLINOIS

Candidates	Votes	%
1 Harold Washington (D)	172,641	97.3
2 Gus Savage (D)	140,827	87.0
Kevin Walker Sparks (R)	20,670	12.8
3 Marty Russo (D)	137,391	74.0
Richard D. Murphy (R)	48,268	26.0
4 George M. O'Brien (R)	79,842	54.6
Michael A. Murer (D)	66,323	45.4
5 William O. Lipinski (D)	110,351	75.4
Daniel J. Partyka (R)	35,970	24.6
6 Henry J. Hyde (R)	97,918	68.4
Leroy E. Kennel (D)	45,237	31.6
7 Cardiss Collins (D)	133,978	86.5
Dansby Cheeks (R)	20,994	13.5
8 Dan Rostenkowski (D)	124,318	83.4
Bonnie Hickey (R)	24,666	16.6
9 Sidney R. Yates (D)	114,083	66.5
Catherine Bertini (R)	54,851	32.0
10 John Edward Porter (R)	90,750	59.0
Eugenia S. Chapman (D)	63,115	41.0
11 Frank Annunzio (D)	134,755	72.6
James F. Moynihan (R)	50,967	27.4
12 Philip M. Crane (R)	86,487	66.2
Daniel G. DeFosse (D)	40,108	30.7
13 John N. Erlenborn (R)	113,423	69.8
Robert Bily (D)	49,105	30.2
14 Tom Corcoran (R)	98,262	64.6
Dan McGrath (D)	53,914	35.4
15 Edward R. Madigan (R)	105,083	66.3
Tim L. Hall (D)	53,303	33.7
16 Lynn Martin (R)	89,405	57.2
Carl R. Schwerdtfeger (D)	66,877	42.8
17 Lane Evans (D)	94,483	52.8
Kenneth G. McMillan (R)	84,347	47.2
18 Robert H. Michel (R)	97,406	51.6
G. Douglas Stephens (D)	91,281	48.4
19 Daniel B. Crane (R)	94,833	52.1
John Gwinn (D)	87,231	47.9
20 Richard J. Durbin (D)	100,758	50.4
Paul Findley (R)	99,348	49.6

Candidates	Votes	%
21 Melvin Price (D)	89,500	63.7
Robert H. Gaffner (R)	46,764	33.3
22 Paul Simon (D)	123,693	66.2
Peter G. Prineas (R)	63,279	33.8

INDIANA

Candidates	Votes	%
1 Katie Hall (D)	87,369	56.3
Thomas H. Krieger (R)	66,921	43.1
2 Philip R. Sharp (D)	107,298	56.2
Ralph W. Van Natta (R)	83,593	43.8
3 John Hiler (R)	86,958	51.2
Richard C. Bodine (D)	83,046	48.8
4 Dan Coats (R)	110,155	64.3
Roger M. Miller (D)	60,054	35.1
5 Elwood Hillis (R)	105,469	61.1
Allen B. Maxwell (D)	67,238	38.9
6 Dan Burton (R)	131,100	64.9
George E. Grabianowski (D)	70,764	35.1
7 John T. Myers (R)	115,884	62.3
Stephen S. Bonney (D)	70,249	37.7
8 Francis X. McCloskey (D)	100,592	51.4
Joel Deckard (R)	94,127	48.1
9 Lee H. Hamilton (D)	121,094	67.1
Floyd E. Coates (R)	58,532	32.4
10 Andrew Jacobs Jr. (D)	114,674	66.7
Michael A. Carroll (R)	56,992	33.2

IOWA

Candidates	Votes	%
1 Jim Leach (R)	89,585	59.2
William E. Gluba (D)	61,734	40.8
2 Tom Tauke (R)	99,478	58.8
Brent Appel (D)	69,539	41.1
3 Cooper Evans (R)	104,072	55.5
Lynn G. Cutler (D)	83,581	44.5
4 Neal Smith (D)	118,849	66.0
Dave Readinger (R)	60,534	33.6
5 Tom Harkin (D)	93,333	58.9
Arlyn E. Danker (R)	65,200	41.1
6 Berkley Bedell (D)	101,690	64.3
Al Bremer (R)	56,487	35.7

KANSAS

Candidates	Votes	%
1 Pat Roberts (R)	115,749	68.4
Kent Roth (D)	51,079	30.2
2 Jim Slattery (D)	86,286	57.4
Morris Kay (R)	63,942	42.6
3 Larry Winn Jr. (R)	82,117	59.2
William L. Kostar (D)	53,140	38.3
4 Dan Glickman (D)	107,326	73.9
Gerald Caywood (R)	35,478	24.4
5 Bob Whittaker (R)	103,551	67.6
Lee Rowe (D)	47,676	31.1

KENTUCKY

Candidates	Votes	%
1 Carroll Hubbard Jr. (D)	48,342	100.0
2 William H. Natcher (D)	49,571	73.8
Mark T. Watson (R)	17,561	26.2
3 Romano L. Mazzoli (D)	92,849	65.1
Carl Brown (R)	45,900	32.2
4 Gene Snyder (R)	74,109	54.2
Terry L. Mann (D)	61,937	45.3
5 Harold Rogers (R)	52,928	65.2
Doye Davenport (D)	28,285	34.8
6 Larry J. Hopkins (R)	68,418	56.8
Don Mills (D)	49,839	41.4
7 Carl D. Perkins (D)	82,463	79.4
Tom Hamby (R)	21,436	20.6

LOUISIANA

Candidates	Votes	%
1 Bob Livingston (R)		100.0
2 Lindy (Mrs. Hale) Boggs (D)		100.0
3 W. J. (Billy) Tauzin (D)		100.0
4 Buddy Roemer (D)		100.0

Footnote, see p. 286.

Candidates	Votes	%
5 Jerry Huckaby (D)		100.0
6 Henson Moore (R)		100.0
7 John B. Breaux (D)		100.0
8 Gillis W. Long (D)		100.0

MAINE

Candidates	Votes	%
1 John R. McKernan Jr. (R)	124,850	50.3
John M. Kerry (D)	118,884	47.9
2 Olympia J. Snowe (R)	136,075	66.6
James Patrick Dunleavy (D)	68,086	33.3

MARYLAND

Candidates	Votes	%
1 Roy Dyson (D)	89,503	69.3
C. A. Porter Hopkins (R)	39,656	30.7
2 Clarence D. Long (D)	83,318	52.6
Helen Delich Bentley (R)	75,062	47.4
3 Barbara A. Mikulski (D)	110,042	74.2
H. Robert Scherr (R)	38,259	25.8
4 Marjorie S. Holt (R)	75,617	61.2
Patricia O'Brien Aiken (D)	47,947	38.8
5 Steny H. Hoyer (D)	83,937	79.6
William P. Guthrie (R)	21,533	20.4
6 Beverly B. Byron (D)	102,596	74.4
Roscoe Bartlett (R)	35,321	25.6
7 Parren J. Mitchell (D)	103,496	87.9
M. Leonora Jones (R)	14,203	12.1
8 Michael D. Barnes (D)	121,761	71.3
Elizabeth W. Spencer (R)	48,910	28.7

MASSACHUSETTS

Candidates	Votes	%
1 Silvio O. Conte (R, D)	145,417	100.0
2 Edward P. Boland (D)	118,215	72.6
Thomas P. Swank (R)	44,544	27.4
3 Joseph D. Early (D)	142,611	100.0
4 Barney Frank (D)	121,802	59.5
Margaret M. Heckler (R)	82,804	40.5
5 James M. Shannon (D)	140,177	84.6
Angelo Laudani (LIBERT)	25,224	15.2
6 Nicholas Mavroules (D)	117,723	57.8
Thomas H. Trimarco (R)	85,849	42.2
7 Edward J. Markey (D)	151,305	77.8
David Basile (R)	43,063	22.2
8 Thomas P. O'Neill Jr. (D)	123,296	74.9
Frank Luke McNamara Jr. (R)	41,370	25.1
9 Joe Moakley (D)	102,665	64.1
Deborah R. Cochran (R)	55,030	34.3
10 Gerry E. Studds (D)	138,418	68.7
John E. Conway (R)	63,014	31.3
11 Brian J. Donnelly (D)	144,132	100.0

MICHIGAN

Candidates	Votes	%
1 John Conyers Jr. (D)	125,517	96.7
2 Carl D. Pursell (R)	106,960	65.5
George Wahr Sallade (D)	53,040	32.5
3 Howard Wolpe (D)	96,842	56.3
Richard L. Milliman (R)	73,315	42.6
4 Mark Siljander (R)	87,489	59.7
David A. Masiokas (D)	56,877	38.8
5 Harold S. Sawyer (R)	98,650	53.1
Stephen V. Monsma (D)	87,229	46.9
6 Bob Carr (D)	84,778	51.4
Jim Dunn (R)	78,388	47.5
7 Dale E. Kildee (D)	118,538	75.4
George R. Darrah (R)	36,303	23.1
8 Bob Traxler (D)	113,515	91.0
Sheila M. Hart (LIBERT)	11,219	9.0
9 Guy Vander Jagt (R)	112,504	64.9
Gerald D. Warner (D)	60,932	35.1
10 Don Albosta (D)	102,048	60.1
Lawrence W. Reed (R)	66,080	38.9
11 Robert W. Davis (R)	106,039	60.5
Kent Bourland (D)	69,181	39.5
12 David E. Bonior (D)	103,851	65.9
Ray Contesti (R)	52,312	33.2

Candidates	Votes	%
13 George W. Crockett Jr. (D)	108,351	88.0
Letty Gupta (R)	13,732	11.1
14 Dennis M. Hertel (D)	116,421	94.9
Harold H. Dunn (LIBERT)	6,175	5.0
15 William D. Ford (D)	94,950	72.8
Mitchell Moran (R)	33,904	26.0
16 John D. Dingell (D)	114,006	73.7
David K. Haskins (R)	39,227	25.3
17 Sander Levin (D)	116,901	66.6
Gerald E. Rosen (R)	55,620	31.7
18 Allen J. Sipher (D)	46,545	25.7
William S. Broomfield (R)	132,902	73.3

MINNESOTA

Candidates	Votes	%
1 Timothy J. Penny (DFL)	109,257	51.2
Tom Hagedorn (I-R)	102,298	47.9
2 Vin Weber (I-R)	123,508	54.5
James W. Nichols (DFL)	103,243	45.5
3 Bill Frenzel (I-R)	166,891	72.2
Joel Saliterman (DFL)	60,993	26.4
4 Bruce F. Vento (DFL)	153,494	73.2
Bill James (I-R)	56,248	26.8
5 Martin Olav Sabo (DFL)	136,634	65.5
Keith W. Johnson (I-R)	61,184	29.4
6 Gerry Sikorski (DFL)	109,246	50.8
Arlen Erdahl (I-R)	105,734	49.2
7 Arlan Stangeland (I-R)	108,254	50.3
Gene Wenstrom (DFL)	107,062	49.7
8 James L. Oberstar (DFL)	176,392	76.7
Marjory L. Luce (I-R)	53,467	23.3

MISSISSIPPI

Candidates	Votes	%
1 Jamie L. Whitten (D)	79,726	70.9
Fran Fawcett (R)	32,750	29.1
2 Webb Franklin (R)	74,450	50.3
Robert G. Clark (D)	71,536	48.4
3 G. V. (Sonny) Montgomery (D)	114,530	93.1
James Bradshaw (I)	8,519	6.9
4 Wayne Dowdy (D)	79,977	52.5
Liles Williams (R)	69,469	45.6
5 Trent Lott (R)	82,884	78.5
Arlon (Blackie) Coate (D)	22,634	21.5

MISSOURI

Candidates	Votes	%
1 William Clay (D)	102,656	66.1
William E. White (R)	52,599	33.9
2 Robert A. Young (D)	100,770	56.5
Harold L. Dielmann (R)	77,433	43.5
3 Richard A. Gephardt (D)	131,566	77.9
Richard Foristel (R)	37,388	22.1
4 Ike Skelton (D)	96,388	54.8
Wendell Bailey (R)	79,565	45.2
5 Alan Wheat (D)	96,059	57.9
John A. Sharp (R)	66,664	40.2
6 E. Thomas Coleman (R)	97,993	55.3
Jim Russell (D)	79,053	44.7
7 Gene Taylor (R)	91,391	50.5
David A. Geisler (D)	89,549	49.5
8 Bill Emerson (R)	86,493	53.1
Jerry Ford (D)	76,413	46.9
9 Harold L. Volkmer (D)	99,228	60.8
Larry E. Mead (R)	63,942	39.2

MONTANA

Candidates	Votes	%
1 Pat Williams (D)	100,087	59.7
Bob Davies (R)	62,402	37.2
2 Howard Lyman (D)	65,815	44.2
Ron Marlenee (R)	79,968	53.7

NEBRASKA

Candidates	Votes	%
1 Douglas K. Bereuter (R)	137,675	75.1
Curt Donaldson (D)	45,676	24.9
2 Hal Daub (R)	92,639	56.7
Richard M. Fellman (D)	70,431	43.1
3 Virginia Smith (R)	171,853	100.0

NEVADA

Candidates	Votes	%
1 Harry Reid (D)	61,901	57.5
Peggy Cavnar (R)	45,675	42.5
2 Barbara Vucanovich (R)	70,188	55.5
Mary Gojack (D)	52,265	41.3

NEW HAMPSHIRE

Candidates	Votes	%
1 Norman E. D'Amours (D)	76,281	54.9
Robert C. Smith (R)	61,876	44.5
2 Judd Gregg (R)	92,098	70.8
Robert L. Dupay (D)	37,906	29.2

NEW JERSEY

Candidates	Votes	%
1 James J. Florio (D)	110,570	73.3
John A. Dramesi (R)	39,501	26.2
2 William J. Hughes (D)	102,826	68.0
John J. Mahoney (R)	47,069	31.1
3 James J. Howard (D)	104,055	62.3
Marie Sheehan Muhler (R)	60,515	36.2
4 Christopher H. Smith (R)	85,660	52.7
Joseph P. Merlino (D)	75,658	46.5
5 Marge Roukema (R)	104,695	65.3
Fritz Cammerzell (D)	53,659	33.5
6 Bernard J. Dwyer (D)	100,419	68.1
Bertram L. Buckler (R)	46,095	31.3
7 Matthew J. Rinaldo (R)	91,837	56.0
Adam K. Levin (D)	70,978	43.3
8 Robert A. Roe (D)	89,980	70.7
Norm Robertson (R)	36,317	28.5
9 Robert G. Torricelli (D)	99,090	53.0
Harold C. Hollenbeck (R)	86,022	46.0
10 Peter W. Rodino Jr. (D)	76,684	82.6
Timothy Lee Jr. (R)	14,551	15.7
11 Joseph G. Minish (D)	105,607	64.3
Rey Redington (R)	57,099	34.8
12 Jim Courter (R)	117,793	66.8
Jeff Connor (D)	57,049	32.3
13 Edwin B. Forsythe (R)	100,061	59.5
George Callas (D)	65,820	39.1
14 Frank J. Guarini (D)	94,021	74.3
Charles J. Catrillo (R)	28,257	22.3

NEW MEXICO

Candidates	Votes	%
1 Manuel Lujan Jr. (R)	74,459	52.4
Jan Alan Hartke (D)	67,534	47.6
2 Joe Skeen (R)	71,021	58.4
Caleb Chandler (D)	50,599	41.6
3 Bill Richardson (D)	84,669	64.5
Marjorie Bell Chambers (R)	46,466	35.4

NEW YORK

Candidates	Votes	%
1 William Carney (R, C, RTL)	88,234	63.9
Ethan C. Eldon (D)	49,787	36.1
2 Thomas J. Downey (D)	80,951	63.9
Paul G. Costello (R, C)	42,790	33.8
3 Robert J. Mrazek (D)	93,846	51.8
John LeBoutillier (R, C)	83,238	46.0
4 Norman F. Lent (R, C)	105,241	60.4
Robert P. Zimmerman (D, L)	63,390	36.4
5 Raymond J. McGrath (R, C)	100,485	58.1
Arnold J. Miller (D, L)	67,002	38.8
6 Joseph P. Addabbo (D, R, L)	95,483	95.9
7 Benjamin S. Rosenthal (D, L)	84,013	77.2
Albert Lemishow (R, C, RTL)	24,832	22.8
8 James H. Scheuer (D, L)	91,830	89.5
John T. Blume (C)	10,741	10.5
9 Geraldine A. Ferraro (D)	75,286	73.2
John J. Weigandt (R)	20,352	19.8
Ralph G. Groves (C, RTL)	6,011	5.9
10 Charles E. Schumer (D, L)	89,852	79.2
Stephen Marks (R, C)	21,726	19.2
11 Edolphus Towns (D)	39,357	83.7
James W. Smith (R)	4,449	9.5
12 Major R. Owens (D, L)	44,586	90.5
David Katan Sr. (R)	3,215	6.5
13 Stephen J. Solarz (D, L)	68,549	80.5
Leon F. Nadrowski (R, RTL)	14,257	16.7
14 Guy V. Molinari (R, C, RTL)	67,626	56.1
Leo C. Zeferetti (D)	51,728	42.9
15 Bill Green (R)	66,262	53.6
Betty G. Lall (D, L)	55,483	44.9
16 Charles B. Rangel (D, R, L)	76,626	97.5
17 Ted Weiss (D, L)	113,172	85.0
Louis S. Antonelli (R, C, RTL)	19,928	15.0
18 Robert Garcia (D, R, L)	57,009	98.9
19 Mario Biaggi (D, R, L, RTL)	118,803	93.7
Michael J. McSherry (C)	7,438	5.9
20 Richard L. Ottinger (D)	98,425	56.5
Jon S. Fossel (R, C)	72,005	41.3
21 Hamilton Fish Jr. (R, C)	117,460	75.2
J. Morgan Strong (D)	38,664	24.8
22 Benjamin A. Gilman (R)	92,266	52.9
Peter A. Peyser (D)	73,124	42.0
23 Samuel S. Stratton (D)	164,427	76.1
Frank Wicks (R, NF)	41,386	19.2
24 Gerald B. H. Solomon (R, C, RTL)	140,296	73.9
Roy Esiason (D)	49,441	26.1
25 Sherwood L. Boehlert (R)	93,071	55.8
Anita Maxwell (D)	70,793	42.4
26 David O'B. Martin (R, C)	108,962	71.6
David P. Landy (D)	43,208	28.4
27 George C. Wortley (R)	95,290	53.2
Elaine Lytel (D, L)	79,209	44.2
28 Matthew F. McHugh (D, L)	100,665	56.3
David F. Crowley (R, C)	75,991	42.5
29 Frank Horton (R)	104,412	66.4
William C. Larsen (D)	47,463	30.2
30 Barber B. Conable Jr. (R)	119,105	68.2
Bill Benet (D)	48,764	27.9
31 Jack F. Kemp (R, C)	133,462	75.3
James A. Martin (D, L)	43,843	24.7
32 John J. LaFalce (D, L)	116,386	91.4
Raymond R. Walker (R, C)	8,638	6.8
33 Henry J. Nowak (D, L)	126,091	84.1
Walter J. Pillich (R, C)	19,791	13.2
34 Stanley N. Lundine (D)	99,502	60.2
James J. Snyder (R, C)	63,972	38.7

NORTH CAROLINA

Candidates	Votes	%
1 Walter B. Jones (D)	79,954	81.3
James F. McIntyre III (R)	17,478	17.8
2 I. T. (Tim) Valentine Jr. (D)	59,617	53.6
John W. Marin (R)	34,293	30.8
H. M. Michaux Jr. (WRITE IN)	15,990	14.4
3 Charles Whitley (D)	68,936	63.6
Eugene (Red) McDaniel (R)	39,046	36.0
4 Ike Andrews (D)	70,369	51.3
William Cobey Jr. (R)	64,955	47.4
5 Stephen L. Neal (D)	87,819	60.3
Anne Bagnal (R)	57,083	39.2
6 Charles Robin Britt (D)	68,696	53.8
Eugene Johnston (R)	58,244	45.6
7 Charlie Rose (D)	68,529	71.0
Edward Johnson (R)	27,015	28.0
8 W. G. (Bill) Hefner (D)	71,691	57.4
Harris D. Blake (R)	52,417	42.0
9 James G. Martin (R)	64,297	57.0
Preston Cornelius (D)	47,258	41.9
10 James T. Broyhill (R)	80,904	92.7
Jhon Rankin (LIBERT)	6,360	7.3
11 James McClure Clarke (D)	85,410	49.9
Bill Hendon (R)	84,085	49.2

NORTH DAKOTA

Candidates	Votes	%
AL Byron L. Dorgan (D)	186,534	71.6
Kent H. Jones (R)	72,241	27.7

OHIO

Candidates	Votes	%
1 Thomas A. Luken (D)	99,143	63.5
John (Jake) Held (R)	52,658	33.7
2 Bill Gradison (R)	97,434	62.7
William J. Luttmer (D)	53,169	34.2
3 Tony P. Hall (D)	119,926	87.7
Kathryn E. Brown (LIBERT)	16,828	12.3
4 Michael G. Oxley (R)	105,087	64.6
Robert W. Moon (D)	57,564	35.4
5 Delbert L. Latta (R)	86,450	55.2
James R. Sherck (D)	70,120	44.8
6 Bob McEwen (R)	92,135	59.2
Lynn Alan Grimshaw (D)	63,435	40.8
7 Michael Dewine (R)	87,842	56.3
Roger D. Tackett (D)	65,543	42.0
8 Thomas N. Kindness (R)	98,527	66.4
John W. Griffin (D)	49,877	33.6
9 Marcy Kaptur (D)	95,162	57.9
Ed Weber (R)	64,459	39.3
10 Clarence E. Miller (R)	100,044	63.3
John M. Buchanan (D)	57,983	36.7
11 Dennis E. Eckart (D)	93,302	60.9
Glen W. Warner (R)	56,616	36.9
12 John R. Kasich (R)	88,335	50.5
Bob Shamansky (D)	82,753	47.3
13 Don J. Pease (D)	92,296	61.2
Timothy Paul Martin (R)	53,376	35.4
14 John F. Seiberling (D)	115,629	70.5
Louis A. Mangels (R)	48,421	29.5
15 Chalmers P. Wylie (R)	104,678	66.3
Greg Kostelac (D)	47,070	29.8
16 Ralph Regula (R)	110,485	65.8
Jeffrey R. Orenstein (D)	57,386	34.2
17 Lyle Williams (R)	98,476	55.1
George D. Tablack (D)	80,375	44.9
18 Douglas Applegate (D)	128,665	100.0
19 Edward F. Feighan (D)	111,760	58.8
Richard G. Anter II (R)	72,682	38.3
20 Mary Rose Oakar (D)	133,603	85.6
Paris T. LeJeune (R)	17,675	11.3
21 Louis Stokes (D)	132,544	86.1
Alan G. Shatteen (R)	21,332	13.9

Special Election

Candidates	Votes	%
17 Jean Ashbrook (R)	18,106	73.4
Jack Koelbe (D)	6,385	25.9

OKLAHOMA

Candidates	Votes	%
1 James R. Jones (D)	76,379	54.1
Richard C. Freeman (R)	64,704	45.9
2 Mike Synar (D)	111,895	72.6
Lou Striegel (R)	42,298	27.4
3 Wes Watkins (D)	121,670	82.2
Patrick K. Miller (R)	26,335	17.8
4 Dave McCurdy (D)	84,205	65.0
Howard Rutledge (R)	44,351	34.2
5 Mickey Edwards (R)	98,979	67.2
Dan Lane (D)	42,453	28.8
6 Glenn English (D)	102,811	75.4
Ed Moore (R)	33,519	24.6

OREGON

Candidates	Votes	%
1 Les AuCoin (D)	118,638	53.8
Bill Moshofsky (R)	101,720	46.2
2 Bob Smith (R)	106,912	55.6
Larryann Willis (D)	85,495	44.4
3 Ron Wyden (D)	159,416	78.3
Thomas H. Phelan (R)	44,162	21.7
4 James Weaver (D)	115,448	59.0
Ross Anthony (R)	80,054	40.9
5 Denny Smith (R)	103,906	51.2
J. Ruth McFarland (D)	98,952	48.8

PENNSYLVANIA

Candidates	Votes	%
1 Thomas M. Foglietta (D)	103,626	72.3
Michael Marino (R)	38,155	26.6
2 William H. Gray III (D)	120,744	76.1
Milton Street (I)	35,205	22.2
3 Robert A. Borski (D)	97,161	50.1
Charles F. Dougherty (R)	94,497	48.7
4 Joseph P. Kolter (D)	100,481	60.1
Eugene V. Atkinson (R)	64,539	38.6
5 Richard T. Schulze (R)	90,648	67.2
Bob Burger (D)	44,170	32.8
6 Gus Yatron (D)	108,230	72.0
Harry B. Martin (R)	42,155	28.0
7 Robert W. Edgar (D)	105,775	55.4
Steve Joachim (R)	85,023	44.6
8 Peter H. Kostmayer (D)	83,242	50.3
Jim Coyne (R)	80,928	48.9
9 Bud Shuster (R)	92,322	65.1
Eugene J. Duncan (D)	49,583	34.9
10 Joseph M. McDade (R)	103,617	67.5
Robert J. Rafalko (D)	49,868	32.5
11 Frank Harrison (D)	90,371	53.5
James L. Nelligan (R)	78,485	46.5
12 John P. Murtha (D)	96,369	61.1
William N. Tuscano (R)	54,212	34.4
13 Lawrence Coughlin (R)	109,198	64.3
Martin J. Cunningham Jr. (D)	59,709	35.2
14 William J. Coyne (D)	120,980	74.9
John R. Clark (R)	32,780	20.3
15 Don Ritter (R)	79,455	57.8
Richard J. Orloski (D)	58,002	42.2
16 Robert S. Walker (R)	93,034	71.3
Jean D. Mowery (D)	37,364	28.7
17 George W. Gekas (R)	84,291	57.6
Larry J. Hochendoner (D)	61,974	42.4
18 Doug Walgren (D)	101,807	54.2
Ted Jacob (R)	84,428	45.0
19 Bill Goodling (R)	101,163	70.8
Larry Becker (D)	41,787	29.2
20 Joseph M. Gaydos (D)	127,281	76.0
Terry T. Ray (R)	38,212	22.8
21 Thomas J. Ridge (R)	80,180	50.2
Anthony (Buzz) Andrezeski (D)	79,451	49.8
22 Austin J. Murphy (D)	123,716	78.7
Frank J. Paterra (R)	32,176	20.5
23 William F. Clinger Jr. (R)	92,424	65.2
Joseph J. Calla Jr. (D)	49,297	34.8

RHODE ISLAND

Candidates	Votes	%
1 Fernand J. St Germain (D)	97,254	60.7
Burton Stallwood (R)	61,253	38.3
2 Claudine Schneider (R)	96,282	55.6
James V. Aukerman (D)	76,769	44.4

SOUTH CAROLINA

Candidates	Votes	%
1 Thomas F. Hartnett (R)	63,945	54.3
W. Mullins McLeod (D)	52,916	44.9
2 Floyd Spence (R)	71,569	58.5
Ken Mosely (D)	50,749	41.5
3 Butler Derrick (D)	77,125	90.4
Gordon T. Davis (LIBERT)	8,214	9.6
4 Carroll A. Campbell Jr. (R)	69,802	63.3
Marion E. Tyus (D)	40,394	36.7
5 John Spratt (D)	69,345	67.6
John S. Wilkerson (R)	33,191	32.4
6 Robert M. Tallon Jr. (D)	62,582	52.5
John L. Napier (R)	56,653	47.5

SOUTH DAKOTA

Candidates	Votes	%
AL Thomas A. Daschle (D)	142,122	51.6
Clint Roberts (R)	133,530	48.4

TENNESSEE

Candidates	Votes	%
1 James H. Quillen (R)	89,497	74.1
Jessie J. Cable (D)	27,580	22.8
2 John J. Duncan (R)	109,045	100.0
3 Marilyn Lloyd Bouquard (D)	84,967	61.8
Glen Byers (R)	49,885	36.3
4 Jim Cooper (D)	93,453	66.1
Cissy Baker (R)	47,865	33.9
5 Bill Boner (D)	109,282	80.1
Laural Steinhice (R)	27,061	19.8
6 Albert Gore Jr. (D)	104,094	100.0
7 Don Sundquist (R)	73,835	50.5
Bob Clement (D)	72,359	49.5
8 Ed Jones (D)	93,945	74.9
Bruce Benson (R)	31,527	25.1
9 Harold E. Ford (D)	112,143	72.4
Joe Crawford (R)	40,812	26.4

TEXAS

Candidates	Votes	%
1 Sam B. Hall Jr. (D)	100,685	97.5
2 Charles Wilson (D)	91,762	94.3
Ed Richbourg (LIBERT)	5,584	5.7
3 Steve Bartlett (R)	99,852	77.1
James L. McNees Jr. (D)	28,223	21.8
4 Ralph M. Hall (D)	94,134	73.8
Peter J. Collumb (R)	32,221	25.3
5 John Bryant (D)	52,214	64.8
Joe Devaney (R)	27,121	33.7
6 Phil Gramm (D)	91,546	94.5
Ron Hard (LIBERT)	5,288	5.5
7 Bill Archer (R)	108,718	85.0
Dennis Scoggins (D)	17,866	14.0
8 Jack Fields (R)	50,630	56.7
Henry E. Allee (D)	38,041	42.6
9 Jack Brooks (D)	78,965	67.6
John W. Lewis (R)	35,422	30.3
10 J. J. Pickle (D)	121,030	90.1
William C. Kelsey (LIBERT)	8,735	6.5
11 Marvin Leath (D)	83,236	96.3
12 Jim Wright (D)	78,913	68.9
Jim Ryan (R)	34,879	30.5
13 Jack Hightower (D)	86,376	63.6
Ron Slover (R)	47,877	35.3
14 Bill Patman (D)	76,851	60.7
Joe Wyatt Jr. (R)	48,942	38.6
15 E. (Kika) de la Garza (D)	76,544	95.7
16 Ronald Coleman (D)	44,024	53.9
Pat B. Haggerty (R)	36,064	44.2
17 Charles W. Stenholm (D)	109,359	97.1
18 Mickey Leland (D)	68,014	82.6
C. Leon Pickett (R)	12,104	14.7
19 Kent Hance (D)	89,702	81.6
E. L. Hicks (R)	19,062	17.3
20 Henry B. Gonzalez (D)	68,544	91.5
Roger V. Gary (LIBERT)	4,163	5.6
21 Tom Loeffler (R)	106,515	74.6
Charles S. Stough (D)	35,112	24.6
22 Ron Paul (R)	66,536	100.0
23 Abraham Kazen Jr. (D)	51,690	55.3
Jeff Wentworth (R)	41,363	44.2
24 Martin Frost (D)	63,857	72.9
Lucy P. Patterson (R)	22,798	26.0
25 Mike Andrews (D)	63,974	60.4
Mike Faubion (R)	40,112	37.9
26 Tom Vandergriff (D)	69,782	50.1
Jim Bradshaw (R)	69,438	49.9
27 Solomon P. Ortiz (D)	66,604	64.0
Jason Luby (R)	35,209	33.8

UTAH

Candidates	Votes	%
1 James V. Hansen (R)	111,416	62.8
A. Stephen Dirks (D)	66,006	37.2
2 Dan Marriott (R)	92,109	53.8
Frances Farley (D)	78,981	46.2
3 Howard C. Nielson (R)	108,478	76.9
Henry A. Huish (I)	32,661	23.1

VERMONT

Candidates	Votes	%
AL James M. Jeffords (R)	114,191	69.2
Mark A. Kaplan (D)	38,296	23.2

VIRGINIA

Candidates	Votes	%
1 Herbert H. Bateman (R)	76,926	53.9
John J. McGlennon (D)	62,379	43.7
2 G. William Whitehurst (R)	78,108	99.9
3 Thomas J. Bliley Jr. (R)	92,928	59.2
John A. Waldrop Jr. (D)	63,946	40.8
4 Norman Sisisky (D)	80,695	54.4
Robert W. Daniel Jr. (R)	67,708	45.6
5 Dan Daniel (D)	88,293	100.0
6 James R. Olin (D)	68,192	49.7
Kevin G. Miller (R)	66,537	48.5
7 J. Kenneth Robinson (R)	76,752	59.9
Lindsay G. Dorrier Jr. (D)	46,514	36.3
8 Stan Parris (R)	69,620	49.7
Herbert E. Harris II (D)	68,071	48.6
9 Frederick C. Boucher (D)	76,205	50.4
William C. Wampler (R)	75,082	49.6
10 Frank R. Wolf (R)	86,506	52.7
Ira M. Lechner (D)	75,361	45.9

WASHINGTON

	Votes	%
1 Joel Pritchard (R)	123,956	67.6
Brian Long (D)	59,444	32.4

Candidates	Votes	%
2 Al Swift (D)	101,383	59.6
Joan Houchen (R)	68,622	40.4
3 Don Bonker (D)	97,323	60.1
J. T. Quigg (R)	59,686	36.8
4 Sid Morrison (R)	112,148	69.8
Charles D. Kilbury (D)	45,990	28.6
5 Thomas S. Foley (D)	109,549	64.3
John Sonneland (R)	60,816	35.7
6 Norman D. Dicks (D)	89,985	62.5
Ted Haley (R)	47,720	33.2
7 Mike Lowry (D)	126,313	70.9
Bob Dorse (R)	51,759	29.1
8 Rodney Chandler (R)	79,209	57.0
Beth Bland (D)	59,824	43.0

WEST VIRGINIA

	Votes	%
1 Alan B. Mollohan (D)	79,529	53.2
John F. McCuskey (R)	70,069	46.8
2 Harley O. Staggers Jr. (D)	87,904	64.0
J. D. Hinkle Jr. (R)	49,413	36.0
3 Bob Wise (D)	84,619	57.9
David Michael Staton (R)	60,844	41.6
4 Nick J. Rahall II (D)	91,184	80.5
Homer L. Harris (R)	22,054	19.5

WISCONSIN

Candidates	Votes	%
1 Les Aspin (D)	95,055	61.0
Peter N. Jannson (R)	59,309	38.1
2 Robert W. Kastenmeier (D)	112,677	60.6
Jim Johnson (R)	71,989	38.7
3 Steve Gunderson (R)	99,304	56.6
Paul Offner (D)	75,132	42.8
4 Clement J. Zablocki (D)	129,557	94.6
5 Jim Moody (D)	99,713	63.5
Rod K. Johnston (R)	54,826	34.9
6 Thomas E. Petri (R)	111,348	65.0
Gordon E. Loehr (D)	59,922	35.0
7 David R. Obey (D)	122,124	68.0
Bernard A. Zimmerman (R)	57,535	32.0
8 Toby Roth (R)	101,379	57.2
Ruth C. Clusen (D)	74,436	42.0
9 F. James Sensenbrenner Jr. (R)	111,503	100.0

WYOMING

	Votes	%
AL Dick Cheney (R)	113,236	71.1
Ted Hommel (D)	46,041	28.9

1982 Elections

1. For the 1982 House elections in Louisiana, an open primary election was held with candidates from all parties running on the same ballot. Any candidate who received a majority was elected unopposed, with no further appearance on the general election ballot. If no candidate received 50 percent, a runoff was held between the two top finishers.

1983 House Elections

CALIFORNIA

Candidates	Votes	%
Special Election		
5 Sala Burton (D)	44,790	56.9
Dunan Howard (R)	18,305	23.3
Richard Doyle (D)	6,582	8.4

COLORADO

	Votes	%
Special Election		
6 Daniel S. Schaefer (R)	49,816	63.3
Steve Hogan (D)	27,779	35.3

GEORGIA

Special Election (Non-partisan)

Candidates	Votes	%
7 Kathryn McDonald	25,468	30.6
George W. (Buddy) Darden	22,894	27.6
George A. Sellers	20,970	25.2
George Pullen	4,578	5.5
Dan H. Fincher	4,278	5.1

Special Runoff Election (Non-partisan)

	Votes	%
7 George W. (Buddy) Darden	56,267	59.1
Kathryn McDonald	38,949	40.9

ILLINOIS

Special Election

	Votes	%
1 Charles A. Hayes (D)	39,623	93.7
Diane Preacely (R)	2,272	5.4

NEW YORK

Candidates	Votes	%
Special Election		
7 Gary L. Ackerman (D, L)	18,388	48.7
Albert Lemishow (R, C)	8,331	22.1
Douglas F. Schoen (NEIGH)	5,997	15.9
Sheldon Loeffler (I)	4,318	11.4

TEXAS

Special Election

	Votes	%
6 Phil Gramm (R)	46,371	55.3
Dan Kubiak (D)	33,201	39.6

1984 House Elections

ALABAMA

	Candidates	Votes	%
1	Sonny Callahan (R)	102,479	51.0
	Frank McRight (D)	98,455	49.0
2	William L. Dickinson (R)	118,153	60.3
	Larry Lee (D)	75,506	38.6
3	Bill Nichols (D)	120,357	96.2
4	Tom Bevill (D)	120,106	100.0
5	Ronnie G. Flippo (D)	140,542	95.9
6	Ben Erdreich (D)	130,973	59.6
	J. T. (Jabo) Waggoner (R)	87,550	39.8
7	Richard C. Shelby (D)	135,834	96.8

ALASKA

	Candidates	Votes	%
AL	Don Young (R)	113,582	55.0
	Pegge Begich (D)	86,052	41.7

ARIZONA

	Candidates	Votes	%
1	John McCain (R)	162,418	78.1
	Harry W. Braun III (D)	45,609	21.9
2	Morris K. Udall (D)	106,332	87.7
	Lorenzo Torrez (I)	14,869	12.3
3	Bob Stump (R)	156,686	71.8
	Bob Schuster (D)	57,748	26.4
4	Eldon Rudd (R)	167,558	100.0
5	Jim Kolbe (R)	116,075	50.9
	James F. McNulty Jr. (D)	109,871	48.2

ARKANSAS

	Candidates	Votes	%
1	Bill Alexander (D)	121,047	97.2
2	Tommy F. Robinson (D)	103,165	47.1
	Judy Petty (R)	90,841	41.5
	Jim Taylor (I)	25,073	11.4
3	John Paul Hammerschmidt (R)		100.0
4	Beryl Anthony Jr. (D)	117,123	97.9

CALIFORNIA

	Candidates	Votes	%
1	Douglas H. Bosco (D)	157,037	62.3
	David Redick (R)	95,186	37.7
2	Gene Chappie (R)	158,679	69.5
	Harry Cozad (D)	69,793	30.5
3	Robert T. Matsui (D)	131,369	100.0
4	Vic Fazio (D)	130,109	61.4
	Roger Canfield (R)	77,773	36.7
5	Sala Burton (D)	139,692	72.3
	Tom Spinosa (R)	45,930	23.8
6	Barbara Boxer (D)	162,511	68.0
	Douglas Binderup (R)	71,011	29.7
7	George Miller (D)	158,306	66.7
	Rosemary Thakar (R)	78,985	33.3
8	Ronald V. Dellums (D)	144,316	60.3
	Charles Connor (R)	94,907	39.7
9	Fortney H. (Pete) Stark (D)	136,511	69.9
	J. T. Eager Beaver (R)	51,399	26.3
10	Don Edwards (D)	102,469	62.4
	Robert P. Herriott (R)	56,256	34.3
11	Tom Lantos (D)	147,607	69.9
	John J. Hickey (R)	59,625	28.3
12	Ed Zschau (R)	155,795	61.7
	Martin Carnoy (D)	91,026	36.0
13	Norman Y. Mineta (D)	139,851	65.2
	John D. Williams (R)	70,666	33.0
14	Norman D. Shumway (R)	179,238	73.3
	Ruth (Paula) Carlson (D)	58,384	23.9
15	Tony Coelho (D)	109,590	65.5
	Carol Harner (R)	54,730	32.7
16	Leon E. Panetta (D)	153,377	70.8
	Patricia Smith Ramsey (R)	60,065	27.7
17	Charles Pashayan Jr. (R)	128,802	72.5
	Simon Lakritz (D)	48,888	27.5
18	Richard H. Lehman (D)	128,186	67.3

	Candidates	Votes	%
	Dale L. Ewen (R)	62,339	32.7
19	Robert J. Lagomarsino (R)	153,187	67.3
	James C. Carey Jr. (D)	70,278	30.9
20	William M. Thomas (R)	151,732	70.9
	Mike LeSage (D)	62,307	29.1
21	Bobbi Fiedler (R)	173,504	72.3
	Charles Davis (D)	62,085	25.9
22	Carlos J. Moorhead (R)	184,981	85.2
	Michael B. Yauch (LIBERT)	32,036	14.8
23	Anthony C. Beilenson (D)	140,461	61.6
	Claude Parrish (R)	84,093	36.9
24	Henry A. Waxman (D)	97,340	63.4
	Jerry Zerg (R)	51,010	33.2
25	Edward R. Roybal (D)	74,261	71.7
	Roy D. (Bill) Bloxom (R)	24,968	24.1
26	Howard L. Berman (D)	117,080	62.8
	Miriam Ojeda (R)	69,372	37.2
27	Mel Levine (D)	116,933	54.9
	Robert B. Scribner (R)	88,896	41.8
28	Julian C. Dixon (D)	113,076	75.6
	Beatrice M. Jett (R)	33,511	22.4
29	Augustus F. Hawkins (D)	108,777	86.6
	Echo Y. Goto (R)	16,781	13.4
30	Matthew G. Martinez (D)	64,378	51.8
	Richard Gomez (R)	53,900	43.3
31	Mervyn M. Dymally (D)	100,658	70.7
	Henry C. Minturn (R)	41,691	29.3
32	Glenn M. Anderson (D)	102,961	60.7
	Roger E. Fiola (R)	62,176	36.6
33	David Dreier (R)	147,363	70.6
	Claire K. McDonald (D)	54,147	26.0
34	Esteban Edward Torres (D)	87,060	59.8
	Paul R. Jackson (R)	58,467	40.2
35	Jerry Lewis (R)	176,477	85.5
	Kevin Akin (PFP)	29,990	14.5
36	George E. Brown Jr. (D)	104,438	56.6
	John Paul Stark (R)	80,212	43.4
37	Al McCandless (R)	149,955	63.6
	David E. Skinner (D)	85,908	36.4
38	Bob Dornan (R)	86,545	53.2
	Jerry M. Patterson (D)	73,231	45.0
39	William E. Dannemeyer (R)	175,788	76.2
	Robert E. Ward (D)	54,889	23.8
40	Robert E. Badham (R)	164,257	64.4
	Carol Ann Bradford (D)	86,748	34.0
41	Bill Lowery (R)	161,068	63.4
	Robert L. Simmons (D)	85,475	33.7
42	Dan Lungren (R)	177,783	73.0
	Mary Lou Brophy (D)	60,025	24.6
43	Ron Packard (R)	165,643	74.1
	Lois E. Humphreys (D)	50,996	22.8
44	Jim Bates (D)	99,378	69.7
	Neill Campbell (R)	39,977	28.0
45	Duncan L. Hunter (R)	149,011	75.1
	David W. Guthrie (D)	45,325	22.9

COLORADO

	Candidates	Votes	%
1	Patricia Schroeder (D)	126,348	62.0
	Mary Downs (R)	73,993	36.3
2	Timothy E. Wirth (D)	118,580	53.2
	Michael J. Norton (R)	101,488	45.5
3	Mike Strang (R)	122,669	57.1
	W. Mitchell (D)	90,063	41.9
4	Hank Brown (R)	146,469	71.1
	Mary Fagan Bates (D)	56,462	27.4
5	Ken Kramer (R)	163,654	78.6
	William Geffen (D)	44,588	21.4
6	Dan L. Schaefer (R)	171,427	89.4
	John Heckman (I)	20,333	10.6

CONNECTICUT

	Candidates	Votes	%
1	Barbara B. Kennelly (D)	147,748	61.7
	Herschel A. Klein (R)	90,823	37.9
2	Sam Gejdenson (D)	124,110	54.4
	Roberta F. Koontz (R)	103,119	45.2

	Candidates	Votes	%
3	Bruce A. Morrison (D)	129,230	52.6
	Lawrence J. DeNardis (R)	115,939	47.2
4	Stewart B. McKinney (R)	165,644	70.4
	John M. Ormon (D)	69,666	29.6
5	John G. Rowland (R)	130,700	54.3
	William R. Ratchford (D)	109,425	45.5
6	Nancy L. Johnson (R)	155,422	64.0
	Arthur H. House (D)	87,489	36.0

DELAWARE

	Candidates	Votes	%
AL	Thomas R. Carper (D)	142,070	58.5
	Elise R. W. du Pont (R)	100,650	41.4

FLORIDA

	Candidates	Votes	%
1	Earl Hutto (D)		100.0
2	Don Fuqua (D)		100.0
3	Charles E. Bennett (D)		100.0
4	Bill Chappell Jr. (D)	134,694	64.8
	Alton H. (Bill) Starling (R)	73,218	35.2
5	Bill McCollum (R)		100.0
6	Buddy MacKay (D)	167,409	99.3
7	Sam Gibbons (D)	100,430	58.8
	Michael N. Kavouklis (R)	70,280	41.2
8	C. W. Bill Young (R)	184,553	80.3
	Robert Kent (D)	45,393	19.7
9	Michael Bilirakis (R)	191,343	78.6
	Jack Wilson (D)	52,150	21.4
10	Andy Ireland (R)	126,206	61.9
	Patricia M. Glass (D)	77,635	38.1
11	Bill Nelson (D)	145,764	60.5
	Rob Quartel (R)	95,115	39.5
12	Tom Lewis (R)		100.0
13	Connie Mack (R)		100.0
14	Daniel A. Mica (D)	153,935	55.4
	Don Ross	123,926	44.6
15	E. Clay Shaw Jr. (R)	128,097	65.7
	Bill Humphrey (D)	66,833	34.3
16	Larry Smith (D)	108,410	56.4
	Tom Bush (R)	83,903	43.6
17	William Lehman (D)		100.0
18	Claude Pepper (D)	76,404	60.5
	Ricardo Nunez (R)	49,818	39.5
19	Dante B. Fascell (D)	115,631	64.3
	Bill Flanagan (R)	64,317	35.7

GEORGIA

	Candidates	Votes	%
1	Robert Lindsay Thomas (D)	126,082	81.6
	Erie Lee Downing (R)	28,460	18.4
2	Charles Hatcher (D)	110,561	100.0
3	Richard Ray (D)	111,061	81.4
	Mitchell Cantu (R)	25,410	18.6
4	Pat Swindall (R)	120,456	53.1
	Elliott H. Levitas (D)	106,376	46.9
5	Wyche Fowler Jr. (D)	151,233	100.0
6	Newt Gingrich (R)	116,655	69.1
	Gerald Johnson (D)	52,061	30.9
7	George (Buddy) Darden (D)	106,586	55.2
	William E. Bronson (R)	86,431	44.8
8	J. Roy Rowland (D)	100,936	100.0
9	Ed Jenkins (D)	109,422	67.5
	Frank H. Cofer Jr. (R)	52,731	32.5
10	Doug Barnard Jr. (D)	116,364	100.0

HAWAII

	Candidates	Votes	%
1	Cecil Heftel (D)	114,844	82.7
	William F. Beard (R)	20,608	14.8
2	Daniel K. Akaka (D)	112,377	82.2
	A. D. Shipley (R)	20,000	14.6

IDAHO

	Candidates	Votes	%
1	Larry E. Craig (R)	139,085	68.6
	Bill Hellar (D)	63,591	31.4

Candidates	Votes	%
2 Richard H. Stallings (D)	101,287	50.0
George Hansen (R)	101,117	50.0

ILLINOIS

Candidates	Votes	%
1 Charles A. Hayes (D)	177,438	95.6
2 Gus Savage (D)	155,349	83.0
Dale F. Harman (R)	31,865	17.0
3 Marty Russo (D)	143,363	64.4
Richard D. Murphy (R)	79,218	35.6
4 George M. O'Brien (R)	121,744	64.0
Dennis E. Marlow (D)	68,547	36.0
5 William O. Lipinski (D)	106,597	63.6
John M. Paczkowski (R)	61,109	36.4
6 Henry J. Hyde (R)	157,370	75.1
Robert H. Renshaw (D)	52,189	24.9
7 Cardiss Collins (D)	135,493	78.4
James L. Bevel (R)	37,411	21.6
8 Dan Rostenkowski (D)	114,385	71.3
Spiro F. Georgeson (R)	46,030	28.7
9 Sidney R. Yates (D)	144,879	67.5
Herbert Sohn (R)	69,613	32.5
10 John Edward Porter (R)	153,330	72.6
Ruth C. Braver (D)	57,809	27.4
11 Frank Annunzio (D)	138,171	62.6
Charles J. Theusch (R)	82,518	37.4
12 Philip M. Crane (R)	159,582	77.8
Edward J. LaFlamme (D)	45,537	22.2
13 Harris W. Fawell (R)	157,603	67.0
Michael J. Donohue (D)	77,623	33.0
14 John E. Grotberg (R)	135,967	62.2
Dan McGrath (D)	82,756	37.8
15 Edward R. Madigan (R)	149,096	73.2
John M. Hoffman (D)	54,516	26.8
16 Lynn Martin (R)	127,684	58.4
Carl R. Schwerdtfeger (D)	90,850	41.6
17 Lane Evans (D)	128,273	56.7
Kenneth G. McMillan (R)	98,069	43.3
18 Robert H. Michel (R)	136,183	61.0
Gerald A. Bradley (D)	86,884	38.9
19 Terry L. Bruce (D)	117,634	52.3
Daniel B. Crane (R)	107,463	47.7
20 Richard J. Durbin (D)	145,092	61.3
Richard G. Austin (R)	91,728	38.7
21 Melvin Price (D)	127,046	60.2
Robert H. Gaffner (R)	84,148	39.8
22 Kenneth J. Gray (D)	116,952	50.3
Randy Patchett (R)	115,775	49.7

INDIANA

Candidates	Votes	%
1 Peter J. Visclosky (D)	147,035	70.7
Joseph B. Grenchik (R)	59,986	28.8
2 Philip R. Sharp (D)	118,965	53.4
Ken MacKenzie (R)	103,061	46.3
3 John Hiler (R)	115,139	52.4
Michael P. Barnes (D)	103,961	47.3
4 Dan Coats (R)	129,674	60.8
Michael H. Barnard (D)	82,053	38.5
5 Elwood Hillis (R)	143,560	67.9
Allen B. Maxwell (D)	66,631	31.5
6 Dan Burton (R)	178,814	72.7
Howard O. Campbell (D)	65,772	26.8
7 John T. Myers (R)	147,787	67.3
Arthur E. Smith (D)	69,097	31.5
8[1] Richard D. McIntyre (R)	114,278	49.9
Frank McCloskey (D)	113,860	49.8
9 Lee H. Hamilton (D)	137,018	65.1
Floyd E. Coates (R)	72,652	34.5
10 Andrew Jacobs Jr. (D)	115,274	59.0
Joseph P. Watkins (R)	79,342	40.6

IOWA

Candidates	Votes	%
1 Jim Leach (R)	131,182	66.8
Kevin Ready (D)	65,293	33.2
2 Tom Tauke (R)	136,893	63.9
Joe Welsh (D)	77,335	36.1
3 Cooper Evans (R)	133,737	60.7
Joe Johnston (D)	86,574	39.3

Candidates	Votes	%
4 Neal Smith (D)	136,922	60.7
Robert R. Lockard (R)	88,717	39.3
5 Jim Lightfoot (R)	104,632	50.8
Jerome D. Fitzgerald (D)	101,435	49.2
6 Berkley Bedell (D)	127,706	62.0
Darrel Rensink (R)	78,182	38.0

KANSAS

Candidates	Votes	%
1 Pat Roberts (R)	159,931	76.0
Darrell Ringer (D)	49,015	23.3
2 Jim Slattery (D)	112,263	60.0
Jim Van Slyke (R)	73,045	39.1
3 Jan Meyers (R)	117,159	54.8
John E. Reardon (D)	85,441	39.9
John S. Ralph Jr. (I)	11,302	5.3
4 Dan Glickman (D)	138,917	74.4
William V. Krause (R)	47,776	25.6
5 Bob Whittaker (R)	144,075	73.5
John A. Barnes (D)	49,435	25.2

KENTUCKY

Candidates	Votes	%
1 Carroll Hubbard Jr. (D)	112,180	100.0
2 William H. Natcher (D)	93,042	62.1
Timothy A. Morrison (R)	56,700	37.9
3 Romano L. Mazzoli (D)	145,680	67.7
Suzanne M. Warner (R)	68,185	31.7
4 Gene Snyder (R)	108,398	53.7
William P. Mulloy II (D)	93,640	46.3
5 Harold Rogers (R)	125,164	75.9
Sherman W. McIntosh (D)	39,783	24.1
6 Larry J. Hopkins (R)	126,525	71.4
Jerry Hammond (D)	49,657	28.0
7[2] Carl C. (Chris) Perkins (D)	122,679	73.7
Aubrey Russell (R)	43,890	26.3

LOUISIANA[3]

Candidates	Votes	%
1 Bob Livingston (R)		100.0
2 Lindy (Mrs. Hale) Boggs (D)		100.0
3 W. J. (Billy) Tauzin (D)		100.0
4 Buddy Roemer (D)		100.0
5 Jerry Huckaby (D)		100.0
6 W. Henson Moore (R)		100.0
7 John B. Breaux (D)		100.0
8 Gillis W. Long (D)		100.0

MAINE

Candidates	Votes	%
1 John R. McKernan Jr. (R)	182,785	63.5
Barry J. Hobbins (D)	104,972	36.5
2 Olympia J. Snowe (R)	192,166	75.7
Chipman C. Bull (D)	57,347	22.6

MARYLAND

Candidates	Votes	%
1 Roy Dyson (D)	96,673	58.4
Harlan C. Williams (R)	68,865	41.6
2 Helen Delich Bentley (R)	111,517	51.4
Clarence D. Long (D)	105,571	48.6
3 Barbara A. Mikulski (D)	133,189	68.2
Ross Z. Pierpont (R)	59,493	30.5
4 Marjorie S. Holt (R)	114,430	66.2
Howard M. Greenebaum (D)	58,312	33.8
5 Steny H. Hoyer (D)	116,310	72.2
John E. Ritchie (R)	44,839	27.8
6 Beverly B. Byron (D)	123,383	65.1
Robin Ficker (R)	66,056	34.9
7 Parren J. Mitchell (D)	139,488	100.0
8 Michael D. Barnes (D)	181,947	71.5
Albert Ceccone (R)	70,715	27.8

MASSACHUSETTS

Candidates	Votes	%
1 Silvio O. Conte (R)	162,646	72.9
Mary L. Wentworth (D)	60,372	27.1

Candidates	Votes	%
2 Edward P. Boland (D)	132,693	68.7
Thomas P. Swank (R)	60,463	31.3
3 Joseph D. Early (D)	148,461	67.4
Kenneth J. Redding (R)	71,765	32.6
4 Barney Frank (D)	172,903	74.2
Jim Forte (R)	60,121	25.8
5 Chester G. Atkins (D)	120,008	53.4
Gregory S. Hyatt (R)	104,912	46.6
6 Nicholas Mavroules (D)	168,662	70.4
Frederick S. Leber (R)	63,363	26.4
7 Edward J. Markey (D)	167,211	71.4
S. Lester Ralph (R)	66,930	28.6
8 Thomas P. O'Neill Jr. (D)	179,617	91.8
Laura Ross (COM)	15,810	8.1
9 Joe Moakley (D)	153,132	99.9
10 Gerry E. Studds (D)	143,062	55.7
Lewis Crampton (R)	113,745	44.3
11 Brian J. Donnelly (D)	172,010	100.0

MICHIGAN

Candidates	Votes	%
1 John Conyers Jr. (D)	152,432	89.4
Edward J. Mack (R)	17,393	10.2
2 Carl D. Pursell (R)	140,688	68.6
Mike McCauley (D)	62,374	30.4
3 Howard Wolpe (D)	106,505	52.9
Jackie McGregor (R)	94,714	47.1
4 Mark D. Siljander (R)	127,907	66.9
Charles S. Rodebaugh (D)	63,159	33.1
5 Paul B. Henry (R)	140,131	61.8
Gary J. McInerney (D)	85,232	37.6
6 Bob Carr (D)	106,705	52.4
Tom Ritter (R)	95,113	46.7
7 Dale E. Kildee (D)	145,070	93.1
Samuel Johnston (I)	10,663	6.8
8 Bob Traxler (D)	126,161	64.4
John Heussner (R)	69,683	35.6
9 Guy Vander Jagt (R)	150,885	70.9
John M. Senger (D)	61,233	28.8
10 Bill Schuette (R)	104,950	50.1
Donald J. Albosta (D)	103,636	49.4
11 Robert W. Davis (R)	126,992	58.6
Tom Stewart (D)	89,640	41.4
12 David E. Bonior (D)	113,772	58.3
Eugene J. Tyza (R)	79,824	40.9
13 George W. Crockett Jr. (D)	132,222	86.6
Robert Murphy (R)	20,416	13.4
14 Dennis M. Hertel (D)	113,610	59.1
John Lauve (R)	77,427	40.3
15 William D. Ford (D)	98,973	59.9
Gerald R. Carlson (R)	66,172	40.1
16 John D. Dingell (D)	121,463	63.7
Frank Grzywacki (R)	68,116	35.7
17 Sander M. Levin (D)	133,064	100.0
18 William S. Broomfield (R)	186,505	79.4
Vivian H. Smargon (D)	46,191	19.7

MINNESOTA[4]

Candidates	Votes	%
1 Timothy J. Penny (DFL)	140,095	57.0
Keith Spicer (I-R)	105,723	43.0
2 Vin Weber (I-R)	153,308	63.1
Todd Lundquist (DFL)	89,770	36.9
3 Bill Frenzel (I-R)	207,819	73.2
Dave Peterson (DFL)	76,132	26.8
4 Bruce F. Vento (DFL)	167,678	73.5
Mary Jane Rachner (I-R)	57,450	25.2
5 Martin Olav Sabo (DFL)	165,075	70.1
Richard D. Wieblen (I-R)	62,642	26.6
6 Gerry Sikorski (DFL)	154,603	60.5
Patrick Trueman (I-R)	101,058	39.5
7 Arlan Stangeland (I-R)	135,087	57.0
Collin C. Peterson (DFL)	101,720	42.9
8 James L. Oberstar (DFL)	165,727	67.2
Dave Rued (I-R)	79,181	32.1

MISSISSIPPI

Candidates	Votes	%
1 Jamie L. Whitten (D)	136,530	88.4
John Hargett (I)	17,991	11.6

Footnotes, see p. 291.

Candidates	Votes	%
2 Webb Franklin (R)	92,392	50.6
Robert G. Clark (D)	89,154	48.9
3 G. V. (Sonny) Montgomery (D)	158,002	100.0
4 Wayne Dowdy (D)	113,635	55.3
David Armstrong (R)	91,797	45.6
5 Trent Lott (R)	142,637	84.7
Arlon (Blackie) Coate (D)	25,840	15.3

MISSOURI

Candidates	Votes	%
1 William L. Clay (D)	147,436	68.3
Eric Rathbone (R)	68,538	31.7
2 Robert A. Young (D)	139,123	51.8
John Buechner (R)	127,710	47.5
3 Richard A. Gephardt (D)	193,537	100.0
4 Ike Skelton (D)	150,624	66.9
Carl D. Russell (R)	74,434	33.1
5 Alan Wheat (D)	150,675	66.0
Jim Kenworthy (R)	72,477	31.8
6 E. Thomas Coleman (R)	150,996	64.8
Kenneth C. Hensley (D)	81,917	35.2
7 Gene Taylor (R)	164,586	69.6
Ken Young (D)	71,867	30.4
8 Bill Emerson (R)	134,186	65.4
Bill Blue (D)	70,922	34.6
9 Harold L. Volkmer (D)	123,588	52.9
Carrie Francke (R)	110,100	47.1

MONTANA

Candidates	Votes	%
1 Pat Williams (D)	126,998	65.6
Gary K. Carlson (R)	61,794	31.9
2 Ron Marlenee (R)	116,932	65.9
Chet Blaylock (D)	60,445	34.1

NEBRASKA

Candidates	Votes	%
1 Doug Bereuter (R)	158,836	74.1
Monica Bauer (D)	55,508	25.9
2 Hal Daub (R)	139,384	64.9
Thomas F. Cavanaugh (D)	75,210	35.0
3 Virginia Smith (R)	183,901	83.3
Tom Vickers (D)	36,899	16.7

NEVADA

Candidates	Votes	%
1 Harry Reid (D)	73,242	56.1
Peggy Cavnar (R)	55,391	42.4
2 Barbara F. Vucanovich (R)	99,775	71.2
Andrew Barbano (D)	36,130	25.8

NEW HAMPSHIRE

Candidates	Votes	%
1 Robert C. Smith (R)	111,627	58.6
Dudley Dudley (D)	76,854	40.3
2 Judd Gregg (R)	138,975	76.2
Larry Converse (D)	42,257	23.2

NEW JERSEY

Candidates	Votes	%
1 James J. Florio (D)	152,125	71.9
Frederick A. Busch Jr. (R)	58,800	27.8
2 William J. Hughes (D)	132,841	63.2
Raymond G. Massie (R)	77,231	36.7
3 James J. Howard (D)	122,291	53.3
Brian T. Kennedy (R)	105,024	45.8
4 Christopher H. Smith (R)	139,295	61.3
James C. Hedden (D)	87,908	38.7
5 Marge Roukema (R)	171,979	71.2
Rose Brunetto (D)	69,666	28.8
6 Bernard J. Dwyer (D)	118,532	55.9
Dennis Adams (R)	90,862	42.8
7 Matthew J. Rinaldo (R)	165,685	74.2
John F. Feeley (D)	56,798	25.4
8 Robert A. Roe (D)	118,793	62.7
Marguerite A. Page (R)	69,973	36.9

Candidates	Votes	%
9 Robert G. Torricelli (D)	149,493	62.6
Neil Romano (R)	89,166	37.4
10 Peter W. Rodino Jr. (D)	111,244	83.7
Howard E. Berkeley (R)	21,712	16.3
11 Dean A. Gallo (R)	133,662	55.8
Joseph G. Minish (D)	106,038	44.2
12 Jim Courter (R)	148,042	65.0
Peter Bearse (D)	78,167	34.3
13⁵ H. James Saxton (R)	141,136	60.7
James B. Smith (D)	89,307	38.4
14 Frank J. Guarini (D)	115,117	65.7
Edward T. Magee (R)	58,265	33.3

NEW MEXICO

Candidates	Votes	%
1 Manuel Lujan Jr. (R)	115,808	64.9
Charles Ted Asbury (D)	60,598	34.0
2 Joe Skeen (R)	116,006	74.3
Peter R. York (D)	40,063	25.7
3 Bill Richardson (D)	100,470	60.8
Louis H. Gallegos (R)	62,351	37.7

NEW YORK

Candidates	Votes	%
1 William Carney (R, C, RTL)	107,029	53.1
George J. Hochbrueckner (D, RP)	94,551	46.9
2 Thomas J. Downey (D, IP)	97,648	54.7
Paul Aniboli (R, C, RTL)	80,855	45.3
3 Robert J. Mrazek (D)	120,191	51.0
Robert P. Quinn (R)	112,909	47.9
4 Norman F. Lent (R, C)	154,875	68.9
Sheldon Engelhard (D, L)	65,678	29.2
5 Raymond J. McGrath (R, C)	138,560	62.4
Michael d'Innocenzo (D, IV)	78,429	35.3
6 Joseph P. Addabbo (D)	120,098	82.7
Philip J. Veltre (R, C, RTL)	25,040	17.3
7 Gary L. Ackerman (D, L)	97,674	69.3
Gustave A. Reifenkugel (R, C)	43,370	30.7
8 James H. Scheuer (D, L)	104,558	62.8
Robert L. Brandofino (R, C)	62,015	37.2
9 Thomas J. Manton (D)	71,420	52.8
Serphin R. Maltese (R, C, RTL)	63,910	47.2
10 Charles E. Schumer (D, L)	115,867	72.4
John H. Fox (R, C)	42,009	26.3
11 Edolphus Towns (D, L)	81,002	85.2
Nathaniel Hendricks (R)	12,494	13.1
12 Major R. Owens (D, L)	82,047	90.5
Joseph N. O. Caesar (R, C, RTL)	8,609	9.5
13 Stephen J. Solarz (D, L)	82,610	65.9
Lew Y. Levin (R, C, RTL)	42,737	34.1
14 Guy V. Molinari (R, C, RTL)	117,041	70.2
Kevin L. Sheehy (D)	49,776	29.8
15 Bill Green (R, I)	107,644	56.1
Andrew J. Stein (D, L)	84,404	43.9
16 Charles B. Rangel (D, R)	117,759	97.0
17 Ted Weiss (D, L)	162,489	81.5
Kenneth Katzman (R)	33,316	16.7
18 Robert Garcia (D, L)	85,960	89.2
Curtis Johnson (R)	8,970	9.3
19 Mario Biaggi (D, R, L, RTL)	155,067	94.8
Alice Farrell (C)	8,472	5.2
20 Joseph J. DioGuardi (R, C)	106,958	50.1
Oren J. Teicher (D)	102,842	48.2
21 Hamilton Fish Jr. (R, C, RTL)	160,053	78.3
Lawrence W. Grunberger (D)	44,274	21.7
22 Benjamin A. Gilman (R)	144,278	68.5
Bruce M. Levine (D, L)	57,934	27.5
23 Samuel S. Stratton (D)	188,144	77.8
Frank Wicks (R, NF)	53,060	21.9
24 Gerald B. H. Solomon (R, C, RTL)	164,019	73.2
Edward J. Bloch (D)	60,188	26.8
25 Sherwood Boehlert (R)	140,256	72.8
James J. Ball (D)	52,434	27.2
26 David O'B. Martin (R, C)	131,257	70.6
Bernard J. Lammers (D)	54,663	29.4

Candidates	Votes	%
27 George C. Wortley (R, C)	122,215	56.6
Thomas C. Buckel Jr. (D, L)	93,601	43.4
28 Matthew F. McHugh (D)	123,334	56.6
Constance E. Cook (R)	90,324	41.4
29 Frank Horton (R)	138,362	69.6
James R. Toole (D)	48,301	24.3
30 Fred J. Eckert (R, C, RTL)	119,844	54.4
W. Douglas Call (D)	100,066	45.4
31 Jack F. Kemp (R, C, RTL)	168,332	75.0
Peter J. Martinelli (D, L)	56,156	25.0
32 John J. LaFalce (D, L)	139,979	69.4
Anthony J. Murty (R, C, RTL)	61,797	30.6
33 Henry J. Nowak (D, L)	155,198	77.6
David S. Lewandowski (R, C, RTL)	44,880	22.4
34 Stan Lundine (D)	110,902	54.2
Jill Houghton Emery (R, C)	91,016	44.5

NORTH CAROLINA

Candidates	Votes	%
1 Walter B. Jones (D)	122,815	67.1
Herbert W. Lee (R)	60,153	32.9
2 Tim Valentine (D)	122,292	67.7
Frank H. Hill (R)	58,312	32.3
3 Charles Whitley (D)	100,185	64.1
Danny G. Moody (R)	56,096	35.9
4 Bill Cobey (R)	117,436	50.6
Ike Andrews (D)	114,462	49.4
5 Stephen L. Neal (D)	109,831	50.7
Stuart Epperson (R)	106,599	49.3
6 Howard Coble (R)	102,925	50.6
Robin Britt (D)	100,263	49.3
7 Charlie Rose (D)	92,157	59.2
S. Thomas Rhodes (R)	63,625	40.8
8 W. G. (Bill) Hefner (D)	99,731	50.9
Harris D. Blake (R)	96,354	49.1
9 J. Alex McMillan (R)	109,420	50.1
D. G. Martin (D)	109,099	49.9
10 James T. Broyhill (R)	142,873	73.4
Ted A. Poovey (D)	51,860	26.6
11 Bill Hendon (R)	112,598	51.0
James McClure Clarke (D)	108,284	49.0

NORTH DAKOTA

Candidates	Votes	%
AL Byron L. Dorgan (D)	242,968	78.7
Lois Ivers Altenburg (R)	65,761	21.3

OHIO

Candidates	Votes	%
1 Thomas A. Luken (D)	121,577	55.1
Norman A. Murdock (R)	88,859	40.3
2 Bill Gradison (R)	149,856	68.6
Thomas D. Porter (D)	68,597	31.4
3 Tony P. Hall (D)	151,398	100.0
4 Michael G. Oxley (R)	162,199	77.5
William O. Sutton (D)	47,018	22.5
5 Delbert L. Latta (R)	132,582	62.7
James R. Sherck (D)	78,809	37.3
6 Bob McEwen (R)	150,101	74.0
Bob Smith (D)	52,727	26.0
7 Michael DeWine (R)	147,885	76.7
Donald E. Scott (D)	40,621	21.1
8 Thomas N. Kindness (R)	155,200	76.9
John T. Francis (D)	46,673	23.1
9 Marcy Kaptur (D)	117,985	54.9
Frank Venner (R)	93,210	43.4
10 Clarence E. Miller (R)	149,337	73.0
John M. Buchanan (D)	55,172	27.0
11 Dennis E. Eckart (D)	133,096	66.8
Dean Beagle (R)	66,278	33.2
12 John R. Kasich (R)	148,899	69.5
Richard Sloan (D)	65,215	30.5
13 Don J. Pease (D)	131,923	66.4
William G. Schaffner (R)	59,610	30.0
14 John F. Seiberling (D)	155,729	71.4
Jean E. Bender (R)	62,366	28.6
15 Chalmers P. Wylie (R)	148,311	71.6
Duane Jager (D)	58,870	28.4

	Candidates	Votes	%
16	Ralph Regula (R)	152,399	72.4
	James Gwin (D)	58,048	27.6
17	James A. Traficant Jr. (D)	123,014	53.3
	Lyle Williams (R)	105,449	45.7
18	Douglas Applegate (D)	155,759	75.9
	Kenneth P. Burt Jr. (R)	49,356	24.1
19	Edward F. Feighan (D)	139,605	55.2
	Matthew J. Hatchadorian (R)	107,957	42.7
20	Mary Rose Oakar (D)	167,115	100.0
21	Louis Stokes (D)	165,247	82.4
	Robert L. Woodall (R)	29,500	14.7

OKLAHOMA

	Candidates	Votes	%
1	James R. Jones (D)	113,919	52.2
	Frank Keating (R)	103,098	47.3
2	Mike Synar (D)	148,124	74.1
	Gary K. Rice (R)	51,889	25.9
3	Wes Watkins (D)	137,964	77.8
	Patrick K. Miller (R)	39,454	22.2
4	Dave McCurdy (D)	109,447	63.6
	Jerry Smith (R)	60,844	35.4
5	Mickey Edwards (R)	135,167	75.6
	Allen Greeson (D)	39,089	21.9
6	Glenn English (D)	96,994	58.9
	Craig Dodd (R)	67,601	41.1

OREGON

	Candidates	Votes	%
1	Les AuCoin (D)	138,393	53.1
	Bill Moshofsky (R)	122,247	46.9
2	Robert F. Smith (R)	132,649	57.0
	Larryann C. Willis (D)	100,152	43.0
3	Ron Wyden (D)	173,438	72.3
	Drew Davis (R)	66,394	27.7
4	James Weaver (D)	134,190	58.2
	Bruce Long (R)	96,487	41.8
	Ruth McFarland (D)	108,919	45.5
5	Denny Smith (R)	130,424	54.5

PENNSYLVANIA

	Candidates	Votes	%
1	Thomas M. Foglietta (D)	148,123	74.9
	Carmine DiBiase (R)	49,559	25.1
2	William H. Gray III (D)	200,484	91.0
	Ronald J. Sharper (R)	18,224	8.3
3	Robert A. Borski (D)	152,598	63.9
	Flora L. Becker (R)	85,358	35.7
4	Joe Kolter (D)	114,040	56.8
	James Kunder (R)	86,769	43.2
5	Richard T. Schulze (R)	141,965	72.6
	Louis J. Fanti (D)	53,586	27.4
6	Gus Yatron (D)	181,165	100.0
7	Bob Edgar (D)	124,458	50.1
	Curt Weldon (R)	124,046	49.9
8	Peter H. Kostmayer (D)	112,648	50.9
	David A. Christian (R)	108,696	49.1
9	Bud Shuster (R)	118,437	66.5
	Nancy Kulp (D)	59,549	33.5
10	Joseph M. McDade (R)	150,166	77.1
	Gene Basalyga (D)	44,571	22.9
11	Paul E. Kanjorski (D)	108,430	58.6
	Robert P. Hudock (R)	76,692	41.4
12	John P. Murtha (D)	134,384	69.1
	Thomas J. Fullard III (R)	57,466	29.5
13	Lawrence Coughlin (R)	133,948	56.1
	Joseph M. Hoeffel (D)	104,756	43.9
14	William J. Coyne (D)	163,818	76.6
	John Robert Clark (R)	42,616	19.9
15	Don Ritter (R)	110,338	58.1
	Jane Wells-Schooley (D)	79,490	41.9
16	Robert S. Walker (R)	138,477	77.8
	Martin L. Bard (D)	39,515	22.2
17	George W. Gekas (R)	129,716	80.3
	Stephen A. Anderson (D)	31,770	19.7
18	Doug Walgren (D)	149,628	62.7
	John G. Maxwell (R)	87,521	36.7
19	Bill Goodling (R)	141,196	75.6
	F. John Rarig (D)	44,117	23.6
20	Joseph M. Gaydos (D)	158,751	76.0
	Daniel Lloyd (R)	50,247	24.0

	Candidates	Votes	%
21	Tom Ridge (R)	125,730	65.4
	James A. Young (D)	65,594	34.1
22	Austin J. Murphy (D)	153,514	79.0
	Nancy S. Pryor (R)	39,752	20.0
23	William F. Clinger Jr. (R)	94,952	51.6
	Bill Wachob (D)	88,957	48.4

RHODE ISLAND

	Candidates	Votes	%
1	Fernand J. St Germain (D)	130,584	68.5
	Alfred Rego Jr. (R)	60,026	31.5
2	Claudine Schneider (R)	135,161	67.7
	Richard Sinapi (D)	64,341	32.3

SOUTH CAROLINA

	Candidates	Votes	%
1	Thomas F. Hartnett (R)	103,288	61.7
	Ed Pendarvis (D)	64,022	38.3
2	Floyd Spence (R)	108,085	62.1
	Ken Mosely (D)	63,932	36.7
3	Butler Derrick (D)	88,917	58.4
	Clarence E. Taylor (R)	61,739	40.6
4	Carroll A. Campbell Jr. (R)	105,139	63.9
	Jeff Smith (D)	57,854	35.2
5	John M. Spratt Jr. (D)	98,513	96.3
6	Robin Tallon (D)	97,329	59.9
	Lois Eargle (R)	63,005	38.8

SOUTH DAKOTA

	Candidates	Votes	%
AL	Thomas A. Daschle (D)	181,401	57.4
	Dale Bell (R)	134,821	42.6

TENNESSEE

	Candidates	Votes	%
1	James H. Quillen (R)	113,407	100.0
2	John J. Duncan (R)	132,604	77.3
	John F. Bowen (D)	38,846	22.7
3	Marilyn Lloyd (D)	99,465	52.4
	John Davis (R)	90,216	47.6
4	Jim Cooper (D)	93,848	75.2
	James Beau Seigneur (R)	31,011	24.8
5	Bill Boner (D)	138,233	100.0
6	Bart Gordon (D)	103,989	62.8
	Joe Simpkins (R)	61,559	37.2
7	Don Sundquist (R)	107,257	100.0
8	Ed Jones (D)	118,653	100.0
9	Harold E. Ford (D)	133,428	71.5
	William B. Thompson Jr. (R)	53,064	28.5

TEXAS

	Candidates	Votes	%
1	Sam B. Hall Jr. (D)	139,829	100.0
2	Charles Wilson (D)	113,225	59.3
	Louis Dugas Jr. (R)	77,842	40.7
3	Steve Bartlett (R)	228,819	83.0
	Jim Westbrook (D)	46,890	17.0
4	Ralph M. Hall (D)	120,749	58.0
	Thomas Blow (R)	87,553	42.0
5	John Bryant (D)	94,391	100.0
6	Joe L. Barton (R)	131,482	56.6
	Dan Kubiak (D)	100,799	43.4
7	Bill Archer (R)	213,480	86.7
	Billy Willibey (D)	32,835	13.3
8	Jack Fields (R)	113,031	64.6
	Don Buford (D)	62,072	35.4
9	Jack Brooks (D)	120,559	58.9
	Jim Mahan (R)	84,306	41.2
10	J. J. Pickle (D)	186,447	99.8
11	Marvin Leath (D)	112,940	100.0
12	Jim Wright (D)	106,299	100.0
13	Beau Boulter (R)	107,600	53.0
	Jack Hightower (D)	95,367	47.0
14	Mac Sweeney (R)	104,181	51.3
	Bill Patman (D)	98,885	48.7
15	E. (Kika) de la Garza (D)	104,863	100.0
16	Ronald D. Coleman (D)	76,375	57.4
	Jack Hammond (R)	56,589	42.6

	Candidates	Votes	%
17	Charles W. Stenholm (D)	143,012	100.0
18	Mickey Leland (D)	109,626	78.8
	Glen E. Beaman (R)	26,400	19.0
19	Larry Combest (R)	102,805	58.1
	Don R. Richards (D)	74,044	41.9
20	Henry B. Gonzalez (D)	100,443	100.0
21	Tom Loeffler (R)	199,909	80.6
	Joe Sullivan (D)	48,039	19.4
22	Thomas D. DeLay (R)	125,225	65.3
	Doug Williams (D)	66,495	34.7
23	Albert G. Bustamante (D)	95,721	100.0
24	Martin Frost (D)	105,210	59.5
	Bob Burk (R)	71,703	40.5
25	Michael A. Andrews (D)	113,946	64.0
	Jerry Patterson (R)	63,974	36.0
26	Dick Armey (R)	126,641	51.3
	Tom Vandergriff (D)	120,451	48.7
27	Solomon P. Ortiz (D)	105,516	63.6
	Richard Moore (R)	60,283	36.4

UTAH

	Candidates	Votes	%
1	James V. Hansen (R)	142,952	71.2
	Milton C. Abrams (D)	56,619	28.2
2	David S. Monson (R)	105,540	49.4
	Frances Farley (D)	105,044	49.1
3	Howard C. Nielson (R)	138,918	74.5
	Bruce R. Baird (D)	46,560	25.0

VERMONT

	Candidates	Votes	%
AL	James M. Jeffords (R)	148,025	65.4
	Anthony Pollina (D)	60,360	26.7

VIRGINIA

	Candidates	Votes	%
1	Herbert H. Bateman (R)	118,085	59.1
	John McGlennon (D)	79,577	39.8
2	G. William Whitehurst (R)	136,632	99.8
3	Thomas J. Bliley Jr. (R)	169,987	85.6
	Roger L. Coffey (I)	28,556	14.4
4	Norman Sisisky (D)	120,093	99.9
5	Dan Daniel (D)	117,738	100.0
6	James R. Olin (D)	105,207	53.5
	Ray Garland (R)	91,344	46.5
7	D. French Slaughter Jr. (R)	109,110	56.5
	Lewis M. Costello (D)	77,624	40.2
8	Stan Parris (R)	125,015	55.8
	Richard L. Saslaw (D)	97,250	43.4
9	Frederick C. Boucher (D)	102,446	52.0
	Jefferson Stafford (R)	94,510	48.0
10	Frank R. Wolf (R)	158,528	62.5
	John P. Flannery II (D)	95,074	37.5

WASHINGTON

	Candidates	Votes	%
1	John R. Miller (R)	147,926	56.3
	Brock Evans (D)	115,001	43.7
2	Al Swift (D)	142,065	58.6
	Jim Klauder (R)	93,472	38.6
3	Don Bonker (D)	150,432	71.1
	Herb Elder (R)	61,219	28.9
4	Sid Morrison (R)	150,322	76.1
	Mark Epperson (D)	47,158	23.9
5	Thomas S. Foley (D)	154,988	69.7
	Jack Hebner (R)	67,438	30.3
6	Norman D. Dicks (D)	124,367	66.1
	Mike Lonergan (R)	60,721	32.3
7	Mike Lowry (D)	174,560	70.4
	Robert O. Dorse (R)	71,576	28.9
8	Rod Chandler (R)	146,891	62.4
	Bob Lamson (D)	88,379	37.6

WEST VIRGINIA

	Candidates	Votes	%
1	Alan B. Mollohan (D)	104,639	54.4
	James Altmeyer (R)	87,622	45.6
2	Harley O. Staggers Jr. (D)	100,345	56.0
	Cleve Benedict (R)	78,936	44.0

	Candidates	Votes	%
3	Bob Wise (D)	125,306	67.9
	Margaret Miller (R)	59,128	32.1
4	Nick J. Rahall II (D)	98,919	66.7
	Jess T. Shumate (R)	49,474	33.3

WISCONSIN

	Candidates	Votes	%
1	Les Aspin (D)	127,184	56.2
	Pete Jansson (R)	99,080	43.8
2	Robert W. Kastenmeier (D)	159,987	63.6
	Albert E. Wiley Jr. (R)	91,345	36.3

	Candidates	Votes	%
3	Steve Gunderson (R)	160,437	68.4
	Charles F. Dahl (D)	74,253	31.6
4	Gerald D. Kleczka (D)	158,722	66.6
	Robert V. Nolan (R)	78,056	32.8
5	Jim Moody (D)	175,243	98.0
6	Thomas E. Petri (R)	170,271	75.8
	David L. Iaquinta (D)	54,266	24.2
7	David R. Obey (D)	146,131	61.2
	Mark G. Michaelsen (R)	92,507	38.8
8	Toby Roth (R)	161,005	67.9
	Paul Willems (D)	73,090	30.8

	Candidates	Votes	%
9	F. James Sensenbrenner Jr. (R)	180,247	73.4
	John Krause (D)	64,157	26.1

Special Election

		Votes	%
4	Gerald D. Kleczka (D)	76,384	65.0
	Robert V. Nolan (R)	41,007	34.9

WYOMING

		Votes	%
AL	Dick Cheney (R)	138,234	73.6
	Hugh B. McFadden Jr. (D)	45,857	24.4

1984 Elections

1. Contested election. A recount by a House Administration Committee task force determined that McCloskey defeated McIntyre by a four-vote margin, 116,645 (50.00085 percent) to 116,641 (49.99914 percent). On May 1, 1985, the House voted 236-190 to seat McCloskey.

2. A special election was held in conjunction with the November election. Perkins was elected to fill both the unexpired term of his father, Rep. Carl D. Perkins, D, who died Aug. 3, 1984, and the two-year term beginning Jan. 3, 1985.

3. For the 1984 House elections in Louisiana, an open primary election was held with candidates from all parties running on the same ballot. Any candidate who received a majority

was elected unopposed, with no further appearance on the general election ballot. If no candidate received 50 percent, a runoff was held between the two top finishers.

4. In Minnesota the Democratic Party is known as the Democratic-Farmer-Labor Party and the Republican Party as the Independent-Republican Party; candidates appear on the ballot with these designations.

5. A special election was held in conjunction with the November election. Saxton was elected to serve both the unexpired term of Rep. Edwin B. Forsythe, R, who died March 29, 1984, and the two-year term beginning Jan. 3, 1985.

1985 House Elections

LOUISIANA

Special Election [1]

	Candidates	Votes	%
8	Cathy (Mrs. Gillis) Long (D)	61,791	55.7
	John E. (Jock) Scott (D)	27,138	24.5
	Clyde C. Holloway (R)	18,013	16.3

TEXAS

Special Election [2]

	Candidates	Votes	%
1	Edd Hargett (R)	29,720	42.0
	Jim Chapman (D)	21,382	30.2
	Sam Russell (D)	13,090	18.5

Special Runoff Election

		Votes	%
1	Jim Chapman (D)	52,665	50.9
	Edd Hargett (R)	50,741	49.1

1985 Elections

1. Long was elected to serve the unexpired term of her husband, Rep. Gillis W. Long, D, who died Jan. 20, 1985.

2. A special election was held to fill the unexpired term of Rep. Sam B. Hall Jr., D, who resigned May 27, 1985, to accept a federal judgeship.

House Candidates Index

For an index of all House candidates listed in this section (pages 192-324), see pages 340-371. Instructions for use of the House Candidates Index appear on page 340.

1986 House Elections

ALABAMA

	Candidates	Votes	%
1	Sonny Callahan (R)	96,469	100.0
2	William L. Dickinson (R)	115,302	66.7
	Mercer Stone (D)	57,568	33.3
3	Bill Nichols (D)	115,127	80.6
	Whit Guerin (R)	27,769	19.4
4	Tom Bevill (D)	132,881	77.5
	Al DeShazo (R)	38,588	22.5
5	Ronnie G. Flippo (D)	125,406	78.9
	Herb McCarley (R)	33,528	21.1
6	Ben Erdreich (D)	139,608	72.7
	L. Morgan Williams (R)	51,924	27.1
7	Claude Harris (D)	108,126	59.8
	Bill McFarland (R)	72,777	40.2

ALASKA

		Votes	%
AL	Don Young (R)	101,799	56.5
	Pegge Begich (D)	74,053	41.1

ARIZONA

		Votes	%
1	John J. Rhodes III (R)	127,370	71.3
	Harry Braun III (D)	51,163	28.7
2	Morris K. Udall (D)	77,239	73.3
	Sheldon Clark (R)	24,522	23.3
3	Bob Stump (R)	146,462	100.0
4	Jon Kyl (R)	121,939	43.6
	Philip R. Davis (D)	66,894	35.4
5	Jim Kolbe (R)	119,647	64.9
	Joel Ireland (D)	64,848	35.1

ARKANSAS

		Votes	%
1	Bill Alexander (D)	105,773	64.2
	Rick H. Albin (R)	58,937	35.8
2	Tommy F. Robinson (D)	128,814	75.7
	Keith Hamaker (R)	41,244	24.2
3	John Hammerschmidt (R)	145,113	79.8
	Su Sargent (D)	36,726	20.2
4	Beryl Anthony Jr. (D)	115,335	77.5
	Lamar Keels (R)	22,980	15.4
	Stephen A. Bitely (I)	10,604	7.1

CALIFORNIA

		Votes	%
1	Douglas H. Bosco (D)	138,174	67.5
	Floyd G. Sampson (R)	54,436	26.6
	Elden McFarland (PFP)	12,149	5.9
2	Wally Herger (R)	109,758	58.3
	Stephen C. Swendiman (D)	74,602	39.6
3	Robert T. Matsui (D)	158,709	75.9
	Lowell P. Landowski (R)	50,265	24.1
4	Vic Fazio (D)	128,364	70.2
	Jack D. Hite (R)	54,596	29.8
5	Sala Burton (D)	122,688	75.1
	Mike Garza (R)	36,039	22.1
6	Barbara Boxer (D)	142,946	73.9
	Franklin H. Ernst III (R)	50,606	26.1
7	George Miller (D)	124,174	66.6
	Rosemary Thakar (R)	62,379	33.4
8	Ronald V. Dellums (D)	121,790	60.0
	Steven Eigenberg (R)	76,850	37.9
9	Fortney H. Stark (D)	113,490	69.7
	David M. Williams (R)	49,300	30.3
10	Don Edwards (D)	84,240	70.5
	Michael R. La Crone (R)	31,826	26.6
11	Tom Lantos (D)	112,380	74.1
	G. M. ''Bill'' Quraishi (R)	39,315	25.9
12	Ernest L. Konnyu (R)	111,252	59.5
	Lance T. Weil (D)	69,564	37.2

	Candidates	Votes	%
13	Norman Y. Mineta (D)	107,696	69.7
	Bob Nash (R)	46,754	30.3
14	Norman D. Shumway (R)	146,906	71.6
	Bill Steele (D)	53,597	26.1
15	Tony Coelho (D)	93,600	71.0
	Carol Harner (R)	35,793	27.2
16	Leon E. Panetta (D)	128,151	78.4
	Louis Darrigo (R)	31,386	19.2
17	Charles Pashayan Jr. (R)	88,787	60.2
	John Hartnett (D)	58,682	39.8
18	Richard H. Lehman (D)	101,480	71.3
	David C. Crevelt (R)	40,907	28.7
19	Robert J. Lagomarsino (R)	122,578	71.9
	Wayne B. Norris (D)	45,619	26.7
20	William M. Thomas (R)	129,989	72.6
	Jules H. Moquin (D)	49,027	27.4
21	Elton Gallegly (R)	132,090	68.4
	Gilbert R. Saldana (D)	54,497	28.2
22	Carlos J. Moorhead (R)	141,096	73.8
	John G. Simmons (D)	44,036	23.1
23	Anthony C. Beilenson (D)	121,468	65.7
	George Woolverton (R)	58,746	31.8
24	Henry A. Waxman (D)	103,914	87.9
	George Abrahams (LIBERT)	8,871	7.5
25	Edward R. Roybal (D)	62,692	76.1
	Gregory L. Hardy (R)	17,558	21.3
26	Howard L. Berman (D)	98,091	65.1
	Robert M. Kerns (R)	52,662	34.9
27	Mel Levine (D)	110,403	63.7
	Robert B. Scribner (R)	59,410	34.3
28	Julian C. Dixon (D)	92,635	76.4
	George Z. Adams (R)	25,858	21.3
29	Augustus F. Hawkins (D)	78,132	84.6
	John Van de Brooke (R)	13,432	14.5
30	Matthew G. Martinez (D)	59,369	62.5
	John W. Almquist (R)	33,705	35.5
31	Mervyn M. Dymally (D)	77,126	70.3
	Jack McMurray (R)	30,322	27.6
32	Glenn M. Anderson (D)	90,739	68.5
	Joyce M. Robertson (R)	39,003	29.4
33	David Dreier (R)	118,541	71.7
	Monty Hempel (D)	44,312	26.8
34	Esteban E. Torres (D)	66,404	60.3
	Charles M. House (R)	43,659	39.7
35	Jerry Lewis (R)	127,235	76.9
	R. ''Sarge'' Hall (D)	38,322	23.1
36	George E. Brown Jr. (D)	78,118	57.1
	Bob Henley (R)	58,660	42.9
37	Al McCandless (R)	122,416	63.7
	David E. Skinner (D)	69,808	36.3
38	Bob Dornan (R)	66,032	55.3
	Richard Robinson (D)	50,625	42.4
39	William E. Dannemeyer (R)	137,603	74.5
	David D. Vest (D)	42,377	24.0
40	Robert E. Badham (R)	119,829	59.8
	Bruce W. Sumner (D)	75,664	37.7
41	Bill Lowery (R)	133,566	67.8
	Dan Kripke (D)	59,816	30.4
42	Dan Lungren (R)	140,364	72.8
	Michael P. Blackburn (D)	47,586	24.7
43	Ron Packard (R)	137,341	73.1
	Joseph Chirra (D)	45,078	24.0
44	Jim Bates (D)	70,557	64.3
	Bill Mitchell (R)	36,359	33.1
45	Duncan Hunter (R)	118,900	76.9
	Hewitt Fitts Ryan (D)	32,800	21.2

COLORADO

		Votes	%
1	Patricia Schroeder (D)	106,113	68.4
	Joy Wood (R)	49,095	31.6
2	David E. Skaggs (D)	91,223	51.5
	Michael J. Norton (R)	86,032	48.5
3	Ben Nighthorse Campbell (D)	95,353	51.9

	Candidates	Votes	%
	Mike Strang (R)	88,508	48.1
4	Hank Brown (R)	117,089	69.8
	David Sprague (D)	50,672	30.2
5	Joel Hefley (R)	121,153	69.8
	Bill Story (D)	52,488	30.2
6	Dan Schaefer (R)	104,359	65.0
	Chuck Norris (D)	53,834	33.5

CONNECTICUT

		Votes	%
1	Barbara B. Kennelly (D)	128,930	74.2
	Herschel A. Klein (R)	44,122	25.4
2	Sam Gejdenson (D)	109,229	67.4
	Francis M. ''Bud'' Mullen (R)	52,869	32.6
3	Bruce A. Morrison (D)	114,276	69.6
	Ernest J. Diette Jr. (R)	49,806	30.4
4	Stewart B. McKinney (R)	77,212	53.5
	Christine M. Niedermeier (D)	66,999	46.5
5	John G. Rowland (R)	98,664	60.9
	Jim Cohen (D)	63,371	39.1
6	Nancy L. Johnson (R)	111,304	64.2
	Paul S. Amenta (D)	62,133	35.8

DELAWARE

		Votes	%
AL	Thomas R. Carper (D)	106,351	66.2
	Thomas Stephen Neuberger (R)	53,767	33.4

FLORIDA

		Votes	%
1	Earl Hutto (D)	97,465	63.8
	Greg Neubeck (R)	55,415	36.2
2	Bill Grant (D)	110,120	99.4
3	Charles E. Bennett (D)		100.0
4	Bill Chappell Jr. (D)		100.0
5	Bill McCollum (R)		100.0
6	Buddy MacKay (D)	143,583	70.2
	Larry Gallagher (R)	61,053	29.8
7	Sam Gibbons (D)		100.0
8	C. W. Bill Young (R)		100.0
9	Michael Bilirakis (R)	166,504	70.8
	Gabe Cazares (D)	68,574	29.2
10	Andy Ireland (R)	122,368	71.2
	David B. Higginbottom (D)	49,559	28.8
11	Bill Nelson (D)	149,036	72.7
	Scott Ellis (R)	55,904	27.3
12	Tom Lewis (R)	150,222	99.4
13	Connie Mack (R)	187,794	75.0
	Addison S. Gilbert III (D)	62,694	25.0
14	Daniel A. Mica (D)	171,961	73.8
	Rick Martin (R)	61,185	26.2
15	E. Clay Shaw Jr. (R)		100.0
16	Lawrence J. Smith (D)	121,213	69.7
	Mary Collins (R)	52,807	30.3
17	William Lehman (D)		100.0
18	Claude Pepper (D)	80,047	73.5
	Tom Brodie (R)	28,803	26.5
19	Dante B. Fascell (D)	99,203	69.1
	Bill Flanagan (R)	44,455	30.9

GEORGIA

		Votes	%
1	Lindsay Thomas (D)	69,440	100.0
2	Charles Hatcher (D)	72,482	100.0
3	Richard Ray (D)	75,850	99.7
4	Pat Swindall (R)	86,366	53.2
	Ben Jones (D)	75,892	46.8
5	John Lewis (D)	93,229	75.3
	Portia A. Scott (R)	30,562	24.7
6	Newt Gingrich (R)	75,583	59.5
	Crandle Bray (D)	51,352	40.5
7	George ''Buddy'' Darden (D)	88,636	66.4

Candidates	Votes	%
Joe Morecraft (R)	44,891	33.6
8 J. Roy Rowland (D)	82,254	86.4
Eddie McDowell (R)	12,952	13.6
9 Ed Jenkins (D)	84,303	100.0
10 Doug Barnard Jr. (D)	79,548	67.3
Jim Hill (R)	38,714	32.7

HAWAII

	Votes	%
1 Patricia Saiki (R)	99,683	59.2
Mufi Hannemann (D)	63,061	37.5
2 Daniel K. Akaka (D)	123,830	76.1
Maria M. Hustace (R)	35,371	21.7

Special Election [1]

	Votes	%
1 Neil Abercrombie (D)	42,031	29.9
Patricia Saiki (R)	41,067	29.2
Mufi Hannemann (D)	39,800	28.3
Steve Cobb (D)	16,721	11.9

IDAHO

	Votes	%
1 Larry E. Craig (R)	120,553	65.1
Bill Currie (D)	59,723	32.3
2 Richard H. Stallings (D)	103,035	54.4
Mel Richardson (R)	86,528	45.6

ILLINOIS

	Votes	%
1 Charles A. Hayes (D)	122,376	96.4
2 Gus Savage (D)	99,268	83.8
Ron Taylor (R)	19,149	16.2
3 Marty Russo (D)	102,949	66.2
James J. Tierney (R)	52,618	33.8
4 Jack Davis (R)	61,633	51.6
Shawn Collins (D)	57,925	48.4
5 William O. Lipinski (D)	82,466	70.4
Daniel John Sobieski (R)	34,738	29.6
6 Henry J. Hyde (R)	98,196	75.4
Robert H. Renshaw (D)	32,064	24.6
7 Cardiss Collins (D)	90,761	80.2
Caroline K. Kallas (R)	21,055	18.6
8 Dan Rostenkowski (D)	82,873	78.7
Thomas J. DeFazio (R)	22,383	21.3
9 Sidney R. Yates (D)	92,738	71.6
Herbert Sohn (R)	36,715	28.4
10 John Edward Porter (R)	87,531	75.1
Robert A. Cleland (D)	28,990	24.9
11 Frank Annunzio (D)	106,970	70.7
George S. Gottlieb (R)	44,341	29.3
12 Philip M. Crane (R)	89,044	77.7
John A. Leonardi (D)	25,536	22.3
13 Harris W. Fawell (R)	107,227	73.4
Dominick J. Jeffrey (D)	38,874	26.6
14 Dennis Hastert (R)	77,288	52.4
Mary Lou Kearns (D)	70,293	47.6
15 Edward R. Madigan (R)	115,284	100.0
16 Lynn Martin (R)	92,982	66.9
Kenneth F. Bohnsack (D)	46,087	33.1
17 Lane Evans (D)	85,442	55.6
Sam McHard (R)	68,101	44.4
18 Robert H. Michel (R)	94,308	62.6
Jim Dawson (D)	56,331	37.4
19 Terry L. Bruce (D)	111,105	66.4
Al Salvi (R)	56,186	33.6
20 Richard J. Durbin (D)	126,556	68.1
Kevin B. McCarthy (R)	59,291	31.9
21 Melvin Price (D)	65,722	50.4
Robert H. Gaffner (R)	64,779	49.6
22 Kenneth J. Gray (D)	97,585	53.2
Randy Patchett (R)	85,733	46.8

INDIANA

	Votes	%
1 Peter J. Visclosky (D)	86,983	73.4
William Costas (R)	30,395	25.7
2 Philip R. Sharp (D)	102,456	61.9
Donald J. Lynch (R)	62,013	37.4

Candidates	Votes	%
3 John Hiler (R)	75,979	49.8
Thomas W. Ward (D)	75,932	49.8
4 Daniel R. Coats (R)	99,865	69.6
Gregory Alan Scher (D)	43,105	30.0
5 Jim Jontz (D)	80,772	51.4
James R. Butcher (R)	75,507	48.1
6 Dan Burton (R)	118,363	68.3
Thomas F. McKenna (D)	53,431	30.9
7 John T. Myers (R)	104,965	66.8
L. Eugene Smith (D)	49,675	31.6
8 Frank McCloskey (D)	106,662	53.0
Richard D. McIntyre (R)	93,586	46.5
9 Lee H. Hamilton (D)	120,586	71.9
Robert Walter Kilroy (R)	46,398	27.7
10 Andrew Jacobs Jr. (D)	68,817	57.7
Jim Eynon (R)	49,064	41.2

IOWA

	Votes	%
1 Jim Leach (R)	86,834	66.4
John R. Whitaker (D)	43,985	33.6
2 Tom Tauke (R)	88,708	61.3
Eric Tabor (D)	55,903	38.7
3 David R. Nagle (D)	83,504	54.6
John McIntee (R)	69,386	45.4
4 Neal Smith (D)	107,271	68.4
Bob Lockard (R)	49,641	31.6
5 Jim Ross Lightfoot (R)	85,025	59.2
Scott Hughes (D)	58,552	40.8
6 Fred Grandy (R)	81,861	50.9
Clayton Hodgson (D)	78,807	49.0

KANSAS

	Votes	%
1 Pat Roberts (R)	141,297	76.5
Dale Lyon (D)	43,359	23.5
2 Jim Slattery (D)	110,737	70.6
Phill Kline (R)	46,029	29.4
3 Jan Meyers (R)	109,266	100.0
4 Dan Glickman (D)	111,164	64.5
Bob Knight (R)	61,178	35.5
5 Bob Whittaker (R)	116,800	71.1
Kym E. Myers (D)	47,540	28.9

KENTUCKY

	Votes	%
1 Carroll Hubbard Jr. (D)	64,315	100.0
2 William H. Natcher (D)	57,644	100.0
3 Romano L. Mazzoli (D)	81,943	73.0
Lee Holmes (R)	29,348	26.2
4 Jim Bunning (R)	67,626	55.1
Terry L. Mann (D)	53,906	43.9
5 Harold Rogers (R)	56,760	100.0
6 Larry J. Hopkins (R)	75,906	74.3
Jerry W. Hammond (D)	26,315	25.7
7 Carl C. Perkins (D)	90,619	79.6
James T. Polley (R)	23,209	20.4

LOUISIANA [2]

	Votes	%
1 Robert L. Livingston (R)		100.0
2 Lindy (Mrs. Hale) Boggs (D)		100.0
3 W. J. "Billy" Tauzin (D)		100.0
4 Buddy Roemer (D)		100.0
5 Jerry Huckaby (D)		100.0
6 Richard H. Baker (R)		100.0
7 Jimmy Hayes (D)	109,205	57.0
Margaret Lowenthal (D)	82,293	43.0
8 Clyde C. Holloway (R)	102,276	51.4
Faye Williams (D)	96,864	48.6

MAINE

	Votes	%
1 Joseph E. Brennan (D)	121,848	53.2
H. Rollin Ives (R)	100,260	43.7
2 Olympia J. Snowe (R)	148,770	77.3
Richard R. Charette (D)	43,614	22.7

MARYLAND

Candidates	Votes	%
1 Roy Dyson (D)	88,113	66.8
Harlan C. Williams (R)	43,764	33.2
2 Helen Delich Bentley (R)	96,745	58.7
Kathleen Kennedy Townsend (D)	68,200	41.3
3 Benjamin L. Cardin (D)	100,161	79.1
Ross Z. Pierpont (R)	26,452	20.9
4 Tom McMillen (D)	65,075	50.2
Robert R. Neall (R)	64,651	49.8
5 Steny H. Hoyer (D)	82,098	81.9
John Eugene Sellner (R)	18,102	18.1
6 Beverly B. Byron (D)	102,975	72.2
John Vandenberge (R)	39,600	27.8
7 Kweisi Mfume (D)	79,226	86.7
Saint George I. B. Crosse III (R)	12,170	13.3
8 Constance A. Morella (R)	92,917	52.9
Stewart Bainum Jr. (D)	82,825	47.1

MASSACHUSETTS

	Votes	%
1 Silvio O. Conte (R)	113,653	77.8
Robert S. Weiner (D)	32,396	22.2
2 Edward P. Boland (D)	91,033	65.9
Brian P. Lees (R)	47,022	34.1
3 Joseph D. Early (D)	120,222	100.0
4 Barney Frank (D)	134,387	88.8
Thomas D. DeVisscher (AM)	16,857	11.2
5 Chester G. Atkins (D)	113,690	99.9
6 Nicholas Mavroules (D)	131,051	99.9
7 Edward J. Markey (D)	124,183	100.0
8 Joseph P. Kennedy II (D)	104,651	72.0
Clark C. Abt (R)	40,259	27.7
9 Joe Moakley (D)	110,026	83.8
Robert W. Horan (I)	21,292	16.2
10 Gerry E. Studds (D)	121,578	65.1
Ricardo M. Barros (R)	49,451	26.5
Alexander Byron (I)	15,687	8.4
11 Brian J. Donnelly (D)	114,926	100.0

MICHIGAN

	Votes	%
1 John Conyers Jr. (D)	94,307	89.2
Bill Ashe (R)	10,407	9.8
2 Carl D. Pursell (R)	79,567	59.0
Dean Baker (D)	55,204	41.0
3 Howard Wolpe (D)	78,720	60.4
Jackie McGregor (R)	51,678	39.6
4 Fred Upton (R)	70,331	61.9
Dan Roche (D)	41,624	36.6
5 Paul B. Henry (R)	100,577	71.2
Teresa S. Decker (D)	40,608	28.8
6 Bob Carr (D)	74,927	56.7
Jim Dunn (R)	57,283	43.3
7 Dale E. Kildee (D)	101,225	79.6
Trudie Callihan (R)	24,848	19.5
8 Bob Traxler (D)	97,406	72.6
John A. Levi (R)	36,695	27.4
9 Guy Vander Jagt (R)	89,991	64.4
Richard J. Anderson (D)	49,702	35.6
10 Bill Schuette (R)	78,475	51.2
Donald J. Albosta (D)	74,941	48.8
11 Robert W. Davis (R)	91,575	63.0
Robert C. Anderson (D)	53,180	36.6
12 David E. Bonior (D)	87,643	66.4
Candice S. Miller (R)	44,442	33.6
13 George W. Crockett Jr. (D)	76,435	85.2
Mary Griffin (R)	12,395	13.8
14 Dennis M. Hertel (D)	92,328	72.9
Stanley T. Grot (R)	33,831	26.7
15 William D. Ford (D)	77,950	75.2
Glen Kassel (R)	25,078	24.2
16 John D. Dingell (D)	101,659	77.8
Frank W. Grzywacki (R)	28,971	22.2
17 Sander M. Levin (D)	105,031	76.4
Calvin Williams (R)	30,879	22.5
18 William S. Broomfield (R)	110,099	73.8
Gary L. Kohut (D)	39,144	26.2

Footnotes, see p. 296.

MINNESOTA [3]

Candidates	Votes	%
1 Timothy J. Penny (DFL)	125,115	72.4
Paul H. Grawe (I-R)	47,750	27.6
2 Vin Weber (I-R)	100,249	51.6
Dave Johnson (DFL)	94,048	48.4
3 Bill Frenzel (I-R)	127,434	70.1
Ray Stock (DFL)	54,261	29.9
4 Bruce F. Vento (DFL)	112,662	72.9
Harold Stassen (I-R)	41,926	27.1
5 Martin Olav Sabo (DFL)	105,410	72.7
Rick Serra (I-R)	37,583	25.9
6 Gerry Sikorski (DFL)	110,598	65.8
Barbara Zwach Sykora (I-R)	57,460	34.2
7 Arlan Stangeland (I-R)	94,024	49.7
Collin C. Peterson (DFL)	93,903	49.6
8 James L. Oberstar (DFL)	135,718	72.6
Dave Rued (I-R)	51,315	27.4

MISSISSIPPI

Candidates	Votes	%
1 Jamie L. Whitten (D)	59,870	66.4
Larry Cobb (R)	30,267	33.6
2 Mike Espy (D)	73,119	51.7
Webb Franklin (R)	68,292	48.3
3 G. V. "Sonny" Montgomery (D)	80,575	100.0
4 Wayne Dowdy (D)	85,819	71.5
Gail Healy (R)	34,190	28.5
5 Trent Lott (R)	75,288	82.3
Larry L. Albritton (D)	16,143	17.7

MISSOURI

Candidates	Votes	%
1 William L. Clay (D)	91,044	66.1
Robert J. Wittmann (R)	46,599	33.9
2 Jack Buechner (R)	101,010	51.9
Robert A. Young (D)	93,538	48.1
3 Richard A. Gephardt (D)	116,403	69.0
4 Ike Skelton (D)	129,471	100.0
5 Alan Wheat (D)	101,030	70.9
Greg Fisher (R)	39,340	27.6
6 E. Thomas Coleman (R)	95,865	56.7
Doug R. Hughes (D)	73,155	43.3
7 Gene Taylor (R)	114,210	67.0
Ken Young (D)	56,291	33.0
8 Bill Emerson (R)	79,142	52.5
Wayne Cryts (D)	71,532	47.5
9 Harold L. Volkmer (D)	95,939	57.5
Ralph Uthlaut Jr. (R)	70,972	42.5

MONTANA

Candidates	Votes	%
1 Pat Williams (D)	98,501	61.7
Don Allen (R)	61,230	38.3
2 Ron Marlenee (R)	84,548	53.5
Richard "Buck" O'Brien (D)	73,583	46.5

NEBRASKA

Candidates	Votes	%
1 Doug Bereuter (R)	121,772	64.4
Steve Burns (D)	67,137	35.5
2 Hal Daub (R)	99,569	58.5
Walter M. Calinger (D)	70,372	41.3
3 Virginia Smith (R)	136,985	69.8
Scott E. Sidwell (D)	59,182	30.2

NEVADA

Candidates	Votes	%
1 James H. Bilbray (D)	61,830	54.1
Bob Ryan (R)	50,342	44.0
2 Barbara F. Vucanovich (R)	83,479	58.4
Pete Sferrazza (D)	59,433	41.6

NEW HAMPSHIRE

Candidates	Votes	%
1 Robert C. Smith (R)	70,739	56.4
James M. Demers (D)	54,787	43.6
2 Judd Gregg (R)	85,479	74.2
Laurence Craig-Green (D)	29,688	25.8

NEW JERSEY

Candidates	Votes	%
1 James J. Florio (D)	93,497	75.6
Fred A. Busch (R)	29,175	23.6
2 William J. Hughes (D)	83,821	68.3
Alfred J. Bennington Jr. (R)	35,167	28.6
3 James J. Howard (D)	73,743	58.7
Brian T. Kennedy (R)	51,882	41.3
4 Christopher H. Smith (R)	78,699	61.1
Jeffrey Laurenti (D)	49,290	38.3
5 Marge Roukema (R)	94,253	74.6
H. Vernon Jolley (D)	32,145	25.4
6 Bernard J. Dwyer (D)	67,460	69.0
John D. Scalamonti (R)	28,286	28.9
7 Matthew J. Rinaldo (R)	92,254	79.0
June S. Fischer (D)	24,462	21.0
8 Robert A. Roe (D)	57,820	62.8
Thomas P. Zampino (R)	34,268	37.2
9 Robert G. Torricelli (D)	89,634	69.0
Arthur F. Jones (R)	40,226	31.0
10 Peter W. Rodino Jr. (D)	46,666	95.9
11 Dean A. Gallo (R)	75,037	68.0
Frank Askin (D)	35,280	32.0
12 Jim Courter (R)	72,966	63.5
David B. Crabiel (D)	41,967	36.5
13 H. James Saxton (R)	82,866	65.4
John Wydra (D)	43,920	34.6
14 Frank J. Guarini (D)	63,057	70.7
Albio Sires (R)	23,822	26.7

NEW MEXICO

Candidates	Votes	%
1 Manuel Lujan Jr. (R)	90,476	70.9
Manny Garcia (D)	37,138	29.1
2 Joe Skeen (R)	77,787	62.9
Mike Runnels (D)	45,924	37.1
3 Bill Richardson (D)	95,760	71.3
David F. Cargo (R)	38,552	28.7

NEW YORK

Candidates	Votes	%
1 George J. Hochbrueckner (D)	67,139	51.2
Gregory J. Blass (R)	55,413	42.3
2 Thomas J. Downey (D)	69,771	64.3
Jeffrey A. Butzke (R, C)	35,132	32.4
3 Robert J. Mrazek (D)	83,985	56.4
Joseph A. Guarino (R, C)	60,367	40.6
4 Norman F. Lent (R, C)	92,214	64.8
Patricia Sullivan (D, L)	43,581	30.6
5 Raymond J. McGrath (R, C)	93,473	65.3
Michael T. Sullivan (D, L, RTL)	49,728	34.7
6 Floyd H. Flake (D)	58,317	67.7
Richard Dietl (R, C)	27,773	32.3
7 Gary L. Ackerman (D)	62,836	77.4
Edward Nelson Rodriguez (R, C)	18,384	22.6
8 James H. Scheuer (D, L)	70,605	90.2
Gustave Reifenkugel (C)	7,679	9.8
9 Thomas J. Manton (D)	50,738	69.4
Salvatore J. Calise (R)	18,040	24.7
Thomas V. Ognibene (C)	4,348	5.9
10 Charles E. Schumer (D, L)	76,318	93.3
Alice E. Gaffney (C)	5,472	6.7
11 Edolphus Towns (D, L)	41,689	89.4
Nathaniel Hendricks (R)	4,053	8.7
12 Major R. Owens (D, L)	42,138	91.5
Owen Augustin (R)	2,752	6.0
13 Stephen J. Solarz (D, L)	61,089	82.4
Leon Nadrowski (R)	10,941	14.8
14 Guy V. Molinari (R, C)	64,647	68.8
Barbara Walla (D)	27,950	29.7
15 Bill Green (R)	58,214	58.0
George A. Hirsch (D, L)	42,147	42.0
16 Charles B. Rangel (D, R, L)	61,262	96.4
17 Ted Weiss (D, L)	95,094	85.5

Candidates	Votes	%
Thomas A. Chorba (R, C)	15,587	14.0
18 Robert Garcia (D, L)	43,343	93.5
Melanie Chase (C)	2,479	5.4
19 Mario Biaggi (D, R, L)	87,774	90.2
Alice Farrell (C)	6,906	7.1
20 Joseph J. DioGuardi (R, C)	80,220	53.9
Bella S. Abzug (D)	66,359	44.5
21 Hamilton Fish Jr. (R, C)	102,070	76.5
Lawrence W. Grunberger (D)	28,339	21.3
22 Benjamin A. Gilman (R)	94,244	69.5
Eleanor F. Burlingham (D)	36,852	27.2
23 Samuel S. Stratton (D)	140,759	96.4
24 Gerald B. H. Solomon (R, C, RTL)	117,285	70.4
Ed Bloch (D)	49,225	29.6
25 Sherwood Boehlert (R)	104,216	69.0
Kevin J. Conway (D)	33,864	22.4
Robert S. Barstow (C, RTL)	12,999	8.6
26 David O'B. Martin (R, C)	94,840	100.0
27 George C. Wortley (R, C)	83,430	49.7
Rosemary S. Pooler (D)	82,491	49.1
28 Matthew F. McHugh (D)	103,908	68.3
Mark R. Masterson (R, C, RTL)	48,213	31.7
29 Frank Horton (R)	99,704	70.7
James R. Vogel (D)	34,194	24.2
30 Louise M. Slaughter (D)	86,777	51.0
Fred J. Eckert (R, C)	83,402	49.0
31 Jack F. Kemp (R, C, RTL)	92,508	57.4
James P. Keane (D)	67,574	42.0
32 John J. LaFalce (D, L)	99,745	91.0
Dean L. Walker (C)	6,234	5.7
33 Henry J. Nowak (D, L)	109,256	85.1
Charles A. Walker (R, C)	19,147	14.9
34 Amo Houghton (R, C)	85,856	60.1
Larry M. Himelein (D)	56,898	39.9

Special Election [4]

Candidates	Votes	%
6 Alton R. Waldon Jr. (D)	12,654	31.0
Floyd H. Flake (UT)	12,376	30.3
Richard Dietl (R, C)	8,700	21.3
Kevin McCabe (GOOD GOV)	3,738	9.2
Andrew Jenkins (L)	3,323	8.1

NORTH CAROLINA

Candidates	Votes	%
1 Walter B. Jones (D)	91,122	69.5
Howard Moye (R)	39,912	30.5
2 Tim Valentine (D)	95,320	74.6
Bud McElhaney (R)	32,515	25.4
3 H. Martin Lancaster (D)	71,460	64.5
Gerald B. Hurst (R)	39,408	35.5
4 David E. Price (D)	92,216	55.7
William Cobey Jr. (R)	73,469	44.3
5 Stephen L. Neal (D)	86,410	54.1
Stuart Epperson (R)	73,261	45.9
6 Howard Coble (R)	72,329	50.0
Robin Britt (D)	72,250	50.0
7 Charlie Rose (D)	70,471	64.2
Thomas J. Harrelson (R)	39,289	35.8
8 W. G. "Bill" Hefner (D)	80,959	57.9
William G. Hamby Jr. (R)	58,941	42.1
9 Alex McMillan (R)	80,352	51.3
D. G. Martin (D)	76,240	48.7
10 Cass Ballenger (R)	83,902	57.5
Lester D. Roark (D)	62,035	42.5
11 James McClure Clarke (D)	91,575	50.7
Bill Hendon (R)	89,069	49.3

Special Election [5]

Candidates	Votes	%
10 Cass Ballenger (R)	82,973	57.5
Lester D. Roark (D)	61,205	42.5

NORTH DAKOTA

Candidates	Votes	%
AL Byron L. Dorgan (D)	216,258	75.5
Syver Vinje (R)	66,989	23.4

Footnote, see p. 296.

OHIO

Candidates	Votes	%
1 Thomas A. Luken (D)	90,477	61.7
Fred E. Morr (R)	56,100	38.3
2 Bill Gradison (R)	105,061	70.7
William F. Stineman (D)	43,448	29.3
3 Tony P. Hall (D)	98,311	73.7
Ron Crutcher (R)	35,167	26.3
4 Michael G. Oxley (R)	115,751	75.1
Clem T. Cratty (D)	26,320	17.1
Raven L. Workman (I)	11,997	7.8
5 Delbert L. Latta (R)	102,016	65.0
Tom Murray (D)	54,864	35.0
6 Bob McEwen (R)	106,354	70.3
Gordon Roberts (D)	42,155	27.8
7 Michael DeWine (R)	119,238	100.0
8 Donald E. Lukens (R)	98,475	68.1
John W. Griffin (D)	46,195	31.9
9 Marcy Kaptur (D)	105,646	77.5
Mike Shufeldt (R)	30,643	22.5
10 Clarence E. Miller (R)	106,870	70.4
John M. Buchanan (D)	44,847	29.6
11 Dennis E. Eckart (D)	104,740	72.4
Margaret Mueller (R)	35,944	24.9
12 John R. Kasich (R)	117,905	73.4
Timothy C. Jochim (D)	42,727	26.6
13 Don J. Pease (D)	88,612	62.8
William D. Nielsen (R)	52,452	37.2
14 Thomas C. Sawyer (D)	83,257	53.7
Lynn Slaby (R)	71,713	46.3
15 Chalmers P. Wylie (R)	97,745	63.7
David L. Jackson (D)	55,750	36.3
16 Ralph Regula (R)	118,206	76.3
William J. Kennick (D)	36,639	23.7
17 James A. Traficant Jr. (D)	112,855	72.3
James H. Fulks (R)	43,334	27.7
18 Douglas Applegate (D)	126,526	100.0
19 Edward F. Feighan (D)	97,814	54.8
Gary C. Suhadolnik (R)	80,743	45.2
20 Mary Rose Oakar (D)	110,976	84.9
Bill Smith (R)	19,794	15.1
21 Louis Stokes (D)	99,878	81.6
Franklin H. Roski (R)	22,594	18.4

OKLAHOMA

Candidates	Votes	%
1 James M. Inhofe (R)	78,919	54.8
Gary D. Allison (D)	61,663	42.8
2 Mike Synar (D)	114,543	73.3
Gary K. Rice (R)	41,795	26.7
3 Wes Watkins (D)	114,008	78.1
Patrick K. Miller (R)	31,913	21.9
4 Dave McCurdy (D)	94,984	76.2
Larry Humphreys (R)	29,697	23.8
5 Mickey Edwards (R)	108,774	70.6
Donna Compton (D)	45,256	29.4
6 Glenn English (D)		100.0

OREGON

Candidates	Votes	%
1 Les AuCoin (D)	141,585	61.7
Tony Meeker (R)	87,874	38.3
2 Robert F. Smith (R)	113,566	60.2
Larry Tuttle (D)	75,124	39.8
3 Ron Wyden (D)	180,067	85.9
Thomas H. Phelan (R)	29,321	14.0
4 Peter A. DeFazio (D)	105,697	54.1
Bruce Long (R)	89,795	45.9
5 Denny Smith (R)	125,906	60.5
Barbara Ross (D)	82,290	39.5

PENNSYLVANIA

Candidates	Votes	%
1 Thomas M. Foglietta (D)	88,224	74.7
Anthony J. Mucciolo (R)	29,811	25.3
2 William H. Gray III (D)	128,399	98.4
3 Robert A. Borski (D)	107,804	61.8
Robert A. Rovner (R)	66,693	38.2
4 Joe Kolter (D)	86,133	60.4
Al Lindsay (R)	55,165	38.7
5 Richard T. Schulze (R)	87,593	65.7
Tim Ringgold (D)	45,648	34.3
6 Gus Yatron (D)	98,142	69.1
Norm Bertasavage (R)	43,858	30.9
7 Curt Weldon (R)	110,118	61.3
Bill Spingler (D)	69,557	38.7
8 Peter H. Kostmayer (D)	85,731	55.0
David A. Christian (R)	70,047	45.0
9 Bud Shuster (R)	120,890	100.0
10 Joseph M. McDade (R)	118,603	74.7
Robert C. Bolus (D)	40,248	25.3
11 Paul E. Kanjorski (D)	112,405	70.6
Marc Holtzman (R)	46,785	29.4
12 John P. Murtha (D)	97,135	67.4
Kathy Holtzman (R)	46,937	32.6
13 Lawrence Coughlin (R)	100,701	58.5
Joseph M. Hoeffel (D)	71,381	41.5
14 William J. Coyne (D)	104,726	89.6
Richard Edward Caligiuri (LIBERT)	6,058	5.2
15 Don Ritter (R)	74,829	56.8
Joe Simonetta (D)	56,972	43.2
16 Robert S. Walker (R)	100,784	74.6
James D. Hagelgans (D)	34,399	25.4
17 George W. Gekas (R)	101,027	73.6
Michael S. Ogden (D)	36,157	26.4
18 Doug Walgren (D)	104,164	63.0
Ernie Buckman (R)	61,164	37.0
19 Bill Goodling (R)	100,055	72.9
Richard F. Thornton (D)	37,223	27.1
20 Joseph M. Gaydos (D)	136,638	98.5
21 Tom Ridge (R)	111,148	80.9
Joylyn Blackwell (D)	26,324	19.1
22 Austin J. Murphy (D)	131,650	100.0
23 William F. Clinger Jr. (R)	79,595	55.5
Bill Wachob (D)	63,875	44.5

RHODE ISLAND

Candidates	Votes	%
1 Fernand J. St Germain (D)	85,077	57.7
John A. Holmes Jr. (R)	62,397	42.3
2 Claudine Schneider (R)	113,603	71.8
Donald J. Ferry (D)	44,586	28.2

SOUTH CAROLINA

Candidates	Votes	%
1 Arthur Ravenel Jr. (R)	59,969	52.0
Jimmy Stuckey (D)	55,262	48.0
2 Floyd D. Spence (R)	73,455	53.6
Fred Zeigler (D)	63,592	46.4
3 Butler Derrick (D)	79,109	68.4
Richard Dickison (R)	36,495	31.5
4 Liz J. Patterson (D)	67,012	51.4
Bill Workman (R)	61,648	47.3
5 John M. Spratt Jr. (D)	95,859	99.7
6 Robin Tallon (D)	92,398	75.5
Robbie Cunningham (R)	29,922	24.5

SOUTH DAKOTA

Candidates	Votes	%
AL Tim Johnson (D)	171,462	59.2
Dale Bell (R)	118,261	40.8

TENNESSEE

Candidates	Votes	%
1 James H. Quillen (R)	80,289	68.9
John B. Russell (D)	36,278	31.1
2 John J. Duncan (R)	96,396	76.2
John F. Bowen (D)	30,088	23.8
3 Marilyn Lloyd (D)	75,034	53.9
Jim Golden (R)	64,084	46.1
4 Jim Cooper (D)	86,997	100.0
5 Bill Boner (D)	85,126	57.9
Terry Holcomb (R)	58,701	39.9
6 Bart Gordon (D)	102,180	76.8
Fred Vail (R)	30,823	23.2
7 Don Sundquist (R)	93,902	72.3
M. Lloyd Hiler (D)	35,966	27.7
8 Ed Jones (D)	101,699	80.4
Dan H. Campbell (R)	24,792	19.6
9 Harold E. Ford (D)	83,006	83.4
Isaac Richmond (I)	16,221	16.3

TEXAS

Candidates	Votes	%
1 Jim Chapman (D)	84,445	100.0
2 Charles Wilson (D)	78,529	56.7
Julian Gordon (R)	55,986	40.5
3 Steve Bartlett (R)	143,381	94.1
4 Ralph M. Hall (D)	97,540	71.7
Thomas Blow (R)	38,578	28.3
5 John Bryant (D)	57,410	58.5
Tom Carter (R)	39,945	40.7
6 Joe L. Barton (R)	86,190	55.8
Pete Geren (D)	68,270	44.2
7 Bill Archer (R)	129,673	87.4
Harry Kniffen (D)	17,635	11.9
8 Jack Fields (R)	66,280	68.4
Blaine Mann (D)	30,617	31.6
9 Jack Brooks (D)	73,285	61.5
Lisa D. Duperier (R)	45,834	38.5
10 J. J. "Jake" Pickle (D)	135,863	72.3
Carole Keeton Rylander (R)	52,000	27.7
11 Marvin Leath (D)	84,201	100.0
12 Jim Wright (D)	84,831	68.7
Don McNeil (R)	38,620	31.3
13 Beau Boulter (R)	84,980	64.9
Doug Seal (D)	45,907	35.1
14 Mac Sweeney (R)	74,471	52.3
Greg H. Laughlin (D)	67,852	47.7
15 E. "Kika" de la Garza (D)	70,777	100.0
16 Ronald D. Coleman (D)	50,590	65.7
Roy Gillia (R)	26,421	34.3
17 Charles W. Stenholm (D)	97,791	100.0
18 Mickey Leland (D)	63,335	90.2
Joanne Kuniansky (I)	6,884	9.8
19 Larry Combest (R)	68,695	62.0
Gerald McCathern (D)	42,129	38.0
20 Henry B. Gonzalez (D)	55,363	100.0
21 Lamar Smith (R)	100,346	60.6
Pete Snelson (D)	63,779	38.5
22 Thomas D. DeLay (R)	76,459	71.8
Susan Director (D)	30,079	28.2
23 Albert G. Bustamante (D)	68,131	90.7
Ken Hendrix (LIBERT)	7,001	9.3
24 Martin Frost (D)	69,368	67.2
Bob Burk (R)	33,819	32.8
25 Michael A. Andrews (D)	67,435	100.0
26 Dick Armey (R)	101,735	68.1
George Richardson (D)	47,651	31.9
27 Solomon P. Ortiz (D)	64,165	100.0

UTAH

Candidates	Votes	%
1 James V. Hansen (R)	82,151	51.6
Gunn McKay (D)	77,180	48.4
2 Wayne Owens (D)	76,921	55.2
Tom Shimizu (R)	60,967	43.7
3 Howard C. Nielson (R)	86,599	66.6
Dale F. Gardiner (D)	42,582	32.7

VERMONT

Candidates	Votes	%
AL James M. Jeffords (R)	168,403	89.1

VIRGINIA

Candidates	Votes	%
1 Herbert H. Bateman (R)	80,713	56.0
Robert C. Scott (D)	63,364	44.0
2 Owen B. Pickett (D)	54,491	49.5
A. J. "Joe" Canada Jr. (R)	46,131	41.9
Stephen P. Shao (I)	9,492	8.6
3 Thomas J. Bliley Jr. (R)	74,525	67.0
Kenneth E. Powell (D)	32,961	29.7
4 Norman Sisisky (D)	64,699	99.8
5 Dan Daniel (D)	73,085	81.5
J. F. "Frank" Cole (I)	16,551	18.5

	Candidates	Votes	%
6	Jim Olin (D)	88,230	69.9
	Flo Neher Traywick (R)	38,051	30.1
7	D. French Slaughter Jr. (R)	58,927	98.3
8	Stan Parris (R)	72,670	61.8
	James H. Boren (D)	44,965	38.2
9	Rick Boucher (D)	59,864	99.0
10	Frank R. Wolf (R)	95,724	60.2
	John G. Milliken (D)	63,292	39.8

WASHINGTON

	Candidates	Votes	%
1	John R. Miller (R)	97,969	51.4
	Reese Lindquist (D)	92,697	48.6
2	Al Swift (D)	124,840	72.2
	Thomas S. Talman (R)	48,077	27.8
3	Don Bonker (D)	114,775	73.6
	Joe Illing (R)	41,275	26.4
4	Sid Morrison (R)	107,593	72.1
	Robert Goedecke (D)	41,709	27.9
5	Thomas S. Foley (D)	121,732	74.7
	Floyd L. Wakefield (R)	41,179	25.3

	Candidates	Votes	%
6	Norm Dicks (D)	90,063	71.2
	Kenneth W. Braaten (R)	36,410	28.8
7	Mike Lowry (D)	124,317	72.6
	Don McDonald (R)	46,831	27.4
8	Rod Chandler (R)	107,824	65.2
	David E. Giles (D)	57,545	34.8

WEST VIRGINIA

	Candidates	Votes	%
1	Alan B. Mollohan (D)	90,715	100.0
2	Harley O. Staggers Jr. (D)	76,355	69.5
	Michele Golden (R)	33,554	30.5
3	Bob Wise (D)	73,669	64.9
	Tim Sharp (R)	39,820	35.1
4	Nick J. Rahall II (D)	58,217	71.3
	Martin Miller (R)	23,490	28.7

WISCONSIN

	Candidates	Votes	%
1	Les Aspin (D)	106,288	74.3
	Iris Peterson (R)	34,495	24.1

	Candidates	Votes	%
2	Robert W. Kastenmeier (D)	106,919	55.6
	Ann J. Haney (R)	85,156	44.2
3	Steve Gunderson (R)	104,393	64.1
	Leland E. Mulder (D)	58,445	35.9
4	Gerald D. Kleczka (D)	120,354	99.6
5	Jim Moody (D)	109,506	99.0
6	Thomas E. Petri (R)	124,328	96.7
7	David R. Obey (D)	106,700	62.2
	Kevin J. Hermening (R)	63,408	36.9
8	Toby Roth (R)	118,162	67.4
	Paul F. Willems (D)	57,265	32.6
9	F. James Sensenbrenner Jr. (R)	138,766	78.2
	Thomas G. Popp (D)	38,636	21.8

WYOMING

	Candidates	Votes	%
AL	Dick Cheney (R)	111,007	69.5
	Rick Gilmore (D)	48,780	30.5

1986 Elections

1. A special election was held to fill the unexpired term of Rep. Cecil Heftel (D), who resigned July 11, 1986.

2. For the 1986 House elections in Louisiana, an open primary election was held with candidates from all parties running on the same ballot. Any candidate who received a majority was elected unopposed, with no further appearance on the general election ballot. If no candidate received 50 percent, a runoff was held between the two top finishers.

3. In Minnesota the Democratic Party is known as the Democratic-Farmer-Labor Party and the Republican Party as the Independent-Republican Party; candidates appear on the ballot with these designations.

4. A special election was held to fill the unexpired term of Rep. Joseph P. Addabbo (D), who died April 10, 1986.

5. A special election was held to fill the unexpired term of Rep. James T. Broyhill (R), who resigned in July 1986, having been appointed to the Senate.

1987 House Elections

CALIFORNIA

Special Election [1]

	Candidates	Votes	%
5	Nancy Pelosi (D)	46,428	63.3
	Harriet Ross (R)	22,478	30.7

CONNECTICUT

Special Election [2]

	Candidates	Votes	%
4	Christopher Shays (R)	50,518	57.2
	Christine M. Niedermeier (D)	37,293	42.2

1987 Elections

1. A special election was held to fill the unexpired term of Rep. Sala Burton (D), who died Feb. 1, 1987.

2. A special election was held to fill the unexpired term of Rep. Stewart B. McKinney (R), who died May 7, 1987.

1988 House Elections

ALABAMA

	Candidates	Votes	%
1	Sonny Callahan (R)	115,173	59.2
	John M. Tyson Jr. (D)	77,670	40.0
2	Bill Dickinson (R)	120,408	94.2
	Brooke King (LIBERT)	7,352	5.8
3	Bill Nichols (D)	117,514	96.1
	Shockley (LIBERT)	4,793	3.9
4	Tom Bevill (D)	131,880	96.2
	John Sebastian (LIBERT)	5,264	3.8
5	Ronnie G. Flippo (D)	120,142	64.4
	Stan McDonald (R)	64,491	34.5
6	Ben Erdreich (D)	138,920	66.5
	Charles Caddis (R)	68,788	32.9
7	Claude Harris (D)	136,074	67.7
	James E. "Jim" Bacon (R)	63,372	31.5

ALASKA

		Votes	%
AL	Don Young (R)	120,595	62.5
	Peter Gruenstein (D)	71,881	37.3

ARIZONA

		Votes	%
1	John J. Rhodes III (R)	184,639	72.1
	John M. Fillmore (D)	71,388	27.9
2	Morris K. Udall (D)	99,895	73.3
	Joseph D. Sweeney (R)	36,309	26.7
3	Bob Stump (R)	174,453	68.9
	Dave Moss (D)	72,417	28.6
4	Jon Kyl (R)	206,248	87.1
	Gary Sprunk (LIBERT)	30,430	12.9
5	Jim Kolbe (R)	164,462	67.8
	Judith E. Belcher (D)	78,115	32.2

ARKANSAS

		Votes	%
1	Bill Alexander (D)		100.0
2	Tommy F. Robinson (D)	168,889	83.5
	Warren D. Carpenter (R)	33,475	16.5
3	John Paul Hammerschmidt (R)	161,623	74.7
	David Stewart (D)	54,767	25.3
4	Beryl Anthony Jr. (D)	129,508	69.2
	Roger N. Bell (R)	57,658	30.8

CALIFORNIA

		Votes	%
1	Douglas H. Bosco (D)	159,815	62.9
	Samuel "Mark" Vanderbilt (R)	72,189	28.4
	Eric Fried (PFP)	22,150	8.7
2	Wally Herger (R)	139,010	58.8
	Wayne Meyer (D)	91,088	38.5
3	Robert T. Matsui (D)	183,470	71.2
	Lowell P. Landowski (R)	74,296	28.8
4	Vic Fazio (D)	181,184	99.3
5	Nancy Pelosi (D)	133,530	76.4
	Bruce Michael O'Neill (R)	33,692	19.3
6	Barbara Boxer (D)	176,645	73.4
	William Steinmetz (R)	64,174	26.6
7	George Miller (D)	170,006	68.4
	Jean Last (R)	78,478	31.6
8	Ronald V. Dellums (D)	163,221	66.6
	John J. Cuddihy Jr. (R)	76,531	31.2
9	Pete Stark (D)	152,866	73.0
	Howard Hertz (R)	56,656	27.0
10	Don Edwards (D)	142,500	86.2
	Kennita Watson (LIBERT)	22,801	13.8
11	Tom Lantos (D)	145,484	71.0
	G. M. "Bill" Quraishi (R)	50,050	24.4
12	Tom Campbell (R)	136,384	51.7
	Anna G. Eshoo (D)	121,523	46.0
13	Norman Y. Mineta (D)	143,980	67.1

Candidates	Votes	%
Luke Sommer (R)	63,959	29.8
14 Norman D. Shumway (R)	173,876	62.6
Patricia Malberg (D)	103,899	37.4
15 Tony Coelho (D)	118,710	69.7
Carol Harner (R)	47,957	28.2
16 Leon E. Panetta (D)	177,452	78.6
Stanley Monteith (R)	48,375	21.4
17 Charles Pashayan Jr. (R)	129,568	71.5
Vincent Lavery (D)	51,730	28.5
18 Richard H. Lehman (D)	125,715	69.9
David A. Linn (R)	54,034	30.1
19 Robert J. Lagomarsino (R)	116,026	50.2
Gary K. Hart (D)	112,033	48.5
20 William M. Thomas (R)	162,779	71.1
Lita Reid (D)	62,037	27.1
21 Elton Gallegly (R)	181,413	69.1
Donald E. Stevens (D)	75,739	28.8
22 Carlos J. Moorhead (R)	164,699	69.5
John G. Simmons (D)	61,555	26.0
23 Anthony C. Beilenson (D)	147,858	63.5
Jim Salomon (R)	77,184	33.1
24 Henry A. Waxman (D)	112,038	72.3
John N. Cowles (R)	36,835	23.7
25 Edward R. Roybal (D)	85,378	85.5
Raul Reyes (PFP)	8,746	8.8
John C. Thie (LIBERT)	5,752	5.8
26 Howard L. Berman (D)	126,930	70.3
G. C. "Brodie" Broderson (R)	53,518	29.7
27 Mel Levine (D)	148,814	67.5
Dennis Galbraith (R)	65,307	29.6
28 Julian C. Dixon (D)	109,801	76.1
George Z. Adams (R)	28,645	19.8
29 Augustus F. Hawkins (D)	88,169	82.8
Reuben D. Franco (R)	14,543	13.7
30 Matthew G. Martinez (D)	72,253	59.9
Ralph R. Ramirez (R)	43,833	36.3
31 Mervyn M. Dymally (D)	100,919	71.6
Arnold C. May (R)	36,017	25.5
32 Glenn M. Anderson (D)	114,666	66.9
Sanford W. Kahn (R)	50,710	29.6
33 David Dreier (R)	151,704	69.2
Nelson Gentry (D)	57,586	26.2
34 Esteban E. Torres (D)	92,087	63.2
Charles M. House (R)	50,954	35.0
35 Jerry Lewis (R)	181,203	70.4
Paul Sweeney (D)	71,186	27.7
36 George E. Brown Jr. (D)	103,493	54.0
John Paul Stark (R)	81,413	42.5
37 Al McCandless (R)	174,284	64.3
Johnny Pearson (D)	89,666	33.1
38 Robert K. Dornan (R)	87,690	59.5
Jerry Yudelson (D)	52,399	35.6
39 William E. Dannemeyer (R)	169,360	73.8
Don E. Marquis (D)	52,162	22.7
40 C. Christopher Cox (R)	181,269	67.0
Lida Lenney (D)	80,782	29.9
41 Bill Lowery (R)	187,380	65.6
Dan Kripke (D)	88,192	30.8
42 Dana Rohrabacher (R)	153,280	64.2
Guy C. Kimbrough (D)	78,778	33.0
43 Ron Packard (R)	202,478	71.7
Howard Greenebaum (D)	72,499	25.6
44 Jim Bates (D)	90,796	59.7
Rob Butterfield (R)	55,511	36.5
45 Duncan Hunter (R)	166,451	74.0
Pete Lepiscopo (D)	54,012	24.0

COLORADO

		Votes	%
1	Patricia Schroeder (D)	133,922	69.9
	Joy Wood (R)	57,587	30.1
2	David E. Skaggs (D)	147,437	62.7
	David Bath (R)	87,578	37.3
3	Ben Nighthorse Campbell (D)	169,284	78.0
	Jim Zartman (R)	47,625	22.0

Candidates	Votes	%
4 Hank Brown (R)	156,202	73.1
Charles S. Vigil (D)	57,552	26.9
5 Joel Hefley (R)	181,612	75.1
John J. Mitchell (D)	60,116	24.9
6 Dan Schaefer (R)	136,487	63.0
Martha M. Ezzard (D)	77,158	35.6

CONNECTICUT

		Votes	%
1	Barbara B. Kennelly (D)	176,463	77.2
	Mario Robles Jr. (R)	51,985	22.8
2	Sam Gejdenson (D)	143,326	63.6
	Glenn Carberry (R)	81,965	36.4
3	Bruce A. Morrison (D)	147,394	66.5
	Gerard B. Patton (R)	74,275	33.5
4	Christopher Shays (R)	147,843	71.8
	Roger Pearson (D)	55,751	27.1
5	John G. Rowland (R)	163,729	73.6
	Joseph Marinan Jr. (D)	58,612	26.4
6	Nancy L. Johnson (R)	157,020	66.3
	James L. Griffin (D)	78,814	33.3

DELAWARE

		Votes	%
AL	Thomas R. Carper (D)	158,338	67.5
	James P. Krapf Sr. (R)	76,179	32.5

FLORIDA

		Votes	%
1	Earl Hutto (D)	142,449	66.9
	E. D. Armbruster (R)	70,534	33.1
2	Bill Grant (D)	134,269	99.7
3	Charles E. Bennett (D)		100.0
4	Craig T. James (R)	125,608	50.2
	Bill Chappell Jr. (D)	124,817	49.8
5	Bill McCollum (R)		100.0
6	Cliff Stearns (R)	136,415	53.5
	Jon Mills (D)	118,756	46.5
7	Sam Gibbons (D)		100.0
8	C. W. Bill Young (R)	169,165	73.0
	C. Bette Wimbish (D)	62,539	27.0
9	Michael Bilirakis (R)	223,925	99.9
10	Andy Ireland (R)	156,563	73.5
	David B. Higginbottom (D)	56,536	26.5
11	Bill Nelson (D)	168,390	60.8
	Bill Tolley (R)	108,373	39.2
12	Tom Lewis (R)		100.0
13	Porter J. Goss (R)	231,170	71.2
	Jack Conway (D)	93,700	28.8
14	Harry A. Johnston (D)	173,292	54.9
	Ken Adams (R)	142,635	45.1
15	E. Clay Shaw Jr. (R)	132,090	66.1
	Michael A. "Mike" Kuhle (D)	67,746	33.9
16	Lawrence J. Smith (D)	153,032	69.4
	Joseph Smith (R)	67,461	30.6
17	William Lehman (D)		100.0
18	Claude Pepper (D)		100.0
19	Dante B. Fascell (D)	135,355	72.4
	Ralph Carlos Rocheteau (R)	51,628	27.6

GEORGIA

		Votes	%
1	Lindsay Thomas (D)	94,531	67.0
	Chris Meredith (R)	46,552	33.0
2	Charles Hatcher (D)	85,029	61.7
	Ralph T. Hudgens (R)	52,807	38.3
3	Richard Ray (D)	97,663	100.0
4	Ben Jones (D)	148,394	60.3
	Pat Swindall (R)	97,745	39.7
5	John Lewis (D)	135,194	78.2
	J. W. Tibbs Jr. (R)	37,693	21.8
6	Newt Gingrich (R)	110,169	58.9
	David Worley (D)	76,824	41.1
7	George "Buddy" Darden (D)	135,056	64.8

Candidates	Votes	%
Robert Lamutt (R)	73,425	35.2
8 J. Roy Rowland (D)	102,696	100.0
9 Ed Jenkins (D)	121,800	62.9
Joe Hoffman (R)	71,905	37.1
10 Doug Barnard Jr. (D)	118,156	64.0
Mark Myers (R)	66,521	36.0

HAWAII

Candidates	Votes	%
1 Patricia Saiki (R)	96,848	54.7
Mary Bitterman (D)	76,394	43.2
2 Daniel K. Akaka (D)	144,802	88.9
Lloyd "Jeff" Mallan (LIBERT)	18,006	11.1

IDAHO

Candidates	Votes	%
1 Larry E. Craig (R)	135,221	65.8
Jeanne Givens (D)	70,328	34.2
2 Richard H. Stallings (D)	127,956	63.4
Dane Watkins (R)	68,226	33.8

ILLINOIS

Candidates	Votes	%
1 Charles A. Hayes (D)	164,125	96.0
2 Gus Savage (D)	138,256	82.7
William T. Hespel (R)	28,831	17.3
3 Marty Russo (D)	132,111	62.2
Joseph J. McCarthy (R)	80,181	37.8
4 George E. Sangmeister (D)	91,282	50.3
Jack Davis (R)	90,243	49.7
5 William O. Lipinski (D)	93,567	61.3
John J. Holowinski (R)	59,128	38.7
6 Henry J. Hyde (R)	153,425	73.7
William J. Andrle (D)	54,804	26.3
7 Cardiss Collins (D)	135,331	100.0
8 Dan Rostenkowski (D)	107,728	74.6
V. Stephen Vetter (R)	34,659	24.0
9 Sidney R. Yates (D)	135,583	66.1
Herbert Sohn (R)	67,604	32.9
10 John Edward Porter (R)	158,519	72.5
Eugene F. Friedman (D)	60,187	27.5
11 Frank Annunzio (D)	131,753	64.5
George S. Gottlieb (R)	72,489	35.5
12 Philip M. Crane (R)	165,913	75.2
John A. Leonardi (D)	54,769	24.8
13 Harris W. Fawell (R)	174,992	70.2
Evelyn E. Craig (D)	74,424	29.8
14 Dennis Hastert (R)	161,146	73.7
Stephen Youhanaie (D)	57,482	26.3
15 Edward R. Madigan (R)	140,171	71.7
Thomas J. "Tom" Curl (D)	55,260	28.3
16 Lynn Martin (R)	128,365	63.9
Steven E. Mahan (D)	72,431	36.1
17 Lane Evans (D)	132,130	64.9
William E. Stewart (R)	71,560	35.1
18 Robert H. Michel (R)	114,458	54.7
G. Douglas Stephens (D)	94,763	45.3
19 Terry L. Bruce (D)	132,889	64.2
Robert F. Kerans (R)	73,981	35.8
20 Richard J. Durbin (D)	153,341	68.9
Paul E. Jurgens (R)	69,303	31.1
21 Jerry F. Costello (D)	105,836	52.6
Robert H. Gaffner (R)	95,385	47.4
22 Glenn Poshard (D)	139,392	64.9
Patrick J. Kelley (R)	75,462	35.1

Special Election [1]

	Votes	%
21 Jerry F. Costello (D)	33,144	51.5
Robert H. Gaffner (R)	31,257	48.5

INDIANA

Candidates	Votes	%
1 Peter J. Visclosky (D)	138,251	77.1
Owen W. Crumpacker (R)	41,076	22.9
2 Philip R. Sharp (D)	116,915	53.2
Mike Pence (R)	102,846	46.8
3 John Hiler (R)	116,309	54.3

Candidates	Votes	%
Thomas W. Ward (D)	97,934	45.7
4 Daniel R. Coats (R)	132,843	62.1
Jill Long (D)	80,915	37.9
5 Jim Jontz (D)	116,240	56.3
Patricia L. Williams (R)	90,163	43.7
6 Dan Burton (R)	192,064	72.9
George Thomas Holland (D)	71,447	27.1
7 John T. Myers (R)	130,578	61.8
Mark Richard Waterfill (D)	80,738	38.2
8 Frank McCloskey (D)	141,355	61.8
John L. Myers (R)	87,321	38.2
9 Lee H. Hamilton (D)	147,193	70.7
Floyd Eugene Coates (R)	60,946	29.3
10 Andrew Jacobs Jr. (D)	105,846	60.5
James C. Cummings (R)	68,978	39.5

IOWA

Candidates	Votes	%
1 Jim Leach (R)	112,746	60.7
Bill Gluba (D)	71,280	38.4
2 Tom Tauke (R)	113,543	56.8
Eric Tabor (D)	86,438	43.2
3 Dave Nagle (D)	129,204	63.4
Donald B. Redfern (R)	74,682	36.6
4 Neal Smith (D)	157,065	71.6
Paul Lunde (R)	62,056	28.3
5 Jim Ross Lightfoot (R)	117,761	63.9
Gene Freund (D)	66,599	36.1
6 Fred Grandy (R)	125,859	64.4
Dave O'Brien (D)	69,614	35.6

KANSAS

Candidates	Votes	%
1 Pat Roberts (R)	168,700	100.0
2 Jim Slattery (D)	135,694	73.3
Phil Meinhardt (R)	49,498	26.7
3 Jan Meyers (R)	150,223	73.6
Lionel Kunst (D)	53,959	26.4
4 Dan Glickman (D)	122,777	64.0
Lee Thompson (R)	69,165	36.0
5 Bob Whittaker (R)	127,722	70.2
John A. Barnes (D)	54,327	29.8

KENTUCKY

Candidates	Votes	%
1 Carroll Hubbard Jr. (D)	117,288	95.0
2 William H. Natcher (D)	92,184	60.6
Martin A. Tori (R)	59,907	39.4
3 Romano L. Mazzoli (D)	131,981	69.7
Philip Dunnagan (R)	57,387	30.3
4 Jim Bunning (R)	145,609	74.2
Richard V. Beliles (D)	50,575	25.8
5 Harold Rogers (R)	104,467	100.0
6 Larry J. Hopkins (R)	128,898	74.0
Milton Patton (D)	45,339	26.0
7 Carl C. Perkins (D)	96,946	58.7
Will T. Scott (R)	68,165	41.3

LOUISIANA [2]

Candidates	Votes	%
1 Robert L. Livingston (R)		100.0
2 Lindy (Mrs. Hale) Boggs (D)		100.0
3 W. J. "Billy" Tauzin (D)		100.0
4 Jim McCrery (R)		100.0
5 Jerry Huckaby (D)		100.0
6 Richard H. Baker (R)		100.0
7 Jimmy Hayes (D)		100.0
8 Clyde C. Holloway (R)	116,241	56.8
Faye Williams (D)	88,564	43.2

Special Election [3]

	Votes	%
4 Jim McCrery (R)	63,590	50.5
Foster Campbell (D)	62,214	49.5

MAINE

Candidates	Votes	%
1 Joseph E. Brennan (D)	190,989	63.2
Edward S. O'Meara Jr. (R)	111,125	36.8
2 Olympia J. Snowe (R)	167,229	66.2
Kenneth P. Hayes (D)	85,346	33.8

MARYLAND

	Votes	%
1 Roy Dyson (D)	96,128	50.4
Wayne T. Gilchrest (R)	94,588	49.6
2 Helen Delich Bentley (R)	157,956	71.5
Joseph Bartenfelder (D)	63,114	28.5
3 Benjamin L. Cardin (D)	133,779	72.9
Ross Z. Pierpont (R)	49,733	27.1
4 Tom McMillen (D)	128,624	68.3
Bradlyn McClanahan (R)	59,688	31.7
5 Steny H. Hoyer (D)	128,437	78.6
John Eugene Sellner (R)	34,909	21.4
6 Beverly B. Byron (D)	166,753	75.4
Kenneth W. Halsey (R)	54,528	24.6
7 Kweisi Mfume (D)	117,650	100.0
8 Constance A. Morella (R)	172,619	62.7
Peter Franchot (D)	102,478	37.3

MASSACHUSETTS

	Votes	%
1 Silvio O. Conte (R)	186,356	82.7
John R. Arden (D)	38,907	17.3
2 Richard E. Neal (D)	156,262	80.2
Louis R. Godena (I)	38,446	19.7
3 Joseph D. Early (D)	191,005	99.8
4 Barney Frank (D)	169,729	70.3
Debra R. Tucker (R)	71,661	29.7
5 Chester G. Atkins (D)	181,860	84.1
T. David Hudson (LIBERT)	34,339	15.9
6 Nicholas Mavroules (D)	177,643	69.6
Paul McCarthy (R)	77,186	30.3
7 Edward J. Markey (D)	188,647	100.0
8 Joseph P. Kennedy II (D)	165,745	80.4
Glenn W. Fiscus (R)	40,316	19.6
9 Joe Moakley (D)	160,799	99.8
10 Gerry E. Studds (D)	187,178	66.7
Jon L. Bryan (R)	93,564	33.3
11 Brian J. Donnelly (D)	169,692	80.8
Michael C. Gilleran (R)	40,277	19.2

MICHIGAN

	Votes	%
1 John Conyers Jr. (D)	127,800	91.2
Bill Ashe (R)	10,979	7.8
2 Carl D. Pursell (R)	120,070	54.7
Lana Pollack (D)	98,290	44.7
3 Howard Wolpe (D)	112,605	57.3
Cal Allgaier (R)	83,769	42.7
4 Fred Upton (R)	132,270	70.8
Norman J. Rivers (D)	54,428	29.2
5 Paul B. Henry (R)	166,569	72.6
James M. Catchick (D)	62,868	27.4
6 Bob Carr (D)	120,581	58.9
Scott Schultz (R)	81,079	39.6
7 Dale E. Kildee (D)	150,832	75.8
Jeff Coad (R)	47,071	23.6
8 Bob Traxler (D)	139,904	72.1
Lloyd F. Buhl (R)	54,195	27.9
9 Guy Vander Jagt (R)	149,748	69.8
David John Gawron (D)	64,843	30.2
10 Bill Schuette (R)	152,646	72.7
Mathias G. Forbes (D)	55,398	26.4
11 Robert W. Davis (R)	129,085	59.6
Mitch Irwin (D)	86,526	40.0
12 David E. Bonior (D)	108,158	53.6
Douglas Carl (R)	91,780	45.5
13 George W. Crockett Jr. (D)	99,751	87.0
John Wright Savage II (R)	13,196	11.5
14 Dennis M. Hertel (D)	111,612	62.6
Kenneth C. McNealy (R)	64,750	36.3
15 William D. Ford (D)	104,596	63.8
Burl C. Adkins (R)	56,963	34.8

Footnotes, see p. 301.

	Candidates	Votes	%
16	John D. Dingell (D)	132,775	97.4
17	Sander M. Levin (D)	135,493	70.2
	Dennis M. Flessland (R)	55,197	28.6
18	William S. Broomfield (R)	195,579	76.0
	Gary L. Kohut (D)	57,643	22.4

MINNESOTA [4]

		Votes	%
1	Timothy J. Penny (DFL)	161,118	70.1
	Curt Schrimpf (I-R)	67,709	29.5
2	Vin Weber (I-R)	131,639	57.8
	Doug Peterson (DFL)	96,016	42.2
3	Bill Frenzel (I-R)	215,322	68.2
	Dave Carlson (DFL)	99,770	31.6
4	Bruce F. Vento (DFL)	181,227	72.4
	Ian Maitland (I-R)	67,073	26.8
5	Martin Olav Sabo (DFL)	174,416	72.1
	Raymond C. Gilbertson (I-R)	60,646	25.1
6	Gerry Sikorski (DFL)	169,486	65.4
	Ray Ploetz (I-R)	89,209	34.4
7	Arlan Stangeland (I-R)	121,396	54.6
	Marv Hanson (DFL)	101,011	45.4
8	James L. Oberstar (DFL)	165,656	74.5
	Jerry Shuster (I-R)	56,630	25.5

MISSISSIPPI

		Votes	%
1	Jamie L. Whitten (D)	137,445	78.2
	Jim Bush (R)	38,381	21.8
2	Mike Espy (D)	112,401	64.7
	Jack Coleman (R)	59,827	34.5
3	G. V. "Sonny" Montgomery (D)	164,651	88.8
	Jimmie Ray Bourland (R)	20,729	11.2
4	Mike Parker (D)	110,184	54.8
	Thomas Collins (R)	88,433	44.0
5	Larkin Smith (R)	100,185	55.0
	Gene Taylor (D)	82,034	45.0

MISSOURI

		Votes	%
1	William L. Clay (D)	140,751	71.6
	Joseph A. Schwan (R)	53,109	27.0
2	Jack Buechner (R)	186,450	66.3
	Bob Feigenbaum (D)	91,645	32.6
3	Richard A. Gephardt (D)	150,205	62.8
	Mark F. "Thor" Hearne (R)	86,763	36.3
4	Ike Skelton (D)	166,480	71.8
	David Eyerly (R)	65,393	28.2
5	Alan Wheat (D)	149,166	70.3
	Mary Ellen Lobb (R)	60,453	28.5
6	E. Thomas Coleman (R)	135,883	59.3
	Doug R. Hughes (D)	93,128	40.7
7	Mel Hancock (R)	127,939	53.1
	Max E. Bacon (D)	111,244	46.2
8	Bill Emerson (R)	117,601	58.1
	Wayne Cryts (D)	84,801	41.9
9	Harold L. Volkmer (D)	160,872	67.9
	Ken Dudley (R)	76,008	32.1

MONTANA

		Votes	%
1	Pat Williams (D)	115,278	60.8
	Jim Fenlason (R)	74,405	39.2
2	Ron Marlenee (R)	97,465	55.5
	Richard "Buck" O'Brien (D)	78,069	44.5

NEBRASKA

		Votes	%
1	Doug Bereuter (R)	146,231	66.9
	Corky Jones (D)	72,167	33.0
2	Peter Hoagland (D)	112,174	50.5
	Jerry Schenken (R)	109,193	49.1
3	Virginia Smith (R)	170,302	79.0
	John D. Racek (D)	45,183	21.0

NEVADA

	Candidates	Votes	%
1	James H. Bilbray (D)	101,764	64.0
	Lucille Lusk (R)	53,588	33.7
2	Barbara F. Vucanovich (R)	105,981	57.3
	James Spoo (D)	75,163	40.6

NEW HAMPSHIRE

		Votes	%
1	Robert C. Smith (R)	131,824	60.3
	Joseph F. Keefe (D)	86,623	39.6
2	Chuck Douglas (R)	119,742	56.8
	James W. Donchess (D)	89,677	42.5

NEW JERSEY

		Votes	%
1	James J. Florio (D)	141,988	69.9
	Frank A. Cristaudo (R)	60,037	29.5
2	William J. Hughes (D)	134,505	65.7
	Kirk W. Conover (R)	67,759	33.1
3	Frank Pallone Jr. (D)	117,024	51.6
	Joseph Azzolina (R)	107,479	47.4
4	Christopher H. Smith (R)	155,283	65.7
	Betty Holland (D)	79,006	33.4
5	Marge Roukema (R)	175,562	75.7
	Lee Monaco (D)	54,828	23.6
6	Bernard J. Dwyer (D)	120,125	61.1
	Peter J. Sica (R)	74,824	38.1
7	Matthew J. Rinaldo (R)	153,350	74.6
	James Hely (D)	52,189	25.4
8	Robert A. Roe (D)	96,036	100.0
9	Robert G. Torricelli (D)	142,012	67.1
	Roger J. Lane (R)	68,363	32.3
10	Donald M. Payne (D)	84,681	77.4
	Michael Webb (R)	13,848	12.6
	Anthony Imperiale (I)	5,422	5.0
11	Dean A. Gallo (R)	154,654	70.5
	John C. Shaw (D)	64,773	29.5
12	Jim Courter (R)	165,918	69.3
	Norman J. Weinstein (D)	71,596	29.9
13	H. James Saxton (R)	167,470	69.5
	James B. Smith (D)	73,561	30.5
14	Frank J. Guarini (D)	104,001	67.3
	Fred J. Theemling Jr. (R)	47,293	30.6

Special Election [5]

		Votes	%
3	Frank Pallone Jr. (D)	116,988	52.0
	Joseph Azzolina (R)	106,489	47.3

NEW MEXICO

		Votes	%
1	Steven H. Schiff (R)	89,985	50.6
	Tom Udall (D)	84,138	47.3
2	Joe Skeen (R)	100,324	100.0
3	Bill Richardson (D)	124,938	73.1
	Cecilia M. Salazar (R)	45,954	26.9

NEW YORK

		Votes	%
1	George J. Hochbrueckner (D)	105,624	50.8
	Edward P. Romaine (R, C, RTL)	102,327	49.2
2	Thomas J. Downey (D)	107,646	61.6
	Joseph Cardino Jr. (R, C, RTL)	66,972	38.4
3	Robert J. Mrazek (D)	128,336	57.2
	Robert Previdi (R, C)	91,122	40.6
4	Norman F. Lent (R, C)	151,038	70.1
	Francis T. Goban (D, L)	59,479	27.6
5	Raymond J. McGrath (R, C)	134,881	65.1
	William G. Kelly (D)	68,930	33.2
6	Floyd H. Flake (D, L)	94,506	85.9
	Robert L. Brandofino (C)	15,547	14.1
7	Gary L. Ackerman (D, L)	93,120	100.0
8	James H. Scheuer (D, L)	100,240	100.0
9	Thomas J. Manton (D)	72,851	100.0
10	Charles E. Schumer (D, L)	107,056	78.4
	George S. Popielarski (R)	24,313	17.8

	Candidates	Votes	%
11	Edolphus Towns (D, L)	73,755	88.7
	Riaz B. Hussain (R)	7,418	8.9
12	Major R. Owens (D, L)	74,304	93.0
	Owen Augustin (R, C)	5,582	7.0
13	Stephen J. Solarz (D, L)	81,305	74.7
	Anthony M. Curci (R, C)	27,536	25.3
14	Guy V. Molinari (R, C, RTL)	99,179	63.3
	Jerome X. O'Donovan (D)	57,503	36.7
15	Bill Green (R)	107,599	61.3
	Peter G. Doukas (D)	64,425	36.7
16	Charles B. Rangel (D, R, L)	107,620	97.1
17	Ted Weiss (D, L)	157,339	84.4
	Myrna C. Albert (R, C)	29,156	15.6
18	Robert Garcia (D, L)	75,459	91.1
	Fred Brown (R)	5,764	6.9
19	Eliot L. Engel (D, L)	77,158	56.0
	Mario Biaggi (D)	37,454	27.2
	Martin J. O'Grady (RTL)	11,271	8.2
	Robert Blumetti (C)	11,182	8.1
20	Nita M. Lowey (D)	102,235	50.3
	Joseph J. DioGuardi (R, C)	96,465	47.5
21	Hamilton Fish Jr. (R, C)	150,443	74.6
	Lawrence D. Grunberger (D)	47,294	23.5
22	Benjamin A. Gilman (R)	144,227	70.8
	Eleanor F. Burlingham (D)	54,312	26.7
23	Michael R. McNulty (D)	145,040	61.7
	Peter M. Bakal (R, C)	89,858	38.3
24	Gerald B. H. Solomon (R, C, RTL)	162,962	72.4
	Fred Baye (D)	62,177	27.6
25	Sherwood Boehlert (R)	130,122	100.0
26	David O'B. Martin (R, C)	131,043	75.0
	Donald R. Ravenscroft (D)	43,585	25.0
27	James T. Walsh (R)	124,928	57.5
	Rosemary S. Pooler (D)	90,854	41.8
28	Matthew F. McHugh (D)	141,976	93.2
	Mary C. Dixon (RTL)	10,395	6.8
29	Frank Horton (R)	132,608	68.8
	James R. Vogel (D)	51,243	26.6
30	Louise M. Slaughter (D)	128,364	56.9
	John D. Bouchard (R)	89,126	39.5
31	Bill Paxon (R, C, RTL)	117,710	53.4
	David J. Swarts (D)	102,777	46.6
32	John J. LaFalce (D, L)	133,917	72.7
	Emil K. Everett (R, C, RTL)	50,229	27.3
33	Henry J. Nowak (D, L)	139,604	100.0
34	Amo Houghton (R, C)	131,078	96.5

NORTH CAROLINA

		Votes	%
1	Walter B. Jones (D)	118,027	65.2
	Howard Moye (R)	63,013	34.8
2	Tim Valentine (D)	128,832	100.0
3	H. Martin Lancaster (D)	95,323	100.0
4	David E. Price (D)	131,896	58.0
	Tom Fetzer (R)	95,482	42.0
5	Stephen L. Neal (D)	110,516	52.6
	Lyons Gray (R)	99,540	47.4
6	Howard Coble (R)	116,534	62.5
	Tom Gilmore (D)	70,008	37.5
7	Charlie Rose (D)	102,392	67.3
	George "Jerry" Thompson (R)	49,855	32.7
8	W. G. "Bill" Hefner (D)	99,214	51.5
	Ted Blanton (R)	93,463	48.5
9	Alex McMillan (R)	139,014	65.9
	Mark Sholander (D)	71,802	34.1
10	Cass Ballenger (R)	112,554	61.0
	Jack L. Rhyne (D)	71,865	39.0
11	James McClure Clarke (D)	108,436	50.4
	Charles H. Taylor (R)	106,907	49.6

NORTH DAKOTA

		Votes	%
AL	Byron L. Dorgan (D)	212,583	70.9
	Steve Sydness (R)	84,475	28.1

OHIO

	Candidates	Votes	%
1	Thomas A. Luken (D)	117,682	56.5
	Steve Chabot (R)	90,738	43.5
2	Bill Gradison (R)	153,162	72.3
	Chuck R. Stidham (D)	58,637	27.7
3	Tony P. Hall (D)	141,953	76.9
	Ron Crutcher (R)	42,664	23.1
4	Michael G. Oxley (R)	160,099	99.7
5	Paul E. Gillmor (R)	123,838	60.7
	Tom Murray (D)	80,292	39.3
6	Bob McEwen (R)	152,235	74.3
	Gordon Roberts (D)	52,635	25.7
7	Michael DeWine (R)	142,597	73.9
	Jack Schira (D)	50,423	26.1
8	Donald E. Lukens (R)	154,164	75.9
	John W. Griffin (D)	49,084	24.1
9	Marcy Kaptur (D)	157,557	81.3
	Al Hawkins (R)	36,183	18.7
10	Clarence E. Miller (R)	143,673	71.6
	John M. Buchanan (D)	56,893	28.4
11	Dennis E. Eckart (D)	124,600	61.5
	Margaret Mueller (R)	78,028	38.5
12	John R. Kasich (R)	154,727	79.0
	Mark P. Brown (D)	41,178	21.0
13	Don J. Pease (D)	137,074	69.8
	Dwight Brown (R)	59,287	30.2
14	Thomas C. Sawyer (D)	148,951	74.7
	Loretta A. Lang (R)	50,356	25.3
15	Chalmers P. Wylie (R)	146,854	74.8
	Mark S. Froehlich (D)	49,441	25.2
16	Ralph Regula (R)	158,824	78.6
	Melvin J. Gravely (D)	43,356	21.4
17	James A. Traficant Jr. (D)	162,526	77.2
	Frederick W. Lenz (R)	47,929	22.8
18	Douglas Applegate (D)	151,306	76.6
	William C. Abraham (R)	46,130	23.4
19	Edward F. Feighan (D)	168,065	70.5
	Noel F. Roberts (R)	70,359	29.5
20	Mary Rose Oakar (D)	146,715	82.6
	Michael Sajna (R)	30,944	17.4
21	Louis Stokes (D)	148,388	85.7
	Franklin H. Roski (R)	24,804	14.3

OKLAHOMA

	Candidates	Votes	%
1	James M. Inhofe (R)	103,458	52.6
	Kurt Glassco (D)	93,101	47.4
2	Mike Synar (D)	136,009	64.9
	Ira Phillips (R)	73,659	35.1
3	Wes Watkins (D)		100.0
4	Dave McCurdy (D)		100.0
5	Mickey Edwards (R)	139,182	72.2
	Terry J. Montgomery (D)	53,668	27.8
6	Glenn English (D)	122,887	73.1
	Mike Brown (R)	45,239	26.9

OREGON

	Candidates	Votes	%
1	Les AuCoin (D)	179,915	69.6
	Earl Molander (R)	78,626	30.4
2	Robert F. Smith (R)	125,366	62.7
	Larry Tuttle (D)	74,700	37.3
3	Ron Wyden (D)	190,684	99.4
4	Peter A. DeFazio (D)	108,483	72.0
	Jim Howard (R)	42,220	28.0
5	Denny Smith (R)	111,489	50.2
	Mike Kopetski (D)	110,782	49.8

PENNSYLVANIA

	Candidates	Votes	%
1	Thomas M. Foglietta (D)	128,076	76.3
	William J. O'Brien (R)	39,749	23.7
2	William H. Gray III (D)	184,322	93.7
	Richard L. Harsch (R)	12,365	6.3
3	Robert A. Borski (D)	135,590	63.2
	Mark Matthews (R)	78,909	36.8
4	Joe Kolter (D)	124,041	69.8
	Gordon R. Johnston (R)	52,402	29.5
5	Richard T. Schulze (R)	153,453	78.2
	Donald A. Hadley (D)	42,758	21.8
6	Gus Yatron (D)	114,119	63.1
	James R. Erwin (R)	65,278	36.1
7	Curt Weldon (R)	155,387	67.8
	David Landau (D)	73,745	32.2
8	Peter H. Kostmayer (D)	128,153	56.8
	Ed Howard (R)	93,648	41.5
9	Bud Shuster (R, D)	158,702	100.0
10	Joseph M. McDade (R)	140,096	73.2
	Robert C. Cordaro (D)	51,179	26.8
11	Paul E. Kanjorski (D)	120,706	100.0
12	John P. Murtha (D)	133,081	100.0
13	Lawrence Coughlin (R)	152,191	66.6
	Bernard Tomkin (D)	76,424	33.4
14	William J. Coyne (D)	135,181	78.6
	Richard Edward Caligiuri (D)	36,719	21.4
15	Don Ritter (R)	106,951	57.5
	Ed Reibman (D)	79,127	42.5
16	Robert S. Walker (R)	136,944	74.0
	Ernest Eric Guyll (D)	48,169	26.0
17	George W. Gekas (R, D)	166,289	100.0
18	Doug Walgren (D)	136,924	62.7
	John A. Newman (R)	80,975	37.0
19	Bill Goodling (R)	145,381	77.2
	Paul E. Ritchey (D)	42,819	22.8
20	Joseph M. Gaydos (D)	137,472	98.5
21	Tom Ridge (R)	141,832	78.7
	George R. H. Elder (D)	38,288	21.3
22	Austin J. Murphy (D)	123,428	72.4
	William Hodgkiss (R)	47,039	27.6
23	William F. Clinger Jr. (R)	105,575	62.0
	Howard Shakespeare (D)	63,476	37.3

RHODE ISLAND

	Candidates	Votes	%
1	Ronald K. Machtley (R)	105,506	55.6
	Fernand J. St Germain (D)	84,141	44.4
2	Claudine Schneider (R)	145,218	72.1
	Ruth S. Morgenthau (D)	56,129	27.9

SOUTH CAROLINA

	Candidates	Votes	%
1	Arthur Ravenel Jr. (R)	101,572	63.8
	Wheeler Tillman (D)	57,691	36.2
2	Floyd D. Spence (R)	94,960	52.8
	Jim Leventis (D)	83,978	46.6
3	Butler Derrick (D)	89,071	53.7
	Henry S. Jordan (R)	75,571	45.6
4	Liz J. Patterson (D)	90,234	52.2
	Knox White (R)	82,793	47.8
5	John M. Spratt Jr. (D)	107,959	69.8
	Robert K. "Bob" Carley (R)	46,622	30.2
6	Robin Tallon (D)	120,719	76.1
	Robert Cunningham Sr. (R)	37,958	23.9

SOUTH DAKOTA

	Candidates	Votes	%
AL	Tim Johnson (D)	223,759	71.7
	David Volk (R)	88,157	28.3

TENNESSEE

	Candidates	Votes	%
1	James H. Quillen (R)	119,526	80.2
	Sidney S. Smith (D)	29,469	19.8
2	John J. Duncan (R)	99,631	56.2
	Dudley W. Taylor (D)	77,540	43.8
3	Marilyn Lloyd (D)	108,264	57.4
	Harold L. Coker (R)	80,372	42.6
4	Jim Cooper (D)	94,129	100.0
5	Bob Clement (D)	155,068	100.0
6	Bart Gordon (D)	123,652	76.5
	Wallace Embry (R)	38,033	23.5
7	Don Sundquist (R)	142,025	80.1
	Ken Bloodworth (D)	35,237	19.9
8	John Tanner (D)	94,571	62.4
	Ed Bryant (R)	56,893	37.6
9	Harold E. Ford (D)	126,280	81.6
	Isaac Richmond (I)	28,522	18.4

	Candidates	Votes	%
	Special Elections		
2	John J. "Jimmy" Duncan Jr. [6] (R)	92,929	56.1
	Dudley W. Taylor (D)	70,576	42.6
5	Bob Clement (D) [7]	56,323	62.2
	Terry Holcomb (R)	32,847	36.3

TEXAS

	Candidates	Votes	%
1	Jim Chapman (D)	122,566	62.2
	Horace McQueen (R)	74,357	37.8
2	Charles Wilson (D)	145,614	87.7
	Gary W. Nelson (LIBERT)	20,475	12.3
3	Steve Bartlett (R)	227,882	81.8
	Blake Cowden (D)	50,627	18.2
4	Ralph M. Hall (D)	139,379	66.4
	Randy Sutton (R)	67,337	32.1
5	John Bryant (D)	95,376	60.7
	Lon Williams (R)	59,877	38.1
6	Joe L. Barton (R)	164,692	67.6
	N. P. "Pat" Kendrick (D)	78,786	32.4
7	Bill Archer (R)	185,203	79.1
	Diane Richards (D)	48,824	20.9
8	Jack Fields (R)	90,503	100.0
9	Jack Brooks (D)	137,270	100.0
10	J. J. "Jake" Pickle (D)	232,213	93.4
	Vincent J. May (LIBERT)	16,281	6.6
11	Marvin Leath (D)	134,207	95.4
12	Jim Wright (D)	135,459	99.3
13	Bill Sarpalius (D)	98,345	52.5
	Larry S. Milner (R)	89,105	47.5
14	Greg H. Laughlin (D)	111,395	53.2
	Mac Sweeney (R)	96,042	45.9
15	E. "Kika" de la Garza (D)	93,672	93.9
	Gloria Joyce Hendrix (LIBERT)	6,133	6.1
16	Ronald D. Coleman (D)	104,514	100.0
17	Charles W. Stenholm (D)	149,064	100.0
18	Mickey Leland (D)	94,408	92.9
	J. Alejandro Snead (LIBERT)	7,235	7.1
19	Larry Combest (R)	113,068	67.7
	Gerald McCathern (D)	53,932	32.3
20	Henry B. Gonzalez (D)	94,527	70.7
	Lee Trevino (R)	36,801	27.5
21	Lamar Smith (R)	203,989	93.2
	James A. Robinson (LIBERT)	14,801	6.8
22	Thomas D. DeLay (R)	125,733	67.4
	Wayne Walker (D)	58,471	31.4
23	Albert G. Bustamante (D)	116,423	64.5
	Jerome L. Gonzales (R)	60,559	33.6
24	Martin Frost (D)	135,794	92.6
	Leo Sadovy (LIBERT)	10,841	7.4
25	Michael A. Andrews (D)	113,499	71.4
	George H. Loefflor Jr. (R)	44,043	27.7
26	Dick Armey (R)	194,944	69.3
	Jo Ann Reyes (D)	86,490	30.7
27	Solomon P. Ortiz (D)	105,085	100.0

UTAH

	Candidates	Votes	%
1	James V. Hansen (R)	130,893	59.8
	Gunn McKay (D)	87,976	40.2
2	Wayne Owens (D)	112,129	57.4
	Richard Snelgrove (R)	80,212	41.1
3	Howard C. Nielson (R)	129,951	66.8
	Robert W. Stringham (D)	60,018	30.9

VERMONT

	Candidates	Votes	%
AL	Peter Smith (R)	98,937	41.2
	Bernard Sanders (I)	90,026	37.5
	Paul N. Poirier (D)	45,330	18.9

VIRGINIA

	Candidates	Votes	%
1	Herbert H. Bateman (R)	135,937	73.3
	James S. Ellenson (D)	49,614	26.7
2	Owen B. Pickett (D)	106,666	60.5

Candidates	Votes	%
Jerry R. Curry (R)	62,564	35.5
Stephen P. Shao (I)	4,255	2.4
Robert A. Smith (I)	2,691	1.5
3 Thomas J. Bliley Jr. (R)	187,354	99.7
4 Norman Sisisky (D)	134,786	99.9
5 Lewis F. Payne Jr. (D)	97,242	54.2
Charles Hawkins (R)	78,396	43.7
6 Jim Olin (D)	118,369	63.9
Charles E. Judd (R)	66,935	36.1
7 D. French Slaughter Jr. (R)	136,988	99.6
8 Stan Parris (R)	154,761	62.3
David G. Brickley (D)	93,561	37.7
9 Rick Boucher (D)	113,309	63.4
John C. Brown (R)	65,410	36.6
10 Frank R. Wolf (R)	188,550	68.1
Robert L. Weinberg (D)	88,284	31.9

Special Election [8]

5 Lewis F. Payne Jr. (D)	55,469	59.3
Linda Arey (R)	38,063	40.7

WASHINGTON

1 John R. Miller (R)	152,265	55.4
Reese Lindquist (D)	122,646	44.6

Candidates	Votes	%
2 Al Swift (D)	175,191	100.0
3 Jolene Unsoeld (D)	109,412	50.1
Bill Wight (R)	108,794	49.9
4 Sid Morrison (R)	142,938	74.5
J. Richard Golob (D)	48,850	25.5
5 Thomas S. Foley (D)	160,654	76.4
Marlyn A. Derby (R)	49,657	23.6
6 Norm Dicks (D)	125,904	67.6
Kevin P. Cook (R)	60,346	32.4
7 Jim McDermott (D)	173,809	76.3
Robert Edwards (R)	53,902	23.7
8 Rod Chandler (R)	174,942	70.9
Jim Kean (D)	71,920	29.1

WEST VIRGINIA

1 Alan B. Mollohan (D)	119,256	74.5
Howard K. Tuck (R)	40,732	25.5
2 Harley O. Staggers Jr. (D)	118,356	100.0
3 Bob Wise (D)	120,192	74.3
Paul W. Hart (R)	41,478	25.7
4 Nick J. Rahall II (D)	78,812	61.3
Marianne R. Brewster (R)	49,753	38.7

WISCONSIN

Candidates	Votes	%
1 Les Aspin (D)	158,552	76.2
Bernie Weaver (R)	49,620	23.8
2 Robert W. Kastenmeier (D)	151,501	58.5
Ann J. Haney (R)	107,457	41.5
3 Steve Gunderson (R)	157,513	68.3
Karl E. Krueger (D)	72,935	31.6
4 Gerald D. Kleczka (D)	177,283	99.7
5 Jim Moody (D)	140,518	64.1
Helen Barnhill (R)	78,307	35.7
6 Thomas E. Petri (R)	165,923	74.2
Joe Garrett (D)	57,552	25.8
7 David R. Obey (D)	142,197	61.8
Kevin J. Hermening (R)	86,077	37.4
8 Toby Roth (R)	167,275	69.7
Robert Baron (D)	72,708	30.3
9 F. James Sensenbrenner Jr. (R)	185,093	74.9
Tom Hickey (D)	62,003	25.1

WYOMING

AL Dick Cheney (R)	118,350	66.6
Bryan Sharratt (D)	56,527	31.8

1988 Elections

1. A special election was held to fill the unexpired term of Rep. Melvin Price (D), who died April 22, 1988.

2. For the 1988 House elections in Louisiana, an open primary election was held with candidates from all parties running on the same ballot. Any candidate who received a majority was elected unopposed, with no further appearance on the general election ballot. If no candidate received 50 percent, a runoff was held between the two top finishers.

3. A special election was held to fill the unexpired term of Rep. Buddy Roemer (D), who resigned March 14, 1988, having been elected governor.

4. In Minnesota the Democratic Party is known as the Democratic-Farmer-Labor Party and the Republican Party as the Independent-Republican Party; candidates appear on the ballot with these designations.

5. A special election was held to fill the unexpired term of Rep. James J. Howard (D), who died March 25, 1988.

6. A special election was held to fill the unexpired term of Rep. John J. Duncan (R), who died June 21, 1988.

7. A special election was held to fill the unexpired term of Rep. Bill Bonor (D), who resigned Oct. 5, 1987, having been elected mayor of Nashville.

8. A special election was held to fill the unexpired term of Rep. W. C. Daniel (D), who died Jan. 23, 1988.

1989 House Elections

ALABAMA

Special Election [1]

Candidates	Votes	%
3 Glen Browder (D)	47,294	65.3
John Rice (R)	25,142	34.7

CALIFORNIA

Special Election [2]

	Votes	%
15 Gary Condit (D)	51,543	57.1
Clare Berryhill (R)	1,592	35.0

FLORIDA

Special Election [3]

	Votes	%
18 Ileana Ros-Lehtinen (R)	49,298	53.3
Gerald Richman (D)	43,274	46.7

INDIANA

Special Election [4]

	Votes	%
4 Jill L. Long (D)	65,272	50.7
Dan Heath (R)	63,494	49.3

MISSISSIPPI

Special Election [5]

Candidates	Votes	%
5 Gene Taylor (D)	51,561	42.0
Tom Anderson Jr. (R)	45,727	37.2
Mike Moore (D)	25,579	20.8

Special Runoff Election

	Votes	%
5 Gene Taylor (D)	83,296	65.2
Tom Anderson Jr. (R)	44,494	34.8

TEXAS [6]

Special Election [7]

	Votes	%
12 Bob Lanier (R)	21,978	39.4
Pete Geren (D)	17,751	31.8
Jim Lane (D)	12,308	22.1

Special Runoff Election

Candidates	Votes	%
12 Pete Geren (D)	40,210	51.0
Bob Lanier (R)	38,590	49.0

Special Election [8]

	Votes	%
18 Craig Washington (D)	27,367	41.3
Anthony Hall (D)	22,797	34.4
Ron Wilson (D)	4,948	7.5

Special Runoff Election

	Votes	%
18 Craig Washington (D)	24,140	56.6
Anthony Hall (D)	18,484	43.4

WYOMING

Special Election [9]

	Votes	%
AL Craig Thomas (R)	74,384	52.5
John P. Vinich (D)	60,845	43.0

1989 Elections

1. A special election was held to fill the unexpired term of Rep. Bill Nichols (D), who died Dec. 13, 1988.

2. A special election was held to fill the unexpired term of Rep. Tony Coelho (D), who resigned June 15, 1989.

3. A special election was held to fill the unexpired term of Rep. Claude Pepper (D), who died May 30, 1989.

4. A special election was held to fill the unexpired term of Rep. Daniel R. Coats (R), who resigned in January 1989, having been appointed to the U.S. Senate.

5. A special election was held to fill the unexpired term of Rep. Larkin Smith (R), who died

Aug. 15, 1989.

6. Texas election law required all candidates in special elections to run against each other, regardless of party. If no candidate received a majority, a special runoff election was held between the two candidates receiving the most votes in the special election.

7. A special election was held to fill the unexpired term of Rep. Jim Wright (D), who resigned June 30, 1989.

8. A special election was held to fill the unexpired term of Rep. Mickey Leland (D), who died Aug. 7, 1989.

9. A special election was held to fill the unexpired term of Rep. Dick Cheney (R), who resigned March 17, 1989, having been appointed defense secretary.

1990 House Elections

ALABAMA

	Candidates	Votes	%
1	Sonny Callahan (R)	82,185	99.6
2	Bill Dickinson (R)	87,649	51.3
	Faye Baggiano (D)	83,243	48.7
3	Glen Browder (D)	101,923	73.7
	Don Sledge (R)	36,317	26.3
4	Tom Bevill (D)	129,872	99.7
5	Robert E. "Bud" Cramer (D)	113,047	67.1
	Albert McDonald (R)	55,326	32.9
6	Ben Erdreich (D)	134,412	92.8
	David A. Alvarez (I)	8,640	6.0
7	Claude Harris (D)	127,490	70.5
	Michael D. Barker (R)	53,258	29.5

ALASKA

		Votes	%
AL	Don Young (R)	99,003	51.7
	John E. Devens (D)	91,677	47.8

ARIZONA

		Votes	%
1	John J. Rhodes III (R)	166,223	99.5
2	Morris K. Udall (D)	76,549	65.9
	Joseph D. Sweeney (R)	39,586	34.1
3	Bob Stump (R)	134,279	56.6
	Roger Hartstone (D)	103,018	43.4
4	Jon Kyl (R)	141,843	61.3
	Mark Ivey Jr. (D)	89,395	38.7
5	Jim Kolbe (R)	138,975	64.8
	Chuck Phillips (D)	75,642	35.2

ARKANSAS

		Votes	%
1	Bill Alexander (D)	101,026	64.3
	Terry Hayes (R)	56,071	35.7
2	Ray Thornton (D)	103,471	60.4
	Jim Keet (R)	67,800	39.6
3	John Paul Hammerschmidt (R)	129,876	70.5
	Dan Ivy (D)	54,332	29.5
4	Beryl Anthony Jr. (D)	110,365	72.4
	Roy Rood (R)	42,130	27.6

CALIFORNIA

		Votes	%
1	Frank Riggs (R)	99,782	43.3
	Douglas H. Bosco (D)	96,468	41.9
	Darlene G. Comingore (PF)	34,011	14.8
2	Wally Herger (R)	133,315	63.7
	Erwin E. "Bill" Rush (D)	65,333	31.2
	Ross Crain (LIBERT)	10,753	5.1
3	Robert T. Matsui (D)	132,143	60.3
	Lowell P. Landowski (D)	76,148	34.8
4	Vic Fazio (D)	115,090	54.7
	Mark Baughman (R)	82,738	39.3
	Bryce Bigwood (LIBERT)	12,626	6.0
5	Nancy Pelosi (D)	120,633	77.2
	Alan Nichols (R)	35,671	22.8
6	Barbara Boxer (D)	137,306	68.1
	Bill Boerum (R)	64,402	31.9
7	George Miller (D)	121,080	60.5
	Roger A. Payton (R)	79,031	39.5
8	Ronald V. Dellums (D)	119,645	61.3
	Barbara Galewski (R)	75,544	38.7
9	Pete Stark (D)	94,739	58.4
	Victor Romero (R)	67,412	41.6
10	Don Edwards (D)	81,875	62.7
	Mark Patrosso (R)	48,747	37.3
11	Tom Lantos (D)	105,029	65.9
	G. M. "Bill" Quraishi (R)	45,818	28.8
	June R. Genis (LIBERT)	8,518	5.3
12	Tom Campbell (R)	125,157	60.8
	Robert Palmer (D)	69,270	33.7

	Candidates	Votes	%
	Chuck Olson (LIBERT)	11,271	5.5
13	Norman Y. Mineta (D)	97,286	58.0
	David E. Smith (R)	59,773	35.7
	John H. Webster (LIBERT)	10,587	6.3
14	John T. Doolittle (R)	128,309	51.5
	Patricia Malberg (D)	120,742	48.5
15	Gary Condit (D)	97,147	66.2
	Cliff Burris (R)	49,634	33.8
16	Leon E. Panetta (D)	134,236	74.2
	Jerry M. Reiss (R)	39,885	22.0
17	Calvin Dooley (D)	82,611	54.5
	Charles Pashayan Jr. (R)	68,848	45.5
18	Richard H. Lehman (D)	98,804	100
19	Robert J. Lagomarsino (R)	94,599	54.6
	Anita Perez Ferguson (D)	76,991	44.4
20	William M. Thomas (R)	112,962	59.8
	Michael A. Thomas (D)	65,101	34.4
	William H. Dilbeck (LIBERT)	10,555	5.6
21	Elton Gallegly (R)	118,326	58.4
	Richard D. Freiman (D)	68,921	34.0
	Peggy Christensen (LIBERT)	15,364	7.6
22	Carlos J. Moorhead (R)	108,634	60.0
	David Bayer (D)	61,630	34.1
23	Anthony C. Beilenson (D)	103,141	61.7
	Jim Salomon (R)	57,118	34.2
24	Henry A. Waxman (D)	71,562	68.9
	John N. Cowles (R)	26,607	25.6
	Maggie Phair (PF)	5,706	5.5
25	Edward R. Roybal (D)	48,120	70.0
	Steven J. Renshaw (R)	17,021	24.8
	Robert H. Scott (LIBERT)	3,576	5.2
26	Howard L. Berman (D)	78,031	61.1
	Roy Dahlson (R)	44,492	34.8
27	Mel Levine (D)	90,857	58.2
	David Barrett Cohen (R)	58,140	37.2
28	Julian C. Dixon (D)	69,482	72.7
	George Z. Adams (R)	21,245	22.2
29	Maxine Waters (D)	51,350	79.4
	Bill DeWitt (R)	12,054	18.6
30	Matthew G. Martinez (D)	45,456	58.2
	Reuben D. Franco (R)	28,914	37.0
31	Mervyn M. Dymally (D)	56,394	67.1
	Eunice A. Sato (R)	27,593	32.9
32	Glenn M. Anderson (D)	68,268	61.5
	Sanford W. Kahn (R)	42,692	38.5
33	David Dreier (R)	101,336	63.7
	Georgia Houston Webb (D)	49,981	31.4
34	Esteban E. Torres (D)	55,646	60.7
	John Eastman (R)	36,024	39.3
35	Jerry Lewis (R)	121,602	60.6
	Barry Norton (D)	66,100	32.9
	Jerry Johnson (LIBERT)	13,020	6.5
36	George E. Brown Jr. (D)	72,409	52.7
	Robert Hammock (D)	64,961	47.3
37	Al McCandless (R)	115,469	49.7
	Ralph Waite (D)	103,961	44.8
38	Robert K. Dornan (R)	60,561	58.1
	Barbara Jackson (D)	43,693	41.9
39	William E. Dannemeyer (R)	113,849	65.3
	Francis X. Hoffman (D)	53,670	30.8
40	C. Christopher Cox (R)	142,299	67.6
	Eugene C. Gratz (D)	68,087	32.4
41	Bill Lowery (R)	105,723	49.2
	Dan Kripke (D)	93,586	43.6
	Karen S. R. Works (PF)	15,428	7.2
42	Dana Rohrabacher (R)	109,353	59.3
	Guy C. Kimbrough (D)	67,189	36.5
43	Ron Packard (R)	151,206	68.1
	Doug Hansen (PF)	40,212	18.1
	Richard L. Arnold (LIBERT)	30,720	13.8
44	Randy "Duke" Cunningham (R)	50,377	46.3
	Jim Bates (D)	48,712	44.8
45	Duncan Hunter (R)	123,591	72.8
	Joe Shea (LIBERT)	46,068	27.2

COLORADO

	Candidates	Votes	%
1	Patricia Schroeder (D)	82,176	63.7
	Gloria Gonzales Roemer (R)	46,802	36.3
2	David E. Skaggs (D)	105,248	60.7
	Jason Lewis (R)	68,226	39.3
3	Ben Nighthorse Campbell (D)	124,487	70.2
	Bob Ellis (R)	49,961	28.2
4	Wayne Allard (R)	89,285	54.1
	Dick Bond (D)	75,901	45.9
5	Joel Hefley (R)	127,740	66.4
	Cal Johnston (D)	57,776	30.0
6	Dan Schaefer (R)	105,312	64.5
	Don Jarrett (D)	57,961	35.5

CONNECTICUT

		Votes	%
1	Barbara B. Kennelly (D)	126,566	71.4
	James M. Garvey (R)	50,690	28.6
2	Sam Gejdenson (D)	105,085	59.7
	John M. Ragsdale (R)	70,922	40.3
3	Rosa DeLauro (D)	90,772	52.1
	Thomas Scott (R)	83,440	47.9
4	Christopher Shays (R)	105,682	76.5
	Al Smith (D)	32,352	23.4
5	Gary Franks (R)	93,912	51.7
	Toby Moffett (D)	85,803	47.2
6	Nancy L. Johnson (R)	141,105	74.4
	Paul Kulas (D)	48,628	25.6

DELAWARE

		Votes	%
AL	Thomas R. Carper (D)	116,274	65.5
	Ralph O. Williams (R)	58,037	32.7

FLORIDA

		Votes	%
1	Earl Hutto (D)	88,416	52.2
	Terry Ketchel (R)	80,851	47.8
2	Pete Peterson (D)	103,032	56.9
	Bill Grant (R)	77,939	43.1
3	Charles E. Bennett (D)	84,280	72.7
	Rod Sullivan (R)	31,727	27.3
4	Craig T. James (R)	120,895	55.9
	Reid Hughes (D)	95,320	44.1
5	Bill McCollum (R)	94,453	59.9
	Bob Fletcher (D)	63,253	40.1
6	Cliff Stearns (R)	138,588	59.2
	Art Johnson (D)	95,421	40.8
7	Sam Gibbons (D)	99,464	67.6
	Charles D. Prout (R)	47,765	32.4
8	C. W. Bill Young (R)		100.0
9	Michael Bilirakis (R)	142,163	58.1
	Cheryl Davis Knapp (D)	102,503	41.9
10	Andy Ireland (R)		100.0
11	Jim Bacchus (D)	120,991	51.9
	Bill Tolley (R)	111,970	48.1
12	Tom Lewis (R)		100.0
13	Porter J. Goss (R)		100.0
14	Harry A. Johnston (D)	156,055	66.0
	Scott Shore (R)	80,249	34.0
15	E. Clay Shaw Jr. (R)	104,295	97.8
16	Lawrence J. Smith (D)		100.0
17	William Lehman (D)	79,569	78.3
	Earl Rodney (R)	22,029	21.7
18	Ileana Ros-Lehtinen (R)	56,364	60.4
	Bernard Anscher (D)	36,978	39.6
19	Dante B. Fascell (D)	87,696	62.0
	Bob Allen (R)	53,796	38.0

GEORGIA

	Candidates	Votes	%
1	Lindsay Thomas (D)	80,515	71.2
	Chris Meredith (R)	32,532	28.8
2	Charles Hatcher (D)	77,910	73.0
	Jonathan Perry Waters (R)	28,781	27.0
3	Richard Ray (D)	72,961	63.2
	Paul Broun (R)	42,561	36.8
4	Ben Jones (D)	96,526	52.4
	John Linder (R)	87,569	47.6
5	John Lewis (D)	86,037	75.6
	J. W. Tibbs Jr. (R)	27,781	24.4
6	Newt Gingrich (R)	78,768	50.3
	David Worley (D)	77,794	49.7
7	George "Buddy" Darden (D)	95,817	60.1
	Al Beverly (R)	63,588	39.9
8	J. Roy Rowland (D)	81,344	68.7
	Bob Cunningham (R)	36,980	31.3
9	Ed Jenkins (D)	96,191	55.8
	Joe Hoffman (R)	76,121	44.2
10	Doug Barnard Jr. (D)	89,683	58.3
	Sam Jones (R)	64,184	41.7

HAWAII

	Candidates	Votes	%
1	Neil Abercrombie (D)	97,622	60.0
	Mike Liu (R)	62,982	38.7
2	Patsy T. Mink (D)	118,155	66.3
	Andy Poepoe (R)	54,625	30.6

Special Election [1]

		Votes	%
2	Patsy T. Mink (D)	51,841	37.4
	Mufi Hannemann (D)	50,164	36.1
	Ron Menor (D)	23,629	17.0
	Andy Poepoe (R)	8,872	6.4

IDAHO

		Votes	%
1	Larry LaRocco (D)	85,054	53.0
	C. A. "Skip" Smyser (R)	75,406	47.0
2	Richard H. Stallings (D)	98,008	63.6
	Sean McDevitt (R)	56,044	36.4

ILLINOIS

		Votes	%
1	Charles A. Hayes (D)	100,890	93.8
	Babette Peyton (R)	6,708	6.2
2	Gus Savage (D)	80,245	78.2
	William T. Hespel (R)	22,350	21.8
3	Marty Russo (D)	110,512	70.9
	Carl L. Klein (R)	45,299	29.1
4	George E. Sangmeister (D)	77,290	59.2
	Manny Hoffman (R)	53,258	40.8
5	William O. Lipinski (D)	73,805	66.3
	David J. Shestokas (R)	34,440	31.0
6	Henry J. Hyde (R)	96,410	66.7
	Robert J. Cassidy (D)	48,155	33.3
7	Cardiss Collins (D)	80,021	79.9
	Michael Dooley (R)	20,099	20.1
8	Dan Rostenkowski (D)	70,151	79.1
	Robert Marshall (LIBERT)	18,529	20.9
9	Sidney R. Yates (D)	96,557	71.2
	Herbert Sohn (R)	39,031	28.8
10	John Edward Porter (R)	104,070	67.7
	Peg McNamara (D)	47,286	30.8
11	Frank Annunzio (D)	82,703	53.6
	Walter W. Dudycz (R)	68,850	44.6
	Larry Saska (IS)	2,692	1.7
12	Philip M. Crane (R)	113,081	82.2
	Steve Pedersen (IS)	24,450	17.8
13	Harris W. Fawell (R)	116,048	65.8
	Steven Thomas (D)	60,305	34.2
14	Dennis Hastert (R)	112,383	66.9
	Donald J. Westphal (D)	55,592	33.1
15	Edward R. Madigan (R)	119,812	100
16	John W. Cox Jr. (D)	83,061	54.6
	John W. Hallock Jr. (R)	69,105	45.4

	Candidates	Votes	%
17	Lane Evans (D)	102,062	66.5
	Dan Lee (R)	51,380	33.5
18	Robert H. Michel (R)	105,693	98.4
19	Terry L. Bruce (D)	113,958	66.3
	Robert F. Kerans (R)	55,680	32.4
20	Richard J. Durbin (D)	130,114	66.2
	Paul E. Jurgens (R)	66,433	33.8
21	Jerry F. Costello (D)	95,208	66.0
	Robert H. Gaffner (R)	48,949	34.0
22	Glenn Poshard (D)	138,425	83.7
	Jim Wham (I)	26,896	16.3

INDIANA

		Votes	%
1	Peter J. Visclosky (D)	68,920	66.0
	William Costas (R)	35,450	34.0
2	Philip R. Sharp (D)	93,495	59.4
	Mike Pence (R)	63,980	40.6
3	Tim Roemer (D)	80,740	50.9
	John Hiler (R)	77,911	49.1
4	Jill Long (D)	99,347	60.7
	Rick Hawks (R)	64,415	39.3
5	Jim Jontz (D)	81,373	53.1
	John A. Johnson (R)	71,750	46.9
6	Dan Burton (R)	116,470	63.5
	James P. Fadely (D)	67,024	36.5
7	John T. Myers (R)	88,598	57.6
	John W. Riley Sr. (D)	65,248	42.4
8	Frank McCloskey (D)	97,465	54.7
	Richard E. Mourdock (R)	80,645	45.3
9	Lee H. Hamilton (D)	107,526	69.0
	Floyd Eugene Coates (R)	48,325	31.0
10	Andrew Jacobs Jr. (D)	69,362	66.4
	Janos Horvath (R)	35,049	33.6

IOWA

		Votes	%
1	Jim Leach (R)	90,042	99.8
2	Jim Nussle (R)	82,650	49.8
	Eric Tabor (D)	81,008	48.8
3	David R. Nagle (D)	100,947	99.2
4	Neal Smith (D)	127,812	97.9
5	Jim Ross Lightfoot (R)	99,978	68.0
	Rod Powell (D)	47,022	32.0
6	Fred Grandy (R)	112,333	71.8
	Mike D. Earll (D)	44,063	28.2

KANSAS

		Votes	%
1	Pat Roberts (R)	102,974	62.6
	Duane West (D)	61,396	37.4
2	Jim Slattery (D)	99,093	62.8
	Scott Morgan (R)	58,643	37.2
3	Jan Meyers (R)	88,725	60.1
	Leroy Jones (D)	58,923	39.9
4	Dan Glickman (D)	112,015	70.8
	Roger M. Grund (R)	46,283	29.2
5	Dick Nichols (R)	90,555	59.3
	George Wingert (D)	62,244	40.7

KENTUCKY

		Votes	%
1	Carroll Hubbard Jr. (D)	85,323	86.9
	Marvin H. Seat (POP)	12,879	13.1
2	William H. Natcher (D)	77,057	66.0
	Martin A. Tori (R)	39,624	34.0
3	Romano L. Mazzoli (D)	84,750	60.6
	Al Brown (R)	55,188	39.4
4	Jim Bunning (R)	101,680	69.3
	Galen Martin (D)	44,979	30.7
5	Harold Rogers (R)	64,660	100
6	Larry J. Hopkins (R)	76,859	100
7	Carl C. Perkins (D)	61,330	50.8
	Will T. Scott (R)	59,377	49.2

LOUISIANA [2]

	Candidates	Votes	%
1	Bob Livingston (R)	X	X
2	William J. Jefferson (D)	55,621	52.5
	Marc H. Morial (D)	50,232	47.5
3	W. J. "Billy" Tauzin (D)		X
4	Jim McCrery (R)		100.0
5	Jerry Huckaby (D)		100.0
6	Richard H. Baker (R)		100.0
7	Jimmy Hayes (D)		100.0
8	Clyde C. Holloway (R)		100.0

MAINE

		Votes	%
1	Thomas H. Andrews (D)	167,623	60.1
	David F. Emery (R)	110,836	39.7
2	Olympia J. Snowe (R)	121,704	51.0
	Patrick K. McGowan (D)	116,798	49.0

MARYLAND

		Votes	%
1	Wayne T. Gilchrest (R)	88,920	56.8
	Roy Dyson (D)	67,518	43.2
2	Helen Delich Bentley (R)	115,398	74.4
	Ronald P. Bowers (D)	39,785	25.6
3	Benjamin L. Cardin (D)	82,545	69.7
	Harwood Nichols (R)	35,841	30.3
4	Tom McMillen (D)	85,601	58.9
	Robert P. Duckworth (R)	59,846	41.1
5	Steny H. Hoyer (D)	84,747	80.7
	Lee F. Breuer (R)	20,314	19.3
6	Beverly B. Byron (D)	106,502	65.3
	Christopher P. Fiotes Jr. (R)	56,479	34.7
7	Kweisi Mfume (D)	59,628	85.0
	Kenneth Kondner (R)	10,529	15.0
8	Constance A. Morella (R)	130,059	73.5
	James Walker Jr. (R)	39,343	22.2

MASSACHUSETTS

		Votes	%
1	Silvio O. Conte (R)	150,748	77.5
	John R. Arden (D)	43,611	22.4
2	Richard E. Neal (D)	134,152	99.8
3	Joseph D. Early (D)	150,992	99.4
4	Barney Frank (D)	143,473	65.5
	John R. Soto (R)	75,454	34.5
5	Chester G. Atkins (D)	110,232	52.2
	John F. MacGovern (R)	101,017	47.8
6	Nicholas Mavroules (D)	149,284	65.0
	Edgar L. Kelley (R)	80,177	34.9
7	Edward J. Markey (D)	155,380	99.9
8	Joseph P. Kennedy II (D)	125,479	72.2
	Glenn W. Fiscus (R)	39,310	22.6
	Susan C. Davies (NA)	8,806	5.1
9	Joe Moakley (D)	124,534	70.3
	Robert W. Horan (I)	52,660	29.7
10	Larry E. Studds (D)	137,805	53.4
	Jon L. Bryan (R)	120,217	46.6
11	Brian J. Donnelly (D)	145,480	99.7

MICHIGAN

		Votes	%
1	John Conyers Jr. (D)	76,556	89.3
	Ray Shoulders (R)	7,298	8.5
2	Carl D. Pursell (R)	95,962	64.1
	Elmer White (D)	49,678	33.2
3	Howard Wolpe (D)	82,376	57.9
	Brad Haskins (R)	60,007	42.1
4	Fred Upton (R)	75,850	57.8
	JoAnne McFarland (D)	55,449	42.2
5	Paul B. Henry (R)	126,308	75.4
	Thomas Trzybinski (D)	41,170	24.6
6	Bob Carr (D)	97,547	99.8
7	Dale E. Kildee (D)	90,307	68.4
	David J. Morrill (R)	41,759	31.6
8	Bob Traxler (D)	98,903	68.6
	James White (R)	45,259	31.4
9	Guy Vander Jagt (R)	89,078	54.8

Footnotes, see p. 307.

Candidates	Votes	%
Geraldine Greene (D)	73,604	45.2
10 Dave Camp (R)	99,952	65.0
Joan Louise Dennison (D)	50,923	33.1
11 Robert W. Davis (R)	94,555	61.3
Marcia Gould (D)	59,759	38.7
12 David E. Bonior (D)	98,232	64.7
Jim Dingeman (R)	51,119	33.7
13 Barbara-Rose Collins (D)	54,345	80.1
Carl R. Edwards Sr. (R)	11,203	16.5
14 Dennis M. Hertel (D)	78,506	63.6
Kenneth C. McNealy (R)	40,499	32.8
15 William D. Ford (D)	68,742	61.2
Burl C. Adkins (R)	41,092	36.6
16 John D. Dingell (D)	88,962	66.6
Frank Beaumont (R)	42,629	31.9
17 Sander M. Levin (D)	92,205	69.7
Blaine L. Lankford (R)	40,100	30.3
18 William S. Broomfield (R)	126,629	66.4
Walter Briggs (D)	64,185	33.6

MINNESOTA [3]

1 Timothy J. Penny (DFL)	156,749	78.1
Doug Andersen (I-R)	43,856	21.9
2 Vin Weber (I-R)	126,367	61.8
Jim Stone (DFL)	77,935	38.1
3 Jim Ramstad (I-R)	195,833	66.9
Lewis DeMars (DFL)	96,395	32.9
4 Bruce F. Vento (DFL)	143,353	64.7
Ian Maitland (I-R)	77,639	35.1
5 Martin Olav Sabo (DFL)	144,682	72.9
Raymond C. Gilbertson (I-R)	53,720	27.1
6 Gerry Sikorski (DFL)	164,816	64.6
Bruce D. Anderson (I-R)	90,138	35.3
7 Collin C. Peterson (DFL)	107,126	53.5
Arlan Stangeland (I-R)	92,876	46.4
8 James L. Oberstar (DFL)	151,145	72.9
Jerry Shuster (I-R)	56,068	27.0

MISSISSIPPI

1 Jamie L. Whitten (D)	43,668	64.9
Bill Bowlin (R)	23,650	35.1
2 Mike Espy (D)	59,393	84.1
Dorothy Benford (R)	11,224	15.9
3 G. V. "Sonny" Montgomery (D)	49,162	100.0
4 Mike Parker (D)	57,137	80.6
Jerry "Rev" Parks (R)	13,754	19.4
5 Gene Taylor (D)	89,926	81.4
Sheila Smith (R)	20,588	18.6

MISSOURI

1 William L. Clay (D)	62,550	60.9
Wayne G. Piotrowski (R)	40,160	39.1
2 Joan Kelly Horn (D)	94,378	50.0
Jack Buechner (R)	94,324	50.0
3 Richard A. Gephardt (D)	88,950	56.8
Malcolm L. Holekamp (R)	67,659	43.2
4 Ike Skelton (D)	105,527	61.8
David Eyerly (R)	65,095	38.2
5 Alan Wheat (D)	71,890	62.1
Robert H. Gardner (R)	43,897	37.9
6 E. Thomas Coleman (R)	78,956	51.9
Bob McClure (D)	73,093	48.1
7 Mel Hancock (R)	83,609	52.1
Thomas Patrick Deaton (D)	76,725	47.9
8 Bill Emerson (R)	81,452	57.3
Russ Carnahan (D)	60,751	42.7
9 Harold L. Volkmer (D)	94,156	57.5
Don Curtis (R)	69,514	42.5

MONTANA

1 Pat Williams (D)	100,409	61.1
Brad Johnson (R)	63,837	38.9
2 Ron Marlenee (R)	96,449	63.0
Don Burris (D)	56,739	37.0

NEBRASKA

Candidates	Votes	%
1 Doug Bereuter (R)	129,654	64.7
Larry Hall (D)	70,587	35.2
2 Peter Hoagland (D)	111,903	57.9
Ally Milder (R)	80,845	41.8
3 Bill Barrett (R)	98,607	51.1
Sandra K. Scofield (D)	94,234	48.8

NEVADA

1 James H. Bilbray (D)	84,650	61.4
Bob Dickinson (R)	47,377	34.4
2 Barbara F. Vucanovich (R)	103,508	59.1
Jane Wisdom (D)	59,581	34.0
Dan Becan (LIBERT)	12,120	6.9

NEW HAMPSHIRE

1 Bill Zeliff (R)	81,684	55.1
Joseph F. Keefe (D)	66,176	44.6
2 Dick Swett (D)	74,829	52.7
Chuck Douglas (R)	67,063	47.2

NEW JERSEY

1 Robert E. Andrews (D)	73,522	54.3
Daniel J. Mangini (R)	57,801	42.7
2 William J. Hughes (D)	98,734	88.2
William A. Kanengiser (POP)	13,246	11.8
3 Frank Pallone Jr. (D)	77,709	49.1
Paul A. Kapalko (R)	73,451	46.4
4 Christopher H. Smith (R)	101,508	62.9
Mark Setaro (D)	55,454	34.4
5 Marge Roukema (R)	118,101	75.7
Lawrence Wayne Olsen (D)	35,010	22.4
6 Bernard J. Dwyer (D)	63,696	50.5
Paul Danielczyk (R)	58,209	46.2
7 Matthew J. Rinaldo (R)	100,274	74.6
Bruce H. Bergen (D)	31,114	23.2
8 Robert A. Roe (D)	55,212	76.9
Stephen Sibilia (IC)	13,239	18.4
9 Robert G. Torricelli (D)	82,736	57.0
Peter J. Russo (R)	59,759	41.2
10 Donald M. Payne (D)	42,616	81.5
Howard E. Berkeley (R)	9,072	17.3
11 Dean A. Gallo (R)	95,198	64.9
Michael Gordon (D)	47,782	32.6
12 Dick Zimmer (R)	108,173	64.0
Marguerite Chandler (D)	52,498	31.1
13 H. James Saxton (R)	100,537	58.1
John H. Adler (D)	68,286	39.5
14 Frank J. Guarini (D)	57,581	66.1
Fred J. Theemling Jr. (R)	25,473	29.2

Special Election [4]

1 Robert E. Andrews (D)	72,324	55.3
Daniel J. Mangini (R)	58,671	44.7

NEW MEXICO

1 Steven H. Schiff (R)	97,375	70.2
Rebecca Vigil-Giron (D)	41,306	29.8
2 Joe Skeen (R)	80,677	100.0
3 Bill Richardson (D)	104,225	74.5
Phil T. Archuletta (R)	35,751	25.5

NEW YORK

1 George J. Hochbrueckner (D, Tax Break)	75,211	56.3
Francis W. Creighton (R)	46,380	34.7
Clayton Baldwin Jr. (C)	6,883	5.2
2 Thomas J. Downey (D)	56,722	55.8
John W. Bugler (R, RTL, Tax Cut)	36,859	36.2

Candidates	Votes	%
Dominic A. Curcio (C)	8,150	8.0
3 Robert J. Mrazek (D, L)	73,029	53.3
Robert Previdi (R, C)	59,089	43.1
4 Norman F. Lent (R, C)	79,304	61.2
Francis T. Goban (D)	41,308	31.8
John J. Dunkle (RTL)	6,706	5.2
5 Raymond J. McGrath (R, C)	71,948	54.6
Mark S. Epstein (D, L)	53,920	40.9
6 Floyd H. Flake (D, L)	44,306	73.1
William Sampol (R)	13,224	21.8
John Cronin (RTL)	3,111	5.1
7 Gary L. Ackerman (D, L)	51,091	100
8 James H. Scheuer (D, L)	56,396	72.3
Gustave Reifenkugel (R)	21,646	27.7
9 Thomas J. Manton (D)	35,177	64.4
Ann Pfoser Darby (R, AC)	13,330	24.4
Thomas V. Ognibene (R)	6,137	11.2
10 Charles E. Schumer (D, L)	61,468	80.4
Patrick J. Kinsella (R, C)	14,963	19.6
11 Edolphus Towns (D, L)	36,286	92.9
12 Major R. Owens (D, L)	40,570	94.9
13 Stephen J. Solarz (D, L)	47,446	80.4
Edwin Ramos (R, C)	11,557	19.6
14 Susan Molinari (R, C)	58,616	60.0
Anthony J. Pocchia (D, L, SIS)	34,625	35.5
15 Bill Green (R)	52,919	58.8
Frances L. Reiter (D)	33,464	37.2
16 Charles B. Rangel (D, R, L)	55,882	97.2
Alvaader Frazier (NA)	1,592	2.8
17 Ted Weiss (D, L)	79,161	80.4
William W. Koeppel (R)	15,219	15.5
18 Jose E. Serrano (D, L)	38,024	93.2
19 Eliot L. Engel (D, L)	45,758	61.2
William J. Gouldman (R)	17,135	22.9
Kevin Brawley (C, RTL)	11,868	15.9
20 Nita M. Lowey (D, L)	82,203	62.8
Glenn D. Belitto (R)	35,575	27.2
John M. Schafer (C, RTL)	13,030	10.0
21 Hamilton Fish Jr. (R, C)	99,866	71.4
Richard J. Barbuto (D)	34,128	24.4
22 Benjamin A. Gilman (R, C)	95,495	68.6
John G. Dow (D)	37,034	26.6
23 Michael R. McNulty (D, C)	117,239	64.1
Margaret B. Buhrmaster (R)	65,760	35.9
24 Gerald B. H. Solomon (R, C, RTL)	121,206	68.1
Bob Lawrence (D)	56,671	31.9
25 Sherwood Boehlert (R)	91,348	83.9
William L. Griffen (L)	17,481	16.1
26 David O'B. Martin (R, C)	97,340	100
27 James T. Walsh (R, C)	95,220	63.2
Peggy L. Murray (D, L)	52,438	34.8
28 Matthew F. McHugh (D)	97,815	64.8
Seymour Krieger (R)	53,077	35.2
29 Frank Horton (R)	89,105	63.0
Alton F. Eber (D)	34,835	24.6
Peter DeMauro (C)	12,599	8.9
30 Louise M. Slaughter (D)	97,280	59.0
John M. Regan Jr. (R, C, RTL)	67,534	41.0
31 Bill Paxon (R, C, RTL)	90,237	56.6
Kevin P. Gaughan (D, L)	69,328	43.4
32 John J. LaFalce (D, L)	68,367	55.0
Michael T. Waring (R)	39,053	31.4
Kenneth J. Kowalski (C, RTL)	16,853	13.6
33 Henry J. Nowak (D, L)	84,905	77.5
Thomas K. Kepfer (R)	18,181	16.6
Louis P. Corrigan Jr. (C)	6,460	5.9
34 Amo Houghton (R, C)	89,831	69.6
Joseph P. Leahey (D)	37,421	29.0

Special Elections

14 Susan Molinari (R) [5]	29,336	59.0
Robert Gigante (D)	17,302	34.8
Barbara Bollaert (RTL)	2,649	5.3
18 Jose E. Serrano (D, L) [6]	26,928	92.4
Simeon Golar (R)	2,079	7.1

Footnotes, see p. 307.

NORTH CAROLINA

	Candidates	Votes	%
1	Walter B. Jones (D)	105,832	64.8
	Howard Moye (R)	57,526	35.2
2	Tim Valentine (D)	130,979	74.7
	Hal C. Sharpe (R)	44,263	25.3
3	H. Martin Lancaster (D)	83,930	59.3
	Don Davis (R)	57,605	40.7
4	David E. Price (D)	139,396	58.1
	John Carrington (R)	100,661	41.9
5	Stephen L. Neal (D)	113,814	59.1
	Ken Bell (R)	78,747	40.9
6	Howard Coble (R)	125,392	66.6
	Helen R. Allegrone (D)	62,913	33.4
7	Charlie Rose (D)	94,946	65.6
	Robert C. Anderson (R)	49,681	34.4
8	W. G. ''Bill'' Hefner (D)	98,700	55.0
	Ted Blanton (R)	80,852	45.0
9	Alex McMillan (R)	131,936	62.0
	David P. McKnight (D)	80,802	38.0
10	Cass Ballenger (R)	106,400	61.8
	Daniel R. Green Jr. (D)	65,710	38.2
11	Charles H. Taylor (R)	101,991	50.7
	James McClure Clarke (D)	99,318	49.3

NORTH DAKOTA

		Votes	%
AL	Byron L. Dorgan (D)	152,530	65.2
	Edward T. Schafer (R)	81,443	34.8

OHIO

		Votes	%
1	Charles Luken (D)	83,932	51.1
	J. Kenneth Blackwell (R)	80,362	48.9
2	Bill Gradison (R)	103,817	64.4
	Tyrone K. Yates (D)	57,345	35.6
3	Tony P. Hall (D)	116,797	100
4	Michael G. Oxley (R)	103,897	61.7
	Thomas E. Burkhart (D)	64,467	38.3
5	Paul E. Gillmor (R)	113,615	68.5
	P. Scott Mange (D)	41,693	25.1
	John E. Jackson (I)	10,612	6.4
6	Bob McEwen (R)	117,220	71.2
	Ray Mitchell (D)	47,415	28.8
7	David L. Hobson (R)	97,123	62.1
	Jack Schira (D)	59,349	37.9
8	John A. Boehner (R)	99,955	61.1
	Gregory V. Jolivette (D)	63,584	38.9
9	Marcy Kaptur (D)	117,681	77.7
	Jerry D. Lammers (R)	33,791	22.3
10	Clarence E. Miller (R)	106,009	63.2
	John M. Buchanan (D)	61,656	36.8
11	Dennis E. Eckart (D)	111,923	65.7
	Margaret Mueller (R)	58,372	34.3
12	John R. Kasich (R)	130,495	72.0
	Mike Gelpi (D)	50,784	28.0
13	Don J. Pease (D)	93,431	56.7
	William D. Nielsen (R)	60,925	36.9
	John Michael Ryan (I)	10,506	6.4
14	Thomas C. Sawyer (D)	97,875	59.6
	Jean E. Bender (R)	66,460	40.4
15	Chalmers P. Wylie (R)	99,251	59.1
	Thomas V. Erney (D)	68,510	40.8
16	Ralph Regula (R)	101,097	58.9
	Warner D. Mendenhall (D)	70,516	41.1
17	James A. Traficant Jr. (D)	133,207	77.7
	Robert R. DeJulio Jr. (R)	38,199	22.3
18	Douglas Applegate (D)	120,782	74.3
	John A. Hales (R)	41,823	25.7
19	Edward F. Feighan (D)	132,951	64.8
	Susan M. Lawko (R)	72,315	35.2
20	Mary Rose Oakar (D)	109,390	73.3
	Bill Smith (R)	39,749	26.7
21	Louis Stokes (D)	103,338	80.0
	Franklin H. Roski (R)	25,906	20.0

OKLAHOMA

	Candidates	Votes	%
1	James M. Inhofe (R)	75,618	56.0
	Kurt Glassco (D)	59,521	44.0
2	Mike Synar (D)	90,820	61.3
	Terry M. Gorham (R)	57,331	38.7
3	Bill Brewster (D)	107,641	80.4
	Patrick K. Miller (R)	26,261	19.6
4	Dave McCurdy (D)	100,879	73.6
	Howard Bell (R)	36,232	26.4
5	Mickey Edwards (R)	114,608	69.6
	Bryce Baggett (D)	50,086	30.4
6	Glenn English (D)	110,100	80.0
	Robert Burns (R)	27,540	20.0

OREGON

		Votes	%
1	Les AuCoin (D)	150,292	63.1
	Earl Molander (R)	72,382	30.4
	Rick Livingston (I)	15,585	6.5
2	Robert F. Smith (R)	127,998	68.0
	Jim Smiley (D)	60,131	32.0
3	Ron Wyden (D)	169,731	80.8
	Philip E. Mooney (R)	40,216	19.1
4	Peter A. DeFazio (D)	162,494	85.8
	Tonie Nathan (LIBERT)	26,432	14.0
5	Mike Kopetski (D)	124,610	55.0
	Denny Smith (R)	101,650	44.9

PENNSYLVANIA

		Votes	%
1	Thomas M. Foglietta (D)	73,423	79.4
	James Love Jackson (R)	19,018	20.6
2	William H. Gray III (D)	94,584	92.1
	Donald Bakove (R)	8,118	7.9
3	Robert A. Borski (D)	89,908	60.0
	Joseph Marc McColgan (R)	59,901	40.0
4	Joe Kolter (D)	74,114	55.9
	Gordon R. Johnston (R)	58,469	44.1
5	Richard T. Schulze (R)	75,097	57.1
	Samuel C. Stretton (D)	50,597	38.5
6	Gus Yatron (D)	74,394	57.0
	John F. Hicks (R)	56,093	43.0
7	Curt Weldon (R)	105,868	65.3
	John Innelli (D)	56,292	34.7
8	Peter H. Kostmayer (D)	85,015	56.6
	Audrie Zettick Schaller (R)	65,100	43.4
9	Bud Shuster (R, D)	106,632	100.0
10	Joseph M. McDade (R, D)	113,490	100.0
11	Paul E. Kanjorski (D)	88,219	100.0
12	John P. Murtha (D)	80,686	61.7
	William Choby (R)	50,007	38.3
13	Lawrence Coughlin (R)	89,577	60.3
	Bernard Tomkin (D)	58,967	39.7
14	William J. Coyne (D)	77,636	71.8
	Richard Edward Caligiuri (R)	30,497	28.2
15	Don Ritter (R)	77,178	60.6
	Richard J. Orloski (D)	50,233	39.4
16	Robert S. Walker (R)	85,596	66.1
	Ernest Eric Guyll (D)	43,849	33.9
17	George W. Gekas (R, D)	110,317	100
18	Rick Santorum (R)	85,697	51.4
	Doug Walgren (D)	80,880	48.6
19	Bill Goodling (R)	96,336	100.0
20	Joseph M. Gaydos (D)	82,080	65.6
	Robert C. Lee (R)	43,054	34.4
21	Tom Ridge (R)	92,732	100.0
22	Austin J. Murphy (D)	78,375	63.3
	Suzanne Hayden (R)	45,509	36.7
23	William F. Clinger Jr. (R)	78,189	59.4
	Daniel J. Shannon (D)	53,465	40.6

RHODE ISLAND

		Votes	%
1	Ronald K. Machtley (R)	89,963	55.2
	Scott Wolf (D)	73,131	44.8
2	Jack Reed (D)	108,818	59.2
	Gertrude M. ''Trudy'' Coxe (R)	74,953	40.8

SOUTH CAROLINA

	Candidates	Votes	%
1	Arthur Ravenel Jr. (R)	80,839	65.5
	Eugene Platt (D)	42,555	34.5
2	Floyd D. Spence (R)	90,054	88.7
	Geb Sommer (LIBERT)	11,101	10.9
3	Butler Derrick (D)	72,561	58.0
	Ray Haskett (R)	52,419	41.9
4	Liz J. Patterson (D)	81,927	61.4
	Terry E. Haskins (R)	51,338	38.4
5	John M. Spratt Jr. (D)	91,775	99.9
6	Robin Tallon (D)	94,121	99.6

SOUTH DAKOTA

		Votes	%
AL	Tim Johnson (D)	173,814	67.6
	Don Frankenfeld (R)	83,484	32.4

TENNESSEE

		Votes	%
1	James H. Quillen (R)	47,796	99.9
2	John J. Duncan (R)	62,797	80.6
	Peter Hebert (I)	15,127	19.4
3	Marilyn Lloyd (D)	49,662	53.0
	Grady L. Rhoden (R)	36,855	39.3
	Peter T. Melcher (I)	5,598	6.0
4	Jim Cooper (D)	52,101	67.4
	Claiborne ''Clay'' Sanders (R)	22,890	29.6
5	Bob Clement (D)	55,607	72.4
	Tom Stone (I)	13,577	17.7
	Al Borgman (I)	5,383	7.0
6	Bart Gordon (D)	60,538	66.7
	Gregory Cochran (R)	26,424	29.1
7	Don Sundquist (R)	66,141	62.0
	Ken Bloodworth (D)	40,516	38.0
8	John Tanner (D)	62,241	100.0
9	Harold E. Ford (D)	48,629	58.1
	Aaron C. Davis (R)	25,730	30.8
	Thomas M. Davidson (I)	7,249	8.7

TEXAS

		Votes	%
1	Jim Chapman (D)	89,241	61.0
	Hamp Hodges (R)	56,954	39.0
2	Charles Wilson (D)	76,974	55.6
	Donna Peterson (R)	61,555	44.4
3	Steve Bartlett (R)	153,857	99.6
4	Ralph M. Hall (D)	108,300	99.6
5	John Bryant (D)	65,228	59.6
	Jerry Rucker (R)	41,307	37.7
6	Joe L. Barton (R)	125,049	66.5
	John E. Welch (D)	62,344	33.1
7	Jack Archer (R)	114,254	100.0
8	Jack Fields (R)	60,603	100.0
9	Jack Brooks (D)	79,786	57.7
	Maury Meyers (R)	58,399	42.3
10	J. J. ''Jake'' Pickle (D)	152,784	64.9
	David Beilharz (R)	73,766	31.3
11	Chet Edwards (D)	73,810	53.5
	Hugh D. Shine (R)	64,269	46.5
12	Pete Geren (D)	98,026	71.3
	Mike McGinn (R)	39,438	28.7
13	Bill Sarpalius (D)	81,815	56.5
	Dick Waterfield (R)	63,045	43.5
14	Greg H. Laughlin (D)	89,251	54.3
	Joe Dial (R)	75,098	45.7
15	E. ''Kika'' de la Garza (D)	72,461	100.0
16	Ronald D. Coleman (D)	62,455	95.6
17	Charles W. Stenholm (D)	104,100	100.0
18	Craig Washington (D)	54,477	99.6
19	Larry Combest (R)	83,795	100.0
20	Henry B. Gonzalez (D)	56,318	100.0
21	Lamar Smith (R)	144,570	74.8
	Kirby J. Roberts (D)	48,585	25.2
22	Thomas D. DeLay (R)	93,425	71.2
	Bruce Director (D)	37,721	28.8
23	Albert G. Bustamante (D)	71,052	63.5
	Jerome L. Gonzales (R)	40,856	36.5
24	Martin Frost (D)	86,297	100.0

	Candidates	Votes	%
25	Michael A. Andrews (D)	67,427	100.0
26	Dick Armey (R)	147,856	70.4
	John Wayne Caton (D)	62,158	29.6
27	Solomon P. Ortiz (D)	62,822	100.0

UTAH

		Votes	%
1	James V. Hansen (R)	82,746	52.1
	Kenley Brunsdale (D)	69,491	43.8
2	Wayne Owens (D)	85,167	57.6
	Genevieve Atwood (R)	58,869	39.8
3	Bill Orton (D)	79,163	58.3
	Karl Snow (R)	49,452	36.4

VERMONT

		Votes	%
AL	Bernard Sanders (I)	117,522	56.0
	Peter Smith (R)	82,938	39.5

VIRGINIA

		Votes	%
1	Herbert H. Bateman (R)	72,000	51.0
	Andrew H. Fox (D)	69,194	49.0
2	Owen B. Pickett (D)	55,179	75.0
	Harry G. Broskie (I)	15,915	21.6
3	Thomas J. Bliley Jr. (R)	77,125	65.3
	Jay Starke (D)	36,253	30.7
4	Norman Sisisky (D)	71,051	78.3
	Don L. Reynolds (I)	12,295	13.6
	Loretta F. Chandler (I)	7,102	7.8
5	Lewis F. Payne Jr. (D)	66,532	99.4

	Candidates	Votes	%
6	Jim Olin (D)	92,968	82.7
	Gerald E. Berg (I)	18,148	16.1
7	D. French Slaughter Jr. (R)	81,688	58.1
	David M. Smith (D)	58,684	41.7
8	James P. Moran Jr. (D)	88,475	51.7
	Stan Parris (R)	76,367	44.6
9	Rick Boucher (D)	67,215	97.1
10	Frank R. Wolf (R)	103,761	61.5
	N. MacKenzie Canter III (D)	57,249	33.9

WASHINGTON

		Votes	%
1	John R. Miller (R)	100,339	52.0
	Cynthia Sullivan (D)	92,447	48.0
2	Al Swift (D)	92,837	50.5
	Doug Smith (R)	75,669	41.2
	William L. McCord (LIBERT)	15,165	8.3
3	Jolene Unsoeld (D)	95,645	53.8
	Bob Williams (R)	82,269	46.2
4	Sid Morrison (R)	106,545	70.7
	Ole Hougen (D)	44,241	29.3
5	Thomas S. Foley (D)	110,234	68.8
	Marlyn A. Derby (R)	49,965	31.2
6	Norm Dicks (D)	79,079	61.4
	Norbert Mueller (R)	49,786	38.6
7	Jim McDermott (D)	106,761	72.3
	Larry Penberthy (R)	35,511	24.1
8	Rod Chandler (R)	96,323	56.2
	David E. Giles (D)	75,031	43.8

WEST VIRGINIA

	Candidates	Votes	%
1	Alan B. Mollohan (D)	72,849	67.1
	Howard K. Tuck (R)	35,657	32.9
2	Harley O. Staggers Jr. (D)	63,174	55.5
	Oliver Luck (R)	50,708	44.5
3	Bob Wise (D)	75,327	100.0
4	Nick J. Rahall II (D)	39,948	52.0
	Marianne R. Brewster (R)	36,946	48.0

WISCONSIN

		Votes	%
1	Les Aspin (D)	93,961	99.4
2	Scott L. Klug (R)	96,938	53.2
	Robert W. Kastenmeier (D)	85,156	46.8
3	Steve Gunderson (R)	94,509	61.0
	James L. Ziegeweid (D)	60,409	39.0
4	Gerald D. Kleczka (D)	96,981	69.2
	Joseph L. Cook (R)	43,001	30.7
5	Jim Moody (D)	77,557	68.0
	Donalda Hammersmith (R)	31,255	27.4
6	Thomas E. Petri (R)	111,036	99.5
7	David R. Obey (D)	100,069	62.1
	John L. McEwen (R)	60,961	37.9
8	Toby Roth (R)	95,902	53.5
	Jerome Van Sistine (D)	83,199	46.4
9	F. James Sensenbrenner Jr. (R)	117,967	99.7

WYOMING

		Votes	%
AL	Craig Thomas (R)	87,078	55.1
	Pete Maxfield (D)	70,977	44.9

1990 Elections

1. A special election was held to fill the unexpired term of Rep. Daniel K. Akaka (D), who resigned May 16, 1990, having been appointed to the U.S. Senate.

2. For the 1990 House elections in Louisiana, an open primary election was held with candidates from all parties running on the same ballot. Any candidate who received a majority was elected unopposed, with no further appearance on the general election ballot. If no candidate received 50 percent, a runoff was held between the two top finishers.

3. In Minnesota the Democratic Party is known as the Democratic-Farmer-Labor Party and

the Republican Party as the Independent-Republican Party; candidates appear on the ballot with these designations.

4. A special election was held to fill the unexpired term of Rep. James J. Florio (D), who resigned Jan. 16, 1990, having been elected governor.

5. A special election was held to fill the unexpired term of Rep. Guy V. Molinari (R), who resigned Jan. 1, 1990.

6. A special election was held to fill the unexpired term of Rep. Robert Garcia (D), who resigned Jan. 7, 1990.

1991 House Elections

ARIZONA

Special Election [1]

Candidates	Votes	%
2 Ed Pastor (D)	32,289	*55.5*
Pat Conner (R)	25,814	*44.4*

MASSACHUSETTS

Special Election [3]

Candidates	Votes	%
1 John Olver (D)	70,022	*49.6*
Steven D. Pierce (R)	68,052	*48.2*

TEXAS

Special Election [5]

Candidates	Votes	%
3 Sam Johnson (R)	24,004	*52.6*
Tom Pauken (R)	21,647	*47.4*

PENNSYLVANIA

Special Election [4]

	Votes	%
2 Lucien E. Blackwell (D)	51,820	*39.2*
Chaka Fattah (D)	37,068	*28.0*
John F. White Jr. (D)	36,469	*27.6*
Nadine G. Smith-Bulford (R)	6,928	*5.2*

ILLINOIS

Special Election [2]

	Votes	%
15 Thomas W. Ewing (R)	25,675	*66.4*
Gerald Bradley (D)	13,011	*33.6*

VIRGINIA

Special Election [6]

	Votes	%
7 George F. Allen (R)	106,745	*62.0*
Kay Slaughter (D)	59,655	*34.7*

1991 Elections

1. A special election was held to fill the unexpired term of Rep. Morris K. Udall (D), who resigned May 4, 1991.

2. A special election was held to fill the unexpired term of Rep. Edward R. Madigan (R), who resigned March 8, 1991, having been appointed agriculture secretary.

3. A special election was held to fill the unexpired term of Rep. Silvio O. Conte (R), who died Feb. 8, 1991.

4. A special election was held to fill the unexpired term of Rep. William H. Gray III (D), who resigned Sept. 11, 1991.

5. A special election was held to fill the unexpired term of Rep. Steve Bartlett (R), who resigned March 11, 1991.

6. A special election was held to fill the unexpired term of Rep. D. French Slaughter Jr. (R), who resigned Nov. 5, 1991.

House Candidates Index

For an index of all House candidates listed in this section (pages 192-324), see pages 340-371. Instructions for use of the House Candidates Index appear on page 340.

1992 House Elections

ALABAMA

	Candidates	Votes	%
1	Sonny Callahan (R)	128,874	60.2
	William A. Brewer (D)	78,742	36.8
2	Terry Everett (R)	112,906	49.5
	George C. Wallace Jr. (D)	109,335	47.9
3	Glen Browder (D)	119,175	60.3
	Don Sledge (R)	73,800	37.4
4	Tom Bevill (D)	157,907	68.5
	Mickey Strickland (R)	66,934	29.0
5	Robert E. "Bud" Cramer (D)	160,060	65.6
	Terry Smith (R)	77,951	31.9
6	Spencer Bachus (R)	146,599	52.4
	Ben Erdreich (D)	126,062	45.0
7	Earl F. Hilliard (D)	144,320	69.5
	Kervin Jones (R)	36,086	17.4
	James M. Lewis (I)	12,461	6.0
	James Chambliss (I)	11,466	5.5

ALASKA

	Candidates	Votes	%
AL	Don Young (R)	111,849	46.8
	John E. Devens (D)	102,378	42.8
	Michael A. States (ALI)	15,049	6.3

ARIZONA

	Candidates	Votes	%
1	Sam Coppersmith (D)	130,715	51.3
	John J. Rhodes III (R)	113,613	44.6
2	Ed Pastor (D)	90,693	66.0
	Don Shooter (R)	41,257	30.0
3	Bob Stump (R)	158,906	61.5
	Roger Hartstone (D)	88,830	34.4
4	Jon Kyl (R)	156,330	59.2
	Walter R. Mybeck II (D)	70,572	26.7
	Debbie Collings (I)	25,553	9.7
5	Jim Kolbe (R)	172,867	66.5
	Jim Toevs (D)	77,256	29.7
6	Karan English (D)	124,251	53.0
	Doug Wead (R)	97,074	41.4
	Sarah Stannard (I)	13,047	5.6

ARKANSAS

	Candidates	Votes	%
1	Blanche Lambert (D)	149,558	69.8
	Terry Hayes (R)	64,618	30.2
2	Ray Thornton (D)	154,946	74.2
	Dennis Scott (R)	53,978	25.8
3	Tim Hutchinson (R)	125,295	50.2
	John VanWinkle (D)	117,775	47.2
4	Jay Dickey (R)	113,009	52.3
	W. J. "Bill" McCuen (D)	102,918	47.7

CALIFORNIA

	Candidates	Votes	%
1	Dan Hamburg (D)	119,676	47.6
	Frank Riggs (R)	113,266	45.1
	Elliot Roy Freedman (D)	71,780	28.0
	Harry H. Pendery (LIBERT)	17,529	6.8
2	Wally Herger (R)	167,247	65.2
3	Vic Fazio (D)	122,149	51.2
	H. L. "Bill" Richardson (R)	96,092	40.3
	Ross Crain (LIBERT)	20,444	8.6
4	John T. Doolittle (R)	141,155	49.8
	Patricia Malberg (D)	129,489	45.7
5	Robert T. Matsui (D)	158,250	68.6
	Robert S. Dinsmore (R)	58,698	25.5
6	Lynn Woolsey (D)	190,322	65.2
	Bill Filante (R)	98,171	33.6
7	George Miller (D)	153,320	70.3
	Dave Scholl (R)	54,822	25.1
8	Nancy Pelosi (D)	191,906	82.5
	Marc Wolin (R)	25,693	11.0

	Candidates	Votes	%
9	Ronald V. Dellums (D)	164,265	71.9
	G. William Hunter (R)	53,707	23.5
10	Bill Baker (R)	145,702	52.0
	Wendell H. Williams (D)	134,568	48.0
11	Richard W. Pombo (R)	94,453	47.6
	Patricia Garamendi (D)	90,539	45.6
	Christine Roberts (LIBERT)	13,498	6.8
12	Tom Lantos (D)	157,205	68.8
	Jim Tomlin (R)	53,278	23.3
13	Pete Stark (D)	123,795	60.2
	Verne Teyler (R)	64,953	31.6
	Roslyn A. Allen (PFP)	16,768	8.2
14	Anna G. Eshoo (D)	146,873	56.7
	Tom Huening (R)	101,202	39.0
15	Norman Y. Mineta (D)	168,617	63.5
	Robert Wick (R)	82,875	31.2
	Duggan Dieterly (LIBERT)	13,293	5.0
16	Don Edwards (D)	96,661	62.0
	Ted Bundesen (R)	49,843	32.0
	Amani S. Kuumba (PFP)	9,370	6.0
17	Leon E. Panetta (D)	151,565	72.0
	Bill McCampbell (R)	49,947	23.7
18	Gary Condit (D)	139,704	84.7
	Kim R. Almstrom (LIBERT)	25,307	15.3
19	Richard H. Lehman (D)	101,619	46.9
	Tal L. Cloud (R)	100,590	46.4
	Dorothy L. Wells (PFP)	13,334	6.2
20	Calvin Dooley (D)	72,679	64.9
	Ed Hunt (R)	39,388	35.1
21	William M. Thomas (R)	127,758	65.2
	Deborah A. Vollmer (D)	68,058	34.7
22	Michael Huffington (R)	131,242	52.5
	Gloria Ochoa (D)	87,328	34.9
	Mindy Lorenz (GREEN)	23,699	9.5
23	Elton Gallegly (R)	115,504	54.3
	Anita Perez Ferguson (D)	88,225	41.4
24	Anthony C. Beilenson (D)	141,742	55.5
	Tom McClintock (R)	99,835	39.1
	John Paul Lindblad (PFP)	13,690	5.4
25	Howard P. "Buck" McKeon (R)	113,611	51.9
	James H. "Gil" Gilmartin (D)	72,233	33.0
	Rick Pamplin (I)	13,930	6.4
26	Howard L. Berman (D)	73,807	61.0
	Gary Forsch (R)	36,453	30.1
	Margery Hinds (PFP)	7,180	5.9
27	Carlos J. Moorhead (R)	105,521	49.7
	Doug Kahn (D)	83,805	39.4
	Jesse A. Moorman (GREEN)	11,003	5.2
28	David Dreier (R)	122,353	58.4
	Al Wachtel (D)	76,525	36.5
29	Henry A. Waxman (D)	160,312	61.3
	Mark A. Robbins (R)	67,141	25.7
	David Davis (I)	15,445	5.9
	Susan C. Davies (PFP)	13,888	5.3
30	Xavier Becerra (D)	48,800	58.4
	Morry Waksberg (R)	20,034	24.0
	Blase Bonpane (GREEN)	6,315	7.6
	Elizabeth A. Nakano (PFP)	6,173	7.4
31	Matthew G. Martinez (D)	68,324	62.6
	Reuben D. Franco (R)	40,873	37.4
32	Julian C. Dixon (D)	150,644	87.2
	Bob Weber (LIBERT)	12,384	7.2
	William R. Williams (PFP)	9,782	5.7
33	Lucille Roybal-Allard (D)	32,010	63.0
	Robert Guzman (R)	15,428	30.4
34	Esteban E. Torres (D)	91,738	61.3
	J. "Jay" Hernandez (R)	50,907	34.0
35	Maxine Waters (D)	102,941	82.5
	Nate Truman (R)	17,417	14.0
36	Jane Harman (D)	125,751	48.4
	Joan Milke Flores (R)	109,684	42.2
	Richard H. Greene (GREEN)	13,297	5.1
37	Walter R. Tucker (D)	97,159	85.7
	B. Kwaku Duren (PFP)	16,178	14.3
38	Steve Horn (R)	92,038	48.6

	Candidates	Votes	%
	Evan Anderson Braude (D)	82,108	43.4
39	Ed Royce (R)	122,472	57.3
	Molly McClanahan (D)	81,728	38.2
40	Jerry Lewis (R)	129,563	63.1
	Donald M. Rusk (D)	63,881	31.1
	Margie Akin (PFP)	11,839	5.8
41	Jay C. Kim (R)	101,753	59.6
	Bob Baker (D)	58,777	34.4
	Mike Noonan (PFP)	10,136	5.9
42	George E. Brown Jr. (D)	79,780	50.7
	Dick Rutan (R)	69,251	44.0
	Fritz R. Ward (LIBERT)	8,424	5.4
43	Ken Calvert (R)	88,987	46.7
	Mark A. Takano (D)	88,468	46.4
44	Al McCandless (R)	110,333	54.2
	Georgia Smith (D)	81,693	40.1
	Phil Turner (LIBERT)	11,515	5.7
45	Dana Rohrabacher (R)	123,731	54.5
	Patricia McCabe (D)	88,508	39.0
	Gary D. Copeland (LIBERT)	14,777	6.5
46	Robert K. Dornan (R)	55,659	50.2
	Robert John Banuelos (D)	45,435	41.0
	Richard G. Newhouse (LIBERT)	9,712	8.8
47	C. Christopher Cox (R)	165,004	64.9
	John F. Anwiler (D)	76,924	30.3
48	Ron Packard (R)	140,935	61.1
	Michael Farber (D)	67,415	29.2
	Donna White (PFP)	13,396	5.8
49	Lynn Schenk (D)	127,280	51.1
	Judy Jarvis (R)	106,170	42.7
50	Bob Filner (D)	77,293	56.6
	Tony Valencia (R)	39,531	28.9
	Barbara Hutchinson (LIBERT)	15,489	11.3
51	Randy "Duke" Cunningham (R)	141,890	56.1
	Bea Herbert (D)	85,148	33.7
52	Duncan Hunter (R)	112,995	52.9
	Janet M. Gastil (D)	88,076	41.2

COLORADO

	Candidates	Votes	%
1	Patricia Schroeder (D)	156,629	68.8
	Raymond Diaz Aragon (R)	70,902	31.2
2	David E. Skaggs (D)	164,790	60.7
	Bryan Day (R)	88,470	32.6
	Vern Tharp (AGA)	18,101	6.7
3	Scott McInnis (R)	143,293	54.7
	Mike Callihan (D)	114,480	43.7
4	Wayne Allard (R)	139,884	57.8
	Tom Redder (D)	101,957	42.2
5	Joel Hefley (R)	173,096	71.1
	Charles A. Oriez (D)	62,550	25.7
6	Dan Schaefer (R)	142,021	60.9
	Tom Kolbe (D)	91,073	39.1

CONNECTICUT

	Candidates	Votes	%
1	Barbara B. Kennelly (D, ACP)	164,735	67.1
	Philip L. Steele (R)	75,113	30.6
2	Sam Gejdenson (D, ACP)	123,291	50.8
	Edward W. Munster (R)	119,416	49.2
3	Rosa DeLauro (D, ACP)	162,568	65.7
	Thomas Scott (R)	84,952	34.3
4	Christopher Shays (R)	147,816	67.3
	Dave Schropfer (D)	58,666	26.7
	Al Smith (ACP)	11,679	5.3
5	Gary Franks (R)	104,891	43.7
	James J. Lawlor (D)	74,791	31.1
	Lynn H. Taborsak (ACP)	54,022	22.5
6	Nancy L. Johnson (R)	166,967	69.7
	Eugene F. Slason (D)	60,373	25.2

DELAWARE

Candidates	Votes	%
AL Michael N. Castle (R)	153,037	55.4
S. B. Woo (D)	117,426	42.5

FLORIDA

Candidates	Votes	%
1 Earl Hutto (D)	118,941	52.0
Terry Ketchel (R)	100,349	43.9
2 Pete Peterson (D)	167,215	73.4
Ray Wagner (R)	60,425	26.5
3 Corrine Brown (D)	91,915	59.3
Don Weidner (R)	63,115	40.7
4 Tillie Fowler (R)	135,883	56.7
Mattox Hair (D)	103,531	43.2
5 Karen L. Thurman (D)	129,698	49.2
Tom Hogan (R)	114,356	43.4
Cindy Munkittrick (I)	19,462	7.4
6 Cliff Stearns (R)	144,195	65.4
Phil Denton (D)	76,419	34.6
7 John L. Mica (R)	125,823	56.4
Dan Webster (D)	96,945	43.5
8 Bill McCollum (R)	141,977	68.5
Chuck Kovaleski (D)	65,145	31.5
9 Michael Bilirakis (R)	158,028	58.9
Cheryl Davis Knapp (D)	110,135	41.1
10 C. W. Bill Young (R)	149,606	56.6
Karen Moffitt (D)	114,809	43.4
11 Sam Gibbons (D)	100,984	52.8
Mark Sharpe (R)	77,640	40.6
Joe De Minico (I)	12,730	6.7
12 Charles T. Canady (R)	100,484	52.1
Tom Mims (D)	92,346	47.9
13 Dan Miller (R)	158,881	57.8
Rand Snell (D)	115,767	42.2
14 Porter J. Goss (R)	220,351	82.1
James H. King (I)	48,160	17.9
15 Jim Bacchus (D)	132,412	50.7
Bill Tolley (R)	128,873	49.3
16 Tom Lewis (R)	157,322	60.8
John P. Comerford (D)	101,237	39.2
17 Carrie Meek (D)	102,784	100.0
18 Ileana Ros-Lehtinen (R)	104,755	66.8
Magda Montiel Davis (D)	52,142	33.2
19 Harry A. Johnston (D)	177,423	63.1
Larry Metz (R)	103,867	36.9
20 Peter Deutsch (D)	130,959	55.1
Beverly Kennedy (R)	91,589	38.5
James M. Blackburn (I)	15,341	6.4
21 Lincoln Diaz-Balart (R)		100.0
22 E. Clay Shaw Jr. (R)	128,400	52.0
Gwen Margolis (D)	91,625	37.1
Richard "Even" Stephens (I)	15,469	6.3
23 Alcee L. Hastings (D)	84,249	58.5
Ed Fielding (R)	44,807	31.1
Al Woods (I)	14,879	10.3

GEORGIA

Candidates	Votes	%
1 Jack Kingston (R)	103,932	57.8
Barbara Christmas (D)	75,808	42.2
2 Sanford Bishop (D)	95,789	63.7
Jim Dudley (R)	54,593	36.3
3 Mac Collins (R)	114,107	54.8
Richard Ray (D)	94,271	45.2
4 John Linder (R)	126,495	50.5
Cathey Steinberg (D)	123,819	49.5
5 John Lewis (D)	147,445	72.1
Paul R. Stabler (R)	56,960	27.9
6 Newt Gingrich (R)	158,761	57.7
Tony Center (D)	116,196	42.3
7 George "Buddy" Darden (D)	111,374	57.3
Al Beverly (R)	82,915	42.7
8 J. Roy Rowland (D)	108,472	55.7
Bob Cunningham (R)	86,220	44.3
9 Nathan Deal (D)	113,024	59.2
Daniel Becker (R)	77,919	40.8
10 Don Johnson (D)	108,426	53.8
Ralph T. Hudgens (R)	93,059	46.2

Candidates	Votes	%
11 Cynthia McKinney (D)	120,168	73.1
Woodrow Lovett (R)	44,221	26.9

HAWAII

Candidates	Votes	%
1 Neil Abercrombie (D)	129,332	72.9
Warner C. Kimo Sutton (R)	41,575	23.4
2 Patsy T. Mink (D)	131,454	72.6
Kamuela Price (R)	40,070	22.1
Lloyd "Jeff" Mallan (LIBERT)	9,431	5.2

IDAHO

Candidates	Votes	%
1 Larry LaRocco (D)	140,985	58.1
Rachel S. Gilbert (R)	90,983	37.5
2 Michael D. Crapo (R)	139,783	60.8
J. D. Williams (D)	81,450	35.4

ILLINOIS

Candidates	Votes	%
1 Bobby L. Rush (D)	209,258	82.8
Jay Walker (R)	43,453	17.2
2 Mel Reynolds (D)	182,614	78.1
Ron Blackstone (R)	31,957	13.7
Louanner Peters (I)	19,293	8.2
3 William O. Lipinski (D)	162,165	63.5
Harry C. Lepinske (R)	93,128	36.5
4 Luis V. Gutierrez (D)	90,452	77.6
Hildegarde Rodriguez-Schieman (R)	26,154	22.4
5 Dan Rostenkowski (D)	132,889	57.3
Elias R. Zenkich (R)	90,738	39.1
6 Henry J. Hyde (R)	165,009	65.5
Barry W. Watkins (D)	86,891	34.5
7 Cardiss Collins (D)	182,811	81.1
Norman G. Boccio (R)	35,346	15.7
8 Philip M. Crane (R)	132,887	55.7
Sheila A. Smith (D)	96,419	40.4
9 Sidney R. Yates (D)	162,942	68.0
Herbert Sohn (R)	64,760	27.0
Sheila A. Jones (ECR)	12,001	5.0
10 John Edward Porter (R)	155,230	64.5
Michael J. Kennedy (D)	85,400	35.5
11 George E. Sangmeister (D)	135,387	55.7
Robert T. Herbolsheimer (R)	107,860	44.3
12 Jerry F. Costello (D)	168,762	71.2
Mike Starr (R)	68,115	28.8
13 Harris W. Fawell (R)	179,257	68.4
Dennis Michael Temple (D)	82,985	31.6
14 Dennis Hastert (R)	155,271	67.3
Jonathan Abram Reich (D)	75,294	32.6
15 Thomas W. Ewing (R)	142,167	59.3
Charles D. Mattis (D)	97,190	40.6
16 Donald Manzullo (R)	142,388	55.6
John W. Cox Jr. (D)	113,555	44.4
17 Lane Evans (D)	156,233	60.1
Ken Schloemer (R)	103,719	39.9
18 Robert H. Michel (R)	156,533	57.8
Ronald C. Hawkins (D)	114,413	42.2
19 Glenn Poshard (D)	187,156	69.1
Douglas E. Lee (R)	83,526	30.9
20 Richard J. Durbin (D)	154,869	56.5
John M. Shimkus (R)	119,219	43.5

INDIANA

Candidates	Votes	%
1 Peter J. Visclosky (D)	147,054	69.4
David J. Vucich (R)	64,770	30.6
2 Philip R. Sharp (D)	130,881	57.1
William G. Frazier (R)	90,593	39.5
3 Tim Roemer (D)	121,269	57.4
Carl H. Baxmeyer (R)	89,834	42.6
4 Jill Long (D)	134,907	62.1
Charles W. Pierson (R)	82,468	37.9
5 Steve Buyer (R)	112,492	51.0
Jim Jontz (D)	107,973	49.0
6 Dan Burton (R)	186,499	72.2
Natalie M. Bruner (D)	71,952	27.8

Candidates	Votes	%
7 John T. Myers (R)	129,189	59.5
Ellen E. Wedum (D)	88,005	40.5
8 Frank McCloskey (D)	125,244	52.5
Richard E. Mourdock (R)	108,054	45.3
9 Lee H. Hamilton (D)	160,980	69.7
Michael E. Bailey (R)	70,057	30.3
10 Andrew Jacobs Jr. (D)	117,604	64.0
Janos Horvath (R)	64,378	35.0

IOWA

Candidates	Votes	%
1 Jim Leach (R)	178,042	68.1
Jan J. Zonneveld (D)	81,600	31.2
2 Jim Nussle (R)	134,536	50.2
David R. Nagle (D)	131,570	49.1
3 Jim Ross Lightfoot (R)	125,931	48.9
Elaine Baxter (D)	121,063	47.1
4 Neal Smith (D)	158,610	61.6
Paul Lunde (R)	94,045	36.5
5 Fred Grandy (R)	196,942	99.3

KANSAS

Candidates	Votes	%
1 Pat Roberts (R)	194,912	68.3
Duane West (D)	83,620	29.3
2 Jim Slattery (D)	151,019	56.2
Jim Van Slyke (R)	109,801	40.8
3 Jan Meyers (R)	169,929	58.0
Tom Love (D)	110,076	37.6
4 Dan Glickman (D)	143,671	51.7
Eric R. Yost (R)	117,070	42.1
Seth L. Warren (LIBERT)	17,275	6.2

KENTUCKY

Candidates	Votes	%
1 Tom Barlow (D)	128,524	60.5
Steve Hamrick (R)	83,088	39.1
2 William H. Natcher (D)	126,894	61.4
Bruce R. Bartley (R)	79,684	38.6
3 Romano L. Mazzoli (D)	148,066	52.7
Susan B. Stokes (R)	132,689	47.3
4 Jim Bunning (R)	139,634	61.6
Dr. Floyd G. Poore (D)	86,890	38.4
5 Harold Rogers (R)	115,255	54.6
John Doug Hays (D)	95,760	45.4
6 Scotty Baesler (D)	135,613	60.7
Charles W. Ellinger (R)	87,816	39.3

LOUISIANA [1]

Candidates	Votes	%
1 Robert L. Livingston (R)		100.0
2 William J. Jefferson (D)		100.0
3 W. J. "Billy" Tauzin (D)		100.0
4 Cleo Fields (D)	143,980	73.9
Charles Jones (D)	50,851	26.1
5 Jim McCrery (R)	153,501	63.0
Jerry Huckaby (D)	90,079	37.0
6 Richard H. Baker (R)	123,953	50.6
Clyde C. Holloway (R)	121,225	49.4
7 Jimmy Hayes (D)		100.0

MAINE

Candidates	Votes	%
1 Thomas H. Andrews (D)	232,696	65.0
Linda Bean (R)	125,236	35.0
2 Olympia J. Snowe (R)	153,022	49.1
Patrick K. McGowan (D)	130,824	42.0
Jonathan K. Carter (GREEN)	27,526	8.8

MARYLAND

Candidates	Votes	%
1 Wayne T. Gilchrest (R)	120,084	51.6
Tom McMillen (D)	112,771	48.4
2 Helen Delich Bentley (R)	165,443	65.1
Michael C. Hickey Jr. (D)	88,658	34.9
3 Benjamin L. Cardin (D)	163,354	73.5
William T. S. Bricker (R)	58,869	26.5
4 Albert R. Wynn (D)	136,902	75.2

Footnote, see p. 313.

Candidates	Votes	%
Michele Dyson (R)	45,166	24.8
5 Steny H. Hoyer (D)	118,312	53.0
Lawrence J. Hogan Jr. (R)	97,982	43.9
6 Roscoe G. Bartlett (R)	125,564	54.2
Thomas H. Hattery (D)	106,224	45.8
7 Kweisi Mfume (D)	152,689	85.3
Kenneth Kondner (R)	26,304	14.7
8 Constance A. Morella (R)	203,377	72.5
Edward J. Heffernan (D)	77,042	27.5

MASSACHUSETTS

Candidates	Votes	%
1 John W. Olver (D)	135,049	51.5
Patrick Larkin (R)	113,828	43.4
2 Richard E. Neal (D)	131,215	53.1
Anthony W. Ravosa Jr. (R)	76,795	31.1
Thomas R. Sheehan (FTP)	38,963	15.8
3 Peter I. Blute (R)	131,473	50.4
Joseph D. Early (D)	115,587	44.3
4 Barney Frank (D)	182,633	67.7
Edward J. McCormick III (R)	70,665	26.2
Luke Lumina (IV)	13,670	5.1
5 Martin T. Meehan (D)	133,844	52.2
Paul W. Cronin (R)	96,206	37.5
Mary J. Farinelli (I)	19,077	7.4
6 Peter G. Torkildsen (R)	159,165	54.8
Nicholas Mavroules (D)	130,248	44.9
7 Edward J. Markey (D)	174,837	62.1
Stephen A. Sohn (R)	78,262	27.8
Robert B. Antonelli (I)	28,421	10.1
8 Joseph P. Kennedy II (D)	149,903	83.1
Alice Harriett Nakash (I)	30,402	16.8
9 Joe Moakley (D)	175,550	69.2
Martin D. Conboy (R)	54,291	21.4
Lawrence C. Mackin (I)	15,637	6.2
10 Gerry E. Studds (D)	189,342	60.8
Daniel W. Daly (R)	75,887	24.4
Jon L. Bryan (I)	39,265	12.6

MICHIGAN

Candidates	Votes	%
1 Bart Stupak (D)	144,857	53.9
Philip E. Ruppe (R)	117,056	43.6
2 Peter Hoekstra (R)	155,577	63.0
John H. Miltner (D)	86,265	35.0
3 Paul B. Henry (R)	162,451	61.3
Carol S. Kooistra (D)	95,927	36.2
4 Dave Camp (R)	157,337	62.5
Lisa A. Donaldson (D)	87,573	34.8
5 James A. Barcia (D)	147,618	60.3
Keith Muxlow (R)	93,098	38.0
6 Fred Upton (R)	144,083	61.8
Andy Davis (D)	89,020	38.2
7 Nick Smith (R)	133,972	87.6
Kenneth Proctor (LIBERT)	18,751	12.3
8 Bob Carr (D)	135,517	47.6
Dick Chrysler (R)	131,906	46.3
9 Dale E. Kildee (D)	133,956	53.7
Megan O'Neill (R)	111,798	44.8
10 David E. Bonior (D)	138,193	53.1
Douglas Carl (R)	114,918	44.2
11 Joe Knollenberg (R)	168,940	57.6
Walter Briggs (D)	117,725	40.2
12 Sander M. Levin (D)	137,514	52.6
John Pappageorge (R)	119,357	45.7
13 William D. Ford (D)	127,642	51.9
R. Robert Geake (R)	105,169	42.8
14 John Conyers Jr. (D)	165,496	82.4
John W. Gordon (R)	32,036	15.9
15 Barbara-Rose Collins (D)	148,908	80.5
Charles C. Vincent (R)	31,849	17.2
16 John D. Dingell (D)	156,964	65.1
Frank Beaumont (R)	75,694	31.4

MINNESOTA [2]

Candidates	Votes	%
1 Timothy J. Penny (DFL)	206,369	73.9
Timothy R. Droogsma (I-R)	72,367	25.9
2 David Minge (DFL)	132,156	47.8
Cal R. Ludeman (I-R)	131,587	47.6
3 Jim Ramstad (I-R)	200,240	63.6
Paul Mandell (DFL)	104,606	33.2
4 Bruce F. Vento (DFL)	159,796	57.5
Ian Maitland (I-R)	101,744	36.6
5 Martin Olav Sabo (DFL)	174,139	62.8
Stephen A. Moriarty (I-R)	77,093	27.8
6 Rod Grams (I-R)	133,564	44.4
Gerry Sikorski (DFL)	100,016	33.2
Dean Barkley (I)	48,329	16.1
James H. Peterson (IFP)	16,411	5.5
7 Collin C. Peterson (DFL)	133,886	50.4
Bernie Omann (I-R)	130,396	49.1
8 James L. Oberstar (DFL)	167,104	59.0
Phil Herwig (I-R)	83,823	29.6
Harry Robb Welty (Perot Choice)	22,619	8.0

MISSISSIPPI

Candidates	Votes	%
1 Jamie L. Whitten (D)	121,664	59.5
Clyde E. Whitaker (R)	82,952	40.5
2 Mike Espy (D)	133,361	76.4
Dorothy Benford (R)	41,248	23.6
3 G. V. "Sonny" Montgomery (D)	162,864	81.2
Michael E. Williams (R)	37,710	18.8
4 Mike Parker (D)	130,927	67.3
Jack L. McMillan (R)	43,705	22.5
Liz Gilchrist (I)	10,523	5.4
5 Gene Taylor (D)	120,766	63.2
Paul Harvey (R)	67,619	35.4

MISSOURI

Candidates	Votes	%
1 William L. Clay (D)	158,693	68.1
Arthur S. Montgomery (R)	74,482	31.9
2 James M. Talent (R)	157,594	50.4
Joan Kelly Horn (D)	148,729	47.6
3 Richard A. Gephardt (D)	174,000	64.0
Malcolm L. Holekamp (R)	90,006	33.1
4 Ike Skelton (D)	176,977	70.4
John Carley (R)	74,475	29.6
5 Alan Wheat (D)	151,014	59.1
Edward "Gomer" Moody (R)	93,562	36.6
6 Pat Danner (D)	148,887	55.4
E. Thomas Coleman (R)	119,637	44.6
7 Mel Hancock (R)	160,303	61.6
Thomas Patrick Deaton (D)	99,762	38.4
8 Bill Emerson (R)	147,398	62.9
Thad Bullock (D)	86,730	37.0
9 Harold L. Volkmer (D)	124,694	47.7
Rick Hardy (R)	118,811	45.5

MONTANA

Candidates	Votes	%
AL Pat Williams (D)	203,711	50.5
Ron Marlenee (R)	189,570	47.0

NEBRASKA

Candidates	Votes	%
1 Doug Bereuter (R)	142,713	59.7
Gerry Finnegan (D)	96,309	40.3
2 Peter Hoagland (D)	119,512	51.2
Ronald L. Staskiewicz (R)	113,828	48.8
3 Bill Barrett (R)	170,857	71.7
Lowell Fisher (D)	67,457	28.3

NEVADA

Candidates	Votes	%
1 James H. Bilbray (D)	128,278	57.9
J. Coy Pettyjohn (R)	84,217	38.0
2 Barbara F. Vucanovich (R)	129,575	47.9
Pete Sferrazza (D)	117,199	43.3

NEW HAMPSHIRE

Candidates	Votes	%
1 Bill Zeliff (R)	135,936	53.1
Bob Preston (D)	108,578	42.4
2 Dick Swett (D)	157,328	61.7
Bill Hatch (R)	91,126	35.7

NEW JERSEY

Candidates	Votes	%
1 Robert E. Andrews (D)	153,525	67.3
Lee A. Solomon (R)	65,123	28.6
2 William J. Hughes (D)	132,465	55.9
Frank A. LoBiondo (R)	98,315	41.5
3 H. James Saxton (R)	151,368	59.2
Timothy E. Ryan (D)	94,012	36.8
4 Christopher H. Smith (R)	149,095	61.8
Brian M. Hughes (D)	84,514	35.0
5 Marge Roukema (R)	196,198	71.5
Frank R. Lucas (D)	67,579	24.6
6 Frank Pallone Jr. (D)	118,266	52.3
Joseph M. Kyrillos (R)	100,949	44.6
7 Bob Franks (R)	132,174	53.3
Leonard R. Sendelsky (D)	105,761	42.6
8 Herbert C. Klein (D)	96,742	47.0
Joseph L. Bubba (R)	84,674	41.1
Gloria J. Kolodziej (IFC)	16,170	7.9
9 Robert G. Torricelli (D)	139,188	58.3
Patrick J. Roma (R)	88,179	36.9
10 Donald M. Payne (D)	117,287	78.4
Alfred D. Palermo (R)	30,160	20.2
11 Dean A. Gallo (R)	188,165	70.1
Ona Spiridellis (D)	68,871	25.7
12 Dick Zimmer (R)	174,216	63.9
Frank Abate (D)	83,035	30.4
13 Robert Menendez (D)	93,670	64.3
Fred J. Theemling Jr. (R)	44,529	30.6

NEW MEXICO

Candidates	Votes	%
1 Steven H. Schiff (R)	128,426	62.6
Robert J. Aragon (D)	76,600	37.3
2 Joe Skeen (R)	94,838	56.4
Dan Sosa Jr. (D)	73,157	43.5
3 Bill Richardson (D)	122,850	67.4
F. Gregg Bemis Jr. (R)	54,569	29.9

NEW YORK

Candidates	Votes	%
1 George J. Hochbrueckner (D, LIF)	117,940	51.7
Edward P. Romaine (R, C, RTL, TCP-LI)	110,043	48.3
2 Rick A. Lazio (R, C, TCP-LI)	109,386	53.2
Thomas J. Downey (D, LIF)	96,328	46.8
3 Peter T. King (R, C)	124,727	49.6
Steve A. Orlins (D)	116,915	46.5
4 David A. Levy (R, C)	110,710	50.2
Philip Schiliro (D, L)	100,386	45.5
5 Gary L. Ackerman (D, L)	110,476	52.4
Allan E. Binder (R, C)	94,907	45.0
6 Floyd H. Flake (D)	96,972	81.0
Dianand D. Bhagwandin (R, C)	22,687	19.0
7 Thomas J. Manton (D)	72,280	56.9
Dennis C. Shea (R, C)	54,639	43.1
8 Jerrold Nadler (D, L)	138,296	81.2
David L. Askren (D)	25,548	15.0
9 Charles E. Schumer (D, L)	116,545	88.6
Alice E. Gaffney (C)	14,985	11.4
10 Edolphus Towns (D, L)	97,509	95.8
11 Major R. Owens (D, L)	80,028	93.6
Michael Gaffney (C)	4,287	5.0
12 Nydia M. Velázquez (D)	55,926	76.5
Angel Diaz (R, C, RTL)	14,976	20.5
13 Susan Molinari (R, C)	107,903	56.1
Sal F. Albanese (D, L)	73,520	38.2
Kathleen M. Murphy (RTL)	10,825	5.6

Footnote, see p. 313.

	Candidates	Votes	%
14	Carolyn B. Maloney (D, L)	101,652	50.4
	Bill Green (R, INS)	97,215	48.2
15	Charles B. Rangel (D)	105,011	94.9
16	Jose E. Serrano (D, L)	85,222	91.4
	Michael Walters (R, C)	7,975	8.6
17	Eliot L. Engel (D, L)	98,068	80.1
	Martin Richman (R)	16,511	13.5
18	Nita M. Lowey (D)	115,841	55.6
	Joseph J. DioGuardi (R, C, RTL)	92,687	44.4
19	Hamilton Fish Jr. (R, C)	139,610	60.1
	Neil McCarthy (D)	92,854	39.9
20	Benjamin A. Gilman (R)	150,301	66.1
	Jonathan L. Levine (D)	66,826	29.4
21	Michael R. McNulty (D, C)	166,371	62.7
	Nancy Norman (R, L)	91,184	34.4
22	Gerald B. H. Solomon (R, C, RTL)	164,436	65.4
	David Roberts (D)	86,896	34.6
23	Sherwood Boehlert (R)	139,774	63.6
	Paula DiPerna (D)	61,835	28.2
24	John M. McHugh (R, VR)	122,257	60.8
	Margaret M. Ravenscroft (D)	47,675	23.7
	Morrison J. Hosley Jr. (C, RTL)	26,763	13.3
25	James T. Walsh (R, C)	135,076	55.7
	Rhea Jezer (D, CS)	107,310	44.3
26	Maurice D. Hinchey (D, L)	119,557	50.4
	Bob Moppert (R, C)	110,738	46.7
27	Bill Paxon (R, C, RTL)	156,596	63.5
	W. Douglas Call (D)	89,906	36.5
28	Louise M. Slaughter (D)	140,908	55.2
	William P. Polito (R, C)	112,273	44.0
29	John J. LaFalce (D, L)	128,230	54.5
	William E. Miller Jr. (R, C)	98,031	41.6
30	Jack Quinn (R, CC)	125,734	51.7
	Dennis Gorski (D, C)	111,445	45.8
31	Amo Houghton (R, C)	150,696	70.6
	Joseph P. Leahey (D)	52,010	24.4
	Gretchen S. McManus (RTL)	10,848	5.1

Special Election [3]

	Candidates	Votes	%
17	Jerrold Nadler (D, L)	151,122	100.0

NORTH CAROLINA

	Candidates	Votes	%
1	Eva Clayton (D)	116,078	67.0
	Ted Tyler (R)	54,457	31.4
2	Tim Valentine (D)	113,693	53.7
	Don Davis (R)	93,893	44.4
3	H. Martin Lancaster (D)	101,739	54.4
	Tommy Pollard (R)	80,759	43.2
4	David E. Price (D)	171,299	64.6
	LaVinia "Vicky" Rothrock Goudie (R)	89,345	33.7
5	Stephen L. Neal (D)	117,835	52.7
	Richard M. Burr (R)	102,086	45.6
6	Howard Coble (R)	162,822	70.8
	Robin Hood (D)	67,200	29.2
7	Charlie Rose (D)	92,414	56.7
	Robert C. Anderson (R)	66,536	40.8
8	W. G. "Bill" Hefner (D)	113,162	59.3
	Coy C. Privette (R)	71,842	37.6
9	Alex McMillan (R)	153,650	67.3
	Rory Blake (D)	74,583	32.7
10	Cass Ballenger (R)	149,033	63.4
	Ben Neill (D)	79,206	33.7
11	Charles H. Taylor (R)	130,158	54.7
	John S. Stevens (D)	108,003	45.3
12	Melvin Watt (D)	127,262	70.4
	Barbara Gore Washington (R)	49,402	27.3

Special Election [4]

	Candidates	Votes	%
1	Eva Clayton (D)	118,324	56.7
	Ted Tyler (R)	86,273	41.3

NORTH DAKOTA

	Candidates	Votes	%
AL	Earl Pomeroy (D)	169,273	56.8
	John T. Korsmo (R)	117,442	39.4

OHIO

	Candidates	Votes	%
1	David Mann (D)	120,190	51.3
	Steve Grote (I)	101,498	43.3
	James A. Berns (I)	12,734	5.4
2	Bill Gradison (R)	177,720	70.1
	Thomas R. Chandler (D)	75,924	29.9
3	Tony P. Hall (D)	146,072	59.7
	Peter W. Davis (R)	98,733	40.3
4	Michael G. Oxley (R)	147,346	61.3
	Raymond M. Ball (D)	92,608	38.5
5	Paul E. Gillmor (R)	187,860	100.0
6	Ted Strickland (D)	122,720	50.7
	Bob McEwen (R)	119,252	49.3
7	David L. Hobson (R)	164,195	71.3
	Clifford S. Heskett (D)	66,237	28.7
8	John A. Boehner (R)	176,362	74.0
	Fred Sennet (D)	62,033	26.0
9	Marcy Kaptur (D)	178,879	73.6
	Ken D. Brown (R)	53,011	21.8
10	Martin R. Hoke (R)	136,433	56.8
	Mary Rose Oakar (D)	103,788	43.2
11	Louis Stokes (D)	154,718	69.2
	Beryl E. Rothschild (R)	43,866	19.6
	Edmund Gudenas (I)	19,773	8.8
12	John R. Kasich (R)	170,297	71.2
	Bob Fitrakis (D)	68,761	28.8
13	Sherrod Brown (D)	134,486	53.3
	Margaret Mueller (R)	88,889	35.2
	Mark Miller (I)	20,320	8.1
14	Thomas C. Sawyer (D)	165,335	67.8
	Robert Morgan (R)	78,659	32.2
15	Deborah Pryce (R)	110,390	44.1
	Richard Cordray (D)	94,907	37.9
	Linda S. Reidelbach (I)	44,906	17.9
16	Ralph Regula (R)	158,489	63.7
	Warner D. Mendenhall (D)	90,224	36.3
17	James A. Traficant Jr. (D)	216,503	84.2
	Salvatore Pansino (R)	40,743	15.8
18	Douglas Applegate (D)	166,189	68.3
	Bill Ress (R)	77,229	31.7
19	Eric D. Fingerhut (D)	138,465	52.6
	Robert A. Gardner (R)	124,606	47.4

OKLAHOMA

	Candidates	Votes	%
1	James M. Inhofe (R)	119,211	52.8
	John Selph (D)	106,619	47.2
2	Mike Synar (D)	118,542	55.5
	Jerry Hill (R)	87,657	41.1
3	Bill Brewster (D)	155,934	75.1
	Robert W. Stokes (R)	51,725	24.9
4	Dave McCurdy (D)	140,841	70.7
	Howard Bell (R)	58,235	29.3
5	Ernest Jim Istook (R)	123,237	53.4
	Laurie Williams (D)	107,579	46.6
6	Glenn English (D)	134,734	67.8
	Bob Anthony (R)	64,068	32.2

OREGON

	Candidates	Votes	%
1	Elizabeth Furse (D)	152,917	52.0
	Tony Meeker (R)	140,986	47.9
2	Robert F. Smith (R)	184,163	67.1
	Denzel Ferguson (D)	90,036	32.8
3	Ron Wyden (D)	208,028	77.1
	Al Ritter (R)	50,235	18.6
4	Peter A. DeFazio (D)	199,372	71.4
	Richard L. Schulz (R)	79,733	28.5
5	Mike Kopetski (D)	174,443	63.9
	Jim Seagraves (R)	97,984	35.9

PENNSYLVANIA

	Candidates	Votes	%
1	Thomas M. Foglietta (D)	150,172	80.9
	Craig Snyder (R)	35,419	19.1
2	Lucien E. Blackwell (D)	164,355	76.8
	Larry Hollin (R)	47,906	22.4
3	Robert A. Borski (D)	130,828	58.9
	Charles F. Dougherty (R)	86,787	39.1
4	Ron Klink (D)	186,684	78.5
	Gordon R. Johnston (R)	48,484	20.4
5	William F. Clinger Jr. (R, D)	188,911	100.0
6	Tim Holden (D)	108,312	52.1
	John E. Jones (R)	99,694	47.9
7	Curt Weldon (R)	180,648	66.0
	Frank Daly (D)	91,623	33.5
8	Jim Greenwood (R)	129,593	51.9
	Peter H. Kostmayer (D)	114,095	45.7
9	Bud Shuster (R, D)	182,406	100.0
10	Joseph M. McDade (R, D)	189,414	90.4
	Albert A. Smith (LIBERT)	20,134	9.6
11	Paul E. Kanjorski (D)	138,875	67.1
	Michael A. Fescina (R)	68,112	32.9
12	John P. Murtha (D)	166,916	100.0
13	Marjorie Margolies-Mezvinsky (D)	127,685	50.3
	Jon D. Fox (R)	126,312	49.7
14	William J. Coyne (D)	165,633	72.3
	Byron W. King (R)	61,311	26.8
15	Paul McHale (D)	111,419	52.2
	Don Ritter (R)	99,520	46.7
16	Robert S. Walker (R)	137,823	64.8
	Robert Peters (D)	74,741	35.2
17	George W. Gekas (R)	150,158	69.5
	Bill Sturges (D)	65,881	30.5
18	Rick Santorum (R)	154,024	60.6
	Frank A. Pecora (D)	96,655	38.0
19	Bill Goodling (R)	98,599	45.3
	Paul V. Kilker (D)	74,798	34.4
	Thomas M. Humbert (I)	44,190	20.3
20	Austin J. Murphy (D)	114,898	50.7
	Bill Townsend (R)	111,591	49.3
21	Tom Ridge (R)	150,729	68.0
	John C. Harkins (D)	70,802	32.0

RHODE ISLAND

	Candidates	Votes	%
1	Ronald K. Machtley (R)	135,982	70.1
	David R. Carlin Jr. (D)	48,092	24.8
	Frederick E. Dick (RPI)	6,012	3.1
	Norman J. Jacques (I)	4,003	2.1
2	Jack Reed (D)	144,450	70.7
	James W. Bell (R)	49,998	24.5

SOUTH CAROLINA

	Candidates	Votes	%
1	Arthur Ravenel Jr. (R)	121,938	66.1
	Bill Oberst Jr. (D)	59,908	32.5
2	Floyd D. Spence (R)	148,667	87.6
	Geb Sommer (LIBERT)	20,816	12.3
3	Butler Derrick (D)	119,119	61.1
	Jim Bland (R)	75,660	38.8
4	Bob Inglis (R)	99,879	50.3
	Liz J. Patterson (D)	94,182	47.5
5	John M. Spratt Jr. (D)	112,031	61.2
	Bill Horne (R)	70,866	38.7
6	James E. Clyburn (D)	120,647	65.3
	John Chase (R)	64,149	34.7

SOUTH DAKOTA

	Candidates	Votes	%
AL	Tim Johnson (D)	230,070	69.1
	John Timmer (R)	89,375	26.8

TENNESSEE

	Candidates	Votes	%
1	James H. Quillen (R)	114,797	67.5
	J. Carr "Jack" Christian (D)	47,809	28.1

Candidates	Votes	%
2 John J. Duncan (R)	148,377	72.2
Troy Goodale (D)	52,887	25.7
3 Marilyn Lloyd (D)	105,693	48.8
Zach Wamp (R)	102,763	47.5
4 Jim Cooper (D)	98,984	64.1
Dale Johnson (R)	50,340	32.6
5 Bob Clement (D)	125,233	66.8
Tom Stone (R)	49,417	26.3
6 Bart Gordon (D)	120,177	56.6
Marsha Blackburn (R)	86,289	40.6
7 Don Sundquist (R)	125,101	61.7
David R. Davis (D)	72,062	35.5
8 John Tanner (D)	136,852	83.7
Lawrence J. Barnes (I)	9,605	5.9
9 Harold E. Ford (D)	123,276	57.9
Charles L. Black (R)	60,606	28.5
Richard Liptock (I)	14,075	6.6
James Vandergriff (I)	12,265	5.8

TEXAS

Candidates	Votes	%
1 Jim Chapman (D)	152,209	100.0
2 Charles Wilson (D)	118,625	56.1
Donna Peterson (R)	92,176	43.6
3 Sam Johnson (R)	201,569	86.1
Noel Kopala (LIBERT)	32,570	13.9
4 Ralph M. Hall (D)	128,008	58.1
David L. Bridges (R)	83,875	38.1
5 John Bryant (D)	98,567	58.9
Richard Stokley (R)	62,419	37.3
6 Joe L. Barton (R)	189,140	71.9
John Dietrich (D)	73,933	28.1
7 Bill Archer (R)	169,407	100.0
8 Jack Fields (R)	179,349	77.0
Chas. Robinson (D)	53,473	23.0
9 Jack Brooks (D)	118,690	53.6
Steve Stockman (R)	96,270	43.5
10 J. J. "Jake" Pickle (D)	177,233	67.7
Herbert Spiro (R)	68,646	26.2
11 Chet Edwards (D)	119,999	67.4
James W. Broyles (R)	58,033	32.6
12 Pete Geren (D)	125,492	62.8
David Hobbs (R)	74,432	37.2
13 Bill Sarpalius (D)	117,892	60.3
Beau Boulter (R)	77,514	39.7
14 Greg H. Laughlin (D)	135,930	68.1
Humberto J. Garza (R)	54,412	27.3
15 E. "Kika" de la Garza (D)	86,351	60.4
Tom Haughey (R)	56,549	39.6
16 Ronald D. Coleman (D)	66,731	51.9
Chip Taberski (R)	61,870	48.1
17 Charles W. Stenholm (D)	136,213	66.1
Jeannie Sadowski (R)	69,958	33.9
18 Craig Washington (D)	111,422	64.7
Edward Blum (R)	56,080	32.6
19 Larry Combest (R)	162,057	77.4
Terry Lee Moser (D)	47,325	22.6
20 Henry B. Gonzalez (D)	103,755	100.0
21 Lamar Smith (R)	190,979	72.2
James M. Gaddy (D)	62,827	23.7
22 Thomas D. DeLay (R)	150,221	68.9
Richard Konrad (D)	67,812	31.1
23 Henry Bonilla (R)	98,259	59.1
Albert G. Bustamante (D)	63,797	38.4
24 Martin Frost (D)	104,174	59.8
Steve Masterson (R)	70,042	40.2
25 Michael A. Andrews (D)	98,975	56.0
Dolly Madison McKenna (R)	73,192	41.4
26 Dick Armey (R)	150,209	73.1
John Wayne Caton (D)	55,237	26.9
27 Solomon P. Ortiz (D)	87,022	55.5
Jay Kimbrough (R)	66,853	42.6
28 Frank Tejeda (D)	122,457	87.1
David C. Slatter (LIBERT)	18,128	12.9
29 Gene Green (D)	64,064	64.9
Clark Kent Ervin (R)	34,609	35.1
30 Eddie Bernice Johnson (D)	107,831	71.5
Lucy Cain (R)	37,853	25.1

UTAH

Candidates	Votes	%
1 James V. Hansen (R)	160,037	65.3
Ron Holt (D)	68,712	28.0
William J. Lawrence (IP)	16,505	6.7
2 Karen Shepherd (D)	127,738	50.5
Enid Greene (R)	118,307	46.8
3 Bill Orton (D)	135,029	58.9
Richard R. Harrington (R)	84,019	36.7

VERMONT

Candidates	Votes	%
AL Bernard Sanders (I)	162,724	57.8
Tim Philbin (R)	86,901	30.9
Lewis E. Young (D)	22,279	7.9

VIRGINIA

Candidates	Votes	%
1 Herbert H. Bateman (R)	133,537	57.5
Andrew H. Fox (D)	89,814	38.7
2 Owen B. Pickett (D)	99,253	56.0
J.L. "Jim" Chapman IV (R)	77,797	43.9
3 Robert C. Scott (D)	132,442	78.6
Daniel Jenkins (R)	35,780	21.2
4 Norman Sisisky (D)	147,649	68.4
A.J. "Tony" Zevgolis (R)	68,286	31.6
5 Lewis F. Payne Jr. (D)	133,031	68.9
W. A. "Bill" Hurlburt (R)	60,030	31.1
6 Robert W. Goodlatte (R)	127,309	60.0
Stephen Alan Musselwhite (D)	84,618	39.9
7 Thomas J. Bliley Jr. (R)	211,618	82.9
Gerald E. Berg (I)	43,267	16.9
8 James P. Moran Jr. (D)	138,542	56.1
Kyle E. McSlarrow (R)	102,717	41.6
9 Rick Boucher (D)	133,284	63.1
L. Garrett Weddle (R)	77,985	36.9
10 Frank R. Wolf (R)	144,471	63.6
Raymond E. Vickery (D)	75,775	33.4
11 Leslie L. Byrne (D)	114,172	50.0
Henry N. Butler (R)	103,119	45.2

WASHINGTON

Candidates	Votes	%
1 Maria Cantwell (D)	148,844	54.9
Gary Nelson (R)	113,897	42.0
2 Al Swift (D)	133,207	52.1
Jack Metcalf (R)	107,365	42.0
3 Jolene Unsoeld (D)	138,043	56.0
Pat Fiske (R)	108,583	44.0
4 Jay Inslee (D)	106,556	50.8
Richard "Doc" Hastings (R)	103,028	49.2
5 Thomas S. Foley (D)	135,965	55.2
John Sonneland (R)	110,443	44.8
6 Norm Dicks (D)	152,933	64.2
Lauri J. Phillips (R)	66,664	28.0
Tom Donnelly (I)	14,490	6.1
7 Jim McDermott (D)	222,604	78.4
Glenn C. Hampson (R)	54,149	19.1
8 Jennifer Dunn (R)	155,874	60.4
George O. Tamblyn (D)	87,611	33.9
Bob Adams (I)	14,686	5.7
9 Mike Kreidler (D)	110,902	52.1
Pete von Reichbauer (R)	91,910	43.2

WEST VIRGINIA

Candidates	Votes	%
1 Alan B. Mollohan (D)	172,924	100.0
2 Bob Wise (D)	143,988	70.9
Samuel A. Cravotta (R)	59,102	29.1
3 Nick J. Rahall II (D)	122,279	65.6
Ben Waldman (R)	64,012	34.4

WISCONSIN

Candidates	Votes	%
1 Les Aspin (D)	147,495	57.6
Mark Neumann (R)	104,352	40.7
2 Scott L. Klug (R)	183,366	62.6
Ada E. Deer (D)	108,291	37.0
3 Steve Gunderson (R)	146,903	56.4
Paul Sacia (D)	108,664	41.7
4 Gerald D. Kleczka (D)	173,482	65.8
Joseph L. Cook (R)	84,872	32.2
5 Thomas M. Barrett (D)	162,344	69.3
Donalda Hammersmith (R)	71,085	30.4
6 Thomas E. Petri (R)	143,875	52.9
Peggy A. Lautenschlager (D)	128,232	47.1
7 David R. Obey (D)	166,200	64.4
Dale R. Vannes (R)	91,772	35.6
8 Toby Roth (R)	191,704	70.1
Catherine L. Helms (D)	81,792	29.9
9 F. James Sensenbrenner Jr. (R)	192,898	69.7
Ingrid K. Buxton (D)	77,362	28.0

WYOMING

Candidates	Votes	%
AL Craig Thomas (R)	113,882	57.8
Jon Herschler (D)	77,418	39.3

1992 Elections

1. For the 1992 House elections in Louisiana, an open primary election was held with candidates from all parties running on the same ballot. Any candidate who received a majority was elected unopposed, with no further appearance on the general election ballot. If no candidate received 50 percent, a runoff was held between the two top finishers.

2. In Minnesota the Democratic Party is known as the Democratic-Farmer-Labor Party and the Republican Party as the Independent-Republican Party; candidates appear on the ballot with these designations.

3. A special election was held in conjunction with the November election. Nadler was elected to serve both the unexpired term of Rep. Ted Weiss, D, who died Sept. 14, 1992, and the two-year term beginning Jan. 5, 1993 in a newly renumbered district.

4. A special election was held in conjunction with the November election. Clayton was elected to serve both the unexpired term of Rep. Walter B. Jones, who died Sept. 15, 1992, and the two-year term beginning Jan. 5, 1993.

1993 House Elections

CALIFORNIA

Special Election [1]

	Candidates	Votes	%
17	Sam Farr (D)	53,675	*52.3*
	Bill McCampbell (R)	43,774	*42.6*

MICHIGAN

Special Election [2]

	Candidates	Votes	%
3	Vernon J. Ehlers (R)	57,484	*66.4*
	Dale R. Sprik (D)	19,993	*23.1*
	Dawn Ida Krupp (I)	8,759	*10.1*

MISSISSIPPI

Special Election [3]

	Candidates	Votes	%
2	Bennie Thompson (D)	72,561	*55.2*
	Hayes Dent (R)	58,995	*44.8*

OHIO

Special Election [4]

	Candidates	Votes	%
2	Rob Portman (R)	53,020	*70.1*
	Lee Hornberger (D)	22,652	*29.9*

WISCONSIN

Special Election [5]

	Candidates	Votes	%
1	Peter W. Barca (D)	55,605	*49.9*
	Mark W. Neumann (R)	54,930	*49.3*

1993 Elections

1. A special election was held to fill the unexpired term of Rep. Leon E. Panetta (D), who resigned Jan. 21, 1993, having been appointed director of the White House Office of Management and Budget.

2. A special election was held to fill the unexpired term of Rep. Paul B. Henry (R), who died July 31, 1993.

3. A special election was held to fill the unexpired term of Rep. Mike Espy (D), who resigned Jan. 21, 1993, having been appointed agriculture secretary.

4. A special election was held to fill the unexpired term of Rep. Bill Gradison (R), who resigned Jan. 31, 1993.

5. A special election was held to fill the unexpired term of Rep. Les Aspin (D), who resigned Jan. 20, 1993, having been appointed defense secretary.

1994 House Elections

ALABAMA

	Candidates	Votes	%
1	Sonny Callahan (R)	103,431	67.3
	Don Womack (D)	50,227	32.7
2	Terry Everett (R)	124,465	73.6
	Brian Dowling (D)	44,694	26.4
3	Glen Browder (D)	93,924	63.6
	Ben Hand (R)	53,757	36.4
4	Tom Bevill (D)	119,436	98.5
5	Robert E. "Bud Cramer (D)	88,693	50.5
	Wayne Parker (R)	86,923	49.5
6	Spencer Bachus (R)	155,047	79.0
	Larry Fortenberry (D)	41,030	20.9
7	Earl F. Hilliard (D)	116,150	76.9
	Alfred J. MiddletonSr. (R)	34,814	23.0

ALASKA

		Votes	%
AL	Don Young (R)	118,537	56.9
	Tony Smith (D)	68,172	32.7
	Jonni Whitmore (GREEN)	21,277	10.2

ARIZONA

		Votes	%
1	Matt Salmon (R)	101,350	56.0
	Chuck Blanchard (D)	70,627	39.0
2	Ed Pastor (D)	62,589	62.3
	Robert MacDonald (R)	32,797	32.7
	James Bertrand (LIBERT)	5,060	5.0
3	Bob Stump (R)	145,396	70.1
	Howard Lee Sprague (D)	61,939	29.9
4	John Shadegg (R)	116,714	60.2
	Carol Cure (D)	69,760	36.0
5	Jim Kolbe (R)	149,514	67.7
	Gary Auerbach (D)	63,436	28.7
6	J. D. Hayworth (R)	107,060	54.6
	Karan English (D)	81,321	41.5

ARKANSAS

		Votes	%
1	Blanche Lambert (D)	95,290	53.4
	Warren Dupwe (R)	83,147	46.6
2	Ray Thornton (D)	97,580	57.4
	Bill Powell (R)	72,473	42.6
3	Tim Hutchinson (R)	129,800	67.7
	Berta L. Seitz (D)	61,883	32.3
4	Jay Dickey (R)	87,469	51.8
	Jay Bradford (D)	81,370	48.2

CALIFORNIA

		Votes	%
1	Frank Riggs (R)	106,870	53.3
	Dan Hamburg (D)	93,717	46.7
2	Wally Herger (R)	137,863	64.2
	Mary Jacobs (D)	55,958	26.1
	Devvy Kidd (AMI)	15,569	7.2
3	Vic Fazio (D)	97,093	49.8
	Tim Lefever (R)	89,964	46.1
4	John T. Doolittle (R)	144,936	61.3
	Katie Hirning (D)	82,505	34.9
5	Robert T. Matsui (D)	125,042	68.5
	Robert S. Dinsmore (R)	52,905	29.0
6	Lynn Woolsey (D)	137,642	58.1
	Michael J. Nugent (R)	88,940	37.6
7	George Miller (D)	116,105	69.7
	Charles V. Hughes (R)	45,698	27.4
8	Nancy Pelosi (D)	137,642	81.8
	Elsa C. Cheung (R)	30,528	18.2
9	Ronald V. Dellums (D)	129,233	72.2
	Deborah Wright (R)	40,448	22.6
	Emma Wong Mar (PFP)	9,194	5.1
10	Bill Baker (R)	138,916	59.3
	Ellen Schwartz (D)	90,523	38.6
11	Richard W. Pombo (R)	99,302	62.1

	Candidates	Votes	%
	Randy A. Perry (D)	55,794	34.9
12	Tom Lantos (D)	118,408	67.4
	Deborah Wilder (R)	57,228	32.6
13	Pete Stark (D)	97,344	64.6
	Larry Molton (R)	45,555	30.2
	Robert "Bob" Gough (LIBERT)	7,743	5.1
14	Anna G. Eshoo (D)	120,713	60.6
	Ben Brink (R)	78,475	39.4
15	Norman Y. Mineta (D)	119,921	59.9
	Robert Wick (R)	80,266	40.1
16	Zoe Lofgren (D)	74,935	65.0
	Lyle J. Smith (R)	40,409	35.0
17	Sam Farr (D)	87,222	52.2
	Bill McCampbell (R)	74,380	44.5
18	Gary A. Condit (D)	91,105	65.5
	Tom Carter (R)	44,046	31.7
19	George P. Radanovich (R)	104,435	56.8
	Richard H. Lehman (D)	72,912	39.6
20	Cal Dooley (D)	57,394	56.7
	Paul Young (R)	43,836	43.3
21	Bill Thomas (R)	116,874	68.1
	John L. Evans (D)	47,517	27.7
22	Andrea Seastrand (R)	102,987	49.3
	Walter Holden Capps (D)	101,424	48.5
23	Elton Gallegly (R)	114,043	66.2
	Kevin Ready (D)	47,345	27.5
24	Anthony C. Beilenson (D)	95,342	49.4
	Rich Sybert (R)	91,806	47.5
25	Howard P. "Buck" McKeon (R)	110,301	64.9
	James H. Gilmartin (D)	53,445	31.4
26	Howard L. Berman (D)	55,145	62.6
	Gary E. Forsch (R)	28,423	32.2
	Erich D. Miller (LIBERT)	4,570	5.2
27	Carlos J. Moorhead (R)	88,341	53.0
	Doug Kahn (D)	70,267	42.1
28	David Dreier (R)	110,179	67.1
	Tommy Randle (D)	50,022	30.4
29	Henry A. Waxman (D)	129,413	68.0
	Paul Stepanek (R)	53,801	28.3
30	Xavier Becerra (D)	43,943	66.2
	David A. Ramirez (R)	18,741	28.2
	R. William Weilburg (LIBERT)	3,741	5.6
31	Matthew G. Martinez (D)	50,541	59.1
	John V. Flores (R)	34,926	40.9
32	Julian C. Dixon (D)	98,017	77.6
	Ernie A. Farhat (R)	22,190	17.6
33	Lucille Roybal-Allard (D)	33,814	81.5
	Kermit Booker (PFP)	7,694	18.5
34	Esteban E. Torres (D)	72,439	61.7
	Albert J. Nunez (R)	40,068	34.1
35	Maxine Waters (D)	65,688	78.1
	Nate Truman (R)	18,390	21.9
36	Jane Harman (D)	93,939	48.0
	Susan M. Brooks (R)	93,127	47.6
37	Walter R. Tucker III (D)	64,166	77.4
	Guy Wilson (LIBERT)	18,502	22.3
38	Steve Horn (R)	85,225	58.5
	Peter Mathews (D)	53,681	36.8
39	Ed Royce (R)	113,037	66.4
	R. O. "Bob" Davis (D)	49,459	29.0
40	Jerry Lewis (R)	115,728	70.7
	Donald M. "Don" Rusk (D)	48,003	29.3
41	Jay C. Kim (R)	81,854	62.1
	Ed Tessier (D)	49,924	37.9
42	George E. Brown Jr. (D)	58,888	51.1
	Rob Guzman (R)	56,259	48.8
43	Ken Calvert (R)	84,500	54.7
	Mark A. Takano (D)	59,342	38.4
	Gene L. Berkman (LIBERT)	9,636	6.2
44	Sonny Bono (R)	95,521	55.6
	Steve Clute (D)	65,370	38.1
	Donald Cochran (AMI)	10,885	6.3
45	Dana Rohrabacher (R)	124,006	69.1
	Brett Williamson (D)	55,489	30.9

	Candidates	Votes	%
46	Robert K. Dornan (R)	50,126	57.1
	Michael Farber (D)	32,577	37.1
	Richard G. Newhouse (LIBERT)	5,018	5.7
47	Christopher Cox (R)	152,413	71.7
	Gary Kingsbury (D)	53,035	24.9
48	Ron Packard (R)	143,275	73.4
	Andrei Leschick (D)	43,446	22.3
49	Brian P. Bilbray (R)	90,283	48.5
	Lynn Schenk (D)	85,597	46.0
50	Bob Filner (D)	59,214	56.7
	Mary Alice Acevedo (R)	36,955	35.4
51	Randy "Duke" Cunningham (R)	138,547	66.9
	Rita K. Tamerius (D)	57,374	27.7
52	Duncan Hunter (R)	109,201	64.0
	Janet M. Gastil (D)	53,024	31.1

COLORADO

		Votes	%
1	Patricia Schroeder (D)	93,123	60.0
	William Eggert (R)	61,978	39.9
2	David E. Skaggs (D)	105,938	56.8
	Patricia "Pat" Miller (R)	80,723	43.2
3	Scott McInnis (R)	145,365	69.6
	Linda Powers (D)	63,427	30.4
4	Wayne Allard (R)	136,251	72.3
	Cathy Kipp (D)	52,202	27.7
5	Joel Hefley (R)		100.0
6	Dan Schaefer (R)	124,079	69.8
	John Hallen (D)	49,701	28.0

CONNECTICUT

		Votes	%
1	Barbara B. Kennelly (D,ACP)	138,637	73.4
	Douglas T. Putnam (R)	46,865	24.8
2	Sam Gejdenson (D)	79,188	42.6
	Edward W. Munster (R)	79,167	42.5
	David Bingham (ACP)	27,716	14.9
3	Rosa L. DeLauro (D)	111,261	63.4
	Susan E. Johnson (R,ACP)	64,094	36.6
4	Christopher Shays (R)	109,436	74.4
	Jonathan D. Kantrowitz (D)	34,962	23.8
5	Gary A. Franks (R)	93,471	52.2
	James H. Maloney (D,ACP)	81,523	45.5
6	Nancy L. Johnson (R)	123,101	63.9
	Charlotte Koskoff (D,ACP)	60,701	31.5

DELAWARE

		Votes	%
AL	Michael N. Castle (R)	137,960	70.7
	Carol Ann DeSantis (D)	51,803	26.6

FLORIDA

		Votes	%
1	Joe Scarborough (R)	112,901	61.6
	Vince Whibbs Jr. (D)	70,389	38.4
2	Pete Peterson (D)	117,404	61.3
	Carole Griffin (R)	74,011	38.7
3	Corrine Brown (D)	63,845	57.7
	Marc Little (R)	46,895	42.3
4	Tillie Fowler (R)		100.0
5	Karen L. Thurman (D)	125,780	57.2
	"Big Daddy" Don Garlits (R)	94,093	42.8
6	Cliff Stearns (R)	148,698	99.1
7	John L. Mica (R)	131,711	73.4
	Edward D. Goddard (D)	47,747	26.6
8	Bill McCollum (R)	131,376	99.7
9	Michael Bilirakis (R)	177,253	99.9
10	C. W. Bill Young (R)		100.0
11	Sam M. Gibbons (D)	76,814	51.6
	Mark Sharpe (R)	72,119	48.4
12	Charles T. Canady (R)	106,123	65.0
	Robert Connors (D)	57,203	35.0

	Candidates	Votes	%
13	Dan Miller (R)		100.0
14	Porter J. Goss (R)		100.0
15	Dave Weldon (R)	117,027	53.7
	Sue Munsey (D)	100,513	46.1
16	Mark Foley (R)	122,734	58.1
	John Comerford (D)	88,646	41.9
17	Carrie P. Meek (D)		100.0
18	Ileana Ros-Lehtinen (R)		100.0
19	Harry A. Johnston (D)	147,591	66.1
	Peter J. Tsakanikas (R)	75,779	33.9
20	Peter Deutsch (D)	114,615	61.2
	Beverly "Bev" Kennedy (R)	72,516	38.8
21	Lincoln Diaz-Balart (R)		100.0
22	E. Clay Shaw Jr. (R)	119,690	63.4
	Hermine L. Wiener (D)	69,215	36.6
23	Alcee L. Hastings (D)		100.0

GEORGIA

	Candidates	Votes	%
1	Jack Kingston (R)	88,788	76.6
	Raymond Beckworth (D)	27,197	23.4
2	Sanford D. Bishop Jr. (D)	65,383	66.2
	John Clayton (R)	33,429	33.8
3	Mac Collins (R)	94,717	65.5
	Fred Overby (D)	49,828	34.5
4	John Linder (R)	90,063	57.9
	Comer Yates (D)	65,566	42.1
5	John Lewis (D)	85,094	69.1
	Dale Dixon (R)	37,999	30.9
6	Newt Gingrich (R)	119,432	64.2
	Ben Jones (D)	66,700	35.8
7	Bob Barr (R)	71,265	51.9
	George "Buddy" Darden (D)	65,978	48.1
8	Saxby Chambliss (R)	89,591	62.7
	Craig Mathis (D)	53,408	37.3
9	Nathan Deal (R)	79,145	57.9
	Robert L. Castello (R)	57,568	42.1
10	Charlie Norwood (R)	96,099	65.2
	Don Johnson (D)	51,192	34.8
11	Cynthia A. McKinney (D)	71,560	65.6
	Woodrow Lovett (R)	37,533	34.4

HAWAII

	Candidates	Votes	%
1	Neil Abercrombie (D)	94,754	53.6
	Orson Swindle (R)	76,623	43.4
2	Patsy T. Mink (D)	124,431	70.1
	Robert H. Garner (R)	42,891	24.2
	Lawrence R. Bartley (LIBERT)	10,074	5.7

IDAHO

	Candidates	Votes	%
1	Helen Chenoweth (R)	111,728	55.4
	Larry LaRocco (D)	89,826	44.6
2	Michael D. Crapo (R)	143,593	75.0
	Penny Fletcher (D)	47,936	25.0

ILLINOIS

	Candidates	Votes	%
1	Bobby L. Rush (D)	112,474	75.7
	William J. Kelly (R)	36,038	24.3
2	Mel Reynolds (D)	93,998	98.1
3	William O. Lipinski (D)	92,353	54.2
	Jim Nalepa (R)	78,163	45.8
4	Luis V. Gutierrez (D)	46,695	75.2
	Steven Valtierra (R)	15,384	24.8
5	Michael Patrick Flanagan (R)	75,328	54.4
	Dan Rostenkowski (D)	63,065	45.6
6	Henry J. Hyde (R)	115,664	73.5
	Tom Berry (D)	37,163	23.6
7	Cardiss Collins (D)	93,457	79.6
	Charles "Chuck" Mobley	24,011	20.4
8	Philip M. Crane (R)	88,225	64.9
	Robert C. Walberg (D)	47,654	35.1
9	Sidney R. Yates (D)	94,404	66.1
	George Edward Larney (R)	48,419	33.9
10	John Edward Porter (R)	114,884	75.1
	Andrew M. Krupp (D)	38,191	24.9
11	Gerald C. "Jerry" Weller (R)	97,241	60.6
	Frank Giglio (D)	63,150	39.4
12	Jerry F. Costello (D)	101,391	65.9
	Jan Morris (R)	52,419	34.1
13	Harris W. Fawell (R)	124,312	73.1
	William A. Riley (D)	45,709	26.9
14	Dennis Hastert (R)	110,204	76.5
	Steve Denari (D)	33,891	23.5
15	Thomas W. Ewing (R)	108,857	68.2
	Paul Alexander (D)	50,874	31.8
16	Donald Manzullo (R)	117,238	70.6
	Pete Sullivan (D)	48,736	29.4
17	Lane Evans (D)	95,312	54.5
	Jim Anderson (R)	79,471	45.5
18	Ray LaHood (R)	119,838	60.2
	G. Douglas Stephens (D)	78,332	39.3
19	Glenn Poshard (D)	115,045	58.4
	Brent Winters (R)	81,995	41.6
20	Richard J. Durbin (D)	108,034	54.8
	Bill Owens (R)	88,964	45.2

INDIANA

	Candidates	Votes	%
1	Peter J. Visclosky (D)	68,612	56.5
	John Larson (R)	52,920	43.5
2	David M. McIntosh (R)	93,592	54.5
	Joseph H. Hogsett (D)	78,241	45.5
3	Tim Roemer (D)	72,497	55.2
	Richard Burkett (R)	58,878	44.8
4	Mark Edward Souder (R)	88,584	55.4
	Jill L. Long (D)	71,235	44.6
5	Steve Buyer (R)	111,031	69.5
	J. D. Beatty (D)	45,224	28.3
6	Dan Burton (R)	136,876	77.0
	Natalie M. Bruner (D)	40,815	23.0
7	John T. Myers (R)	104,359	65.1
	Michael M. Harmless (D)	55,941	34.9
8	John Hostettler (R)	93,529	52.4
	Frank McCloskey (D)	84,857	47.6
9	Lee H. Hamilton (D)	91,459	52.0
	Jean Leising (R)	84,315	48.0
10	Andrew Jacobs Jr. (D)	58,573	53.5
	Marvin Bailey Scott (R)	50,998	46.5

IOWA

	Candidates	Votes	%
1	Jim Leach (R)	110,448	60.2
	Glen Winekauf (D)	69,461	37.9
2	Jim Nussle (R)	111,076	56.0
	Dave Nagle (D)	86,087	43.9
3	Jim Ross Lightfoot (R)	111,862	57.8
	Elaine Baxter (D)	79,310	41.0
4	Greg Ganske (R)	111,935	52.5
	Neal Smith (D)	98,824	46.4
5	Tom Latham (R)	114,796	60.8
	Sheila McGuire (D)	73,627	39.0

KANSAS

	Candidates	Votes	%
1	Pat Roberts (R)	169,531	77.4
	Terry L. Nichols (D)	49,477	22.6
2	Sam Brownback (R)	135,725	65.6
	John Carlin (D)	71,025	34.4
3	Jan Meyers (R)	102,218	56.6
	Judy Hancock (D)	78,401	43.4
4	Todd Tiahrt (R)	111,653	52.9
	Dan Glickman (D)	99,366	47.1

KENTUCKY

	Candidates	Votes	%
1	Edward Whitfield (R)	64,849	51.0
	Tom Barlow (D)	62,387	49.0
2	Ron Lewis (R)	90,535	59.8
	David Adkisson (D)	60,867	40.2
3	Mike Ward (D)	67,663	44.4
	Susan B. Stokes (R)	67,238	44.1
	Richard Lewis (KTAX)	17,591	11.5
4	Jim Bunning (R)	96,695	74.1
	Sally Harris Skaggs (D)	33,717	25.9
5	Harold Rogers (R)	82,291	79.4
	Walter "Doc" Blevins (D)	21,318	20.6
6	Scotty Baesler (D)	70,085	58.8
	Matthew Eric Wills (R)	49,032	41.2

Special Election[1]

	Candidates	Votes	%
2	Ron Lewis (R)	40,126	55.2
	Joseph E. Prather (D)	32,625	44.8

LOUISIANA[2]

	Candidates	Votes	%
1	Robert L. Livingston (R)		100.0
2	William J. Jefferson (D)		100.0
3	W. J. "Billy" Tauzin (D)		100.0
4	Cleo Fields (D)		100.0
5	Jim McCrery (R)		100.0
6	Richard H. Baker (R)		100.0
7	Jimmy Hayes (D)		100.0

MAINE

	Candidates	Votes	%
1	James B. Longley Jr. (R)	136,316	51.9
	Dennis L. Dutremble (D)	126,373	48.1
2	John Baldacci (D)	109,615	45.7
	Richard A. Bennett (R)	97,754	40.7
	John M. Michael (I)	21,117	8.8

MARYLAND

	Candidates	Votes	%
1	Wayne T. Gilchrest (R)	120,975	67.7
	Ralph T. Gies (D)	57,712	32.3
2	Robert L. Ehrlich Jr. (R)	125,162	62.7
	Gerry L. Brewster (D)	74,275	37.2
3	Benjamin L. Cardin (D)	117,269	71.0
	Robert Ryan Tousey (R)	47,966	29.0
4	Albert R. Wynn (D)	93,148	75.0
	Michele Dyson (R)	30,999	25.0
5	Steny H. Hoyer (D)	98,821	58.8
	Donald Devine (R)	69,211	41.2
6	Roscoe G. Bartlett (R)	122,809	65.9
	Paul Muldowney (D)	63,411	34.1
7	Kwesi Mfume (D)	97,016	81.5
	Kenneth Kondner (R)	22,007	18.5
8	Constance A. Morella (R)	143,449	70.3
	Steven Van Grack (D)	60,660	29.7

MASSACHUSETTS

	Candidates	Votes	%
1	John W. Olver (D)	150,047	99.4
2	Richard E. Neal (D)	117,178	58.6
	John M. Briare (R)	72,732	36.3
	Kate Ross (NL)	10,167	5.1
3	Peter I. Blute (R)	115,810	54.6
	Kevin O'Sullivan (D)	93,689	44.2
4	Barney Frank (D)	168,942	99.5
5	Martin T. Meehan (D)	140,725	69.8
	David E. Coleman (R)	60,734	30.1
6	Peter G. Torkildsen (R)	120,952	50.5
	John F. Tierney (D)	113,481	47.4
7	Edward J. Markey (D)	146,246	64.4
	Brad Bailey (R)	80,674	35.5
8	Joseph P. Kennedy II (D)	113,224	99.0
9	Joe Moakley (D)	146,287	69.8
	Michael M. Murphy (R)	63,369	30.2
10	Gerry E. Studds (D)	172,753	68.7
	Keith Jason Hemeon (R)	78,487	31.2

MICHIGAN

	Candidates	Votes	%
1	Bart Stupak (D)	121,433	56.9
	Gil Ziegler (R)	89,660	42.0
2	Peter Hoekstra (R)	146,164	75.3
	Marcus Pete Hoover (D)	46,097	23.7
3	Vernon J. Ehlers (R)	136,711	73.9
	Betsy J. Flory (D)	43,580	23.5
4	Dave Camp (R)	145,176	73.1
	Damion Frasier (D)	50,544	25.5
5	James A. Barcia (D)	126,456	65.5

Footnotes, see p. 319.

Candidates	Votes	%
William T. Anderson (R)	61,342	31.8
6 Fred Upton (R)	121,923	73.5
David Taylor (D)	42,348	25.5
7 Nick Smith (R)	115,621	65.1
Kim McCaughtry (D)	57,326	32.3
8 Dick Chrysler (R)	109,663	51.6
Bob Mitchell (D)	95,383	44.9
9 Dale E. Kildee (D)	97,096	51.2
Megan O'Neill (R)	89,148	47.0
10 David E. Bonior (D)	121,876	62.2
Donald J. Lobsinger (R)	73,862	37.7
11 Joe Knollenberg (R)	154,696	68.2
Mike Breshgold (D)	69,168	30.5
12 Sander M. Levin (D)	103,508	52.0
John Pappageorge (R)	92,762	46.6
13 Lynn Nancy Rivers (D)	89,573	51.9
John A. Schall (R)	77,908	45.1
14 John Conyers Jr. (D)	128,463	81.5
Richard Charles Fornier (R)	26,215	16.6
15 Barbara-Rose Collins (D)	119,442	84.1
John W. Savage II (R)	20,074	14.1
16 John D. Dingell (D)	105,849	59.1
Ken Larkin (R)	71,159	39.8

MINNESOTA

Candidates	Votes	%
1 Gil Gutknecht (R)	117,613	55.2
John C. Hottinger (D)	95,328	44.7
2 David Minge (D)	114,289	52.0
Gary B. Revier (R)	98,881	45.0
3 Jim Ramstad (R)	173,223	73.2
Bob Olson (D)	62,211	26.3
4 Bruce F. Vento (D)	115,638	54.9
Dennis Newinski (R)	88,344	41.9
5 Martin Olav Sabo (D)	121,515	61.9
Dorothy LeGrand (R)	73,258	37.3
6 William P. "Bill" Luther (D)	113,740	49.9
Tad Jude (R)	113,190	49.7
7 Collin C. Peterson (D)	108,023	51.2
Bernie Omann (R)	102,623	48.6
8 James L. Oberstar (D)	153,161	65.7
Phil Herwig (R)	79,818	34.2

MISSISSIPPI

Candidates	Votes	%
1 Roger Wicker (R)	80,553	63.1
Bill Wheeler (D)	47,192	36.9
2 Bennie Thompson (D)	68,014	53.7
Bill Jordan (R)	49,270	38.9
Vince Thornton (MSTAX)	9,408	7.4
3 G. V. "Sonny" Montgomery (D)	83,163	67.6
Dutch Dabbs (R)	39,826	32.4
4 Mike Parker (D)	82,939	68.5
Mike Wood (R)	38,200	31.5
5 Gene Taylor (D)	73,179	60.1
George Barlos (R)	48,575	39.9

MISSOURI

Candidates	Votes	%
1 William L. Clay (D)	97,061	63.4
Donald R. Counts (R)	50,303	32.9
2 James M. Talent (R)	154,882	67.3
Pat Kelly (D)	70,480	30.6
3 Richard A. Gephardt (D)	117,601	57.7
Gary Gill (R)	80,977	39.7
4 Ike Skelton (D)	137,876	67.8
James A. Noland Jr. (R)	65,616	32.2
5 Karen McCarthy (D)	100,391	56.6
Ron Freeman (R)	77,120	43.4
6 Pat Danner (D)	140,108	66.1
Tina Tucker (R)	71,709	33.9
7 Mel Hancock (R)	112,228	57.3
James R. Fossard (D)	77,836	39.7
8 Bill Emerson (R)	129,320	70.1
James L. "Jay" Thompson (D)	48,987	26.5
9 Harold L. Volkmer (D)	103,443	50.5
Kenny Hulshof (R)	92,301	45.0

MONTANA

Candidates	Votes	%
AL Pat Williams (D)	171,372	48.7
Cy Jamison (R)	148,715	42.2
Steve Kelly (I)	32,046	9.1

NEBRASKA

Candidates	Votes	%
1 Doug Bereuter (R)	117,967	62.6
Patrick Combs (D)	70,369	37.3
2 Jon Christensen (R)	92,516	49.9
Peter Hoagland (D)	90,750	49.0
3 Bill Barrett (R)	154,919	78.7
Gil Chapin (D)	41,943	21.3

NEVADA

Candidates	Votes	%
1 John Ensign (R)	73,769	48.5
James Bilbray (D)	72,333	47.5
2 Barbara F. Vucanovich (R)	142,202	63.5
Janet Greeson (D)	65,390	29.2

NEW HAMPSHIRE

Candidates	Votes	%
1 Bill Zeliff (R)	97,017	65.6
Bill Verge (D)	42,481	28.7
2 Charles Bass (R)	83,121	51.4
Dick Swett (D)	74,243	46.0

NEW JERSEY

Candidates	Votes	%
1 Robert E. Andrews (D)	108,155	72.3
James N. Hogan (R)	41,505	27.7
2 Frank A. LoBiondo (R)	102,566	64.6
Louis N. Magazzu (D)	56,151	35.4
3 H. James Saxton (R)	115,750	66.4
James Smith (D)	54,441	31.2
4 Christopher H. Smith (R)	109,818	67.9
Ralph Walsh (D)	49,537	30.6
5 Marge Roukema (R)	139,964	74.2
Bill Auer (D)	41,275	21.9
6 Frank Pallone Jr. (D)	88,922	60.4
Mike Herson (R)	55,287	37.5
7 Bob Franks (R)	98,814	59.6
Karen Carroll (D)	64,231	38.7
8 Bill Martini (R)	70,494	49.9
Herb Klein (D)	68,661	48.6
9 Robert G. Torricelli (D)	99,984	62.5
Peter J. Russo (R)	57,651	36.1
10 Donald M. Payne (D)	74,622	75.9
Jim Ford (D)	21,524	21.9
11 Rodney Frelinghuysen (R)	127,868	71.2
Frank Herbert (D)	50,211	28.0
12 Dick Zimmer (R)	125,939	68.3
Joseph D. Youssouf (D)	55,977	30.4
13 Robert Menendez (D)	67,688	70.9
Fernando A. Alonso (R)	24,071	25.2

NEW MEXICO

Candidates	Votes	%
1 Steven H. Schiff (R)	119,996	73.9
Peter L. Zollinger (D)	42,316	26.1
2 Joe Skeen (R)	89,966	63.3
Benjamin Anthony Chavez (D)	45,316	31.9
3 Bill Richardson (D)	99,900	63.6
F. Gregg Bemis Jr. (R)	53,515	34.1

NEW YORK

Candidates	Votes	%
1 Michael P. Forbes (R,C,RTL,WTP)	90,491	52.5
George J. Hochbrueckner (D,LIF)	80,146	46.5
2 Rick A. Lazio (R,C,WTP)	100,107	68.2
James Manfre (D,LIF)	41,102	28.0
3 Peter T. King (R,C)	115,236	59.2
Norma Grill (D)	77,774	40.0
4 Daniel Frisa (R)	87,815	50.2
Philip M. Schiliro (D)	65,286	37.3

Candidates	Votes	%
David A. Levy (C)	15,173	8.7
5 Gary Ackerman (D,L)	93,896	55.0
Grant M. Lally (R,C)	73,884	43.3
6 Floyd H. Flake (D)	68,596	80.4
Denny D. Bhagwandin (R,C)	16,675	19.6
7 Thomas J. Manton (D)	58,935	87.1
Robert E. Hurley (C)	8,698	12.9
8 Jerrold Nadler (D,L)	109,946	82.0
David L. Askren (D)	21,132	15.8
9 Charles E. Schumer (D,L)	95,139	72.6
James McCall (R,C)	35,880	27.4
10 Edolphus Towns (D,L)	77,026	89.0
Amelia Smith Parker (R)	7,995	9.2
11 Major R. Owens (D,L)	61,945	88.9
Gary S. Popkin (R,LIBERT)	6,605	9.5
12 Nydia M. Velazquez (D,L)	39,929	92.3
Genevieve R. Brennan (C)	2,747	6.3
13 Susan Molinari (R,C)	96,491	71.4
Tyrone G. Butler (D,L)	33,937	25.1
14 Carolyn B. Maloney (D,IN)	98,479	64.2
Charles Millard (R,L)	54,277	35.4
15 Charles B. Rangel (D,L)	77,830	96.5
16 Jose E. Serrano (D,L)	58,572	96.3
17 Eliot L. Engel (D,L)	73,321	77.6
Edward T. Marshall (R)	16,896	17.9
18 Nita M. Lowey (D,L)	91,663	57.3
Andrew C. Hartzell Jr. (R,C)	65,517	40.9
19 Sue W. Kelly (R)	100,173	52.1
Hamilton Fish Jr. (D)	70,696	36.8
Joseph J. DioGuardi (C,RTL)	19,761	10.3
20 Benjamin A. Gilman (R)	120,334	67.5
Gregory B. Julian (D)	52,345	29.4
21 Michael R. McNulty (D,C)	147,804	67.0
Joseph A. Gomez (R)	68,745	31.2
22 Gerald B. H. Solomo (R,C,RTL)	157,717	73.4
L. Robert Lawrence (D)	57,064	26.6
23 Sherwood Boehlert (R)	124,486	70.5
Charles W. Skeele Jr. (D)	40,786	23.1
Donald J. Thomas (RTL)	11,216	6.4
24 John M. McHugh (R,C)	124,645	78.6
Danny M. Francis (D)	34,032	21.4
25 James T. Walsh (R,C)	113,949	57.6
Rhea Jezer (D,CHGC)	83,853	42.4
26 Maurice D. Hinchey (D,L)	95,492	49.1
Bob Moppert (R,C)	94,244	48.5
27 Bill Paxon (R,C,RTL)	152,610	74.5
William A. Long Jr. (D)	52,160	25.5
28 Louise M. Slaughter (D)	110,987	56.6
Renee Forgensi Davison (R,C)	78,516	40.1
29 John J. LaFalce (D,L)	103,053	55.2
William E. Miller (R,C)	80,355	43.0
30 Jack Quinn (R,C)	124,738	67.0
David A. Franczyk (D,L)	61,392	33.0
31 Amo Houghton (R,C)	121,178	84.8
Gretchen S. McManus (RTL)	21,747	15.2

NORTH CAROLINA

Candidates	Votes	%
1 Eva Clayton (D)	66,827	61.1
Ted Tyler (R)	42,602	38.9
2 David Funderburk (R)	79,207	56.0
Richard Moore (D)	62,122	44.0
3 Walter B. Jones Jr. (R)	72,464	52.7
H. Martin Lancaster (D)	65,013	47.3
4 Frederick Kenneth Heineman (R)	77,773	50.4
David Price (D)	76,558	49.6
5 Richard Burr (R)	84,741	57.3
A. P. "Sandy" Sands (D)	63,194	42.7
6 Howard Coble (R)		100.0
7 Charlie Rose (D)	62,670	51.6
Robert C. Anderson (R)	58,849	48.4
8 W. G. "Bill" Hefner (D)	62,845	52.4
Sherrill Morgan (R)	57,140	47.6
9 Sue Myrick (R)	82,374	65.0
Rory Blake (D)	44,379	35.0
10 Cass Ballenger (R)	107,829	71.5

	Candidates	Votes	%
	Robert Wayne Avery (D)	42,939	28.5
11	Charles H. Taylor (R)	115,826	60.1
	Maggie Palmer Lauterer (D)	76,862	39.9
12	Melvin Watt (D)	57,655	65.8
	Joseph A. "Joe" Martino (R)	29,933	34.2

NORTH DAKOTA

	Candidates	Votes	%
AL	Earl Pomeroy (D)	123,134	52.3
	Gary Porter (R)	105,988	45.0

OHIO

	Candidates	Votes	%
1	Steve Chabot (R)	92,997	56.1
	David Mann (D)	72,822	43.9
2	Rob Portman (R)	150,128	77.4
	Les Mann (D)	43,730	22.6
3	Tony P. Hall (D)	105,342	59.3
	David A. Westbrock (R)	72,314	40.7
4	Michael G. Oxley (R)		100.0
5	Paul E. Gillmor (R)	135,879	73.4
	Jarrod Tudor (D)	49,335	26.6
6	Frank A. Cremeans (R)	91,263	50.9
	Ted Strickland (D)	87,861	49.1
7	David L. Hobson (R)		100.0
8	John A. Boehner (R)	148,338	99.9
9	Marcy Kaptur (D)	118,120	75.3
	R. Randy Whitman (R)	38,665	24.7
10	Martin R. Hoke (R)	95,226	51.9
	Francis E. Gaul (D)	70,918	38.6
	Joseph J. Jacobs Jr. (I)	17,495	9.5
11	Louis Stokes (D)	114,220	77.2
	James J. Sykora (R)	33,705	22.8
12	John R. Kasich (R)	114,608	66.5
	Cynthia L. Ruccia (D)	57,294	33.2
13	Sherrod Brown (D)	93,147	49.1
	Gregory A. White (R)	86,422	45.5
14	Tom Sawyer (D)	96,274	51.9
	Lynn Slaby (R)	89,106	48.1
15	Deborah Pryce (R)	112,912	70.7
	Bill Buckel (D)	46,480	29.1
16	Ralph Regula (R)	137,322	75.0
	J. Michael Finn (D)	45,781	25.0
17	James A. Traficant Jr. (D)	149,004	77.4
	Mike G. Meister (R)	43,490	22.6
18	Bob Ney (R)	103,115	54.0
	Greg L. DiDonato (D)	87,926	46.0
19	Steven C. LaTourette (R)	99,997	48.5
	Eric D. Fingerhut (D)	89,701	43.5
	Ronald E. Young (I)	11,364	5.5

OKLAHOMA

	Candidates	Votes	%
1	Steve Largent (R)	107,085	62.7
	Stuart Price (D)	63,753	37.3
2	Tom Coburn (R)	82,479	52.1
	Virgil R. Cooper (D)	75,943	47.9
3	Bill Brewster (D)	115,731	73.8
	Darrel Dewayne Tallant (R)	41,147	26.2
4	J. C. Watts (R)	80,251	51.6
	David Perryman (D)	67,237	43.3
	Bill Tiffee (I)	7,913	5.1
5	Ernest Jim Istook (R)	136,877	78.1
	Tom Keith (I)	38,270	21.9
6	Frank D. Lucas (R)	106,961	70.2
	Jeffrey S. Tollett (D)	45,399	29.8

Special Election3

	Candidates	Votes	%
6	Frank D. Lucas (R)	71,354	54.2
	Dan Webber Jr. (D)	60,411	45.8

OREGON

	Candidates	Votes	%
1	Elizabeth Furse (D)	121,147	47.7
	Bill Witt (R)	120,846	47.6
2	Wes Cooley (R)	134,255	57.3
	Sue C. Kupillas (D)	90,822	38.7
3	Ron Wyden (D)	161,624	72.5

	Candidates	Votes	%
	Everett Hall (R)	43,211	19.4
	Mark Brunelle (I)	13,550	6.1
4	Peter A. DeFazio (D)	158,981	66.8
	John D. Newkirk (R)	78,947	33.2
5	Jim Bunn (R)	121,369	49.8
	Catherine Webber (D)	114,015	46.8

PENNSYLVANIA

	Candidates	Votes	%
1	Thomas M. Foglietta (D)	99,669	81.5
	Roger F. Gordon (R)	22,595	18.5
2	Chaka Fattah (D)	120,553	85.9
	Lawrence R. Watson (R)	19,824	14.1
3	Robert A. Borski (D)	92,702	62.7
	James C. Hasher (R)	55,209	37.3
4	Ron Klink (D)	119,115	64.2
	Ed Peglow (R)	66,509	35.8
5	William F. Clinger (R)	145,335	99.9
6	Tim Holden (D)	90,023	56.7
	Fred Levering (R)	68,610	43.3
7	Curt Weldon (R)	137,480	69.7
	Sara Nichols (D)	59,845	30.3
8	James C. Greenwood (R)	110,499	66.1
	John P. Murray (D)	44,559	26.7
9	Bud Shuster (R)	146,688	99.7
10	Joseph M. McDade (R)	106,992	65.7
	Daniel J. Schreffler (D)	50,635	31.1
11	Paul E. Kanjorski (D)	101,966	66.5
	J. Andrew Podolak (R)	51,295	33.5
12	John P. Murtha (D)	117,825	68.9
	Bill Choby (R)	53,147	31.1
13	Jon D. Fox (R)	96,254	49.4
	Marjorie Margolies-Mezvinsky (D)	88,073	45.2
14	William J. Coyne (D)	105,310	64.1
	John Robert Clark (R)	53,221	32.4
15	Paul McHale (D)	72,073	47.8
	Jim Yeager (R)	71,602	47.4
16	Robert S. Walker (R)	109,759	69.7
	Bill Chertok (D)	47,680	30.3
17	George W. Gekas (R)	133,788	99.9
18	Mike Doyle (D)	101,784	54.8
	John McCarty (R)	83,881	45.2
19	Bill Goodling (R)	124,496	99.5
20	Frank R. Mascara (D)	95,251	53.1
	Mike McCormick (R)	84,156	46.9
21	Phil English (R)	89,439	49.5
	Bill Leavens (D)	84,796	46.9

RHODE ISLAND

	Candidates	Votes	%
1	Patrick J. Kennedy (D)	89,832	54.1
	Kevin Vigilante (R)	76,069	45.9
2	Jack Reed (D)	119,659	68.0
	A. John Elliot (R)	56,348	32.0

SOUTH CAROLINA

	Candidates	Votes	%
1	Marshall "Mark" Sanford (R)	973,03	66.3
	Robert Barber (D)	47,769	32.4
2	Floyd D. Spence (R)	133,307	99.8
3	Lindsey Graham (R)	90,123	60.1
	James Bryan (D)	59,932	39.9
4	Bob Inglis (R)	109,626	73.5
	Jerry Fowler (D)	39,396	26.4
5	John M. Spratt Jr. (D)	77,311	52.1
	Larry Bigham (R)	70,967	47.8
6	James E. Clyburn (D)	88,635	63.8
	Gary McLeod (R)	50,259	36.2

SOUTH DAKOTA

	Candidates	Votes	%
AL	Tim Johnson (D)	183,036	59.8
	Jan Berkhout (R)	112,054	36.6

TENNESSEE

	Candidates	Votes	%
1	James H. Quillen (R)	102,947	72.9
	J. Carr "Jack" Christian (D)	34,691	24.6

	Candidates	Votes	%
2	John J. "Jimmy" Duncan Jr. (R)	128,937	90.5
3	Zach Wamp (R)	84,583	52.3
	Randy Button (D)	73,839	45.6
4	Van Hilleary (R)	81,539	56.6
	Jeff Whorley (D)	60,489	42.0
5	Bob Clement (D)	95,953	60.2
	John Osborne (R)	61,692	38.7
6	Bart Gordon (D)	90,933	50.6
	Steve Gill (R)	88,759	49.4
7	Ed Bryant (R)	102,587	60.2
	Harold Byrd (D)	65,851	38.6
8	John Tanner (D)	97,951	63.8
	Neal R. Morris (R)	55,573	36.2
9	Harold E. Ford (D)	94,805	57.8
	Rod DeBerry (R)	69,226	42.2

TEXAS

	Candidates	Votes	%
1	Jim Chapman (D)	86,480	55.3
	Mike Blankenship (R)	63,911	40.9
2	Charles Wilson (D)	87,709	57.0
	Donna Peterson (R)	66,071	43.0
3	Sam Johnson (R)	157,011	91.0
	Tom Donahue (LIBERT)	15,611	9.0
4	Ralph M. Hall (D)	99,303	58.8
	David L. Bridges (R)	67,267	39.8
5	John Bryant (D)	61,877	50.1
	Pete Sessions (R)	58,521	47.3
6	Joe L. Barton (R)	152,038	75.6
	Terry Jesmore (D)	44,286	22.0
7	Bill Archer (R)		100.0
8	Jack Fields (R)	148,473	92.0
	Russ Klecka (I)	12,831	8.0
9	Steve Stockman (R)	81,353	51.9
	Jack Brooks (D)	71,643	45.7
10	Lloyd Doggett (D)	113,738	56.3
	A. Jo Baylor (R)	80,382	39.8
11	Chet Edwards (D)	76,667	59.2
	Jim Broyles (R)	52,876	40.8
12	Pete Geren (D)	96,372	68.7
	Ernest J. Anderson Jr. (R)	43,959	31.3
13	William M. "Mac" Thornberry (R)	79,466	55.4
	Bill Sarpalius (D)	63,923	44.6
14	Greg Laughlin (D)	86,175	55.6
	Jim Deats (R)	68,793	44.4
15	E. "Kika" de la Garza (D)	61,527	59.0
	Tom Haughey (R)	41,119	39.4
16	Ronald D. Coleman (D)	49,815	57.1
	Bobby Ortiz (R)	37,409	42.9
17	Charles W. Stenholm (D)	83,497	53.7
	Phil Boone (R)	72,108	46.3
18	Sheila Jackson Lee (D)	84,790	73.5
	Jerry Burley (R)	28,153	24.4
19	Larry Combest (R)		100.0
20	Henry B. Gonzalez (D)	60,114	62.5
	Carl Bill Colyer (R)	36,035	37.5
21	Lamar Smith (R)	165,595	90.0
	Kerry Lowry (I)	18,480	10.0
22	Tom DeLay (R)	120,302	73.7
	Scott Douglas Cunningham (D)	38,826	23.8
23	Henry Bonilla (R)	73,815	62.6
	Rolando L. Rios (D)	44,101	37.4
24	Martin Frost (D)	65,019	52.8
	Ed Harrison (R)	58,062	47.2
25	Ken Bentsen (D)	61,959	52.3
	Gene Fontenot (R)	53,321	45.0
26	Dick Armey (R)	135,398	76.4
	LeEarl Ann Bryant (D)	39,763	22.4
27	Solomon P. Ortiz (D)	65,325	59.4
	Erol A. Stone (R)	44,693	40.6
28	Frank Tejeda (D)	73,986	70.9
	David C. Slatter (R)	28,777	27.6
29	Gene Green (D)	44,102	73.4
	Harold "Oilman" Eide (R)	15,952	26.6
30	Eddie Bernice Johnson (D)	73,166	72.6
	Lucy Cain (R)	25,848	25.7

Footnotes, see p. 319.

UTAH

	Candidates	Votes	%
1	James V. Hansen (R)	104,954	64.5
	Bobbie Coray (D)	57,644	35.5
2	Enid Greene Waldholtz (R)	85,507	45.8
	Karen Shepherd (D)	66,911	35.9
	Merrill Cook (I)	34,167	18.3
3	Bill Orton (D)	91,505	59.0
	Dixie Thompson (R)	61,839	39.9

VERMONT

	Candidates	Votes	%
AL	Bernard Sanders (I)	105,502	49.9
	John Carroll (R)	98,523	46.6

VIRGINIA

	Candidates	Votes	%
1	Herbert H. Bateman (R)	142,930	74.3
	Mary Sinclair (D)	45,173	23.5
2	Owen Pickett (D)	81,372	59.0
	Jim Chapman (R)	56,375	40.9
3	Robert C. Scott (D)	108,532	79.4
	Tom Ward (R)	28,080	20.6
4	Norman Sisisky (D)	115,055	61.6
	George Sweet (R)	71,678	38.4
5	Lewis F. Payne Jr. (D)	95,308	53.3
	George C. Landrith III (R)	83,555	46.7
6	Robert W. Goodlatte (R)	126,455	99.9
7	Thomas J. Bliley Jr. (R)	176,941	84.0
	Gerald E. "Jerry" Berg (I)	33,220	15.8
8	James P. Moran (D)	120,281	59.3
	Kyle E. McSlarrow (R)	79,568	39.3

	Candidates	Votes	%
9	Rick Boucher (D)	102,876	58.8
	Steve Fast (R)	72,133	41.2
10	Frank R. Wolf (R)	153,311	87.3
	Alan R. Ogden (I)	13,687	7.8
11	Thomas M. Davis III (R)	98,216	52.9
	Leslie L. Byrne (D)	84,104	45.3

WASHINGTON

	Candidates	Votes	%
1	Rick White (R)	100,554	51.7
	Maria Cantwell (D)	94,110	48.3
2	Jack Metcalf (R)	107,430	54.7
	Harriet A. Spanel (D)	89,096	45.3
3	Linda Smith (R)	100,188	52.0
	Jolene Unsoeld (D)	85,826	44.6
4	Doc Hastings (R)	92,828	53.3
	Jay Inslee (D)	81,198	46.7
5	George Nethercutt (R)	110,057	50.9
	Thomas S. Foley (D)	106,074	49.1
6	Norm Dicks (D)	105,480	58.3
	Benjamin Gregg (R)	75,322	41.7
7	Jim McDermott (D)	148,353	75.1
	Keith Harris (R)	49,091	24.9
8	Jennifer Dunn (R)	140,409	76.1
	Jim Wyrick (D)	44,165	23.9
9	Randy Tate (R)	77,833	51.8
	Mike Kreidler (D)	72,451	48.2

WEST VIRGINIA

	Candidates	Votes	%
1	Alan B. Mollohan (D)	103,177	70.3
	Sally Rossy Riley (R)	43,590	29.7

	Candidates	Votes	%
2	Bob Wise (D)	90,757	63.7
	Sam Cravotta (R)	51,691	36.3
3	Nick J. Rahall II (D)	74,967	63.9
	Ben Waldman (R)	42,382	36.1

WISCONSIN

	Candidates	Votes	%
1	Mark W. Neumann (R)	83,937	49.4
	Peter W. Barca (D)	82,817	48.8
2	Scott L. Klug (R)	133,734	69.2
	Thomas C. Hecht (D)	55,406	28.7
3	Steve Gunderson (R)	89,338	55.7
	Harvey Stower (D)	65,758	41.0
4	Gerald D. Kleczka (D)	93,789	53.7
	Tom Reynolds (R)	78,225	44.8
5	Thomas M. Barrett (D)	87,806	62.4
	Stephen B. Hollingshead (R)	51,145	36.4
6	Tom Petri (R)	119,384	99.5
7	David R. Obey (D)	97,184	54.3
	Scott West (R)	81,706	45.7
8	Toby Roth (R)	114,319	63.7
	Stan Gruszynski (D)	65,065	36.3
9	F. James Sensenbrenner (R)	141,617	99.8

WYOMING

	Candidates	Votes	%
AL	Barbara Cubin (R)	104,426	53.2
	Bob Schuster (D)	81,022	41.3
	Dave Dawson (LIBERT)	10,749	5.5

1994 Elections

1. A special election was held to fill the unexpired term of Rep. William H. Natcher (D), who died March 29, 1994.

2. For the 1994 House elections in Louisiana, an open primary election was held with candidates from all parties running on the same ballot. Any candidate who received a majority was elected unopposed, with no further appearance on the general election ballot. If no candidate received 50 percent, a runoff was held between the two top finishers.

3. A special election was held to fill the unexpired term of Rep. Glen English (D), who resigned Jan. 7, 1994.

1995 House Elections

CALIFORNIA

Special Election[1]

	Candidates	Votes	%
15	Tom Campbell (R)	54,372	58.9
	Jerry Estruth (D)	33,051	35.8
	Linh Kieu Dao (I)	4,922	5.3

ILLINOIS

Special Election[2]

	Candidates	Votes	%
2	Jesse Jackson Jr. (D)	48,145	76.0
	Thomas "T. J." Somer (R)	15,171	24.0

1995 Elections

1. A special election was held to fill the unexpired term of Rep. Norman Y. Mineta (D), who resigned Oct. 10, 1995.

2. A special election was held to fill the unexpired term of Rep. Mel Reynolds (D), who resigned Oct. 1, 1995.

1996 House Elections

ALABAMA

	Candidates	Votes	%
1	Sonny Callahan (R)	132,206	64.4
	Don Womack (D)	69,470	33.8
2	Terry Everett (R)	132,563	63.2
	Bob E. Gaines (D)	74,317	35.4
3	Bob Riley (R)	98,353	50.4
	T. D "Ted" Little (D)	92,325	47.3
4	Robert B. Aderholt (R)	102,741	49.9
	Robert T. "Bob" Wilson (D)	99,250	48.2
5	Robert E. "Bud" Cramer (D)	114,442	55.7
	Wayne Parker (R)	86,727	42.2
6	Spencer Bachus (R)	180,781	70.9
	Mary Lynn Bates (D)	69,592	27.3
7	Earl F. Hilliard (D)	136,651	71.1
	Joe Powell (R)	52,142	27.1

ALASKA

	Candidates	Votes	%
AL	Don Young (R)	138,834	59.4
	Georgianna Lincoln (D)	85,114	36.4

ARIZONA

	Candidates	Votes	%
1	Matt Salmon (R)	135,634	60.2
	John Cox (D)	89,738	39.8
2	Ed Pastor (D)	81,982	65.0
	Jim Buster (R)	38,786	30.8
3	Bob Stump (R)	175,231	66.5
	Alexander "Big Al" Schneider (D)	88,214	33.5
4	John Shadegg (R)	150,486	66.8
	Maria Elena Milton (D)	74,857	33.2
5	Jim Kolbe (R)	179,349	68.7
	Mort Nelson (D)	67,597	25.9
6	J. D Hayworth (R)	121,431	47.6
	Steve Owens (D)	118,957	46.6
	Robert Anderson (LIBERT)	14,899	5.8

ARKANSAS

	Candidates	Votes	%
1	Marion Berry (D)	105,280	52.8
	Warren Dupwe (R)	88,436	44.3
2	Vic Snyder (D)	114,841	52.3
	Bud Cummins (R)	104,548	47.7
3	Asa Hutchinson (R)	137,093	55.7
	Ann Henry (D)	102,994	41.8
4	Jay Dickey (R)	125,956	63.5
	Vincent Tolliver (D)	72,391	36.5

CALIFORNIA

	Candidates	Votes	%
1	Frank Riggs (R)	110,242	49.6
	Michela Alioto (D)	96,522	43.5
	Emil Rossi (LIBERT)	15,354	6.9
2	Wally Herger (R)	144,913	60.8
	Roberts A. Braden (D)	80,401	33.7
3	Vic Fazio (D)	118,663	53.5
	Tim LeFever (R)	91,134	41.1
4	John T. Doolittle (R)	164,048	60.5
	Katie Hirning (D)	97,948	36.1
5	Robert T. Matsui (D)	142,618	70.4
	Robert S. Dinsmore (R)	52,940	26.1
6	Lynn Woolsey (D)	156,958	61.8
	Duane C. Hughes (R)	86,278	34.0
7	George Miller (D)	137,089	71.8
	Norman H. Reece (R)	42,542	22.3
8	Nancy Pelosi (D)	175,216	84.3
	Justin Raimondo (R)	25,739	12.4
9	Ronald V. Dellums (D)	154,806	77.0
	Deborah Wright (R)	37,126	18.5
10	Ellen O. Tauscher (D)	137,726	48.6
	Bill Baker (R)	133,633	47.2
11	Richard W. Pombo (R)	107,477	59.3
	Jason Silva (D)	65,536	36.2

	Candidates	Votes	%
12	Tom Lantos (D)	149,052	71.7
	Storm Jenkins (R)	49,278	23.7
13	Pete Stark (D)	114,408	65.2
	James S. Fay (R)	53,385	30.4
14	Anna G. Eshoo (D)	149,313	64.9
	Ben Brink (R)	71,573	31.1
15	Tom Campbell (R)	132,737	58.5
	Dick Lane (D)	79,048	34.8
16	Zoe Lofgren (D)	94,020	65.7
	Chuck Wojslaw (R)	43,197	30.2
17	Sam Farr (D)	115,116	58.9
	Jess Brown (R)	73,856	37.8
18	Gary A. Condit (D)	108,827	65.7
	Bill Conrad (R)	52,695	31.8
19	George P. Radanovich (R)	137,402	66.6
	Paul Barile (D)	58,452	28.3
20	Cal Dooley (D)	65,381	56.5
	Trice Harvey (R)	45,276	39.1
21	Bill Thomas (R)	125,916	65.8
	Deborah A. Vollmer (D)	50,694	26.5
22	Walter Holden Capps (D)	118,299	48.4
	Andrea Seastrand (R)	107,987	44.2
23	Elton Gallegly (R)	118,880	59.6
	Robert R. Unruhe (D)	70,035	35.1
24	Brad Sherman (D)	106,193	49.4
	Rich Sybert (R)	93,629	43.6
25	Howard P. "Buck" McKeon (R)	122,428	62.4
	Diane Trautman (D)	65,089	33.2
26	Howard L. Berman (D)	67,525	65.9
	Bill Glass (R)	29,332	28.6
27	James E. Rogan (R)	95,310	50.2
	Doug Kahn (D)	82,014	43.2
28	David Dreier (R)	113,389	60.7
	David Levering (D)	69,037	36.9
29	Henry A. Waxman (D)	145,278	67.6
	Paul Stepanek (R)	52,857	24.6
30	Xavier Becerra (D)	58,283	72.3
	Patricia Jean Parker (R)	15,078	18.7
31	Matthew G. Martinez (D)	69,285	67.5
	John V. Flores (R)	28,705	28.0
32	Julian C. Dixon (D)	124,712	82.4
	Larry Ardito (R)	18,768	12.4
33	Lucille Roybal-Allard (D)	47,478	82.1
	John P. Leonard (R)	8,147	14.1
34	Esteban E. Torres (D)	94,730	68.4
	David G. Nunez (R)	36,852	26.6
35	Maxine Waters (D)	92,762	85.5
	Eric Carlson (R)	13,116	12.1
36	Jane Harman (D)	117,752	52.5
	Susan Brooks (R)	98,538	43.9
37	Juanita Millender McDonald (D)	87,247	85.0
	Michael E. Voetee (R)	15,399	15.0
38	Steve Horn (R)	88,136	52.6
	Rick Zbur (D)	71,627	42.7
39	Ed Royce (R)	120,761	62.8
	R. O "Bob" Davis (D)	61,392	31.9
	Jack Dean (LIBERT)	10,137	5.3
40	Jerry Lewis (R)	98,821	64.9
	Robert "Bob" Conaway (D)	44,102	29.0
41	Jay C. Kim (R)	83,934	58.5
	Richard L. Waldron (D)	47,346	33.0
42	George E. Brown Jr. (D)	52,166	50.5
	Linda M. Wilde (R)	51,170	49.5
43	Ken Calvert (R)	97,247	54.7
	Guy C. Kimbrough (D)	67,422	37.9
44	Sonny Bono (R)	110,643	57.7
	Anita Rufus (D)	73,844	38.5
45	Dana Rohrabacher (R)	125,326	61.0
	Sally J. Alexander (D)	68,312	33.2
46	Loretta Sanchez (D)	47,964	46.8
	Robert K. Dornan (R)	46,980	45.8
47	Christopher Cox (R)	160,078	65.7
	Tina Louise Laine (D)	70,362	28.9
48	Ron Packard (R)	145,814	65.9

	Candidates	Votes	%
	Dan Farrell (D)	59,558	26.9
49	Brian P. Bilbray (R)	108,806	52.6
	Peter Navarro (D)	86,657	41.9
50	Bob Filner (D)	73,200	61.9
	Jim Baize (R)	38,351	32.4
51	Randy "Duke" Cunningham (R)	149,032	65.1
	Rita Tamerius (D)	66,250	28.9
52	Duncan Hunter (R)	116,746	65.5
	Darity Wesley (D)	53,104	29.8

Special Election[1]

		Votes	%
37	Juanita Millender-McDonald (D)	13,868	27.3
	Willard H. Murray Jr. (D)	10,396	20.4
	Omar Bradley (D)	6,975	13.7
	Paul H. Richards (D)	6,035	11.9
	Robert M. Sausedo (D)	4,495	8.8
	Robin Tucker (D)	3,661	7.2
	Charles Davis (D)	2,555	5.0

COLORADO

		Votes	%
1	Diana DeGette (D)	112,631	56.9
	Joe Rogers (R)	79,540	40.2
2	David E. Skaggs (D)	145,894	57.0
	Pat Miller (R)	97,865	38.3
3	Scott McInnis (R)	183,523	68.9
	Al Gurule (D)	82,953	31.1
4	Bob Schaffer (R)	137,012	56.1
	Guy Kelley (D)	92,837	38.1
5	Joel Hefley (R)	188,805	71.9
	Mike Robinson (D)	73,660	28.1
6	Dan Schaefer (R)	146,018	62.2
	Joan Fitz-Gerald (D)	88,600	37.8

CONNECTICUT

		Votes	%
1	Barbara B. Kennelly (D,ACP)	158,222	73.5
	Kent Sleath (R)	53,666	24.9
2	Sam Gejdenson (D,ACP)	115,175	51.6
	Edward W. Munster (R)	100,332	44.9
3	Rosa DeLauro (D,ACP)	150,798	71.3
	John Coppola (R)	59,335	28.1
4	Christopher Shays (R)	121,949	60.5
	Bill Finch (D)	75,902	37.6
5	Jim Maloney (D,ACP)	111,974	52.0
	Gary A. Franks (R)	98,782	45.9
6	Nancy L. Johnson (R)	113,020	49.6
	Charlotte Koskoff (D,ACP)	111,433	48.9

DELAWARE

		Votes	%
AL	Michael N. Castle (R)	185,576	69.5
	Dennis E. Williams (D)	73,253	27.5

FLORIDA

		Votes	%
1	Joe Scarborough (R)	175,946	72.5
	Kevin Beck (D)	66,495	27.4
2	Allen Boyd (D)	138,151	59.4
	Bill Sutton (R)	94,122	40.5
3	Corrine Brown (D)	98,085	61.2
	Preston James Fields (R)	62,196	38.8
4	Tillie Fowler (R)		100.0
5	Karen L. Thurman (D)	161,050	61.7
	Dave Gentry (R)	100,051	38.3
6	Cliff Stearns (R)	161,527	67.2
	Newell O'Brien (D)	78,908	32.8
7	John L. Mica (R)	143,667	62.0
	George Stuart Jr. (D)	87,832	37.9
8	Bill McCollum (R)	136,515	67.5

Footnote, see p. 324.

Candidates	Votes	%
Al Krulick (D)	65,794	32.5
9 Michael Bilirakis (R)	161,708	68.7
Jerry Provenzano (D)	73,809	31.3
10 C. W Bill Young (R)	114,443	66.6
Henry Green (D)	57,375	33.4
11 Jim Davis (D)	108,522	57.9
Mark Sharpe (R)	78,881	42.0
12 Charles T. Canady (R)	122,584	61.6
Mike Canady (D)	76,513	38.4
13 Dan Miller (R)	173,671	64.3
Sanford Gordon (D)	96,098	35.6
14 Porter J. Goss (R)	176,992	73.5
Jim Nolan (D)	63,842	26.5
15 Dave Weldon (R)	139,014	51.4
John L. Byron (D)	115,981	42.9
David Golding (I)	15,349	5.7
16 Mark Foley (R)	175,714	64.0
Jim Stuber (D)	98,827	36.0
17 Carrie P. Meek (D)	114,638	88.8
Wellington Rolle (R)	14,525	11.2
18 Ileana Ros-Lehtinen (R)	123,659	100.0
19 Robert Wexler (D)	188,766	65.6
Beverly "Bev" Kennedy (R)	99,101	34.4
20 Peter Deutsch (D)	159,256	65.0
Jim Jacobs (R)	85,777	35.0
21 Lincoln Diaz-Balart (R)	125,469	100.0
22 E. Clay Shaw Jr. (R)	137,098	61.9
Kenneth D. Cooper (D)	84,517	38.1
23 Alcee L. Hastings (D)	102,161	73.5
Robert Paul Brown (R)	36,907	26.5

GEORGIA

Candidates	Votes	%
1 Jack Kingston (R)	108,616	68.2
Rosemary Kaszans (D)	50,622	31.8
2 Sanford D. Bishop Jr. (D)	88,256	54.0
Darrel Ealum (R)	75,282	46.0
3 Mac Collins (R)	120,251	61.1
Jim Chafin (D)	76,538	38.9
4 Cynthia A. McKinney (D)	127,157	57.8
John Mitnick (R)	92,985	42.2
5 John Lewis (D)	136,555	100.0
6 Newt Gingrich (R)	174,155	57.8
Michael Coles (D)	127,135	42.2
7 Bob Barr (R)	112,009	57.8
Charlie Watts (D)	81,765	42.2
8 Saxby Chambliss (R)	93,619	52.6
Jim Wiggins (D)	84,506	47.4
9 Nathan Deal (R)	132,532	65.5
McCracken "Ken" Poston (D)	69,662	34.5
10 Charlie Norwood (R)	96,723	52.3
David Bell (D)	88,054	47.7
11 John Linder (R)	145,821	64.3
Tommy Stephenson (D)	80,940	35.7

HAWAII

Candidates	Votes	%
1 Neil Abercrombie (D)	86,732	50.4
Orson Swindle (R)	80,053	46.5
2 Patsy T. Mink (D)	109,178	60.3
Tom Pico Jr. (R)	55,729	30.8

IDAHO

Candidates	Votes	%
1 Helen Chenoweth (R)	132,344	50.0
Dan Williams (D)	125,899	47.5
2 Michael D. Crapo (R)	157,646	68.8
John D. Seidl (D)	67,625	29.5

ILLINOIS

Candidates	Votes	%
1 Bobby L. Rush (D)	174,005	85.7
Noel Naughton (R)	25,659	12.6
2 Jesse L. Jackson Jr. (D)	172,648	94.1
Frank H. Stratman (LIBERT)	10,880	5.9
3 William O. Lipinski (D)	137,153	65.3
Jim Nalepa (R)	67,214	32.0
4 Luis V. Gutierrez (D)	85,278	93.6

Candidates	Votes	%
William Passmore (LIBERT)	5,857	6.4
5 Rod R. Blagojevich (D)	117,544	64.1
Michael Patrick Flanagan (R)	65,768	35.9
6 Henry J. Hyde (R)	132,401	64.3
Stephen de la Rosa (D)	68,807	33.4
7 Danny K. Davis (D)	149,568	82.6
Randy Borow (R)	27,241	15.0
8 Philip M. Crane (R)	127,763	62.2
Elizabeth Ann "Betty" Hull (D)	74,068	36.1
9 Sidney R. Yates (D)	124,319	63.4
Joseph Walsh (R)	71,763	36.6
10 John Edward Porter (R)	145,626	69.1
Philip R. Torf (D)	65,144	30.9
11 Gerald C. "Jerry" Weller (R)	109,896	51.8
Clem Balanoff (D)	102,388	48.2
12 Jerry F. Costello (D)	150,005	71.6
Shapley R. Hunter (R)	55,690	26.6
13 Harris W. Fawell (R)	141,651	59.9
Susan W. Hynes (D)	94,693	40.1
14 Dennis Hastert (R)	134,432	64.4
Doug Mains (D)	74,332	35.6
15 Thomas W. Ewing (R)	121,019	57.3
Laurel Lunt Prussing (D)	90,065	42.7
16 Donald Manzullo (R)	137,523	60.3
Catherine M. Lee (D)	90,575	39.7
17 Lane Evans (D)	120,008	51.9
Mark Baker (R)	109,240	47.3
18 Ray LaHood (R)	143,110	59.3
Mike Curran (D)	98,413	40.7
19 Glenn Poshard (D)	158,668	66.7
Brent Winters (R)	75,751	31.8
20 John M. Shimkus (R)	120,926	50.3
Jay C. Hoffman (D)	119,688	49.7

INDIANA

Candidates	Votes	%
1 Peter J. Visclosky (D)	133,553	69.2
Michael Edward Petyo (R)	56,418	29.2
2 David M. McIntosh (R)	123,113	57.8
R. Marc "Marc" Carmichael (D)	85,105	40.0
3 Tim Roemer (D)	114,288	57.9
Joe Zakas (R)	80,699	40.9
4 Mark E. Souder (R)	121,344	58.4
Gerald L. Houseman (D)	81,740	39.3
5 Steve Buyer (R)	125,191	59.3
Douglas L. Clark (D)	63,578	30.1
6 Dan Burton (R)	193,193	74.9
Carrie J. Dillard Trammell (D)	59,661	23.1
7 Ed Pease (R)	130,010	62.0
Robert F. Hellmann (D)	72,705	34.6
8 John Hostettler (R)	109,860	50.0
Jonathan Weinzapfel (D)	106,201	48.3
9 Lee H. Hamilton (D)	128,123	56.5
Jean Leising (R)	96,442	42.5
10 Julia Carson (D)	85,965	52.9
Virginia Blankenbaker (R)	72,796	44.8

IOWA

Candidates	Votes	%
1 Jim Leach (R)	129,242	52.8
Bob Rush (D)	111,595	45.6
2 Jim Nussle (R)	127,827	53.4
Donna L. Smith (D)	109,731	45.9
3 Leonard L. Boswell (D)	115,914	49.4
Mike Mahaffey (R)	111,895	47.6
4 Greg Ganske (R)	133,419	52.0
Connie McBurney (D)	119,790	46.7
5 Tom Latham (R)	147,576	65.5
MacDonald Smith (D)	75,785	33.6

KANSAS

Candidates	Votes	%
1 Jerry Moran (R)	191,899	73.5
John Divine (D)	63,948	24.5
2 Jim Ryun (R)	131,592	52.2

Candidates	Votes	%
John Frieden (D)	114,644	45.5
3 Vince Snowbarger (R)	139,169	49.8
Judy Hancock (D)	126,848	45.4
4 Todd Tiahrt (R)	128,486	50.1
Randy Rathbun (D)	119,544	46.6

KENTUCKY

Candidates	Votes	%
1 Edward Whitfield (R)	111,473	53.6
Dennis L. Null (D)	96,684	46.4
2 Ron Lewis (R)	125,433	58.1
Joe Wright (D)	90,483	41.9
3 Anne M. Northup (R)	126,625	50.3
Mike Ward (D)	125,326	49.7
4 Jim Bunning (R)	149,135	68.4
Denny Bowman (D)	68,939	31.6
5 Harold Rogers (R)	117,842	100.0
6 Scotty Baesler (D)	125,999	55.7
Ernest Fletcher (R)	100,231	44.3

LOUISIANA [2]

Candidates	Votes	%
1 Robert L. Livingston (R)		100.0
2 William J. Jefferson (D)		100.0
3 W. J "Billy" Tauzin (R)		100.0
4 Jim McCrery (R)		100.0
5 John Cooksey (R)	135,990	58.3
Francis Thompson (D)	97,363	41.7
6 Richard H. Baker (R)		100.0
7 Chris John (D)	128,449	53.1
Hunter Lundy (D)	113,351	46.9

MAINE

Candidates	Votes	%
1 Tom Allen (D)	173,745	55.3
James B. Longley Jr. (R)	140,354	44.7
2 John Baldacci (D)	205,439	71.9
Paul R. Young (R)	70,856	24.8

MARYLAND

Candidates	Votes	%
1 Wayne T. Gilchrest (R)	131,033	61.6
Steven R. Eastaugh (D)	81,825	38.4
2 Robert L. Ehrlich Jr. (R)	143,075	61.8
Connie Galiazzo DeJuliis (D)	88,344	38.2
3 Benjamin L. Cardin (D)	130,204	67.3
Patrick L. McDonough (R)	63,229	32.7
4 Albert R. Wynn (D)	142,094	85.2
John B. Kimble (R)	24,700	14.8
5 Steny H. Hoyer (D)	121,288	56.9
John S. Morgan (R)	91,806	43.1
6 Roscoe G. Bartlett (R)	132,853	56.8
Stephen Crawford (D)	100,910	43.2
7 Elijah E. Cummings (D)	115,764	83.5
Kenneth Kondner (R)	22,929	16.5
8 Constance A. Morella (R)	152,538	61.2
Don Mooers (D)	96,442	38.6

Special Election[3]

Candidates	Votes	%
7 Elijah E. Cummings (D)	18,870	80.9
Kenneth Konder (R)	4,449	19.1

MASSACHUSETTS

Candidates	Votes	%
1 John W. Olver (D)	129,232	52.7
Jane Swift (R)	115,801	47.2
2 Richard E. Neal (D)	162,995	71.7
Mark Steele (R)	49,885	21.9
3 Jim McGovern (D)	135,047	52.9
Peter I. Blute (R)	115,695	45.4
4 Barney Frank (D)	183,854	71.6
Jonathan Raymond (R)	72,707	28.3
5 Martin T. Meehan (D)	183,457	99.1
6 John F. Tierney (D)	133,684	48.2
Peter G. Torkildsen (R)	132,318	48.1
7 Edward J. Markey (D)	177,053	69.8
Patricia Long (R)	76,407	30.1
8 Joseph P. Kennedy II (D)	147,246	84.3

Footnotes, see p. 324.

Candidates	Votes	%
R. Philip Hyde (R)	27,315	15.6
9 Joe Moakley (D)	172,012	72.2
Paul Gryska (R)	66,080	27.7
10 Bill Delahunt (D)	160,747	54.3
Edward Teague (R)	123,523	41.7

MICHIGAN

Candidates	Votes	%
1 Bart Stupak (D)	181,486	70.7
Bob Carr (R)	69,957	27.2
2 Peter Hoekstra (R)	165,608	65.3
Dan Kruszynski (D)	83,603	33.0
3 Vernon J. Ehlers (R)	169,466	68.6
Betsy J. Flory (D)	72,791	29.5
4 Dave Camp (R)	159,561	65.5
Lisa A. Donaldson (D)	79,691	32.7
5 James A. Barcia (D)	162,675	70.0
Lawrence Sims	65,542	28.2
6 Fred Upton (R)	146,170	67.7
Clarence J. Annen (D)	66,243	30.7
7 Nick Smith (R)	120,227	55.0
Kim H. Tunnicliff (D)	93,725	42.9
8 Debbie Stabenow (D)	141,086	53.8
Dick Chrysler (R)	115,836	44.1
9 Dale E. Kildee (D)	136,856	59.2
Patrick M. Nowak (R)	89,733	38.8
10 David E. Bonior (D)	132,829	54.4
Susy Heintz (R)	106,444	43.6
11 Joe Knollenberg (R)	169,165	61.2
Morris Frumin (D)	99,303	35.9
12 Sander M. Levin (D)	133,436	57.4
John Pappageorge (R)	94,235	40.5
13 Lynn Rivers (D)	123,133	56.6
Joe Fitzsimmons (R)	89,907	41.3
14 John Conyers Jr. (D)	157,722	85.9
William A. Ashe (R)	22,152	12.1
15 Carolyn Cheeks Kilpatrick (D)	143,683	88.4
Stephen Hume (R)	16,009	9.8
16 John D. Dingell (D)	136,854	62.0
James R. DeSana (R)	78,723	35.7

MINNESOTA

Candidates	Votes	%
1 Gil Gutknecht (R)	137,545	52.7
Mary Rieder (D)	123,188	47.2
2 David Minge (D)	144,083	54.9
Gary B. Revier (R)	107,807	41.1
3 Jim Ramstad (R)	205,845	70.1
Stanley J. Leino (D)	87,359	29.8
4 Bruce F. Vento (D)	145,831	57.0
Dennis Newinski (R)	94,110	36.8
5 Martin Olav Sabo (D)	158,275	64.3
Jack Uldrich (R)	70,115	28.5
Erika Anderson (GR)	13,102	5.3
6 William P. "Bill" Luther (D)	164,921	55.8
Tad Jude (R)	129,989	44.0
7 Collin C. Peterson (D)	170,936	67.9
Darrell McKigney (R)	80,132	31.8
8 James L. Oberstar (D)	185,333	67.3
Andy Larson (R)	69,460	25.2
Stan Estes (REF)	16,639	6.0

MISSISSIPPI

Candidates	Votes	%
1 Roger Wicker (R)	123,724	67.6
Henry Boyd Jr. (D)	55,998	30.6
2 Bennie Thompson (D)	102,503	59.6
Danny Covington (R)	65,263	38.0
3 Charles W. "Chip" Pickering Jr. (R)	115,443	61.4
John Arthur Eaves Jr. (D)	68,658	36.5
4 Mike Parker (R)	112,444	61.2
Kevin Antoine (D)	66,836	36.4
5 Gene Taylor (D)	103,415	58.3
Dennis Dollar (R)	71,114	40.1

MISSOURI

Candidates	Votes	%
1 William L. Clay (D)	131,659	70.2
Daniel F. O'Sullivan Jr. (R)	51,857	27.6
2 James M. Talent (R)	165,999	61.3
Joan Kelly Horn (D)	100,372	37.1
3 Richard A. Gephardt (D)	137,300	59.0
Deborah Lynn Wheelehan (R)	90,202	38.8
4 Ike Skelton (D)	153,566	63.8
Bill Phelps (R)	81,650	33.9
5 Karen McCarthy (D)	144,223	67.4
Penny Bennett (R)	61,803	28.9
6 Pat Danner (D)	169,006	68.6
Jeff Bailey (R)	72,064	29.3
7 Roy Blunt (R)	162,558	64.9
Ruth Bamberger (D)	79,306	31.6
8 Jo Ann Emerson (I)	112,472	50.5
Emily Firebaugh (D)	83,084	37.3
Richard A. Kline (R)	23,477	10.5
9 Kenny Hulshof (R)	123,580	49.4
Harold L. Volkmer (D)	117,685	47.0

Special Election[4]

Candidates	Votes	%
8 Jo Ann Emerson (I)	132,804	63.3
Emily Firebaugh (D)	71,625	34.1

MONTANA

Candidates	Votes	%
AL Rick Hill (R)	211,975	52.4
Bill Yellowtail (D)	174,516	43.2

NEBRASKA

Candidates	Votes	%
1 Doug Bereuter (R)	157,108	70.0
Patrick J. Combs (D)	67,152	29.9
2 Jon Christensen (R)	125,201	56.8
James Martin Davis (D)	88,447	40.1
3 Bill Barrett (R)	167,758	77.4
John Webster (D)	48,833	22.5

NEVADA

Candidates	Votes	%
1 John Ensign (R)	86,472	50.1
Bob Coffin (D)	75,081	43.5
2 Jim Gibbons (R)	162,310	58.6
Thomas Wilson (D)	97,742	35.3

NEW HAMPSHIRE

Candidates	Votes	%
1 John E. Sununu (R)	123,939	50.0
Joseph F. Keefe (D)	115,462	46.6
2 Charles Bass (R)	123,001	50.5
Deborah "Arnie" Arnesen (D)	105,867	43.5

NEW JERSEY

Candidates	Votes	%
1 Robert E. Andrews (D)	160,415	76.1
Mel Suplee (R)	44,286	21.0
2 Frank A. LoBiondo (R)	133,130	60.3
Ruth Katz (D)	83,912	38.0
3 H. James Saxton (R)	157,503	64.2
John Leonardi (D)	81,590	33.3
4 Christopher H. Smith (R)	146,404	63.6
Kevin John Meara (D)	77,565	33.7
5 Marge Roukema (R)	181,323	71.3
Bill Auer (D)	62,956	24.8
6 Frank Pallone Jr. (D)	124,635	61.3
Steven J. Corodemus (R)	73,402	36.1
7 Bob Franks (R)	128,817	55.4
Larry Lerner (D)	97,283	41.8
8 Bill J. Pascrell Jr. (D)	98,853	51.2
Bill Martini (R)	92,604	47.7
9 Steve R. Rothman (D)	117,646	55.8
Kathleen A. Donovan (R)	89,005	42.2
10 Donald M. Payne (D)	127,126	84.2
Vanessa Williams (R)	22,086	14.6
11 Rodney Frelinghuysen (R)	169,091	66.3
Chris Evangel (D)	78,742	30.9
12 Michael Pappas (R)	135,811	50.4
David N. Del Vecchio (D)	125,594	46.7

Candidates	Votes	%
13 Robert Menendez (D)	115,457	78.8
Carlos E. Munoz (R)	25,426	17.4

NEW MEXICO

Candidates	Votes	%
1 Steven H. Schiff (R)	109,290	56.6
John Wertheim (D)	71,635	37.1
2 Joe Skeen (R)	95,091	55.9
E. Shirley Baca (D)	74,915	44.1
3 Bill Richardson (D)	124,594	67.2
Bill Redmond (R)	56,580	30.5

NEW YORK

Candidates	Votes	%
1 Michael P. Forbes (R,C,INDC,RTL)	116,620	54.7
Nora Bredes (D,SM)	96,496	45.3
2 Rick A. Lazio (R,C)	112,135	64.2
Kenneth J. Herman (D,INDC)	57,953	33.2
3 Peter T. King (R,C,FDM)	127,972	55.3
Dal LaMagna (D,INDC)	97,518	42.1
4 Carolyn McCarthy (D,INDC)	127,060	57.5
Daniel Frisa (R,C,FDM)	89,542	40.5
5 Gary L. Ackerman (D,L,INDC)	125,918	63.7
Grant M. Lally (R,C,FDM)	69,244	35.0
6 Floyd H. Flake (D)	102,799	84.9
Jorawar Misir R,C,INDC,FDM	18,348	15.1
7 Thomas J. Manton (D)	78,848	71.1
Rose Birtley (R,C,INDC)	32,092	28.9
8 Jerrold Nadler (D,L)	131,943	82.3
Michael Benjamin (R,FDM)	26,028	16.2
9 Charles E. Schumer (D,L)	107,107	74.8
Robert J. Verga (R,INDC,FDM)	30,488	21.3
10 Edolphus Towns (D,L)	99,889	91.3
Amelia Smith Parker (R,C,FDM)	8,660	7.9
11 Major R. Owens (D,L)	89,905	92.0
Claudette Hayle (R,C,INDC,FDM)	7,866	8.0
12 Nydia M. Velazquez (D,L)	61,913	84.6
Miguel I. Prado (R,C,RTL)	9,978	13.6
13 Susan Molinari (R,C,FDM)	94,660	61.6
Tyrone G. Butler (D,L)	53,376	34.7
14 Carolyn B. Maloney (D,L)	130,175	72.4
Jeffrey E. Livingston (R)	42,641	23.7
15 Charles B. Rangel (D,L)	113,898	91.3
Jose E. Serrano (D,L)	95,568	96.3
16 Jose E. Serrano (D,L)	95,568	96.3
17 Eliot L. Engel (D,L)	101,287	85.0
Denis McCarthy (R,C,RTL)	15,892	13.3
18 Nita M. Lowey (D)	118,194	63.6
Kerry J. Katsorhis (R,C)	59,487	32.0
19 Sue W. Kelly (R,FDM)	102,142	46.3
Richard S. Klein (D,L)	86,926	39.4
Joseph J. DioGuardi (C,RTL)	27,424	12.4
20 Benjamin A. Gilman (R)	122,479	57.1
Yash P. Aggarwal (D,L)	80,761	37.6
21 Michael R. McNulty (D,C,INDC)	158,491	66.1
Nancy Norman (R,FDM)	64,471	26.9
Lee H. Wasserman (L)	16,794	7.0
22 Gerald B. H Solomon (R,C,RTL,FDM)	144,125	60.5
Steve James (D)	94,192	39.5
23 Sherwood Boehlert (R,FDM)	124,626	64.3
Bruce W. Hapanowicz (D)	50,436	26.0
Thomas E. Loughlin Jr. (INDC)	10,835	5.6
24 John M. McHugh (R,C)	124,240	71.1
Donald Ravenscroft (D)	43,692	25.0
25 James T. Walsh (R,C,INDC,FDM)	126,691	55.1
Marty Mack (D)	103,199	44.9
26 Maurice D. Hinchey (D,L)	122,850	55.2
Sue Wittig (R,C,RTL,FDM)	94,125	42.3
27 Bill Paxon (R,C,RTL,FDM)	142,568	59.9
Thomas M. Fricano (D,SM)	95,503	40.1

Footnote, see p. 324.

	Candidates	Votes	%
28	Louise M. Slaughter (D)	133,084	57.3
	Geoffrey Rosenberge (R,C,FDM)	99,366	42.7
29	John J. LaFalce (D,L)	132,317	62.0
	David B. Callard (R,C,RTL,FDM)	81,135	38.0
30	Jack Quinn (R,C,INDC,FDM)	121,369	54.8
	Francis Pordum (D,PS)	100,040	45.2
31	Amo Houghton (R,C,FDM)	139,734	71.6
	Bruce D. MacBain (D)	49,502	25.4

NORTH CAROLINA

	Candidates	Votes	%
1	Eva Clayton (D)	108,759	65.9
	Ted Tyler (R)	54,666	33.1
2	Bob Etheridge (D)	113,820	52.5
	David Funderburk (R)	98,951	45.7
3	Walter B. Jones Jr. (R)	118,159	62.7
	George Parrott (D)	68,887	36.5
4	David E. Price (D)	157,194	54.4
	Fred Heineman (R)	126,466	43.8
5	Richard M. Burr (R)	130,177	62.1
	Neil Grist Cashion Jr. (D)	74,320	35.4
6	Howard Coble (R)	167,828	73.4
	Mark Costley (D)	58,022	25.4
7	Mike McIntyre (D)	87,487	52.9
	Bill Caster (R)	75,811	45.8
8	W. G "Bill" Hefner (D)	103,129	55.2
	Curtis Blackwood (R)	81,676	43.7
9	Sue Myrick (R)	147,755	63.0
	Michel C. "Mike" Daisley (D)	83,078	35.4
10	Cass Ballenger (R)	158,585	70.0
	Ben Neill (D)	65,103	28.7
11	Charles H. Taylor (R)	132,860	58.3
	James Mark Ferguson (D)	91,257	40.0
12	Melvin Watt (D)	124,675	71.5
	Joseph A. "Joe" Martino Jr. (R)	46,581	26.7

NORTH DAKOTA

	Candidates	Votes	%
AL	Earl Pomeroy (D)	144,833	55.1
	Kevin Cramer (R)	113,684	43.2

OHIO

	Candidates	Votes	%
1	Steve Chabot (R)	118,324	54.2
	Mark P. Longabaugh (D)	94,719	43.4
2	Rob Portman (R)	186,853	72.0
	Thomas R. Chandler (D)	58,715	22.6
	Kathleen M. McKnight (NL)	13,905	5.4
3	Tony P. Hall (D)	144,583	63.6
	David A. Westbrock (R)	75,732	33.3
4	Michael G. Oxley (R)	147,608	64.8
	Paul McClain (D)	69,096	30.3
5	Paul E. Gillmor (R)	145,692	61.1
	Annie Saunders (D)	81,170	34.1
6	Ted Strickland (D)	118,003	51.3
	Frank A. Cremeans (R)	111,907	48.7
7	David L. Hobson (R)	158,087	67.8
	Richard K. Blain (D)	61,419	26.4
	Dawn Marie Johnson (NL)	13,478	5.8
8	John A. Boehner (R)	165,815	70.3
	Jeffrey D. Kitchen (D)	61,515	26.1
9	Marcy Kaptur (D)	170,617	77.1
	Randy Whitman (R)	46,040	20.8
10	Dennis J. Kucinich (D)	110,723	49.1
	Martin R. Hoke (R)	104,546	46.3
11	Louis Stokes (D)	153,546	81.2
	James J. Sykora (R)	28,821	15.2
12	John R. Kasich (R)	151,667	63.9
	Cynthia L. Ruccia (D)	78,762	33.2
13	Sherrod Brown (D)	146,690	60.5
	Kenneth C. Blair Jr. (R)	87,108	35.9
14	Tom Sawyer (D)	124,136	54.3
	Joyce George (R)	95,307	41.7
15	Deborah Pryce (R)	156,776	70.8
	Cliff Arnebeck (D)	64,665	29.2

	Candidates	Votes	%
16	Ralph Regula (R)	159,314	68.7
	Thomas E. Burkhart (D)	64,902	28.0
17	James A. Traficant Jr. (D)	218,283	91.0
	James M. Cahaney (NL)	21,685	9.0
18	Bob Ney (R)	117,365	50.2
	Robert L. Burch (D)	108,332	46.3
19	Steven C. LaTourette (R)	135,012	54.7
	Tom Coyne Jr. (D)	101,152	41.0

OKLAHOMA

	Candidates	Votes	%
1	Steve Largent (R)	143,415	68.2
	Randolph John Amen (D)	57,996	27.6
2	Tom Coburn (R)	112,273	55.5
	Glen D. Johnson (D)	90,120	44.5
3	Wes Watkins (R)	98,526	51.4
	Darryl Roberts (D)	86,647	45.2
4	J. C Watts (R)	106,923	57.7
	Ed Crocker (D)	73,950	39.9
5	Ernest Jim Istook Jr. (R)	148,362	69.7
	James L. Forsythe (D)	57,594	27.1
6	Frank D. Lucas (R)	113,499	63.9
	Paul M. Barby (D)	64,173	36.1

OREGON

	Candidates	Votes	%
1	Elizabeth Furse (D)	144,588	51.9
	Bill Witt (R)	126,146	45.3
2	Bob Smith (R)	164,062	61.7
	Mike Dugan (D)	97,195	36.5
3	Earl Blumenauer (D)	165,922	66.9
	Scott Bruun (R)	65,259	26.3
4	Peter A. DeFazio (D)	177,270	65.7
	John D. Newkirk (R)	76,649	28.4
5	Darlene Hooley (D)	139,521	51.2
	Jim Bunn (R)	125,409	46.0

Special Election[5]

	Candidates	Votes	%
3	Earl Blumenauer (D)	50,125	69.9
	Mark Brunelle (R)	17,085	23.8

PENNSYLVANIA

	Candidates	Votes	%
1	Thomas M. Foglietta (D)	145,210	87.5
	James D. Cella (R)	20,734	12.5
2	Chaka Fattah (D)	168,887	88.0
	Larry G. Murphy (R)	23,047	12.0
3	Robert A. Borski (D)	121,120	68.9
	Joseph M. McColgan (R)	54,681	31.1
4	Ron Klink (D)	142,621	64.2
	Paul T. Adametz (R)	79,448	35.8
5	John E. Peterson (R)	116,303	60.2
	Ruth C. Rudy (D)	76,627	39.7
6	Tim Holden (D)	115,193	58.6
	Christian Y. Leinbach (R)	80,061	40.7
7	Curt Weldon (R)	165,087	66.9
	John Innelli (D)	79,875	32.4
8	James C. Greenwood (R)	133,749	59.1
	John P. Murray (D)	79,856	35.3
9	Bud Shuster (R)	142,105	73.7
	Monte Kemmler (D)	50,650	26.3
10	Joseph M. McDade (R)	124,670	59.8
	Joe Cullen (D)	75,536	36.2
11	Paul E. Kanjorski (D)	128,258	68.0
	Stephen A. Urban (R)	60,339	32.0
12	John P. Murtha (D)	136,815	70.0
	Bill Choby (R)	58,643	30.0
13	Jon D. Fox (R)	120,304	48.9
	Joseph M. Hoeffel (D)	120,220	48.9
14	William J. Coyne (D)	122,922	60.7
	Bill Ravotti (R)	78,921	39.0
15	Paul McHale (D)	109,812	54.8
	Bob Kilbanks (R)	82,803	41.3
16	Joseph R. Pitts (R)	124,511	59.4
	James G. Blaine (D)	78,598	37.5
17	George W. Gekas (R)	150,678	72.2
	Paul Kettl (D)	57,911	27.8
18	Mike Doyle (D)	120,410	56.0

	Candidates	Votes	%
	David B. Fawcett (R)	86,829	40.4
19	Bill Goodling (R)	130,716	62.6
	Scott L. Chronister (D)	74,944	35.9
20	Frank R. Mascara (D)	113,394	53.9
	Mike McCormick (R)	97,004	46.1
21	Phil English (R)	106,875	50.7
	Ronald A. DiNicola (D)	104,004	49.3

RHODE ISLAND

	Candidates	Votes	%
1	Patrick J. Kennedy (D)	121,781	69.4
	Giovanni D. Cicione (R)	49,199	28.0
2	Bob Weygand (D)	118,827	64.5
	Rick Wild (R)	58,458	31.7

SOUTH CAROLINA

	Candidates	Votes	%
1	Mark Sanford (R)	138,467	96.4
2	Floyd D. Spence (R)	158,229	89.8
	Maurice T. Raiford (NL)	17,713	10.0
3	Lindsey Graham (R)	114,273	60.3
	Debbie Dorn (D)	73,417	38.7
4	Bob Inglis (R)	138,165	70.9
	Darrell E. Curry (D)	54,126	27.8
5	John M. Spratt Jr. (D)	97,335	54.1
	Larry L. Bigham (R)	81,455	45.3
6	James E. Clyburn (D)	120,132	69.4
	Gary McLeod (R)	51,974	30.0

SOUTH DAKOTA

	Candidates	Votes	%
AL	John Thune (R)	186,393	57.7
	Rick Weiland (D)	119,547	37.0

TENNESSEE

	Candidates	Votes	%
1	Bill Jenkins (R)	117,676	64.8
	Kay C. Smith (D)	58,657	33.3
2	John J. "Jimmy" Duncan Jr. (R)	150,953	70.7
	Stephen Smith (D)	61,020	28.6
3	Zach Wamp (R)	113,408	56.3
	Charles "Chuck" Jolly (D)	85,714	42.6
4	Van Hilleary (R)	103,091	57.9
	Mark Stewart (D)	73,331	41.2
5	Bob Clement (D)	140,264	72.4
	Steven L. Edmondson (R)	46,201	23.8
6	Bart Gordon (D)	123,846	54.4
	Steve Gill (R)	94,599	41.6
7	Ed Bryant (R)	136,643	64.1
	Don Trotter (D)	73,629	34.6
8	John Tanner (D)	123,681	67.3
	Tom Watson (R)	55,024	29.9
9	Harold E. Ford Jr. (D)	116,345	61.1
	Rod DeBerry (R)	70,951	37.3

TEXAS [6]

	Candidates	Votes	%
1	Max Sandlin (D)	102,697	51.6
	Ed Merritt (R)	93,105	46.7
2	Jim Turner (D)	102,908	52.2
	Brian Babin (R)	89,838	45.6
3	Sam Johnson (R)	142,325	73.0
	Lee Cole (D)	47,654	24.4
4	Ralph M. Hall (D)	132,126	63.8
	Jerry Ray Hall (R)	71,065	34.3
5	Pete Sessions (R)	80,196	53.1
	John Pouland (D)	70,922	47.0
6	Joe L. Barton (R)	160,800	77.1
	Janet Carroll "Skeet" Richardson (I)	26,713	12.8
	Catherine A. Anderson (L)	14,456	6.9
7	Bill Archer (R)	152,024	81.4
	Al J. K Siegmund (D)	28,187	15.1
8[6]	Kevin Brady (R)	80,325	41.5
	Gene Fontenot (R)	75,399	38.9
	Cynthia "C. J" Newman (D)	26,246	13.6
	Robert Musemeche (D)	11,689	6.0
9[6]	Steve Stockman (R)	88,171	46.4
	Nick Lampson (D)	83,782	44.1

Footnotes, see p. 324.

Candidates	Votes	%
Geraldine Sam (D)	17,887	9.4
10 Lloyd Doggett (D)	132,066	56.2
Teresa Doggett (R)	97,204	41.4
11 Chet Edwards (D)	99,990	56.8
Jay Mathis (R)	74,549	42.4
12 Kay Granger (R)	98,349	57.8
Hugh Parmer (D)	69,859	41.0
13 William M. "Mac" Thornberry (R)	116,098	66.9
Samuel Brown Silverman (D)	56,066	32.3
14 Ron Paul (R)	99,961	51.1
Charles "Lefty" Morris (D)	93,200	47.6
15 Ruben Hinojosa (D)	86,347	62.3
Tom Haughey (R)	50,914	36.7
16 Silvestre Reyes (D)	90,260	70.6
Rick Ledesma (R)	35,271	27.6
17 Charles W. Stenholm (D)	99,678	51.6
Rudy Izzard (R)	91,429	47.4
18 Sheila Jackson-Lee (D)	106,111	77.1
Larry White (R)	13,956	10.1
Jerry Burley (R)	7,877	5.7
19 Larry Combest (R)	156,910	80.4
John W. Sawyer (D)	38,316	19.6
20 Henry B. Gonzalez (D)	88,190	63.7
James D. Walker (R)	47,616	34.4
21 Lamar Smith (R)	205,830	76.4
Gordon H. Wharton (D)	60,338	22.4
22 Tom DeLay (R)	126,056	68.1
Scott Douglas Cunningham (D)	59,030	31.9
23 Henry Bonilla (R)	101,332	61.8
Charles P. Jones (D)	59,596	36.4
24 Martin Frost (D)	77,847	55.7
Ed Harrison (R)	54,551	39.1
25[6] Ken Bentsen (D)	43,701	34.0
Dolly Madison McKenna (R)	21,898	17.1
Beverley Clark (D)	21,699	16.9
Brent Perry (R)	16,737	13.0
John Devine (R)	9,070	7.1
John M. Sanchez (R)	8,984	7.0
26 Dick Armey (R)	163,708	73.6
Jerry Frankel (D)	58,623	26.4
27 Solomon P. Ortiz (D)	97,350	64.6
Joe Gardner (R)	50,964	33.8
28 Frank Tejeda (D)	110,148	75.4
Mark Lynn Cude (R)	34,191	23.4
29 Gene Green (D)	61,751	67.5
Jack Rodriguez (R)	28,381	31.0
30 Eddie Bernice Johnson (D)	61,723	54.6
John Hendry (R)	20,664	18.3
James L. Sweatt (D)	9,909	8.8
Marvin E. Crenshaw (D)	7,765	6.9
Lisa Anne Kitterman (R)	7,761	6.9

Special Runoff Elections[6]

Candidates	Votes	%
8 Kevin Brady (R)	30,366	59.1
Gene Fontenot (R)	21,004	40.9
9 Nick Lampson (D)	59,225	52.8
Steve Stockman (R)	52,870	47.2
25 Ken Bentsen (D)	29,396	57.3
Dolly Madison McKenna (R)	21,892	42.7

UTAH

	Votes	%
1 James V. Hansen (R)	150,126	68.3
Gregory J. Sanders (D)	65,866	30.0
2 Merrill Cook (R)	129,963	55.0
Ross Anderson (D)	100,283	42.4
3 Christopher B. Cannon (R)	106,220	51.1
Bill Orton (D)	98,178	47.3

VERMONT

	Votes	%
AL Bernard Sanders (I)	140,678	55.2
Susan Sweetser (R)	83,021	32.6
Jack Long (D)	23,830	9.4

VIRGINIA

	Votes	%
1 Herbert H. Bateman (R)	165,574	99.0
2 Owen B. Pickett (D)	106,215	64.8
John Tate (R)	57,586	35.1
3 Robert C. Scott (D)	118,603	82.1
Elsie Holland (R)	25,781	17.9
4 Norman Sisisky (D)	160,100	78.6
A. J "Tony" Zevgolis (R)	43,516	21.4
5 Virgil H. Goode Jr. (D)	120,323	60.8
George C. Landrith III (R)	70,869	35.8
6 Robert W. Goodlatte (R)	133,576	67.0
Jeffrey Grey (D)	61,485	30.8
7 Thomas J. Bliley Jr. (R)	189,644	75.1
Roderic H. Slayton (D)	51,206	20.3
8 James P. Moran (D)	152,334	66.4
John Otey (R)	64,562	28.1
9 Rick Boucher (D)	122,908	65.0
Patrick Muldoon (R)	58,055	30.7
10 Frank R. Wolf (R)	169,266	72.0
Robert L. Weinberg (D)	59,145	25.2
11 Thomas M. Davis III (R)	138,758	64.1
Tom Horton (D)	74,701	34.5

WASHINGTON

	Votes	%
1 Rick White (R)	141,948	53.7
Jeffrey Coopersmith (D)	122,187	46.3
2 Jack Metcalf (R)	124,655	48.5

Candidates	Votes	%
Kevin Quigley (D)	122,728	47.8
3 Linda Smith (R)	123,117	50.2
Brian Baird (D)	122,230	49.8
4 Richard "Doc" Hastings (R)	108,647	53.0
Rick Locke (D)	96,502	47.0
5 George Nethercutt (R)	131,618	55.6
Judy Olson (D)	105,166	44.4
6 Norm Dicks (D)	155,467	65.9
Bill Tinsley (R)	71,337	30.2
7 Jim McDermott (D)	209,753	81.0
Frank Kleschen (R)	49,341	19.0
8 Jennifer Dunn (R)	170,691	65.4
Dave Little (D)	90,340	34.6
9 Adam Smith (D)	105,236	50.1
Randy Tate (R)	99,199	47.3

WEST VIRGINIA

	Votes	%
1 Alan B. Mollohan (D)	171,334	100.0
2 Bob Wise (D)	141,551	68.9
Greg Morris (R)	63,933	31.1
3 Nick J. Rahall II (D)	145,550	100.0

WISCONSIN

	Votes	%
1 Mark W. Neumann (R)	118,408	50.9
Lydia C. Spottswood (D)	114,148	49.0
2 Scott L. Klug (R)	154,557	57.4
Paul R. Soglin (D)	110,467	41.0
3 Ron Kind (D)	121,967	52.0
Jim Harsdorf (R)	112,146	47.8
4 Gerald D. Kleczka (D)	134,470	57.6
Tom Reynolds (R)	98,438	42.2
5 Thomas M. Barrett (D)	141,179	73.3
Paul D. Melotik (R)	47,384	24.6
6 Tom Petri (R)	169,213	73.0
Alver Lindskoog (D)	55,377	23.9
7 David R. Obey (D)	137,428	57.0
Scott West (R)	103,365	42.9
8 Jay W. Johnson (D)	129,551	52.0
David T. Prosser Jr. (R)	119,398	48.0
9 F. James Sensenbrenner Jr. (R)	197,910	74.4
Floyd Brenholt (D)	67,740	25.5

WYOMING

	Votes	%
AL Barbara Cubin (R)	116,004	55.2
Pete Maxfield (D)	85,724	40.8

1996 Elections

1. A special election was held to fill the unexpired term of Rep. Walter R. Tucker III (D), who resigned Dec. 15, 1995. No runoff was required because only Democrats filed for the primary.

2. For the 1996 House elections in Louisiana, an open primary election was held with candidates from all parties running on the same ballot. Any candidate who received a majority was elected unopposed, with no further appearance on the general election ballot. If no candidate received 50 percent, a runoff was held between the two top finishers.

3. A special election was held to fill the unexpired term of Rep. Kweisi Mfume (D), who resigned Feb. 15, 1996.

4. A special election was held in conjunction with the November election. Emerson was elected to serve both the unexpired term of Bill Emerson (R), who died June 22, 1996, and the two-year term beginning Jan. 7, 1997.

5. A special election was held to fill the unexpired term of Ron Wyden (D), who resigned Feb. 5, 1996, having been elected to the U.S. Senate.

6. In July 1996 a panel of federal judges declared that three Texas districts were unconstitutionally drawn. The three districts and an additional ten surrounding ones were redrawn, invalidating the March 1996 primary results for the districts. In November, candidates in the thirteen districts ran in open primaries, with only those capturing a majority of the vote winning outright. Special runoff elections were held in December for the top two finishers in the districts where no candidate received a majority of the votes cast.

House Returns: Other Sources

In the preceding pages of House popular election returns *(pp. 192-324)* the symbol # is used to denote returns for the years 1946-1973 that were taken from a source other than the Inter-University Consortium for Political and Social Research (ICPSR). This page lists the source for each of those returns. *(For description of ICPSR data, see p. 190.)*

The two most frequently used alternative sources were *Statistics of the Congressional Elections of _____.*

published by the Clerk of the House of Representatives for every general election year since 1920, and the Elections Research Center, which compiled the biennial *America Votes* series under the direction of Richard M. Scammon and Alice V. McGillivray.

For elections 1974-1996, Congressional Quarterly obtained the returns for the state secretaries of state. Where discrepancies existed between these figures and *America Votes*, the latter's figures were used.

1946—Georgia (5th District); **Nebraska** (3rd District):
Statistics of the Congressional Election of Nov. 5, 1946.

1950—Tennessee (5th District):
Statistics of the Congressional Election of Nov. 4, 1950.

1950—Texas (18th District special):
Texas Secretary of State.

1951—Missouri (11th District special):
Missouri Secretary of State.

1959—Iowa (4th District special):
Iowa Secretary of State.

1960—Indiana (5th District):
Richard M. Scammon (ed.), *America Votes 4* (Pittsburgh: University of Pittsburgh Press, 1962), p. 123.

1961—Arizona, Arkansas, Michigan, Tennessee (special elections):
Elections Research Center.

1962—Michigan (14th District special); **New York** (6th District special); **South Carolina** (2nd District special)
Elections Research Center.

1963—North Dakota, Pennsylvania, Texas (special elections):
Elections Research Center.

1964—Pennsylvania (5th District special): **Tennessee** (2nd District special):
Elections Research Center.

1964—Pennsylvania (6th District):
Pennsylvania Secretary of State.

1965—South Carolina (2nd District special)
Elections Research Center.

1966—California (4th District special); **Texas** (8th District special):
Elections Research Center.

1967—California (11th District special primary):
California Secretary of State.

1967—California (11th District special):
Elections Research Center.

1967—New York, Rhode Island (special elections):
Elections Research Center.

1968—New York (7th District):
Richard M. Scammon (ed.), *America Votes 8* (Washington, D.C.: Congressional Quarterly, 1970), p. 274.

1968—New York (13th District special); **Texas** (3rd District special):
Elections Research Center.

1968—Mississippi (3rd District special):
Mississippi Secretary of State.

1969—California (27th District special primary):
California Secretary of State.

1969—Massachusetts; Montana; Tennessee (special elections):
Elections Research Center.

1970—Texas (2nd District):
Texas Secretary of State.

1971—Kentucky (6th District special):
Kentucky Secretary of State.

1972—Pennsylvania (27th District special):
Pennsylvania Secretary of State.

1972—Vermont (AL District special):
Elections Research Center.

1973—Illinois (7th District special):
Illinois Secretary of State.

Political Party Abbreviations

The following list provides a key to the political party abbreviations used in *Congressional Elections 1946-1996*. This list was developed by Congressional Quarterly from three sources for party designations: the Inter-University Consortium for Political and Social Research (ICPSR), for most election returns up to 1973; and Richard M. Scammon and Alice V. McGillivray's *America Votes* series, for most election returns from 1974 to 1990; and the *Congressional Quarterly Weekly Report* for most election returns from 1992 to 1996. In cases of discrepancy, the ICPSR party designation was used.

The election data obtained from the ICPSR contain hundreds of different party labels. In many cases the party labels represent combinations of multi-party support received by individual candidates. However, in preparing the returns for publication, many of the party labels were eliminated because the candidate(s) did not receive at least 5 percent of the votes cast. The names of the parties appear below in the form they were obtained from ICPSR and Scammon.

AC	Anti-Corruption	FTP	For the People	NL	Natural Law
ACP	A Connecticut Party	GOOD GOV	Good Government	NON PART	Non Partisan
AGA	American Grassroots Alternative	GREEN	Green	NP	National Prohibition
AIP	American Independent	I	Independent	P	Prohibition
ALI	Alaskan Independent	IA	Independent American	PEROT CHOICE	Perot Choice
ALL PP	All Peoples	I ALNC	Independent Alliance	PF, PFP	Peace and Freedom
AM	American	ID	Independent Democrat	POP	Populist
AM I	American Independent			PP	People's
AM LAB	American Labor	IFC	Independents for Change	PROG	Progressive
C	Conservative			PS	Protect Seniors
CC	Change Congress	IFP	Independents for Perot	R	Republican
CIT	Citizens	IND	Independent	R-D	Republican-Democrat
CLEAN GV	Clean Government	INDC	Independence	REF	Reform
CLUNEY	Cluney Taxpayers Good Government	INS	Independent Neighbors	RP	Rate Payers Against LILCO
COM	Communist	IPP CH	Independent People's Choice	RPI	Ross Perot Independent
CONST	Constitution	I PROG	Independent Progressive	RTL	Right to Life
CP	Commonwealth	IR, I-R	Independent Republican	SILENT	Silent Majority
CR	Conservative Republican	IV	Independent Voters	SIS	Staten Island Secession
CS	Common Sense	I VT	Independent Vermonters	SM	Save Medicare
CST	Constitutional	KTAX	Taxpayers Party of Kentucky	SOC	Socialist
D	Democrat			SOCIAL D	Social Democrat
DFL	Democrat Farmer-Labor	L	Liberal	SOC WORK	Socialist Workers
D & P	Democrat and Prohibition	LIBERT	Libertarian	TCN	Tax Cut Now
		LIF	Long Island First	TCP-LI	Tax Cut Party-Long Island
D & PROG	Democrat and Progressive	LLJ	Life-Liberty-Justice		
		LRU	La Raza Unida	U CIT	United Citizen
D-IP	Democrat-Independent Progressive	LU	Liberty Union	USLP	U.S. Labor Party
		MINN TAX	Minnesota Taxpayers	UT	Unity
DODD I	Dodd Independent	MSTAX	Mississippi Taxpayers	U TAX	United Taxpayers
D-R	Democratic-Republican	NA	New Alliance	VETS F	Veterans Farmer
ECR	Economic Recovery	NDPA	National Democratic Party of Alabama	VETS V	Veterans Victory
EJ	Economic Justice			VR	Voter Rights
ENVIRON	Environment	NEIGH	Neighborhood	WRITE IN	Write in
FDM	Freedom	NEW I	New Independent	WTP	We The People
FF	Four Freedoms	NF	Nuclear Freeze	YOUNGMAN	Youngman

Bibliography

Books

Abramowitz, Alan I., and Jeffrey A. Segal. *Senate Elections.* Ann Arbor: University of Michigan Press, 1992.

Barone, Michael, and Grant Ujifusa. *The Almanac of American Politics, 1998.* Rev. ed. Washington, D.C.: National Journal, 1997.

Bartley, Numan V., and Hugh D. Graham. *Southern Elections: County and Precinct Data, 1950–1972.* Baton Rouge: Louisiana State University Press, 1977.

Bass, Jack, and Walter DeVries. *Transformation of Southern Politics: Social Change and Political Consequence Since 1945.* Athens: University of Georgia Press, 1995.

Benjamin, Gerald, and Michael J. Malbin. *Limiting Legislative Terms.* Washington, D.C.: Congressional Quarterly, 1992.

Campbell, James E. *The Presidential Pulse of Congressional Elections.* Lexington: University Press of Kentucky, 1993.

Crane, Edward H., and Roger Pilon, eds. *The Politics and Law of Term Limits.* Washington, D.C.: Cato Institute, 1994.

Congressional Quarterly. *American Leaders 1789–1994* Washington, D.C.: Congressional Quarterly, 1994.

___. *Congressional Districts in the 1990s.* Washington, D.C.: Congressional Quarterly, 1993.

___. *Guide to Congress.* 4th ed. Washington, D.C.: Congressional Quarterly, 1992.

___. *Politics in America 1998.* Washington, D.C.: Congressional Quarterly, 1997.

Cook, Rhodes. *America Votes: A Handbook of Contemporary Election Statistics.* Vol. 22. Washington, D.C.: Congressional Quarterly, 1997.

——, and Alice V. McGillivray. *U.S. Primary Elections: 1995–1996.* Washington, D.C.: Congressional Quarterly, 1997.

Davidson, Roger H., and Walter J. Oleszek. *Congress and Its Members.* 6th ed. Washington, D.C.: CQ Press, 1997.

Dodd, Lawrence D., and Bruce I Oppenheimer, ed. *Congress Reconsidered.* 6th ed. Washington, D.C.: CQ Press, 1997.

Election Data Book: A Statistical Portrait of Voting in America. Lanham, Md.: Bernan Press, 1993.

Ewing, Cortez A. *Primary Elections in the South: Study in Uniparty Politics.* 1953. Reprint. Westport, Conn.: Greenwood Press, 1980.

Falco, Maria J. *Bigotry: Ethnic, Machine and Sexual Politics in a Senatorial Election.* Westport, Conn.: Greenwood Press, 1980.

Fenno, Richard F., Jr. *Home Style: House Members in Their Districts.* Boston: Little, Brown, 1978.

Fiorina, Morris P. *Congress: Keystone of the Washington Establishment.* 2nd ed. New Haven, Conn.: Yale University Press, 1989.

Galloway, George B. *History of the House of Representatives.* 2nd. ed. New York: Crowell, 1976.

Grantham, Dewey W. *Democratic South.* 1963. Reprint. New York: Norton, 1965.

Grofman, Bernard, et al. *Reapportionment Policy.* Urbana: Policy Studies Organization, University of Illinois at Urbana-Champagne, 1981.

Herrnson, Paul S. *Congressional Elections: Campaigning at Home and in Washington.* Washington, D.C.: CQ Press, 1997.

Jacobson, Gary C. *The Electoral Origins of Divided Government: Competition in U.S. House Elections, 1946–1988.* Boulder, Colo.: Westview, 1990.

___. *The Politics of Congressional Elections.* 3rd ed. New York: HarperCollins, 1991.

Key, V. O., Jr. *Southern Politics in State and Nation.* Knoxville: University of Tennessee Press, 1984.

Krasno, Jonathan S. *Challengers, Competition, and Reelection: Comparing Senate and House Elections.* New Haven, Conn.: Yale University Press, 1994

Lamis, Alexander P. *The Two-Party South.* 2nd ed. New York: Oxford University Press, 1990.

Mann, Thomas E. *Unsafe at Any Margin: Interpreting Congressional Elections.* Washington, D.C.: American Enterprise Institute, 1978.

——, and Norman J. Ornstein. *Renewing Congress.* Washington, D.C.: Brookings, 1993.

Martin, Fenton S., and Robert U. Goehlert. *How to Research Congress.* Washington, D.C.: Congressional Quarterly, 1996.

Martis, Kenneth C. *The Historical Atlas of United States Congressional Districts 1789–1983.* New York: The Free Press, 1982.

Matteson, David M. *The Organization of the Government under the Constitution.* New York: Da Capo Press, 1970.

Matthews, Donald R. *U.S. Senators and Their World.* 1960. Reprint. Westport, Conn.: Greenwood Press, 1980.

Maurine, Christopher. *Black Americans in Congress.* New York: Crowell, 1976.

McGillivray, Alice V. *Congressional and Gubernatorial Primaries: 1993–1994: A Handbook of Election Statistics.* Washington, D.C.: Congressional Quarterly, 1995.

Miller, Warren, Arthur Miller and Edward Schneider. *American National Election Studies Data Sourcebook, 1952–1986.* Cambridge, Mass.: Harvard University Press, 1989.

O'Rourke, Timothy. *The Impact of Reapportionment.* New Brunswick, N. J.: Transaction Books, 1980.

Ornstein, Norman J., Thomas E. Mann and Michael J. Malbin. *Vital Statistics on Congress 1997–1998.* Washington, D.C.: Congressional Quarterly, 1997.

Pomper, Gerald M., ed. *The Election of 1992: Reports and Interpretations.* Chatham, N. J.: Chatham House, 1993.

Reichley, A. James, ed. *Elections American Style.* Washington, D.C.: Brookings, 1987.

Rohde, David W. *Parties and Leaders in the Postreform House.* Chicago: University of Chicago Press, 1991.

Sale, Kirkpatrick. *Power Shift: The Rise of the Southern Rim and Its Challenge to the Eastern Establishment.* New York: Random House, 1975.

Scammon, Richard M. *America Votes: A Handbook of Contemporary Election Statistics.* Vols. 1–2. New York: Macmillan, 1956, 1958. *America Votes.* Vols. 3–5. Pittsburgh: University of Pittsburgh, 1959, 1962, and 1964. *America Votes.* Vols. 6–11. Washington, D.C.: Congressional Quarterly, 1966–1975.

___. and Alice V. McGillivray. *America Votes.* Vols. 12–21. Washington, D.C.: Congressional Quarterly, 1977–1995.

Schneier, Edward V., and Bertram Gross. *Congress Today.* New York: St. Martin's Press, 1993.

Tindale, George B. *The Disruption of the Solid South.* New York: W. W. Norton, 1972.

Will, George F. *Restoration: Congress, Term Limits, and the Recovery of a Deliberative Democracy.* New York: Free Press, 1992.

Articles

Abramowitz, Alan I. "Choices and Echoes in the 1978 U.S. Senate Elections: A Research Note." *American Journal of Political Science* 25 (February 1981): 112–118.

___. "A Comparison of Voting for U.S. Senator and Representative in 1978." *American Political Science Review* 74 (September 1980): 633–640.

Abramson, Paul R., John H. Aldrich and David W. Rohde. "Progressive Ambition among United States Senators: 1972–1988." *Journal of Politics* 49 (February 1987): 3–35.

Alford, John R., and John R. Hibbing. "Increased Incumbency Advantage in the House." *Journal of Politics* 43 (November 1981): 1042–1061.

Bernstein, Robert A. "Divisive Primaries Do Hurt: U.S. Senate Races, 1956–1972." *American Political Science Review* 71 (June 1977): 540–545.

Black, Merle, and Earl Black. "Republican Party Development in the South: The Rise of the Contested Primary." *Social Science Quarterly* (December 1976): 566–578.

Bond, Jon R. "The Influence of Constituency Diversity on Electoral Competition in Voting for Congress, 1974–1978." *Legislative Studies Quarterly* 8 (May 1983): 201–217.

Born, Richard. "Generational Replacement and the Growth of Incumbent Reelection Margins in the U.S. House." *American Political Science Review* 73 (September 1979): 811–817.

___. "The Influence of House Primary Election Divisiveness on General Election Margins, 1962–1976." *Journal of Politics* 43 (August 1981): 640–661.

___. "Reassessing the Decline of Presidential Coalitions: U.S. House Elections from 1952–80," *Journal of Politics* 46 (February 1984): 60–79.

Brookshire, Robert G., and Dean F. Duncan III. "Congressional Career Patterns and Party Systems." *Legislative Studies Quarterly* 8 (February 1983): 65–78.

Bullock, Charles S., III, and David W. Brady. "Party Constituency and Roll Call Voting in the U.S. Senate." *Legislative Studies Quarterly* 8 (February 1983): 29–43.

Collie, Melissa P. "Incumbency, Electoral Safety and Turnover in the House of Representatives." *American Political Science Review* 75 (March 1981): 119–131.

"Congress in the Thicket: The Congressional Redistricting Bill of 1967." *George Washington Law Review* 36 (1967): 224–234.

"Congressional Redistricting: One Man, One Vote Demands Near Mathematical Precision." *De Paul Law Review* (Autumn 1969): 152–171.

Cosman, Bernard. "Republican in the South: Goldwater's Impact Upon Voting Alignment in Congressional, Gubernatorial and Senatorial Races." *Southwestern Social Science Quarterly* (June 1967): 13–23.

Delli Carpini, Michael X., and Ester R. Fuchs. "The Year of the Woman? Candidates, Voters, and the 1992 Elections." *Political Science Quarterly* 108 (Spring 1993): 29–36.

Eisenberg, Ralph. "1966 Politics in Virginia: The Democratic Senatorial Primary." *University of Virginia News Letter* (Jan. 15, 1967).

Elving, Ronald D. "Redistricting: Drawing Power with a Map," *Editorial Research Reports*, Feb. 15, 1991, 99.

"Equal Representation and the Weighted Vote Alternative." *Yale Law Review* (Spring 1970): 311–321.

Fenno, Richard F., Jr. *Home Style: House Members in Their Districts*. Boston: Little, Brown, 1978.

Gross, Donald A. "Representative Styles and Legislative Behavior." *Western Political Quarterly* 31 (September 1978): 359–371.

Irwin, William P. "Representation and Apportionment." *Parliamentary Affairs* (Summer 1968): 226–245.

Katz, Ellis. "Apportionment and Majority Rule." *Publius* (1971): 141–161.

Kostroski, Warren. "The Effect of Number of Terms on the Re-Election of Senators, 1920–1970." *Journal of Politics* 40 (May 1978): 488–497.

Kuklinski, James H., and Darrell M. West. "Economic Expectations and Voting Behavior in the United States House and Senate Elections." *American Political Science Review* 75 (June 1981): 436–447.

Linton, Robert N. "Further Exploration in the Political Thicket: The Gerrymander and the Constitution." *Loyola Law Review* (October 1973): 1–47.

Lipset, Seymour Martin. "The Significance of the 1992 Election." *PS: Political Science and Politics* 26 (March 1993): 7–16.

Mann, Thomas E., and Raymond E. Wolfinger. "Candidates and Parties in Congressional Elections." *American Political Science Review* 74 (September 1980): 617–632.

Payne, James L. "Career Intentions and Electoral Performance of Members of the U.S. House." *Legislative Studies Quarterly* 7 (February 1982): 93–99.

Robeck, Bruce W. "State Legislator Candidacies for the U.S. House: Prospect for Success." *Legislative Studies Quarterly* 7 (November 1982): 507–514.

Rohde, David W. "Risk-Bearing and Progressive Ambition: The Case of the United States House of Representatives." *American Journal of Political Science* 23 (February 1979): 1–26.

Sigelman, Lee. "Special Elections to the U.S. House: Some Descriptive Generalizations." *Legislative Studies Quarterly* (November 1981): 577–588.

Stone, Walter J. "The Dynamics of Constituency: Electoral Control in the House." *American Politics Quarterly* 8 (October 1980): 399–424.

Sullivan, John L. "Electoral Choice and Popular Control of Policy: The Case of the 1966 House Elections." *American Political Science Review* (December 1972): 1256–1268.

Tuchel, Peter. "The Initial Re-election Chances of Appointed and Elected United States Senators." *Polity* 16 (Fall 1983): 138–142.

Uslaner, Eric M. "Party Reform and Electoral Disaggregation: A Paradox in Congress." *Policy Studies Journal* 5 (Summer 1977): 454–459.

Wattenberg, Martin P. "From Parties to Candidates: Examining the Role of the Media." *Public Opinion Quarterly* 46 (Summer 1982): 216–227.

Westlye, Mark C. "Competitiveness of Senate Seats and Voting Behavior in Senate Elections." *American Journal of Political Science* 27 (May 1983): 253–283.

Wollock, Andrea J. "Reapportionment Now." *State Legislatures* (January 1982): 7–13.

Worsnop, Richard L. "Changing Southern Politics." *Editorial Research Reports* 1 (Jan. 19, 1966): 43–59.

Senate
Candidates Index

The Senate Candidates Index includes all candidates appearing in Senate Popular Vote Returns, 1946-1996. The index includes candidates' names followed by state abbreviations and the years of candidacy. To locate a candidate's returns, turn to pages 81-100 where the returns are arranged alphabetically by state and in chronological order by class of senator for each state. *(Explanation of Senate classes, p. 61; State Abbreviations, below)* For other references to Senate candidates in the *Congressional Elections 1946-1996*, see the General Index, pages 372-375.

A

Aandahl, Fred G. (ND) - 1952
Abdnor, James (SD) - 1980, 1986
Abel, Hazel H. (NE) - 1954
Abourezk, James (SD) - 1972
Abraham, Spencer (MI) - 1994
Abrams, Robert (NY) - 1992
Adams, Brock (WA) - 1986
Aiken, George D. (VT) - 1950, 1956, 1962, 1968
Aiken, Paul (KS) - 1950
Akaka, Daniel K. (HI) - 1990, 1994
Alexander, Archibald S. (NJ) - 1948, 1952
Alexander, W. H. Bill (OK) - 1950
Allard, Wayne (CO) - 1996
Allen, Jim (AL) - 1968, 1974
Allott, Gordon (CO) - 1954, 1960, 1966, 1972
Anaya, Toney (NM) - 1978
Andersen, Bill (TN) - 1988
Anderson, Clinton P. (NM) - 1948, 1954, 1960, 1966
Anderson, Wendell R. (MN) - 1978
Andrews, Jackson M. (KY) - 1986
Andrews, Lloyd J. (WA) - 1964
Andrews, Mark (ND) - 1980, 1986
Andrews, Thomas H. (ME) - 1994
Archambault, Raoul (RI) - 1960
Arndt, Raymond W. (NE) - 1964
Ashcroft, John (MO) - 1994
Ashe, Victor (TN) - 1984
Atchley, Forrest S. (NM) - 1958
Atkins, Hobart F. (TN) - 1952, 1956, 1958
AuCoin, Les (OR) - 1992
Aylward Paul L. (KS) - 1962

B

Babbitt, Wayne H. (AR) - 1972
Babcock, Tim (MT) - 1966
Backus, Jan (VT) - 1994
Baker, Howard H. Jr. (TN) - 1964, 1966, 1972, 1978
Baker, Stuart D. (VA) - 1960
Baldwin, Raymond E. (CT) - 1946
Ball, Joseph H. (MN) - 1948

Bantz, William B. (WA) - 1958
Barbour, Haley (MS) - 1982
Bard, Guy Kurtz (PA) - 1952
Barkley, Alben W. (KY) - 1954
Barkley, Dean M. (MN) - 1994, 1996
Barnett, Don (SD) - 1978
Barrett, Frank A. (WY) - 1952, 1958
Bartlett, Dewey F. (OK) - 1972
Bartlett, E. L. (AK) - 1958, 1960, 1966
Barton, Joe L. (TX) - 1993
Bass, Perkins (NH) - 1962
Bass, Ross (TN) - 1964
Baucus, Max (MT) - 1978, 1984, 1990, 1996
Bauman, Rick (OR) - 1986
Baxter, James H. (DE) - 1978
Bayard, A. I. du Pont (DE) - 1952
Bayh, Birch (IN) - 1962, 1968, 1974, 1980
Beall, J. Glenn (MD) - 1952, 1958, 1964
Beall, J. Glenn Jr. (MD) - 1970, 1976
Beard, Robin L. (TN) - 1976
Beasley, Michael (AK) - 1990
Bedford, Roger (AL) - 1996
Bell, Jeffrey (NJ) - 1978
Bellmon, Henry (OK) - 1968, 1974
Benavides, Tom R. (NM) - 1990
Bender, George H. (OH) - 1954, 1956
Benedict, Cleveland K. (WV) - 1982
Benedict, Cooper P. (WV) - 1964
Bennett, Robert F. (UT) - 1992
Bennett, Wallace F. (UT) - 1950, 1956, 1962, 1968
Bentley, Alvin M. (MI) - 1960
Benton, William (CT) - 1950, 1952
Bentsen, Lloyd (TX) - 1970, 1976, 1982, 1988
Berman, Dan (UT) - 1980
Bernard, Charles (AR) - 1968
Beshear, Steven L. (KY) - 1996
Bethune, Ed (AR) - 1984
Betley, Stanley J. (NH) - 1954
Betts, James E. (OH) - 1980
Bible, Alan (NV) - 1954, 1956, 1962, 1968
Biden, Joseph R. Jr. (DE) - 1972, 1978, 1984, 1990, 1996
Bigelow, James E. (VT) - 1950
Bilbo, Theodore G. (MS) - 1946
Bingaman, Jeff (NM) - 1982, 1988, 1994
Bishop, Neil S. (ME) - 1970
Bjornson, Val (MN) - 1954

Black, John G. (AR) - 1978
Blakley, William A. (TX) - 1961
Blanton, Ray (TN) - 1972
Blatt, Genevieve (PA) - 1964
Blewett, Alex (MT) - 1964
Blount, Winton M. "Red" (AL) - 1972
Boggs, J. Caleb (DE) - 1960, 1966, 1972
Bond, Christopher S. (MO) - 1986, 1992
Bontrager, D. Russell (IN) - 1964
Booth, John P. (FL) - 1950
Boren, David L. (OK) - 1978, 1984, 1990
Boren, Jim (OK) - 1996
Borough, Reuben W. (CA) - 1952
Boschwitz, Rudy (MN) - 1978, 1984, 1990, 1996
Bottum, Joe (SD) - 1962
Boulter, Beau (TX) - 1988
Boxer, Barbara (CA) - 1992
Bradley, Bill (NJ) - 1978, 1984, 1990
Bradshaw, Jean Paul (MO) - 1964
Brady, M. Jane (DE) - 1990
Brannen, James H. (CT) - 1974
Breaux, John B. (LA) - 1990, 1992
Breeding, J. Floyd (KS) - 1966
Brekke, Gerald W. (MN) - 1976
Brennan, Joseph E. (ME) - 1996
Brewster, Daniel B. (MD) - 1962, 1968
Brewster, Ralph O. (ME) - 1946
Bricker, John W. (OH) - 1946, 1952, 1958
Bridges, Styles (NH) - 1948, 1954, 1960
Briggs, Frank (MO) - 1946
Briggs, Ruth M. (RI) - 1966
Briley, John Marshall (OH) - 1962
Brock, Bill (TN) - 1970, 1976 ; (MD) - 1994
Brockett, Bruce (AZ) - 1950
Brooke, Edward W. (MA) - 1966, 1972, 1978
Brooks, C. Wayland (IL) - 1948
Broughton, J. Melville (NC) - 1948
Brown, Clarence J. (HI) - 1982
Brown, Cooper (HI) - 1980
Brown, Edgar A. (SC) - 1954
Brown, Ernest S. (NV) - 1954
Brown, George M. (WA) - 1976
Brown, Hank (CO) - 1990
Brown, John Young (KY) - 1946, 1966
Brownback, Sam (KS) - 1996
Broyhill, James T. (NC) - 1986
Bruggere, Tom (OR) - 1996
Brunner, George E. (NJ) - 1946
Bryan, Richard H. (NV) - 1988, 1994

Bryant, Winston (AR) - 1996
Buchanan, Mary E. (CO) - 1980
Buck, Clayton Douglass (DE) - 1948
Buckley, James L. (CT) - 1980
Buckley, James L. (NY) - 1968, 1970, 1976
Bumpers, Dale (AR) - 1974, 1980, 1990, 1992
Bunker, Berkeley L. (NV) - 1946
Burdick, Quentin N. (ND) - 1956, 1960, 1964, 1970, 1976, 1982, 1988
Burditt, George M. (IL) - 1974
Burger, Stanley C. (MT) - 1976
Burke, Thomas A. (OH) - 1954
Burks, Betty A. (WV) - 1996
Burns, Conrad (MT) - 1988, 1994
Burris, John M. (DE) - 1984
Burtenshaw, Claude J. (ID) - 1950
Burton, Laurence J. (UT) - 1970
Busch, Peter M. (ID) - 1984
Bush, George (TX) - 1964, 1970
Bush, Gwenyfred (SC) - 1974
Bush, Prescott S. (CT) - 1950, 1952, 1956
Butler, Hugh (NE) - 1946, 1952
Butler, John Marshall (MD) - 1950, 1956
Byrd, Harry F. (VA) - 1946, 1952, 1958, 1964
Byrd, Harry F. Jr. (VA) - 1966, 1970, 1976
Byrd, Robert C. (WV) - 1958, 1964, 1970, 1976, 1982, 1988, 1994

C

Cabaniss, Bill (AL) - 1990
Cain, Harry P. (WA) - 1946, 1952
Campbell, Alex M. (IN) - 1950
Campbell, Ben Nighthorse (CO) - 1992
Cannon, Howard W. (NV) - 1958, 1964, 1970, 1976, 1982
Capehart, Homer E. (IN) - 1950, 1956, 1962
Carlson, Frank (KS) - 1950, 1956, 1962
Carlson, William E. (MN) - 1952
Carmichael, Gil (MS) - 1972
Carpenter, Terry (NE) - 1948, 1972
Carr, Bob (MI) - 1994
Carr, Waggoner (TX) - 1966
Carroll, John A. (CO) - 1950, 1954, 1956, 1962
Carter, Anderson (NM) - 1966, 1970
Carter, John W. (VA) - 1966

Senate Primary Candidates Index

The Senate Primary Candidates Index includes all candidates appearing in Senate Primary Returns 1946-1996. The index includes candidates' names followed by state abbreviations and the years of candidacy. To locate a candidate's returns, turn to pages 103-164 where the returns are arranged alphabetically by state and in chronological order by class of senator for each state. *(Explanation of Senate classes, p. 61; State Abbreviations, below)* For other references to Senate primary candidates in the *Congressional Elections 1946-1996*, see the General Index, pages 372-375.

A

Abbott, John H. (CA) - 1986, 1988
Abdnor, James (SD) - 1980, 1986
Abercrombie, Neil (HI) - 1970
Abourezk, James (SD) - 1972
Abraham, Spencer (MI) - 1994
Abrams, Robert (NY) - 1992
Abzug, Bella (NY) - 1976
Accardo, Nick J. (LA) - 1992
Adams, Brock (WA) - 1986
Adams, Thomas B. (MA) - 1966
Addington, W. H. (KS) - 1986
Aiken, George D. (VT) - 1956, 1962, 1968
Airy, Frederic W. (NJ) - 1960
Akaka, Daniel K. (HI) - 1990, 1994
Albough, William A. (MD) - 1964, 1982
Albright, Ernest G. (OK) - 1956
Alderson, Fleming N. (WV) - 1958
Alexander, Lee (NY) - 1974
Algood, Alice W. (TN) - 1988
Alioto, Kathleen Sullivan (MA) - 1978
Allard, Wayne (CO) - 1996
Allen, Frank Tunney (LA) - 1972
Allen, James B. Jr. (AL) - 1986
Allen, Jim (AL) - 1968, 1974
Allen, Maryon Pittman (AL) - 1978
Allen, Melba T. (AL) - 1972
Allen, William B. (CA) - 1992
Allott, Gordon (CO) - 1960, 1966, 1972
Allred, Thomas L. (NC) - 1984
Altvater, George (OR) - 1960
Anaya, Toney (NM) - 1978
Anderson, Andy (NV) - 1992
Anderson, Anson (ND) - 1958
Anderson, Ava A. (KS) - 1966
Anderson, Bill (TN) - 1988
Anderson, Blanche (MT) - 1958
Anderson, Clinton P. (NM) - 1960, 1966
Anderson, Doug (UT) - 1992
Anderson, Fred (NV) - 1958
Anderson, Le Roy (MT) - 1960
Anderson, Mark E. (UT) - 1968
Anderson, Steve (OR) - 1978, 1986, 1990
Anderson, Tom (PA) - 1980
Anderson, Wendell R. (MN) - 1978
Andrews, Jackson M. (KY) - 1980, 1986
Andrews, Lloyd J. (WA) - 1964
Andrews, Mark (ND) - 1980, 1986

Andrews, Michael A. (TX) - 1994
Andrews, Thomas H. (ME) - 1994
Andromidas, Ted J. (CA) - 1994
Angell, Wayne (KS) - 1978
Annanders, David Louis (OK) - 1996
Antonovich, Michael D. (CA) - 1986
Apodaca, Jerry (NM) - 1982
Applegate, Ralph A. (OH) - 1988, 1994
Aragona, Xavier A. (MD) - 1974
Archambault, Raoul (RI) - 1960
Armstrong, Hepburn T. (WY) - 1958
Armstrong, William L. (CO) - 1978, 1984
Arn, Edward F. (KS) - 1962
Arndt, Raymond W. (NE) - 1964, 1966
Arnold, Burleigh (MO) - 1982
Aron, Ruthann (MD) - 1994
Arvidson, Gene (OR) - 1980
Ashcroft, John (MO) - 1994
Ashe, Victor (TN) - 1984
Askew, James J. (MO) - 1986
Atchley, Forrest S. (NM) - 1958
Atkins, Hobart F. (TN) - 1958
AuCoin, Les (OR) - 1992
Austin, Richard H. (MI) - 1976
Auvil, Ken (WV) - 1984
Avery, William (KS) - 1968
Aylward, Paul (KS) - 1956, 1962

B

Babb, Leslie R. (NH) - 1974
Babbitt, Wayne H. (AR) - 1972
Babcock, C. H. (NC) - 1962
Babcock, Tim M. (MT) - 1966
Bacaloff, James (OR) - 1966
Backus, Jan (VT) - 1994
Bagley, E. J. (GA) - 1980
Bailey, Don (PA) - 1986
Baker, Albert J. (NE) - 1960
Baker, Deane (MI) - 1976, 1982
Baker, Gerald (IA) - 1978
Baker, Howard H. Jr. (TN) - 1964, 1966, 1972, 1978
Baker, John (AL) - 1978
Baker, John (TN) - 1994
Ball, Albert T. (OH) - 1962
Ballard, John S. (OH) - 1962
Ballenger, William S. (MI) - 1982

Bangerter, Bruce (UT) - 1974
Bantz, William B. (WA) - 1958
Banuelos, Robert J. (CA) - 1988
Barbour, Haley (MS) - 1982
Barilla, Bruce (WV) - 1996
Barkley, Dean (MN) - 1996
Barlow, Tom (KY) - 1996
Barnes, Bill (AK) - 1986
Barnes, John (KS) - 1980
Barnes, Michael D. (MD) - 1986
Barnett, Don (SD) - 1978
Baron, Murray (NY) - 1968
Barr, Bob (GA) - 1992
Barrasso, John (WY) - 1996
Barrett, Frank A. (WY) - 1958, 1960
Barron, Elizabeth Cervantes (CA) - 1994
Barrows, Gordon H. (WY) - 1978
Bartlett, Dewey F. (OK) - 1972
Bartlett, E. L. (AK) - 1958, 1960, 1966
Bartlett, Roscoe G. (MD) - 1980
Bartley, David M. (MA) - 1984
Bass, Doris M. (MO) - 1970
Bass, Perkins (NH) - 1962
Bass, Ross (TN) - 1964, 1966
Batchelor, George M. (UT) - 1980
Bates, Joe B. (KY) - 1956
Battle, Laurie C. (AL) - 1954
Baucom, John D. (MN) - 1970
Baucus, Max S. (MT) - 1978, 1984, 1990, 1996
Bauman, Rick (OR) - 1986
Baxter, James H. (DE) - 1978
Bayh, Birch (IN) - 1980
Beall, Forest W. (OK) - 1964
Beall, J. Glenn (MD) - 1958, 1964, 1970, 1976
Beals, Manny (NV) - 1986
Beard, Robin L. (TN) - 1982
Beard, Samuel S. (DE) - 1988
Beasley, Michael (AK) - 1984, 1990, 1996
Beck, Paul V. (OK) - 1956
Beck, Rodney W. (ID) - 1992
Beckjord, Walter E. (OH) - 1982
Beckworth, Lindley (TX) - 1952
Bedford, Roger (AL) - 1996
Beilenson, Anthony C. (CA) - 1968
Belk, William I. (NC) - 1986
Bell, Alphonzo E. (CA) - 1976
Bell, Bob (OR) - 1992

Bell, Dale (SD) - 1980
Bell, Jeffrey (NJ) - 1978, 1982
Bellmon, Henry (OK) - 1968, 1974
Belluso, Nick M. (GA) - 1980
Benavides, Tom R. (NM) - 1990
Bender, George H. (OH) - 1956
Benedict, Cleveland K. (WV) - 1982
Benedict, Cooper P. (WV) - 1964
Bennett (SC) - 1948
Bennett, James G. (MD) - 1988
Bennett, Robert F. (UT) - 1992
Bennett, Terry (NH) - 1992
Bennett, Wallace F. (UT) - 1956, 1962, 1968
Bennett, William M. (CA) - 1968
Bentivegna, Joe (CT) - 1994
Bentley, Alvin M. (MI) - 1960
Bentsen, Lloyd (TX) - 1970, 1976, 1982, 1988
Bergeson, Rollo (IA) - 1960
Bergland, David (CA) - 1980
Beringer, Raymond Warren (OH) - 1962
Berman, Dan (UT) - 1980
Bernard, Charles T. (AR) - 1968
Bernard, Sherman A. (LA) - 1974
Bernier-Nachtwey, E. F. (HI) - 1980, 1982
Bernstein, Mert (MO) - 1992
Bertroche, Joe (IA) - 1978
Beshear, Steven L. (KY) - 1996
Bethune, Ed (AR) - 1984
Betts, James E. (OH) - 1980
Bible, Alan (NV) - 1956, 1962, 1968
Bichsel, T. J. (AK) - 1966
Biddle, Walter I. (KS) - 1956
Biden, Joseph R. (DE) - 1984, 1990, 1996
Bilbo, Theodore G. (MS) - 1946
Binford, Hugh (WY) - 1978
Bingaman, Jeff (NM) - 1982, 1988, 1994
Bird, Robert M. (AK) - 1990
Bishop, Neil S. (ME) - 1970
Blair, Thomas L. (MD) - 1988
Blake, Henry J. Jr. (AK) - 1996
Blake, Jimmy (AL) - 1996
Blakeney, Ance (MS) - 1960
Blakley, William A. (TX) - 1958
Blanche, Maurice P. (LA) - 1968
Blanton, Ray (TN) - 1972
Blatt, Genevieve (PA) - 1964
Blauvelt, Ronald I. (NE) - 1972

State Abbreviations

Alabama	AL	**Illinois**	IL	**Montana**	MT	**Rhode Island**	RI
Alaska	AK	**Indiana**	IN	**Nebraska**	NE	**South Carolina**	SC
Arizona	AZ	**Iowa**	IA	**Nevada**	NV	**South Dakota**	SD
Arkansas	AR	**Kansas**	KS	**New Hampshire**	NH	**Tennessee**	TN
California	CA	**Kentucky**	KY	**New Jersey**	NJ	**Texas**	TX
Colorado	CO	**Louisiana**	LA	**New Mexico**	NM	**Utah**	UT
Connecticut	CT	**Maine**	ME	**New York**	NY	**Vermont**	VT
Delaware	DE	**Maryland**	MD	**North Carolina**	NC	**Virginia**	VA
Florida	FL	**Massachusetts**	MA	**North Dakota**	ND	**Washington**	WA
Georgia	GA	**Michigan**	MI	**Ohio**	OH	**West Virginia**	WV
Hawaii	HI	**Minnesota**	MN	**Oklahoma**	OK	**Wisconsin**	WI
Idaho	ID	**Mississippi**	MS	**Oregon**	OR	**Wyoming**	WY
		Missouri	MO	**Pennsylvania**	PA		

Dougherty, Dudley T. (TX) - 1954
Douglas, Herbert (MO) - 1956
Douglas, James H. (VT) - 1992
Douglas, Paul H. (IL) - 1960, 1966
Douglass, Steve (PA) - 1988
Douglass, Robert L. (MD) - 1980
Dowdy, Wayne (MS) - 1988
Doyle, Howard J. (IL) - 1966
Driscoll, John (MT) - 1978, 1990
Droney, John J. (MA) - 1972
Drum, Dave (MT) - 1976
Duesenberg, Walter D. (NV) - 1970
Duff, James H. (PA) - 1956
Duffey, Joseph D. (CT) - 1970
Duffy, Clyde (ND) - 1958
Du Haime, Richard A. (NJ) - 1996
Duke, David E. (LA) - 1990, 1996
Duncan, Morris D. (MO) - 1962, 1964, 1968, 1970, 1980
Duncan, Robert B. (OR) - 1966, 1968, 1972
Dunn, Jim (MI) - 1984, 1988
Dunn, Pete (AZ) - 1982
Dunn, Thomas C. (OK) - 1960
Dupay, Robert L. (NH) - 1986
Durant, Clark (MI) - 1990
Durbin, Richard J. (IL) - 1996
Durenberger, Dave (MN) - 1978, 1982, 1988
Durkin, John A. (NH) - 1974, 1980, 1990
Durno, Edwin R. (OR) - 1962
Duval, Clive L. (VA) - 1970
Dwinell, Lane (NH) - 1966
Dworshak, Henry C. (ID) - 1960
Dwyer, Bill (OR) - 1996
Dyas, Hess (NE) - 1976
Dyrstad, Joanell M. (MN) - 1994
Dyson, John S. (NY) - 1986

E

Eagleton, Thomas F. (MO) - 1968, 1974, 1980
Earl, Anthony S. (WI) - 1988
Easley, Mike (NC) - 1990
Easley, W. W. III (MS) - 1984
East, John P. (NC) - 1980
Eastland, Hiram (MS) - 1994
Eastland, James O. (MS) - 1948, 1954, 1960, 1966, 1972
Eckerd, Jack M. (FL) - 1974
Eckman, Harold (NH) - 1992
Eden, Charles H. (RI) - 1966
Edgar, Robert W. (PA) - 1986
Edmondson, Ed (OK) - 1972, 1974, 1978
Edmondson, J. Howard (OK) - 1964
Edwards, Richard B. (NM) - 1970
Elder, George R. H. (PA) - 1986
Elias, Brenda J. (NH) - 1992
Elicker, Charles W. (WA) - 1970
Ellender, Allen J. (LA) - 1948, 1954, 1960, 1966, 1972
Ellis (MS) - 1946
Ellis, Frank B. (LA) - 1954
Ellsworth, R. F. (KS) - 1966
Elson, Roy L. (AZ) - 1964, 1968
Emerson, Lee E. (VT) - 1958
Emery, David F. (ME) - 1982
Engdahl, Lynn (OR) - 1972
Engeleiter, Susan (WI) - 1988
Engle, Clair (CA) - 1958
Enzi, Michael B. (WY) - 1996
Erhart, Milton E. (ID) - 1992
Erickson, John E. (WI) - 1970
Ervin, Sam J. Jr. (NC) - 1954, 1956, 1962, 1968
Esch, Marvin L. (MI) - 1976
Eskind, Jane (TN) - 1978
Espinoza, Reginaldo (NM) - 1958
Esser, Fred (AZ) - 1980
Etchison, Lenore R. (NE) - 1978
Evans, Dan (WA) - 1983
Evans, John V. (ID) - 1986
Evans, R. M. (IA) - 1956
Evslin, Tom (VT) - 1980
Ewing, Bayard (RI) - 1958
Exon, J. James (NE) - 1978, 1984, 1990

F

Faircloth, Earl (FL) - 1968
Faircloth, Lauch (NC) - 1992
Faircloth, Sean F. (ME) - 1996
Fannin, Paul (AZ) - 1964, 1970
Faranda, Tom (MT) - 1988
Farrell, Bill (MT) - 1990
Fasi, Frank F. (HI) - 1959
Faulkner, Roger W. (WI) - 1992

Fayette, Frederick J. (VT) - 1958, 1964
Feighan, William M. (AZ) - 1974
Fein, Jill (WA) - 1986
Feingold, Russell D. (WI) - 1992
Feinstein, Dianne (CA) - 1992, 1994
Fenwick, Millicent (NJ) - 1982
Ferguson, Joel (MI) - 1994
Ferraro, Geraldine A. (NY) - 1992
Fiedler, Bobbi (CA) - 1986
Fike, Ed (NV) - 1968
Fillmore, Herb (MO) - 1980
Finch, Cliff (MS) - 1978
Finch, Donovan B. (MD) - 1982
Finch, Robert H. (CA) - 1976
Finch, Walter G. (MD) - 1968, 1970, 1974
Finney, Joan (KS) - 1996
Fisher, Richard (TX) - 1994
Fithian, Floyd (IN) - 1982
Fitzpatrick, Patrick M. (NV) - 1988
Fitzpatrick, Thomas M. (WI) - 1994
Fjare, Orvin B. (MT) - 1960
Flaherty, Peter (PA) - 1974, 1980
Flowers, Walter (AL) - 1978
Flynn, Helen E. (RI) - 1982
Flynn, Matthew J. (WI) - 1986
Foley, Stephen J. (NJ) - 1976
Foley, Tom (MN) - 1994
Folsom, James E. (AL) - 1968
Folsom, Jim Jr. (AL) - 1980
Fondren, Louis (MS) - 1972
Fong, Hiram L. (HI) - 1959, 1964, 1970
Ford, Wendell H. (KY) - 1974, 1980, 1986, 1992
Fore, Rick (NV) - 1982
Forsythe, Robert A. (MN) - 1966
Foust, Mary Louise (KY) - 1980
Fowler, Harry C. (OR) - 1960
Fowler, Wyche (GA) - 1986, 1992
Fox, John G. (WV) - 1956
Fox, Milton E. (TX) - 1988
Fox, Ora J. (OK) - 1956
Frahm, Sheila (KS) - 1996
Francis, E. Lee (NM) - 1972
Franklin, Marvin (HI) - 1986
Franklin, Nick (NM) - 1984
Franklin, Ralph E. (MN) - 1966
Franks, Ronald (MD) - 1994
Franson, Dick (MN) - 1996
Franson, Richard W. (MN) - 1976
Fraser, Donald M. (MN) - 1978
Frazier, A. Bradley (TN) - 1960
Freeburg, Rosanne (IA) - 1992
Freiberger, Lawrence (AK) - 1996
Freind, Stephen F. (PA) - 1992
Frey, Louis (FL) - 1980
Frist, Bill (TN) - 1994
Fritchell, William E. (WY) - 1972
Fritz, John P. (HI) - 1980
Frost, David (NJ) - 1966
Frothingham, Nathaniel (VT) - 1974
Fry, Charles E. (OH) - 1962
Fuhrig, Joseph (CA) - 1982
Fulbright, J. William (AR) - 1950, 1956, 1962, 1968, 1974
Fuller, James M. (WV) - 1994
Fullmer, Larry (ID) - 1980
Funderburk, David B. (NC) - 1986
Furcolo, Foster (MA) - 1960
Furman, Hal (NV) - 1994

G

Gaar, Norman E. (KS) - 1978
Gable, Robert E. (KY) - 1972
Gaby, Daniel M. (NJ) - 1972
Galifianakis, Nick (NC) - 1972, 1974
Galloway, Sam J. (TN) - 1964
Gambrell, David H. (GA) - 1972
Gann, Paul (CA) - 1980
Gantt, Harvey B. (NC) - 1990, 1996
Garcia, Gloria (CA) - 1988
Gardner, Earl S. (VT) - 1980, 1982
Gardner, Kenneth C. (ND) - 1988
Garn, Jake (UT) - 1974
Garry, Joseph R. (ID) - 1960
Gartin, Carroll (MS) - 1954
Garvey, Edward R. (WI) - 1986, 1988
Gary, Raymond (OK) - 1964
Gaston, William A. (FL) - 1952
Gathings, John T. (NC) - 1968
Gavin, George (AZ) - 1964
Gavin, Joseph T. (NJ) - 1970
Gaydosh, Frank W. (PA) - 1970
Gayle, Dennard A. (MD) - 1994
Genis, June R. (CA) - 1992
Gentry, George (OK) - 1986
George, Gary R. (WI) - 1986
George, Walter F. (GA) - 1950
Gerard, Sumner (MT) - 1960
Gerth, Charles L. (LA) - 1948

Gifford, Howard L. (CA) - 1974
Gigler, Robert Alan (AK) - 1996
Gil, Don (RI) - 1996
Gilbert, Charles E. (OR) - 1962
Gilbert, Larry L. (MT) - 1976
Gilbert, William L. (MS) - 1984
Gilbreath, Wes (TX) - 1988
Gill, Thomas P. (HI) - 1964
Gilligan, John J. (OH) - 1968
Gilster, Richard (NV) - 1986
Gindin, Arthur (WV) - 1994
Glassner, Richard M. (NJ) - 1960
Gleason, James P. (MD) - 1962, 1964
Glebe, Otis (NE) - 1970, 1990
Glenn, John (OH) - 1964, 1970, 1974, 1980, 1986, 1992
Glister, Richard A. (NV) - 1980
Glover, John H. (MN) - 1976
Gojack, Mary (NV) - 1980
Golden, Julian H. (KY) - 1956
Goldner, Herman W. (FL) - 1968
Goldstein, Louis L. (MD) - 1964
Goldwater, Barry (AZ) - 1958, 1968, 1974, 1980
Goldwater, Barry M. Jr. (CA) - 1982
Goode, Virgil H. (VA) - 1994
Goodell, Charles E. (NY) - 1970
Goodloe, William C. (WA) - 1988
Gordon, Houston (TN) - 1996
Gordon, Slade (WA) - 1986, 1988
Gore, Albert (TN) - 1952, 1958, 1964, 1970
Gore, Albert Jr. (TN) - 1984, 1990
Gore, Bob (NV) - 1992
Gorton, Slade (WA) - 1980, 1994
Gourley, Ray (CA) - 1956
Grady, John (FL) - 1976
Graham, Bob (FL) - 1986, 1992
Graham, Frank P. (NC) - 1950
Graham, Gar (OK) - 1984
Grainge, Jim H. (KS) - 1980
Grainger, Scott (AZ) - 1994
Gramm, Phil (TX) - 1976, 1984, 1990, 1996
Grams, Rod (MN) - 1994
Grant, Bill (FL) - 1992
Grant, Charles B. (NV) - 1962
Grassley, Charles E. (IA) - 1980, 1986, 1992
Gravel, Mike (AK) - 1968, 1974, 1980
Graves, Cody L. (OK) - 1994
Gray, William (VT) - 1988
Green, Gabriel (CA) - 1962
Green, Robert A. "Lex" (FL) - 1946
Green, William J. III (PA) - 1976
Greene, Abbott O. (ME) - 1970
Greene, Charles (CA) - 1986, 1988
Greene, Claude R. (NC) - 1962
Greenspan, Elliot (NJ) - 1984
Gregg, Judd (NH) - 1992
Gregory, Robert W. (NC) - 1960
Greiner, Raymond J. (RI) - 1978
Greuel, Richard J. (AK) - 1974
Griffes, Mike (VT) - 1988
Griffin, James C. (CA) - 1980
Griffin, Robert P. (MI) - 1966, 1972, 1978
Griffis, Erle (FL) - 1956
Grogan, John J. (NJ) - 1958
Gropper, John L. (VT) - 1992
Grosby, Hiram (MO) - 1958
Gross, Nelson G. (NJ) - 1974
Grossman, Sam (AZ) - 1970
Grover, Henry C. "Hank" (TX) - 1996
Growe, Joan Anderson (MN) - 1984
Grubbs, Steve (IA) - 1996
Gruening, Clark S. (AK) - 1980
Gruening, Ernest (AK) - 1958, 1962, 1968
Guarini, Frank J. (NJ) - 1970
Gubbrud, Archie M. (SD) - 1968
Guenther, Louie (KY) - 1978
Guess, Gene (AK) - 1972, 1974
Guest, James A. (VT) - 1982
Guice, Troyce E. (LA) - 1966
Gulick, Ray E. (MT) - 1976
Gunderson, Barbara B. (SD) - 1974
Gunderson, Matthew (WI) - 1994
Gunter, Bill (FL) - 1988
Gunter, William D. Jr. (FL) - 1974
Gurney, Edward J. (FL) - 1968
Gutmann, Abraham J. (NM) - 1996
Guy, William L. (ND) - 1974
Guzzi, Paul (MA) - 1978

H

Haabestad, Bud (PA) - 1980
Haar, Charlene (SD) - 1992
Hagel, Chuck (NE) - 1996
Hager, Edward B. (NH) - 1980
Haggard, Clarence (ND) - 1976
Hahn, Kenneth (CA) - 1970
Hales, Patrick K. (TN) - 1990

Hall, Fred (CA) - 1964
Hallmark, Donald G. (AL) - 1962
Halloway, Harry (WI) - 1958
Hamburg, Al (WY) - 1984, 1990
Hamilton, James E. (OK) - 1980
Hamlin, Thurman (KY) - 1984
Hamlin, Thurman J. (KY) - 1962, 1974, 1978, 1986
Hamm, Philip J. (AL) - 1948
Hampshire, Larry D. (CA) - 1994
Hance, Kent (TX) - 1984
Hancock, Mel (MO) - 1982
Hansen, Clifford P. (WY) - 1966, 1972
Hansen, George (ID) - 1962, 1968, 1972
Hansen, Phil L. (UT) - 1968
Hansen, Philip (MN) - 1972
Hansman, Gregory (MO) - 1974, 1976, 1980
Hanson, Warren (WA) - 1976, 1994
Harbaugh, John J. (MD) - 1964
Hardage, Sam (KS) - 1978
Hardin, Lu (AR) - 1996
Harding, Ralph R. (ID) - 1966
Hardman, Scott (WA) - 1994
Harker, C. Roger (KY) - 1984
Harker, Robert H. (HI) - 1994
Harkin, Tom (IA) - 1984, 1990, 1996
Harmer, John L. (CA) - 1976
Harper, Ken (MS) - 1994
Harrington, Larry E. (NC) - 1992
Harris, Fred R. (OK) - 1964, 1966
Harris, Homer L. (WV) - 1984
Harris, Thomas J. (OK) - 1964
Hart, Gary (CO) - 1974, 1980
Hart, George (KS) - 1956, 1974
Hart, James P. Jr. (VA) - 1948
Hart, Philip A. (MI) - 1958, 1964, 1970
Hartke, R. Vance (IN) - 1976
Hartnett, Thomas F. (SC) - 1992
Haskell, Floyd (CO) - 1972, 1978
Hastings, Al (FL) - 1970
Hastings, Lawrence (MO) - 1958
Hatch, Orrin G. (UT) - 1976, 1994
Hatfield, Mark O. (OR) - 1966, 1972, 1978, 1984, 1990
Hatfield, Paul (MT) - 1978
Hathaway, W. John (ME) - 1996
Hathaway, William D. (ME) - 1972, 1978
Hatheway, Louis A. (ID) - 1984
Havelock, John E. (AK) - 1984
Hawkins, Bert W. (OR) - 1978
Hawkins, John P. (RI) - 1976
Hawkins, Paula (FL) - 1974, 1980, 1986
Hawkins, William R. (TN) - 1990
Hawley, Jack (ID) - 1962
Hay, Jean (ME) - 1996
Hayakawa, S. I. (CA) - 1976
Hayden, Carl (AZ) - 1956, 1962
Hayden, Tom (CA) - 1976
Hayes, Bobby K. (AR) - 1968
Hayes, Jimmy (LA) - 1996
Hayes, Kyle (NC) - 1960
Hayes, Philip H. (IN) - 1976
Haytaian, Garabed (NJ) - 1994
Healy, Bernadine (OH) - 1994
Hearnes, Warren E. (MO) - 1976
Heath, Josie (CO) - 1990, 1992
Hecht, Chic (NV) - 1982, 1988
Heen, William H. (HI) - 1959
Heflin, Howell (AL) - 1978, 1984, 1990
Heftel, Cecil ((HI) - 1970
Heinz, John (PA) - 1976, 1982, 1988
Helling, Kathy (WY) - 1990
Helm, Paul (MN) - 1978
Helms, Jesse (NC) - 1972, 1978, 1984, 1990, 1996
Henderson, Henry M. (GA) - 1962
Hendricksen, Margie (OR) - 1984
Henkle, Joseph W. (KS) - 1960
Hennings, Thomas C. Jr. (MO) - 1956
Henry, Doyle W. (WY) - 1972, 1976
Hensel, Helen S. (FL) - 1976
Hensley, William L. (AK) - 1992
Herbert, Dick (AZ) - 1968
Herbert, R. B. (SC) - 1960
Herd, Harold S. (KS) - 1966
Herschbach, Kent S. (MN) - 1988
Herschensohn, Bruce (CA) - 1986, 1992
Herzing, Philip (OH) - 1982
Hewes, Henry F. (NY) - 1994
Hewlett, Addison (NC) - 1960
Heyburn, Weldon B. (PA) - 1958
Hibbard, Henry S. (MT) - 1972
Hickenlooper, Bourke B. (IA) - 1956, 1962
Hickey, J. J. (WY) - 1962
Hicks, Mike (GA) - 1984
Hill, Baron P. (IN) - 1990
Hill, Herbert W. (NH) - 1964
Hill, Lister (AL) - 1956, 1962
Hill, Philip H. (WV) - 1956
Hill, Tim (WA) - 1992

House
Candidates Index

The House Candidates Index includes all candidates appearing in House Popular Vote Returns, 1946-1996. The index includes candidates' names followed by state abbreviations and the years of candidacy. To locate a candidate's returns, turn to pages 192-324 where the returns are arranged chronologically by year and alphabetically by state for each year. State abbreviations appear below. For other references to House candidates in the *Congressional Elections 1946-1996*, see the General Index, pages 372-375.

A

Aandahl, Fred G. (ND) - 1950
Aarons, Morris (NY) - 1960
Abate, Frank (NJ) - 1992
Abbitt, Watkins M. (VA) - 1948, 1950, 1952, 1954, 1956, 1958, 1960, 1962, 1964, 1966, 1968, 1970
Abbot, William S. (MA) - 1968
Abdella, James (NY) - 1980
Abdnor, James (SD) - 1972, 1974, 1976, 1978
Abele, Homer E. (OH) - 1958, 1962, 1964
Abercrombie, Neil (HI) - 1986, 1990, 1992, 1994, 1996
Abernethy, Thomas G. (MS) - 1946, 1948, 1950, 1952, 1954, 1956, 1958, 1960, 1962, 1964, 1966, 1968, 1970
Abernethy, Tom (AL) - 1962
Abourezk, James (SD) - 1970
Abraham, William C. (OH) - 1988
Abrahams, George (CA) - 1986
Abrams, Milton C. (UT) - 1984
Abramson, R. S. (LA) - 1972
Abt, Clark C. (MA) - 1986
Abzug, Bella S. (NY) - 1970, 1972, 1974, 1978, 1986
Acer, Christopher T. (NY) - 1970, 1974
Acevedo, Mary Alice (CA) - 1994
Ackerman, Gary L. (NY) - 1983, 1984, 1986, 1988, 1990, 1992, 1994, 1996
Ackerman, J. Waldo Jr. (IL) - 1960
Ackerman, Johann S. (IL) - 1956
Ackerman, Luther H. (PA) - 1958
Ackerson, Nels J. (IN) - 1980
Acklin, George W. (PA) - 1998
Adair, E. Ross (IN) - 1950, 1952, 1954, 1956, 1958, 1960, 1962, 1964, 1966, 1968, 1970
Adair, J. Carlton (NV) - 1962
Adair, Verdell (MD) - 1972
Adametz, Paul T. (PA) - 1996
Adams, Alfred (TN) - 1972
Adams, Alva B. (CO) - 1954, 1956
Adams, Billy (GA) - 1976
Adams, Bob (WA) - 1992
Adams, Brock (WA) - 1964, 1966, 1968, 1970, 1972, 1974, 1976
Adams, Clifford R. (MN) - 1970
Adams, Clyde (FL) - 1976

Adams, Dennis (NJ) - 1984
Adams, Dennis Sr. (NJ) - 1976
Adams, Edson (CA) - 1974
Adams, Edward R. (NY) - 1996
Adams, George Z. (CA) - 1986, 1988, 1990
Adams, James A. (WI) - 1972
Adams, John (NH) - 1976
Adams, Ken (FL) - 1988
Adams, L. S. (AZ) - 1954
Adams, Mike (TN) - 1980
Adams, Norman W. (OH) - 1946
Adams, Stanley G. (VA) - 1948
Adams, Thomas J. (NY) - 1968
Adams, Wayne N. (WA) - 1968
Adanti, Michael J. (CT) - 1976
Addabbo, Joseph P. (NY) - 1960, 1962, 1964, 1966, 1968, 1970, 1972, 1974, 1976, 1978, 1980, 1982, 1984
Addonizio, G. George (NJ) - 1956, 1958
Addonizio, Hugh J. (NJ) - 1948, 1950, 1952, 1954, 1956, 1958, 1960
Adelman, Lynn S. (WI) - 1974
Adelman, William J. (IL) - 1970
Aderholt, Robert (AL) - 1996
Adkins, Burl C. (MI) - 1988, 1990
Adkins, Stockton (TN) - 1972
Adkinson, Ray (CA) - 1946
Adkisson, David (KY) - 1994
Adler, John H. (NJ) - 1990
Adler, John R. (CA) - 1980
Adler, Milton H. (NY) - 1956, 1958
Afflis, Margaret A. (IN) - 1946
Aggarwal, Yash P. (NY) - 1996
Agnew, Arnie W. (WI) - 1952
Ahearn, John (AZ) - 1964
Ahern, D. Patrick (CA) - 1960
Aiken, Patricia O'Brien (MD) - 1982
Ain, Stewart L. (NY) - 1978
Ainlay, Charles W. (IN) - 1962
Ajello, Michael V. (NY) - 1968, 1974
Akaka, Daniel K. (HI) - 1976, 1978, 1980, 1982, 1984, 1986, 1988
Akers, Anthony B. (NY) - 1954, 1956, 1958
Akin, Kevin (CA) - 1984
Akin, Margie (CA) - 1992
Aland, David S. (MD) - 1970
Albanese, Andrew (NY) - 1980
Albanese, Sal F. (NY) - 1992
Albert, Carl (OK) - 1946, 1948, 1950, 1952, 1954, 1956, 1958, 1960, 1962, 1964, 1966, 1968, 1970, 1972, 1974

Albert, Myrna C. (NY) - 1988
Albin, Rick H. (AR) - 1986
Albosta, Donald J. (MI) - 1976, 1978, 1980, 1982, 1984, 1986
Albright, Miles (PA) - 1960
Albritton, Larry L. (MS) - 1986
Aldrich, Richard S. (NY) - 1962
Alexander, Bill (AR) - 1968, 1970, 1972, 1974, 1976, 1978, 1980, 1982, 1984, 1986, 1988, 1990
Alexander, Edwin J. (WA) - 1962
Alexander, Horace V. (CA) - 1952
Alexander, Hugh Q. (NC) - 1952, 1954, 1956, 1958, 1960, 1962
Alexander, Lee (NY) - 1962
Alexander, Lowell H. (PA) - 1946
Alexander, Paul (IL) - 1994
Alexander, Sally J. (CA) - 1996
Alexander, W. B. (MS) - 1960
Alexander, W. J. (TX) - 1968
Alfange, Dean (NY) - 1948
Alford, T. Dale (AR) - 1958, 1960
Alfson, George (MN) - 1952
Alger, Bruce (TX) - 1954, 1956, 1958, 1960, 1962, 1964
Aliberti, Joan M. (MA) - 1972
Alioto, Michela (CA) - 1996
Alissandratos, A. D. (TN) - 1976
Allard, Wayne (CO) - 1990, 1992, 1994
Allee, Henry E. (TX) - 1982
Allegrone, Helen R. (NC) - 1990
Allegrucci, Donald L. (KS) - 1978
Allen, A. Leonard (LA) - 1946, 1948, 1950
Allen, Bob (FL) - 1990
Allen, Calhoun Jr. (LA) - 1956
Allen, Clifford R. (TN) - 1975, 1976
Allen, Daniel W. (NJ) - 1958
Allen, Don (MT) - 1986
Allen, Edward P. (IL) - 1946
Allen, Fred (IL) - 1956
Allen, George F. (VA) - 1991
Allen, John J. Jr. (CA) - 1946, 1948, 1950, 1952, 1954, 1956, 1958
Allen, Joseph C. (OH) - 1948
Allen, Leo E. (IL) - 1946, 1948, 1950, 1952, 1954, 1956, 1958
Allen, Oliver S. (MA) - 1946
Allen, Philip A. (IA) - 1944
Allen, Richard J. (MI) - 1980
Allen, Robert F. (NJ) - 1966, 1968
Allen, Robert S. (CA) - 1978

Allen, Roslyn A. (CA) - 1992
Allen, Tom (ME) - 1996
Allgaier, Cal (MI) - 1988
Allison, Gary D. (OK) - 1986
Allmon, Jack (SD) - 1966
Almeida, John Jr. (MA) - 1958
Almond, J. Lindsay Jr. (VA) - 1946
Almond, Lincoln C. (RI) - 1968
Almquist, John W. (CA) - 1986
Almstrom, Kim R. (CA) - 1992
Alonso, Fernando A. (NJ) - 1994
Alschuler, Benjamin P. (IL) - 1968
Altenburg, Lois Ivers (ND) - 1984
Altham, James F. Jr. (CT) - 1974
Altmeyer, Stephen A. (PA) - 1984
Alton, Duane (WA) - 1976, 1978
Alvarez, David A. (AL) - 1990
Alvarez, Ida (CA) - 1952
Ambro, Jerome A. Jr. (NY) - 1974, 1976, 1978, 1980
Ambrosio, Gabriel (NJ) - 1980
Amen, Randolph John (OK) - 1996
Amenta, Paul S. (CT) - 1986
Ammerman, Joseph S. (PA) - 1976, 1978
Amster, Daniel (NJ) - 1956
Anastasi, Joseph G. (MD) - 1972
Anderko, Joseph J. (PA) - 1974
Andersen, Doug (MN) - 1990
Andersen, H. Carl (MN) - 1946, 1948, 1950, 1952, 1954, 1956, 1958, 1960
Anderson, Anson J. (ND) - 1960
Anderson, Bruce D. (MN) - 1990
Anderson, Catherine A. (TX) - 1996
Anderson, Erika (MN) - 1996
Anderson, Ernest J. Jr. (TX) - 1994
Anderson, Fred (CA) - 1980
Anderson, Fred E. (CO) - 1968
Anderson, Glenn G. (PA) - 1970
Anderson, Glenn M. (CA) - 1968, 1970, 1972, 1974, 1976, 1978, 1980, 1982, 1984, 1986, 1988, 1990
Anderson, Harold L. (WA) - 1964
Anderson, J. Edward (MN) - 1946
Anderson, J. R. (TX) - 1960
Anderson, James (MN) - 1976
Anderson, Jim (IL) - 1994
Anderson, John B. (IL) - 1960, 1962, 1964, 1966, 1968, 1970, 1972, 1974, 1976, 1978
Anderson, John T. (IL) - 1978, 1980
Anderson, John Z. (CA) - 1946, 1948, 1950

Levitt, William (NY) - 1966
Levy, Annette Flatto (NY) - 1972
Levy, Barnett (NY) - 1950
Levy, David A. (NY) - 1992, 1994
Lewandowski, David S. (NY) - 1984
Lewis, Brian (WA) - 1970
Lewis, Donald J. (OH) - 1966, 1968
Lewis, Earl R. (OH) - 1946, 1948
Lewis, Edward (IN) - 1952
Lewis, James M. (AL) - 1992
Lewis, Jason (CO) - 1990
Lewis, Jerry (CA) - 1978, 1980, 1982, 1984, 1986, 1988, 1990, 1992, 1994, 1996
Lewis, John (GA) - 1977, 1986, 1988, 1990, 1992, 1994, 1996
Lewis, John W. (IN) - 1966
Lewis, John W. (TX) - 1982
Lewis, John W. Jr. (LA) - 1962
Lewis, Joseph (OH) - 1970
Lewis, Richard (KY) - 1994
Lewis, Ron (KY) - 1994, 1996
Lewis, Tom (FL) - 1982, 1984, 1986, 1988, 1990, 1992
Leys, Helen Benson (IL) - 1956
Libonati, Roland V. (IL) - 1956, 1958, 1960, 1962
Libous, Alfred J. (NY) - 1974
Lichtenwalter, Franklin H. (PA) - 1948
Lieberg, Prescott O. (CA) - 1958
Lieberman, Joseph I. (CT) - 1980
Lieblong, Warren (AR) - 1962
Liff, Joseph (NY) - 1952
Ligham, Chester K. (NJ) - 1956
Lightburn, Joseph B. (WV) - 1954
Lightfoot, Jim Ross (IA) - 1984, 1986, 1988, 1990, 1992, 1994
Limehouse, J. Sidi (SC) - 1972
Limes, Leonard L. (LA) - 1966
Liming, Richard E. (OH) - 1960
Lincoln, Georgianna (AK) - 1996
Lind, James F. (PA) - 1948, 1950, 1952
Lindblad, John Paul (CA) - 1992
Linder, John (GA) - 1990, 1992, 1994, 1996
Lindgren, Don (CA) - 1968
Lindheim, Irma (NY) - 1948
Lindley, Alfred D. (MN) - 1950
Lindquist, Leonard E. (MN) - 1958
Lindquist, Reese (WA) - 1986, 1988
Lindsay, Al (PA) - 1986
Lindsay, George G. (PA) - 1956
Lindsay, John V. (NY) - 1958, 1960, 1962, 1964
Lindsey, Archie (GA) - 1966
Lindsey, Jack B. (CA) - 1969
Lindskoog, Alver (WI) - 1996
Linehan, Neil J. (IL) - 1948, 1950, 1952
Linford, Velma (WY) - 1968
Link, Arthur A. (ND) - 1970
Link, William W. (IL) - 1946
Linn, David A. (CA) - 1988
Linsky, Martin A. (MA) - 1972
Lionett, David J. (MA) - 1974
Lipinski, William O. (IL) - 1982, 1984, 1986, 1988, 1990, 1992, 1994, 1996
Lipscomb, Glenard P. (CA) - 1954, 1956, 1958, 1960, 1962, 1964, 1966, 1968
Liptock, Richard (TN) - 1992
Lisoni, Joseph L. (CA) - 1980
Lisoski, Edward V. (NY) - 1958, 1960
Litke, William W. (PA) - 1962
Litsey, James P. (KS) - 1978
Little, Dave (WA) - 1996
Little, Erick P. (NC) - 1972
Little, John T. (WA) - 1946
Little, Marc (FL) - 1994
Little, T.D. "Ted" (AL) - 1996
Little, Ted (WA) - 1996
Litton, Jerry (MO) - 1972, 1974
Liu, Mike (HI) - 1990
Livingston, Clyde B. (SC) - 1976
Livingston, Jeffrey E. (NY) - 1996
Livingston, Rick (OR) - 1990
Livingston, Robert L. "Bob" (LA) - 1976, 1977, 1978, 1980, 1982, 1984, 1986, 1988, 1990, 1992, 1994, 1996
Livingston, Tally R. (TN) - 1962
Lloyd, Daniel (PA) - 1984
Lloyd, Jim (CA) - 1974, 1976, 1978, 1980
Lloyd, Marilyn (TN) - 1974, 1976, 1978, 1980, 1982, 1984, 1986, 1988, 1990, 1992
Lloyd, Robin (VT) - 1980
Lloyd, Sherman P. (UT) - 1960, 1962, 1966, 1968, 1970, 1972
Lobb, Mary Ellen (MO) - 1988
LoBiondo, Frank A. (NJ) - 1992, 1994, 1996
Lobsinger, Donald J. (MI) - 1994
Lockard, Robert R. (IA) - 1984, 1986
Locke, Bobby (TX) - 1980
Locke, Bobby A. (TX) - 1976

Locke, Rick (WA) - 1996
Locker, Dale (OH) - 1981
Lockley, Sidney L. (PA) - 1956
Lodge, John Davis (CT) - 1946, 1948
LoDico, Carl C. (IL) - 1978
Lodise, Carmen (CA) - 1980
Loeb, Charles H. (OH) - 1956
Loebl, James D. (CA) - 1974
Loeffler, Tom (TX) - 1978, 1980, 1982, 1984
Loefflor, George H. Jr. (TX) - 1988
Loehr, Gordon E. (WI) - 1982
Lofgren, Zoe (CA) - 1994, 1996
Logan, R. G. (IL) - 1970
Logan, Ralph H. (KY) - 1948
Logue, John J. (PA) - 1966
Lombardi, Peter O. (HI) - 1968
Lonergan, Mike (WA) - 1984
Long, Brian (WA) - 1982
Long, Bruce (OR) - 1984, 1986
Long, Cathy (Mrs. Gillis) (LA) - 1985
Long, Charles W. (IN) - 1950
Long, Clarence D. (MD) - 1962, 1964, 1966, 1968, 1970, 1972, 1974, 1976, 1978, 1980, 1982, 1984
Long, George S. (LA) - 1952, 1954, 1956
Long, Gillis W. (LA) - 1962, 1972, 1974, 1976, 1978, 1980, 1982, 1984
Long, Jack (VT) - 1996
Long, Jill (IN) - 1988, 1989, 1990, 1992, 1994
Long, M. M. (VA) - 1952
Long, Patricia (WA) - 1996
Long, Speedy O. (LA) - 1964, 1966, 1968, 1970
Long, Stanley D. (NE) - 1946
Long, William A. Jr. (NY) - 1994
Longabaugh, Mark P. (OH) - 1996
Longe, William T. (PA) - 1954
Longhi, Vincent J. (NY) - 1946, 1948, 1950
Longley, James B. Jr. (ME) - 1994, 1996
Longshore, W. L. Jr. (AL) - 1956
Lopez, Junio (NM) - 1962
Lore, Marvin E. (IL) - 1956
Lorenz, Mindy (CA) - 1992
Lorusso, Anthony P. (NY) - 1972
Loser, J. Carlton (TN) - 1956, 1958, 1960, 1962
Loss, Frank L. (MN) - 1970
Loth, John (PA) - 1964, 1970
Lott, Trent (MS) - 1972, 1974, 1976, 1978, 1980, 1982, 1984, 1986
Lotz, Charles E. (PA) - 1954, 1958
Louchery, Daniel L. (WV) - 1956
Loughlin, Thomas E. Jr. (NY) - 1996
Love, Francis J. (WV) - 1946, 1948, 1950, 1952
Love, Frank (WV) - 1952
Love, Rodney M. (OH) - 1964, 1966
Love, Tom (KS) - 1992
Love, W. T. (NC) - 1954
Love, Walter B. (NC) - 1952
Loveless, Herschel C. (IA) - 1954
Lovell, Christopher (NY) - 1980
Lovett, Woodrow (GA) - 1992, 1994
Lovingood, Joe Z. (FL) - 1966, 1968, 1970, 1974
Lovitt, Craig (IL) - 1968
Lovre, Harold O. (SD) - 1948, 1950, 1952, 1954, 1956
Lowe, Bob (CA) - 1972
Lowe, Kenneth K. (MO) - 1960
Lowe, Lynn (AR) - 1966
Lowe, Wyman C. (GA) - 1974
Lowenstein, Allard K. (NY) - 1968, 1970, 1972, 1974, 1976
Lowenthal, Margaret (LA) - 1986
Lowery, Bill (CA) - 1980, 1982, 1984, 1986, 1988, 1990
Lowery, Thomas J. (NY) - 1956
Lowey, Nita M. (NY) - 1988, 1990, 1992, 1994, 1996
Lowry, H. Graham (MA) - 1978
Lowry, J. M. (MO) - 1954
Lowry, James W. (KS) - 1946
Lowry, Kerry (TX) - 1994
Lowry, Mike (WA) - 1978, 1980, 1982, 1984, 1986
Lowry, Thomas C. (WA) - 1972
Loy, William H. (WV) - 1974
Luby, Jason (TX) - 1982
Lucas, Charles P. (OH) - 1968
Lucas, Frank D. (OK) - 1994, 1996
Lucas, Frank R. (NJ) - 1992
Lucas, Wingate H. (TX) - 1946, 1948, 1950, 1952
Lucca, Mariano A. (NY) - 1954, 1958, 1960
Luce, Marjory L. (MN) - 1982
Lucey, Patrick J. (WI) - 1950
Luck, Oliver (WV) - 1990
Ludeman, Cal R. (MN) - 1992
Ludlow, Louis (IN) - 1946
Ludlow, Willis H. (ID) - 1972

Ludwig, Earl (OH) - 1948
Lujan, Manuel Jr. (NM) - 1968, 1970, 1972, 1974, 1976, 1978, 1980, 1982, 1984, 1986
Luke, George W. (NJ) - 1968
Luken, Charles (OH) - 1990
Luken, Thomas A. (OH) - 1974, 1976, 1978, 1980, 1982, 1984, 1986, 1988
Lukens, Donald E. (OH) - 1966, 1968, 1986, 1988
Lukson, Lee (WA) - 1968
Lumina, Luke (MA) - 1992
Lund, Arnold L. (FL) - 1956
Lunde, Paul (IA) - 1988, 1992
Lundeen, B. A. (MN) - 1970
Lundine, Stanley N. (NY) - 1976, 1978, 1980, 1982, 1984
Lundquist, Todd (MN) - 1984
Lundstrom, Milton A. (IL) - 1958
Lundy, Daniel F. (NJ) - 1970
Lundy, Hunter (LA) - 1996
Lundy, Rayfield (CA) - 1964, 1968, 1972
Lungren, Brian (CA) - 1982
Lungren, Dan (CA) - 1980, 1984, 1986
Lungren, Daniel E. (CA) - 1976, 1978
Lupton, John M. (CT) - 1962
Lupton, William R. (NY) - 1946
Lusk, Georgia L. (NM) - 1946
Lusk, Lucille (NV) - 1988
Lustig, Wayne (VA) - 1964
Luther, Ernest M. (NE) - 1954
Luther, William P. "Bill" (MN) - 1994, 1996
Luttmer, William J. (WI) - 1982
Lutton, John M. (CA) - 1980
Lutz, Earle (IA) - 1946
Luxford, Richard (CO) - 1950
Lyford, Joseph P. (CT) - 1952, 1954
Lyle, John E. Jr. (TX) - 1946, 1948, 1950, 1952
Lyman, Asael (ID) - 1948
Lyman, Howard (MT) - 1982
Lynch, Daniel C. (NB) - 1974
Lynch, Donald J. (IN) - 1986
Lynch, Emmett (CA) - 1982
Lynch, J. Gregory (CT) - 1950
Lynch, T. Joseph (NY) - 1956, 1958, 1960, 1962
Lynch, Walter A. (NY) - 1946, 1948
Lynch, Walter A. Jr. (NY) - 1958
Lyon, Dale (KS) - 1986
Lyons, Charlton H. (LA) - 1961
Lyons, Hall M. (LA) - 1966
Lytel, Elaine (NY) - 1982

M

Macaluso, Michael (NY) - 1976
MacBain, Bruce D. (NY) - 1996
Macchio, Nicholas R. (NY) - 1972
MacDonald, Robert (AZ) - 1994
MacDonald, Torbert H. (MA) - 1954, 1956, 1958, 1960, 1962, 1964, 1966, 1968, 1970, 1972, 1974
MacGovern, John F. (MA) - 1990
MacGregor, Clark (MN) - 1960, 1962, 1964, 1966, 1968
Machen, Hervey G. (MD) - 1964, 1966, 1968
Machrowicz, Thaddeus M. (MI) - 1950, 1952, 1954, 1956, 1958, 1960
Machtley, Ronald K. (RI) - 1988, 1990, 1992
Mack, Bill (OH) - 1970, 1974, 1978
Mack, Connie (FL) - 1982, 1984, 1986
Mack, Edward J. (MI) - 1984
Mack, Joseph S. (MI) - 1956, 1958
Mack, Marty (NY) - 1996
Mack, Peter F. Jr. (IL) - 1948, 1950, 1952, 1954, 1956, 1958, 1960, 1962, 1974, 1976
Mack, Russell V. (WA) - 1948, 1950, 1952, 1954, 1956, 1958
MacKaig, Milton R. (CA) - 1982
MacKay, Buddy (FL) - 1986
MacKay, J. Alan (MA) - 1974
MacKay, James A. (GA) - 1964, 1966, 1968
MacKay, Kenneth H. "Buddy" (FL) - 1982, 1984
Macken, Terry R. (CA) - 1966
MacKenzie, A. E. (NV) - 1950
MacKenzie, Ken (IN) - 1984
Mackie, John C. (MI) - 1964, 1966
Mackie, John G. (CO) - 1958
Mackin, Lawrence C. (MA) - 1992
MacKinnon Daniel F. (CT) - 1978
MacKinnon, George (MN) - 1946, 1948
MacLaren, Joseph R. (NY) - 1954
MacLeod, Charles Kevin (MA) - 1978
Macleod, Kenneth P. (ME) - 1964
Maclin, Earl (TN) - 1964
MacMullen, Leon C. (PA) - 1950

MacVicar, James A. (ME) - 1948
Macy, W. Kingsland (NY) - 1946, 1948, 1950
Madden, Charles F. Jr. (OH) - 1966
Madden, Ray J. (IN) - 1946, 1948, 1950, 1952, 1954, 1956, 1958, 1960, 1962, 1964, 1966, 1968, 1970, 1972, 1974
Madden, William C. (MA) - 1960
Maddox, Henry J. (MS) - 1952
Madigan, Edward R. (IL) - 1972, 1974, 1976, 1978, 1980, 1982, 1984, 1986, 1988, 1990
Madrid, Jim (CA) - 1976
Magazzu, Louis N. (NJ) - 1994
Magee, Clare (MO) - 1948, 1950
Magee, Edward T. (NJ) - 1984
Maginnis, John J. (MA) - 1948
Magli, Vito (NY) - 1952
Magnuson, Don (WA) - 1952, 1954, 1956, 1958, 1960, 1962
Magrann, Thomas J. (PA) - 1980
Maguire, Andrew (NJ) - 1974, 1976, 1978, 1980
Maguire, Crispin M. (NY) - 1978
Maguire, Robert C. (MA) - 1968
Mahaffey, Dan (CA) - 1980
Mahaffey, Mike (IA) - 1996
Mahan, Jim (TX) - 1984
Mahan, Steven E. (IL) - 1988
Maher, Phillip V. (MO) - 1962
Mahler, George (WA) - 1966
Mahon, Don (IA) - 1966, 1968, 1970
Mahon, George (TX) - 1946, 1948, 1950, 1952, 1954, 1956, 1958, 1960, 1962, 1964, 1966, 1968, 1970, 1972, 1974, 1976
Mahoney, Elmo J. (KS) - 1954, 1956, 1958
Mahoney, John J. (NJ) - 1982
Mahoney, William P. Jr. (AZ) - 1956
Maickel, Aloysius J. (NY) - 1946
Maietta, Julia L. (PA) - 1948, 1958
Mailliard, William S. (CA) - 1948, 1952, 1954, 1956, 1958, 1960, 1962, 1964, 1966, 1968, 1970, 1972
Mailloux, Raymond A. (RI) - 1946
Mains, Doug (IL) - 1996
Maitland, Ian (MN) - 1988, 1990, 1992
Major, Stan (IL) - 1968
Malang, Robert J. (NY) - 1964
Malberg, Patricia (CA) - 1988, 1990, 1992
Malinowsky, Winifred H. (PA) - 1962
Malkus, Frederick C. (MD) - 1973
Mallan, Lloyd "Jeff" (HI) - 1988, 1992
Mallary, Richard W. (VT) - 1972
Mallonee, Walter L. (CA) - 1970
Malone, George W. (NV) - 1960
Malone, Richard T. (MN) - 1952
Maloney, Carolyn B. (NY) - 1992, 1994, 1996
Maloney, Franklin J. (PA) - 1946, 1948
Maloney, James H. (CT) - 1994, 1996
Maloney, John J. Jr. (ME) - 1950
Maloney, John R. (NY) - 1976
Malpass, C. Dana (NC) - 1956, 1958
Maltese, Serphin R. (NY) - 1984
Manasco, Carter (AL) - 1946
Mandel, William M. (NY) - 1950
Mandell, Alvin (MA) - 1974
Mandell, Luther (CA) - 1972
Mandell, Paul (MN) - 1992
Manes, Panny (OH) - 1972
Manfre, James (NY) - 1994
Mange, P. Scott (OH) - 1990
Mangels, Louis A. (OH) - 1980, 1982
Mangini, Daniel J. (NJ) - 1990
Manion, Albert F. (IL) - 1966
Mankin, Helen Douglas (GA) - 1946
Mankin, Jack H. (IN) - 1950, 1952
Mankus, Louis A. (WY) - 1962
Mann, Blaine (TX) - 1986
Mann, David (OH) - 1992, 1994
Mann, James R. (IL) - 1946
Mann, James R. (SC) - 1968, 1970, 1972, 1974, 1976
Mann, Les (OH) - 1994
Mann, Terry L. (KY) - 1982, 1986
Manning, Darrell (ID) - 1968
Manning, Howard (IL) - 1950
Manning, Thomas R. (MA) - 1974
Manno, Francis J. (PA) - 1948
Mansfield, Joseph C. (PA) - 1954
Mansfield, Joseph J. (TX) - 1946
Mansfield, Mike (MT) - 1946, 1948, 1950
Mansi, Salvatore T. (NJ) - 1970
Manti, Alfred A. (NY) - 1954
Mantis, James H. (PA) - 1960
Manton, Thomas J. (NY) - 1984, 1986, 1988, 1990, 1992, 1994, 1996
Mantovani, Andrew (NY) - 1968
Manus, Albert H. Jr. (IL) - 1948

Neill, Ben (NC) - 1992, 1996
Nelligan, James L. (PA) - 1980, 1982
Nelsen, Ancher (MN) - 1958, 1960, 1962, 1964, 1968, 1970, 1972
Nelson, Ancher (MN) - 1966
Nelson, Bill (FL) - 1978, 1980, 1982, 1984, 1986, 1988
Nelson, Charles P. (ME) - 1948, 1950, 1952, 1954
Nelson, Ed (AL) - 1972
Nelson, Edwin M. (IL) - 1960
Nelson, G. M. (FL) - 1956
Nelson, Gary (WA) - 1992
Nelson, Gary W. (TX) - 1988
Nelson, Gaylord A. (WI) - 1954
Nelson, Mort (AZ) - 1996
Nelson, Patrick L. (OH) - 1974
Nelson, Robert L. (NY) - 1964
Nelson, Thomas F. (WI) - 1962
Nelson, Verner (MN) - 1946
Nelson, Will L. Jr. (MO) - 1946
Nero, Frank R. (NJ) - 1976
Nesemeier, Edward (ND) - 1952
Nesmith, Robert (TX) - 1958, 1960
Nethercutt, George (WA) - 1994, 1996
Neubauer, Bruce J. (GA) - 1980
Neubeck, Greg (FL) - 1986
Neuberger, Thomas Stephen (DE) - 1986
Neumann, Mark W. (WI) - 1992, 1993, 1994, 1996
Neutze, George F. (NJ) - 1946
New, Joe (NC) - 1954, 1956
Newcomb, Guy (AR) - 1968
Newcomb, James (NC) - 1978
Newhouse, Richard G. (CA) - 1992, 1994
Newinski, Dennis (MN) - 1994, 1996
Newkirk, John D. (OR) - 1994, 1996
Newman, Cynthia "C. J." (TX) - 1996
Newman, Don M. (IN) - 1970, 1972
Newman, Frank J. (CA) - 1966
Newman, John A. (PA) - 1988
Newmann, F. S. (TX) - 1960
Newmyer, John A. (CA) - 1982
Newstetter, Wilber I. Jr. (PA) - 1950
Newton, Blake T. (VA) - 1950
Newton, Huey P. (CA) - 1968
Ney, Bob (OH) - 1994, 1996
Nice, Mary Louise (NY) - 1948, 1950
Nicholas, Dimitri (OH) - 1972
Nichols, Alan (CA) - 1990
Nichols, Benjamin (NY) - 1968
Nichols, Bill (AL) - 1966, 1968, 1970, 1972, 1974, 1976, 1978, 1980, 1982, 1984, 1986, 1988
Nichols, Dick (KS) - 1990
Nichols, Franklin (NY) - 1972
Nichols, Glenn W. (ID) - 1980
Nichols, Harwood (MD) - 1990
Nichols, James W. (MN) - 1982
Nichols, Nelson (PA) - 1948
Nichols, Sara (PA) - 1994
Nichols, Terry L. (KS) - 1994
Nichols, Thomas H. (OH) - 1954
Nicholson, Donald W. (MA) - 1948, 1950, 1952, 1954, 1956
Nicholson, James M. (IN) - 1966
Nicholson, Richard (KY) - 1966
Nicholson, Scott (FL) - 1980
Nickell, James D. (KY) - 1968
Nicolay, Edward P. (NJ) - 1946
Nicosia, Salvatore (NY) - 1976
Niedermeier, Christine M. (CT) - 1986, 1987
Niedner, Robert V. (MO) - 1948
Nielsen, William D. (OH) - 1986, 1990
Nielson, Howard C. (UT) - 1982, 1984, 1986, 1988
Niemeyer, Ernest (IN) - 1980
Niemi, Janice (WA) - 1978
Nieten, Edgar (MI) - 1978
Nighswonger, William A. (CA) - 1972
Nigliazzo, Carl (TX) - 1972, 1974
Nigro, Russell M. (PA) - 1974
Nilson, Douglas C. Jr. (CA) - 1976
Nims, Stuart V. (NH) - 1958, 1960
Nimtz, F. Jay (IN) - 1956, 1958, 1960
Nine, Louis (NY) - 1978
Nix, Edmund A. (WI) - 1964
Nix, Robert N. C. (PA) - 1958, 1960, 1962, 1964, 1966, 1968, 1970, 1972, 1974, 1976
Nixon, John E. (WI) - 1968
Nixon, Richard M. (CA) - 1946, 1948
Noble, Aloma Keen (HI) - 1980
Noble, David D. (OH) - 1974
Noblitt, Harding C. (MN) - 1962
Nodar, Robert J. Jr. (NY) - 1946, 1948
Nolan, Jim (FL) - 1996
Nolan, Monica (OH) - 1962
Nolan, Richard (MN) - 1978
Nolan, Richard M. (MN) - 1972, 1974, 1976
Nolan, Robert V. (WI) - 1984
Nolan, Tom (TX) - 1954
Noland, James A. Jr. (MO) - 1974, 1994
Noland, James E. (IN) - 1946, 1948, 1950
Noll, Richard P. (PA) - 1972, 1976, 1980
Noonan, J. C. (TX) - 1960
Noonan, L. W. "Red" (AL) - 1978
Noonan, Mike (CA) - 1992
Norblad, Walter (OR) - 1946, 1948, 1950, 1952, 1954, 1956, 1958, 1960, 1962
Nordhougen, Orris G. (ND) - 1958
Nordquist, Dale M. (WA) - 1960
Nordvall, Stephen L. (IL) - 1972, 1974
Norem, Ralph A. (WI) - 1952
Norgard, Sterling J. (CA) - 1948
Norman, Fred (WA) - 1946
Norman, Nancy (NY) - 1992, 1996
Norrell, William F. (AR) - 1946, 1948, 1950, 1952, 1954, 1956, 1958, 1960
Norris, Chuck (CO) - 1986
Norris, Ivan (CA) - 1964
Norris, Wayne B. (CA) - 1986
Norsworthy, Ernie (GA) - 1978
North, David S. (NJ) - 1958
Northern, Eugene E. (MO) - 1968
Northup, Anne Meagher (KY) - 1996
Norton, Barry (CA) - 1990
Norton, Mary T. (NJ) - 1946, 1948
Norton, Michael J. (CO) - 1984, 1986
Norton, William J. (IN) - 1968
Norwood, Charlie (GA) - 1994, 1996
Norwood, D. C. (TX) - 1966
Notti, Emil (AK) - 1973
Notz, Edward V. (IL) - 1968
Novak, Mark S. (CA) - 1972
Nowak, Henry J. (NY) - 1974, 1976, 1978, 1980, 1982, 1984, 1986, 1988, 1990
Nowak, Patrick M. (MI) - 1996
Nugent, Michael J. (CA) - 1994
Null, Dennis L. (KY) - 1996
Nulty, Francis X. (NY) - 1946
Nunez, Albert J. (CA) - 1994
Nunez, David G. (CA) - 1996
Nunez, Ricardo (FL) - 1982, 1984
Nussle, Jim (IA) - 1990, 1992, 1994, 1996
Nutter, Raymond (AL) - 1971
Nygaard, Hjalmar C. (ND) - 1960, 1962

O

Oakar, Mary Rose (OH) - 1976, 1978, 1980, 1982, 1984, 1986, 1988, 1990, 1992
Oakes, Dave (TX) - 1964
Oakes, Paul R. (IN) - 1966
Oakman, Charles G. (MI) - 1952, 1954
Oaks, Dave Dr. (TX) - 1962
O'Benshain, Richard D. (VA) - 1964
Oberst, Bill Jr. (SC) - 1992
Oberstar, James L. (MN) - 1974, 1976, 1978, 1980, 1982, 1984, 1986, 1988, 1990, 1992, 1994, 1996
Obert, Walter E. (OH) - 1946
Obey, David R. (WI) - 1970, 1972, 1974, 1976, 1978, 1980, 1982, 1984, 1986, 1988, 1990, 1992, 1994, 1996
Obley, Fred A. (PA) - 1960
O'Brien, Dave (IA) - 1988
O'Brien, David V. (NY) - 1968
O'Brien, Donald E. (IA) - 1958, 1960
O'Brien, Dorothy G. (IL) - 1958, 1960
O'Brien, F. T. (TX) - 1946
O'Brien, George D. (MI) - 1946, 1948, 1950, 1952
O'Brien, George M. (IL) - 1972, 1974, 1976, 1978, 1980, 1982, 1984
O'Brien, J. W. "Billy" (VA) - 1976
O'Brien, J. William (VT) - 1972
O'Brien, James P. (PA) - 1958
O'Brien, John A. (PA) - 1964
O'Brien, Leo W. (NY) - 1952, 1954, 1956, 1958, 1960, 1962, 1964
O'Brien, Michael P. (OH) - 1952
O'Brien, Newell (FL) - 1996
O'Brien, Richard "Buck" (MT) - 1986, 1988
O'Brien, Thomas J. (IL) - 1946, 1948, 1950, 1952, 1954, 1956, 1958, 1960, 1962
O'Brien, Walter A. (MA) - 1948
O'Brien, William J. (PA) - 1988
O'Bryant, Henri Jr. (CA) - 1966
O'Callaghan, Jeremiah J. (NJ) - 1954, 1968
O'Callaghan, Jerry A. (WY) - 1956
O'Callaghan, L. J. (GA) - 1962, 1964
O'Callaghan, Thomas P. (NY) - 1960
Ocasek, Oliver (OH) - 1962, 1968
Occhiogrosso, Frank J. (NY) - 1970
Ochenkowski, Edmund W. (IL) - 1970
Ochoa, Gloria (CA) - 1992
O'Connell, Bernard J. (NY) - 1952
O'Connell, John A. (CA) - 1962
O'Connell, John J. (WA) - 1952
O'Connell, John M. (TX) - 1964
O'Connell, Walter J. (NJ) - 1954
O'Connor, Colleen M. (CA) - 1974
O'Connor, Donald J. (NY) - 1948, 1950, 1952
O'Connor, Ed (CA) - 1966
O'Connor, Eugene (NY) - 1968
O'Connor, James H. (NY) - 1954
O'Connor, John (IA) - 1954
O'Connor, John F. (NY) - 1970
Oddo, Salvatore E. (IL) - 1974
Oddstad, Elma D. (CA) - 1958
Odegard, Robert J. (MN) - 1962, 1964
O'Dell, Tracy (CA) - 1966
Oder, Henry A. Jr. (VA) - 1958
Odlum, Jacqueline Cochran (CA) - 1956
Odman, Robert (WA) - 1958
O'Doherty, Kieran (NY) - 1964
Odom, Archie C. (SC) - 1966
Odom, Christine P. (NC) - 1954
O'Donnell, Pierce (CA) - 1980
O'Donovan, Jerome X. (NY) - 1988
O'Dwyer, Paul (NY) - 1948
Officer, Charles B. (NH) - 1964, 1972
Offner, Paul (WI) - 1982
Ogdahl, Harmon T. (MN) - 1968
Ogden, A. R. (VA) - 1974, 1976
Ogden, Alan R. (VA) - 1978, 1994
Ogden, Dan (CO) - 1976
Ogden, Michael S. (PA) - 1986
Ognibene, Thomas V. (NY) - 1986, 1990
O'Grady, Jack J. (IN) - 1948
O'Grady, Martin J. (NY) - 1988
O'Halloran, Edward J. (PA) - 1968
O'Hara, Barratt (IL) - 1948, 1950, 1952, 1954, 1956, 1958, 1960, 1962, 1964, 1966
O'Hara, Frederic S. (IL) - 1956
O'Hara, James F. (NY) - 1950
O'Hara, James G. (MI) - 1958, 1960, 1962, 1964, 1966, 1968, 1970, 1972, 1974
O'Hara, John Grady (TN) - 1958
O'Hara, Joseph P. (MN) - 1946, 1948, 1950, 1952, 1954, 1956
Ohlendorf, Howard C. (MO) - 1964, 1974
Ojala, William R. (MN) - 1975
Ojeda, Miriam (CA) - 1984
O'Keefe, Dan (CA) - 1978
O'Keefe, Richard B. (MA) - 1946
Okicki, Joseph F. (PA) - 1970
Okonski, Alvin E. (WI) - 1946, 1948, 1950, 1952, 1954, 1956, 1958, 1960, 1962, 1964, 1966, 1968, 1970, 1972
O'Laughlin, Joseph M. (MA) - 1976
O'Leary, Richard A. (NY) - 1952
Olessker, Karl (IN) - 1964
Olin, James R. (VA) - 1982, 1984
Olin, Jim (VA) - 1986, 1988, 1990
Olin, Vernon E. (NY) - 1954
Oliver, James C. (ME) - 1954, 1956, 1958, 1960
Oliver, Robert C. (IN) - 1948
Olsen, Arnold (MT) - 1960, 1962, 1964, 1966, 1968, 1970, 1972
Olsen, Bob (TN) - 1975
Olsen, John E. (MI) - 1976
Olsen, Jon D. (HI) - 1968
Olsen, Kirsten (CA) - 1978, 1980
Olsen, Lawrence Wayne (NJ) - 1990
Olsen, Leslie O. (MO) - 1970
Olson, Alec G. (MN) - 1962, 1964, 1966
Olson, Bob (MN) - 1994
Olson, Chuck (CA) - 1990
Olson, Curtiss T. (MN) - 1950, 1952
Olson, Dawn (WA) - 1962
Olson, Judy (WA) - 1996
Olson, Larry H. (MI) - 1972
Olson, Leslie O. (MO) - 1968
Olson, Robert C. (MN) - 1954
Olson, Robert C. Jr. (MN) - 1976
Olson, Virgil L. (KS) - 1976
Olver, John W. (MA) - 1991, 1992, 1994, 1996
O'Malley, Patrick J. (MA) - 1948
Omann, Bernie (MN) - 1992, 1994
O'Mara, Bill (NV) - 1978
Omdahl, Lloyd (ND) - 1976
O'Meara, Edward S. Jr. (ME) - 1988
O'Meara, John R. (MI) - 1958
O'Merberg, Maynard J. (CA) - 1948
O'Neal, Emmet (KY) - 1946
O'Neal, Maston (GA) - 1964, 1966, 1968
O'Neil, Frank M. (PA) - 1962
O'Neil, James F. (MI) - 1962
O'Neil, Patrick M. (NY) - 1972
O'Neill, Bruce Michael (CA) - 1988
O'Neill, Eugene T. (NY) - 1946
O'Neill, Harry P. (PA) - 1948, 1950, 1952
O'Neill, James F. (MA) - 1952, 1954
O'Neill, Megan (MI) - 1992, 1994
O'Neill, Paul J. (FL) - 1964
O'Neill, Thomas P. Jr. (MA) - 1952, 1954, 1956, 1958, 1960, 1962, 1964, 1966, 1968, 1972, 1974, 1976, 1978, 1980, 1982, 1984
O'Neill, Vincent E. (MI) - 1952
Oppenheim, J. Philip (IN) - 1978
Orchard, Ernest R. (MN) - 1952
Orchard, Ernie (MN) - 1954
O'Reilly, Gerald (NY) - 1946
O'Reilly, Kathleen F. (MI) - 1980
O'Reilly, Maurice (IA) - 1950
O'Reilly, T. Bronson (NY) - 1956
O'Reilly, Timothy I. (CA) - 1954
Orenstein, Jeffrey R. (OH) - 1982
Oriez, Charles A. (CO) - 1992
Orlins, Steve A. (NY) - 1992
Orloski, Richard J. (PA) - 1982, 1990
Ormon, John M. (CT) - 1984
Ormsby, Walter M. (NY) - 1962
Ornstein, Franklin (NY) - 1974
O'Rourke, Jerome F. (MI) - 1960
O'Rourke, Peter (MI) - 1968
O'Rourke, Philip A. (CA) - 1954
O'Rourke, Vernon A. (PA) - 1946
Orozco, Bill (CA) - 1966, 1968
Orr, James W. (TX) - 1964
Ortiz, Bobby (TX) - 1994
Ortiz, Solomon P. (TX) - 1982, 1984, 1986, 1988, 1990, 1992, 1994, 1996
Orton, Bill (UT) - 1990, 1992, 1994, 1996
Orton, Duane (IA) - 1960
Osborn, Michael (TN) - 1970
Osborne, Bartley P. (PA) - 1960
Osborne, John (TN) - 1994
Osborne, W. Ted (OH) - 1958, 1960
O'Scannlain, Diarmuid (OR) - 1974
Osgood, Jim (CA) - 1974
O'Shea, Bernard (VT) - 1970
O'Shea, Bernard G. (VT) - 1964
O'Shea, George J. (MA) - 1962
O'Shea, Robert S. (IL) - 1972
Oshel, Val (IL) - 1968, 1974
O'Shinskie, John (PA) - 1948
Oshlo, Richard (IA) - 1968
Osmers, Frank C. Jr. (NJ) - 1952, 1954, 1956, 1958, 1960, 1962, 1964, 1966
Osser, Maurice S. (PA) - 1948, 1950
Osteen, William L. (NC) - 1968
Ostertag, Harold C. (NY) - 1950, 1952, 1954, 1956, 1958, 1960, 1962
O'Sullivan, Daniel F. Jr. (MO) - 1996
O'Sullivan, Eugene D. (NE) - 1948, 1950
O'Sullivan, Frank P. (CA) - 1954
O'Sullivan, Jerry (IA) - 1968
O'Sullivan, Kevin (MA) - 1994
O'Sullivan, William Jr. (NJ) - 1980
Oswald, Louis William (IL) - 1946
Otey, John (VA) - 1996
O'Toole, Donald L. (NY) - 1946, 1948, 1950, 1952, 1954, 1956
O'Toole, Thomas J. (PA) - 1952
O'Toole, Thomas P. (CA) - 1964
Ottinger, Richard L. (NY) - 1964, 1966, 1968, 1972, 1974, 1976, 1978, 1980, 1982
Outland, George E. (CA) - 1946, 1948
Overby, Fred (GA) - 1994
Overstreet, Russell (OK) - 1948
Owen, John L. (MI) - 1970
Owen, William E. (WI) - 1954
Owens, Bill (IL) - 1994
Owens, Dusty (FL) - 1976
Owens, J. Henry (MI) - 1954
Owens, John M. (NY) - 1980
Owens, Leon (VA) - 1962
Owens, Major R. (NY) - 1982, 1984, 1986, 1988, 1990, 1992, 1994, 1996
Owens, Marv (OR) - 1960
Owens, Steve (AZ) - 1996
Owens, Thomas A. (PA) - 1946
Owens, Thomas L. (IL) - 1946
Owens, Wayne (UT) - 1972, 1986, 1988, 1990
Owensby, Don W. (MO) - 1958
Owings, Theodore R. (CA) - 1954
Oxley, Michael G. (OH) - 1981, 1982, 1984, 1986, 1988, 1990, 1992, 1994, 1996
Ozols, Gunars (NY) - 1980
Ozols, Gunars M. (NY) - 1978

P

Pace, Stephen (GA) - 1946, 1948
Pachios, Harold C. (ME) - 1980
Pacht, Jerry (CA) - 1960
Packard, Ron (CA) - 1982, 1984, 1986, 1988, 1990, 1992, 1994, 1996
Paczkowski, John M. (IL) - 1984
Padrutt, Arthur L. (WI) - 1953
Page, Douglas R. (CA) - 1960
Page, Marguerite A. (NJ) - 1984
Page, Ronnie (TN) - 1968
Page, Winfield E. (MT) - 1954

Richards, Ernest (MI) - 1962
Richards, James P. (SC) - 1946, 1948, 1950
Richards, Joseph C. (OH) - 1972
Richards, Paul H. (CA) - 1996
Richards, Richard (UT) - 1970
Richards, Robert R. (VA) - 1974
Richardson, Bill (NM) - 1980, 1982, 1984, 1986, 1988, 1990, 1992, 1994, 1996
Richardson, Bobby (SC) - 1976
Richardson, Gary (OK) - 1980
Richardson, Gary L. (OK) - 1978
Richardson, George (TX) - 1986
Richardson, H. L. "Bill" (CA) - 1992
Richardson, H. L. (CA) - 1962
Richardson, Janet Carroll "Skeet" (TX) - 1996
Richardson, Jed J. (UT) - 1978
Richardson, John A. (CA) - 1966
Richardson, Mel (ID) - 1986
Richardson, Robert O. (MO) - 1952
Richardson, Roy M. D. (NY) - 1946
Richbourg, Ed (TX) - 1982
Richey, Homer G. (VA) - 1952
Richey, Tom (AZ) - 1978
Richman, Gerald (FL) - 1989
Richman, Martin (NY) - 1992
Richman, Philip (PA) - 1952
Richmond, Fred (NY) - 1980
Richmond, Frederick W. (NY) - 1974, 1976, 1978
Richmond, Isaac (TN) - 1986, 1988
Richter, Francis C. (SD) - 1966
Richter, Leonard G. (OH) - 1960, 1962
Riddering Albert A. (MI) - 1946
Ridge, Tom (PA) - 1982, 1984, 1986, 1988, 1990, 1992
Rieder, Mary (MN) - 1996
Riegle, Donald W. Jr. (MI) - 1966, 1968, 1970, 1972, 1974
Riehlman, R. Walter (NY) - 1946, 1948, 1950, 1952, 1954, 1956, 1958, 1960, 1962, 1964
Riehm, Curtis G. (IA) - 1960
Riemer, Wolfgang J. (NY) - 1962
Riggle, Paul (PA) - 1964, 1966, 1968
Riggs, Bob (MN) - 1974
Riggs, Frank (CA) - 1990, 1992, 1994, 1996
Riggs, L. Alton (AZ) - 1966
Riley, Bob (AL) - 1996
Riley, Corinne B. (SC) - 1962
Riley, James J. (MD) - 1980
Riley, John J. (SC) - 1946, 1950, 1952, 1954, 1956, 1958, 1960
Riley, John W. (IN) - 1990
Riley, Robert A. (OH) - 1962
Riley, Sally Rossy (WV) - 1994
Riley, Tom (IA) - 1968, 1974, 1976
Riley, William A. (IL) - 1994
Rinaldo, Matthew J. (NJ) - 1972, 1974, 1976, 1978, 1980, 1982, 1984, 1986, 1988, 1990
Ring, Carl E. (NJ) - 1950
Ring, James H. (PA) - 1970
Ringer, Darrell (KS) - 1984
Ringgold, Tim (PA) - 1986
Rinker, Glenn (FL) - 1982
Riordan, Obrien (CA) - 1970
Rios, Rolando L. (TX) - 1994
Ripple, James L. (OH) - 1974
Rippon, Donald J. (PA) - 1968, 1972
Rippon, Thomas R. (PA) - 1978
Risenhoover, Theodore (OK) - 1974, 976
Ristow, Harold C. (WI) - 1964
Ritchey, Paul E. (PA) - 1988
Ritchie, Jess M. (CA) - 1954
Ritchie, John E. (MD) - 1984
Ritchie, R. S. (NC) - 1974
Ritenauer, Fred M. (OH) - 1974
Rittenband, Richard M. (CT) - 1972
Rittenhouse, E. Stanley (VA) - 1976
Ritter, Al (OR) - 1992
Ritter, Donald L. (PA) - 1978, 1980, 1982, 1984, 1986, 1988, 1990, 1992
Ritter, Milo (OK) - 1958
Ritter, Tom (MI) - 1984
Rivers, L. Mendel (SC) - 1946, 1948, 1950, 1952, 1954, 1956, 1958, 1960, 1962, 1964, 1966, 1968, 1970
Rivers, Lynn (MI) - 1994, 1996
Rivers, Norman J. (MI) - 1988
Rivers, Ralph J. (AK) - 1958, 1960, 1962, 1964, 1966
Rizley, Ross (OK) - 1946
Roach, John L. (IL) - 1952
Roach, William D. (IN) - 1970
Roark, Lester D. (NC) - 1986
Robb, Holland L. (NC) - 1960
Robb, John H. (NM) - 1960
Robb, Scotty (OK) - 1978
Robbie, Joseph (MN) - 1956, 1958
Robbins, Mark A. (CA) - 1992
Robbins, Robert J. (MI) - 1960
Roberts, Charles H. (PA) - 1970
Roberts, Christine (CA) - 1992
Roberts, Clint (SD) - 1980, 1982
Roberts, Clyde M. (NC) - 1964
Roberts, Courtney (TX) - 1972
Roberts, Darryl (OK) - 1996
Roberts, David (NY) - 1992
Roberts, David G. (ME) - 1960
Roberts, Elmer C. (KY) - 1950
Roberts, Frederick M. (CA) - 1946
Roberts, Gordon (OH) - 1986, 1988
Roberts, Harry (WY) - 1970
Roberts, Jack E. (CA) - 1974
Roberts, Kenneth A. (AL) - 1950, 1952, 1954, 1956, 1958, 1960, 1962, 1964
Roberts, Kirby J. (TX) - 1990
Roberts, Noel F. (OH) - 1988
Roberts, Pat (KS) - 1980, 1982, 1984, 1986, 1988, 1990, 1992, 1994
Roberts, Ray (TX) - 1961, 1962, 1964, 1966, 1968, 1970, 1972, 1974, 1976, 1978
Roberts, Thomas J. (KY) - 1968
Roberts, Victor W. (IL) - 1978
Robertson, Charles R. (ND) - 1946
Robertson, Ernest (VA) - 1954
Robertson, Harrison M. (KY) - 1954
Robertson, Joyce M. (CA) - 1986
Robertson, Norm (NJ) - 1982
Robertson, Paul (MD) - 1946
Robeson, Edward J. Jr. (VA) - 1950, 1952, 1954, 1956
Robinson, Blackwell P. (NC) - 1962
Robinson, Chas. (TX) - 1992
Robinson, David L. (IL) - 1980
Robinson, Gilbert A. (NY) - 1962
Robinson, Harvey R. (PA) - 1962
Robinson, J. Chester (AL) - 1962
Robinson, J. Kenneth (VA) - 1962, 1970, 1972, 1974, 1976, 1978, 1980, 1982
Robinson, J. Will (UT) - 1946
Robinson, James A. (TX) - 1988
Robinson, James C. (FL) - 1968
Robinson, Joel (FL) - 1982
Robinson, Mike (CO) - 1996
Robinson, Richard (CA) - 1986
Robinson, Tommy F. (AR) - 1984, 1986, 1988
Robinson, William I. (KS) - 1960
Robison, Howard W. (NY) - 1958, 1960, 1962, 1964, 1966, 1968, 1970, 1972
Robles, Ernest Z. (CA) - 1972
Robles, Mario Jr. (CT) - 1988
Robsion, John M. (KY) - 1946
Roche, Anthony M. (MA) - 1946, 1948
Roche, Dan (MI) - 1986
Rocheteau, Ralph Carlos (FL) - 1988
Rochford, Dennis J. (PA) - 1980
Rock, Sherman T. (NC) - 1964
Rockhold, Loyd J. (LA) - 1968
Rockwell, Robert F. (CO) - 1946, 1948
Rodebaugh, Charles S. (MI) - 1984
Rodebush, Johnie (MI) - 1981
Rodey, Patrick (AK) - 1978
Rodger, Ronald A. (IL) - 1974, 1976
Rodgers, Bernard F. (NJ) - 1962, 1964
Rodgers, H. Edmund (NC) - 1946
Rodino, Peter W. Jr. (NJ) - 1946, 1948, 1950, 1952, 1954, 1956, 1958, 1960, 1962, 1964, 1966, 1968, 1970, 1972, 1974, 1976, 1978, 1980, 1982, 1984, 1986
Rodman, Samuel S. (MA) - 1962
Rodney, Earl (FL) - 1990
Rodriguez, Edward Nelson (NY) - 1986
Rodriguez, Jack (TX) - 1996
Rodriguez, Pedro Luis (NY) - 1966
Rodriguez-Schieman, Hildegarde (IL) - 1992
Roe, Dudley George (MD) - 1946, 1952
Roe, Robert A. (NJ) - 1969, 1970, 1972, 1974, 1976, 1978, 1980, 1982, 1984, 1986, 1988, 1990
Roemer, Buddy (LA) - 1980, 1982, 1984, 1986
Roemer, Charles H. (NJ) - 1950
Roemer, Gloria Gonzales (CO) - 1990
Roemer, Tim (IN) - 1990, 1992, 1994, 1996
Rogan, James E. (CA) - 1996
Rogells, F. Onell (FL) - 1962
Rogers, Ben A. (MO) - 1964, 1966
Rogers, Byron G. (CO) - 1950, 1952, 1954, 1956, 1958, 1960, 1962, 1964, 1966, 1968
Rogers, Charles Arthur (MI) - 1970
Rogers, Dwight L. (FL) - 1946, 1948, 1950, 1952, 1954
Rogers, Edith Nourse (MA) - 1946, 1948, 1950, 1952, 1954, 1956, 1958
Rogers, Edmund T. (PA) - 1954
Rogers, George F. (NY) - 1946, 1948
Rogers, Harold (KY) - 1980, 1982, 1984, 1986, 1988, 1990, 1992, 1994, 1996
Rogers, James W. (KY) - 1972
Rogers, Jesse A. (MA) - 1952
Rogers, Jim (WY) - 1980
Rogers, Joe (CO) - 1996
Rogers, Louis G. (NC) - 1950
Rogers, P. D. (TX) - 1960
Rogers, Paul G. (FL) - 1956, 1958, 1960, 1962, 1964, 1966, 1968, 1970, 1972, 1974, 1976
Rogers, T. Y. (AL) - 1970
Rogers, Thomas F. (KY) - 1974
Rogers, W. D. (KY) - 1946
Rogers, Walter (TX) - 1950, 1952, 1954, 1956, 1958, 1960, 1962, 1964
Rohlfing, Fred W. (HI) - 1972, 1976
Rohm, J. Robert (PA) - 1966
Rohrabacher, Dana (CA) - 1988, 1990, 1992, 1994, 1996
Rohrbough, Edward G. (WV) - 1946, 1948
Roland, Frederick P. (NY) - 1966, 1968
Rolander, Robert D. (CO) - 1960
Rolle, Wellington (FL) - 1996
Rollman, Heinz (NC) - 1960
Rolvaag, Karl F. (MN) - 1946, 1948, 1952
Roma, Patrick J. (NJ) - 1992
Romack, William H. (CA) - 1966
Romaine, Edward P. (NY) - 1988, 1992
Romano, Frank R. (PA) - 1970
Romano, Neil (NJ) - 1984
Romanyak, James A. (IL) - 1978
Romero, Victor (CA) - 1990
Romig, Ralph H. (OH) - 1974
Ronan, Daniel J. (IL) - 1964, 1966, 1968
Roncalio, Teno (WY) - 1964, 1970, 1972, 1974, 1976
Roncallo, Angelo D. (NY) - 1972, 1974
Rood, Roy (AR) - 1990
Rooney, Fred B. (PA) - 1964, 1966, 1968, 1970, 1972, 1974, 1976, 1978
Rooney, George H. (NY) - 1946
Rooney, John J. (NY) - 1946, 1948, 1950, 1952, 1954, 1956, 1958, 1960, 1962, 1964, 1966, 1968, 1970, 1972
Roosevelt, Franklin D. Jr. (NY) - 1949, 1950, 1952
Roosevelt, James (CA) - 1954, 1956, 1958, 1960, 1962, 1964
Root, Gerald (NY) - 1950
Root, Marv (O) - 1968
Roque, Manuel R. (NY) - 1964
Ros-Lehtinen, Ileana (FL) - 1989, 1990, 1992, 1994, 1996
Rosario, Carlos (NY) - 1966
Rose, Charles (NC) - 1972, 1974, 1976
Rose, Charlie (NC) - 1978, 1980, 1982, 1984, 1986, 1988, 1990, 1992, 1994
Rose, Henry (NY) - 1954, 1956, 1964
Rose, John D. (NJ) - 1972
Rose, Robert A. (NY) - 1954
Rosen, Bernard (OH) - 1956
Rosen, Gerald E. (MI) - 1982
Rosen, Julius J. (NY) - 1960
Rosenberg, Irwin A. (NY) - 1966
Rosenberger, Geoffrey (NY) - 1996
Rosenblatt, Elias (NY) - 1954, 1956
Rosenblum, Everett A. (NY) - 1978
Rosenstein, Stephen L. (MD) - 1966
Rosenthal, Benjamin S. (NY) - 1962, 1964, 1966, 1968, 1970, 1972, 1974, 1976, 1978, 1980, 1982
Rosier, Joseph A. (FL) - 1976
Roskam, William E. (CA) - 1954
Roski, Franklin H. (OH) - 1986, 1988, 1990
Rosof, Murray (NY) - 1948
Ross, Alonzo A. (AR) - 1952
Ross, Barbara (OR) - 1986
Ross, Don (FL) - 1984
Ross, Galen J. (UT) - 1968
Ross, Harriet (CA) - 1987
Ross, Kate (MA) - 1994
Ross, Laura (MA) - 1975
Ross, Lyman (OR) - 1946
Ross, Rhecha R. (MI) - 1966
Ross, Robert R. Jr. (WY) - 1952
Ross, Robert Tripp (NY) - 1946, 1948, 1950, 1951, 1952
Ross, Ronald R. (IN) - 1962
Rossi, Emil (CA) - 1996
Rostenkowski, Dan (IL) - 1958, 1960, 1962, 1964, 1966, 1968, 1970, 1972, 1974, 1976, 1978, 1980, 1982, 1984, 1986, 1988, 1990, 1992, 1994
Rostron, William E. (MI) - 1970, 1972, 1976
Rotenberg, Joe (MA) - 1974
Roth, Charles III (NY) - 1978
Roth, Kent (KS) - 1982
Roth, Norman (NJ) - 1954
Roth, Norman H. (NH) - 1956
Roth, Phil J. (OR) - 1956
Roth, Tobias A. (WI) - 1978
Roth, Toby (WI) - 1980, 1982, 1984, 1986, 1988, 1990, 1992, 1994
Roth, W. A. "Jack" (CA) - 1980
Roth, William V. (DE) - 1966, 1968
Rothfuss, Paul A. (PA) - 1950
Rothman, Melvyn M. (NY) - 1962
Rothman, Steve R. (NJ) - 1996
Rothschild, Beryl E. (OH) - 1992
Rotondo, Vincent J. (RI) - 1974
Roudebush, Richard L. (IN) - 1960, 1962, 1964, 1966, 1968
Roukema, Marge (NJ) - 1978, 1980, 1982, 1984, 1986, 1988, 1990, 1992, 1994, 1996
Rourke, Russell A. (NY) - 1974
Roush, J. Edward (IN) - 1958, 1960, 1962, 1964, 1966, 1968, 1970, 1972, 1974, 1976
Rousselot, John H. (CA) - 1960, 1962, 1970, 1972, 1974, 1976, 1978, 1980, 1982
Rovner, Edward H. (PA) - 1964
Rovner, Robert A. (PA) - 1986
Rowan, Robert P. (IL) - 1970
Rowan, William A. (IL) - 1946, 1954
Rowe, Douglas J. (MA) - 1974
Rowe, Ed (OH) - 1948
Rowe, Lee (KS) - 1982
Rowell, Lonnie (SC) - 1976
Rowland, Herbert (KY) - 1960
Rowland, J. Roy (GA) - 1982, 1986, 1988, 1990, 1992
Rowland, John G. (CT) - 1984, 1986, 1988
Rowland, Mike (TN) - 1976
Rowland, Roy (GA) - 1984
Rowland, William D. (FL) - 1974
Roy, Alphonse (NH) - 1958
Roy, Archibald (CA) - 1967
Roy, John R. (IL) - 1952
Roy, William R. (KS) - 1970, 1972
Roybal, Edward R. (CA) - 1962, 1964, 1966, 1968, 1970, 1972, 1974, 1976, 1978, 1980, 1982, 1984, 1986, 1988, 1990
Roybal-Allard, Lucille (CA) - 1992, 1994, 1996
Royce, Ed (CA) - 1992, 1994, 1996
Royer, Bill (CA) - 1979, 1980, 1982
Roylance, Susan (WA) - 1978
Rubens, Jack (NY) - 1972
Rubenstein, Alan B. (PA) - 1978
Rubin, Ellis S. (FL) - 1972
Rubin, Rose L. (NY) - 1968, 1970
Rubinstein, Annette T. (NY) - 1949
Ruccia, Cynthia L. (OH) - 1994, 1996
Rucker, Jerry (TX) - 1990
Rudd, Eldon (AZ) - 1976, 1978, 1980, 1982, 1984
Rudd, Ralph (OH) - 1970
Ruddick, John Paul (VA) - 1954
Rudy, Ruth C. (PA) - 1996
Ruebenacker, Paul C. (NY) - 1978
Ruebush, Glenn W. (VA) - 1952
Rued, Dave (MN) - 1984, 1986
Rufus, Anita (CA) - 1996
Ruhala, Richard J. (MI) - 1970
Rule, Victor A. (FL) - 1962
Rumsfeld, Donald (IL) - 1962, 1964, 1966, 1968
Runnels, Dorothy (NM) - 1980
Runnels, Harold (NM) - 1970, 1972, 1974, 1976, 1978
Runnels, Joe (TX) - 1970
Runnels, Mike (NM) - 1986
Rupp, Charles Edward (NJ) - 1952
Ruppe, Philip E. (MI) - 1966, 1968, 1970, 1972, 1974, 1976, 1992
Ruppert, James D. (OH) - 1970, 1972
Rush, Bob (IA) - 1996
Rush, Bobby L. (IL) - 1992, 1994, 1996
Rush, Erwin E. "Bill" (CA) - 1990
Rusk, Donald M. (CA) - 1980, 1986, 1994
Russell, Allen (OH) - 1952
Russell, Aubrey (KY) - 1984
Russell, Carl D. (MO) - 1984
Russell, Charles H. (NV) - 1946, 1948
Russell, Howard E. Jr. (RI) - 1968
Russell, James (TX) - 1972
Russell, Jim (MO) - 1982
Russell, Joe W. (IL) - 1950
Russell, John B. (TN) - 1986
Russell, Reb (KS) - 1964
Russell, Reece L. (OK) - 1954
Russell, Richard M. (MA) - 1950
Russo, Gaetano A. Jr. (CT) - 1968
Russo, Lawrence P. (NY) - 1972
Russo, Martin A. (IL) - 1974, 1976
Russo, Marty (IL) - 1978, 1980, 1982, 1984, 1986, 1988, 1990
Russo, Peter J. (NJ) - 1990, 1994

Rust, Gary (MO) - 1970
Rust, Robert W. (FL) - 1968
Rutan, Dick (CA) - 1992
Ruth, Earl B. (NC) - 1968, 1970, 1972, 1974
Rutherford, J. T. (TX) - 1954, 1956, 1958, 1960, 1962
Rutledge, Howard (OK) - 1980, 1982
Rutta, Philip Robert (CA) - 1972
Ryan, Aileen B. (NY) - 1966
Ryan, Bob (NV) - 1986
Ryan, Dan J. P. (IA) - 1946, 1948
Ryan, Donald P. (RI) - 1972
Ryan, Edward J. (MD) - 1954
Ryan, Fran (OH) - 1974, 1976
Ryan, Harold M. (MI) - 1962
Ryan, Herbert F. (NY) - 1966
Ryan, Hewitt Fitts (CA) - 1986
Ryan, Jim (TX) - 1982
Ryan, John F. Jr. (NY) - 1972
Ryan, John Michael (OH) - 1972, 1990
Ryan, Leo J. (CA) - 1972, 1974, 1976, 1978
Ryan, Matthew (IL) - 1976
Ryan, Priscilla M. (NY) - 1972
Ryan, Timothy E. (NJ) - 1992
Ryan, William F. (NY) - 1960, 1962, 1964, 1966, 1968, 1970
Ryan, William J. (VT) - 1966
Rybacki, Ray J. (IL) - 1964, 1966
Ryder, Richard R. (VA) - 1958
Rylander, Carole Keeton (TX) - 1986
Ryler, Joseph F. (CT) - 1946
Ryun, Jim (KS) - 1996

S

Saad, Paul A. (FL) - 1968
Saar, T. D. Jr. (KS) - 1970
Saari, Gene A. (MI) - 1948
Sabath, Adolph J. (IL) - 1946, 1948, 1950, 1952
Sabo, Martin Olav (MN) - 1978, 1980, 1982, 1984, 1986, 1988, 1990, 1992, 1994, 1996
Sabol, John (MI) - 1950
Sabol, Joseph Jr. (PA) - 1966, 1968
Sacia, Paul (WI) - 1992
Sacks, Alexander (NY) - 1968
Sadlak, Anton N. (CT) - 1946, 1948, 1950, 1952, 1954, 1956, 1958, 1960
Sadler, Claude E. (MI) - 1964
Sadler, Gareth W. (CA) - 1960
Sadovy, Leo (TX) - 1988
Sadowski, George G. (MI) - 1946, 1948
Sadowski, Jeannie (TX) - 1992
Safranek, Frank A. (CO) - 1946
Saiki, Patricia (HI) - 1986, 1988
Saintamour, Camille E. (VT) - 1956
Sajna, Michael (OH) - 1988
Saks, Carl (NY) - 1970
Salazar, Cecilia M. (NM) - 1988
Saldana, Gilbert R. (CA) - 1986
Salem, Robert J. (IA) - 1956
Salerno, Joseph A. (IL) - 1962
Salisbury, D. L. (WV) - 1948
Salisbury, William (MD) - 1976
Saliterman, Joel (MN) - 1980, 1982
Sallade, George Wahr (MI) - 1982
Sallah, Donald R. (NY) - 1974
Salley, Robert L. (CA) - 1976
Salloum, Robert J. (MI) - 1978
Salmon, Matt (AZ) - 1994, 1996
Salmona, Stelio (CT) - 1966, 1968
Salomon, Jim (CA) - 1988, 1990
Salter, Leslie E. (IL) - 1948
Saltonstall, John L. (MA) - 1958
Saltonstall, William (MA) - 1969
Salvi, Al (IL) - 1986
Salvi, Albert S. (IL) - 1968
Salyers, Willis Earl (MO) - 1966
Sam, Geraldine (TX) - 1996
Sammartino, Everett C. (RI) - 1966
Sampol, William (NY) - 1970, 1972, 1990
Sampson, Floyd G. (CA) - 1986
Sams, W. Harold (NC) - 1958
Samuel, Ralph O. (PA) - 1964
Samuels, David L. (NY) - 1950
Samuelson, Bob (SD) - 1978
Sanborn, John C. (ID) - 1946, 1948
Sanchez, John M. (TX) - 1996
Sanchez, Loretta (CA) - 1996
Sanchez, Phillip V. (CA) - 1970
Sand, H. A. (OH) - 1960, 1962, 1964
Sandegren, Andrew Sandy (MO) - 1952
Sander, Richard W. (OH) - 1978
Sanders, Barefoot (TX) - 1958
Sanders, Bernard (VT) - 1988, 1990, 1992, 1994, 1996
Sanders, Claiborne "Clay" (TN) - 1990
Sanders, Emma (MS) - 1966
Sanders, Gregory J. (UT) - 1996
Sanders, Hartley (WV) - 1946, 1948
Sanders, Herman (NY) - 1960, 1964
Sanders, J. M. (AZ) - 1974
Sanders, Jessie E. (SD) - 1948
Sanders, Marion K. (NY) - 1952
Sanders, William H. (WV) - 1956
Sandlin, Max (TX) - 1996
Sandman, Charles W. Jr. (NJ) - 1966, 1968, 1970, 1972, 1974
Sands, A. P. "Sandy" (NC) - 1994
Sanford, Mark (SC) - 1994, 1996
Sanford, William K. (NY) - 1946
Sangmeister, George E. (IL) - 1988, 1990, 1992
Santangelo, Alfred E. (NY) - 1956, 1958, 1960, 1962
Santini, James (NV) - 1974, 1976, 1978, 1980
Santorum, Rick (PA) - 1990, 1992
Santry, Horace A. (KS) - 1952
Sarasin, Ronald A. (CT) - 1972, 1974, 1976
Sarbacher, George W. Jr. (PA) - 1946, 1948, 1950
Sarbanes, Paul S. (MD) - 1970, 1972, 1974
Sargent, Aaron A. (CA) - 1971
Sargent, Su (AR) - 1986
Sarpalius, Bill (TX) - 1988, 1990, 1992, 1994
Sarsfield, George P. (MT) - 1960
Sarsoun, Lawrence C. (IL) - 1980
Saska, Larry (IL) - 1990
Saslaw, Richard L. (VA) - 1984
Sasscer, Lansdale G. (MD) - 1946, 1948, 1950
Sato, Eunice A. (CA) - 1990
Satterfield, David E. III (VA) - 1964, 1966, 1968, 1970, 1972, 1974, 1976, 1978
Satterlee, Ray (SD) - 1954
Satterthwaite, Cameron B. (IL) - 1966
Saund, Dalip S. (CA) - 1956, 1958, 1960, 1962
Saunders, Annie (OH) - 1996
Saunders, Francis C. (NY) - 1970
Saunders, JoAnn (FL) - 1974, 1976
Saunders, Vince (NV) - 1980
Saunders, Warren D. (VA) - 1974, 1976
Sausedo, Robert M. (CA) - 1996
Savage, Carl (GA) - 1974
Savage, Charles R. (WA) - 1946, 1948
Savage, Gus (IL) - 1980, 1982, 1984, 1986, 1988, 1990
Savage, John W. II (MI) - 1988, 1994
Savage, Wallace (TX) - 1954
Savin, Moses A. (CT) - 1962
Savino, Frank A. (WI) - 1976
Savoie, Gene (AZ) - 1972
Sawyer, Arthur T. (NY) - 1948
Sawyer, Harold S. (MI) - 1976, 1978, 1980, 1982
Sawyer, John W. (TX) - 1996
Sawyer, Thomas C. (OH) - 1986, 1988, 1990, 1992, 1994, 1996
Sawyer, William C. (MA) - 1980
Sawyers, William Orr "Tom" (MO) - 1946
Saxton, H. James (NJ) - 1984, 1986, 1988, 1990, 1992, 1994, 1996
Saylor, John P. (PA) - 1950, 1952, 1954, 1956, 1958, 1960, 1962, 1964, 1966, 1968, 1970, 1972
Sayre, Woodrow Wilson (CA) - 1952
Scalamonti, John D. (NJ) - 1986
Scalf, Charles E. (PA) - 1962
Scalf, W. D. (KY) - 1952, 1956, 1958
Scalzitti, Clement R. (PA) - 1974
Scanlan, Charles V. (NY) - 1954, 1958
Scanlon, Michael T. (OH) - 1976
Scannel, Joseph J. (DE) - 1952
Scannell, William F. (IL) - 1964
Scarborough, Joe (FL) - 1994, 1996
Schade, Terrence J. (PA) - 1976
Schade, W. John Jr. (IL) - 1974
Schadeberg, Henry C. (WI) - 1960, 1962, 1964, 1966, 1968, 1970
Schaefer, Dan L. (CO) - 1983, 1984, 1986, 1988, 1990, 1992, 1994, 1996
Schaefer, Howard G. (CA) - 1978
Schaefer, Mike (CA) - 1968
Schaeffer, Tim (TN) - 1974
Schaeffer, William R. Jr. (NY) - 1978
Schafer, Edward T. (ND) - 1990
Schafer, John C. (WI) - 1952, 1954
Schafer, John M. (NY) - 1990
Schaffenegger, John (IL) - 1952
Schaffer, Robert W. (CO) - 1996
Schaffer, Russell T. (MD) - 1980
Schaffner, William G. (OH) - 1984
Schall, John A. (MI) - 1994
Schaller, Audrie Zettick (PA) - 1990
Schaux, Nicolas (CT) - 1980
Schellenger, Waldo E. (IL) - 1956
Schenck, Paul F. (OH) - 1950, 1952, 1954, 1956, 1958, 1960, 1962, 1964
Schendel, Harry (MO) - 1951
Schenk, Lynn (CA) - 1992, 1994
Schenken, Jerry (NE) - 1988
Scher, David (NY) - 1946
Scher, Gregory Alan (IN) - 1986
Scherer, Gordon H. (OH) - 1952, 1954, 1956, 1958, 1960
Scherle, William J. (IA) - 1966, 1968, 1970, 1972, 1974
Scherr, J. Robert (MD) - 1982
Scheuer, James H. (NY) - 1964, 1966, 1968, 1970, 1974, 1976, 1978, 1980, 1982, 1984, 1986, 1988, 1990
Scheuermann, David H. Sr. (LA) - 1976
Schiaffo, Alfred D. (NJ) - 1972
Schiemann, Fred E. (NY) - 1950
Schiff, Steven H. (NM) - 1988, 1990, 1992, 1994, 1996
Schifrin, Louis (NY) - 1952, 1954
Schiliro, Philip M. (NY) - 1992, 1994
Schilson, Donald L. (IL) - 1968
Schira, Jack (OH) - 1988, 1990
Schisler, Gale (IL) - 1964, 1966
Schissler, James J. (PA) - 1956
Schlafly, Phyllis Stewart (IL) - 1952, 1960, 1970
Schlessel, Bennett I. (NY) - 1950
Schlessinger, Gary (CA) - 1969
Schlingheyde, Leslie B. (CA) - 1952
Schlitz, Lester E. (VA) - 1974
Schloemer, Ken (IL) - 1992
Schlossberg, David A. (NY) - 1946
Schluter, William E. (NJ) - 1976
Schmarkey, John C. (AL) - 1970
Schmauch, Ray (KY) - 1946
Schmidhauser, John R. (IA) - 1964, 1966, 1968
Schmidt, Herman (NJ) - 1974
Schmidt, William F. H. (IL) - 1958
Schmitt, William Patrick (OK) - 1972
Schmitz, John G. (CA) - 1970
Schneck, Robert M. (NY) - 1970
Schneebeli, Herman T. (PA) - 1960, 1962, 1964, 1966, 1968, 1970, 1972, 1974
Schneider, Alexander (AZ) - 1996
Schneider, Claudine (RI) - 1978, 1980, 1982, 1984, 1986, 1988
Schneider, Jerome P. (NY) - 1958, 1960
Schneider, Robert (TX) - 1968
Schneir, Ned (NY) - 1976
Schnur, Warren L. (NY) - 1954
Schoen, Douglas F. (NY) - 1983
Scholl, Dave (CA) - 1992
Scholl, Inez M. (IN) - 1954
Scholle, August (MI) - 1970
Schooley, Thomas M. Jr. (PA) - 1964
Schoonard, Forest A. (MI) - 1950
Schrader, Digter J. (AL) - 1972
Schreffler, Daniel J. (PA) - 1994
Schreiber, Ed (CO) - 1980
Schrimpf, Curt (MN) - 1988
Schroeder, Anthony C. (MO) - 1958, 1960, 1962, 1964, 1966, 1970
Schroeder, Lou (OH) - 1978
Schroeder, Patricia (CO) - 1972, 1974, 1976, 1978, 1980, 1982, 1984, 1986, 1988, 1990, 1992, 1994
Schroeder, Raymond W. (NJ) - 1964
Schropfer, Dave (CT) - 1992
Schrump, Raymond C. (NC) - 1978
Schuette, Bill (MI) - 1984, 1986, 1988
Schuh, David W. (CA) - 1968
Schultz, Edward A. (PA) - 1946
Schultz, Malvern E. (OH) - 1958
Schultz, Robert C. (WI) - 1952
Schultz, Scott (MI) - 1988
Schulz, Richard L. (OR) - 1992
Schulz, William Adams (NY) - 1952
Schulze, Richard T. (PA) - 1974, 1976, 1978, 1980, 1982, 1984, 1986, 1988, 1990
Schumacher, Ervin (ND) - 1950
Schumer, Charles E. (NY) - 1980, 1982, 1984, 1986, 1988, 1990, 1992, 1994, 1996
Schuster, Bob (AZ) - 1984
Schuster, Bob (WY) - 1994
Schwab, Frank X. (NY) - 1966
Schwabe, George B. (OK) - 1946, 1948, 1950
Schwabe, Max (MO) - 1946, 1948, 1950, 1952
Schwan, Joseph A. (MO) - 1988
Schwandt, Russel (MN) - 1960
Schwartz, Ellen (CA) - 1994
Schwartz, Emmett A. (CA) - 1960
Schwartz, Irving A. (NY) - 1980
Schwartz, Morton L. (MO) - 1960
Schwartz, Ron (CA) - 1980
Schweiker, Richard S. (PA) - 1960, 1962, 1964, 1966
Schweinhaut, Margaret C. (MD) - 1968
Schwengel, Fred (IA) - 1954, 1956, 1958, 1960, 1962, 1964, 1966, 1968, 1970, 1972
Schwerdtfeger, Carl R. (IL) - 1982, 1984
Schwiebert, Erwin H. (ID) - 1954, 1962
Schwinger, Louis C. (MI) - 1948
Schwolsky, Harry (CT) - 1950
Scialabba, Samuel R. (NY) - 1946
Scimeca, Anthony (NY) - 1946
Scoblick, James P. (PA) - 1946
Scofield, Glenni W. (PA) - 1972
Scofield, Sandra K. (NE) - 1990
Scoggins, Dennis (TX) - 1982
Scola, Robert N. (MA) - 1960
Sconing, C. L. (PA) - 1974
Scott, Anna Wall (IL) - 1976
Scott, Audrey (MD) - 1981
Scott, Dennis (AR) - 1992
Scott, Donald E. (OH) - 1984
Scott, Ed (CO) - 1976, 1978
Scott, Edward W. (MS) - 1960
Scott, Hardie (PA) - 1946, 1948, 1950
Scott, Horace C. (PA) - 1956
Scott, Hugh (MO) - 1968
Scott, Hugh D. Jr. (PA) - 1946, 1948, 1950, 1952, 1954, 1956
Scott, Jerry C. (NC) - 1972
Scott, John E. "Jock" (LA) - 1984, 1985
Scott, John W. (ND) - 1963
Scott, Mark Elliott (NY) - 1978
Scott, Marvin Bailey (IN) - 1994
Scott, Portia A. (GA) - 1986
Scott, Ralph J. (NC) - 1956, 1958, 1960, 1962, 1964
Scott, Robert C. (VA) - 1986, 1992, 1994, 1996
Scott, Robert H. (CA) - 1990
Scott, Samuel J. (IL) - 1956
Scott, Thomas (CT) - 1990, 1992
Scott, Uric (MN) - 1974
Scott, Will T. (KY) - 1988, 1990
Scott, William Lloyd (VA) - 1966, 1968, 1970
Scranton, William W. (PA) - 1960
Scribner, Robert B. (CA) - 1984, 1986
Scrivner, Errett P. (KS) - 1946, 1948, 1950, 1952, 1954, 1956, 1958
Scudder, Hubert B. (CA) - 1948, 1950, 1952, 1954, 1956
Scull, David (MD) - 1964
Seagraves, Jim (OR) - 1992
Seal, Doug (TX) - 1986
Seale, Jack (TX) - 1962
Seals, Marilyn (CA) - 1976
Sealy, Albert H. (OH) - 1980
Searcy, Donald (NE) - 1970
Searle, William D. (PA) - 1964, 1966
Seastrand, Andrea (CA) - 1994, 1996
Seastrand, Eric (CA) - 1978
Seat, Marvin H. (KY) - 1990
Seay, Pamella A. (MI) - 1980
Sebastian, John (AL) - 1988
Sebastian, Robert M. (PA) - 1950
Sebelius, Keith G. (KS) - 1968, 1970, 1972, 1974, 1976, 1978
Sebree, William T. (IN) - 1974
Secrest, Robert T. (OH) - 1946, 1948, 1950, 1952, 1962, 1964, 1966
Sedberry, J. C. (NC) - 1954
See, C. F. (KY) - 1966
See, M. J. (KY) - 1954
Seely-Brown, Horace Jr. (CT) - 1946, 1948, 1950, 1952, 1954, 1956, 1958, 1960
Seep, Joseph A. (WI) - 1954
Seiberling, John F. (OH) - 1970, 1972, 1974, 1976, 1978, 1980, 1982, 1984
Seidl, John D. (ID) - 1996
Seielstad, George A. (CA) - 1974
Seigneur, James Beau (TN) - 1980, 1984
Seitz, Berta L. (AR) - 1994
Seiverling, Daniel S. (PA) - 1980
Selby, Norm (MN) - 1972
Selden, Armstead I. Jr. (AL) - 1952, 1954, 1956, 1958, 1960, 1962, 1964, 1966
Seldin, Abe (NY) - 1968
Selland, Arthur L. (CA) - 1962
Sellars, Lee T. (PA) - 1952, 1958
Sellers, Dave (GA) - 1982
Sellner, John Eugene (MD) - 1986, 1988
Selph, John (OK) - 1992
Semrow, Harry H. (IL) - 1954
Sendak, Theodore L. (IN) - 1948
Sendelsky, Leonard R. (NJ) - 1992
Seney, John M. (MD) - 1974, 1976
Senger, John M. (MI) - 1984
Senner, George F. Jr. (AZ) - 1962, 1964, 1966
Sennet, Fred (OH) - 1992

Winston, Daniel (OH) - 1958, 1960
Winterberg, Edward J. (KY) - 1976
Winters, Brent (IL) - 1994, 1996
Wirth, Russell Jr. (WI) - 1956
Wirth, Timothy E. (CO) - 1974, 1976, 1978, 1980, 1982, 1984
Wirth, Timothy E. (CO) - 1980, 1982, 1984
Wisdom, Jane (NV) - 1990
Wise, Bob (WV) - 1982, 1984, 1986, 1988, 1990, 1992, 1994, 1996
Wise, S. B. (MS) - 1966
Wishnofsky, Helen (NY) - 1950
Witbeck, George H. Jr. (NY) - 1958
Withers, Garrett L. (KY) - 1952
Withers, Harold J. Jr. (NY) - 1978
Witherspoon, Robert L. (MO) - 1976
Withrow, Gardner R. (WI) - 1948, 1950, 1952, 1954, 1956, 1958
Withrow, Pat B. Jr. (WV) - 1954
Witkin, Morton (PA) - 1952
Witmer, Ed (OH) - 1962
Witt, Bill (OR) - 1994, 1996
Witt, Richard C. (PA) - 1956
Witteck, Charles Jr. (NY) - 1968
Wittig, Sue (NY) - 1996
Wittmann, Robert J. (MO) - 1986
Wofford, Louise (GA) - 1976
Wognum, James (IL) - 1978
Wohlfarth, John R. (PA) - 1966
Wojslaw, Chuck (CA) - 1996
Wojtkowiak, Bernard J. (NY) - 1954
Wolbank, Edward (IL) - 1970
Wolcott, Jesse P. (MI) - 1946, 1948, 1950, 1952, 1954
Wold, John (WY) - 1968
Wolf, Frank R. (VA) - 1978, 1980, 1982, 1984, 1986, 1988, 1990, 1992, 1994, 1996
Wolf, Leonard G. (IA) - 1956, 1958, 1960
Wolf, Scott (RI) - 1990
Wolfe, Bruce P. (CA) - 1972
Wolfe, Louis E. (NY) - 1960
Wolfe, Richard R. (IL) - 1966
Wolfe, Thomas E. (OH) - 1966
Wolff, Lester L. (NY) - 1964, 1966, 1968, 1970, 1972, 1974, 1976, 1978, 1980
Wolff, Nelson W. (TX) - 1978
Wolfram, Ray (IL) - 1964
Wolin, Marc (CA) - 1992
Wolpe, Howard (MI) - 1976, 1978, 1980, 1982, 1984, 1986, 1988, 1990
Wolterman, Edward W. (OH) - 1974
Wolthuis, Robert K. (UT) - 1972
Wolverton, Charles A. (NJ) - 1946, 1948, 1950, 1952, 1954, 1956
Womack, Don (AL) - 1994, 1996
Wong, Emma Mar (CA) - 1994
Woo, S. B. (DE) - 1992
Wood, Dave (WA) - 1976
Wood, Jim (GA) - 1982
Wood, John S. (GA) - 1946, 1948, 1950
Wood, John T. (ID) - 1950, 1952
Wood, Joy (CO) - 1986, 1988
Wood, Leonard V. (FL) - 1970
Wood, Leslie E. (CA) - 1952
Wood, Lloyd Allen (OH) - 1974
Wood, Louis A. (OR) - 1946
Wood, Mike (MS) - 1994

Wood, P. H. (TN) - 1956
Wood, Roberta Lynn (CA) - 1972
Woodall, Robert L. (OH) - 1980, 1984
Woodcock, James A. (PA) - 1980
Woodhouse, Chase Going (CT) - 1946, 1948, 1950
Woodruff, Roy O. (MI) - 1946, 1948, 1950
Woods, Al (FL) - 1992
Woods, Jesse W. Jr. (PA) - 1974, 1976
Woods, Max E. (CA) - 1960
Woodward, Harold C. (IL) - 1946
Woodward, M. H. (AL) - 1946
Woodworth, Thomas B. (MI) - 1950
Woolley, M. M. (FL) - 1962
Woolsey, Cecil T. (NJ) - 1964
Woolsey, Lynn (CA) - 1992, 1994, 1996
Woolverton, George (CA) - 1986
Workman, Bill (SC) - 1986
Workman, Raven L. (OH) - 1986
Works, Karen S. R. (CA) - 1990
Worley, David (GA) - 1988, 1990
Worley, Eugene (TX) - 1946, 1948
Worley, Francis (PA) - 1950
Worrell, T. Eugene (VA) - 1948
Wortley, George C. (NY) - 1976, 1980, 1982, 1984, 1986
Worton, Joseph Edward (FL) - 1950
Worzel, Harold W. (NY) - 1948
Woskow, Herman (NY) - 1950, 1952
Wozniak, Theodore (IL) - 1958
Wren, G. Louie (OH) - 1954
Wrenn, Thomas (AL) - 1968
Wright, Alan D. (OH) - 1968
Wright, Branson (IL) - 1954
Wright, Carl E. Jr. (IL) - 1946
Wright, Chester M. (CA) - 1970
Wright, Crispus (CA) - 1958
Wright, Deborah (CA) - 1994, 1996
Wright, Donald (MN) - 1972
Wright, Herbert William Jr. (OK) - 1958, 1962
Wright, James A. (WI) - 1978, 1980
Wright, Jim (TX) - 1954, 1956, 1958, 1960, 1962, 1964, 1966, 1968, 1970, 1972, 1974, 1976, 1978, 1980, 1982, 1984, 1986, 1988
Wright, Joe (KY) - 1996
Wright, John H. (TX) - 1980
Wright, Sam H. (TX) - 1976
Wright, Victor O. (IL) - 1956
Wright, Vivian S. (NC) - 1980
Wright, W. Clyde (NY) - 1960
Wright, William A. (VA) - 1950
Wulster, Emil M. (NJ) - 1950
Wurst, Henry E. (MO) - 1964
Wyatt, Cecil (AL) - 1980
Wyatt, Joe (TX) - 1978
Wyatt, Joe Jr. (TX) - 1982
Wyatt, Wendell (OR) - 1964, 1966, 1968, 1970, 1972
Wyckoff, Ted (AZ) - 1972
Wyden, Ron (OR) - 1980, 1982, 1984, 1986, 1988, 1990, 1992, 1994
Wydler, John W. (NY) - 1962, 1964, 1966, 1968, 1970, 1972, 1974, 1976, 1978
Wydra, John (NJ) - 1986

Wylie, Chalmers P. (OH) - 1966, 1968, 1970, 1972, 1974, 1976, 1978, 1980, 1982, 1984, 1986, 1988, 1990
Wyman, Louis C. (NH) - 1962, 1964, 1966, 1968, 1970, 1972
Wynell, Dorothy (TX) - 1958, 1960
Wynn, Albert R. (MD) - 1992, 1994, 1996
Wynne, Peter (NY) - 1946
Wyrick, James Douglas (TN) - 1946
Wyrick, Jim (WA) - 1994

Y

Yaffe, Bertram A. (MA) - 1970
Yambrek, Leopold (AL) - 1982
Yarbrough, Willard V. (TN) - 1964
Yates, Charles B. (NJ) - 1970, 1974
Yates, Comer (GA) - 1994
Yates, Joy (TX) - 1978
Yates, Sidney R. (IL) - 1948, 1950, 1952, 1954, 1956, 1958, 1960, 1964, 1966, 1968, 1970, 1972, 1974, 1976, 1978, 1980, 1982, 1984, 1986, 1988, 1990, 1992, 1994, 1996
Yates, Tyrone K. (OH) - 1990
Yatron, Gus (PA) - 1968, 1970, 1972, 1974, 1976, 1978, 1980, 1982, 1984, 1986, 1988, 1990
Yauch, Michael B. (CA) - 1984
Yeager, Jim (PA) - 1994
Yellowtail, Bill (MT) - 1996
Yemen, Arpo (MI) - 1966
Yerger, Brower B. (PA) - 1972
Yoder, Fred (WA) - 1954
Yonavick, Peter (PA) - 1968
York, Peter R. (NM) - 1984
Yorty, Samuel William (CA) - 1950, 1952
Yost, Eric R. (KS) - 1992
Youhanaie, Stephen (IL) - 1988
Young, Andrew (GA) - 1970, 1972, 1974, 1976
Young, Arthur L. (CA) - 1962
Young, C. W. Bill (FL) - 1970, 1972, 1974, 1976, 1978, 1980, 1982, 1984, 1986, 1988, 1990, 1992, 1994, 1996
Young, Clifford O. (CA) - 1976
Young, Clifton (NV) - 1952, 1954
Young, Don (AK) - 1972, 1973, 1974, 1976, 1978, 1980, 1982, 1984, 1986, 1988, 1990, 1992, 1994, 1996
Young, Donald C. (IA) - 1980
Young, Edward L. (SC) - 1972, 1974, 1976
Young, Francis E. (OH) - 1954
Young, George E. (OK) - 1948, 1954
Young, Glenn O. (OK) - 1950
Young, James A. (PA) - 1984
Young, John (TX) - 1956, 1958, 1960, 1962, 1964, 1968, 1970, 1972, 1974, 1976
Young, John A. (PA) - 1964
Young, Ken (MO) - 1980, 1984, 1986
Young, Lewis E. (VT) - 1992
Young, Martin J. (WI) - 1946, 1948
Young, Paul (CA) - 1994
Young, Paul R. (ME) - 1996
Young, Robert A. (MO) - 1976, 1978, 1980, 1982, 1984, 1986
Young, Ronald E. (OH) - 1994
Young, Samuel H. (IL) - 1972, 1974, 1976

Young, Stephen M. (OH) - 1948, 1950
Young, Thomas H. (PA) - 1968, 1972
Young, Truman R. (CA) - 1946
Young, W. Hall (NC) - 1964, 1966
Young, William A. (IL) - 1974
Youngblood, Harold F. (MI) - 1946, 1948, 1956
Youngdale, James M. (MN) - 1948, 1952
Younger, J. Arthur (CA) - 1952, 1954, 1956, 1958, 1960, 1962, 1964, 1966
Youssouf, Joseph D. (NJ) - 1994
Yowell, Randy D. (KS) - 1976
Yudelson, Jerry (CA) - 1988
Yunker, Donald E. (OH) - 1980

Z

Zablocki, Clement J. (WI) - 1948, 1950, 1952, 1954, 1956, 1958, 1960, 1962, 1964, 1966, 1968, 1970, 1972, 1974, 1976, 1978, 1980, 1982
Zablotny, John J. (NY) - 1954
Zabrosky, Alex J. (IL) - 1970
Zadrozny, Mitchell G. (IL) - 1974
Zafris, James G. Jr. (MA) - 1964
Zakas, Joe (IN) - 1996
Zamos, Jerome (CA) - 1978
Zampino, Thomas P. (NJ) - 1986
Zanillo, Michael R. (IL) - 1980
Zartman, Jim (CO) - 1988
Zbur, Rick (CA) - 1996
Zealor, Murray P. (PA) - 1952, 1978
Zeferetti, Leo C. (NY) - 1974, 1976, 1978, 1980, 1982
Zeigler, Fred (SC) - 1986
Zelenko, Herbert (NY) - 1954, 1956, 1958, 1960
Zeliff, Bill (NH) - 1990, 1992, 1994
Zemmol, Allen (MI) - 1968
Zenkich, Elias R. (IL) - 1992
Zerg, Jerry (CA) - 1982, 1984
Zetterberg, Steve (CA) - 1950
Zevgolis, A. J. "Tony" (VA) - 1992, 1996
Ziccardi, Joseph S. (PA) - 1970
Ziebarth, Wayne W. (NB) - 1974
Ziegeweid, James L. (WI) - 1990
Ziegler, Gil (MI) - 1994
Ziegler, Jerome M. (IL) - 1962, 1964
Zietlow, Charlotte (IN) - 1978
Zilke, Walter F. (IL) - 1980
Zimmer, Dick (NJ) - 1990, 1992, 1994
Zimmer, Harry T. Jr. (PA) - 1958
Zimmerman, Bernard A. (WI) - 1982
Zimmerman, Orville (MO) - 1946
Zimmerman, Robert P. (NY) - 1982
Zimmermann, John W. (NJ) - 1946, 1952
Zinzell, Robert A. (FL) - 1970
Zion, Roger H. (IN) - 1964, 1966, 1968, 1970, 1972, 1974
Zipf, Henry (AZ) - 1954
Zirin, Lester (NY) - 1950
Zollinger, Peter L. (NM) - 1994
Zonneveld, Jan J. (IA) - 1992
Zupp, Harold (MN) - 1956
Zurick, William P. (PA) - 1970
Zwach, John M. (MN) - 1966, 1968, 1970, 1972
Zwick, Donald J. (OH) - 1980

General Index

The General Index includes page references to all section of *Congressional Elections 1946-1996*, except for the popular vote returns, which are indexed separately in the candidate indexes. The three candidate indexes are: Senate Candidate Index, pages 329-332; Senate Primary Candidate Index, pages 333-339; and House Candidate Index, pages 340-371.